Lecture Notes in Artificial Intelligence 7926

Subseries of Lecture Notes in Computer Science

H. Chad Lane Kalina Yacef Jack Mostow
Philip Pavlik (Eds.)

Artificial Intelligence in Education

16th International Conference, AIED 2013
Memphis, TN, USA, July 9-13, 2013
Proceedings

Springer

Volume Editors

H. Chad Lane
University of Southern California, Institute for Creative Technologies
Playa Vista, CA 90094, USA
E-mail: lane@ict.usc.edu

Kalina Yacef
University of Sydney, School of Information Technologies
Sydney, NSW 2006, Australia
E-mail: kalina@it.usyd.edu.au

Jack Mostow
Carnegie Mellon University, School of Computer Science
Pittsburgh, PA 15213, USA
E-mail: mostow@cs.cmu.edu

Philip Pavlik
University of Memphis, Department of Psychology
Memphis, TN 38152, USA
E-mail: ppavlik@memphis.edu

ISSN 0302-9743 e-ISSN 1611-3349
ISBN 978-3-642-39111-8 e-ISBN 978-3-642-39112-5
DOI 10.1007/978-3-642-39112-5
Springer Heidelberg Dordrecht London New York

Library of Congress Control Number: 2013941034

CR Subject Classification (1998): I.2, K.3, H.4, H.5

LNCS Sublibrary: SL 7 – Artificial Intelligence

Typesetting: Camera-ready by author, data conversion by Scientific Publishing Services, Chennai, India

Printed on acid-free paper

Springer is part of Springer Science+Business Media (www.springer.com)

Preface

The 16th International Conference on Artificial Intelligence in Education (AIED 2013) was held July 9–13, 2013, in Memphis, USA. As the biennial conference of the International Artificial Intelligence in Education Society (http://iaied.org), it has a longstanding reputation for high-quality research in intelligent systems and cognitive science for educational computing applications. The conference provides opportunities for the cross-fertilization of approaches, techniques, and ideas from the many fields that comprise the multidisciplinary field of AIED, including computer science, cognitive and learning sciences, education, game design, psychology, sociology, linguistics, as well as many domain-specific areas for which AIED systems have been designed and evaluated.

Since the first AIED meeting 30 years ago, both the breadth of the research and the reach of the technologies have expanded in dramatic ways. The theme of AIED2013 sought to capture this evolution—From education to lifelong learning: constructing ubiquitous and enduring environments for learning. In line with this theme of expansion, AIED2013 welcomed a new category for Industry and Innovation papers that sought to capture the challenges, solutions, and results from the transition of AIED technologies in the commercial sector.

We received a total of 168 submissions from 37 countries all over the globe, reflecting the wide international presence of AIED: 18 European countries, 9 Asian countries, 5 American countries, 3 African countries, and 2 Oceania countries. Of these, 55 were accepted as full papers (32.7%) and 73 as posters. The full papers were allotted 10 pages in the proceedings and the posters, which report high-quality yet perhaps less mature research, were allotted 4 pages. These papers cover a wide range of established as well as emerging topics in AIED, with many papers covering several of these. The conference program was arranged in sessions on student modeling and personalization, open-learner modeling, affective computing and engagement, educational data mining, learning together (collaborative learning and social computing), natural language processing, pedagogical agents, metacognition and self-regulated learning, feedback and scaffolding, designed learning activities, educational games and narrative, and outreach and scaling up.

The new Industry and Innovation track received six submissions, of which one full paper and one poster appear in these proceedings, preceded by a summary of the contributions by the Industry and Innovation Track Chairs. Following its long tradition of collegial community, and in particular for nurturing younger researchers, the conference included a Young Research Track. This important track provides a forum for PhD students to get feedback and mentoring from more established AIED researchers, and to exchange peer feedback with other young scholars. Out of the 22 YRT submissions received, 15 were accepted and included in the proceedings. The proceedings also include eight abstracts of

Interactive Events, which enable AIED attendees to experiment with new and emerging AIED technologies. Finally, nine workshops were organized on the days before and after the conference to bring together people working on emerging and/or very specialized topics. A brief description of each workshop is included.

We were delighted to invite three keynote speakers to start each day of the conference: Jack Mostow, Research Professor at Carnegie Mellon University in Pittsburgh, USA, offering an overview of his lessons learned during his 20+ years of work on Project LISTEN; Maria Roussou, Interaction Designer at make-believe design in Marousi, Greece, presenting her research in the commercial sector on virtual learning environments and informal learning; Doug Clark, Associate Professor at Vanderbilt University in Nashville, USA, discussing educational games for science learning. Abstracts of their presentations are included in these proceedings.

Peer review remains one of the most established and rigorous forms of decision-making that human history has ever seen. We strived to ensure a high quality of the review process. AIED2013 was fortunate to have dedicated Program Committees of international experts for each of its tracks. The main conference utilized a Senior Program Committee (SPC), a Program Committee (PC), and additional reviewers, who were called upon when necessary and supervised by members of the SPC and PC. The matching of reviewers' expertise and interests with papers was optimized thanks to an abstract bidding process before allocating papers for review. Conflicts of interest were identified so that no paper was assigned to a reviewer who is a close collaborator or institution colleague of any of the papers' authors. Each paper was blind-reviewed by three or four reviewers, half SPC members and the other half PC members. Reviewers were strongly encouraged to provide detailed, insightful feedback to authors on how to improve their papers. For each paper, a member of the SPC headed a week-long discussion phase with the other reviewers assigned to that paper to help reach a decision advice, and summarized it in a meta-review. The Program Chairs made the final decisions for acceptance on the basis of the reviews, discussions, and meta-reviews. When needed, the Program Chairs carefully read the papers and sought additional reviews to resolve inconsistencies.

Conferences and proceedings are never successful because of the work of just a few. We thank the many people who contributed and volunteered their time to make AIED2013 a success. We especially thank the SPC and PC for their diligence in reviewing and providing high-quality, useful, detailed, and constructive feedback. Most of them were allocated five to six papers each for the main track, as well as one to two for YRT. Overall, the committees did an outstanding job and made a significant contribution to the quality of this conference program. We thank the Local Arrangements Chairs and team for their tremendous work on all organizational aspects of AIED, and also for their (southern) hospitality. We also thank the other members of the Organizing Committee for their invaluable help, dedication, and professionalism in putting this conference program together: the Poster Chairs, YRT Chairs, Industry and Innovation Track Chairs, Workshop Chairs, Interactive Events Chairs, and Panel Chairs. We are also grateful to the researchers who volunteered to organize a workshop in conjunction with the conference. We express our gratitude to the past organizers of AIED and ITS conferences for their kind help and tips. We would like to extend our appreciation to the creators of EasyChair for the free management of the review process and the preparation of the proceedings. Last but not least, we thank the authors who submitted their work to AIED and whose papers appear in these proceedings.

This volume contains all the accepted full papers as well as the rest of the AIED 2013 program, including the invited talks, posters, industry and innovation papers, description summaries of the workshops (held on July 9 and 13), interactive event summaries, and YRT papers. We hope you enjoy these proceedings! It has been our pleasure to assemble them and have a small part in making AIED 2013 important and memorable.

May 2013

H. Chad Lane
Kalina Yacef
Jack Mostow
Phil Pavlik

Organization

International Artificial Intelligence in Education Society Management Board

Advisory Board

IAIED Society Executive Committee

Rosemary Luckin	London Knowledge Lab, UK
Bruce McLaren	Carnegie Mellon University, USA
Antonija Mitrovic	University of Canterbury, New Zealand
Riichiro Mizoguchi	Osaka University, Japan
Jack Mostow	Carnegie Mellon University, USA
Helen Pain	University of Edinburgh, UK
Julita Vassileva	University of Saskatchewan, Canada
Beverly P. Woolf	University of Massachusetts, USA

Organizing Committee

General Chair

Jack Mostow	Carnegie Mellon University, USA

Local Arrangements Chairs

Art Graesser	University of Memphis, USA
Andrew Olney	University of Memphis, USA
Phil Pavlik	University of Memphis, USA

Program Chairs

H. Chad Lane	University of Southern California, USA
Kalina Yacef	University of Sydney, Australia

Poster Chairs

Jihie Kim	University of Southern California, USA
Bruce McLaren	Carnegie Mellon University, USA

Industry and Innovation Track Chairs

Lewis Johnson	Alelo Inc., USA
Ari Bader-Natal	Minvera Project, USA

Young Researcher Track Chairs

Cristina Conati	University of British Columbia, Canada
Sidney D'Mello	University of Notre Dame, USA

Interactive Event Chairs

Vania Dimitrova	University of Leeds, UK
Fazel Keshtkar	University of Memphis, USA

Workshop Chairs

Chee-Kit Looi	Nanyang Technological University, Singapore
Erin Walker	Arizona State University, USA

Panel Chairs

Mike Sharples	The Open University, UK
Julita Vassileva	University of Saskatchewan, Canada

Awards Chairs

Ryan Baker	Columbia University Teachers College, USA
Rosemary Luckin	London Knowledge Lab, UK

Sponsorship Chair

John Stamper	Carnegie Mellon University, USA

Program Committee

Senior Program Committee

Vincent Aleven	Carnegie Mellon University, USA
Ivon Arroyo	University of Massachusetts Amherst, USA
Kevin Ashley	University of Pittsburgh, USA
Roger Azevedo	McGill University, Canada
Ryan Baker	Columbia University Teachers College, USA
Gautam Biswas	Vanderbilt University, USA
Jacqueline Bourdeau	TELU-UQAM, Canada
Bert Bredeweg	University of Amsterdam, The Netherlands
Peter Brusilovsky	University of Pittsburgh, USA
Susan Bull	University of Birmingham, UK
Tak-Wai Chan	National Central University, Taiwan
Cristina Conati	University of British Columbia, Canada
Albert Corbett	Carnegie Mellon University, USA
Sidney D'Mello	University of Notre Dame, USA
Vania Dimitrova	University of Leeds, UK
Benedict Du Boulay	University of Sussex, UK
Jim Greer	University of Saskatchewan, Canada
Neil Heffernan	Worcester Polytechnic Institute, USA
Tsukasa Hirashima	Hiroshima University, Japan
Ulrich Hoppe	University Duisburg-Essen, Germany
Lewis Johnson	Alelo Inc., USA
Akihiro Kashihara	University of Electro-Communications, Japan
Judy Kay	University of Sydney, Australia
Jihie Kim	University of Southern California, USA
Kenneth Koedinger	Carnegie Mellon University, USA
Susanne Lajoie	McGill University, Canada

James Lester	North Carolina State University, USA
Diane Litman	University of Pittsburgh, USA
Chee-Kit Looi	Nanyang Technological University, Singapore
Rose Luckin	London Knowledge Lab, UK
Gordon McCalla	University of Saskatchewan, Canada
Bruce McLaren	Carnegie Mellon University, USA
Tanja Mitrovic	University of Canterbury, New Zealand
Riichiro Mizoguchi	University of Osaka, Japan
Jack Mostow	Carnegie Mellon University, USA
Stellan Ohlsson	University of Illinois at Chicago, USA
Helen Pain	University of Edinburgh, UK
Phil Pavlik	University of Memphis, USA
Niels Pinkwart	Clausthal University of Technology, Germany
Steven Ritter	Carnegie Learning Inc., USA
Ido Roll	University of British Columbia, Canada
Carolyn Rose	Carnegie Mellon University, USA
Peter Sloep	Open Universiteit, The Netherlands
John Stamper	Carnegie Mellon University, USA
Pierre Tchounikine	University of Grenoble, France
Wouter Van Joolingen	University of Twente, The Netherlands
Kurt Vanlehn	Arizona State University, USA
Julita Vassileva	University of Saskatchewan, Canada
Felisa Verdejo	Universidad Nacional de Educacion a Distancia, Spain
Gerhard Weber	University of Education Freiburg, Germany
Beverly P. Woolf	University of Massachusetts, USA

Program Committee

Fabio Akhras	Elizabeth Kemp
Ari Bader-Natal	Fazel Keshtkar
Nilufar Baghaei	Jean-Marc Labat
Tiffany Barnes	Krittaya Leelawong
Paul Brna	Vanda Luengo
Winslow Burleson	Noboru Matsuda
Maiga Chang	Alessandro Micarelli
Chih-Kai Chang	Alain Mille
Mark Core	Marcelo Milrad
Scotty Craig	Kazuhisa Miwa
Alexandra Cristea	Kiyoshi Nakanayashi
Elisabeth Delozanne	Roger Nkambou
Barbara DiEugenio	Toshio Okamoto
Darina Dicheva	Andrew Olney
Peter Dolog	Zachary Pardos
Aude Dufresne	Chris Quintana
Matthew Easterday	Peter Reimann

Isabel Fernandez-Castro
Elena Gaudioso
Stephen Gilbert
Ashok Goel
Monique Grandbastien
Agneta Gulz
Susan Haller
Matthew Hays
Pentti Hietala
Sridhar Iyer
G. Tanner Jackson
Russell Johnson
Demetrios Sampson
Olga C. Santos
Andreas Schmidt
Pratim Sengupta
Pramudi Suraweera
Andre Tricot
Rosa Vicari
Erin Walker
Aisha Walker
Amali Weerasinghe
Diego Zapata-Rivera

Additional Reviewers

Bunmi Adewoyin
Ainhoa Alvarez
Nicolas Balacheff
Satabdi Basu
Emmanuel G. Blanchard
Denis Bouhineau
Acey Boyce
Whitney Cade
Veronica Catete
John Champaign
Maria Chavez-Echeagaray
Lin Chen
Kyle Cheney
Carrie Demmans Epp
Dimoklis Despotakis
Christo Dichev
Yang Fu-Yu
Sergio GÃşmez
Nick Green
Peter Griffin
Magnus Haake
Rachel Harsley
Yugo Hayashi
Tobias Hecking
Drew Hicks
Tomoya Horiguchi
Yun Huang
Johnson Iyilade
Samad Kardan
Fazel Keshtkar
John Kinnebrew
Sven Manske
Maite Martn
Noriyuki Matsuda
Shitanshu Mishra
Jonathan Mitchall
Brent Morgan
Junya Morita
Behrooz Mostafavi
Sayooran Nagulendra
AmirShareghi Najar
Silvia M.B. Navarro
Rita Orji
Hercules Panoutsopoulos
Barry Peddycord
Dominique Py
Dovan Rai
Ramkumar Rajendran
Kelly Rivers
Shaghayegh Sahebi
Hitomi Saito
Filippo Sciarrone
James Segedy
Mayya Sharipova
Erica Snow
Eliane Stampfer
Christina M. Steiner
Ming-Hui Tai
Hitoshi Terai
Dhavalkumar Thakker
Maite Urreavizcaya
Martin van Velsen

Lydia Lau
Nguyen-Thinh Le
Marie Lefevre
Blair Lehman
Nan Li
Carla Limongelli
Bob Loblaw
Yanjin Long
Christopher MacLellan
Laura Varner
Iro Voulgari
Yutao Wang
Mike Wixon
Longkai Wu
Nesra Yannier
Amel Yessad
Panagiotis Zervas

YRT Program Committee

Fabio Akhras
Roger Azevedo
Tiffany Barnes
Jacqueline Bourdeau
Peter Brusilovsky
Winslow Burleson
Mark Core
Alexandra Cristea
Darina Dicheva
Peter Dolog
Benedict Du Boulay
Elena Gaudioso
Stephen Gilbert
Monique Grandbastien
Agneta Gulz
Tsukasa Hirashima
G. Tanner Jackson
W. Lewis Johnson
Judy Kay
Jihie Kim
Jean-Marc Labat
Krittaya Leelawong
James Lester
Vanda Luengo
Noboru Matsuda
Gordon McCalla
Bruce Mclaren
Alain Mille
Riichiro Mizoguchi
Jack Mostow
Kiyoshi Nakanayashi
Roger Nkambou
Helen Pain
Zachary Pardos
Philip I. Pavlik Jr.
Niels Pinkwart
Carolyn Rose
Ryan Baker
Alicia Sagae
Olga C. Santos
Andreas Schmidt
Mike Van Lent
Erin Walker
Amali Weerasinghe

Industry and Innovation Track Program Committee

Jared Bernstein
Chris Brannigan
John Carney
Jared Freeman
Neil Heffernan
David Kuntz
Garrett Pelton
Sowmya Ramachandran
Steve Ritter
Alicia Sagae
Mike Van Lent

Sponsors

Institute for Intelligent Systems

Carney Labs LLC

The University of Memphis

International Artificial Intelligence in Education Society

Pearson

USC ICT Institute for Creative Technologies

Table of Contents

Affective Computing and Engagement

Learning Together

Student Modeling and Personalisation

Open-Learner Modeling

Metacognition and Self-Regulated Learning

Natural Language Processing

Pedagogical Agents

Designed Learning Activities

Educational Games and Narrative

Educational Data Mining

Assessment and Evaluation

Outreach and Scaling Up

Feedback and Scaffolding

Invited Talks

Industry and Innovation Track

Posters

Young Researchers Track

Interactive Events

Workshops

Embodied Affect in Tutorial Dialogue: Student Gesture and Posture

Joseph F. Grafsgaard[1], Joseph B. Wiggins[1], Kristy Elizabeth Boyer[1], Eric N. Wiebe[2], and James C. Lester[1]

[1] Department of Computer Science, North Carolina State University
[2] Department of STEM Education, North Carolina State University
Raleigh, North Carolina, USA
{jfgrafsg,jbwiggi3,keboyer,wiebe,lester}@ncsu.edu

Abstract. Recent years have seen a growing recognition of the central role of affect and motivation in learning. In particular, nonverbal behaviors such as posture and gesture provide key channels signaling affective and motivational states. Developing a clear understanding of these mechanisms will inform the development of personalized learning environments that promote successful affective and motivational outcomes. This paper investigates posture and gesture in computer-mediated tutorial dialogue using automated techniques to track posture and hand-to-face gestures. Annotated dialogue transcripts were analyzed to identify the relationships between student posture, student gesture, and tutor and student dialogue. The results indicate that posture and hand-to-face gestures are significantly associated with particular tutorial dialogue moves. Additionally, two-hands-to-face gestures occurred significantly more frequently among students with low self-efficacy. The results shed light on the cognitive-affective mechanisms that underlie these nonverbal behaviors. Collectively, the findings provide insight into the interdependencies among tutorial dialogue, posture, and gesture, revealing a new avenue for automated tracking of embodied affect during learning.

Keywords: Affect, gesture, posture, tutorial dialogue.

1 Introduction

Recent years have seen a growing recognition of the central role of affect and motivation in learning. In particular, nonverbal behaviors such as posture and gesture provide key channels signaling affective and motivational states. Insights into how systems may leverage these nonverbal behaviors for intelligent interaction are offered by a growing body of literature [1–5]. Within the intelligent tutoring systems literature, nonverbal behaviors have been linked to cognitive-affective states that impact learning [6–8].

A rich body of work has explored the moment-by-moment effects of these learning-centered affective states. Numerous techniques and tools have been applied to recognize affect, including human judgments [6, 9], computer vision techniques [4, 9, 10], sensors

K. Yacef et al. (Eds.): AIED 2013, LNAI 7926, pp. 1–10, 2013.

[11], and speech [8]. There has even been work toward identifying affect in the absence of rich data streams, instead using interaction log data [12]. The abundant utility of these techniques has been illustrated by their use in a number of affectively adaptive tutoring systems [7, 8].

Although there has been substantial progress toward integrating affective data streams into intelligent learning environments, the field does not yet have a clear understanding of affective expression across multiple modalities. Some modalities, such as facial expression, are relatively well-explored [1, 3], while others are subjects of significant active research. For instance, posture has been used as an affective feature in multiple systems, but interpretation of postural movements is very complex [2, 9]. Early work focused on postural movement as a signal; for example, pressure-sensitive chairs have long been used for fine-grained measurement of posture [7, 13]. Early studies of posture have indicated that the signal is involved in numerous cognitive-affective states, such as boredom, focus, and frustration [7, 13]. Over the years, a replicated result in analyses of postural movement has arisen: increases in postural movement are linked with negative affect or disengagement [6, 7, 9, 14, 15]. There have also been recent developments in techniques for tracking postural movement. Posture can now be tracked in both two-dimensional [9, 14] and three-dimensional video [15] using computer vision. These computer vision-based approaches have the advantage of directly identifying postural components such as body lean angle and slouch factor [14] that were indirectly measured in the signals from pressure-sensitive chairs.

In contrast to posture, affective gestural displays have recently begun to be investigated. There is abundant cultural and anecdotal evidence for the importance of gestures [16], yet empirical research results on the cognitive-affective states underlying gesture are sparse. A system trained on acted expressions of cognitive-affective states relied on combinations of facial expression and gesture features [4], with meaning ascribed by human judges. Gestures have also been tangentially reported on in the intelligent tutoring systems community [6, 7, 17], but other phenomena were the primary focus of those studies. A recent study investigated different categories of hand-over-face gestures, with the researchers providing possible interpretations ranging over cognitive-affective states such as thinking, frustration, or boredom [5]. More recently, a hand-to-face gesture tracking algorithm was developed using the Kinect depth camera [15]. This algorithm distinguishes between one or two hands contacting the lower face. Initial analyses of these hand-to-face gestures indicated that one-hand-to-face gestures may be associated with less negative affect, while two-hands-to-face gestures may be indicative of reduced focus [15].

This paper presents an analysis of posture and gesture within computer-mediated textual tutorial dialogue. Utilizing automated algorithms that measure postural quantity of motion, one-hand-to-face gestures, and two-hands-to-face gestures, we examine the interdependencies between dialogue acts and student posture and gesture in order to identify ways in which the nonverbal behaviors may influence or be influenced by dialogue. Additionally, we report groupwise differences in nonverbal behavior displays, finding that students with lower self-efficacy tend to produce more two-hands-to-face gestures. We discuss the implications of these findings as a step toward understanding the embodied affect that intertwines with tutorial dialogue.

2 Corpus Annotation and Nonverbal Behavior Tracking

The corpus consists of computer-mediated tutorial dialogue for introductory computer science. Students (*N*=42) and tutors interacted through a web-based interface that provided learning tasks, an interface for computer programming, and textual dialogue. The participants were university students in the United States, with average age of 18.5 years (*stdev*=1.5). The students voluntarily participated for course credit in an introductory engineering course, with no computer science knowledge required. Substantial self-reported prior programming experience was an exclusion criterion. Each student was paired with a tutor for a total of six sessions on different days, limited to forty minutes each session. Recordings of the sessions included database logs, webcam video, skin conductance, and Kinect depth video. The Kinect recording rate was set to approximately 8 frames per second to reduce storage requirements. The student workstation configuration and tutoring interface are shown in Figure 1.

Fig. 1. JavaTutor student workstation and tutoring interface

Prior to the first session, students completed a main pretest and pre-survey, which included an instrument for domain-specific self-efficacy (six Likert-scale items adapted from [18]). Before each session, students completed a content-based pretest. After each session, students answered a post-session survey and posttest (identical to the pretest). This paper presents analyses of data from the first session.

Dialogue acts were annotated using a parallel coding scheme that was applied to both tutor and student utterances. The coding scheme used here is an update to a prior task-oriented dialogue annotation scheme [19]. Three annotators tagged a subset of the corpus (*N*=36). Fourteen percent of these annotated sessions were doubly annotated, with a resulting average agreement across dialogue acts of Cohen's κ=0.73. The dialogue act tags and frequencies in the corpus are shown in Table 1.

Table 1. Dialogue act tags ordered by frequency in the corpus (*S*=student, *T*=tutor)

Act	Example Tutor Utterances	*S*	*T*
STATEMENT	*"java does things in the order you say."*	282	1255
QUESTION	*"Any questions so far?"*	213	630
POSITIVE FEEDBACK	*"great debugging!"*	2	539
DIRECTIVE	*"change that in all three places"*	-	252
HINT	*"it is missing a semicolon."*	-	223
ANSWER	*"yes, now line 1 is a comment."*	547	162
ACKNOWLEDGMENT	*"alright" "okay" "Yes"*	323	68
LUKEWARM FEEDBACK	*"Right, nearly there"*	-	32
NEGATIVE FEEDBACK	*"no" "nope"*	-	19
CORRECTION	Repairing a prior utterance: *"*can use"*	11	15
REQUEST CONFIRMATION	*"Make sense?" "okay?"*	6	14
OTHER	*"LOL"*	11	6
REQUEST FOR FEEDBACK	*"How does that look?"*	11	1

Recently developed posture and gesture tracking techniques were applied to the recorded Kinect depth images. The posture tracking algorithm compares depth pixels in three regions at the center of the depth image (head, mid torso, and lower torso) and selects depth pixel distances representative of each region. The gesture detection algorithm performs a surface propagation across the head and connected surfaces to identify hand-to-face gestures. The posture tracking algorithm was previously evaluated to be 92.4% accurate, while gesture tracking was found to be 92.6% accurate [15]. The tracking algorithms were run on all sessions, but four sessions had no Kinect recordings due to human error (*N*=38). The combined corpus of dialogue acts and nonverbal tracking data contains 32 sessions. Sample output of posture and gesture tracking is shown in Figure 2.

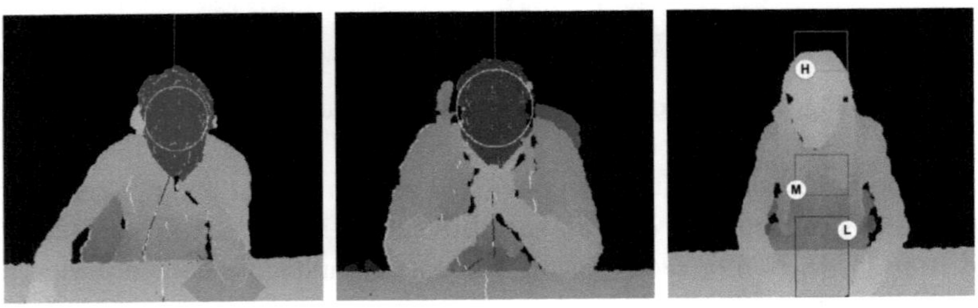

Fig. 2. Tracked gestures (one-hand-to-face, two-hands-to-face) and posture

The posture tracking values were converted into a "postural shift" feature, a discrete representation of *quantity of motion* [14]. Postural shifts were identified through tracked head distances as follows. The median head distance of students at each workstation was selected as the "center" postural position. Distances at one standard deviation (or more) closer or farther than "center" were labeled as "near" or "far," respectively. Postural shifts were labeled when a student moved from one positional category to another (e.g., from "near" to "center"). Both postural shift and gesture events were smoothed by removing those with duration of less than one second. This smoothing mitigated the problem of jitter at decision boundaries (e.g., slight movements at the boundary between "center" and "far" postural positions that cause rapid swapping of both labels). The nonverbal behaviors will hereafter be referenced with the labels ONEHAND, TWOHANDS, and PSHIFT.

3 Tutorial Dialogue and Nonverbal Behavior

Tutorial dialogue and nonverbal behavior have both been extensively examined separately from each other, but there are few investigations of their interactions [20]. We focused on a series of analyses to identify co-dependencies between tutorial dialogue and nonverbal behavior. First, we ran a series of comparisons between overall dialogue act frequencies and dialogue act frequencies conditioned on presence of nonverbal displays. Then, a series of groupwise comparisons identified whether differences existed between students based on gender, prior knowledge, and domain-specific self-efficacy. Statistically significant results are shown in bold.

The first analyses consider the frequency of dialogue acts given that a nonverbal behavior occurred either before or after a dialogue act. An empirically determined fifteen-second interval was used to tabulate occurrence of nonverbal behavior events both before and after dialogue acts. The frequencies were normalized for individuals and averaged across the corpus. Thus, the values shown in the analyses below are average relative frequencies. Dialogue acts with overall average relative frequency below 1% were excluded from the analyses.

The analyses of student dialogue acts consider two situations for each nonverbal behavior. The first examines student dialogue acts given that a nonverbal behavior occurred prior to a dialogue act. This may show how student dialogue moves are affected by the nonverbal behaviors. The second situation considers student dialogue acts given that a nonverbal behavior followed. This represents differences in how a student proceeded following their own dialogue act. In both situations, the nonverbal context may provide insight into the dialogue.

The analyses of student dialogue acts conditioned on prior ONEHAND events revealed a statistically significantly lower frequency of student QUESTIONS following ONEHAND gestures. There was also a trend of more student answers following ONEHAND gestures (Table 2).

Table 2. Analyses of student dialogue acts preceded by ONEHAND gesture

Student Dialogue Act	**Relative Freq. of Stud. Act (*stdev*)**	**Rel. Freq. of Stud. Act with ONEHAND Prior (*stdev*)**	***p*-value (paired *t*-test, two-tailed, *N*=30)**
ANSWER	0.42 (*0.16*)	0.50 (*0.27*)	0.114
ACKNOWLEDGMENT	0.22 (*0.08*)	0.22 (*0.23*)	0.878
QUESTION	**0.14 (*0.09*)**	**0.08 (*0.16*)**	**0.048**
STATEMENT	0.18 (*0.09*)	0.18 (*0.22*)	0.896

The analyses of student dialogue acts followed by PSHIFT events showed a statistically significant lower frequency of student questions followed by PSHIFT (Table 3).

Table 3. Analyses of student dialogue acts followed by PSHIFT postural event

Student Dialogue Act	**Relative Freq. of Stud. Act (*stdev*)**	**Rel. Freq. of Stud. Act Followed by PSHIFT (*stdev*)**	***p*-value (paired *t*-test, two-tailed, *N*=24)**
ANSWER	0.40 (*0.13*)	0.43 (*0.33*)	0.649
ACKNOWLEDGMENT	0.23 (*0.09*)	0.29 (*0.29*)	0.296
QUESTION	**0.15 (*0.09*)**	**0.08 (*0.12*)**	**0.019**
STATEMENT	0.20 (*0.11*)	0.16 (*0.20*)	0.246

The analyses of tutor dialogue acts are conditioned on student nonverbal behaviors present after a tutor move, which may show how students reacted to tutor moves. The analyses of tutor dialogue acts followed by posture identified statistically significant lower frequencies of tutor DIRECTIVEs and tutor POSITIVE FEEDBACK followed by PSHIFT (Table 4). The analyses of tutor dialogue acts followed by TWOHANDS revealed statistically significant lower frequencies of tutor ANSWERs and tutor DIRECTIVEs followed by TWOHANDS (Table 5). Additionally, there was a trend of greater frequency of questions followed by TWOHANDS.

Table 4. Analyses of tutor dialogue acts followed by PSHIFT postural event

Tutor Dialogue Act	**Relative Freq. of Tutor Act (*stdev*)**	**Rel. Freq. of Tutor Act Followed by PSHIFT (*stdev*)**	***p*-value (paired *t*-test, two-tailed, *N*=24)**
ANSWER	0.04 (*0.03*)	0.04 (*0.07*)	0.722
ACKNOWLEDGMENT	0.03 (*0.03*)	0.06 (*0.13*)	0.162
DIRECTIVE	**0.08 (*0.04*)**	**0.05 (*0.06*)**	**0.012**
HINT	0.07 (*0.05*)	0.11 (*0.20*)	0.350
POSITIVE FDBK	**0.18 (*0.05*)**	**0.13 (*0.10*)**	**0.033**
QUESTION	0.21 (*0.07*)	0.26 (*0.24*)	0.359
STATEMENT	0.36 (*0.10*)	0.32 (*0.23*)	0.419

Table 5. Analyses of tutor dialogue acts followed by TWOHANDS gesture

Tutor Dialogue Act	**Relative Freq. of Tutor Act (*stdev*)**	**Rel. Freq. of Tutor Act Followed by TWOHANDS (*stdev*)**	***p*-value (paired *t*-test, two-tailed, *N*=23)**
ANSWER	**0.05 (*0.03*)**	**0.01 (*0.03*)**	**<0.001**
ACKNOWLEDGMENT	0.03 (*0.03*)	0.01 (*0.04*)	0.258
DIRECTIVE	**0.08 (*0.03*)**	**0.03 (*0.05*)**	**<0.001**
HINT	0.06 (*0.05*)	0.04 (*0.11*)	0.382
POSITIVE FDBK	0.18 (*0.05*)	0.21 (*0.18*)	0.524
QUESTION	0.19 (*0.07*)	0.26 (*0.25*)	0.135
STATEMENT	0.39 (*0.09*)	0.39 (*0.30*)	0.977

The primary focus of the above analyses was to investigate the relationships between tutorial dialogue and student nonverbal behaviors. However, the broader nature of nonverbal behavior in tutoring can be explored through analyses conditioned upon student characteristics. For this purpose, three groupwise analyses were conducted to examine gender and domain-specific self-efficacy. First, students were grouped into categories of male (N=28) and female (N=10). Comparisons of PSHIFT, ONEHAND, and TWOHANDS yielded no significant differences (t-tests with unequal variance, two-tailed). Second, students were grouped through a median split on pretest score, with high prior knowledge (N=19) and low prior knowledge (N=19). Comparisons of PSHIFT, ONEHAND, and TWOHANDS yielded no significant differences (t-tests with unequal variance, two-tailed). Finally, a median split on domain-specific self-efficacy was performed to create groups of high self-efficacy (N=19) and low self-efficacy (N=19). No differences were found in ONEHAND or PSHIFT across the groups (t-tests with unequal variance, two-tailed). However, students who reported low self-efficacy were found to display more TWOHANDS gestures (t-test with unequal variance, two-tailed). Students in the low self-efficacy group had an average of 0.53 TWOHANDS displays per minute (N=19, $stdev$=0.52), while the high self-efficacy group had an average of 0.20 TWOHANDS displays per minute (N=19, $stdev$=0.34). This result was statistically significant with p=0.029.

4 Discussion

The hand-to-face gestures examined here are in a class different from those involved in social conversation and face-to-face tutoring. In face-to-face interaction, social communication guides the nonverbal interaction [16]. Objects in the surrounding environment and spoken concepts form a common substrate that is referenced in conversational gestures. In the case of computer-mediated tutoring, social displays are greatly reduced [15]. Thus, hand-to-face gestures may be more representative of the cognitive-affective states that accompany them compared to communicative or social gestures.

One-hand-to-face gestures are often thought of as embodiments of a thoughtful state.[1] Here, student questions were found to be less frequent following a one-hand-to-face gesture. It may be that students who presented one-hand-to-face gestures had fewer questions to ask. Only fifteen percent of one-hand-to-face gestures occurred before student utterances. Additionally, one-hand-to-face gestures most frequently occurred before student answers. Students are likely to think before providing an answer and in work on task outside of the dialogue. The occurrence of one-hand-to-face gestures coincides with both of these thought-provoking events. Thus, our corpus supports interpretation of one-hand-to-face gestures as a nonverbal behavior with an underlying thoughtful state.

The groupwise self-efficacy analysis presented here showed that students with lower self-efficacy tend to produce more two-hands-to-face gestures. Coupled with a

[1] One such gesture has even been cast in bronze as a timeless exemplar, "The Thinker."

prior result [15] that found two-hands-to-face gestures to be negatively correlated with focus, a picture emerges of this gesture as an embodiment of reduced focus and lower confidence. Here, tutor answers and tutor directives were less likely to be followed by two-hands-to-face displays. This appears to indicate that students were more focused after these tutor moves. Both tutor answers and directives provide responsive instruction to the student. In the case of answers, the student would have asked a question, and thus would be attentively waiting for the tutor's answer. With directives, the tutor is supplying the student with direct task solution steps that the student must then act upon. The interface did not allow tutors to edit students' computer programming code, so tutor directives imply subsequent student work.

Postural shifts have been linked with disengagement or negative affect. Studies in different contexts agree: whether it is a child playing a game with a robot [14] or a student interacting with a tutoring system [6, 7, 9], postural shifting has repeatedly been shown to co-occur with disengaged or negative cognitive-affective states. Thus, the postural shifts examined in these analyses most likely indicate a disengaged affective state. In this case, we find that less disengagement followed student questions, tutor answers, and tutor positive feedback. Each of these dialogue acts is directly related to collaborative tutorial interaction in which the student is more likely to be engaged. In the case of student questions and tutor answers, the student has posed the question and subsequently received a response. The student clearly plays an active role in this pattern, so it is not surprising that their body reflects this. With tutor positive feedback, the tutor has praised the student for completing a sub-task. The student was actively engaged in the computer programming task, so this result shows that both the student's body and tutor praise reflect the student's engagement.

4.1 Limitations

As noted in [5], there are many variants of hand-to-face and hand-over-face gestures. The hand-to-face gestures tracked here consider contact between hands and the lower face, without more detail as to how the hand is touching the face (e.g., the difference between holding one's chin and leaning on the palm of a hand). Additionally, temporal characteristics of these gestures may be important. An individual may stroke his or her chin, as opposed to resting on a hand. Thus, the present analyses aggregate an array of more specific gestures into categories of one-hand-to-face or two-hands-to-face. Further development efforts are needed to provide tracking algorithms that distinguish between the spatiotemporal subtleties of hand and face [2].

5 Conclusion

Posture and gesture are fundamental components of embodied affect, with ties to cognitive-affective states that may help or hinder learning. Posture and gesture in computer-mediated tutorial dialogue were investigated using automated techniques to track posture and hand-to-face gestures. Annotated dialogue transcripts were analyzed to identify the relationships between student posture, student gesture, and tutor and student dialogue. The results indicate that posture and hand-to-face gestures are significantly associated with student questions, tutor answers, tutor directives and tutor positive feedback. Additionally, two-hands-to-face gestures occurred significantly more frequently among students with low self-efficacy. The results shed light on the cognitive-affective mechanisms that underlie these nonverbal behaviors. Collectively, the findings provide novel insight into the interdependencies among tutorial dialogue, posture, and gesture, revealing a new avenue for automated tracking of embodied affect during learning.

An important emerging trend in intelligent tutoring systems research is that models of nonverbal behaviors are gradually being integrated into runtime diagnostic models. Gesture is a particularly promising modality for informing runtime behavior of tutoring. Gesture and posture constitute key components of a holistic model of nonverbal behavior and embodied affect during learning. Together, they provide a basis for the next generation of affect-informed personalized learning technologies.

Acknowledgments. This work is supported in part by the North Carolina State University Department of Computer Science and the National Science Foundation through Grant DRL-1007962 and the STARS Alliance Grant CNS-1042468. Any opinions, findings, conclusions, or recommendations expressed in this report are those of the participants, and do not necessarily represent the official views, opinions, or policy of the National Science Foundation.

References

1. Zeng, Z., Pantic, M., Roisman, G.I., Huang, T.S.: A Survey of Affect Recognition Methods: Audio, Visual, and Spontaneous Expressions. IEEE Transactions on Pattern Analysis and Machine Intelligence 31, 39–58 (2009)
2. Kleinsmith, A., Bianchi-Berthouze, N.: Affective Body Expression Perception and Recognition: A Survey. IEEE Transactions on Affective Computing (2012)
3. Calvo, R.A., D'Mello, S.K.: Affect Detection: An Interdisciplinary Review of Models, Methods, and Their Applications. IEEE Transactions on Affective Computing 1, 18–37 (2010)
4. El Kaliouby, R., Robinson, P.: The Emotional Hearing Aid: an Assistive Tool for Children with Asperger Syndrome. Universal Access in the Information Society 4, 121–134 (2005)
5. Mahmoud, M., Robinson, P.: Interpreting Hand-Over-Face Gestures. In: D'Mello, S., Graesser, A., Schuller, B., Martin, J.-C. (eds.) ACII 2011, Part II. LNCS, vol. 6975, pp. 248–255. Springer, Heidelberg (2011)
6. Rodrigo, M.M.T., Baker, R.S.J.d.: Comparing Learners' Affect while using an Intelligent Tutor and an Educational Game. Research and Practice in Technology Enhanced Learning 6, 43–66 (2011)
7. Woolf, B.P., Burleson, W., Arroyo, I., Dragon, T., Cooper, D.G., Picard, R.W.: Affect-Aware Tutors: Recognising and Responding to Student Affect. International Journal of Learning Technology 4, 129–164 (2009)
8. Forbes-Riley, K., Litman, D.: Benefits and Challenges of Real-Time Uncertainty Detection and Adaptation in a Spoken Dialogue Computer Tutor. Speech Communication 53, 1115–1136 (2011)

9. D'Mello, S., Dale, R., Graesser, A.: Disequilibrium in the Mind, Disharmony in the Body. Cognition & Emotion 26, 362–374 (2012)
10. Baltrusaitis, T., McDuff, D., Banda, N., Mahmoud, M., El Kaliouby, R., Robinson, P., Picard, R.: Real-Time Inference of Mental States from Facial Expressions and Upper Body Gestures. In: Proceedings of the IEEE International Conference on Automatic Face and Gesture Recognition, pp. 909–914 (2011)
11. Brawner, K.W., Goldberg, B.S.: Real-Time Monitoring of ECG and GSR Signals during Computer-Based Training. In: Cerri, S.A., Clancey, W.J., Papadourakis, G., Panourgia, K. (eds.) ITS 2012. LNCS, vol. 7315, pp. 72–77. Springer, Heidelberg (2012)
12. Baker, R.S.J.d., Gowda, S.M., Wixon, M., Kalka, J., Wagner, A.Z., Salvi, A., Aleven, V., Kusbit, G.W., Ocumpaugh, J., Rossi, L.: Towards Sensor-Free Affect Detection in Cognitive Tutor Algebra. In: Proceedings of the 5th International Conference on Educational Data Mining, pp. 126–133 (2012)
13. Kapoor, A., Burleson, W., Picard, R.W.: Automatic Prediction of Frustration. International Journal of Human-Computer Studies 65, 724–736 (2007)
14. Sanghvi, J., Castellano, G., Leite, I., Pereira, A., McOwan, P.W., Paiva, A.: Automatic Analysis of Affective Postures and Body Motion to Detect Engagement with a Game Companion. In: Proceedings of the ACM/IEEE International Conference on Human-Robot Interaction, pp. 305–311 (2011)
15. Grafsgaard, J.F., Fulton, R.M., Boyer, K.E., Wiebe, E.N., Lester, J.C.: Multimodal Analysis of the Implicit Affective Channel in Computer-Mediated Textual Communication. In: Proceedings of the 14th ACM International Conference on Multimodal Interaction, pp. 145–152 (2012)
16. McNeill, D.: Gesture & Thought. The University of Chicago Press, Chicago (2005)
17. Grafsgaard, J.F., Boyer, K.E., Phillips, R., Lester, J.C.: Modeling Confusion: Facial Expression, Task, and Discourse in Task-Oriented Tutorial Dialogue. In: Biswas, G., Bull, S., Kay, J., Mitrovic, A. (eds.) AIED 2011. LNCS, vol. 6738, pp. 98–105. Springer, Heidelberg (2011)
18. Bandura, A.: Guide for Constructing Self-Efficacy Scales. In: Pajares, F., Urdan, T. (eds.) Self-Efficacy Beliefs of Adolescents, pp. 307–337. Information Age Publishing, Greenwich (2006)
19. Boyer, K.E., Phillips, R., Ingram, A., Ha, E.Y., Wallis, M., Vouk, M., Lester, J.: Characterizing the Effectiveness of Tutorial Dialogue with Hidden Markov Models. In: Aleven, V., Kay, J., Mostow, J. (eds.) ITS 2010, Part I. LNCS, vol. 6094, pp. 55–64. Springer, Heidelberg (2010)
20. Ha, E.Y., Grafsgaard, J.F., Mitchell, C.M., Boyer, K.E., Lester, J.C.: Combining Verbal and Nonverbal Features to Overcome the "Information Gap" in Task-Oriented Dialogue. In: Proceedings of the Thirteenth Annual SIGDIAL Meeting on Discourse and Dialogue, pp. 247–256 (2012)

What Emotions Do Novices Experience during Their First Computer Programming Learning Session?

Nigel Bosch[1], Sidney D'Mello[1,2], and Caitlin Mills[2]

[1] Departments of Computer Science
[2] Psychology, University of Notre Dame, Notre Dame, IN 46556
{pbosch1,sdmello,cmills4}@nd.edu

Abstract. We conducted a study to track the emotions, their behavioral correlates, and relationship with performance when novice programmers learned the basics of computer programming in the Python language. Twenty-nine participants without prior programming experience completed the study, which consisted of a 25 minute scaffolding phase (with explanations and hints) and a 15 minute fadeout phase (no explanations or hints) with a computerized learning environment. Emotional states were tracked via retrospective self-reports in which learners viewed videos of their faces and computer screens recorded during the learning session and made judgments about their emotions at approximately 100 points. The results indicated that flow/engaged (23%), confusion (22%), frustration (14%), and boredom (12%) were the major emotions students experienced, while curiosity, happiness, anxiety, surprise, anger, disgust, fear, and sadness were comparatively rare. The emotions varied as a function of instructional scaffolds and were systematically linked to different student behaviors (idling, constructing code, running code). Boredom, flow/engaged, and confusion were also correlated with performance outcomes. Implications of our findings for affect-sensitive learning interventions are discussed.

1 Introduction

Computer science (CS) remains a difficult degree to complete and has some of the highest attrition rates in undergraduate universities in the U.S. [1]. There has been some research aimed at identifying the factors that contribute to the eventual success or failure of students in computer programming classes. Some of this research has focused on individual differences like mathematical ability, programming aptitude, and psychological traits of non-cognitive factors like temperament and motivation [2–5]. Many of these factors have proven to be somewhat influential in predicting a student's decision to enroll in a computer programming course, as well as their eventual success in such courses, but these trait-based measures are very coarse grained and assume fixed dispositions instead of malleable factors.

Taking a somewhat different approach, the present paper focuses on the emotions that students experience during their first encounter with computer programming. It is expected that flow/engagement is the ideal affective state in which students tend to be most capable of acquiring meaningful information through the learning process [6, 7].

K. Yacef et al. (Eds.): AIED 2013, LNAI 7926, pp. 11–20, 2013.

However, other emotions interact with flow/engagement and augment or detract from learning. For example confusion and frustration are expected to arise quickly when the results of a program do not match expectations (confusion) or the student has no idea how to proceed and gets stuck at a logical impasse (frustration). Persistent failure is associated with frustration [8] and lower self-efficacy, which can lead to boredom and disengagement [9], and ultimately attrition [10]. Therefore, our working hypothesis is that emotional factors play an instrumental role in the process of learning to program and can influence both immediate (failing an exam) and long-term outcomes (dropping out of a CS course).

There has been some research that has investigated the emotions that students experience while learning programming, as well as the effect of those emotions on eventual success in a CS class [11–13]. For example, [12] used two human observers to code student affect (boredom, confusion, delight, surprise, frustration, flow, or the neutral state) during 50-minute lab sessions. They found that confusion, boredom, and on-task conversation (i.e. asking for help) were negative significant predictors of performance on a midterm exam.

More recently, [14] collected several data sources while students conversed with a human tutor about the exercises they were completing via a computer-mediated interface. They found that frustration reported by students correlated (r = .53) with confusion reported by the tutor. Additionally, tutor reports of student confusion and frustration were correlated (r = .59), and confusion was negatively correlated with posttest scores (r = -.38).

These studies have provided some important insights into the emotions that arise when students learn to program and the influence of these emotions on performance. The long-term goal of this research is to develop advanced learning environments that detect and respond to student emotions. However, much more basic research on the emotions themselves is needed before such an affect-sensitive learning environment can be successfully engineered. As an initial step in this direction, the present study systematically tracks student emotions during computer programming. It builds upon and extends previous research in this area in the following ways. First, we delve more deeply into the emotions experienced by novice programmers by tracking emotion at a fine-grained level (every 20 seconds) during a 40 minute programming session. Second, we focus on tracking emotions during students' *first* programming experience. This was accomplished by carefully screening participants to remove those with prior programming experience and those who are majoring in computer science. Third, our focus is one-on-one human-computer programming experiences without interference, distractions, or social pressures that may become factors when teachers or peers are involved in the learning process. Our emphasis was on the following three questions regarding the emotions of novice programming students: (1) which emotions are most prevalent overall and at various phases in the session, (2) how are student behaviors linked to their emotions, and (3) what is the relationship between emotion and performance?

2 Methods

2.1 Participants

Participants were undergraduate students selected from the Psychology Subject Pool at a private Midwest university in the U.S. 35 participants completed the study, but 6 were removed from consideration due to self-reported prior experience with computer programming, thereby resulting in a sample of 29 novices. We chose to eliminate students with prior experience so that the sample would be representative of novices, who may or may not eventually become programmers.

2.2 Learning Environment

The computerized learning environment consisted of four main components: an instructional area with texts and diagrams, a coding area with syntax highlighting, a hint display area, and an output console area. Participants were able to test their code via "Run" and "Stop" buttons. They used the "Submit" button to move to the next exercise, which executed their code non-interactively, using predefined inputs to determine code correctness. Participants were then given non-elaborated feedback about whether or not their submission was correct, and if correct they would automatically proceed to the next exercise. Hints were available via a "Show Hint" button. The possible score for each exercise was set to be the number of hints for that exercise plus one. Using a hint resulted in a deduction of one point from the exercise and the cumulative score was always displayed to the participants. Hints were made available on a variable time delay ranging from 45 to 90 seconds relative to the start of the exercise or the previous hint request. This delay was used so that participants would be encouraged to think about exercises instead of simply using hints to solve them quickly. Additionally, hints were only available for selected exercises as discussed below.

2.3 Procedure

Participants were individually tested in a two-hour session. The study consisted of three main phases as discussed below. A webcam built into the bezel of the monitor recorded the face of participants, while screen capture software recorded videos of the learning environment. The learning environment kept logs of the participants' interactions, including actions like key presses, button presses, and code snapshots.

Phase 1: Scaffolding Phase (25 minutes). The goal of the scaffolding phase was to provide foundational knowledge that could be applied in the fadeout phase. The scaffolding phase consisted of a set of 18 programming exercises. Each exercise had a problem statement, an explanatory text, and a set of hints. Participants needed to write working Python code to solve the problem in each exercise. Hints ranged from further instructional explanation of the key concept(s) in an exercise, code examples illustrating the concept(s), up to complete solutions for an exercise (bottom-out hint).

The exercises were predominately math-based geometry problems with numeric inputs. This topic was chosen because it is often used in introductory programming courses. Complexity and difficulty of exercises increased throughout the scaffolding phase. This was accomplished by introducing one new concept or incrementally adding to previous concepts. Explanations were precise but not exhaustive enough for participants to solve the exercises without thinking of some possible solutions, experimenting with code, or resorting to using hints when they became stuck.

One example of an exercise participants would encounter during the experiment is as follows: "Suppose you want to calculate the mileage you are getting in your car easily. Create a program to assist in this, first by prompting for *Miles driven:* and then *Gallons of gas used:* Store each of these values in a variable and print out the resulting miles per gallon." This exercise represents an incremental step from reading user input and storing it as a variable (previous exercise) to reading two different inputs into different variables (current exercise).

Participants could complete as many exercises as possible in the 20 minute time limit for the scaffolding phase before being automatically directed to the fadeout phase. On average, participants completed 16 exercises (*SD* = 3.40).

Phase 2: Fadeout (15 minutes). The fadeout phase consisted of two exercises that integrated the individual concepts covered in the scaffolding phase. The exercises in this phase were considerably more difficult compared to the scaffolding phase. No hints or explanation were available during the fadeout phase to encourage unscaffolded problem solving. The first fadeout exercise was a debugging exercise, in which participants were given code containing a variety of errors and were asked to correct the code. Five minutes were allocated for this debugging task. The second component of the fadeout phase consisted of a difficult programming exercise requiring participants to produce eleven lines of code. It also required the use of an output formatting technique that the participants were not familiar with, thereby ensuring every participant would encounter at least one logical impasse during this phase. Ten minutes were allocated for this exercise, but no student completed the exercise in that time.

Phase 3: Retrospective Affect Judgment. The retrospective affect judgment phase commenced immediately after the programming session. It involved the participant providing judgments of their emotions while viewing synchronized videos of their face and screen recorded during the session. Participants provided judgments on 13 emotions, which were mostly selected from Pekrun's taxonomy of academic emotions [15]. These included basic emotions (anger, disgust, fear, sadness, surprise, happiness), learning-centered emotions (anxiety, boredom, frustration, flow/engaged, curiosity, confusion/uncertainty) and neutral (no apparent feeling).

Emotion ratings were made at 100 points over the course of viewing the videos. The judgment points were roughly chosen to correspond with interaction events such as key presses, running of code, or displaying a new exercise. Rating points were pseudo-randomly selected with a minimum of 20 seconds between points to alleviate annoyance from making judgments in quick succession. At each rating point participants were required to select an emotion as the primary emotion they were experiencing at the time, and were also given the choice of reporting a secondary emotion.

It is important to mention three points pertaining to the affect judgment methodology. This procedure was adopted because it affords monitoring participants' affective states at multiple points, with minimal task interference, and without participants knowing that these states are being monitored while they complete the learning task. Second, this retrospective affect-judgment method has been previously validated [16], and analyses comparing these offline affect judgments with online measures including self-reports and observations by judges have produced similar distributions of emotions [17, 18]. Third, the offline affect annotations obtained via this protocol correlate with online recordings of facial activity and body movements in expected directions [19]. Although no method is without its limitations, the present method appears to be a viable approach to track emotions at a relatively fine-grained temporal resolution.

2.4 Assessing Performance

The participants' cumulative score (see above) was used as a measure of performance in the scaffolding phase. The highest possible score was 67, while the lowest possible score was a 0. Scores for the fadeout phase of the study were calculated differently because there were no hints. Instead, we considered the number of lines of code in a participant's solution that corresponded semantically to lines in a "correct" solution. The correct solution was very specific in the debugging task since participants were given code with predetermined errors. Thus, we were able to use a text processing script to remove formatting differences and determine the number of lines correctly debugged, which was used as the score (maximum of 9). For the coding portion of the fadeout phase, two trained human judges compared lines from participants' code against a correct solution to determine the score (maximum of 11). The human judges independently scored every solution and resolved any differences.

3 Results and Discussion

Which Emotions Are Most Prevalent Overall and across Different Phases? A total of 3,035 affect judgments were collected from the 29 participants. Only 589 of the judgments included a secondary affect rating, and five of the participants never reported a secondary emotion at any point. Because of the paucity of secondary emotion reports, we will not consider them any further in these results.

The analyses proceeded by computing proportion scores for each participant's primary emotion reports. The distribution of emotion proportions violated assumptions of normality, so nonparametric tests are used for all analyses. Table 1 presents mean proportions of emotion reports overall and across the two phases of the study.

The results indicated that flow/engaged, confusion/uncertainty, frustration and boredom (henceforth referred to as frequent emotions) plus neutral accounted for approximately 86% of all affect judgments, while the other eight emotions (curiosity, happiness, anxiety, surprise, anger, disgust, fear, and sadness) only accounted for 14% of the emotion reports. Moreover, Wilcoxon signed rank tests (with a Bonferroni correction of .00125 to account for multiple tests) indicated that the four frequent emotions and neutral occured at significantly ($p < .05$ unless specified otherwise) higher rates than the eight less frequent emotions. This finding is in line with previous research suggesting that boredom, engagement/flow, confusion, and frustration are the emotions that routinely occur during learning with technology [20]. Hence, the subsequent analyses will focus on these four states as well as neutral.

We compared the emotions reported during the two phases of the study (scaffolding and fadeout). Five Wilcoxon signed rank tests, one for each emotion (plus neutral), revealed that there were significant differences for frustration and neutral. There was also a marginally significant difference for boredom. Results indicated there was more neutral reported in the scaffolding phase ($M = .187$, $SD = .187$) compared to the fadeout phase ($M = .097$, $SD = .178$), ($Z = -3.01$, $p = .003$). A different pattern was revealed for frustration in that there was less frustration reported in the scaffolding phase ($M = .109$, $SD = .085$) than the fadeout phase ($M = .184$, $SD = .152$), ($Z = -2.56$, $p = .010$). Similarly, there was less boredom reported in the scaffolding phase ($M = .104$, $SD = .131$) compared to the fadeout phase ($M = .146$, $SD = .210$), ($Z = -1.71$, $p = .088$). These findings are particularly interesting because of the differences in the two phases. The scaffolding phase gave students hints and explanations, while the fadeout phase did not provide any assistance. This might have caused more frustration in the fadeout phase since there was no easy way to resolve any difficulties encountered, though other factors such as increased problem difficulty and time within the session may also be influential here.

Table 1. Proportion of emotions made in retrospective affect judgment

Emotion	Overall	Scaffolding	Fadeout
Flow/Engaged	.231	.233	.229
Confusion/Uncertainty	.217	.207	.235
Frustration	.139	.109	.184
Boredom	.118	.104	.147
Curiosity	.059	.073	.034
Happiness	.030	.042	.011
Anxiety	.022	.013	.038
Surprise	.014	.019	.004
Anger	.009	.004	.018
Disgust	.006	.008	.003
Fear	.000	.001	.000
Sadness	.000	.001	.000
Neutral	.153	.187	.097

How Are Student Behaviors Linked to Their Emotions? To investigate this question, we grouped the different student behaviors into three broad categories: *idling*, *constructing,* and *running*. When participants were entering code into the learning environment interface, they were *constructing*. When executing code either via a Run or Submit interaction event, they were *running* code, and they were *idling* when otherwise not interacting with the interface.

We computed proportional scores for each emotion and neutral with respect to each of these three behaviors (see Table 2 for mean proportions of emotions for these behaviors). We then computed five separate Friedman tests for each emotion and neutral in order to test for differences in emotions based on the three types of student behavior. Tests for differences in flow/engagement, frustration, and boredom were significant, $p < .01$. There was also a trend in differences for confusion, $\chi2(2, N = 29) = 4.42$, $p = .110$. Post-hoc comparisons in the form of Wilcoxon signed rank tests with a Bonferroni adjustment ($\alpha = .016$) were conducted in order to further probe these differences. The results indicated that flow/engagement was reported at higher rates when students were *constructing*, followed by *running*, and *idling* (constructing > running > idling). There was significantly more boredom when students were *idling* compared to *running* (idling > running). Frustration was greater when students were *running* compared to when students were *constructing* or *idling*, which were statistically equivalent (running > constructing = idling). Finally, confusion was greater when students were *idling* compared to *constructing*, while both were similar to *running* (idling > constructing).

These patterns were quite revealing about the types of emotions that occurred based on the behavior exhibited. Students experienced more engagement but also frustration when they were engaging in behaviors that require some activity (e.g., running and constructing). Idling might be indicative of two different emotions, namely boredom or confusion. On one hand, students might stop interacting to idle because they are disengaged. On the other, idling might indicate confusion that requires some processing before moving forward. A finer-grained analysis of behavior is needed to resolve these two alternatives.

Table 2. Means and standard deviations (in parentheses) for the proportion of emotions and neutral for each type of student behavior

Emotion	Constructing	Idling	Running
Boredom	.117 (.162)	.156 (.162)	.087 (.135)
Confusion	.176 (.127)	.236 (.134)	.241 (.144)
Flow/Engaged	.303 (.245)	.220 (.181)	.151 (.145)
Frustration	.119 (.100)	.124 (.110)	.193 (.124)
Neutral	.189 (.214)	.150 (.165)	.126 (.138)

What Is the Relationship between Emotion and Performance? On average, students scored 52.1 ($SD = 4.24$) out of the maximum scaffolding score of 67 (77.6%). Scores were considerably lower for the more difficult fadeout debugging ($M = 4.24$, $SD = 2.64$; 47.1% out of maximum 9), and fadeout coding ($M = 5.66$, $SD = 3.64$; 51.5% out of a maximum of 11) portions of the study. We correlated these scores with the proportion of emotions reported at corresponding portions of the study and the resultant Spearman correlation matrix is presented in Table 3. It should be noted that although we tested the significance of the correlational coefficients, our small sample size of 29 participants does not yield sufficient statistical power to detect small ($rho \approx .1$) and medium sized effects ($rho \approx .3$). Hence, in addition to discussing significant effects we also consider non-significant correlations of .2 or higher to be meaningful because these might be significant with a larger sample.

Table 3. Correlations between emotions and performance

Emotion	Scaffolding	Fadeout: Debugging	Fadeout: Programming
Boredom	.239	*-.341	**-.459
Flow/Engaged	-.061	.254	**.512
Confusion/Uncertainty	**-.407	-.001	-.207
Frustration	-.031	.041	-.026
Neutral	.188	-.087	-.036

Note. **$p < .05$; *$p < .10$.

The results were illuminating in a number of respects. Consistent with our expectations, boredom was negatively correlated with performance during both parts of the fadeout phase. However, boredom was positively correlated with performance during the scaffolding phase, which was contrary to our expectations. This might be attributed to students finding the exercises in the scaffolding phase to be less challenging, presumably due to the presence of hints and explanations. Flow/engagement was not correlated with performance during the scaffolding phase, but was a positive predictor of performance in both the debugging and programming parts of the fadeout phase, which is what we might expect.

Confusion/uncertainty had a large negative effect on performance during the scaffolding phase, suggesting that much of the confusion went unresolved. Confusion was not correlated with performance in the debugging portion of the fadeout phase, but had a smaller negative correlation with performance during the programming part of the fadeout phase. Finally, we were surprised to discover that frustration was not correlated with performance during both the scaffolding and fadeout phases, a finding (or lack thereof) that warrants further analysis.

4 General Discussion

We performed a fine-grained analysis of the emotional states of novice computer programming students with an eye for applying any insights gleaned towards the development of computerized interventions that respond to emotion in addition to cognition. We found that flow/engaged, confusion, frustration and boredom represented the majority of emotion self-reports, thereby suggesting that an affect-sensitive intervention should focus on these states. We also found that the emotions varied as a function of instructional scaffolds and were systematically linked to different student behaviors (idling, constructing code, running code), a finding which would pave the way for developing automated interactional- and contextual-based methods to track these emotions. Finally, our results revealed that the emotions were not merely incidental to the learning process; they also correlated with performance in expected and surprising ways. In general, but noting exceptions discussed above, performance was negatively correlated with boredom and confusion, positively correlated with flow/engaged and not correlated with frustration.

There are some limitations with the present study that need to be addressed in the future. First, self-reports are biased by the honesty of the participants, so future studies should combine additional method in addition to or in lieu of self-reports. Possible methods include trained observers, physiological sensors, and peers that may be able to pick up on more nuanced indicators of affective states. Second, the sample size was also quite small, which limited the statistical power required to detect smaller effects. Third, the participants were sampled from a single university, which might not be reflective of the body of novice computer programmers as a whole. Fourth, the course-grained nature of some of the logs made it difficult to disambiguate when students read explanations from other idling activities. This can be resolved by redesigning the interface or by using an eye tracker to determine what part of the interface students are focusing on while not interacting.

Future work will focus on collecting additional data to alleviate the limitations discussed above. We will also use log data (e.g. keystrokes, syntax errors, hint usage) and video recordings to build models that detect novice programmer emotions, using established computer vision and machine learning techniques [21]. The long-term goal is to use these detectors to trigger automated interventions that are informed by affect. It is our hope that an affect-sensitive learning environment for novice computer programmers equipped with intelligent handling of emotions might contribute to a more technical workforce to handle the demands of the age of Big Data.

Acknowledgment. This research was supported by the National Science Foundation (NSF) (ITR 0325428, HCC 0834847, DRL 1235958). Any opinions, findings and conclusions, or recommendations expressed in this paper are those of the authors and do not necessarily reflect the views of NSF.

References

1. Haungs, M., Clark, C., Clements, J., Janzen, D.: Improving first-year success and retention through interest-based CS0 courses. In: Proceedings of the 43rd ACM Technical Symposium on Computer Science Education, pp. 589–594. ACM, New York (2012)
2. Alspaugh, C.A.: Identification of Some Components of Computer Programming Aptitude. Journal for Research in Mathematics Education 3, 89–98 (1972)
3. Blignaut, P., Naude, A.: The influence of temperament style on a student's choice of and performance in a computer programming course. Computers in Human Behavior 24, 1010–1020 (2008)
4. Law, K.M.Y., Lee, V.C.S., Yu, Y.T.: Learning motivation in e-learning facilitated computer programming courses. Computers & Education 55, 218–228 (2010)
5. Shute, V.J., Kyllonen, P.C.: Modeling Individual Differences in Programming Skill Acquisition. Technical report no. AFHRL-TP-90-76, Air Force Human Resources Laboratory, Brooks AFB, TX (1990)

6. Csikszentmihalyi, M.: Flow: The psychology of optimal experience. Harper and Row, New York (1990)
7. Lee, D.M.C., Rodrigo, M.M.T., Baker, R.S.J.d., Sugay, J.O., Coronel, A.: Exploring the Relationship between Novice Programmer Confusion and Achievement. In: D'Mello, S., Graesser, A., Schuller, B., Martin, J.-C. (eds.) ACII 2011, Part I. LNCS, vol. 6974, pp. 175–184. Springer, Heidelberg (2011)
8. Burleson, W., Picard, R.W.: Affective agents: Sustaining motivation to learn through failure and a state of stuck. In: Social and Emotional Intelligence in Learning Environments Workshop In Conjunction with the 7th International Conference on Intelligent Tutoring Systems, Maceio-Alagoas, Brasil (2004)
9. D'Mello, S., Graesser, A.: Dynamics of affective states during complex learning. Learning and Instruction 22, 145–157 (2012)
10. Larson, R.W., Richards, M.H.: Boredom in the middle school years: Blaming schools versus blaming students. American Journal of Education 99, 418–443 (1991)
11. Khan, I.A., Hierons, R.M., Brinkman, W.P.: Mood independent programming. In: Proceedings of the 14th European Conference on Cognitive Ergonomics: Invent! Explore!, London, United Kingdom, pp. 28–31 (2007)
12. Rodrigo, M.M.T., Baker, R.S.J.d.: Coarse-grained detection of student frustration in an introductory programming course. In: Proceedings of the Fifth International Workshop on Computing Education Research, pp. 75–80. ACM, New York (2009)
13. Rodrigo, M.M.T., Baker, R.S.J.d., Jadud, M.C., Amarra, A.C.M., Dy, T., Espejo-Lahoz, M.B.V., Lim, S.A.L., Pascua, S.A.M.S., Sugay, J.O., Tabanao, E.S.: Affective and behavioral predictors of novice programmer achievement. SIGCSE Bulletin 41, 156–160 (2009)
14. Grafsgaard, J.F., Fulton, R.M., Boyer, K.E., Wiebe, E.N., Lester, J.C.: Multimodal analysis of the implicit affective channel in computer-mediated textual communication. In: Proceedings of the 14th ACM International Conference on Multimodal Interaction, pp. 145–152. ACM, New York (2012)
15. Pekrun, R., Stephens, E.J.: Academic emotions. In: Harris, K.R., Graham, S., Urdan, T., Graham, S., Royer, J.M., Zeidner, M. (eds.) APA Educational Psychology Handbook. Individual differences and cultural and contextual factors, vol. 2, pp. 3–31. American Psychological Association, Washington, DC (2012)
16. Rosenberg, E.L., Ekman, P.: Coherence between expressive and experiential systems in emotion. Cognition & Emotion 8, 201–229 (1994)
17. Craig, S., D'Mello, S., Witherspoon, A., Graesser, A.: Emote aloud during learning with AutoTutor: Applying the Facial Action Coding System to cognitive–affective states during learning. Cognition & Emotion 22, 777–788 (2008)
18. Craig, S., Graesser, A., Sullins, J., Gholson, B.: Affect and learning: An exploratory look into the role of affect in learning with AutoTutor. Journal of Educational Media 29, 241–250 (2004)
19. D'Mello, S.K., Graesser, A.: Multimodal semi-automated affect detection from conversational cues, gross body language, and facial features. User Modeling and User-Adapted Interaction 20, 147–187 (2010)
20. D'Mello, S.: A selective meta-analysis on the relative incidence of discrete affective states during learning with technology (in review)
21. Blikstein, P.: Using learning analytics to assess students' behavior in open-ended programming tasks. In: Proceedings of the 1st International Conference on Learning Analytics and Knowledge, pp. 110–116. ACM, New York (2011)

Defining the Behavior of an Affective Learning Companion in the Affective Meta-tutor Project

Sylvie Girard, Maria Elena Chavez-Echeagaray, Javier Gonzalez-Sanchez, Yoalli Hidalgo-Pontet, Lishan Zhang, Winslow Burleson, and Kurt VanLehn

Arizona State University, Computing, Informatics, and Decision Systems Engineering, Tempe, AZ, 85281, U.S.A.
{sylvie.girard,helenchavez,javiergs,lzhang90,yhidalgo, winslow.burleson,kurt.vanlehn}@asu.edu

Abstract. Research in affective computing and educational technology has shown the potential of affective interventions to increase student's self-concept and motivation while learning. Our project aims to investigate whether the use of affective interventions in a meta-cognitive tutor can help students achieve deeper modeling of dynamic systems by being persistent in their use of meta-cognitive strategies during and after tutoring. This article is an experience report on how we designed and implemented the affective intervention. (The meta-tutor is described in a separate paper.) We briefly describe the theories of affect underlying the design and how the agent's affective behavior is defined and implemented. Finally, the evaluation of a detector-driven categorization of student behavior, that guides the agent's affective interventions, against a categorization performed by human coders, is presented.

Keywords: affective computing, affective learning companion, intelligent tutoring system, robust learning, meta-cognition.

1 Introduction

Research in AIED has taken interest in the potential of using interventions of affective nature in intelligent tutoring systems to improve learning [2, 19, 23] and motivation [8, 13, 20] and to reduce undesirable behaviors such as gaming [3-5] and undesirable affective states such as disengagement [17]. The interventions have been designed to either respond to student' specific behavior [14, 19], or to elicit a certain emotional state in the student [9], often by providing cognitive support and scaffolds within the learning environment.

The hypothesis of our project [24] is that affective interventions in a meta-cognitive tutor can help students achieve robust learning by being persistent in their use of meta-cognitive strategies during and after tutoring. In order to test this hypothesis, an affective intervention was designed, using an affective learning companion to convey the affective message. This article describes the design of the affective intervention. In the first section, a three-dimensional design space of affective interventions is outlined, along with our choice along each dimension. The second

K. Yacef et al. (Eds.): AIED 2013, LNAI 7926, pp. 21–30, 2013.

section describes the implementation of the design using categorization of student behavior based on log data detectors. The last section describes an empirical evaluation of the classification accuracy.

2 Design of the Affective Intervention

2.1 Definition of the Affective Intervention

Over the past decade, numerous affective interventions have been designed and evaluated with respect to alternate techniques in the field of educational technology. In order to define a design space of the affective intervention for the AMT project, a review of current research was performed. The design space has three dimensions: mechanism for delivery of the affective intervention, timing of the intervention, and type of message delivered during the intervention. We briefly describe each dimension, then indicate where along it our design falls.

***Mechanism:* How Is the Intervention Message Conveyed?**

There are various ways to intervene affectively in tutoring systems, ranging from the presentation of an affective message via a user-interface component [2, 19], to the use of bio-feedback and affect-sensitive tutors that respond to the user's emotional state [9]. Some results [2,8,12,23] have shown the potential of using pedagogical agents, or Affective Learning Companion (ALC), to portray the affective message. These interventions involve design decisions concerning the different components of a pedagogical agent that can impact learning, such as the presence of facial expressions or deictic gestures [2,14], vocal intonation [6], gender [2,8,16], or ethnicity and student's cultural background [12,19].

In this phase of our project affective messages in the form of pop-up text messages are provided by a pedagogical agent, represented by an image with neutral facial expression. The agent is a humanoid comic-like gendered character, representing a student of a similar age to our target population (16-21 yrs olds). This decision took into account the results from [12] for the agent's image type, and [2, 23] where pairing students' gender to the agent's gender was found beneficial for user's self-concept and learning.

***Timing*: When Is the Affective Intervention Happening in the Learning Process?**

The affective intervention can happen before any tutoring takes place, between learning tasks during the tutoring, and at different moments while a learner is performing a specific task or learning a specific set of skills. In order to describe when the affective intervention occurs, we first must describe the instruction.

The AMT software teaches students how to create and test a model of a dynamic system. The instruction is divided into three phases: (1) an *introduction* phase where students learn basic concepts of dynamic system model construction and how to use the interface; (2) a *training* phase where students are guided by a tutor and a meta-tutor to create several models; and (3) a *transfer* phase where all scaffolding is removed from software and students are free to model as they wish. The tutor gives feedback and corrections on domain mistakes. The meta-tutor requires students to follow a goal-reduction problem solving strategy, using the Target Node Strategy [24], which decomposes the overall modeling problem into a series of "atomic" modeling problems whose small scope encourages students to engage in deep modeling rather than shallow guess-based modeling strategies. Using various measures of deep and shallow learning [5], an experiment demonstrated that requiring students to follow this strategy during training did indeed increase the frequency of deep modeling compared to students who were not required to follow the strategy. However, the effect was not strong, and the amount of deep modeling could certainly be improved. The goal of the ALC is to encourage students to do even more deep modeling.

The pedagogical agent conveying the affective message in AMT intervenes at three different moments of software interaction:

- *At the beginning and the end of the introduction*: These interventions aim to introduce the agent and its role in the instruction, as well as building rapport between the student and the ALC which has been shown in [7] to help keep students motivated and on task.
- *Between each modeling task in the training phase*: The main purpose of these interventions is to invite the student to reflect on his/her actions and decisions during the task, as well as maintain the interest of the student. As performing a given task can require from 3 to 15 minutes, the ALC intervenes after each task rather than intervening after a pre-defined number of tasks as in [1,2,23].
- *At the end of the training phase*: This intervention tries to convince the student to persevere in the use of the deep modeling strategy during the forthcoming transfer phase.

Type: What Type of Message Is Given/Transmitted During the Intervention?

Finally, the third dimension of the intervention represents its affective or motivational content: what does the ALC say and what emotional tone does it use when saying it? Our design is based on the following policies:

- Baylor and Kim [6] showed that a combination of cognitive and affective interventions (the "Mentor") led to better student self-regulation and self-efficacy than the presence of either type of intervention alone. Our meta-tutor and tutor already provide cognitive information without affect (like the "Expert" of [6]). To avoid boring redundancy, the ALC presents as little cognitive and meta-cognitive content as possible (just enough to maintain context) while presenting motivational messages (described below) in a friendly, encouraging manner.

The content of the intervention has been designed to help low-achievers and shallow learners get back on track and avoid gaming [3-5, 9, 19], while not interrupting high-achievers who might not benefit from an affective intervention [2, 19, 23]. It involves the following theories:

- *Dweck's "the mind is a muscle" theory* [10]: the more you exercise your mind, the more competent you become. Before the introduction phase, all students read a text introducing this theory. The between-task interventions reinforce the message by mentioning passages of the reading and referring to how different activities help to improve the brain's function.
- *Attribution theory* [21]: failures should be attributed to the difficulty of the task or lack of preparation, whereas success should be attributed to the student's effort.
- *Theory of reflection* [15]: Students have been found to be more receptive after completing a problem rather than during problem solving [15]. Every time a task is finished the ALC invites students to reflect on what they have experienced. It encourages them to replicate the action if it was positive or to change the action if it was negative.
- *Use of a meta-cognitive representation of student's modeling depth* [1, 22]: Alongside the ALC is a bar showing the depth of the student's modeling while working on the current task. That is, it shows the proportion of student actions that were classified as deep, based on the detectors described in [11]. ALC messages often refer to the modeling depth bar in combination with the other theories listed above.

The following section illustrates how we defined the ALC behavior by using learners' prior interactions with the system.

3 Implementing the ALC's Behavior

While students learn, their motivation and attention to detail can fluctuate. In the context of a problem solving activity requiring modeling skills, the depth of the modeling techniques used by students can also vary. The ALC should adapt to these fluctuations, presenting different affective messages depending on the student's recent behavior. Simply mapping the student's behavior onto competence would not suffice, so we defined several behavioral classifications such as "engaged," "gaming" and "lack of planning." We then defined log data detectors relevant to each behavioral classification. We also paired affective messages with each behavioral classification. In the first subsection, the detectors that measure the user's behavior are described. The second sub-section then describes the behavioral classification, how they were created and how they are mapped to the detectors' output.

3.1 How to Detect Shallow Modeling Practices?

The detectors process a stream of user interface activity (log data) and output behavioral measures. The detectors require no human intervention and run in real time, because they will eventually be used to regulate the system's responses to the student. Our detectors extend the gaming detectors of [4] by including measures relevant to depth of modeling and other constructs.

Nine detectors were defined. The first six detectors were based on classifying and counting segments in the log, where a segment corresponds roughly to a correct step in the construction or debugging of a model. Each segment holds the value of the detector that best represents the situation, for example a student showing both a single_answer and good_method behavior would be defined as following a good_method behavior for this segment. The output per task for each detector is a proportion: the number of segments meeting its criteria divided by the total number of segments in the log for the task. Based on an extensive video analysis of student's past actions and HCI task modeling techniques [11], six segmental detectors were defined:

- GOOD_METHOD: The students followed a deep method in their modeling. They used the help tools[1] provided appropriately including the one for planning each part of the model.
- VERIFY_INFO: Before checking their step for correctness, students looked back at the problem description, the information provided by the instruction slides, or the meta-tutor agent.
- SINGLE_ANSWER: The student's initial response for this step was correct, and the student did not change it.
- SEVERAL_ANSWERS: The student made more than one attempt at completing the step. This includes guessing and gaming the system.
- UNDO_GOOD_WORK: This action suggests a modeling misconception on the students' part. One example is when students try to run the model when not all of the nodes are fully defined.
- GIVEUP: The student gave up on finding the answer and clicked on the "give up" button.

A limitation of the above detectors is the inability to distinguish between a student trying hard to complete a step but making a lot of errors versus a student gaming or guessing a lot. This led to the development of two additional detectors based on earlier work in detecting robust learning and gaming [5, 9, 18, 23]: (1) the time spent on task and (2) the number of times the learner misused the "run model" button. While the former is self-explanatory and commonly used in ITSs, the latter is specific to the AMT software. As students construct a system dynamics model, they can reach a point where all elements are sufficiently defined to "run the model" (the model is correct in terms of syntax) and therefore test whether its semantics corresponds to the system they were asked to model. Students clicking on this button before the model's syntax is correct, or clicking repetitively on the model without making changes once it is correct in syntax but not in semantics, is considered shallow behavior that shows a lack of planning, a lack of understanding of the task to perform, or a tendency to guess/game the answer rather than think it through.

---

[1] Two help systems are available to users: (1) referring back to the instructions always available for viewing, and (2) looking at the problem situation where all details of the dynamic system to model are described.

The ninth and last detector is a function of the six segmental detectors. It is intended to measure the overall depth of the students' modeling. Although it is used as an outcome measure in the transfer phase, it helps drive the ALC during the training phase. It is based on considering two measures (GOOD_ANSWER, VERIFY_INFO) to indicate deep modeling, one measure (SINGLE_ANSWER) to be neutral, and three measures (SEVERAL_ANSWERS, UNDO_GOOD_WORK, and GIVE_UP) to indicate shallow modeling.

In order to facilitate writing rules that defined the students' behavioral category (e.g., engaged, gaming, etc.) in terms of the detector outputs, we triaged the output of each detector so it reports its output as either low, medium and high. The rules are mostly driven by the values: low and high. To implement the triage, we collected logs from 23 students. For each of the nine detectors, we determine the 33rd and 66th percentile points and used them as thresholds. Thus, for each detector, roughly a third of the 23 students were reported as low, as medium and as high. Because the tasks vary in complexity, different thresholds were calculated for each task.

3.2 From Shallow Learning Detection to the ALC Intervention

A series of 6 types of ALC behavioral categories were defined using video analysis of past user's actions on software. Human coders reviewed screen-capture videos and verbal protocols of a pool of 20 students using the meta-cognitive tutor. Following their recommendations and a review of messages transmitted in affective interventions in the literature, the following set of ALC categories was defined:

- *Good Modeling*: The students think about their steps, do not hesitate to go back to the introduction or the situation to look for answers, use the plan feature judiciously in their creation of nodes, and have a minimum of guessing and wrong actions performed on task.
- *Engaged*: The students respond by thinking about the problem rather than guessing, refer back to the instructions or problem situation when they find themselves stuck rather than trying all possible answers. The students take a medium to a high amount of time to complete the task, favoring reflection to quick decisions.
- *Lack of Planning*: The students answer quickly, relying heavily on the feedback given in the interface to get the next steps. While the students sometimes refer to instructions and the situation, they only use the features when they are stuck, not when planning the modeling activity.
- *Help Avoidance*: The students attempt a lot of answers without referring back to the instructions or the problem situation. They rarely make use of the information filled in the plan tab and try to skip the meta-tutor instructions. Instead of using help when they are confused, they spend a lot of time trying to get the interface green or give up rather than thinking about the problem.
- *Gaming*: The students try multiple possible answers within the interface without pausing long enough to think about the problem. They may give up when this random guessing doesn't work. They rarely refer to the instructions or the problem situation and pay little attention to the plan tab or the meta-tutor instructions.
- *Shallow Modeling (default, not recognized as the above mentioned categories)*: The students tend to try several answers on the interface rather than pausing and thinking about the problem. They sometimes refer back to the instructions and problem situation, but not frequently.

Table 1. Examples of ALC intervention between-task

Behavior	Example
Good Modeling	You're a Green Master! What was your secret? I know… you make your reading count and thus your brain is getting rewired.
Engaged	Even though it might take a little bit longer, it is worth it to explore the available resources. You are giving your brain a great workout. Look at that green bar! Keep up the good work!
Lack of Planning	Going fast is good, but it doesn't always help you reach your potential… Why don't you stop and think about what you want to model when you are confused. To make more of the bar green, try re-reading the problem description and noting what it asks you to do.
Help Avoidance	It might be worth rereading the problem description and paying more attention to the suggestions presented by the pop-up messages. Our brain needs to engage the material deeply so it can create good connections. That's how we can get more of the bar green!
Gaming	Hmmm! It seems that you need to put quality time into your tasks. Maybe "trial and error" is not always the best strategy. Although you might move quickly through the problem, your brain doesn't get a workout, and it shows in the length of the green bar.
Shallow Modeling (default)	You are getting there! Look at that bar! But remember that to strengthen your brain you have to engage the problem and all its details.

Once these six behaviors were defined, human coders applied them to a sample of 100 tasks and students. The outputs of the detectors on the sample were obtained, and rules were defined to map their values to the behavioral categories.

Using the theories of affect defined in section 2, ALC messages were created for each behavior in order to provide affective support to the learner. A stereotypical message was first created, as illustrated in table 1, for each behavior. The research group then created many synonymous versions of each message, so that the ALC would not repeat itself and thus reduce the student's perception of the ALC as an artificial agent. A separate message was produced for the first and last task performed by the user in the training phase, in order to introduce and wrap-up the ALC interventions.

4 Evaluation of the Behavior's Accuracy

Before working with students, we first tested the detectors and behavioral categorizer via test cases. We wrote scenarios of software use that typified each of the six behavioral categories. A member of the research group enacted each scenario, and we confirmed that the detector outputs fell in the anticipated range (low, typical or high) and that the rules assigned the anticipated behavioral classification.

The second part of the validation of ALC behaviors involved pilot subjects and human coders. Seven college students used the AMT system with the ALC turned on. They were asked to speak aloud as they worked. Their voice and screen were recorded as videos. A sample video was made from screen recordings. It included 15 tasks. Three human coders watched each task, paying attention to the depth of modeling shown by the student's actions. Independently of what the software chose, they chose the ALC intervention that they felt best matched the student's modeling practices. A multi-rater and pairwise kappa was then performed, and showed a sufficient level of inter-reliance with a level of .896.

5 Conclusion and Future Work

This article described the development of an affective intervention based on an affective learning companion (ALC) that works with a meta-tutor and a tutor. It described the theories of affect underlying the interventions, and how we defined and implemented the ALC's behavior. The ALC's messages were based on deciding which of six behavioral categories best represented the student's work on the most recently completed task. This categorization was driven by log data. When compared to human coders working with screen captures and verbal reports of students, the detector-driven categorizations agreed with the human coding with a kappa of .896.

The next step in the research is to measure the benefits of this version of the ALC in a two-condition experiment. One group of students will use the system with the ALC turned on during the training phase, and the other will used it without the ALC turned on. We hypothesize that this will cause measurable differences in the depth of students' modeling during the transfer phase.

The forthcoming evaluation will also have students wear physiological sensors while they work so that we can collect calibration data that will be used to supplement the detectors' assessment of the students' affective state. This extra information will be used to help define affective interventions not only between tasks but also while the learner performs on task.

Acknowledgements. This material is based upon work supported by the National Science Foundation under Grant No. 0910221.

References

1. Arroyo, I., Ferguson, K., Johns, J., Dragon, T., Meheranian, H., Fisher, D., et al.: Repairing disengagement with non-invasive interventions. Frontiers in Artificial Intelligence and Applications, vol. 158, p. 195 (2007)
2. Arroyo, I., Woolf, B.P., Cooper, D.G., Burleson, W., Muldner, K.: The Impact of Animated Pedagogical Agents on Girls' and Boys' Emotions, Attitudes, Behaviors and Learning. In: Proceedings of the 2011 IEEE 11th International Conference on Advanced Learning Technologies. Proceedings from ICALT 2011, Washington, DC, USA (2011)
3. Baker, R.S.J.d., et al.: Adapting to when students game an intelligent tutoring system. In: Ikeda, M., Ashley, K.D., Chan, T.-W. (eds.) ITS 2006. LNCS, vol. 4053, pp. 392–401. Springer, Heidelberg (2006)
4. Baker, R.S.J.d., Gowda, S.M., Corbett, A.T.: Towards predicting future transfer of learning. In: Biswas, G., Bull, S., Kay, J., Mitrovic, A. (eds.) AIED 2011. LNCS, vol. 6738, pp. 23–30. Springer, Heidelberg (2011)

5. Baker, R.S.J.d., Gowda, S.M., Corbett, A.T., Ocumpaugh, J.: Towards automatically detecting whether student learning is shallow. In: Cerri, S.A., Clancey, W.J., Papadourakis, G., Panourgia, K. (eds.) ITS 2012. LNCS, vol. 7315, pp. 444–453. Springer, Heidelberg (2012)
6. Baylor, A.L., Kim, Y.: Simulating instructional roles through pedagogical agents. International Journal of Artificial Intelligence in Education 15(2), 95–115 (2005)
7. Bickmore, T.W., Picard, R.W.: Establishing and maintaining long-term human-computer relationships. ACM Transactions on Computer-Human Interaction (TOCHI) 12(2), 293–327 (2005)
8. Burleson, W., Picard, R.W.: Gender-Specific Approaches to Developing Emotionally Intelligent Learning Companions. IEEE Intelligent Systems 22(4), 62–69 (2007), doi:10.1109/MIS.2007.69
9. D'Mello, S.K., Lehman, B., Person, N.: Monitoring affect states during effortful problem solving activities. International Journal of Artificial Intelligence in Education 20(4), 361–389 (2010), doi:10.3233/JAI-2010-012
10. Dweck, C.: Self-Theories: Their role in motivation, personality and development. Psychology Press, Philadelphia (2000)
11. Girard, S., Zhang, L., Hidalgo-Pontet, Y., VanLehn, K., Burleson, W., Chavez-Echeagary, M.E., Gonzalez-Sanchez, J.: Using HCI task modeling techniques to measure how deeply students model. In: Chad Lane, H., Yacef, K., Mostow, J., Pavlik, P. (eds.) AIED 2013. LNCS (LNAI), vol. 7926, pp. 766–769. Springer, Heidelberg (2013)
12. Gulz, A.: Benefits of Virtual Characters in Computer Based Learning Environments: Claims and Evidences. International Journal of Artificial Intelligence in Education 14(3), 313–334 (2004)
13. Gulz, A., Haake, M., Silvervarg, A.: Extending a teachable agent with a social conversation module – effects on student experiences and learning. In: Biswas, G., Bull, S., Kay, J., Mitrovic, A. (eds.) AIED 2011. LNCS, vol. 6738, pp. 106–114. Springer, Heidelberg (2011)
14. Hayashi, Y.: On pedagogical effects of learner-support agents in collaborative interaction. In: Cerri, S.A., Clancey, W.J., Papadourakis, G., Panourgia, K. (eds.) ITS 2012. LNCS, vol. 7315, pp. 22–32. Springer, Heidelberg (2012)
15. Katz, S., Connelly, J., Wilson, C.: Out of the lab and into the classroom: An evaluation of reflective dialogue in Andes. In: Proceeding of the 2007 Conference on Artificial Intelligence in Education: Building Technology Rich Learning Contexts That Work, pp. 425–432 (2007)
16. Kim, Y., Baylor, A., Shen, E.: Pedagogical agents as learning companions: the impact of agent emotion and gender. Journal of Computer Assisted Learning 23(3), 220–234 (2007)
17. Lehman, B., D'Mello, S., Graesser, A.: Interventions to regulate confusion during Learning. In: Cerri, S.A., Clancey, W.J., Papadourakis, G., Panourgia, K. (eds.) ITS 2012. LNCS, vol. 7315, pp. 576–578. Springer, Heidelberg (2012)
18. Muldner, K., Burleson, W., Van de Sande, B., VanLehn, K.: An analysis of students' gaming behaviors in an intelligent tutoring system: predictors and impacts. User Modeling and User-Adapted Interaction 21(1-2), 99m–135m (2011), doi:10.1007/s11257-010-9086-0
19. Rodrigo, M.M.T., Baker, R.S.J.d., Agapito, J., Nabo, J., Repalam, M.C., Reyes, S.S., San Pedro, M.O.C.Z.: The Effects of an Interactive Software Agent on Student Affective Dynamics while Using an Intelligent Tutoring System. IEEE Transactions on Affective Computing 3, 224–236 (2012), doi:http://doi.ieeecomputersociety.org/10.1109/T-AFFC.2011.41

20. Wang, N., Johnson, W.L., Mayer, R.E., Rizzo, P., Shaw, E., Collins, H.: The politeness effect: Pedagogical agents and learning outcomes. International Journal of Human-Computer Studies 66(2), 98–112 (2008), doi:10.1016/j.ijhcs.2007.09.003
21. Weiner, B.: An attributional theory of achievement motivation and emotion. Psychological Review 92(4), 548 (1985)
22. Walonoski, J.A., Heffernan, N.T.: Prevention of off-task gaming behavior in intelligent tutoring systems. In: Ikeda, M., Ashley, K.D., Chan, T.-W. (eds.) ITS 2006. LNCS, vol. 4053, pp. 722–724. Springer, Heidelberg (2006)
23. Woolf, B.P., Arroyo, I., Muldner, K., Burleson, W., Cooper, D.G., Dolan, R., Christopherson, R.M.: The Effect of Motivational Learning Companions on Low Achieving Students and Students with Disabilities. In: Aleven, V., Kay, J., Mostow, J. (eds.) ITS 2010, Part I. LNCS, vol. 6094, pp. 327–337. Springer, Heidelberg (2010)
24. Zhang, L., Burleson, W., Chavez-Echeagaray, M.E., Girard, S., Gonzalez-Sanchez, J., Hidalgo-Pontet, Y., VanLehn, K.: Evaluation of a meta-tutor for constructing models of dynamic systems. In: Chad Lane, H., Yacef, K., Mostow, J., Pavlik, P. (eds.) AIED 2013. LNCS (LNAI), vol. 7926, pp. 666–669. Springer, Heidelberg (2013)

Exploring the Relationships between Design, Students' Affective States, and Disengaged Behaviors within an ITS

Lakshmi S. Doddannara[1], Sujith M. Gowda[1], Ryan S.J.d. Baker[2], Supreeth M. Gowda[1], and Adriana M.J.B. de Carvalho[3]

[1] Worcester Polytechnic Institute, Worcester MA 01609
[2] Teacher's College, Columbia University, New York NY 10027
[3] Carnegie Mellon University, Pittsburgh, PA 15213
{Lakshmi1023,dikajoazeirodebaker}@gmail.com,
{sujithmg,smgowda}@wpi.edu,
baker2@exchange.tc.columbia.edu

Abstract. Recent research has shown that differences in software design and content are associated with differences in how much students game the system and go off-task. In particular the design features of a tutor have found to predict substantial amounts of variance in gaming and off-task behavior. However, it is not yet understood how this influence takes place. In this paper we investigate the relationship between a student's affective state, their tendency to engage in disengaged behavior, and the design aspects of the learning environments, towards understanding the role that affect plays in this process. To investigate this question, we integrate an existing taxonomy of the features of tutor lessons [3] with automated detectors of affect [8]. We find that confusion and frustration are significantly associated with lesson features which were found to be associated with disengaged behavior in past research. At the same time, we find that the affective state of engaged concentration is significantly associated with features associated with lower frequencies of disengaged behavior. This analysis suggests that simple re-designs of tutors along these lines may lead to both better affect and less disengaged behavior.

Keywords: Educational Data Mining, Intelligent Tutoring System, design features, affect, Gaming the System, Off-task behavior.

1 Introduction

There has been considerable research into students' disengaged behaviors in intelligent tutoring systems over the last few years [6, 7, 10, 11, 13, 15, 21, 29, 32]. This work has generally found that a range of disengaged behaviors are associated with negative learning outcomes, including both gaming the system and off-task behavior [cf. 1, 15, 30].

Early work on why students became disengaged investigated whether fairly non-malleable factors such as goal orientation or motivation could predict disengaged behaviors [e.g. 10, 11]. However, recent research has suggested that differences in the

K. Yacef et al. (Eds.): AIED 2013, LNAI 7926, pp. 31–40, 2013.

design of intelligent tutoring systems can also have substantial impacts on student engagement. Relatively simple aspects of design such as the concreteness of problem scenarios and hints were found to predict a considerable proportion of the variance in gaming the system among a group of students using Cognitive Tutor Algebra over the course of a year [6]. Off-task behavior has also been found to vary according to design features such as presence or absence of problem scenarios [3]. These findings suggest that design aspects of tutor lessons may play a significant role in influencing the prevalence of disengaged behavior.

However, we do not yet understand the mechanisms through which differences in the design of tutor lessons may influence disengaged behavior. One mechanism hypothesized in those earlier papers was that affect might be mediating the relationship between tutor design and disengaged behavior. There is evidence for reasonably strong relationships between affect and disengaged behavior. Research in Aplusix and The Incredible Machine (an ITS and a puzzle game) found that boredom preceded and co-occurred with a student's choice to game the system [7]. Boredom has also been found to precede off-task behavior [9] and off-task behavior within the learning environment (also called WTF/"without thinking fastidiously" behavior) within intelligent tutoring systems [32]. There is also evidence that boredom leads to future off-task behavior, within both the Chemistry Virtual Laboratory [9] and Science ASSISTments [22]. However, it is not yet known how strong the relationships are between intelligent tutor design features and affect.

Understanding the factors leading to differences in affect is important by itself as well. There is increasing evidence that differences in affect during use of educational software can have a substantial impact on learning. Craig and colleagues [16] investigated the relationships between learning gains and affect state and found that confusion and flow were positively associated with learning gains but boredom was negatively associated with learning. Pardos and colleagues [30] also found that affect in intelligent tutors can predict not just local learning, but longer-term learning outcomes (state standardized exam scores) as well, specifically finding that boredom is negatively associated with longer-term learning outcomes while engaged concentration (e.g. flow) and frustration were positively associated with learning gains. Evidence in that paper suggested that the context of affect matters more than the overall prevalence, with the relationship between boredom and learning outcomes reversing and becoming positive if the boredom occurs during scaffolding. Other work has suggested that the duration of affect also matters, with brief confusion correlating positively with learning but lengthy confusion correlating negatively with learning [26]. Flow/engaged concentration has also been shown to be associated with longer-term engagement with specific domains [17] One possible explanation for this finding is that positive affect may lead to increased situational interest [23], which in turn has been theorized to lead to greater long term personal interest in the content domain [25].

Given the relationship between disengaged behavior and affect, and the importance of affect in general, it may be worth considering the ways in which tutor design features drive not just disengaged behaviors, but affect as well. In this paper we study the relationships between these three factors. We use an existing taxonomy of the features of tutor lessons [6] to express the differences between lessons. Taxonomies of this nature, also referred to as "design pattern languages" [34], can be useful tools for studying and understanding design. We integrate data from the application of this taxonomy to a set of lessons from an algebra tutor, with predictions from previously published automated detectors of affect [8] and disengaged behaviors [4, 5]. We then conduct correlation mining (with post-hoc controls) to study the relationships between these variables.

2 Data Set

Data was obtained from the PSLC DataShop (dataset: Algebra I 2005-2006 Hampton Only; this data set was chosen because it is readily available in the DataShop and has been studied in other research as well), for 58 students' use of Cognitive Tutor Algebra during an entire school year. A full description of the Cognitive Tutor used in this study can be found in [24]. The data set was composed of approximately 437,000 student transactions (entering an answer or requesting help) in the tutor software. All of the students were enrolled in algebra classes in one high school in the Pittsburgh suburbs which used Cognitive Tutors two days a week, as part of their regular mathematics curriculum. None of the classes were composed predominantly of gifted or special needs students. The students were in the 9th and 10th grades (approximately 14-16 years old). The Cognitive Tutor Algebra curriculum involves 32 lessons, covering a complete selection of topics in algebra, including formulating expressions for word problems, equation solving, and algebraic function graphing.

Data from 10 lessons was eliminated from consideration, to match the original analysis of this data in [6], where the relationship between tutor design and gaming the system was studied. In that original study, lessons were eliminated due to having insufficient data to be able to conduct a sufficient number of text replays to effectively measure gaming the system. On average, each student completed 9.9 tutor lessons (among the set of lessons considered), for a total of 577 student/lesson pairs.

3 Method

In describing the methods sections, first we will describe taxonomic feature generation process and then describe affect detection process used to build machine learned affect models which were in-turn used in this analysis to obtain affect predictions.

3.1 The Cognitive Tutor Lesson Variation Space (CTLVS)

The enumeration of the ways that Cognitive Tutor lessons can differ from one another was originally developed in [6]. This enumeration, in its current form, is called the Cognitive Tutor Lesson Variation Space version 1.2 (CTLVS1.2). The CTLVS was developed by a six member design team with diverse expertise, including three Cognitive Tutor designers (with expertise in cognitive psychology and artificial intelligence), a researcher specializing in the study of gaming the system, a mathematics teacher with several years of experience using Cognitive Tutors in class, and a designer of non-computerized curricula who had not previously used a Cognitive Tutor.

During the first step of the design process, the six member design team generated a list with 569 features. In the next step a list of criteria for features that would be worth coding, were developed. Finally the list was narrowed down to a more tractable size of 79 features. Inter-rater reliability checks were not conducted, owing to the hypothesis-generating nature of this study. Then CTLVS1 was labeled with reference to the 21 lessons studied in this paper by a combination of educational data mining and hand coding by the educational designer and mathematics teacher. The 10 features among 79 within the CTLVS1.1 which were significant predictors of disengaged behaviors in [3, 6] are shown in Table 1.

After initial publication of the results [e.g. 3, 6], using the CTLVS 1.1, additional coding was conducted by the gaming the system researcher and the designer of non-computerized curricula resulting in the addition of 5 more features, shown in Table 2. This produced a total of 84 quantitative and binary features within the CTLVS1.2.

Table 1. Design features which were significant predictors of disengaged behaviors in [3, 6]

1. Lesson is an equation-solver lesson, where a student is given an equation to solve mathematically (with no story problem)
2. Avg. amount that reading on-demand hints improves performance on future opportunities to use skill (using model from [12])
3. % of hint sequences with final "bottom-out" hint that explicitly tells student what to enter [cf. 1]
4. Reference in problem statement to interface component that does not exist (ever occurs)
5. Not immediately apparent what icons in toolbar mean
6. Hint requests that student perform some action
7. % of hints that explicitly refer to abstract principles
8. % of problem statements that use same numeric value for two constructs
9. % of problem statements with text not directly related to problem-solving task (typically included to increase interest)
10. Any hint gives directional feedback (example: "try a larger number")

3.2 Affect Detection Process

In order to study the relationship between students' affect and tutor design, we used previously developed detectors of student affect within Cognitive Tutor Algebra [cf. 8]. See [8] for a full discussion of the detectors. Unlike many of the pioneering efforts to detect student affect in intelligent tutoring systems [2, 18, 27], this work does not make use of any visual, audio or physiological sensors such as webcams, pressure sensing keyboard and mice, pressure sensitive seat pads and back pads, or wireless conductance bracelets in detecting affect. Instead, affect is detected solely from log files, supporting scalable analyses. These affect detectors were originally developed by labeling a set of students' affective states with field observations and then using those labels to create machine-learned models which automatically detect the student's affective state. Affect detectors were developed for the states of boredom, confusion, frustration, and engaged concentration (the affect associated with the flow state [cf. 7]. A separate detector was developed for each affective state. The goodness of the detectors (under student-level cross-validation) is given in Table 3; the detectors agree with human coders approximately half as well as human coders agree with each other. Note that the A' values for the models are lower than presented in the original paper [8]. This is because the implementation of AUC in RapidMiner 4.6 [28] was used to compute the A' values. This implementation has a bug, where estimates of A' are inflated, if multiple data points have the same confidence. In this paper we report estimates computed through directly computing the A'/Wilcoxon statistic, which is more computationally intensive but mathematically simpler (involving a set of pairwise comparisons rather than integrating under a complex function), using the code at http://www.columbia.edu/~rsb2162/edmtools.html .

Table 2. The design features added in CTLVS1.2

1. % of hints with requests for students with politeness indicators
2. % of scenarios with text not directly related to problem-solving task
3. Maximum number of times any skill is used in problem
4. Average number of times any skill is used in problem
5. Were any of the problem scenarios lengthy and with extraneous text? (Long Extraneous Text)

Table 3. Goodness of the affect models [cf. 8]

Affect	**Algorithm**	**Kappa**	**A'**
Engaged Concentration	K*	0.31	0.67
Boredom	Naïve Bayes	0.28	0.69
Confusion	JRip	0.40	0.71
Frustration	REPTree	0.23	0.64

To apply the machine-learned models to the data set used in this paper, we computed the features which were used in the models. The data was divided into "clips", of 20 second intervals of student behavior (the same grain-size used in the original observations which were used to build the detector), using the absolute time of each student action. Next, the 15 features used in the detectors [cf. 8] were computed for each clip. Finally RapidMiner 4.6 [28] was used to load each of the affect models and then each of the affect models were applied on the algebra data set to obtain assessments of affect for each clip, which were then aggregated to compute each student's proportion of each affective state in each lesson.

4 Results

For each lesson in the data set, we computed values for each of the 84 taxonomical features discussed in the data section. The value of each taxonomic feature was then correlated to the proportion of each of the four affective states (engaged concentration, boredom, confusion and frustration) detected within the log data for the lesson. As this represents a substantial number of statistical analyses (84*4 = 336), we controlled for multiple comparisons. In specific, the analyses in this study utilize the false discovery rate (FDR) [14] paradigm for post-hoc hypothesis testing, using Storey's method [33]. This method produces a substitute or p-values, termed q-values, driven by controlling the proportion of false positives obtained via a set of tests. Whereas a p-value expresses that 5% of all tests may include false positives, a q-value indicates that 5% of significant tests may include false positives. As such, the FDR method does not guarantee each test's significance, but guarantees a low overall proportion of false positives. This avoids the substantial Type II errors (over-conservatism) associated with the better-known Bonferroni correction [see 31 for a discussion of current statistical thought on the Bonferroni correction]. The FDR calculations in the results section were made using the QVALUE software package [33] within the R statistical software environment.

Across the features, only the five following tutor design features achieved statistically significant correlation to any of the affective states.

1. Lesson is an Equation Solver lesson (Equation Solver)
2. % of problem statements with text not directly related to problem-solving task (Extraneous Text),
3. % of problem statements which involve concrete people/places/things (Concrete Problem Statements),
4. Were any of the problem scenarios lengthy and with extraneous text? (Long Extraneous Text)
5. Average percent error in problem (Percent Error)

Table 4 summarizes the results. Equation Solver was statistically significantly positively associated with Concentration, $r=0.728$, $t(1,19)=4.622$, $q<0.01$; on the other hand 2 of the features Concrete Problem Statements and Long Extraneous Text were statistically significantly negatively associated with Concentration; Concrete Problem Statements $r= -0.604$, $t(1,19)= -3.31$, $q=0.013$; Long Extraneous Text $r= -0.538$, $t(1,19)= -2.78$, $q=0.032$.

Table 4. Statistical Significant results with q-values from FDR analysis

Design Features	Affect	r	Q
Equation Solver	Concentration	0.728	<0.01
Extraneous Text	Confusion	0.787	<0.001
Concrete Problem Statements	Concentration	-0.604	0.013
Concrete Problem Statements	Confusion	0.644	<0.01
Long Extraneous Text	Concentration	-0.538	0.032
Long Extraneous Text	Confusion	0.716	<0.01
Percent Error	Frustration	-0.718	<0.01

Three of the features were statistically significantly positively associated with Confusion, Concrete Problem Statement r=0.644, t(1,19)=3.67, q<0.01; Long Extraneous Text r=0.716, t(1,19)=4.47, q<0.0; Extraneous Text r=0.787, t(1,19)=5.56, q<0.001.

Only one of the features, Percent Error was statistically significantly negatively associated with Frustration, r= -0.718, t(1,19)= -4.5, q<0.01.

None of the features showed significant association with Boredom. The strongest correlation was achieved by "Hint gives directional feedback (example: "try a larger number")", r=0.50, t(1,19) = 2.5, q=0.30. It is worth noting that the original p value, before post-hoc correction, was p=0.02; hence, it may be worth considering this feature in future research, but there is insufficient evidence to make a conclusive inference about it at this point.

In terms of past features associated with gaming (in [6], it was hypothesized that this relationship was mediated by boredom), boredom appeared to be weakly correlated with Extraneous Text r=0.160, t(1,19) = 0.71, q=0.78 and Long Extraneous Text r=0.264, t(1,19)=1.19, q=0.64 and appeared to be moderately correlated with Concrete Problem Statements, r=0.335, t(1,19)= 1.55, q=0.64. None of these relationships, however, would be statistically significant even without post-hoc controls.

5 Discussion and Conclusions

The result here suggests that there are significant relationships between affect state of students, and the taxonomic features of an intelligent tutoring system. Five out of 84 taxonomic features were found to be statistically significantly associated with three affective states, engaged concentration, frustration, and confusion. These findings correspond in interesting ways to prior results regarding the relationship between disengaged behaviors and these same taxonomic features [cf. 3, 6].

Students were found to be concentrating significantly more during equation-solver lessons. These same lessons have also been found to be associated with a lower degree of off-task behavior and gaming the system in the previous research [3, 6].

We also found that students' concentration was reduced when the student encountered lessons with substantial extraneous text, as well as or problem statements and scenarios with concrete people, places or things. These same features were also associated with increased confusion. These are somewhat surprising findings, as extraneous text was also associated with gaming the system in earlier research [6]. Since gaming is thought to be negatively associated with engaged concentration [7], it is surprising that the same features of an interface are associated both with gaming and less engaged concentration. This finding clearly calls for greater research to understand its full implications.

At the same time, the connection between substantial extraneous text and concrete scenarios, and confusion, accords well to past findings in other contexts. The details in these long concrete scenarios could be considered "seductive details" – details which draw student attention away from the content. Seductive details have been found to be associated with poorer learning in laboratory studies [20]; the initial interpretation of [6] seemed to contradict this finding, but our results here seem more in keeping with it. Of course, it also may be that tutor designers have chosen (whether consciously or not) to increase the complexity of the scenarios when material is more confusing; as such, it would take an experimental study to be fully confident of the hypothesis generated here.

One unexpected finding was negative correlation between percent error and frustration, which should be investigated further. In a different intelligent tutor, frustration was found to be positively correlated with learning, suggesting that frustration's role in learning may be somewhat different than typically hypothesized [cf. 30].

Another surprising finding is that none of the taxonomic features were significantly associated with boredom, a persistent affect state within several types of learning environments [7]. We had earlier hypothesized that the negative relationship between gaming and lengthier scenarios would be mediated by boredom [e.g. 6], a finding not obtained here. Though we found some appearance of correlation between boredom and lengthier scenarios as well as other features known to be associated with gaming, these associations were not significant even without taking post-hoc adjustment into account, suggesting that it is unlikely that boredom is a key mediator between these tutor design features and gaming the system.

One valuable area of future work would be to extend the research here to additional affective states, such as delight, disgust, and anxiety. The affective states chosen in this research were selected because relevant detectors already existed, and because these states have high theoretical importance and/or are known to correlate with differences in learning outcomes and engagement; extending to additional affective states would help to create a fuller picture of the relationships between affect and tutor design.

One of the final things that can be noted from this analysis is that the designs of educational interfaces can have a considerable impact on student affect. Although only a relatively small number of relationship remained significant after post-hoc testing, it is worth noting that the conservatism of post-hoc approaches meant that the relationships that remained significant had extremely high correlations (in the 0.7 range). This finding implies that relatively small differences in intelligent tutors may result in substantial impacts on student experiences.

Acknowledgments. The authors thank the Pittsburgh Science of Learning Center (National Science Foundation) via grant "Toward a Decade of PSLC Research", award number SBE- 0836012.

References

1. Aleven, V., McLaren, B., Roll, I., Koedinger, K.R.: Toward tutoring help seeking: Applying cognitive modeling to meta-cognitive skills. In: Lester, J.C., Vicari, R.M., Paraguaçu, F. (eds.) ITS 2004. LNCS, vol. 3220, pp. 227–239. Springer, Heidelberg (2004)
2. Arroyo, I., Woolf, B.P., Cooper, D., Burleson, W., Muldner, K., Christopherson, R.: Emotion Sensors Go To School. In: Proc. of the 14th International Conference on Artificial Intelligence in Education (2009)
3. Baker, R.S.J.d.: Differences Between Intelligent Tutor Lessons, and the Choice to Go Off-Task. In: Proc. of the 2nd Int'l. Conference on Educational Data Mining, pp. 11–20 (2009)
4. Baker, R.S.J.d.: Modeling and understanding students' off-task behavior in intelligent tutoring systems. In: Proceedings of the SIGCHI Conference on Human Factors in Computing Systems, pp. 1059–1068 (2007)
5. Baker, R.S.J.d., de Carvalho, A.M.J.A.: Labeling Student Behavior Faster and More Precisely with Text Replays. In: Proceedings of the 1st International Conference on Educational Data Mining, pp. 38–47 (2008)
6. Baker, R.S.J.d., de Carvalho, A.M.J.A., Raspat, J., Aleven, V., Corbett, A.T., Koedinger, K.R.: Educational Software Features that Encourage and Discourage "Gaming the System". In: Proc. of the 14th Int'l. Conf. on Artificial Intelligence in Education, pp. 475–482 (2009)
7. Baker, R.S.J.d., D'Mello, S.K., Rodrigo, M.M.T., Graesser, A.C.: Better to Be Frustrated than Bored: The Incidence, Persistence, and Impact of Learners' Cognitive-Affective States during Interactions with Three Different Computer-Based Learning Environments. International Journal of Human-Computer Studies 68(4), 223–241 (2010)
8. Baker, R.S.J.d., Gowda, S.M., Wixon, M., Kalka, J., Wagner, A.Z., Salvi, A., Aleven, V., Kusbit, G., Ocumpaugh, J., Rossi, L.: Sensor-free automated detection of affect in a Cognitive Tutor for Algebra. In: Proceedings of the 5th International Conference on Educational Data Mining, pp. 126–133 (2012)
9. Baker, R.S.J.d., Moore, G.R., Wagner, A.Z., Kalka, J., Salvi, A., Karabinos, M., Ashe, C.A., Yaron, D.: The Dynamics Between Student Affect and Behavior Occuring Outside of Educational Software. In: D'Mello, S., Graesser, A., Schuller, B., Martin, J.-C. (eds.) ACII 2011, Part I. LNCS, vol. 6974, pp. 14–24. Springer, Heidelberg (2011)
10. Baker, R.S.J.d., Walonoski, J., Heffernan, N., Roll, I., Corbett, A., Koedinger, K.: Why Students Engage in "Gaming the System" Behavior in Interactive Learning Environments. Journal of Interactive Learning Research 19(2), 185–224 (2008)
11. Beal, C.R., Qu, L., Lee, H.: Mathematics motivation and achievement as predictors of high school students' guessing and help-seeking with instructional software. Journal of Computer Assisted Learning 24(6), 507–514 (2008)
12. Beck, J.E., Chang, K.-M., Mostow, J., Corbett, A.: Does Help Help? Introducing the Bayesian Evaluation and Assessment Methodology. In: Woolf, B.P., Aïmeur, E., Nkambou, R., Lajoie, S. (eds.) ITS 2008. LNCS, vol. 5091, pp. 383–394. Springer, Heidelberg (2008)
13. Beck, J.: Engagement tracing: using response times to model student disengagement. In: Proc. of 12th Int'l Conference on Artificial Intelligence in Education, pp. 88–95 (2005)
14. Benjamini, Y., Hochberg, Y.: Controlling the false discovery rate: A practical and powerful approach to multiple testing. Journal of the Royal Statistical Society, Series B 57, 289–300 (1995)
15. Cocea, M., Hershkovitz, A., Baker, R.S.J.d.: The Impact of Off-task and Gaming Behaviors on Learning: Immediate or Aggregate? In: Proceedings of the 14th International Conference on Artificial Intelligence in Education, pp. 507–514 (2009)
16. Craig, S.D., Graesser, A.C., Sullins, J., Gholson, B.: Affect and learning: an exploratory look into the role of affect in learning. J. of Educational Media 29, 241–250 (2004)
17. Csikszentmihalyi, M., Schneider, B.: Becoming Adult. Basic Books, New York (2001)

18. D'Mello, S.K., Graesser, A.C.: Multimodal semiautomated affect detection from conversational cues, gross body language, and facial features. User Modeling and User-adapted Interaction 20(2), 147–187 (2010)
19. D'Mello, S.K., Taylor, R., Graesser, A.C.: Monitoring Affective Trajectories during Complex Learning. In: Proc. of the 29th Annual Conf. of the Cognitive Science Society, pp. 203–208 (2007)
20. Harp, S.F., Mayer, R.E.: How seductive details do their damage: a theory of cognitive interest in science learning. Journal of Educational Psychology 90, 414–434 (1998)
21. Hastings, P., Arnott-Hill, E., Allbritton, D.: Squeezing out gaming behavior in a dialog-based ITS. In: Aleven, V., Kay, J., Mostow, J. (eds.) ITS 2010, Part I. LNCS, vol. 6094, pp. 204–213. Springer, Heidelberg (2010)
22. Hershkovitz, A., Baker, R.S.J.d., Gobert, J., Nakama, A.: A Data-driven Path Model of Student Attributes, Affect, and Engagement in a Computer-based Science Inquiry Microworld. In: Proceedings of the International Conference on the Learning Sciences (2012)
23. Hidi, S., Anderson, V.: Situational interest and its impact on reading and expository writing. In: Renninger, K.A., Hidi, S., Krapp, A. (eds.) The Role of Interest in Learning and Development, pp. 215–238. Erlbaum, Hillsdale (1992)
24. Koedinger, K., Corbett, A.: Cognitive Tutors: Technology bringing learning science to the classroom. In: Sawyer, K. (ed.) The Cambridge Handbook of the Learning Sciences, pp. 61–78. Cambridge University Press (2006)
25. Krapp, A.: Structural and dynamic aspects of interest development: theoretical considerations from an ontogenetic perspective. Learning and Instruction 12(4), 383–409 (2002)
26. Lee, D.M.C., Rodrigo, M.M.T., Baker, R.S.J.d., Sugay, J.O., Coronel, A.: Exploring the Relationship between Novice Programmer Confusion and Achievement. In: D'Mello, S., Graesser, A., Schuller, B., Martin, J.-C. (eds.) ACII 2011, Part I. LNCS, vol. 6974, pp. 175–184. Springer, Heidelberg (2011)
27. Litman, D.J., Forbes-Riley, K.: Recognizing Student Emotions and Attitudes on the Basis of Utterances in Spoken Tutoring Dialogues with both Human and Computer Tutors. Speech Communication 48(5), 559–590 (2006)
28. Mierswa, I., Wurst, M., Klinkenberg, R., Scholz, M., Euler, T.: Yale: rapid prototyping for complex data mining tasks. In: Proceedings of the 12th ACM SIGKDD International Conference on Knowledge Discovery and Data Mining, pp. 935–940 (2006)
29. Murray, R.C., VanLehn, K.: Effects of dissuading unnecessary help requests while providing proactive help. In: Proc. of the Int'l Conf. on Artificial Intelligence in Education (2005)
30. Pardos, Z., Baker, R.S.J.d., San Pedro, M.O.Z., Gowda, S.M., Gowda, S.: Affective states and state tests: Investigating how affect throughout the school year predicts end of year learning outcomes. In: To Appear in Proceedings of the 3rd International Conference on Learning Analytics and Knowledge (in press)
31. Perneger, T.V.: What's wrong with Bonferroni adjustments. British Medical Journal 316, 1236–1238 (1998)
32. Sabourin, J., Rowe, J.P., Mott, B.W., Lester, J.C.: When Off-Task is On-Task: The Affective Role of Off-Task Behavior in Narrative-Centered Learning Environments. In: Biswas, G., Bull, S., Kay, J., Mitrovic, A. (eds.) AIED 2011. LNCS, vol. 6738, pp. 534–536. Springer, Heidelberg (2011)
33. Storey, J.D., Taylor, J.E., Siegmund, D.: Strong control, conservative point estimation, and simultaneous conservative consistency of false discovery rates: A unified approach. Journal of the Royal Statistical Society, Series B 66(1), 187–205 (2004)
34. Van Duyne, D.K., Landay, J.A., Hong, J.I.: The design of sites patterns for creating winning web sites, Upper Saddle River, NY (2008)

Towards an Understanding of Affect and Knowledge from Student Interaction with an Intelligent Tutoring System

Maria Ofelia Z. San Pedro[1], Ryan S.J.d. Baker[1], Sujith M. Gowda[2], and Neil T. Heffernan[2]

[1] Teachers College, Columbia University, New York, NY
[2] Worcester Polytechnic Institute, Worcester, MA
mzs2106@tc.columbia.edu, baker2@exchange.tc.columbia.edu, mgsujith@gmail.com, nth@wpi.edu

Abstract. Csikszentmihalyi's Flow theory states that a balance between challenge and skill leads to high engagement, overwhelming challenge leads to anxiety or frustration, and insufficient challenge leads to boredom. In this paper, we test this theory within the context of student interaction with an intelligent tutoring system. Automated detectors of student affect and knowledge were developed, validated, and applied to a large data set. The results did not match Flow theory: boredom was more common for poorly-known material, and frustration was common both for very difficult material and very easy material. These results suggest that design for optimal engagement within online learning may require further study of the factors leading students to become bored on difficult material, and frustrated on very well-known material.

Keywords: Affect Modeling, Prior Knowledge, Intelligent Tutoring System, Boredom, Frustration, Engaged Concentration.

1 Introduction

In recent years, substantial work has gone into increasing the sensitivity and responsiveness of intelligent tutoring systems (ITSs) to differences in student affect [10, 11]. One theory that has inspired design in education [cf. 28] is Csikszentmihalyi's Flow theory [8]. This theory details the attributes of optimal experience during activity, making a number of specific claims that can be investigated, tested, and leveraged within design when a person is engaged in an activity with clear goals, with immediate feedback, and when balance is achieved between the person's perception of task difficulty and perception of one's own skills to do the task [8]. Empirical work in classrooms using traditional approaches (e.g., not ITS) has found that high school students experience the highest engagement when students perceive both challenge and their skill as high [28]. Csikszentmihalyi [8, 9] also hypothesized that specific affective states (emotion in context [cf. 7]) emerge depending on the degree of challenge and skill that is present for an activity. His theory indicates that when an

K. Yacef et al. (Eds.): AIED 2013, LNAI 7926, pp. 41–50, 2013.

activity is perceived to be too easy one becomes bored, and when the task is too difficult one gets anxious [8]. An additional hypothesis is that the same conditions that lead to anxiety also lead to frustration [13], implying that challenge is higher than skill, leading some researchers to use frustration rather than anxiety in applying Csikszentmihalyi's theory [cf. 20, 25].

Flow theory, when applied to the context of education, asserts that a learning activity should be perceived as challenging but not too difficult [27]. As such, non-adaptive learning materials are likely to fail in producing flow for most students, as materials at a specific difficulty level are likely to be boring for students with higher skill, and frustrating for students with lower skill [cf. 26]. However, a learning system that accurately infers student skill – as modern intelligent tutoring systems do – may be able to specifically select problems of appropriate difficulty, in an attempt to balance challenge with skill level [18].

However, there is still not sufficient empirical evidence that Flow theory's account of the consequences of failing to achieve a balance between difficulty and skill are as predicted. In particular, recent research has suggested that boredom is often characteristic of the least successful students rather than students who have already achieved mastery [1, 7, 19]. This same research finds that frustration does not appear to be strongly connected with the poorest students [7, 22, 23]. These studies have the limitation of investigating these issues at a fairly coarse grain-size, looking solely at overall prevalence of affective states and long-term measures of learning. By studying these issues at a finer grain-size, we can understand these relationships better.

In this paper, we operationalize boredom, frustration, and engaged concentration during online learning in the fashion proposed in [3, 7]. In this paradigm, affective states are conceptualized as atomic and distinct from one another. Of particular importance to Flow theory are boredom [8, 15], frustration [13], and engaged concentration [cf. 3], which is the affect associated with Csikszentmihalyi's construct of flow but does not involve the inherent task-related aspects of flow – clear goals, immediate feedback, and balance between challenge and skill.

We conduct this research in a data set of 8,454 students learning online for a year apiece in the ASSISTment system [21], a free web-based tutoring system for middle school mathematics. Within ASSISTments, students complete mathematics problems and are formatively assessed – providing detailed information on their knowledge to their teachers – while being assisted with scaffolding, help, and feedback. Items in ASSISTments are designed to correspond to the skills and concepts taught in relevant state standardized examinations. Teachers have the ability to assign students questions on a particular skill and typically select the problems or problem sets their students receive (though mastery learning can also be activated by the teacher for some problem sets). As shown in Figure 1, the ASSISTment system provides feedback on incorrect answers. When a student answers a problem incorrectly, they are provided with scaffolding questions breaking the problem into its component steps. Hints are provided at each step and the student can ask for a bottom-out hint that eventually tells the answer.

Within this paper, we use automated detectors of student affect within the ASSISTment system (published in previous work [16]) to operationalize student affect within the ASSISTment system. These detectors, developed and validated using data from 229 students, are then applied to the full data set of 8,454 students. We combine these detectors with data from models of student knowledge in order to analyze the conditions under which each affective state occurs, and whether the relationship between affect and the difficulty of a problem for a specific student accords with Flow theory. We conclude with a discussion of potential implications for the design of interactive educational systems.

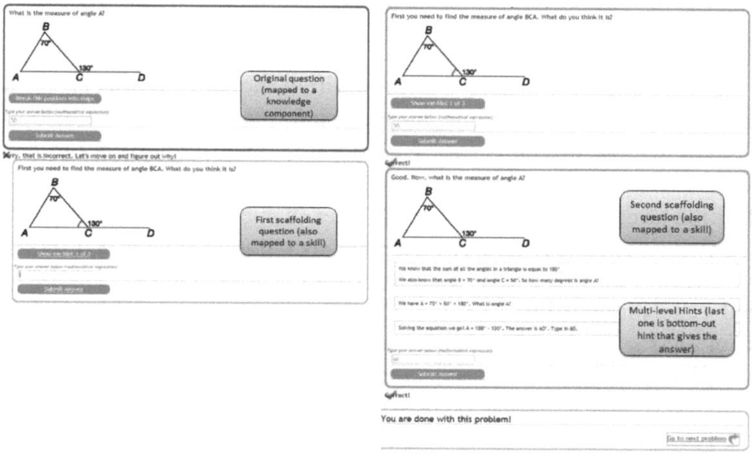

a) b)

Fig. 1. Example of an ASSISTment. a) If a student gets it incorrect, hints and scaffolding problems are there to aid the student in eventually getting the correct answer. b) Example of Scaffolding and Hints in an ASSISTment.

2 Measures Used

2.1 Affect Detectors

Within this paper, we leverage existing detectors of student affect within the ASSISTment system [16], to help us understand student affect across contexts. Detectors of three affective states are utilized: engaged concentration, boredom, and frustration. The detectors of engaged concentration and boredom used in this paper are identical to the detectors used in [16]. After publishing [16], we discovered a minor computation error in one of the features used in the frustration detector. Hence, a re-computed model is used here (the goodness of the detector is almost exactly identical between the [16] and this paper). Though anxiety plays a prominent role in Csikszentmihalyi's Theory of Flow, no detector of anxiety in ASSISTments was available, in part because anxiety has been observed so rarely in classroom use of intelligent tutoring systems as to not merit its own coding category [12, 14, 23].

These detectors were developed using a two-stage process: first, student affect was labeled for a sample of 3,075 field observations [cf. 3] of 229 students conducted by two coders using an Android app, and then those labels were used to create automated detectors that can be applied to log files at scale. An inter-rater reliability session was conducted, where the two coders coded the same student at the same time (they observed multiple students, but observed each student together). They conducted 51 simultaneous observations, achieving a Cohen's Kappa of 0.72, indicating agreement 72% better than chance. The detectors were created by synchronizing log files generated by the ASSISTments system with field observations conducted at the same time. To enhance scalability, only log data was used as the basis of the detectors, instead of using physical sensors (and indeed, the research presented in this paper could not have been conducted if physical sensors were used). The detectors were constructed using only log data from student actions within the software occurring at the same time as or before the observations. By using information only from before and during the observation, our detectors can be used for automated interventions, as well as the discovery with models analyses presented in this paper.

All of the affect detectors performed better than chance. Detector goodness within ASSISTments was at the high end of previous reports of published models inferring student affect in an ITS solely from log files [cf. 4, 5, 11, 24]. The best detector of engaged concentration involved the K* algorithm, achieving an A' of 0.678 and a Kappa of 0.358. The best boredom detector was found using the JRip algorithm, achieving an A' of 0.632 and a Kappa of 0.229. The best frustration detector achieved an A' of 0.681 and a Kappa of 0.301, using the J48 algorithm. These levels of detector goodness indicate models that are clearly informative, though there is still considerable room for improvement.

Within the original observations, boredom was observed 17.7% of the time, frustration was observed 4.4% of the time, and engaged concentration 53.0% of the time, with other affective states representing the remainder of student time. The detectors emerging from the data mining process had some systematic error in prediction, where the average confidence of the resultant models was systematically higher or lower than the proportion of the affective states in the original data set. This type of bias does not affect correlation to other variables since relative order of predictions is unaffected, but it can reduce model interpretability. To increase model interpretability, model confidences were rescaled to have the same mean as the original distribution, using linear interpolation. Rescaling the confidences this way does not impact model A' or Kappa, as it does not change the relative ordering of model assessments.

2.2 Prior Knowledge Assessment

Estimates of student knowledge were used as a proxy for Flow theory's "balance between challenge and skill." These estimates were computed using Bayesian Knowledge Tracing (BKT) [6], a model used in several ITSs to estimate a student's latent knowledge based on his/her observable performance. This model can predict how difficult the current problem will be for the current student, based on the skills required for that problem. As such, this model can implicitly capture the tradeoff between difficulty and skill for the current context. This model can inform us whether student skill is higher than current difficulty (resulting in a high probability of correctness), when current difficulty is higher than student skill (resulting in a low probability of correctness), and when difficulty and skill are in balance (medium probabilities of correctness). To assess student skill, BKT infers student knowledge by continually updating the estimated probability a student knows a skill every time the student gives a first response to a new problem. It uses four parameters, each estimated separately per skill: L_O, the initial probability the student knows the skill; T, the probability of learning the skill at each opportunity to use that a skill; G, the probability that the student will give a correct answer despite not knowing the skill; and S, the probability that the student will give an incorrect answer despite knowing the skill. In this model, the four parameters for each skill are held constant across contexts and students (variants of BKT relax these assumptions). BKT uses Bayesian algorithms after each student's first response to a problem in order to re-calculate the probability that the student knew the skill before the response. Then the algorithm accounts for the possibility that the student learned the skill during the problem in order to compute the probability the student will know the skill after the problem [6]. With the data from the logs, BKT parameters were fit by employing brute-force grid search [cf. 2].

After obtaining the assessments of student affect and prior knowledge at each problem, we assessed the relationship between the two. The following section shows both qualitative and quantitative estimates of these relationships for each affective state. Since our models provide confidences in their predictions as well as overall predictions, we conduct analyses using the confidences of the affect predictions rather than the proportion of binary predictions.

3 Studying the Relationship between Affect and Knowledge

3.1 Data Set

The detectors of student affect and student knowledge were applied to a data set consisting of five years of student usage of the ASSISTment system by four schools in New England, from 2004-2005 to 2008-2009. These four schools represent a diverse sample of students in terms of ethnicity and socio-economic status. Two districts were urban with many students requiring free or reduced-price lunches due to poverty, relatively low scores on state standardized examinations, and many students learning English as a second language. The other two districts were suburban, serving relatively wealthier populations. The affect models were applied to this much larger dataset. This data set included 8,454 students and a total of 1,568,974 student actions within the learning software.

3.2 Boredom and Student Knowledge

Boredom is less common when student skill is higher, as shown in Figure 2. This finding contrasts with predictions by Csikszentmihalyi [8] and Shernoff et al. [28], which would suggest that boredom should mostly occur when material is too easy relative to student skill. The linear trend is fairly modest (a difference of 5% in average boredom between material where the student has a high probability of knowing

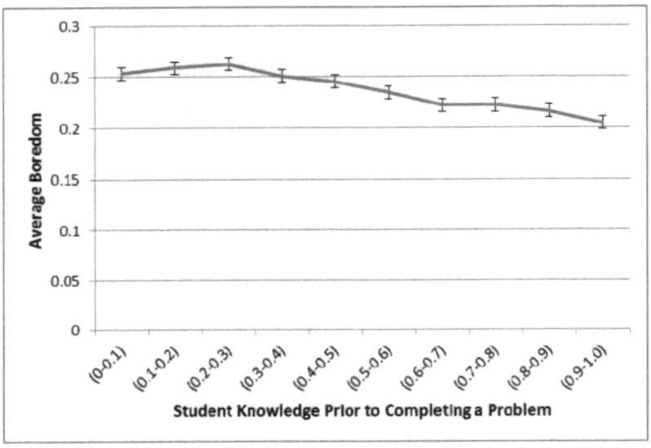

Fig. 2. The relationship between boredom and the probability that the student knows the skill. Note that the X axis denotes difficulty for the current problem for the current student, prior to the student completing the problems; i.e., the contextually hardest problems are on the left, and the contextually easiest problems are on the right.

the skill and material where the student has a very low probability of knowing the skill). However, due to the large sample size, the negative linear trend is statistically significant ($r = -0.157$, $F(1, 1560519) = 14223.174$, $p < 0.0001$). Note that a student term was included in the model (and all the statistical tests in this paper) to avoid violation of statistical independence.

3.3 Frustration and Student Knowledge

The relationship between frustration and student skill, shown in Figure 3, appears non-linear. Frustration appears to be significantly more common for students with very low skill and for students with very high skill, than for other students. When we fit a linear curve, there is a significant but small correlation between frustration and prior knowledge ($r = 0.093$, $F(1, 1560519) = 11647$, $p < 0.0001$). A parabolic curve

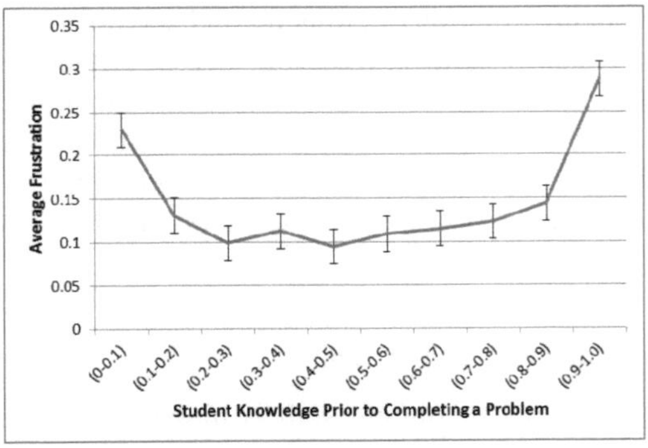

Fig. 3. The relationship between frustration and the probability that the student knows the skill

(i.e., Frustration = (Knowledge – Mean(Knowledge))^2) achieves better fit (r = 0.222, F(1, 1560519) = 63989, p < 0.0001). The difference in BiC' values between these two models is 65,667, indicating that the parabolic curve fits the data substantially better than the linear function (differences in BiC' of ten or greater indicate substantial differences between models). The relationship between low skill and frustration accords with Flow theory, but the relationship between high skill and frustration is surprising, indicating that students may become frustrated when repeatedly given easy items.

3.4 Engaged Concentration and Student Knowledge

The incidence of engaged concentration is higher for more skilled students, as shown in Figure 4. The linear trend is fairly modest (a difference of 6% in average engaged concentration between material where the student has a high probability of knowing the skill and material where the student has a very low probability of knowing the skill). However, due to the large sample size, the linear trend is statistically significant (r = 0.184, F(1, 1560519) = 13660.477, p < 0.0001). In accordance with past studies [3, 24], engaged concentration is the most common affect when using ASSISTments regardless of student skill level.

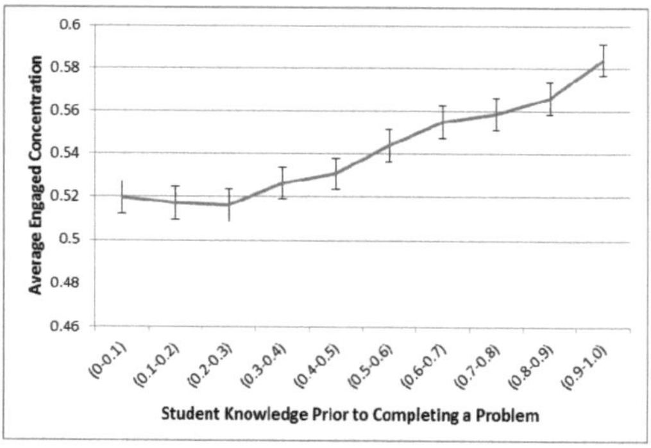

Fig. 4. The relationship between engaged concentration and the probability that the student knows the skill

4 Discussion and Conclusion

Flow theory has emphasized the importance of achieving a balance between perceived challenge of a task and perceived skill for that task, to produce optimal student engagement (i.e., flow). In these models, an imbalance between challenge and skill would result in either boredom or frustration (or anxiety, which is not studied here).

In this paper, we study the relationship between these student affect and student knowledge within the context of an ITS, towards providing a concrete test of one aspect of Flow theory. We do so by applying automated detectors of student affect and knowledge to data from the ASSISTment system, a widely used intelligent tutoring system for middle school mathematics. By integrating these two types of detectors, we can analyze the frequency of each affective state for students with different levels of knowledge.

A limitation in this paper is that the model used for difficulty measures looked at estimations of actual knowledge and difficulty rather than a student's self-perceptions (as in from Flow theory). A challenge in obtaining measures of self-perception is that they may change the student's emotions and learning if obtained in real-time, and may be prone to memory limitations if obtained retrospectively. They also present some risk of demand effects. However, replicating this research with self-report measures would be a valuable step for future work.

Overall, we find that engaged concentration is the most likely affect, regardless of difficulty. This result shows that completing problems in ASSISTments is generally engaging, even when the problems are too easy or too difficult. Beyond this, problems are seen to become more engaging as student mastery increases, which contrasts somewhat with predictions made in Flow theory, which would predict that engagement would be reduced for the most challenging problems. (However, this result replicates a result seen in [17]). Flow theory predicts that these highly challenging problems will result in student frustration. Indeed, higher frustration is seen for the most challenging problems. However, higher boredom is also seen for these highly challenging problems, contrary to Flow theory. Boredom is generally lower for easy problems than hard problems, also contrary to Flow theory. In addition, higher frustration is seen for easy problems than for problems of middling difficulty, a finding that cannot be easily explained with Flow theory.

Given that these results are different from earlier predictions, it is worth thinking about their interpretation. There have been reports of boredom being associated with poorer learning [7, 19] and with disengaged behaviors that in turn lead to poorer learning [3]. Recent studies using other methods have also found that students become bored and disengaged when they find items difficult [1, 19]. These results accord with our findings that boredom is characteristic of less successful students rather than highly successful students. Perhaps these students are bored because they have given up on succeeding with the material, but must continue to work with the software. It may be that this type of boredom is more common in intelligent tutoring systems than boredom resulting from overly low challenge – especially since many tutors such as ASSISTments are designed to advance students when they reach mastery.

One possibility is that the relatively low boredom seen for easy items and the unexpected frustration seen on these items is due to the student's lack of control over problem difficulty. Perhaps a student who wishes to receive more challenging problems, but cannot obtain these problems within the software, becomes frustrated and upset with the software. In general, further research may be necessary in order to understand why students become frustrated with easy material. One possible approach would be to pop-up an automated question in this situation (detected frustration on easy material), asking students if they are frustrated and why. An interesting aspect of the current finding on frustration and student knowledge is that this result provides an account for a surprising result from previous studies. Past research has failed to find significant relationships between frustration and learning outcomes [cf.7, 22], contrary to theoretical predictions [13]. If unsuccessful students are not more likely to become frustrated, one would not expect to see such a relationship. In general, frustration appears to be a more complex construct than originally thought [cf. 13].

Overall, our findings suggest that there may be substantial holes in our understanding of the situations where different affective states emerge, during human-computer interaction. Current theory does not explain these results, and makes predictions that are in some cases contrary to the findings presented here. It is important to note that these findings only involve one intelligent tutor, and rely upon imperfect detectors of both affect and knowledge (though each of these detectors is approximately as good as the current state-of-the-art for sensor-free detection of these constructs). Replicating these results (or failing to) in other learning software will be an important step towards understanding the generality of these findings, and towards creating general principles for how intelligent tutoring systems should respond to users when they demonstrate these affective states. It is likely that we will find that each of the affective states can emerge in multiple situations, driven by differences in tutor design, and perhaps by individual differences as well. Hence, further investigation of the contexts of affect will be needed to fully understand these relationships.

Acknowledgements. This research was supported by grants NSF #DRL-1031398, NSF #SBE-0836012, and grant #OPP1048577 from the Bill & Melinda Gates Foundation. We also thank Zak Rogoff, Adam Nakama, Aatish Salvi, Adam Goldstein, and Sue Donas for their assistance in conducting the study.

References

1. Acee, T.W., Kim, H., Kim, H.J., Kim, J., Hsiang-Ning, R.C., Kim, M.: Academic Boredom in Under- and Overchallenging Situations. Contemporary Ed. Psy. 35, 17–27 (2010)
2. Baker, R.S.J.d., Corbett, A.T., Gowda, S.M., Wagner, A.Z., MacLaren, B.A., Kauffman, L.R., Mitchell, A.P., Giguere, S.: Contextual Slip and Prediction of Student Performance after Use of an Intelligent Tutor. In: De Bra, P., Kobsa, A., Chin, D. (eds.) UMAP 2010. LNCS, vol. 6075, pp. 52–63. Springer, Heidelberg (2010)
3. Baker, R.S.J.d., D'Mello, S.K., Rodrigo, M.M.T., Graesser, A.C.: Better to Be Frustrated than Bored: The Incidence, Persistence, and Impact of Learners' Cognitive-Affective States during Interactions with Three Different Computer-Based Learning Environments. Int'l. J. Human-Computer Studies 68(4), 223–241 (2010)
4. Baker, R.S.J.d., Gowda, S.M., Wixon, M., Kalka, J., Wagner, A.Z., Salvi, A., Aleven, V., Kusbit, G., Ocumpaugh, J., Rossi, L.: Towards Sensor-Free Affect Detection in Cognitive Tutor Algebra. In: EDM 2012, pp. 126–133 (2012)
5. Conati, C., Maclaren, H.: Empirically Building and Evaluating a Probabilistic Model of User Affect. User Modeling and User-Adapted Interaction 19(3), 267–303 (2009)
6. Corbett, A.T., Anderson, J.R.: Knowledge Tracing: Modeling the Acquisition of Procedural Knowledge. User Modeling and User-Adapted Interaction 4(4), 253–278 (1995)
7. Craig, S.D., Graesser, A.C., Sullins, J., Gholson, B.: Affect and Learning: An Exploratory Look into the Role of Affect in Learning. J. of Educational Media 29, 241–250 (2004)
8. Csikszentmihalyi, M.: Flow: The Psychology of Optimal Experience. Harper-Row (1990)
9. Csikszentmihalyi, M., Csikszentmihalyi, I.S.: Optimal Experience: Psychological Studies of Flow in Consciousness. Cambridge University, Cambridge (1988)

10. D'Mello, S.K., Craig, S.K., Gholson, B., Franklin, S., Picard, R.W., Graesser, A.C.: Integrating Affect Sensors in an Intelligent Tutoring System. In: Intelligent User Interface 2005. AMC Press (2005)
11. D'Mello, S.K., Craig, S.D., Witherspoon, A.W., McDaniel, B.T., Graesser, A.C.: Automatic Detection of Learner's Affect from Conversational Cues. User Modeling and User-Adapted Interaction 18(1-2), 45–80 (2008)
12. Dragon, T., Arroyo, I., Woolf, B.P., Burleson, W., el Kaliouby, R., Eydgahi, H.: Viewing Student Affect and Learning through Classroom Observation and Physical Sensors. In: Woolf, B.P., Aïmeur, E., Nkambou, R., Lajoie, S. (eds.) ITS 2008. LNCS, vol. 5091, pp. 29–39. Springer, Heidelberg (2008)
13. Kort, B., Reilly, R., Picard, R.: An Affective Model of Interplay between Emotions and Learning: Reengineering Educational Pedagogy—Building A Learning Companion. In: IEEE Int'l. Conf. on Advanced Learning Technology 2001, pp. 43–48 (2001)
14. Lehman, B., D'Mello, S.K., Person, N.: All Alone with your Emotions: An Analysis of Student Emotions during Effortful Problem Solving Activities. In: Workshop on Emotional and Cognitive Issues in ITS, Int'l Conf. on Intelligent Tutoring Systems (2008)
15. Miserandino, M.: Children Who Do Well in School: Individual Differences in Perceived Competence and Autonomy in Above-Average Children. J. Ed. Psych. 88, 203–214 (1996)
16. Pardos, Z., Baker, R.S.J.d., San Pedro, M.O.Z., Gowda, S.M., Gowda, S.: Affective States and State Tests: Investigating How Affect throughout the School Year Predicts End of Year Learning Outcomes. In: Learning Analytics and Knowledge (in press)
17. Pavlik Jr., P.I.: The Microeconomics of Learning: Optimizing Paired-Associate Memory. Doctoral Dissertation, Carnegie Mellon University (2005)
18. Pavlik Jr., P.I., Presson, N., Dozzi, G., Wu, S., MacWhinney, B., Koedinger, K.R.: The FaCT (Fact and Concept Training) System: A New Tool Linking Cognitive Science with Educators. In: Proc. Cognitive Science Society 2007, 397–402 (2007)
19. Pekrun, R., Goetz, T., Daniels, L.M., Stupnisky, R.H., Perry, R.P.: Boredom in Achievement Settings: Exploring Control-Value Antecedents and Performance Outcomes of a Neglected Emotion. J. Educational Psychology 102(3), 531–549 (2010)
20. Pilke, E.M.: Flow Experiences in Information Technology Use. Int'l. J. Human-Computer Studies 61(3), 347–357 (2004)
21. Razzaq, L., Feng, M., Nuzzo-Jones, G., Heffernan, N.T.: The Assistment Project: Blending Assessment and Assisting. In: AIED 2005, pp. 555–562 (2005)
22. Rodrigo, M.M.T., Baker, R.S.J.d.: Coarse-Grained Detection of Student Frustration in an Introductory Programming Course. In: ACM ICER 2009 (2009)
23. Rodrigo, M.M.T., Baker, R., Jadud, M., Amarra, A., Dy, T., Espejo-Lahoz, M., Lim, S., Pascua, S., Sugay, J.: Affective and Behavioral Predictors of Novice Programmer Achievement. In: ACM-SIGCSE 2009, pp. 156–160 (2009)
24. Sabourin, J., Mott, B., Lester, J.: Modeling Learner Affect with Theoretically Grounded Dynamic Bayesian Networks. In: D'Mello, S., Graesser, A., Schuller, B., Martin, J.-C. (eds.) ACII 2011, Part I. LNCS, vol. 6974, pp. 286–295. Springer, Heidelberg (2011)
25. Sedighian, K.: Challenge-Driven Learning: A Model for Children's Multimedia Mathematics Learning Environments. In: ED-MEDIA 1997 (1997)
26. Sessink, O., Beeftink, H., Tramper, J., Hartog, R.: Proteus: A Lecturer-Friendly Adaptive Tutoring System. J. Interactive Learning Research 18(4), 533–554 (2007)
27. Shernoff, D.J., Csikszentmihalyi, M.: Flow in Schools: Cultivating Engaged Learners and Optimal Learning Environments. In: Gilman, R., Huebner, E.S., Furlong, M. (eds.) Handbook of Positive Psychology in Schools, pp. 131–145. Routledge, New York (2009)
28. Shernoff, D.J., Csikszentmihalyi, M., Shneider, B., Shernoff, E.S.: Student Engagement in High School Classrooms from the Perspective of Flow Theory. School Psychology Quarterly 18(2), 158 (2003)

Who Benefits from Confusion Induction during Learning? An Individual Differences Cluster Analysis

Blair Lehman[1], Sidney D'Mello[2], and Art Graesser[1]

[1] University of Memphis, Memphis, TN 38152, USA
{balehman,graesser}@memphis.edu
[2] University of Notre Dame, Notre Dame, IN 46556, USA
sdmello@nd.edu

Abstract. Recent research has indicated that learning environments that intentionally induce confusion to promote deep inquiry can be beneficial for learning if students engage in confusion resolution processes and if relevant scaffolds are provided. However, it is unlikely that these environments will benefit all students, so it is necessary to identify the student profiles that most benefit from confusion induction. We investigated how individual differences (e.g., prior knowledge, interest, attributional complexity) impacted confusion and learning outcomes in an environment that induced confusion via false system feedback (e.g., negative feedback after a correct response). A *k*-means cluster analysis revealed four clusters that varied on cognitive ability and cognitive drive. We found that students in the high cognitive ability + high cognitive drive cluster reported more confusion after receiving false feedback compared to the other clusters. These students also performed better on tasks requiring knowledge transfer, but only when they were meaningfully confused.

Keywords: confusion, individual differences, cluster analysis, false feedback, intelligent tutoring systems, learning.

1 Introduction

Recent research has shown that intelligent tutoring systems (ITS) are an effective and comparable alternative to novice as well as accomplished (or expert) human tutors [1]. ITSs are effective because they are interactive, provide immediate feedback, and provide individualized instruction, which are similar to the techniques used by human tutors [2-4]. ITSs must attend to both student cognition and affect in order to provide effective, individualized instruction. Recently many ITSs have adopted this approach and provide individualized instruction that focuses on the affective states of the student in addition to their cognitive states (e.g., [5-9]).

Confusion is one affective state that is particularly important to the learning process. Confusion is an epistemic or knowledge affective state [10-11] that occurs when students confront contradictions, anomalies, and discrepant events that create impasses and when students are uncertain about how to proceed [12-14]. In other words, confusion signals that there is something wrong with the state of one's

K. Yacef et al. (Eds.): AIED 2013, LNAI 7926, pp. 51–60, 2013.

knowledge [15]. Increased experiences of confusion have been linked to learning at deeper levels [16-17]. Importantly, it is not the mere experience of confusion that presumably benefits learning; instead it is the effortful cognitive activities inspired by confusion resolution (e.g., reflection, deliberation) that underlie improvements in learning [14,18]. However, all experiences of confusion are not expected to be beneficial for learning. Learning is unlikely to occur when students are unable to resolve their confusion either due to a lack of motivation, ability, or instructional scaffolds. This type of unresolved or hopeless confusion should be contrasted with productive confusion, which can eventually be resolved [18].

It has been suggested that ITSs can capitalize on the benefits of confusion by adaptively responding to natural occurrences of confusion. For example, UNC-ITSpoke is a novel ITS that provides adaptive feedback and instruction based on the correctness and level of certainty in a student's spoken response [8]. Similarly, the *Affective AutoTutor* provides motivational and supportive statements to help students persist in the learning task when it senses that they are confused [19]. Both systems have been shown to be more effective than non-affective counterparts, but only for a subset of students. This suggests that affective response strategies must take into consideration individual differences, an idea that is at the core of this paper.

A somewhat different approach to *reactively* capitalizing on opportunities afforded by naturally occurring confusion, is a *proactive* approach in which learning environments create learning opportunities through confusion induction. We have experimented with this approach and had some success with confusion induction through the presentation of system breakdowns [20], contradictory information [21-22], and false system feedback [23]. Space limitations preclude a detailed discussion of these studies, however, they all revealed that confusion induction and regulation was a successful learning strategy, but only for a subset of students. It is important, then, to understand the individual differences that influence the incidence of confusion itself, attempts at confusion resolution, and learning outcomes associated with these processes. In line with this, the present paper investigates the impact of individual differences in a learning environment that induces confusion via false feedback.

Our focus is on the analysis of a data set collected from a study in which students attempted to learn research methods while interacting with an animated tutor agent [23]. Students diagnosed the flaws in research case studies and received feedback (accurate or inaccurate) on the quality of the flaw diagnosis. The false feedback was expected to trigger confusion, which would inspire deeper processing, and the learning environment provided explanatory texts to aid confusion resolution. We found that students learned the most when they received false feedback and were successfully confused by the feedback. The previous paper [23] did not analyze individual differences associated with successful learning in this environment. To address this issue, we investigated whether individual differences impacted (1) the effectiveness of false feedback as a method of confusion induction and (2) learning gains in a false feedback learning environment. The individual difference measures included in the present paper were prior knowledge, confidence in the ability to learn from a computer tutor, perceptions of research methods (interest, willingness to put in effort to learn), the School Failure Tolerance scale (SFT, [24]), the Attributional

Complexity scale (ACS, [25]), and the Theory of Intelligence scale (TOI, [26]). These measures were selected because they assess preferences for challenging material and responses to academic challenges like those posed by confusion inducing stimuli.

2 Method

2.1 Participants

Participants (called students for the remainder of the paper) were 167 undergraduate students from a mid-south university in the US who received course credit for participation. Data from eleven students was not included in the present analyses because they did not complete the individual difference measures (described below). There were 115 females and 41 males in the sample, 62% of which were African-American, 32% Caucasian, 4% Hispanic, and 2% Asian.

2.2 Design and Manipulation

The experiment had a within-subjects design with four conditions, one on each research method topic (control group, experimenter bias, random assignment, replication): *positive-positive*, *positive-negative*, *negative-negative*, and *negative-positive*. Students completed two learning sessions in which they received accurate feedback and two sessions of false feedback. It was not guaranteed, however, that each student would be in all four conditions due to the fact that condition assignment was partially dependent upon student responses. Order of feedback condition, order of topics, and assignment of topics to conditions were counterbalanced across students with a Graeco-Latin Square.

False feedback was delivered during dialogues with an animated tutor agent over the course of identifying flaws in research case studies. Each study contained one subtle methodological flaw pertaining to one of four topics. The four feedback conditions were based on student response quality (*positive*: correct and *negative*: incorrect) and tutor agent feedback (*positive*: "Yes, that's right" and *negative*: "No, that's not right"). Students who responded correctly either received accurate, positive feedback (*positive-positive*) or inaccurate, negative feedback (*positive-negative*). Students in the *negative-negative* condition received accurate, negative feedback, whereas those in the *negative-positive* condition received inaccurate, positive feedback. It should be noted that all misleading information presented via false feedback was corrected at the end of each dialogue and participants were fully debriefed at the end of the experiment.

2.3 Procedure

The experiment occurred over two phases: (1) knowledge assessments and learning sessions and (2) individual difference measures.

Knowledge Tests. Research methods knowledge was assessed with a multiple-choice definition test and flaw identification task. The definition test consisted of eight multiple-choice questions. There was one question pertaining to each topic that was discussed in the learning sessions. In addition, there were four questions that pertained to topics not covered in the learning sessions (construct validity, correlational studies, generalizability, measure quality). The definition test was presented before and after all of the learning sessions had been completed (pretest and posttest, respectively). Two versions of the test were created and order of presentation was counterbalanced across students.

The flaw identification task consisted of a description of a previously unseen study and students were asked to identify flaw(s) in the study by selecting as many items as they wanted from a list of eight research methods topics. The list included four topics that could potentially be flawed (i.e., discussed in the learning sessions) and four distractor topics (i.e., not discussed in the learning sessions). Students also had the option of selecting that there was no flaw, although each study contained one flaw. Near and far transfer versions of studies were presented to students. The near transfer studies differed from the studies discussed in the learning sessions on surface features, whereas the far transfer studies differed on both surface and structural features. Each topic discussed during the learning sessions had one near and one far transfer study, resulting in eight transfer studies in all.

Learning Sessions. First, students signed an informed consent, completed a brief demographics questionnaire, and completed the pretest. Students then read a short introductory text on research methods. Next, students completed a survey about their perceptions of learning research methods (PLRM). These questions assessed student *interest* in and willingness to put in *effort* when learning about research methods and student *confidence* in the ability to learn from a computer tutor.

Students then began the first of four learning sessions. Each learning session consisted of four phases: manipulation, assumption check, remediation, and post-remediation. For the present paper only the manipulation and remediation phases are relevant and the others are not discussed here. The manipulation phase began with students reading a description of the study that was being discussed. Next, students were presented with a forced-choice question to diagnose the flaw in that study. When discussing the study with replication as its flaw, for example, the tutor agent asked the student "Was this a good or bad replication?" Students then selected one of the three response options: *target* (correct), *thematic miss* (incorrect but generally related to the concept), and *irrelevant distractor* (incorrect and not related to the concept). Students also rated whether they were confident or not confident in the correctness of their response prior to receiving feedback. The majority of students (80%) were confident in the correctness of their response [23]. The tutor agent then provided feedback about the quality of the response. Based on the condition, the feedback delivered could either be accurate or inaccurate, regardless of the actual quality of the response.

After receiving feedback, students were prompted to make a *post-feedback confusion judgment*. Students were prompted to indicate whether a classmate would be confused or not confused at this point in the learning session. The confusion prompt was phrased in this manner to avoid potential biases due to students' negative perceptions of being in a state of confusion [21]. Reports of confusion were found to be significantly related to increased student processing time after feedback [23]. Student processing time was assessed by asking students to indicate when they were ready to proceed with the learning session after receiving feedback.

In the remediation phase students were presented with an explanatory text to potentially alleviate their confusion. The texts were adapted from the electronic textbook that accompanies the *Operation ARA!* ITS [27]. Longer text reading times were considered to indicate greater depth of processing [28], which is ostensibly related to increased effort to resolve confusion. Post-feedback confusion judgments and explanatory text read times served as the learning process measures.

Individual Difference Measures. In addition to the PLRM (see above), students also completed three individual difference measures after the posttest: SFT [24], ACS [25], and TOI [26]. The SFT consists of three subscales: prefer difficult material, experience negative affect after failure, and take action after failure. These subscales describe the type of material students generally prefer (difficult vs. easy; *prefer difficult*) as well as the affective states that they experience (negative vs. positive; *negative affect*) and how they respond after failure (take action vs. avoid; *take action*).

The ACS consists of seven subscales. Only four of the subscales were used in the present analyses due to reliability issues within the current sample (see below). The four subscales used were motivation, metacognition, complex contemporary external explanations, and use of temporal dimension. These subscales assess the degree to which students look for (*motivation*) and monitor their own behavior for (*metacognition*) multiple explanations and prefer complex external explanations that are either temporally close (*contemporary*) or distant (*temporal*) from an event. The TOI has two subscales that represent either a theory that intelligence can be increased through effort and training (*incremental mindset*) or that people have a certain level of intelligence that cannot be altered (*entity mindset*). Reliability (Cronbach's alpha) for the nine subscales included in the analyses ranged from .616 to .915.

3 Results and Discussion

The analyses are divided into two sections. First, we conducted a *k*-means cluster analysis to group students with similar characteristics. Second, we investigated differences between clusters for the learning process and learning outcome measures.

3.1 Cluster Analysis

We used a *k*-means clustering method to group the 156 students into clusters. Students were grouped based on 14 attributes that included their pretest score; self-reported ACT score; interest, effort, and confidence from the PLRM; and the nine subscales from the SFT, ACS, and TOI. The *k* value was set to 4 based on an exploratory factor analysis and a hierarchical cluster analysis. We also experimented with *k's* of 3 and 5; however, the clusters were most distinct with $k = 4$.

ANOVAs indicated that 10 out of the 14 measures used to create the clusters significantly discriminated between clusters (p*'s* $< .05$). *Incremental mindset* (TOI) was only marginally significant ($p < .1$), while *entity mindset* (TOI), *confidence* (PLRM), and *negative affect* (SFT) did not discriminate between clusters (p*'s* $> .1$).

We correlated the individual clusters (dummy coded) and the 10 aforementioned measures in an attempt to name the clusters. Table 1 shows the pattern of correlations and the *N* for each cluster. *Cognitive Ability* (CA) and *Cognitive Drive* (CD) appeared to be the latent factors that distinguished the clusters. CA included pretest and ACT scores, whereas CD encompassed characteristics related to interest, effort, motivation, determination, and persistence. Thus the four clusters were named High CA + High CD (cluster 3), High CA + Low CD (cluster 1), Low CA + High CD (cluster 2), and Low CA + Low CD (cluster 4).

Table 1. Patterns in correlation matrix used for cluster naming

	Cluster 1 High CA + Low CD ($N = 12$)	**Cluster 2** Low CA + High CD ($N = 68$)	**Cluster 3** High CA + High CD ($N = 32$)	**Cluster 4** Low CA + Low CD ($N = 44$)
Cognitive Ability				
Pretest Score			+	-
ACT Score	+	-	+	-
Cognitive Drive				
PLRM: Interest		+	+	-
PLRM: Effort	-	+		
SFT: Prefer Difficult		+		-
SFT: Action	-	+	-	
ACS: Motivation	-		+	-
ACS: Metacognition	-			
ACS: Contemporary	-	+	+	
ACS: Temporal	-			

Notes. +'s or –'s indicate positive or negative correlations at $p < .10$.

3.2 Differences between Clusters

Next, we investigated differences between clusters for the learning process and learning outcome measures. Analyses were conducted separately for each type of learning session: positive-positive, positive-negative, negative-negative, and negative-positive. The High CA + Low CD cluster was not included in the present analyses due to the low N of 12. We conducted non-parametric Kruskal-Wallis tests with Mann-Whitney U post hoc tests when the variables were not normally distributed and ANOVAs with Bonferroni post hoc tests otherwise.

There were no significant cluster differences for the accurate feedback learning sessions (positive-positive, negative-negative). Thus, the discussion will focus on the false feedback learning sessions (positive-negative, negative-positive).

Learning Process Measures. There were marginally significant differences between clusters for the post-feedback confusion judgments in both false feedback learning sessions: positive-negative: $\chi^2(2, N = 119) = 5.47$, $p = .065$; negative-positive: $\chi^2(2, N = 99) = 4.56$, $p = .102$ (see Table 2). For the positive-negative sessions the High CA + High CD cluster reported significantly more confusion than the Low CA + Low CD cluster ($p = .034$). The other cluster comparisons were not significant. For the negative-positive sessions, the High CA + High CD cluster reported more confusion than the Low CA + High CD cluster ($p = .045$) and was the only significant cluster difference. These findings suggest that students must know enough and be sufficiently driven to recognize that there is a discrepancy in the system feedback.

Table 2. Descriptives for learning process measures

Measure	High CA + High CD	Low CA + High CD	Low CA + Low CD
Confusion (Proportion)			
Positive-Negative	.704	.475	.636
Negative-Positive	.630	.381	.412
Text Read Time M(SD) in secs			
Positive-Negative	75.5 (36.7)	68.5 (41.8)	78.2 (45.2)
Negative-Positive	97.9 (45.8)	78.2 (52.6)	62.6 (46.9)

There was a significant cluster difference in explanatory text reading times for the negative-positive sessions, $F(2, 96) = 3.55$, $p = .032$ but not for the positive-negative sessions ($p = .528$) (see Table 2). For the negative-positive sessions, the High CA + High CD cluster read for longer than Low CA + Low CD cluster ($p = .027$). The other cluster comparisons were not significant.

Learning Outcome Measures. Student performance on the definition posttest was assessed by selection of the correct answer option. For both transfer tasks student performance was assessed with hits (correctly identifying the presence of a flaw). There were no significant differences on the definition posttest for either of the false feedback learning sessions (*p's* > .1).

However, there were significant cluster differences on the flaw identification task (see Table 3). For the near transfer task, there were significant differences between clusters for the positive-negative sessions, $\chi^2(2, N = 118) = 6.24$, $p = .044$. The High CA + High CD ($p = .033$) and Low CA + High CD ($p = .026$) clusters performed better than the Low CA + Low CD cluster. The High CA + High CD and Low CA + High CD clusters did not significantly differ. There was not a significant difference between clusters for the negative-positive sessions ($p = .568$).

Table 3. Proportion of correct flaw detection for the flaw identification task

Measure	High CA + High CD	Low CA + High CD	Low CA + Low CD
Near Transfer			
Positive-Negative	.538	.466	.273
Negative-Positive	.500	.583	.471
Far Transfer			
Positive-Negative	.315	.169	.182
Negative-Positive	.545	.226	.318

There were significant differences between clusters for the negative-positive sessions for the far transfer task, $\chi^2(2, N = 97) = 7.32$, $p = .026$. The only significant cluster difference was that the High CA + High CD cluster performed better than the Low CA + High CD cluster ($p = .008$). There was not a significant cluster difference for the positive-negative sessions ($p = .248$).

These findings show that false feedback can promote learning at a deeper level, but that false feedback was most beneficial for a particular group of students (i.e., High CA + High CD). It is interesting, however, that the High CA + High CD cluster only performed better on the near transfer task when in the positive-negative learning sessions and the far transfer task when in the negative-positive learning sessions. We hypothesized that the increased performance on the transfer tasks could be related to the increased effort to resolve confusion (i.e., longer text read times) by the High CA + High CD cluster when in the false feedback learning sessions.

To address this hypothesis, we explored cluster differences on the transfer tasks when students were divided into those who read the text more quickly and read more slowly via a median split. There were no significant cluster differences when students read more quickly (p's > .05). However, when students read for longer, the High CA + High CD cluster performed better than the Low CA + Low CD cluster on the near transfer task, $\chi^2(2, N = 61) = 6.92, p = .031$, and better than the Low CA + High CD cluster on the far transfer task, $\chi^2(2, N = 62) = 5.88, p = .053$, for the positive-negative sessions. A similar pattern was found for the far transfer task in the negative-positive sessions, $\chi^2(2, N = 48) = 6.72, p = .035$, with the High CA + High CD cluster outperforming the Low CA + High CD cluster. These findings suggest that effortful attempts at confusion resolution were needed to perform well on the transfer tasks.

4 General Discussion

Recent research has focused on developing ITSs that promote learning through adaptive scaffolding based on both student cognition and affect [5-9]. It is also important, however, to determine the individual differences (e.g., interest, prior knowledge, learning styles) that influence the effectiveness of these affect-aware learning interventions because there is no one-size-fits-all approach to learning. As a step in this direction, we investigated the relationship between individual differences, confusion, and learning within a learning environment that proactively induces confusion as a means to promote deep inquiry.

A cluster analysis on a number of individual difference measures indicated that students differed with respect to cognitive ability and cognitive drive. We found that students with a combination of high cognitive ability and high cognitive drive benefited the most from the current learning environment. These students were successfully confused by the false feedback (induction) and performed better on the transfer tasks (learning). It is critically important to note that the high cognitive ability and high cognitive drive cluster did not simply learn more than the other clusters in all learning sessions. This cluster of students only outperformed the other clusters on transfer tasks when they received false feedback. Moreover, these students only outperformed the other clusters on the difficult far transfer task when they received false feedback and read the text for longer in an effort to resolve their confusion.

Despite these promising findings, some critics might object to the use of false feedback due to the potential for negative impacts on learning. This is a valid concern for more authentic learning contexts and for this reason it is important to understand which students do and do not benefit from this method of confusion induction.

However, it is important to note that previous analyses showed that inaccurate feedback did not negatively impact learning in the present experimental research [23].

Now that we have identified which students benefited from false feedback in the present learning environment, the next step is to determine how to help other students benefit from experiences of confusion during learning. There are two aspects of the learning environment that can be targeted. First, false feedback is not the only method of confusion induction. It may be the case that productive confusion is triggered by different stimuli for different students (e.g., system breakdowns [20], contradictory information [21-22]). Second, presentation of an explanatory text may not have been the most appropriate method of confusion remediation for all students. Students who are lower in cognitive ability and cognitive drive may need more adaptive, targeted scaffolding (e.g., critical information [8] or encouragement [19]). Or perhaps, it is simply better to avoid confusing these students and rely on more explanation-focused pedagogical approaches. Future research will need to differentially adapt both confusion induction and remediation strategies for different individual differences to maximize learning for all students.

Acknowledgments. This research was supported by the National Science Foundation (NSF) (ITR 0325428, HCC 0834847, DRL 1235958). Any opinions, findings and conclusions, or recommendations expressed in this paper are those of the authors and do not necessarily reflect the views of NSF.

References

1. VanLehn, K.: The relative effectiveness of human tutoring, intelligent tutoring systems, and other tutoring systems. Educational Psychologist 46, 197–221 (2011)
2. D'Mello, S., Lehman, B., Person, N.: Expert tutors feedback is immediate, direct, and discriminating. In: Murray, C., Guesgen, H. (eds.) Proceedings of the 23rd Florida Artificial Intelligence Research Society Conference, pp. 595–660. AAAI Press, Menlo Park (2010)
3. Graesser, A., Person, K., Magliano, J.: Collaborative dialogue patterns in naturalistic one-to-one tutoring. Applied Cognitive Psychology 9, 495–522 (1995)
4. Lepper, M., Woolverton, M.: The wisdom of practice: Lessons learned from the study of highly effective tutors. In: Aronson, J. (ed.) Improving Academic Achievement: Impact of Psychological Factors on Education, pp. 135–158. Academic Press, Orlando (2002)
5. Arroyo, I., Woolf, B., Cooper, D., Burleson, W., Muldner, K., Christopherson, R.: Emotion sensors go to school. In: Dimitrova, V., Mizoguchi, R., Du Boulay, B., Graesser, A. (eds.) Proceedings of 14th International Conference on Artificial Intelligence in Education, pp. 17–24. IOS Press, Amsterdam (2009)
6. Conati, C., Maclaren, H.: Empirically building and evaluating a probabilistic model of user affect. User Modeling and User-Adapted Interaction 19(3), 267–303 (2009)
7. D'Mello, S., Craig, S., Fike, K., Graesser, A.: Responding to learners' cognitive-affective states with supportive and shakeup dialogues. In: Jacko, J.A. (ed.) HCI International 2009, Part III. LNCS, vol. 5612, pp. 595–604. Springer, Heidelberg (2009)
8. Forbes-Riley, K., Litman, D.: Benefits and challenges of real-time uncertainty detection and adaptation in a spoken dialogue computer tutor. Speech Communication 53, 1115–1136 (2011)

9. Robison, J., McQuiggan, S., Lester, J.: Evaluating the consequences of affective feedback in intelligent tutoring systems. In: Muhl, C., Heylen, D., Nijholt, A. (eds.) Proceedings of International Conference on Affective Computing & Intelligent Interaction, pp. 37–42. IEEE Computer Society Press, Los Alamitos (2009)
10. Pekrun, R., Stephens, E.: Academic emotions. In: Urdan, T. (ed.) APA Educational Psychology Handbook, vol. 2, pp. 3–31. American Psychological Association, Washington, DC (2012)
11. Silvia, P.: Confusion and interest: The role of knowledge emotions in aesthetic experience. Psychology of Aesthetics, Creativity, and the Arts 4, 75–80 (2010)
12. Carroll, J., Kay, D.: Prompting, feedback and error correction in the design of a scenario machine. International Journal of Man-Machine Studies 28, 11–27 (1988)
13. D'Mello, S., Graesser, A.: Confusion. In: Pekrun, R., Linnenbrink-Garcia, L. (eds.) Handbook of Emotions and Education. Taylor & Francis, New York (in press)
14. VanLehn, K., Siler, S., Murray, C., Yamauchi, T., Baggett, W.: Why do only some events cause learning during human tutoring? Cognition and Instruction 21, 209–249 (2003)
15. Piaget, J.: The origins of intelligence. International University Press, New York (1952)
16. Craig, S., Graesser, A., Sullins, J., Gholson, B.: Affect and Learning: An exploratory look into the role of affect in learning. Journal of Educational Media 29, 241–250 (2004)
17. Graesser, A., Chipman, P., King, B., McDaniel, B., D'Mello, S.: Emotions and learning with AutoTutor. In: Luckin, R., Koedinger, K., Greer, J. (eds.) Proceedings of the 13th International Conference on Artificial Intelligence in Education, pp. 569–571. IOS Press, Amsterdam (2007)
18. D'Mello, S., Graesser, A.: Dynamics of affective states during complex learning. Learning and Instruction 22, 145–157 (2012)
19. D'Mello, S., Lehman, B., Sullins, J., Daigle, R., Combs, R., Vogt, K., Perkins, L., Graesser, A.: A time for emoting: When affect-sensitivity is and isn't effective at promoting deep learning. In: Aleven, V., Kay, J., Mostow, J. (eds.) ITS 2010, Part I. LNCS, vol. 6094, pp. 245–254. Springer, Heidelberg (2010)
20. D'Mello, S., Graesser, A.: Inducing and tracking confusion and cognitive disequilibrium with breakdown scenarios (in review)
21. D'Mello, S., Lehman, B., Pekrun, R., Graesser, A.: Confusion can be beneficial for learning. Learning and Instruction (in press)
22. Lehman, B., D'Mello, S., Strain, A., Mills, C., Gross, M., Dobbins, A., Wallace, P., et al.: Inducing and tracking confusion with contradictions during complex learning. International Journal of Artificial Intelligence in Education (in press)
23. Lehman, B., D'Mello, S., Graesser, A.: False feedback can improve learning when you're productively confused (in review)
24. Clifford, M.: Failure tolerance and academic risk-taking in ten- to twelve-year-old students. British Journal of Educational Psychology 58, 268–294 (1988)
25. Fletcher, G., Danilovics, P., Fernandez, G., Peterson, D., Reeder, G.: Attributional complexity: An individual differences measure. Journal of Personality and Social Psychology 51, 875–884 (1986)
26. Dweck, C.: Self theories: Their role in motivation, personality and development. Taylor & Francis/Psychology Press, Philadelphia (1999)
27. Halper, D., Millis, K., Graesser, A., Butler, H., Forsyth, C., Cai, Z.: Operation ARA: A computerized learning game that teaches critical thinking and scientific reasoning. Thinking Skills and Creativity 7, 93–100 (2012)
28. Craik, F., Tulving, E.: Depth of processing and the retention of words in episodic memory. Journal of Experimental Psychology: General 104, 268–294 (1975)

Aligning and Comparing Data on Emotions Experienced during Learning with MetaTutor

Jason M. Harley, François Bouchet, and Roger Azevedo

McGill University, Laboratory for the Study of Metacognition and Advanced Learning Technologies, Montreal, Canada
jason.harley@mail.mcgill.ca

Abstract. In this study we aligned and compared self-report and on-line emotions data on 67 college students' emotions at five different points in time over the course of their interactions with MetaTutor. Self-reported emotion data as well as facial expression data were converged and analyzed. Results across channels revealed that neutral and positively-valenced basic and learner-centered emotional states represented the majority of emotional states experienced with MetaTutor. The self-report results revealed a decline in the intensity of positively-valenced and neutral states across the learning session. The facial expression results revealed a substantial decrease in the number of learners' with neutral facial expressions from time one to time two, but a fairly stable pattern for the remainder of the session, with participants who experienced other basic emotional states, transitioning back to a state of neutral between self-reports. Agreement between channels was 75.6%.

Keywords: Emotions, affect, intelligent tutoring systems, pedagogical agents.

1 Emotions during Learning with ITSs

Effective learning and students' experience of emotions are critically related [e.g., 1,2]. For ITS research, this translates into a recognized need to design systems with embodied pedagogical agents (PAs) that use AI algorithms to detect, model, and adapt to changes in learners' emotional fluctuations, in order to promote adaptive emotional states that will facilitate learning [3-5]. Despite the recent surge in interdisciplinary research on emotions and affective computing [6], little is known about many important facets of learners' emotional experiences with ITSs, such as how learners' emotions fluctuate over time (e.g., over the course of a learning session) and how different components (behavioral, physiological, and experiential) of emotions align. Identifying patterns in learners' emotional experiences over time is critical to understanding how learners' feel as they progress temporally through the learning session. In particular, such finer-grained analyses provide valuable diagnostic information regarding events or time segments to focus system changes on, such as changes to the rules used to determine system dynamics or the creation of new PA-delivered emotional interventions. It is equally paramount to assess the convergence of different methods for measuring emotions in order to establish convergent

K. Yacef et al. (Eds.): AIED 2013, LNAI 7926, pp. 61–70, 2013.

validity between methodologies and to further our psychological theories of emotions regarding, for example, the loose or tight coupling of different emotional expression components [7]. Answering these questions will help ITS researchers design more effective emotionally adaptive ITSs with improved calibration between the emotion-regulating prompts provided by PAs and learners' emotional states. Furthermore, this important user-diagnostic information will also help reduce the negative outcomes associated with mis-calibrations between participants' experienced emotional states and ITSs' understanding of them [3-5].

1.1 Research Objectives

There were three primary purposes of this study. (1) To examine learners' emotional responses across the MetaTutor learning session to determine which emotions were most prominently experienced and whether they changed as the learning session unfolded. (2) To examine whether significant differences in learners' emotional experiences existed between MetaTutor's two PAs scaffolding conditions: prompt and feedback (PF) and control (C). (3) To examine whether there was convergent evidence of learners' emotional experiences between the two emotion measurement methods we used: automatic facial expression analysis (FaceReader 5.0 [8]), and an in-session, concurrent, emotional state self-report measure (Emotions-Value questionnaire).

2 Methods

2.1 Participants

67 undergraduate students from a large, public university in North America participated in this study. Participants (82.8% female, 72.4% Caucasian) were randomly assigned to either the C or PF condition.

2.2 MetaTutor and Apparatus

MetaTutor [9] is a multi-agent ITS and hypermedia learning environment which consists of 38 pages of text and static diagrams organized by a table of contents displayed in the left pane of the environment. The version of MetaTutor used in this experiment is comprised of material on the human circulatory system, which it is designed to teach participants about during their interactions with four embedded, pedagogical agents (PAs). The four PAs' instructional scaffolding varied depending on the experimental condition learners were assigned to (aside from PA scaffolding, the C and PF conditions were identical). In the PF condition, learners were prompted by the PAs to use specific self-regulatory processes (e.g., to metacognitively monitor their emerging understanding of the topic or deploy a specific cognitive learning strategy such as re-reading or coordinating informational sources), and were given feedback about their use of those processes. In the C condition, participants did not receive prompts or feedback.

A Logitech Orbit AF webcam was used to record the participants' faces during their interaction with MetaTutor. In accordance with FaceReader's guidelines, the camera was mounted above the monitor of the computer participants were using, in order to capture their faces, but not obstruct the screen. Videos were recorded as WMV files with a resolution of 1600x1200, and 12.1 frames per second on average.

2.3 Measures and Materials

FaceReader 5.0. FaceReader [8] analyzes participants' facial expressions and provides a classification of their emotional states using an Active Appearance Model which models participants' facial expressions, and an artificial neural network with seven discrete outputs, corresponding to Ekman and Friesen's six basic emotions [10] in addition to neutral, that classifies participants' constellations of facial expressions. FaceReader has been validated through comparison with human coders [11]. Videos recorded during the two sessions of the experiment (with an average length of 40 and 100 minutes respectively) were imported and used to calibrate FaceReader with General or Asian face models. Videos of the second session (when the learning occurred) were then analyzed with the "smoothen classification" parameter enabled.

Emotions-Value Questionnaire (EV). During the learning session, participants were asked on five occasions (see section 2.4) by a PA to complete the EV questionnaire, for which each participant responded to 20 items: 19 items on emotions and 1 item on task value which was not considered in this analysis. These items were on a 5-point Likert scale ranging from "Strongly Disagree" to "Strongly Agree." One example item is: "right now I feel engaged." The 19 emotions that are measured using the EV represent an exhaustive list of discrete basic and learner-centered emotions that appear in the research and theories of a variety of emotion researchers [e.g., 2, 12]. Definitions, based on these researchers' work and operationalizations of these emotions, were used to create a digital, definition hand out that was provided in a side panel to participants every time they filled out an electronic version of the EV embedded in MetaTutor. The instructions and wording of the questions were based on a subscale of Pekrun et al. [13] academic emotions questionnaire (AEQ) which assesses participants' concurrent, 'right now' state-emotions as opposed to emotions generated from prospective or retrospective focal points. The majority of the 19 emotions can be conceptualized into different quadrants along the axis of valence (positive/negative) and activation (activating/deactivating) [2, 13].

2.4 Experimental Procedure

During Day One of the experiment, which took approximately 30 minutes, participants read and signed the informed consent form, took a pretest on the human circulatory system, completed a demographics questionnaire, and several self-report measures (e.g., AEQ trait emotions) on a computer with their face being video recorded. For Day Two, we collected video, audio, eye-tracking, and physiological data on each participant while they used MetaTutor for about 90 min to learn about the human circulatory system. At the beginning of the learning session participants set up two sub goals for learning about the human circulatory system and proceeded to interact with MetaTutor and its learning content for one hour; half-way through, they were asked to complete the concurrent state AEQ and then invited to take a five-minute break. At the end of their learning session, learners filled out the post-test measure and a series of self-report measures, including the retrospective state AEQ. Days One and Two occurred at least one hour apart from each other and no more than four days apart. The first time participants filled out the EV was at the beginning of the learning session after they had successfully set two sub goals. The following occasions occurred regularly every 14 minutes during the on hour learning session, with the fifth EV being administered just before learners' took the post-test. Participants had as much time as necessary to fill out the EV on each occasion.

2.5 Data Analysis

FaceReader 5.0. FaceReader provides a score between 0 and 1, for each frame of each participant's video for each of Ekman's six basic emotions, in addition to neutral. FaceReader also provides information about the dominant emotional state (computed with a proprietary algorithm using the scores of the seven emotional states in the previous frames) and timestamp information regarding the on and offset of the hierarchical rankings of these states. In these analyses, we aligned FaceReader's dominant state with the EV by extracting log information corresponding to the 10 seconds of video footage of participants right before they were asked to fill in each of the EVs. We selected the primary dominant state defined as the state reported as dominant during the majority of the 10 seconds. In 80.7% of the cases, no other unique emotion was dominant for more than 3s, which makes it unnecessary to consider the possibility of a secondary co-occurring emotion [14]. Moreover, in 92.9% of the remaining situations, neutral was either the primary or secondary dominant emotion.

67 participants were analyzed, but nine of them were excluded from our sample because their dominant state in the 10s for at least three of the five EVs were identified as "Unknown" by FaceReader (this situation generally occurs when the participant's face is not sufficiently oriented towards the webcam, e.g. when they look down to type on the keyboard).

In order to evaluate the agreement between the self-reported emotions in the 5 EVs and the dominant emotion identified by FaceReader during the 10s before, we started by defining a mapping between the 13 non-basic emotions from the EV onto the 6 basic emotions in addition to neutral that are used by FaceReader to classify participants' emotions. Using work from Pekrun et al. [2, 13] on the AEQ, (1) all positively valenced activating emotions (enjoyment, hope, pride, curiosity and eureka) were associated with happy; among the negatively valenced activating emotions, (2) frustration was grouped with anger, (3) anxiety with fear and (4) contempt with disgust, and (5) all negatively valenced deactivating emotions (hopelessness and boredom) were associated with sadness, while the (6 and 7) non-valenced emotions (neutral and surprise) were kept as two distinct categories. Two additional emotions (confusion and shame) used in the EV could not be associated to any basic emotions and were therefore discarded for this analysis.

Given these seven groups of emotions, we defined that there was an agreement between FaceReader's dominant emotion and the EV if and only if one of the emotions associated to FaceReader's dominant emotion was rated with a score of 3 or more (out of 5) in the EV (e.g., if the dominant emotion according to FaceReader is anger, either anger or frustration need to have a score of 3 or more in the EV). The 20 (out of 290) occurrences of "Unknown" were excluded from this analysis.

EV. Several scores on different emotions on the EV measure were identified as univariate outliers with standardized scores exceeding z = +/- 3.29 and were therefore replaced with the next most outlying values for each variable [15]. Several variables were identified as being skewed with values exceeding z = +/- 3.20. Only emotion variables that were skewed across all five EVs were transformed, including fear, shame, hopelessness, disgust, sadness, and eureka. Square root, logarithmic, and inverse transformations were performed, but did not normalize the distributions for all variables (only hopelessness and eureka). Two to three of the five EV variables for anger, contempt, surprise, and confusion were skewed, but were not transformed in order to maintain consistency across the measures of each emotion.

3 Results

3.1 Which Emotions Were Most Prominent in Learners' Experience with MetaTutor and Did They Change during a One-Hour Learning Session?

Emotion-Value Questionnaire. We ran 19 repeated measure ANOVAs on the level of each self-reported emotion between the two conditions and across the five EVs. Table 1 provides the means and standard deviations (SDs) of each of the 19 emotions for each of the five EVs. Neutral (M = 3.36; SD = 0.64), curiosity (M = 2.93; SD = 0.71), and hope (M = 2.89; SD = 0.54) had the highest mean levels when averaging all the EVs together. The inferential results of the repeated measure ANOVAs, summarized in Table 2, illustrate that the administration of the EV exerted a significant main effect on learners' experience of happiness, enjoyment, hope, pride, anger, frustration, surprise, confusion, curiosity, and neutral. In the interest of space, only significant results are reported in Table 2. Pairwise difference tests, conducted using a Bonferoni correction, revealed which EVs learners' emotions significantly differed between.

FaceReader. Table 3 provides a summary of the results obtained from FaceReader in which the frequencies and proportions of participants' dominant emotions are reported for each EV. Figure 1 illustrates the proportions from Table 3 using different gradients of circle sizes. Line gradients represent the number of participants who transition from one basic emotion state to another. For example, in the 10 sec. before participants reported their emotions on EV1, more than 50% of them (which we know to be 77.6% from Table 3) had a neutral facial expression. The thin solid blue lines show

Table 1. Summary of means and standard deviations on emotions using the Evs

Emotion	*1*		*2*		*3*		*4*		*5*		*Avg.*	
	M	*SD*	*M*	*SD*	*M*	*SD*	*M*	*SD*	*M*	*SD*	*M*	*SD*
Happy	3.03	0.67	2.90	1.00	2.62	0.93	2.59	0.97	2.59	1.12	2.74	0.48
Enjoy.	3.07	0.95	2.91	1.14	2.66	1.00	2.57	1.06	2.50	1.05	2.74	0.52
Hope	3.38	0.88	3.07	1.06	2.74	0.94	2.69	1.05	2.57	0.06	2.89	0.54
Pride	2.74	0.81	2.67	0.98	2.38	0.95	2.48	1.05	2.40	0.97	2.53	0.51
Anger	1.41	0.72	1.67	0.91	1.74	1.02	1.95	1.08	1.62	0.95	1.68	0.41
Frust.	1.99	1.25	2.16	1.27	2.41	1.41	2.60	1.34	2.28	1.36	2.29	0.63
Anx.	2.34	1.09	2.31	1.26	2.34	1.34	2.19	1.25	2.24	1.22	2.29	0.62
Fear	1.36	0.61	1.24	0.43	1.29	0.65	1.28	0.56	1.34	0.63	1.30	0.21
Shame	1.60	0.90	1.59	0.88	1.52	0.90	1.40	0.84	1.57	0.88	1.53	0.34
Hopel.	1.48	0.80	1.52	0.86	1.72	1.07	1.76	1.08	1.67	1.07	1.63	0.40
Bored	2.47	1.16	2.69	1.13	2.66	1.37	2.64	1.44	2.57	1.42	2.60	0.69
Surp.	1.90	1.02	2.03	1.14	1.43	0.70	1.66	0.89	1.52	0.80	1.71	0.56
Cntmpt.	1.84	1.14	1.78	1.12	1.76	1.16	1.95	1.18	1.72	1.18	1.81	0.42
Disgust	1.16	0.37	1.26	0.55	1.21	0.55	1.22	0.56	1.34	0.69	1.24	0.17
Confus.	1.91	0.94	2.10	1.13	2.09	1.11	1.76	0.98	1.72	0.99	1.92	0.52
Curios.	3.57	1.06	3.05	1.23	2.86	1.15	2.71	1.24	2.48	1.20	2.93	0.71
Sad	1.26	0.55	1.36	0.64	1.28	0.59	1.28	0.56	1.44	0.78	1.32	0.25
Eureka	1.50	0.78	1.74	1.09	1.66	0.98	1.67	1.05	1.57	0.98	1.63	0.34
Neutral	3.88	1.04	3.26	1.25	3.24	1.26	3.31	1.25	3.12	1.30	3.36	0.64

Table 2. Summary of Significant Repeated Measure ANOVA Results Using EVs

Emot.	*df*	*F*	*P*	η_p^2	**Pairwise difference ($p < .05$)?**									
					1,2	**1,3**	**1,4**	**1,5**	**2,3**	**2,4**	**2,5**	**3,4**	**3,5**	**4,5**
Happy	3.2, 177.9	5.77	0.01*	0.09		>	>	>						
Enjoy.	4, 224	7.77	0.00*	0.12		>	>	>			>			
Hope	3.3, 182.8	15.30	0.00*	0.22		>	>	>		>	>			
Pride	4, 224	3.52	0.01*	0.06										
Anger	4, 224	5.76	0.00*	0.09				<						>
Frust.	3.3, 184.9	4.57	0.00*	0.08			<			<				
Surp.	3.2, 179.2	6.54	0.00*	0.11		>			>		>			
Confus.	4, 224	3.50	0.01*	0.06										
Curios	3.3, 186.6	14.55	0.00*	0.21	>	>	>	>			>		>	
Neutral	4,224	7.32	0.00*	0.12	>	>	>	>						

* $p < 0.05$. Note: Greater than signs indicate which emotion's mean for each EV was larger

that between five and nine of these participants transitioned to a state of surprise or happiness before taking the second EV; the dotted blue line indicates that four or less transitioned to a state of sadness; and the thick, solid blue line indicates that 10 or more also had neutral facial expressions, once again, prior to filling out the EV2.

Table 3. Frequencies and Proportions of Emotions using FaceReader in the 10s before each EV

Emotion	1		2		3		4		5	
	Freq.	%	Freq.	%	Freq.	%	Freq.	%	Freq.	%
Neutral	45	77.6	30	51.7	31	53.4	33	56.9	32	55.2
Happy	5	8.6	11	19.0	12	20.7	17	29.3	11	19.0
Surprise	2	3.4	7	12.1	1	1.7	1	1.7	3	5.2
Fear	-	-	-	-	-	-	-	-	-	-
Anger	2	3.4	-	-	2	3.4	2	3.4	3	5.2
Sad	2	3.4	4	6.9	7	12.1	3	5.2	3	5.2
Disgust	-	-	-	-	-	-	1	1.7	-	-
Unknown	2	3.4	6	10.3	5	8.6	1	1.7	6	10.3
Sum	58	100	58	100	58	100	58	100	58	100

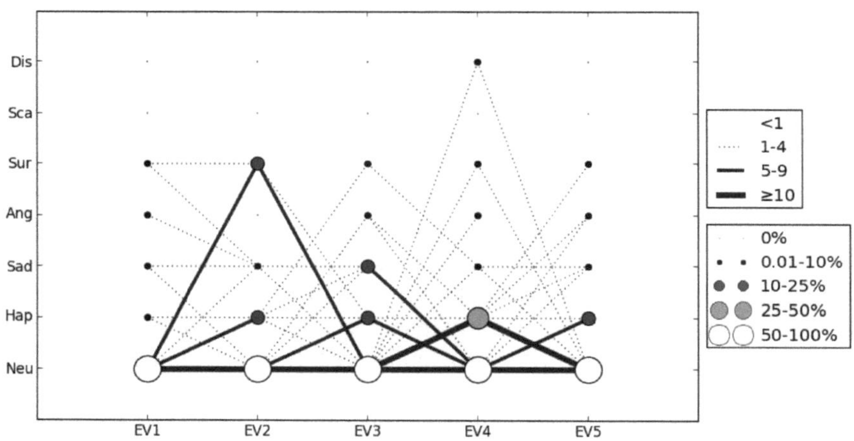

Fig. 1. Transitions between basic emotions using FaceReader data

3.2 Were There Significant Differences in Learners' Emotional Experiences between MetaTutor's Two PAs Scaffolding Conditions?

One of the previously described repeated measure ANOVAs revealed a significant main effect of condition on learners' self-reported emotional states: neutral, $F(1, 56) = 5.87$, $p <. 02$, $n^2_p = 0.10$. A second repeated measure ANOVA, found a significant interaction effect between EV and condition for sadness $F(3.01, 168.70) = 2.73$, $p < .05$, $n^2_p = 0.05$. Levene's test of equality of error variances was violated for three of the five EV self-reports for sadness, however, therefore this effect should be interpreted with caution. No other significant effects of condition were found.

3.3 Is There Converging Evidence of Learners' Emotional Experiences between Self-report and On-Line Measures?

Using the method described above to compare self-reported and classified (through FaceReader) emotions, we established an agreement rate[1] of 75.6%, suggesting that FaceReader can be used reasonably well to assess learner's emotions, even if it cannot provide a fine-grained identification of non-basic (i.e., learner-centered) emotions.

4 Discussion

In response to our first research question (which emotions are most prominent in learners' experience with MetaTutor and do they change as the learning session unfolds?) we found that neutral, curiosity and hope had the highest mean levels when averaging all the EVs together. We also noted that of the 19 emotions assessed using the EV, learners' experience of happiness, enjoyment, hope, pride, anger, frustration, surprise, confusion, curiosity, and neutral meaningfully differed across the learning session, while the others remained more stable. In looking at these fluctuations more closely a pattern emerges in which learners' positive, activating emotions and neutral states tended to decline as the session progressed, most notably, between the administration of EV1 and EV3. These patterns draw our attention to a need for an intervention to sustain higher levels of positive emotions (e.g., curiosity, engagement) and neutral states. Another pattern that ran in the opposite direction was the negative, activating emotions anger and frustration, which gradually increased as the session progressed and peaked just before participants filled out the EV4.

In examining the results from FaceReader we observed, similarly, that neutral and a positive activating emotion, happiness, made up the largest proportions of participants' emotional experiences. In particular, most participants embodied a neutral state at each of the EVs, though a substantial proportion of them transitioned to a positive state; the majority of which either transitioned back to a state of neutral or another emotional state before the next EV was administered. It is notable that, similar to the EV self-report analyses in which participants reported low mean levels of negative emotions, few participants facially embodied negative emotions and those who did didn't tend to remain fixed in that state. For example, all of the participants who embodied a sad facial expression before EV3 transitioned to a neutral state before EV4. In summary, these results are favorable, especially considering that MetaTutor is not presently designed using gamification features (e.g., points, story elements) or to provide interventions that specifically aim to improve or sustain learners' (adaptive) emotions. Furthermore, most students were not biology majors[2] and the content was not designed to be related to a specific course for those who were.

In general, the answer to our second research question, did significant differences in learners' emotional experiences exist between MetaTutor's two PAs

[1] Because learners were not asked to provide their dominant emotion among the 19 proposed, it is not possible to provide a kappa value.

[2] 93% of students majored in non-biology fields (e.g., psychology, economics, engineering).

scaffolding conditions, is no. Overall, given the low level of negative emotions reported and observed facially, this suggests that at the very least, the more advanced and adaptive feedback that MetaTutor's PAs are providing are not being responded to with negative feelings.

This study also demonstrated that different emotion (behavioral and experiential) measurement methodologies (facial expressions analyses and self-report) can be effectively aligned and produce convergent results. This is particularly notable because of the differences between these two measures. Specifically, the EV assesses the level (e.g., intensity) of a set of potential emotional experiences concurrently, while FaceReader assesses which emotional state learners' are in based on fit with pre-learned facial expressions. Furthermore, these two methods are based on different theories of emotion and use different sub sets of discrete emotions. As a result, despite the strong agreement rate (75.6%), there are some differences in terms of the overall patterns, such as the decline in mean levels of positive activating emotions when they are measured separately with the EV vs. the increase in learners' facial expressions of happiness (up to EV 4). This apparent variation in patterns may be the result of subtle differences between the facial embodiment of an emotion and its psychological experience and corresponding self-report. For example, a participant may smile and self-report a 3 on the EV regarding a feeling of pride. In this example, the learner reported experiencing a moderate intensity level of a positive activating emotion (pride) related to FaceReader's classification of happiness as the dominant emotional state, which would be counted as an agreement between the methods.

In conclusion, the high agreement rate we found between methods and convergent results (e.g., that neutral and positively-valenced basic and learner-centered emotional states represented the majority of emotional states experienced with MetaTutor) bolsters the validity of our emotion assessments and provides a strong foundation to make valid and reliable diagnostic examinations of learners' emotions at discrete points during learning with MetaTutor. Conceptually and theoretically, our results provide evidence that the experiential and behavioral components of emotions are tightly coupled. Educationally, improved measurement strategies of emotions will lead to better calibrated interventions that can be designed to support and sustain adaptive emotional states during learning with ITSs.

Acknowledgements. The research presented in this paper has been supported by a doctoral fellowship from the Fonds Québécois de recherche - Société et culture (FQRSC) awarded to the first author and the National Science Foundation (DRL 1008282) awarded to the third author.

References

1. Chauncey Strain, A., Azevedo, R., D'Mello, S.K.: Using a False Biofeed-back Methodology to Explore Relationships Among Learners' Affect, Metacognition, and Performance. Contemporary Ed. Psych. 38, 22–39 (2013)
2. Pekrun, R., Goetz, T., Frenzel-Anne, C., Petra, B., Perry, R.P.: Measuring Emotions in Students' Learning and Performance: The Achievement Emotions Questionnaire (AEQ). Contemporary Ed. Psych. 36, 34–48 (2011)

3. D'Mello, S.K., Lehman, B., Graesser, A.: A Motivationally Supportive Affect-Sensitive AutoTutor. In: Calvo, R.A., D'Mello, S.K. (eds.) New Perspectives on Affect and Learning Tech., pp. 113–126. Springer, NY (2011)
4. Robinson, J., McGuiggan, S.W., Lester, J.: Evaluating the Consequences of Affective Feedback in ITSs. In: Cohn, J., Nijholt, A., Pantic, M. (eds.) Proceedings of the 3rd Int. Conference on Affective Computing & Intelligent Interaction, pp. 37–42. IEEE, Amsterdam (2009)
5. Woolf, B.P., Arroyo, I., Muldner, K., Burleson, W., Cooper, D.G., Dolan, R., Christopherson, R.M.: The Effect of Motivational Learning Companions on Low Achieving Students and Students with Disabilities. In: Aleven, V., Kay, J., Mostow, J. (eds.) ITS 2010, Part I. LNCS, vol. 6094, pp. 327–337. Springer, Heidelberg (2010)
6. Calvo, R.A., D'Mello, S.K. (eds.): New Perspectives on Affect and Learning Technologies. Springer, Amsterdam (2011)
7. Gross, J.J., Barret, L.F.: Emotion Generation and Emotion Regulation: One or Two Depends on Your Point of View. Emotion Rev. 3, 8–16 (2011)
8. VicarVision: FaceReader 5.0 [Computer software]. Noldus Information Technology, Wageningen, The Netherlands (2012)
9. Azevedo, R., Behnagh, R., Duffy, M., Harley, J., Trevors, G.: Metacognition and SRL in Student-Centered Leaning Environments. In: Jonassen, D., Land, S. (eds.) Theoretical Foundations of Student-centered Learning Environments, 2nd edn., pp. 171–197. Routledge, New York (2012)
10. Ekman, P.: An Argument for Basic Emotions. Cognition & Emotion 6, 169–200 (1992)
11. Terzis, V., Moridis, C.N., Economides, A.A.: Measuring Instant Emotions During a Self-Assessment Test: The Use of FaceReader. In: Proceedings of the 7th Inter. Conf. on Methods and Techniques in Behavioral Research, pp. 18:1–18:4. ACM, New York (2010)
12. D'Mello, S.K., Lehman, B., Person, N.: Monitoring Affective States During Effortful Problem Solving Activities. International Journal of Artificial Intelligence in Education 20, 361–389 (2010)
13. Pekrun, R., Goetz, T., Titz, W., Perry, R.: Academic Achievement Emotions in Students' Self-Regulated Learning and Achievement: A Program of Quantitative and Qualitative Research. Ed. Psychologist 37, 91–206 (2002)
14. Harley, J.M., Bouchet, F., Azevedo, R.: Measuring learners' co-occurring emotional responses during their interaction with a pedagogical agent in MetaTutor. In: Cerri, S.A., Clancey, W.J., Papadourakis, G., Panourgia, K. (eds.) ITS 2012. LNCS, vol. 7315, pp. 40–45. Springer, Heidelberg (2012)
15. Tabachnick, B.G., Fidell, L.S.: Using Multivariate Statistics, 5th edn. Pearson Education/Allyn and Bacon, Boston, MA (2007)

What Makes Learning Fun? Exploring the Influence of Choice and Difficulty on Mind Wandering and Engagement during Learning

Caitlin Mills[1], Sidney D'Mello[1, 2], Blair Lehman[3], Nigel Bosch[2], Amber Strain[3], and Art Graesser[3]

[1] Departments of Psychology
[2] Computer Science, University of Notre Dame Notre Dame, IN 46556, USA
{cmills4,sdmello,pbosch}@nd.edu
[3] Department of Psychology and Institute for Intelligent Systems, University of Memphis, Memphis, TN 38152, USA
{dchuncey,balehman,a-graesser}@memphis.edu

Abstract. Maintaining learner engagement is critical for all types of learning technologies. This study investigated how choice over a learning topic and the difficulty of the materials influenced mind wandering, engagement, and learning during a computerized learning task. 59 participants were randomly assigned to a text difficulty and choice condition (i.e., self-selected or experimenter-selected topic) and measures of mind wandering and engagement were collected during learning. Participants who studied the difficult version of the texts reported significantly higher rates of mind wandering (d = .41) and lower arousal both during (d = .52) and after the learning session (d = .48). Mind wandering and arousal were not affected by choice. However, participants who were assigned to study the topic they selected reported significantly more positive valence during (d = .57) but not after learning. These participants also scored substantially higher on a subsequent knowledge test (d = 1.27). These results suggest that choice and text difficulty differentially impact mind wandering, engagement, and learning and provide important considerations for the design of ITSs and serious games with a reading component.

Keywords: engagement, mind wandering, reading, serious games, affect.

1 Introduction

Keeping learners attentive and engaged has long been an important challenge for computerized learning systems. Although learners might begin a session with some enthusiasm and involvement, engagement wanes as time passes [1–3] and learners start to disengage by zoning out or engaging in unproductive, off-task behaviors [4–6]. These types of behaviors have been linked to negligible learning, lowered interest, and attrition in academic contexts [6–8]. The problem of diminished or outright disengagement during a learning session threatens the effectiveness of educational technologies because engagement is a necessary (but not sufficient) condition for

K. Yacef et al. (Eds.): AIED 2013, LNAI 7926, pp. 71–80, 2013.

learning, particularly at deeper levels. Therefore, advances in uncovering and detecting the factors that trigger disengagement are sorely needed.

Engagement is a complex meta-construct with behavioral, affective, and cognitive components that vary both situationally and dispositionally [9]. Effort and task persistence constitute some of the behavioral components of engagement [9], while the affective components include valence, arousal, and discrete emotions like interest and curiosity. The cognitive components of engagement include attention, concentration, and the use of learning strategies. There have been an increasing number of studies that focus on the behavioral and affective components of engagement [10–12], yet very little attention has been given to some of the cognitive components.

One such component is the phenomenon of mind wandering (or zoning out or daydreaming). Mind wandering is the attentional shift away from processing external, task-related information towards the processing of internal, task-unrelated information [13]. Mind wandering is detrimental to a range of educational activities as reviewed by [14]. This is because active comprehension involves extracting information from the learning environment and aligning this information with existing mental models that are ultimately consolidated into long term memory structures [15–18]. A coupling between external information (task) and internal representations (existing mental model) is essential for meaningful comprehension of the material. Mind wandering signals a breakdown in this coupling process [19-20].

To date, very little research in the AIED and ITS communities have been devoted to the study of mind wandering. One notable exception is a study by [4] that focused on using acoustic-prosodic and lexical features to detect self-reported instances of zoning out during a spoken learning session. Hence, the present paper consists of some basic research to identify the factors that influence engagement and mind wandering during a computerized learning task.

One important factor that might play a role in maintaining engagement during learning sessions is the difficulty of the material. For example, [21] reported that mind wandering was more frequent when participants read difficult texts compared to easy texts and that mind wandering also had a more negative impact on comprehension for the difficult texts. However, this study used narrative texts, so there is the question of whether these findings generalize to learning from academic texts.

Another factor that might impact engagement is the perception of choice over the learning material. The control-value theory of emotion posits that learners' appraisals of subjective control and value about an activity predict the emotions that will arise during a learning session [3, 22]. Engagement is hypothesized to be higher when learners have control and some autonomy over the learning task [23-24]. One pioneering study by [25] provided some evidence to support this claim. They gave learners choices over non-instructional components of a serious game (e.g., character icons and names). Learners who were given choices liked the system better, wanted more time with the system, and performed better on a math test. More recently, [26] found that when children had control over an interactive storybook, they showed more interest and less dramatic declines in attention, compared to when adults were in control. Another study by [27] found that more interest was reported when learners chose the order in which texts were presented. Interest, in turn, influenced affect, learning, and persistence.

The studies discussed above have focused on the influence of choice and difficulty on promoting engagement. However, these factors have been studied in isolation, so there is the question of whether these factors interact to influence engagement. For example, are difficult topics more engaging when learners perceive a choice over the topics? In line with these questions, the goal of the present research was to investigate how text difficulty and perceived choice affect engagement and learning during a computerized learning task consisting of reading instructional texts. We focused on text reading because students arguably spend more time studying from textbooks than other learning activities and reading is often considered to be non-interactive and boring. Reading is therefore an excellent context to investigate engagement.

The texts used in the present study were modified versions of materials from a serious game called *Operation ARIES!* [28]. *Operation ARIES!* teaches scientific critical thinking through a series of modules, including reading about core concepts from an online textbook and having conversations with animated pedagogical agents. We focused on the reading portion, because it lacks interactivity and it is solely up to the learner to maintain attention during reading in order to learn the material.

The current experiment had a 2 × 2 (text difficulty × perceived choice) between subjects design. For the difficulty manipulation, participants received an easy or difficult version of a scientific reasoning text. For the choice manipulation, participants were given a choice of two text titles, and either received the text they selected to read (self-selected) or the text they did not select (experimenter-selected). Engagement was measured in two ways: (1) self-reported levels of valence and arousal (affective component) and (2) mind wandering reports via auditory probes, which is a standard way to track mind wandering [13, 29]. We focus on three research questions: (1) What is the rate of mind wandering during a computerized learning task?, (2) What is the impact of perceived choice and text difficulty on mind wandering, valence, and arousal?, and (3) Do perceived choice and text difficulty affect text comprehension?

2 Method

2.1 Participants and Design

There were 59 participants recruited from Amazon's Mechanical Turk™ (AMT). AMT allows individuals to receive monetary compensation for completing Human Intelligence Tasks online. Participation was limited to native English speakers at least 18 years of age. The mean age was 38.4 years old (SD = 12.3). On average, the study lasted 22 minutes and participants were compensated $1.75. Past research suggests AMT is a reliable and valid source for collecting experimental data [30-31]. There are also some advantages to using AMT with respect to diversity, at least when compared to typical undergraduate samples used in many research studies.

The experiment had a 2 × 2 between subjects design in which choice (self- selected vs. experimenter-selected) and text difficulty (easy vs. difficult) were randomly assigned. Details on these manipulations are given below.

2.2 Materials

Text Manipulations. The experimental texts were adapted from two texts about research methods used in the serious game, *Operation ARIES!* [28]. Both texts focused on a research methods concept: (1) the dependent variable and (2) making causal claims. Texts began with a case study that demonstrated how the respective concept applies to real world situations and followed with explanations and examples demonstrating uses for the concept.

Easy and difficult versions were created for each text by manipulating the two texts on the following dimensions: narrativity, sentence length, word frequency, syntactic simplicity, and referential cohesion. These were identified by [32] as the textual features that contribute to text difficulty and conceptual clarity. Easy versions were created to be more narrative, with shorter sentences and fewer low frequency words. They were also made more cohesive by replacing ambiguous pronouns with proper nouns. Difficult texts had longer, more complex sentences with more low frequency words. Both versions, however, had the same conceptual content and were approximately 1500 words.

Significant differences in text difficulty were assessed by comparing easy and difficult texts via three measures: (1) Flesch-Kincaid Grade Level (FKGL), (2) Coh-Metrix (a text-analysis software) indices of difficulty [33], and (3) subjective human ratings. First, we ensured that the FKGL were at least two grade levels different. Easy texts were at grade 9 and difficult texts were grade 11. Second, we looked at a more systematic assessment of difficulty based on the Coh-Metrix indices of difficulty (narrativity, referential cohesion, deep cohesion, and syntactic simplicity). Higher values of each index indicate that a text is easier to read. Easy and difficult texts were significantly different based on these four indices in the expected direction (average $p < .05$). Finally, we completed a pilot study to make sure that humans perceived the texts to differ in levels of difficulty. Humans rated the difficult texts to be significantly more difficult after reading ($d = .93$), $p < .05$. There were also no differences between the two texts (e.g., easy dependent variable text compared to easy causal claims text) among these three dimensions.

Learning Measures. Learning was measured through multiple-choice deep reasoning questions (nine questions per text). These questions were developed in adherence to the Graesser-Person question asking taxonomy [34] specifically targeting logical, causal, or goal-oriented reasoning. Each participant received a three-question pretest and a six-question posttest, which corresponded to the specific text they read.

2.3 Procedure

After filling out an electronic consent form, participants completed a pretest that consisted of three deep reasoning questions to assess prior knowledge, followed by instructions for the self-paced learning task. Self-paced reading was adopted for this task to eliminate any pressures from time constraints.

The choice feedback manipulation occurred before participants began reading the text. First, participants were presented with two different headlines (one for each text) and were asked to choose which one they would like to read. The headlines were:

(dependent variable) "Are you being controlled by subliminal messages hidden in plain sight?" and (making causal claims) "Wipe that tired expression off your face! This new energy pill is bound to put some pep in your step!"

After selecting a headline, participants were immediately given feedback to indicate whether or not they would be given their selected text to read. Participants were randomly assigned to either receive the text they selected (self-selected) or the text they did not select (experimenter-selected). Participants who received the self-selected text were given the message, "Good news for you! You'll read the text you wanted to read!" Alternatively, participants who received the experimenter-selected text received the following message: "Unfortunately, you'll be reading the text you did not choose. Too bad." This feedback manipulation explicitly informed participants about whether or not their headline selection influenced the text they received.

Prior to engaging in the self-paced reading, participants were informed that an auditory probe (i.e., a beep) would periodically sound during reading. At the time of the probe, they were instructed to indicate whether or not they were currently mind wandering by hitting "Y" (yes) or "N" (no) on the keyboard. The following description of mind wandering, taken from previous studies [13, 21], was provided to the participants to aid in distinguishing mind wandering episodes: "At some point during reading, you may realize you have no idea what you just read. Not only were you not thinking about the text, you were thinking about something else altogether." A total of ten auditory mind wandering probes were inserted in each text. The probes corresponded to pages that contained content that was relevant to the learning measure. A sentence-by-sentence reading paradigm allowed probes to be located at more precisely controlled content locations across easy and difficult texts.

In addition to the mind wandering probes, participants were asked to report levels of valence and arousal at three separate points: before, during (the middle), and after reading the text. Valence was measured on a 6-point scale from 1 (very negative) to 6 (very positive). Arousal was measured with a similar scale ranging from 1 (very sleepy) to 6 (very active). Finally, a six-item posttest was completed after the learning session.

3 Results and Discussion

3.1 Mind Wandering

There were a total of 590 mind wandering probes across the 59 participants. The distribution of mind wandering proportions was non-normal, so non-parametric statistics were used for significance testing involving this variable. The mean proportion of probes to which participants responded "yes" was .354, indicating that mind wandering occurred approximately one third of the time participants were probed. Indeed, this finding reveals that participants reported mind wandering over 30% of the time during this computerized learning task, highlighting an important concern for the prevalence of this phenomenon.

There is a question of whether perceived choice and text difficulty influenced levels of mind wandering. A Mann-Whitney U Test revealed that there was significantly more mind wandering in the difficult condition (33.7%) compared to the easy condition (20.3%), $Z = -1.95$, $p = .051$. Perceived choice, however, did not impact rates of mind wandering, $p = .654$ (see Table 1 for descriptive statistics on mind wandering).

3.2 Valence and Arousal

Participants reported their valence and arousal levels at three different points: before, during, and after reading. Delta valence and arousal scores were computed by subtracting before scores from *during* and *after* scores (delta during and after valence and arousal). These two delta measures were used in order to control for participants' baseline valence and arousal levels. Table 1 provides descriptive statistics for the delta valence and arousal measures.

Univariate analyses of variance (ANOVAs) revealed a main effect of perceived choice on delta valence during reading, $F(1, 55) = 4.52$, $p = .038$, partial $\eta^2 = .076$. Participants who read the self-selected text reported negligible changes in valence *during* reading ($M = .029$, $SD = .674$) compared to the participants who read the experimenter-assigned text ($M = -.360$, $SD = .700$). However, there was no perceived choice effect for the change in valence *after* reading, $F(1, 55) = 1.10$, $p = .300$.

Interestingly, the main effect of text difficulty yielded quite different patterns for valence and arousal. Whereas perceived choice influenced valence, text difficulty impacted arousal. There was a marginally significant main effect of text difficulty on delta arousal *during* reading, $F(1, 55) = 3.74$, p = .058, partial $\eta^2 = .064$. Participants who read the difficult text ($M = -.233$, $SD = .897$) showed a larger drop in arousal in the middle of the reading compared to the participants who read an easy text; arousal actually increased for those participants who read an easy text ($M = .172$, $SD = .658$). Similarly, there was a marginally significant effect of text difficulty on delta arousal *after* reading, $F(1, 55) = 3.40$, $p = .071$, partial $\eta^2 = .058$. There was a larger drop in arousal for participants who read a difficult text ($M =-.300$, $SD = 1.06$) compared to an easy text ($M =.138$, $SD = .743$) *after* reading. However, text difficulty did not impact valence either *during* or *after* reading.

These findings indicate that perceived choice and text difficulty differentially impacted valence and arousal. Perceived choice increased valence *during* reading ($d = .57$), whereas text difficulty was associated with a decrease in arousal *during* ($d = .52$) and *after* reading ($d = .48$). There were no interactions of perceived choice and text difficulty with respect to valence and arousal.

It is also worth noting that delta valence and arousal *during* and *after* reading were negatively correlated with mind wandering. Non-parametric correlations indicated that mind wandering was negatively correlated with delta arousal *during* ($r_s = -.256$, $p = .050$) and *after* ($r_s = -.329$, $p = .011$) reading. Similarly, delta valence *during* ($r_s = -.100$, p = .453) and *after* ($r_s = -.317$, $p = .015$) reading were also negatively correlated with mind wandering.

3.3 Text Comprehension

Participants' performance on the pretest and posttest were computed as the proportion of items answered correctly. In order to control for prior knowledge, corrected learning gains were calculated from these scores as: (Posttest – Pretest)/ (1 – Pretest). A univariate ANOVA indicated that participants who read the self-selected text (M = .473, SD = .300) had significantly higher learning gains compared to those who read the experimenter-assigned text (M = -.153, SD = .628), F (1, 54) = 24.6, $p < .001$. Text difficulty did not impact learning gains nor did it interact with perceived choice.

This finding further supports the control-value theory of emotions and previous work on autonomy and choice. Those participants who felt as if they had a choice in the learning material performed significantly better on the comprehension test compared to those who did not perceive a choice (d = 1.27). A heightened sense of subjective value might be inherent in the ability to choose learning materials, leading to deeper engagement and learning.

Table 1. Descriptive Statistics (*M*) for Mind Wandering, Valence, Arousal, and Corrected Learning Gains based on Text Difficulty and Perceived Choice

	Text Difficulty			**Perceived Choice**		
	Easy	**Diff**	***d***	**Self**	**Exp**	***d***
Mind Wandering (Proportion)	.244	.461	.413	.357	.351	.012
Valence During	-.172	-.100	.102	.029	-.360	.567
Valence After	-.310	-.267	.046	-.177	-.440	.271
Arousal During	.172	-.233	-.515	-.088	.040	-.154
Arousal After	.138	-.300	-.480	-.059	.886	.064
Corrected Learning Gains	.238	.192	-.083	.473	-.153	1.27

4 General Discussion

Sustaining students' engagement over time in any ITS or serious game is still an important concern. This paper provides insight for how two factors, namely text difficulty and perceived choice, impact engagement during a non-interactive reading task. Results suggest giving learners choices about their learning material might be a simple way for systems to advantageously maintain engagement, specifically capitalizing on the control aspect in the control-value theory of emotions [22]. One idea is to focus on the choice of certain materials over others (e.g., choose between these two texts), rather than the choice of the order of materials (e.g., choose the order you will read these texts). Specifically, systems could employ this technique and facilitate engagement by creating the illusion of choice. The selection options can be highly ambiguous (more or less interchangeable), such that the target learning material can be presented regardless of the option that was selected. For example, if the target learning material is a text on the scientific method, two headlines can be presented that both could feasibly align with the text. Regardless of which headline the participant selects, the same text could then be presented, giving the participant a greater sense of control by having made a choice.

The results of the present study also indicated that the difficult texts were associated with lowered engagement levels. Therefore, it is important to design learning materials that will adequately challenge learners, without being so difficult that attention cannot be sustained. Texts that are too difficult might induce lower engagement, as well as increase the risk of attentional lapses from the external environment, which is obviously undesirable for the duration of a learning session. The importance of difficulty of the learning material is not a novel idea [16-17]; however, this study is the first evaluation of how text difficulty and perceived choice affect mind wandering in a computerized learning task with academic texts.

It is important to note the limitations of this study. For example, a longer text would allow us to track how these factors affect engagement over a longer period of time. Another limitation is that we did not measure any individual differences of topic and situational interest, which have been previously related to choice manipulations [27]. Understanding individual differences, such as these, might improve models of engagement by incorporating how learners' traits interact with factors from the learning environment. Also, although previous research found a negative relationship between mind wandering and learning [21], we did not replicate this finding. This warrants further testing with different sets of academic texts over different time domains, as this learning session was relatively short (about 1500 words).

Lastly, since our study was conducted online, we were unable to collect any eye tracking or physiological measurements of engagement. These additional measures could aid in developing a more fine-grained model of mind wandering and engagement. Combining task factors like the ones in this experiment with physiological measures and eye tracking can be an initial step towards predicting when a learner begins to mind wander and/or disengage from a text. Interventions can then be put into place in order to restore attentional focus to the current learning task.

Acknowledgment. This research was supported by the National Science Foundation (NSF) (ITR 0325428, HCC 0834847, DRL 1235958). Any opinions, findings and conclusions, or recommendations expressed in this paper are those of the authors and do not necessarily reflect the views of NSF.

References

1. Csikszentmihalyi, M.: Flow: The psychology of optimal performance. Cambridge University Press, New York (1990)
2. D'Mello, S., Graesser, A.: The half-life of cognitive-affective states during complex learning. Cognition & Emotion 25, 1299–1308 (2011)

3. Pekrun, R., Goetz, T., Daniels, L., Stupnisky, R., Perry, R.: Boredom in achievement settings: Exploring control–value antecedents and performance outcomes of a neglected emotion. Journal of Educational Psychology 102, 531 (2010)
4. Drummond, J., Litman, D.: In the zone: Towards detecting student zoning out using supervised machine learning. In: Aleven, V., Kay, J., Mostow, J. (eds.) ITS 2010, Part II. LNCS, vol. 6095, pp. 306–309. Springer, Heidelberg (2010)
5. Forbes-Riley, K., Litman, D.: When does disengagement correlate with learning in spoken dialog computer tutoring? In: Biswas, G., Bull, S., Kay, J., Mitrovic, A. (eds.) AIED 2011. LNCS, vol. 6738, pp. 81–89. Springer, Heidelberg (2011)
6. Mann, S., Robinson, A.: Boredom in the lecture theatre: An investigation into the contributors, moderators and outcomes of boredom amongst university students. British Educational Research Journal 35, 243–258 (2009)
7. Baker, R., D'Mello, S., Rodrigo, M., Graesser, A.: Better to be frustrated than bored: The incidence, persistence, and impact of learners' cognitive–affective states during interactions with three different computer-based learning environments. International Journal of Human-Computer Studies 68, 223–241 (2010)
8. Larson, R., Richards, M.: Boredom in the middle school years: Blaming schools versus blaming students. American Journal of Education 99, 418–443 (1991)
9. Fredricks, J., Blumenfeld, P., Paris, A.: School engagement: Potential of the concept, state of the evidence. Review of Educational Research 74, 59–109 (2004)
10. Arroyo, I., Ferguson, K., Johns, J., Dragon, T., Meheranian, H., Fisher, D., et al.: Repairing disengagement with non-invasive interventions. Frontiers in Artificial Intelligence and Applications, vol. 158, p. 195 (2007)
11. D'Mello, S., Chipman, P., Graesser, A.: Posture as a predictor of learner's affective engagement. In: Proceedings of the 29th Annual Meeting of the Cognitive Science Society, pp. 905–910 (2007)
12. Joseph, E.: Engagement tracing: Using response times to model student disengagement. In: Artificial Intelligence in Education: Supporting Learning Through Intelligent and Socially Informed Technology, vol. 125, p. 88 (2005)
13. Smallwood, J., Schooler, J.: The restless mind. Psychological Bulletin 132, 946 (2006)
14. Smallwood, J., Fishman, D., Schooler, J.: Counting the cost of an absent mind: Mind wandering as an underrecognized influence on educational performance. Psychonomic Bulletin & Review 14, 230–236 (2007)
15. Graesser, A.: Constructing inferences during narrative text comprehension. Psychological Review 101, 371–395 (1994)
16. McNamara, D., Kintsch, W.: Learning from texts: Effects of prior knowledge and text coherence. Discourse Processes 22, 247–288 (1996)
17. Ozuru, Y., Dempsey, K., McNamara, D.: Prior knowledge, reading skill, and text cohesion in the comprehension of science texts. Learning and Instruction 19, 228–242 (2009)
18. Zwaan, R., Radvansky, G.: Situation models in language comprehension and memory. Psychological Bulletin 123, 162 (1998)
19. Schooler, J., Smallwood, J., Christoff, K., Handy, T., Reichle, E., Sayette, M.: Meta-awareness, perceptual decoupling and the wandering mind. Trends in Cognitive Sciences 15, 319–326 (2011)
20. Smallwood, J., McSpadden, M., Schooler, J.: The lights are on but no one's home: Meta-awareness and the decoupling of attention when the mind wanders. Psychonomic Bulletin & Review 14, 527–533 (2007)
21. Feng, S., D'Mello, S., Graesser, A.: Mind wandering while reading easy and difficult texts. Psychonomic Bulletin and Review (in press)

22. Pekrun, R.: The control-value theory of achievement emotions: Assumptions, corollaries, and implications for educational research and practice. Educational Psychology Review 18, 315–341 (2006)
23. Deci, E., Ryan, R.: Intrinsic motivation and self-determination in human behavior. Plenum, New York (1985)
24. Hidi, S., Renninger, K.: The four-phase model of interest development. Educational Psychologist 41, 111–127 (2006)
25. Cordova, D., Lepper, M.: Intrinsic motivation and the process of learning: Beneficial effects of contextualization, personalization, and choice. Journal of Educational Psychology 88, 715 (1996)
26. Calvert, S., Strong, B., Gallagher, L.: Control as an engagement feature for young children's attention to and learning of computer content. The American Behavioral Scientist 48, 578 (2005)
27. Ainley, M., Hidi, S., Berndorff, D.: Interest, learning, and the psychological processes that mediate their relationship. Journal of Educational Psychology 94, 545 (2002)
28. Millis, K., Forsyth, C., Butler, H., Wallace, P., Graesser, A., Halpern, D.: Operation ARIES!: A serious game for teaching scientific inquiry. In: Serious Games and Edutainment Applications, pp. 169–195. Springer, London (2011)
29. Smilek, D., Carriere, J., Cheyne, J.: Out of mind, out of sight Eye blinking as indicator and embodiment of mind wandering. Psychological Science 21, 786–789 (2010)
30. Buhrmester, M., Kwang, T., Gosling, S.: Amazon's Mechanical Turk a new source of inexpensive, yet high-quality, data? Perspectives on Psychological Science 6, 3–5 (2011)
31. Mason, W., Suri, S.: Conducting behavioral research on Amazon's Mechanical Turk. Behavior Research Methods 44, 1–23 (2012)
32. Graesser, A., McNamara, D., Kulikowich, J.: Coh-Metrix providing multilevel analyses of text characteristics. Educational Researcher 40, 223–234 (2011)
33. McNamara, D., Louwerse, M., McCarthy, P., Graesser, A.: Coh-Metrix: Capturing linguistic features of cohesion. Discourse Processes 47, 292–330 (2010)
34. Graesser, A., Person, N.: Question asking during tutoring. American Educational Research Journal 31, 104–137 (1994)

Automatically Generating Discussion Questions

David Adamson[1], Divyanshu Bhartiya[2], Biman Gujral[3], Radhika Kedia[3], Ashudeep Singh[2], and Carolyn P. Rosé[1]

[1] Carnegie Mellon University, Pittsburgh PA 15213, USA
{dadamson,cprose}@cs.cmu.edu
[2] IIT Kanpur, Uttar Pradesh, India
{divbhar,ashudeep}@iitk.ac.in
[3] DA-IICT, Gandhinagar, Gujarat, India
{biman_gujral,radhika_kedia}@daiict.ac.in

Abstract. Automatic question generation can support instruction and learning. However, work to date has produced mostly "shallow" questions that fall short of supporting deep learning and discussion. We propose an extension to a state-of-the-art question generation system that allows it to produce deep, subjective questions suitable for group discussion. We evaluate the questions generated by this system against a panel of experienced judges, and find that our approach fares significantly better than the baseline system.

Keywords: question generation, facilitation, subjectivity, computer-supported collaborative learning.

1 Introduction

Recent work, built on observations of expert classroom instruction, has advocated strategies for reading and knowledge-building that move beyond simple comprehension and into questioning and reasoning [1]. Additionally, deep reasoning questions in tutorial environments have been shown to be correlated with student learning [2,3,4]. Such questions offer opportunities for evaluation, multiple perspectives and opinions, and synthesis, corresponding to the higher ("deeper") levels of Bloom's taxonomy [5,6]. Effective automated support for deep learning should be able to produce contextually suitable deep questions . However, producing such questions automatically for a new text or domain has remained an unanswered challenge.

Automatic question generation can indeed support instruction and learning in computer-based settings [7,8,9]. Work to date has produced mostly shallow questions that are not intended to promote deep thought or discussion, or that depend on special features of a particular domain. In this paper, we propose an extension to a state-of-the-art question generation system [10], allowing it to produce deep, subjective questions suitable for group discussion.

In the section that follows, we review the literature and prior work in the areas of discussion-oriented learning, deep questions, and question generation.

K. Yacef et al. (Eds.): AIED 2013, LNAI 7926, pp. 81–90, 2013.

Sec. 3 describes our improvements to a baseline question generation system. Our evaluation method and analysis of results are described in Sec. 4 and 5, followed by discussion of the results and directions for future work.

2 Theoretical Framework

2.1 Discussion and Instruction

The literature of instructional practices has advocated strategies for reading and knowledge-building that move beyond comprehension into questioning and reasoning [1], including Questioning the Author [11], Reciprocal Teaching [12], and Collaborative Reasoning [13]. Drawing on observations and analysis of successful classroom instruction, Michaels, O'Connor, and Resnick describe a framework for academically productive talk [14,15] as a collection of discussion-facilitating questions that a teacher can use to promote rich student-centered conversation and collaboration. In a study with teachers employing similar strategies, students have shown steep growth in achievement on standardized math scores, transfer to reading test scores, and retention of transfer for up to 3 years [16]. The success of these approaches hinges on skillful use of elicitation strategies like deep questions to invite the kind of discussion that leads to learning.

2.2 Deep Discussion Questions

Deep questions, allowing for multiple perspectives and reflective answers, are associated with the "deep learning" levels of Bloom's taxonomy [5]. Past work has shown the use of deep-reasoning questions [6] to be significantly correlated with student learning. Several recent studies [2,3,4] have shown high-quality discussion questions and reflective knowledge-building activities to be associated with positive learning outcomes. Further work [17,18] argues that text comprehension can be significantly improved by replacing traditional IRE instruction (Intiation-Reply-Evaluation [19]) with discussion-based activities where students have opportunities to summarize, challenge, make predictions on questions that allow multiple answers, and respond to questions that require them to draw upon evidence from both the text and their own personal perspectives.

Questions containing a greater proportion of highly subjective words - that is, words expressing opinions and evaluations - allow for multiple answers and personal perspective [20]. Responses to such questions offer opportunities to be challenged and built upon. Work in this sphere has produced the SentiWordNet database [21], where word senses are associated with subjectivity scores. While measures of subjectivity have largely been used for opinion mining, the measure of the subjective potential of a question may serve as a convenient proxy for deepness. More objective questions may be "shallower" in that they may be answered simply and factually, whereas more subjective questions leave room for justification and opinion, aligning with the "deep" questions described above.

2.3 Question Generation

Recent work in question generation has focused on generating objectively answerable, fill-in-the-blank or multiple-choice questions [8,9,10]. These basic questions can be generated with some success, but do not necessarily promote discussion. Present methods prefer clear, answerable questions - but to promote discussion, multiple answers and perspectives must be possible.

Heilman [10] describes a system for producing reading questions from a text. Leveraging off-the-shelf NLP tools, each declarative sentence passes through a set of general-purpose structural transformations to produce a collection of candidate questions. These questions are then ranked by a model trained on human judgements, using lexical and structural features of the question. While this method creates reading comprehension questions that are reliably grammatical, they are recall-oriented, and are not intended as "deep questions".

Although there has been some preliminary work in generating more probing questions from a text, the questions thus generated are limited in scope and depend on particularities of the domain. For example, Wang [8] employs question templates specific to the domain of medical texts, and Liu [22] uses the structure of citations in an academic paper to produce questions that address argumentation style.

3 Generating Questions for Discussion

We describe changes to baseline sentence selection and question generation methods [10] in order to promote deeper, more subjective questions drawn from a text. Instead of over-generating questions from all sentences in the summary, we instead select a subset of sentences based on one of three models of sentence "relevance". In all cases, including our application of the baseline system, questions are generated from sentences selected from a human-generated summary of a longer "original" text. Two of our selection models also utilize information from the original text. A summary is a more suitable source for discussion questions because individual sentences are more likely to contain abstractions or synthesis of ideas from the original text. After generating questions from this reduced set of candidate sentences, we apply the baseline system's method for generating questions. We then apply a set of transformations to the result to produce a set of questions more suitable for discussion. A measure of question-level subjectivity allows us to anticipate these questions' potential for deeper reasoning and rich discussion.

3.1 Selecting Sentences

We examine three methods for sentence selection, drawing on the fields of text categorization [23,24], information retrieval [25], and summarization [26,27,28]. Each of these embodies a different intuition as to what makes a sentence particularly salient, as described in each subsection below.

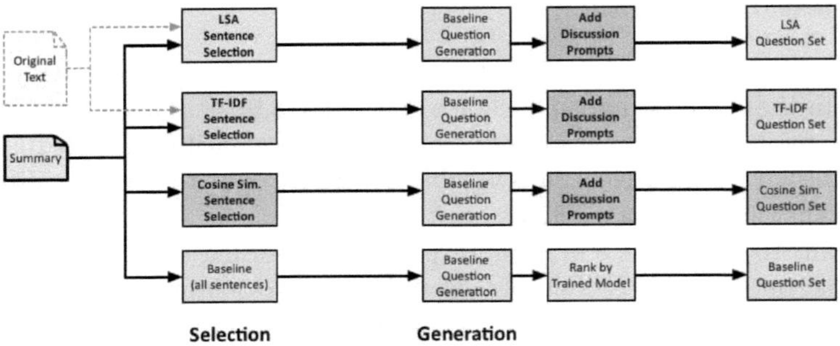

Fig. 1. System architecture, contrasted with the baseline system

Cosine Similarity. This method identifies sentence candidates from the summary using only the summary text. Considering each sentence as a "bag of words" vector, the cosine distance between two sentences is the angle between their word-vectors [24]. The smaller the cosine distance, the greater the similarity. Recognizing that the summary may highlight and build upon key concepts within its own structure, we calculate cosine similarity between each sentence of the summary text and the sentence preceding it. Sentences with high similarity to their immediate predecessors may be interpreted as marking an important concept, and as such are selected as candidates for question generation.

LSA Content Scores. Latent Semantic Analysis [23] is a technique designed to analyze the relationships between a set of documents (sentences, in our case) and the terms they contain. Each sentence is represented as an N-dimensional vector, where each dimension's value roughly corresponds to a sentence's weight for a "topic" in the original document set. We reduce the term-sentence matrix of the original text to an N-dimensional LSA space (N=5 in our case, although we did not tune this value), and also transform each sentence from the summary into its own vector in this space. Our goal, comparable to a text summarization task [26,27], is to select sentences most representative of each dimension. We select those sentences with the highest weight in each of the "topic" dimensions, producing N sets of candidate sentences from the summary.

TF-IDF Uniqueness. Term Frequency-Inverse Document Frequency is a metric used in information retrieval to measure the importance of a word [25]. In a given document (a candidate sentence in the summary text), the TF-IDF score of a word is the count of its occurrences in that document, multiplied by a factor (the inverse document frequency) that discounts its appearances in the entire corpus (in our case, the original text). Here TF-IDF is being applied as a measure of uniqueness, preferring those sentences in the summary with higher averaged per-word TF-IDF scores. Sentences from the summary with a high TF-IDF score contain a greater proportion of "rare" words relative to the source text, and thus may contain new ideas that are not literally present in the original.

3.2 Transforming and Ranking Questions

We further transform some of the more factoid-like questions generated by the baseline system into more subjective questions. When a simple yes-or-no question is extracted by the original system, we transform it into a "why" question, for example "(Why) does psychological manipulation prevent the common animals from doubting the pigs' abilities?". Other factoid questions are transformed by prompting for justification or elaboration, for example the question "What was inscribed on the side of the barn?" is appended with "Discuss in detail." While these transformations are nearly trivial to apply, they do transfer the responsibility of evaluation from the asker to the answerer. Such simple moves can empower students and promote productive discussion [14].

To rank the questions on the basis of abstraction and ability to trigger discussion, we calculate a *subjectivity* score for each question. Subjectivity may stand as a measure for "deepness", as described in Section 2.2. Question subjectivity is taken as an average of the subjectivity values of each word in the sentence, as given by SentiWordNet [21]. SentiWordNet is a database of words-senses, differentiated by part-of-speech, with subjectivity scores assigned to each. In the case where a word has more than one sense for a given part of speech, we take the average of its senses' subjectivity values.

4 Evaluation

We generated 50 questions using the baseline method [10] from an analysis and summary [29] of George Orwell's *Animal Farm* [30]. These were the top 50 questions as ranked by the system's trained model. We also generated questions using the methods described in this paper, and selected 50 of these at random. For discussion of texts in literature courses, we can rely on the bounty of existing human-authored summaries and analyses (like SparkNotes) to draw our questions from, although in future work we would like to incorporate an automatic summarization method.

A group of four teachers served as judges and evaluated this combined set of questions. Each judge received the questions in a random order. For each generated question, the judges rated their agreement with six statements about the question on a Likert scale, from 1-7. The first three of these statements

Table 1. Question evaluation dimensions

1 This question lends itself to multiple answers.
2 Answering this question could engage a student's personal values or perspective.
3 This question would be valuable for stimulating discussion among students.
4 This question touches upon important themes from the story.
5 This question is comprehensible.
6 This question is grammatical.

(shown in Table 1) correspond to Bloom's [5] and Graesser's [6] descriptions of the sort of deep-level questions that have been shown to be effective in tutorial settings [2]. The fourth statement probes the suitability of the question content. The last two dimensions are indicators of quality of the question's form. While none of these dimensions is inherently more important than another, a method for generating high-quality discussion questions should receive high scores in all dimensions.

5 Results and Analysis

In order to evaluate the relative quality of questions generated with our approach in comparison with the baseline method, as well as to compare among different selection criteria used by our method, we used an ANCOVA model for each of the six dimensions evaluated by the judges. For each dimension, the dependent measure was the rating assigned by the judge for that dimension. The independent variable was binary, indicating whether the rating was assigned to a question generated with the baseline approach or one of the experimental approaches. In order to differentiate among the three selection methods used by the experimental approach, we included a three-way categorical variable nested within the main independent variable. This allows us to test simultaneously whether the experimental approach is better than the control condition, and whether there are differences between the experimental approach's selection methods. In order to control for systematic differences between judges, we included a categorical control variable indicating which of the four judges assigned the score. A summary of the human ratings is displayed in Fig. 2. The Subjectivity score was used as a covariate in order to evaluate the effect of using Subjectivity as part of a selection criteria for discussion questions.

Multiple Answers. In terms of potential for eliciting multiple student answers, the judges rated the set of experimental approaches significantly better than the baseline approach $F(1, 288) = 12.3, p < .0005$, effect size .64 s.d. There were also significant differences between experimental approaches $F(2, 288) = 3.74, p < .05$ such that LSA and Cosine were significantly better than TF-IDF,

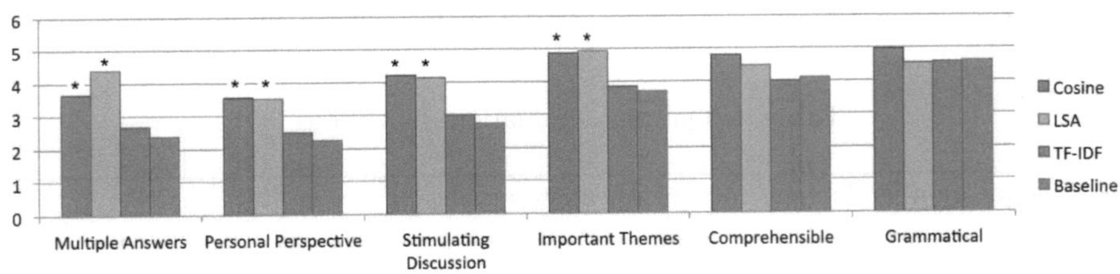

Fig. 2. Average rating per selection method for each dimension. A star (⋆) indicates values which are significantly better than the baseline.

and TF-IDF was not significantly different from baseline. There was a marginal positive correlation between Subjectivity and the dependent measure ($p = .1$), indicating some support for using a subjectivity score as part of a selection method for discussion questions.

Personal Perspective. The results for a questions' potential to engage personal perspective were consistent with those for eliciting multiple answers. The judges rated the set of experimental approaches significantly better than the baseline $F(1, 288) = 8.2, p < .005$, effect size .39 s.d. There were also significant differences between experimental approaches $F(2, 288) = 3.02, p < .05$ such that LSA and Cosine were significantly better than TF-IDF, and TF-IDF was not significantly different from baseline. For this dimension, there was a significant positive correlation between Subjectivity and the dependent measure ($R = .13, p < .05$), suggesting that questions scored as more subjective offer students more opportunity to express their personal perspective.

Stimulating Discussion. Again, results for potential to stimulate discussion were the same. The judges rated the set of experimental approaches significantly better than the baseline approach $F(1, 288) = 9.6, p < .005$, effect size .43 s.d. There were also significant differences between experimental approaches $F(2, 288) = 3.28, p < .05$ such that LSA and Cosine were significantly better than TF-IDF, and TF-IDF was not significantly different from baseline. Again, there was a significant positive correlation between Subjectivity and the dependent measure ($R = .11, p < .05$), suggesting that questions that are scored as more subjective are rated as more stimulating for discussion.

Important Themes. Results for capturing important themes were distinct, although they still favored the experimental approach. This time, Subjectivity had no effect, and there were no significant distinctions among experimental approaches. However, there was a significant advantage attributed to the experimental approaches as a set over that of the baseline approach, $F(1, 288) = 7.05, p < .05$, effect size .37 s.d.

Comprehensibility. In terms of comprehensibility, the experimental approaches as a set were rated as marginally better than the baseline approach $F(1, 288) = 3.22, p < .1$. There were no differences among experimental approaches. And, in contrast to the other metrics, Subjectivity had a negative correlation with comprehensibility ($R = .19, p < .0005$).

Grammaticality. In terms of grammaticality, there were no significant differences among approaches. However, similar to the comprehensibility rating, Subjectivity had a negative correlation with grammaticality ($R = .17, p < .005$).

6 Discussion and Future Work

Broadly, we find that our method for generating questions from a summary text significantly outperforms the baseline system on those dimensions related to their suitability for classroom discussion. Table 2 illustrates some representative questions and scores produced by the three selection methods of our approach, as well as the baseline system.

Table 2. Representative questions generated by our system and the baseline on each of the 6 dimensions presented in Sec. 4 *Subj.* is determined as per Sec. 3.2

Selection Method	Question	Subj. Score	1 MA	2 PP	3 SD	4 ITT	5 Com	6 Gra
Cosine Sim.	Why does psychological manipulation unite the animals against a supposed enemy ?	0.26	5.5	5.75	6.25	6.25	6.5	6.5
TF-IDF	Whose idealism leads to his downfall?	0.29	3.25	2.75	2.75	4.5	7	7
LSA	What does the increasing frequency of the rituals bespeak? Discuss in detail.	0.18	5.5	4.5	5.25	5.5	5.25	4
Baseline	Who gathers the animals of the Manor Farm for a meeting in the big barn?	0.09	1	1.25	1.25	2.75	7	7

We note that although the questions generated from sentences selected by the LSA and by Cosine Similarity methods are rated nearly identically in each dimension, the set of questions they generate are quite different from each other. The Cosine Similarity selection method relies on the structure of the summary to highlight concepts worthy of discussion, and in so doing captures repeating elements - not just story words like "animals" and "windmill", but more abstract themes developed in the summary. The LSA method, by contrast, selects a set of sentences from the summary that most strongly echo the latent "topics" of the original text, which can include both chronological associations (the character of Snowball is much more prevalent in the early story) and repeated themes ("Animalism", "pigs", "men", "power", and "equal" are favored by a single LSA-space dimension, highlighting the recurring contrast between the animals' society and the humans'). The TF-IDF selection method favors sentences that are unique in comparison to the original document, which could potentially highlight those sentences which synthesize or abstract ideas not made explicit in the story. In practice however, the questions produced from the sentences selected by this method are short and specific, picking up on details in individual sentences that have less relationship to the story as a whole. It is thus unsurprising that this selection method fares no better than the baseline.

To evaluate the suitability of discussion questions in an educational setting, a prototype conversational agent has been implemented. Adapting the "revoicing" behavior described by Dyke and colleagues [31], the agent facilitates discussion on a given text by prompting the group with discussion questions (drawn from any one of the methods described in this paper) that are similar to statements made by the students (the details of this system is beyond the scope of this paper). In addition to piloting this system with students, future work might explore ways to scaffold a discussion session, perhaps by starting with more concrete questions, with lower subjectivity scores, and transition to deeper, more subjective questions as the discussion progressed.

References

1. Palincsar, A.: Collaborative approaches to comprehension instruction. In: Rethinking Reading Comprehension, pp. 99–114 (2003)
2. Graesser, A., Person, N.: Question asking during tutoring. American Educational Research Journal 31(1), 104–137 (1994)
3. Craig, S., Sullins, J., Witherspoon, A., Gholson, B.: The deep-level-reasoning-question effect: The role of dialogue and deep-level-reasoning questions during vicarious learning. Cognition and Instruction 24(4), 565–591 (2006)
4. Roscoe, R., Chi, M.: Understanding tutor learning: Knowledge-building and knowledge-telling in peer tutors explanations and questions. Review of Educational Research 77(4), 534–574 (2007)
5. Bloom, B., Engelhart, M., Furst, E., Hill, W., Krathwohl, D.: Taxonomy of educational objectives: Handbook i: Cognitive domain, vol. 19, p. 56. David McKay, New York (1956)
6. Graesser, A., Rus, V., Cai, Z.: Question classification schemes. In: Proc. of the Workshop on Question Generation (2008)
7. Brown, J., Frishkoff, G., Eskenazi, M.: Automatic question generation for vocabulary assessment. In: Proceedings of the Conference on Human Language Technology and Empirical Methods in Natural Language Processing, pp. 819–826. Association for Computational Linguistics (2005)
8. Wang, W.-M., Hao, T., Liu, W.: Automatic question generation for learning evaluation in medicine. In: Leung, H., Li, F., Lau, R., Li, Q. (eds.) ICWL 2007. LNCS, vol. 4823, pp. 242–251. Springer, Heidelberg (2008)
9. Agarwal, M., Mannem, P.: Automatic gap-fill question generation from text books. In: Proceedings of the 6th Workshop on Innovative Use of NLP for Building Educational Applications, pp. 56–64. Association for Computational Linguistics (2011)
10. Heilman, M., Smith, N.: Question generation via overgenerating transformations and ranking. Technical report, DTIC Document (2009)
11. Beck, I., et al.: Questioning the Author: An Approach for Enhancing Student Engagement with Text. ERIC (1997)
12. Palinscar, A., Brown, A.: Reciprocal teaching of comprehension-fostering and comprehension-monitoring activities. Cognition and Instruction 1(2), 117–175 (1984)
13. Chinn, C., Anderson, R., Waggoner, M.: Patterns of discourse in two kinds of literature discussion. Reading Research Quarterly 36(4), 378–411 (2001)
14. Michaels, S., O'Connor, C., Resnick, L.: Deliberative discourse idealized and realized: Accountable talk in the classroom and in civic life. Studies in Philosophy and Education 27(4), 283–297 (2008)

15. Resnick, L., Michaels, S., O'Connor, C.: How (well structured) talk builds the mind. In: Innovations in Educational Psychology: Perspectives on Learning, Teaching and Human Development, pp. 163–194 (2010)
16. Adey, P., Shayer, M.: An exploration of long-term far-transfer effects following an extended intervention program in the high school science curriculum. Cognition and Instruction 11(1), 1–29 (1993)
17. Langer, J.: Envisioning Literature: Literary Understanding and Literature Instruction. Language and Literacy Series. ERIC (1995)
18. Applebee, A., Langer, J., Nystrand, M., Gamoran, A.: Discussion-based approaches to developing understanding: Classroom instruction and student performance in middle and high school English. American Educational Research Journal 40(3), 685–730 (2003)
19. Cazden, C.B.: Classroom Discourse: The Language of Teaching and Learning. Heinemann, Portsmouth (1988)
20. Wiebe, J., Mihalcea, R.: Word sense and subjectivity. In: Proceedings of the 21st International Conference on Computational Linguistics and the 44th Annual Meeting of the Association for Computational Linguistics, pp. 1065–1072. Association for Computational Linguistics (2006)
21. Baccianella, S., Esuli, A., Sebastiani, F.: Sentiwordnet 3.0: An enhanced lexical resource for sentiment analysis and opinion mining. In: Proceedings of the Seventh Conference on International Language Resources and Evaluation (LREC 2010), Valletta, Malta. European Language Resources Association, ELRA (May 2010)
22. Liu, M., Calvo, R.A., Rus, V.: Automatic question generation for literature review writing support. In: Aleven, V., Kay, J., Mostow, J. (eds.) ITS 2010, Part I. LNCS, vol. 6094, pp. 45–54. Springer, Heidelberg (2010)
23. Dumais, S.T.: Latent semantic analysis. Annual Review of Information Science and Technology 38(1), 188–230 (2004)
24. Huang, A.: Similarity measures for text document clustering. In: Proceedings of the Sixth New Zealand Computer Science Research Student Conference (NZCSRSC 2008), Christchurch, New Zealand, pp. 49–56 (2008)
25. Wu, H.C., Luk, R.W.P., Wong, K.F., Kwok, K.L.: Interpreting tf-idf term weights as making relevance decisions. ACM Trans. Inf. Syst. 26(3), 13:1–13:37 (2008)
26. Wang, D., Zhu, S., Li, T., Gong, Y.: Multi-document summarization using sentence-based topic models. In: Proceedings of the ACL-IJCNLP 2009 Conference Short Papers, pp. 297–300. Association for Computational Linguistics (2009)
27. Dredze, M., Wallach, H., Puller, D., Pereira, F.: Generating summary keywords for emails using topics. In: Proceedings of the 13th International Conference on Intelligent User Interfaces, pp. 199–206. ACM (2008)
28. Hu, M., Sun, A., Lim, E.: Comments-oriented blog summarization by sentence extraction. In: Proceedings of the Sixteenth ACM Conference on Information and Knowledge Management, pp. 901–904. ACM (2007)
29. SparkNotes: SparkNote on Animal Farm (2007), `http://www.sparknotes.com/lit/animalfarm/` (accessed January 3, 2013)
30. Orwell, G.: Animal Farm (1945), `http://gutenberg.net.au/ebooks01/0100011.txt` (accessed January 3, 2013)
31. Dyke, G., Adamson, D., Howley, I., Rosé, C.: Enhancing scientific reasoning and explanation skills with conversational agents. Submitted to the IEEE Journal on Transactions on Learning Technologies Special Issue on Learning Systems for Science and Technology Education

Identifying Localization in Peer Reviews of Argument Diagrams

Huy V. Nguyen and Diane J. Litman

University of Pittsburgh, Pittsburgh, PA, 15260
{huynv,litman}@cs.pitt.edu

Abstract. Peer-review systems such as SWoRD lack intelligence for detecting and responding to problems with students' reviewing performance. While prior work has demonstrated the feasibility of automatically identifying desirable feedback features in free-text reviews of student papers, similar methods have not yet been developed for feedback regarding argument diagrams. One desirable feedback feature is problem localization, which has been shown to positively correlate with feedback implementation in both student papers and argument diagrams. In this paper we demonstrate that features previously developed for identifying localization in paper reviews do not work well when applied to peer reviews of argument diagrams. We develop a novel algorithm tailored for reviews of argument diagrams, and demonstrate significant performance improvements in identifying problem localization in an experimental evaluation.

Keywords: peer review, argument diagrams, localization, localization pattern algorithm, natural language processing, SWoRD, LASAD.

1 Introduction

To facilitate writing and reviewing practices for students, web-based reciprocal peer-review systems such as SWoRD [3] have been built to manage typical activity cycles[1] such as writing, reviewing, back-evaluating, and rewriting. While some features of SWoRD are aimed at reducing potential drawbacks of novice reviewing (e.g., displaying review rating reliability indices, asking authors' to back-evaluate peer reviews), SWoRD does not automatically detect problems with student feedback, which in turn could be used to intelligently scaffold and tutor students to write better reviews. Prior work has shown that localization, which refers to pinpointing the source or location of a problem and/or solution, was one desirable feature of feedback regarding student writing, as it was significantly related to feedback implementation [5]. As the first step towards enriching SWoRD with such an automated assessment of student reviewing performance, Xiong and Litman [8] demonstrated the feasibility of using natural language processing (NLP) and machine learning to automatically predict localization in free-text feedback to student papers. In this paper we have a similar

[1] A basic function of SWoRD is to automatically distribute papers to reviewers and reviews back to authors given an instructor-defined number of reviews that each paper will receive.

K. Yacef et al. (Eds.): AIED 2013, LNAI 7926, pp. 91–100, 2013.

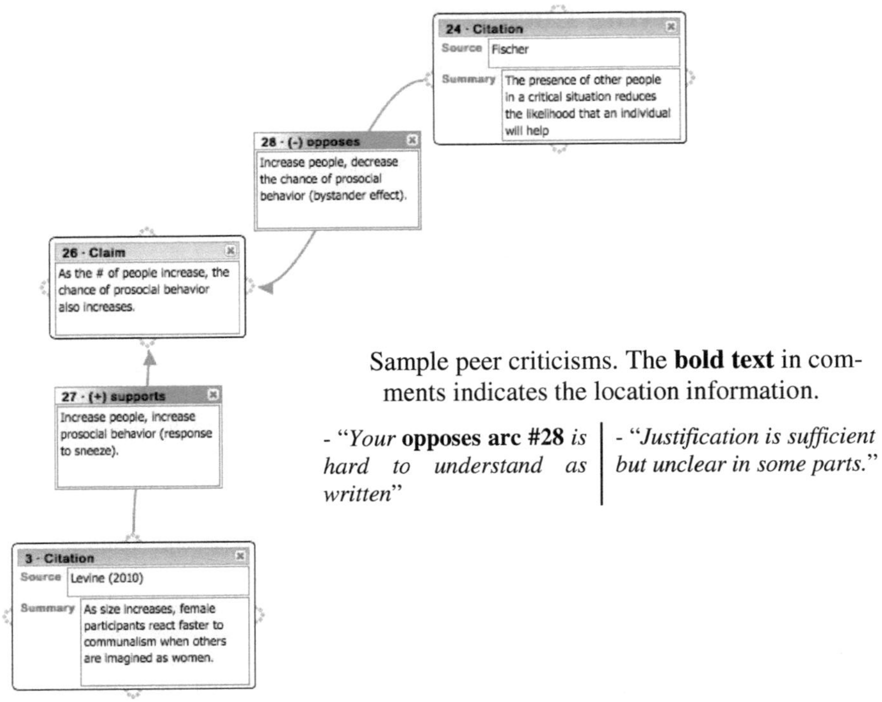

Fig. 1. Excerpt from a student argument diagram, and samples of localized (left) and not localized (right) peer-review comments

interest in predicting localization, but in feedback regarding student *argument diagrams* rather than student papers.

There is increasing interest in developing software tools such as LASAD [6, 7] to support the learning of argumentation skills through graphical representations (see O. Scheuer at el. 2010 [7] for a recent review). In graphical argumentation, students create argument diagrams in which boxes represent statements and links represent argumentative or rhetorical relations between statements. Figure 1 shows an example LASAD diagram excerpt from our corpus. Recently, the idea of combining such graphical argumentation systems with peer-review systems has been proposed [1]. In such a combined system, student authors use argument diagramming to prepare or summarize their arguments; student argument diagrams are then distributed through a peer-review system to student reviewers for comment. Two example review comments associated with the LASAD argument diagram are also shown in Figure 1. Lippman et al. [4] studied such peer-review feedback comments to student argument diagrams, and showed that as with paper reviews, the presence of localization in feedback comments is strongly related to student implementation of peer feedback.

In this paper we present a new localization identification algorithm tailored to identifying localization in free-text peer feedback comments[2] to student argument diagrams. Experimental results show that when testing on a corpus of argument diagram reviews, our proposed algorithm outperforms a prior algorithm designed for feedback to student papers [8].

Section 2 introduces the corpus of argument diagrams and associated free-text review comments used in our study. Section 3 reviews the prior algorithm for identifying localization in paper reviews. Sections 4 and 5 next motivate and formalize our new algorithm for identifying localization in argument diagram reviews. Section 6 evaluates our algorithm. Finally, Sections 7 and 8 summarize our contributions and discuss future research.

2 Argument Diagram Review Corpus

Our corpus of peer-review textual feedback comments to student argument diagrams was collected in a Research Methods Lab at the University of Pittsburgh during Fall 2011. The Lab provided students with an opportunity to conduct psychological research and to write associated papers. To help students organize their thinking and create effective arguments, students were asked to create argument diagrams justifying their hypotheses using LASAD. LASAD argument diagrams consist of nodes and arcs from an instructor-defined ontology. The ontology for Research Methods consists of 4 node types (*current study, hypothesis, claim,* and *citation*) and 4 arc types (*comparison, undefined, supports,* and *opposes*). The diagram in Fig. 1, for example, contains three nodes (two citations and one claim) and 2 arcs (supports and opposes). Argument diagrams were later distributed via SWoRD to be reviewed by peer reviewers, using an instructor-defined rubric. Each student reviewer was asked to give textual feedback (the focus of our study), and to also grade the assigned diagrams on five dimensions using a 7-point scale. On average, each argument diagram was reviewed by 3 peers, with 19 textual comment units (defined below) per diagram.

The textual review feedback was segmented into 1104 comment units (defined as contiguous feedback referring to a single topic), then all comments were manually coded by two independent annotators (not the authors of this paper) for various coding schemes, two of which are relevant to our study. Each comment was first coded for the type of issue that it mentioned: *praise, summary, problem, solution, problem and solution (both), uncodeable*. Only comments having issue types of *problem,*

---

[2] SWoRD supports end-written comments as it is believed that a simple clicking interface that allows reviewers to point to a node/arc when providing a comment is too simple to address the localization issue. In diagram reviews, we have seen that reviewers may refer to more than one diagram component, or some missing node or arc. It is common in our corpus that reviewers mention groups of nodes and/or arcs when commenting on a line of argumentation. In such situations, reviewers may have trouble in pointing to the most appropriate node/arc expressing their comments. Moreover, click-to-point interfaces tend to lead reviewers to focus on low-level writing problems rather than evaluating the argumentation [5]. Due to such issues of direct annotations, we wish to support end-note written localizations.

solution, or *both* were further coded for localization; the localization values *yes* or *no* represented whether or not the exact location of the issue was mentioned in the comment. Inter-rater reliability for the two coding schemes is high with kappas of 0.87 for issue type and 0.84 for localization [4]. Our study focuses on the 590 comment units coded for localization (437 *yes*, 153 *no*). Fig. 1 shows an example localized comment (left) and an example not-localized comment (right).

In addition to the review comments, our corpus contains 56 student argument diagrams that were the targets of the 590 comments. While student papers were used to construct features for predicting localization in [8], we instead will extract features from student argument diagrams. In the next sections, we first review features used to predict localization in comments regarding papers [8], then describe our proposed algorithm that is tailored for predicting localization in reviews of argument diagrams.

3 Predicting Localization in Peer Reviews of Student Papers

Xiong and Litman [8] used NLP to develop features for predicting localization in peer-review comments of student papers. The class label was actually named pLocalization as it was coded for presence of problem localization in criticism feedback. Since this approach will serve as a baseline for evaluating our proposed algorithm, here we briefly describe this feature set.

Regular expression (**reg**) is a Boolean feature that indicates whether any of a predefined set of regular expressions are matched in a given comment. The regular expressions were manually created to match the structure of student papers, e.g. `on page 5`, `the section about`.

Domain word count (**dw_cnt**) is a numerical feature indicating the number of domain words present in a given comment, where the dictionary of domain words is automatically extracted from the set of papers being reviewed using statistical NLP techniques [8]. For our argument diagram review corpus, the domain words will instead be extracted from the textual content associated with the nodes and arcs in the set of student argument diagrams, e.g. `As the # of people increase, the chance of prosocial behavior also increases`, in the claim node of Fig. 1.

Syntactic properties of a comment are represented using two features. The Boolean feature **so_domain** indicates whether any domain word occurs between the subject and object of any sentence in the comment. **Det_count** indicates the number of demonstrative determiners (*this, that, these,* and *those*) in the comment.

Finally, the numerical features window size (**wnd_size**) and number of overlapped words (**overlap_num**) are constructed using an overlapping window algorithm for searching for the common text span between a comment and a student paper. The algorithm iteratively searches through the paper for the referred windows of the most likely text span in the comment, and merges any two windows that are found to overlap. The algorithm returns the length of the maximal window and the number of window's words present in the comment.

We use the original code developed in [8] to compute features from our corpus without any modification. It is likely that the regular expressions defined in [8] will not be particularly applicable to our corpus of argument diagram reviews. However, all features are extracted automatically from data and we can easily compute them using our corpus (substituting the text extracted from the argument diagrams wherever the student paper text was previously used). We will thus examine the predictive utility of our new algorithm both in isolation, as well as in conjunction with the original feature set.

4 Patterns of Localization in Argument Diagram Reviews

Obviously, inherent differences in the structure of papers and argument diagrams makes the problem of identifying localization in diagram reviews different than identifying localization in paper reviews. For example, we observe that the graph structure of argument diagrams seems to make it more convenient for reviewers to include location information in their comments. In the paper review corpus studied in [8], only 53% of the review comments were coded as localized. In our diagram review corpus, in contrast, 74% of the comments are labeled as localized. Not only does the frequency of localization differ, but the way that localization is realized in review text differs when commenting on diagrams rather than papers. We hypothesize that a model tailored to the following observations regarding localization in argument diagram review will work better than simply applying the features in [8] to our corpus.

Pattern 1: Numbered Ontology Type. Every node or arc that is added to a LASAD argument diagram must have a header consisting of both a numerical ID, and a node/arc type from the ontology (headers are visually displayed in the colored bars in Fig. 1). It is very common in our corpus that reviewers identify a diagram component by referring to its node/arc type followed by its ID number, e.g. `hypothesis 1`, `claim 4`, `supports arc 27`.

Pattern 2: Textual Component Content. As the diagram is a summarized graphical representation of an argument, students usually make the text in the node and arc bodies very concise. Reviewers often use this text in conjunction with node and arc types to identify specific diagram components, e.g. `claim that women are more polite than men`, `gender hypothesis`, `your Levine citation`.

Pattern 3: Unique Component. Because a localized comment must be tied to a particular node or arc in the argument diagram, when there is a unique node or arc of a given type, localization can be done using a definite noun phrase expressing the node/arc type, e.g. `the opposing arc` (assuming there is only one opposes arc).

Pattern 4: Connected Component. It is possible to localize a component in a diagram by expressing its connection to another component, e.g. `support for the time of day hypothesis` (as the mentioned support node can be located accurately), `claim node in between the opposes and support arcs 28 and 27`.

Pattern 5: Typical Numerical Regular Expression. Due to the fact that all nodes and arcs are numbered, there are typical numerical expressions used by reviewers to express localization, e.g. `the first hypothesis`, `H1` (hypothesis 1), `[14]` (node or arc 14), `#28` (node or arc 28).

5 The Localization Pattern Algorithm (LPA)

The basic idea of our algorithm is that if **location information** expressed in a peer comment helps the author of an argument diagram pinpoint a unique part of the diagram, then that location information is a possible signal that the review comment is localized. Patterns for detecting such location information involve a **diagram component keyword** surrounded by **supporting word(s)**.

A diagram component keyword can be the word *node*, *arc*, or any of the words defining the node and arc types from the diagram ontology. Recall that ontologies are defined by instructors, and may differ across courses. For our corpus, the keywords from the ontology include the node and arc types introduced in Section 2: *current study, hypothesis, claim, citation, comparison, undefined, supports,* and *opposes*. Our algorithm has been implemented to extract such keywords automatically by parsing the ontology.

In general, supporting word(s) are one or more words in proximity of a keyword, that help readers locate the diagram component(s) mentioned in a review comment. For example, the noun phrase `gender hypothesis` has the word `hypothesis` as its keyword; the word `gender` plays a supporting role when it distinguishes the mentioned hypothesis from other hypotheses that may exist in the diagram. For the noun phrase `gender hypothesis` to express location information in a peer comment, there must be a hypothesis node in the diagram and that node must have gender in its textual content.

To search for location information using patterns, we first segment peer-review comments into sentences, remove stop-words, and extract the keywords in each sentence. For each keyword found in a sentence, we collect all remaining non-keywords in the sentence that also appear in the text of a node or arc that is consistent with the keyword. We note that all keywords and content words are stemmed before being fed to a word matching procedure. To determine whether such words are supporting words that indicate localization, we then apply rules representing the 5 types of localization patterns noted above.

For the first pattern, we define supporting words as a number or list of numbers occurring right after the keyword, where the numbers match diagram component IDs.

The second pattern involves two cases. First, supporting words must occur before the keyword, e.g. `gender hypothesis`. This case requires that the nearest supporting word is right before the keyword. Second, supporting words can be after the keyword, e.g. `claim that women are more polite than men`. This case requires that the nearest supporting word must have distance less than 3 from the keyword, and the number of supporting words is at least 3.

For pattern 3, we count the number of nodes and arcs of each type when parsing the argument diagram, to easily determine whether or not the found keyword refers to a unique component of the diagram.

Pattern 4 can be addressed by doing reference resolution in the argument diagram. For each node and arc of the diagram, we extend its original textual content by adding sections that contain exactly the text of the node and/or arc to which it connects. While searching for common words between a review sentence and a diagram node/arc, we tag a matching phrase as support if it is in the added sections of the component. The rule is that the matching phrase in the original text must be a keyword, and the matching phrase in added sections must be location information.

Finally, pattern 5 was created by looking for typical regular expressions seen in the held-out set of development data to be described next.

As our localization pattern algorithm is rule-based, it was important to have development data to learn the localization patterns and create the rules for identifying those patterns. Fortunately, there was a data segment from the Fall 2011 Research Methods Lab which was not coded for localization, and was thus not included in our testing corpus. The first author collected 200 phrases[3] representing references to locations from that data segment. Those 200 localized phrases were used to learn the patterns and refine the parameters for the localization pattern algorithm. Note that the localization annotation described in Section 2 required comments to have an issue type of only problem, solution, or both; annotators were also instructed to look at the target diagram to verify location information. The first author did not follow those instructions, and collected location information from comments of all issue types, without the diagrams.

6 Experimental Results

We evaluate the predictive performance of two models that use LPA to identify localization in peer reviews of student argument diagrams, by comparing their performance to two baselines: a model (pLocalization) learned using only the paper review features [8] described in Section 3, and a model (Majority) that simply determines the most common class (localized) in the data and assigns every instance that class label. Our first proposed model directly uses LPA as the classifier for localization; if LPA can extract location information from a comment by matching at least one of its patterns, then the comment is classified as localized, otherwise it is classified as not-localized. Our second proposed model (Combined) adds the binary value returned by LPA as an additional feature to the original pLocalization feature set.

Table 1. Performance of 4 models for identifying localization. * denotes significantly better than the majority baseline with $p < 0.05$.

Metric	Majority	pLocalization	LPA	Combined
Accuracy (%)	74.07	73.98	80.34*	83.78*
Kappa	0	< 0.01	0.54*	0.56*
Weighted Precision	0.55	0.55	0.83*	0.84*
Weighted Recall	0.74	0.74	0.80*	0.84*

Table 1 shows the predictive performance for these 4 localization classifiers. To make the experiment consistent with [8], models involving pLocalization features are learned using the WEKA[4] J48 decision tree algorithm; testing with other algorithms (e.g. SVM and Logistic) did not yield significantly different results. All models are evaluated via 10-fold cross validation. Our results show that while the pLocalization

[3] Some phrases are used as examples in Section 4.

[4] `www.cs.waikato.ac.nz/ml/weka`. Algorithms in our experiments use parameters set to the defaults.

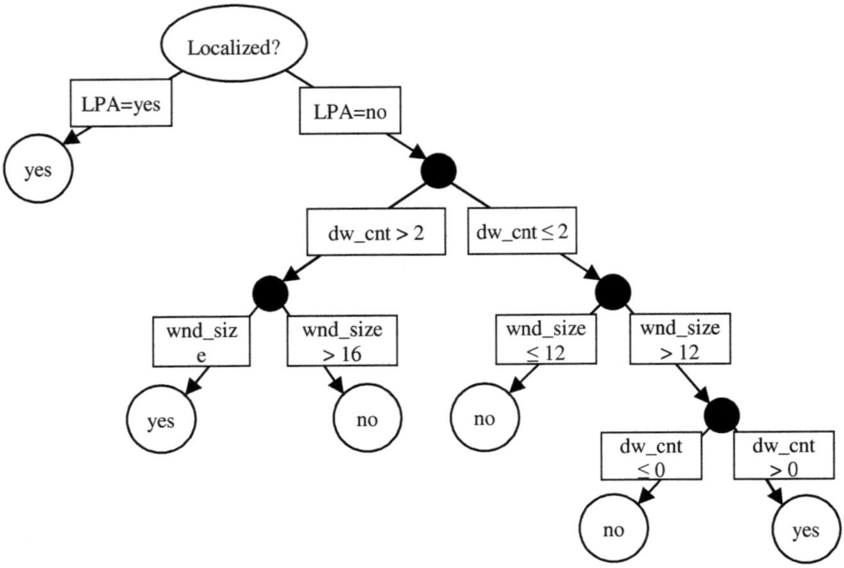

Fig. 2. Learned decision tree for predicting localization of argument-diagram reviews, leaves are prediction outputs, conditions are in rectangle boxes

model does not outperform Majority for any metric, LPA alone significantly outperforms Majority for all metrics. The significant improvement in precision, recall and kappa shows that LPA can predict efficiently the minor class which the baseline models fail to predict. Furthermore, the Combined model yields the best results of all, with accuracy and weighted recall values significantly better than LPA alone ($p < 0.05$).

Fig. 2 presents the decision tree learned for the Combined model. The LPA feature appears at the root, with comments classified as localized if LPA outputs *yes*. Two features from [8] (domain word count (dw_cnt) and window size (wnd_size)) are used to refine the cases in which LPA outputs *no*. Note that the regular expression feature (reg), which was the most predictive feature for paper reviews [8], is not predictive for diagram reviews. This result shows the advantage of diagram-tailored features.

7 Related Work

Research has been conducted to understand what type of feedback is the most helpful, and why it is helpful. Nelson and Schunn [5] studied relationships between feedback features, potential internal mediators and feedback helpfulness in terms of the likelihood of implementation. Their assumption was that feedback features may not directly affect implementation, but instead do so through internal mediators because of the complex nature of writing performance. The corpus consisted of peer reviews of student papers in a History class, which were coded for feedback features, e.g. localization. The authors' back-review regarding peers' comment were coded for internal mediators, e.g. problem understanding. Nelson and Schunn found that localization in review was significantly related to problem understanding which is an effective mediator that significantly relates to implementation.

Unlike Nelson and Schunn's study on peer reviews of student papers [5], Lippman et al. [4] studied what influences the implementation of peer reviews of student argument diagrams. Peer reviews were collected from a Research Method Lab in which students were asked to give feedback, and rate argument diagrams of their peers. The authors coded peer feedback for various features, e.g. problem, solution, localization. Their finding was consistent with Nelson and Schunn [5] to an extent, and showed that issue type (problem, solution, or both) and localization have distinct, non-interacting influence on the implementation of peer feedback. In addition, results in [4] also suggested that location information helps student implement peer feedback when the focus of the critique is more complex as opposed to more superficial.

Cho [2] further investigated the relationship between feedback features and feedback helpfulness, but using a machine-learning approach. Peer reviews were collected from a Physics class using SWoRD, and were human-coded for various issue types, e.g. problem detection, solution suggestion. Each review was then labeled as helpful or not helpful in terms of these issue types. Experimental results showed that peer reviews can be classified regarding helpfulness with accuracy up to 67% using simple NLP techniques. While Cho's work strengthened the understanding of some feedback features regarding peer review helpfulness, our work instead aims to automatically identify one important aspect, i.e. localization; we also focus on diagram reviews rather than paper reviews, and use different NLP techniques for feature construction.

Given findings of previous studies showing that localization is an important indicator of feedback helpfulness, Xiong and Litman [8] used NLP techniques and supervised machine learning to automatically identify the problem localization in peer feedback. Their work is different from ours firstly at the data domain. While Xiong and Litman studied peer reviews of student papers, the data domain in our study is peer reviews of student argument diagrams. The second difference between our work and [8] is at the syntactic level of features extracted from the textual content. Xiong and Litman proposed using features from the parsed dependency tree of the sentence to abstract their intuition regarding the structure of localized reviews. In this study, we however focus only on the word level by considering common words between peer reviews and student diagram. Our intuition regarding structure of localized reviews is formulated simply through the relative order between keywords and supporting words.

8 Conclusion and Future Work

This paper presents the LPA algorithm for identifying localization in peer reviews of argument diagrams. Experimental results show that LPA outperforms a model developed for student papers with respect to a number of evaluation metrics, and that combining the two approaches works best of all. The combined model has the LPA feature appear at the root of the learned decision tree. Even though the location patterns were defined manually based on the development data, they show potential generality by yielding significantly high accuracy on the test data. Recall that the development data and test data are non-overlapping which means all reviewers in the development set are not those in the test set. Moreover, the only domain-specific features used in our combined model are keywords and domain-words lists which can be extracted automatically by parsing instructor-defined ontologies and student-generated diagrams. Therefore we expect the model will work well with new argument diagram reviews from other courses with different ontologies and content domains.

In future work, we aim to apply advanced learning techniques to automatically learn the type of rules and regular expressions used in LPA, rather than use our cur-rent hand-engineered approach. We also plan to evaluate the generality of our LPA and Combined models, by testing them on data currently being collected from courses with different argument diagram ontologies. In addition we are incorporating the Combined model into SWoRD and will be evaluating its use for intelligent scaffolding. Finally, we plan to adapt the lessons learned from developing LPA back to the area of paper reviews. It is more challenging to learn keywords and supporting words from paper comments, but we expect that the task will be feasible when localization patterns can be learned automatically.

Acknowledgements. This material is based upon work supported by the National Science Foundation under Grant No. 1122504. We are grateful to J. Lippman and our other colleagues for providing us with the annotated corpus. We thank members of both the ArgumentPeer and ITSPOKE projects for commenting on our research, W. Xiong and M. Lipschultz for providing feedback regarding this paper, and the reviewers for their many constructive comments.

References

1. Ashley, K.D., Goldin, I.M.: Toward AI-enhanced Computer-supported Peer Review in Legal Education. In: Proceedings of JURIX 2011, pp. 3–12 (2011)
2. Cho, K.: Machine classification of peer comments in physics. In: Proceedings of the Educational Data Mining 2008, pp. 192–196 (2008)
3. Cho, K., Schunn, C.D.: Scaffolded writing and rewriting in the discipline: A web-based reciprocal peer review system. Computers and Education 48(3), 409–426 (2007)
4. Lippman, J., Elfenbein, M., Diabes, M., Luchau, C., Lynch, C., Ashley, K.D., Schunn, C.D.: To Revise or Not To Revise: What Influences Undergrad Authors to Implement Peer Critiques of Their Argument Diagrams? In: ISPST 2012 Conf., poster (2012)
5. Nelson, M.M., Schunn, C.D.: The nature of feedback: How different types of peer feedback affect writing performance. Instructional Science 37(4), 375–401 (2009)
6. Scheuer, O., McLaren, B.M., Loll, F., Pinkwart, N.: An Analysis and Feedback Infrastructure for Argumentation Learning Systems. In: Proceedings of AIED 2009, pp. 629–631 (2009)
7. Scheuer, O., Loll, F., Pinkwart, N., McLaren, B.M.: Computer-supported argumentation: A review of the state of the art. International Journal of Computer-Supported Collaborative Learning 5(1), 43–102 (2010)
8. Xiong, W., Litman, D.: Identifying Problem Localization in Peer-Review Feedback. In: Aleven, V., Kay, J., Mostow, J. (eds.) ITS 2010, Part II. LNCS, vol. 6095, pp. 429–431. Springer, Heidelberg (2010)

An Automatic Approach for Mining Patterns of Collaboration around an Interactive Tabletop

Roberto Martinez-Maldonado, Judy Kay, and Kalina Yacef

School of Information Technologies, University of Sydney, NSW 2006, Australia
{roberto,judy,kalina}@it.usyd.edu.au

Abstract. Learning to collaborate is important. But how does one learn to collaborate face-to-face? What are the actions and strategies to follow for a group of students who start a task? We analyse aspects of students' collaboration when working around a multi-touch tabletop enriched with sensors for identifying users, their actions and their verbal interactions. We provide a technological infrastructure to help understand how highly collaborative groups work compared to less collaborative ones. The contributions of this paper are (1) an *automatic approach* to distinguish, discover and distil salient common patterns of interaction within groups, by mining the logs of students' tabletop touches and detected speech; and (2) the *instantiation* of this approach in a particular study. We use three data mining techniques: a classification model, sequence mining, and hierarchical clustering. We validated our approach in a study of 20 triads building solutions to a posed question at an interactive tabletop. We demonstrate that our approach can be used to discover patterns that may be associated with strategies that differentiate high and low collaboration groups.

Keywords: Data Mining, CSCL, Face-to-face Collaboration, Tabletops.

1 Introduction

When students collaborate on a task, the triggering of specific cognitive mechanisms, such as argumentation, debating and building of shared understanding, increases the likelihood that learning may occur [2]. Developing skills for effective collaboration is crucial not only in educational settings but also to meet other real-world challenges [17]. In particular, face-to-face collaboration skills provides benefits that are not easy to find in other forms of group work [5]. Without adequate support, however, group members do not always naturally collaborate to complete their joint task or they may find out that it requires too much time and additional effort [2]. This means that in collaborative learning environments, it is important for the teacher to be aware of students' collaboration in order to provide this support [14].

New technologies can provide meaningful collaborative learning experiences for students but also open new ways to help teachers enhance their awareness of students' collaborative processes and potential group issues. We use two emerging technologies in order to *automatically* capture and analyse students' collaborative interactions: multi-touch tabletops and data mining. We argue that enriched interactive tabletops

K. Yacef et al. (Eds.): AIED 2013, LNAI 7926, pp. 101–110, 2013.

have the potential to capture students' verbal and touch activity that can be analysed using data mining techniques to discover effective group collaboration strategies.

This paper describes the design of an automatic approach to distinguish, discover and distil patterns of interaction that can be associated with groups' strategies. We apply three data mining techniques: a classification model to detect periods of collaboration; sequential pattern mining, to find sequences that differentiate groups; and hierarchical clustering. We demonstrate our approach with a study involving 20 triads of students building a shared artefact at an enriched tabletop that can automatically and unobtrusively capture students' activity. The main contribution of the paper is our approach to automatically discover patterns of verbal interactions between peers and touch actions on the shared device, which can be associated with strategies that distinguish high from low collaboration groups.

The paper is organised as follows. First, we describe a summary of research at the intersection of educational data mining and interactive tabletops. Then, we outline the context of the study and the software and hardware used. Section 4 describes the data mining approach. Section 5 presents the results found in our study and Section 6 concludes with a discussion of the results and future research directions.

2 Related Work

There has been little prior research on using Artificial Intelligence (AI) techniques for collaborative learning through a shared device. In previous work, we introduced a semi-supervised technique to mine frequent students' actions using a pen-based tabletop [11]. However, that work did not consider verbal activity, an essential aspect of face-to-face collaboration. By contrast, Roman et al. [16] explored patterns of collaborative conversation at a non-interactive table. Even without AI techniques, they showed that simple measures of speech presence can help distinguish outstanding groups in terms of collaboration. In a similar setting, we proposed a technique to detect periods of collaboration at a multi-display setting using classification algorithms and taking into account the aggregation of both manually captured verbal utterances and actions performed on personal computers [10]. However, no previous work in the area has explored the fine-grained interweaving of students' speech and touch activity when working at an interactive tabletop.

A number of research projects have used AI techniques in networked collaborative settings. For example, Anaya et al. [1] presented an approach to cluster and classify students according to their collaborative activity. Duque et al. [3] proposed a fuzzy model that generates rules to classify the different forms of collaboration that leads to solutions of a certain quality. Soller et al. [18] used Hidden-Markov Models to identify moments of knowledge sharing at a constrained and scaffolded interactive networked system. In these three projects, the learning setting was such that all communication during the learning task was mediated by the system, making it possible to automatically log all the students' actions compared with face-to-face environments, where communication occurs simultaneously also verbally.

3 Context of the Study

A total of 60 students, mostly enrolled in science courses, participated in the study. Their learning goal was to enhance and share their understanding of the types of food that should be included in a balanced diet, as recommended by the Dietary Guidelines 2011 published by the National Health and Medical Research Council of Australia. First, each student read the guidelines and then created a *concept map* to represent their understanding. A concept map is a directed graph in which nodes represent the main *concepts* of a given topic and the edges are labelled with a linking word to form a meaningful statement called *proposition* [13]. These maps were first built individually, using a desktop editor called CmapTools. For this, they were provided with an informative text and received basic training in building concept maps. Then, students were organised into groups of three and were given 30-35 minutes to build a joint concept map at a tabletop. Next, we describe the tools the students used to create a group concept map and, simultaneously, capture information of their interactions.

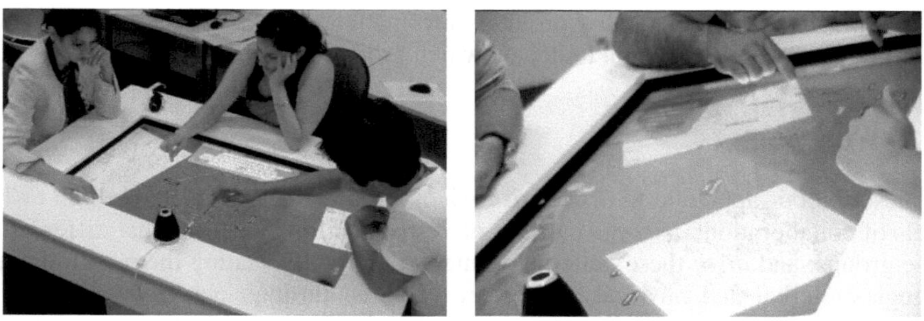

Fig. 1. Interactive tabletop learning environment for collaborative concept mapping

3.1 Collaborative Learning Tabletop Environment

We used Cmate [9], a tabletop application that allows learners to represent their collective understanding of a topic in the form of a concept map (Figure 1). Cmate provides students with personalised menus to add the concepts or linking words they used in their individual concept map created with CmapTools. At any time they can create new concepts and links. Students can also have access to a screenshot of their individual map to recall or share it with others. Students can decide to collaborate, work separately, build upon their previous maps or create a totally new group artefact.

To capture students' differentiated verbal and touch activity, we used Collaid [7]. Collaid extends ordinary interactive tabletop hardware to unobtrusively differentiate students' input by associating each touch performed on the interactive surface with a specific student tracked through an overhead depth sensor[1]. Additionally, we capture the presence of verbal participations by each learner and verbal turn-taking through an array of microphones[2] situated on one of the edges of the tabletop.

[1] `http://www.xbox.com/kinect`
[2] `http://www.dev-audio.com`

3.2 Qualitative Assessments

The 20 groups were assessed by an external observer, following the method proposed by Meier et al. [12] which quantifies nine qualitative dimensions of collaboration. These are: mutual understanding, dialogue management, information pooling, consensus, task division, time management, technical coordination, reciprocal interaction and task orientation. Each dimension is quantified with a number between -2 (very bad) and 2 (very good). We summed the nine dimensions to obtain a single score. Groups with an overall negative score were considered as having low collaboration (10 groups had scores ranging from -10 to 0). Groups with positive scores were considered as having high collaboration (10 groups had scores ranging from 5 to 19).

3.3 Research Question of the Study

In this study, we aimed to address the following research question: *can we distinguish high from low collaboration groups by identifying patterns of interaction, based on their interwoven verbal and touch actions*? Addressing this question can help build a system that may automatically provide information to classroom teachers about multiple groups, enabling them to decide which group most needs attention.

4 Approach

We describe our approach to *distinguish* which groups of students show high or low levels of collaboration; *discover* patterns of verbal and touch activity that differentiate these groups; and *distil* these patterns of interaction by associating them with groups' strategies. Verbal and physical actions are captured through our environment. The analysis is based on three data mining techniques. First, a classification model detects periods of collaboration within each group to generate two datasets of high and low collaboration. We aim to obtain group assessments similarly to the one described in section 3.2 with no human intervention. Second, a sequential mining technique extracts patterns more frequently found in either high or low groups. Finally, hierarchical clustering is used to group similar patterns and facilitate their interpretation. Next, we describe the details of each technique in the context of our research question.

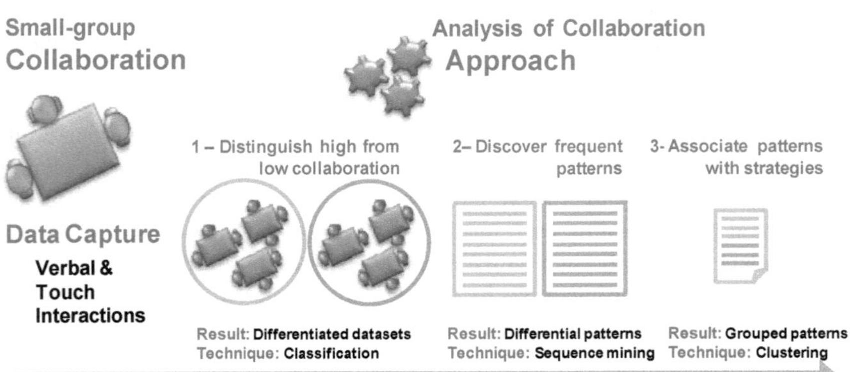

Fig. 2. Analysis of collaboration approach using three data mining techniques

4.1 Distinguishing from Groups' High and Low Collaboration

To determine the level of collaboration we implemented a method proposed by Martinez-Maldonado et al. [8]. This begins by splitting the continuous group session into blocks. Then, a Best-First decision tree is produced and used to classify each period of group work according to a set of features of verbal and physical activity. It was implemented as follows: 1) the audio and touch actions of each triad are grouped in *blocks* of period of time *t* (*t*=30 seconds as recommended by [8]); 2) a defined set of indicators of interaction are calculated per block, including: *total time* of all learners' speech, total number of *utterances*, distribution of verbal participation among the students measured with the Gini coefficient [10] (*symmetry of speech)*, total number of *touch actions* and *symmetry of these actions*; 3) the algorithm generates a decision tree based on these features to classify each block as matching one of three possible values: *high (H)*, *medium (M)* or *low (L)* collaboration; finally, 4) the group is labelled overall as having either high or low collaboration based on the proportion of blocks that appears more often.

This method was trained on a dataset captured from a multi-display setting where learners had the same opportunities of participation and no roles assigned. The approach was further extended to multi-touch tabletop systems [10]. This work explored a few tabletop sessions and proposed the description of this model in terms of simplified rules. They report that highly collaborative groups are characterised by high levels of symmetric conversation, fewer physical actions and some asymmetry in touch activity. By contrast, low collaboration groups present low levels of talk, asymmetry in the conversation and more physical actions.

4.2 Discovering Frequent Patterns

One technique that takes account of the order of system's events and that has been used to identify patterns differentiating students' behaviours in groups is sequential pattern mining. Perera et. al. [15] analysed teamwork interactions through an online management system by proposing a series of alphabets to represent sequential events. Martinez-Maldonado et al. [11] also extracted sequential patterns of physical actions at a pen-based tabletop and mapped similar patterns to group strategies. Kinnebrew et al. [6] presented the *differential sequence mining* (DSM) technique which looks for patterns that differentiate two datasets. These authors also included contextual data of the actions in the sequence mining algorithm. We implemented a mixed technique by using the DSM algorithm [6] and designing our own alphabet that considers verbal and touch actions performed by multiple students [11, 15].

Alphabet definition. The DSM algorithm works on encoded students' actions that contain contextual information as defined by an alphabet. The *initial raw data* of each group consists of two long sequences of actions: verbal and touch, defined as: {*Resource, ActionType, Author, Time, Duration*}, where ActionType can be: *Add* (create a concept or link), *Del* (delete), *Mov* (move), *Chg* (edit), *Open* or *Close* (an individual map). Resources can be: *Conc* (concept), *Link* (proposition), *Indmap* (individual map) or *Speech* (utterance). Author is the learner who performed the action, Time is the timestamp when the action occurred, and Duration is the time taken to complete it.

Then, we encode each action using the alphabet in Table 1. The coding for a touch action has *one keyword from each level.* The first two levels correspond to *Resource* and *ActionType*. Levels 3 and 4 add contextual information. First, we inspect the important aspect of speech flow between students. Level 3 indicates whether there was speech occurring with touch actions. It includes the next keywords: *Sauthor*, which indicates that the same learner was talking and performing the touch action; *Sother*, when another learner was talking while the author was performing the action; and *Nospeech*, when the action was performed with no speech from any learner. Then, we focus on *touch actions,* taking into account the time, order and author of each touch to explore if only one student was building the solution or if their individual work was more reciprocal (by either taking turns or modifying the solution in parallel).

Table 1. Alphabet

Alphabet: Touch-Verbal participation				
Level 1: Resource	**Level 2: Action type**		**Level 3: Speech during touch**	**Level 4: Previous action**
Link	Add	Rem	Nospeech	Tsame
Conc	Chg	Mov	Sauthor	Tother
Indmap	*Open	*Close	Sother	Tparallel
Speech	Shrt	Full		

* Applies to INDMAP object only

Level 4 distinguishes the learner who performed the previous touch action and possible parallelism. It includes the next keywords: *Tsame*, when the previous action was performed by the same learner; *Tother*, when the previous action was performed by a different learner; and *Tparallel*, when the previous action was performed by a different learner less than one second earlier. The utterances (*Speech*) that did not happen in parallel with any touch actions are coded in the same sequence, with 2 keywords: *Shrt* and *Full* for utterances shorter or longer than u seconds respectively (u=2). Some examples or encoded actions are: {*Conc-Add-Tother-Sother*} for an *add a concept* action performed while another learner was talking; {*Link-Add-Tsame-Sauthor*} if the same learner who performed the previous action added a link while speaking; and {*Speech-Full*} if one of the learners starts speaking while none of learners interact with the tabletop. The sequence obtained for each group contained from 434 to 1467 *physical actions* and from 83 to 627 *utterances.*

The algorithm. In order to extract patterns of activity that differentiate high from low collaboration groups, we applied the DSM algorithm [6] on our encoded datasets. A sequential pattern is a consecutive or non-consecutive ordered sub-set of a sequence of events that is considered frequent when it meets a minimum support criteria [4]. For DSM this is called sequence-support (*s-support*) and corresponds to the number of sequences in which the pattern occurs, regardless of how often it appears within each sequence. For this study, we set the *s-support* to 0.5 (similarly to [6]). The algorithm also calculates repeated patterns within the dataset of sequences. This is called instance support (*i-support*). We also set the error threshold to 1 to allow the matching of patterns with up to one action different (similarly to [6, 11]). The output of this algorithm is a list of frequent patterns in each dataset that distinguish high from low collaboration groups based on their *i-support* ($p<0.1$).

4.3 Clustering Frequent Patterns

As a result of applying the DSM technique it may be possible to find *too many* differential patterns or some that are very *similar*. Therefore, it may not be simple to determine the higher level meaning of such findings without further processing. To alleviate these redundancy and dimension issues, we clustered the resulting patterns based on their *similarity,* as we did in [11]. We designed a modified version of the Agglomerative Nesting (AGNES) hierarchical clustering algorithm. It was implemented as follows: 1) Due to the multi-dimensionality of each sequence item, (each item can have up to 4 keywords) we define a *similarity criterion* to drive the clustering. This is performed by configuring the level of keywords that will be used to measure the similarity between 2 patterns. We explored two similarity criteria: i) focused on speech (*speech*, *nospeech*, *sauthor* and *sother* keywords), or ii) focused on touch (*tsame*, *tother* and *tparallel* keywords). 2) The hierarchical clustering step is performed in an iterative process that starts by considering each single pattern as a cluster. Then, a similarity matrix among clusters is generated by calculating the average average-link inter-clustering distance between sequences of each pair of clusters focusing on the keywords selected in the previous step. The algorithm merges the most similar clusters into new clusters recalculating the similarity matrix and continuing with the process until it produces one single cluster that contains all the sequences in the dataset. 3) To choose an *adequate* number of clusters we stop the iterations when their number matches the max threshold (parameter $m<=10$). The clusters that are still similar are merged (only if the intra-clustering distance of the new cluster is not higher than the maximum internal distance of the largest cluster). 4) For each cluster, the sequence that has an *average length* and contains the *majority of the top keywords* found within each cluster is chosen as the *representative sequence* of the cluster. Clusters with only one sequence are not included in the results. The result is a short list of clusters of sequences within each dataset (high and low collaboration).

5 Study Results

Detecting Level of Collaboration. The classification model to detect blocks that are collaborative was trained on an external dataset [8] and then applied to each of the half a minute blocks of tabletop activity. This dataset included audio and activity logs captured from a multi display collaborative environment. As a result, 17 out of the 20 (85%) group sessions were correctly identified as either highly or not very collaborative according to the aggregation of their classified blocks (around 60-70 in each group) and the qualitative assessment described in Section 3.2. Table 2 presents the distribution of blocks according to groups' collaboration. We can observe an increasing trend to highly collaborative blocks in the high collaboration groups (30, 17 and 12 blocks classified as high, medium and low collaboration). Groups with low collaboration levels presented more medium than low collaboration blocks, but very few highly collaborative blocks (H=8, M=35, L= 29). Some of the indicators of *quality of collaboration* are not easy to determine even through human judgment, and in consequence more challenging to measure automatically. These results show that it is possible to approximately detect the overall level of collaboration with simple rules using only quantitative indicators.

Table 2. Average number of classified blocks for high and low collaboration groups

Mean proportions of collaborative blocks			
Collaboration	**High**	**Medium**	**Low**
High	30 s=10	17 s=6	12 s=4
Low	8 s=4	35 s=9	29 s=10

Differential sequence mining and clustering. Then, the DSM algorithm was applied on the dataset of high and low collaboration groups that was originally assessed *qualitatively.* The result of this process was a total of 453 and 88 frequent patterns respectively that were differential ($p<0.1$). The next step was to cluster similar patterns using the AGNES clustering technique described above. Table 3 shows the resulting clusters using two similarity criteria: i) focused on speech, and ii) focused on parallelism and turn taking. First, regarding the role of speech in learners' strategies at the tabletop, highly collaborative groups had two main clusters: cluster-c1 that contains sequenced speech actions (utterances, highlighted in Table 3) and cluster-c2 that shows an interweaving of physical actions with speech performed by other learners (*Sother* keyword). For low collaboration groups, the clusters were: c3 that contains mostly sequences of touch actions without speech (*Nospeech*, highlighted in Table 3) and, to a much lesser extent compared with the highly collaborative groups, clusters

Table 3. Clusters generated

Clusters: focused on speech		
High collaboration Representative sequences	Strategy	#
C1-{Con-Mov-Sother}>{**Speech**}>{**Speech**}>{**Speech**}>{**Speech**}>{**Speech**}	Chain of conversation	269
C2-{Speech}>{Speech}>{Con-Mov-**Sother**}>{Link-Add-**Sother**}	Actions and others' speech	144
Low collaboration		
C3-{Con-Mov-**Nospeech**}>{Link-Add-**Nospeech**}>{Con-Mov-**Nospeech**}	Actions with no speech	72
C4-{**Speech**}>{**Speech**}>{Con-Mov-**Nospeech**}	Speech and actions	9
C5-{Con-Mov-Sauthor}>{**Speech**}>{**Speech**}>{**Speech**}>{**Speech**}	Chain of conversation	4
C6-{Con-Mov-**Sother**}>{Con-Mov-**Sother**}	Actions and others' speech	3
Clusters: focused on turn-taking and parallelism		
High collaboration Representative sequences	Strategy	#
C7-{Speech}>{Speech}>{Speech}>{Speech}>{Speech}>{Speech}>{Speech}	Long conversation	246
C8-{Speech}>{Con-Mov-Tsame}>{Speech}>{Speech}>{Speech}	Chain of conversation	145
C9-{Con-Mov-**Tsame**}>{Link-Add-**Tsame**}>{Link-Chg-**Tsame**}	1 learner actions	36
C10-{Speech}>{Con-Mov-Tsame}>{Link-Add-Tsame}>{Speech}>{Speech}	1 learner actions and speech	20
C11-{Link-Add-**Tsame**}>{Con-Mov-**Tother**}>{Link-Mov-**Tother**}	Turn-taking	6
Low collaboration		
C12-{Con-Mov-**Tparallel**}>{Link-Mov-**Tother**}>{Con-Mov-**Tparallel**}	Parallelism	34
C13-{Con-Mov-**Tother**}>{Con-Mov-**Tother**}>{Link-Add-**Tsame**}	Turn-taking	27
C14-{**Speech**}>{Con-Mov-**Tparallel**}>{**Speech**}	Speech and parallelism	5
C15-{Con-Mov-Tother}>{Speech}>{Speech}>{Speech}>{Speech}	Chain of conversation	4

number of frequent patterns included in the cluster

that can be associated with conversational patterns and interweaving of actions with some speech (c5 and c6). In the case of clusters obtained by focusing on the sequence and authorship of touch actions, we found 5 clusters for the highly collaborative groups (c7-11). Similarly to the previous case, the two larger clusters are associated with long chains of conversation (c7) or conversation accompanied with some touch actions (c8). Clusters c9 and c10 show chains of actions performed by the same learner in a row. This information is shown by the presence of the keyword *Tsame* (highlighted in Table 3) in the sequences. The smaller cluster is c11 that shows sequences of actions performed by different learners; an indication of what we call *turn-taking* (*Tother* keyword). In the case of low collaboration groups the size of the clusters had the opposite order compared to highly collaborative groups. The largest clusters mostly contain sequenced actions with the keywords *Tparallel* and *Tother* (c12 and c13), pointing to the presence of more parallelism and turn-taking in low collaboration groups than in highly collaborative groups. Cluster c-15 shows some conversational patterns in these groups.

6 Discussion and Conclusions

We presented the design of our approach for *automatically* distinguishing groups according to their level of collaboration, mining the frequent sequential patterns that differentiate these, and then grouping the patterns to associate them with higher level strategies. We implemented this process by analysing the *verbal and touch traces* of learners' interaction at an interactive tabletop. We validated our approach through a study that involved the participation of 20 triads building concept maps on a tabletop.

We used a decision tree to classify blocks of activity based on quantitative indicators of verbal and touch actions and how symmetric these were. This method proved effective in identifying the level of collaboration of 85% of the triads. The classification was not infallible but had an acceptable rate, suggesting a reasonable method for automatic differentiation of groups' activity. We applied the DSM [6] technique which generated a large number of patterns, especially for the highly collaborative groups. Our AGNES hierarchical clustering algorithm served to analyse the relationship of speech and touch and address our research question. We found some strategies that differentiate groups based on the sequences of actions of speech with *and* without physical activity, which characterised the highly collaborative groups. On the other hand, we found that the sequenced actions with higher rates of parallelism, turn taking and touch activity with less speech characterised the low collaboration groups.

Our approach can serve as a basis for the implementation of a system that can automatically and unobtrusively capture verbal and physical activity at the tabletop in order to alert teachers of possible issues in small-groups activities. It can provide them with key information to enhance their awareness of and highlight good collaboration practices. Our future work includes the design of the presentation layer for a teachers' dashboard displaying a suitable form of this information. We also plan to include different contextual information in the data analysis, for example, indicators obtained from the group artefact and the content of the learners' utterances.

References

1. Anaya, A., Boticario, J.: Application of machine learning techniques to analyse student interactions and improve the collaboration process. Expert Systems with Applications 38(2), 1171–1181 (2011)
2. Dillenbourg, P.: What do you mean by 'collaborative learning'? In: Collaborative Learning: Cognitive and Computational Approaches. Advances in Learning and Instruction Series, pp. 1–19. Elsevier Science, Oxford (1998)
3. Duque, R., Bravo, C.: A Method to Classify Collaboration in CSCL Systems. In: Beliczynski, B., Dzielinski, A., Iwanowski, M., Ribeiro, B. (eds.) ICANNGA 2007. LNCS, vol. 4431, pp. 649–656. Springer, Heidelberg (2007)
4. Jiang, L., Hamilton, H.J.: Methods for Mining Frequent Sequential Patterns. In: Xiang, Y., Chaib-draa, B. (eds.) AI 2003. LNCS (LNAI), vol. 2671, pp. 486–491. Springer, Heidelberg (2003)
5. Johnson, D.M., Sutton, P., Poon, J.: Face-to-Face vs. CMC: Student communication in a technologically rich learning environment. In: Proc. ASCILITE 2000, pp. 509–520 (2000)
6. Kinnebrew, J.S., Loretz, K.M., Biswas, G.: A Contextualized, Differential Sequence Mining Method to Derive Students' Learning Behavior Patterns. Journal of Educational Data Mining, JEDM (2012)
7. Martinez-Maldonado, R., Collins, A., Kay, J., Yacef, K.: Who did what? who said that? Collaid: an environment for capturing traces of collaborative learning at the tabletop. In: Proc. International Conference on Interactive Tabletops and Surfaces, pp. 172–181 (2011)
8. Martinez, R., Kay, J., Wallace, J.R., Yacef, K.: Modelling symmetry of activity as an indicator of collocated group collaboration. In: Konstan, J.A., Conejo, R., Marzo, J.L., Oliver, N. (eds.) UMAP 2011. LNCS, vol. 6787, pp. 207–218. Springer, Heidelberg (2011)
9. Martinez-Maldonado, R., Kay, J., Yacef, K.: Collaborative concept mapping at the tabletop. In: Proc. International Conference on Interactive Tabletops and Surfaces, pp. 207–210 (2010)
10. Martinez, R., Wallace, J.R., Kay, J., Yacef, K.: Modelling and identifying collaborative situations in a collocated multi-display groupware setting. In: Biswas, G., Bull, S., Kay, J., Mitrovic, A. (eds.) AIED 2011. LNCS, vol. 6738, pp. 196–204. Springer, Heidelberg (2011)
11. Martinez-Maldonado, R., Yacef, K., Kay, J., Kharrufa, A., Al-Qaraghuli, A.: Analysing frequent sequential patterns of collaborative learning activity around an interactive tabletop. In: Proc. EDM 2011, pp. 111–120 (2011)
12. Meier, A., Spada, H., Rummel, N.: A rating scheme for assessing the quality of computer-supported collaboration processes. International Journal of Computer-Supported Collaborative Learning (ijCSCL) 2(1), 63–86 (2007)
13. Novak, J., Cañas, A.: The Theory Underlying Concept Maps and How to Construct and Use Them. Florida Institute for Human and Machine Cognition (2008)
14. O'Donnell, A.M.: The Role of Peers and Group Learning. In: Handbook of Educational Psychology, pp. 781–802. Lawrence Erlbaum Associates (2006)
15. Perera, D., Kay, J., Koprinska, I., Yacef, K., Zaiane, O.: Clustering and Sequential Pattern Mining of Online Collaborative Learning Data. IEEE Transactions on Knowledge and Data Engineering 21(6), 759–772 (2009)
16. Roman, F., Mastrogiacomo, S., Mlotkowski, D., Kaplan, F., Dillenbourg, P.: Can a table regulate participation in top level managers' meetings? In: Proc. Conference on Supporting Group Work (GROUP 2012), pp. 1–10 (2012)
17. Scheuer, O., Loll, F., Pinkwart, N., McLaren, B.: Computer-supported argumentation: A review of the state of the art. International Journal of Computer-Supported Collaborative Learning (ijCSCL) 5(1), 43–102 (2010)
18. Soller, A., Wiebe, J., Lesgold, A.: A machine learning approach to assessing knowledge sharing during collaborative learning activities. In: Proc. CSCL 2002, pp. 128–137 (2002)

A Learning Environment That Combines Problem-Posing and Problem-Solving Activities

Kazuhisa Miwa[1], Hitoshi Terai[1], Shoma Okamoto[1], and Ryuichi Nakaike[2]

[1] Nagoya University, Nagoya, 464-8601, Japan
miwa@is.nagoya-u.ac.jp
[2] Kyoto University, Kyoto, 606-8501, Japan

Abstract. We developed a learning environment to combine problem-posing and problem-solving activities. The participants learned a formal logic system, natural deduction, by alternating between the problem-posing and problem-solving phases. In the problem posing-phase, the participants posed original problems and presented them on a shared problem database called "Forum," which was accessible to other group members. During the problem-solving phase, the participants solved the problems presented on Forum. This first round of problem posing and solving was followed by a second round of problem posing. We performed two practices for evaluation. The results showed that the participants successfully posed more advanced problems in the second round of problem posing as compared to the first. The empirical data gathered from the two practices indicated a significant relationship between problem-solving and problem-posing abilities.

Keywords: problem posing, problem solving, natural deduction, production system.

1 Introduction

In addition to problem solving, problem posing (i.e., learners generating original problems) is an effective method of learning. Computer-based learning enviornments for problem posing have been developed in the AIED community [14] [6]. Learning with problem posing has been actively performed, especially in mathematical education. Silver discussed the functions of problem posing with other learning activities such as creative activities, inquiry learning, and improvement of problem-solving performances [11]. English indicated that problem posing has learning effects such as improving problem-solving abilities, training divergent thinking, discovering erroneous concepts, and improving attitudes toward mathematics [3].

Conversely, learning with problem posing also presents difficulties. Problem posing is generally more difficult than problem solving, especially for introductory students. In problem posing, students must generate a variety of problems; however, most introductory students tend to generate limited types of problems. English instructed elementary school students to pose problems consistent with

K. Yacef et al. (Eds.): AIED 2013, LNAI 7926, pp. 111–120, 2013.

a specific equation within a context by presenting photographs and stories [4]. This resulted in the construction of limited types of problems. Even after three months of class practice, this tendency was not notably improved. Mestre required university students to pose problems in kinetics by presenting physical concepts such as Newton's second law of motion and the law of conservation of energy within a problem-posing context [7]. The result was that many representative problems similar to example problems in textbooks were generated.

Problems generated in learning through problem posing were not deductively constructed from given conditions. Learners must add additional constraints and assume contexts while problem posing. Thus, problem posing is a creative thinking activity. In fact, problem posing is often used as an item in creative thinking tests. In psychological studies of creative thinking, researchers have utilized abstract experimental tasks such as imagining aliens from unknown planets and inventing original furniture for the near future [5]. In the preceding studies, it was recognized that reality and practicality along with originality were important criteria fulfilled by creative products. Practicality in learning with problem posing implies that invented problems must be mathematically valid. Such constraints were especially important in problem-posing activities. When considering learning support in problem posing, it may be a key to have learners specifically focus on originality and validity.

The first aim of the current study is to design and develop a unified learning environment for learning through problem posing, and to evaluate its utility empirically through class practices. The characteristics of our learning environment are as follows:

Simultaneously Learning Problem Posing and Problem Solving: Generally, problem posing is recognized as a more advanced learning activity than problem solving. Therefore, learning through problem posing usually follows learning through problem solving. In our learning environment, these two types of learning develop simultaneously, and one activity reinforces the other by linking the problem-posing and problem-solving training.

Learning Problem Posing through Group Activities: We proposed an instructional design for group learning called Learning through Intermediate Problems (LtIP) [9] [8]. LtIP makes differences in the implicit knowledge of group members explicit through intermediate problems generated by participants and motivates the members to overcome these differences. Learning is achieved during the group activities. The learning environment in the current study is an example of a learning design based on LtIP.

The former characteristic enables the gathering of rich empirical data about both problem-posing and problem-solving activities. Problem posing is divergent thinking, while problem solving is convergent thinking; each has an opposite flow in its cognitive information processing, and the relationship between the two has drawn the attention of cognitive and learning scientists. Preceding studies have indicated large gaps between the two cognitive activities. For example, studies in second language acquisition have investigated the relationship between sentence recognition and sentence production. Although learners may acquire relatively high skills for sentence recognition, they face challenges in sentence production. Takakuwa suggested through his ESL education practices that sentence recognition and production performances are based on different types of cognitive processing in learners [13]. Furthermore, training in one activity does not contribute to an improvement in the other. A similar phenomenon was confirmed in the skill acquisition of computer programming languages. Anderson et al. indicated only slight transfer of ability from reading program codes to writing them [12]. The second aim of this study is to examine the relationship between such opposing types of cognitive processing as problem posing and problem solving and to accumulate empirical data about the activities through class practices.

2 Learning Environment

Lessons in our learning environment were conducted with university students. We used an authentic task, natural deduction (ND), as a learning material.

ND is a proof calculus in which logical reasoning is expressed by inference rules that are closely related to natural methods of reasoning [2]. Participants learn inference rules and strategies for applying these rules, such as strategies for inferring a proposition $\neg Q \to \neg P$ from a premise $P \to Q$. Several universities include ND in their curricula to teach the basics of logical thinking and formal reasoning.

The following is an example of a solution process:

(1) $P \to Q$	Premised
(2) $\neg Q$	Assumption
(3) P	Assumption
(4) $P \to Q$	Reiteration of (1)
(5) Q	$\to$ Elimination from (3) and (4)
(6) $\neg Q$	Reiteration of (2)
(7) $\neg P$	$\neg$ Introduction from (3), (5), and (6)
(8) $\neg Q \to \neg P$	$\to$ Introduction from (2) and (7)

Participants learn in a small group consisting of approximately ten members. Learning is developed by alternating between the problem-posing and problem-solving phases. Figure 1 shows an overview of our learning environment that consists of (1) "Forum," a shared problem database, (2) the problem-posing editor, and (3) the problem-solving support system.

In the problem-posing phase, participants pose original problems using the problem-posing editor and share them on Forum, which were accessible to other group members. In the problem-solving phase, participants solve the problems presented on Forum.

A key factor in our learning environment is the linkage between problem posing and problem solving. Participants learn through two types of linkages between problem-posing and problem-solving activities. The first is an intrapersonal linkage functioning within an individual. Participants self-check the validity of their original problem before presenting it on Forum, and as they pose

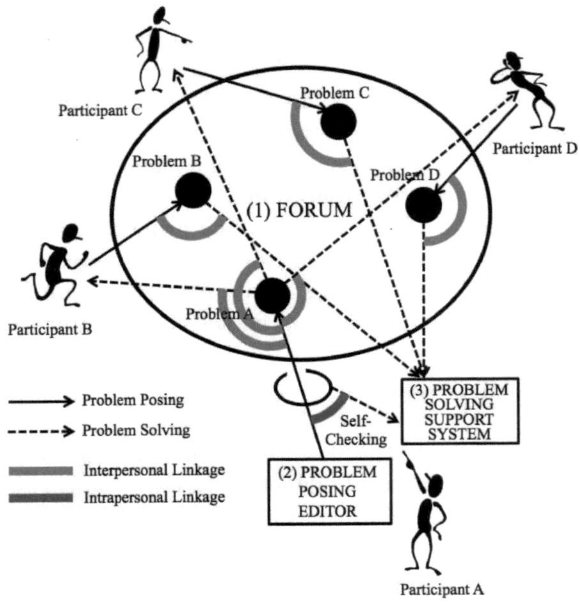

Fig. 1. An overview of the learning environment

more complex and difficult problems, they are required to solve them independently. The second linkage is an interpersonal linkage functioning among the group members. As the group members pose more sophisticated problems in the problem-posing phase, the quality of problems shared in Forum increases, engaging the group members in advanced problem-solving activities during the problem-solving phase. Thus, participants who experienced advanced problem solving are expected to establish footholds for more advanced problem posing in the second problem-posing phase.

In our learning environment, learning supports are provided for problem-solving activities. A complete problem solver that can solve any ND problem must be built in the problem-solving support system because problems that the system encounters are not determined prior to class activities. This problem-solving support system was developed in our preceding study [10]. The system is used for both self-checking original problems in the problem-posing phase and solving problems in the problem-solving phase.

3 Practices

3.1 Participants and Procedures

We performed two practices: one for undergraduates in a liberal arts college and the other for graduates in a graduate school of information science.

Practice 1: In Practice 1, 32 students (juniors and seniors) in a liberal arts college joined our practice. They were divided into four groups, including groups of seven and nine students as well as two groups of eight students. The ND system comprised thirteen inference rules and eight solution strategies. In Practice 1, a subset of nine rules and two strategies was used for introductory students.

Practice 1 was performed during three lessons of a cognitive science class. The participants learned the basics of formal reasoning systems and psychology of human reasoning and the basics of natural deduction from printed material. Subsequently, they used the problem-solving support system to solve eight example problems. In the final phase of the three classes, two printed test problems were solved to measure the participants' problem solving abilities.

Following the class activities, the problem-posing practice was performed. The first round of problem posing was performed over 23 minutes, followed by a 32-minute problem-solving phase. Then, the second round of problem posing was also performed over 23 minutes. We evaluated the effects of our learning environment by comparing the problems posed in the first and second rounds of problem posing. In addition, we discussed the relationship between the participants' problem-posing and problem-solving abilities by comparing their problem-solving test scores and the quality of the original problems in the problem-posing phase.

Practice 2: Practice 2 investigates more advanced problem-posing activities than Practice 1, and was performed in a laboratory setting. Twenty-five graduates in a graduate school of information science were recruited for the practice, and each was compensated JPY 8000 if they participated in all sessions of the practice. The participants were divided into four groups, including three groups of six and one group of seven participants. A full set of ND system consisting of thirteen inference rules and eight solution strategies was used.

The experimental procedure was almost identical to that in Practice 1. Basic instructions were provided to each group. The participants used the problem-solving support system to solve nine problems. This training was performed individually at each participant's residence. The system was provided as a web-based software. On the other hand, for problem posing, the participants were gathered in a laboratory, where each group engaged in the problem-posing and problem-solving activities. Prior to the activities, two test problems were solved to measure the participants' problem-solving abilities; these problems were more difficult than those used in Practice 1.

3.2 Comparisons of Problems in 1st and 2nd Round Problem Posing

The quality of problems posed was measured on the basis of the number of steps required to solve the problems and the required number of inference rules and solution strategies. We admit problems with larger numbers in these indexes as more complex and higher in quality. Figure 2 shows a comparison of the average number of solution steps for the problems posed in the first and second rounds ($t(31) = 3.25$, $p < 0.01$ in Practice 1 and $t(24) = 2.90$, $p < 0.01$ in Practice 2) and Figure 3 shows a comparison of the average number of rules and strategies

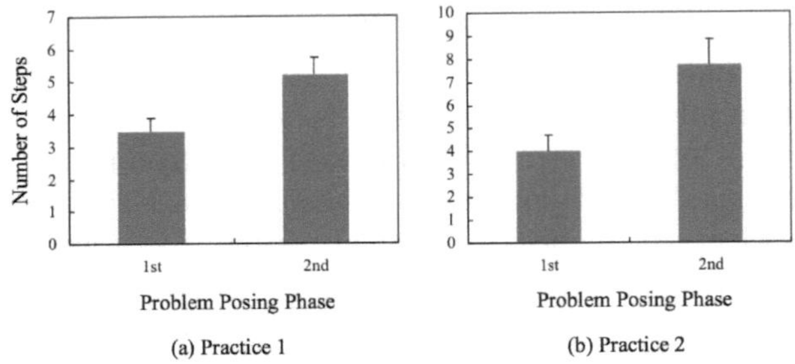

Fig. 2. Number of steps required to solve problems posed in the first and second rounds of problem posing

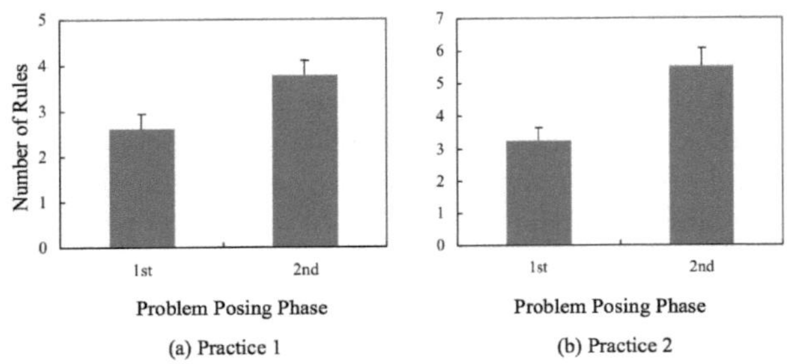

Fig. 3. Number of rules and strategies required to solve problems posed in the first and second rounds of problem posing

to solve the problems ($t(31) = 3.53$, $p < 0.01$ in Practice 1 and $t(24) = 3.33$, $p < 0.01$ in Practice 2). The results indicate that the quality of posed problems increased from the first to second phase in both Practice 1 and Practice 2.

For more detailed analysis, we categorized the relationship between rules (and strategies) required to solve the problems posed in the first round and those in the second round into five types, as illustrated in Figure 4. The results of the analysis are shown in Table 1 (Practice 1) and Table 2 (Practice 2), which indicate that most participants posed advanced problems in the second round; they used rules and strategies that had not been employed in the first round of problem posing in both Practice 1 and Practice 2.

Figure 5 indicates the degree to which the rules and strategies that the group members utilized for posing problems covered the full set of ND system in Practice 2 and the aforementioned subset in Practice 1. The results show that in Practice 1, the covering rate reached almost 100% in the first round of problem posing. However, in Practice 2, less than 50% of the rules and strategies were used in the first round, and the rate increased in the second round. This suggests that, especially in more advanced learning in Practice 2, the participants were successfully guided to adopting more rules and strategies through a group activity by referring to other members' problems in the preceding problem-solving phase.

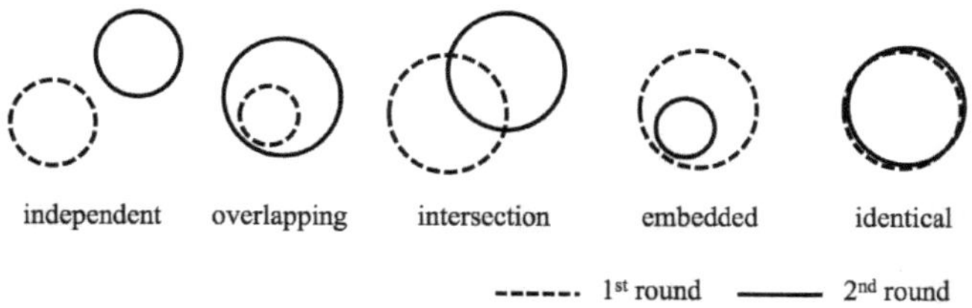

Fig. 4. Relationship between problems posed in the first and second rounds of problem posing

Table 1. Distribution of relationship between problems posed in the first and second rounds of problem posing (Practice 1)

	Independent	Overlapping	Intersection	Embedded	Identical
Group 1	5	2	1	1	0
Group 2	2	0	3	0	1
Group 3	4	2	2	0	0
Group 4	2	2	4	0	0
Total	13	6	10	1	1

Table 2. Distribution of relationship between problems posed in the first and second rounds of problem posing (Practice 2)

	Independent	Overlapping	Intersection	Embedded	Identical
Group 1	3	1	2	0	0
Group 2	1	3	3	0	0
Group 3	0	4	2	0	0
Group 4	2	1	2	1	0
Total	6	9	9	1	0

3.3 Comparison between Problems Posed and Problem-Solving Test

Figure 6 shows a correlation between the average number of solution steps for the problems posed in the second round and the average score of the two problems in the problem-solving test ($r = 0.57$, $p < 0.01$ in Practice 1 and $r = 0.37$, $p < 0.10$ in Practice 2). Furthermore, Figure 7 shows a correlation between the average number of rules and strategies required to solve the problems and the average score of the two problems in the problem-solving test ($r = 0.58$, $p < 0.01$ in Practice 1 and not significant in Practice 2). Thus, the results from Practice 1 indicate a significant relationship between problem-solving and problem-posing abilities.

Contrary to Practice 1, neither correlation was significant in Practice 2, since there were participants who achieved a high score in the problem-solving test but were unable to pose a high quality problem. These participants are distributed to the lower right area of the graphs in Figures 6 (b) and 7 (b). Conversely, there

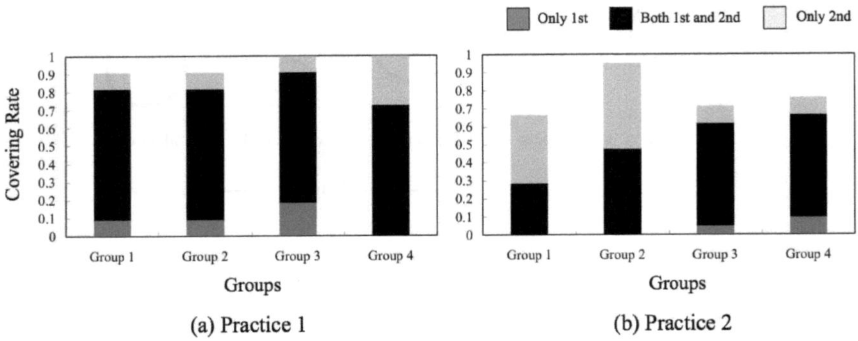

Fig. 5. Covering rate of rules and strategies used in the first and second rounds of problem posing

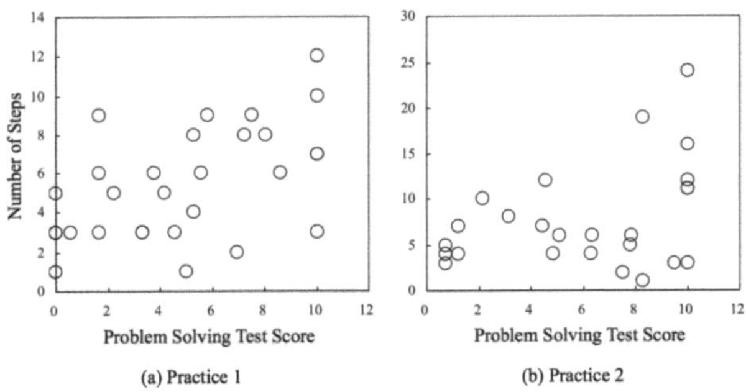

Fig. 6. Correlation between the number of problem-solving steps and the score of the problem-solving test

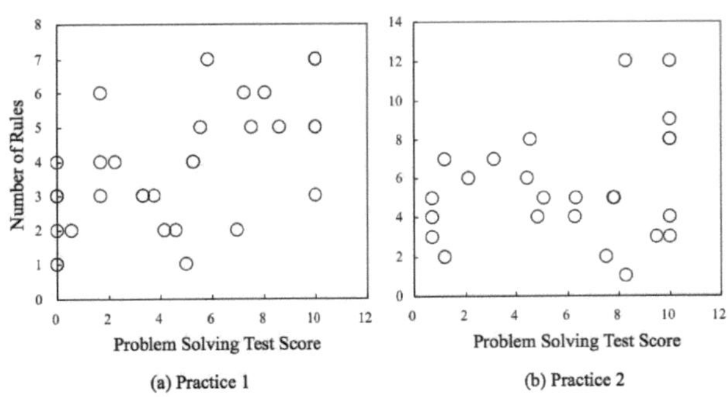

Fig. 7. Correlation between the number of rules and strategies and the score of the problem-solving test

were no participants distributed to the upper left area of the graphs, indicating that all participants who posed high quality problems acquired high problem-solving abilities. Thus, acquiring a high problem-solving ability is required for a high capability for problem posing.

4 Discussion and Conclusions

This study adopted the LtIP framework to develop a unified learning support environment for teaching ND, in which participants learn while referring to problems posed by other participants. In addition, this study evaluated the utility of this environment.

The results of our practices indicated that the participants posed more advanced problems after solving other members' problems presented on Forum. A question remains regarding the degree to which referring to other problems contributes to this improvement. Is a similar effect obtained even when participants solve problems that teachers systematically select and offer instead of the mutual references of shared problems? The answer is likely YES. Nevertheless, the advantages of our learning environment, which includes mutual references of problems, still remain.

The relationship between learning to solve problems from teachers and learning through other members' problems corresponds to the relationship between learning in which teachers directly instruct students and learning in which students construct knowledge by themselves through mutual interactions. A representative example of the latter is the jigsaw learning [1]. Previous practices using the jigsaw method indicated that group members constructively acquired meta-level knowledge by exchanging their knowledge. Since an individual responsibility was assigned to each member, contributions of each member to the group activities were promoted. In addition, affective effects such as an increase in interest and enjoyable learning experience were also confirmed.

Certain advanced problems that are not included in published textbooks were included in the problems posed in Practice 2. The validity of all problems saved in Forum was verified, and their fundamental natures such as the required inference rules and solution steps are recorded in the database as the problems were solved by the problem-solving support system before being presented on Forum. Thus, the problem database itself is valuable as a set of problems for learning ND. Developing systematic methods of using the constructed database may be an important focus for future research.

Next, we discussed the relationship between problem-solving and problem-posing abilities based on the empirical data obtained through the practices. The analyses indicated a correlation between the two abilities in Practice 1 but not in Practice 2. However, in Practice 2, it was confirmed that problem-solving ability is required for advanced problem posing.

In both practices, we analyzed the quality of problems posed on the basis of the required number of solution steps and inference rules and strategies. Thus, we evaluated the quality from the viewpoint of complexity and difficulty. However, some participants, especially in Practice 2, may have been interested in the originality of their problem. For example, a participant in Practice 2 posed the following problem: deduct $\neg(\neg P)$ from a premise P. This problem was constructed by reversing the premise and conclusion of the following problem: deduct P from $\neg(\neg P)$. The latter was an inference rule rather than a problem, and was solved through merely one step. On the other hand, to solve the former problem, one of the most advanced solution strategies, the reductio ad absurdum, should be utilized. Four solution steps are required for the problem; therefore, from the viewpoint of solution steps, it is not highly difficult. However, it may be a creative problem because an insight is required to invent this problem. More detailed analysis from multiple viewpoints is our important future work.

References

1. Aronson, E., Patnoe, S.: The jigsaw classroom: Building cooperation in the classroom. Addison Wesley Longman, New York (1996)
2. Barwise, J., Etchemendy, J.: Language, Proof and Logic. CSLI publications (2003)
3. English, L.D.: Promoting a problem-posing classroom. Teaching Children Mathematics 4, 172–179 (1997)
4. English, L.D.: Children's problem posing within formal and informal contexts. Journal for Research in Mathematics Education 29, 83–106 (1998)
5. Finke, R.A., Ward, T.B., Smith, S.M.: Creative cognition: Theory, research, and applications. MIT Press (1992)
6. Hirashima, T., Kurayama, M.: Learning by problem-posing for reverse-thinking problems. In: Biswas, G., Bull, S., Kay, J., Mitrovic, A. (eds.) AIED 2011. LNCS, vol. 6738, pp. 123–130. Springer, Heidelberg (2011)
7. Mestre, J.P.: Probing adults' conceptual understanding and transfer of learning via problem posing. Journal of Applied Developmental Psychology 23, 9–50 (2002)
8. Miwa, K., Morita, J., Nakaike, R., Terai, H.: Learning through intermediate problems in creating cognitive models. Interactive Learning Environments (in press)
9. Miwa, K., Nakaike, R., Morita, J., Terai, H.: Development of production system for anywhere and class practice. In: Proceedings of the 14th International Conference of Artificial Intelligence in Education, pp. 91–99 (2009)
10. Miwa, K., Terai, H., Kanzaki, N., Nakaike, R.: Development and evaluation of an intelligent tutoring system for teaching natural deduction. In: Proceedings of the 20th International Conference on Computers in Education, pp. 41–45 (2012)
11. Silver, E.A.: On mathematical problem posing. For the Learning of Mathematics 14, 19–28 (1994)
12. Singley, M.K., Anderson, J.R.: The Transfer of Cognitive Skill. Harvard University Press, Cambridge (1989)
13. Takakuwa, J.: Japanese efc learners' syntactic analyses: Focusing on learners' sentence comprehension and production. Annual Review of English Language Education in Japan 12, 11–20 (2001)
14. Yu, F., Liu, Y.H., Chan, T.W.: A networked question-posing and peer assessment learning system: a cognitive enhancing tool. Journal of Educational Technology Systems 32, 211–226 (2003)

ViewS in User Generated Content for Enriching Learning Environments: A Semantic Sensing Approach

Dimoklis Despotakis[1], Vania Dimitrova[1], Lydia Lau[1], Dhavalkumar Thakker[1], Antonio Ascolese[2], and Lucia Pannese[2]

[1] School of Computing, University of Leeds, Leeds, LS2 9JT, United Kingdom
{scdd,V.G.Dimitrova,l.m.s.lau,D.Thakker}@leeds.ac.uk
[2] Imaginary Srl, Milan, 50 - 20124, Italy
{antonio.ascolese,lucia.pannese}@i-maginary.it

Abstract. Social user-generated content (e.g. comments, blogs) will play a key role in learning environments providing a rich source for capturing diverse viewpoints; and is particularly beneficial in ill-defined domains that encompass diverse interpretations. This paper presents ViewS - a framework for capturing viewpoints from user-generated textual content following a semantic sensing approach. It performs semantic augmentation using existing ontologies and presents the resultant semantic spaces in a visual way. ViewS was instantiated for interpersonal communication and validated in a study with comments on job interview videos, achieving over 82% precision. The potential of ViewS for enriching learning environments is illustrated in an exploratory study by analysing micro-blogging content collected within a learning simulator for interpersonal communication. A group interview with simulator designers evinced benefits for gaining insights into learner reactions and further simulator improvement.

Keywords: Social content, Semantic Augmentation and Analysis, Viewpoints, Interpersonal Communication, Simulated Environments for Learning.

1 Introduction

Social spaces are radically transforming the educational landscape. A new wave of intelligent learning environments that exploit social interactions to enrich learning environments is forming[1]. Notable successes include using socially generated content to augment learning experiences [2], facilitate search[3], aid informal learning through knowledge discovery or interactive exploration of social content [4], facilitate organisational learning and knowledge maturing. In the same line, social contributions are becoming invaluable source to augment existing systems, e.g. [5-7] and to build open user models [8-9]. Social spaces and user generated content provide a wealth of authentic and unbiased collection of different perspectives resulting from diverse backgrounds and personal experiences. This can bring new opportunities for informal learning of soft skills (e.g. communicating, planning, managing, advising,

K. Yacef et al. (Eds.): AIED 2013, LNAI 7926, pp. 121–130, 2013.

negotiating), which are ill-defined domains requiring awareness of multiple interpretations and viewpoints [10]. There is a pressing demand for robust methods to get an insight into user generated content to empower learning of soft skills. Such a method is presented in this paper, exploiting ontologies and semantic augmentation.

While semantic analysis of social content is revolutionizing human practices in the many areas (e.g. policy making, disaster response, open government), little attention has been paid at exploiting semantic technologies to gain an understanding of social content in order to empower learning environments. The approach presented in this paper is a step in this direction. We present a *semantic social sensing* approach which explores ontologies and semantic augmentation of social content to get an insight into diversity and identify interesting aspects that can be helpful for enriching a learning environment. While the approach can be seen as resembling open learner models of social interactions (e.g.[8-9, 11], it has crucial differences - we link social user generated content to ontology entities and provide interactive visualizations in the form of semantic maps for exploring such content.

The work presented here is conducted within the EU project ImREAL[1] which examines the use of digital traces from social spaces to augment simulated environments for learning. We present a semantic social sensing approach adapted for user generated content on interpersonal communication (Sections 2 and 3), focusing on non-verbal communication (body language and emotion). This contributes to newly establishing research in social knowledge management for learning. The approach is then applied to one of the ImREAL use cases – a simulator for interpersonal communication in business settings (Section 4). We examine the potential for gaining an understanding of user reactions with the simulation and extending the simulation content. Our approach offers a new dimension in the established research strand on evaluating and extending simulated environments for learning by adding a novel way of *sensing* learners and content, in addition to traditional methods of log data analysis [12-13], measuring the learning effect [14-15] or eye tracking[16].

2 The ViewS Framework

ViewS (short for Viewpoint Semantics) - is a framework for capturing the semantics of textual user generated content (e.g. comments, stories, blogs). ViewS utilises existing semantic repositories (in the form of ontologies) with corresponding techniques for semantic augmentation of text input, and comprises of two phases (see Figure 1).

Phase 1: Text Processing. This involves: (i) Extraction of text surface form (SF) from the input text using Natural Language Processing (NLP) modules. The Stanford NLP[2] parser is utilised for these modules for tokenisation, sentence splitting, part-of-speech tagging and typed dependency extraction. The extracted SF includes exact text tokens (spans), stemmed tokens, and multi-token terms from the typed dependencies (negations are also included). (ii) Linguistic and semantic enrichment of the SF to provide enriched surface form (ESF). Freely available generic language resources are

[1] `http://www.imreal-project.eu`

[2] Stanford Parser: `http://nlp.stanford.edu/software/lex-parser.shtml`

used: a) WordNet[3] for lexical derivations and extraction of synonyms and antonyms (presented with negation); b) DISCO[4] corpus for deriving similar words based on co-occurrences in textual corpus by using the similarity queries; and c) Suggested Upper Merged Ontology - SUMO[5], for detecting relevant senses by using lexical categories and semantic mappings of terms identified from WordNet. The resultant ESF allows for a broader set of textual terms to be mapped to ontologies.

Phase 2: Semantic Annotation. The semantic annotation concerns the mapping of both SF and ESF to ontology entities, using one or more ontologies. Each ontology represents a specific dimension of the domain which we wish to analyse the view-points expressed in user generated content. For example, emotion and body language are the two chosen dimensions for examining user generated content in the domain of interpersonal communication. The algorithm for annotation prioritises the mapping of the SF. The result of the semantic annotation is a set of XML elements which semantically augment the textual content with ontology entities. These elements include the annotated textual token(s), the ontology entity URI, a negation operator (when such exists), the WordNet sense for the specific token (based on the SUMO mapping) and the corresponding ontology name.

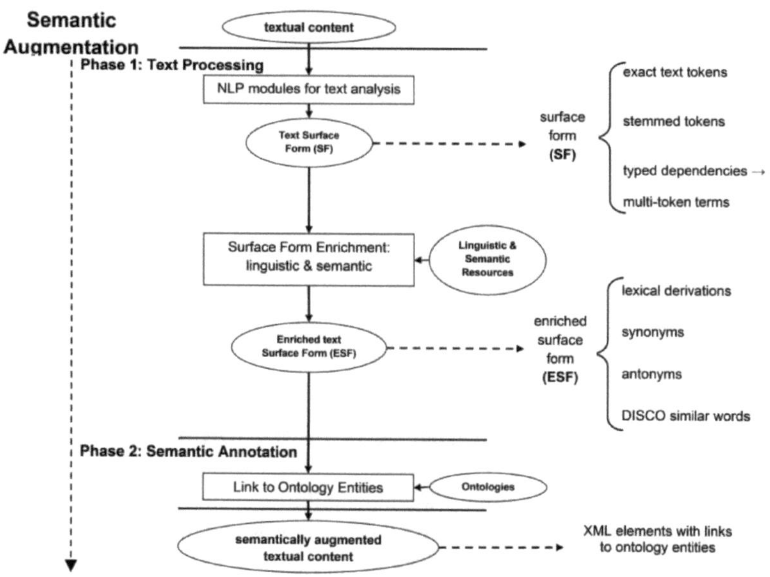

Fig. 1. The ViewS[6] semantic augmentation pipeline: a text surface form is extracted and enriched from the text processing Phase 1 and in Phase 2 is linked to ontologies

[3] WordNet: `http://wordnet.princeton.edu/`
[4] DISCO: `http://www.linguatools.de/disco/disco_en.html`
[5] SUMO: `http://www.ontologyportal.org/`
[6] Demo of the ViewS Semantic augmentation is available at: `http://imash.leeds.ac.uk/services/ViewS`

Instantiation of ViewS for Interpersonal Communication with a Focus on Social Signals. In this paper, the domain interpersonal communication (IC) is chosen with the focus on two dimensions of social signals (emotion and body language). WordNet lexical categories and SUMO concepts for sense detection relevant to IC and social signals were selected[7]. For the semantic annotation phase we utilised two ontologies: (i) WordNet-Affect, which comprises a rich taxonomy of emotions with 304 concepts. The original XML format of WordNet-Affect was transformed to RDF/XML[8] to enable semantic processing. (ii) A body language ontology[9] which was built as part of the Activity Modelling Ontology [17] developed within the ImREAL EU Project. This body language ontology combined concepts in a survey article for social signal processing [18], a personal development site for business communications skills[10], and a portion of SUMO. An example of a user comment on a job interview video, and the corresponding set of annotations, is shown in Table 1.

Table 1. The annotation set of an example comment

Comment	" *The applicant is not anxious. She appears very confident, although she is not greeting the interviewer and then sits and crosses her legs. She does not respect the interviewer. The interviewer might feel discomfort with the applicant's manners.* "
Text Token(s)	**(ontology entity, {Ontologies presenting dimensions})**
{not, anxious}	(¬ anxiousness,{WNAffect, Body Language}),(¬ nervousness, {Body Language}),
appears	(facial_expression, {Body Language}), (face, {Body Language})
confident	(confidence, {WNAffect, Body Language}), (authority, {Body Language})
Sits	(sitting , {Body Language})
{not, greeting}	(¬ greeting, {Body Language})
Legs	(legs, {Body Language})
respect	(¬ regard, {WNAffect}), (¬ admiration, {WNAffect})
discomfort	(nausea, {WNAffect}), (distress, {WNAffect}), (frustration, {WNAffect}), (anxiety, {WNAffect}), (¬comfortableness, {WNAffect}), (confusion, {WNAffect})
{crosses, legs}	(crossed_legs_sitting, {Body Language})

3 Validation of the Semantic Augmentation Mechanism

An experimental study was conducted to validate the precision of the semantic augmentation with ViewS in the above instantiation. Content was collected using a system which presented selected YouTube videos showing interesting job interview situations and asked users to comment at any point in the videos on interesting aspects they saw in the videos or could relate to their personal experience. The study involved 10 participants (5 male and 5 female). 183 user comments were collected. 1526 annotations were extracted

[7] The selection was made by a social scientist expert in manual annotation of content for IC.

[8] The WNAffect taxonomy: `http://imash.leeds.ac.uk/ontologies/WNAffect/WNAffect.owl`

[9] BodyLanguage ontology: `http://imash.leeds.ac.uk/ontologies/BodyLanguage/BodyLanguage.owl`

[10] `http://www.businessballs.com/body-language.htm`

with ViewS (average of 8.3 annotations per comment). Three expert annotators (two social scientists with experience in content annotation and activity modelling and one psychologist) examined each comment and the corresponding semantic augmentation produced by ViewS. The average pair-wise inter-annotator specific agreement[11] for correct annotation was 80%. The system achieved 89.97% micro-averaging precision[12] (i.e. the precision of the annotations for the whole corpus of comments) for correct ontology entity extraction (for WNAffect 96.84% and for Body Language 92.65% - entities are shared between the two ontologies) and 82.5% for correct identification of textual terms important to describe the textual comment (see Table 2 for a summary), considering the majority of responses by the three annotators. For these annotations the enrichment methods followed were more favorable than the surface form based (73% compared to 27%). The macro-averaging precision (i.e. the average of the precision for each comment) was 89.55% for correct ontology entity extraction and 82.72% for correctly identifying text terms to describe the comment.

Table 2. Summary of the annotated content (183 user comments) over the two ontologies

		SF	ESF	Total
Annotations	**WNAffect**	28	321	349
	Body Language	318	859	1117
Distinct Ontology Entities	**WNAffect**	12	89	101 (33.2% of 304)
	Body Language	82	142	224 (42.5% of 526)

The validation study showed that ViewS performed very well with the instantiation for emotion and body language (see Section 2). The high precision (over 82% in different annotation aspects) signifies a reliable semantic augmentation mechanism to enable semantic analysis of IC related content.

4 Application of ViewS for Enriching an IC Simulator

4.1 The Simulator and Study Setup

To examine the potential of exploiting the semantic output of ViewS for enriching learning environments, we conducted an exploratory study that collected social content within an existing simulator for interpersonal communication in business settings. The simulator is developed by imaginary Srl within the framework of the ImREAL EU project. The study involved one of the simulation scenarios – the learner is a host who organises a business dinner involving several people from different nationalities. The interaction with the simulator is expected to promote awareness of the importance of cultural variations in IC, focusing on differences in social norms and use of

[11] The prevalence of responses by the annotators lead to imbalanced distribution which results to low Kappa, even though the observed agreement (Po) is high. The specific agreement was reported following: D. V. Cicchetti and A. R. Feinstein, "High agreement but low kappa: II. Resolving the paradoxes," Journal of Clinical Epidemiology, vol. 43, pp. 551-558, 1990.

[12] For details regarding precision calculation please refer to: Sebastiani, F.: Machine learning in automated text categorization. ACM Comput. Surv. 34, 1-47 (2002).

Fig. 2. Example learner interaction screen – the simulated situation is in the Dinner episode where the host has to decide about ordering food for his business guests

body language, and how this may influence a person's expectations and emotions. It also aims to promote reflection on personal experiences in relevant IC contexts.

The simulated scenario includes **four episodes**: *Greetings* (situations embed arriving on time, different norms about greetings, first impression, and use of body language), *Dinner* (situations embed use of body language and different preferences about food and drink), *Bill* (situations embed use of body language and different norms about payment), *Goodbye* (situations embed use of body language and different norms about greetings). Figure 2 illustrates the interface and the interaction features provided to the leaner to select a response and read/write micro-blogging comments.

The simulator was used by 39 users who attended interactive sessions at learning technology workshops or responded to invitations sent to learning forums in Europe. The data was collected during the period 29 Oct 2012 – 15 Jan 2013. Micro-blogging comments (total of 193) were provided by 25 of the users, and were semantically augmented with ViewS for IC (see Table 3 for a summary).

Table 3. Summary of the ViewS annotation of the micro-blogging content in the study

	Episode	**Greetings**	**Dinner**	**Bill**	**Goodbye**	**All**
Annotations	**WNAffect**	82	84	18	8	192
	Body Language	311	236	100	76	723
Distinct Ontology Entities	**WNAffect**	36	36	11	5	57
	Body Language	76	63	43	33	106

The output of ViewS was shown to two simulator designers (with background in Psychology) who were involved in the creation and improvement of the simulated scenario. The semantic augmentation output was visualised in the form of semantic maps to enable exploration of both ontologies - WNAffect and Body language-, and identification of ontology entities that linked to user comments and their location over the ontologies (see examples in Figures 3, 4). The exploration allowed filtering based on episodes and user groups, and comparison of the resultant semantic maps.

4.2 Semantic Social Sensing with ViewS

The simulator designers were shown semantic maps providing: (i) overview of the annotations for each episode; (ii) comparison between different episodes; and (iii) exploration and comparison of user groups. For each semantic map, the designers were asked if they could see anything interesting and, if so, how it could be helpful for them. Designers' observations and feedback were driven by the key challenges they were facing: (i) getting an insight of the user reactions with the simulator; and (ii) improving the simulation scenario to make it more realistic and engaging. Identified benefits and limitations of ViewS for simulator enrichment are sumarised below.

Overview. The simulator designers were first shown an overview of the annotations of comments from all users for each simulation episode.

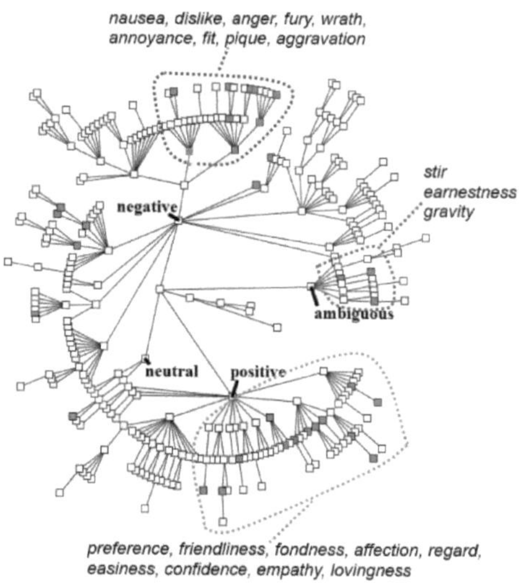

Fig. 3. The semantic map of annotations (highlighted nodes) for all comments on the Greetings episode. It shows a cluster of negative emotions around dislike and anger (top, centre), a cluster of positive emotions, and few ambiguous emotions on the right side.

Exploring the semantic maps, the designers noted that: (i) there were several clusters of positive and negative emotions in WNAffect (Figure 3); this *confirmed the designers' expectation that the simulation experience should trigger links to these emotions*; (ii) the body language entities clustered around social interaction and psychological process, which was also seen as an *indication of the desired effect of the simulation;* (iii) the formed ontology clusters were also characterised by the designers as *"hot-topics" on which more attention could be given* in the simulation (e.g. by extending the feedback or by adding more situations); (iv) the ontology hierarchy was helpful to see the depth (abstract or specific) of the emotions and body language entities - the designers commented that this could give them *suggestions for the range of emotions they could include* in further situations or for improving the existing situations.

Gateway to Comments. In addition to the semantic overview, the designers pointed out the need for examining the learners' comments in order to get deeper insight into the content. The ontology clusters facilitated the examination of user comments in semantically close groups related to specific ontology regions. The designers were specifically interested whether the comments were related to personal experience or to the simulated situation, which was not possible to analyse with ViewS. Manual inspection of several groups of comments indicated that most comments referred to either personal experience or rules the learners were following (see examples in Table 4). Some of the comments were seen as helpful to enrich the feedback provided to the learner or to add more options for response in the simulator.

Table 4. Example comments and annotated WNAffect entities in the Greetings episode

Negative	*Just two days ago I discussed with a friend of mine because he was really late...I felt so angry!*	**anger, fury**
Positive	*Being on-time helps to build confidence especially when meeting new people for the first or second time*	**confidence**

Comparison between Episodes. Comparison of semantic maps enabled comparing different episodes. For example, the content related to the Bill episode did not refer to many WNAffect entities (Figure 4, left), compared with the Greetings episode (Figure 3). The designers found such comparison useful because it provided a *sensor of which simulation parts would require further improvement and in what direction* (e.g. the designers noted that the Bill episode could be improved as it did not have many branches and situations, and hence did not provoke much user comments linking to emotion entities). Furthermore, semantic maps for the same episode were compared (an example is shown in Figure 4, right). The designers found such comparisons helpful for *balancing elements of the simulation in the same or different situations.*

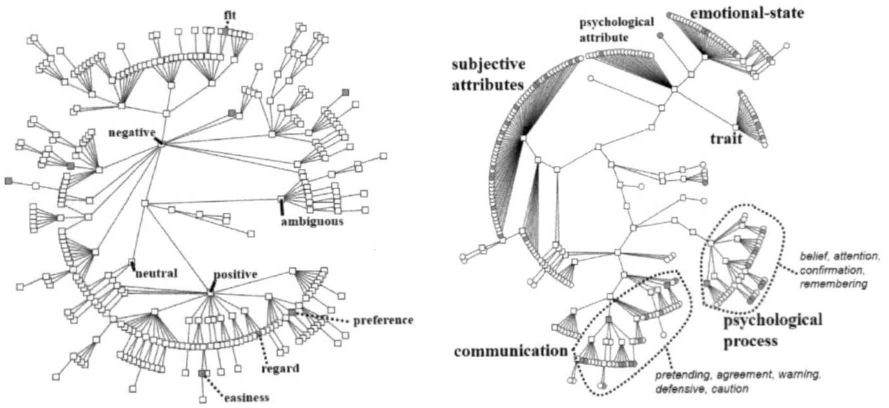

Fig. 4. The WNAffect (left) and body language signal meaning (right) semantic maps of annotations (highlighted nodes) for the Bill episode

Example comment	WNAffect	Body Language
You can make a softer gesture with your palm when you want someone to hold and relax while you take care of things.	easiness	gesture, relaxation, attention, interest, caution

Comparison between User Groups. The designers were able to spatially examine the contributions from different user groups and see the distribution in the semantic map. Interesting observations were made. Comparing the semantic maps with WNAffect annotations of comments by 17-26 years old users and over 27 years old users, it was noted that WNAffect entities by the second user group *were broader and covered different levels of abstraction, while the first group linked to a more limited set of entities*. Similarly, comparison was made between male and female users, and was noted that the former *referred to a broader set of WNAffect entities*. The designers were reluctant to draw any conclusions regarding user groups. They noted however that the comparison between user groups could be useful when *thinking of the target audiences during the simulation design process*.

In sum, there was overall a positive feedback about the potential of semantic exploration of social content to provide various ways of sensing what emotions or body language meanings the users noticed in the simulation and recalled from their personal experiences. This could be used to check the designers' expectations for learners' reactions with the simulator, or to identify areas for further improvement of the simulation situations, interaction, and feedback. The groupings of content were particularly helpful, and there was a strong desire to explore comments together with ontology concepts. Further text analysis to identify clusters of comments regarding textual content (e.g. personal experiences, rules, simulation feedback) could be helpful.

5 Conclusions

The paper presented a framework, called ViewS, which exploits ontologies and semantic augmentation techniques to analyse social user generated content and to explore diverse viewpoints presented in such content. ViewS provides a semantic sensing approach to get an insight into social content diversity and to identify interesting aspects that can be helpful for enriching a learning environment. ViewS has been validated in the ill-defined domain of interpersonal communication, focusing on social signals. ViewS distinguishes from other approaches by utilising a rich taxonomy of emotions and a prototypical ontology to describe body language for semantic annotation exploiting different enrichment methods.

The potential of the approach for enriching learning environments was examined in an exploratory study with a simulated environment for interpersonal communication in business settings. Our immediate future work includes further experimental studies to examine the benefits of ViewS, which will include deeper evaluation with a broader range of simulator designers and relating comments to the learner performance and individual profiles. Further zooming into the content will be also investigated by exploiting different ontologies to capture ViewS on various dimensions (e.g. in the example presented in the paper, food habits were mentioned but not captured by the semantic augmentation). We are also currently implementing algorithms for semantic aggregation of annotations and content to enable semantic zooming and exploration at different abstraction levels of the semantic output generated by ViewS.

Acknowledgments. The research leading to these results has received funding from the EU 7th Framework Programme under grant ICT 257831 (ImREAL project).

References

1. Vassileva, J.: Toward Social Learning Environments. IEEE Transactions on Learning Technologies 1, 199–214 (2008)
2. Dragon, T., Floryan, M., Woolf, B., Murray, T.: Recognizing Dialogue Content in Student Collaborative Conversation. In: Aleven, V., Kay, J., Mostow, J. (eds.) ITS 2010, Part II. LNCS, vol. 6095, pp. 113–122. Springer, Heidelberg (2010)
3. Nejdl, W.: Exploiting User Generated Content to Improve Search. In: Proceedings of the 2009 Conference on Artificial Intelligence in Education: Building Learning Systems that Care: From Knowledge Representation to Affective Modelling, p. 5. IOS Press (2009)
4. Thakker, D., Despotakis, D., Dimitrova, V., Lau, L., Brna, P.: Taming digital traces for informal learning: a semantic-driven approach. In: Proceedings of the 7th ECTEL (2012)
5. Ziebarth, S., Malzahn, N., Hoppe, H.U.: Matchballs – A Multi-Agent-System for Ontology-Based Collaborative Learning Games. In: Herskovic, V., Hoppe, H.U., Jansen, M., Ziegler, J. (eds.) CRIWG 2012. LNCS, vol. 7493, pp. 208–222. Springer, Heidelberg (2012)
6. Ammari, A., Lau, L., Dimitrova, V.: Deriving Group Profiles from Social Media to Facilitate the Design of Simulated Environments for Learning. In: LAK (2012)
7. Kazai, G., Eickhoff, C., Brusilovsky, P.: Report on BooksOnline'11: 4th workshop on online books, complementary social media, and crowdsourcing. In: SIGIR, vol. 46, pp. 43–50 (2012)
8. Vatrapu, R., Teplovs, C., Fujita, N., Bull, S.: Towards visual analytics for teachers' dynamic diagnostic pedagogical decision-making. In: Proceedings of the 1st International Conference on LAK, pp. 93–98. ACM (2011)
9. Brusilovsky, P., Hsiao, I.-H., Folajimi, Y.: QuizMap: Open Social Student Modeling and Adaptive Navigation Support with TreeMaps. In: Delgado Kloos, C., Gillet, D., Crespo García, R.M., Wild, F., Wolpers, M. (eds.) EC-TEL 2011. LNCS, vol. 6964, pp. 71–82. Springer, Heidelberg (2011)
10. Lynch, C., Ashley, K.D., Pinkwart, N., Aleven, V.: Concepts, Structures, and Goals: Redefining Ill-Definedness. Int. J. Artif. Intell. Ed. 19, 253–266 (2009)
11. Mazza, R., Dimitrova, V.: CourseVis: A graphical student monitoring tool for supporting instructors in web-based distance courses. IJHCS 65, 125–139 (2007)
12. Thomas, P., Labat, J.-M., Muratet, M., Yessad, A.: How to Evaluate Competencies in Game-Based Learning Systems Automatically? In: Cerri, S.A., Clancey, W.J., Papadourakis, G., Panourgia, K. (eds.) ITS 2012. LNCS, vol. 7315, pp. 168–173. Springer, Heidelberg (2012)
13. Johnson, W.L., Ashish, N., Bodnar, S., Sagae, A.: Expecting the Unexpected: Warehousing and Analyzing Data from ITS Field Use. In: Aleven, V., Kay, J., Mostow, J. (eds.) ITS 2010, Part II. LNCS, vol. 6095, pp. 352–354. Springer, Heidelberg (2010)
14. Hays, M., Lane, H.C., Auerbach, D., Core, M.G., Gomboc, D., Rosenberg, M.: Feedback Specificity and the Learning of Intercultural Communication Skills. In: Proceedings of the 2009 Conference on Artificial Intelligence in Education: Building Learning Systems that Care: From Knowledge Representation to Affective Modelling, pp. 391–398 (2009)
15. Wang, N., Pynadath, D.V., Marsella, S.C.: Toward Automatic Verification of Multiagent Systems for Training Simulations. In: Cerri, S.A., Clancey, W.J., Papadourakis, G., Panourgia, K. (eds.) ITS 2012. LNCS, vol. 7315, pp. 151–161. Springer, Heidelberg (2012)
16. Muir, M., Conati, C.: An Analysis of Attention to Student – Adaptive Hints in an Educational Game. In: Cerri, S.A., Clancey, W.J., Papadourakis, G., Panourgia, K. (eds.) ITS 2012. LNCS, vol. 7315, pp. 112–122. Springer, Heidelberg (2012)
17. Thakker, D., Dimitrova, V., Lau, L., Denaux, R., Karanasios, S., Yang-Turner, F.: A priori ontology modularisation in ill-defined domains. In: Proceedings of the 7th ICSS, pp. 167–170. ACM, Graz (2011)
18. Vinciarelli, A., Pantic, M., Bourlard, H.: Social signal processing: Survey of an emerging domain. Image Vision Comput. 27, 1743–1759 (2009)

Tangible Collaborative Learning with a Mixed-Reality Game: EarthShake

Nesra Yannier, Kenneth R. Koedinger, and Scott E. Hudson

Human Computer Interaction Institute, Carnegie Mellon University,
5000 Forbes Avenue, Pittsburgh, PA 15213, USA
{nyannier,kkoedinger,scott.hudson}@cs.cmu.edu

Abstract. We explore the potential of bringing together the advantages of computer games and the physical world to increase engagement, collaboration and learning. We introduce EarthShake: A tangible interface and mixed-reality game consisting of an interactive multimodal earthquake table, block towers and a computer game synchronized with the physical world via depth camera sensing. EarthShake helps kids discover physics principles while experimenting with real blocks in a physical environment supported with audio and visual feedback. Students interactively make predictions, see results, grapple with disconfirming evidence and formulate explanations in forms of general principles. We report on a preliminary user study with 12 children, ages 4-8, indicating that EarthShake produces large and significant learning gains, improvement in explanation of physics concepts, and clear signs of productive collaboration and high engagement.

Keywords: Tangible interfaces, Learning technologies, Educational Games.

1 Introduction

Children are often attracted to computer games. Modern computer games show potential for engaging and entertaining users while also promoting learning [6], provided by their feedback mechanisms [10]. Computer games have also been demonstrated to have motivational benefits with their compelling narratives [7] as well as providing long term learning gains [5]. However, the computer also has a tendency to pull people away from their physical environment and make them physically and socially isolated. Roe and Mujis have found some justification to associate frequent gamers with social isolation and less positive behavior towards society [11]. Researchers at USC have shown that family time has decreased by more than thirty percent due to computer usage at home [1].

The physical environment can help children play, discover, experiment and learn together in an engaging way. Montessori has observed that young children are highly attracted to sensory development apparatuses and that they used physical materials spontaneously, independently, and repeatedly with deep concentration [9]. Theories of embodied cognition and situated learning have also shown that mind and body are deeply integrated in the process of producing learning and reasoning [4]. Our work aims to bring together the advantages of computer games – consisting of engaging

K. Yacef et al. (Eds.): AIED 2013, LNAI 7926, pp. 131–140, 2013.

Fig. 1. A classroom activity with EarthShake. The pictures indicate the engagement we observed including frequent shouts of excitement (left picture) or disappointment (right picture) when the predicted tower fell or not, respectively.

characters, fantasy settings, compelling scenarios, guided experimentation, and immediate feedback – with the advantages of the physical environment – tangible learning, face to face social interaction, collaboration, physical experimentation and discovery – for better learning and increased human-human social interaction.

In theory, tangible interfaces help learning because they encourage sensory engagement, active manipulation and physical activity. Despite this promise there has been little empirical evidence demonstrating these environments' benefits [13]. Fitzmaurice *et al.* suggest that tangible interfaces allow for more parallel input specification by the user, thereby improving the expressiveness or the communication capacity of the computer. Tangible interfaces also take advantage of well-developed, everyday skills for physical object manipulations and spatial reasoning, externalize traditionally internal computer representations and afford multi-person collaborative use [3]. Schneider *et al.* have shown that tangible interfaces bringing together physical and virtual objects helped people perform the task better and achieve a higher learning gain than screen-based multi-touch surface [12]. Yannier *et al.* have also shown that using a haptic augmented virtual environment helped people learn the cause and effect relationships in climate data better than using a solely virtual environment [14].

With the introduction of the inexpensive depth cameras such as Microsoft Kinect, there is opportunity for new paradigms for interaction with physical objects, since having computation within the objects themselves can be expensive and non-scalable. Our work utilizes the Kinect camera to combine tangible and virtual worlds for better learning and collaboration in an affordable and practical way.

We introduce EarthShake: a mixed reality game consisting of a multimodal interactive earthquake table, physical towers made of blocks integrated with an educational computer game via Kinect and our specialized computer vision algorithm. The game asks the users to make a prediction about which of the block towers on the earthquake table they think will fall first when the table shakes. When the user shakes the earthquake table, it detects which of the towers in the physical setup falls first and gives visual and audio feedback accordingly. It targets children in Kindergarten through third grade [ages 4-8] and is aimed to teach physics principles of stability and balance, which are listed in the NRC Framework &Asset Science Curriculum for this age group [8].

1.1 Physical Setup and Vision Algorithm to Detect Blocks

The setup consists of an earthquake table, physical towers (made of blocks that stick together) placed on top of the table, Kinect color and depth cameras facing the towers, a projector and a screen where the computer game is displayed, as shown in Figure 2. When the earthquake table shakes, the physical towers start shaking. When the towers fall, our specialized computer vision algorithm, using input from the Kinect color and depth cameras, detects the fall. The computer game, which is in sync with what is happening in the physical world gets the information provided by the camera and gives visual and audio feedback accordingly, which is then projected onto the screen.

Our computer vision algorithm uses color segmentation and depth information to distinguish between two towers and detect when a tower falls. Depth information is used to reliably segregate the blocks from the background (which can contain similar colors). This depth segmentation creates a mask that is used to select a subset of the color image that corresponds with the towers. Blob tracking is then used to track each segment of the colored blocks. Each tower consists of four colors. The start and end of the horizontal and vertical span of each color segment in the tower is calculated by scanning the pixels, which determines the size and location of the color blobs. These color blobs are then used to provide a depiction of the live state of the blocks on the screen (see Figure 3). Finally, falls are detected when all blobs for a tower are below a minimum height above the table.

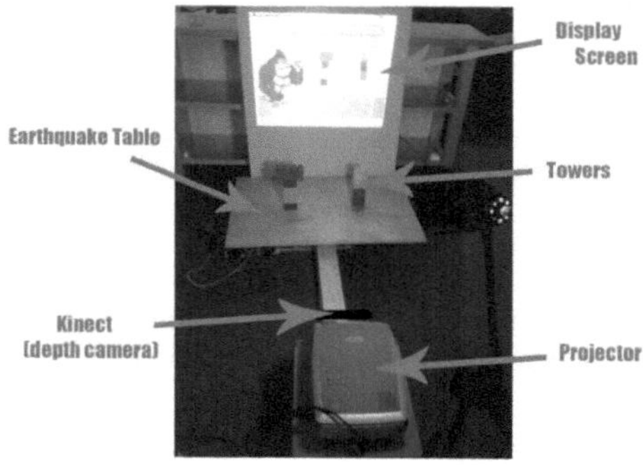

Fig. 2. EarthShake physical setup

1.2 Scenario

In the scenario of the game (Figure 3), there is a gorilla, which asks the students which of the towers will fall first or if they will fall at the same time when he shakes the table. The users can see the physical towers on the real earthquake table and the virtual representation of the towers on the screen behind the table at the same time. They make a prediction and click on the tower that they think will fall first. Then the gorilla asks the users to discuss with their partner why they chose this tower and explain why they think this tower will fall first. The users make a hypothesis and discuss why they think this tower will fall first. When they are done discussing, they click the shake button. When they click shake, the physical earthquake table starts shaking and the virtual table on the screen starts having a shaking animation simultaneously with the gorilla moving it back and forth. When one of the towers falls, the vision algorithm determines this and the gorilla gives feedback to the users. If their choice was right and the tower they had predicted falls first, he says: "Good job! Your hypothesis was right. Why do you think this tower fell first?" If they were wrong, he says: "Oh oh you were wrong! Why do you think this tower fell first?" So, the users are asked to explain the reason again. This time there are six multiple-choice answers that the users can choose from to explain why they think this tower fell first. They can choose one of the following: “Because it is smaller”, “Because it is taller”, “Because it has more weight on top than bottom”, “Because it has a wider base”, “Because it is not symmetrical”, “Because it has a thinner base”. The multiple-choice answers have spoken output on mouse-overs. The scenario is repeated for ten contrasting cases with different towers (see Figure 4) targeting height, wide base, symmetry and center of mass principles.

Fig. 3. The game scenario involves soliciting a prediction (left), asking for a hypothesis and starting an experiment (middle), and seeing the result and explaining it (right)

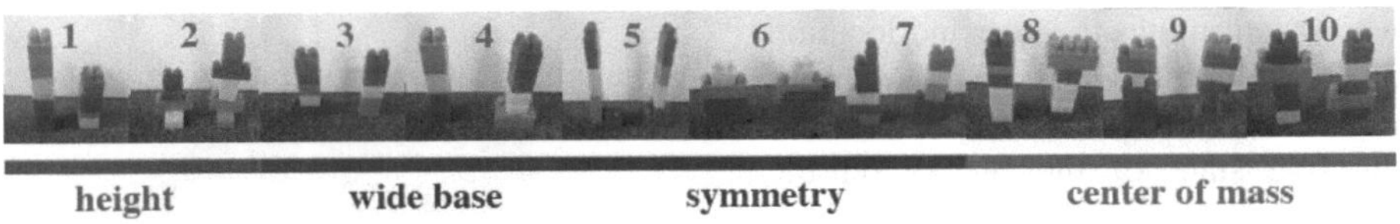

Fig. 4. Contrasting cases used in EarthShake are designed to maintain irrelevant surface features and change just one relevant feature to emphasize Physics principles of stability

1.3 Preliminary Study Informing Design Choices

Toward designing EarthShake, we first conducted a preliminary study in a local Elementary School with a diverse population of students in grades K-3. We used the earthquake table solely (with no projected game) and asked students to predict which of the towers would fall first. We observed that children have a harder time with the center of mass and symmetry principles and that those who had a basic understanding of the center of mass principle would explain it as: “having more weight on top than bottom”. Children tended to have an easier time predicting which of the towers would fall first than explaining the reasons behind it. These observations informed our design choices for EarthShake. We created the contrasting case items accordingly, having more items that target center of mass and symmetry. We also designed an explanation menu consisting of six items of explanations in children’s terms (including “having more weight on top than bottom”).

2 User Study

We conducted a user study to evaluate the effects of EarthShake on usability, collaboration, engagement and learning. Twelve children, five female and seven male, ranging from kindergarten to 3rd grade participated. Six of them interacted with

EarthShake in a classroom setting as a group, while the other six were divided into three pairs, where each pair interacted with EarthShake in our lab. All pairs were siblings, where one of them was two or three years older than the other. The classroom study was conducted in a local elementary school with a diverse student population in a class with mixed-age students.

2.1 Methodology

We first gave children a paper pretest on stability and balance principles. The paper pre- and post-tests were created taking into account the science goals listed in the NRC Framework & Asset Science Curriculum [8]. There were prediction and explanation items in the test. In the prediction items, there was a picture of a table with two towers standing on it, and the student was asked to predict what would happen when the table shook by circling one of the multiple-choice answers. In the explanation items students were asked to explain the reason behind their answers to the prediction items.

We then gave each pair a bag of seventeen blocks that stick together and told them to build the most stable tower they could using all the blocks, but with the constraint of using a particular block on the bottom of the tower as the base. We then tested their tower on the earthquake table to see if it would fall down when the table shakes. The purpose of this activity was to assess the types of towers children built before playing with EarthShake.

After the paper and physical pretests, children played with EarthShake for approximately thirty minutes, which consisted of ten contrasting cases (Figure 4), targeting the wide base, height, center of mass and symmetry principles. For each case, they were asked to predict which tower would fall first and discuss with their partner why they thought so. Then they observed what happened in real life by shaking the table and saw if their prediction was right or wrong. Finally, they were asked to explain the reason behind what they observed.

After the EarthShake activity, they were given a bag of seventeen blocks and asked to build a tower again with the same constraints as before. Then their tower was again tested on the earthquake table side by side with the previous tower they had built to see which one stood up longer on the shaking table. Finally, they were given a paper posttest consisting of questions matched to those in the pretest.

All the activities were video recorded. At the end of the activities, the participants were given a survey, asking how they liked the activity (they could circle one of the three choices: "I liked it", "It was so-so" and "I didn't like it"). They were also interviewed about their experiences and asked to provide any suggestions they might have.

3 Results

On the multiple-choice questions in the paper tests, an average of 62% were answered correctly in the pretest, and 78% in the posttest (see Figure 5a). A paired samples t-test indicates this gain is statistically significant ($t(11)=4.2$, $p<0.002$) and the effect size, $d=0.78$, indicates it is substantial. For the explanation items, 17% were answered correctly in the pretest, and 71% in the posttest. Here too, the paired t-test is significant ($t(11)=9$, $p<0.001$) and the effect size, $d=2.98$, is large. We also see a significant learning gain from the pre and post towers kids made (Figure 5b). For all of the six pairs that built a tower together, the post tower was more stable (with a lower center of mass for all and more symmetrical for one of them) and stood up longer when placed on the earthquake table.

In the survey, 10 out of 12 kids circled "I liked it" whereas 2 kids circled between "I liked it" and "It was so-so". Kids commented that they liked to see the table shake, "knocking the blocks" and "watching the real block show". They also pointed out that they liked the gorilla and that they enjoyed building their own towers. Many of the kids asked if they could play the game again while some others asked if they could have the earthquake table as a birthday present!

We also analyzed our video data to better understand the dynamics involved in the learning gains from EarthShake and look for evidence for or against engagement, collaboration, and learning.

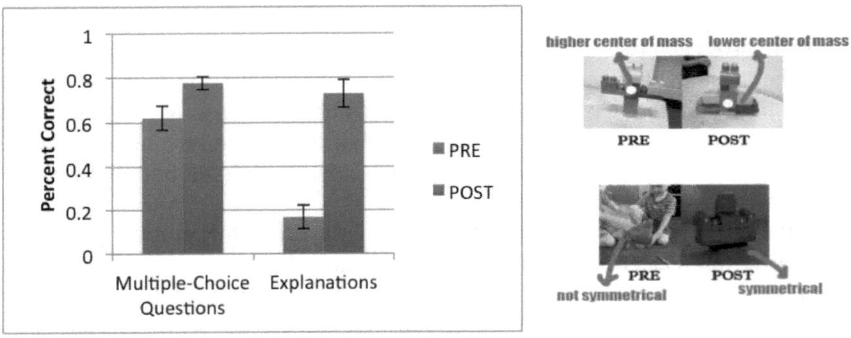

Fig. 5. (a) Results of the paper pre/post tests. (b) Two examples of pre/post towers.

3.1 Engagement

We observed that kids were highly engaged with the physical earthquake table and the EarthShake game. The motion of the earthquake table knocking the towers down seemed to have an especially strong positive effect on engagement. During the game after kids made a prediction, they watched attentively to see what would happen when the gorilla shook the table. If their prediction was right they often said: "Yesss!" jumping up with their hands in the air. (Figure 6c) When they were wrong, they showed their disappointment, for example, by putting their hands on their head.

We also observed that kids were very engaged when they were asked to build their own towers. They concentrated while building their tower, discussing thoroughly how to build it so that it would withstand the earthquake. In the classroom setting, when all the towers were put on the table and shaken to see whose towers would stay up, the teams whose towers did not fall down started jumping up and down, cheering and yelling, while the groups whose towers fell down asked if they can try it again. The motion of the earthquake table and the noise, as well as the scenario with the gorilla in the game seemed to play an effective role in the engagement.

3.2 Collaboration and Joint Explanation Development

We saw a lot of collaboration going on between the children during the game and the building activity. They seemed to be learning by building on each other's ideas and explaining to each other. In one case (9th case in Figure 4), "Bob" (the older sibling) predicted the second tower would fall first saying: "I'm betting that one because it has more weight on top" whereas "Steve" (the younger sibling) thought they would fall at the same time saying: "Wait, they're the same on top". Then Bob said "No, look…" pointing at the top of the second tower where there were more blocks and tried to explain to his brother that the second one had more weight on top than the first one. When they got the answer right, they said "Yeah we were right!"

While building their towers, the partners seemed to be collaborating well. In one case, the younger kid first tried to put more blocks on one side of the tower. His partner warned him saying: "No, don't put all the blocks on one side, that would make it unbalanced. We want it to be the same on each side". Then the younger kid said "Maybe we can try this" and put the blocks on each side of the tower evenly. The older kid said: "Good idea!" After a while, the older kid tried to put two blocks on the same side of the tower. This time the younger kid warned his brother saying: "No, but it's unbalanced, see…" showing the other side of the tower. Their final tower was symmetrical and very stable.

The mom of one pair commented that her sons do not usually collaborate so well. "There was pretty good interaction between them, it was very cooperative. They do a lot of Legos at home. The tendency is that Bob is three years older so he is like I'm just doing it, he doesn't usually let Steve do his thing. Given that tendency I think they did pretty well at cooperation. Bob actually listened to Steve and said 'Oh OK that's is a good idea!'"

The tangibility of the earthquake table seemed to be facilitating collaboration during the pair and classroom activities as two or more kids (six in the classroom) could sit around a table seeing the physical setup simultaneously and could interact with the physical blocks together, where as with a screen-only game this would be impossible or, at least, quite difficult.

For the building activity the classroom group was divided into 3 pairs where each pair made their own tower. When everyone had built their towers, all the towers were placed on the earthquake table together to see whose tower would stay up longest when the table shakes. This activity created a lot of bonding and cooperation within the pairs. One of the pairs expressed their team spirit explicitly. After placing their tower on the table, one said: "Let's hope that will stay up". The other added: "It's gotta work, it's gotta work, keep our fingers crossed!" as they sat down facing their tower with their fingers crossed.

Fig. 6. a) Older sister explaining why the tower fell first. b) Seeing the multiple-choice explanations on the screen projected behind the towers prompts them to understand the reason behind what happens. c) Excitement of kids as they watch whose tower stays up longest.

3.3 Physicality and Believability

The physicality of EarthShake and the building activity also seemed to play an important role to facilitate the collaboration and learning. While building their own towers, kids were able to place blocks simultaneously, which facilitated collaboration (unlike on a screen where they wouldn't be able to place blocks at the same time via one mouse). They also seemed to be experimenting with physical manipulation while building their own towers feeling the weight and stability with their hands. Furthermore, we saw indications that children may believe what was happening more in real life than on a screen-based game. One of the kids commented: "You can actually see what happens rather than the computer telling you what happened. I liked the fact that it was on the computer but it was actually happening in real life."

3.4 Aha Moments and Signs of Learning

During the game, we observed some signs of learning and aha-moments. When a result differed from their prediction students showed their surprise. We observed that seeing the menu with the multiple choice explanations, which appeared on the screen behind the falling towers, seemed to prompt thinking, leading to aha moments. For example, in one of the pairs, for the 8th contrasting case (Figure 4), the kids predicted that both of the towers would fall at the same time, because they had the same base. When the gorilla shook the table, they saw that the T-shaped tower fell first. As soon as the menu with the explanation choices appeared, one of the kids shouted: "Cause the top has more weight!" while the other kid followed saying: "Oooohhh". For another question they had a similar reaction when they saw the menu: "Now I get it! Now I get why that one fell first. Because it is not symmetrical!"

We also observed signs of learning while kids were building their own towers after playing with EarthShake, brainstorming about what they had learned from the game. One of the pairs had this conversation: "More weight on bottom! Put more weight on bottom!" "Yes, let's put all the weight blocks on the bottom and all the not-weight blocks on top. This way it has more weight on the bottom than the top!"

3.5 Natural Interaction

Kids appeared to have a very natural interaction with EarthShake. Most of them did not even realize that there was a camera in the set up; they assumed that the gorilla could in effect see the real blocks. This natural interaction is an important achievement: Good technology should be there transparent to users. It reflects well on the reliability and efficiency of the vision algorithm we developed, which detected the identity of the towers and which tower fell.

4 Discussion

Bringing together the physical and virtual worlds, EarthShake suggests a new kind of collaborative tangible learning. While playing with EarthShake, children learn to think critically by making predictions, observing direct physical evidence, formulating hypotheses by explaining their reasoning, and collaborating with others.

The quantitative learning gains measured by the pre and post paper tests, the changes observed in the towers built before and after playing with the game, and the signs of learning captured qualitatively during the studies all suggest that the tangible system facilitates learning while also giving way to engagement and collaboration.

We can compare certain learning outcomes of EarthShake to outcomes from a study of RumbleBlocks: a screen-based computer game designed by our collaborators. The game is designed to give kids of the same age group practice on the same physics principles as EarthShake. Students engage in a similar task where the goal is to build towers of blocks that will survive an earthquake simulation [2]. Like Earthshake, part of the RumbleBlocks game involves contrasting cases of two towers where the player is asked to predict which of the towers will stay up after the earthquake. Unlike EarthShake this game is an on-screen only, single-player game, and does not involve explanation of the answers as EarthShake does.

RumbleBlocks was tested as a formative evaluation with 174 kids in K-3 grade at the same school where EarthShake was tested. Our collaborators provided us with the results from this study, where the pre and post-tests consisted of a subset of the questions used in the pre and post-tests of the EarthShake study (the same multiple-choice items targeting a single principle). The pre-to-post learning gains from RumbleBlocks were modest (from 62% to 66% correct) but statistically reliable ($t(173)=2.13$, $p=.04$, $d=0.2$), as indicated by a paired t-test. Although we should be cautious about interpreting cross-study comparisons, the contrast with the learning gains from EarthShake is striking. Taking into account only the twelve common questions used in the pre/posttests of both games, the pre-to-post learning gains from EarthShake are higher (from 69% to 82%, $t(11)=2.6$, $p=0.026$, $d=0.68$). EarthShake students had a higher average pre-test score than RumbleBlocks students and one might think that perhaps they learned more because they were better prepared. However, in fact, a better-matched group of lower performing EarthShake students (the nine students under 90% on the pre-test), gained as much or more, 61% to 80% ($t(8)=3.7$, $p<0.01$, $d=1.40$) as the group as a whole.

5 Conclusion and Future Work

We presented EarthShake, a mixed-reality educational game to teach kids physics principles. We have seen the boosted learning gains created by the combination of tangibility, collaboration, explanations and engagement in EarthShake compared with the screen-based computer game, Rumble Blocks, targeting the same content goals. Our future goal is to better isolate the effect of tangibility and collaboration in an experiment with a tightly matched screen-based game used as a control condition. A technical goal is to generalize this system and create a platform with intelligent sensing for developing tangible educational games in other content areas as well. Our preliminary evidence indicates that combining physical experimentation and engagement created by tangible environments, with the compelling scenario and interactive feedback of computer games shows promise for a substantial impact on young children's learning of and engagement in science.

Acknowledgements. We would like to thank Cathy Chase, Vincent Aleven, Eakta Jain, Erik Harpstead, Kelly Rivers and the ENGAGE team for their kind help with this work. We would also like to thank the participating teachers and students. This research is supported by contract ONR N00014-12-C-0284 (awarded by DARPA), "Learning to Solve Problems, Solving Problems to Learn." Any opinions expressed in this paper represent those of the authors, not ONR or DARPA.

References

1. Center for the Digital Future. The 2009 digital future report: Surveying the digital future-year eight. USC Annenberg School Center for the Digital Future, Los Angeles (2009)
2. Christel, M.G., Stevens, S.M., et al.: RumbleBlocks: Teaching Science Concepts to Young Children through a Unity Game. In: CGames, 162–166 (2012)
3. Fitzmaurice, G.W., Ishii, H., Buxton, W.: Bricks: laying the foundations for graspable user interfaces. In: Proceedings of the SIGCHI Conference on Human Factors in Computing Systems (CHI 1995), pp. 442–449. ACM Press (1995)
4. Henning, P.: Everyday Cognition and Situated Learning. In: Jonassen, D. (ed.) Handbook of Research on Educational Communications and Technology, 2nd edn. Simon & Schuster, New York (1998)
5. Jackson, G.T., Dempsey, K.B., McNamara, D.S.: Short and Long Term Benefits of enjoyment and Learning within a Serious Game. In: Biswas, G., Bull, S., Kay, J., Mitrovic, A. (eds.) AIED 2011. LNCS, vol. 6738, pp. 139–146. Springer, Heidelberg (2011)
6. Johnson, W.L., Vilhjalmsson, H., Marsella, S.: Serious Games for Language Learning: How Much Game, How Much AI? In: AIED 2005 Proceedings of the 2005 Conference on Artificial Intelligence in Education, pp. 306–313 (2005)
7. McQuiggan, S.W., Rowe, J.P., Lee, S., Lester, J.C.: Story-based learning: The impact of narrative on learning experiences and outcomes. In: Woolf, B.P., Aïmeur, E., Nkambou, R., Lajoie, S. (eds.) ITS 2008. LNCS, vol. 5091, pp. 530–539. Springer, Heidelberg (2008)
8. Quinn, H., et al.: A Framework for K-12 Science Education: Practices, Crosscutting Concepts, and Core Ideas. The National Academies Press (2012)
9. O'Malley, C., Stanton-Fraser, D.: Literature review in learning with tangible technologies. Nesta FutureLab Series, report 12 (2004)
10. Prensky, M.: Digital game-based learning. McGraw-Hill, New York (2001)
11. Roe, K., Mujis, D.: Children and computer games – a profile of the heavy user. European Journal of Communication 13(2), 181–200 (1998)
12. Schneider, B., Jermann, P., Zufferey, G., Dillenbourg, P.: Benefits of a Tangible Interface for Collaborative Learning and Interaction. IEEE Transactions on Learning Technologies 4, 222–232 (2011)
13. Walker, E., Burleson, W.: Using Need Validation to Design an Intelligent Tangible Learning Environment. In: Proceeding CHI 2012 Extended Abstracts on Human Factors in Computing Systems, pp. 2123–2128 (2012)
14. Yannier, N., Basdogan, C., Tasiran, S., Sen, O.L.: Using Haptics to Convey Cause and Effect Relations in Climate Visualization. IEEE Transactions on Haptics 1(2), 130–141 (2009)

From a Customizable ITS to an Adaptive ITS

Nathalie Guin and Marie Lefevre

Université de Lyon, CNRS
Université Lyon 1, LIRIS, UMR5205, F-69622, France
{Nathalie.Guin,Marie.Lefevre}@liris.univ-lyon1.fr

Abstract. The personalization of learning remains a major challenge for research in Intelligent Tutoring Systems (ITS). We report in this article how we used the Adapte tool to make AMBRE-add adaptive. AMBRE-add is an ITS designed to teach a problem solving method. This ITS includes a module that analyzes the learner's activity traces in order to compute a learner profile. Furthermore a problem generator enables us to specify activities proposed to the student. In order to design an automated process of personalizing activities according to the learner profile, we used the Adapte system. This is a generic system enabling the definition of a personalization strategy and its application to an external ITS. In this article we present how this tool provides real assistance to an ITS designer wishing to make his/her system adaptive.

Keywords: personalization, adaptation, adaptive ITS, teaching strategy, support to the ITS designer.

1 Introduction

One of the main advantages of using an Intelligent Tutoring System (ITS) compared to a situation of traditional teaching is the ability to individualize learning more easily, an ITS having the ability to adapt itself to the pace and skills of each student. We are therefore interested in the issue of the personalization of learning, and particularly to how to assist a designer who wants to turn a Technology Enhanced Learning system (TEL system) into an adaptive one. For this purpose, we conducted a case study on the use of the Adapte tool [1] by the designer of the AMBRE-add ITS [2] who intended to turn this learning system into an adaptive one.

We chose the AMBRE-add ITS, intended to teach a method of problem solving, because it is a customizable ITS, meaning that a module dedicated to the teacher and including a problem generator [3] allows customization of the ITS and the building of sequences of problems that meet the teacher's need. This ITS also has a module that analyzes traces of learners' interactions in order to compute a profile of each student. So we wanted to use these two modules to automatically adapt the sequences of problems proposed in AMBRE-add to the profile of each student.

As it is essential for teachers to be able to adapt the tool that their students will use, we wanted the teacher who uses AMBRE-add in the classroom to be able to act on how the ITS automatically adapts itself to the profile of the student. This is why we

K. Yacef et al. (Eds.): AIED 2013, LNAI 7926, pp. 141–150, 2013.

chose the Adapte tool, which allows externalized customization of an ITS and enables the teacher to define a strategy for personalization.

In Figure 1 we present the way we envision the automated adaptation to the learner of AMBRE-add educational activities: from traces of the learner's interactions with AMBRE-add, the existing module of trace analysis computes (and updates) a learner profile. Using the personalization strategy previously defined by the designer of the adaptation (and that the teacher can afterwards modify), the Adapte tool provides the AMBRE problems generator with constraints for the construction of a working session with AMBRE-add adapted to the learner profile. By analyzing the traces of the learner's interactions during this new working session with AMBRE-add, the system updates his/her profile and builds the next session, and so on.

This article is structured as follows: in Section 2 we describe the AMBRE-add ITS, the problem generator of the teacher module which is associated with, and the module that analyzes traces to compute students' profiles. In Section 3, we present the Adapte tool and the different types of knowledge that the user must provide in order to personalize an ITS. Section 4 describes the case study carried out on the use of Adapte to render AMBRE-add adaptive: the knowledge expressed by the user, the time required for each step, and the results obtained. We discuss lessons learned from this case study in Section 5, comparing this approach to the state of the art, before presenting a conclusion and opening research perspectives.

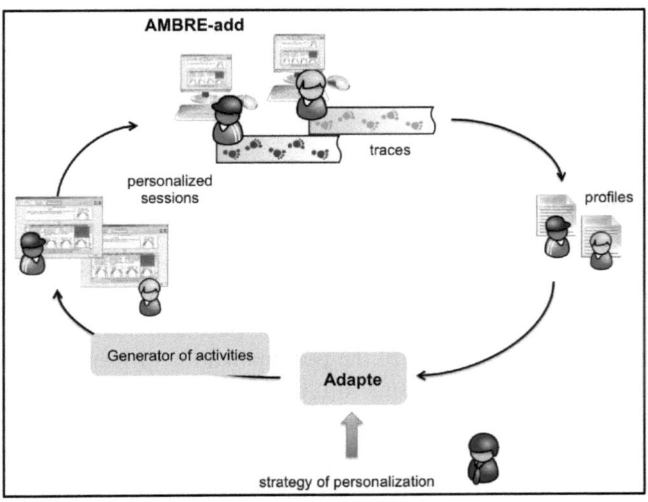

Fig. 1. Adaptation of AMBRE-add ITS to profiles of learners, using the Adapte tool

2 AMBRE-add: A Customizable ITS

The AMBRE-add ITS [2] was designed to teach a problem solving method based on classes of problems and the solving techniques associated with those classes in the domain of arithmetic. Arithmetic problems for seven-year-old to nine-year-old children describe a concrete situation such as a game of marbles: "Brad went to school with marbles. He gave thirteen of his marbles to Luke during the day. In the evening, he had fifty-six left. How many marbles did he have when he went to school?".

In order to help learners to acquire classes of problems and the techniques associated with those classes, they are first presented with a few typical solved problems. Then they are assisted in solving new problems. The environment directs the learner toward steps inspired by the Case-Based Reasoning cycle, as follows: (1) the learner reformulates the problem using a schema, in order to identify structure features of the problem; (2) then, he/she chooses a typical problem similar to the problem to solve among the solved problems he/she has been presented with; (3) next, he/she adapts the typical problem solution to the problem to be solved; (4) finally, he/she stores the new problem with the typical one, which represents a class of problems.

Using this analogical reasoning helps students to build more abstract knowledge corresponding to classes of problems [4].

2.1 A Problem Generator for AMBRE-add

In order to allow teachers to adapt AMBRE-add to their needs and their pedagogical strategies, we developed AMBRE-teacher [3]. This module enables a teacher to configure the software intended for his/her students and to create the sequence of problems he/she wants them to solve. This makes it possible to personalize the sequence designed for each student. This personalization can address the type of problems to solve, the number and the order of these problems, and the functionality of the software used by the student during the sequence.

To enable the teacher to configure the nature of the problems proposed to the student, AMBRE-teacher includes a module for generating problems: GenAMBRE. From the teacher's standpoint, generating a problem consists in fixing some characteristics for the exercise to generate, that is to say, describing a set of constraints that specify the problem. As the problems are created by the system GenAMBRE from these constraints, the result of the generation is not only a wording in natural language, but also a model of the problem to be understood by the solver used by the software for the student. The problem generation can be more or less automated depending on the teacher's choice: he/she may specify all the characteristics of the problem to obtain a precise wording, only some, or otherwise none. The fewer constraints, the more varied the generated problems will be.

Constraints that the teacher may define fall into four categories: structural features, surface features, values and complication. The structure of a problem to be generated corresponds to its class, defined by several attributes that can be set or not. Surface features are elements like objects and characters of the wording. The teacher can also choose the values of the data that will be used in the problems or define an interval for each required value and for the difference between the values, and he can also allow the carry over or not. Complication concerns all options proposed to complicate the wording of the problem to adapt it to the students' level. Designing this part required close collaboration with teachers to identify their needs. The environment proposes language complications (complexity of the vocabulary and of turn of phrase) and complications of the wording itself (writing numbers in full, modification of the sentences order, addition of distractor sentences, addition of non pertinent data). Not all constraints are mandatory for the exercise creation. Constraints not specified by the teacher will be randomly defined by the system.

2.2 Analyzing Traces to Build Profiles

As we are seeking an automated process for customizing AMBRE-add, it is necessary to have available profiles of students using the ITS. We have designed a module that computes such profiles by analyzing the traces of the students' interaction.

The activity of students using AMBRE-add is fully tracked: the traces contain all the learner's actions at each step in solving a problem. All the answers, requests for assistance or diagnostic, uses of specific calculation tools, and all of the ITS feedbacks (hints and diagnostics) can be found in the traces, all of these observed elements being time-stamped.

From all of the data in these traces, the software computes some indicators. The profile consists of two parts: first personal data on the student that may be indicated by the teacher, and secondly skills and behavior determined by the software.

Regarding skills, the program determines if the learner can solve an arithmetic problem, in general, but especially according to the class of the problem. The impact of certain parameters (use of large numbers, of carry over, writing numbers in words, adding unnecessary values or unnecessary sentences) on the success of the learner in solving problems is also studied. The learner's success in specific steps of the resolution, for example calculation, is also examined.

3 The Adapte Tool

Thus for AMBRE-add, a module computing learners' profiles and a way using AMBRE-teacher to customize the working sessions for each learner were available. This customization required the intervention of a teacher who had to carry out a very heavy task. For this reason, AMBRE-add could not really at this time be considered as an ITS (that is supposed to be adaptive) but more as a TEL system. We decided to design an automatic process that, based on the content of the profile of each learner, provides GenAMBRE with constraints needed to build a customized session of work. That is why we considered using Adapte [1], a system allowing to define personalization strategies and able to apply them to an external ITS. Adapte requires two types of knowledge: knowledge about how it is possible to customize the ITS, and knowledge of how you want to personalize it based on the content of the profiles.

3.1 Acquisition of Knowledge about the ITS to Be Personalized

In order to personalize any ITS (noted X), Adapte needs to have a model of this ITS. An expert familiar with the ITS X must define this model, firstly by defining a set of pedagogical knowledge on the activities of the ITS X and secondly by defining technical knowledge about the files used to configure the ITS X.

To perform this knowledge acquisition from experts, the Adapte software relies on a meta-model described in [5] which will be instantiated for each ITS. Thus the expert must define the type of activities offered in the ITS and how it is possible to select or generate activities of this ITS. He/she may also describe how to set the sequences of activities as well as the functionalities or the interface of the ITS. Regarding technical knowledge, the expert describes how to act concretely on the system: path of the system, path of the exercises generator or of the exercise base, path and content of the configuration files and rules to complete these files.

From the model thus created for the ITS X, Adapte tool dynamically generates a specific interface allowing each teacher using Adapte to adapt the content and functionalities of this ITS and to define a pedagogical strategy for personalizing the ITS.

3.2 Acquisition of Personalization Strategies

Once the expert has given Adapte knowledge about an ITS X, a teacher wishing to use this ITS with his/her students and having their profiles available can define how he/she wants to customize the learning sessions according to the profiles.

Defining a pedagogical strategy to personalize an ITS X with Adapte consists in defining adaptation rules specifying which activities to generate or to choose depending on the content of the learner profile. For this, a first step consists in defining structures of activities specifying (using constraints) the activities to select or to generate. It is in this step that the model of the ITS X allows the system to propose a specific interface for customizing this ITS. Then, in a second step, the teacher sets constraints on the learner profile. An assignment rule binds constraints on the profile to one or more structures of activities. The pedagogical strategy consists of a set of assignment rules that are ordered according to the priority given to them by the teacher.

This approach was applied to enable teachers to personalize several ITS [1] [5]. In this article where the design of an automated process of personalization is required, the ITS designer defined a personalization strategy that a teacher can still modify if he/she wishes to.

4 Using Adapte to Personalize AMBRE-add

We now describe how we used Adapte to implement an automated process of personalization of the sequences of problems within AMBRE-add. The person we call *the user* in this case study is a person who participated in the design team of AMBRE-add ITS, but who had never used the Adapte tool. However, this person had global knowledge of the concepts needed to use Adapte and therefore a good overview of the process she will have to perform and that we presented in Section 3.

4.1 Importing AMBRE-add Profiles in EPROFILEA

Adapte is a module of the EPROFILEA environment [6]. This environment allows a teacher to manage learners' profiles produced by various sources, regardless of discipline or level of education. EPROFILEA is made up of two parts: the first one is intended to obtain profiles usable within the environment; the second one allows exploiting these profiles, especially using Adapte.

Before using Adapte, the user therefore had to specify the import process of existing AMBRE-add profiles within EPROFILEA. This is achieved in two steps within

EPROFILEA: the definition of a profile model in conformity with EPROFILEA environment and then the creation of a process for converting existing profiles into profiles in accordance with this profile model.

It took the user fifty minutes to create a profile model for AMBRE-add within EPROFILEA. All elements of the original profile have not been reported, but only those that the user thought she needed to adapt the ITS. This model consists of:

- Information that may be indicated by the teacher, such as the learner's level in reading and calculation.
- Ability to solve the problems of each of the thirteen existing classes in AMBRE-add. These thirteen classes have been grouped into four categories: very easy, easy, difficult, and very difficult. We notice that this categorization does not exist in AMBRE-add profiles, and that the user introduced this notion of class difficulty in order to prepare her personalization strategy.
- Mastering the step of problem reformulation using a diagram, in general, but also according to the complication elements introduced in the wording of the problem (number in words, unnecessary sentences or unnecessary values, complex situations or complex vocabulary, etc.).
- The level of calculation (computed by the system), in general, and in difficult cases (carry over, large numbers).
- The frequency of use of calculating tools by the learner.

The user then took an hour and ten minutes to create a converter to import existing AMBRE-add profiles into EPROFILEA. To achieve this, for each element of the profile model defined during the previous step, she had to show to the system where the information was in an AMBRE-add profile. Using this mapping, the system created a converter able to import all the students' profiles.

In addition to information about the position of the value of each element of the profile, in some cases the user also provided knowledge about converting these values. For example, she defined how to translate a success rate, expressed as a percentage, in a mastery within the equivalent profile in EPROFILEA, expressed by an enumerated type: mastered, partly mastered, not mastered.

After these two steps, the user thus had an automated process for importing AMBRE-add profiles in EPROFILEA, as they are updated. Thus, the initialization process took the user two hours, but the profile import is now possible in a few seconds. It is then possible to use these profiles to personalize AMBRE-add using Adapte. As presented in Section 3, using Adapte requires two steps: defining a model of AMBRE-add and then defining a personalization strategy.

4.2 Defining a Model of the AMBRE-add ITS

In order to offer the teacher an interface to define a strategy for personalization, Adapte requires knowledge about the ITS to customize: pedagogical properties, pedagogical rules, technical properties and technical rules. This step must be performed only once for a given ITS and must be performed by an expert. In our study on AMBRE-add, it took the user two hours.

Pedagogical properties are the features of pedagogical activities proposed in the ITS, so here for AMBRE-add, the features of the problems to solve. The user thus defined the elements of the problems on which we can act with GenAMBRE generator: the class of the problem, the presence of carry over in the calculation, the values of the numbers, the difference between the numbers, the complexity of the vocabulary of the wording, of the situation described in the wording, the number of unnecessary sentences, the level of unnecessary sentences, etc. She also defined properties that do not exist in GenAMBRE but which make it possible to combine the above properties, in preparation for the definition of her personalization strategy: the difficulty of a class of problems, the difficulty of the calculation, and the level of complication of the wording. All of these properties were separated into three categories: those related to the structure of the problem (*i.e.* the class), those related to the calculation and those related to the complication of the wording.

Pedagogical rules make it possible to define relations between values of pedagogical property. Thus the user defined: the difficulty associated with each class of problems; the difficulty in calculating according to the values of three pedagogical properties that are the carry over, the number values and the difference between the numbers; and difficulty of the complication of the wording according to the values of seven pedagogical properties (complexity of vocabulary, unnecessary sentences, etc.).

For the technical properties, the user defined the path of the AMBRE-add executable, and relative path of the GenAMBRE generator, of files defining generation constraints that GenAMBRE takes as input, and of session files to customize.

Technical rules enabled the user to specify, from pedagogical properties set in Adapte, how to modify the file describing the generation constraints provided to GenAMBRE, and from the sequences thus constructed by GenAMBRE, how to assign them to each learner.

4.3 Defining the Personalization Strategy

Once the model of the ITS is defined by the expert, the system generates an interface that allows a teacher to define his/her strategy for personalization. For our study about AMBRE-add, it was the designer of an adaptive version of the ITS who used this interface, and proposed a personalization strategy. A teacher can later modify this strategy if he/she wishes.

A personalization strategy consists of a list of assignment rules of the form: IF <constraints on profile> THEN <structure(s) of activity(ies)> ELSE <structure(s) of activity(ies)>, the ELSE part being optional. A priority is associated with each rule in the case where several rules can be applied.

As a first step, the user defined a personalization strategy manually, using rules but without using Adapte. It took the user forty minutes to define a set of ten rules. Two of them relate to the learner's reading level (*e.g.* IF reading level = very low THEN never offer a complication level of the wording greater than 1). Three of them concern the learner's level in calculation (*e.g.* IF calculating in general is partially mastered or mastered THEN propose a calculation with difficulty greater than 2). The five other rules concern the difficulty of the class of problems (*e.g.*IF very easy classes = mastered and easy classes = partially mastered THEN provide very easy classes with complication = 2 and / or easy or difficult classes with complication = 1).

When the user wanted to define this personalization strategy set manually with the Adapte tool, she faced several difficulties:

- It is not possible to use an OR in the THEN part of a rule (*e.g.* easy OR difficult class). She had therefore to create two rules.
- Problems are assigned one after the other; it is therefore not possible to reason about the whole sequence (*e.g.* offer a majority of easy classes and some difficult ones). It is therefore necessary to create two rules and to use priority rules, which does not give exactly the same result.
- To express the learner's progress with regard to levels of difficulty, the user would have liked to use IF - THEN - ELSEIF rules. However, this is not possible in Adapte because rules have to be independent of each other. Therefore, the user had to write more rules with more complex conditions to take into account all the cases, using different conditions with conjunctions and negations.
- The user considered independently on one hand the part of her manual strategy related to the choice of the difficulty of the class of the problem, and on the other hand the choices related to the level of reading and the level of calculation. The rules related to potential difficulties in reading or calculation should be able to change the outcome of the rules on the difficulty of the problem (for example by changing the level of complication of the wording), which is not possible with Adapte. The solution to this limitation was to increase the number of rules by combining different conditions to take all cases into account.

Thus, the user was able to express her personalization strategy, although some limitations were encountered, which were overcome by increasing the number of rules.

To this personalization strategy proposed by the user designing the ITS, each teacher will be able to associate one or more contexts of use. Each context of use contains a list of students involved in the learning session, as well as their profiles. It also contains information about the duration of the session or the number of exercises required. As for the personalization strategy, the designer of the ITS may provide a default context of use for sessions taking place outside the school context, and therefore without a teacher.

4.4 Synthesis of the Study

By associating the Adapte tool with the AMBRE-add ITS, the user was able to define rules to make AMBRE-add adaptive. For this, three steps were required: two hours to define the process of integration of AMBRE-add profiles in the system including the Adapte tool; two hours to define the knowledge enabling Adapte to know and act on the configuration of the AMBRE-add ITS; about one hour and a half to define a personalization strategy which will be proposed to teachers.

The pair AMBRE-add/Adapte thus built is now an adaptive ITS, meaning that it is automatically adapted to each student. Furthermore, this adaptivity is adaptable by each teacher. Indeed, a teacher may either use the personalization strategy and the context of use provided by default, or change the strategy according to his/her needs, or redefine his/her own personalization strategy following the proposed model.

5 Discussion and Related Work

Allowing teachers to define strategies to adapt working sessions proposed on ITS according to their own purposes/needs is not new. Some authoring tools provide teachers creating educational software or adaptive hypermedia with the ability to customize models for teaching strategies [7-8]. These teaching strategies are then implemented when the learner uses the system created. With this solution, when the teacher wants to change strategy, he/she must generate the system again. He/she will then have as many versions of the system as teaching strategies.

Some of these authoring tools separate educational content from adaptation rules in order to make these rules reusable. Thus, the KBT-MM meta-model [9] allows to build ITS containing several pedagogical strategies for a given educational content. Similarly, the LAOS model [10] enables to define adaptation rules that are reusable for several adaptive hypermedia.

Like the Adapte tool, these approaches are based on the same principle of separation between content and teaching strategies, but the model implemented in Adapte generalizes the principles of KBT-MM or LAOS. Indeed, Adapte makes it possible to outsource the definition of teaching strategies, not in an authoring tool, but in a tool used as an interface between the user and the various educational programs to customize [5]. This outsourcing enables customizing of much existing educational software, whatever their origin (systems designed from authoring tools or directly). These systems just need to describe teaching strategy using configuration files that the user has rights to access and write.

6 Conclusion and Research Perspectives

We reported in this article how a designer was able to use the Adapte tool to make an ITS adaptive, what were the steps of the process and the necessary knowledge. To make an existing TEL system adaptive using Adapte, it is firstly necessary for the system to be adaptable, and secondly to have a regularly updated learner profile.

In this study conducted on the AMBRE-add ITS, the design process of the adaptive version of the ITS took about six hours, which represents a time saving compared with the time that would have needed the design and implementation of an ad-hoc module that would have driven the GenAMBRE generator according to the data contained in the profiles. Furthermore, the use of Adapte for this design did not require programming skills on the part of the user. Indeed, the Adapte user has to be able to write IF-THEN rules, and needs to have deep knowledge of the TEL system he/she wants to personalize, but does not need knowledge about any programming language. Being able to use a single system to make several ITS adaptive is also time-saving for a designer who would not have to get used to different tools.

This study also generated feedback on the use of Adapte. Some usability problems were identified, particularly concerning the import of profiles and the definition of the pedagogical strategy, which allows us to propose improvements to the tool.

A next step in this work would be to conduct experiments using this adaptive version of AMBRE-add, the classic version of the ILE having already been tested in about ten classes [4]. We could thus investigate whether an adaptive version arouses greater satisfaction or interest from students and teachers than a classic version, and if it brings a gain on learning. It would also be interesting to study if and how teachers adapt the ITS adaptability *i.e.* personalize the adaptation strategy proposed by the designer according to their needs.

References

1. Lefevre, M., Cordier, A., Jean-Daubias, S., Guin, N.: A Teacher-dedicated Tool Supporting Personalization of Activities. In: ED-MEDIA 2009, Honolulu, pp. 1136–1141 (2009)
2. Nogry, S., Guin, N., Jean-Daubias, S.: AMBRE-add: An ITS to Teach Solving Arithmetic Word Problems. Technology, Instruction, Cognition and Learning 6(1), 53–61 (2008)
3. Jean-Daubias, S., Guin, N.: AMBRE-teacher: a module helping teachers to generate problems. In: 2nd Workshop on Question Generation, AIED 2009, Brighton, pp. 43–47 (2009)
4. Nogry, S., Jean-Daubias, S., Duclosson, N.: ITS Evaluation in Classroom: The Case of AMBRE-AWP. In: Lester, J.C., Vicari, R.M., Paraguaçu, F. (eds.) ITS 2004. LNCS, vol. 3220, pp. 511–520. Springer, Heidelberg (2004)
5. Lefevre, M., Mille, A., Jean-Daubias, S., Guin, N.: A Meta-Model to Acquire Relevant Knowledge for Interactive Learning Environments Personalization. In: Adaptive 2009, Athènes, pp. 78–85 (2009) ISBN 978-0-7695-3862-4
6. Eyssautier-Bavay, C., Jean-Daubias, S., Pernin, J.-P.: A model of learners profiles management process. In: AIED 2009. Frontiers in Artificial Intelligence and Applications, pp. 265–272. IOS Press, Brighton (2009)
7. Murray, T.: Eon: Authoring Tools for Content, Instructional Strategy, Student Model, and Interface Design. In: Authoring Tools for Advanced Technology Learning Environments, ch. 11, vol. 200. Kluwer Academic Publisher (2003)
8. Cristea, A.: Authoring of Adaptative Hypermedia. Educational Technology & Society 8(3), 6–8 (2005)
9. Murray, T.: Principles for Pedagogy-oriented Knowledge Based Tutor Authoring Systems: Lessons Learned and a Design Meta-Model. In: Authoring Tools for Advanced Technology Learning Environments, ch. 15. Kluwer Academic Publisher (2003)
10. Cristea, A., De Mooij, L.: LAOS: Layered WWW AHS Authoring Model and their corresponding Algebraic Operators. In: WWW 2003, Alternate Track on Education (2003)

Class vs. Student in a Bayesian Network Student Model

Yutao Wang and Joseph Beck

Worcester Polytechnic Institute
{yutaowang,josephbeck}@wpi.edu

Abstract. For decades, intelligent tutoring systems researchers have been developing various methods of student modeling. Most of the models, including two of the most popular approaches: Knowledge Tracing model and Performance Factor Analysis, all have similar assumption: the information needed to model the student is the student's performance. However, there are other sources of information that are not utilized, such as the performance on other students in same class. This paper extends the Student-Skill extension of Knowledge Tracing, to take into account the class information, and learns four parameters: prior knowledge, learn, guess and slip for each class of students enrolled in the system. The paper then compares the accuracy using the four parameters for each class versus the four parameters for each student to find out which parameter set works better in predicting student performance. The result shows that modeling at coarser grain sizes can actually result in higher predictive accuracy, and data about classmates' performance is results in a higher predictive accuracy on unseen test data.

Keywords: Bayesian Networks, Knowledge Tracing, Individualization, student-skill model, class-skill model.

1 Introduction

Student modeling is crucial for Intelligent Tutoring Systems (ITS) to improve and to provide better tutoring for students. For decades, researchers in ITS have been developing various methods of modeling students. Two of the most popular approaches are Bayesian Knowledge Tracing (KT) [1], which uses a dynamic Bayesian Network to model student learning, and Performance Factor Analysis (PFA) [2], which uses a logistic regression to predict student performance. Both techniques have a similar underlying assumption that two things are needed to model the student: one component concerns the domain, such as skill information in KT and PFA models, or item information in the PFA model; the other component is the student's problem solving performance on the skill.

However, there are other sources of knowledge that are not utilized, such as the performance of other students in the same class. Instead, only *this* student's previous performances are taken into account. Imagine there is a class of 20 students, 19 of whom get the first item on a skill wrong, and you want to predict the performance of the 20th student's first item on the skill. Intuitively, predicting that this student would also respond incorrectly seems like a safe bet. However, current student models such

K. Yacef et al. (Eds.): AIED 2013, LNAI 7926, pp. 151–160, 2013.

as KT and PFA will not be affected by those 19 incorrect responses, as they were all made by other students. What would the effect on predictive accuracy be if which class a student is currently in was factored into student models? Our intuition is that class perhaps contains important information such as the student's prior knowledge about a skill. Since all students in a class share a common teacher, curriculum, and assigned homework problems, we should expect similarities in performance. Our goal is to capitalize on this dependency to improve student modeling.

In fact, the US Institute for Educational Sciences requires grant proposals' power analyses to discount the sample size if there are multiple students in the same classroom, due to their lack of independence from each other (most statistical tests require each sample to be independent). Given that we know this dependence effect exists statistically, why not make use of it? In this paper, we are focusing on utilizing the class information to improve student modeling and trying to determine under which circumstances, using other students' information could be more beneficial than using current student's individual information.

Section 2 introduces the model and dataset we are using in our experiments. Section 3 shows the experimental results. In section 4 and 5 we discuss the conclusions and future directions for our work.

2 Approach

This section briefly introduces the Student Skill model and the modification of it in order to allow class level individualization. The modified model also allows us to run experiments on various combinations of student and class information to determine whether or not the class information is better than the student information for each parameter.

2.1 Model

Knowledge Tracing is one of the most popular methods for modeling student knowledge. The original Knowledge Tracing model do not allow for individualization, and assumes that all students have the same probability of knowing a particular skill at their first opportunity, or slipping (making a careless mistake) on a skill, or learning a particular skill. This assumption is almost certainly invalid, as students are likely to differ in these aspects. Several researchers have tried to show the power of individualization [4, 5]. The model we use in this work is build upon one of the individualization model called the Student Skill model [4]. The idea of the Student Skill model is that rather than estimating a learning rate for each skill, instead view learning rate as being a function of the skill and of this individual learner. Perhaps some skills are learned more quickly or slowly than others, and perhaps some students learn more quickly or slowly than others. By combining both effects, it is possible to more accurately model the student.

The Student Skill model structure is shown in Fig.1. The goal of the Student Skill model is to add individualization into the original Knowledge Tracing model. It can learn four student parameters and four skill parameters simultaneously. The lowest two levels of this model is the same as the original Knowledge Tracing model (nodes

K1…Kn and Q1…Qn in Fig. 1). The Student Skill model adds upper levels to represent the student and skill information and their interaction. Two multinomial nodes are used to represent the identity of each student (node St in Fig.1) and each skill (node Sk in Fig.1). Instead of pointing the student identity and the skill identity nodes directly to the knowledge nodes, which will result in an exponentially increasing number of parameters, we instead added a level of nodes to represent the four student parameters (node StP, StG, StS and StL in Fig.1) and the four skill parameters (node SkP, SkG, SkS and SkL in Fig.1). Those parameter nodes are binary nodes which represents the high/low level of the corresponding parameters. For example, if the StP node is 1 for a student, means the student has high level of prior knowledge, and if the StP node is 0 for a student, means the student has low level of prior knowledge. Then the next level combines the influence of the student parameters and the skill parameters and generated four standard Knowledge Tracing parameters (node P, G, S and L in Fig.1) to be used in the lowest two levels. In this way, we generate a knowledge tracing model that is custom-fit to each learner and for each skill.

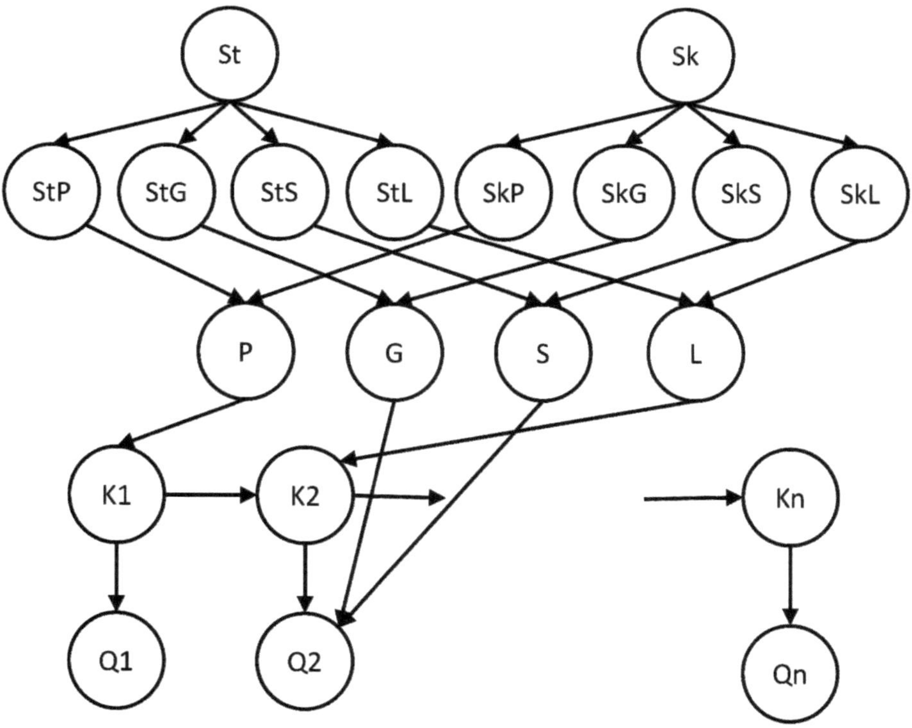

Fig. 1. The Student Skill model

One drawback of the Student Skill model is that it requires a large number of parameters. In addition to estimating four parameters per skill, it must also estimate four parameters per student. Given that many datasets have considerably more users than skills, this inflation in the number of parameters is a large concern. Therefore, we considered methods for reducing the number of parameters in our model, to enable them to better generalize to unseen data. One approach is, rather than modeling the students as individuals, to instead model which mathematics class the student is enrolled in. Students within the same class have the same teacher, textbook, homework, and may even be grouped by ability in the subject. Given that, in our datasets, there are typically about 24 students per class, modeling class-level effects has 24 times as much data to estimate parameters. In addition, if we only model class parameters, we only have to estimate 1 set of parameters for each *class* of students, rather than 1 set for each individual students. Thus, the use of class information can be seen as a coarser grain-size individualization compared to the Student Skill model. We demonstrate the Class Skill model in figure 2, and the nodes are identified as follows:

- St: A multinomial node represents each student's identity, observable.
- Sk: A multinomial node represents each skill's identity, observable.
- StP: Student Prior Knowledge, binary node, latent.
- StG: Student Guess rate, binary node, latent.
- StS: Student Slip rate, binary node, latent.
- StL: Student Learning rate, binary node, latent.
- SkP: Skill Prior Knowledge, binary node, latent.
- SkG: Skill Guess rate, binary node, latent.
- SkS: Skill Slip rate, binary node, latent.
- SkL: Skill Learning rate, binary node, latent.
- P: Prior Knowledge of a particular student and a particular skill, binary node, latent.
- G: Guess rate of a particular student and a particular skill, binary node, latent.
- S: Slip rate of a particular student and a particular skill, binary node, latent.
- L: Learning of a particular student and a particular skill, binary node, latent.
- K1~Kn: Knowledge, binary node, latent.
- Q1~Qn: Question performance, binary node, latent.

The Student Skill model can easily be changed to consider the class information rather than the student information by replacing the St node to be a class node (Cl), and the parameters StP, StG, StS and StL will be turned into class prior (ClP), class guess (ClG), class slip (ClS) and class learning rate (ClL).

Instead of simply using class information to replace the student information, which is still considering only one resource of information, this paper combines these two models together to explore whether knowing which class a student is in is a better predictor than knowing which student, for each parameter in the model. For example, perhaps slip rate is best modeled at the individual student level, while learning rate is best estimated at the class level? Therefore, we have run experiments with different ways of combine the two resources of information trying to determine which parameter is best modeled using which source of information.

As shown in Fig. 2, the model is almost the same as the Student Skill model in Fig. 1. The only difference is the addition of the class (Cl) node, which is a multinomial node, represents which class a student is in. Nodes StP, StG, StS, StL turns into StP/ClP, StG/ClG, StS/ClS, StL/ClL, which means the nodes can either be a student level parameter or a class level parameter. The dash line between node Cl and node StP/ClP is a potential relationship in the model, as well as the dash line between node St and node Stp/ClP. If we choose one of these two dash lines, the other one will be ignored as if it does not exist. For example, if we choose to use class information for prior knowledge, the dash line between St and node StP/ClP is ignored, and the node StP/ClP only contains the class prior (ClP). The same assumption is hold for all the other dash lines and parameters of class and student: StS/ClS, StG/ClG, StL/ClL.

Based on this model, by choosing different dash lines, we can test the best combination of class and student parameters and find the variability.

In our experiment, we used the Bayes Net Toolbox for Matlab developed by Murphy [6] to implement the Bayesian network student models and the Expectation Maximization (EM) algorithm to fit the model parameters to the dataset. The EM algorithm finds a set of parameters that maximize the likelihood of the data by iteratively running an expectation step to calculate expected likelihood given student performance data and a maximization step to compute the parameters that maximize that expected likelihood.

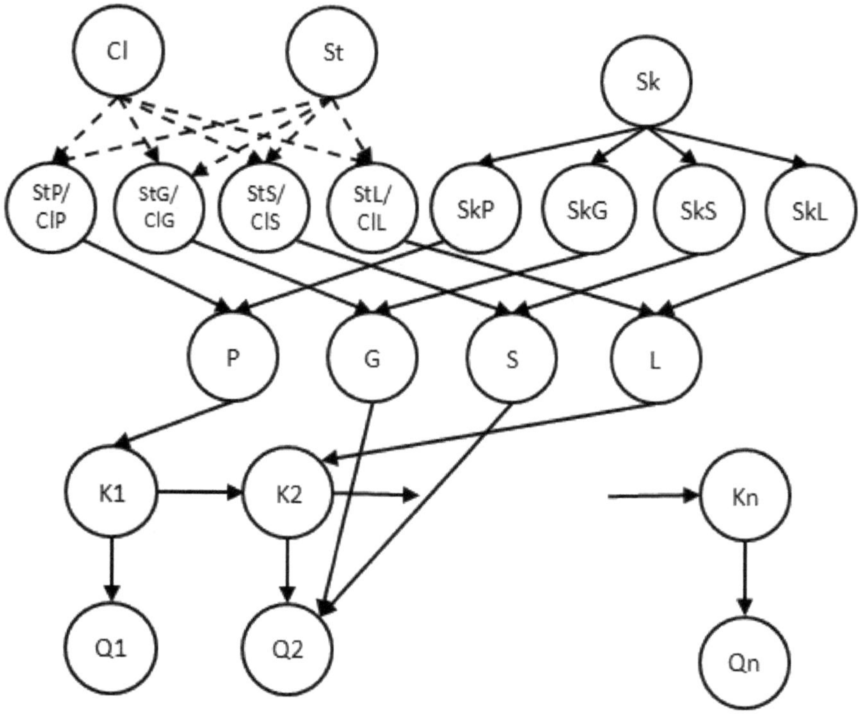

Fig. 2. Combination of Class Skill model and Student Skill model

2.2 Data and Model-Fitting

The data used in the analysis presented here came from the ASSISTments platform (www.assistments.org), a freely available web-based tutoring system for 4th through 10th grade mathematics. The performance of a question is marked as wrong if the first response is incorrect, or if the student asks for help.

We randomly sampled data of one hundred 12-14 year old 8th grade students from 4 classes and fifty skills from the school year September 2010 to September 2011. There are in total 53,450 problem solved in the dataset.

To make sure there were sufficient data in the training set to estimate parameters for students and skills, we divide the dataset into a training set and a test set using the following strategy: for each student, for every skill that she was practicing we flipped a coin and assigned this student-skill pair into either the training set or into the testing set. This process enables us to have a broad coverage of students and skills in the training set, to enable generalization to the testing set. However, we do not have data for the same student-skill pair in both the training and in the testing data. In this way, we maintain a relatively independent test set, but still enable our approach to see enough types of data to estimate all of the required parameters.

In the experiment, we estimate each knowledge tracing parameter using data about the skill, and either data about this student's or the student's classmates' performance on this skill. Thus, for each parameter we tried two ways of estimating its value. We examined each combination of settings for all four knowledge tracing parameters (P,G,S,L) To simplify the problem, we group the performance parameters, guess and slip, together. This leaves us in total $2^3 = 8$ different combinations in parameters. The models and experimental results are shown in the next section.

3 Results

The accuracy of the predictions was evaluated in terms of the Root Mean Squared Error (RMSE), with lower values meaning higher accuracy. We compared different models to analyze the best individualization level for prior Knowledge (K0), learning rate (L) and Guess and Slip (G/S) respectively. That is, for each of the parameters (K0, L, G/S), we choose Class level individualization or Student level individualization, there are in total 8 possible combinations. The different combination models and their RMSE results on the test set are shown in Table 1.

The first column shows which parameter is chosen for the prior knowledge, the second column shows which parameter is chosen for the learning rate, the third column shows which parameter is chosen for the performance parameters (guess and slip), the fourth column shows the RMSE result of each model on the test dataset. We order the rows in this table based on the RMSE on the test set, with the top rows representing higher accuracy on the test set.

Table 1. RMSE result on test and training data

K0	L	G/S	RMSE
Class	Student	Class	0.413
Class	Class	Class	0.415
Class	Student	Student	0.417
Class	Class	Student	0.419
Student	Student	Student	0.421
Student	Student	Class	0.423
Student	Class	Class	0.424
Student	Class	Student	0.425

For comparison, the standard Knowledge Tracing model produces an RMSE of 0.428 on the test data, which is less accurate than all of the models we experimented with in Table 1. Therefore, it appears that both of the class level and the student level individualization can help improve Knowledge Tracing's predictive accuracy.

A second point of comparison is our baseline Student Skill model, represented in the 5th row in this table (underlined), which represents estimating all of the parameters using information about each student. Thus, each student has a customized estimate of prior knowledge (K0), learning (L), and guess (G) and slip (S), as they are derived from the student node. In this case, model in Fig. 2 degenerates to be the same as the Student Skill model in Fig. 1. The fact that this model is only at the middle of the table shows that, it is not as strong as other methods of estimating parameters.

In other words, sometimes it is better to use the class information rather than using individual student information. This result could occur if students within a class do not vary very much on a particular parameters. In that case, it would be better to estimate that parameter for the entire class to take advantage of the larger quantity of data. For example, the fact that the 4th row, which has prior and learning comes from class information, and guess and slip comes from the student information results in lower RMSE value on the test data than the 5th row, indicates that the prior knowledge and learning rate may be better estimated through the class information rather than estimated from completely individualization of student. Back to the example at the beginning of this paper, this means that for prior knowledge, and guess and slip rate, knowing the information of all of the other students in the class may be slightly more beneficial than only knowing the information of the current student. If all of the other students in the class do not know a skill initially, it is more likely the current student do not know the skill either, no matter how good the student is on other skills.

Among all of these models, the best mode (the first row in the table) is the one with prior knowledge (K0) and performance parameters (guess and slip) derived from the class information, and the learning rate (L) is derived from individual student information. The result seems plausible because all students in a class normally get the same instruction, thus might have similar prior knowledge (K0) about a particular skill, and some students learn faster than others, thus the learning rate (L) would be beneficial from individual student information. To be clear, we are not asserting that all students have the same prior knowledge, as some students will not complete homework or might not pay attention in class. However, within a class, prior knowledge varies less than the other parameters, and, at least in this instance, the potential benefit of customizing K0 to each student is not worth the additional parameters.

Besides finding the best combination of grain-sizes for estimating various parameters, there are also some interesting general trends visible in Table 1. The most interesting one is that prior knowledge (K0) is always better modeled at the class level: the top 4 rows are all with class information used to estimate the K0 parameter. This result confirms our intuition that all students in a class tend to have similar prior knowledge, which could be caused by the fact that they are going through similar instructions, or the fact that similar students are tend to be assigned to the same classroom.

The trend in learning rate (L) is the opposite as the trend for prior knowledge. Since the bottom two rows both have class information as the resource for learning rate, student information seems to be a more powerful resource. Therefore, within a class, students' ability to learn mathematics appears to vary more than their prior knowledge. However, these differences appear to be rather small: comparing the first and second lines results in a difference in RMSE of 0.002; similarly, comparing the third and fourth lines also results in a difference in RMSE of 0.002. This difference is rather small, so estimating learning rate at the class level or at the student level works approximately equally well.

As for the performance parameters (guess and slip), there seems to be a general advantage to modeling these effects at the class level, but the trend is not completely clear. We expected guess and slip behaviors to vary considerably within a class, and to be better modeled at the student level. Therefore, we found this result somewhat surprising.

4 Contributions, Future Work, and Conclusions

This paper makes three main contributions. Philosophically, it considers the learner's classmates as a viable source of information for predicting the learner's behavior. This source of information seems to have been overlooked by the ITS community.

The second contribution this paper makes computational, as it extends the Bayesian knowledge tracing framework to take into account the class information. Our model structure enables us to model parameters at the class- or student-level, and to mix and match grain sizes within an experiment. In a similar effort, a PFA-like model was modified to account for class-level information [7].

The third contribution this paper makes is empirical. Our results suggest that initial knowledge of a skill is probably best modeled at the class level. Prior work either assumed the initial knowledge is determined either by the skill itself or a combination of the student and skill. This paper's experimental results suggest that student modelers should consider additional sources of power for understanding learners.

Currently, the way we utilize the student and class information is to consider using either class parameters or student parameters. That is, each of the models we compared considered using one source of power for each of the parameters, but not both. It is possible that we can look at both sources information simultaneously and even take into account the fact that a student is a member of a class, to build a hierarchically structured model that blends the two sources of information together. In this model, class could be the parent node of different students. The model is easy for people to understand and interpret, yet we are not sure if a complex Bayesian Network representation of this model can be properly built and learn back the expected parameters. Both experiments with real and simulated data will be helpful for evaluating such approaches. It is also unclear if the model will be practical given the large number of parameters required.

One issue that we have not yet addressed is whether the performance parameters (guess and slip) should be grouped together. In this paper, we group the performance parameters together to simplify the experiments based on the assumption that these two parameters are both related to performance and should have similar properties with respect to the best grain size for modeling. Yet, it is likely that guess and slip behaves very differently at the class level compared to the student level. For example, some type of instruction may cause all students in the class very likely to guess the correct answer for some skills, even though the students do not fully understand the skill. We suspect that slip is best modeled at the individual level. The mixed result in the performance parameters in section 3 could perhaps become more clear if we run more experiments with separate guess and slip parameters.

Another question that we are interested in exploring is whether the results about class-level parameters transfer across years? Currently, our evaluation looks at only one year's data and generates the test and training set from that year. This approach has the normal cold start problem, that if it is the start of a new school year and we have no information about the class yet, what would be a reasonable information to use to build the student model? One possible solution that we are interested in is to use the class information of previous school years. If we can find a class that we have data from previous years that is similar to a current class, we might be able to use the information from that class to start building the model for the current class. How to define similarity of different classes, however, is a challenging question. We could look at the teacher or use the very first performance of each student in the class as an estimate of prior knowledge. We could also choose a set of similar previous classes and use the average of their parameters instead of choose only one from all. Or, we could use whichever prior class has the highest predictive accuracy for this student, as in [3].

Finally, from a broader perspective, class can be seen as a group of students, thus is a natural way of clustering students. There are literatures that focus on clustering in student modeling such as [8,9]. What are the differences and connections between using class and using other clustering methods? Class could be an effect of the teacher or ability grouping; in this case, using clustering algorithms on features such as teacher and student ability could result in similar clusters as classes. There are also other levels of abstraction and natural clustering, such as which grade or school a student is in, exploring models that utilizing these new sources of information is also new and interesting.

In summary, this paper introduces a framework for using a dynamic Bayesian network to model parameters as a combination of student-skill effects, or class-skill effects. We have found that using either source of knowledge is more accurate than a standard knowledge tracing model. By selectively estimating some parameters at a coarser grain size, we are able to improve accuracy a bit over the class-skill model.

Acknowledgements. This work was supported by the National Science Foundation (grant DRL-1109483) to Worcester Polytechnic Institute. The opinions expressed are those of the authors and do not necessarily represent the views of the Foundation.

References

1. Corbett, A., Anderson, J.: Knowledge Tracing: Modeling the Acquisition of Procedural Knowledge. User Modeling and User-Adapted Interaction 4, 253–278 (1995)
2. Pavlik, P.I., Cen, H., Koedinger, K.: Performance Factors Analysis – A New Alternative to Knowledge. In: Proceedings of the 14th International Conference on Artificial Intelligence in Education, pp. 531–538 (2009)
3. Gong, Y., Beck, J.E., Ruiz, C.: Modeling Multiple Distributions of Student Performances to Improve Predictive Accuracy. In: Masthoff, J., Mobasher, B., Desmarais, M.C., Nkambou, R. (eds.) UMAP 2012. LNCS, vol. 7379, pp. 102–113. Springer, Heidelberg (2012)

4. Wang, Y., Heffernan, N.T.: The Student Skill Model. In: Cerri, S.A., Clancey, W.J., Papadourakis, G., Panourgia, K. (eds.) ITS 2012. LNCS, vol. 7315, pp. 399–404. Springer, Heidelberg (2012)
5. Pardos, Z.A., Heffernan, N.T.: Modeling Individualization in a Bayesian Networks Implementation of Knowledge Tracing. In: De Bra, P., Kobsa, A., Chin, D. (eds.) UMAP 2010. LNCS, vol. 6075, pp. 255–266. Springer, Heidelberg (2010)
6. Murphy, K.P.: The Bayes Net Toolbox for Matlab, Computing Science and Statistics. Proceedings of Interface 33 (2001)
7. Xiong, X., Beck, J.E., Li, S.: Class distinctions: Leveraging class-level features to predict student retention performance. In: Chad Lane, H., Yacef, K., Mostow, J., Pavlik, P. (eds.) AIED 2013. LNCS (LNAI), vol. 7926, pp. 820–823. Springer, Heidelberg (2013)
8. Trivedi, S., Pardos, Z.A., Heffernan, N.T.: The Utility of Clustering in Prediction Tasks. In: Proceedings of the 17th Conference on Knowledge Discovery and Data Mining (2011)
9. Song, F., Sarkozy, G.N., Trivedi, S., Wang, Y., Heffernan, N.T.: Applying Clustering to the Problem of Predicting Retention within an ITS: Comparing Regularity Clustering with Traditional Methods. Accepted by the 24th FLAIRS

Comparing Student Models in Different Formalisms by Predicting Their Impact on Help Success

Sébastien Lallé[1,2,3], Jack Mostow[3], Vanda Luengo[1], and Nathalie Guin[2]

[1] LIG METAH, Joseph Fourier University, Grenoble, France
[2] LIRIS, University of Lyon 1, CNRS, Lyon, France
[3] Carnegie Mellon University, Pittsburgh PA, United States of America
{sebastien.lalle,vanda.luengo}@imag.fr, mostow@cs.cmu.edu, Nathalie.Guin@liris.univ-lyon1.fr

Abstract. We describe a method to evaluate how student models affect ITS decision quality – their raison d'être. Given logs of randomized tutorial decisions and ensuing student performance, we train a classifier to predict tutor decision outcomes (success or failure) based on situation features, such as student and task. We define a decision policy that selects whichever tutor action the trained classifier predicts in the current situation is likeliest to lead to a successful outcome. The ideal but costly way to evaluate such a policy is to implement it in the tutor and collect new data, which may require months of tutor use by hundreds of students. Instead, we use historical data to simulate a policy by extrapolating its effects from the subset of randomized decisions that happened to follow the policy. We then compare policies based on alternative student models by their simulated impact on the success rate of tutorial decisions. We test the method on data logged by Project LISTEN's Reading Tutor, which chooses randomly which type of help to give on a word. We report the cross-validated accuracy of predictions based on four types of student models, and compare the resulting policies' expected success and coverage. The method provides a utility-relevant metric to compare student models expressed in different formalisms.

Keywords: Student models, knowledge tracing, classification, help policy.

1 Introduction

A challenge in the field of Intelligent Tutoring Systems (ITS) is to evaluate student models by their impact on the success of an ITS's decisions – in particular, about which type of help to give students. Individualized help can have a strong impact on learning [1]. The better the tutor adapts its help to the student and situation, the likelier the student will learn from it.

This paper shows how to use logged tutor data and a student model to learn what help to provide in a given situation, and how to compare alternative student models based on the resulting help policies. The paper is organized as follows. Section 2 reviews prior work on learning help policies. Section 3 describes the student models we used in the study. Section 4 discusses the data. Section 5 presents the algorithm for learning a help policy. Section 6 reports results. Section 7 concludes.

K. Yacef et al. (Eds.): AIED 2013, LNAI 7926, pp. 161–170, 2013.

2 Relation to Prior Work

Several papers report positive results from learning individualized help policies.

Andes [7] used a Bayesian network to adapt hints to the student, the problem, and the context, but required human-designed sequences of hint templates; we do not.

ADVISOR [4] and later work [2, 6, 7] used reinforcement learning to adapt a pedagogical agent to optimize student performance metrics such as the time to solve problems. The agent could give hints or to select the next exercise. ADVISOR used only one student model; in contrast, we compare alternative student models. Only Chi *et al.* [6] included features of system behavior, which they found affected feedback success more than task or student features. Barnes and Stamper [2, 7] derived policies from effects of student decisions; in contrast, we learn from tutor decisions.

Project LISTEN's Reading Tutor [19] chose randomly among different types of help on a word. Heiner et al. [13] compared their success rates based on how often the student read a word acceptably at the next encounter. We use this and other information plus a student model to train a policy, not just compare overall success rates.

Razzaq and Heffernan [22] compared two types of feedback, namely scaffolds and hints, and found that students who got scaffolds learned more than students who got hints with pre and post tests, although the difference was not statistically significant. Like Heiner, they compared rates, but between groups rather than within-subject.

Recommender systems can be used to recommend suitable learning resources to a given student in an ITS or web-based learning. Verbert et al. [26] predicted the success of recommendations (in terms of student satisfaction) from student activities. In contrast, we predict the success of help (in terms of student performance) from student traits, task features, help type, and a student model of estimated skills.

Table 1. Summary of prior work on help or hint selection, in terms of features and evaluation

Work	Features used to select help or hints	Methodology to validate learned policy
Gertner *et al.* [11]	Problem goal + current problem state + context + student's mastery of skills	Experiments (pre and post tests)
Beck *et al.* [4]	Student model + current problem state	Simulation (check if probability of success increases with the help) and experiments
Heiner *et al.* [13]	Student level + word difficulty	Use historical data (expected increase in success for unseen students)
Barnes, Stamper *et al.* [3, 23]	Student model + current problem state	Experiments (number of solved problems, errors, and number of hints given with the generated policy vs. default policy)
Chi *et al.* [6]	Student features + domain features + system behavior features	Experiments (pre and post test)
This paper	Student features + domain features + system behavior features	Use historical data (expected increase in success for unseen students)

Table 1 summarizes all this work in terms of the features used in the help or hint policy, and how it was evaluated using on-line experiments or off-line simulation.

Prior research has explored various ways to compare student models [17]. Several papers [5, 12, 21, 27] compare different knowledge tracing models based on goodness of fit. That work frames student modeling as a prediction problem, where the goal is to predict the next observation of student performance (correct or incorrect). Other papers compared the accuracy of models based on constraint-based modeling [14] or Item Response Theory [9]. Results depend on the domain, the datasets, and the model-fitting method. For instance, Pavlik *et al.* found that Performance Factor Models (PFM) beat Bayesian Knowledge Tracing [21], but Gong *et al.* found the opposite, leaving uncertain the reason for this divergence in results [12]. Moreover, we know of no prior quantitative comparisons of different types of student models.

3 Student Models

We now describe the three types of student models we compare in this paper.

Knowledge Tracing [8] is based on a *cognitive model*, which specifies the skills underlying students' successive observable actions. Knowledge tracing uses these observations to update estimated probabilities of the student knowing the skills, based on the *knew* probability of having a skill beforehand, the *learn* probability of acquiring the skill at any given step, the *guess* probability of responding correctly without knowing a skill, and the *slip* probability of responding incorrectly despite knowing it. Knowledge Tracing uses a Bayesian update, while the *Performance Factor Model* (PFM) [21] uses a linear combination of skill difficulty, student proficiency, and past performance (number of previous successes and failures on a given skill).

Constraint-based modeling [20] has no cognitive model of skills underlying steps. Instead, it represents domain constraints whose violation reveals missing knowledge or misconceptions that call for corrective feedback. A constraint-based model represents domain knowledge as a set of constraints (Cr, Cs), where Cr specifies the situations where the constraint is relevant, and Cs specifies the correct answer in those situations. The constraint-based model can infer student knowledge from students' observed actions as the probability of satisfying a constraint when it is relevant.

Finally, the *Control-based Approach* [16] (based on cKc [2]) represents domain knowledge as a set of problems, operators for solving the problems, indicators of how a problem or operator is represented (e.g. as proof vs. diagram in geometry), and skills for deciding whether an answer or action is correct, represented as nodes in a Dynamic Bayesian Network. The Control-based Approach uses observed student actions to update the conditional probability of knowing the skill given the problem, the representation indicators, the operator used, and whether the action is correct.

4 Experimental Data

We use data from Project LISTEN's Reading Tutor [19], which displays text and listens to a child to read it aloud. The Reading Tutor uses automatic speech recognition (ASR) to classify each text word as read correctly or not, and to measure the latency before reading each word. We label a word as *fluent* if the Reading Tutor recognized it as read correctly without help or hesitation. The Reading Tutor can give several types of help on a word, such as say it, give a rhyming hint (e.g., *rhymes with cat*), or sound out its successive phonemes (*/K/ /AE/ /T/*) [13]. Some types of help are infeasible or infelicitous on some words, such as rhyming hints for rhymeless words, syllabifying a one-syllable word, or sounding out a word longer than 4 phonemes. The Reading Tutor chooses randomly among types of help suitable for a given word.

Each such decision generates one randomized controlled trial. To test whether the help helped the child learn the word, we define the outcome of the trial as whether the child read the same word fluently at the next encounter on a later day, thereby excluding recency and scaffolding effects. Thus if a student gets help on word *W* on day *i*, its outcome is the first encounter of word *W* on day *j* where *j*>*i*, as Figure 1 shows. Our data for this paper consist of 30,838 such trials logged by the Reading Tutor in the 2002-2003 school year, from 96 students and 1078 distinct words. To simplify analysis, we omitted trials where a child got help on word *W* more than once on day *i*.

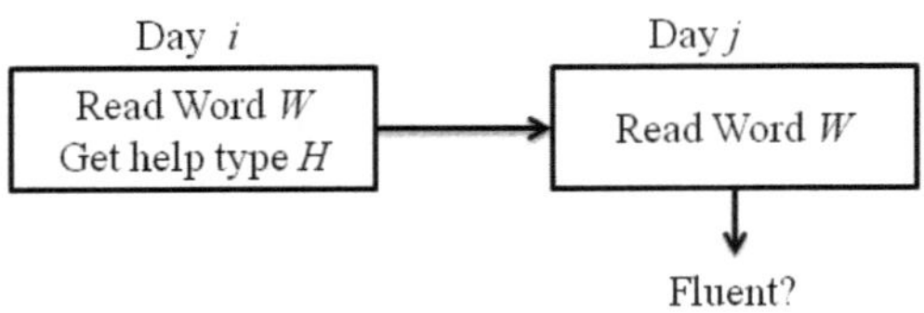

Fig. 1. Help type H on word *W* on day *i* succeeds if *W* is fluent at the first encounter on day *j*

5 Method for Training a Help Policy

We train a help policy as follows. First annotate the logged trials with information from a student model. Then select a set of features (such as student reading level or word length) that affect help success, according to a linear model. Next, use the logged trials, student model, and selected features to learn when help will succeed. Finally, derive a policy from the learned classifier to choose help likeliest to succeed.

5.1 Using Student Models to Annotate Logged Trials

Knowledge diagnosis is the process of inferring or updating a student model from student interactions with an ITS [25]. We considered four knowledge diagnosis techniques: Performance Factor Modeling [21], Bayesian Knowledge Tracing [8], constraint-based modeling [18], and a Control-based model based on cKc [16] (see Table 2). These techniques are generic, so that it is possible to use them on our domain. Diagnosis techniques use various methods to update the student model, such as Bayesian inference or logistic regression. Updating a student model means updating the estimated probability of knowing different skills, based on students' observed performance (such as correct or incorrect answers). These estimates make it possible to predict future performance on those skills.

Table 2. Summary of the four types of student models used in this work

Type of student model	Update method	Output (prediction)	Ref
Performance Factor Model	Linear regression	Probability of answering correctly	[21]
Bayesian Knowledge Tracing	Hidden Markov Model	Probability of answering correctly	[8]
Constraint-based	Constraints	Probability of violating constraints	[18]
Control-based	Dynamic Bayesian Network	Probability of using skills or not, correctly or not	[16]

Constraint-based models are typically updated at the end of exercises. To update them online instead, we associate a power law function with each constraint (knowledge), fit these functions to observed student performance so far, and use them to predict subsequent performance. Another difficulty in our data is that the skills are not directly observable. Our model of oral reading represents a skill as mapping a grapheme to a phoneme. For instance, the word *chemist* maps *ch*→/K/, *e*→/EH/, *m*→/M/, *i*→/IH/, *s*→/S/, and *t*→/T/. However, our speech recognizer only recognizes words. Thus, we used a multiskill approach, meaning that a single observed step (reading a word) may require multiple skills . We estimate each skill independently, predict performance conjunctively (i.e. multiply the estimates of all the skills used in a step), and update each skill separately as if assigning it sole responsibility for the step's success or failure [27].

To fit models that maximize data likelihood, we use EM for Bayesian Knowledge Tracing and Control-based models, and R's stats and igraph packages for Performance Factors Models and Constraint-based models.

5.2 Selecting Features

Help type H on word *W* on day *i* succeeds if *W* is fluent at the first encounter on day *j*. To find which features best predict success, we use stepwise linear regression with success as response variable and features as predictors, and optimize AIC, defined as:

$$\text{AIC} = 2 \times \text{k} - 2 \times \ln(\text{L})$$

Here *k* is the number of parameters of the model and *L* the data likelihood. A one-way ANOVA tests if the features significantly ($p<0.01$) explain success. The initial features were all selected: student's reading level, student proficiency (% of words accepted as fluent when first seen each day), story's difficulty level, word length, word frequency in English, word position in the story, the number of prior encounters of the word, and the word class, defined by which Reading Tutor interventions apply to it.

5.3 Learning Classifiers to Predict Help Success

To predict based on the student model, the selected features, and the type of help whether help will succeed, i.e. lead to reading the word fluently at the next encounter (cf. Figure 1), we trained three types of classifiers – two based on rules (Part [10] and JRip [7]) and one on random trees, using Weka[1]. Here is an example of a learned rule:

[1] `http://www.cs.waikato.ac.nz/ml/weka`

```
1) Word = c145
2) AND Story_Level = B
3) AND Student_Model_Prediction > 0.6
4) AND Help_Type = "SayWord"
      ⇨ Fluent (22/22)
```

Clause 1 specifies that the rule applies to words in the class "c145," for which the feasible help types (described in [13]) are 1 ("Autophonics"), 4 ("Recue"), and 5 ("RhymesWith"). Clause 2 specifies that the story is at a grade 2 level. Clause 3 specifies that based on prior data, the student model estimates probability over 0.6 that the student will read the word fluently. Clause 4 specifies help type. We compute confidence in a rule as the frequency of success in the training instances to which the rule applies. The rule here predicts with confidence 22/22 that "SayWord" help will succeed. We prune rules with confidence below 0.75 (Weka's default).

5.4 Using a Predictor of Help Success as a Decision Policy for What Help to Pick

The decision policy based on the trained classifier works as follows: Choose the type of help specified by whichever rule applies to the current situation and has the highest confidence according to the training data. If there is more than one such rule, pick randomly among them. An alternative is to train a separate model to predict success for each type of help, and pick a type with the maximum probability of success.

6 Experimental Results

We evaluated our method on Reading Tutor data (cf. section 4). To split the data into two sets, one to train a student model and one to train and test a success predictor, we first sorted the data alphabetically by student initials, and used the first 60% to train a student model. Then we used the remaining 40% to train and test success predictors using 10-fold cross-validation. That is, we partitioned the students into 10 disjoint folds, pooled 9 of them to train a predictor, and tested it on the remaining fold. We repeated this procedure for each fold, and averaged the results. To test how well a student model fit the data, we used it to predict each time the Reading Tutor gave help on a word whether the student read the word fluently at the next encounter of it.

We measure model accuracy as percentage of correct predictions, which Table 3 lists from highest to lowest. We score a probabilistic prediction as correct if it rates the true outcome of the next encounter as likelier than 50%. Varying this probability threshold trades off false positive and false negative errors along an ROC curve. The area under the ROC Curve (AUC) measures the probability that given a fluent and non-fluent instance, the model will correctly identify which is which. AUC of 1 means the model is perfect; AUC of 0.5 means the model is no better than chance.

AIC (defined in section 5.2) measures the goodness of fit to training data based on data likelihood, penalized by the number of parameters k. Here k is the number of model parameters multiplied by the number of skills and the number of students.

Table 3. Predictive accuracy of each student model, and of help success prediction based on it

Type of student model	Predictiveness of student models			Predictors of help success		
	Accuracy	AUC	AIC	Coverage	Accuracy	
Bayesian Knowledge Tracing	84% (± 2.6%)	0.68	5.1 E+4	32%	75% (± 4.1%)	} **
Control-based model	83% (± 2.9%)	0.67	7.2 E+4	34%	73% (± 4.4%)	} ***
Performance Factor model	81% (± 3%)	0.65	5.5 E+4	26%	68% (± 4.4%)	} ***
Constraint-based model	80% (± 2.8%)	0.65	5.6 E+4	25%	65% (± 4.3%)	

Significance on McNemar's test: ** $0.01 < p < 0.05$; *** $p \leq 0.01$

All 4 diagnostic techniques beat the majority class (76% fluent words in our data). These results are consistent with a previous evaluation of Knowledge Tracing [27] on a different set of Reading Tutor data, which found accuracies ranging from 72% to 87%, but below 35% on non-fluent instances – which might explain why AUC, which measures a model's accuracy in distinguishing positive from negative instances [24], was 0.68 or worse in our data. AIC rated Bayesian Knowledge Tracing highest, penalizing the control-based model because it has more parameters than the other models.

Table 3 evaluates each success predictor by its cross-validated accuracy on help given to held-out students. We show results only from JRip, because it beat the other two classifier methods (by less than 2%). Bayesian Knowledge Tracing did best. Coverage is the proportion of words in the test set to which a rule of a policy applies.

Predictors of help success were less accurate than the student models they used. Evidently, predicting whether a student will read a word fluently at the next encounter is easier than predicting whether help on that word will succeed. A possible reason is data sparseness: we predict success of each help type from the training instances where the Reading Tutor happened to give that type, which may be very few.

To test the statistical reliability of accuracy differences between predictors of help success rate, we used McNemar's test, which checks for significant differences between two classifiers C1 and C2 on the same data using this formula:

$$\chi^2 = (d_1 - d_2)^2 / (d_1 + d_2)$$

Here d_1 is the number of instances classified as positive by C1 but negative by *C2*, and d_2 is the number of instances classified as positive by C2 but negative by C1. The sum $d_1 + d_2$ exceeds 80 in our data, well over the minimum of 10 specified by McNemar [15], so this test can be approximated as a Chi-squared distribution. Each two consecutive predictors in Table 3 differ significantly ($p<0.025$), assuming negligible effects of statistical dependencies among trials with the same student or word.

Finally, we computed the expected percentage of words read fluently at the next encounter after help based on each learned policy. The difference between expected and actual percentages represents the simulated increase in help success, shown in Table 4. (Simulated means based on historical data rather than on new experiments.) The last row shows results when solely picking types of help with the highest success rate in the training set. We compute the expected help success rate E:

$$E(Fluent \mid h^{*}, S, F)$$

Here S is the student model, F is the set of student and domain features, and h^* is the type of help with the highest estimated probability of success in that situation:

$$h^{*} = \text{argmax}_{h} E(Fluent \mid h, S, F)$$

Table 4. Expected absolute percentage increase in (simulated) help success

Diagnosis technique (type of student model)	Expected increase in help success	Coverage (% of test set covered by rules)
Bayesian Knowledge Tracing	5.2%	32%
Control-based model	5.1%	34%
Performance Factor Model	4.7%	26%
Constraint-based model	4.5%	25%
Average success in the training set	2.4%	

7 Conclusion

This paper presents new methods to compare student models and induce help policies. Prior work compared the predictive accuracy of student models expressed in the same formalism, e.g. cognitive modeling or Item Response Theory. In contrast, we compare the impact of student models on expected success of tutorial decisions based on them, a measure more directly relevant to utility than predictive accuracy is. We believe quantitative comparison of student models across different formalisms is novel.

We described a method to learn a policy for picking which type of help to give in a given situation, based on types of help, student features, domain features, and a student model, by using this information to learn the probability that help will succeed, and then picking the type of help likeliest to succeed in a given situation. Using data from Project LISTEN's Reading Tutor, we showed that success predictors differ significantly, depending on the student model used. All four learned policies improved the Reading Tutor's expected success compared to its original randomized decisions. A 5.2% increase despite only 32% coverage implies 16.3% increase on the covered test instances; thus better-generalized policies could potentially triple help success.

Our approach has several limitations. It applies only to tutors that decide among multiple types of applicable help. It assumes that the logged decisions were randomized, and that their outcomes can be computed from the ensuing tutorial interactions. The learned policy's coverage and accuracy in predicting whether a given type of help will succeed in a given situation are limited by the number of observations in the logged training data of the tutor giving that type of help in that situation. Thus the method can only learn policies followed sufficiently often in the data to estimate their success. The learned policy is therefore vulnerable to under-covering and over-fitting. The accuracy of the cross-validated estimate of the learned policy's expected success is similarly limited by the number of observations of each situation-decision pair in the held-out test data. Both the policy and the estimate of its success assume that the outcomes of the held-out logged instances are representative of future unseen cases. This inductive leap is the price we pay for evaluating the policy based on its simulated rather than actual success. Future work includes trying more accurate student models such as LR-DBN [26], more powerful classifiers such as Support Vector Machines (SVM) or Random Forests, analysis of how student model accuracy affects the accuracy of predicting the success of help, learning more general policies to increase coverage and reduce overfitting, and experiments to test how accurately expected success predicts actual success in practice.

Acknowledgements. This work was supported by the first author's PhD scholarship and travel grant from the Rhône-Alpes Region in France, and by the Institute of Education Sciences, U.S. Department of Education, through Grant R305A080628 to Carnegie Mellon University. The opinions expressed are those of the authors and do not necessarily represent the views of the Institute or U.S. Department of Education. We thank the children, schools, and LISTENers who generated, collected, and organized Reading Tutor data.

References

1. Anderson, J.R., Gluck, K.: What role do cognitive architectures play in intelligent tutoring systems. In: Cognition and Instruction: Twenty-Five Years of Progress, pp. 227–262. Lawrence Erlbaum, Mahwah (2001)
2. Balacheff, N., Gaudin, N.: Students conceptions: an introduction to a formal characterization. Cahier Leibniz 65, 1–21 (2002)
3. Barnes, T., Stamper, J., Lehman, L., Croy, M.: A pilot study on logic proof tutoring using hints generated from historical student data. In: Procs. of the 1st International Conference on Educational Data Mining, Montréal, Canada, pp. 552–557 (2008)
4. Beck, J.E., Woolf, B.P., Beal, C.R.: ADVISOR: a machine-learning architecture for intelligent tutor construction. In: Procs. of the 17th AAAI Conference on Artificial Intelligence, Boston, MA, pp. 552–557 (2000)
5. Cen, H., Koedinger, K., Junker, B.: Comparing two IRT models for conjunctive skills. In: Woolf, B.P., Aïmeur, E., Nkambou, R., Lajoie, S. (eds.) ITS 2008. LNCS, vol. 5091, pp. 796–798. Springer, Heidelberg (2008)
6. Chi, M., VanLehn, K., Litman, D., Jordan, P.: Inducing effective pedagogical strategies using learning context features. In: De Bra, P., Kobsa, A., Chin, D. (eds.) UMAP 2010. LNCS, vol. 6075, pp. 147–158. Springer, Heidelberg (2010)
7. Cohen, W.W.: Fast Effective Rule Induction. In: Procs. of the 12th International Conference on Machine Learning, Tahoe City, CA, pp. 115–123 (1995)
8. Corbett, A.T., Anderson, J.R.: Knowledge tracing: Modeling the acquisition of procedural knowledge. User Modelling and User-Adapted Interaction 4, 253–278 (1995)
9. Desmarais, M.C.: Performance comparison of item-to-item skills models with the IRT single latent trait model. In: Konstan, J.A., Conejo, R., Marzo, J.L., Oliver, N. (eds.) UMAP 2011. LNCS, vol. 6787, pp. 75–86. Springer, Heidelberg (2011)
10. Frank, E., Witten, I.H.: Generating accurate rule sets without global optimization. In: Procs. of the 15th International Conference on Machine Learning, Madison, WI, pp. 144–151 (1998)
11. Gertner, A.S., Conati, C., VanLehn, K.: Procedural help in Andes: Generating hints using a Bayesian network student model. In: Procs. of the 15th National Conference on Artificial Intelligence, Madison, WI, pp. 106–111 (1998)

12. Gong, Y., Beck, J.E., Heffernan, N.T.: How to Construct More Accurate Student Models: Comparing and Optimizing Knowledge Tracing and Performance Factor Analysis. International Journal of Artificial Intelligence in Education 21(1), 27–46 (2011)
13. Heiner, C., Beck, J., Mostow, J.: Improving the help selection policy in a Reading Tutor that listens. In: Procs. of the InSTIL/ICALL 2004 Symposium on NLP and Speech Technologies in Advanced Language Learning Systems, Venice, Italy, pp. 195–198 (2004)
14. Le, N.-T., Pinkwart, N.: Can Soft Computing Techniques Enhance the Error Diagnosis Accuracy for Intelligent Tutors? In: Cerri, S.A., Clancey, W.J., Papadourakis, G., Panourgia, K. (eds.) ITS 2012. LNCS, vol. 7315, pp. 320–329. Springer, Heidelberg (2012)
15. McNemar, Q.: Note on the sampling error of the difference between correlated proportions or percentages. Psychometrika 12(2), 153–157 (1947)
16. Minh Chieu, V., Luengo, V., Vadcard, L., Tonetti, J.: Student modeling in complex domains: Exploiting symbiosis between temporal Bayesian networks and fine-grained didactical analysis. International Journal of Artificial Intelligence in Education 20(3), 269–301 (2010)
17. Mitrovic, A., Koedinger, K., Martin, B.: A comparative analysis of cognitive tutoring and constraint-based modeling. In: Procs. of the 9th International Conference on User Modeling, Johnstown, PA, pp. 313–322 (2003)
18. Mitrovic, A., Ohlsson, S.: Evaluation of a Constraint-Based Tutor for a Database. International Journal of Artificial Intelligence in Education 10(3-4), 238–256 (1999)
19. Mostow, J., Aist, G.: Evaluating tutors that listen: An overview of Project LISTEN. In: Smart Machines in Education: The Coming Revolution in Educational Technology, pp. 169–234. MIT/AAAI Press, Cambridge, MA (2001)
20. Ohlsson, S.: Constraint-based student modeling. NATO ASI Series F Computer and Systems Sciences, vol. 125, pp. 167–189 (1994)
21. Pavlik, P.I., Cen, H., Koedinger, K.: Performance Factors Analysis–A New Alternative to Knowledge Tracing. In: Procs. of the 15th International Conference on Artificial Intelligence in Education, Auckland, New Zealand, pp. 531–538 (2009)
22. Razzaq, L., Heffernan, N.T.: Scaffolding vs. Hints in the Assistment System. In: Ikeda, M., Ashley, K.D., Chan, T.-W. (eds.) ITS 2006. LNCS, vol. 4053, pp. 635–644. Springer, Heidelberg (2006)
23. Stamper, J., Barnes, T., Lehmann, L., Croy, M.: The hint factory: Automatic generation of contextualized help for existing computer aided instruction. In: Procs. of the International 9th Conference on Intelligent Tutoring Systems Young Researchers Track, Montréal, Canada, pp. 71–78 (2008)
24. Swets, J.A.: Measuring the accuracy of diagnostic systems. Science 240(4857), 1285–1293 (1988)
25. VanLehn, K.: Student modeling. In: Foundations of Intelligent Tutoring Systems, pp. 55–78. Lawrence Erlbaum, Mahwah (1988)
26. Verbert, K., Drachsler, H., Manouselis, N., Wolpers, M., Vuorikari, R., Duval, E.: Dataset-driven research for improving recommender systems for learning. In: Procs. of the 1st International Conference on Learning Analytics and Knowledge, Banff, Canada, pp. 44–53 (2011)
27. Xu, Y., Mostow, J.: Comparison of methods to trace multiple subskills: Is LR-DBN best? In: Procs. of the 5th International Conference on Educational Data Mining, Chania, Greece, pp. 41–48 (2012)

Individualized Bayesian Knowledge Tracing Models

Michael V. Yudelson, Kenneth R. Koedinger, and Geoffrey J. Gordon

Carnegie Mellon University,
5000 Forbes Ave., Pittsburgh, PA 15213, USA
{yudelson,koedinger}@cmu.edu, ggordon@cs.cmu.edu

Abstract. Bayesian Knowledge Tracing (BKT)[1] is a user modeling method extensively used in the area of Intelligent Tutoring Systems. In the standard BKT implementation, there are only skill-specific parameters. However, a large body of research strongly suggests that student-specific variability in the data, when accounted for, could enhance model accuracy [5,6,8]. In this work, we revisit the problem of introducing student-specific parameters into BKT on a larger scale. We show that student-specific parameters lead to a tangible improvement when predicting the data of unseen students, and that parameterizing students' speed of learning is more beneficial than parameterizing a priori knowledge.

Keywords: Bayesian knowledge tracing, model fitting, model selection, student-specific model parameters.

1 Introduction

Modeling student knowledge as a latent variable is a popular approach. The latent variable is updated based on the correctness of the observed student opportunities to apply the skill in question. In general case, this modeling approach is called a Hidden Markov Model. A special case of the approach is known as Bayesian Knowledge Tracing (BKT) [1]. BKT assumes that student knowledge is represented as a set of binary variables – one per skill (the skill is either mastered by the student or not). Observations in BKT are also binary: a student gets a problem [step] either right or wrong.

BKT has a long history of being actively used in Intelligent Tutoring Systems (ITS) in the context of mastery learning and problem sequencing. In its standard implementation that is still in predominant use today, BKT only has skill-specific parameters. Starting with the original publication on BKT [1] and including more recent works (e.g. [5]), there exist strong indicators that BKT models (often called individualized BKT models) that somehow account for student variance are superior to the standard BKT model.

Prior work on individualized BKT models (e.g. [1], [5]), and [8]) describes quite different approaches to defining and learning student-specific parameters as well as report radically different performance measures. In this paper, we

K. Yacef et al. (Eds.): AIED 2013, LNAI 7926, pp. 171–180, 2013.

approach the problem of introducing student-specific parameters in a more systematic manner. We build several individualized BKT models in an incremental manner (adding student-specific parameters in batches) and examine the effect each addition has on the model's cross-validation performance.

We find that BKT parameters corresponding to the a priori student knowledge give BKT models only a marginal cross-validation performance improvement. At the same time, student-specific speed of learning parameters result in a considerable boost in the model prediction accuracy.

2 Related Work

2.1 Bayesian Knowledge Tracing

There are four types of model parameters used in Bayesian Knowledge Tracing: initial probability of knowing the skill a priori – $p(L_0)$ (or *p-init*), probability of student's knowledge of a skill transitioning from *not known* to *known* state after an opportunity to apply it – $p(T)$ (or *p-transit*), probability to make a mistake when applying a known skill – $p(S)$ (or *p-slip*), and probability of correctly applying a not-known skill – $p(G)$ (or *p-guess*). Given that parameters are set for all skills, the formulae used to update student knowledge of skills are as follows. The initial probability of student u mastering skill k is set to the p-init parameter for that skill Equation (1a). Depending on whether the student u applied skill k correctly or incorrectly, the conditional probability is computed either using Equation (1b) or Equation (1c). The conditional probability is used to update the probability of skill mastery according to Equation (1d). To compute the probability of student u applying the skill k correctly on an upcoming practice opportunity one uses Equation (1e).

$$p(L_1)_u^k = p(L_0)^k, \tag{1a}$$

$$p(L_{t+1}|obs = correct)_u^k = \frac{p(L_t)_u^k \cdot (1 - p(S)^k)}{p(L_t)_u^k \cdot (1 - p(S)^k) + (1 - p(L_t)_u^k) \cdot p(G)^k}, \tag{1b}$$

$$p(L_{t+1}|obs = wrong)_u^k = \frac{p(L_t)_u^k \cdot p(S)^k}{p(L_t)_u^k \cdot p(S)^k + (1 - p(L_t)_u^k) \cdot (1 - p(G)^k)}, \tag{1c}$$

$$p(L_{t+1})_u^k = p(L_{t+1}|obs)_u^k + (1 - p(L_{t+1}|obs)_u^k) \cdot p(T)^k, \tag{1d}$$

$$p(C_{t+1})_u^k = p(L_t)_u^k \cdot (1 - p(S)^k) + (1 - p(L_t)_u^k) \cdot p(G)^k \tag{1e}$$

In the standard BKT model, we use one copy of each of the above four parameters $\langle\ p(L_0),\ p(T),\ p(S),\ p(G)\ \rangle$ per skill. BKT models are usually fit using the expectation maximization method (EM) [2], Conjugate Gradient Search [1], or discretized brute-force search [7].

2.2 Student-Specific Parameters in Bayesian Knowledge Tracing

In the area of building cognitive models of practice, student-specific parameters have been used for quite some time. The logistic regression based Rasch model [3] (also known as 1PL IRT) and its descendant the Additive Factors Model [6] both include a 'student proficiency' parameter to account for variability in student a priori abilities. In our prior work, we found that the inclusion of student-specific parameters has a significant positive effect on prediction accuracy and interpretability, as well as reduces over-fitting [4].

Prior work introducing student-specific parameters to BKT is limited. Corbett and Anderson, in the original BKT paper [1], discussed fitting all four BKT parameters for students (e.g. $p(T)_u$) as well as skills (e.g. $p(T)^k$). Namely, data of all students practicing skill k would be used to fit four BKT parameters for that skill, and all data of student u would be used to fit four BKT parameters for that student. The student and skill parameters would then be combined using a special function to yield a value (here $p(T)_u^k$) to be used for updating the probability of skill mastery. The individualized BKT model led to better correlation between actual and expected accuracy across students when compared to the same correlation for the non-individualized BKT model. However, accuracy of predicting student test scores (after a period of working with a tutoring system) did not improve tangibly.

Pardos and Heffernan [5] individualized the initial probability of mastery $p(L_0)^k$ by assigning according to a set of heuristics: randomly, by selecting from two pre-set values based on first student response correctness, by using overall percent correct. The 'prior per-student' models fit better than traditional BKT on a significant fraction of the problem sets authors considered.

Lee and Brunskill [8] investigated individualizing all four BKT parameters. However, in contrast to [1], the student-specific parameters were fit differently. Instead of fitting per skill and per-student BKT parameters to be combined later, they only fit per-student parameters for each student (assuming there is one skill all students have to learn). Lee and Brunskill did not discuss goodness of fit of their individualized models. Their focus was whether the individualized model, when used in an intelligent tutoring system, would schedule fewer or more practice opportunities than the traditional BKT skill-specific model (or *population* model as authors referred to it). The results showed that a considerable fraction of students, as judged by individualized model, would have received too few or too many practice opportunities (although no confidence intervals were given).

Although the [potential] benefits of individualized BKT models are visible, the results are unclear about the ideal configuration of student-specific parameters (4 per student [1], 1 heuristic value per student [5], 4 per student [8]), are limited in the evidence for improved mode prediction and are hard to operationalize for the purpose of implementing in an ITS. The original work on BKT [1] pointed out that operationalization of the discussed individualized BKT model could be problematic. Work by Pardos and Heffernan [5] showed that their prior-per-student BKT does not always win over traditional BKT. Lee and Brunskill [8] made a practically important derivation that using individualized model parameters could save time for stronger students and could allocate more time for struggling ones. However, this derivation assumed that individualized BKT models predict student data better which was not tested.

Table 1. BKT parameters in matrix form

(a) Priors (Π)

known	$p(L_0)$
unknown	1-$p(L_0)$

(b) Transitions (A)

	to known	to unknown
from known	1	0
from unknown	$p(T)$	$1 - p(T)$

(c) Observations (B)

	right	wrong
known	1-$p(S)$	$p(S)$
unknown	$p(G)$	1-$p(G)$

3 Methods

Our goal is to unify and extend prior work on individualized BKT models. We construct four variants of individualized BKT models varying the number of student-specific parameters. and we rank the constructed models with respect to predictive accuracy on unseen data.

3.1 Bayesian Knowledge Tracing with Student-Specific Parameters

Instead of a traditional Expectation Maximization (EM) method for learning BKT parameters, we base our method on the so-called *optimization techniques* approach described in [2] for the following reasons. First, EM does not directly optimize a likelihood of the student observations given BKT parameters (a standard metric for HMM). As a result, the EM algorithm could make adjustments to BKT parameters that would actually worsen the fit. Second, using the gradient-based optimization techniques allows us to introduce student-specific parameters to BKT without expanding the structure of the underlying HMM (cf. [5]). Keeping the structure of the underlying HMM unchanged permits us to lower the computational cost of fitting.

Table 1 shows BKT parameters defined in matrix format, as they are normally represented in HMM. A priori probability of mastery $p(L_0)$ belongs in the *Priors* matrix $\Pi = \{\pi_i\}$ in an HMM, $i \in [1, N]$ (N is the number of hidden states, in our case two), learning probability $p(T)$ is in the *Transitions* matrix $A = \{a_{ij}\}$, $i, j \in [1, N]$ (note that there is no forgetting – transition from known to unknown is zero), probabilities of slipping and guessing belong to the *Observations* matrix $B = \{b_j(m)\}$, $j \in [1, N]$, $m \in [1, M]$ (M is the number of observations, in our case two). These matrices follow two constraints: all of the elements should be non-negative, and the priors vector and the rows of transitions and observations matrices should sum to one.

To successfully implement our BKT models, we need to solve two problems. First, the *evaluation problem*: given BKT parameters $\lambda = \{\Pi, A, B\}$ and a sequence of observations (practice attempts) $O = \{o_t\}$, $t \in [1, T]$, what is the probability that the observations are generated given BKT model, or formally $p\{O|\lambda\}$. Second, the *learning problem*: given BKT parameters λ and a sequence of observations O, how should λ be adjusted to maximize $p\{O|\lambda\}$.

The objective function we use in our method is negative log likelihood, or $J = -log(L_{tot})$, where L_{tot} is the sum of all likelihoods $p\{O|\lambda\}$ for all student-skill practice sequences in our data. We will define our search for better λ parameters of the BKT as gradient search (cf. Equation 2a, where η is the search step size). Here, gradients with respect to our matrices from Table 1 are defined in terms of the so-called *forward* variables α (cf. Equation 2b and 2c) and *backward* variables β (cf. Equation 2d and 2e). Gradients with respect to BKT parameters are given in Equation 2f, 2g, and 2h. For detailed discussion of forward and backward variables as well as derivations of the gradients see [2].

$$\lambda^{new} = \lambda^{old} - \eta \left[\frac{\partial J}{\partial \lambda}\right]_{\lambda=\lambda old} \tag{2a}$$

$$\alpha_1(j) = \pi_j b_j(o_1), j \in [1, N] \tag{2b}$$

$$\alpha_{t+1}(j) = b_j(o_{t+1}) \sum_{i=1}^{N} \alpha_t(i) a_{ij}, j \in [1, N], t \in [1, T] \tag{2c}$$

$$\beta_T(i) = 1, i \in [1, N] \tag{2d}$$

$$\beta_t(i) = \sum_{j=1}^{N} \beta_{t+1}(j) a_{ij} b_j(o_{t+1}), i \in [1, N], t \in [1, T-1] \tag{2e}$$

$$\frac{\partial J}{\partial \pi_i} = -\frac{1}{L_{tot}} \beta_1(i) b_i(o_1) \tag{2f}$$

$$\frac{\partial J}{\partial a_{ij}} = -\frac{1}{L_{tot}} \sum_{t=2}^{T} \beta_t(j) b_j(o_t) \alpha_{t-1}(i) \tag{2g}$$

$$\frac{\partial J}{\partial b_j(o_t)} = -\frac{1}{L_{tot}} \frac{\alpha_t(j)\beta_t(j)}{b_j(o_t)} \tag{2h}$$

$$\tag{2i}$$

We have defined how to compute gradients with respect to traditional BKT parameters. To introduce student-specific parameters we *split* the skill-specific BKT parameters into two components the following way. Using w to substitute for each of the corresponding skill-specific BKT parameters (π_i, a_{ij}, or $b_j(m)$), we define it in terms of both student- and skill-specific parameters as shown in Equation 3a. Here, w^k is the skill-specific component of the parameter, w^u is the student-specific component, $l(p) = log[p/(1-p)]$ is a logit function, and $\sigma(x) = 1/(1+e^{-x})$ is a sigmoid function (inverse of logit). Not that in summing logistic functions in Equation 3b to combine student and skill parameters we are incorporating the compensatory logic behind the IRT and AFM family of models [3,6]. Updating parameter gradients is possible using the chain rule (illustrated in Equation 3b for the student-specific component of the parameter w), since both the sigmoid and logit functions are differentiable.

$$w = \sigma(l(w^k) + l(w^u)) \quad (3a)$$

$$\frac{\partial J}{\partial w^u} = \frac{\partial J}{\partial w}\frac{\partial w}{\partial w^u} \quad (3b)$$

The importance of having all the gradients' derivations in Equations 2f to 2h is two-fold. First of all, freely available specialized HMM toolkits usually target general purpose Bayesian inference algorithms (most often EM) that are more computationally intensive. Second, without computing the gradients explicitly, a general-purpose optimization packages (part of tools like Matlab and R) would have to make computationally inefficient approximations.

3.2 Data

We used the datasets from the KDD Cup 2010 Educational Datamining Challenge (`http://pslcdatashop.web.cmu.edu/KDDCup`). The data was donated by Carnegie Learning Inc., a publisher of math curricula and a producer of intelligent tutoring systems for middle school and high school. There are two datasets, Algebra I, and Bridge to Algebra, both collected in 2008-2009 school year. Each dataset is a log of students' step-by-step performance (correctness and timing) during problem solving and was tagged with two alternative skill models.

The Algebra I dataset has 8,918,054 rows covering practice attempts of 3,310 students. 4,419,705 rows of the Algebra I dataset are tagged with 515 distinct skills from skill model 1 (used for problem sequencing in an ITS) and 6,442,137 rows are tagged with 541 distinct skills from an alternative skill model 2. The Bridge to Algebra dataset contains data of 6,043 students comprised of 20,012,498 rows, 11,239,188 and 12,350,449 of which are tagged with skills from skill model 1 (807 distinct skills) and model 2 (933 distinct skills) respectively. It is worth underlining the sheer size of each of the datasets. Except for the prior-per-student model reported in [5], none of the BKT models were ever tried on the dataset of this size, and prior-per-student has been individualized by using simple heuristics including random, correctness of first response defines the choice of one of two pre-set priors, and overall per-student percent correct.

3.3 Fitting Procedures

We created a tool capable of fitting and cross-validating standard and individualized BKT models using the derivations discussed in Section 3.1. To facilitate efficiency, it was implemented in C/C++. The tool is capable of fitting classical BKT models using the EM method, as well as fitting classical and individualized BKT models using the gradient descent method (using linear step size search) and a set of versions of conjugate gradient descent method.

We tested four different model variants on four different dataset-skill model combinations. We chose gradient descent method, since, although conjugate gradient methods are expected to yield better fits, the actual advantage was minimal to non-existent. When fitting individualized models, the coordinate descent method was used: two blocks of parameters – skill-specific and student-specific – by interleaving fits if one block at a time. The BKT model variants we fit were:

1. Standard BKT model,
2. Individualized BKT with student-specific $p(L_0)$,
3. Individualized BKT with student-specific $p(T)$,
4. Individualized BKT with student-specific $p(L_0)$ and $p(T)$.

While constructing the models, we constrained model values for all guess and slip parameters to prevent the occurrence of a phenomenon called model degeneracy (cf. [7]). All of the models were cross-validated using 10 randomly assigned user-stratified folds. For each of the cross-validation results we computed root mean squared error (RMSE) and accuracy (number of correctly predicted student successes and failures).

Our tool is implemented to handle large datasets in an efficient manner. For example, 10-fold cross-validation of the simplest standard BKT model on Algebra I dataset with skill model 1 takes under 2.5 minutes, for the most complex model 4 in the list above on the larger Bridge to Algebra dataset and skill model 2 the running time is under 70 minutes.

4 Results

Table 2 is a summary of cross-validation results for the standard BKT and the three individualized BKT models. For each dataset - skill model pair, in addition to RMSE and Accuracy, the contrasts to other BKT model variants are given in terms of fewer/more correct predictions. The correctness is computed using model's prediction (rounded toward 0 or 1 using 0.5 as threshold) and the actual correctness of student step in the data.

Across both datasets and both skill models, student-specific a priori probability of mastery ($p(L_0)$) in model 2 has no effect on model performance. On the other hand, introduction of student specific speed of learning ($p(T)$) in model 3 results in a consistent and more pronounced advantage over models 1 and 2. Moreover, the improvement in model accuracy resulting from adding individualized $p(L_0)$ on top of individualized $p(T)$ (going from model 3 to model 4) is even smaller than when adding individualized $p(L_0)$ to the standard BKT model (going from model 1 to model 2), despite the fact that model 3 has half as many student specific parameters as model 4. Given that, model 3 with individualized $p(T)$ can be considered superior to the standard BKT and other individualized models.

Bear in mind that results in Table 2 are for student-stratified validation. Namely, individualized BKT models are making predictions on data from unseen students unable to use their learnt student-specific parameters. Considering a potential operationalization of our findings, this shows a valuable property of model 3 (and model 4): producing *cleaner* skill-specific parameters (read, devoid of student-specific noise/variability). In an incremental ITS design cycle it would mean that, even if the core system only has a standard BKT implemented, it is

Table 2. Model cross-validation statistics for datasets Algebra I (A) and Bridge to Algebra (B) and skill models 1 and 2. Subscripts next to RMSE and Accuracy denote respective rank. The correct predictions difference tables show how many more correct predictions a model in the row makes over the model in the column header (a negative number means a model makes fewer correct predictions).

(a) Dataset A, skill model 1

model	RMSE	Accuracy	Correct rows	Correct predictions difference model 1	model 2	model 3	model 4
1	0.36273^4	0.827550^3	3,657,527	0	348	-6232	-5972
2	0.36265^3	0.827471^4	3,657,179	-348	0	-6580	-6320
3	0.36116^1	0.828960^1	3,663,759	6232	6580	0	260
4	0.36119^2	0.828901^2	3,663,499	5972	6320	-260	0

(b) Dataset A, skill model 2

model	RMSE	Accuracy	Correct rows	Correct predictions difference model 1	model 2	model 3	model 4
1	0.34187^4	0.84914^3	5,470,279	0	783	-6390	-6594
2	0.34180^3	0.84902^4	5,469,496	-783	0	-7173	-7377
3	0.34065^2	0.85013^2	5,476,669	6390	7173	0	-204
4	0.34060^1	0.85016^1	5,476,873	6594	7377	204	0

(c) Dataset B, skill model 1

model	RMSE	Accuracy	Correct rows	Correct predictions difference model 1	model 2	model 3	model 4
1	0.36294^4	0.82261^4	9,245,493	0	-6638	-78249	-76805
2	0.36255^3	0.82320^3	9,252,131	6638	0	-71611	-70167
3	0.35851^1	0.82957^1	9,323,742	78249	71611	0	1444
4	0.35854^2	0.82945^2	9,322,298	76805	70167	-1444	0

(d) Dataset B, skill model 2

model	RMSE	Accuracy	Correct rows	Correct predictions difference model 1	model 2	model 3	model 4
1	0.35895^4	0.82757^4	10,220,891	0	-7122	-78339	-77993
2	0.35857^3	0.82815^3	10,228,013	7122	0	-71217	-70871
3	0.35484^2	0.83392^2	10,299,230	78339	71217	0	346
4	0.35482^1	0.83389^1	10,298,884	77993	70871	-346	0

possible to improve overall student model accuracy by incrementally updating the skill-specific weights once a new group of students finishes a course or a course unit.

5 Conclusions

In this paper we presented an approach to building individualized Bayesian Knowledge Tracing models that are capable of accounting for student differences with respect to initial mastery probabilities and skill learning probabilities. Our approach does not require the underlying Hidden Markov Model to be changed. It is based on gradients of prior (Π), transition (A), and observation (B) parameter matrices and can be used together with a wide range of existing gradient descent algorithms. Our own implementation includes a conjugate gradient method with a variety of kernel formulas for computing the direction of parameter updates.

As we were able to show, our implementation of individualized BKT models is capable of tangibly improving the accuracy of predicting the success of student work in an intelligent tutoring system. An interesting finding was that adding student-specific probability of learning (*pLearn*) is more beneficial for the model accuracy than adding student-specific probability of initial mastery (*pInit*). In an alternative realm of models of learning practice that are based on logistic regression (for example, Item Response Theory), the analog of initial probability of mastery is student proficiency, which is thought to be critical for the model performance. Could it be in those models that individualizing learning rate is better than individualizing proficiency.

It is out intent to continue developing the instrumental framework for fitting standard and individualized BKT models as well as to persist with its empirical evaluation on real-world and synthetic datasets. As part of this work we intend to include item-stratified and unstratified cross-validation to the currently implemented student-stratified and to extend individualization features to currently not covered observation matrix parameters – *pSlip* and *pGuess*.

Acknowledgments. This research was supported by the Learnlab DataShop team, Carnegie Learning Inc., and National Science Foundation (NSF award #SBE-0836012).

References

1. Corbett, A.T., Anderson, J.R.: Knowledge tracing: Modeling the acquisition of procedural knowledge. User Modeling and User-Adapted Interaction 4(4), 253–278 (1995)
2. Levinson, S.E., Rabiner, L.R., Sondhi, M.M.: An Introduction to the Application of the Theory of Probabilistic Functions of a Markov Process to Automatic Speech Recognition. Bell System Technical Journal 62(4), 1035–1074 (1983)
3. van der Linden, W.J., Hambleton, R.K.: Handbook of Modern Item Response Theory. Springer, New York (1997)
4. Yudelson, M., Pavlik Jr., P.I., Koedinger, K.R.: User Modeling – A Notoriously Black Art. In: Konstan, J.A., Conejo, R., Marzo, J.L., Oliver, N. (eds.) UMAP 2011. LNCS, vol. 6787, pp. 317–328. Springer, Heidelberg (2011)

5. Pardos, Z.A., Heffernan, N.T.: Modeling Individualization in a Bayesian Networks Implementation of Knowledge Tracing. In: De Bra, P., Kobsa, A., Chin, D. (eds.) UMAP 2010. LNCS, vol. 6075, pp. 255–266. Springer, Heidelberg (2010)
6. Cen, H., Koedinger, K.R., Junker, B.: Comparing Two IRT Models for Conjunctive Skills. In: Woolf, B.P., Aïmeur, E., Nkambou, R., Lajoie, S. (eds.) ITS 2008. LNCS, vol. 5091, pp. 796–798. Springer, Heidelberg (2008)
7. Baker, R.S.J., Corbett, A.T., Aleven, V.: More Accurate Student Modeling through Contextual Estimation of Slip and Guess Probabilities in Bayesian Knowledge Tracing. In: Woolf, B.P., Aïmeur, E., Nkambou, R., Lajoie, S. (eds.) ITS 2008. LNCS, vol. 5091, pp. 406–415. Springer, Heidelberg (2008)
8. Lee, J.I., Brunskill, E.: The Impact on Individualizing Student Models on Necessary Practice Opportunities. In: Yacef, K., Zaïane, O.R., Hershkovitz, A., Yudelson, M., Stamper, J.C. (eds.) Proceedings of the 5th International Conference on Educational Data Mining (EDM 2012), pp. 118–125 (2012)

Extending Knowledge Tracing to Allow Partial Credit: Using Continuous versus Binary Nodes

Yutao Wang and Neil Heffernan

Worcester Polytechnic Institute
{yutaowang,nth}@wpi.edu

Abstract. Both Knowledge Tracing and Performance Factors Analysis, are examples of student modeling frameworks commonly used in AIED systems (i.e., Intelligent Tutoring Systems). Both of them use student correctness as a binary input, but student performance on a question might better be represented with a continuous value representing a type of partial credit. Intuitively, a student who has to make more attempts, or has to ask for more hints, deserves a score closer to zero, while students who asks for no hints and just needs to make a second attempt on a question should get a score close to one. In this work, we present a simple change to the Knowledge Tracing model and a simple (non-optimized) method for assigning partial credit. We report our real data experiment result in which we compared the original Knowledge Tracing (OKT) model with this new Knowledge Tracing model that uses partial credit as input (KTPC). The new model outperforms the traditional model reliably. The practical implication of this work is that this new technique can be widely used easily, as it is a small change from the traditional way of fitting KT models.

Keywords: Knowledge Tracing, Intelligent Tutoring Systems, Student Responses, Partial Credit.

1 Introduction

In many important student models, such as the Knowledge Tracing model and the Performance Factor Analysis (Pavlik, Cen and Koedinger 2009), student performance is presented as a binary value of correct or incorrect. The amount of assistance a student needed to eventually get a problem correct is ignored in these models. Feng and Heffernan (2010) showed that we can predict student performance better by accounting for amount of assistance they received, but they did not provide the field with a model that could be used in "run time" to predict individual responses. Arroyo, et al.(2010) showed how to use this information to predict learning gains. Their work suggests that using hints and attempts to model student behavior online could be effective.

There is good work in the psychometric literature on using partial credit, which goes back 30 years. Psychometricians have shown that different multiple choice answers might worth different credits [6, 10]. For instance, choice A might be totally wrong but choice B is close, choice C is the correct answer.

K. Yacef et al. (Eds.): AIED 2013, LNAI 7926, pp. 181–188, 2013.

More recently, a new type of partial credit is coming online. For instance, Attila and Powers (2010) at the Educational Testing Service showed they could better predict student GRE scores if they let students make multiple attempts. Their score on a question would go down by a third for each attempt (students could only make three attempts). Our work generalizes their work in two ways. First, we show how to incorporate the partial credit score into a model with learning (i.e., Knowledge Tracing) as their model did not model learning. Second, we show how to incorporate penalties for each hint student request.

In our previous work (Wang and Heffernan, 2010), we presented a naïve algorithm to assign partial credit, and showed it accounts for some variance in student knowledge. But in that work, we did not present a model that could do this task. In this paper we want to see if we can improve one of the dominant methods of student modeling (i.e., the Knowledge Tracing model) by relaxing the assumption of binary correctness: replacing the discrete performance node with continuous partial credit node.

In the next section, we describe our modification to the original Knowledge Tracing (OKT) model, and the method we use to make the correctness continuous. Section 3 describes the tutoring system and dataset used in our experiments and the experiment result. In Sections 5 and 6 we discuss our conclusions and future directions for our work.

2 Approach

2.1 Knowledge Tracing with Continuous Performance Node

The Knowledge Tracing model shown in Fig.1 has been widely used in ITS to model student knowledge and learning over time. It has become the dominant method of student modeling and many variants have been developed to improve its performance (Baker et al., 2010, Pardos and Heffernan 2010). Knowledge Tracing uses one latent and one observable dynamic Bayesian network to model student learning. As shown in Fig.1, four parameters are used for each skill, with two for student knowledge (initial knowledge and probability of learning the skill) and the other two for student performance (the probability of guessing correctly when the student doesn't know the skill and the probability of slipping when the student does know the skill).

The structure of the Knowledge Tracing model with a continuous performance node is the same as the original Knowledge Tracing model. The only difference is how we set up the "Student Performance" node. The idea is straight forward, yet there has never been positive result reported in this field. Some other Intelligent Tutoring System groups, such as LISTEN (http://www.cs.cmu.edu/~listen/) tried this approach before but failed for unknown reasons.

In this model, instead of assign the "*Guess*" and "*Slip*" parameters in a CPT table as the original Knowledge Tracing model, we assigned two Gaussian distributions for "*Guess*" and "*Slip*" with given standard deviations. Four parameters: *guess_mu*, *guess_sigma*, *slip_mu*, *slip_sigma*, are used to describe the two Gaussian distributions.

Similarly, when we predict student performance, we also get a Gaussian distribution with a mean value and a standard deviation value, in which the mean value will be the prediction and the standard deviation contains the information of how good the prediction is. In this work, we are not using the standard deviation of the prediction, but it has potential to be useful in the future to determine how confident we are in our prediction.

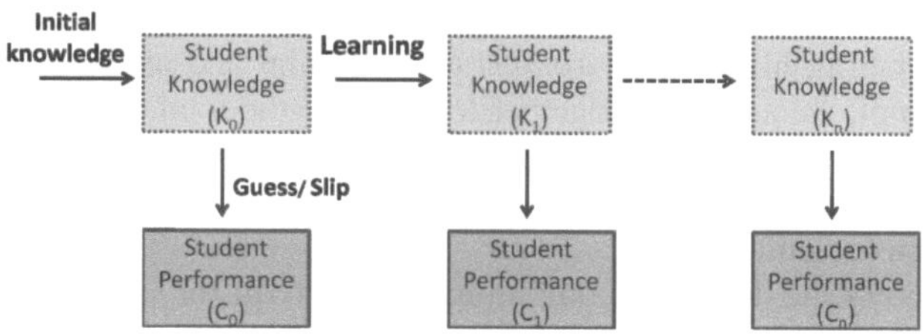

Fig. 1. Knowledge Tracing model
(Figure comes from Gong, Beck et al. 2010)

In our experiment, we used the Bayes Net Toolbox for Matlab developed by Murphy (2001) to implement Knowledge Tracing and the Expectation Maximization (EM) algorithm. The EM algorithm finds a set of parameters that maximizes the likelihood of the data. Since EM can be sensitive to initial conditions (Pardos and Heffernan 2010b), we report the initial settings. We used *initial knowledge* = 0.5, *learning* = 0.1, *guess_mu* = 0.1, *guess_sigma* = 0.02, *slip_mu* = 0.1, *slip_sigma* = 0.02 for the KTPC model, and *knowledge* = 0.5, *learning* = 0.1, *guess* = 0.1, *slip* = 0.1 for the OKT model.

2.2 Make the Correctness Continuous: Partial Credit

Partial credit can be assigned in different ways. In our experiment, we are using the algorithm that was mentioned in our previous poster [11] to make the correctness to be continuous. Since we never introduce the algorithm completely, it is described in this section in detail.

In a model with binary performance, a student would get a '1' if he/she answered the problem correctly on the attempt without asking for a hint and '0' otherwise. For the purpose of this paper we "made up" a scoring method that would give students a score between '0' and '1' according to how many attempts and how many hints they required to answer a question correctly based on intuition. We are well aware that this method could be optimized in lots of ways, for example, should each hint cost the same, or should the first hint cost less? As shown in our result, this simple method is effective and we leave to others different ways to optimize it.

Intuitively, the more hints that are asked for, the less likely it is that the student understands the skill, so we penalize a student for each hint asked for by what we call the hint penalty, which is 1 divided by the total number of hints available. For example, if there are 4 hints possible and a student asks for three of them and then gets the problem correct he/she would get a .25 score. In a similar manner, more attempts indicate a lower possibility of understanding the required skill, and we penalize each attempt. The size of the penalty depends upon whether the question type is "multiple choice" or "Fill in the Blank". In our data set, we have about 80% questions that are "Fill in the Blank" questions, for which we picked a penalty 0.1 for each wrong attempt. For multiple choice questions with x choices, the penalty was computed by one over the number of remaining multiple choice options minus one. So a true false question will have a penalty of one if a student guessed wrong. If there were 4 choices, a student's first wrong attempt would get a penalty of 1/3, a second wrong attempt would get a penalty of ½, and a third wrong attempt would get a penalty of 1.

After computing hint penalty (*phint*) for each hint and attempt penalty (*pattempt*) for each attempt, we add them together to compute the total hint penalty (*total_phint*) and the total attempt penalty (*total_pattempt*) for this problem. If the number is less than zero we make it zero. The last column of Table 2 shows two examples of formula doing this calculation.

Table 1 shows the details of computing partial credit for scaffolding questions. Our dataset has a special type of feedback called scaffolding. Since it's only a small amount of our data this detail might not be that important. But for completeness, we wanted to describe this. (Please note that all of our code and data are available at *http://users.wpi.edu/~yutaowang/* so that others can attempt to improve upon our work). For those problems with scaffolding questions, if a student gets the original question wrong, the system will give the student a series of questions we call "scaffolding" that walk the student through the steps. Each of these scaffolding questions has hints and so can be scored with this partial credit function just like normal questions. The only question left is how to score the "original question". If a student gets a question wrong and is given three scaffolding questions, the total credit of the whole problem is computed by averaging the partial credit scores of the three scaffolding questions and penalized by 10% for answering the original question incorrectly. If a student got the original question wrong but then got all the scaffolding questions correct, he/she should get a score close to 1, which in our method would be 0.9. Again these parameters such as 0.9 are not optimized and could be learned from data in future work.

Table 1. The algorithm of computing partial credit

```
function pc = partial_credit(problem){

    if first attempt correct then
        return pc = 1
    else if problem has no scaffold then
        pc = 1 - #hint * phint – total_pattempt
        if pc<0 then return pc = 0
        return pc
    else
        for each scaffold question i in the problem do
            pc_scaffold(i)  =  partial_credit(scaffold(i))
        end for
        pc = 0.9 * average(pc_scaffold(i))
        return pc
}
```

The algorithm is used only for testing the effect of relaxing the assumption of binary correctness in a Knowledge Tracing model.

3 Evaluation

3.1 The Tutoring System and Dataset

Our dataset consisted of student responses from ASSISTments, a web based tutoring system for 7th-12th grade students that provides preparation for the state standardized test by using released math items from previous years' tests as questions. The tutorial helps the student learn the required knowledge by breaking the problem into sub questions called scaffolding or giving the student hints on how to solve the question. Fig.2. shows an example of a hint. A second type of assistance is presented if the student clicks on (or types in) an incorrect answer, at which point the student is given feedback that he/she answered incorrectly (sometimes, but by no means always, the student will get a context-sensitive message called "buggy message"). Examples can be seen at "tinyurl.com/buaesc2".

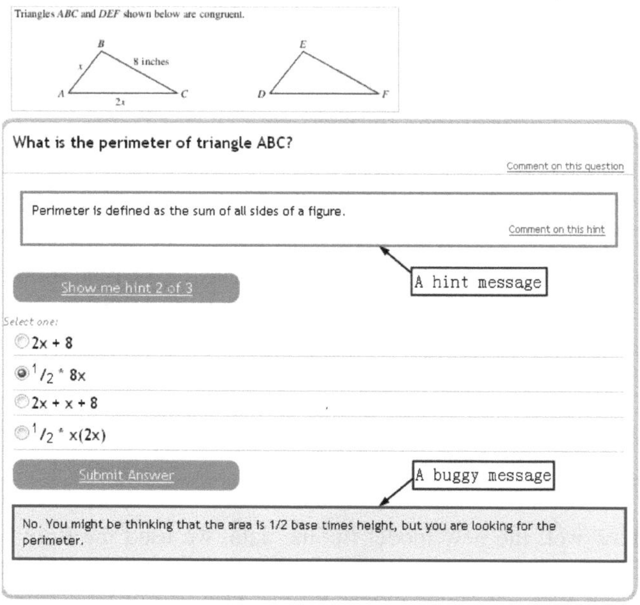

Fig. 2. Assistance in ASSISTment

The data we analyzed was drawn from ASSISTments. It comes from 72 twelve-through fourteen-year old 8th grade students in a school district of the Northeast United States. There were 106 skills (e.g., area of polygon, Venn diagram, division, etc.) that students were working on. The data consisted of 52,529 log records during the period Jan 2009-Feb 2009 where each log record is similar to one row in Table 2, which shows the details of one problem done by one student. We use the same data format as the KDD

Cup 2010: Educational Data Mining Challenge (https://pslcdatashop.web.cmu.edu/KDDCup/FAQ/#data-format). Table 2 shows an example of the type of data we used. There are in total 12 columns, the first 9 columns in the table are straight from the KDD Cup data format (https://pslcdatashop.web. cmu.edu/KDDCup/rules_data_format.jsp), and we added three extra columns, which are used for partial credit. In particular, column 10 "Number of Choices (if Multiple Choice)" was added to describe if the problem is multiple choice problem or not, and how many choices there are. Total number of hints available for the problem is put in column 11, to help compute the partial penalty per hint. The last hint always gives away the answer, so if a student asked for all of the hints, their score should be zero. This column allows us to give a bigger penalty for hints if the number of total available hints is small. Column 12 is for showing how we compute the partial credit score, a continuous value between 0 and 1 that the student would get given the data log. Note that the original KT model will only use the 7th column, "Error Rate", as model input; while the KT with partial credit model will only use the 12th column, "Partial Credit". The 7th column is generated as 1 if the student answered the problem correctly, otherwise 0.

Table 2. An example of a few rows of data, showing how we calculate partial credit

1.Row	2.Student	3.Problem	4.Step	5.Incorrects	6.Hints	7.Error Rate
1	S01	WATERING _VEGGIES	(WATERED-AREA Q1)	0	0	0
2	S01	WATERING _VEGGIES	(TOTAL-GARDEN Q1)	2	1	1

8.Knowledge component	9.Opportunity Count	10.Number of Choices (If Multiple Choice)	11.Total Hints Available	12.Partial Credit
Circle-Area	1	4 Choice Multiple Choice	2	1
Rectangle-Area	1	Fill in the Blank	3	1-2*0.1-1*1/3=0.46

3.2 Results

To evaluate how well the new model fits the data, we used the Root Mean Squared Error (RMSE) to examine the predictive performance on an unseen test set. Lower values for RMSE indicate better model fitting. There were randomly 2,313 student data in the test set and 3,297 students in the training set.

Table 3 shows the result of the comparison of the two different models, the original Knowledge Tracing(OKT) model and the Knowledge Tracing with partial credit(KTPC) model.

We compared the RMSE in predicting the partial credit performance and in predicting the traditional binary performance respectively. The Knowledge Tracing with partial credit model has lower RMSE value in both situations. The lower left column shows that KTPC does a great job in predicting partial credit scores, which is expected. The top left cell shows that OKT can do some reasonable job of predicting partial credit scores. The more interesting result is the right column, which shows that OKT has higher RMSE than the KTPC in predicting binary performances.

Table 3. Original KT (OKT) vs KT with partial credit (KTPC)

Model	**RMSE**	
	Partial Credit	**Binary Performance**
OKT	0.4128	0.4637
KTPC	0.2824	0.4572

We determined whether the difference between these two models is statistically reliable by computing the RMSE value for each student to account for the non-independence of student actions, and then compared these two models using a two tailed paired t-test.

The t-test p value of the RMSE between using the original Knowledge Tracing model and the Knowledge Tracing with partial credit model to predict the partial credit is 0. The p value between using the original Knowledge Tracing model and the Knowledge Tracing with partial credit model to predict the binary performance is $p<.001$. The degree of freedom of the t-test is 2,312 (since we are doing a student level t-test, the degree of freedom is the same as the number of students in the test set). Thus, the Knowledge Tracing with partial credit model is statistically reliably better at predicting student performance than the original Knowledge Tracing model.

4 Conclusions and Future Work

In this paper, we extended Bayesian Network student modeling to include continuous performance node. The effectiveness is demonstrated by incorporating a partial credit algorithm that assigns continuous performance given detailed student responses. Experiment results show that relaxing the assumption of binary correctness in student modeling can help improve predictions of student performance. This also proves that our intuition based heuristic for partial credit might be broadly applicable.

One topic we are interested in exploring is other partial credit schemes, for example, a method to refine the algorithm to generate partial credits that can better fit student data and more accurately infer student knowledge. Also, since we observed some abnormal parameters in the performance parameters (guess/slip), we are interested in finding out why the parameters are so different compare to normal Knowledge Tracing model.

5 Contributions

Moving from binary performance to continuous performance could make Intelligent Tutoring Systems more flexible. In this paper, on one hand, we extended the Knowledge Tracing framework to include a continuous performance node. This allows the Knowledge Tracing model to combine with all possible continuous performances such as essay score, speech recognition score. On the other hand, we presented an understandable and easy to refine algorithm to assign partial credit according to detailed student responses. This algorithm is one of many possible ways to convert student detailed responses into a continuous value.

The model presented in this paper enhanced student model accuracy by improving upon the classic Knowledge Tracing model. The result shows that the new model makes statistical reliably improvement in predicting both students' partial credit performances and binary performances. Also, freely available code is shared online, which could be useful for researchers that are trying to do the same task.

Acknowledgements. This research was made possible by the U.S. Department of Education, Institute of Education Science (IES) grants #R305K03140 and #R305A070440, the Office of Naval Research grant # N00014-03-1-0221, NSF CAREER award to Neil Heffernan, and the Spencer Foundation. All the opinions, findings, and conclusions expressed in this article are those of the authors, and do not reflect the views of any of the funders.

References

1. Arroyo, I., Cooper, D.G., Burleson, W., Woolf, B.P.: Bayesian Networks and Linear Regression Models of Students' Goals, Moods, and Emotions. In: Handbook of Educational Data Mining, pp. 323–338. CRC Press, Boca Raton (2010)
2. Attali, Y., Powers, D.: Immediate feedback and opportunity to revise answers to open-end questions. Educational and Psychological Measures 70(1), 22–35 (2010)
3. Baker, R.S.J.d., Corbett, A.T., Gowda, S.M., Wagner, A.Z., MacLaren, B.A., Kauffman, L.R., Mitchell, A.P., Giguere, S.: Contextual Slip and Prediction of Student Performance after Use of an Intelligent Tutor. In: De Bra, P., Kobsa, A., Chin, D. (eds.) UMAP 2010. LNCS, vol. 6075, pp. 52–63. Springer, Heidelberg (2010)
4. Corbett, A., Anderson, J.: Knowledge Tracing: Modeling the Acquisition of Procedural Knowledge. User Modeling and User-Adapted Interaction 4, 253–278 (1995)
5. Feng, M., Heffernan, N.: Can We Get Better Assessment from a Tutoring System Compared to Traditional Paper Testing? Can We Have Our Cake (Better Assessment) and Eat It too (Student Learning during the Test)? In: Aleven, V., Kay, J., Mostow, J. (eds.) ITS 2010, Part II. LNCS, vol. 6095, pp. 309–311. Springer, Heidelberg (2010)
6. Masters, G.N.: A rasch model for partial credit scoring. Psychometrica 47, 149–174 (1982)
7. Pardos, Z.A., Heffernan, N.T.: Modeling individualization in a bayesian networks implementation of knowledge tracing. In: De Bra, P., Kobsa, A., Chin, D. (eds.) UMAP 2010. LNCS, vol. 6075, pp. 255–266. Springer, Heidelberg (2010a)
8. Pardos, Z.A., Heffernan, N.T.: Navigating the parameter space of Bayesian Knowledge Tracing models: Visualization of the convergence of the Expectation Maximization algorithm. In: Proceedings of the 3rd International Conference on EDM (2010b)
9. Pavlik, P.I., Cen, H., Koedinger, K.: Performance Factors Analysis – A New Alternative to Knowledge. In: Proceedings of the 14th International Conference on Artificial Intelligence in Education, pp. 531–538 (2009)
10. Tang, K.L.: Polytomous item response theory (IRT) models and their applications in large-scale testing problems: Review of the literature. Educational Testing Service Technical Report (1996), http://www.ets.org/Media/Research/pdf/RM-96-08.pdf
11. Wang, Y., Heffernan, N.T., Beck, J.E.: Representing Student Performance with Partial Credit. In: Proceedings of the 3rd International Conference on Educational Data Mining, Pittsburgh, PA (2010)

Using Learner Modeling to Determine Effective Conditions of Learning for Optimal Transfer

Jaclyn K. Maass and Philip I. Pavlik Jr.

Institute for Intelligent Systems and Department of Psychology, University of Memphis, Memphis, TN, USA
{jkmaass,ppavlik}@memphis.edu

Abstract. Semantic network theories of knowledge organization support the idea that recall of organized information depends on how well a learner encodes the connections between the items in the semantic network. However, there is need for more research into what this implies for configuring instruction so that strong semantic network learning is supported with the goal of creating an integrated mental model in the student's mind. We investigate this question in the context of map learning, where country names are encoded relative to geographic border, internal features, or external features. The main hypothesis was that external features as cues would encourage transfer, since students would practice a network of relationships. The results primarily supported a theory of "cue reinstatement", where transfer occurred when cues present at learning were present at testing. These effects were analyzed with a mixed effects logistic regression learner model of trial-by-trial learning.

Keywords: Learner modeling, transfer, contextual effects, student strategies.

1 Introduction

1.1 Semantic Network Models

In the original theory of a cognitive network model set by Collins and Quillian [1], the basic components were nodes, which held concepts or words, and links, which connected the nodes and encoded relationships between them. Their original model was structured hierarchically with the number of links between nodes being negatively correlated with their degree of relatedness. In other words, the farther you had to travel from one node to another, the less similar those two concepts were said to be.

However, not all of the experimental evidence supported the Collins and Quillian model. Later experiments showed that rather than following a strictly hierarchical pattern, property and category verification times varied with the prototypicality of the probe item; the model lacked an ability to represent typicality [2]. These results spurred Collins and Loftus [3] to create a modified network model in which the strict hierarchical sense was stripped and the length of the link now represented the strength of the relationship between two nodes.

K. Yacef et al. (Eds.): AIED 2013, LNAI 7926, pp. 189–198, 2013.

Another set of research that highlights the importance of how we bundle the information we obtain is that of schemas and scripts [4-5]. Schema and script theories are based on the notion that knowledge is packaged in integrated conceptual structures. Scripts are typical action sequences (e.g., the characteristic routine for going to a restaurant) whereas schemas are specific organized knowledge structures (e.g., your knowledge of cognitive psychology). It is likely that both are encoded similarly but with the former referencing actions and the latter referencing features.

1.2 Categorical Organization

A related area of research involves organization by categories. There are many examples of studies showing the effect of categorization on learning. For example, in a Tulving and Pearlstone [6] study, subjects were taught words that were designated as belonging to different conceptual categories. The results showed that if you don't have cues during a time of recall, previously learnt organization (categorization) can be used as an implicit cue. This can also be explained by category knowledge spreading to enhance item recall and provides evidence that activating related information boosts recall and enhances learning.

Categorization and the organization of knowledge are important aspects of learning; for many cognitive psychologists, change of such structures is generally considered to be synonymous with learning [7]. The perspective of cognitive constructivism is widely regarded as a strong theory of knowledge acquisition which places upmost importance on the individual's active role in the learning process [7-8]. Much qualitative research exists on knowledge acquisition and how schemas are transformed and built as new information is acquired [9-10], but less quantitative research exists on how the constructivist approach is best implemented in learning environments [7]. It is one thing to say that knowledge is built upon previous knowledge, and new knowledge can either change a previous schema or create a new one, but it is quite another to explain what the best step by step actions are that lead to this. The current work does not intend to come up with an all-inclusive answer to this issue, but rather attempts to find some (of many) optimal conditions under which constructivist learning can occur.

1.3 Testing for Transferable Learning

A key aspect in the evaluation of learning gains is transfer of knowledge from one situation to another. Educators want students to be able to apply what they learn to situations that differ in context from what they were originally exposed to. Much research has been done on different learning environments that promote transfer. For example, studying problems: from multiple viewpoints [11], in a problem solving context [12], or with an emphasis on metacognition [13]. However, there seems to be less literature available on the effects of learning different network structures, or different levels of contextual information, on transfer, which is what the present study sought to investigate.

1.4 The Current Study

Based on this research, we know that information is organized, likely into semantic networks and categories. However, semantic network theories and categorization theories tell a different story about how learning might proceed in specific domains. One such domain is map learning, which the current study was centered around. With map learning, semantic network theory might suggest we need to build the relationships between the items in the network (countries in the map), while categorization theories may suggest that we need to build up examples within the category (cities/features in the country). The current experiment sought to expand research along these lines in an exploratory fashion by asking how learning the different components of the map stimuli would affect transfer to other stimuli with or without the same components that were presented during learning. This research sought to build upon constructivist ideas by providing insight into optimal sequencing of complex organized factual materials. The different stimuli components, which the learners may have used to learn the country names, were geographic border (shape), internal features (interior city cues), or external features (surrounding country cues). The main hypothesis favored a semantic network hypothesis, because the map domain seemed particularly well suited for network representation. We hypothesized that external features would encourage transfer, since the participants would practice a network of relationships with strong spreading activation.

2 Methods

2.1 Participants

Participants consisted of 75 (23 male; 52 female) University of Memphis undergraduate students who were enrolled in an Introductory Psychology course in the fall semester of 2012. Students participated in the experiment for course credit. Ages ranged from 18 to 58 years of age.

2.2 Materials

A computerized flashcard tutor on world countries, built using the FaCT (Fact and Concept Training) System [14], was created in order to test the effect of using different cues from within a network on learning. The countries stimuli originated from the United States Central Intelligence Agency [15] and included an image of the target country, with its interior cities, capitals, and deserts labeled (herein referred to as interior city cues). Immediate surrounding countries, without their interior cities, were also labeled (herein referred to as surrounding country cues). The countries stimuli were chosen due to their applied educational nature as well as their clearly defined levels of contextual information within the network (interior cities and exterior, surrounding countries). The countries stimuli were also ideal due to the large amount of both interior and exterior contextual information available for cueing during learning and recall. The continent of Africa was selected as a result of having an adequate amount of countries with which to test participants. We separated the continent into Northern and Southern countries so that we could split the continent into two groups for counterbalancing the pretest and learning phases.

2.3 Procedure

The experiment consisted of three phases: a pretest, a tutoring or learning phase, and a posttest, all completed within a single one-hour session. The pretest lasted approximately five minutes, the tutoring phase 30 minutes, and the posttest approximately 15 minutes. All three were completed through a computer interface. The tutoring phase was a between-subjects 2 (presence of interior city cues) x 2 (presence of surrounding country cues) design. Therefore, the four conditions were interior city cues only, surrounding country cues only, all cues, and shape cues only. The shape cues only condition was with neither interior city cues nor surrounding country cues (i.e., with only the geographic borders, or shape, present).

The pretest consisted of eight of the 16 countries from either North or South Africa (counterbalanced) which were presented to the participants in random order in each of the four conditions for a total of 32 items. The directions instructed participants to enter in the name of the country in an answer box to the right of the country image on the computer screen. No corrective feedback was given during this phase.

The next phase, the tutoring phase, used the 16 African countries from whichever region was not used in the pretest in order to avoid carryover effects from the pretest. Participants were randomly assigned to one of the four conditions for this portion. The tutor gave corrective feedback during this phase. For incorrect responses, a period of review followed, providing the participants with the correct answer and allowing them to study the image with its correct country name. Each student decided when their review period would end, after which the next image would appear on the screen. This phase lasted for either 30 minutes or until the participant received 90 points (with one point given for each correct response). This was done as an incentive for students to try their best in the tutoring phase in order to possibly finish early.

The final phase was the posttest which was the same format as the pretest, but using the same region of Africa as was learnt during the tutoring phase as a measure of recall. Every participant was tested once on each of the four conditions of each of the 16 countries for a total of 64 test items. No corrective feedback was given. The dependent variable for all three phases was the number of correct responses. A short questionnaire was given after the posttest. The questionnaire consisted of an open-ended and a closed-ended question regarding strategy use as well as questions about demographics.

3 Results and Discussion

3.1 Repeated Measures ANOVA

The results of a repeated measures analysis of variance on the posttest with a 2 (presence of surrounding country cues during learning) x 2 (presence of interior city cues during learning) x 2 (North or South African region during learning and testing) x 2 (presence of surrounding country cues during testing) x 2 (presence of interior city cues during testing) design, using the pretest scores as a covariate, revealed a total of seven significant effects. Seventy-one participants produced usable data. Three participants' data were thrown out due to being two standard deviations below the mean score during the tutoring phase, and one for technical reasons. See Table 1 for means and standard deviations for the four conditions in each of the three experimental phases. There were two significant main effects: the presence of surrounding country cues during the tutoring session, F (1, 63) = 50.26, p = 1.40e^{-9}, and the presence of interior city cues during the tutoring session, F (1, 63) = 44.42, p = 7.64e^{-9}. In both cases, with surrounding country cues and interior city cues, participants performed better when the cues were present.

Four two-way interactions were detected. The presence of surrounding country cues during the tutoring phase interacted with the presence of surrounding country cues during the testing (posttest) phase, F (1, 63) = 50.26, p = 1.40e^{-9}. Those receiving surrounding country cues during tutoring performed better when they also received the surrounding country cues during testing. The presence of interior city cues during tutoring interacted with the presence of interior city cues during testing, F (1, 63) = 58.73, p = 1.38e^{-10}. This means that those who received interior city cues during tutoring had higher performance in the testing phase when they were given interior city cues again. It appears that in these two situations, participants relied on the types of cues they had seen during learning.

The presence of surrounding country cues during the tutoring phase interacted with the presence of interior city cues during the testing phase, F (1, 63) = 6.72, p = .012. Those receiving surrounding country cues during tutoring performed better on the posttest when not receiving interior city cues rather than when receiving interior city cues, but this effect is likely driven by the 3-way interaction, which is similar but more specific (see below). Also, the presence of interior city cues during the tutoring phase interacted with the presence of surrounding country cues in the testing phase, F (1, 63) = 5.22, p = .026. Those who received interior city cues in the tutoring phase performed worse than those who did not receive such cues during tutoring when presented with country cues during testing. This is most likely because in the all cues condition (which had interior city cues in tutoring) the students had to divide the learning benefit from additional cues among both cue sources in the stimuli. In other words, if training was with surrounding country cues only, more benefit was gained to the surrounding country cue testing condition than if learning attention was split across both types of cues.

There was also one significant three-way interaction between the presence of interior city cues during tutoring, surrounding country cues during tutoring, and interior city cues during testing, F (1, 63) = 5.81, p = .019. When testing on the no interior city cues items, those who had the interior city cues during learning performed very poorly, but when combined with surrounding country cue learning (the all cues condition), this deficit was greatly reduced. This supports the idea that interior city cues (or internal, featural cues in general) might not be best to learn first; apparently, if they are learned first, people come to rely on them, taking away from learning of the broader structure of the material.

Table 1. Means and Standard Deviations for Each Phase

Condition	Pretest Phase Mean *(SD)*	Tutoring Phase Mean *(SD)*	Posttest Phase Mean *(SD)*
Interior cues only	.0347 *(.055)*	.5569 *(.158)*	.5044 *(.139)*
Surrounding cues only	.0694 *(.125)*	.5647 *(.204)*	.5197 *(.185)*
All cues	.0368 *(.056)*	.6471 *(.138)*	.5864 *(.112)*
Shape cues only	.0399 *(.060)*	.5064 *(.181)*	.5012 *(.187)*

3.2 Learning Modeling Analysis

A logistic mixed effects model was created to analyze the transfer effects. This model was based on an Additive Factors Model (AFM) [16] where we predict subsequent trials in the sequence for each participant as a function of the count of prior practices. After testing various models, it became clear that we were getting the best performance out of a rather standard compensatory Q-matrix model of transfer following the Q-matrix in Table 2. In addition to this we found an improved AIC and BIC when we used a Performance Factors Analysis (PFA) model version which credits successes and failures with different learning effects [17]. We have broken up the task of naming countries into three basic knowledge component features: geographic borders, internal features, and external features. The Q-matrix in Table 2 indicates which knowledge component features are assigned to which conditions. A knowledge component is defined as any domain-specific information or concept that is necessary to complete a task [18], in this case naming the target country. The Q-matrix indicates that, for example, practice of any stimuli will cause learning of the geographic border component, while only surrounding country cues or all cues items provide practice with the external features component. Similarly, this matrix shows that if we test with a surrounding country cues item we apply prior practice from any items that caused either geographic border or external features learning.

Table 2. Matrix assigning knowledge component features to conditions

		Knowledge Component Features		
		Geographic Borders	Internal Features	External Features
Item Conditions	All Cues	1	1	1
	Shape only cues	1	0	0
	Surrounding country cues	1	0	1
	Interior city cues	1	1	0

Due to the different procedure and mixed stimuli (inclusion of all of the conditions) in the posttest, we also included an adjustment parameter in our model for our prediction of post-test trials. We expected the change in the posttest to mixed stimuli would make the overall posttest results a bit lower due to interference between items within the varied context of the posttest. Furthermore, our sum of prior practice did not include these posttest trials since they were not repeated and did not include feedback, nor did the sum of prior practice include pretest items since those items were for the other region of Africa. Finally, the model included correlated subject random effect intercepts and subject random effect learning slopes. Equation 1 summarizes the linear function for the logistic prediction.

$$\text{answer} = Y_{\text{Posttest}} + B_S + B_F + I_S + I_F + E_S + E_F + U + V \qquad \text{(Equation 1)}$$

where:

Y_{Posttest} – adjustment for posttest section
B_S – borders learning, after a correct response (success)
B_F – borders learning, after an incorrect response (failure)
I_S – internal feature learning, after a correct response (success)
I_F – internal feature learning, after an incorrect response (failure)
E_S – external features learning, after a correct response (success)
E_F – external features learning, after an incorrect response (failure)
U – random effect learning slope for each student
V – random effect intercept for each student

Seventy-one participants produced usable data. Four participants' data were thrown out for the same reasons as stated previously. Table 3 summarizes the parameter values from the final model. The final model had an R^2 equal to .29, with 15049 total observations. *AIC* was 15936 and *BIC* was 16020. While in the simple model (not shown) where we counted only number of opportunities and not success and failures, there was strong learning of all three knowledge components but significantly less learning (about 1/3 less) for interior cues, the PFA model in Table 3 shows a categorically different result.

Table 3. Summary of Fixed and Random Effects

Parameter	Parameter estimate	p-value†	
$\beta_{Posttest}$	-.42	$1.1e^{-06}$	***
B_S	.018	$< 2e^{-16}$	***
B_F	.0087	$7.6e^{-06}$	***
E_S	.012	$2.9e^{-06}$	***
E_F	.0066	.0098	**
I_S	.031	$< 2e^{-16}$	***
I_F	-.0025	0.35	
U_i	$1.7e^{-01}$		
V_i	$6.2e^{-05}$		

† Significance codes: . -$p \leq .1$, *-$p \leq .05$, **-$p \leq .01$, ***-$p \leq .001$

First, note that because the PFA model is stabilized by fitting random effects for both subject prior knowledge (intercept random effect) and for subject learning rate difference (slope random effect) the model might be expected to capture the actual learning difference between practice types, rather than tracking individual differences. Some main effects in Table 3 are quite clear. First we see that failure results in dramatically less learning overall (however this may be due to the procedure which allowed as little review study time for each drill as students chose). Second we see that geographic border learning is stronger (t = 1.91, p =.057) for successes compared to external features learning. While the effect is marginal, this implies that the country shape is more salient and perhaps more easily learned. This is similar to what we found in the simple model (not shown) mentioned above.

More interesting is the dramatic contrast revealed for success and failure with internal features. This result means that following a success when cities are present, there is strong learning of the cities knowledge. In contrast, when there is a failure of a trial with cities present, nothing is learned about the cities. This result seems to reveal that students do not find the internal cues to be that useful (perhaps because they are unfamiliar) and so do not study them during the review after an unsuccessful trial. However, they do show learning of these cues when answering correctly during the initial recall process. It appears that during this successful recall, participants were implicitly learning the city information and apparently strengthening its association with each stimulus.

This interesting finding has implications for sequencing learning of complex information. Specifically, it implies an order advantage for learning that begins by presenting organizational information (borders and external cues), since these cues are learned much more easily upon failure than the internal cues. In contrast, featural (internal cue) information seems to be better to present late in learning, since it appears to be picked up very easily once a person is responding correctly.

Due to the fact that standard cross-validation requires a held-out test fold, it conflicts with mixed-effect models which simultaneously estimate the random effects for the entire data set. Since cross validation works by showing that the pattern in the bulk of the data is similar to the pattern in the held out folds, we decided to validate our mixed-effect model using a similar but slightly weaker fold based process where we split the data into five folds to create five separate models. We did this 20 times with different fold randomizations to get a set of 100 estimates that allow us to bootstrap small sample confidence intervals for the parameters in small samples. Since other important effects in the model were confirmed by inferential statistics, we focused this comparison on validating the interesting difference for success and failure when learning with internal cues (having a difference of about .032). Validity of this important difference in small samples was confirmed, with interior success learning having a small-sample average coefficient of .0273 per trial (SE =.00149) and interior failure learning having a small-sample average coefficient of .00459 (SE =.00177).

4 Conclusions

In summary, our hypothesis that external features (i.e., surrounding country cues) would encourage transfer appears to be partially supported by aspects of both the repeated measures ANOVA and PFA model results. Both sets of results imply that presenting the shape and surrounding country cues early on, while students are still having more failures than successes might aid transfer since the external cues were found to be more helpful after incorrect responses than internal cues. After students had learned the overall structure of the material, their best strategy was to turn their focus to the specific features. This shift may be suggestive of implicit learning since the students cannot help but notice the internal features while using the other cues; they may then incorporate the internal features into learning in a more automatic fashion.

The results of the current experiment indicated that when students are first starting to study, and thus have a higher number of incorrect responses, the two conditions with less features showed a better effect on learning. In our model, once the students started to respond successfully (correctly) we began to see a benefit for those items high in internal features (specifically the interior city cue condition). These results may transfer into the use of advance organizers [20], which are used to start students off with more of the structural, organizational features of a topic prior to giving the specifics of that topic. These results support the notion that "the best test of advance organizers occurs when material is unfamiliar, technical or otherwise difficult for the learner to relate to his or her existing knowledge" (p.372) [20].

These conclusions may help to enhance constructivist theories by giving a more detailed quantitative account of how new knowledge should be added to existing knowledge. If replication can provide further support for the theories proposed by the current work, notions in the sequencing of learning materials may be enhanced by focusing on more abstract or structural features early in learning. It should be noted that we do not intend this sort of analysis to occur every time a researcher builds a learning system; rather, we are searching for a domain general model of complex display learning to be used in educational systems. The most logical next step for this line of research would be to test two ordering sequences, one being the recommended problem order (external cues prior to internal cues) and the other being a less preferred problem order, to test whether the preferred problem sequence yields significantly more transfer than the other sequencing. Another route for future work may include testing the current model of learning in a manner that is less applied, or less specific, than map learning. Future work may also benefit from training students in specific strategies as the current work did not control for students' strategies, thus limiting our conclusions about what conditions are optimal.

References

1. Collins, A.M., Quillian, M.R.: Retrieval Time from Semantic Memory. Journal of Verbal Learning and Verbal Behavior 8, 240–247 (1969)
2. Rogers, T.: Computational Models of Semantic Memory. In: The Cambridge Handbook of Computational Psychology, pp. 226–267. Cambridge University Press, Cambridge (2008)
3. Collins, A.M., Loftus, E.F.: A Spreading-Activation Theory of Semantic Processing. Psychological Review 82, 407–428 (1975)

4. Bartlett, F.C.: Remembering: A Study in Experimental and Social Psychology. Cambridge University Press, Cambridge (1932)
5. Schank, R.C., Abelson, R.P.: Scripts, Plans, Goals and Understanding: An Inquiry into Human Knowledge Structures. Erlbaum, Hillsdale (1977)
6. Tulving, E., Pearlstone, Z.: Availability Versus Accessibility of Information in Memory for Words. Journal of Verbal Learning & Verbal Behavior 5, 381–391 (1966)
7. Dole, J.A., Sinatra, G.M.: Reconceptualizing Change in the Cognitive Construction of Knowledge. Educational Psychologist 33, 109–128 (1998)
8. Cobb, P.: Constructivism in Mathematics and Science Education. Educational Researcher 23, 4 (1994)
9. Chi, M.T.: Conceptual Change within and across Ontological Categories: Examples from Learning and Discovery in Science. In: Cognitive Models of Science: Minnesota Studies in the Philosophy of Science, pp. 129–160 (1992)
10. Vosniadou, S., Brewer, W.F.: Theories of Knowledge Restructuring in Development. Review of Educational Research 57, 51–67 (1987)
11. Bransford, J.D., Vye, N., Kinzer, C., Risko, V.: Teaching Thinking and Content Knowledge: Toward an Integrated Approach. In: Jones, B.F., Idol, L. (eds.) Dimensions of Thinking and Cognitive Instruction: Implications for Educational Reform, vol. 1, pp. 381–413. Erlbaum, Hillsdale (1990)
12. Michael, A.L., Klee, T., Bransford, J.D., Warren, S.F.: The Transition Form Theory to Therapy: Test of Two Instructional Methods. Applied Cognitive Psychology 7, 139–153 (1993)
13. White, B.Y., Frederiksen, J.R.: Inquiry, Modeling, and Metacognition: Making Science Accessible to All Students. Cognition and Instruction 16, 3–118 (1998)
14. Pavlik Jr., P.I., Presson, N., Dozzi, G., Wu, S., MacWhinney, B., Koedinger, K.R.: The FaCT (Fact and Concept Training) System: A New Tool Linking Cognitive Science with Educators. In: McNamara, D., Trafton, G. (eds.) Proceedings of the Twenty-Ninth Annual Conference of the Cognitive Science Society, pp. 397–402. Lawrence Erlbaum, Mahwah (2007)
15. Central Intelligence Agency, `https://www.cia.gov/library/publications/the-world-factbook/`
16. Draney, K.L., Pirolli, P., Wilson, M.: A Measurement Model for a Complex Cognitive Skill. In: Nichols, P.D., Chipman, S.F., Brennan, R.L. (eds.) Cognitively Diagnostic Assessment, pp. 103–125 (1995)
17. Pavlik Jr., P.I., Cen, H., Koedinger, K.R.: Performance Factors Analysis – A New Alternative to Knowledge Tracing. In: Dimitrova, V., Mizoguchi, R., du Boulay, B., Graesser, A. (eds.) Proceedings of the 14th International Conference on Artificial Intelligence in Education, Brighton, England, pp. 531–538 (2009)
18. VanLehn, K.: The Behavior of Tutoring Systems. International Journal of Artificial Intelligence in Education 16, 227–265 (2006)
19. Son, J.Y., Smith, L.B., Goldstone, R.L.: Simplicity and Generalization: Short-Cutting Abstraction in Children's Object Categorizations. Cognition 108, 626 (2008)
20. Mayer, R.E.: Can Advance Organizers Influence Meaningful Learning? Review of Educational Research 49, 371–383 (1979)

Visualising Multiple Data Sources in an Independent Open Learner Model

Susan Bull[1], Matthew.D. Johnson[1], Mohammad Alotaibi[1], Will Byrne[1], and Gabi Cierniak[2]

[1] Electronic, Electrical and Computer Engineering, University of Birmingham, UK
[2] Knowledge Media Research Center, Tuebingen, Germany
s.bull@bham.ac.uk

Abstract. This paper introduces the Next-TELL independent open learner model which is constructed based on data from a range of sources. An example is presented for a university course, with the learner model built from the main activities undertaken during the course. Use of the Next-TELL open learner model over a five week period is described for this group of students, suggesting that independent open learner models built from multiple sources of data may have much to offer in supporting students' understanding of their learning, and could potentially be used to encourage greater peer interaction.

Keywords: Open learner model, multiple data sources, visualisation.

1 Introduction

Adaptive learning environments enable personalisation of the interaction to suit the needs of the individual student, according to the data in their learner model. Environments with an *open learner model* (OLM) allow that data to be externalised to the learner, in one or more learner model views that are user-interpretable [4]. *Independent OLMs* (IOLM) are not attached to a specific tutoring system: their focus is usually to facilitate metacognitive processes [6], where the learner takes decisions more traditionally handled by the tutoring component of an adaptive system. Aims of such visualisation of the learner model include raising learner awareness and prompting reflection on understanding and learning; acting as a starting point for planning; facilitating independent learning; encouraging collaborative interaction and problem-solving; and helping learners to take greater responsibility for their learning. These differ from the recent work on learning analytics and dashboards (see e.g. [24]) primarily in this focus on the learner model: learning analytics more typically show activity data (e.g. interaction time in forums; links in social networks; or a range of participation, usage or performance data).

Deployment of OLMs and IOLMs in university courses has recently become more prevalent (e.g. [5];[10];[13];[19];[21]). With the additional increasing use of a range of technologies in today's classrooms and beyond, recent work suggests bringing together data sources and learner modelling in novel ways. For example: a framework for exchanging learner profiles between various sources, including the evidence for

K. Yacef et al. (Eds.): AIED 2013, LNAI 7926, pp. 199–208, 2013.

data that will allow another system to interpret its meaning appropriately [11]; the combination of e-portfolios and IOLMs as a means to provide data for other learner models, thus requiring learner modelling across multiple applications [22]; a tool to integrate and edit models, which is supplemented with a separate OLM to interact with other learner models based on different learning resources - i.e. a generic approach [9]; and environments designed to include diverse data from different sources in the OLM [18];[20];[23]. In line with this direction of research, we introduce the Next-TELL (http://www.next-tell.eu/) IOLM built from multiple data sources, and present results from university students using the IOLM in practice, during a course.

2 The Next-TELL Independent Open Learner Model

The Next-TELL project integrates multiple aspects of teaching, from support for teachers' planning, use of an e-portfolio, to visualisations of the learner model to help students and instructors interpret information about learning, coming from a variety of sources [23]. This paper focuses on the latter area of the project. We present two aspects of the Next-TELL IOLM: the sources of data and the IOLM visualisations.

2.1 Data Sources

(I)OLMs have often been described with reference to a single activity or activity type, or in conjunction with a single system. As indicated above, there have been calls to incorporate different data sources in an OLM [18];[20]. We here consider students' use and acceptance of an IOLM based on multiple data sources. The course in which we illustrate the Next-TELL IOLM is an "Adaptive Learning Environments" course at university level. The activities providing data for the learner model were:

- Student self-assessments;
- OLMlets [5]: an open learner model based on multiple choice questions;
- Chat facility embedded into OLMlets;
- Facebook discussion of students' understanding as revealed by OLMlets;
- Students' text addressing core aspects of the course (revisions possible);
- Practice open-ended test questions (revisions possible);
- Test (open-ended questions) covering the complete course content.

The nature of the activities in this course mean that most require manual input to the learner model. The exception to this is OLMlets. However, at the time of the study, the API integration was not available, so the instructor manually input the OLMlets data to contribute to the Next-TELL model at intervals during the course, to illustrate the feasibility of combined manual and automated data. (Automated data transfer is now possible, as is use of the Next-TELL ProNIFA (probabilistic non-invasive formative assessment) tool to facilitate semi-automated input of data [7].

By default, the most recent data from the various sources has higher weighting, according to the following algorithm, but allows instructors to alter the weightings of the activities contributing to the learner model, using a slider.

new_value = new_data x depreciation_factor + old_value x (1 - depreciation_factor)

In addition to numerical data that contributes to the learner model (e.g. star input top of Figure 1, automatically generated Google spreadsheet centre of Figure 1), input may be in the form of text feedback from the instructor (relating to student strengths, and guidance for further development). This feedback is not transformed by the modelling process, but is available for viewing by the student, and used in conjunction with the model data it can support their understanding of their OLM. A hyperlink may also link to evidence supporting a specific assessment, for example, a learning-based artefact stored in the Next-TELL e-portfolio, in Moodle, or a Google document. Drilling down through the OLM will ultimately arrive at these artefacts. The bottom of Figure 1 illustrates how this feedback is displayed. In this case the numerical data indicated by the skill meters comes from a student's self assessment, with additional text feedback on strengths and further guidance from the instructor.

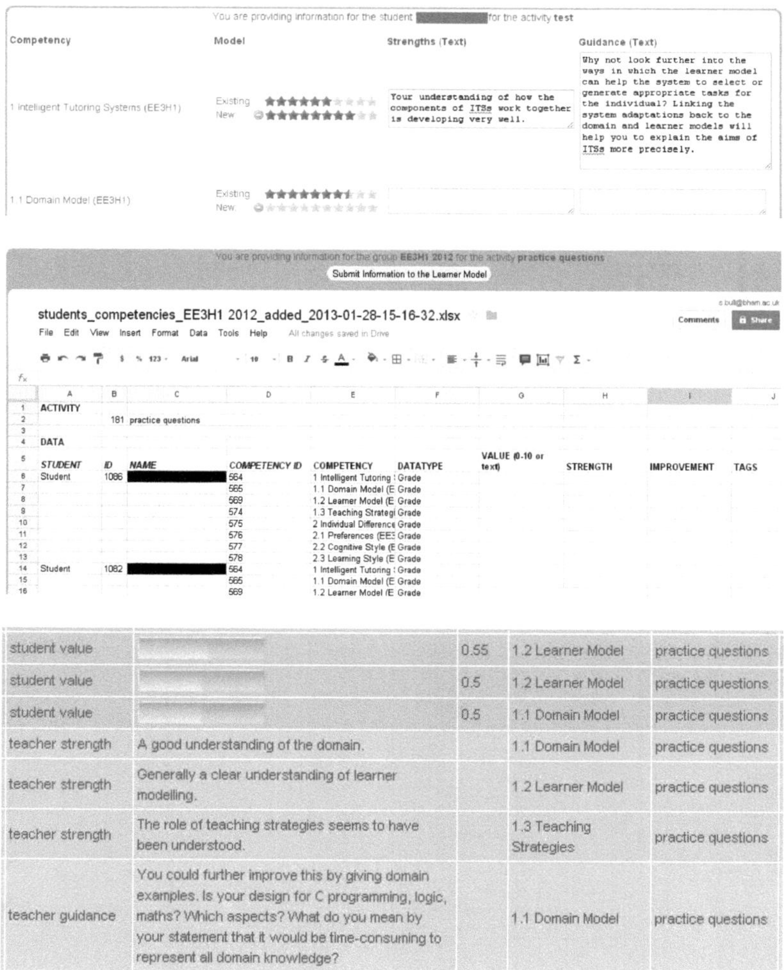

Fig. 1. Adding data manually to the OLM

2.2 Visualisation

Various OLM presentation examples have been described for university students in the literature. The most common visualisations used in courses include skill meters [5];[19];[25]; concept maps [16];[21]; and hierarchical tree structures [8];[14];[16]. Recently, tree map overview-zoom-filter approaches to open learner modelling have also appeared [2];[15]. However, there is, as yet, no generally agreed set of OLM visualisations and, indeed, this may depend on a variety of factors. For example, eye-tracking studies have suggested that the most useful visualisation may depend on the context in which the OLM is used [17]; or user preference for the visualisation itself [3]. Some preference towards skill meters over more complex visualisations has also been found [12]. The range of potential (human and technology-gathered) data sources in the Next-TELL context demands methods of model externalisation that can either be adapted according to the specific data sources, or methods that are sufficiently generic to be applicable in the range of cases. As previously argued for generic open learner model contexts [1], Next-TELL takes the latter approach.

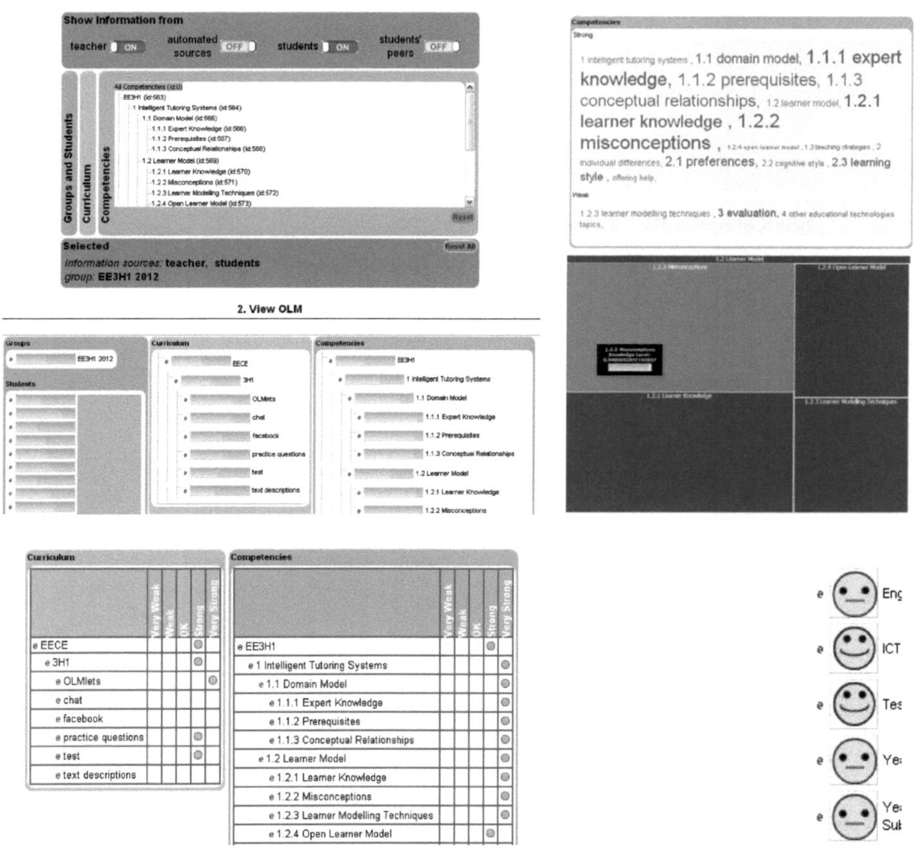

Fig. 2. Next-TELL OLM visualisations

Multiple views have previously been found useful, as learners do not necessarily have the same visualisation preferences, but appear able to select a method of viewing the learner model that suits their current task or purpose of inspecting their model [4]. The Next-TELL IOLM uses several visualisations, as illustrated in Figure 2. The skill meters are shown here as seen by the instructor, with the overview of level of understanding for each student shown in the left set of skill meters (student names are hidden); the level of contribution of each activity to the model in the centre; and the level of understanding of each topic in the skill meters on the right. Instructors can also view this information applied to a specific individual and/or activity and/or topic or competency; and students can see their own models in this way, using the filters above the skill meters (competency/topic is shown in Figure 2). The word cloud separates strongly from weakly (or not) understood topics. The topics in the upper group are coloured blue, with the relative level of understanding indicated by text size; the topics in the lower group are coloured red, with the weakest of these indicated by the larger size of the text. The treemap shows level of understanding of topics by the size of the corresponding square, with subtopics appearing in a similar way when a user clicks on a topic. The table illustrates the knowledge level of an individual student (here shown for a specific student), including the activity and topic/competency data. The smilies also show level of understanding (intended primarily for child users).

3 Students' Use of the Next-TELL OLM

This section presents a study investigating student use of the Next-TELL IOLM, to determine the likely perceptions, uptake and benefits of this type of IOLM in courses.

3.1 Participants, Materials and Methods

11 students volunteered to take part in the study: most of those enrolled on the course. They were in their third year studying for a 3 year BEng or a 4 year MEng degree in Computer Systems Engineering or Computer Interactive Systems. Only the test activity was summatively examined. Data from 5 weeks during the course contributed to the individual learner models built from the activities listed as data sources in Section 2.1. Students were introduced to the Next-TELL IOLM during a lab, and were already familiar with the notion of OLMs from a theoretical perspective as this topic formed part of the course content; and from a practical perspective from their use of OLMlets in this and other courses. A questionnaire was administered at the end of the course, with response options on a five-point scale (with strongly agree and agree / strongly disagree and disagree combined here for clarity of reporting). The questionnaire was completed by 8 participants attending a session reviewing the overall course content. The system log data and the Facebook and chat records were examined.

3.2 Results

In total there were 1169 OLM student events logged (mean 106; median 94; range 25-300). These include viewing, adding and filtering information into and from the learner model. Figure 3 (left) shows the general (combined) pattern of interaction across the 5 weeks, indicating that the interactions were spread across this period. There were 57 instances of students adding evidence/self-assessments, and 196 student accesses to the learner model views and text feedback provided by the instructor. Accesses to the views and feedback were as shown in the centre of Figure 3. Of the learner model views, the skill meters were used the most frequently (29% of learner model accesses), followed by the table (19%). Smilies, wordcloud and treemap were also used, at similar levels (11-12%). The text feedback from the instructor (not contributing data to the learner model) accounted for 18% of accesses.

Participants viewed their level of understanding in their learner model in overview (unfiltered form), or with reference to a specific competency/topic and/or associated with a specific activity, as on the right of Figure 3. In most cases they viewed their understanding of the topics with all activities contributing to their learner model (34%); followed by viewing knowledge level with reference to a specific activity (30%). In some cases students filtered both activity and topic, to see something specific in their model (21%), or used no filters (overview of all information: 15%).

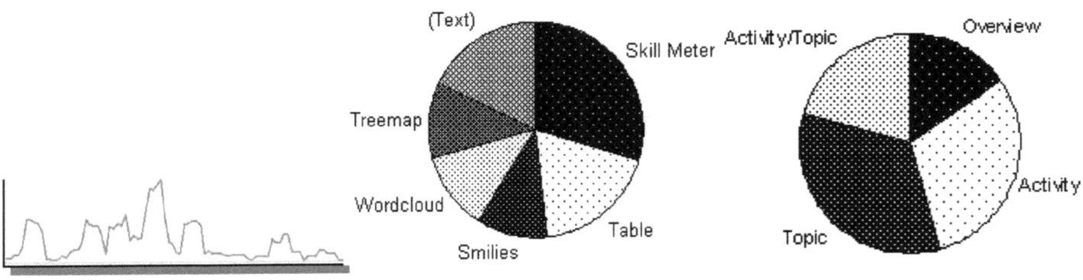

Fig. 3. OLM events logged (left); learner model views (centre) and ways of viewing (right)

Table 1. OLM filter by topic

Times	0	1	3-4	9-11
Users	4	2	2	3

Table 2. OLM filter by activity

Times	0	2	5	15
Users	5	2	3	1

Table 3. OLM filter by both

Times	0	1-3	9-10
Users	7	2	2

Tables 1-3 give the breakdown of viewing by topic and activity, by individuals. Table 1 shows the data for individuals looking at the data in specific topics (i.e. they clicked on the topic/competency to receive OLM information for that topic only). Seven users took this approach, with two of these doing this only once, two users doing this 3 and 4 times, and three viewing their learner model by specific topic/competency 9 to 11 times. Six users filtered the information by activity, as shown in Table 2, with most of these doing this between 2 and 5 times, and one, 15 times. Four students filtered by both topic and activity, two between 1 and 3 times, and two 9-10 times, as in Table 3. All other viewings were 'overview', i.e. no filters were applied: 9 users, 1-3 times. Comparing this information shows that individuals used more than one approach.

The questionnaires included items on perceived utility of the learner model visualisations. Figure 4 shows that, in general, respondents reported the written feedback, table and skill meters to be useful, as well as the facility to perform self-assessment. Half (4) found the smilies and word cloud to be helpful, while only 2 gave a positive response for the treemap. Users were also asked whether they thought that peer assessments would be helpful in a future version: this was generally positive (6).

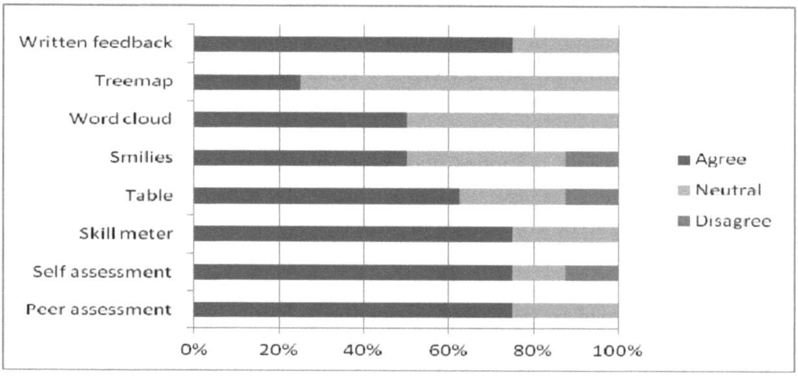

Fig. 4. Perceived utility of IOLM views and interaction

The Facebook and chat interactions consisted mostly of students asking a question prompted by a difficulty they had experienced with one or more OLMlets questions: *Facebook Post: do you think the expert knowledge may be represented as misconceptions?*

- *Comment 1: u mad boi? expert knowledge is the domain knowledge.*
- *Comment 2: but i think that expert knowledge could not represent the misconceptions since EK represent the conceptual facts*
- *Comment 3: the domain is where the right answers are stored (which is the Expert Knowledge). They do not represent misconceptions.*

Student texts, practice questions and test were more traditionally content-focussed in nature, and so are not described further here.

3.3 Discussion

Given that the Next-TELL IOLM is designed to build up learner data over time and, in this case, draws on activities that are for the most part repeated (OLMlets, Facebook discussion, student text revisions, open-ended practice questions, student self-assessments), it is expected that students would consult the IOLM intermittently rather than regularly and/or frequently. This is shown in Figure 3: while the first usage peak occurred when the IOLM was introduced, use continued through the five week period, decreasing towards the end of the course when students started preparing more intensively for their summative test. Therefore, the 196 accesses to learner model data occurred at different points. Thus, we have shown that students *will* use an IOLM based on multiple data sources throughout a course, for formative guidance.

As argued above, students may have different preferences for how to view their learner model, and this was also identified in this study. We have not considered in detail, whether individuals prefer specific views or use multiple views, but it has been demonstrated that multiple views are also used in this context. Furthermore, for contexts in which it is feasible in practice, such as smaller groups: provision of text feedback in addition to multiple IOLM views, is recommended. This may help students to understand the learner model representations more fully.

Another new finding in this study is that, if available: students will look at their learner model from the perspective of specific topics or competencies; according to specific activities; filtered by both topic and activity; or generally as summary of all information. Although we have not here investigated at what points students used filters, we do know that some users did, and so presumably perceived some benefit from this. Therefore, we suggest that where multiple activities and data sources may contribute to the learner model: allowing students to access the learner model by topic/competency, activity/data source, or both, is likely to be considered helpful by users.

The questionnaire responses reinforce the above, with reference to students' perceptions of the utility of the various learner model views. Similarly, as suggested by the logs, students claimed to find the text feedback helpful. Also in line with the log data, the facility for self-assessment was considered useful. In addition, students were asked whether they believed that peer assessment would be beneficial in a future version of the IOLM, with the responses showing as much interest in this as for self-assessments. This is particularly promising given the potential for the Facebook interactions or chat to reveal more detail about students' understanding. For example, the Facebook post shows a misconception (relating to the OLMlets questions about the Domain Model topic). Students sometimes think that, because the domain model represents 'expert' knowledge, it must also know what misconceptions exist because a human expert would know this. The first two comments do link the domain model to expert knowledge in the sense of a domain representation. However, the third comment reveals a further misconception (also quite common), that the domain is equivalent to correct answers. While such discussion reveals greater detail to the instructor about students' viewpoints, which can then be manually transferred to the Next-TELL IOLM, it might also help encourage peer assessments in the Next-TELL IOLM and, as a result, greater collaboration. The OLMlets chat facility is now also embedded in the Next-TELL IOLM, with the aim of encouraging discussion also in situations where students will not be using Facebook, such as in school classes. In addition to collaborative interaction and further data for the IOLM, this can also help address issues of instructor time in groups where numbers of students are larger, as students will have more opportunity to discover and work out their difficulties.

In summary, the Next-TELL IOLM aims to flexibly support the way instructors wish and need to work in their own contexts. In large groups with much data from various applications, etc., this can be amalgamated into individual open learner models with no, or relatively little (e.g. [7]) intervention from the instructor. Self and peer assessments can complement this data, if the teacher chooses to permit this. Direct instructor input is also possible, and additional feedback can be helpful for groups producing drafts or work that can benefit from greater detail. Future work can investigate the inclusion of further automated methods of providing feedback on learners' artefacts as well as data into the learner model.

4 Summary

This paper has introduced the Next-TELL IOLM, which can take a range of sources of data for visualisation to the learner. A study of use of the IOLM in a university course shows the feasibility of this approach in practice, while also demonstrating ways in which students might use an IOLM of this kind with reference to how they explore their learner model. It also illustrates how learner model information from combined sources can provide greater insight on students' general learning to instructors, and points towards possibilities for encouraging greater peer interaction in learning, both issues being interesting directions for future research.

Acknowledgement. This project is supported by the European Community (EC) under the Information Society Technology priority of the 7th Framework Programme for R&D under contract no 258114 NEXT-TELL. This document does not represent the opinion of the EC and the EC is not responsible for any use that might be made of its content.

References

1. Albert, D., Nussbaumer, A., Steiner, C.M.: Towards Generic Visualisation Tools and Techniques for Adaptive E-Learning. In: Wong, S.L., et al. (eds.) International Conference on Computers in Education, Putrajaya, Malaysia, pp. 61–65. Asia-Pacific Society for Computers in Education (2010)
2. Bakalov, F., Hsiao, I.-H., Brusilovsky, P., Koenig-Ries, B.: Visualizing Student Models for Social Learning with Parallel Introspective Views. In: Workshop on Visual Interfaces to the Social Semantic Web, ACM IUI 2011, Palo Alto, US (2011)
3. Bull, S., Cooke, N., Mabbott, A.: Visual Attention in Open Learner Model Presentations: An Eye-Tracking Investigation. In: Conati, C., McCoy, K., Paliouras, G. (eds.) UM 2007. LNCS (LNAI), vol. 4511, pp. 177–186. Springer, Heidelberg (2007)
4. Bull, S., Gakhal, I., Grundy, D., Johnson, M., Mabbott, A., Xu, J.: Preferences in Multiple-View Open Learner Models. In: Wolpers, M., Kirschner, P.A., Scheffel, M., Lindstaedt, S., Dimitrova, V. (eds.) EC-TEL 2010. LNCS, vol. 6383, pp. 476–481. Springer, Heidelberg (2010)
5. Bull, S., Jackson, T., Lancaster, M.: Students' Interest in their Misconceptions in First Year Electrical Circuits and Mathematics Courses. International Journal of Electrical Engineering Education 47(3), 307–318 (2010b)
6. Bull, S., Kay, J.: Open Learner Models as Drivers for Metacognitive Processes. In: Azevedo, R., Aleven, V. (eds.) International Handbook on Metacognition and Learning Technologies (in press)
7. Bull, S., Wasson, B., Kickmeier-Rust, M., Johnson, M.D., Moe, E., Hansen, C., Meissl-Egghart, G., Hammermuller, K.: Assessing English as a Second Language: From Classroom Data to a Competence-Based Open Learner Model. In: International Conference on Computers in Education (2012)
8. Conejo, R., Trella, M., Cruces, I., Garcia, R.: INGRID: A Web Service Tool for Hierarchical Open Learner Model Visualization. In: Ardissono, L., Kuflik, T. (eds.) UMAP 2011 Workshops. LNCS, vol. 7138, pp. 406–409. Springer, Heidelberg (2012), http://www.umap2011.org/proceedings/posters/paper_241.pdf
9. Cruces, I., Trella, M., Conejo, R., Galvez, J.: Student Modeling Services for Hybrid Web Applications. In: International Workshop on Architectures and Building Blocks of Web-Based User-Adaptive Systems (2010), http://ceur-ws.org/Vol-609/paper1.pdf

10. Demmans Epp, C., McCalla, G.: ProTutor: Historic Open Learner Models for Pronunciation Tutoring. In: Biswas, G., Bull, S., Kay, J., Mitrovic, A. (eds.) AIED 2011. LNCS, vol. 6738, pp. 441–443. Springer, Heidelberg (2011)
11. Dolog, P., Schaefer, M.: Learner Modeling on the Semantic Web. In: Workshop on Personalization on the Semantic Web, User Modeling 2005 (2005), http://www.win.tue.nl/persweb/full-proceedings.pdf
12. Duan, D., Mitrovic, A., Churcher, N.: Evaluating the Effectiveness of Multiple Open Student Models in EER-Tutor. In: Wong, S.L., et al. (eds.) International Conference on Computers in Education, Putrajaya, Malaysia, pp. 86–88. Asia-Pacific Society for Computers in Education (2010)
13. Hsiao, I.-H., Bakalov, F., Brusilovsky, P., König-Ries, B.: Open Social Student Modeling: Visualizing Student Models with Parallel IntrospectiveViews. In: Konstan, J.A., Conejo, R., Marzo, J.L., Oliver, N. (eds.) UMAP 2011. LNCS, vol. 6787, pp. 171–182. Springer, Heidelberg (2011)
14. Kay, J.: Learner Know Thyself: Student Models to Give Learner Control and Responsibility. In: Halim, Z., Ottomann, T., Razak, Z. (eds.) ICCE, pp. 17–24. AACE (1997)
15. Kump, B., Seifert, C., Beham, G., Lindstaedt, S.N., Ley, T.: Seeing What the System Thinks You Know - Visualizing Evidence in an Open Learner Model. In: Proceedings of LAK 2012. ACM (2012)
16. Mabbott, A., Bull, S.: Student Preferences for Editing, Persuading, and Negotiating the Open Learner Model. In: Ikeda, M., Ashley, K., Chan, T.-W. (eds.) ITS 2006. LNCS, vol. 4053, pp. 481–490. Springer, Heidelberg (2006)
17. Mathews, M., Mitrovic, A., Lin, B., Holland, J., Churcher, N.: Do Your Eyes Give It Away? Using Eye Tracking Data to Understand Students' Attitudes towards Open Student Model Representations. In: Cerri, S.A., Clancey, W.J., Papadourakis, G., Panourgia, K. (eds.) ITS 2012. LNCS, vol. 7315, pp. 422–427. Springer, Heidelberg (2012)
18. Mazzola, L., Mazza, R.: GVIS: A Facility for Adaptively Mashing Up and Representing Open Learner Models. In: Wolpers, M., Kirschner, P.A., Scheffel, M., Lindstaedt, S., Dimitrova, V. (eds.) EC-TEL 2010. LNCS, vol. 6383, pp. 554–559. Springer, Heidelberg (2010)
19. Mitrovic, A., Martin, B.: Evaluating the Effect of Open Student Models on Self-Assessment. Int. J. of Artificial Intelligence in Education 17(2), 121–144 (2007)
20. Morales, R., Van Labeke, N., Brna, P., Chan, M.E.: Open Learner Modelling as the Keystone of the Next generation of Adaptive Learning Environments. In: Mourlas, C., Germanakos, P. (eds.) Intelligent User Interfaces, pp. 288–312. Information Science Reference, ICI Global, London (2009)
21. Perez-Marin, D., Pascual-Nieto, I.: Showing Automatically Generated Students' Conceptual Models to Students and Teachers. Int. J. of Artificial Intelligence in Education 20(1), 47–72 (2010)
22. Raybourn, E.M., Regan, D.: Exploring e-portfolios and Independent Open Learner Models: Toward Army Learning Concept 2015. In: Interservice/Industry Training, Simulation, and Education Conference Proceedings, Florida, USA (2011)
23. Reimann, P., Bull, S., Halb, W., Johnson, M.: Design of a Computer-Assisted Assessment System for Classroom Formative Assessment. In: CAF 2011. IEEE (2011)
24. Verbert, K., Duval, E., Klerkx, J., Govaerts, S., Santos, J.L.: Learning Analytics Dashboard Applications, American Behavioral Scientist, early online version February 28 (2013), doi:10.1177/0002764213479363
25. Weber, G., Brusilovsky, P.: ELM-ART: An Adaptive Versatile System for Web-Based Instruction. Int. Journal of Artificial Intelligence in Education 12(4), 351–384 (2001)

Discovering Behavior Patterns of Self-Regulated Learners in an Inquiry-Based Learning Environment

Jennifer Sabourin, Bradford Mott, and James Lester

North Carolina State University, Raleigh, North Carolina
{jlrobiso,bwmott,lester}@ncsu.edu

Abstract. Inquiry-based learning has been proposed as a natural and authentic way for students to engage with science. Inquiry-based learning environments typically require students to guide their own learning and inquiry processes as they gather data, make and test hypotheses and draw conclusions. Some students are highly self-regulated learners and are able to guide and monitor their own learning activities effectively. Unfortunately, many students lack these skills and are consequently less successful in open-ended, inquiry-based environments. This work examines differences in inquiry behavior patterns in an open-ended, game-based learning environment, CRYSTAL ISLAND. Differential sequence mining is used to identify meaningful behavior patterns utilized by Low, Medium, and High self-regulated learners. Results indicate that self-regulated learners engage in more effective problem solving behaviors and demonstrate different patterns of use of the provided cognitive tools. The identified patterns help provide further insight into the role of SRL in inquiry-based learning and inform future approaches for scaffolding.

Keywords: Self-regulation, inquiry-based learning, game-based learning.

1 Introduction

Inquiry-based learning has been the focus of recent attention in both traditional classrooms [1, 2] and intelligent tutoring systems [3–5]. Inquiry-based learning has achieved this popularity primarily due to its use of authentic problem-solving scenarios and because the student is put in control of her own learning. During this process, the student is expected to play an active part in "making observations, formulating hypotheses, gathering and analyzing data, and forming conclusions from that data" [5]. However, inquiry-based learning environments are naturally very open-ended and may provide little guidance to students on when and how to engage in these behaviors. Without sufficient guidance, students are less likely to learn effectively [1, 2].

To be successful in open-ended, inquiry-based environments students must be capable of setting meaningful learning objectives [6]. They must then identify activities, behaviors, and strategies that may achieve these learning goals, monitor and evaluate their progress and alter their behavior and strategies accordingly. Together these skills form the foundation of self-regulated learning. Self-regulated learning (SRL) can be described as "the process by which students activate and sustain cognitions,

K. Yacef et al. (Eds.): AIED 2013, LNAI 7926, pp. 209–218, 2013.

behaviors, and affects that are systematically directed toward the attainment of goals" [7]. Unfortunately, students can demonstrate a wide range of fluency in their SRL behaviors [8], with some students lagging behind their peers in their ability to appropriately set and monitor learning goals.

This work seeks to identify the patterns of inquiry behaviors characteristic of self-regulated learners during game-based learning. It investigates these behaviors in the context of the CRYSTAL ISLAND game-based learning environment. CRYSTAL ISLAND is an open-ended game for middle school science in which students engage in inquiry behaviors of gathering evidence, forming and testing hypothesis, and reporting conclusions. Students are classified as Low, Medium, or High self-regulated learners based on evidence of goal setting and monitoring behaviors. Differential sequence mining [9] techniques are used to identify patterns of behavior that occur at statistically different frequencies between the classes of self-regulated learners. Results suggest differences in how students use tools, monitor their progress, and draw conclusions based on relevant information. These findings suggest that self-regulated learners engage in fundamentally different types of inquiry behaviors and point to methods for supporting the inquiry of students who do not have strong SRL skills.

2 Background

The ability to set learning goals, identify successful strategies, and evaluate personal success is the hallmark of self-regulated learning. Students who exhibit self-regulated learning (SRL) skills are able to drive their own learning and are often more successful in learning tasks and academic settings [10]. While SRL skills can be taught and often improve with practice [11], students who have not yet developed appropriate SRL strategies are more likely to flounder in self-guided, inquiry-based learning environments [6]. However, there is evidence that with appropriate scaffolding, these environments can improve learning as well as aid in development of SRL and inquiry skills [5, 12, 13].

Consequently, identifying and scaffolding metacognitive behaviors such as self-regulated learning (SRL) in open-ended environments has been a focus of much work in the intelligent tutoring systems community. For example, in MetaTutor, a hypermedia environment for learning biology, think-aloud protocols have been used to examine which regulatory strategies students use, while analysis of students' navigation through the hypermedia environment helps to identify profiles of self-regulated learners [13]. Similarly, researchers have identified patterns of behavior in the Betty's Brain system that are indicative of self-regulation [14] and utilized sequence mining techniques to further explore successful learning patterns [9].

Prior work exploring self-regulated learning in CRYSTAL ISLAND has utilized evidence of goal setting and monitoring to distinguish Low, Medium, and High classifications of SRL tendencies [15]. Further analyses demonstrated that Medium and High SRL students have both higher prior knowledge and higher learning gains than Low SRL students. This suggests that Low SRL students start with some disadvantage and that the overall gap in knowledge is increased after interactions with CRYSTAL

ISLAND. Though all groups have significant learning gains, Low SRL students are not experiencing the same benefits of interaction with CRYSTAL ISLAND. Further analyses suggest that High SRL students may be making better use of the curricular resources in CRYSTAL ISLAND than Medium or Low SRL students. These findings have highlighted the need to better understand the inquiry behaviors of High self-regulated learners and how these patterns can be used to inform scaffolding of the Low SRL students.

3 Method

The investigation of SRL behaviors was conducted with students from two North Carolina middle schools interacting with CRYSTAL ISLAND, an open-ended game-based learning environment being developed for the domain of microbiology that is aligned with the North Carolina Standard Course of Study for eighth grade science [16].

3.1 CRYSTAL ISLAND

CRYSTAL ISLAND features a science mystery set on a recently discovered volcanic island. The student plays the role of a visitor who recently arrived on the island in order to see her sick father. However, the student gets drawn into a mission to save the entire research team from a spreading outbreak. The student explores the research camp from a first-person viewpoint and manipulates virtual objects, converses with characters, and uses lab equipment and other resources to solve the mystery. As the student investigates the mystery, she completes an in-game diagnosis worksheet in order to record findings, hypotheses, and a final diagnosis. This worksheet is designed

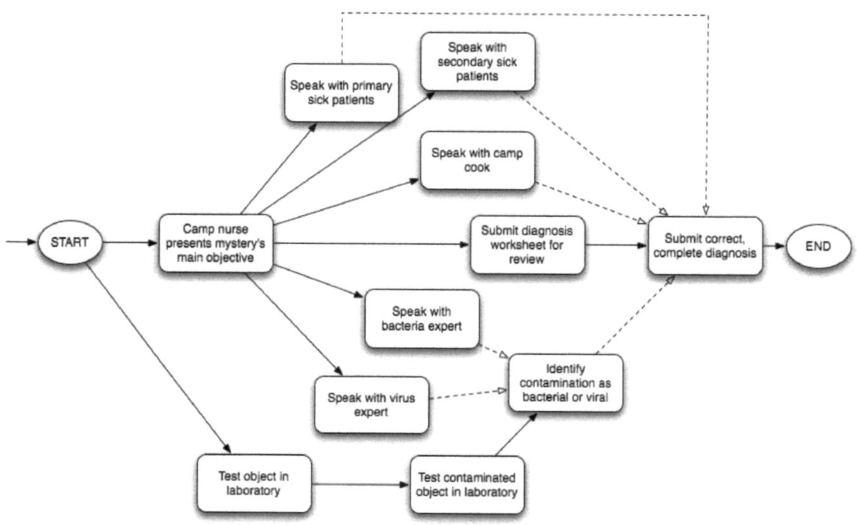

Fig. 1. Goal ordering in CRYSTAL ISLAND

to scaffold the student's problem-solving process and provide a space for the student to offload any findings gathered about the illness. The mystery is solved when the student submits a complete, correct diagnosis and treatment plan to the camp nurse.

To successfully complete the mystery, students must achieve several partially ordered goals (Figure 1). The goal topology indicates that many data-collection tasks are encouraged for students. They should converse with subject matter experts to learn about the underlying science content. They should discuss symptoms and possible sources of the outbreak with sick characters. They should read posters and books about different illnesses to help narrow down which diseases match the patients' symptoms. As students work towards solving the problem, they have two primary means to test their hypotheses. The first is through equipment in the camp's laboratory where students run tests on food objects to see if they are contaminated with pathogens, mutagens, or carcinogens. The second is through the diagnosis worksheet where they keep track of their hypothesized source and type of illness. This worksheet can be checked by the camp nurse for correctness.

While there is a subset of tasks that are strictly necessary to solve the mystery, there are a variety of tasks that are optional, but beneficial, for learning and problem-solving activities. For example, the diagnosis worksheet contains many fields to help students keep track of their hypotheses and thoughts, though only one small portion is required for reporting their final conclusions. Additionally, reading posters and books and talking with subject matter experts are helpful but not required to solve the mystery. Understanding how students choose to use these features of the learning environment is important for understanding effective inquiry strategies and how these strategies relate to self-regulated learning.

3.2 Study Procedure

A study with 450 eighth grade students interacting with the CRYSTAL ISLAND environment was conducted. After removing subjects with incomplete data or who experienced logging errors, there were 400 students remaining. Among the remaining students, there were 193 male and 207 female participants varying in age and ethnicity. Participants interacted with CRYSTAL ISLAND in their school classroom, although the study was not directly integrated into their regular classroom activities. Pre-study materials were completed during the week prior to interacting with CRYSTAL ISLAND. The pre-study materials included a demographic survey, researcher-generated CRYSTAL ISLAND curriculum test, and several personality questionnaires.

Immediately after solving the mystery, or after 55 minutes of interaction, students moved to a different room in order to complete several post-study questionnaires including the curriculum post-test. Students also completed two questionnaires aimed to measure students' interest and involvement with CRYSTAL ISLAND.

During the interaction students were prompted every seven minutes to self-report their current mood and status through an in-game smartphone device. Students selected one emotion from a set of seven options, which included the following: anxious, bored, confused, curious, excited, focused, and frustrated. After selecting an emotion, students were instructed to type a few words about their current status in the game, similarly to how they might update their status in an online social network. These typed statements were tagged for evidence of goal setting and monitoring and used to classify students as High ($n=131$), Medium ($n=120$), or Low ($n=149$) SRL. (See [15] for more details.)

4 Identifying Behavior Patterns

Prior findings [15] on the differences in learning between Low, Medium, and High SRL students in CRYSTAL ISLAND prompted the current work to investigate differences in behavior patterns and inquiry strategies. Specifically, we sought to determine whether students interacted with CRYSTAL ISLAND in measurably different ways given their level of SRL skills. We also hoped to discover effective patterns utilized by High self-regulated learners that could be used to inform scaffolding for less skilled students. The exploratory nature of these questions and the desire to compare patterns across groups motivated the use of the differential sequence mining approach described by Kinnebrew et al. [9].

4.1 Action Abstraction

The first step to identify meaningful behavior patterns was to transform the highly detailed trace logs from interactions with CRYSTAL ISLAND into a more abstract representation of the overall behaviors being performed. This involved removing irrelevant or uninteresting actions (e.g., entering buildings, or manipulating individual objects) and grouping together instance of similar behaviors (e.g., reading a book on influenza and then a book on ebola).

In total, four general action types were identified as important distinguishing behaviors: TALK, READ, TEST, and WORKSHEET (Figure 2). The first two actions represent the primary source of gathering data in the environment, while the second two represent the primary problem-solving tasks and hypothesis testing tasks. These behaviors are central to the inquiry-based problem-solving in CRYSTAL ISLAND. Additional details were also considered for each action and are described below:

- **TALK:** One of the primary ways students gather information is through talking with in-game characters. Students may talk with patients to learn about the symptoms of their illness (TALKSYM). There are also experts on pathogens, bacteria, and viruses that students may talk to (TALKPATH, TALKBAC, TALKVIR). Finally, some of the characters also describe the nature of the illness and how it spread to students and provide details about the specific problem solving task (TALKPROB).
- **READ:** There are several books and posters scattered around the environment that students may use for additional information. Many of these resources cover the same topics as conversations with experts on the island (READPATH, READBAC, READVIR). There is also a variety of books and posters that describe specific diseases (READDIS).

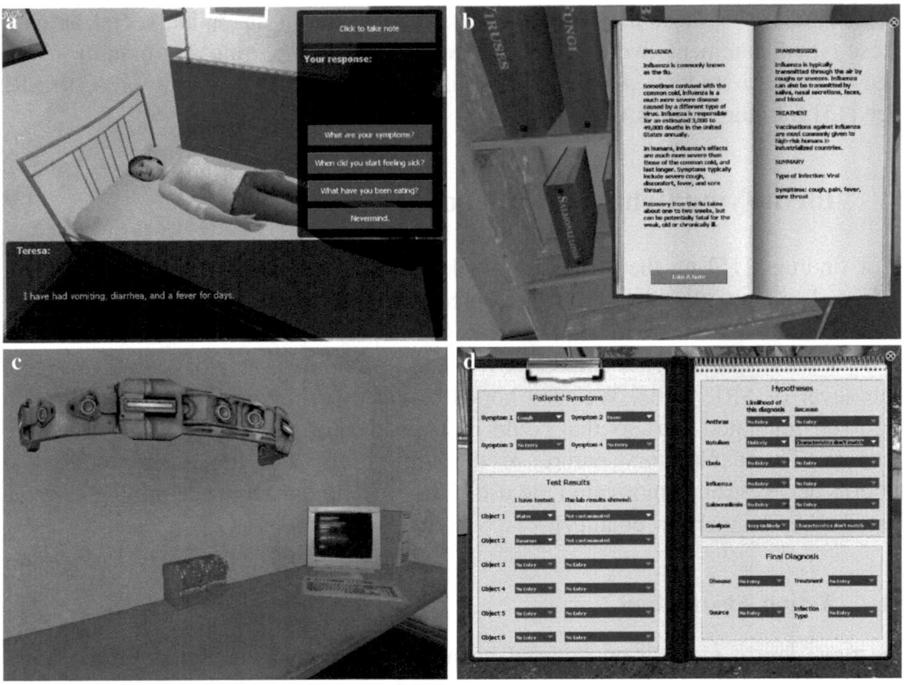

Fig. 2. Targeted behaviors (a) TALK, (b) READ, (c) TEST, (d) WORKSHEET

- **TEST:** To identify contaminated items students must run tests on individual food items. They must also specify whether they are testing the item for a pathogen, mutagen or carcinogen. Based on the nature of the illness, students should rule out mutagen or carcinogen as possible sources and testing for this is considered irrelevant (TESTIRR). Tests for pathogens are identified as correct (TESTCORR) if the proper food item was selected and incorrect (TESTINC) otherwise.
- **WORKSHEET (WS):** The diagnosis worksheet is where students keep notes about their findings and hypotheses. There are several sections of information that can be filled out. They can record symptoms of patients (WSSYM) and the results of their tests (WSTEST). They can also keep track of hypotheses (WSHYP) about individual diseases and their reasoning. The final section of the worksheet (WSREP) is used to report their final conclusions to the nurse in order to complete the mystery.

4.2 Differential Sequence Mining

To identify patterns of behavior which were statistically different between Low, Medium, and High SRL students we utilized a differential sequence mining algorithm adapted from Kinnebrew et al. [9]. This approach identifies two metrics for representing the frequency of a pattern in different groups. The sequence support (*s-support*) metric refers to the percentage of sequences the pattern occurs in, regardless of frequency. Alternatively, the instance support *(i-support)* metric represents the average number of times the pattern occurs per sequence. The primary adaption was to allow for comparison across the three groups where the original algorithm only compares between two populations. The adapted algorithm can be summarized in the following steps:

- *Identify frequent patterns.* Patterns included sequences of 2-5 actions. To ensure patterns considered for analysis were meaningful we only consider patterns that occur for at least 20% of students in a group. This threshold is the same as described in [9].
- *Calculate s-support and i-support metrics for each pattern.* Metrics were calculated for each group using the definition described above.
- *Identify statistically significant differences in frequency.* T-tests with a Bonferroni correction were conducted to compare the *s-support* and *i-support* metrics across each pair of SRL classifications. The Bonferroni correction was conducted for 95% confidence across the three pairwise tests but did not account for the multiple comparisons across patterns. This approach was employed because the primary purpose of our investigation was to identify meaningful patterns, not to prove statistical differences between populations [9].

5 Results

In total, 137 sequences were identified as frequent, occurring in more than 20% of student traces. Of these 29 were identified as having a significant difference in frequency between Low, Medium, or High SRL students. Further interpretation of these sequences suggested 6 general behavior patterns that occurred at different frequencies between the groups (Table 1). Of these, 3 patterns were more frequently displayed by High SRL students, while the remaining 3 patterns were more frequent among Low SRL students. These general patterns of behavior provide important insight into how students differentially interact with the environment given their level of SRL skill.

For instance, patterns **P1** and **P3** both highlight High SRL students' usage of the diagnosis worksheet. Specifically, these students are more likely to keep track of information as they receive it. Both the hypothesis and symptoms area of the diagnosis worksheet are optional, suggesting that High SRL students are choosing to use the resource to help themselves keep track of their ideas. Additionally, while the symptoms section of the worksheet involves simple recording of facts, the hypothesis area requires students to synthesize what they know and make inferences about the likelihood of different hypotheses, indicating strong inquiry skills. Together these patterns indicate that High SRL students are utilizing resources to keep track of what they know and are actively reflecting on the inquiry process.

In contrast, pattern **P5**, which is demonstrated more frequently by Low SRL students, indicates poor planning and inquiry skills. This pattern involves students reading about diseases, then visiting patients to ask about their symptoms, and repeating this process. This pattern suggests that Low SRL students are gathering data "just in time." They are repeatedly checking the information from patients against the information in books and posters to arrive at a hypothesis. These students are not keeping

Table 1. Differential patterns of behavior

	Sample Sequences	s-support			i-support		
		L	M	H	L	M	H
High SRL Students	**P1: Reading about diseases and updating hypotheses in worksheet**						
	READDIS-WSHYP-READDIS-WSHYP-READDIS	0.10	0.19	0.26	0.28	0.53	0.74
	WSHYP-READDIS-WSHYP-READDIS-WSHYP	0.11	0.18	0.24	0.31	0.54	0.70
	P2: Talk about problem and learn about pathogens						
	TALKPROB-TALKPATH-TALKPROB	0.75	0.80	0.88	0.83	0.95	0.98
	TALKPROB-TALKPATH-READPATH	0.15	0.25	0.27	0.16	0.26	0.27
	P3: Talk about symptoms and update symptoms in worksheet						
	TALKSYM-WSSYM	0.42	0.61	0.61	0.74	1.16	1.13
	TALKSYM-TALKPROB-WSSYM	0.03	0.08	0.12	0.03	0.08	0.13
Low SRL Students	**P4: Alternating incorrect and irrelevant tests**						
	TESTIRR-TESTINC-TESTIRR	0.61	0.55	0.47	1.79	1.55	1.01
	TESTINC-TESTIRR	0.71	0.71	0.66	2.27	2.04	1.50
	P5: Read about diseases and ask about symptoms						
	TALKSYM-READDIS-TALKSYM-READDIS	0.39	0.26	0.23	0.39	0.31	0.25
	READDIS-TALKSYM-READDIS-TALKSYM-TALKPROB	0.35	0.19	0.18	0.35	0.22	0.19
	P6: Learn about pathogens and run irrelevant tests						
	READPATH-TESTIRR-TESTINC	0.33	0.29	0.18	0.44	0.34	0.24
	TALKPROB-TALKPATH-TESTIRR	0.28	0.25	0.21	0.34	0.32	0.24

track of this information in their diagnosis worksheet and consequently are going back and forth between the books and posters on diseases to the infirmary with the patients. This represents a much less effective approach to problem solving when compared with the High SRL students. Additionally, these students are likely experiencing an increased cognitive load as they are trying to recall all the details they have gathered without the aid of the in-game resources. These patterns indicate that Low SRL students may need scaffolding for effective organization of knowledge and use of external cognitive tools, which is an important component of self-regulated learning [6, 10].

Another important distinction concerns students making connections about the type of illness affecting the patients. Specifically, students learn that the illness was spread through food that the camp members ate (TALKPROB). Students should also learn (through TALKPATH or READPATH) that a pathogen is a type of illness that can be spread through food or contact, whereas mutagens and carcinogens are not spread from person to person. Students should consequently conclude that the illness is a form of pathogen. This may be what is occurring in pattern **P2** demonstrated by High SRL students. These students are alternating between finding out information about the nature of the illness and about pathogens and are likely using this information to draw the conclusion that the illness is a form of pathogen. Additionally, the back-and-forth nature of these activities suggests goal-driven behavior perhaps to inform their testing strategies.

When running tests in the lab, students select whether they are testing for pathogens, mutagens or carcinogens. Knowledge of the pathogens and the nature of the illness should preclude students from running tests on carcinogens or mutagens ($TEST_{IRR}$); however, pattern **P6** indicates that Low SRL students are not making this connection or choose to ignore it. Additionally, **P4** suggests that Low SRL students may not be carefully selecting their testing strategy based on prior knowledge and may be trying any form of test to get a positive result. This suggests that Low SRL students may need more guidance in making the connection between the nature of the problem and type of illness. Additionally, they should be encouraged to identify whether the source is a pathogen, mutagen, or carcinogen before beginning to test.

6 Conclusion

Open-ended, inquiry-based learning environments are powerful tools for engaging students in scientific thinking and authentic problem solving. However, not all students are successfully able to navigate these environments and learn effectively. Self-regulated learning behaviors such as goal setting, progress monitoring, and effective tool use are critical for optimizing learning outcomes. Students lacing these skills have a disadvantage, but may be able to overcome this with additional guidance and support.

This work utilized differential sequence mining techniques to identify patterns of inquiry behaviors associated with self-regulated learning skills. Results indicated that students with more developed SRL skills utilize in-game resources more effectively to help reduce cognitive load. They also appear to be able to more effectively draw inferences and use them to inform future behaviors and strategies. These differences highlight areas for scaffolding students with less-developed regulatory skills. Specifically, Low SRL students can be encouraged and guided through the use of cognitive tools. Hopefully by clearly demonstrating how these tools can be successfully used, students will be more likely and more effective at using the resources. Additionally, it may be important to highlight ties between different sources of information and present specific learning goals related to each component of the problem solving activity. An important area for future work will be to incorporate these scaffolding strategies and to measure the impact on behavior patterns and overall learning for students who are not already strong self-regulated learners.

Acknowledgements. The authors wish to thank members of the IntelliMedia Group for their assistance, Omer Sturlovich and Pavel Turzo for use of their 3D model libraries, and Valve Software for access to the Source™ engine and SDK. This research was supported by the National Science Foundation under Grants DRL-0822200, IIS-0812291, and CNS-0739216. This material is based upon work supported under a National Science Foundation Graduate Research Fellowship.

References

1. Alfieri, L., Brooks, P., Aldrich, N., Tenenbaum, H.: Does Discovery-Based Instruction Enhance Learning. Journal of Education Psychology, 103, 1–18 (2011)
2. Kirschner, P.A., Sweller, J., Clark, R.E.: Why Minimal Guidance during instruction does not work: An analysis of the Failure of Constructivist, Discovery, Problem-Based, Experiential, and Inquiry-Based Teaching. Educational Psychologist 41, 75–86 (2006)
3. Roll, I., Aleven, V., Koedinger, K.R.: The Invention Lab: Using a Hybrid of Model Tracing and Constraint-Based Modeling to Offer Intelligent Support in Inquiry Environments. In: Aleven, V., Kay, J., Mostow, J. (eds.) ITS 2010, Part I. LNCS, vol. 6094, pp. 115–124. Springer, Heidelberg (2010)
4. Woolf, B.P., et al.: Critical Thinking Environments for Science Education. In: Proceedings of the 12th International Conference on Artificial Intelligence in Education, pp. 515–522 (2005)
5. Ketelhut, D.J.: The impact of student self-efficacy on scientific inquiry skills: An exploratory investigation in "River City", a multi-user virtual environment. Journal of Science Education and Technology 16, 99–111 (2007)
6. Land, S.: Cognitive requirements for learning with open-ended learning environments. Educational Technology Research and Development 48, 61–78 (2000)
7. Schunk, D.H.: Attributions as Motivators of Self-Regulated Learning. In: Motivation and Self-Regulated Learning: Theory, Research, and Applications, pp. 245–266 (2008)
8. Ellis, D., Zimmerman, B.J.: Enhancing self-monitoring during self-regulated learning of speech, pp. 205–228 (2001)
9. Kinnebrew, J.S., Loretz, K.M., Biswas, G.: A Contextualized, Differential Sequence Mining Method to Derive Students' Learning Behavior Patterns. Journal of Educational Data Mining (in press)
10. Zimmerman, B.J.: Self-regulated learning and academic achievement: An overview. Educational Psychologist 25, 3–17 (1990)
11. Kostons, D., van Gog, T., Paas, F.: Training Self-Assessment and Task-Selection Skills: A Cognitive Approach to Improving Self-Regulated Learning. Learning and Instruction 22, 121–132 (2012)
12. Cuevas, P., Lee, O., Hart, J., Deaktor, R.: Improving Science Inquiry with Elementary Students of Diverse Backgrounds. Journal of Research in Science Teaching 42, 337–357 (2005)
13. Azevedo, R., Cromley, J.G., Winters, F.I., Moos, D.C., Greene, J.A.: Adaptive human scaffolding facilitates adolescents' self-regulated learning with hypermedia. Instructional Science 33, 381–412 (2005)
14. Biswas, G., Jeong, H., Roscoe, R., Sulcer, B.: Promoting Motivation and Self-Regulated Learning Skills through Social Interactions in Agent-Based Learning Environments. In: 2009 AAAI Fall Symposium on Cognitive and Metacognitive Educational Systems (2009)
15. Sabourin, J., Shores, L.R., Mott, B.W., Lester, J.C.: Predicting Student Self-regulation Strategies in Game-Based Learning Environments. In: Cerri, S.A., Clancey, W.J., Papadourakis, G., Panourgia, K. (eds.) ITS 2012. LNCS, vol. 7315, pp. 141–150. Springer, Heidelberg (2012)
16. Rowe, J.P., Shores, L.R., Mott, B.W., Lester, J.C.: Integrating Learning, Problem Solving, and Engagement in Narrative-Centered Learning Environments. International Journal of Artificial Intelligence in Education, 166–177 (2011)

Supporting Students' Self-Regulated Learning with an Open Learner Model in a Linear Equation Tutor

Yanjin Long and Vincent Aleven

Human Computer Interaction Institute, Carnegie Mellon University,
5000 Forbes Avenue, Pittsburgh, PA 15213, USA
{ylong,aleven}@cs.cmu.edu

Abstract. Self-assessment and study choice are two important metacognitive processes involved in Self-Regulated Learning. Yet not much empirical work has been conducted in ITSs to investigate how we can best support these two processes and improve students' learning outcomes. The present work redesigned an Open Learner Model (OLM) with three features aimed at supporting self-assessment (self-assessment prompts, delaying the update of the skill bars and progress information on the problem type level). We also added a problem selection feature. A 2x2 experiment with 62 7th graders using variations of an ITS for linear equation solving found that students who had access to the OLM performed significantly better on the post-test. To the best of our knowledge, the study is the first experimental study that shows an OLM enhances students' learning outcomes with an ITS. It also helps establish that self-assessment has key influence on student learning of problem solving tasks.

Keywords: Self-regulated learning, open learner model, self-assessment, study choice, intelligent tutoring system, classroom evaluation.

1 Introduction

Theories of Self-Regulated Learning (SRL) emphasize that students are active learners [13]. Different metacognitive processes are involved in SRL, such as goal setting, self-assessment, help-seeking, self-monitoring, study choice, etc. Two common metacognitive processes are self-assessment and study choice. Self-assessment refers to students' ability to evaluate how well they are learning/have learned. Study choice means that students make their own decisions with respect to the learning materials they study. More accurate self-assessment can lead to better study choice, which can further result in more efficient and effective learning [13]. Studies conducted with memory tasks and reading comprehension have found some ways to scaffold students' self-assessment and study choice, such as generating delayed key words [5]. Nevertheless, not much such work has been conducted with problem solving tasks, which is an area that Intelligent Tutoring Systems (ITSs) frequently focus on. The mechanism of self-assessing for solving math problems could be significantly different from memory task and reading comprehension.

K. Yacef et al. (Eds.): AIED 2013, LNAI 7926, pp. 219–228, 2013.

ITS researchers have been interested in the potential of Open Learner Models (OLM) to prompt students' reflection and metacognition [3]. Many ITSs have a learner model that intelligently tracks students' learning progress or their skill mastery. An OLM affords students access to part/all of progress information, often in different formats, which may help them reflect on what they know well and not so well. Bull and colleagues [4] found that first year college students were interested in viewing their misconceptions in an OLM, and believed that viewing such information could help them better assess their learning and allocate efforts. Hartley and Mitrovic [6] compared students' learning gains when with or without access to an inspectable OLM, but found no significant effect on the learning gains due to the OLM [6]. In our own prior work, we conducted surveys and interviews with experienced Cognitive Tutor users and found that they inspect the tutor's OLM (the Skillometer) quite frequently but do not actively use it to help them reflect or self-assess [8]. Similar work has also been conducted in the field of adaptive hypermedia. Brusilovsky et al. [2] found that with adaptive navigation support in QuizGuide (an adaptive system provides students self-assessment quizzes), students' participation was increased in the system, as well as their final academic performance. The adaptive navigation support has similar features as the OLMs, as it highlights to the students the important topics and topics that need more practice. Thus, as Bull et al. [3] point out, more empirical studies are needed to investigate how we can design an OLM to effectively facilitate students' metacognition, such as self-assessment and study choice. Moreover, it is also worth investigating to what extent access to an OLM and particular features of OLMs can significantly increase students' learning gains.

There has been limited prior work on study choice within ITS; typically, the ITS is responsible for selecting problems for the students. Mitrovic and Martin [9] found that in an ITS for SQL, lower-performing students learned in a "faded" condition in which they went from system-selected problems to student-selected problems. However, this study did not establish a statistically significant difference with other problem selection methods (fully system-selected or fully student-selected) [9]. The effect of problem selection on students' learning outcomes is still open for further investigation.

In the current work, we redesigned the Skillometer (OLM) of an ITS for linear equation solving so that it facilitates students' self-assessment. Specifically, we designed and implemented three new features for the Skillometer to support a brief self-assessment phase at the end of each tutor problem: self-assessment prompts, delaying the update of the skill bars (so that the updating of the skill bars can function as feedback on students' self-assessment) and showing students' progress on the problem type level in addition to on the skill level (to give students an overview of their progress in the tutor). We also implemented a problem selection feature in the tutor that lets students select their next problem.

We hypothesize that 1) having access to the redesigned OLM can enhance students' learning outcomes and self-assessment accuracy; 2) letting students select their own problems in the tutor could afford them opportunities to apply the results of their self-assessment and improve their learning outcomes even further. We conducted a 2x2 classroom experiment with 62 7th graders with the linear equation tutor to investigate the hypotheses.

2 Methods

2.1 Linear Equation Tutor and the Open Learner Model

We investigate the relationship between OLM, self-assessment and study choice within an ITS for linear equations. This tutor is an example-tracing tutor built using the Cognitive Tutor Authoring Tools [1, 11]. It was first designed and implemented by Maaike Waalkens [11] and has been used in two prior studies with around 150 students from grades 7 and 8. The tutor teaches five types of linear equations of varying difficulty levels (see Table 1). Figure 1 shows the main interface of the tutor: in addition to solving the equations, students need to self-explain each main step. The tutor provides step-by-step guidance for each problem. It also applies knowledge tracing and mastery learning to adaptively select problems for each student, so as to make sure the student reaches mastery on all targeted skills.

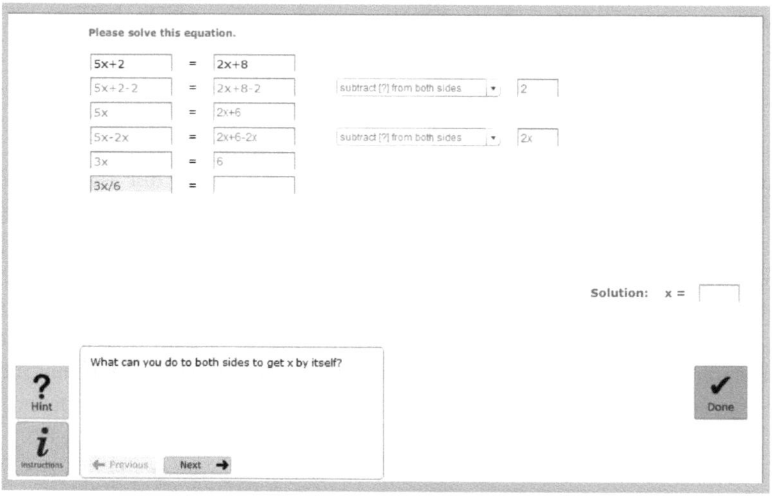

Fig. 1. The interface of the linear equation tutor

Table 1. Five types of equations in the linear equation tutor

Equations	Example	Level
One Step	x+5 = 7	Level 1
Two Steps	2x+1=7	Level 2
Multiple Steps	3x+1=x+5	Level 3
Parentheses	2(x+1)=8	Level 4
Parentheses, more difficult	2(x+1)+1=5	Level 5

As discussed in the introduction, we redesigned the OLM so as to support students' self-assessment and reflection at the end of each problem. We used a user-centered design approach to redesign the OLM. We started with building paper and digital prototypes for the OLM based on literature review. To refine the initial prototypes, we conducted think-aloud sessions with these prototypes in a local middle school with 7 students. Based on the findings from the think-alouds, we finalized the design as shown in Figure 2 and Figure 3. The five types of equations were categorized from level 1 to level 5 based on the skills involved, in order to more systematically reflect students' learning progress in the OLM. We implemented two views of the OLM with three new features: self-assessment prompts, delaying the update of the skill bars and showing progress on the problem type level. We also implemented a problem selection feature in the tutor to let students select their next problem.

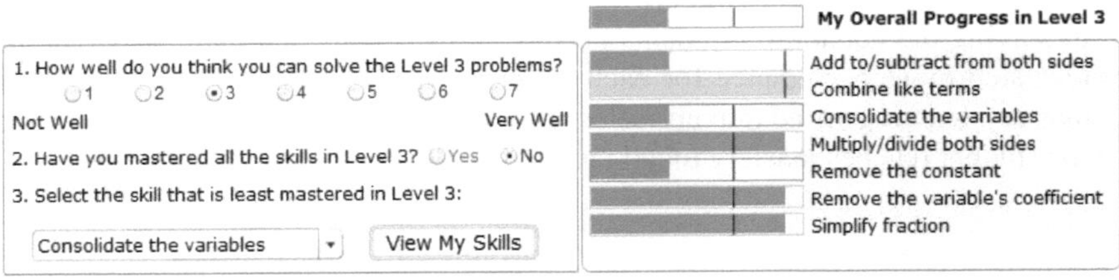

Fig. 2. View-1 of the OLM

Self-Assessment Prompts. View-1 of the OLM is initially hidden on the tutor interface but is revealed after the student finishes the problem. After students complete each problem, three self-assessment prompts are shown one by one (see Figure 2). (The level and skill bars on the right in Figure 2 are not displayed yet at this point in time, so that students answer the self-assessment questions unaided by the skill bars.) Students are asked to rate how well they think they can solve the problems in the current level on a scale from 1 to 7, then answer whether in their own assessment they have mastered the skills in the current level, and finally select the skill that they think is least mastered at this time. After that, the "View My Skills" button appears.

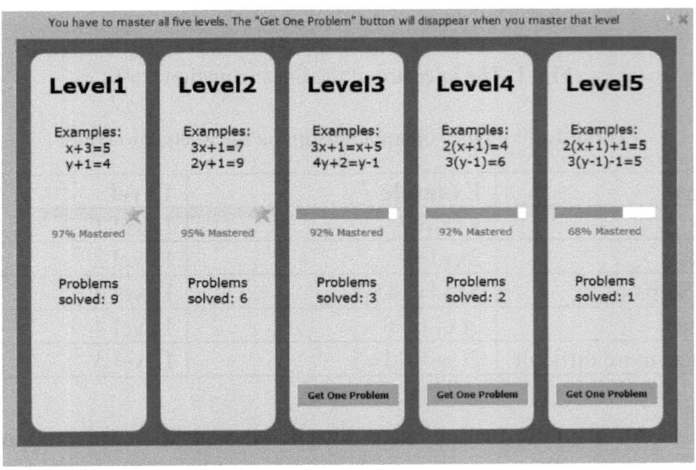

Fig. 3. View-2 of the OLM

Delaying the Update of the Skill Bars. Once students click the "View My Skills" button, the level and skill bars (on the right of Figure 2) are shown and start updating after 1 second (i.e., they move to their new positions, based on the student's performance on the problem they just completed). The updating of the bars serves as feedback on students' responses to the self-assessment prompts. The black vertical lines allow for a before/after comparison.

Showing Progress on the Problem Type Level. Figure 3 shows View-2 of the OLM, which is displayed to students in between problems (when they click the done button after the skill bars have finished updating). View-2 shows a summary of their progress with respect to each level as well as how many problems they have solved at that level.

Selecting the Next Problem. Further, on View-2, students can select the level they want to work on next by clicking the "Get One Problem" button for the preferred level. If a level is fully mastered, the "Get One Problem" button is hidden, so students can only select levels that contain unmastered skills. To complete the tutor they must master all levels.

2.2 Experimental Design, Participants, Procedure and Measurements

We conducted a 2x2 experiment with independent factors OLM (whether or not both views of the OLM are shown to the students) and PS (whether or not students could select their next problem from an unfinished level) with 62 7th grade students from one teacher's three classes at a local public middle school in Pittsburgh. The participants were randomly assigned to one of the four conditions. The OLM+PS condition used the interfaces we introduced in 2.1. The other three conditions used versions of the interfaces that were modified to match the manipulation. Specifically, for the OLM+noPS condition, View-1 of the OLM was unchanged, but View-2 was revised to have only a single "Get One Problem" button, rather than one for each level. Students in this condition were given problems from level 1 to 5 sequentially (they needed to finish level 1 first and then get problems from level 2, and so on). For the noOLM+PS condition, View-1 was not shown to the students. On View-2, all progress information was hidden (i.e., the progress bars and the number of problems completed for each level), but students could freely select their next problem from unmastered levels. Lastly, for the noOLM+noPS condition, View-1 was also not shown. For View-2, the progress information was hidden and there was only one single "Get One Problem" button.

The four conditions followed the same procedure. They all completed a paper pre-test on the same day for around 25 minutes, and started to work with the tutor in their computer lab from the next day for five consecutive days. On each day, all students worked on the tutor for one class period of 41 minutes. If a student finished early (in less than 5 periods), they were directed to work in a Geometry unit. After the five days, all conditions again completed an immediate paper post-test on the same day in one class period.

The pre- and post-tests were in similar format and measured students' knowledge of solving linear equations. We created two equivalent test forms and administered them in counterbalanced orders. There were two types of test items on both tests: procedural and conceptual items. Procedural items were the same five types of equations students had practiced in the tutor. Conceptual items were True/False questions measuring the knowledge and understanding of the key concepts involved in equations. We also measured students' self-assessment accuracy for the procedural items on both tests. Students were asked to rate from 1 to 7 regarding how well they think they can solve each equation before they actually solved it. Formula 1 calculates the absolute accuracy of students' self-assessment [10], where "N" represents the number of tasks, "c" stands for students' confidence ratings on their ability to finish the task while "p" represents their actual performance on that task.

$$\text{Absolute Accuracy Index} = \frac{1}{N}\sum_{i=1}^{N}(c_i - p_i)^2 \tag{1}$$

Besides the pre- and post-tests, we analyzed tutor log data to determine if there were differences between the conditions in students' learning behaviors in the tutor.

3 Results

56 students finished all five levels (reached mastery) after 5 class periods. We analyzed the 56 students' pre-test and post-test performance, tutor log data and their self-assessment data. We report the p-values and effect sizes (partial η^2) for the main effects and interactions. An effect size partial η^2 of .01 corresponds to a small effect, .06 to a medium effect, and .14 to a large effect (Cohen's guidelines for effect sizes).

Learning Effects of the Linear Equation Tutor. There were 7 procedural items and 12 conceptual items on both tests. The procedural items were graded from 0 to 1, with partial credit given where appropriate. Cronbach's Alpha for the 7 procedural items on the pre-test is .794, and .669 on the post-test. For the conceptual items, the Cronbach's Alphas are .626 and .672 for pre- and post-test respectively.

Table 2. Means and SDs for the test performance for all four conditions

Conditions	Pre-Test (Procedural)	Post-Test (Procedural)	Pre-Test (Conceptual)	Post-Test (Conceptual)
OLM+PS	.439 (.263)	.711 (.230)	.483 (.215)	.515 (.188)
OLM+noPS	.555 (.347)	.684 (.222)	.472 (.166)	.541 (.230)
noOLM+PS	.358 (.201)	.625 (.237)	.391 (.216)	.357 (.195)
noOLM+noPS	.490 (.204)	.634 (.290)	.436 (.164)	.462 (.202)

A 1-way ANOVA shows that there were no significant differences between the conditions on the pre-test. To examine the learning gains from pre- to post-test, we ran repeated measures ANOVAs (with OLM and PS as independent variables) on procedural items, conceptual items and the sum of the two (the overall test score). The results reveal that the conditions together improved significantly from pre- to post-test on the test as a whole (F (1, 52) = 13.927, p = .000, η^2 = .211) and on the procedural items separately (F (1. 52) = 35.239, p = .000, η^2 = .404), both with effect sizes considered to be very large. No significant improvement on conceptual items was found.

Effects of Open Learner Model (OLM). We also ran ANOVAs (with OLM and PS as independent variables) for the post-test results. There was a significant main effect of OLM on the overall test scores (F (3, 52) = 4.903, p = .031, η^2 = .078), as well as on the conceptual items (F (3, 52) = 5.212, p = .026, η^2 = .082). No significant main effect was found for the procedural items. In short, the two OLM conditions performed better on the post-test than the two groups who did not have access to the OLM. We then looked at process measures from the tutor log data to determine whether having access to the OLM significantly influenced students' behaviors while learning with the tutor. The process measures shown in Table 3 are commonly used in Cognitive Tutor studies [7]. As shown in Table 3, the two OLM conditions made fewer incorrect attempts, requested fewer hints and had a lower average assistance score ((hints + incorrect attempts) / total steps). ANOVAs (with OLM and PS as independent variables) show that there was a marginally significant main effect of OLM on incorrect attempts (F (3, 52) = 3.608, p = .062, η^2 = .059), and a significant main effect of OLM on average assistance score (F (3, 52) = 3.292, p = .009, η^2 = .116). There was no significant main effect of OLM on the number of hints.

Table 3. Means and SDs of process measures for all four conditions

	OLM+PS	OLM+noPS	noOLM+PS	noOLM+noPS
Total number of problems	32.80 (9.15)	36.93 (11.50)	34.23 (6.51)	39.31 (9.30)
Incorrect attempts per step	.248 (.180)	.261 (.164)	.337 (.256)	.364 (.182)
Hints per step	.157 (.138)	.190 (.178)	.221 (.197)	.268 (.433)
Average assistance score	.260 (.178)	.268 (.166)	.321 (.123)	.532 (.368)

Effects of Problem Selection (PS). ANOVAs (with OLM and PS as independent variables) found no significant main effect of PS on the overall post-test score or on the two categories of post-test items separately. For log data, the students in the PS conditions made fewer incorrect attempts, requested fewer hints, had a lower average assistance score, and needed fewer problems to reach mastery in the tutor. The effect of PS was marginally significant on the average assistance score (F (3, 52) = 3.292, p = .075, η^2 = .056), but was not significant for the other dependent measures mentioned above.

Effects of the Interaction between OLM and PS. We did not find any significant interactions between OLM and PS on the post-test results. From the log data, we found an interaction that was on the borderline of significance for the average assistance score (ANOVA, F (3, 52) = 2.804, p = .100, η^2 = .049). Specifically, when students did *not* have access to the OLM, control over problem selection led to a lower assistance score, whereas with access to the OLM, their assistance score was the same regardless of whether they had control over problem selection.

Self-Assessment (SA) Accuracy. We also evaluated students' self-assessment accuracy. Figure 4 shows the frequencies of each self-assessment score (on the left) as well as how students' actual test performance relates to their self-assessment score (on the right). For both pre- and post-tests, the actual test scores increase as the self-assessment scores increase. We also compared students' self-assessment scores on the pre- and post-tests. A repeated measures ANOVA reveals that students' self-assessment scores increased significantly from pre- to post-test ($F(1, 52) = 13.078$, $p = .001$, $\eta^2 = .201$; pre-test Mean = 4.706, post-test Mean = 5.270). No significant differences were found between the conditions.

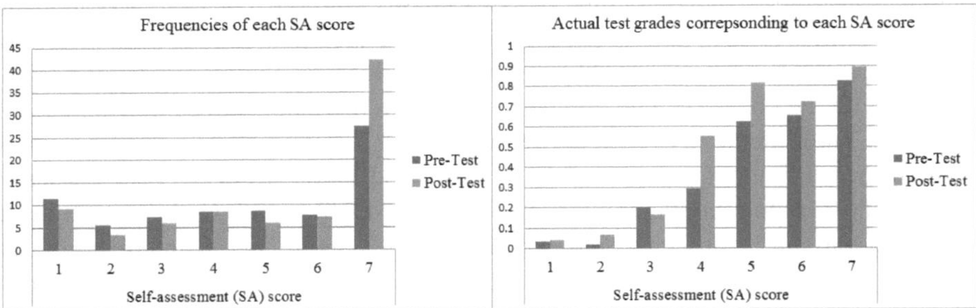

Fig. 4. The frequencies of different SA scores and the distribution of the test performance

Table 4 shows students' absolute accuracy of self-assessment (the lower the index, the better students' self-assessment). An absolute accuracy index of .14 means that a student answers a question correctly and s/he is 62.6% confident (according to Schraw [10], 50% confident is considered to be moderately accurate). Therefore, as shown in Table 4, the students had moderate to high accuracy of self-assessment. No significant differences were found among the conditions.

Table 4. The absolute self-assessment (SA) accuracy for different conditions

	OLM+PS	OLM+noPS	noOLM+PS	noOLM+noPS
Pre-test SA accuracy	.186 (.163)	.146 (.145)	.147 (.128)	.143 (.146)
Post-test SA accuracy	.127 (.115)	.127 (.088)	.166 (.077)	.106 (.084)

4 Discussion, Conclusion and Future Work

We conducted a controlled classroom experiment to investigate the effectiveness of having access to an OLM and having problem selection in an ITS, an area where not much empirical work has been conducted. Firstly, the pre- and post-test results reveal that students' knowledge of solving linear equations improved significantly, with large effect sizes on both the procedural problems and whole test, affirming the effectiveness of the tutor. Secondly, having access to an OLM resulted in better performance on the post-test. OLMs are a common feature in ITS. Although much effort has been put into the design and evaluation of the OLMs, and it has often been theorized that OLMs enhance the effectiveness of ITSs, we know of no prior experimental studies that had demonstrated an OLM significantly enhances student learning compared to a noOLM condition. The advantage of our OLM conditions suggests that the reflective self-assessment activities scaffolded by the OLM can significantly enhance students' learning outcomes, similar to the paper-based support in White and Frederiksen [12]. Specifically, students were prompted to reflect and self-assess on their learning status after each problem, with the display and updating of the OLM functioning as implicit feedback on their self-assessment. In this way, students might have been reminded of the errors and difficulties they had while solving each problem, as well as how they had corrected/resolved them. Such reflective process could enhance their understanding and help them learn from their errors. In addition, being exposed to their progress could also keep the students alerted the whole time. They would be more careful and motivated to stay focused on the learning. As revealed by the log data, the students with the OLM needed significantly less assistance from the system and made marginally significantly fewer incorrect attempts.

Thirdly, we did not find any significant main effect of PS on post-test results. In the log data, we only found that the students in the PS conditions had a marginally significant lower assistance score, suggesting that having control over problem selection leads to a somewhat smoother experience when solving problems. We also found the interaction between OLM and PS was on the borderline of significance for the average assistance score. When students had to select their own problems, they might be spurred to be more careful and active in their learning process, as evidenced by the lower assistance score. However, the fact that no significant results were found on the post-test suggests that more studies are still needed to investigate whether and how problem selection can enhance students' learning outcome in ITSs.

In regard to self-assessment, we found that students' self-assessment scores (confidence ratings) increased significantly from pre- to post-test, with a large effect size. Another interesting finding is that the participating students generally had moderate to high accuracy of self-assessment on the procedural problems, which is different from what have been observed in lots of prior work focusing on memory tasks and reading comprehension [5]. One explanation could be that the superficial features of equations correspond well with their difficulty levels, i.e. equations with more terms (or with parentheses) normally are more difficult. Consequently, it might be easier for the students to make accurate self-assessment on these questions. However, the mechanisms of self-assessment for different learning tasks need to be clarified in future research. Regardless, the increased self-assessment, especially given that it was accurate, should be viewed as positive result in its own right; arguably, learning is not truly robust if not accompanied by accurate self-assessment.

In sum, the present study shows that having an OLM while learning with a tutor leads to better learning outcomes, while the effects of having control over problem selection still need further investigation. Our findings help establish that reflective self-assessment is beneficial for students learning with math problem solving tasks in ITSs. To the best of our knowledge, our study is the first controlled experiment that supports the theoretical claim that OLMs can enhance students' learning outcomes. The future design of effective OLMs should consider incorporating features that can facilitate students' self-assessment to better support metacognition and Self-Regulated Learning.

Acknowledgements. We thank Jonathan Sewall, Borg Lojasiewicz, Octav Popescu, Brett Leber, Gail Kusbit and Emily Zacchero for their kind help with this work. We would also like to thank the participating teacher and students. This work is funded by an NSF grant to the Pittsburgh Science of Learning Center (NSF Award SBE0354420).

References

1. Aleven, V., et al.: A New Paradigm for Intelligent Tutoring Systems: Example-Tracing Tutors. International Journal of Artificial Intelligence in Education 19, 105–154 (2009)
2. Brusilovsky, P., Sosnovsky, S., Shcherbinina, O.: QuizGuide: Increasing the Educational Value of Individualized Self-Assessment Quizzes with Adaptive Navigation Support. In: Nall, J., Robson, R. (eds.) Proceedings of World Conference on E-Learning, E-Learn 2004, pp. 1806–1813. AACE (2004)
3. Bull, S., Dimitrova, V., McCalla, G.: Open Learner Models: Research Questions (Special Issue of IJAIED Part 1). International Journal of Artificial Intelligence in Education 17(2), 83–87 (2007)
4. Bull, S., Jackson, T., Lancaster, M.: Students' Interest in Their Misconceptions in First Year Electrical Circuits and Mathematics Courses. International Journal of Electrical Engineering Education 47(3), 307–318 (2010)
5. Dunlosky, J., Lipko, A.: Metacomprehension: A Brief History and How to Improve Its Accuracy. Current Directions in Psychological Science 16, 228–232 (2007)
6. Hartley, D., Mitrovic, A.: Supporting Learning by Opening the Student Model. In: Cerri, S.A., Gouardères, G., Paraguaçu, F. (eds.) ITS 2002. LNCS, vol. 2363, pp. 453–462. Springer, Heidelberg (2002)
7. Koedinger, K.R., Baker, R.S.J.d., Cunningham, K., Skogsholm, A., Leber, B., Stamper, J.: A Data Repository for the EDM Community: The PSLC DataShop. In: Romero, C., Ventura, S., Pechenizkiy, M., Baker, R.S.J.d. (eds.) Handbook of Educational Data Mining. CRC Press, Boca Raton (2010)
8. Long, Y., Aleven, V.: Students' Understanding of Their Student Model. In: Biswas, G., Bull, S., Kay, J., Mitrovic, A. (eds.) AIED 2011. LNCS, vol. 6738, pp. 179–186. Springer, Heidelberg (2011)
9. Mitrovic, A., Martin, B.: Scaffolding and Fading Problem Selection in SQL-Tutor. In: Hoppe, U., Verdejo, F., Kay, J. (eds.) Proceedings of the 11th International Conference on Artificial Intelligence in Education, pp. 479–481. Springer, Berlin (2003)
10. Schraw, G.: A Conceptual Analysis of Five Measures of Metacognitive Monitoring. Metacognition and Learning 4(1), 33–45 (2009)
11. Waalkens, M., Aleven, V., Taatgen, N.: Does Supporting Multiple Student Strategies Lead to Greater Learning and Motivation? Investigating a Source of Complexity in the Architecture of Intelligent Tutoring Systems. Computers & Education 60, 159–171 (2013)
12. White, B.C., Fredrickson, J.: Inquiry, Modeling, and Metacognition: Making Science Accessible to All Students. Cognition and Instruction 16, 39–66 (1998)
13. Zimmerman, B.J.: Investigating Self-Regulation and Motivation: Historical Background, Methodological Developments, and Future Prospects. American Educational Research Journal 45(1), 166–183 (2008)

Inferring Learning from Gaze Data during Interaction with an Environment to Support Self-Regulated Learning

Daria Bondareva[1], Cristina Conati[1], Reza Feyzi-Behnagh[2], Jason M. Harley[2], Roger Azevedo[2], François Bouchet[2]

[1] University of British Columbia
[2] McGill University
{bondaria,conati}@cs.ubc.ca,
{reza.feyzibehnagh,jason.harley}@mail.mcgill.ca,
{roger.azevedo,francois.bouchet}@mcgill.ca

Abstract. In this paper, we explore the potential of gaze data as a source of information to predict learning as students interact with MetaTutor, an ITS that scaffolds self-regulated learning. Using data from 47 college students, we show that a classifier using a variety of gaze features achieves considerable accuracy in predicting student learning after seeing gaze data from the complete interaction. We also show promising results on the classifier ability to detect learning in real-time during interaction.

Keywords: student modeling, eye-tracking, self-regulated learning.

1 Introduction

Student modeling is known to be a difficult problem because there is often a large gap between students behaviors observable by an Intelligent Tutoring Systems (ITS) and the students' states and processes that the ITS needs to model in order to provide personalized instruction. One approach that is being explored to address this problem is to investigate the use of sensors that can help reduce the gap between the student's relevant states and what an ITS can observe about them.

This paper contributes to this body of research by exploring the value of eye-tracking data (also referred to as *gaze data* from now on) in assessing student learning during interactions with MetaTutor, a multi-agent ITS that scaffolds self-regulated learning (SRL) while students study material on the human circulatory system [1]. This research is part of a larger endeavor to understand and model the relations among affect, cognition and meta-cognition in learning with MetaTutor, by leveraging multi-channel data sources including think-aloud protocols, eye-tracking, human-agent dialogue, log-file, embedded quizzes, galvanic skin response, and face recognition. We decided to start by focusing on gaze data, because there is already evidence that it can provide useful information on all the student modeling dimensions we are interested in: cognitive [e.g. 2–4], metacognitive [5] and affective [6, 7]. We start by investigating if and how gaze data can be used to predict learning in MetaTutor because tracking whether a student is learning is important for a tutoring agent to decide when to provide personalized instruction.

K. Yacef et al. (Eds.): AIED 2013, LNAI 7926, pp. 229–238, 2013.

The main contribution of this paper are results showing that gaze data can indeed be a useful source of information to predict student learning with MetaTutor. This result is especially important because it does not exist in isolation. Similar research using a different type of learning environment (an interactive simulation to support learning by exploration), also found that gaze data was a good predictor of student learning [3]. Therefore, the results reported here contribute to confirm the importance of gaze data as a predictor of learning across different types of learning environments, that can be leveraged for providing real-time personalized support.

In the rest of the paper, Section 2 summarizes related work. Section 3 describes MetaTutor, and the study that generated the data used in this paper. Section 4 describes how we trained classifiers on eye-tracking data to predict student learning. Section 5 reports the classification results, followed by conclusions and future work.

2 Related Work

Eye-tracking has been the focus of increasing interest in student modeling, as a way to track user's states and processes at the cognitive, meta-cognitive and affective level. At the cognitive level, in addition to [3], discussed above, Gluck and Anderson [4] used gaze data to assess student problem-solving behaviors within an ITS for algebra, including attention shifts, problem disambiguation and processing of error messages. Sibert et al. [8] explored gaze tracking to assess reading performance in a system for automated reading remediation that provides support if a user gaze patterns indicate difficulties in reading a word. D'Mello et al. [2] show that tracking a student's attention toward a Pedagogical Agent in a dialogue-based ITS and generating prompts to guide this attention, improves student learning. At the meta-cognitive level, [5] shows that using gaze data improves a student model's ability to track students' self-explanation behaviors (i.e. generating explanations to one-self to improve one's understanding), and consequent learning. At the affective level, Qu and Johnson [6] leveraged gaze data to assess student motivation in an ITS for teaching engineering skills. Muldner et al. [7] looked at pupil dilation to detect relevant student affective and meta-cognitive states during the interaction with an ITS that supports analogical problem solving.

In the context of modeling students' SRL processes, so far researchers have mainly relied on mining action logs. For instance, Kinnebrew and Biswas [9], used sequence mining on action logs to identify effective and ineffective behaviors in students interacting with Betty's Brain, an ITS for scaffolding SRL via teachable agents. Bouchet et al. [10] performed similar work with MetaTutor, the ITS used in this paper. Sabourin et al. [11], mined both actions and students self-reports on their affective states for the early prediction of SRL processes during interaction with Crystal Island, a narrative-based and inquiry-oriented serious game for science.

3 MetaTutor Study

MetaTutor is an adaptive hypermedia learning environment which includes 38 pages of text and diagrams, organized by a table of contents displayed in the left pane of the environment (see Figure 1[1]) [1]. Text and diagrams are displayed separately in the two central panels of the interface. In addition to providing structured access to relevant content, MetaTutor also includes a variety of components designed to scaffold learners' use of SRL processes and their learning of science topics, such as the human circulatory system. Four pedagogical agents (PAs) are displayed in turn in the upper right-hand corner of the environment. Each agent provides spoken prompts and feedback on various SRL processes. For example, one PA assists the student in establishing two learning sub-goals related to the overall learning goal for the session (see top horizontal panel in Figure 1, with sub-goal panel right below). The shading of the sub-goal bars in the corresponding panel shows the student's current progress towards completing that sub-goal as the interaction proceeds.

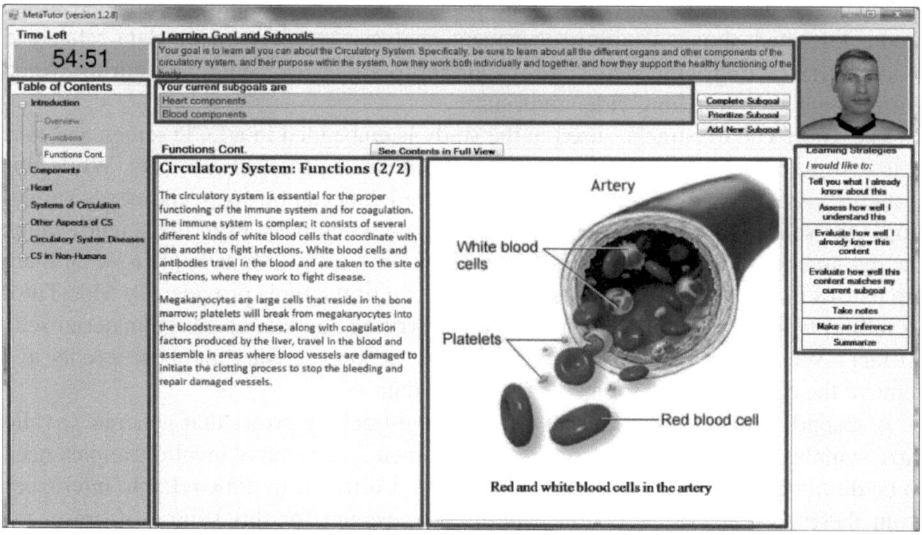

Fig. 1. Sample MetaTutor interface

Other SRL processes supported by the PAs include taking notes, writing summaries of the viewed content, evaluating one's current understanding, etc., and they can be initiated via the learning strategy palette displayed in the right interface pane.

A study was conducted in 2012 with the goal of collecting multi-channel data to examine the role of cognitive, metacognitive, and affective processes during learning with MetaTutor [12]. The study included two conditions: one (adaptive) in which the Meta-Tutor's PAs provided prompts and feedback adapted to each student's performance; another (non-adaptive) in which prompts and feedback were generic. The study consisted of two sessions. In the first, participants (university students who were randomly assigned to the two study conditions) completed a pre-test on the

[1] The boxed areas in the figure indicate Areas of Interest used for eye-tracking, as described in Section 4.

circulatory system and demographics questionnaires. The second session started with the calibration of apparatuses, including a Tobii T60 eye-tracker[2]. Next, each participant watched video tutorials on SRL processes and related interface functionalities, and was then asked to set two sub-goals for the session. After that, the participant interacted with MetaTutor for one hour, followed by a post-test. In this paper, we focus on exploring whether the gaze data collected in the study can be leveraged to predict student learning, as measured by the study pre- and post-tests The next section describes how we built gaze-based classifiers to achieve this goal.

4 Classification Experiments

For the current work, we used 64 participants with eye-tracking data collected in the study described above. For the subsequent analysis, we focused on data related to students interacting with MetaTutor, excluding parts of the interaction during which participants were watching video tutorials.

The Tobii T60 eye-tracker used in the study is embedded in a LCD screen and thus it is non-intrusive, because it does not constrain participants' movements. While this is a great asset, the down side is that the collected data can be noisy and needs validation. One source of noise is due to participants looking away from the screen, which the eye-tracker interprets as invalid data. These look-away events happen when there are pauses in the session or when students use one of the tools provided by MetaTutor to submit typed text to the system (e.g., while writing summaries on the material seen so far)[3]. We created scripts to parse the study action-log files for these events and remove the corresponding segments from gaze data.

A second source of noise is due to actual eye-tracking errors that generate invalid gaze samples. Participants with gaze data that include too many invalid samples need to be discarded because the missing data makes it difficult to draw reliable inferences from these participants' attention patterns. To account for this source of noise, we adopted the data validation process discussed in [3], which essentially discards participants that have less than 80% valid samples overall, as reported by the eye-tracker (after removing known look-away events). The validation process resulted in discarding 16 users, leaving a total of 48 for the actual classification study.

4.1 Gaze Features

An eye-tracker captures gaze information in terms of *fixations* (i.e., maintaining gaze at one point on the screen) and *saccades* (i.e., a quick movement of gaze from one fixation point to another). Gaze patterns are further defined by measures that represent gaze direction, including *absolute path angles* (i.e., the angle between a saccade and

[2] Precision/accuracy for X are 0.18-0.36°/0.4-0.5°, for Y are 0.18-0.30°/0.4-0.6°. The smallest distinguishable size of Area of Interest is 30 by 30 pixels.

[3] These activities can be reliability tracked using action logs, and will be included as part of our future work.

the horizontal) and *relative path angles* (i.e., the angle between two consecutive saccades). Following the approach suggested in [13], and followed in [3], we computed a large variety of features based on raw gaze data. These are divided into two types. The first type was generated by applying summary statistics such as mean and standard deviation (SD) to the above measures, taken independently of the specific interface layout. This process generated 10 features representing general gaze trends that do not take into account the nature of the interaction with MetaTutor (see Table 1, "no-AOI" column, where AOI stands for Area of Interest). The second type consists of features that do incorporate interface-specific information in terms of salient areas, or AOIs, of the MetaTutor's interface. We defined seven of these AOIs (labeled with rectangles in Figure 1): Text Content, Image Content, Goal, Subgoals, Learning Strategies Pallete, Agent and Table of Contents.

Table 1. Description of gaze-based features

No-AOI Features	AOI-based Features
Rate and Number of Fixations	Fixation rate in AOI
Mean and SD of Fixation Duration	Proportion of fixation time and fixation number in AOI
Mean and SD of Saccade Length	Duration of longest fixation
Mean and SD of Relative Path Angles	Proportion of transitions from every other AOI to the current one (7 different features)
Mean and SD of Abs Path Angles	

For each AOI, we calculated the following features: rate of fixations, proportion of time and number of fixations, and duration of longest fixation. We also included the proportion of transitions from every other AOI to the current one. Proportional measures were used to assess the relative magnitude of attention devoted to each AOI over the course of a complete interaction. In total, there are 77 AOI-based features (summarized in the second column of Table 1). In the classification experiments described next, we trained separate classifiers on each of the two feature sets described above, as well as on a third feature set obtained by combining the two, referred to as the *Full* feature set from now on. Our goal is to ascertain the relative importance of AOI dependent and AOI independent features in predicting student learning.

4.2 Training Classifiers on Gaze Data

A large number of features can lead to over-fitting when only relatively small datasets are available for training. To avoid this issue, we reduced the number of features by performing wrapper feature selection [14]. This approach is based on searching subsets of the available features to find one that gives the classifier with the highest accuracy, where the search is greedy if the initial set of features is large (as is the case for our *Full* and *AOI-based* feature sets). To further reduce the likelihood of over-fitting, the feature selection process was cross-validated. For each of the original feature sets, the final set of features was obtained by discarding all features that appeared in less than 10% of the cross validation folds.

Classification labels were generated by dividing students into High Learners (HL) or Low Learners (LL) based on a median split of their learning performance, measured as proportional learning gains (PLG), namely the ratio of the differences between post and pre-test scores, and between maximum post-test score and pre-test. One outlier was excluded, resulting in a dataset of 47 participants. It should be noted that, in this dataset, we found no significant differences between users from the adaptive and non-adaptive study conditions described in Section 3[4] ($t(45) = -0.77$, $p = 0.45$, Cohen's $d = 0.23$). Thus, for the purpose of our analysis, it makes sense to collapse the two groups. Performing a median split on this dataset resulted in 23 LL (Mean PLG = 0.93, SD = 36.05), and 24 HL (Mean PLG = 67.01, SD = 16.48). Given these labels, we used the WEKA data mining toolkit to train a variety of classifiers with feature selection on our three feature sets: *Full*, *AOI-based* and *no-AOI*. The next section summarizes our results.

5 Results

5.1 Classification Accuracy

Table 2. Accuracy and Kappa[5] scores for different classifiers and feature sets

Full Feature set	**Accuracy (%)**			**Kappa**
	Overall	**LL**	**HL**	
Simple Logistic Regression	78.3	70.43	85.83	0.56
Multinomial Logistic Regression	61.28	66.52	56.25	0.23
Naïve Bayes	71.7	51.3	91.25	0.43
Random Forest	64.48	67.83	61.67	0.29
Multilayer Perceptron	66.59	60.86	72.08	0.33
AOI-based Feature set	**Overall**	**LL**	**HL**	**Kappa**
Simple Logistic Regression	64.47	51.3	77.08	0.28
Multinomial Logistic Regression	54.47	51.3	57.5	0.09
Naïve Bayes	69.57	56.52	82.08	0.39
Random Forest	68.08	72.61	63.75	0.36
Multilayer Perceptron	56.59	51.3	61.67	0.13
No-AOI Feature set	**Overall**	**LL**	**HL**	**Kappa**
Simple Logistic Regression	52.55	60.43	45	0.05
Multinomial Logistic Regression	58.3	60.43	56.25	0.17
Naïve Bayes	52.34	45.65	58.75	0.04
Random Forest	48.93	48.69	49.17	-0.02
Multilayer Perceptron	55.96	54.78	57.08	0.12

[4] There was also no significant difference in PLGs between the two conditions in the original group.

[5] As per [15] kappa: <0.2 is poor; 0.21-0.4 is fair; 0.41-0.6 is moderate; >0.61 is good.

All the results reported here are based on 10-fold cross-validation, with 10 runs per fold, and pertain to the 5 best performing classifiers among the ones we tested (Simple Logistic Regression, Multinomial Logistic Regression, Naïve Bayes, Random Forest and Multilayer Perceptron). Table 2 reports, for each feature set (Full, AOI-based and No-AOI): overall accuracy (percentage of data points correctly classified), accuracy on each class (LL and HL), and kappa scores (another commonly used measure of accuracy that accounts for agreement due to chance)[16].

To ascertain the impact that different feature sets have on classification performance, we performed two, two-way ANOVA with feature set (3 levels) and classifiers (5 levels) as factors on both overall accuracy and kappa-scores. The two analyses generated analogous results, thus here we discuss only results on overall accuracy, because they are easier to interpret in terms of practical classification performance.

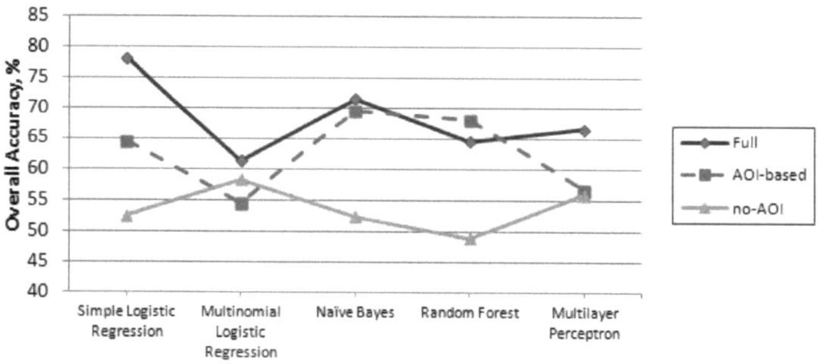

Fig. 2. Overall accuracy of the 5 classifiers over the 3 features sets

Figure 2 shows the mean of overall accuracy for each combination of classifier and feature set. There are significant main effects of both classifier ($F(4, 36) = 9.01$, $p<0.001$, $\eta_p^2 = 0.50$) and feature set, ($F(2, 18) = 112.55$, $p<0.001$, $\eta_p^2 = 0.93$), further qualified by a significant interaction between factors, $F(8, 72) = 16.63$, $p<0.001$, $\eta_p^2=0.65$), showing that classifier type influences the relative accuracy that can be achieved with each feature set. We performed planned contrast analysis (with corresponding Bonferroni adjustments) to gain a better understanding of the relative value of AOI-dependent and AOI independent features. This analysis shows that, in general, the performance of the classifiers that were trained on the Full feature set is significantly better than those trained on AOI-based features ($t(72) = 6.21$, $p<0.001$, Cohen's $d = 1.46$). The latter classifiers, in turn, perform better than those trained on no-AOI ($t(72) = 9.53$, $p<0.001$, Cohen's $d = 2.24$). In particular, the highest overall accuracy is achieved by Simple Logistic Regression on the Full dataset (78.3%, kappa = 0.56), which also shows good balance in class accuracy (70.4% on LL and 85.8% on HL as shown in Table 2).

We see this result as strong evidence of the value of eye-tracking data as a source of rich information in student modeling, because it shows that gaze information can be a good predictor of student learning, even before taking into account other student interaction behaviors (e.g., interface actions). Furthermore, this result seems to generalize across at least some learning environments that are different in nature, because similar accuracies were found in [3], where the authors looked at how gaze data predicts learning with an interactive simulation to support exploratory learning.

Simple Logistic regression on the Full dataset performs significantly better ($t(72)=4.12$, $p<0.001$, Cohen's $d = 0.97$) than the best performing classifier on AOI-only features, namely Naïve Bayes (69.6% accuracy, kappa = 0.39). This classifier is also quite unbalanced in terms of class accuracy (56.5% for LL, and 82% for HL), indicating that AOI-independent features have considerable added value when combined with AOI-dependent ones, although on their own they do not perform that well. It is interesting to see that the importance of having a combination of AOI-dependent and AOI-independent features is confirmed by the results of feature selection. For the Simple Logistic Regression classifier, which showed the best overall accuracy on the Full feature set, 14 features were selected: 4 AOI-independent features (mean and standard deviation of fixation duration, rate of fixations and mean of relative path angles), and 10 AOI-dependent ones. These include:

- 7 features describing proportion of transitions between AOIs: (i) from Table of Contents, Learning Strategies Palette and Text Content to Subgoals; (ii) from Table of Contents to Overall Learning Goal; (iii) from Table of Contents and Image Content to Learning Strategies Palette; (iv) from Text Content to Table of Contents.
- Longest fixation in Overall Learning Goal;
- Proportion of time and number of fixations spent in Subgoals.

It is worth noting that seven out of the ten AOI-based features are related to Overall Learning Goal and Subgoals AOIs, suggesting that attention to these elements is indeed important for assessing learning with MetaTutor. The next most frequent AOI to appear in this set, with two related features, is the Learning Strategies Palette, also supporting the importance of this element in gauging learning with MetaTutor. A notable absence is related to any feature involving the Agent AOI. As described in Section 3, the MetaTutor agents provide spoken feedback and prompts during interaction. The fact that attention to the Agent AOI does not seem to play a role in our classification results may be due either to the fact that learners do not need to always look at an agent to process its audio prompts and feedback or, if they do, to the fact that agents' prompts and feedback do not impact learning enough to help detect it (an explanation supported by the lack of difference in learning between the adaptive and non-adaptive conditions in the original MetaTutor study).

5.2 Accuracy over Time

The results in the previous section show that gaze data can be a rather powerful source of information to predict student learning, when data from the complete interaction with MetaTutor is available. Here we explore whether it can also be a source of information for detecting a student's learning performance *during* interaction with MetaTutor, to support real-time personalized help and feedback when needed. To address this question, we simulated online system conditions by incrementally feeding gaze data from the Full feature set to the best performing classifier from the previous

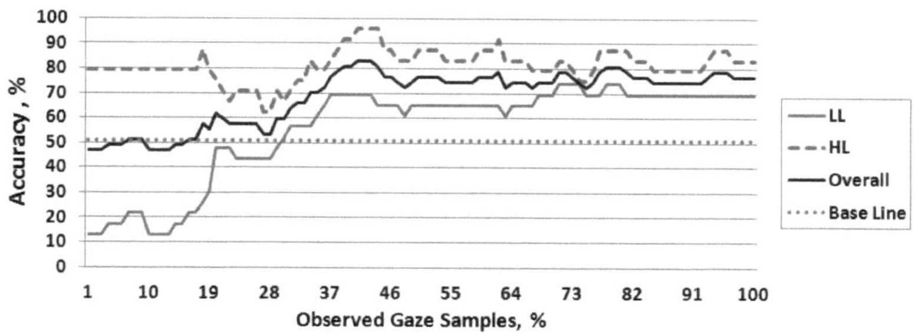

Fig. 3. Accuracy over time (Simple Logistic Regression, Full feature set)

section (Logistic Regression), and calculated overall and class accuracy (cross-validated) at regular intervals of 2 minutes.

Figure 3 shows the result of this process, i.e., the accuracy over time (overall and for each class) of the Logistic Regression classifier on the Full dataset. The classification accuracy starts growing above a baseline that predicts the most likely class (HL) based on a simple median split (51% overall accuracy), after seeing about 28% of the data (28.70 minutes from the beginning of the session). After seeing about 37% of the data (36.61 minutes), overall accuracy stabilizes above 72%, with some small fluctuations. The average accuracy over the session was 68.83%. We argue that these results provide strong support for using eye-tracking data as a source of on-line prediction of student learning, because they are obtained for an interactive system without even considering interface actions. We expect that combining features based on gaze data and features based on interface actions (e.g., taking notes, writing summaries, number of content pages visited, number of sub-goals completed) will boost accuracy over time, a finding that has already been observed in [17], where this approach was used on the interactive simulation discussed in [3].

6 Conclusions and Future Work

We presented research on understanding the value of gaze data to predict student learning during interaction with MetaTutor, an ITS that supports the acquisition of SRL processes. Our results show that gaze data alone achieves 78% classification accuracy on student learning after seeing all data from an interaction, and reaches 72% accuracy after seeing 37% of the data. These results replicate findings obtained by previous research using a different type of learning environment, and confirm the value of using gaze data as a source of information that ITSs can leverage to assess student learning and react accordingly. Our next step will be to combine gaze data with other multi-channel data sources (e.g., interaction logs, facial expressions of emotions), to see how this increases classification accuracy. We also plan to repeat this analysis to predict student states at the affective level (e.g. curiosity, boredom).

References

1. Azevedo, R., Behnagh, R., Duffy, M., Harley, J., Trevors, G.: Metacognition and self-regulated learning in student-centered leaning environments. In: Theoretical Foundations of Student-centered Learning Environments, 2nd edn., pp. 171–197 (2012)
2. D'Mello, S., Olney, A., Williams, C., Hays, P.: Gaze tutor: A gaze-reactive intelligent tutoring system. Int. J. Hum.-Comput. Stud. 70, 377–398 (2012)
3. Kardan, S., Conati, C.: Exploring gaze data for determining user learning with an interactive simulation. In: Masthoff, J., Mobasher, B., Desmarais, M.C., Nkambou, R. (eds.) UMAP 2012. LNCS, vol. 7379, pp. 126–138. Springer, Heidelberg (2012)
4. Anderson, J.R., Gluck, K.: What role do cognitive architectures play in intelligent tutoring systems. In: Cognition & Instruction: Twenty-five Years of Progress, pp. 227–262 (2001)
5. Conati, C., Merten, C.: Eye-tracking for user modeling in exploratory learning environments: An empirical evaluation. Knowledge-Based Systems 20, 557–574 (2007)
6. Qu, L., Johnson, W.L.: Detecting the learner's motivational states in an interactive learning environment. In: Proc. of 12th Int. Conf. on Artificial Intelligence in Education (2005)
7. Muldner, K., Christopherson, R., Atkinson, R., Burleson, W.: Investigating the Utility of Eye-Tracking Information on Affect and Reasoning for User Modeling. In: Houben, G.-J., McCalla, G., Pianesi, F., Zancanaro, M. (eds.) UMAP 2009. LNCS, vol. 5535, pp. 138–149. Springer, Heidelberg (2009)
8. Sibert, J.L., Gokturk, M., Lavine, R.A.: The reading assistant: eye gaze triggered auditory prompting for reading remediation. In: Proc. of the 13th Annual ACM Symposium on User Interface Software and Technology, pp. 101–107 (2000)
9. Kinnebrew, J.S., Biswas, G.: Identifying Learning Behaviors by Contextualizing Differential Sequence Mining with Action Features and Performance Evolution. In: Proc. of EDM, 5th Int. Conf. on Educational Data Mining, pp. 57–64 (2012)
10. Bouchet, F., Azevedo, R., Kinnebrew, J.S., Biswas, G.: Identifying Students' Characteristic Learning Behaviors in an Intelligent Tutoring System Fostering Self-Regulated Learning. In: Proc. of EDM, 5th Int. Conf. on Educational Data Mining, pp. 65–72 (2012)
11. Sabourin, J.L., Mott, B.W., Lester, J.C.: Early Prediction of Student Self-Regulation Strategies by Combining Multiple Models. In: Proc. of EDM, 5th Int. Conf. on Educational Data Mining, pp. 156–159 (2012)
12. Azevedo, R., et al.: The Effectiveness of Pedagogical Agents' Prompting and Feedback in Facilitating Co-adapted Learning with MetaTutor. In: Cerri, S.A., Clancey, W.J., Papadourakis, G., Panourgia, K. (eds.) ITS 2012. LNCS, vol. 7315, pp. 212–221. Springer, Heidelberg (2012)
13. Goldberg, J.H., Helfman, J.I.: Comparing information graphics: a critical look at eye tracking. In: Proc. of BELIV, 3rd Workshop: BEyond time and errors: novel evaLuation methods for Information Visualization, pp. 71–78 (2010)
14. Guyon, I., Elisseeff, A.: An introduction to variable and feature selection. The J. of Machine Learning Research 3, 1157–1182 (2003)
15. Landis, J.R., Koch, G.G.: The measurement of observer agreement for categorical data. Biometrics 33, 159–174 (1977)
16. Ben-David, A.: About the relationship between ROC curves and Cohen's kappa. Engineering Applications of Artificial Intelligence 21, 874–882 (2008)
17. Kardan, S., Conati, C.: Comparing and Combining Eye Gaze and Interface Actions for Determining User Learning with an Interactive Simulation. In: Carberry, S., Weibelzahl, S., Micarelli, A., Semeraro, G. (eds.) UMAP 2013. LNCS, vol. 7899, pp. 215–227. Springer, Heidelberg (2013)

Teammate Relationships Improve Help-Seeking Behavior in an Intelligent Tutoring System

Minghui Tai[1], Ivon Arroyo[2], and Beverly Park Woolf[2]

[1] Department of Teacher Education and Curriculum Studies, University of Massachusetts Amherst
[2] School of Computer Science, University of Massachusetts Amherst
mtai@educ.umass.edu, {ivon,bev}@cs.umass.edu

Abstract. This paper describes a method for improving students' help-seeking behavior by creating a teammate relationship between intelligent tutors and students. Help seeking in intelligent tutors involves student self-regulation as described in learning theory and can be explored from the perspective of social psychology. We describe an experiment in which ninety-seven students were randomly assigned to treatment and control conditions and students in the treatment group were supported to relate to the Wayang Math Tutor as teammates by providing the help button named "Work Together". The result suggests that students who treated the tutor as teammates saw more hints (asked for more hints), exhibited reduced quick-guessing behavior and did not abuse hints while working together to solve math problems.

Keywords: Help seeking, Intelligent tutoring system, Human- computer interaction.

1 Introduction

If students need help while learning in a classroom, they might ask their teacher. Instead, intelligent tutoring systems aim to provide individualized support in the form of adaptive interactive learning environments, where students can work at their own pace [1]. These systems have been widely used in education [2]. One interesting question that has not been asked is "What do students think is the role of the intelligent tutor?" Is it a substitute teacher, a helper, a friend? Do students treat the system as a human or just as a learning tool? Research shows that by manipulating student identity and creating a team relationship between humans and computer, students can be influenced to think that the information from the computer is of better quality and relayed in a more friendly way [3]. In this paper, we explore whether students who are encouraged to build up a teammate relationship with the intelligent tutor, to collaboratively solve math problems with it, are motivated to engage in more productive use of the system, such as effective use of the help-seeking behavior, and whether just attempting to change this relationship with the tutoring system supports improved math learning behavior among students.

This paper describes research to begin to unpack and understand the value of adjusting learning with individualized software for individuals, specific groups of students and

K. Yacef et al. (Eds.): AIED 2013, LNAI 7926, pp. 239–248, 2013.

special social contexts. Since one-size-fits all education does not work, it is important to understand the factors that do influence and bias individual student academic success.

1.1 Background and Related Work

Caring Relationships with Students. Students need caring environments in which to learn [4] [5] and long-term relations with caring individuals. Providing such care once or twice during class is supportive; however, learning is greatly enhanced if that caring includes long-term empathy and support [6]. Caring relationships are associated with high academic performance and various studies have linked interpersonal relationships between human teachers and students to highly motivated outcomes [7]. Additionally, collaboration between friends seems to foster greater development of scientific reasoning and self-efficacy than does collaboration between acquaintances [8][9]. Can this noted human relationship be reproduced, in part, by empathy from a computer character? Apparently the answer is yes [10]. People seem to relate to computers in the same way they relate to humans and some relationships are very similar to real social connections [11]. For example, students continue to engage in frustrating tasks on a computer significantly longer after an empathetic computational response and have immediately lowered stress level (via skin conductance) after empathy and an apology from animated characters.

If computers are to interact naturally with humans to support learning, they must demonstrate social and caring skills, express social competencies and recognize student affect. Affect is central to human cognition and strongly impacts student learning. Many learning theories recognize the need for social learning. For example, activity theory suggests that people are socio-culturally embedded actors (not processors or system components) [12]. Findings from neuroscience suggest that all learning is affective in nature and every person's ideas contain some affective components [13]. Some scholars even suggest that a major weakness in traditional psychology is to separate intellect and affect [12]. Though most intelligent tutoring systems that attempt to build rapport with the learner do so through politeness, actual human peer tutors employ a great deal of impolite and face-threatening behavior [14].

Help-Seeking Behavior and Self-regulation in Intelligent Tutors. Research has shown that effective help-seeking behavior can positively influence students' learning outcomes while working with educational technologies [1][15]. However, existing literature in the help-seeking behavior field has indicated that learners often do not use available help facilities effectively [1]. Research posits two main forms of ineffective help use in intelligent tutoring systems, or help misuse, including help avoidance (the underuse of help) and help abuse (the overuse of help) [1]. Help avoidance describes learning in which help is avoided even though students are obviously in need of help [15][16]. Help abuse describes learning in which help is used too often, possibly so the student can see bottom-out hints and the correct answer without understanding the content of the hints [1][17].

Help seeking is a skill of self-regulation [18]. A successful learner usually has good self-regulatory strategies to control her cognitive processes of learning, including monitoring comprehension, planning what needs to be done, determining how to overcome obstacles and evaluating her progress. Intelligent tutoring systems often provide contextual hints that help students solve problems step-by step [1]. Students should decide how much help they need and ask for different level hints from the tutor to see detailed problem-solving steps in order to solve a problem. Therefore, self-regulation plays an important role in the facilitation of learning outcomes in the context of intelligent tutoring systems.

Existing research builds on cognitive self-regulated learning theory and its focus on having tutors deliver metacognitive feedback to advise students and influence better help-seeking behavior performance [3]. From a social psychological perspective, forming team relationships with the computer makes learners more likely to be influenced by the computer [3]. Little research exists regarding help-seeking behavior from a social psychological perspective in the context of intelligent tutoring systems.

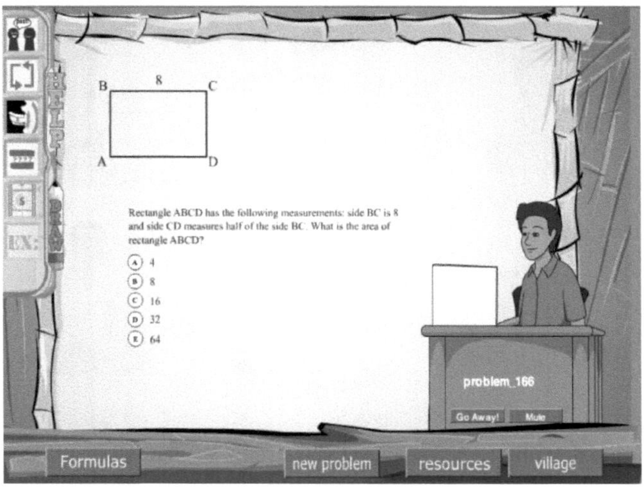

Fig. 1. The Wayang Outpost Math Tutor interface. An animated companion provides individualized comments and help tools are available in the vertical bar (left).

Intelligent Tutoring System Testbed. This research was conducted using the Wayang Mathematics Tutor, see Figure 1. Like a human tutor, the tutor identifies student skills and modifies its presentation to provide missing skills.[1] The tutor uses an adaptive mechanism that tailors the sequencing of problems to identify a student's most critical cognitive skills, adapts the next problem, provides individualized responses and predicts the likelihood of success on future problems [19]. The tutor uses cutting-edge research in cognitive science, interactive and active learning, multiple learning paths, embedded assessment, frequent feedback, and scaffolded learning [19][20]. It identifies the resources that are available to students, including animated color-coded hints with sound, videos, explanations, worked-out examples, and video-game-like adventures to practice real world issues and challenges.

[1] Wayang Outpost is described in detail at `http://wayangoutpost.com`

The tutor begins with skilled student assessment and placement and continues with individualized instruction and problems adapted for student learning needs. This solution has shown great improvement for at-risk students, including underrepresented students (females, minorities and students with disabilities) [21]. The Wayang system provides cultural support for minority students through animated companions that look like minority students (Hispanic and African-American), use expressions from each culture and provide individual help, see Figure 2. In controlled randomized studies, the use of animated companions improved students' math *attitudes*, increased their *motivation* and reduced their *frustration* and *anxiety* [19][20][21]. Females and students with disabilities reported *increased confidence* and *decreased frustration* while working with companions. Gender differences were reported for the impact of animated companions on student affect; for example, matching the gender of students with that of the animated companion is best for all learners and companions are particularly beneficial for girls.

Fig. 2. Multi-cultural animated pedagogical agents show a range of emotion. Companions act out their emotion and talk with students expressing full sentences of cognitive, meta-cognitive and emotional feedback.

The Wayang software provides cultural companions and learner analytics while students solve mathematics problems, see Figure 2. The software identifies students' skills and emotion and adapts its problems and responses to how well each individual student performs with a particular assignment. It determines the level at which students are working and provides appropriate problems. Students receive immediate feedback about how they are doing and make choices about what kind of problem to see next (easier, harder), thus giving weight to their opinions[22].

The system provides real time assessment of student progress and performance involving several existing and validated instruments (e.g., pre and posttests involving state standardized questions; affective surveys and self-reports) [22]. These instruments were used to measure the impact of the tutor on student achievement and on a variety of students' affective states [19][20]. For example, we use log data (e.g., how long students spend solving problems, how many hints they request, etc.) to calculate dependent evaluation variables, such as effort or interest. We use pre- and post-tests to measure performance in mathematics. The system provides careful sequencing, monitoring, and control of the learning process. When students achieve mastery of initial steps in a sequence, they are more likely to make satisfactory progress in subsequent, more advanced steps. Frequent assessment informs teachers and students when additional time is needed to master a particular objective. There is ample evidence that students of all ages and abilities can be taught study skills that can increase their achievement [23]. A student's total learning time and problem completion record is strongly related to future course success. Studies have also shown that the value of doing homework increases significantly when instructors' assessment and comments are presented to students in a timely fashion and along with individualized feedback.

The purpose of this study is to investigate whether students' help-seeking behavior can be enhanced in intelligent tutoring systems by taking a social psychological perspective, specifically, by manipulating students' relationships with a mathematics tutor. We explored two research issues: Do students have better learning outcomes when they learn with a tutor as a teammate and do students engage in effective help-seeking behavior when they work together with a tutor to solve problems as a team.

2 Method

2.1 Design and Participants

Students were randomly assigned to two groups and both groups worked with the Wayang Tutor. One group worked with the tutor manipulated to support a team relationship (treatment group) and the other half of students worked with the non-manipulated tutor (control group). 115 students in four classes were enrolled in this study; one teacher taught two classes each with 28 students and another teacher taught two classes with 34 and 25 students. Students were in Grade 7-8 from one school in a medium size city in Massachusetts. However, 18 students did not complete the posttest (12 out of 57 students in the treatment group and 6 out of 58 students in the control group). Pretest score means from these 18 students in both conditions were not significant with p value =. 091>. 05). Thus, data is analyzed from only 97 students' data (48 female and 49 male).

2.2 Materials

In this study, we rely on Wayang Outpost, an intelligent tutoring system [2] that helps students solve mathematics problems, see Figure 1. These problems commonly appear on Massachusetts's standardized tests. To answer problems in the Wayang interface, participating students choose an answer from a list of multiple-choice options. Wayang provides immediate feedback on students' answers by coloring them red (the answer is incorrect) or green (the answer is correct) in the interface. During problem-solving steps, if students do not know how to solve the problem at hand, they ask the tutor for step-by-step hints by clicking the "Help" button at left side tool bar in the interface, see Figure 1.

2.3 Instruments

Students in the treatment group received a button named "Work Together" instead of a button named "Help". In order to enhance the team relationship they also received the prompt started by "Dear <student's name>." They were prompted to solve math problems with the tutor as a teammate and were advised to "click" the button called "work together" if they didn't know how to solve the problem, so the tutor could help them. Instead, students in the control group were prompted only with "Dear student", without showing a specific student's name [24]. They were prompted to ask for help by clicking on the "Help" button if they did not know how to solve problems. Students in both conditions received the same content of step-by step hints if they asked for help from the tutor. They saw a prompt screen every time they logged in to remind them to ask for help if they did not know how to solve a problem.

2.4 Procedure

Students worked with the Wayang Outpost math tutor during six 50-minute classes during three weeks. Pre and posttests were administered on the first and last day of the series. The Wayang tutor recorded students' pre and posttests scores and detailed interactions with the tutor in the log files.

2.5 Data Analysis

Students' posttest scores were used to analyze students' learning outcome. We also analyzed the difference between students' pretest scores and posttest scores for their learning gain in order to understand their learning improvement. Data from the log files in the Wayang Math Tutor were used to analyze students help-seeking behavior results. The log files recorded total number of problems seen, total hints seen, total problems with abused hints (student rushing through hints to get to the last hint which revealed the correct answer) and total problems that were quick-guessed (quickly making attempts until the correct answer was revealed). An independent-samples t-test was conducted to compare results between treatment and control group.

3 Results

To answer our first research question, do students learn more when they work with the tutor as a team member; an independent-samples t-test was conducted to compare students' posttest scores and learning gains (from pretest scores to posttest scores) in treatment and control conditions. There was no significant difference in the posttest scores for treatment group ($M=69.22$, $SD=27.13$) and control group ($M=71.30$, $SD=23.15$) conditions; $t(95)=-4.07$, $p = 0.69$. Nor was there a difference between treatment group ($M=-4.58$, $SD=23.98$) and control group ($M= 1.11$, $SD=17.52$) conditions with regard to learning gain from pretest scores to posttest scores; $t(95)=-1.35$, $p= 0.18$. These results suggest that changing the interface towards building up a team relationship between a student and Wayang may not have an effect on students' learning outcomes and learning gains.

Table 1. Independent-samples t-test results and effect size (Cohen's *d*)

	Treatment group (N=45)	Control group (N=52)	*t* value	*p* value	Cohen's *d*
Percent Posttest	69.22% (27.13)	71.30 (23.15)	95	0.69	0.08
Learning Gain	-4.58% (23.98)	1.11% (17.52)	95	0.18	0.27
Number of Problems Seen	73 (31.73)	64 (30.34)	95	0.18	0.29
Total Hints Seen	35 (50.46)	16 (20.48)	56	**0.02***	0.50
Percent Hint Abused Problems	5.71% (10.68)	4.98% (7.55)	95	0.70	0.08
Percent Quick Guessed Problems	9.27% (14.36)	15.37% (24.84)	82	0.14	0.30

* p<0.05

The second research question was to evaluate whether a team relationship between a student and Wayang leads to a better help-seeking behavior. An independent-samples t-test was conducted to compare students' help-seeking behavior in treatment and control group conditions. We found significant difference in the total number of hints requested by students for the treatment group (M=35, SD=50.46) and control group (M=16, SD=20.48) conditions; t (56)=2.33, p = 0.02. These results suggest that attempting to build a team relationship between a student and Wayang with a "Work Together" button can affect the number of hints requested by students. Specifically, our results suggest that when students are encouraged to consider the tutor as their teammate they ask for more help from the system and see more hints. There was a lower frequency of quick-guessed problems in the treatment condition; t (82)=-1.50, p= 0.14, though it was not significant. That is, fewer students rushed into providing quick answers to problems: treatment group (M=9.27, SD=14.36) and control group (M=15.37, SD=24.84).

Students in the treatment group saw many more hints, and apparently they were using them in a good way – as there was no significant difference with regard to hint abuses across conditions; t (95) =0.39 p =0.70; treatment group (M=5.71, SD=10.68) and control group (M=4.98, SD=7.55). There was no significant difference with regard to the number of problems seen by students; t (95)=1.36, p= 0.18; though students in the treatment saw more problems: treatment group (M=73, SD=31.73) and control group (M=64, SD=30.34).

4 Discussion

The results in our study show that only by changing the label of a button to encourage building a team relationship between a student and the tutor may not have an effect on students' learning outcomes and learning gains. However, results suggest that such modifications do have an effect on students help-seeking behavior. Our results seemed to confirm a previous study that found an improvement in help-seeking behavior but no improvement in students' learning outcome [25]. Students actually saw more hints (requested more help from the tutor) when they solved math problems with the tutor as a teammate. Fewer students who worked with the tutor as a partner quick-guessed answers to problems, although this difference was not significant. There was no significant difference in abuse of hints, even though students saw more hints. This is a positive improvement of students' help-seeking behavior, since improved help seeking behavior is a first step in improving understanding of mathematics. Perhaps a longer study with more students and a more extensive pre and posttest might show improved learning gain and future studies should address this.

The limitation of the study is a somewhat weak manipulation towards building the team relationship between students and computer. We placed students' names in the prompt screen to make the tutor sound friendlier and changed the name of the "Help" button to "Work Together." We actually are unclear whether students considered the tutor a teammate to work with instead of a learning tool. What kind of relationship and how close the social relationship do students develop with the tutor? Did students think of the tutor as a teammate instead of a supporter and helper? It is very promising to be able to see how small changes such as this one can impact students' help-seeking behaviors. Survey and interviews should be conducted in future studies in order to understand how students see the role of an intelligent tutoring system.

5 Conclusions and Future Work

It is promising to improve students help-seeking behavior in intelligent tutoring systems by introducing the social psychological perspectives. By building up a relationship with a computer, students enhance their own self-regulatory skills. Since improved help seeking behavior is a first step in improving the understanding of math, perhaps a longer study with more students and a more extensive pre and posttest might show an improvement in learning gain.

In future work, we hope to focus on how to strengthen manipulation of the affiliating relationship in human-computer interaction. For example, in this study, we did not manipulate factors involving the companions' gender and ethnicity. In future work, we intend to change features of the companions to strengthen the human-computer interaction. Additionally, redesigning more interactive learning tasks instead of providing only multiple-choices questions will engender more cooperation with the computer [26] and so enhance interdependence [3] with the computer to complete the learning goal. We also hope to move from virtual agents that are merely *friendly* to those that act as *friends*; from those that *inform* to those that also *relate*; and from those that offer *help* to those that truly *care*. One research challenge is to build companions that can gather and use information from one session to the next and apply this deeper understanding to realize an ongoing relationship with learners. We intend to investigate relationships that last over multiple sessions. The learning companion relationships studied to date have been relatively short term and not meant to create the feeling of sustained friendship, interpersonal relationship, or develop any kind of social capital between student and agent. We hope to extend prior work to build companions that use relational behaviors (e.g., empathy and social chat) to establish a social bond with students to maintain engagement over time and keep students returning again and again.

Acknowledgements. This research was funded by an award from the National Science Foundation, NSF REESE #1109642, Personalized Learning: strategies to respond to distress and promote success, Ivon Arroyo, (PI) with Beverly Woolf and Winslow Burleson. Any opinions, findings, conclusions or recommendations expressed in this material are those of the authors and do not necessarily reflect the views of the funding agencies.

References

1. Aleven, V., McLaren, B., Roll, I., Koedinger, K.: Toward meta-cognitive tutoring: A model of help seeking with a Cognitive Tutor. Int. J. Artif. Intell. Educ. 16, 101–128 (2006)
2. Woolf, B.P.: Building Intelligent Interactive Tutors: Bridging Theory and Practice. Morgan Kaufmann (2009)
3. Nass, C., Fogg, B.J., Moon, Y.: Can computers be teammates? Int. J. Hum.-Comput. Stud. 45, 669–678 (1996)
4. Cooper, B.: Care-making the affective leap: More than a concerned interest in a learner's cognitive abilities. Int. J. Artif. Intell. Educ. 13, 3–9 (2003)
5. Self, J.: The defining characteristics of intelligent tutoring systems research: ITSs care, precisely. Int. J. Artif. Intell. Educ. Ijaied. 10, 350–364 (1999)
6. Zimmerman, B.J.: Attaining self-regulation: A social cognitive perspective. In: Handbook of Self-Regulation, pp. 13–39 (2000)
7. Wentzel, K.R., Asher, S.R.: The academic lives of neglected, rejected, popular, and controversial children. Child Dev. 66, 754–763 (1995)
8. Azmitia, M., Montgomery, R.: Friendship, transactive dialogues, and the development of scientific reasoning. Soc. Dev. 2, 202–221 (1993)
9. Hanham, J., McCormick, J.: Group work in schools with close friends and acquaintances: Linking self-processes with group processes. Learn. Instr. 19, 214–227 (2009)
10. Bickmore, T.W., Picard, R.W.: Establishing and maintaining long-term human-computer relationships. ACM Trans. Comput.-Hum. Interact. (TOCHI) 12, 293–327 (2005)
11. Reeves, B., Nass, C.: The media equation: how people treat computers, television, and new media. Cambridge University Press, New York (1996)
12. Vygotsky, L.S.: The Genetic Roots of Thought and Speech. MIT Press, Cambridge (1986)
13. Damasio, A.: Descartes' error: Emotion, reason, and the human brain. Penguin Books, New York (2005)

14. Ogan, A., Finkelstein, S., Walker, E., Carlson, R., Cassell, J.: Rudeness and rapport: Insults and learning gains in peer tutoring. In: Cerri, S.A., Clancey, W.J., Papadourakis, G., Panourgia, K. (eds.) ITS 2012. LNCS, vol. 7315, pp. 11–21. Springer, Heidelberg (2012)
15. Renkl, A.: Worked-out examples: Instructional explanations support learning by self-explanations. Learn. Instr. 12, 529–556 (2002)
16. Karabenick, S.A., Newman, R.S.: Seeking help: Generalizable self-regulatory process and social-cultural barometer. In: Contemp. Motiv. Res. Glob. Local Perspect., pp. 25–48 (2009)
17. Baker, R.S.J.d., Corbett, A.T., Roll, I., Koedinger, K.R.: Developing a generalizable detector of when students game the system. User Model. User-Adapt. Interact. 18, 287–314 (2008)
18. Newman, R.S.: Adaptive help seeking: A role of social interaction in self-regulated learning. In: Karabenick, S.A. (ed.) Strategic Help Seeking: Implications for Learning and Teaching, pp. 13–37 (1998a)
19. Arroyo, I., Cooper, D.G., Burleson, W., Woolf, B.P., Muldner, K., Christopherson, R.: Emotion sensors go to school. In: Proceeding of the 2009 Conference on Artificial Intelligence in Education, Brighton, UK, July 6-10, pp. 17–24. IOS Press (2009)
20. Cooper, D.G., Arroyo, I., Woolf, B.P., Muldner, K., Burleson, W., Christopherson, R.: Sensors model student self concept in the classroom. In: Houben, G.-J., McCalla, G., Pianesi, F., Zancanaro, M. (eds.) UMAP 2009. LNCS, vol. 5535, pp. 30–41. Springer, Heidelberg (2009)
21. Woolf, B.P., Arroyo, I., Muldner, K., Burleson, W., Cooper, D.G., Dolan, R., Christopherson, R.M.: The effect of motivational learning companions on low achieving students and students with disabilities. In: Aleven, V., Kay, J., Mostow, J. (eds.) ITS 2010, Part I. LNCS, vol. 6094, pp. 327–337. Springer, Heidelberg (2010)
22. Rai, D., Arroyo, I., Stephens, L., Lozano, C., Burleson, W., Woolf, B.P., Beck, J.E.: Repairing deactivating negative emotions with student progress pages. In: Chad Lane, H., Yacef, K., Mostow, J., Pavlik, P. (eds.) AIED 2013. LNCS (LNAI), vol. 7926, pp. 795–798. Springer, Heidelberg (2013)
23. Mendicino, M., Razzaq, L., Heffernan, N.T.: A comparison of traditional homework to computer-supported homework. J. Res. Comput. Educ. 41, 331–358 (2009)
24. Cordova, D.I., Lepper, M.R.: Intrinsic motivation and the process of learning: Beneficial effects of contextualization, personalization, and choice. J. Educ. Psychol. 88, 715–730 (1996)
25. Roll, I., Aleven, V., McLaren, B.M., Koedinger, K.R.: Improving students' help-seeking skills using metacognitive feedback in an intelligent tutoring system. Learn. Instr. 21, 267–280 (2011)
26. Ogan, A., Aleven, V., Kim, J., Jones, C.: Intercultural negotiation with virtual humans: The effect of social goals on gameplay and learning. In: Aleven, V., Kay, J., Mostow, J. (eds.) ITS 2010, Part I. LNCS, vol. 6094, pp. 174–183. Springer, Heidelberg (2010)

Skill Diaries: Improve Student Learning in an Intelligent Tutoring System with Periodic Self-Assessment

Yanjin Long and Vincent Aleven

Human Computer Interaction Institute, Carnegie Mellon University,
5000 Forbes Avenue, Pittsburgh, PA 15213, USA
{ylong,aleven}@cs.cmu.edu

Abstract. According to Self-Regulated Learning theories, self-assessment by students can facilitate in-depth reflection and help direct effective self-regulated learning. Yet, not much work has investigated the relation between students' self-assessment and learning outcomes in Intelligent Tutoring Systems (ITSs). This paper investigates this relation with classrooms using the Geometry Cognitive Tutor. We designed a paper-based skill diary that helps students take advantage of the tutor's Open Learner Model to self-assess their problem-solving skills periodically, and investigated whether it can support students' self-assessment and learning. In an experiment with 122 high school students, students in the experimental group were prompted periodically to fill out the skill diaries, whereas the control group answered general questions that did not involve active self-assessment. The experimental group performed better on the post-test, and the skill diaries helped lower-performing students to significantly improve their learning outcomes and self-assessment accuracy. This work is among the first empirical studies that successfully establish the beneficial role of self-assessment in students' learning of problem-solving tasks in ITSs.

Keywords: Skill diaries, problem solving, periodic self-assessment, intelligent tutoring system, open Learner model.

1 Introduction

Researchers of Intelligent Tutoring Systems (ITSs) have been studying how to enhance students' metacognition in order to support their domain-content learning in ITSs, focusing for example on goal setting, self-explanation, help-seeking, gaming the system, and error correction [6, 11]. Some studies demonstrate that metacognitive support in ITSs can significantly improve students' domain level learning outcomes [6]. However, there has not been much work that investigates students' self-assessment in ITSs, which is also a critical metacognitive skill. Self-assessment refers to students' ability to evaluate their learning status (how well they are learning/have learned). It is thought to be important in two ways. First, the process of self-assessing may help students reflect on their learning, which might result in improved learning outcomes [5]. Second, according to theories of self-regulated learning, accurate self-assessment can help students make good future learning plans [13].

K. Yacef et al. (Eds.): AIED 2013, LNAI 7926, pp. 249–258, 2013.

Empirical studies from cognitive and educational psychology have demonstrated a correlation between accurate self-assessment and good learning outcomes. That is, students who assess their own learning more accurately tend to have better learning outcomes [2]. Further, Thiede and colleagues [10] found that improved self-assessment can lead to better re-study choices during learning. However, previous work mainly studied the relationship in the context of memory tests or reading comprehension, whereas ITS researchers tend to focus on problem solving. The nature of self-assessment of problem-solving abilities may well be different from simple memory tests or reading comprehension.

Although not much work has been conducted, some ITS researchers have found interesting and promising results regarding self-assessment. Roll et al. [8] designed a self-assessment tutor that scaffolded students' self-assessment at the start of each section of the tutor curriculum. They found that this tutor improved students' self-assessment on better-mastered problems and that students were able to transfer improved self-assessment in other tutor units [8]. However, this study did not look at whether the self-assessment tutor also enhanced students' domain level learning [8]. Feyzi-Behnagh, Khezri and Azevedo [4] found that by providing metacognitive prompts and feedback, students' self-assessment accuracy improved as well as their learning efficiency (but not the learning effectiveness) when learning with an ITS. Therefore, in spite of these promising initial results it is still an open question how an ITS can support accurate self-assessment in a way that improves robust learning.

A number of researchers have recognized the potential of inspectable Open Learner Models (OLMs) to support students' self-assessment and learning outcomes [1]. However, the promise is not always met. For example, Hartley and Mitrovic [5] compared students' learning gains with or without access to an OLM, but they did not find a significant difference between the two conditions. They only found the less able students' performance improved significantly from pre- to post-test in both conditions [5]. In a previous interview study related to the Geometry Cognitive Tutor [7], a widely-used type of ITS [3], we found that students inspect the tutor's OLM (the "Skillometer") frequently, underlining its potential to support students' self-assessment. We also found, however, that they do not actively use it to reflect or self-assess and that students' self-assessment appears not to be significantly influenced by the Skillometer [7]. Thus, simply presenting an inspectable OLM by itself may not be an effective way to support self-assessment, and additional scaffolding may be necessary. It is an open question what form of scaffolding might be most effective and how interactive it will need to be. White and Frederiksen [12] found that paper-based periodic reflective activities can enhance students' learning significantly. Hence a periodic paper-based method that scaffolds students' use of the Skillometer to help with self-assessing may be similarly effective in an ITS. Therefore, as a first step towards enhancing the Skillometer with self-assessment support, we created a structured, paper skill diary that prompts students to keep track of their skill growth (aided by the Skillometer) while they are learning with a Cognitive Tutor. We conducted a classroom study to test the hypothesis that periodically using the skill diaries can enhance both students' self-assessment accuracy and their learning of math problem-solving skills with the Geometry Cognitive Tutor.

2 Methods

2.1 Participants, Experimental Design, and Procedure

We conducted the study in a local public high school in Pittsburgh in which the Geometry Cognitive Tutor is used as part of the mathematics instruction. A total of 122 students participated and were randomly assigned to two conditions (experimental vs. control). The experimental group periodically filled out skill diaries during their work with the Cognitive Tutor, while the control group periodically answered general questions about the tutor unit they were working on with a control diary. The students came from two math teachers' 6 Geometry Cognitive Tutor classes. For a total of three class periods (around 45 minutes per period), the students covered four sections of the Cognitive Tutor that dealt with volume and surface area of prisms and spheres.

The two groups followed the same procedure: they were first given a pre-test, learned with the Cognitive Tutor for three class periods over consecutive school days, and were then given a post-test following the last tutor class. After the pre-test, the two versions of the diaries (described below) were handed out to the students. During each of the three Cognitive Tutor class periods, the teachers prompted the students to stop twice to fill out the skill/control diaries.

The pre-tests and post-tests were isomorphic and incorporated structurally equivalent Cognitive Tutor problems and transfer problems. There were two parts on both tests. In part I, the to-be-solved problems were shown to the students, while they only needed to rate "How confident are you that you can solve this problem" on a 7-point Likert scale. In part II, students actually solved the problems.

2.2 The Skill Diary and Control Diary

We designed the skill diary to facilitate students' self-assessment both on the skill level and the problem level. There were two kinds of entries in the skill diary: regular entries and end of the day entries. During the three class periods, students were prompted by the teachers to stop and fill out one regular entry twice per class period, and filled out an end of the day entry at the end of each class period. For each of the regular entries, there were three major self-assessment tasks. Firstly, students needed to copy their skill bars from the Skillometer. Secondly, they answered a series of questions in regard to each of the skills listed in the Skillometer, such as "Since the last Tutor problem, this skill has become better/worse/the same?", "Have you had any practice on this skill yet in this unit? Yes/No/Not Sure", and "In your own opinion, do you need more practice on this skill? Yes/No/Not Sure" (Figure 1 shows a filled out diary page for this task). These questions aimed to facilitate students' active self-assessment with the help of the Skillometer. Thirdly, students were asked to rate several specific tutor problems regarding how confident they are in solving these problems based on a 7-point Likert scale (Figure 2 shows an example). The confidence rating on tutor problems was included to enhance students' self-assessment and reflection on the specific problems they encounter in the tutor. It took students about 5 minutes to fill out one regular entry. At the end of each class period, students needed to fill out an end of the day entry that asked them to reflect on their overall learning for that day.

3. Please fill out the table below based on your current learning status in the Tutor:

Skill	Since the last tutor problem, this skill has become.... (check one)	Have you had any practice on this skill yet in this unit? (check one)	In your own opinion, rate your mastery of this skill from 1-7. 1 = poor to 7 = very good	In your own opinion, do you need more practice on this skill? (check one)
Enter given prism height	☐ Better ☐ Same ☐ Worse	☐ Yes ☐ No ☐ Not sure	☐ ☐ ☐ ☐ ☐ ☐ ☐ 1 2 3 4 5 6 7	☐ Yes ☐ No ☐ Not sure
Enter given rectangular prism dimension of base	☐ Better ☐ Same ☐ Worse	☐ Yes ☐ No ☐ Not sure	☐ ☐ ☐ ☐ ☐ ☐ ☐ 1 2 3 4 5 6 7	☐ Yes ☐ No ☐ Not sure
Enter given triangular prism dimension of base	☐ Better ☐ Same ☐ Worse	☐ Yes ☐ No ☐ Not sure	☐ ☐ ☐ ☐ ☐ ☐ ☐ 1 2 3 4 5 6 7	☐ Yes ☐ No ☐ Not sure
Find area of base of rectangular prism	☐ Better ☐ Same ☐ Worse	☐ Yes ☐ No ☐ Not sure	☐ ☐ ☐ ☐ ☐ ☐ ☐ 1 2 3 4 5 6 7	☐ Yes ☐ No ☐ Not sure
Find area of base of triangular prism	☐ Better ☐ Same ☐ Worse	☐ Yes ☐ No ☐ Not sure	☐ ☐ ☐ ☐ ☐ ☐ ☐ 1 2 3 4 5 6 7	☐ Yes ☐ No ☐ Not sure
Find rectangular prism volume	☐ Better ☐ Same ☐ Worse	☐ Yes ☐ No ☐ Not sure	☐ ☐ ☐ ☐ ☐ ☐ ☐ 1 2 3 4 5 6 7	☐ Yes ☐ No ☐ Not sure

Fig. 1. Self-assessment on the skill level in the regular entry of the skill diary

4. Look at problems A, B, C, D, E and F below (do NOT solve them!). Rate how confident you are that you can solve each of them from 1 – 7. (**Circle one number**: 1= Not Confident, 7=Very Confident.)

A. Your aunt makes a fruit cake for a family reunion. The pan she uses is a right rectangular prism. In the prism, CD = 4 centimeters, AD = 2 centimeters, and DH = 3 centimeters, what is the volume of this block?

Not Confident 1	2	3	4	5	6	Very Confident 7

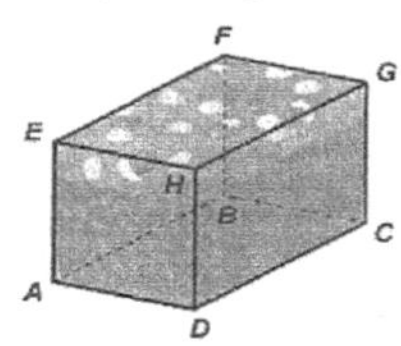

Fig. 2. Self-assessment on the problem level in the regular entry of the skill diary

We also designed a control diary that simply asked students general questions about their learning process, such as "have you seen this problem so far in this unit?" These questions were designed to *not* spur or facilitate active self-assessment. The layouts and structure of the skill diary and control diary were designed as similar as possible to avoid introducing confounding factors between groups.

3 Results

We gathered valid data for 47 students in the control group and 48 in the experimental group. We analyzed students' pre-test and post-test performance, Cognitive Tutor log data and self-assessment accuracy. We report partial η^2 for effect sizes of main effects and interactions. An effect size partial η^2 of .01 corresponds to a small effect, .06 to a medium effect, and .14 to a large effect (Cohen's guidelines for effect sizes).

3.1 Test Performance on Pre and Post Tests

First, we analyzed whether there were significant learning gains from pre-test to post-test. There were 7 problems on the pre-test and 10 problems on the post-test. The pre- and post-tests shared 5 items that were in the same format but had differing numbers. Students' answers were graded from 0 to 1, with partial credit where appropriate.

To assess the students' improvement from pre-test to post-test, we compared their performance on the shared items. Overall, both groups improved significantly from pre- to post-test (repeated measures ANOVA, $F(1, 93) = 13.103$, $p = .000$, $\eta^2 = .123$) on the whole test. The group differences were not significant on the pre-test or the post-test. We then divided the test items into two categories: reproduction (isomorphic to the problems in the tutor) and transfer problems. We found that the experimental group did significantly better than the control group on the reproduction problems on the post-test ($F(1, 93) = 3.861$, $p = .052$, $\eta^2 = .040$), but we found no significant difference between two groups on transfer problems ($F(1, 93) = .056$, $p = .814$, $\eta^2 = .001$)[1]. In sum, scaffolding students' self-assessment with offline skill diaries lead to better learning, although not better transfer of knowledge.

Table 1. Means and SDs for Reproduction and Transfer Problems (Shared Items)

	Pre-Test (Reproduction)	Post-Test (Reproduction)	Pre-Test (Transfer)	Post-Test (Transfer)
Experimental Group	0.545 (.340)	0.620 (.292)	0.499(.217)	0.579(.263)
Control Group	0.456 (.444)	0.494 (.333)	0.464 (.218)	0.567 (.238)

We also investigated the effectiveness of the skill diary for different ability groups. We expected the skill diaries to be especially effective for the lower-performing group, with respect to both domain level learning and self-assessment accuracy. This expectation was based on prior results by Hartley and Mitrovic [5], who found that an inspectable OLM had a stronger influence on the learning of lower-performing students. We used the median pre-test score (.557) to divide the sample into a lower-performing group with 47 students (average pre-test score: .362) and a higher-performing group with 48 students (average pre-test score: .707). Table 2 shows the higher and lower performing students' performance on pre- and post-test. For the lower-performing students, the difference between conditions on post-test reproduction problems was significant ($F(1, 44) = 4.586$, $p = .038$, $\eta^2 = .094$; pre-test reproduction problem score was used as co-variate), whereas no significant condition effect was found within the higher-performing group. No significant condition effects were found for transfer problems within the two ability groups either.

[1] Although we did not find a significant group effect on the pre-test, when we used the pre-test scores as co-variate, the difference between two groups on reproduction problems was on the borderline of significance ($F(1, 92) = 2.747$, $p = .101$, $\eta^2 = .029$), suggesting that part of the difference between the two conditions might be accounted for by pre-test differences.

Table 2. Means and SDs for Reproduction Problems by Ability Groups

	Pre-Test (Experimental)	Pre-Test (Control)	Post-Test (Experimental)	Post-Test (Control)
Lower-Performing Group	0.346 (.451)	0.163 (.350)	0.527 (.468)	0.300(.390)
Higher-Performing Group	0.744 (.409)	0.738 (.752)	0.713 (.382)	0.679 (.414)

3.2 Process Measures from Cognitive Tutor Log Data

Next, we investigated how the scaffolded self-assessment activities (i.e., the skill diaries) may have influenced students' learning processes within the tutor. Metacognitive processes themselves are unobservable, which is why we looked in the log data for learning behaviors that may be strongly related. Specifically, we looked at: 1) the number of tutor hints students requested; 2) the time students spent on each hint they received from the tutor; 3) the number of incorrect attempts in the tutor; 4) the average assistance score ((hints + incorrect attempts)/total number of steps) in the tutor and 5) the average time students spent on each step. Repeated measures ANOVAs were used with these five process measures from the four tutor sections. The condition (experimental or control) was used as the independent variable. Previous Cognitive Tutor learning data indicated that the four targeted sections vary significantly in their difficulty levels. We found that:

1) The control group asked for significantly more hints per step than the experimental group. The main effect of condition was significant ($F(1, 93) = 4.762$, $p = .032$, $\eta^2 = .049$).

2) The experimental group spent significantly more time per hint received. The main effect of condition was significant ($F(1, 138) = 5.265$, $p = .023$, $\eta^2 = .037$).

3) The control group made more incorrect attempts per step. The main effect of condition was marginally significant ($F(1, 93) = 3.006$, $p = .086$, $\eta^2 = .031$).

4) The control group had a significantly higher assistance score. The main effect of condition was significant ($F(1, 93) = 5.388$, $p = .022$, $\eta^2 = .055$). The control group also needed more assistance (compared to the experimental group) in the more difficult sections. The interaction between condition and tutor sections was marginally significant ($F(3, 279) = 2.281$, $p = .080$, $\eta^2 = .024$).

5) The control group spent more time (compared to the experimental group) to finish each step in the more difficult sections. The interaction between condition and tutor sections was significant ($F(3, 279) = 2.624$, $p = .051$, $\eta^2 = .027$).

Correlations between Process Measures and Test Performance. We calculated the Pearson correlations between these measures and students' test scores. These correlations can help us further interpret whether the differences between conditions on the process measures suggest more effective learning for the experimental condition. As shown in Table 3, the number of hints, number of incorrect attempts and average assistance score are highly correlated with students' pre- and post-test scores, and the negative correlations mean that students with better test performance needed less help and made fewer errors in the tutor. Additionally, the time spent on each hint is significantly correlated with post-test scores. The positive correlations between this process measure and test scores point out that students who have better test performance spent more time studying each hint they received.

Table 3. Correlations between Process Measures and Test Performance

	Number of Hints	Time Spent on Each Hint	Number of Incorrect Attempts	Average Assistance Score	Time Spent on Each Step
Pre-Test	-.558 (.000)**	.199 (.087)	-.350 (.000)**	-.519 (.000)**	-.188 (.067)
Post-Test	-.474 (.000)**	.336 (.003)**	-.317 (.002)**	-.466 (.000)**	-.199 (.053)

** indicates significant level <.01

3.3 Accuracy of Self-Assessment

We also looked at whether the skill diaries influenced the accuracy with which students assessed their own problem-solving ability. Schraw [9] summarized two traditional approaches to measure students' self-assessment accuracy: the relative accuracy and absolute accuracy. For relative accuracy, Gamma and Pearson correlations have been widely used by researchers. For absolute accuracy, Schraw introduced the following formula:

$$\text{Absolute Accuracy Index} = \frac{1}{N}\sum_{i=1}^{N}(c_i - p_i)^2 \tag{1}$$

where "N" represents the number of tasks, "c" stands for students' confidence ratings on their ability to finish the task while "p" represents their actual performance on that task. The index thus measures the discrepancy between self-assessed and actual performance. The higher the absolute accuracy index, the worse students' self-assessment is. In this paper we only report the results of absolute accuracy. The Gamma correlations were also calculated and led to similar conclusions.

Table 4 shows the absolute accuracy of self-assessment for both conditions. Repeated measures ANOVAs (with the condition as the independent variable) revealed that both groups improved significantly from pre- to post-tests on accuracy of self-assessment (main effect of test time (pre/post): $F(1, 93) = 4.369$, $p = .039$, $\eta^2 = .045$). The interaction between condition and test time was not significant ($F(1, 93) = .023$, $p = .881$, $\eta^2 = .000$), nor was the main effect of condition ($F(1, 93) = .798$, $p = .374$, $\eta^2 = .009$).

Table 4. Means and SDs of the Two Groups' Absolute Accuracy of Self-Assessment

	Pre-Test	Post-Test
Experimental Group	0.290 (.133)	0.253 (.128)
Control Group	0.270 (.137)	0.238 (.108)

We compared the self-assessment accuracy of higher- and lower-performing students, given previous work that suggests that better students tend to be more accurate in their self-assessment [2]. As shown in Table 5, on both tests the higher-performing group had a lower absolute self-assessment accuracy score, which indicates more accurate self-assessment of their learning. One-way ANOVAs show that the differences between higher- and lower-performing students on pre-test and post-test were both significant ($F(1, 94) = 18.699$, $p = .000$, $\eta^2 = .167$ and $F(1, 94) = 10.064$, $p = .002$, $\eta^2 = .098$). This finding is aligned with previous literature [2].

Table 5. Means and SDs of Absolute Accuracy of Self-Assessment by Ability Groups

	Pre-Test	Post-Test
Lower-Performing Group	0.336 (.153)	0.283 (.109)
Higher-Performing Group	0.226 (.086)	0.209 (.117)

Next we looked at the higher- and lower-performing groups separately. Within the lower-performing group, paired T-Tests revealed that students in the experimental condition improved significantly with respect to self-assessment accuracy from pre-test to post-test ($t(23) = 2.257$, $p = .034$), whereas students in the control group did not. Within the higher-performing group, there were no reliable differences between the conditions.

4 Discussion, Conclusion and Future Work

Theories of self-regulated learning emphasize the importance of accurate self-assessment, but little is known about how self-assessment of problem-solving skills (as opposed to memory or reading comprehension) relates to learning, whether and how supporting self-assessment might lead to better skill acquisition, and what kind of support is most effective. The learner modeling capabilities of ITS would seem to provide unique advantages not shared with other learning technologies, as argued in the introduction, but to what extent is this promise met? We investigated whether skill diaries, designed to help students take advantage of an OLM to self-assess periodically, had beneficial effects with respect to learning outcomes and self-assessment accuracy. The results show that students who learned with skill diaries performed better on post-test reproduction problems, compared to control group students, especially the lower-performing students. The results support the hypothesis that periodic self-assessment scaffolded by an OLM can significantly enhance students' learning. This work is among the first empirical studies that successfully establish the beneficial role of self-assessment in students' learning of problem-solving tasks in ITSs.

To better understand how skill diaries might enhance learning, we analyzed tutor log data to study and compare the learning behaviors of students with and without the skill diaries. This analysis revealed differences in learning behaviors between the conditions. Students who learned with skill diaries needed fewer hints but spent more time on the hints they requested, which pointed to more appropriate use of help from the tutor. Correlation analysis also revealed that the time students spent on each hint positively correlate with their test scores. Furthermore, in more difficult sections of the tutor, the control group spent more time on each step and had a higher average assistance score. Both the time per step and average assistance score correlate negatively with students' test scores, which suggests that the experimental group students learned more effectively and efficiently in harder sections.

The results from log data suggest how the use of a skill diary might enhance students' learning outcomes. Firstly, when prompted to copy their skill bars and answer specific self-assessment questions both on the skill and problem levels, students might be more likely to notice skills that they have not yet mastered, as well as problems they are not yet good at. They might then reflect on the errors they made on these skills and problems, as well as on how they corrected them with help from the tutor or their teachers. Such reflection and self-assessment may be more rare without skill diaries. Secondly, based on theories of self-regulated learning [13], self-assessment can help students to direct attention and effort to address the content that they have not yet mastered. Despite the structured nature of Cognitive Tutors, students can regulate their learning in that they decide when to receive help messages from the tutor. Therefore, when students went back to the tutor after filling out the diary, with their self-assessment in mind, they might use the tutor's hints more deliberately, which could help them master the not-yet-mastered skills. Thirdly, the diaries explicitly directed students' attention to the change of their skill bars, which might help them be more alert and motivated to stay focused on their learning. The fewer incorrect attempts in the tutor may have provided evidence for this change in students' learning behaviors. In the future, we may conduct think-alouds and interviews to further investigate the mechanisms of how the skill diary or periodic self-assessment works to enhance students' learning outcomes.

We also found significant improvement on the accuracy of self-assessment for lower-performing students who used the skill diaries. Previous studies [2] have documented students' overconfidence when self-assessing their learning status, which was more severe for the lower performing students. Skill diaries may have broken the illusion of mastery for the lower-performing students during the learning process, so they could form a more objective view of their learning.

We did not find significant benefits for higher-performing students, with respect to both the learning outcomes and self-assessment accuracy. It is possible that the higher-performing students already possess good self-assessment, so there is not much room for improvement. But it will still be worth investigating in the future why the intervention was more helpful for lower-performing students, and how we can support all students' self-assessment and learning outcomes effectively.

To sum up, both test results and log data from the present study help to empirically establish the beneficial role of self-assessment in learning of problem-solving tasks in ITSs. Although theories of self-regulated learning have emphasized the critical role of self-assessment in learning, our study is among the first rigorous classroom studies which have successfully illustrated the benefits of periodic self-assessment for problem-solving tasks in ITSs. The critical features of the skill diary, namely, prompting students' self-assessment periodically both on the skill level and problem level, can be transferred to build online tools integrated with the OLMs that support students' self-assessment and metacognition in ITSs.

Acknowledgments. We thank Gail Kusbit and Tristan Nixon for their kind help with this work. We would also like to thank the participating teachers and students. This work is funded by an NSF grant to the Pittsburgh Science of Learning Center (NSF Award SBE0354420).

References

1. Bull, S.: Supporting Learning with Open Learner Models. In: Proceedings of 4th Hellenic Conference with International Participation: Information and Communication Technologies in Education, Athens, Greece. Keynote (2004)
2. Chi, M., Bassok, M., Lewis, M., Reimann, P., Glaser, R.: Self-explanations: How students study and use examples in problem solving. Cognitive Science 13, 145–182 (1989)
3. Corbett, A., McLaughlin, M., Scarpinatto, K.: Modeling Student Knowledge: Cognitive Tutors in High School & College. User Modeling and User-Adapted Interaction 10, 81–108 (2000)
4. Feyzi-behnagh, R., Khezri, Z., Azevedo, R.: An Investigation of Accuracy of Metacognitive Judgments during Learning with an Intelligent Multi-Agent Hypermedia Environment. In: The Annual Meeting of the Cognitive Science Society, pp. 96–101. Cognitive Science Society (2011)
5. Hartley, D., Mitrovic, A.: Supporting Learning by Opening the Student Model. In: Cerri, S.A., Gouardères, G., Paraguaçu, F. (eds.) ITS 2002. LNCS, vol. 2363, pp. 453–462. Springer, Heidelberg (2002)
6. Koedinger, K.R., Aleven, V., Roll, I., Baker, R.: In vivo Experiments on Whether Supporting Metacognition in Intelligent Tutoring Systems Yields Robust Learning. In: Hacker, D.J., Dunlosky, J., Graesser, A.C. (eds.) Handbook of Metacognition in Education, pp. 897–964. Routledge, New York (2009)
7. Long, Y., Aleven, V.: Students' Understanding of Their Student Model. In: Biswas, G., Bull, S., Kay, J., Mitrovic, A. (eds.) AIED 2011. LNCS, vol. 6738, pp. 179–186. Springer, Heidelberg (2011)
8. Roll, I., Aleven, V., McLaren, B.M., Koedinger, K.R.: Metacognitive practice makes perfect: Improving students' self-assessment skills with an intelligent tutoring system. In: Biswas, G., Bull, S., Kay, J., Mitrovic, A. (eds.) AIED 2011. LNCS, vol. 6738, pp. 288–295. Springer, Heidelberg (2011)
9. Schraw, G.: A Conceptual Analysis of Five Measures of Metacognitive Monitoring. Metacognition and Learning 4, 33–45 (2009)
10. Thiede, K.W., Anderson, M.C.M., Therriault, D.: Accuracy of Metacognitive Monitoring Affects Learning of Texts. Journal of Educational Psychology 95, 66–73 (2003)
11. Weerasinghe, A., Azevedo, R., Roll, I., du Boulay, B.: The Proceedings of the Fourth Workshop on Self-Regulated Learning in Educational Technology, 11th International Conference on Intelligent Tutoring Systems (2012)
12. White, B.C., Frederiksen, J.: Inquiry, Modeling, and Metacognition: Making Science Accessible to All Students. Cognition and Instruction 16, 39–66 (1998)
13. Winne, P.H., Hadwin, A.F.: Studying as Self-Regulated Learning. In: Hacker, D.J., Dunlosky, J., Graesser, A.C. (eds.) Metacognition in Educational Theory and Practice, pp. 279–306. Erlbaum, Hillsdale (1998)

Feedback and Revising in an Intelligent Tutoring System for Writing Strategies

Rod D. Roscoe[1], Erica L. Snow[1,2], and Danielle S. McNamara[1,2]

[1] Learning Sciences Institute
[2] Department of Psychology, Arizona State University
{rod.roscoe,erica.l.snow,danielle.mcnamara}@asu.edu

Abstract. This study investigates students' essay revising in the context of an intelligent tutoring system called *Writing Pal* (W-Pal), which combines strategy instruction, game-based practice, essay writing practice, and automated formative feedback. We examine how high school students use W-Pal feedback to revise essays in two different contexts: a typical approach that emphasizes intensive writing practice, and an alternative approach that offers less writing practice with more direct strategy instruction. Results indicate that students who wrote fewer essays, but received W-Pal strategy instruction, were more likely to make substantive revisions that implemented specific recommendations conveyed by the automated feedback. Additional analyses consider the role of motivation and perceived learning on students' revising behaviors.

Keywords: intelligent tutoring systems, writing instruction, writing strategies, automated feedback, natural language processing, motivation.

1 Introduction

Writing is a complex process comprising planning, drafting, and revising phases [1-2]. Planning refers to the generation and organization of ideas prior to writing and drafting translates writers' initial ideas into a coherent text that communicates main ideas. Central to the current work, revising entails the refinement of a text to better achieve writers' goals. Skilled writers engage in more substantive revising that addresses deeper organization, meaning, and rhetorical strength (e.g., elaborating and restructuring arguments), which is more likely to improve overall essay quality [3]. However, many students tend to ignore revising or make only unproductive, superficial edits to address spelling, grammar, and mechanical issues [3-6].

Writing Pal (W-Pal) is an intelligent tutoring system developed to improve students' writing and revising [7-8]. Via animated lessons and educational games, W-Pal offers explicit strategy instruction and practice for planning, drafting, and revising. Importantly, students can also author essays and receive automated formative feedback informed by natural language processing (NLP) algorithms [9]. In this study, we investigate students' use of such feedback to revise their essays. Specifically, we consider whether and how students can use automated feedback to guide substantive revisions, and how revising may be influenced by explicit strategy instruction.

K. Yacef et al. (Eds.): AIED 2013, LNAI 7926, pp. 259–268, 2013.

1.1 Revising and Computers

Research on revising indicates that many students rely on superficial edits rather than substantive revisions [3-6]. For example, Bridwell [4] analyzed Grade 12 students' essay revisions at seven grain sizes: surface, words, phrases, clauses, sentences, multiple sentences, and text level. All students revised, but most revisions occurred at the word (31.2%) or surface level (24.8%). Students revised primarily by improving word choice and by correcting mechanical errors. Similarly, Crawford et al. [5] examined the revisions of Grade 5 and Grade 8 students. These elementary and middle school students' revisions also focused on the word (~40%), level (~25%), or punctuation level (~20%), although these edits did lead to moderate increases in essay quality.

Efforts to improve students' revising processes have focused on strategy instruction [3, 10-11] and computer-based scaffolds [12-13]. For example, Midgette et al. [11] provided Grade 5 and Grade 8 students with one of three revising goals: generally improve, elaborate the content, or elaborate the content and consider the audience. Students given an audience goal were better able to revise their essays to address alternative perspectives (i.e., substantive revisions), although essay quality did not differ across conditions. Similarly, Butler and Britt [10] analyzed the revisions of undergraduates given no training, a global revision tutorial (i.e., substantive revisions of sentences, paragraphs, or whole text), an argument revision tutorial (i.e., precise language and addressing counterarguments), or both tutorials. Students who received either tutorial engaged in more substantive revising and improved overall argument quality, whereas students who received no training focused on less-productive superficial edits. Thus, strategy instruction appears to facilitate substantive essay revising.

Other research has explored the benefits of automated writing evaluation (AWE) systems that combine automated scoring with error feedback [12-14]. Such systems seek to improve students' writing and revising by enabling substantially more writing practice than is often feasible given classroom time constraints [13]. In practice, research on AWE has focused on scoring accuracy. Human and computer-assigned scores correlate around .80 to .85, and many systems report 40-60% perfect agreement between human and computer scores, and 90-100% adjacent agreement (i.e., scores within 1 point) [12, 15]. However, accurate scoring does not guarantee that students are able to implement the feedback. For example, *Criterion* [16] utilizes NLP and statistical modeling to automatically score essays and generate feedback related to errors of organization, development, grammar, usage, mechanics, and style. Attali [17] investigated *Criterion* with thousands of Grade 6 through Grade 12 students – over 33,000 essays were submitted to the system. Most of these essays (71%) were not revised. However, analyses showed that students who did revise implemented superficial edits along with occasional substantive revisions to discourse elements.

As computer-based supports for writing gain educational and commercial prominence, it is crucial to explore whether and how students can use automated feedback to revise their essays. Moreover, it is important to consider how explicit strategy instruction and AWE can be synthesized to support revising. To address these questions, we examine essay revising in the context of the W-Pal tutoring system.

1.2 Writing Pal

W-Pal offers writing strategies via eight writing modules comprising instructional videos, narrated by pedagogical agents, and educational practice games (Table 1). The videos provide background information about key writing tasks (e.g., writing a thesis) and decompose the goals and operations for each strategy. Multiple strategies are often organized by acronymic mnemonic devices, which can facilitate students' recall and use of the strategies [18]. Completing the lessons unlocks games that allow students to practice specific strategies. In *identification* games, students examine short texts and essay excerpts to identify strategy applications or exemplars. For example, in *Fix-It*, players attempt to identify problems exhibited in introduction, body, or conclusion paragraphs. In *generative* games, students author short texts while applying one or more strategies. For example, in *Speech Writer*, players help a friend on the debate team by reviewing a "speech" for key problems and then revising that speech.

Table 1. Writing Pal (W-Pal) Writing Strategy Modules, Lesson Videos, and Practice Games

Module	Strategy Lessons	Practice Games
Prologue	*Meet the Student* *Practice Makes Perfect*	
Freewriting	*Figure Out the Prompt* *Ask and Answer Questions* *Support with Evidence* *Think about the Other Side*	*Freewrite Flash*
Planning	*Positions, Arguments, and Evidence* *Outlines* *Flowcharts*	*Planning Passage* *Mastermind Outline*
Introduction Building	*Thesis Statements* *Argument Previews* *Grab the Reader's Attention*	*Essay Launcher* *Dungeon Escape* *Fix It*
Body Building	*Topic Sentences* *Evidence Sentences* *Strengthening Your Evidence*	*RoBoCo* *Fix It*
Conclusion Building	*Summarize the Essay* *Close the Essay* *Hold the Reader's Attention*	*Lockdown* *Dungeon Escape* *Fix It*
Paraphrasing	*Synonym Strategy* *Structure Strategy* *Condensing Strategy* *Splitting Strategy*	*Adventurer's Loot* *Map Conquest*
Cohesion Building	*Signpost Strategy* *Threading* *Connectives Strategy*	*Undefined & Mined* *CON-Artist*
Revising	*Add More* *Removing Irrelevant Details* *Moving Essay Sections* *Substituting Ideas*	*Speech Writer*

Similar to AWE systems, W-Pal also allows students to write and revise prompt-based essays like those on standardized exams. Essays are automatically scored via NLP algorithms developed using Coh-Metrix and related tools [9], which provide a key source of the artificial intelligence of the system. Within technologies that accept natural language as input, students' responses are open-ended and potentially ambiguous. When a user enters natural language into a system and expects useful and intelligent responses, NLP is necessary to interpret that input. In service to these goals, W-Pal utilizes Coh-Metrix to analyze text on multiple dimensions, including co-referential cohesion, causal cohesion, density of connectives, lexical diversity, temporal cohesion, spatial cohesion, and LSA. Coh-Metrix also calculates syntactic complexity and offers psycholinguistic data about words (parts-of-speech, frequency, concreteness, imagability, meaningfulness, familiarity, polysemy, and hypernymy). A variety of methods, including regression, discriminant function analysis, and machine learning, are used to combine indices in models that assign scores (or qualitative thresholds) to essays as a whole or essay sections (e.g., a conclusion paragraph).

In W-Pal, submitted essays receive a holistic rating from *Poor* to *Great* (6-point scale). Essays then receive formative feedback on specific writing goals and strategies, implemented through a series of algorithmic thresholds assessing *Legitimacy, Length*, *Relevance*, *Structure*, *Introduction*, *Body*, *Conclusion*, or *Revising*. Unlike most AWE systems, W-Pal provides no feedback on low-level errors and provides less feedback overall to avoid overwhelming users [14]. W-Pal automatically gives one feedback message on one *Initial Topic* (i.e., the *first* problem detected in the series of checks). Subsequently, students can voluntarily request more feedback on that topic or on one additional *Next Topic* (i.e., the *next* problem detected). Up to ten total feedback messages, five per topic, can be requested by the students. Below is an example of a complete feedback message on the topic of conclusion building:

Skilled writers attempt to hold the reader's attention throughout each segment of the essay. One way to ensure your essay conclusion is interesting to your reader is to use an attention-holding technique.

- These techniques help your reader connect to the essay on a personal level.
- A simple technique is to use personal stories that have not been previously discussed in the essay.
- Consider this prompt: "Is it always better to tell the truth?" A personal anecdote might discuss how, after having hurt your mom's feelings by telling a lie, you learned a lesson about honesty.

In sum, W-Pal strives to integrate strategy instruction and essay-based practice with automated feedback. We hypothesize that strategy instruction will facilitate revising [10-11] by providing students with concrete methods of implementing the automated feedback, and perhaps by influencing their perceived ability to do so [19]. Thus, in this study, we consider 1) whether and how students can use automated feedback to inform substantive essay revisions, and 2) how revising occurs in two contexts: a typical AWE approach that emphasizes intensive writing practice (i.e., writing many essays with automated feedback) and an alternative approach that offers significantly less writing practice (i.e., fewer essays) but with more direct strategy instruction. Additionally, we explore relationships between students' use of feedback to revise and their self-reported motivation and perceptions of the system.

2 Method

2.1 Participants

High school students (n = 65) from an urban area in the southwest United States participated in a 10-session summer program using W-Pal. The average age of students was 16, with 70.8% females. Ethnically, 6.2% of students identified as African-American, 15.4% as Asian, 24.6% as Caucasian, and 44.6% as Hispanic. Average grade level was 10.2 with 35.4% of students reporting a GPA of 3.0 or below. Most students self-identified as native English speakers (n = 38) although many self-identified as English Language Learners (ELL, n = 27). An analysis of prior writing ability found no difference between native speakers and ELLs, $t(62) = 1.05, p = .30$.

2.2 Procedures

Students in the *W-Pal condition* began each session by writing and revising *one* SAT-style persuasive essay and then completing one instructional module (i.e., total of 8 practice essays on different topics). Students were allotted 25 minutes to draft their essay and 10 minutes to revise after receiving feedback. Subsequently, they studied the strategy module of the day and played the educational games. In the *Essay condition* (n = 32), students wrote and revised *two* essays per session (i.e., 16 practice essays), but did not complete any lessons or games. Sessions lasted about 1.5 hours for both conditions with equivalent time on task.

2.3 Data and Coding

Corpus. Students wrote and revised a combined total of 770 essays. Original and revised drafts were contrasted using the Compare Documents tool in a popular word processing program, thus highlighting the additions, deletions, and alterations students made when revising. The automated essay scores assigned to original and revised drafts were logged along with the duration (i.e., time spent writing), number of feedback messages requested, and topics of feedback given.

Revisions. Students' edits were coded in three ways. First, we coded whether students attempted to revise by making *any* edits. Second, we examined whether students attempted substantive revisions to address the Initial Topic of feedback. Students' edits were coded based on whether they implemented any valid strategy to address the specified feedback topic. For example, if a student received feedback related to essay introductions, the essay would be coded as *revised* if an introductory paragraph was added, or if a relevant introductory component was added (e.g., a preview of arguments) or meaningfully modified (e.g., elaborating the thesis statement). To establish coding reliability, the second author and an undergraduate assistant independently coded 120 essays. Reliability of Initial Topic coding was $\kappa = .84$. Finally, the same coding was applied to revisions based on the Next Topic of feedback ($\kappa = .81$).

Daily Surveys. Students completed a motivation survey at the start of each session. Using a 6-point scale, students rated their *enjoyment of the most recent session*, *motivation to participate*, *desire to perform well*, *desire to compete with others*, *perceived learning of writing strategies*, and *perceived improvements in writing quality*. Higher ratings indicated more positive perceptions (e.g., higher enjoyment, greater perceived learning, etc.). These data allow us to consider whether students' motivations or perceptions of W-Pal might have influenced their willingness to revise their essays [19].

3 Results

3.1 All Essays

We first examined writing times, scores, feedback patterns, and revising for the entire corpus of 770 essays. These data are summarized in Table 2.

Table 2. Writing duration, scores, feedback, and revising for all essays

Variable	Mean or Percentage	SD
Duration (minutes)		
Original	21.2	4.7
Revised	5.7	3.1
Score		
Original	2.6	1.0
Revised	2.7	1.0
Feedback Requested		
Total Received	3.4	3.0
1 message[a]	48.5%	
2-5 messages[a]	34.4%	
6+ messages[a]	19.0%	
Revising		
Total Edits	12.0	10.8
Any Revision[a]	97.3%	
Initial Topic Revision[a]	44.1%	
Next Topic Revision[a]	53.8%	

Note. [a]These values indicate a percentage of all essays.

Duration and Scores. On average, students spent 21 minutes composing their original drafts and 6 minutes revising (Table 2). The average score for original drafts was 2.6, which increased very slightly but significantly to 2.7 after revising, $t(769) = 4.21$, $p < .001$, $d = .08$. This result suggests that students essays improved incrementally (i.e., in relation to specific details or features) rather than holistically.

Feedback. On average, students received 3 to 4 feedback messages per essay (Table 2). Because students received one message by default, these data indicate that many students actively requested 2 to 3 additional messages. Six essays did not receive feedback due to system error. The most common Initial Topic categories were Body Building (53.5% of essays), Revising (13.1%), Length (10.6%), and Conclusion Building (7.1%). Students requested Next Topic feedback for 34.0% of their essays. Of the 262 essays that received Next Topic feedback, the most common categories were Revising (17.7%), Introduction Building (7.1%), and Conclusion Building (6.8%). One implication is that students rarely had serious problems with basic essay features such as structure. Rather, students needed help with specific sections of their essays, such as how to introduce, develop, and summarize their arguments.

Revising. Over 97% of essays exhibited some attempt to revise and students made an average of 12.0 edits per essay (Table 2). However, a smaller percentage of essays displayed *substantive revisions* in response to received Initial Topic (44.1%) or Next Topic feedback (53.8%). Overall, students rarely ignored the opportunity to revise, but implemented substantive strategy feedback from W-Pal about half of the time.

3.2 Effects of Instruction and Practice Context

Although all students received feedback, the nature of instruction and practice differed experimentally. The W-Pal condition received strategy lessons, educational games, and wrote eight practice essays with automated feedback. The Essay condition engaged in twice as much writing practice with feedback, but did not complete the lessons or games. In the following analyses, we consider whether revising patterns differed in these two contexts. Because each student composed multiple essays, data for each student were aggregated. This aggregation obscured some of the variance within students and reduced statistical power, but was necessary to use students as the unit of analysis and meet assumptions of independent observations.

Table 3. Comparison of writing duration, scores, feedback, and revising across conditions

	Condition			
Variable	W-Pal	Essay	$F(1,63)$	p
Duration (minutes)				
Original	22.1 (2.9)	20.7 (3.8)	2.63	.11
Revised	6.0 (2.3)	5.5 (2.0)	< 1.00	.35
Score				
Original	2.7 (0.7)	2.5 (0.6)		
Revised	2.8 (0.8)	2.6 (0.6)		
Feedback Requests	3.7 (2.7)	3.2 (2.3)	< 1.00	.44
Revising				
Total Edits	11.4 (8.5)	12.4 (7.1)	< 1.00	.62
Any Revision[a]	98.1 (5.5)	96.8 (4.5)	1.03	.32
Initial Topic Revision[a]	53.7 (30.4)	39.2 (18.8)	5.32	.02
Next Topic Revision[a]	56.0 (40.2)	43.1 (33.4)	1.44	.24

Note. [a]These values are average percentages. They indicate what percentage of students essays were revised in the indicated manner, on average.

Duration and Scores. On average, W-Pal students spent 22 minutes composing their original drafts compared to 21 minutes spent by Essay students. Similarly, W-Pal students spent about 6 minutes revising compared to 5.5 minutes spent by Essay students. Neither difference was statistically significant (Table 3).

A 2 x 2 repeated-measures, mixed-factor ANOVA was conducted to compare original and revised drafts scores (within) by condition (between). A main effect of revision indicated that scores increased very slightly after being revised, $F(1,63) = 13.26$, $p = .001$, $d = .12$. However, there was no effect of condition, $F(1,63) < 1.00$, and no interaction, $F(1,63) < 1.00$. Although essay quality slightly improved as a result of revising, neither condition improved more than the other (Table 3).

Feedback. The conditions did not differ significantly in feedback received. On average, W-Pal students received 3.7 messages and Essay students received 3.2 messages.

Revising. W-Pal and Essay groups made a similar number of edits. Likewise, W-Pal students revised their essays 98% of the time and Essay students revised their essays 97% of the time. For substantive revisions in response to received feedback, W-Pal condition students showed a clear advantage. In response to Initial Topic feedback, W-Pal students made substantive revisions 54% of the time whereas Essay students made substantive revisions only 39% of the time, $F(1,63) = 5.32$, $p = .024$, $d = .57$. In response to Next Topic feedback, W-Pal students made substantive revisions 56% of the time, whereas Essay students made substantive revisions 43% of the time. Although not significant, this followed the same trend as Initial Topic feedback ($d = .35$). The percentage of essays revised in response to Initial Topic ($r = .30$, $p = .015$) or Next Topic feedback ($r = .42$, $p = .003$) was correlated with revised essay scores.

In sum, the groups did not differ in writing time or overall revising, but students who received both explicit strategy instruction and essay-based practice seemed more likely or able to implement automated writing feedback than students who only engaged in intensive essay-based practice.

Table 4. Correlations between motivational ratings and revisions

	Revisions		
Ratings	Any	Initial Topic	Next Topic
Enjoyment of Recent Session	.18	$.32^b$	.12
Motivation to Participate	.08	.19	.01
Desire to Perform Well	.06	.23	.05
Competitiveness	-.04	.10	-.07
Perceived Strategy Learning	$.30^b$	$.31^b$	.16
Perceived Writing Improvement	$.34^a$	$.25^b$	.10

Note $^a p \leq .01$. $^b p \leq .05$.

3.3 Role of Motivation

In further analyses, we considered how students' motivations may have influenced their revising. For each survey item, ratings were averaged across sessions to provide an aggregate rating. Correlations were computed between ratings and students' mean percentage of implementing any revisions, substantive Initial Topic revisions, and substantive Next Topic revisions (Table 4). Due to a logging error, the data for one student in the Essay condition could not be used, reducing the sample size ($n = 64$).

In general, students who perceived that their writing strategies and essay quality were improving seemed more likely to make revisions. Substantive Initial Topic revisions were also moderately correlated with perceived learning and improvement, along with enjoyment of the training sessions. None of the ratings were correlated with substantive Next Topic revisions. Thus, students' perceptions seemed not to affect whether they implemented recommendations beyond the first topic.

4 Discussion

Computer-based writing instruction typically strives to increase the number of essays students write and revise [11]. In this study, we examined how and whether students can revise essays based on automated feedback and how strategy instruction might bolster revising. Results suggest that students can utilize automated formative feedback, and the combination of strategy instruction, educational games, and essay-based practice was more supportive of substantive revising than simply writing and revising many essays. Students in both groups interacted with the same W-Pal writing and feedback tools, and students were able to make small, incremental improvements in essay quality. Thus, the automated feedback provided by W-Pal, guided by natural language algorithms, was moderately helpful to high school students. However, users of the full W-Pal were more willing or able implement substantive revisions. Our interpretation is that strategy instruction and game-based practice helped students to better understand the feedback and how to respond. That is, knowledge of specific strategies helped students understand how to act upon the feedback recommendations.

Importantly, students who perceived that they were learning and improving were also somewhat more likely to revise and make substantive revisions. Strategy instruction perhaps helped students feel more capable in their ability to revise. Students may have been more willing to revise substantively because they felt more equipped to do so. Future research will need to explore how computer-based writing instruction may further encourage students' positive attitudes toward writing and revising.

Acknowledgment. The research reported here was supported by the Institute of Education Sciences, U.S. Department of Education, through Grant R305A090623 to Arizona State University. The opinions expressed are those of the authors and do not represent views of the Institute or the U.S. Department of Education.

References

1. Deane, P., Odendahl, N., Quinlan, T., Fowles, M., Welsh, C., Bivens-Tatum, J.: Cognitive models of writing: writing proficiency as a complex integrated skill. Technical Report No. RR-08-55, Educational Testing Service (2008)

2. Flower, L., Hayes, J.: A cognitive process theory of writing. College Composition and Communication 32, 365–387 (1981)
3. Fitzgerald, J.: Research on revision in writing. Review of Educational Research 57, 481–506 (1987)
4. Bridwell, L.: Revising strategies in twelfth grade students' transactional writing. Research in the Teaching of English 14, 197–222 (1980)
5. Crawford, L., Lloyd, S., Knoth, K.: Analysis of student revisions on a state writing test. Assessment for Effective Intervention 33, 108–119 (2008)
6. Sommers, N.: Revision strategies of student writers and experienced adult writers. College Composition and Communication 31, 378–388 (1980)
7. McNamara, D., Raine, R., Roscoe, R., Crossley, S., Jackson, G., Dai, J., Cai, Z., Renner, A., Brandon, R., Weston, J., Dempsey, K., Carney, D., Sullivan, S., Kim, L., Rus, V., Floyd, R., McCarthy, P., Graesser, A.: The Writing Pal: natural language algorithms to support intelligent tutoring of writing strategies. In: McCarthy, P.M., Boonthum-Denecke, C. (eds.) Applied Natural Language Processing and Content Analysis: Identification, Investigation, and Resolution, pp. 298–311. IGI Global, Hershey (2012)
8. Roscoe, R., Varner, L., Weston, J., Crossley, S., McNamara, D.: The Writing Pal intelligent tutoring system: usability testing and development. Computers and Composition (in press)
9. McNamara, D., Crossley, S., Roscoe, R.: Natural language processing in an intelligent writing strategy tutoring system. Behavior Research Methods (2012), doi:10.3758/s13428-012-0258-1
10. Butler, J., Britt, M.: Investigating instruction for improving revision of argumentative essays. Written Communication 28, 70–96 (2011)
11. Midgette, E., Haria, P., MacArthur, C.: The effects of content and audience awareness goals for revision on the persuasive essays of fifth- and eighth-grade students. Reading and Writing 21, 131–151 (2008)
12. Dikli, S.: An overview of automated scoring of essays. Journal of Technology, Learning, and Assessment 5 (2006), `http://www.jtla.org`
13. Shermis, M., Burstein, J.: Automated essay scoring: a cross-disciplinary perspective. Erlbaum, Mahwah (2003)
14. Grimes, D., Warschauer, M.: Utility in a fallible tool: a multi-site case student of automated writing evaluation. Journal of Technology, Learning, and Assessment 8 (2010), `http://www.jtla.org`
15. Warschauer, M., Ware, P.: Automated writing evaluation: defining the classroom research agenda. Language Teaching Research 10, 1–24 (2006)
16. Burstein, J., Chodorow, M., Leacock, C.: Automated essay evaluation: the Criterion online writing system. AI Magazine 25, 27–36 (2004)
17. Attali, Y.: Exploring the feedback and revision features of Criterion. Paper Presented at the National Council on Measurement in Education, San Diego (April 2004)
18. de la Paz, S., Graham, S.: Explicitly teaching strategies, skills, and knowledge: writing instruction in middle school classrooms. Journal of Educational Psychology 94, 687–698 (2002)
19. Pajares, F., Johnson, M., Usher, E.: Sources of writing self-efficacy beliefs of elementary, middle, and high school students. Research in the Teaching of English 42, 104–120 (2007)

Using Automated Indices of Cohesion to Evaluate an Intelligent Tutoring System and an Automated Writing Evaluation System

Scott A. Crossley[1], Laura K. Varner[2], Rod D. Roscoe[2], and Danielle S. McNamara[2]

[1] Department of Applied Linguistics/ESL, Georgia State University, 34 Peachtree St. Suite 1200, One Park Tower Building, Atlanta, GA 30303, USA
scrossley@gsu.edu
[2] Learning Sciences Institute, Arizona State University, Tempe, AZ 85287
{laura.varner,rod.roscoe}@asu.edu, dsmcnamra1@gmail.com

Abstract. We present an evaluation of the Writing Pal (W-Pal) intelligent tutoring system (ITS) and the W-Pal automated writing evaluation (AWE) system through the use of computational indices related to text cohesion. Sixty-four students participated in this study. Each student was assigned to either the W-Pal ITS condition or the W-Pal AWE condition. The W-Pal ITS includes strategy instruction, game-based practice, and essay-based practice with automated feedback. In the ITS condition, students received strategy training and wrote and revised one essay in each of the 8 training sessions. In the AWE condition, students only interacted with the essay writing and feedback tools. These students wrote and revised two essays in each of the 8 sessions. Indices of local and global cohesion reported by the computational tools Coh-Metrix and the Writing Assessment Tool (WAT) were used to investigate pretest and posttest writing gains. For both the ITS and the AWE systems, training led to the increased use of global cohesion features in essay writing. This study demonstrates that automated indices of text cohesion can be used to evaluate the effects of ITSs and AWE systems and further demonstrates how text cohesion develops as a result of instruction, writing, and automated feedback.

Keywords: Cohesion, Intelligent Tutoring Systems, Natural Language Processing, Corpus Linguistics, Computational Linguistics, Writing Pedagogy.

1 Introduction

For many students, developing writing proficiency is a challenging [1] yet crucial aspect of academic and professional success [2]. To facilitate such writing development, research has emphasized both the teaching of writing strategies [3] and providing students with formative feedback on how to improve writing [4]. For example, local and global cohesion are key linguistic properties of a text that may contribute to the readability and coherence of a text [5-6]. Knowing this, composition instructors might teach students strategies for building cohesion and might offer feedback about "awkward transitions" or "non sequiturs" (i.e., cohesion breaks) in students' written

K. Yacef et al. (Eds.): AIED 2013, LNAI 7926, pp. 269–278, 2013.

work. Such pedagogical principles for strategy instruction and feedback can also be implemented within computer-based technologies for writing instruction, such as intelligent tutoring systems (ITSs) and automated writing evaluation (AWE) systems. The Writing Pal (W-Pal) [7] tutoring system offers strategy instruction and game-based practice across multiple aspects of the writing process. W-Pal also allows students to author original prompt-based essays, which are scored and receive feedback guided by natural language processing (NLP) algorithms.

In W-Pal, and related computer-based systems for writing instruction, automated assessment is a fundamental ingredient of success. NLP algorithms are necessary to detect or diagnose particular strategies or writing errors, such as students' use or omission of cohesive cues. Likewise, algorithms inform the assessment of students' overall writing proficiency or growth. In this study, our goal is to investigate automated indices of cohesion as potential measures of writing growth. This investigation occurs within the context of W-Pal, and uses a variety of automated features of cohesion found in the computational tools Coh-Metrix [8] and the Writing Assessment Tool (WAT) [9]. We specifically examine indices of local cohesion (i.e., connections between smaller text elements, such as sentences) and global cohesion (i.e., connections between larger text elements, such as paragraphs). These indices are employed to contrast writing development across two groups of writers. One group interacted with the complete W-Pal ITS, including strategy instruction, game-based practice, and essay-based practice with automated feedback. A second group used only the essay-based practice and feedback components of W-Pal, but wrote twice as many essays. Our hypothesis is that interacting with the complete W-Pal ITS will lead to the increased use of cohesive devices in student writing over time.

1.1 Cohesion

Cohesion refers to the presence or absence of explicit cues in the text that allow the reader to make connections between the ideas in the text. Cohesion is contrasted with *coherence*, which refers to the understanding that the reader derives from the text. This coherence may be dependent on a number of factors, including linguistic features, background knowledge, and reading skill [10]. Pedagogically, text cohesion is a common theme in writing research [5] and textbooks [6]. Pedagogical perspectives promote the idea that the use of cohesive features in essays increases writing quality. However, empirical support for such assumptions has been mixed.

In two studies, Crossley and McNamara [11-12] investigated the degree to which analytical rubric scores of essay quality (e.g., essay coherence, strength of thesis) predicted holistic essay scores. Results of both studies found that human judgments of text coherence were the most informative predictors of human judgments of essay quality. However, neither of the studies found strong correlations between computational indices of local cohesion (e.g., indices of causal cohesion, spatial cohesion, temporal cohesion, connectives, and word overlap) and human judgments of text coherence. Crossley and McNamara [12], however, found that automated indices of global cohesion (LSA vector between paragraphs) correlated strongly with human judgments of coherence in essays. These studies suggest that *local* cohesive devices may not underlie the development of coherent textual representations of essay quality, but that *global* cohesive devices may contribute.

As measures of writing proficiency rather than text coherence, there are some indications that cohesion features are important in predicting human judgments of essay quality. McNamara et al. [9] found that a cohesion feature related to given information was positively predictive of essay quality. For counterexamples, however, see [13-14], and [9], which demonstrated that cohesion features may not correlate with human ratings or may correlate negatively with such judgments.

1.2 Automated Writing Evaluation

AWE systems provide opportunities for students to practice writing and receive holistic scores and feedback (i.e., deliberate practice) in the absence of a teacher. Deliberate practice is an important aspect of writing development. Like trained musicians and athletes, writers gain from extended practice [15-16] because such practice promotes self-regulation of planning, text generation, and reviewing [16]. However, deliberate practice also requires timely and relevant feedback. In writing instruction, such feedback may be provided by AWE systems, which reduce burdens placed on instructors and offer writers more opportunities to practice writing [17]. The algorithms that underlie AWE systems generally provide accurate scores to users, reporting perfect agreement of 30-60% and adjacent agreement of 85-99% [9, 18].

AWE systems have been critiqued for a variety of reasons. For instance, the scoring reliability of many AWE systems has recently been criticized [18], as has the potential for AWE systems to overlook infrequent writing problems that, while rare for a majority of writers, may be frequent to an individual writer. Such errors will likely not be assessed in an AWE system. Lastly, AWE systems have been criticized for depending on summative feedback at the expense of formative feedback [19].

1.3 The Writing Pal

ITSs that focus on teaching writing strategies adopt a pedagogical focus and are an alternative to strict AWE systems, although they often include AWE systems. W-Pal [7] is an ITS that adopts such a pedagogical focus. Unlike an AWE system that would focus only on essay practice with some supportive instruction, W-Pal emphasizes strategy instruction and targeted strategy practice prior to whole-essay practice. This strategy instruction is intended to facilitate task performance and accelerate skill acquisition and the acquisition of learning strategies, all of which are effective at improving student writing, particularly for adolescent writers [3].

W-Pal teaches writing strategies that cover three phases of the writing process. Each of the writing phases is subdivided into instructional modules: *Freewriting* and *Planning* (prewriting phase); *Introduction Building*, *Body Building*, and *Conclusion Building* (drafting phase); and *Paraphrasing*, *Cohesion Building*, and *Revising* (revising phase). An important component of W-Pal is that it incorporates a suite of games that target specific strategies. The games allow students to practice the strategies in isolation before applying the strategies to the essay writing process. The essay writing component of the system allows students to compose essays and then provides holistic scores and automated, formative feedback based on natural language input.

This feedback depends on the W-Pal AWE system, which focuses on strategies taught in the W-Pal lessons (including cohesion strategies). Thus, within W-Pal, students first view lessons that teach individual strategies; they then practice these strategies via games; lastly, they write practice essays for each of the modules and receive automated feedback from the AWE system on the quality of these essays.

2 Methodology

We collected writing data from two groups of students. The first group interacted with the full W-Pal system described above. The second group wrote and revised essays based only on feedback from the W-Pal AWE system. Both groups wrote pretest and posttest essays. We selected the W-Pal AWE system as a comparison to the full W-Pal system because the AWE system best represents the type of standard practice common in computer-based writing instruction (i.e., students write an essay, receive feedback, and revise the essay). Thus, in this study, we are comparing the benefits of explicit strategy instruction and targeted strategy practice (via games) combined with essay writing to standard computer-based writing instruction.

2.1 Participants

Participants include 64 high school students from the metro Phoenix area. Students ranged in age from 14 to 19 (M = 15.9, SD = 1.3) and ranged in grade level from 9 to 12 (M = 10.2, SD = 1.0). The students participated in one of two conditions: the W-Pal condition (n = 33) or the AWE condition (n = 31). Twenty-seven of the participants self-identified as English Language Learners (ELLs). The remaining participants self-identified as native speakers of English (NS). In the W-Pal condition, 23 participants self-identified as NSs and 10 self-identified as ELLs. In the AWE condition, 14 participants self-identified as NSs and 17 self-identified as ELLs.

2.2 Procedures

Students attended 10 sessions (1 session/day) over a 2-4 week period. Participants wrote a pretest essay during the first session and a posttest essay during the last session. The essays were written on two counterbalanced prompts (i.e., the value of competition/cooperation; the effects of images/impressions). Sessions 2-9 were devoted to training. The students in the W-Pal condition used the full W-Pal. The students in the AWE condition interacted only with the essay writing and automated feedback tools in W-Pal. Thus, a major contrast between the two groups is the number of essays written. Participants in the W-Pal group wrote and received feedback on 8 essays, whereas students in the AWE condition wrote and received feedback on 16 essays (i.e., more essay practice). Time on task in the two conditions was equivalent.

2.3 Corpus and Scoring

The final corpus of essays used in this analysis comprised 128 pretest and posttest essays written by the 64 participants. Descriptive corpus statistics are presented in

Table 1. The essays were scored using the automated scoring algorithm implemented within the W-Pal AWE system. The scoring algorithm assesses essay quality using a combination of computational linguistics and statistical modeling as discussed in [20]. Briefly, the algorithm initially partitions essays into low and high proficiency bins based on number of words and paragraphs thresholds. In subsequent stages, the model presumes that essays that meet and do not meet these thresholds can be characterized by different linguistic features related to lexical sophistication, syntactic complexity, cohesion, semantic categories, and rhetorical elements. Following the initial partition, a number of machine learning algorithms are calculated separately for each group. Each of these algorithms are assigned low proficiency essays a score of 1, 2, or 3 and high proficiency essays a score of 3, 4, 5, or 6.

Table 1. Descriptive statistics for essay corpus: *M* (*SD*)

Paragraphs	Sentences	Words
3.594 (1.359)	21.016 (8.444)	387.211 (129.932)

2.4 Selected Cohesion Indices

We selected a number of local-level cohesion indices (i.e., argument overlap, verb overlap, incidence of *and,* and incidence of all connectives) and global-level cohesion indices (i.e., givenness and incidence of conjuncts) from Coh-Metrix. We also selected newly developed automated indices of global cohesion from the WAT that were created specifically for assessing writing quality. These indices assess cohesion at the paragraph level.

Argument Overlap. Argument overlap refers to the extent to which arguments (nouns, pronouns, and noun phrases) overlap between sentences. Coh-Metrix measures argument overlap between adjacent sentences.

Verb Cohesion. The WAT calculates verb overlap using LSA by computing the average cosine between verbs in adjacent sentences. This index is indicative of the extent to which verbs are repeated across sentences.

Givenness. Given information is information that is recoverable from the preceding discourse. Coh-Metrix calculates text givenness using perpendicular and parallel Latent Semantic Analysis (LSA) vectors [21]. Givenness is computed across a text.

Connectives. Connectives make the relationships among clauses and sentences more explicit. Coh-Metrix assesses negative, positive, additive, temporal, and causal connectives along with conjuncts. These indices are combined into an overall count of connectives. We also include two individual connective scores: incidence of *and* and incidence of conjuncts (e.g., *however* and *in addition*).

Paragraph Cohesion. The WAT measures paragraph cohesion by computing semantic overlap between paragraph types (initial to middle, middle to final, and initial to final). These indices use LSA vectors to compare paragraph types.

2.5 Statistical Analysis

To assess potential differences in prior writing proficiency between NS and ELL participants and between the randomly assigned W-Pal and AWE conditions, we first conducted *t*-tests to compare the automated essay scores at pretest. We also compared scores for the two prompts to ensure that prompt-based effects did not exist. Finally, to assess differences between the pretest and posttest essays for each condition, we conducted mixed-factor analyses of variance (ANOVA) for the selected cohesion indices. We included condition (W-Pal or AWE) as a between-subjects factor.

3 Results

3.1 Differences between NSs and ELL Participants

There was no statistical difference in writing quality as measured by the scoring algorithm between ELL ($M = 2.593$, $SD = .931$) and NS participants ($M = 2.351$, $SD = .887$), ($t = 1.051$, $df = 62$, $p = .297$). This finding indicates that the NS and ELL participants were of equal writing proficiency at the pretest.

3.2 Differences between Conditions

There was no statistical difference in pretest writing quality for the participants in the W-Pal ($M = 2.488$, $SD = 1.064$) and the AWE condition ($M = 2.419$, $SD = .721$), ($t = .286$, $df = 62$, $p = .775$). This finding indicates that the writers in both conditions were of equal writing proficiency at the pretest.

3.3 Differences between Prompts

There was no statistical difference between the writing prompts *Images* ($M = 2.778$, $SD = .906$) and *Competition* ($M = 2.635$, $SD = 1.222$) for all the essays in the corpus, ($t = .894$, $df = 62$, $p = .375$). This finding indicates that there were no prompt-based writing effects for the assigned scores.

3.4 Repeated-Measures ANOVAs for Cohesion Features

There was a significant main effect of test for the following cohesion features: incidence of conjuncts, incidence of *and*s, LSA givenness, LSA middle to middle paragraphs, and LSA middle to final paragraphs. No significant effects were reported for connectives, argument overlap, verb overlap, LSA initial to middle paragraph, and LSA initial to final paragraph (see Table 2 for ANOVA results). These results indicate that participants produced essays that exhibited increased local and global cohesion in the posttest as compared to the pretest (see Table 1 for mean scores in the pretest and posttest). No linguistic features showed a significant interaction between test and condition. These results indicate that the two modes of instruction and practice were equally effective for developing cohesion.

Table 2. Mean (*SD*) and *F* for cohesion indices

Local indices	Pretest	Posttest	*F*
Ands	0.987 (0.557)	1.232 (0.855)	5.147*
All connectives	96.961 (19.894)	98.145 (17.872)	0.199
Argument overlap	0.533 (0.179)	0.497 (0.184)	2.410
Verb overlap	0.107 (0.039)	0.113 (0.035)	1.396

Global indices	Pretest	Posttest	*F*
Conjuncts	0.344 (0.287)	0.519 (0.369)	12.513**
LSA givenness	0.313 (0.043)	0.336 (0.046)	12.292**
LSA I-to-M	0.051 (0.245)	0.166 (0.431)	2.879
LSA I-to-F	0.124 (0.311)	0.196 (0.029)	1.829
LSA M-to-M	0.090 (0.436)	0.281 (0.519)	5.257*
LSA M-to-F	0.097 (0.422)	0.309 (0.605)	4.742*

Note: I = initial paragraph, M = middle paragraph, F = final paragraph
* $p < .050$, ** $p < .001$

4 Discussion

We present an evaluation of the W-Pal ITS through the use of computational indices related to text cohesion. This study demonstrates that automated indices of text cohesion can be used to assess the effects of writing instruction. For both the ITS and the AWE systems, student interaction led to increased use of cohesion features in essay writing. Thus, the use of both the W-Pal ITS and the W-Pal AWE systems can promote writing development, at least with respect to certain cohesive devices.

The students who took part in the W-Pal and the AWE condition demonstrated growth in a variety of cohesion features, including the use of conjuncts, the use of *and*, the increase in given information, and greater semantic overlap between middle paragraphs, and middle and final paragraphs. These findings demonstrate that a mixture of writing instruction, game play, and automated feedback as found in the W-Pal condition led to an increased use of some cohesion features from the pretest to the posttest writing samples. These findings also indicate that intensive writing practice coupled with automated feedback, as found in the AWE condition, also leads to greater production of some cohesion features.

Overall, we found no differences in cohesion scores between the two conditions even though the students in W-Pal condition wrote and revised half as many essays as the essay writing condition. Thus, students who received a mix of writing instruction, practice games, and essay practice with feedback showed similar gains in automated cohesion scores as students who only wrote and revised essays with feedback. Studies have demonstrated that essay-based practice is effective in training writers to increase writing skills [15-16]. However, such practice may be highly repetitive and lower student motivation [20]. The findings from this study suggest that a successful alternative to repetitive essay-based practice is the use of a writing ITS such as W-Pal.

Unlike an AWE system, an ITS provides students not only with the opportunity to practice writing and receive feedback, but also with opportunities to learn writing strategies and play educational games. This mix of options appears to lead to similar gains in cohesion scores as repetitive essay-based practice alone.

The automated cohesion features that demonstrated development over the course of the study are generally related to *global cohesion*. Thus, students in W-Pal and the W-Pal AWE system seemed to develop more global elements of text organization (excluding the increase in the use of *and*) making connections between larger text segments. For instance, conjuncts can not only be used to connect sentences, but also paragraphs. Conjuncts can also be used to provide global organization through enumeration (i.e., *first, second, third*) and summarizing (*to sum up*). Givenness provides information about the use of new and old information across a text. Lastly, our paragraph cohesion indices measure semantic similarity at the global level. Previous research [12] has reported correlations between global cohesion indices and human judgments of text coherence. Such findings along with those reported here suggest that writers working within the W-Pal ITS and AWE systems may begin to develop texts that are more globally coherent. Since indices of global coherence are also linked to essay quality [12], their use may lead to better quality essays.

The majority of the indices that did not demonstrate significant change from pretest to posttest measured *local cohesion* (e.g., general connectives and argument and verb overlap between adjacent sentences). This finding suggests that writers using W-Pal or the W-Pal AWE system do not focus on developing connections between smaller elements of text (i.e., local cohesion). The exceptions were the paragraph cohesion measures that involve the initial paragraphs. Initial paragraphs generally include many textual functions such as an introduction, a claim, and arguments. Thus, initial paragraphs may not overlap strongly with body and conclusion paragraphs because of the number and variety of the textual functions they contain. However, body paragraphs should be semantically related in that they develop similar themes. In addition, conclusion paragraphs should demonstrate greater semantic overlap with body paragraphs because they should include a summary of the body paragraphs.

In general, these findings support earlier research, which has suggested that indices of local cohesion were not significant predictors of essay quality [10], but that indices of global cohesion were [11]. Thus, as writers develop and essay quality increases, we should expect to see a greater development and use of global cohesion in essays, but not in local cohesion.

5 Conclusion

Overall, this study demonstrates how computational indices of cohesion can be used to evaluate ITS and AWE systems. In addition, this study demonstrates how such indices can be used to assess student writing in terms of the development and use of local and global cohesion in essays. Such evaluations can help explain the efficacy of ITSs as compared to AWE systems and help to examine writing development in adolescent learners. In this study, we find that ITS systems are as effective as AWE systems in terms of the development of cohesion strategies even when users of the AWE systems write twice as many essays. We also find that the majority of global cohesion indices show gains between pretest and posttest writing whereas the majority of local cohesion indices do not.

While these findings suggest positive effects of both the W-Pal and the AWE system on writing, additional studies are needed to demonstrate equivalence between the two approaches. Such studies will require a comprehensive investigation of all aspects of the two systems and their effects of writing quality, writing development, system engagement, and participant motivation (to name but a few aspects).

Acknowledgments. This research was supported in part by the Institute for Education Sciences (IES R305A080589 and IES R305G20018-02). Ideas expressed in this material are those of the authors and do not necessarily reflect the views of the IES.

References

1. National Commission on Writing: The Neglected "R". College Entrance Examination Board, New York (2003)
2. Kellogg, R., Raulerson, B.: Improving the Writing Skills of College Students. Psychonomic Bulletin and Review 14, 237–242 (2007)
3. Graham, S., Perin, D.: A meta-analysis of writing instruction for adolescent students. Journal of Educational Psychology 99, 445–476 (2007)
4. McGarrell, H., Verbeem, J.: Motivating revision of drafts through formative feedback. ELT Journal 61, 228–236 (2007)
5. Devillez, R.: Writing: Step by Step. Kendall Hunt, Dubuque (2003)
6. Golightly, K., Sanders, G.: Writing and Reading in the Disciplines, vol. 2. Pearson, New Jersey (2000)
7. McNamara, D., Raine, R., Roscoe, R., Crossley, S., Jackson, G.T., Dai, J., Cai, Z., Renner, A., Brandon, R., Weston, J., Dempsey, K., Carney, D., Sullivan, S., Kim, L., Rus, V., Floyd, R., McCarthy, P., Graesser, A.: The Writing-Pal: Natural Language Algorithms to Support Intelligent Tutoring on Writing Strategies. In: McCarthy, P.M., Boonthum-Denecke, C. (eds.) Applied Natural Language Processing and Content Analysis: Identification, Investigation, and Resolution, pp. 298–311. IGI Global, Hershey (2012)
8. Graesser, A., McNamara, D., Louwerse, M., Cai, Z.: Coh-Metrix: Analysis of Text on Cohesion and Language. Behavioral Research Methods, Instruments and Computers 36, 193–202 (2004)
9. McNamara, D., Crossley, S., Roscoe, R.: Natural Language Processing in an Intelligent Writing Strategy Tutoring System. Behavioral Research Methods, Instruments and Computers (2012) (Advance online publication)
10. McNamara, D., Kintsch, E., Songer, N., Kintsch, W.: Are Good Texts Always Better? Interactions of Text Coherence, Background Knowledge, and Levels of Understanding in Learning from Text. Cognition and Instruction 14, 1–43 (1996)
11. Crossley, S., McNamara, D.: Cohesion, Coherence, and Expert Evaluations of Writing Proficiency. In: Ohlsson, S., Catrambone, R. (eds.) Proceedings of the 32nd Annual Conference of the Cognitive Science Society, pp. 984–989. Cognitive Science Society, Austin (2010)

12. Crossley, S., McNamara, D.: Text Coherence and Judgments of Essay Quality: Models of Quality and Coherence. In: Carlson, L., Hoelscher, C., Shipley, T.F. (eds.) Proceedings of the 29th Annual Conference of the Cognitive Science Society, pp. 1236–1241. Cognitive Science Society, Austin (2011)
13. Crossley, S., Weston, J., Sullivan, S., McNamara, D.: The Development of Writing Proficiency as a Function of Grade Level: A Linguistic Analysis. Written Communication 28, 282–311 (2011)
14. Crossley, S., McNamara, D.: Predicting Second Language Writing Proficiency: The Roles of Cohesion and Linguistic Sophistication. Journal of Research in Reading 53, 115–136 (2012)
15. Johnstone, K.M., Ashbaugh, H., Warfield, T.D.: Effects of repeated practice and contextual-writing experiences on college students' writing skills. Journal of Educational Psychology 94, 305–315 (2002)
16. Kellogg, R.T., Raulerson, B.A.: Improving the writing skills of college students. Psychonomic Bulletin & Review 13(2), 237–242 (2007)
17. Graham, S., Harris, K.R.: The role of self-regulation and transcription skills in writing and writing development. Educational Psychologist 35, 3–12 (2000)
18. Grimes, D., Warschauer, W.: Utility in a Fallible Tool: A Multi-Site Case Study of Automated Writing Evaluation. Journal of Technology, Learning, and Assessment 8, 4–43 (2010)
19. Roscoe, R., Kugler, D., Crossley, S., Weston, J., McNamara, D.: Developing pedagogically-guided threshold algorithms for intelligent automated essay feedback. In: McCarthy, P., Youngblood, Y. (eds.) Proceedings of the 25th International Florida Artificial Intelligence Research Society (FLAIRS) Conference, pp. 466–471. The AAAI Press, Menlo Park (2012)
20. Crossley, S., Roscoe, R., McNamara, D.: Using Natural Language Processing Algorithms to Detect Changes in Student Writing in an Intelligent Tutoring System. Manuscript Submitted to the 26th International Florida Artificial Intelligence Research Society Conference (2013)
21. Hempelmann, C., Dufty, D., McCarthy, P., Graesser, A., Cai, Z., McNamara, D.: Using LSA to Automatically Identify Givenness and Newness of Noun Phrases in Written Discourse. In: Bara, B.G., Bucciarelli, M. (eds.) Proceedings of the 27th Annual Conference of the Cognitive Science Society. Cognitive Science Society, Mahwah (2005)

Combining Semantic Interpretation and Statistical Classification for Improved Explanation Processing in a Tutorial Dialogue System

Myroslava O. Dzikovska, Elaine Farrow, and Johanna D. Moore*

School of Informatics, University of Edinburgh, Edinburgh, United Kingdom
{m.dzikovska,elaine.farrow,j.moore}@ed.ac.uk

Abstract. We present an approach for combining symbolic interpretation and statistical classification in the natural language processing (NLP) component of a tutorial dialogue system. Symbolic NLP approaches support dynamic generation of context-adaptive natural language feedback, but lack robustness. In contrast, statistical classification approaches are robust to ill-formed input but provide less detail for context-specific feedback generation. We describe a system design that combines symbolic interpretation with statistical classification to support context-adaptive, dynamically generated natural language feedback, and show that the combined system significantly improves interpretation quality while retaining the adaptivity benefits of a symbolic interpreter.

Keywords: Tutorial dialogue, natural language processing, Intelligent Tutoring System (ITS), parsing, semantic interpretation.

1 Introduction

In recent years, there has been considerable research on tutorial dialogue systems that accept natural language input and engage in dialogue with students to help them improve their answers [1,4,12,13,15,17,20,23]. Such systems are designed to allow students to express their answers in their own words, thus encouraging knowledge construction and harnessing the power of self-explanation [3].

One of the challenges in developing effective natural language processing (NLP) modules for tutorial dialogue is finding the right balance between level of detail and robustness. Tutorial dialogue systems aim to provide help and feedback in natural language using a wide range of tutoring tactics. Ideally, system responses will be generated dynamically, taking into account multiple factors, including the current answer diagnosis, dialogue history, and information from the student model such as student ability and motivation. In practice, a system's

* This work has been supported in part by US Office of Naval Research grant N000141010085. We would like to thank Natalie Steinhauser, Gwendolyn Campbell, Charlie Scott and Simon Caine for help with data collection and annotation.

K. Yacef et al. (Eds.): AIED 2013, LNAI 7926, pp. 279–288, 2013.

ability to produce such responses depends on the level of detail provided by the NLP component in its analysis of the student answer.

Many existing tutorial dialogue systems use hand-crafted semantic interpreters to link natural language input with their domain models, in order to produce fine-grained representations of student input [1,2,4,11,20]. Such symbolic NLP systems can support dynamic feedback generation by implementing a library of abstract tutorial strategies, and then, for each new problem or situation, producing a feedback message tailored to the context by choosing a strategy to use and instantiating it from the information gathered from the student answer (see Section 2). However, while such systems offer high precision in interpreting user input, they also suffer from recall and robustness problems, and often struggle to achieve adequate performance in large domains.

In contrast, statistical NLP systems use classifiers based on semantic similarity or textual entailment methods to assign student answers to classes corresponding to possible states in a finite-state machine [12,13,17,23]. The classifiers are trained on large corpora, making these methods more robust to unexpected input – an advantage when building systems for large domains. However, the classes they use typically do not provide the fine-grained detail needed to generate natural language feedback dynamically. Therefore, system designers must pre-author feedback messages for each problem and tutoring tactic combination (see Section 3.1), which often limits the range of implemented feedback actions.

In this paper, we investigate how the robustness of a semantic interpreter within a symbolic NLP system can be improved with the addition of a similarity-based statistical classifier. Our goal is to address the robustness issues common in symbolic NLP architectures, making such systems more reliable and easier to use in larger domains. This is the first attempt to integrate statistical classification into an architecture built around dynamic natural language generation. Previous work on combining deep and shallow processing methods in tutorial dialogue [14,21] targeted finite-state systems with manually authored feedback.

We show that our combined system achieves significantly higher performance than the semantic interpreter alone. The best results are achieved by using the classifier to label sentences that the interpreter cannot handle, thus combining the strengths of the two techniques to improve overall system robustness.

The rest of the paper is organized as follows. In Section 2 we describe how semantic interpretation is implemented in the BEETLE II tutorial dialogue system. In Section 3 we examine how statistical classification can be integrated into a system architecture based on symbolic NLP. We then describe the semantic-similarity based classifier we developed and report the results of experimental evaluation in Section 4. We discuss future system improvements in Section 5.

2 Background

As our test environment, we use the BEETLE II tutorial dialogue system [4], developed to teach concepts in basic electricity and electronics to students without prior knowledge of the domain. The system provides a three-hour self-contained course where students read pre-prepared instructional materials and interact with a circuit simulator. During the interaction, they are asked questions about circuit behavior that require one- to two-sentence answers. For example, students may be asked to explain what they observed in the simulator (e.g., "Why was bulb A on when switch Y was open?") or to describe general principles (e.g., "Why does a damaged bulb impact a circuit?"). Over the duration of the course, the system asks 56 different explanation questions, each followed by a remediation dialogue if the student's initial answer is flawed.[1]

The system was designed to support fully automatic feedback generation in a dynamically changing context. Each student answer is parsed by a robust wide-coverage dialogue parser and then mapped into a domain-specific semantic representation using a set of hand-crafted rules [9]. For example, if the student responds to "Why was bulb A on when switch Y was open?" by answering "Bulb A was in a closed path", the representation will be (with some details simplified for exposition purposes) `(Bulb A) (Path p) (is-closed p TRUE) (contains p A)`. This representation is first passed on to the circuit simulator to verify that the named bulb is indeed contained in a closed path. Next, the system checks the explanation content for correctness by matching it against a pattern based on the reference explanation supplied by expert tutors, in this instance `(Bulb ?b) (Battery ?bt) (Path ?p) (is-closed ?p TRUE) (contains ?p ?b) (contains ?p ?bt)`. The resulting diagnosis breaks down the representation of the student answer into correct, missing, contradictory and irrelevant parts [7]. In our example, for a bulb to be lit, it is not enough for it to be in a closed path; there must be a battery in the same path. Therefore, the resulting diagnosis will identify all the objects and relationships mentioned by the student as correct, nothing as contradictory or irrelevant, and will report the missing parts as `(Battery ?bt) (contains p ?bt)`.

The tutorial planner uses the diagnosis to choose from a range of remediation strategies and to instantiate them automatically in context. Most strategies rely on the fine-grained details of the answer analysis for their instantiation; for example, confirming the correct parts of the answer ("Right. The bulb is in a closed path."), hinting at missing bits ("Here's a hint. Your answer should also mention a battery."), or (in another example) explicitly identifying problematic parts ("You said that switch X was closed, but it was open."). But there is also a subset of strategies that require less specific information, such as content-free prompts ("Right, but is that everything?") and suggestions for additional reading. At most points in the interaction, the system can instantiate at least two content-free strategies, and two which require information from the student answer diagnosis and dialogue history. Currently, the system chooses which strategy to use based on past student performance. The general policy is to apply content-free prompts initially, to encourage the students to construct the answer themselves, and provide increasingly more specific remediations if the student is struggling [9]. More complex policies are possible in the future, e.g., adapting the choice of feedback to information in the student model.

[1] In this paper, we use "flawed" to denote any answer class other than "correct".

The use of deep parsing and semantic interpretation provides significant benefits in this application with its dynamically changing simulation environment, because it enables the system to diagnose student input and generate context-specific natural language feedback on the fly. To mitigate robustness issues associated with rule-based processing, the system uses a robust interpretation algorithm and a set of error recovery strategies [6]. This approach is successful on the whole in helping students learn, resulting in significant learning gains between pre- and post-tests [4]. However, natural language interpretation failures are correlated with lower learning gains and lower user satisfaction, and there is substantial room for improvement in interpretation quality [8]. In this paper, we investigate how the quality of natural language interpretation can be improved through a combination of deep and shallow processing without sacrificing the benefits of detailed semantic analysis.

3 System Design

3.1 Answer Classification Approach

The first challenge in developing a statistical classifier to use in a combined system is determining the set of classes to use, balancing the level of detail provided against the feasibility of acquiring training data. It is possible to induce a semantic parser from annotated data [14,16]. However, annotating a large number of sentences with domain-specific logical forms is extremely labor-intensive, and even more complicated when dealing with vague and ill-formed student answers.

Classification approaches that have been implemented in existing tutorial dialogue systems typically map student propositions to classes or "correct answer aspects" [12,18,21], with each class expressing a single complex idea such as "a bulb is in a closed path with a battery".[2] Such classes are represented by one or more exemplar strings, and student answers are assigned to classes based on the closest match, using semantic similarity and textual entailment methods. Because the classes are represented by textual strings and not by structured symbolic representations, class assignment cannot be used directly to generate natural language feedback. Instead, manually authored remediations are associated with each class (i.e., correct answer aspect), and multiple such remediations are needed for the system to adapt to context and dialogue history.

Since we intend to use statistical methods to complement symbolic interpretation, we chose to use a set of problem- and representation-independent classes that support the high-level decision-making structure embedded in the Beetle II tutorial planner. Student answers can be flawed in different ways. They may contain explicit errors, contradicting the expected answer or the state of the world (e.g., saying that a switch is closed when it is open); they may correctly include part of the explanation but miss some crucial aspects; or they may state

[2] A finer-grained, generalizable classification approach has been proposed in [19]. This is a promising avenue of research, but it has not yet been integrated into a running system. We defer further discussion of its applicability until Section 5.

facts that, while true, are not relevant in explaining the phenomenon in question (e.g., stating that a bulb has two terminals does not explain why it is lit).

These different types of flaws are associated with different tutoring strategies in the BEETLE II tutorial planner, based on analysis of human-human tutoring data and strategies suggested in the literature. In general, the system rejects answers containing explicit errors and asks students to try again; provides positive feedback on incomplete answers but requests more information; and redirects students' attention through hints if their explanations lack relevance. For every flaw type, the system provides both detailed feedback strategies and the content-free prompts described in Section 2.

We therefore defined an annotation scheme with 5 classes, to be used in answer classification: "correct", "partially-correct-incomplete", "contradictory", "irrelevant" and "non-domain"[3]. If the fine-grained analysis is unavailable, the tutorial planner can use the class to select an appropriate content-free prompt as a fallback strategy, thus improving its robustness.

3.2 Combining Semantic Interpretation and Classification

Once a suitable classifier is built, we need to decide how to combine its results with the output of the semantic interpreter. To better understand the performance of the BEETLE II interpreter, we previously conducted a system evaluation based on a corpus of paid volunteers interacting with the system. Every student answer was manually annotated using our five class coding scheme ($\kappa = 0.69$), and the associated semantic interpretation and diagnosis output from the BEETLE II system was automatically mapped to the same scheme [5]. This annotation enables us to directly compare the performance of the semantic interpreter with that of the classifier, and identify areas for improvement.

In our previous work, we devised a classifier based on lexical similarity and evaluated it alongside the BEETLE II semantic interpreter [5,10]. The interpreter had a higher precision but substantially lower recall than the statistical classifier, indicating that the two approaches have complementary strengths and weaknesses.

Based on the evaluation results in [10], we identified two key performance issues with the semantic interpreter that we would particularly like to address. First, the interpreter fails to find any interpretation at all for a large proportion of answers to explanation questions (865 out of 2729 instances, or 32%, according to the confusion matrix reported in [10]). We will refer to those cases as "uninterpretable utterances". Second, out of the answers that the system can interpret, a large proportion of "correct" and "contradictory" answers are misinterpreted as "partially-correct-incomplete". Students can feel frustrated if their correct answers are misinterpreted or rejected, and in general when their answers

[3] Students make help requests, social statements and other utterances that do not contribute any domain content to the dialogue, although the tutor has to respond to them nevertheless. These are labeled as "non-domain".

are not understood. Therefore, we attempted to address these issues by testing three combinations of semantic interpretation and statistical classification:[4]

1. `OptimisticCorrect`: if the classifier labels the answer as correct, then the classifier's label is used; otherwise, the label from the semantic interpreter is used. This combination creates a more lenient system that aims to avoid misidentifying correct answers, a known cause of student frustration.
2. `NoReject`: if the semantic interpreter fails to arrive at an interpretation, then the classifier's label is used; otherwise, the label from the semantic interpreter is used. This combination creates a system that never rejects student answers as uninterpretable.
3. `NoRejectCorrect`: if both of the previous conditions hold (the classifier labels the answer as correct and the semantic interpreter fails to find an interpretation), then the classifier's label is used; in all other cases, the label from the semantic interpreter is used. This combination is a more conservative version of the `NoReject` system.

These three different ways of combining the output of the semantic interpreter and the classifier each have advantages and disadvantages. Being more lenient in grading student answers as correct may help improve user satisfaction but risks missing opportunities to correct misconceptions and provide useful remediation. Never rejecting answers as uninterpretable can reduce student frustration. However, uninterpretable utterances often arise from incorrect uses of terminology, and learning to speak in the way expected for the domain has been positively correlated with learning outcomes [22]. The semantic interpreter provides information about the nature of interpretation failures that supports generation of targeted help messages, pointing out problematic wordings not consistent with the domain, such as "Paths cannot be broken, only components can be broken." [6]. Some students may benefit from seeing such rejection messages.

Choosing the best trade-off may depend on the high-level tutoring policy and the application domain. However, it is important to evaluate how different combinations affect the overall quality of natural language interpretation, which affects interaction quality as a whole. This is the focus of the rest of the paper.

4 Evaluation

4.1 Experimental Setup

For this experiment, we used the Beetle portion of the Student Response Analysis task corpus[5], which is an updated version of the gold standard evaluation corpus from [10]. This dataset consists of 3426 student answers to explanation questions collected from the interactions of 35 paid undergraduate volunteers working with the BEETLE II system.

[4] In addition to these rule-based combinations, we also attempted to learn the best combinations directly from the data. Our experiments so far have not resulted in improved performance, so this remains a topic for future work.

[5] `http://www.cs.york.ac.uk/semeval-2013/task7/index.php?id=data`

The BEETLE II semantic interpreter was developed based on transcripts from an earlier version of the system which were not included in our evaluation corpus. Thus, this corpus constitutes unseen data for the semantic interpreter.

We used 10-fold cross-validation to evaluate the performance of the standalone classifier and the combined systems. At every iteration, we used 9 folds to train the statistical classifier, and the 10th fold as a test set for the system using it. We report the per-class precision, recall and F1 scores as evaluation metrics, following [10]. We use the macro-averaged F1 score as the primary evaluation metric because it is suitable for evaluating unbalanced class distributions, requiring that the system performs well on identifying all possible classes and does not only focus on the most frequent cases.

In all our combined systems, we use the simple lexical similarity classifier described in [5]. While more sophisticated approaches are available [18,21], the simple features that we use are fast to compute and do not require additional external resources. Our goal is to produce a lightweight approach that complements the more resource-intensive symbolic interpretation. In future, more advanced features can be considered to further enhance system performance.

4.2 Results

Table 1 shows the performance of the semantic interpreter and our classifier taken alone. Both perform at the same overall level (0.45 macro-averaged F1), but the semantic interpreter has substantially higher precision and lower recall. Thus, the systems have complementary strengths and weaknesses, suggesting that improved performance may be possible by combining the approaches.

Table 2 presents evaluation results for the three combination systems described in Section 3.2. The performance of each of the combined systems differs significantly from the standalone semantic interpreter, with $p < 0.001$ on an approximate randomization test with 10,000 permutations [24].

The best performance improvement is achieved by the `NoReject` system, where the classifier's label is used whenever symbolic interpretation fails, raising the system's macro-averaged F1 from 0.45 to 0.54. Performance improves across all classes, with the largest improvements in "contradictory" and "non-domain". Although this system experiences a drop in precision, resulting in more misidentified classes, it is accompanied by a significant increase in recall, since no utterances are rejected as uninterpretable.

In contrast, the `OptimisticCorrect` system, which always accepts a student answer as correct if the classifier judges it correct, results in significantly reduced performance compared to the semantic interpreter alone (0.43 F1), with precision on identifying correct answers dropping from 0.94 to 0.65, and recall not increasing sufficiently to compensate for the drop. Finally, the more conservative `NoRejectCorrect` system, which only overrides the semantic interpreter if both the interpretation fails and the classifier judges the answer correct, provides a small (though still significant) boost in performance compared to the semantic interpreter alone.

Table 1. Evaluation results for the semantic interpreter alone and the classifier alone

	Semantic interpreter			Statistical classifier		
	P	R	F1	P	R	F1
correct	0.94	0.50	0.66	0.64	0.78	0.70
pc_inc	0.45	0.51	0.48	0.42	0.35	0.38
contra	0.54	0.18	0.27	0.44	0.36	0.40
irrlvnt	0.21	0.21	0.20	0.09	0.03	0.05
nondom	0.90	0.51	0.65	0.63	0.84	0.73
macro avg	0.60	0.38	0.45	0.45	0.47	0.45

Table 2. Evaluation results for three different system combinations

	`OptimisticCorrect`			`NoReject`			`NoRejectCorrect`		
	P	R	F1	P	R	F1	P	R	F1
correct	0.65	0.85	0.74	0.75	0.66	0.70	0.76	0.66	0.70
pc_inc	0.54	0.31	0.40	0.43	0.64	0.51	0.45	0.51	0.48
contra	0.56	0.09	0.16	0.56	0.40	0.46	0.54	0.18	0.28
irrlvnt	0.22	0.19	0.21	0.20	0.24	0.22	0.21	0.21	0.21
nondom	0.93	0.51	0.66	0.76	0.89	0.82	0.90	0.51	0.65
macro avg	0.58	0.39	0.43	**0.54**	**0.57**	**0.54**	0.57	0.42	0.46

These results show that symbolic interpretation and statistical classification can be effectively combined in a system architecture geared towards automatic generation of targeted feedback. We discuss the trade-offs involved and future improvements in the next section.

5 Discussion and Future Work

This paper presents a first attempt at combining a symbolic semantic interpreter and a statistical classifier in the context of a tutorial dialogue system which generates natural language feedback dynamically based on detailed semantic analysis of student contributions. In our evaluation, the rule-based semantic interpreter and the lexical similarity-based statistical classifier perform similarly as stand-alone systems, but can be combined to improve performance significantly by using the statistical classifier to label utterances rejected as uninterpretable by the semantic interpreter.

Unlike previous approaches to statistical natural language understanding in tutorial dialogue, we use a simple set of five correctness classes that apply to all questions, and do not depend on "correct answer aspects" specific to the problem. Assigning one of these classes is sufficient to allow the system to employ a subset of its tutoring strategies, namely, content-free prompts, in situations where the semantic interpreter cannot reliably provide the fine-grained semantic representations necessary for instantiating more specific strategies.

Nielsen et al. [19] show how to obtain more fine-grained information about correct, incorrect and missing parts of student answers using a statistical classification approach. This presents an interesting avenue for future work, as such an approach could potentially enable the system to use a wider range of dynamically generated strategies. However, the finer-grained classification scheme also requires correspondingly more annotation effort, since each student answer must be annotated with 10 labels on average. Our approach is less labor-intensive with respect to annotation, at the cost of having less specific information available.

In the three combination systems that we tried, we found the greatest improvement in language interpretation accuracy when using the classifier only on utterances which the symbolic interpreter rejected as having no interpretation. In contrast, relying on the classifier's "correct" label, which was an attempt to compensate for the large number of correct answers mislabeled by the interpreter, did not improve system performance. This system combination might become more effective if more sophisticated approaches, especially textual entailment methods, were used in the classifier. We are considering the best techniques to use as part of our future work.

The next step in system development is to test the new robust interpreter with users, to see whether improved robustness translates into improvements in end-to-end system performance. While there is clearly a link between interpretation quality and both learning gain and user satisfaction [8], intrinsic evaluation metrics alone are not always good predictors of final outcomes [5]. We are planning to use our robust interpretation module in an upcoming user evaluation, and will assess its contribution by comparing the learning outcomes obtained with the new system to the results of the previous evaluation where less sophisticated NLP was used.

References

1. Aleven, V., Popescu, O., Koedinger, K.R.: Pilot-testing a tutorial dialogue system that supports self-explanation. In: Cerri, S.A., Gouardères, G., Paraguaçu, F. (eds.) ITS 2002. LNCS, vol. 2363, pp. 344–354. Springer, Heidelberg (2002)
2. Callaway, C., Dzikovska, M., Matheson, C., Moore, J., Zinn, C.: Using dialogue to learn math in the LeActiveMath project. In: Proc. of ECAI Workshop on Language-Enhanced Educational Technology, pp. 1–8 (2006)
3. Chi, M.T.H., de Leeuw, N., Chiu, M.H., LaVancher, C.: Eliciting self-explanations improves understanding. Cognitive Science 18(3), 439–477 (1994)
4. Dzikovska, M.O., Bental, D., Moore, J.D., Steinhauser, N.B., Campbell, G.E., Farrow, E., Callaway, C.B.: Intelligent tutoring with natural language support in the BEETLE II system. In: Wolpers, M., Kirschner, P.A., Scheffel, M., Lindstaedt, S., Dimitrova, V. (eds.) EC-TEL 2010. LNCS, vol. 6383, pp. 620–625. Springer, Heidelberg (2010)
5. Dzikovska, M.O., Bell, P., Isard, A., Moore, J.D.: Evaluating language understanding accuracy with respect to objective outcomes in a dialogue system. In: Proc. of EACL 2012 Conference, pp. 471–481 (2012)
6. Dzikovska, M.O., Callaway, C.B., Farrow, E., Moore, J.D., Steinhauser, N.B., Campbell, G.E.: Dealing with interpretation errors in tutorial dialogue. In: Proc. of SIGDIAL 2009 Conference, pp. 38–45 (2009)
7. Dzikovska, M.O., Campbell, G.E., Callaway, C.B., Steinhauser, N.B., Farrow, E., Moore, J.D., Butler, L.A., Matheson, C.: Diagnosing natural language answers to support adaptive tutoring. In: Proc. of 21st Intl. FLAIRS Conference (2008)
8. Dzikovska, M.O., Moore, J.D., Steinhauser, N., Campbell, G.: The impact of interpretation problems on tutorial dialogue. In: Proc. of ACL 2010 Conference Short Papers, pp. 43–48 (2010)

9. Dzikovska, M.O., Moore, J.D., Steinhauser, N., Campbell, G., Farrow, E., Callaway, C.B.: Beetle II: a system for tutoring and computational linguistics experimentation. In: Proc. of ACL 2010 System Demonstrations, pp. 13–18 (2010)
10. Dzikovska, M.O., Nielsen, R.D., Brew, C.: Towards effective tutorial feedback for explanation questions: A dataset and baselines. In: Proc. of 2012 Conference of NAACL: Human Language Technologies, pp. 200–210 (2012)
11. Glass, M.: Processing language input in the CIRCSIM-Tutor intelligent tutoring system. In: Papers from the 2000 AAAI Fall Symposium, pp. 74–79 (2000); Available as AAAI technical report FS-00-01
12. Graesser, A.C., Wiemer-Hastings, K., Wiemer-Hastings, P., Kreuz, R.: Autotutor: A simulation of a human tutor. Cognitive Systems Research 1, 35–51 (1999)
13. Jordan, P., Makatchev, M., Pappuswamy, U., VanLehn, K., Albacete, P.: A natural language tutorial dialogue system for physics. In: Proc. of 19th Intl. FLAIRS Conference, pp. 521–527 (2006)
14. Jordan, P.W., Makatchev, M., VanLehn, K.: Combining competing language understanding approaches in an intelligent tutoring system. In: Lester, J.C., Vicari, R.M., Paraguaçu, F. (eds.) ITS 2004. LNCS, vol. 3220, pp. 346–357. Springer, Heidelberg (2004)
15. Khuwaja, R.A., Evens, M.W., Michael, J.A., Rovick, A.A.: Architecture of CIRCSIM-tutor (v.3): A smart cardiovascular physiology tutor. In: Proc. of 7th Annual IEEE Computer-Based Medical Systems Symposium (1994)
16. Kwiatkowski, T., Zettlemoyer, L., Goldwater, S., Steedman, M.: Inducing probabilistic CCG grammars from logical form with higher-order unification. In: Proc. of EMNLP 2010 Conference, pp. 1223–1233 (2010)
17. Litman, D.J., Silliman, S.: ITSPOKE: an intelligent tutoring spoken dialogue system. In: Demonstration Papers at HLT-NAACL 2004, Boston, Massachusetts, pp. 5–8 (2004)
18. McCarthy, P.M., Rus, V., Crossley, S.A., Graesser, A.C., McNamara, D.S.: Assessing forward-, reverse-, and average-entailment indices on natural language input from the intelligent tutoring system, iSTART. In: Proc. of 21st Intl. FLAIRS Conference, pp. 165–170 (2008)
19. Nielsen, R.D., Ward, W., Martin, J.H.: Learning to assess low-level conceptual understanding. In: Proc. of 21st Intl. FLAIRS Conference, pp. 427–432 (2008)
20. Pon-Barry, H., Clark, B., Schultz, K., Bratt, E.O., Peters, S.: Advantages of spoken language interaction in dialogue-based intelligent tutoring systems. In: Lester, J.C., Vicari, R.M., Paraguaçu, F. (eds.) ITS 2004. LNCS, vol. 3220, pp. 390–400. Springer, Heidelberg (2004)
21. Rosé, C., Vanlehn, K.: An evaluation of a hybrid language understanding approach for robust selection of tutoring goals. Int. J. Artif. Intell. Ed. 15(4), 325–355 (2005)
22. Steinhauser, N.B., Campbell, G.E., Taylor, L.S., Caine, S., Scott, C., Dzikovska, M.O., Moore, J.D.: Talk like an electrician: Student dialogue mimicking behavior in an intelligent tutoring system. In: Biswas, G., Bull, S., Kay, J., Mitrovic, A. (eds.) AIED 2011. LNCS, vol. 6738, pp. 361–368. Springer, Heidelberg (2011)
23. VanLehn, K., Jordan, P., Litman, D.: Developing pedagogically effective tutorial dialogue tactics: Experiments and a testbed. In: Proc. of SLaTE Workshop on Speech and Language Technology in Education, Farmington, PA (October 2007)
24. Yeh, A.: More accurate tests for the statistical significance of result differences. In: Proceedings of the 18th International Conference on Computational Linguistics (COLING 2000), pp. 947–953. Association for Computational Linguistics, Stroudsburg (2000), http://dx.doi.org/10.3115/992730.992783

Can Preschoolers Profit from a Teachable Agent Based Play-and-Learn Game in Mathematics?

Anton Axelsson, Erik Anderberg, and Magnus Haake

Lund University Cognitive Science, Sweden
{Anton.Axelsson.287,Erik.Anderberg.114}@student.lu.se,
Magnus.Haake@lucs.lu.se

Abstract. A large number of studies carried out on pupils aged 8–14 have shown that teachable agent (TA) based games are beneficial for learning. The present pioneering study aimed to initiate research looking at whether TA based games can be used as far down as preschool age. Around the age of four, theory of mind (ToM) is under development and it is not unlikely that a fully developed ToM is necessary to benefit from a TA's socially engaging characteristics. 10 preschool children participated in an experiment of playing a mathematics game. The participants playing a TA-version of the game engaged socially with the TA and were not disturbed by his presence. Thus, this study unveils exciting possibilities for further research of the hypothesised educational benefits in store for preschoolers with regard to play-and-learn games employing TAs.

Keywords: teachable agent, theory of mind, preschoolers, learning by teaching.

1 Introduction

The use of digital equipment has recently made its way into the preschool curriculum. When introducing computers it is vital that we make the best use of them; this calls for innovative software. Lately, much research has gone into what is called *teachable agents*. A teachable agent (TA) can be described as an autonomous, digital student in educational software, where the idea is that the pupil takes the role as *teacher* in order to tutor the TA. This is a modern approach to the framework known as *learning by teaching* [1–3]. This role switching encourages the pupil to take responsibility for someone else's learning [4]. Thus, the pupil learns in order to teach. The main question posed in this paper is whether this pedagogical approach can be used for preschool children as well.

2 Background and Research Aims

It has been shown that teaching others is in fact a very efficient way for a *teacher* to learn [5–8]. Among the underlying mechanisms we find (i) an increased effort in spent time and depth of analysis compared to those who learn for themselves [1, 4, 9]; (ii) that teaching involves an externalisation of one's thoughts and ways of reasoning, which together with questions from the tutee can lead to discoveries of gaps and vagueness in one's own knowledge, that can accordingly be revised and developed [10, 11]; (iii) that

K. Yacef et al. (Eds.): AIED 2013, LNAI 7926, pp. 289–298, 2013.

so called *self-efficacy beliefs* [12], the belief in one's own competence within a given domain, can be positively affected: "I am someone who can teach X".

Some additional advantages of using a *digital* version of learning by teaching over a *non-digital* are: (i) that all pupils can be teachers, including those that are not naturally inclined to take such a role; (ii) that the teaching pupil and tutee can be matched to one-another ensuring an adequate challenge for the pupil; (iii) that no actual tutee will suffer from a poor teacher.

Numerous studies have shown that TA-based software can be powerful in terms of learning outcomes. It has been shown for 8- to 9-year-olds [13, 14]; for 10- to 12-year-olds [15–17] and for 12- to 14-year-olds [4, 18]. Hitherto, no studies have been carried out with pupils younger than 8 years old. The purpose of the pioneering study presented in this paper was to investigate whether the benefits of TA-based games can be extended down to children of preschool age, more specifically, 3- to 5-year-olds.

2.1 Understanding a Teachable Agent

In order to fully understand the concept of teaching someone else, one has to understand that others do not know exactly what I know because they possess a mind, knowledge, and feelings of their own. In other words, one has to have what is often referred to as a *theory of mind* (ToM). Research on the development of children's ToM, or mentalising abilities, begun in the early 1980s and is today one of the most active and fastest growing areas of research within cognitive developmental psychology [19].

The most standardised way of measuring ToM is looking at a persons understanding that others can possess an incorrect or false belief. Clements and Perner [20] showed that some children, although they did not fully pass the false belief tasks, did seem to have an implicit understanding of false beliefs. This finding was later corroborated by Garnham and Perner [21]. This suggests that there are different levels in the development of ToM. At the age of six, all normally developing children have a fully developed ToM, which they can explicitly verbalise.

Metacognition is paid much attention to within the learning sciences. It has an interesting relation with ToM in aspects such as knowledge about one's memory and one's abilities to handle information, problem solving, and learning strategies; one's ability to judge what is easy or difficult to learn, and so forth [22, 23]. Developmental links between early ToM and subsequent metacognitive knowledge have been shown [24].

2.2 Attending to a Teachable Agent

A suggested pedagogical benefit of TA-based games is that they support and stimulate not only problem solving and learning, but also *reflection* on problem solving and learning. This kind of metacognition is usually demanding when one is solving problems on one's own because one is required to both solve a problem, as well as monitor the problem solving. However, this dual task demand can be alleviated by monitoring *somebody else* solving a problem. Thus, one can apply the monitoring process to somebody else's thinking [16]. With teachable agents, it is the teachable agent that is doing the problem solving, which potentially frees up resources for the child's own metacognition.

In order for metacognition to occur in the interaction with a TA, the pupil of course has to really attend to the TA's problem solving and acting. Results from studies with primary school children indicate that they do indeed pay close attention to their teachable agents. This occurs both when they are required to correct or guide their TA, and in the situation where the TA is trying to solve tasks on its own and the pupil cannot interfere. For instance, Lindström and colleagues [25] report a study where 8- to 10-year-olds played a TA-based mathematics game. A rich set of spontaneous utterances from pupils watching their TAs play on their own testify to their attention to their TAs.

2.3 Engaging with a Teachable Agent

Another observation from studies with primary school children is that they show signs of high engagement in terms of emotional utterances and facial as well as gestural excitement when playing TA-based games. Chase and her colleagues [4] conducted a systematic comparison with 10-year-olds, where one group played a TA-based game and another group played the same game without a TA. When a mistake was made, the pupils in the TA-group were significantly more inclined to display affect and engagement than the pupils in the non-TA-group.

2.4 Purpose of Study

At present, there is no data and no studies on children below 8 years of age playing educational games with TAs. Thus, the question is whether benefits from TA-based games can be evidenced already for 3- to 5-year-olds or not. A possible hypothesis is that metacognition, directed to someone else, is only possible for a child that has a sufficiently mature ToM. But in principle it is an open question, and with this study we intend to initiate a first step towards answering it. The present study investigated the interaction between preschoolers, aged 4–5, and a TA. The study explored how the children would respond to a TA-based learning game, and in particular (i) their understanding of a TA in relation to their ToM; (ii) their inclination to attend to a TA; (iii) their engagement with a TA.

3 The System: Rationales for the Game

We chose early mathematics as the learning domain for our TA-game, primarily because we have experience with research and development of TA-based games in this domain for primary school children [13, 14, 18], but also because there are educational arguments, such as the need for teaching rudimentary mathematics early.

One of the key concepts in the area of mathematics for young children is *number sense*. This concept refers to an understanding of the meaning of numbers and an ability to make comparisons, as well as showing proof of fluency with numbers [26], together with an understanding that they relate to quantities [27]. Basic number sense usually emerges in children through social interaction with parents and siblings. If it does not emerge, or if children do not develop it sufficiently during their time at preschool, difficulties in understanding more complex mathematics will most likely occur once the

Fig. 1. Four screen shots of the game with the TA. Pictures 2–4 illustrates the three game modes: self-playing, TA-watching, and TA-playing.

child starts primary school (see e.g., [28, 29]). Number Sense can be taught [27] and for children who have not been exposed to numerical reasoning at home, formal training of Number Sense is essential [30].

3.1 The Game Design

The game used in this study revolves around chicks that fall out of their nests and need help to get back up. One chick at a time holds up a number of feathers representing the branch it lives on. The player's task is to match this number on the keypad of a lift. The idea behind using a lift is that it represents a vertical number line; it gives a good representation of parts of the whole — branches as floors — and higher numbers are further up. It is important to use concepts familiar to the child [27, 31], and lifts are common features with mathematical properties in our society. The game design is depicted in Fig. 1.

The game can be played with or without a TA. In the former, after three rounds of helping chicks, a TA (a panda named Panders) is introduced and observes the player's actions. After another three rounds the TA takes over and the player now guides the TA, correcting him if not agreeing with him. Thus, there are three modes: (i) self-playing, (ii) TA-watching, and (iii) TA-playing (see Fig. 1). If playing without the TA, the player iterates nine rounds of self-playing.

4 Method

4.1 Participants, Design and Measurements

Ten children age 4;1 to 5;2 from a nursery in Southern Sweden participated. A between subjects design was adopted with TA as an independent variable in order to compare: (i) children's inclination to concentrate when playing the game with a TA compared to without a TA, and (ii) their engagement with the game with a TA compared to without a TA. In other words, five children played with the TA and five children played without the TA. Because we were interested in whether a child's ToM would affect her understanding of what a TA is, we strived for homogeneity between the two conditions with respect to participants' ToM as well as gender and age. The variables measured and compared between the two conditions were:

(i) Engagement with the game: how involved the participants appeared to be in playing the game, as manifested through pointing, laughing, an excited tone of voice, and so forth. The opposite would be a participant appearing to be bored by the game, as manifested through sighing, looking away, not saying anything, and so forth.
(ii) Attention to the game: how focused the participants appeared to be on the task at hand, as manifested through signs of absorption in thought, such as starring, not looking away from the screen, wide open mouth, and so forth. The opposite would be a participant who is perceived as engaging in activities irrelevant to the game, as manifested through, for example, attending to things away from the screen.

For the group of children that played the game with a TA, further analysis of their verbal and non-verbal behaviour during the study session was undertaken in order to provide data for the third research question posed in the study: How do children of this age understand and interpret a teachable agent, and does it relate to their ToM?

When playing the game the participants were filmed with an unobtrusive web camera situated above the experiment laptop screen. All mouse events during game play were logged, and audio was captured through the laptop's built-in microphone.

4.2 Procedure

The nursery teacher selected children who fitted the age requirement (3–5) that were not occupied in other activities and who were willing to participate. She escorted them one by one to a secluded part of the nursery where the experiment took place. Before playing the game, a pre-test for screening ToM was conducted. The pre-test was in the form of an adapted Sally-Anne test, devised for testing false belief [32]. To pass the test, the participants would first have to point at the correct box, and also give a coherent account for their choice.

Before starting the game, brief assessment on the participants' counting skills were also carried out. The experiment leader held up eight fingers and asked the children to tell her how many fingers she held up. Those who struggled with counting past five were assigned to play the game with six floors. Those who were able to provide an answer with more ease were assigned eight floors. The rationale behind this is that the focus of this study is on participants engagement with and understanding of a TA and not on mathematical skills. Thus we wanted to avoid that participants would feel discouraged by the level of difficulty. Four children ended up playing with six floors and six children played with eight floors. After the pre-experiment tests, the participant was assigned to play the game either with the TA or without. A balancing sheet was utilised to maintain homogenous groups with respect to the participants' age, gender, and performance on the false belief task.

When a participant finished the game, the preschool teacher was called back into the room and the child was asked to explain to her what the game was about. Those who played with the TA were also asked to explain its role in the game. One of the experimenters noted down the answers with pen and paper. The experiment took on average 11 minutes to complete.

4.3 Coding and Analysis

Each video of the participants playing the game was split into three clips. Each clip consisted of three game rounds. Thus, for participants playing with the TA, the clips matched the three game modes. The resulting 30 clips were muted and randomly distributed between the two experimenters, 15 clips for each experimenter, now acting as coders. All 30 mute clips were also given to two other coders who had never seen any of the participants before. The rationale behind this was that no coder should be able to tell how far a participant had progressed in the game, and also to make it more difficult for the coders to recognise whether a participant was playing with a TA or not. The participants were rated on attention and engagement on a 7-point category scale, where 1 represented fully unattentive/unengaged respectively, and 7 represented fully attentive/engaged respectively.

After this analysis had been completed, the five full-length videos with sound of participants playing with the TA was analysed. All comments and gestures associated with the TA were transcribed.

5 Results

5.1 Understanding of the TA

Participant 1, aged 4;5, pointed correctly in the false belief test (FBT) but could not give an adequate motivation for her choice. She was good at counting and was therefore assigned to play the game with eight floors. When playing the game, she watched very concentrated as the TA introduced himself. Twice during game play, she commented on the TA's suggestions. When the TA asked: "Am I thinking correctly?" the first time she responded: "No he isn't", and the second time she said: "No, it was three in that picture, but the chick is showing two". Once when the TA asked her to show him which button he should have chosen, she pressed the correct button whilst telling him: "That little button". To the post-test question regarding the role of the TA, her answer was that she did not remember.

Participant 2, aged 5;2, did not pass the FBT. She had trouble counting and therefore played the game with six floors. When the TA was introduced, she smiled a lot. Whilst playing with him she was very reluctant to correct him and the experiment leader had to encourage her. After checking the TA's choice, she lit up with a smile and said: "He was correct". To the post-test question of the role of the TA, she responded: "You were supposed to help him".

Participant 5, aged 5;1, passed the FBT and his answer implied that he found the control question silly. He had no trouble counting and played the game with 8 floors. He focused when the TA introduced himself, but paid very little attention to him thereafter and managed to play the game with ease. To the post-test question of the role of the TA, he answered: "Panders was there to help".

Participant 7, aged 4;10, passed the FBT. She counted with ease, and was assigned to play with 8 floors. She said nothing during game play but looked several times at the experimenters for confirmation. To the post-test question of the role of the TA, she answered: "The panda was thinking right or wrong".

Participant 9, aged 4;1, did not pass the FBT. He struggled counting above the number five, and was assigned to play the game with 6 floors. He seemed very reluctant to correct the TA. He continuously pressed the "correct" button in the TA mode, even when the TA had guessed incorrectly, and even when the chick only wanted to go to the third floor. Conversely, he made no errors prior to the TA mode even when presented with the numbers 5 or 6. To the post-test question of the role of the TA, he answered: "The panda is watching".

5.2 Attention and Engagement

When analysing inter-rater reliability for the 30 clips, Spearman's rho revealed that consensus among the coders concerning attention was too low to draw any reliable conclusions. This variable was therefore excluded from analysis. We intend to further investigate the focused attention on a TA with regards to preschoolers, and this will be discussed briefly in Section 6.1.

Regarding engagement, Spearman's rho revealed a significant correlation of inter-rater reliability ($p < 0.01$). From observing the children during the experiment, it was noted that at least three of the five participants were more motivated to play once the TA was introduced. However, this did not surface in an analysis of covariance, which revealed that there were no significant differences in encoded engagement of participants playing with or without a TA.

The qualitative analysis of the video recordings revealed that participants, regardless of condition, in general were pleased with playing the game and seemed to enjoy it. There were a lot of laughters and surprised faces during game play. Though, participant 5 got quite bored with the game and was not shy to make this clear when asked. However, this was one of the oldest participants who, as mentioned above, both counted and passed the FBT with ease.

6 Discussion

This study represents a pioneering examination of how 4 to 5 years old children respond to a teachable agent based educational game. The results showed that engagement — the participants involvement in the game — was evident both with and without the TA. This gives us an indication that the game is in itself engaging. More important, however, is the observation that the children seemed quite at ease in interacting with the TA, and the TA did not impede on engagement to the game and seemed not to be obtrusive.

Unfortunately, the coders could not agree on the participants' inclination to attend to the game. However, the answers the children gave of the TA's role indicated that they indeed had focused on the TA's actions and speech. All of the children either used terms that the TA himself used throughout the game when answering the question as to what they thought the role of the TA was, or responded to him verbally when he asked questions. Judging from the way the participants acted with or commented on the TA, it was also apparent that they did interpret him as a social character that they were supposed to help, or as someone who was there to learn. Especially participant 1 treated the TA as a social entity by promptly responding verbally to his questions.

The results seem to indicate that children can at least engage with social characters without a fully developed ToM. And it was evident that the participants had no trouble playing the game with or without a TA because they were able to help the chicks both by playing alone, and with the TA. Two participants completely failed the false belief task and they were both reluctant to correct the TA. One participant had to be encouraged to give it a try and was successful, the other just kept confirming that the TA was correct when he clearly was not. This participant did have some trouble counting and it could be argued that this was the cause. However, he confirmed the TA even when the TA was incorrect in a round involving the number 3, a task he should have been able to solve considering that he made no errors prior to the TA mode even when presented with numbers as high as 5 or 6. It is tempting to conclude that these two participants' reluctance to correct the TA would be due to an underdeveloped ToM. However, a more extensive assessment of the participants stage in development of ToM would have had to be undertaken before any conclusion could be drawn. An alternative explanation could be that, at least one of the participants lack in executive functions and could therefore not inhibit his urge to press the green confirmation button when the TA was incorrect. We plan to further investigate this (see Section 6.1).

There are three important factors revealed through this study: (i) preschool children are not disturbed by the presence of a teachable agent; (ii) preschool children are able to pay attention to a teachable agent; (iii) it is possible for preschool children to engage in a socio-cognitive interaction with social characters regardless of a fully developed ToM.

6.1 Implications and Future Research

Being a pioneering study with a limited number of participants the study clearly calls for continued research of the potential benefits of using TAs in pedagogical games for preschoolers. A longitudinal study of the learning effects of using TAs with preschoolers is obviously critical. However, such a study is very costly in terms of time and resources, and it is therefore essential to make sure that preschoolers are able to grasp the concept of a TA. An upcoming study will investigate TA-based games with respect to focus of attention among preschoolers. We will study how well preschoolers can inhibit distractions in order to keep focused on the TA, and its relation to the development of ToM and executive functions.

In a larger context, the questions under investigation are crucial. It is well established that metacognitive abilities is a key factor for children's success in their development as learners [33–36], and it is therefore important to further investigate young children in this respect.

Acknowledgments. Special thanks to Lisa Lindberg, Maja Håkansson, and Sanne Bengtsson, collaborators and developers in the study and MSc Layla Husain for quality control of the game. Also thanks to preschool teacher Annika Janz and the children participating in the tests. A special thanks to Professor Daniel Schwarz, Stanford School of Education, for the idea of developing a TA-based game for young children (and TA-based games at all), and Professor Agneta Gulz for supervising work presented in this paper.

References

1. Biswas, G., Leelawong, K., Schwartz, D., Vye, N.: Learning By Teaching: a New Agent Paradigm for Educational Software. Applied Artificial Intelligence 19(3-4), 363–392 (2005)
2. Brophy, S., Biswas, G., Katzlberger, T., Bransford, J., Schwartz, D.: Teachable Agents: Combining Insights from Learning Theory and Computer Science. In: Lajoie, S.P., Vivet, M. (eds.) Artificial Intelligence in Education, pp. 21–28. IOS Press, Amsterdam (1999)
3. Papert, S.: Mindstorms: Children, Computers and Powerful Ideas, 2nd edn. Basic Books, New York (1980)
4. Chase, C.C., Chin, D.B., Oppezzo, M.A., Schwartz, D.L.: Teachable Agents and the Protégé Effect: Increasing the Effort Towards Learning. Journal of Science Education and Technology 18(4), 334–352 (2009)
5. Bargh, J.A., Schul, Y.: On the Cognitive Benefits of Teaching. Journal of Educational Psychology 72(5), 593–604 (1980)
6. Annis, L.F.: The Processes and Effects of Peer Tutoring. Human Learning: Journal of Practical Research & Applications 2(1), 39–47 (1983)
7. Papert, S.: The Children's Machine: Rethinking School in the Age of the Computer. Basic Books, New York (1993)
8. Renkl, A.: Learning for Later Teaching: An Exploration of Mediational Links Between Teaching Expectancy and Learning Results. Learning and Instruction 5(1), 21–36 (1995)
9. Martin, L., Schwartz, D.L.: Prospective Adaptation in the Use of External Representations. Cognition and Instruction 27(4), 370–400 (2009)
10. Graesser, A.C., Person, N.K., Magliano, J.P.: Collaborative Dialogue Patterns in Naturalistic One-to-One Tutoring. Applied Cognitive Psychology 9(6), 495–522 (1995)
11. Roscoe, R.D., Chi, M.T.H.: Tutor Learning: The Role of Explaining and Responding to Questions. Instructional Science 36(4), 321–350 (2008)
12. Bandura, A.: Self-Referent Thought: A Developmental Analysis of Self-Efficacy. In: Flavell, J.H., Ross, L. (eds.) Social Cognitive Development: Frontiers and Possible Futures, pp. 200–239. Cambridge University Press, Cambridge (1981)
13. Pareto, L., Haake, M., Lindström, P., Sjödén, B., Gulz, A.: A Teachable-Agent-Based Game Affording Collaboration and Competition: Evaluating Math Comprehension and Motivation. Educational Technology Research and Development 60(5), 723–751 (2012)
14. Pareto, L., Arvemo, T., Dahl, Y., Haake, M., Gulz, A.: A Teachable-Agent Arithmetic Game's Effects on Mathematics Understanding, Attitude and Self-efficacy. In: Biswas, G., Bull, S., Kay, J., Mitrovic, A. (eds.) AIED 2011. LNCS, vol. 6738, pp. 247–255. Springer, Heidelberg (2011)
15. Schwartz, D., Blair, K.: Animations of Thought: Interactivity in the Teachable Agent Paradigm. In: Lowe, R., Schnotz, W. (eds.) Learning with Animation: Research and Implications for Design, pp. 114–140. Cambrige University Press, Cambridge (2007)
16. Schwartz, D.L., Chase, C., Chin, D., Oppezzo, M., Kwong, H., Okita, S., Biswas, G., Roscoe, R., Jeong, H., Wagster, J.: Interactive Metacognition: Monitoring and Regulating a Teachable Agent. In: Hacker, D., Dunlosky, J., Graesser, A. (eds.) Handbook of Metacognition in Education, pp. 340–358. Routledge Press (2009)
17. Sjödén, B., Tärning, B., Pareto, L., Gulz, A.: Transferring Teaching to Testing – An Unexplored Aspect of Teachable Agents. In: Biswas, G., Bull, S., Kay, J., Mitrovic, A. (eds.) AIED 2011. LNCS, vol. 6738, pp. 337–344. Springer, Heidelberg (2011)
18. Gulz, A., Haake, M., Silvervarg, A.: Extending a Teachable Agent with a Social Conversation Module – Effects on Student Experiences and Learning. In: Biswas, G., Bull, S., Kay, J., Mitrovic, A. (eds.) AIED 2011. LNCS, vol. 6738, pp. 106–114. Springer, Heidelberg (2011)

19. Leudar, I.: Theory of Mind: A Critical Assessment. Theory & Psychology 14(5), 571–578 (2004)
20. Clements, W., Perner, J.: Implicit Understanding of Belief. Cognitive Development 9(4), 377–395 (1994)
21. Garnham, W.A., Perner, J.: Actions Really do Speak Louder than Words – But Only Implicitly: Young Children's Understanding of False Belief in Action. British Journal of Developmental Psychology 19(3), 413–432 (2001)
22. Flavell, J.H.: First Discussant's Comments: What is Memory Development the Development of? Human Development 14(4), 272–278 (1971)
23. Kuhn, D.: Theory of Mind, Metacognition, and Reasoning: A Life-Span Perspective. In: Mitchell, P., Riggs, K.J. (eds.) Children's Reasoning and the Mind, pp. 301–326. Psychology Press, Hove (2000)
24. Schneider, W.: The Development of Metacognitive Knowledge in Children and Adolescents: Major Trends and Implications for Education. Mind, Brain, and Education 2(3), 114–121 (2008)
25. Lindström, P., Gulz, A., Haake, M., Sjödén, B.: Matching and Mismatching Between the Pedagogical Design Principles of a Math Game and the Actual Practices of Play. Journal of Computer Assisted Learning 27(1), 90–102 (2011)
26. Gersten, R., Chard, D.: Number Sense: Rethinking Arithmetic Instruction for Students with Mathematical Disabilities. The Journal of Special Education 33(1), 18–28 (1999)
27. Griffin, S.: Teaching Number Sense. Educational Leadership 65(5), 39–42 (2004)
28. Berch, D.B.: Making Sense of Number Sense: Implications for Children With Mathematical Disabilities. Journal of Learning Disabilities 38(4), 333–339 (2005)
29. Jordan, N.C., Kaplan, D., Nabors Oláh, L., Locuniak, M.N.: Number Sense Growth in Kindergarten: A Longitudinal Investigation of Children at Risk for Mathematics Difficulties. Child Development 77(1), 153–175 (2006)
30. Bruer, J.: Education and the Brain: A Bridge Too Far. Educational Researcher 26(8), 4–16 (1997)
31. Hannula, M.M., Mattinen, A., Lehtinen, E.: Does Social Interaction Influence 3-Year-Old Children's Tendency to Focus on Numerosity? A Quasi-Experimental Study in Day Care. In: De Corte, E., Kanselaar, G., Valcke, M. (eds.) Studia Paedagogica, 41, pp. 63–80. Leuven University Press (2005)
32. Baron-Cohen, S., Leslie, A.M., Frith, U.: Does the Autistic Child have a "Theory of Mind"? Cognition 21(1), 37–46 (1985)
33. Sternberg, R.J., Davidson, J.E.: Insight in the Gifted. Educational Psychologist 18(1), 51–57 (1983)
34. Sternberg, R.J.: Approaches to intelligence. In: Chipman, S.F., Segal, J.W., Glaser, R. (eds.) Thinking and Learning Skills, vol. 2. Erlbaum, Hillsdale (1985)
35. Campione, J.C.: Metacognitive Components of Instructional Research with Problem Learners. In: Weinert, F., Kluwer, R. (eds.) Metacognition, Motivation and Understanding. LEA, Hillsdale (1987)
36. Watson, J.: Reflection Through Interaction: The Classroom Experience of Pupils With Learning Difficulties. Routledge (1996)

Designing a Tangible Learning Environment with a Teachable Agent

Kasia Muldner, Cecil Lozano, Victor Girotto, Winslow Burleson, and Erin Walker

Computing, Informatics & Decision Systems Engineering, Arizona State University
{katarzyna.muldner,cecil.lozano,victor.girotto, winslow.burleson, erin.a.walker}@asu.edu

Abstract. To date, the majority of learning technologies only afford virtual interactions on desktops or tablets, despite evidence that students learn through physical manipulation of their environment. We implemented a tangible system that allows students to solve coordinate geometry problems by interacting in a physical space with digitally augmented devices, using a teachable agent framing. We describe our system and the results from a pilot involving students using our system to teach a virtual agent. Students used a variety of strategies to solve problems that included embodied behaviors, and the majority did feel they were teaching their agent. We discuss the implications of our findings with respect to the design of adaptive tangible teachable systems.

Keywords: tangible learning environments, teachable agents, geometry.

1 Introduction

Research suggests that children construct much of their knowledge through active manipulation of the environment [1], which allows them to connect abstract concepts to something observable [2]. Despite these findings, most educational software, including Intelligent Tutoring Systems (ITSs), has been designed for personal computers [3]. These computers afford little physical interaction, in part because they involve the WIMP (window, icon, menu, pointing device) paradigm that creates an artificial separation between the input device, system output, and underlying real-world representation [4]. Consequently, little is known about how to design novel technologies that step outside of the virtual realm into the physical classroom or their impact on student learning, behaviors and/or perceptions. Our research aims to fill this gap.

As a first step, we implemented a tangible learning environment (TLE) that we call *Tangible Activities for Geometry* (TAG). Students interact with TAG in a physical space with digitally augmented devices to solve geometry problems. In contrast to other TLE work, TAG uses a teachable agent framing, for reasons we explain shortly.

One of the first TLEs was Papert's system, where students used LOGO primitives to control robots [5], for instance to solve geometry problems. Subsequently, other TLEs have been developed, for instance allowing students to interact with balls augmented with acceleration-triggered LEDs during physics activities [6], or using

K. Yacef et al. (Eds.): AIED 2013, LNAI 7926, pp. 299–308, 2013.

digitally-augmented, interactive table tops to support creativity [7] or to facilitate teachers' classroom organization [8]. In general, TLEs afford the manipulation of objects, or sometimes one's own body, that can be mapped to domain concepts students should acquire. For example, in Howison et al.'s TLE [9], students move their hands to different heights to demonstrate different fractions. Another example pertains to classrooms turned into observation centers of seismic activity or orbiting planets [10]. Phenomena occur as class is in session, and students investigate them over multiple sessions. TLEs have also been used in "programming by example" systems, allowing students to record the motion of tangible objects and then play that motion back [11].

Despite TLE's promise, there has been little investigation of their utility. Moreover, while some evaluations have yielded positive results [12], others have shown no difference between tangible and virtual environments [13]. However, TLE's have traditionally provided highly exploratory activities with little structure, despite evidence that explicit support may be needed for learning [14]. TAG aims to address this issue by providing students a set of problems to work on and by using a teachable agent framing. Peer tutoring research suggests that students can learn by teaching because they pay more attention to the material, reflect on misconceptions, and elaborate their knowledge when they construct explanations [15]. Following up on human-human results, computational systems have been developed, and the results are promising: teaching a computer agent can lead to more learning than being taught by an agent [16], and can be more effective than regular classroom instruction [17].

Our goals for the present research were as follows: (1) the design and implementation of a TLE for geometry that includes a teachable agent framing, and (2) evaluation of its impact on student behaviors and perceptions. While TAG relies on sophisticated sensing devices and algorithms to support tangible interactions, the system does not yet include any adaptive support, because we wanted to evaluate TAG before adding more functionalities. In this paper, we begin with a description of TAG and present results from a user study. We conclude with TLE design implications that highlight opportunities for introducing support tailored to students' needs.

2 Tangible Activities for Geometry (TAG)

The TAG system is comprised of three components (see Fig. 1). The *problem space* is a geometry application (Geogebra) that is projected on the ground using a short-throw projector to minimize obstruction by the user. The projection includes a Cartesian plane with zero or more points and the agent - a simulated robot called R2 that is represented by a circle intersected with a line to indicate where it is facing. The *mobile interface* is provided on an iPod touch that (1) displays problems for students to solve, (2) responds to events generated in the *problem space*, and (3) receives student input (provided by tapping and/or its virtual keyboard). The *tangible interface* includes a *hanging pointer*, which acts like a mouse, and which controls the position of the virtual cursor projected onto the ground as the student moves the hanging pointer over the plane; "clicking" is done by pulling the hanging pointer down to the ground to select a click location and then lifting it back up (equivalent to a mouse-up event).

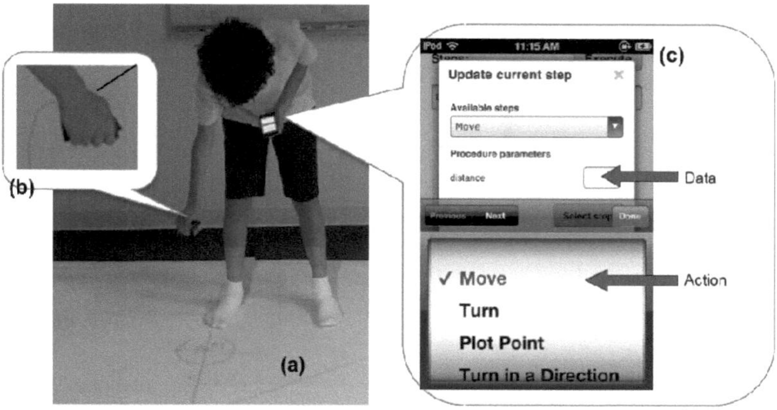

Fig. 1. A student walking in the TAG problem space (a), using the hanging pointer "mouse" to click on projected objects (b) and subsequently select from a menu of iPod actions (c)

When interacting with TAG, students can walk in the problem space and use the hanging pointer to click, which brings up a menu of available actions on the iPod. To illustrate, students can move R2 by positioning the hanging pointer over R2, pulling down on the hanging pointer to simulate a mouse click, and tapping *move* on the menu that appears on the iPod (Fig. 1c). Four actions are provided when a student clicks on R2, including *move* (to move R2 distance *d*), *turn* (to turn R2 *n* degrees), *turn in a direction* (to turn R2 N/S/E/W), and *plot point* (to plot a point in R2's current location). The remaining three actions are shown on the iPod if a student clicks on a point, including *move to a point* (R2 moves to that point), *turn to a point* (R2 turns to that point), and *draw line between points* (R2 draws a line between two user-specified points). For instance, if R2 is located at (0,0) and facing West, plotting the point (2,3) could involve the following sequence of commands (clicking R2 is required to show each command): *turn in a direction* East, *move* 2 units, *turn in a direction* North, *move* 3 units, *plot point*. All commands are automatically added to a list available on the iPod, so that students can watch R2 "execute" a series of commands at once, akin to running a program (commands can also be deleted).

We chose the current task domain because of its conceptual and graphical properties. In theory, as students move over the projected coordinate system and gesture towards particular aspects of the projection, they can physically encode concepts such as how positive and negative coordinates relate to graphical quadrants, and how the rise and run influences the slope of the line.

Figure 2 shows the TAG architecture. All applications communicate with one main computer. The *problem space* is realized by a Geogebra Java applet that includes a JavaScript API. Since the iPod needs to respond to events in the *problem space*, like a click on R2, and then subsequently sent data back to Geogebra (e.g., to plot a new point), a bidirectional communication mechanism is necessary, implemented in TAG with the WebSocket protocol.

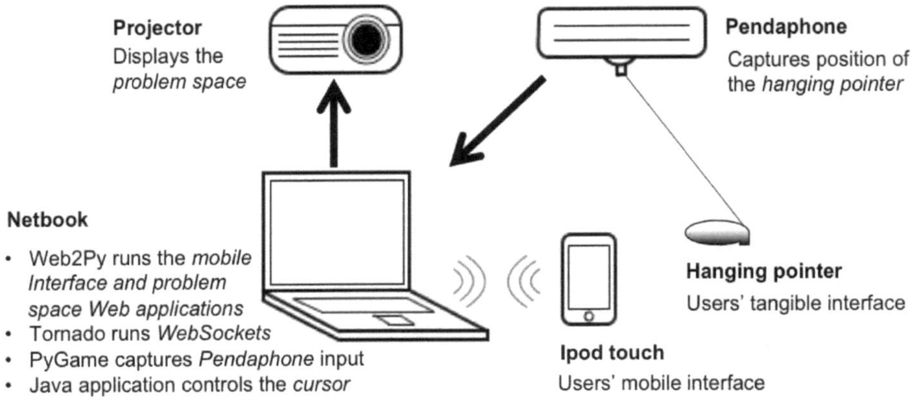

Fig. 2. TAG architecture

The hanging pointer, used to simulate a mouse in a physical space, is attached by wire to a device we call a pendaphone, a modified PS2 Gametrak controller that can detect the x-y-z coordinates of a retractable pointer. When the pendaphone is mounted on the ceiling, it detects the coordinates of students' hand in space as they move the hanging pointer. A Python script is used to send messages between the pendaphone and main computer to indicate when a click event occurs. Prior to use, the hanging pointer must be calibrated, by moving it to three pre-defined points on the projected problem space. This calibration provides information about the projected plane's size relative to (1) the origin of the hanging pointer, using the two vectors made by the three points, and (2) the projected computer screen size, by mapping the physical location of the three points to their known digital locations. This allows TAG to compute the projection onto the coordinate plane of the vector from the pendaphone origin to the physical pointer's endpoint. As students manipulate the hanging pointer, TAG uses the java.awt.Robot library to hijack the mouse cursor and set its location to be the projection of the physical pointer. If a user moves the pointer below a pre-defined threshold, a mousePressed event is generated, followed by a mouseRelease when the pointer is moved above the threshold. The threshold is manually set – in the future we plan to set it automatically during the calibration process.

3 Students' Behaviors in TAG and Perceptions of TAG

We piloted TAG with four participants (S1-S4; one from 6th grade, two from 7th grade, and one from 9th grade). Our key research questions were as follows:

(Q1) What strategies do students use to solve problems in TAG?
(Q2) How does TAG impact students' embodied behaviors and perceptions?
(Q3) How does the teaching framing in TAG influence student perceptions?

All students (1) signed an assent form; (2) filled in a brief background survey; (3) were introduced to TAG (*Training Phase*, ~30 minutes); (4) showed R2 how to solve geometry problems (*Teaching Phase,* 45 minutes); (5) discussed their experience

(*Interview Phase*, ~20 minutes); (6) were compensated ($20). We used the talk aloud protocol for the teaching phase by asking students to verbalize their thoughts and feelings as they worked with TAG. Sessions were conducted individually and were videotaped; two experimenters were present during each session.

To train students on how to use TAG, we asked them to read aloud from a booklet describing the system and also perform the corresponding TAG actions (e.g., plot a point); an experimenter answered any questions that students had. During the teaching phase, we told students to "*tutor R2 about how to solve geometry problems [...] The goal is for R2 to learn enough so that it can solve all kinds of geometry problems. So when you are telling it how to solve a geometry problem, think about what would be most useful*". Students then taught R2 by working through a series of geometry problems related to (1) plotting points in various quadrants; (2) drawing the rise and run for various lines and specifying the slope of those lines; (3) drawing lines with a specified rise and run (only the 9th grader reached these in the time provided). If students got stuck on how to use the system they could refer to the instructions and/or ask the experimenter. Feedback for correctness was provided through a Wizard of Oz technique: When students indicated they were finished with a problem, they heard a sound (one for correct answers and one for incorrect). Students could try a problem as many times as they wished, and if stuck, could ask for help (but only after trying the problem at least once on their own). The help was provided by the experimenter, who used the standard scaffolding technique of starting out with general prompts that became more specific if students required further help. Once 45 minutes elapsed, students participated in a semi-structured interview between the participant and two experimenters. The interview questions were designed to obtain information on students' experience with TAG, the tangible interaction and the teaching framing.

3.1 Analysis and Results

We analyzed the video data from the teaching and interview phases using qualitative description [18], by iteratively deriving codes from the data, organizing these according to emergent themes, and refining these as needed. Our goal with this coding was to provide a qualitative summary of students' experiences and perceptions. In general, subjects found the system easy to use (S1-S4; e.g., "*I can't think of how to make it better, it was pretty easy*" (S4)). We were concerned students might find obstructing the projector distracting, but none of the students mentioned this when asked "what did you find difficult about using TAG?". When asked to compare TAG to other contexts (paper and pencil, and computer), S2 mentioned he preferred TAG over a computer because "*it was more fun*". S3 and S4 chose TAG as their preferred activity due to its embodied and fun nature. For instance, S3 stated that "*you get to walk around and do crazy things*". S3 also mentioned, however, that "*it's a little harder to concentrate on the problem because you have to use all the equipment*" – this may have been a start up problem, since he subsequently said this overload was reduced as time went on.

We now present our results: each section first provides results coming from the *teaching phase*, followed by students' perceptions collected in the *interview phase*.

Problem-Solving Strategies in TAG. Students used a variety of strategies to solve problems in TAG. When plotting points, all students but one first moved along the X-axis first and then the Y-axis. S1 instead was more opportunistic, in that if R2 was already pointing in the necessary direction he would move it that way first; otherwise, he went along the Y-axis first, because he "*preferred to think of rise over run*". Some students chose to minimize the number of actions they had to perform: S2 moved R2 backwards with negative distances, instead of turning R2 and moving it forward. Other strategies to facilitate solution construction included using the cardinal directions (N/E/S/W) instead of numeric angles (all did this except S3, who used the numeric approach for the first 3 problems). Common mistakes on plotting points included moving in the wrong X or Y direction, which students corrected on their own after obtaining the audio feedback for correctness.

In one of the problems, students were provided with two points and asked to draw the rise and the run of the line that included those points. All participants started by drawing a line between the two points (even though it was not necessary), using the closest point to them and R2 as a first reference, by clicking on it (S2 and S3) or by using R2 steps to get to it (S1 and S4). This problem was more challenging for the younger participants (grade 6 and 7) and students did ask for domain hints.

As far as students' perceptions related to strategies they chose, S3 proposed that TAG's scaffolding, which encouraged breaking solutions into small steps, was beneficial: "*it can help you learn why you are doing what you doing, because instead of just looking for the point you are going over and up instead of just diagonal*". S4 echoed these sentiments: "*I'm not very good at geometry but I think breaking it down into little steps has helped me*". In contrast, S1 suggested it would be helpful to combine instructions (e.g., "*I think in the same instructions you should be able to turn and the go again – it should be like on the same page*"). This participant had the highest domain expertise (he was the only grade 9 participant and solved the most problems) and so it is not surprising that he wanted to be able to "chunk" steps [19].

Embodiment: Behaviors and Perceptions. Instead of staying still, students used a range of embodied actions (shown in brackets is the *total number of actions* across all students and *the range of actions* executed by individuals), including *walking around the problem space* in between actions (489; 83-166), *pointing* with some part of the body towards elements in the problem space (169; 24-91) and *sliding/twisting motions* (59; 4-27). These embodied actions appeared to help participants find and physically visualize the strategy to solve the problem before they started to select steps for the agent. For instance, to plot a point, participants would *walk around the problem space,* using their foot *to point* to the places where the point could be plotted, and/or use their foot to outline the path that R2 could take (e.g., moving parallel to the X-axis to the X coordinate). To draw lines corresponding to the rise (or run) of a line *L*, they sometimes would align themselves on the point where the rise and L intercepted and *twisted their body* to orient themselves and so identify the rise line that would be drawn from that point. To specify the slope of a line, they counted the rise and run units by actually stepping while pointing with their hand.

In order to get more insight on the embodied behaviors, we also classified them according to when they occurred, namely during *reading* of the problem, *strategizing* before actually selecting a step for R2, or *action selection* when students moved to click on R2 or a point. Since participants had to approach R2 or a point to perform actions, we expected the majority of embodied behaviors would be in the *action selection* phase and that these would correspond to *walking around the problem space.* While this was true (49%-72%), there was a great deal of variability between subjects in terms of where the embodied actions took place: 12%-39% of total embodied actions took place in the *strategizing phase* and 1%-10% in the *reading phase.*

As far as students' perceptions of the embodied aspect, two explicitly commented on liking the embodied nature of the system (S2, S3). S2 likened it to a game: "*it is kind of like a Wii that is on the floor and you can walk around on a big computer screen that is on the floor and you are the mouse*". This comment highlights that by "becoming the mouse", this student imagined himself to actually be a part of the system. He later added that he liked the projection on the floor because "*you can actually visualize graphing on a line and I think it just fun to walk on it*". While S3 also explicitly mentioned liking "*moving around*", he went on to caution that embodiment might not always be appropriate. Specifically, he believed that when one is first learning the domain, more traditional activities might be better as the technology might be a distraction. S3 also described how he felt TAG's tangible nature influenced his actions, by encouraging him to perform fine grained steps when plotting points, instead of a more direct approach (i.e., "*because you are actually walking you'd use an angle to turn*" and on paper you would "*usually go diagonal*").

Teaching Framing: Behaviors and Perceptions. Although R2 was a projection, participants appeared to connect with it at some level. They followed R2 with their eyes, faced in a similar direction as R2, and even walked around R2 to avoid stepping on the projected circle. Another relevant behavior pertains to students executing the list of actions taught to R2, something referred to as a *testing phase* in other teachable frameworks [16]. S2 did this after finishing a problem, possibly to watch what R2 learned. S3, however, used this for a different purpose: he made a mistake during the solution of one problem, and upon realizing it deleted steps from the iPod list of actions right up to the mistake, essentially allowing him a convenient "restart". S3 was the only participant that did not feel that he was teaching the R2 (see below). It is interesting to note, therefore, that S3 favored the trial and error strategy instead of rethinking the process and so executed the most commands and had less correct responses (60%) than the other students (77%-100%).

When asked if they felt like they were teaching the agent R2, the majority of students responded affirmatively (S1, S2, S4). S4 said this was because he had to "*make the robot do all the actions*" and that without this instruction R2 "*would not know how to do that*". S1 suggested that it was his mistakes that made an impact on R2, i.e., "*I made a mistake so it knows - I forgot to plot a point*". He later suggested R2 might be able to avoid making that mistake. S4 stated R2 was "real", i.e., "*its not fake even though it is not completely real it stills seems like it because it has all the aspects*". However, students felt there were limitations to the "teaching" activity. While all students felt that R2 learned how to plot points and lines (S1-S4), several felt this was due to the R2's "memory". S3 also stated that the agent was not capable of transfer to new problems. Participants went on to say they were telling R2 exactly what to do - e.g., S3 stated that he was "*controlling the robot*", and that R2 had "*no reason to know why I was doing what I was*", while when he was teaching someone, he provided explanations. S2 cited the lack of direct interaction as hindering his "teaching": "*you're not looking at somebody you are looking at a computer screen on the floor*". Another student whose data was lost due to technical issues mirrored this sentiment, indicating that if the agent had a face, then he might feel like he was teaching more.

4 Discussion, Design Implications and Future Work

In this paper, we presented TAG, a tangible teachable agent system for learning concepts related to coordinate geometry. Our pilot study with four users provided promising indications that the embodied aspects of TAG and its teachable agent framework influenced student behaviors and perceptions in ways that could potentially deliver enhanced learning outcomes. When using TAG, student problem-solving process became physical: They would "twist" and "slide" around the environment to identify the distances and orientations needed to solve a problem. These embodied actions encouraged by TAG are consistent with the proposed advantages of TLEs in the literature, where students learn by making abstract concepts physical [2]. Our preliminary results suggest that TAG was successful in achieving a tangible interaction with the problem space. However, in contrast to other TLEs, students in our environment interacted with a teachable agent to solve problems. This agent became an external and physical representation of their problem-solving process, as students encoded their strategies in terms of distances travelled, angles turned, and steps taken by the agent. By merging the teachable agent and the tangible learning environment, students were able to create a physical external representation of their thinking that could move within the environment.

Overall, we saw both advantages and disadvantages to the embodied tangible interactions. Students enjoyed the embodied nature of our system (e.g., using expressions like "*it's awesome*"). However, S3 suggested that tangible nature and its corresponding technologies could interfere with learning new concepts. Research indicates that the degree of cognitive load induced from certain features depends on expertise and that for novices load is reduced once cognitive elements became automated [20]. Although these guidelines are intended for multimedia environments and not TLEs, it is conceivable that some would apply. For instance, there may be an ideal trajectory for learning geometry that involves various contexts, where for learners of a certain expertise, paper and pencil activities may be best, while for others, tangible activities would be preferable. Where exactly in that trajectory TLEs best fit to support learning and foster motivation, and for which learners, is an open question for future work.

Our pilot highlights that to provide ITS-style support in a tangible environment, it is important that the system models physical aspects of students' interaction. Using a ceiling-mounted camera system combined with a depth camera, the TLE may be able to recognize a student by, for instance, a special hat s/he would be asked to wear, and then detect student movements. We plan on improving TAG to adaptively scaffold students in linking their movements to the target concepts they are trying to master. TAG can also demonstrate to students that there are multiple physical strategies that map to the same conceptual outcome. For instance, as described above, only one student realized he could move a negative distance instead of turning the agent 180 degrees before moving it a positive distance. Representing these multiple strategies for navigating around the coordinate space and adaptively drawing student attention to the fact that various actions have the same outcome may give students a better intuitive understanding of graphical concepts and their relationships to each other. Prior work has shown that multiple representations in virtual ITS benefit learning [21]. TLEs could extend representations beyond the symbolic and graphical to the physical.

Another way we plan to introduce artificial intelligence into the system is by extending the agent's support in cognitive and social ways. A current limitation of TAG, as identified by students, is that the agent could only do what it was told. We plan on extending the agent's design by adding inferential ability. For instance, a student could ask R2 to perform two fine-grained steps: *turn an angle / move*, which could be chunked by R2 into one (as suggested by S1). This chunking then would be reflected in the commands on the iPod interface, to highlight that R2 learned. Students could also teach the agent by signaling when it should mimic their behaviors, and having R2 follow the student as s/he moves around in the problem space. This scenario encourages students to take embodied action and to observe the agent actions.

Yet another opportunity for enhancing the design of the agent in a TLE pertains to the affective dimension, by adding behaviors that would build a rapport with the student. We observed students express satisfaction after getting a problem correct by smiling and/or verbal utterances (e.g., "yes!"). Since non-verbal mirroring in virtual environments has been shown to increase motivation, this functionality could be extended to TLEs by having the agent mirror student affect, for instance by twirling around rapidly. This ability requires not only knowing where the student is, but also what he or she is feeling. Incorporating student models of affect and learning is especially critical for TLEs, given that these types of environments inherently encourage exploration. Thus, the TLE needs to rely on a model to understand when to intervene as to not interrupt students at points that might be disruptive to moments of motivation or moments of learning. How to devise such models for physical spaces that involve embodied behaviors, or to orchestrate social interactions between the student and the robot are open questions for future work.

In general, a tangible teachable learning environment that provides cognitive and social support to the learner could potentially be highly effective at engaging students and helping them map their concrete physical understanding to abstract concepts. To conclude, we believe situating a teachable agent within the context of a tangible environment serves as a promising foundation for future exploration.

Acknowledgements. The authors thank the anonymous reviewers for their helpful suggestions and Elissa Thomas for her help with the TAG system and evaluation materials. This research was funded by NSF 1249406: EAGER: A Teachable Robot for Mathematics Learning in Middle School Classrooms and by the CAPES Foundation, Ministry of Education of Brazil, Brasília - DF 70040-020, Brazil.

References

1. Beaty, J.: Skills for Preschool Teachers, Columbus, OH, Merrill (1984)
2. Kaplan, P.: A Child's Odyssey: Child and Adolescent Development, Belmont, CA (2000)
3. Aud, S., Hussar, W., Planty, M., Snyder, T., Bianco, K., Fox, M., Frohlich, L., Kemp, J., Drake, L.: The Condition of Education, Institute of Education Sciences (2010)
4. Ishii, Y., Awaji, M., Watanabe, K.: Stability of Golf Club Motion and EMG When Swinging. In: SICE-ICASE, pp. 2344–2347 (2006)
5. Papert, S.: Mindstorms: Children, Computers, and Powerful Ideas. Basic Books, NY (1980)
6. Resnick, M., Martin, F., Berg, R., Borovoy, R., Colella, V., Kramer, K., Silverman, B.: Digital Manipulatives. In: Human Factors in Computing Systems, CHI (1998)
7. Catala, A., Jaen, J., van Dijk, B., Jordà, S.: Exploring Tabletops as an Effective Tool to Foster Creativity Traits. In: Tangible, Embedded and Embodied Interaction, pp. 143–150 (2012)
8. Do-Lenh, S., Jermann, P., Legge, A., Zufferey, G., Dillenbourg, P.: Tinkerlamp 2.0: Designing and Evaluating Orchestration Technologies for the Classroom. In: 21st Century Learning for 21st Century Skills, pp. 65–78 (2012)
9. Howison, M., Trninic, D., Reinholz, D., Abrahamson, D.: The Mathematical Imagery Trainer: From Embodied Interaction to Conceptual Learning. In: SIGCHI Conference on Human Factors in Computing Systems (CHI), pp. 1989–1998 (2011)
10. Moher, T.: Embedded Phenomena: Supporting Science Learning with Classroom-Sized Distributed Simulations. In: SIGCHI Conference on Human Factors in Computing Systems (CHI), pp. 691–700 (2006)
11. Parkes, A., Raffle, H., Ishii, H.: Topobo in the Wild Longitudinal Evaluations of Educators Appropriating a Tangible Interface. In: SIGCHI Conference on Human Factors in Computing Systems, pp. 1129–1138 (2008)
12. Johnson-Glenberg, M.C., Birchfield, D., Savvides, P., Megowan-Romanowicz, C.: Semi-Virtual Embodied Learning – Real World Stem Assessment. In: Serious Educational Game Assessment: Practical Methods and Models for Educational Games, Simulations and Virtual World, pp. 225–241. Sense Publications, Rotterdam (2010)
13. Klahr, D., Triona, L.M., Williams, C.: Hands on What? The Relative Effectiveness of Physical Vs. Virtual Materials in an Engineering Design Project by Middle School Children. J. of Research in Science Teaching 44, 183–203 (2007)
14. De Jong, T., Van Joolingen, W.R.: Scientific Discovery Learning with Computer Simulations of Conceptual Domains. Rev. of Ed. Research 68(2), 179–201 (1998)
15. Roscoe, R.D., Chi, M.: Understanding Tutor Learning: Knowledge-Building and Knowledge-Telling in Peer Tutors' Explanations and Questions. Rev. of Ed. Research 77(4), 534–574 (2007)
16. Leelawong, K., Biswas, G.: Designing Learning by Teaching Agents: The Betty's Brain System. International J. of Artificial Intelligence in Education 18(3), 181–208 (2008)
17. Pareto, L., Arvemo, T., Dahl, Y., Haake, M., Gulz, A.: A Teachable-Agent Arithmetic Game's Effects on Mathematics Understanding, Attitude and Self-efficacy. In: Biswas, G., Bull, S., Kay, J., Mitrovic, A. (eds.) AIED 2011. LNCS, vol. 6738, pp. 247–255. Springer, Heidelberg (2011)
18. Sandelowski, M.: Whatever Happened to Qualitative Description? Research in Nursing & Health 23, 334–340 (2000)
19. Anderson, J.R.: Rules of the Mind. Psychology Press (1993)
20. Cooper, G., Sweller, J.: Effects of schema acquisition and rule automation on mathematical problem-solving transfer. J. of Ed. Psychology 79(4), 347–362 (1987)
21. Rau, M.A., Aleven, V., Rummel, N.: Intelligent Tutoring Systems with Multiple Representations and Self-Explanation Prompts Support Learning of Fractions. In: Conference on Artificial Intelligence in Education, pp. 441–448 (2009)

The Effects of a Pedagogical Agent for Informal Science Education on Learner Behaviors and Self-efficacy

H. Chad Lane[1], Clara Cahill[2], Susan Foutz[3], Daniel Auerbach[1], Dan Noren[3], Catherine Lussenhop[2], and William Swartout[1]

[1] University of Southern California, Institute for Creative Technologies
Playa Vista, CA USA
{lane,auerbach,swartout}@ict.usc.edu
[2] Boston Museum of Science
Boston, MA USA
{ccahill,clussenhop}@mos.org
[3] Independent Contractor
susanfoutz@gmail.com, dannoren@verizon.net

Abstract. We describe Coach Mike, an animated pedagogical agent for informal computer science education, and report findings from two experiments that provide initial evidence for the efficacy of the system. In the first study, we found that Coach Mike's presence led to 20% longer holding times, increased acceptance of programming challenges, and reduced misuse of the exhibit, but had limited cumulative impact on attitudes, awareness, and knowledge beyond what the host exhibit already achieved. In the second study, we compared two different versions of Coach Mike and found that the use of enthusiasm and self-regulatory feedback led to greater self-efficacy for programming.

Keywords: pedagogical agents, intelligent tutoring systems, informal science education, computer science education, enthusiasm, self-efficacy.

1 Introduction

After over two decades of research, the design, use, and impacts of animated pedagogical agents continue to be topics of much debate for educational technology researchers. Because learning with and from others is a fundamentally social activity, the arguments for using pedagogical agents are compelling: embodied conversational agents allow for a wider range of communicative behaviors, such as nonverbal behaviors, displays of empathy, and more [1]. Further, most research on pedagogical agents has occurred in pursuit of formal learning goals. In this paper, we focus on the use of a pedagogical agent in an informal learning context where self-directed learning is the norm and noncognitive outcomes carry greater importance.

1.1 Cognitive and Social Effects of Pedagogical Agents

Evidence supporting the use of pedagogical agents to promote learning is mixed. Some studies suggest that they can enhance learning and recall [2], while others report

K. Yacef et al. (Eds.): AIED 2013, LNAI 7926, pp. 309–318, 2013.

equivalent learning between conditions that provide learning support with and without an agent [3]. Further, many studies on pedagogical agents lack adequate controls to rule out competing explanations, such as whether learning is due to the *internal* properties of the agent (i.e., pedagogical behaviors) or *external* properties, such as appearance and gestures[4, 5].

Despite mixed findings on learning, the ability of pedagogical agents to achieve social and emotional outcomes is well-established. For example, researchers have determined that some pedagogical agents enhance attitudes and emotions associated with learning [6], increase motivation [7], promote interest and self-efficacy [8], as well as lead to a variety of additional social and emotional outcomes [9].

All of this suggests that it is important to investigate the role pedagogical agents might play in promoting desirable noncognitive outcomes related to learning. And such a focus would not be without empirical merit: seminal work on early-intervention programs by economist James Heckman has shown that promoting noncognitive skills such as perseverance, self-control, grit, motivation, and others have long-term societal benefits [10]. At this time, however, it is not clear how the strengths of pedagogical agents align with broad goals such as Heckman's. Thus, one aim of our work is to begin to disentangle these complex challenges and work towards an understanding of how best to use pedagogical agents for learning.

1.2 Using Pedagogical Agents in Informal Learning Environments

Cognitive and noncognitive skills are both important to consider in informal learning environments such as museums, science centers, and zoos. Such spaces are *designed* to promote understanding, conversations, and positive attitudes about their content. Although knowledge gain is an important goal for informal science educators, it is always accompanied by other important outcomes such as attitude, awareness, interest, and self-efficacy [11]. Choice plays a key role in all phases of a visitor's experience: they decide *what* to see, *when* to engage, and *how* long to stay. In other words, learners have a high degree of control over most aspects of their own learning. This means if an experience is not judged to be of value or sufficiently interesting, the learner will simply disengage and seek another activity.

What does this imply for the design of an intelligent tutoring system or pedagogical agent for informal learning? At the very least, it means that such systems need to go beyond simply focuses on knowledge outcomes. They must take seriously goals such as convincing a visitor to engage, promoting curiosity and interest, and ensuring that a visitor has a positive learning experience. In other words, pedagogical agents for informal learning need to not only act as coach (or teacher), but also as *advocate* (or salesperson). Historically, intelligent tutoring systems rarely address these issues. It is worth noting, however, that the community has radically embraced techniques from affective computing to improve the quality of learning experiences and encourage productive emotional self-regulatory behaviors [12].

Several virtual agents have successfully been deployed in museums, such as the relational agent *Tinker* [13], the conversational guide *Max* [14], and the "Twins," Ada and Grace [15] (who are also at MOS). In each case, these pedagogical agents act as the centerpieces of their exhibits and play a role of guide or teacher. Because they are not designed to support a specific problem solving task, their use of intelligent tutoring techniques is limited. In this paper we consider the use of a pedagogical agent, *Coach Mike*, that uses intelligent tutoring techniques to help visitors acquire basic programming skills in an informal learning setting.

2 Robot Park and Coach Mike

Informal learning experiences are generally more effective when a staff member (or other expert) is available to help visitors, either by answering questions or demonstrating how to interact with exhibits. Staffed spaces have been shown to produce longer *holding times* and improve learning outcomes [16]. We sought to determine if a pedagogical agent would be able to emulate some of the skills and impacts of human guides. In this section, we briefly describe the exhibit that acted as the context for our research and the pedagogical agent, Coach Mike.

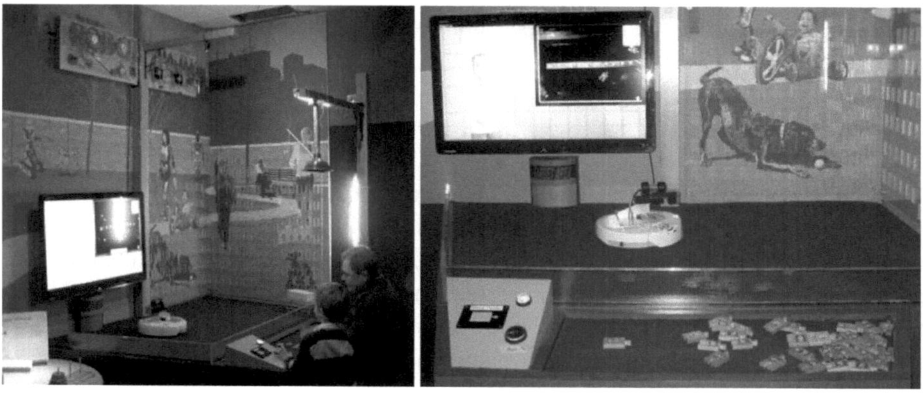

Fig. 1. Robot Park at the Boston Museum of Science. Visitors program a robot using a tangible interface (right) and receive support from a pedagogical agent.

2.1 Robot Park

Located in Cahner's Computer Place at the Museum of Science (MoS), Boston, *Robot Park* is an interactive exhibit where visitors can control an iRobot Create^{TM} robot by assembling jigsaw-like blocks into chains of robot commands. It opened in October of 2007, was used by approximately 20,000 people in its first year [17]. The exhibit was redesigned in 2010 to incorporate a pedagogical agent (figure 1). Each physical block corresponds to a robot action. This set of blocks includes basic movement actions, such as LEFT, FORWARD, and SPIN, while others allow for sound and play, like BEEP, GROWL and SHAKE. Visitors can place blocks on a "tester" which will execute the command immediately or press a "run" button to compile and execute multi-step programs. To create a program, visitors need to attach one or more command blocks to a START block. A push of the run button (1) triggers a camera above to take a snapshot of the work area, (2) recognition of the program steps using fiducial markers on the blocks, and (3) transmission of the steps, sequentially, to the robot. The snapshot is displayed on the screen and each block is highlighted while being executed by the robot (i.e., it steps through the program).

Museum staff members often help visitors by demonstrating these steps and recommending challenges. One of the most common involves writing a program to move the robot touch a target (the metal structure just under the monitor in figure 1). If the robot's magnetic arm touches the target, the Robot Park sign lights up and makes noises. Other challenges, such as turning the robot around or in specific patterns can be found in a small booklet available at the exhibit.

The primary purpose of Robot Park is to give visitors an opportunity to learn programming basics in a fun and engaging context. Ideally, visitors will engage in goal-directed behaviors that involve planning, discussing, writing and debugging programs. According to museum staff, visitors tend to overuse the tester, so they tend to encourage visitors to write full programs instead. Initial studies on Robot Park focused on the benefits of its tangible interface showing that when compared with a point-and-click, graphical interface, using the blocks produced longer holding times, more sophisticated programs, deeper conversations between visitors, and more gender-balanced interest [17].

2.2 Coach Mike

Coach Mike was designed to emulate many of the tactics used by MoS staff. He greets visitors when they arrive and indicates his willingness to help. If visitors start using the exhibit, he will act primarily as a cheerleader by complimenting the programs, encouraging exploration, and reacting to the activities of the robot. At any time, visitors can push "Mike's button" to get his attention, which will trigger his help based on the context. He encourages visitors to do this. For example, upon arrival, he says "Mike is the name and robot programming is my game. Push the button with my picture on it and I'll show you how to get started." Later on, a button press will be an invitation to accept one of his programming challenges, such as to program the robot to move in a square. A constraint base is used to assess progress and provide feedback on three challenge problems. In addition to support for challenge problems, he also spends time explaining how the exhibit works, talking about debugging, and explaining the function of specific programming commands (see [18] for details).

Coach Mike was designed to be approachable and friendly, but also to generate excitement about programming. A creative decision to use a cartoon character was made early in the project because of the intended audience, 7 to 12 year olds. Determining Coach Mike's appearance was a long process, including surveys and voting by museum visitors and staff. Ultimately, a "Pixar-like", younger version of the original creator of Robot Park was the decisive choice of the museum visitors [18]. Further, Ada and Grace [15], Coach Mike's close neighbors, provide a contrast in terms of ethnicity and gender.

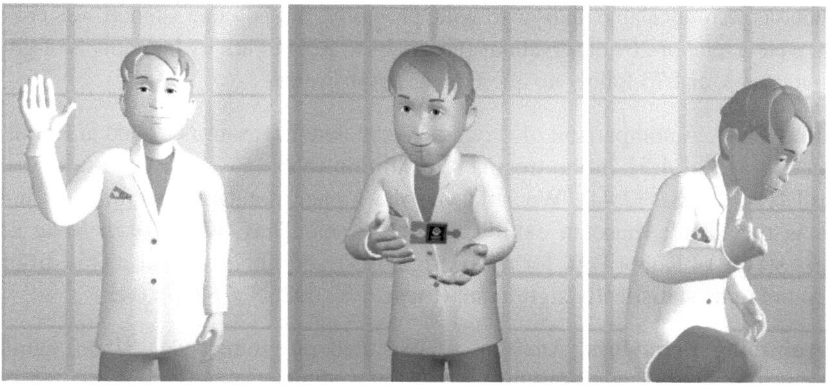

Fig. 2. Coach Mike, a pedagogical agent for computer science education

A variety of techniques were used to give personality to Coach Mike. For example, he can use "magic" to refer to commands – blocks appear and disappear as he refers to them (figure 2, middle). Several animations seek to convey enthusiasm and excitement: when the visitor uses the "growl" command, he will flex his muscles and say that it "makes the robot angry!" Congratulatory feedback is also available, including a fist-pump move (right side of figure 2).

In addition, many of Coach Mike's utterances are intended to be humorous and convey his interest in both the learner and the act of programming. A few examples illustrating Coach Mike's sense of humor are:

- "That was a great square! I think the robot is ready for square dancing!"
- "We've got a regular John Von Neumann on our hands here."
- "You are writing a lot of programs. I think the robot is getting tired! Just kidding, robots don't get tired."

A variety of utterances also encourage visitors to engage more deeply in the exhibit and to not give up. If the visitor is trying out different commands, Coach Mike might say "Keep exploring, I love it!" If a program doesn't correctly solve a challenge, he will sometimes preface his feedback with "Don't worry that program didn't work the first time. That happens to all of us."

3 Experiments with Coach Mike

Our experiments sought to (1) determine the impact of Coach Mike on visitor behaviors at Robot Park, and (2) identify the influence of different kinds of feedback on self-efficacy for computer programming.

3.1 Study 1: Robot Park with and without Coach Mike

Study 1 compared the exhibit with and without the agent (treatment and control, respectively). The control group used Robot Park as-is, with no guidance. Basic instructions were available on how to write programs, but no other support was provided. There were a total of 269 observations (i.e., visits to Robot Park by individuals or groups), 223 interviews, and 75 follow-up questionnaires (answered).

Holding Time. A comparison of stay times revealed that visitors stayed at Robot Park for an average of 4:51 in the treatment condition (N=145, SD=4:12) vs. 4:00 in the control (N=124, SD=2:44). We note that the higher standard deviation for holding times is typical for museum exhibit holding times. Thus, with Coach Mike active, visitors stayed at Robot Park for an average of 51 additional seconds. This difference was found to be statistically significant (t-test: T=2.003, N=269, p=.046).

Programming Behaviors. Analyses of executed programs revealed no significant differences between conditions in terms of the number of programs written or the lengths of programs written during a visit. Coach Mike did influence other visitor behaviors while at Robot Park, however. The likelihood that a visitor would attempt the "touch the target" problem was dependent on the condition ($\chi 2$= 4.858, N=269, p=0.028); treatment visitors were more likely to *attempt* the target challenge. Further, treatment visitors were more likely to *complete* the task ($\chi 2$= 4.553, N=269, p=0.033). A 95% confidence interval shows that between 1% and 24% more visitors will complete the target challenge if Coach Mike is engaged. Also, as time spent at the exhibit increased, the average length of programs written by visitors tended to decrease. This suggests that with Coach Mike, visitors likely spent more of the time revising and creating new programs rather than focusing entirely on program length.

In addition, visitors who attended Robot Park without Coach Mike engaged were more likely to misuse the exhibit, including using the block tester for the majority of movements (as opposed to creating programs), and pushing run without the start block or without creating a program ($\chi 2$ = 12.968, N=269, p=0.000). These specific behaviors reflect visitors' misunderstanding of how to use the exhibit as intended. While engaged, Coach Mike provides tips on how to start and successfully complete a program, and so these initial instructions appeared to be beneficial.

Visitor Ratings. No significant differences were found between conditions in terms of how visitors rated their experience, interest in learning more about computer science, or in how much they discussed the exhibit after leaving the museum. Robot Park was already a highly successful exhibit and since Coach Mike was designed specifically to not overshadow the exhibit, these ceiling effects are perhaps not so surprising. Finally, when asked specifically about Coach Mike, 59% of visitors described him as helpful. This increased to 75% when asked 6-weeks later in the follow-up.

3.2 Study 2: Enthusiastic Feedback and Self-efficacy

One goal of Robot Park is to instill confidence in young visitors that programming is something they can do – that it is not "out of reach". Thus, we chose to investigate the effects of different types of feedback on computer programming self-efficacy, and to explore the relationship between computer programming self-efficacy and behavior. Self-efficacy – the perception of one's own capability to successfully perform tasks in particular content domain – has been shown to be an important predictor of academic achievement. Factors influencing an individual's self-efficacy have been studied extensively in formal learning environments suggesting that self-regulatory feedback - feedback that encourages a learner to reflect on her own cognition, prior knowledge, or problem solving strategies can have a positive impact on self-efficacy [19]. While little research on feedback and self-efficacy in informal settings has been documented, some research suggests that positive feedback, in the form of personal encouragement, can impact task persistence, which is connected to self-efficacy [20].

Design. We developed two variations of Coach Mike for study 2. The first increased the frequency of positive and self-regulatory feedback, as well as general enthusiasm. "Enthusiastic" Mike was given additional utterances and animations to communicate excitement and deliver the additional feedback. Further, when a visitor had trouble following advice or with the exhibit in general, optimistic utterances were added to laud effort and offer encouragement. The second version of Coach Mike, on the other hand, was void of encouragement, excitement, and personality. His delivery of praise was limited using only simple phrases like "OK" and "Correct", with little animation beyond low beat gestures and lip syncing. In short, "serious" Mike was all business and behaved like a cold and mechanical traditional intelligent tutoring system.

For example, serious Mike might prompt a visitor to find a certain block by saying, "Can you find the Start block and place it on the tester?" If the visitor did so, he would move on and say, "Now find the forward block and place it on the tester." In contrast, if the visitor successfully placed the Start block on the tester, enthusiastic Mike would clap and say something like, "I am so impressed," before moving on to the next instruction. During a challenge, where serious Mike would say "The robot will need to make some left or right turns", enthusiastic Mike would give the same instructional feedback, as well as self-regulatory feedback, such as "Think about what you do when you turn around."

Data Collection and Instrument Design. Data about visitor self-efficacy was collected directly through interview questions. The instrument was designed to be short (3-5 minutes), and clear for all visitors age 6 and older. Researchers also collected information about the time spent at Robot Park, number of programs written, and completion of challenges. This allowed for the assessment of any indirect impact of self-efficacy on visitor behavior at the exhibit.

Self-efficacy was assessed with four questions designed to reflect "gradations of challenge", allowing for the creation of a scale that could effectively measure visitors with relatively low and relatively high self-efficacy for computer programming [21]. The four questions asked each visitor to rate on a scale of 0 (not at all confident) to 10 (very confident) how confident she felt in her ability to do two hypothetical tasks with or without support. The first task – programming a LEGO Mindstorms® robot – represented relatively low task difficulty. The second task - writing a smartphone or iPod app – represented higher levels of challenge. In this case, visitors were asked "Do you think you would be able to figure out how to write programs or software, like apps for a smartphone or tablet, from scratch?" To prevent test-retest effects, these questions were administered only after the visit to Robot Park in both conditions.

There were a total of 238 observations (101 for enthusiastic Mike and 137 for serious Mike). 62% of the visitors were male, 54% were between the ages of 6 and 13, and 77% of the groups consisted of adults with children. There were significant differences between the composition of groups (adults only vs. adults with kids), but no differences in terms of prior programming experience or in self-reported interest.

Challenges and Holding Times. There were no significant differences between conditions in terms of challenge attempts, programs written, or successful completions when controlling for participant age. Feedback treatment did not impact the number of challenges attempted or completed by the respondents. Further, no significant difference between conditions was observed in terms of mean holding time. Thus, enthusiastic Mike did not seem to influence task persistence behaviors that might be associated with increased self-efficacy at Robot Park.

Table 1. Impact of enthusiastic Mike on self-efficacy, multiple regression model

	B	Std. Error B
Respondent is 10 or younger (elementary school)	.548*	.210
Respondent is an adult (18 or older)	.540*	.209
Visitor has little or no prior programming experience	-.863***	.169
Visitor successfully completed one "challenge" at Robot Park	.455**	.170
Feedback Treatment	.345*	.164

Notes: *=p<0.05, **=p<0.01, ***=p<0.001; Adjusted R^2=.259; Total n for this analysis=124. Self-efficacy scale is z-scored.

Self Efficacy. A multiple regression model was created to assess the impact of various factors on visitor ratings of self-efficacy for computer programming, and specifically, whether the feedback treatment impacted these ratings. B values in Table 1 relate each of the independent variables to changes in the SD of the sample's self-efficacy scores (which are z-scored). Visitors who spent less than 90 seconds at Robot Park (5% of the sample overall) were removed from the analysis, as these visitors received little feedback from Coach Mike. A regression analysis suggested that chronological age was not associated self-efficacy ratings in a linear manner, when controlling for prior experience. Having little or no computer programming experience predicted self efficacy scores that were nearly a full standard deviation lower (-.86) than visitors who had moderate to high amounts of prior experience. Completion of a challenge was also associated with higher self-efficacy ratings (.46 of a standard deviation).

This model accounts for known differences between the samples (age differences) and other factors that have been shown to directly relate to self-efficacy (prior experience, including reported prior experience and successful challenge completion immediately prior to the interview). Visitors with enthusiastic Mike had self-efficacy scores that were approximately .35 of a standard deviation higher than comparable visitors who used serious Mike (See Table 1). While this difference is quite small, it suggests that, even in a short-duration, open-ended informal science setting, specific types of feedback may be able to impact self-efficacy beliefs.

4 Conclusion

With an average holding time of 3-4 minutes [16], it is a profound challenge to produce meaningful changes in visitors to an exhibit. In study 1, we found some immediate influences on behaviors that seem positive: a 20% increase in holding time, more time spent programming, increased likelihood to accept challenges, and less misuse of the exhibit. Longer term impacts were not detected, however, most likely due to the fact that Robot Park was already considered a highly successful exhibit. In study 2 we sought to understand how Coach Mike's personality and feedback style could impact the learning experience at Robot Park. Although we found no differences in visitor behaviors between conditions, we did detect a modest, but significant increase in visitors' self-reported self-efficacy ratings when Coach Mike was configured to be enthusiastic and to deliver self-regulatory feedback.

A key weakness in the studies was that they did not include a condition providing the feedback content, but without Coach Mike's body. Thus, these findings do not demonstrate the need for an embodied and animated pedagogical agent. Further, Coach Mike's user sensing capabilities are limited only to exhibit actions (e.g., button presses). Affective and learning support could be improved if he could detect user frustration, or know the make-up of different groups who approach. In general, it is well known that expert human tutors apply a variety of affective and motivational tactics [22], and so building on these results and with enhanced interaction capabilities, we believe that pedagogical agents can enhance informal learning outcomes and even reach visitors in new and perhaps previously impossible ways.

Acknowledgments. This material is based upon support by the National Science Foundation under Grant 0813541. We also thank the inspiring staff and volunteers at MoS as well as the extremely creative virtual human and animation teams at ICT.

References

1. Johnson, W.L., et al.: Animated Pedagogical Agents: Face-to-Face Interaction in Interactive Learning Environments. International Journal of Artificial Intelligence in Education 11, 47–48 (2000)
2. Dunsworth, Q., Atkinson, R.K.: Fostering multimedia learning of science: Exploring the role of an animated agent's image. Computers & Education 49, 677–690 (2007)
3. Craig, S.D., et al.: Animated pedagogical agents in multimedia educational environments: Effects of agent properties, picture features, and redundancy. Journal of Educational Psychology 94, 428–434 (2002)
4. Clark, R.E., Choi, S.: Five design principles for experiments on the effects of animated pedagogical agents. Journal of Educational Computing Research 32, 209–225 (2005)

5. Dehn, D.M., van Mulken, S.: The impact of animated interface agents: a review of empirical research. Int. J. Hum.-Comput. Stud. 52, 1–22 (2000)
6. Arroyo, I., et al.: Affective Gendered Learning Companions. In: Dimitrova, V., Mizoguchi, R., du Boulay, B., Graesser, A.C. (eds.) Proc. of the 14th International Conference on Artificial Intelligence in Education, pp. 41–48. IOS Press (2009)
7. Lester, J.C., et al.: The persona effect: affective impact of animated pedagogical agents. In: Proceedings of the SIGCHI Conference on Human Factors in Computing Systems, pp. 359–366. ACM, Atlanta (1997)
8. Kim, Y., et al.: Pedagogical Agents as Learning Companions: The Role of Agent Competency and Type of Interaction. Educational Technology Research and Development 54, 223–243 (2006)
9. Krämer, N., Bente, G.: Personalizing e-Learning. The Social Effects of Pedagogical Agents. Educational Psychology Review 22, 71–87 (2010)
10. Heckman, J.J.: Skill Formation and the Economics of Investing in Disadvantaged Children. Science 312, 1900–1902 (2006)
11. Friedman, A.J. (ed.): Framework for evaluating impacts of informal science education projects. National Science Foundation (2008)
12. Calvo, R.A., D'Mello, S.: New perspectives on affect and learning technologies. Springer, New York (2011)
13. Bickmore, T., Pfeifer, L., Schulman, D.: Relational agents improve engagement and learning in science museum visitors. In: Vilhjálmsson, H.H., Kopp, S., Marsella, S., Thórisson, K.R. (eds.) IVA 2011. LNCS, vol. 6895, pp. 55–67. Springer, Heidelberg (2011)
14. Kopp, S., Gesellensetter, L., Krämer, N.C., Wachsmuth, I.: A Conversational Agent as Museum Guide – Design and Evaluation of a Real-World Application. In: Panayiotopoulos, T., Gratch, J., Aylett, R., Ballin, D., Olivier, P., Rist, T. (eds.) IVA 2005. LNCS (LNAI), vol. 3661, pp. 329–343. Springer, Heidelberg (2005)
15. Swartout, W., et al.: Ada and Grace: Toward Realistic and Engaging Virtual Museum Guides. In: Allbeck, J., Badler, N., Bickmore, T., Pelachaud, C., Safonova, A. (eds.) IVA 2010. LNCS (LNAI), vol. 6356, pp. 286–300. Springer, Heidelberg (2010)
16. Falk, J.H., Dierking, L.D.: Learning from museums: visitor experiences and the making of meaning. AltaMira Press, Walnut Creek (2000)
17. Horn, M.S., et al.: Comparing the use of tangible and graphical programming languages for informal science education. In: Proc. 27th Int. Conf. on Human Factors in Computing Systems, pp. 975–984. ACM, Boston (2009)
18. Lane, H.C., Noren, D., Auerbach, D., Birch, M., Swartout, W.: Intelligent tutoring goes to the museum in the big city: A pedagogical agent for informal science education. In: Biswas, G., Bull, S., Kay, J., Mitrovic, A. (eds.) AIED 2011. LNCS, vol. 6738, pp. 155–162. Springer, Heidelberg (2011)
19. Hattie, J., Timperley, H.: The Power of Feedback. Review of Educational Research 77, 81–112 (2007)
20. Kunz-Kollman, E., Reich, C.: Lessons from observations of educator support at an engineer design activity (No. 2007-9). Museum of Science, Boston (2007)
21. Bandura, A.: Self-efficacy: the exercise of self-control. W.H. Freeman, New York (1997)
22. Lepper, M.R., et al.: Motivational techniques of expert human tutors: Lessons for the design of computer-based tutors. In: Lajoie, S.P., Derry, S.J. (eds.) Computers as Cognitive Tools, pp. 75–105. Lawrence Erlbaum Associates, Inc., Hillsdale (1993)

Differential Impact of Learning Activities Designed to Support Robust Learning in the Genetics Cognitive Tutor

Albert Corbett[1], Ben MacLaren[1], Angela Wagner[1], Linda Kauffman[2], Aaron Mitchell[2], and Ryan S.J.d. Baker[3]

[1] Human-Computer Interaction Inst., Carnegie Mellon Univ., Pittsburgh, PA 15213
{corbett,awagner}@cmu.edu, maclaren@andrew.cmu.edu
[2] Dept. of Biological Sciences, Carnegie Mellon University, Pittsburgh, PA, 15213
lk01@andrew.cmu.edu, apm1@cmu.edu
[3] Dept. of Human Development, Columbia Univ. Teachers College, NY, NY 10027
baker2@exchange.tc.columbia.edu

Abstract. This paper describes two types of Conceptually Grounded Learning Activities designed to foster more robust learning in the Genetics Cognitive Tutor: interleaved worked examples and genetic-process reasoning scaffolds. We report three empirical studies that evaluate the impact of these learning activities on three diverse genetics problem-solving topics in the tutor. We found that interleaved worked examples yielded less basic-skill learning than conventional problem solving, unlike many prior ITS studies of worked examples. We also found preliminary evidence that scaffolded reasoning tasks in conjunction with conventional problem solving leads to more robust understanding than conventional problem solving alone. Implications for the use of contextually grounded learning activities are discussed.

1 Introduction

Problem solving is an essential learning activity across STEM courses. Successful problem solving results in "robust" understanding, grounded in conceptual domain knowledge, that transfers more readily to related problem situations, that is well-retained by students, and that affords more efficient or effective future learning [1]. One of the well-documented risks in problem solving, across STEM domains, is that students can develop superficial knowledge that fails these tests of robust learning. In particular, when students are not well-prepared for problem solving, they can develop problem solving knowledge which focuses on surface elements in problem situations, formal representations, and features of the learning environment itself [2].

This paper describes two types of *Conceptually Grounded Learning Activities* (CGLAs) we have developed to support more robust learning in an intelligent tutoring system for genetics problem solving, and we report the results of three studies that evaluate the impact of these new CGLAs across three problem-solving topics. These two activities are interleaved worked examples, and reasoning scaffolds that link underlying genetics processes with problem solving logic.

K. Yacef et al. (Eds.): AIED 2013, LNAI 7926, pp. 319–328, 2013.

Worked Examples. It is well-documented that integrating worked examples with problem solving serves to decrease total learning time and yields improved learning outcomes.[3], [4]. Recently, several studies have examined the benefits of incorporating worked examples into intelligent tutoring systems (ITSs) for problem solving across a variety of STEM domains [5-10]. In these ITS studies, the chief benefit of incorporating worked examples has been to reduce learning time for a fixed set of activities compared to problem solving, but unlike the classic worked-example literature, these ITS studies generally do not find that the use of worked examples leads to more accurate posttest performance than problem solving alone. Similarly, the evidence that students learn more deeply when worked examples are integrated into ITSs is mixed at best, although [9] found some evidence of greater conceptual transfer in one of two studies. This paper examines the impact of interleaved worked examples in an ITS for genetics problem solving.

Reasoning Scaffolds. Genetics problem solving is characterized by abductive reasoning. In contrast with deductive hypothesis testing, abductive reasoning starts with a set of observations and reasons backwards to infer processes that produced the data (e.g., whether a crossover has occurred between two genes during meiosis). This reasoning task is challenging and there is a risk of shallow learning, since students can learn to solve these types of problems algorithmically, based on the formal properties of the problem representations, without reference to the underlying genetics. As a result, we have developed *process modeling* tasks and *solution construction* tasks that are designed to precede standard genetics problem-solving tasks and to ground students' problem-solving knowledge in the underlying genetics prior to problem solving.

These two types of CGLAs have been developed for three topics in an existing Cognitive Tutor for genetics problem solving [11], which has been successfully piloted in both high school and college classrooms. In the following sections we describe these three problem-solving tasks and the new CGLAs, and report results across three studies that examine the impact of these CGLAs on learning.

1.1 The Domain and Learning Activities

Because of its foundational place in the biological sciences, genetics is a large and growing component of high school biology courses, but it is also viewed as one of the hardest topics in biology by both students and instructors, at the secondary and the post-secondary level. We developed and evaluated CGLAs for three types of genetics problems that represent a diverse range of reasoning tasks: Three-factor crosses, gene interaction, and basic pedigree analysis.

Three-Factor Cross (3FC) Problems. Fig. 1 displays the GCT interface near the end of a *three-factor cross problem*. In these gene-mapping problems, students reason about how crossovers in meiosis reveal the relative positions of genes on a single pair of chromosomes. In each problem, two organisms are crossed, e.g., two fruit flies, and students analyze the relative frequencies of three phenotypic traits among the offspring (displayed in the table on the left of Fig. 1). Each trait is controlled by a single gene and the three genes are located on the same pair of chromosomes. Based on relative frequencies, students infer the order of the three genes on the chromosomes and the relative distance between the three genes.

The basic problem-solving procedure is constant in these problems. The offspring phenotypes fall into four groups and students identify the largest group and smallest group, then identify the middle gene by finding the gene the has switched over relative to the other two, between the two groups. Then students calculate three arithmetic expressions to find the map distances among the pairs of genes.

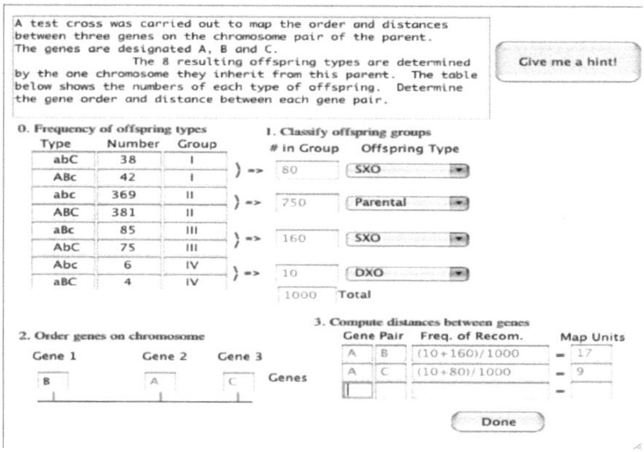

Fig. 1. The GCT interface near the conclusion of a 3FC problem

Gene Interaction and Epistasis (GIE) Problems. These problems extend basic principles of Mendelian transmission to traits controlled by two genes. Fig. 2 displays the GCT interface at the end of a problem. Each problem presents three true-breeding strains of an organism and in each of the three columns across the screen, students cross pairs of strains and intercross the resulting offspring. Based on the ratios of the observed offspring phenotypes, students infer the genotypes of the true-breeding strains and infer the genotype of each of the offspring groups in each of the crosses.

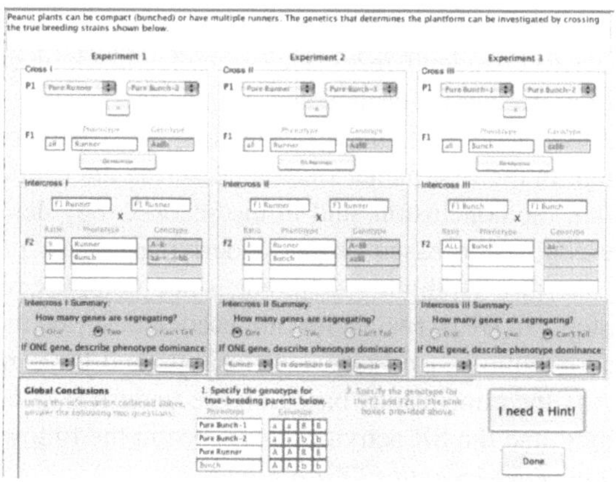

Fig. 2. The GCT interface at the conclusion of a GIE problem

Basic Pedigree Analysis (BPA) Problems. Fig. 3 displays a GCT *pedigree analysis* problem. Each problem displays a family tree, including some individuals who are affected by a rare trait. Females are represented as circles and males as squares. In this family, a single male is affected by the rare trait, as represented by the dark square. The student's task is to determine whether this genetic trait is dominant or recessive, and whether it is X-linked, or transmitted on one of the autosomal chromosomes. The main challenge is to identify the pedigree configurations that identify different transmission modes. Six different conclusions are possible since sometimes the linkage, and/or dominance cannot be determined, and each problem consists of just 2 steps.

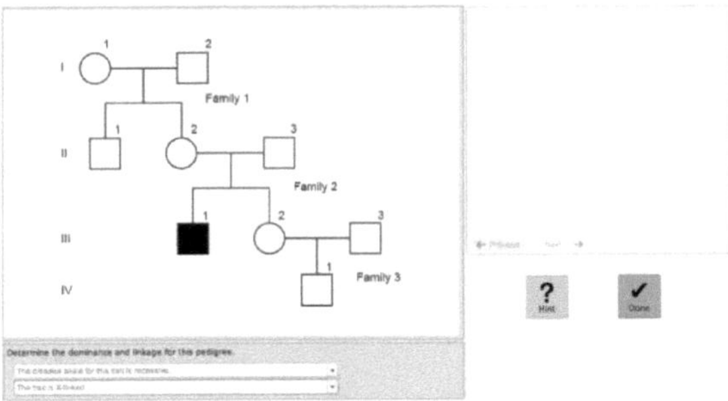

Fig. 3. The GCT Interface for Basic Pedigree Analysis at the end of a problem

Worked Examples

There is a substantial risk of shallow learning in genetics problem solving. In pedigree analysis, for example, students can memorize that when two unaffected parents have an affected child, the trait must be recessive, without any understanding of how the properties of the underlying genetics processes support that conclusion. In this project we developed worked-example learning activities to explicitly ground students' understanding of problem solutions in the underlying genetic processes. In each case, the worked-example interface is constructed around the original problem-solving interface, but includes menus in which students explain the solution steps. As in all Cognitive Tutor activities, students receive accuracy feedback on each menu selection and can ask for help as needed for each menu.

In the 3FC and GIE worked examples, students use two menus to explain each problem-solving step. In the first menu, students describe the features of the empirical evidence that warrant the conclusion, and in the second, they describe why that evidence supports the conclusion based on the underlying genetic processes. The BPA worked examples interface is slightly different, since complex reasoning is packed into just two total steps. In BPA, two menus are used to describe the key pattern in the pedigree that supports both transmission conclusions, and three menus explain how the evidence supports the conclusions based on the underlying genetics. Screenshots of these WE activities, and the SR activities described in the following section, can be viewed at *www.cs.cmu.edu/~genetics/CGLA.html.*

Scaffolded Reasoning. We also developed activities to directly engage students in reasoning about the genetic processes underlying the three types of problem solving tasks. As in all Cognitive Tutor activities, students receive accuracy feedback on each step and can ask for help on each step in these activities.

For the 3FC and GIE topics we developed separate *Forward Modeling* and *Solution Contruction* CGLAs. In abductive reasoning students are given empirical evidence and asked to infer the genetic process that generated the data. In the Forward Modeling tasks, students are given the initial state of a genetic process, and model how the process unfolds to generate empirical data. For example, in 3FC, students are given the ordering and distances among the alleles on the parental chromosomes and model how recombination in meiosis gives rise to offspring phenotypes.

These Forward Modeling activities were coupled with Solution Construction in which students are given both the empirical evidence in a typical problem and the initial state of the underlying process that generated the evidence, and reason through the abductive logic that connects the evidence to the known underlying genetics.

The scaffolded reasoning task was again different for the PA analysis problems. Pilot research showed that students understand the basic transmission genetics that underlie pedigree analysis, so we developed a single Solution Construction activity that scaffolds students' use of that knowledge in solving PA problems. Each problem in this task presents the phenotypes of three family members, two parents and a child. For each of the four possible modes of transmission (autosomal recessive or dominant, X-linked recessive or dominant), the students indicate what the underlying genotype of each family member would have to be, given their phenotypes, and whether the observed pattern of phenotypes is possible under each of the four modes of transmission (i.e., whether the parents have the alleles the child must inherit). Finally, the student summarizes which modes of transmission are possible for the observed phenotype pattern and what final conclusion can be drawn.

2 The Studies

Each study included three conditions defined by the activities described above: a standard problem solving baseline condition (PS), an interleaved worked example condition (WE), and a scaffolded reasoning (SR) condition. Each of the studies included a fourth condition, but these conditions varied across the three studies and are not reported here. A more complete report of all four conditions in the BPA study appears in [12].

The three study procedures varied in specifics, but shared this general structure:

- High school students enrolled in biology courses were recruited through newspaper ads and classroom handouts to participate in the studies.
- The studies were conducted in CMU computer labs and students participated in sessions on two successive days, with each session lasting 2 or 2.5 hours.
- Prior to working with the GCT, students completed a conceptual knowledge pretest and a problem solving pretest.

- After using the GCT, students completed a problem solving posttest and two measures of robust learning: a transfer posttest and a preparation for future (PFL) learning posttest.

Across the three studies, a total of 163 high school students participated in the three treatment conditions reported here. Forty-two students participated in the three-factor cross study; seventy-four students participated in the gene interaction study and forty-seven students participated in the pedigree analysis study. The students participating in each study were randomly assigned to a treatment group.

2.1 Design

The three conditions in each study were defined by students' Cognitive Tutor learning activities in the first study session.

- **Basic Problem Solving (PS):** Students in all three studies only completed standard GCT problems during the first session.
- **Interleaved Worked Examples (WE):** Students completed a problem set in which worked example problems were interleaved with standard problems to solve.
- **Scaffolded Reasoning (SR):** Students completed a block of scaffolded reasoning problems in each study, to prepare them for more robust problem solving. (Students in the 3FC study spent all their time on SR activities in the first session. Students in the GIE and BPA studies spent about 2/3 of their Cognitive Tutor time on SR activities in the first session, followed by standard problem solving)

Students in all conditions within each study concluded their activities with the same block of standard GCT problems to solve.

Students in the 3FC and GIE conditions completed their condition-specific Cognitive Tutor learning activities in the first session. In the second session, students completed a common set of standard Cognitive Tutor problems, followed by the three posttests. The PA problems are intrinsically shorter and students completed all their PA learning activities, including the common block of standard PA problems during the first session. They completed the basic problem solving and transfer posttest the first day and completed their PFL posttest at the beginning of the second session, (followed by additional unrelated Cognitive Tutor activities and tests).

2.2 Tests We Developed Four Types of Paper-and-Pencil Tests for Each Study

- **Problem Solving Tests:** Three forms of a basic problem-solving test were developed for each study. Each student received different forms as the pretest and posttest, with each form serving as the pretest for 1/3 of the students and a posttest for a different 1/3 of the students in each condition.
- **Conceptual Knowledge Tests:** A conceptual knowledge pretest was developed for each study to assess students' understanding of the genetic processes that underlie the problem-solving task.

- **Transfer Tests:** A transfer test was developed for each study, challenging students to extend their understanding to novel, related problem situations without further instruction.
- **Preparation for Future Learning (PFL):** A PFL test was developed for each study. Each test presented 2-3 pages of instruction on a new, but related problem-solving task that builds on the genetics knowledge students were acquiring, then asked students to solve problems.

3 Results

Table 1 displays mean accuracy (probability correct) for the tests administered in the three studies. Students' pretest scores are displayed in the two left columns. Average scores on the conceptual knowledge pretest (CK) varied across studies, but varied little across conditions overall. In an ANOVA with study and condition as factors, the main effect of study was significant, $F(2,154) = 168.51$, $p < .01$, but the main effect of condition, and interaction of condition and study were not significant.

Table 1. Student test accuracy (probability correct)

	Pretests p(C)		**Posttests p(C)**			
	CK	PS1	PS2	PS gain	Transfer	PFL
Overall						
SR	0.60	0.32	0.53	0.21	0.51	0.56
WE	0.58	0.26	0.51	0.25	0.45	0.47
PS	0.61	0.27	0.60	0.33	0.46	0.54
3FC						
SR	0.49	0.14	0.43	0.29	0.54	0.67
WE	0.47	0.15	0.53	0.38	0.55	0.58
PS	0.54	0.17	0.65	0.48	0.51	0.75
GIE						
SR	0.40	0.35	0.68	0.33	0.46	0.65
WE	0.35	0.15	0.43	0.28	0.35	0.51
PS	0.37	0.21	0.67	0.46	0.38	0.55
PA						
SR	0.92	0.47	0.47	0.00	0.54	0.36
WE	0.92	0.49	0.56	0.07	0.46	0.31
PS	0.91	0.43	0.48	0.05	0.47	0.34

Average scores on the Problem Solving pretest (PS1) were much lower overall and again varied across studiess. In an ANOVA, the main effect of study was again significant, $F(2,154) = 44.50$, $p < .01$. The main effect of condition was not significant but the interaction of study and condition was significant, $F(4,154) = 3.04$, $p < .05$, so we treat problem solving pretest score as a covariate in all subsequent ANCOVAs.

Posttest Scores. Students' scores on the basic problem solving posttest, pretest-to-posttest learning gains, and two robust learning posttests are displayed in the four data columns at the right of Table1. As can be seen at the top of the table, students in the conventional problem solving condition are performing about 15% better overall on the basic problem-solving test than the other two groups (0.60 vs. 0.52) and the learning gains in the PS group are about 43% larger than in the other two groups (0.33 vs 0.23). However, students in the SR condition score about 13% better on the transfer tests than students in the other two groups (0.51 vs. 0.45), while on the PFL tests the WE group performs about 14% worse than the other two groups (47% vs 55%).

We performed an ANCOVA on the posttest results, with the three tests as a repeated measure, and study and condition as factors. The most important finding is that the interaction of test type (PS2, transfer & PFL) and condition is significant $F(4, 306) = 3.11$, $p < .05$. The main effect of study is also significant, $F(2,153) = 34.94$, $p < .01$; scores in the pedigree analysis study were substantially lower than in the other two studies. (The main effect of study is significant in all subsequent ANCOVAs at the .01 level; and is not reported separately for subsequent ANCOVAS.) The interaction of study and condition is not significant, while the interaction of test type and study is significant, $F(4,306) = 12.16$, $p < .01$ Finally, the three way interaction of test type, study and treatment condition is significant, $F(8,306) = 2.21$, $p < .05$.

Basic Problem Solving Posttests. Further analyses confirm that the PS condition generally led to better acquisition of basic skill than the other conditions. We performed an ANCOVA on the problem-solving posttest alone, and the main effect of condition is significant, $F(2,153) – 4.01$, $p < .05$. The advantage of PS condition is strongest in the 3FC study and weakest in the BPA study, and this interaction of study and condition is marginal, $F(4,153) = 2.14$, $p < .08$.

We also performed an ANCOVA on basic problem solving scores for each pairwise comparison. For the PS and WE conditions, the main effect of condition is significant $F(1,103) = 4.44$, $p < .05$, while the interaction of condition and study is again marginal, $F(2,103)$, 2.38, $p < .10$. For the PS and SR conditions, the main effect of condition is again significant, $F(1,101) = 7.25$, $p < .01$, while the interaction of study and condition is not significant. Finally, comparing the WE and SR conditions, the main effect of condition is not significant, while the interaction of study and condition is marginal, $F(2,101) = 2.41$, $p < .10$.

Robust Learning Posttests. Finally, we performed an ANCOVA with the two robust learning measures as a repeated measure and the main effect of condition was not significant in this analysis. The only significant result in this ANCOVA was the interaction of test type and study, $F(2,152) = 17.52$, $p < .01$,

However, an inspection of the scores in the individual studies in Table 1 show that in five of six robust learning comparisons, performance in the SR group is higher than in the PS group. Performance in the SR condition is also higher than in the WE condition in five of six comparisons. Both of these patterns are marginally significant in a binomial test, $p = .094$.

Session 1 Total Time. Table 2 displays the average time spent on Session 1 GCT learning activities. As can be seen, students completed the GCT tasks more quickly in the PA study than in the other studies. Within each study, however, the session-1 GCT learning activities were designed to hold time on task constant. Across the three studies, students in the PS and WE conditions spent similar amounts of time on the tutor activities, and students in the SR condition spent about 5% more time.

Table 2. Total time for Session 1 GCT learning activities (min.)

3FC			GIE			BPA		
PS	WE	SR	PS	WE	SR	PS	WE	SR
51	58	53	52	50	55	26	23	27

4 Discussion and Conclusions

In this paper, we present three studies on the use of Cognitively Grounded Learning Activities (CGLAs) in a Cognitive Tutor for Genetics, comparing two CGLAs to a baseline problem-solving condition. While the baseline problem-solving condition led to better acquisition of problem-solving skills than the worked examples or scaffolded reasoning conditions, these studies provide preliminary evidence that reasoning scaffolds that explicitly ground students' problem-solving knowledge in the underlying genetic processes lead to more robust understanding. The benefits in these studies are relatively small; the reasoning scaffolds led to roughly 15% better performance on robust learning measures for GIE and BPA while having little impact for 3FC. Genetic process scaffolding may be less useful in 3FC cross problems because the underlying process in that task is itself relatively simple and the problem-solving procedure is constant across 3FC problems. The underlying genetics processes in the other two domains are more complex and student reasoning varies more across those problems. Therefore grounding student reasoning in the underlying genetic processes may only be helpful when such variation is present

Perhaps the most surprising result across these studies is that interleaved worked examples led to smaller learning gains for basic problem solving than standard problem-solving activities. This may be because the design of the explanations in these studies was too ambitious. Each explanation had two components; students both described the empirical evidence that justified each problem-solving step, and described the underlying genetic processes. The first component is directly relevant to refining procedural problem solving knowledge, but the second component is not. Instead, the genetic process component is intended to ground students' developing problem-solving knowledge in an underlying causal process model. As a result, the genetic process explanations may have represented extraneous cognitive load, essentially time off task, for students who are still actively refining basic procedural knowledge during problem solving. Hence, the preliminary conclusion from these studies is that students may be more likely to benefit from reasoning about underlying causal models when that experience takes the form of explicit scaffolded-reasoning learning activities that precede problem solving.

Acknowledgments. This research was supported by the Institute of Education Sciences award R305A090549 "Promoting Robust Understanding of Genetics with a Cognitive Tutor that Integrates Conceptual Learning with Problem Solving."

References

1. Koedinger, K.R., Corbett, A.T., Perfetti, C.: The Knowledge-Learning-Instruction (KLI) Framework: Bridging the Science-Practice Chasm to Enhance Robust Student Learning. Cognitive Science 36, 757–798 (2012)
2. Bransford, J.D., Brown, A.L., Cocking, R.R.: How People Learn: Brain, Mind, Experience and School. National Academy Press, Washington, DC (2000)
3. Pashler, H., Bain, P., Bottge, B., Graesser, A., Koedinger, K., McDaniel, M., Metcalfe, J.: Organizing Instruction and Study to Improve Student Learning. National Center for Education Research, Institute of Education Sciences, U.S. Department of Education, Washington, DC (2007)
4. Renkl, A., Atkinson, R.K.: Structuring the Transition from Example Study to Problem Solving in Cognitive Skill Acquisition: A Cognitive Load Perspective. Educational Psychologist 38, 15–22 (2003)
5. Corbett, A., MacLaren, B., Wagner, A., Kauffman, L., Mitchell, A., Baker, R., Gowda, S.: Preparing Students for Effective Explaining of Worked Examples in the Genetics Cognitive Tutor. In: Proceedings of the Thirty-third Annual Meeting of the Cognitive Science Society, pp. 1476–1481. Cognitive Science Society, Austin (2011)
6. McLaren, B.M., Lim, S.-J., Koedinger, K.R.: When Is Assistance Helpful to Learning? Results in Combining Worked Examples and Intelligent Tutoring. In: Woolf, B.P., Aïmeur, E., Nkambou, R., Lajoie, S. (eds.) ITS 2008. LNCS, vol. 5091, pp. 677–680. Springer, Heidelberg (2008)
7. Reed, S., Corbett, A., Hoffman, B., Wagner, A., MacLaren, B.: Effect of Worked Examples and Cognitive Tutor Training on Constructing Equations. Instructional Science 41, 1–24 (2013)
8. Salden, R., Aleven, V., Schwonke, R., Renkl, A.: The Expertise Reversal Effect and Worked Examples in Tutored Problem Solving. Instructional Science 38, 289–307 (2010)
9. Schwonke, R., Renkl, A., Salden, R., Aleven, V.: Effects of Different Ratios of Worked Solution Steps and Problem Solving Opportunities on Cognitive Load and Learning Outcomes. Computers in Human Behavior 27, 58–62 (2011)
10. Weitz, R., Salden, R.J.C.M., Kim, R.S., Heffernan, N.T.: Comparing worked examples and tutored problem solving: Pure vs. mixed approaches. In: Proceedings of the Thirty-Second Annual Meeting of the Cognitive Science Society, pp. 2876–2881 (2010)
11. Corbett, A., Kauffman, L., MacLaren, B., Wagner, A., Jones, E.: A Cognitive Tutor for Genetics Problem Solving: Learning Gains and Student Modeling. Journal of Educational Computing Research 42, 219–239 (2010)
12. Corbett, A., MacLaren, B., Wagner, A., Kauffman, L., Mitchell, A., Baker, R.: Enhancing Robust Learning Through Problem Solving in the Genetics Cognitive Tutor. In: Proceedings of the Thirty-fifth Annual Meeting of the Cognitive Science Society (in press)

Complementary Effects of Sense-Making and Fluency-Building Support for Connection Making: A Matter of Sequence?

Martina A. Rau[1], Vincent Aleven[1], and Nikol Rummel[2]

[1] Human-Computer Interaction Institute, Carnegie Mellon University, Pittsburgh, USA
[2] Universität Bochum, Institute of Education, Germany
{marau,aleven}@cs.cmu.edu, nikol.rummel@rub.de

Abstract. Multiple graphical representations can significantly improve students' learning. To acquire robust knowledge of the domain, students need to make connections between the different graphical representations. In doing so, students need to engage in two crucial learning processes: sense-making processes to build up conceptual understanding of the connections, and fluency-building processes to fast and effortlessly make use of perceptual properties in making connections. We present an experimental study which contrasts two hypotheses on how these learning processes interact. Does understanding facilitate fluency-building processes, or does fluency enhance sense-making processes? And consequently, which learning process should intelligent tutoring systems support first? Our results based on test data and tutor logs show an advantage for providing support for sense-making processes before fluency-building processes. To enhance students' robust learning of domain knowledge, ITSs should ensure that students have adequate conceptual understanding of connections between graphical representations before providing fluency-building support for connection making.

Keywords: Multiple graphical representations, connection making, learning processes, intelligent tutoring system.

1 Introduction

Instructional materials almost universally use multiple graphical representations: flow diagrams are used in programming, schemas and tree diagrams in biology, charts and diagrams in math - to mention only a few examples. Intelligent tutoring systems (ITSs) across domains include graphical representations and provide adaptive support on students' interactions with them [e.g., 1, 2]. Fractions are one domain in which multiple graphical representations are used extensively [3], because different graphical representations emphasize complementary conceptual aspects of fractions [4]. To benefit from multiple representations, however, students need to make connections between them [5]. Connection making allows students to integrate different conceptual aspects into one coherent mental model of the domain. Therefore, connection making between representations is key to students' ability to acquire robust knowledge of the domain: knowledge that transfers to novel tasks and lasts over time [6].

K. Yacef et al. (Eds.): AIED 2013, LNAI 7926, pp. 329–338, 2013.

Critical processes in acquiring robust knowledge are sense-making processes and fluency-building processes [6]. Prior research on connection making has mostly focused on supporting students in making sense of connections between representations [e.g., 7, 8]. Sense-making processes in connection making lead to conceptual understanding about how different graphical representations relate to one another by explicitly and verbally reasoning about corresponding components [7] (e.g., how do circle and number line depict the components of numerator and denominator?).

Although support for fluency in retrieving math facts has recently received attention in the ITS literature [9], little research has investigated support for perceptual fluency-building processes in connection making. Fluency-building processes lead to perceptual knowledge about which representations correspond to one another, which can be retrieved fast and effortlessly [10] (e.g., by "just seeing" that a circle and a number line show the same fraction). Being fluent in relating different representations of fractions is recognized as an important foundation for later Algebra learning [3]. Kellman et al. [10] demonstrate the effectiveness of a training for students to gain perceptual experience in finding corresponding math representations.

In prior work, we developed activities for an ITS for fractions that specifically support sense-making processes and fluency-building processes for connection making between multiple graphical representations [11]. In an experiment with the Fractions Tutor, we demonstrate that both types of support for connection making are *necessary* in order for students to benefit from multiple graphical representations [11]: only students who received support for both types of learning processes significantly outperformed a single-representation control condition.

Although we know that sense-making processes and fluency-building processes in making connections between multiple graphical representations interact, we do not know *how* they interact. Does sense-making support enable students to benefit from fluency-building support, or vice versa? The answer to this question has significant implications for the sequence in which instructional support for these learning processes should be provided. We investigate this question in an experiment with the Fractions Tutor.

An analysis of errors that students made during practice with the Fractions Tutor in our earlier experiment [11] yields hypotheses for this question. In this prior study, sense-making support was always provided before fluency-building support. Students who received a combination of sense-making and fluency-building support made fewer errors on fluency-building problems than students who received only fluency-building support. This finding supports the *understanding-first hypothesis* that conceptual understanding of connections equips students with knowledge about the structural correspondences between graphical representations. Such knowledge enables them to attend to relevant aspects of the graphical representations while developing fluency in making connections. According to a contrasting, alternative hypothesis, the *fluency-first hypothesis*, having fluency in making connections frees up cognitive resources that students need in order to engage in sense-making processes [10].

Both hypotheses make different predictions which sequence of support for sense-making processes and fluency-building processes is most effective. According to the understanding-first hypothesis, students should learn better when sense-making support for connection making is provided *before* fluency-building support. By contrast, the fluency-first hypothesis predicts that students should learn better when fluency-building support for connection making is provided *before* sense-making support. Knowing which sequence is most effective will enable designers of ITSs to develop adaptive support for connection making that takes advantage of the complementary effects of sense-making and fluency-building processes.

We contrast these hypotheses in an experiment with the Fractions Tutor, using activities we developed for sense-making support and fluency-building support in connection making between different graphical representations of fractions.

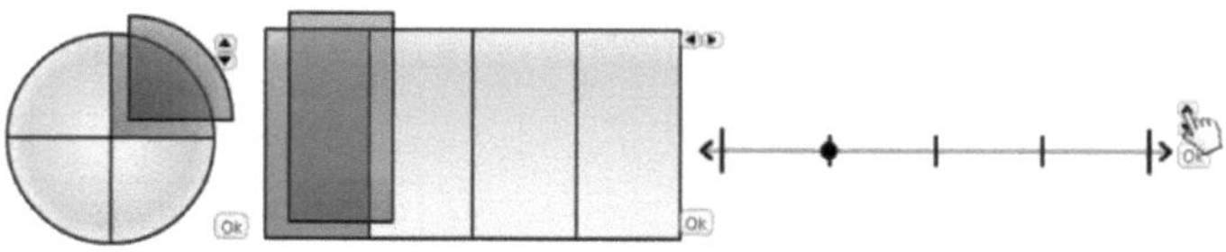

Fig. 1. Interactive representations used in Fractions Tutor: circle, rectangle, number line

2 Methods

2.1 Fractions Tutor

The Fractions Tutor uses three interactive graphical representations of fractions: circles, rectangles, and number lines (see Fig. 1). Each graphical representation emphasizes complementary aspects of fractions as an abstract concept [4]. Circle and rectangle are both area models which depict fractions as parts of a whole. The whole is inherent to the shape of the circle, but not to the rectangle. The number line depicts fractions as measures of parts of a length and can depict fractions larger than 1.

The design of the Fractions Tutor is based on iterative development through a number of classroom experiments with over 3,000 students. Our recent classroom experiment with 599 4th- and 5th-graders provides empirical evidence that it leads to robust learning gains [11]. The entire curriculum of the Fractions Tutor encompasses a range of topics and activities. For the purpose of the present study, we selected a subset of activities which focus on key aspects of students' conceptual understanding of fractions: equivalent fractions and fraction comparison. Specifically, we use activities designed to help students make sense of connections between different graphical representations and to become fluent in making connections.

The design of the *sense-making support* problems makes use of the worked-example principle [12]. Students are first presented with a worked example that uses one of the area models (i.e., circle or rectangle) to demonstrate how to solve a fractions problem. Students complete the last step of the problem and are then presented with an equivalent problem in which they have to use the number line to complete the problem themselves. At the end of the problem, students are prompted to relate the two graphical representations to one another. On all steps, the Fractions Tutor provides adaptive error feedback and hints on demand. Fig. 2 shows an example of a sense-making support problem for equivalent fractions.

The *fluency-building support* problems are based on Kellman et al.'s fluency training for perceptual expertise in connection making [10]. Students are presented with a variety of graphical representations and have to sort them into sets of equivalent fractions (see Fig. 3), or order them from smallest to largest, using drag-and-drop. Students are encouraged to solve the problems by visually estimating the relative size of the fractions, rather than by counting or computationally solving the problems.

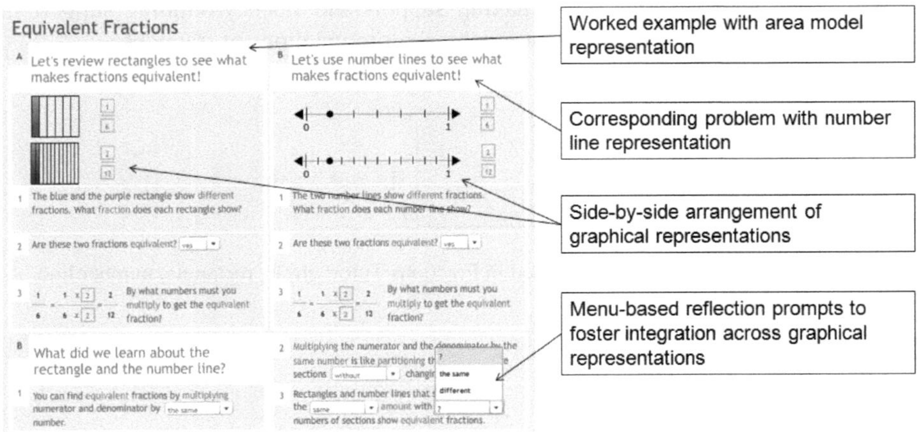

Fig. 2. Sense-making support for connection making

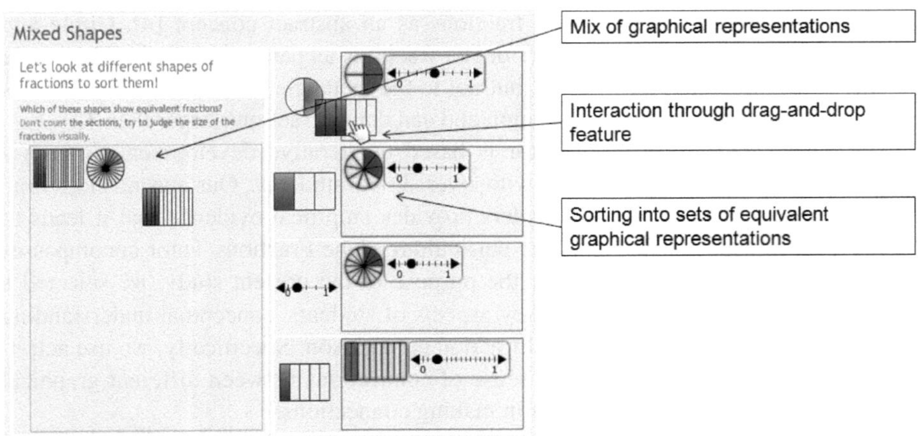

Fig. 3. Fluency-building support for connection making

2.2 Assessments

We assessed *reproduction of fractions knowledge* based on quiz items with circles, rectangles, and number lines, presented in a format identical to the problems in the Fractions Tutor. Specifically, reproduction-understanding items assessed students' conceptual understanding of connections between graphical representations with regard to equivalent fractions and fraction comparison. Reproduction-fluency items assessed students' fluency in making connections with regard to equivalent fractions and fraction comparison. Students' performance on reproduction-understanding items was computed as the proportion of correct responses to the maximum number correct responses. For reproduction-fluency items, we computed efficiency scores to take into account the speed with which students solved the quiz items, following [13]:

$$\text{reproduction-fluency} = \frac{Z\,(\text{proportion correct}) - Z\,(\text{time on quiz items})}{\sqrt{2}}.$$

Higher reproduction-fluency scores indicate higher efficiency at solving reproduction-fluency items correctly.

We assessed students' transfer of fractions knowledge based on equivalent pretests and posttests. A *near transfer* scale assesses students' ability to solve fractions problems with circles, rectangles, and number lines similar to those in the Fractions Tutor, presented in a different format. *Far transfer* items included test items on equivalence and comparison without graphical representations. Students' scores on both transfer scales were computed as the proportion of correct responses to the maximum number correct responses.

2.3 Experimental Design and Procedure

Thirty-nine students from grades 4 and 5 participated in the experiment. Sessions were conducted individually in the lab. Students were randomly assigned to different sequences of sense-making problems and fluency-building problems. In other words, all students worked on the same tutor problems, but in different orders. Students in the *understanding-first condition* received sense-making support before fluency-building support, for each topic (i.e., equivalence and comparison). Specifically,

Table 1. Sequence of activities by experimental condition

Activity Type	Understanding-first condition	Fluency-first condition
Test	Pretest: near / far transfer	Pretest: near / far transfer
Tutor: equivalence	***Sense-making support:*** 4 tutor problems	***Fluency-building support:*** 4 tutor problems
Quiz 1: equivalence	Reproduction-understanding, reproduction-fluency	Reproduction-understanding, reproduction-fluency
Tutor: equivalence	***Fluency-building support:*** 4 tutor problems	***Sense-making support:*** 4 tutor problems
Quiz 2: equivalence	Reproduction-understanding, reproduction-fluency	Reproduction-understanding, reproduction-fluency
Tutor: comparison	***Sense-making support:*** 4 tutor problems	***Fluency-building support:*** 4 tutor problems
Quiz 1: comparison	Reproduction-understanding, reproduction-fluency	Reproduction-understanding, reproduction-fluency
Tutor: comparison	***Fluency-building support:*** 4 tutor problems	***Sense-making support:*** 4 tutor problems
Quiz 2: comparison	Reproduction-understanding, reproduction-fluency	Reproduction-understanding, reproduction-fluency
Test	Posttest: near / far transfer	Posttest: near / far transfer

students in the understanding-first condition first worked on four sense-making problems for equivalent fractions. Next, they worked on four fluency-building problems for equivalent fractions. They then worked on four sense-making problems for fraction comparison, followed by four fluency-building problems for fraction comparison.

By contrast, students in the *fluency-first condition* received fluency-building support before sense-making support, again for each topic. Specifically, students in the fluency-first condition first worked on four fluency-building problems for equivalent fractions, then on four sense-making problems for equivalent fractions. Next, they worked on four fluency-building problems for fraction comparison, followed by four sense-making problems for fraction comparison.

Table 1 details the sequence of assessment problems and tutor problems for each experimental condition. Students first completed a pretest. They then worked on the Fractions Tutor. After every four tutor problems, students completed two quiz items (i.e., reproduction-understanding and reproduction-fluency for the given topic). After completing all tutor problems as well as the last set of quiz items, students were given an immediate posttest.

3 Results

One student was excluded from the analysis because he did not complete both topics of the Fractions Tutor, resulting in $N = 38$ students ($n = 20$ in the understanding-first condition, $n = 18$ in the fluency-first condition). We report partial eta-squared, a standard measure of effect size in the educational psychology literature, with η^2 of .01 corresponding to a small effect, .06 to a medium effect, and .14 to a large effect [14].

3.1 Quiz: Reproduction-Understanding and Reproduction-Fluency

To analyze differences between conditions on the quiz items, which assess reproduction of fractions knowledge, we conducted repeated measures MANCOVAs. We used condition as the independent factor, performance on the near and far transfer pretests as covariates, and quiz time (i.e., first and second quiz for the given topic) as repeated factor. Reproduction-understanding and reproduction-fluency were dependent measures.

Fig. 4 shows students' reproduction-fluency scores per quiz assessment. Results show a significant main effect of quiz time on reproduction-understanding, $F(1,34) = 4.26$, $p < .05$, $\eta^2 = .11$, but not for reproduction-fluency ($F < 1$). There was no significant main effect of condition on reproduction-understanding, $F(1,34) = 1.12$, $p = .30$, nor quiz-fluency ($F < 1$). Yet, there was a significant interaction between quiz time and condition on reproduction-fluency, $F(1,34) = 4.75$, $p < .05$, $\eta^2 = .12$. Pairwise comparisons on reproduction-fluency show that the fluency-first condition marginally significantly outperforms the understanding-first condition at the first assessment of reproduction-fluency, $t(34) = 1.68$, $p = .10$, $\eta^2 = .07$, whereas the understanding-first condition marginally significantly outperforms the fluency-first condition at the second assessment of reproduction-fluency, $t(34) = 1.71$, $p = .10$, $\eta^2 = .08$. This result indicates that the fluency-first condition outperforms the understanding-first condition on the fluency-reproduction quiz *only until* students in the understanding-first condition receive fluency-building support. After having received fluency-building support (at quiz time 2), the understanding-first condition outperforms students in the fluency-first condition on the fluency-reproduction quiz.

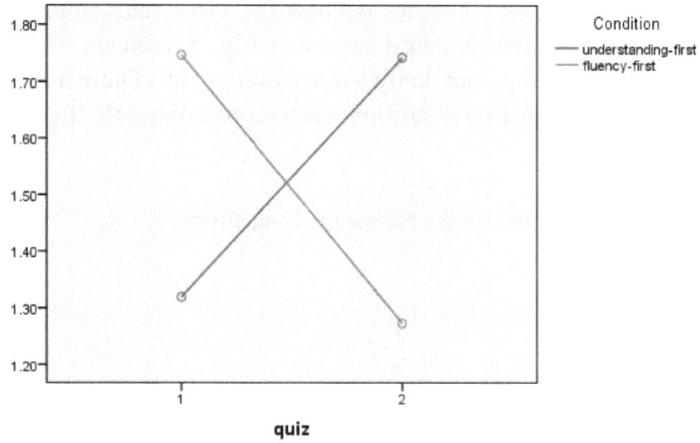

Fig. 4. Reproduction-fluency scores by condition by quiz time

3.2 Posttest: Transfer of Knowledge

To analyze differences between conditions on the posttests, which assess transfer of fractions knowledge, we conducted repeated measures MANOVAs with test time (pretest and posttest) the repeated factor, and near and far transfer performance as dependent measures.

Results demonstrate a significant main effect of test time on near transfer, $F(1,36) = 5.96$, $p < .05$, $\eta^2 = .14$, but not far transfer, $F(1,36) = 2.66$, $p = .11$. There was no significant main effect of condition on near transfer ($F < 1$) nor far transfer, $F(1,36) = 1.18$, $p = .28$, nor a significant interaction between test time and condition (Fs < 1). These findings indicate that both conditions significantly improved their ability to transfer fractions knowledge to novel test items equally.

3.3 Learning Curves: Differences in Rates of Learning

We examined "learning curves" using the DataShop web service [15] which depict the average error rate (across students and knowledge components) as a function of the amount of prior practice (i.e., the number of opportunities a student has had to apply a given knowledge component). Following standard practice in Cognitive Tutors research [6], we viewed each step in a tutor problem as a learning opportunity for the particular knowledge component involved in the step. We used a set of 19 knowledge components as a basis for this analysis. We considered a step in a tutor problem to be correct if the student solved it without hints and errors (i.e., if the student's first action on the step was a correct attempt at solving, as opposed to an error or a hint request).

We expect that, if learning occurs, error rates will decrease with the number of learning opportunities students have encountered.

Fig. 5 shows the aggregate learning curves based on error rates across knowledge components for the understanding-first condition and the fluency-first condition. The error rates decrease for both conditions, but the curves diverge: the understanding-first condition demonstrates a faster decrease in error rates than students in the fluency-first condition. As the standard errors in Fig. 5 indicate, this difference is reliable after the third attempt per knowledge component. These results show that students in the understanding-first condition learn more efficiently than students in the fluency-first condition.

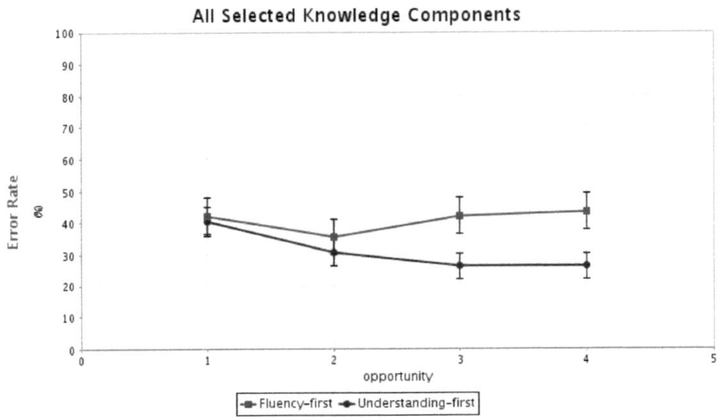

Fig. 5. Learning curves by condition across knowledge components. Bars show standard errors.

4 Discussion and Conclusion

Prior research shows that both sense-making processes and fluency-building processes play an important role in connection making: both learning processes need to be supported in order for students' robust learning of domain knowledge to benefit from multiple graphical representations [11]. Our results shed light into the question of how these learning processes interact. We contrasted two competing hypotheses. On the one hand, the *understanding-first hypothesis* posits that conceptual understanding of connections between graphical representations enables students to acquire fluency by helping them focus on conceptually relevant aspects of graphical representations. According to the *fluency-first hypothesis*, on the other hand, fluency in making connections between representations frees cognitive resources so that students can invest in sense-making processes to develop conceptual understanding of connections between graphical representations.

Our results support the understanding-first hypothesis which predicts that students learn better when sense-making processes are supported *before* fluency-building processes. Students in the understanding-first condition outperformed students in the fluency-first condition on fluency in reproduction of fractions knowledge, with medium effect sizes. Furthermore, an analysis of students' learning rates based on the tutor log data demonstrates that across all knowledge components, students in the understanding-first condition learn more efficiently than students in the fluency-first condition. In addition, students in the understanding-first condition end with a lower error-rate than students in the fluency-first condition. This result is in line with the advantage of the understanding-first condition on the reproduction-fluency quiz. By contrast, our results do not support the fluency-first hypothesis, that perceptual expertise in making connections between graphical representations frees cognitive resources [10] which are needed to make sense of how and why different graphical representations relate to one another. In particular, our findings indicate that students are more likely to acquire fluency in making connections purely based on visual cues, if they have previously acquired conceptual understanding of the connections.

Our results do not show differences between conditions on understanding-reproduction items. This finding indicates that the advantage of the understanding-first condition lies mainly in helping students benefit from fluency-building support, rather than helping students benefit from sense-making support. This interpretation is consistent with the understanding-first hypothesis that conceptual understanding of connections between graphical representations enables students to acquire fluency-building support.

Our results do not show an advantage of the understanding-first condition on near or far transfer assessments. Instead, both conditions improve their ability to transfer knowledge of fractions equally, with medium to large effect sizes. A possible explanation for this finding is that the items on the near and far transfer tests relied more on students' understanding of connections between graphical representations than on their ability to fluently make connections between representations. According to Kellman et al. [10], fluency training promotes students' ability to extract information more efficiently from representations. Future learning of novel graphical representations might benefit from fluency in making connections. However, such test items were not part of the near and far transfer assessments used in the present study. In future research, we will investigate whether there is an advantage of the understanding-first condition over the fluency-first condition in students' ability to learn how to use a novel graphical representation of fractions, such as a set representation.

Taken together, our results indicate that conceptual understanding of connections between multiple graphical representations enhances students' ability to acquire fluency in making connections, rather than vice versa. Consequently, ITSs should provide instructional support for making sense of connections between graphical representations *before* instructional support for fluency-building processes in making connections. Adaptive versions of connection-making support should ensure that students have acquired conceptual understanding of connections between graphical representations before providing fluency-building support. As multiple graphical representations are ubiquitously used across many science and math domains, our results have the potential to impact students' learning across a wide range of settings. We are currently planning a classroom experiment to investigate the extrinsic validity of these findings.

Acknowledgements. This work was supported by the National Science Foundation, REESE-21851-1-1121307, and by the Institute of Education Sciences, R305A120734. We thank Ken Koedinger, Richard Scheines, Brian Junker, Mitchell Nathan, Zelha Tunc-Pekkan, Jay Raspat, Michael Ringenberg, the Datashop and CTAT teams.

References

1. Schwonke, R., Ertelt, A., Renkl, A.: Fostering the translation between external representations. Does it enhance learning with an intelligent tutoring program? In: Zumbach, J., et al. (eds.) Beyond Knowledge: The Legacy of Competence, pp. 117–119. Springer, Netherlands (2008)
2. Koedinger, K.R.: Toward evidence for instructional design principles: Examples from Cognitive Tutor Math 6. In: 24th Annual Meeting of the North American Chapter of the International Group of the Psychology of Mathematics Education. ERIC/CSMEE Publications, Athens (2002)
3. NMAP: Foundations for Success: Report of the National Mathematics Advisory Board Panel. U.S. Government Printing Office (2008)
4. Charalambous, C.Y., Pitta-Pantazi, D.: Drawing on a Theoretical Model to Study Students' Understandings of Fractions. Educational Studies in Mathematics 64, 293–316 (2007)
5. Ainsworth, S.: DeFT: A conceptual framework for considering learning with multiple representations. Learning and Instruction 16, 183–198 (2006)
6. Koedinger, K.R., Corbett, A.T., Perfetti, C.: Knowledge-Learning-Instruction Framework: Bridging the Science-Practice Chasm to Enhance Robust Student Learning. Cognitive Science 36, 757–798 (2012)
7. Seufert, T.: Supporting Coherence Formation in Learning from Multiple Representations. Learning and Instruction 13, 227–237 (2003)
8. Bodemer, D., Ploetzner, R., Feuerlein, I., Spada, H.: The Active Integration of Information during Learning with Dynamic and Interactive Visualisations. Learning and Instruction 14, 325–341 (2004)
9. Arroyo, I., Royer, J.M., Woolf, B.P.: Using an intelligent tutor and math fluency training to improve math performance. I. J. of AIED 21, 135–152 (2011)
10. Kellman, P.J., Massey, C.M., Roth, Z., Burke, T., Zucker, J., Saw, A., Aguero, K., Wise, J.: Perceptual learning and the technology of expertise: Studies in fraction learning and algebra. Pragmatics & Cognition 16, 356–405 (2008)
11. Rau, M.A., Aleven, V., Rummel, N., Rohrbach, S.: Sense Making Alone Doesn't Do It: Fluency Matters Too! ITS Support for Robust Learning with Multiple Representations. In: Cerri, S.A., Clancey, W.J., Papadourakis, G., Panourgia, K. (eds.) ITS 2012. LNCS, vol. 7315, pp. 174–184. Springer, Heidelberg (2012)
12. Renkl, A.: The worked-out example principle in multimedia learning. In: Mayer, R. (ed.) Cambridge Handbook of Multimedia Learning, pp. 229–246. Cambridge University Press, Cambridge (2005)
13. Van Gog, T., Paas, F.: Instructional efficiency: revisiting the original construct in educational research. Educational Psychologist 43, 1–11 (2008)
14. Cohen, J.: Statistical Power Analysis for the Behavioral Sciences. Lawrence Erlbaum Associates, Hillsdale (1988)
15. Koedinger, K.R., Baker, R., Cunningham, K., Skogsholm, A., Leber, B., Stamper, J.: A data repository for the EDM community: The PSLC Data-Shop. In: Romero, C., et al. (eds.) Handbook of Educational Data Mining, pp. 10–12. CRC Press, Boca Raton (2010)

Examples and Tutored Problems: How Can Self-Explanation Make a Difference to Learning?

Amir Shareghi Najar and Antonija Mitrovic

Intelligent Computer Tutoring Group
University of Canterbury, Christchurch, New Zealand
amir.shareghinajar@pg.canterbury.ac.nz,
tanja.mitrovic@canterbury.ac.nz

Abstract. Learning from worked examples has been shown to be superior to unsupported problem solving in numerous studies. Examples reduce the cognitive load on the learner's working memory, thus helping the student to learn faster or deal with more complex questions. Only recently researchers started investigating the worked example effect in Intelligent Tutoring Systems (ITSs). We conducted a study to investigate the effect of using worked examples in combination with supported problem-solving in SQL-Tutor. We had three conditions: Examples Only (EO), Problems Only (PO), and Alternating Examples/Problems (AEP). After completing a problem, students received a self-explanation prompt that focused on the concepts used in the problem, to make sure that students acquire conceptual knowledge. On the other hand, examples were followed by self-explanation prompts that focused on procedural knowledge. The study showed that the AEP and PO conditions outperformed EO in learning gain, while AEP outperformed PO in conceptual knowledge acquisition. Therefore, interleaving examples with supported problems is an optimal choice compared to using examples or supported problems only in SQL-Tutor.

Keywords: worked examples, problem solving, self-explanation, intelligent tutors.

1 Introduction and Related Work

Many studies have shown the worked example effect, in which students who study worked examples learn more than students involved in unsupported problem solving. Sweller et al. [1] explain the worked example effect based on the Cognitive Load Theory (CLT). They show that examples decrease the cognitive load on the learner's working memory. Thereby, learning from worked examples is more helpful for novices who have to deal with an enormous amount of cognitive load.

There has been no agreement on how much assistance should be provided to students during learning. Kirschner et al. [2] show that maximum assistance (e.g. examples) is more efficient than minimal assistance (e.g. unsupported problem-solving) which has been corroborated by prior studies like [3]. Recently researchers focused on different example-based learning strategies. Van Gog et al. [4] investigate the difference between worked examples only (WE), worked examples/problem-solving pairs

K. Yacef et al. (Eds.): AIED 2013, LNAI 7926, pp. 339–348, 2013.

(WE-PS), problem-solving/worked examples pairs (PS-WE) and problem-solving only (PS) for novices. They found that the participants in the WE and WE-PS conditions had higher performances in the post-test than PS and PS-WE. Furthermore, the mental effort training and test rates in WE-PS and WE was lower than PS and PS-WE. In a later study, Van Gog [5] used Modelling Examples (ME) in two conditions PS-ME-PS-ME and ME-PS-ME-PS in the Frog Leap game. A modelling example is a type of example in which an expert illustrates the solution in a video format [6]. After these two sequences of training, students had to work on two tasks, of which the second one was not similar to training tasks. There was no difference in learning performance since the students learnt most after studying the second worked example.

Many prior studies addressed the advantages of example-based strategy against unsupported problem-solving. Koedinger and Aleven [7] criticised those because of the very different amounts of information provided to the two conditions (the unsupported problem-solving condition received no feedback upon submitting solutions). As the response to this criticism, Schwonke et al. [8] compared a standard cognitive tutor (Geometry Tutor) to a new version which was enriched with faded worked examples. Both conditions had the same amount of learning, but the faded example condition led to significantly reduced learning time.

Worked examples are beneficial in ITSs, especially for novices because they do not have adequate prior knowledge to solve problems, and examples can help them obtain the needed information. Therefore, it could be assumed that using a combination of examples and problem-solving might lead to a better result.

Using examples decreases the working memory load. If the freed working memory loads with germane load, learning will improve. One way to increase the germane load is to involve students in self-explanation (e.g. [9]). Self-Explanation (SE) is a metacognitive process in which students give explanations after studying learning materials [10]. Researchers have found evidence that students who generate explanations themselves learn more than students who receive explanations [11].

Few students self-explain spontaneously, and therefore SE prompts can be used to encourage students to explain examples to themselves. SE prompts can be of different nature, according to the knowledge they focus on. For instance, Hausmann et al. [12] compared justification-based prompts (e.g. "what principle is being applied in this step?") and meta-cognitive prompts (e.g. "what new information does each step provide for you?") with a new type called step-focused prompts (e.g. "what does this step mean to you?"). They found that students in the step-focused and justification conditions learnt more from studying examples than students in the meta-cognitive prompts condition. In another study, Chi and VanLehn [13] categorised SE as either procedural explanation (e.g. answer to "Why was this step done"), or derivation SE (e.g. answer to "where did this step come from?").

McLaren and Isotani [14] compared examples only, alternating worked examples with tutored problem solving, and pure problem solving with the ITS. They conducted a study using the Stoichiometry Tutor and modelling examples. The examples were combined with SE prompts in order to involve students in thinking deeper about the examples; the authors refer to such examples as interactive examples [14]. There was no difference in the post-test performance between the conditions, but the group that learnt from examples only had a significantly lower learning time. However, the examples were followed by SE prompts while the problems were not. The authors indicate that this result is interesting at least in some domains, under some conditions.

Our study continues the previous research on comparing learning from worked examples versus supported problem solving; similar to [14], we also investigate learning from Examples Only (EO), Problems Only (PO), and Alternating Examples/Problems (AEP). Since SE is a very effective strategy, we introduced SE prompts not only after examples (as in [14]), but also after problem solving. Our hypothesis is that students in the AEP condition will learn more than the other two groups, and students in the PO condition will learn more than the students in the EO condition (AEP > PO > EO). We also hypothesized that the EO participants would spend less time than the other two groups, as similar findings resulted from prior studies.

We describe our approach in Section 2. Section 3 presents the results of the study, while the conclusions and the directions of future work are presented in Section 4.

2 Study Design and Procedure

The studies discussed in the previous section were conducted in well-defined domains with well-defined tasks. We wanted to study learning from examples in a different context: defining queries in the Structured Query Language (SQL), which is a well-defined domain with ill-defined tasks [15]. Our study was conducted with SQL-Tutor, which is a constraint-based tutor [16] developed and maintained by the Intelligent Computer Tutoring Group (ICTG). SQL-Tutor complements classroom instruction; we assume that students learnt about SQL in lectures, and the system provides numerous practice opportunities. For this study, we developed three versions of SQL-Tutor in which students work with different combinations of examples and problems. In all the three conditions, students were presented with pairs of isomorphic examples and/or problems. That is, students who were in the EO and PO conditions worked with example-example and problem-problem pairs respectively. The students in AEP group interacted with example-problem pairs. There were 10 pairs in all conditions.

We designed 20 problems with ten different levels of complexity, based on the CD collection database, which is one of the databases available in SQL-Tutor. For a problem, SQL-Tutor provides the problem text only. A worked example consists of the problem text, the SQL statement that is the solution and an explanation.

In order to reinforce learning further, we provided SE prompts both after worked examples and after problems. We developed two types of SE prompts. Previous research [8, 17] showed that worked examples increase conceptual knowledge more than problem solving; therefore we provided Procedural-focused Self Explanation (P-SE) prompts after examples to make sure that students pay additional attention to procedural knowledge. P-SE prompts therefore complement learning from examples. On the other hand, working with the ITS is strongly focused on procedural knowledge [17] and therefore after solving problems, students were given Conceptual-focused Self-Explanation (C-SE) prompts in order to ensure that students reflect on the concepts covered in the problem they just completed and acquire conceptual knowledge in that way. Both types of prompts require students to select an answer from a list of options. Figure 1 shows a screenshot of SQL-Tutor when the student has completed a problem, and was then given an SE prompt. In this situation the student's answer was incorrect, and the system provided a correction.

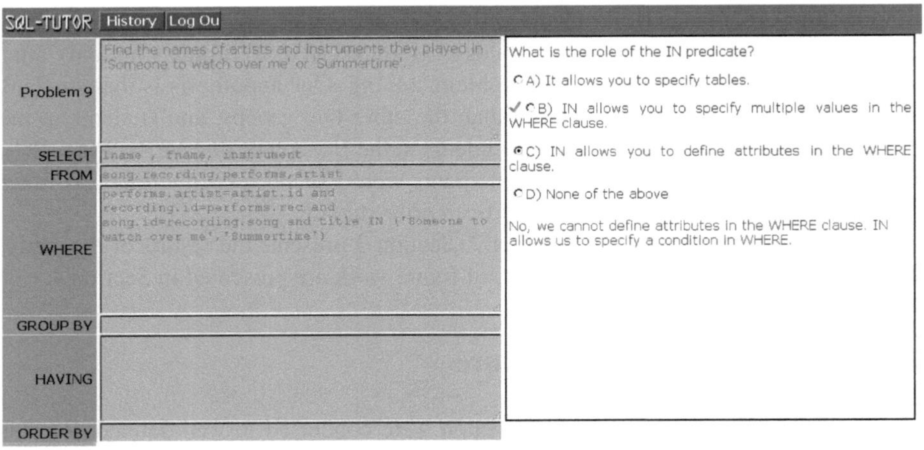

Fig. 1. A C-SE prompt after a problem is solved

Figure 2 shows a screenshot of a P-SE prompt which was provided after the student read an example. In this specific case, the student gave a correct answer which was confirmed by the system.

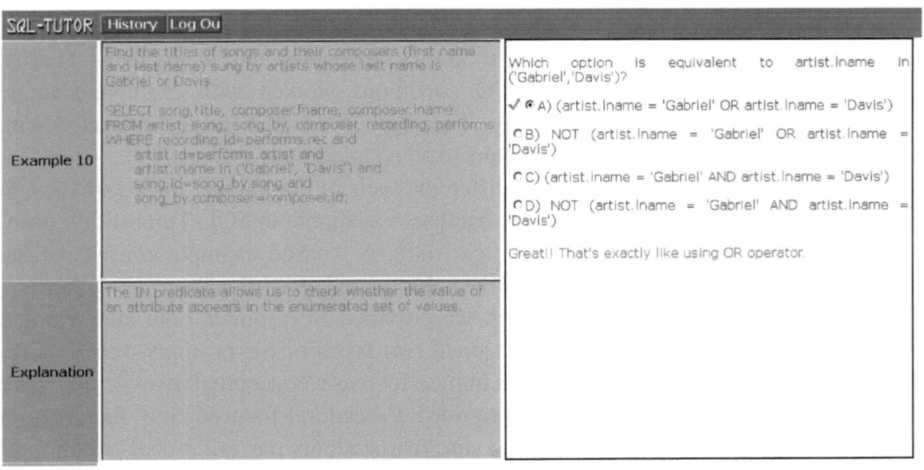

Fig. 2. A screenshot of a P-SE after an example

The participants were 34 students enrolled in the Relational Database Systems course at the University of Canterbury. They learned about SQL in lectures beforehand, and needed to practice in the lab. The students did not receive any inducements for participating in the study, but we told them that working with our system may help them learn SQL. We informed them that they would see ten pairs of problems, and that the tasks in each pair are similar. When students know that the tasks in each pair are isomorphic, they may use them more efficiently.

The students were randomly allocated to one of the conditions, giving sample sizes of 12 in PO, 11 in AEP and 11 in EO. First, the students took a pre-test for 10 minutes. Once the students logged in, SQL-Tutor randomly allocated them to one of the conditions (EO, PO, or AEP). The students then had 90 minutes to work with the system. They could choose to take the post-test at any time during the learning phase to finish the experiment.

The pre-test had five questions, three of which were multiple-choice questions and two were problem-solving questions. The first and the second multiple-choice questions measured conceptual knowledge students had, while the third question measured procedural knowledge. For the fourth and the fifth questions, students had to write a query to answer the question. These two questions measured procedural knowledge and the problem-solving skill of the students. The post-test was similar to the pre-test with one extra question about the difficulty of the tasks. We asked students to answer this question: "How difficult was it for you to complete the tasks in this study?" Students rated the complexity of the tasks on the Likert scale from 1 to 5 (simple to difficult). The maximum score on both tests was 11.

3 Results

The basic statistics about the study are presented in Table 1. There was no significant difference between the pre-test performances of the three groups. ANOVA revealed a significant difference between the post-test results ($p = .02$). The Tukey post-hoc test showed that the performance of the EO group was significantly lower than the AEP group ($p = .02$) and marginally significantly lower than the PO group ($p = .09$), thus confirming our hypothesis. The students in all three conditions improved significantly between the pre- and the post-test, as shown by the paired t-test reported in the Improvement row of Table 1. Correlations between the pre- and post-test scores are also reported in Table 1, but only the PO condition had a significant correlation ($r = .69$).

There was also a significant difference between the mean learning times of the three groups ($p < .01$). The Tukey post-hoc test revealed that the EO group spent significantly shorter time than students in the AEP group and the PO group (both $p < .01$). The EO group participants were free to work with the system for the whole session, but spent much less time than the other two groups. This shows that the EO condition did not engage students like AEP and PO did. One potential explanation for this is that students overestimated their learning based on worked examples, and finished the tasks in a very short time.

There was a marginally significant difference between the three groups in the number of examples/problems they attempted ($p = .05$). The Tukey post-hoc test revealed that the EO group attempted more tasks than PO ($p =.1$) and the AEP group ($p=.07$).

The three groups also differed significantly in the normalised learning gain[1] (p = .01). The Tukey post-hoc test revealed that the EO group learnt significantly less than students in the AEP group (p = .02) and the PO group (p = .03). When we analysed normalised learning gains on the problem-solving questions in the pre/post-tests (questions 4 and 5), we found a significant difference between the groups (p = .01). As we expected, the students in the PO and AEP conditions performed significantly better than the students in the EO condition on problem-solving questions (Tukey post-hoc test: EO and PO p = .01, EO and AEP p=.04), because students in the EO condition were not given any problem-solving tasks during the learning phase.

Table 1. Basic statistics (* denotes the mean difference significant at the 0.05 level)

	PO (12)	**AEP (11)**	**EO (11)**	**p**
Pre-test (%)	41.67 (13.82)	48.76 (13.19)	44 (14.63)	.48
Post-test (%)	72.73 (13.98)	77.69 (16.57)	58.68 (16.57)	*.02
Improvement	*p=.0, t=-9.8	*p=.0, t=-5.1	*p=.03, t=-2.4	
Pre/post-test correlation	*p=.01, r=.69	p=.49, r=.22	p=.43, r=.26	
Learning time (min)	69.67 (11.16)	65.91 (14.53)	38.45 (16.14)	*<.01
Number of attempted problems	14.58 (5.11)	14.09 (5.10)	18.63 (3.23)	.05
Normalised learning gain	.54 (.19)	.55 (.31)	.21 (.35)	*.01
Problem solving gain	.64 (.27)	.58 (.42)	.19 (.37)	*.01
Conceptual knowledge gain	.29 (.39)	.77 (.41)	.54 (.47)	*.03
Procedural knowledge gain	.59 (.22)	.48 (.42)	.13 (.40)	*.01
Perceived task difficulty	3.50 (.80)	3.27 (.90)	2.82 (.75)	

We also analysed the students' conceptual and procedural knowledge separately. Questions 1 and 2 in the tests measured conceptual knowledge, while the remaining three questions focused on procedural knowledge. There was a significant difference on both conceptual and procedural normalised learning gain. The Tukey post-hoc test reveals that the AEP group learned significantly more conceptual knowledge than the PO group (p =.02). We think that examples helped the AEP students to acquire conceptual knowledge. The students in the AEP condition acquired the most conceptual knowledge since they saw both examples and C-SE prompts. That was the only significant difference revealed by the Tukey post-hoc test. There was also a significant difference in the procedural knowledge gain (p = .01); the Tukey post-hoc test revealed a significant difference was between the PO and EO conditions (p=.01), and a marginally significant difference (p=.06) between the AEP and EO conditions.

In the post-test we also asked students about the perceived task difficulty. The Man-Whitney U test indicated that the PO group ranked the problems as more difficult in comparison to the ranking by the EO group; the difference is marginally

[1] Normalised learning gain= (Post test - Pre test) / (Max score - Pre test).

significant (p=.053). This result was expected as problems impose more cognitive load on the working memory than examples [1].

We calculated the effect size based on the normalised learning gain using Cohen's d, reported in Table 2. The effect sizes for both the AEP and PO conditions are large in comparison to the EO condition.

Table 2. The effect size on normalised learning gain between the groups

Conditions		Effect size
AEP	PO	.04
AEP	EO	1.01
PO	EO	1.15

The participants received C-SE prompts after problems and P-SE after examples. Therefore, the AEP group saw half of the C-SE prompts that PO students received, and also half of the P-SE prompts that the EO participants were given. We also analysed the SE success rates for the three conditions, which are reported in Table 3. We found no significant difference between AEP and PO in C-SE, and also no significant difference in P-SE success rate for the students in EO and AEP.

Table 3. SE prompts analysis (* denotes the mean difference significant at the 0.05 level)

	PO	AEP	EO	p
C-SE success rate (%)	88.50 (7.5)	92.84 (10.36)	N/A	.26
P-SE success rate (%)	N/A	77.69 (19.74)	71.36 (11.20)	.37

The students in the PO and AEP groups could select the feedback level[2] when they submitted their solutions, up to the complete solution (the highest level of feedback). Therefore, the participants could transform a problem-solving task to a worked example by asking for the complete solution. For that reason, we analysed help requests submitted for the problems given to the PO and AEP conditions.

Table 4. Maximum hint level analysis

	PO	AEP	
Second problem in pairs	1.08 (1.68)	1.54 (1.69)	p = .51
First problem in pairs	1.33 (1.56)		

Table 4 shows the mean number of problems for which the participants requested complete solutions. Looking at the second problem in each pair (the first row of Table 4), there was no significant difference in this respect between the PO and AEP

[2] SQL-Tutor offers six levels of feedback [16].

conditions. Moreover, we did not see a significant difference in the number of times the PO students requested complete solutions for the first/second problem of each pair ($p = .39$). This result shows the participants from the PO/AEP groups have not converted their problems to worked examples.

Figure 3 depicts the relationship between the normalised learning gain and the learning time. Each data point on this graph represents the mean normalised learning gain of all students who completed their sessions by the specific time. For example, there were three participants from the EO condition who completed their session with SQL-Tutor 22 minutes into the study, and their normalised learning gains were 0.07, 0.11 and 0.14. The corresponding mean normalised learning gain at 22 minutes is therefore 0.11 (this corresponds to the third data point for the EO group). Although the fitted curve is an estimate only, this graph can be used for predicting normalised learning gains for longer learning sessions. The figure shows that the learning gains of the AEP and PO conditions are much higher than those of the EO group. In our study, the participants spent less than 90 minutes learning; the graph shows that the PO condition has the highest predicted learning gain over longer sessions.

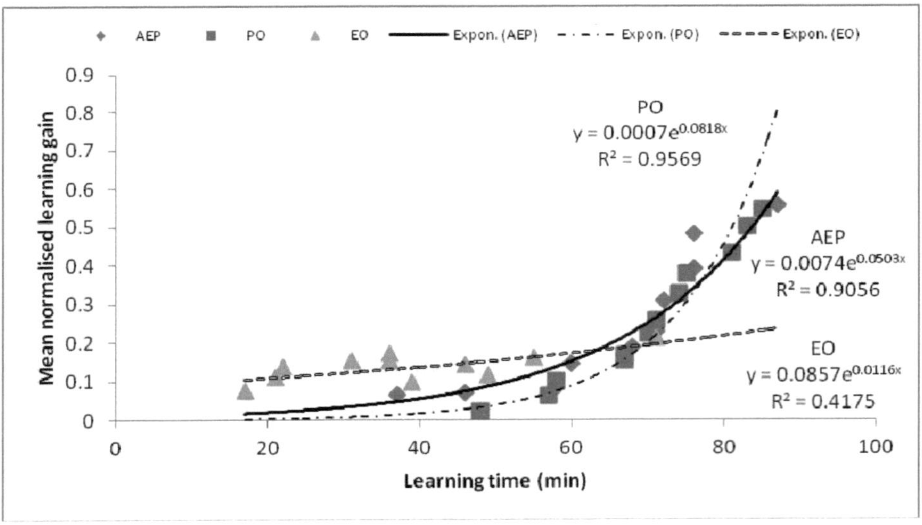

Fig. 3. Learning gain mean growth in time

4 Discussion and Conclusions

Our hypothesis was that the AEP condition would learn more than the PO and EO conditions, and PO would be superior to EO. Our analyses showed that the EO condition learnt significantly less than students in the other two conditions. All students had the same amount of time to work with the system, but the EO condition participants spent a significantly shorter time on reviewing examples. As stated previously, a possible explanation is that the participants could not accurately assess their knowledge after reading examples, even with the addition of scafolded self-explanation. As worked examples do not engage students like problems do, it is necessary to use some additional techniques to engage students to reason deeply about examples. This corroborates our previous finding that students who studied examples learnt less than students who solved problems.

Our results are in contrast with the findings presented in [14]. There are three main differences between the two studies. First, in our study the participants were given self-explanation prompts after problems, not only after worked examples (as in [14]). Moreover, we designed SE prompts to complement problem solving and examples. We provided procedural SE prompts after examples, as examples have been shown to reinforce conceptual knowledge more than procedural knowledge. We also provided conceptual SE prompts after problem solving to reinforce the acquisition of conceptual knowledge. Therefore, both types of SE prompts were designed so to complement the type of learning provided by the main activity (problem solving or learning from examples). The second difference is in the instructional domain used in each study. The instructional task in the McLaren and Isotani's study was simpler, consisting of simple algebraic equations and basic chemistry concepts, while in our study the participants were solving ill-defined design tasks. Thirdly, our constraint-based tutor provided feedback on demand while the Stoichiometry tutor used in [14] provided immediate feedback.

Why are worked examples not as effective as supported problem solving? Worked examples alone do not engage students as much as problem solving, and over time some students become less motivated to put enough effort into learning. Moreover, supported problem solving in contrast with unsupported problems avoid impasses, and is thus less frustrating and more effective. Examples may also induce an illusion of understanding after a certain number of tasks. For instance, students may think they have already learnt the example while they have not; consequently, they pass over the example very fast without spending enough time to process it which causes shallow learning. One potential approach to scaffold learning from worked examples is to provide support for self-assessment like in [18].

We found no significant difference between PO and AEP in the normalised learning gain and learning time. However, the AEP group acquired significantly more conceptual knowledge than the PO group. Consequently, the best instructional condition in our study was AEP, and our hypotheses were confirmed. The AEP participants learnt from the worked examples (the first task in each pair); when they were presented with isomorphic problems, they were already primed and did not have to deal with many unfamiliar details like students in the PO group.

Our study showed that learning from alternating examples with problems is superior to learning from problems or examples only, when the sequence of problems/examples is fixed. The results suggest that instead of just providing problem-solving opportunities, ITSs may provide worked examples followed by isomorphic problem solving. We recently conducted an eye-tracking study to investigate how students process examples. Based on the results of that study, our future research will focus on adding adaptivity to learning from worked examples in ITSs.

References

1. Sweller, J., Ayres, P., Kalyuga, S.: Cognitive load theory. Springer (2011)
2. Kirschner, P.A., Sweller, J., Clark, R.E.: Why Minimal Guidance During Instruction Does Not Work: An Analysis of the Failure of Constructivist, Discovery, Problem-Based, Experiential, and Inquiry-Based Teaching. Educational Psychologist 41, 75–86 (2006)
3. Atkinson, R.K., Derry, S.J., Renkl, A., Wortham, D.: Learning from Examples: Instructional Principles from the Worked Examples Research. Review of Educational Research 70, 181–214 (2000)
4. Van Gog, T., Kester, L., Paas, F.: Effects of worked examples, example-problem, and problem-example pairs on novices' learning. Contemporary Educational Psychology 36, 212–218 (2011)
5. Van Gog, T.: Effects of identical example–problem and problem–example pairs on learning. Computers & Education 57, 1775–1779 (2011)
6. Van Gog, T., Rummel, N.: Example-Based Learning: Integrating Cognitive and Social-Cognitive Research Perspectives. Educational Psychology Review 22, 155–174 (2010)
7. Koedinger, K., Aleven, V.: Exploring the Assistance Dilemma in Experiments with Cognitive Tutors. Educational Psychology Review 19, 239–264 (2007)
8. Schwonke, R., Renkl, A., Krieg, C., Wittwer, J., Aleven, V., Salden, R.: The worked-example effect: Not an artefact of lousy control conditions. Computers in Human Behavior 25, 258–266 (2009)
9. Hilbert, T.S., Renkl, A.: Learning how to use a computer-based concept-mapping tool: Self-explaining examples helps. Computers in Human Behavior 25, 267–274 (2009)
10. Chi, M.T.H., De Leeuw, N., Chiu, M.H., LaVancher, C.: Eliciting self-explanations improves understanding. Cognitive Science 18, 439–477 (1994)
11. Aleven, V., Koedinger, K.R.: An effective metacognitive strategy: Learning by doing and explaining with a computer-based Cognitive Tutor. Cognitive Science 26, 147–179 (2002)
12. Hausmann, R., Nokes, T., VanLehn, K.A., Gershman, S.: The design of self-explanation prompts: The fit hypothesis. In: Proceedings of the 31st Annual Conference of the Cognitive Science Society, pp. 2626–2631 (2009)
13. Chi, M.T.H., VanLehn, K.A.: The content of physics self-explanations. The Journal of the Learning Sciences 1, 69–105 (1991)
14. McLaren, B.M., Isotani, S.: When Is It Best to Learn with All Worked Examples? In: Biswas, G., Bull, S., Kay, J., Mitrovic, A. (eds.) AIED 2011. LNCS, vol. 6738, pp. 222–229. Springer, Heidelberg (2011)
15. Mitrovic, A., Weerasinghe, A.: Revisiting Ill-Definedness and the Consequences for ITSs. In: Mizoguchi, V.D.R. (ed.) The 14th International Conference on Artificial Intelligence in Education, pp. 375–382. IOS Press, Amsterdam (2009)
16. Mitrovic, A.: An Intelligent SQL Tutor on the Web. International Journal of Artificial Intelligence in Education 13, 173–197 (2003)
17. Kim, R.S., Weitz, R., Heffernan, N.T., Krach, N.: Tutored Problem Solving vs. "Pure" Worked Examples. In: Proceedings of the 31st Annual Conference of the Cognitive Science Society, pp. 3121–3126. Cognitive Science Society, Austin (2007)
18. Roll, I., Aleven, V., McLaren, B.M., Koedinger, K.R.: Metacognitive Practice Makes Perfect: Improving Students' Self-Assessment Skills with an Intelligent Tutoring System. In: Biswas, G., Bull, S., Kay, J., Mitrovic, A. (eds.) AIED 2011. LNCS, vol. 6738, pp. 288–295. Springer, Heidelberg (2011)

Improving the Efficiency of Automatic Knowledge Generation through Games and Simulations

Mark Floryan and Beverly Park Woolf

Department of Computer Science, University of Massachusetts, Amherst
140 Governors Dr. Amherst, MA USA
{mfloryan,bev}@cs.umass.edu

Abstract. We have created a generalized algorithm for automatically constructing domain level knowledge bases from student input. This method has demonstrated greater efficiencies than when knowledge is hand crafted by subject matter experts (SMEs). This paper presents two related methods for improving automated knowledge acquisition by leveraging the properties of games and simulations. First, we discuss game mechanics that, when added to our intelligent tutor Rashi, lead to higher quantity and quality of student input. In a separate but related analysis, we present a novel game type called a knowledge refinement game (KRG) to improve the knowledge in an expert knowledge base. This game motivates SMEs to refine the generated knowledge base, especially for data in which the system has low confidence. Utilizing an anonymous agreement policy ensures the quality of SME responses and results show that small amounts of KRG activity leads to noticeable improvements in the quality of the knowledge base. We assert that these two results in unison provide evidence that gaming has a powerful potential role in improving artificial intelligence techniques for education.

Keywords: expert knowledge bases, serious games, game mechanics, ill-defined domains, increased student input.

1 Introduction

Research in educational software is often focused on development of expert knowledge bases that support intelligent algorithms [2], which in turn are intended to improve a student's experience with intelligent tutoring systems (ITS) by offering customized interactions. In contrast, other research communities apply gaming and simulation mechanics to increase the efficacy of educational software, often by increasing user engagement and motivation [1][7][9][22]. This paper describes research to incorporate lessons from game design to optimize a tutor's ability to automatically learn domain level knowledge. In particular, we have developed a set of algorithms that examine student actions while using an intelligent tutor and use this student input to construct an expert knowledge base (for details on this process see [6]). This approach produces relatively small but precise domain models that are useful for generating automatic feedback to students [3].

K. Yacef et al. (Eds.): AIED 2013, LNAI 7926, pp. 349–358, 2013.

The focus of this paper is on applying game mechanics to improve this automated knowledge generation process. We have automatically created a domain knowledge base with greater than 70 percent precision [6] in about 300 student work hours. This paper describes how to improve these precision numbers by incorporating games and simulations into the knowledge generation process. We present two experiments: one focused on *reducing the time* required to automatically build an expert knowledge base and the second on *increasing the quality* of the resulting expert knowledge base.

Our first effort involves incorporating game mechanics into tutors to increase the quantity and quality of student work. If this is accomplished, then we predict that our automatic knowledge generation process can be achieved with greater efficiency because students are contributing more data per hour, and the automatic knowledge acquisition process is directly dependent on the quantity and quality of student data provided. Several researchers have explored the impact of games on digital tutors and many have determined that student engagement and motivation increases [7][9][22].

We also present techniques for *improving the quality* of generated domain models. To this end, we present a novel type of game that invites subject matter experts (SMEs) to correct and vet existing nodes and arcs in the expert knowledge base. We incorporated game mechanics from the nascent field of "games with a purpose" [12]. For example, the ESP Game [13] uses crowd sourcing to support developers' need to collect large amounts of labels for images to improve computer vision algorithms.

This paper provides background information, methods, and results for two experiments. We describe our core tutor and its features in Section 2 and describe the methods and results of an experiment to *reduce the time* needed to develop expert models in Section 3. Specifically we observed that an increase in student motivation led to more student work. Section 4 describes the game to *improve the quality of the expert knowledge base*, while Section 5 describes the results of having SMEs use this game. Section 6 closes with an analysis and discussion of future work.

2 Reducing Knowledge Acquisition Time

This section describes design decisions for game mechanics added in part to improve our tutor's ability to conduct automatic knowledge acquisition. We also examine the impact of these game features on the quantity of student work.

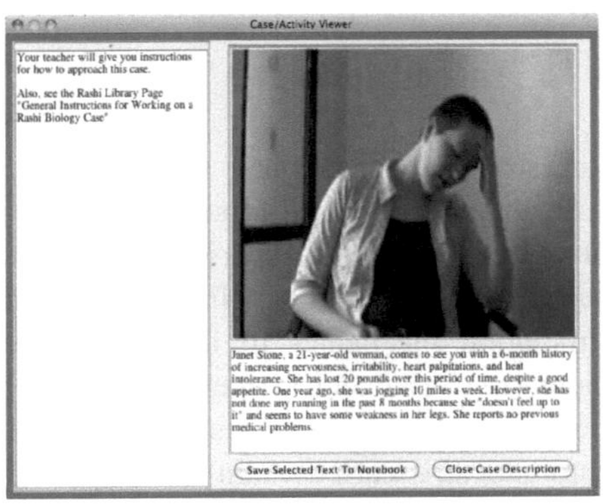

Fig. 1. Case Description. Students question the virtual patient by using the Interview Environment.

This research was conducted within Rashi, an intelligent inquiry tutor used by thousands of students over the past five years to learn human anatomy. In the *Human Biology Tutor,* students evaluate virtual patients and generate hypotheses about their medical condition. The tutor provides case descriptions for students to investigate, along with information about how to approach each problem [4]. Cases are presented as open-ended environments for student exploration and to acquaint students with methods commonly used by professionals in the domain. The basic Rashi tutor is domain independent, but this paper focuses primarily on the *Human Biology* domain.

The system contains two major components: a *procedural core* that supplies data collection mechanisms (e.g., interactive images, interview interfaces, video and dynamic maps) and a *content knowledge base* (e.g., an expert system) with knowledge about individual cases.

We created a methodology for constructing domain-level expert knowledge bases for Rashi automatically through crowdsourcing [6]. This approach involved collecting and analyzing the work of numerous students working within Rashi and using an intelligent algorithm to coalesce data from those student efforts to construct the domain model. We compared the knowledge created in a human crafted expert knowledge base (HEKB) with that resulting from our automated construction of the expert system to judge its quality and found that our algorithm does well and that the evolving expert knowledge base (EEKB) models can be generated in significantly less time [6]. However, we still need to optimize the quality of this generated model (we measured between 70 and 80 percent precision on average) and to further decrease the necessary build time (currently measured around 300 student work hours).

Game Mechanism to Reduce Knowledge Acquisition Time

We added game mechanics to Rashi to optimize the fantasy, urgency, and sense of reward [10]. We added a patient status panel, located within the main Rashi window that provides students with an easy way to monitor, in real time, the condition of the patient, see Figure 2. The patient status panel consists of three parts:

> ***Patient Character:*** *This animated character shows a visual representation of the patient, including a few emotions that are loosely correlated with his or her health.*
>
> ***Health Bar:*** *The health bar displays a quantifiable view of the patient's health. The bar is color coded to display healthy (green), sick (yellow), or critical (red) conditions. This health bar is dynamically updated depending on the patient's current condition and any currently applied treatment.*
>
> ***Treatment:*** *This panel displays a text representation of the condition for which proper treatment is currently being administered. Thus, once students set the treatment for the patient, they can observe both the treatment and its effects in unison.*

Students are also provided with a new *treatment button*. Upon pressing this button, the patient status panel is immediately updated to reflect that the patient is being treated for a condition. The treatment selected directly affects the "health" of the patient, reflected by the patient status panel. The effects of the treatment are revealed slowly, and the result of treatment is not monotonic. While students are waiting for the results of their treatment to become apparent, they are encouraged to explore other potential diagnoses.

These features are game mechanics primarily because they provide a concrete goal (making the patient well), incorporate urgency (fear the patient may be lost despite the fact that this is impossible in Rashi) and fantasy (the feeling of achieving victory when the patient is treated correctly) [10]. Previous Rashi versions asked students to construct arguments for diagnosis, but treatment or even formal diagnosis was not a part of the system. We posit that this sense of responsibility encourages students to be motivated differently than when these features are absent.

Methods and Results to Reduce Knowledge Acquisition Time

Our goal was to identify whether game mechanics led students to produce higher quantity and quality data in Rashi. To study this possibility, we selected two data sets that differed only in the presence of the game mechanics described above. The selected data sets were both from a large rural university class in Biology 101 in 2011 (no game features) and 2012 (game features) and were equivalent in virtually every other respect. Students were taught by the same teachers, used similar pedagogies, and evidenced a similar caliber of introductory biology knowledge. We first aimed to show that the 2012 class produced more Rashi data than did the 2011 class. We compared work produced by students in each class (Table 1). Student work includes generating hypotheses (e.g., "Patient has hypothyroidism") and relations between hypotheses and evidence (e.g., "Elevated TSH supports patient has hypothyroidism.").

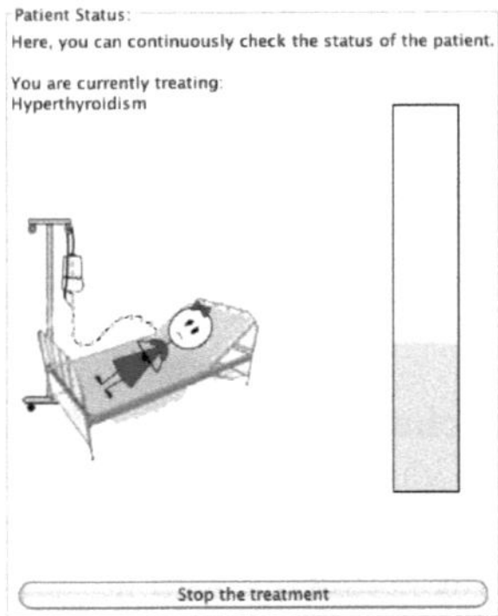

Fig. 2. A cartoon patient is presented to Rashi users along with a health bar

We see that students who used the game mechanics contributed more work per student than did the control group. Namely, we see a 59.5 percent increase in the raw amount of data contributed by students who used Rashi with additional game mechanics. Our previous work found that we needed 300 student work hours to create our EEKB, thus it appears that adding game mechanics to Rashi has the potential to decrease the number of student hours necessary to build our expert system automatically by up to 59 percent. This represents a vast improvement in efficiency.

Table 1. Amount of work contributed by students in similar university courses with and without game mechanics

Year	*Num Students*	*Num Data / Relations*	*Num Hypotheses*	*Total*	*Contributions / Student*
2011 (no game)	396	4342	2111	6453	**16.295**
2012 (game)	539	9328	4683	14011	**25.994**

Additionally, we wish to confirm that the quality of this additional work is not less than that of its counterpart. Therefore, we developed an estimated argument quality metric for judging the strength of student created arguments. Because Rashi teaches in ill-defined domains, we cannot strictly judge the quality of work, but can make strong estimations based on several factors. The formula for estimated work quality is:

$$\text{Grade} = [\text{Correct}(H) / |H|]*W_1 + [\text{Correct}(R) / |R|]*W_2 + [|R| / |H|]*W_3 + [|H|]*W_4$$

Where:

H = the set of student hypotheses

R = the set of student relations

Correct: a function that returns the number of items in the input set that match to the expert knowledge base.

W = A weight ($0<=W_i<=1$) for each term of the grade. $W_1+W_2+W_3+W_4 = 1.0$

We estimated the quality of each student's argument using the metric above. Figure 3 provides a summary of the difference between each group. We see that the student's provided with Rashi game mechanics actually contributed higher quality work, in addition to the increased quantity reported above.

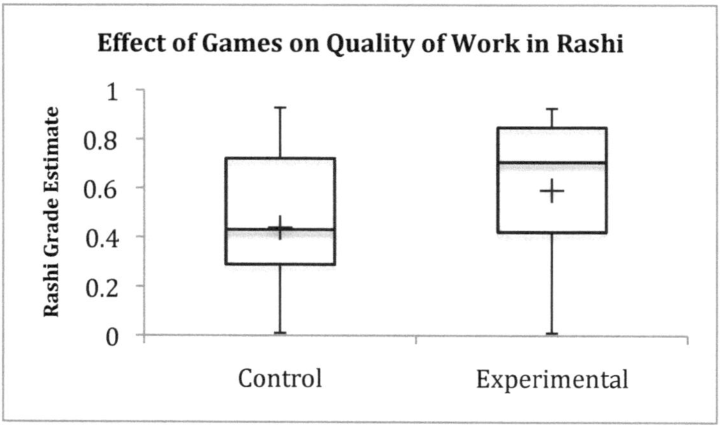

Fig. 3. Estimated student grades in Rashi across groups that contained and did not contain the new Rashi game mechanics *($p < 0.01$)

3 Improving Knowledge Acquisition Quality

Once an expert model is constructed automatically (as described in [6]), it is in our interest to examine its contents and modify the data in places where the knowledge base might have low confidence in the data. In this section, we present our design for a knowledge refinement game (KRG) we call "Dr. Doctor". We define a knowledge refinement game as any game that incorporates game mechanics and whose purpose is to alter the underlying structure of a data model.

The knowledge refinement game performs three major non-trivial tasks. First it analyzes the evolving knowledge base to identify areas of low confidence (improvement detection). Then, it represents expert system knowledge as questions (question generation). Thirdly, it updates the expert system with the knowledge provided in the SME's response (model update). Every EEKB entry (node or relation) has a confidence property with default value of 10% and this confidence rises linearly with every successive student who provides evidence of this entry.

The three step process is repeated for as long as the expert wishes to continue (Figure 4). SMEs are given a score and a level depending on the amount and quality of their contributions.

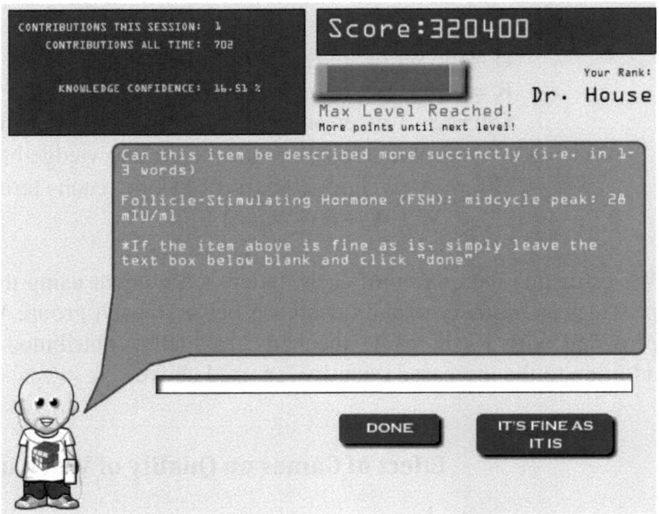

Fig. 4. Screenshot of 'Dr. Doctor', a Knowledge-Refinement Game that accepts input from players and improves the quality of the Rashi evolving knowledge base

The game creates varying types of questions in each phase as described below. The questions are completed for each phase before moving on to questions in the next phase because of dependent relationships that exist between question type and aspects of the knowledge that are not vetted beforehand.

> ***Phase 1. Verify Nodes:*** *Nodes in the expert knowledge base that have a relatively low confidence are retrieved so the SME can confirm whether or not they belong in the EEKB. An example questions of this form: "Is this hypothesis valid for this domain: <Patient is pregnant>?"*
>
> ***Phase 2. Verify Relationships:*** *Once the Nodes are verified, the same is done for the relationships between those nodes. The relationships are presented to the SME and the responses are reflected in updated confidence values. For example, "Reduced TSH" strongly supports "Patient has hypothyroidism"*
>
> ***Phase 3. Combine Similar Nodes:*** *The game uses string search techniques to estimate whether pairs of nodes reflect the same semantic data. The SMEs are presented with such pairs and asked if they are indeed the same topic or idea, and whether they should be combined in the EEKB.*

Dialogue between SME and Refinement Game

After asking the SME a particular question and receiving the response, the system dynamically adjusts the evolving knowledge base to reflect this information, on the assumption that an expert response is generally accurate. The game phrases its queries to require only yes / no responses, and so the system must only deal with the responses from this constrained interaction.

Table 2 summarizes the question types, responses, and reactions within the knowledge refinement game. We see that the expert responses directly impact the probabilistic confidence values of the EEKB data.

Table 2. A simplified summary of the Knowledge-Refinement Game's question types, potential expert answers, and responses made by the game

Phase	Question Type	SME Answer	Response of KRG System
1	Node Verify	*YES*	Increase node confidence
		NO	Decrease node confidence
2	Relation Clarify	*YES*	Increase relation confidence
		NO	Decrease relation confidence
3	Combine Nodes	*YES*	Combine nodes into single node
		NO	Don't ask about these nodes again

In the next section, we discuss the game elements woven into 'Dr. Doctor,' and argue that these game mechanics are essential in promoting accurate SME feedback.

Game Mechanics in the KRG

Dr. Doctor incorporates game mechanics in order to motivate SMEs to work longer and to make the experience more enjoyable [10]. In particular, these mechanics are designed to accomplish two goals: motivate SMEs to continue contributing for extended periods of time and offer incentives for SMEs to provide accurate information [12].

Feedback Statistics: *Dr. Doctor displays dynamically changing statistics regarding experts' contributions, Figure 3, top left. This includes the number of all time contributions these SMEs have made to the expert system, the confidence of the EEKB, and the percent increases for which these players are responsible.*

Points: *Players are awarded points for answering questions, Figure 3, top right. This provides rewards to SMEs for their contributions and motivates them to continue*

Levels: *SMEs progress through increasing levels as they garner points, e.g., undergraduate, graduate, professor, and players are given a higher status at each increasing level.*

Agreement Bonus: *Players are rewarded with a score bonus when their answers are in agreement with other SMEs.*

An anonymous agreement policy is implemented through the agreement bonus described above. This policy helps ensure quality input by forcing a first order optimal strategy of agreeing with fellow SMEs. Since other player's identities are anonymous, the optimal strategy then becomes to input truthful responses. In addition, the application does not update the knowledge base permanently unless multiple SMEs have agreed on the validity of a change.

Methods and Results to Increase Knowledge Acquisition Quality

To evaluate the knowledge refinement game, we posted the application on the web, making it accessible on demand. We then recruited three teaching assistants from the biology department of a large rural university who agreed to play the game at their leisure over the course of one week. We asked that participants contribute at least 100 responses within the game. Two of the participants were upper-level undergraduates, while the other was a graduate student. Additionally, in order to contextualize the game features of 'Dr. Doctor', we offered a prize (gift card) to the participant who achieved the highest score within the game.

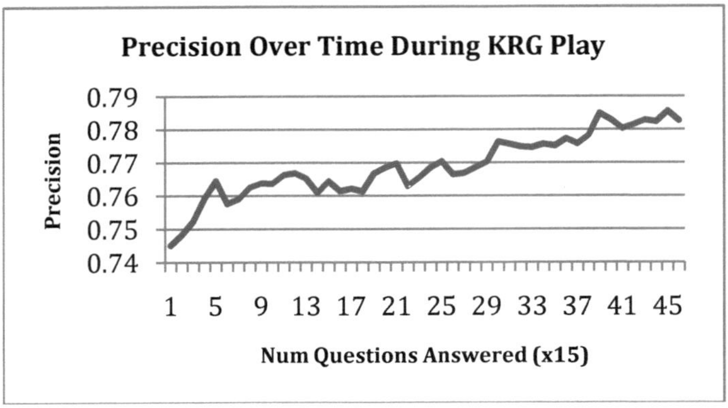

Fig. 5. Precision of the generated knowledge base over time as three SMEs play Dr. Doctor

After one week of the game being available, two of the three participants contributed more responses than asked for, answering 250 and 235 questions respectively. The third participant answered just above the minimum, logging 105 questions answered. We analyzed how the quality of the evolving expert knowledge base changed over time by saving the state of the knowledge after every 15 inputs. For every snapshot of the knowledge base, we judged quality using two metrics. The first was *precision*, which is calculated as the percentage of the generated knowledge that is in agreement with knowledge created by a human expert. More information on precision can be found in [6].

We found that as students played our game, the precision of the evolving knowledge rose. We observed a four percent increase in precision (Figure 5). We also measured knowledge *recall* or the breadth of knowledge acquired through our automated knowledge generation process, see [6] for more information. A display of the change in recall over time can be seen in Figure 6. We observed a nine percent increase in knowledge recall as our participants played Dr. Doctor.

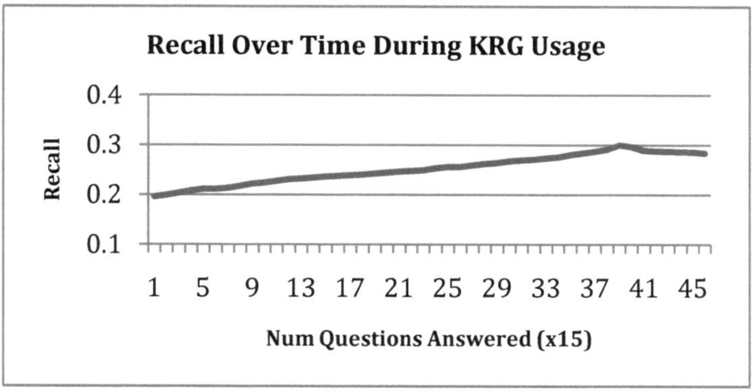

Fig. 6. Recall (breadth of knowledge acquired) over time as SMEs played Dr. Doctor

4 Conclusions and Future Work

In conclusion, this paper presented two experiments that highlight opportunities for applying games to benefit automatic knowledge acquisition within intelligent tutoring systems. We first presented game mechanics that led to higher quantities and quality of student input within an inquiry tutor. Because students contribute more data when presented with game mechanics, automatic knowledge acquisition [6] can be accomplished more efficiently.

Games can also be applied to help optimize the quality of automatically generated knowledge. We presented a novel game called a knowledge refinement game (KRG) that motivates SMEs to judge the quality of generated knowledge. Although the game was designed for SME players, we tested the game with upper class undergraduate and graduate students. We observe that a small amount of KRG game play leads to a four percent increase in the quality of the knowledge base, and a nine percent increase in the breadth of acquired knowledge. We also observe that two of our three participants contributed more than twice the amount of data requested.

Although we present our results on a single example tutor, we believe that these approaches can generalize to an array of tutors that utilize various expert models. It is easy to see that incorporating game approaches can be beneficial for a variety of tutors. In addition to this, knowledge refinement games can be applied to many models. In particular, the KRG requires three essential steps. First the game must be able to identify and locate areas in an expert model that require updating. Then the game must be able to construct a question from this identification, and lastly be able to update the model appropriately once an answer is provided. Any tutor / model that can accommodate these three stages is capable of benefitting from this approach.

Our future work in this area will focus on extending the process of automatic knowledge acquisition and refinement, both to domains outside of Human Biology as well as to additional iterations of the knowledge building process within Rashi. We hope to provide further evidence that large amounts of student data can be obtained automatically from students within tutors, and that knowledge can be efficiently refined and improved by players of knowledge refinement games. We also hope to provide evidence that knowledge refinement games can be effective when played by non-subject matter experts, in an attempt to widen their potential usage and application. Lastly, we wish to explore more deeply the necessity and benefit of game mechanics on the successful usage of the KRG. We believe that the game mechanics had a direct effect on the success of our experiment, but wish to confirm these beliefs experimentally.

Acknowledgements. This research was funded by an award from the National Science Foundation, NSF 0632769, IIS CSE, Effective Collaborative Role-playing Environments, (PI) Beverly Woolf, with Merle Bruno and Daniel Suthers. Any opinions, findings, conclusions or recommendations expressed in this material are those of the authors and do not necessarily reflect the views of the funding agencies.

References

1. Bader-Natal, A.: Incorporating Game Mechanics into a Network of Online Study Groups. In: Proceedings of the Workshop on Intelligent Educational Games 2009, Brighton, England (2009)
2. Dragon, T.: The Impact of Integrated Coaching and Collaboration within an Inquiry Learning Environment. Doctoral Dissertation. University of Massachusetts, Amherst (2013)
3. Dragon, T., Floryan, M., Woolf, B., Murray, T.: Recognizing Dialogue Content in Student Collaborative Conversation. In: Aleven, V., Kay, J., Mostow, J. (eds.) ITS 2010, Part II. LNCS, vol. 6095, pp. 113–122. Springer, Heidelberg (2010)
4. Dragon, T., Park Woolf, B., Marshall, D., Murray, T.: Coaching within a domain independent inquiry environment. In: Ikeda, M., Ashley, K.D., Chan, T.-W. (eds.) ITS 2006. LNCS, vol. 4053, pp. 144–153. Springer, Heidelberg (2006)
5. Floryan, M., Woolf, B.P.: Rashi Game: Towards an Effective Educational 3D Gaming Experience. In: Proceedings of the IEEE International Conference on Advanced Learning Technologies, Athens, GA (2011)
6. Floryan, M., Woolf, B.P.: Authoring Expert Knowledge Bases for Intelligent Tutors through Crowdsourcing. In: Chad Lane, H., Yacef, K., Mostow, J., Pavlik, P. (eds.) AIED 2013. LNCS (LNAI), vol. 7926, pp. 640–643. Springer, Heidelberg (2013)
7. Hallinen, N., Walker, E., Wylie, R., Ogan, A., Jones, C.: I Was Playing When I Learned: A Narrative Game for French Aspectual Distinctions. In: Proceedings of the Workshop on Intelligent Educational Games 2009, Brighton, England (2009)
8. Lynch, C., Ashley, K.D., Pinkwart, N., Aleven, V.: Concepts, Structures, and Goals: Redefining Ill-Definedness. International Journal of AI in Education; Special Issue on Ill-Defined Domains 19(3), 253–266 (2009); Aleven, V., Lynch, C. Pinkwart, N., Ashley, K. (eds.)
9. McAlinden, R., Gordon, A.S., Lane, H.C., Pynadath, D.: UrbanSim: A Game-based Simulation for Counterinsurgency and Stability-focused Operations. In: Proceedings of the Workshop on Intelligent Educational Games 2009, Brighton, England (2009)
10. Prensky, M.: Digital Game-Based Learning. McGraw-Hill (2001)
11. Rowe, J.P., Mott, B.W., McQuiggan, S.W., et al.: Crystal Island: A Narrative-Centered Learning Environment for Eighth Grade Microbiology. In: Proceedings of the Workshop on Intelligent Educational Games 2009, Brighton, England (2009)
12. Siorpaes, K., Hepp, M.: Games with a purpose for the semantic web. IEEE Intelligent Systems 23(3), 50–60 (2008)
13. Von Ahn, L., Dabbish, L.: Labeling Images with a Computer Game. In: Proc. ACM CHI (2004)

Expectations of Technology: A Factor to Consider in Game-Based Learning Environments

Erica L. Snow, G. Tanner Jackson, Laura K. Varner, and Danielle S. McNamara

Department of Psychology, Learning Sciences Institute, Arizona State University, Tempe, AZ, 85287
{Erica.L.Snow,TannerJackson,Laura.Varner,Dsmcnama}@asu.edu

Abstract. This study investigates how students' prior expectations of technology affect overall learning outcomes across two adaptive systems, one game-based (iSTART-ME) and one non-game based (iSTART-Regular). The current study (n=83) is part of a larger study (n=124) intended to teach reading comprehension strategies to high school students. Results revealed that students' prior expectations impacted learning outcomes, but only for students who had engaged in the game-based system. Students who reported positive expectations of computer helpfulness at pretest showed significantly higher learning outcomes in the game-based system compared to students who had low expectations of computer helpfulness. The authors discuss how the incorporation of game-based features in an adaptive system may negatively impact the learning outcomes of students with low technology expectations.

Keywords: Artificial Intelligence, student expectations, learning, motivation, educational technology, game-based features.

1 Introduction

The field of Artificial Intelligence in Education (AIED) promotes the design of so-phisticated learning environments that adapt to students' individual learning needs and abilities [1]. Recently, AIED developers have begun to investigate the relation between students' expectations, engagement, and learning outcomes within these educational learning environments [2-3]. These systems can vary widely in terms of complexity, user control, and interface features, each of which may affect outcomes differently based on students' prior perceptions. For example, incorporating game-based elements within a system has a positive impact on students' perception of a system [4]. Although previous work has shown that game-based features impact students' affect, relatively little work has investigated how these components interact with students' prior expectations to impact overall learning outcomes. To gain a deeper understanding of these relations, this study examines how the impact of students' prior expectations of technology on immediate and long-term learning outcomes depends on whether they engage with a game-based or non-game educational system.

K. Yacef et al. (Eds.): AIED 2013, LNAI 7926, pp. 359–368, 2013.

1.1 Perceptions and Expectations within Technology

We expect the influence of students' attitudes toward technology to be a crucial factor in developing a more complete understanding of user affect and engagement within educational systems [2], [5]. In line with this assumption, the Technology Acceptance Model (TAM) is a model that accounts for how students' attitudes toward technology potentially impact their behaviors within a system [3], [6]. The key notion underlining this model is that students' expectations of a system's usefulness and ease of use are good predictors of their acceptance of the system [6].

Researchers have also begun to investigate how perceptions of technology relate to student motivation and performance within Intelligent Tutoring Systems (ITSs) [5], [2]. For instance, Jackson et al. (2009) found that students' prior expectations of computers' helpfulness predicted their ratings of the ITS after training. Similarly, Corbett and Anderson (2001) found that students' posttest perception of their experience was significantly related to the amount of help (i.e., feedback) they received from an ITS during training. These few studies are in line with the TAM model, providing preliminary evidence that students' expectations and perceptions of technology impact the way in which they view and interact with an ITS. Additional work is clearly needed to better understand these relations and to further investigate how learning goals (e.g., reading strategies, math skills, writing strategies) are affected by system characteristics and students' prior expectations.

1.2 Game Features within Technology

One recent question regarding interactive learning environments has regarded the effects of games and game-based features [7- 8]. Integrating game-based features into a system is typically intended to improve students' engagement and interest while completing target tasks. For example, previous research has indicated that incorporating game-like elements can positively impact students' enjoyment, engagement, and motivation [4], [8]. Providing interactive elements within a system affords students a high locus of control over their individual learning paths as well as increases personal investment and identification with a system [4]. Similarly, research has shown that the inclusion of game-based elements is positively related to increases in student engagement [8]. Leveraging these and similar results, researchers have developed game-based learning environments that incorporate game-based elements into ITSs. This study utilizes two different learning environments (game vs. non-game) to examine how the interaction between system features and prior expectations impacts students' learning outcomes.

1.3 iSTART

The Interactive Strategy Training for Active Reading and Thinking (iSTART) tutor is a traditional ITS designed to enhance students' reading comprehension skills. iSTART focuses on improving students' content comprehension through the use of reading comprehension strategies, including self-explanation [9]. Students who use self-explanation strategies are more successful at problem solving, generating inferences and developing a deeper overall understanding of the meaning of the text [10].

The iSTART system includes three modules: introduction, demonstration, and practice. During the introduction module, three animated agents (a teacher and two students) discuss the concept of self-explanation and how it can be combined with the additional iSTART reading strategies: comprehension monitoring, predicting, paraphrasing, elaborating, and bridging. After the agents discuss each reading strategy, students are given short quizzes intended to formatively assess their understanding of the previously discussed strategies. In the demonstration module, students watch as two animated agents (one teacher and one student) apply various strategies to science texts. Students are then asked to specify which strategy was used in each example. Finally, in the practice module students are given two science texts and asked to apply self-explanation and comprehension strategies to target sentences. A teacher agent then provides each student with formative feedback designed to improve the quality of the self-explanations.

iSTART also contains an extended practice module, called Coached Practice, that begins immediately after students complete the first three phases (see Figure 1 for screenshot). This module functions in the same manner as the first two practice texts (i.e., students generate self-explanations and receive formative feedback). iSTART's extended practice phase is designed to provide a prolonged interaction across weeks or months and allows students to develop mastery by applying the iSTART strategies across a range of texts.

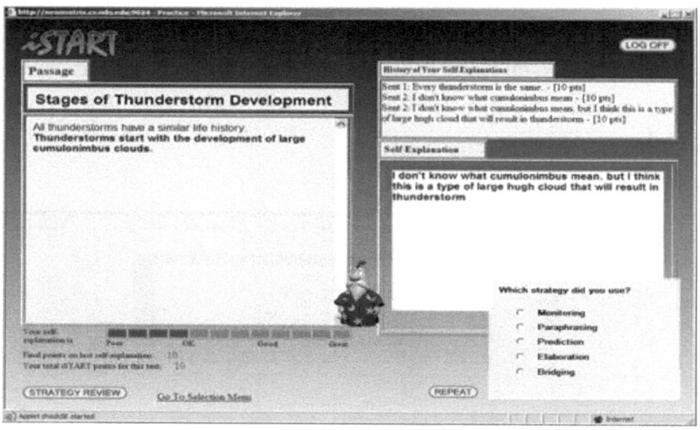

Fig. 1. Screen shot of the Coached Practice Module

The iSTART system provides feedback about strategy usage through an algorithm that assesses the quality of students' generated self-explanations. This feedback algorithm assesses students' self-explanations utilizing a combination of word-based measures and latent semantic analysis (LSA), [11]. The scores range from 0 to 3, describing a range of explanation quality from very poor (e.g., irrelevant, too short) to very good (i.e., incorporating information about the text or prior knowledge at a global level).

1.4 iSTART-ME

Studies with iSTART have demonstrated significant improvements for students' reading comprehension across time [12]. However, the repetitive nature of the extended practice module can occasionally result in student disengagement [13]. iSTART-ME (Motivationally Enhanced) was designed to address this problem by incorporating game-based elements into the original extended practice module [12]. The design and elements incorporated into iSTART-ME were based on previous research indicating a positive relation between specific mechanisms and their effects on motivation, engagement, and learning [14].

Both of the iSTART systems (iSTART-ME and iSTART-Regular) provide identical training through the first three modules: introduction, demonstration, and practice. The difference between the two systems occurs in the extended practice module, where iSTART-ME introduces game-based elements. Within iSTART-ME, the ex-tended practice module is controlled through an interactive selection menu where students can choose to self-explain new texts, personalize features within the interface, or play mini-games (see Figure 2). In addition, this menu allows students to view their advancement in the system through personal progress screens. These screens update students on their achievement level, number of points, and trophies earned within the system.

Students earn points in the system by interacting with three different types of generative practice: Coached Practice, Showdown, and Map Conquest. Coached Practice is a non-game-based method of practice, and is the same environment used within iSTART-Regular extended practice. In addition, Showdown and Map Conquest incorporate the same self-explanation assessment algorithm within two different game environments. As students engage with these generative practice environments, they accumulate more points within the system and subsequently progress to higher achievement levels.

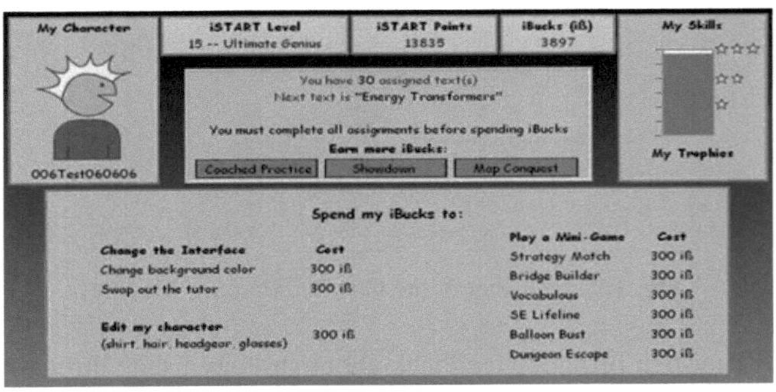

Fig. 2. Screen Shot of iSTART-ME Menu

Students' earned points also serve as currency (iBucks), which they can use to purchase incentives within the system. Students have four options on how to spend their earned iBucks. The first three options allow the user to personalize their experience by customizing an avatar, selecting a new tutor agent, or applying new color themes to the overall interface. All three of these options provide students with control over the environment through a variety of choices.

The fourth option for spending iBucks allows students to select and play one of six mini-games. Each mini-game allows students to engage in play while still practicing reading comprehension strategies from the system. After students complete each mini-game, they are given a score based on their performance and, if applicable, a trophy. Students can accumulate trophies throughout their time in the system and view them at any time through their personal progress screens on the main interface menu. The iSTART-ME system has been found to increase students' motivation and engagement over time, while remaining equally as effective at training students to use self-explanation strategies as the original iSTART system [15].

2 Methods

Participants in this study included 83 high-school students from a mid-south urban environment. The sample included in the current work is a subset of 124 students who participated in a larger study that compared learning outcomes across three conditions: iSTART-ME, iSTART-Regular, and no-tutoring control. This study solely focuses on the students who were randomly assigned to the game (iSTART-ME) and non-game (iSTART-Regular) conditions.

The current study consisted of 11-sessions in which all students completed a pre-test, 8 training sessions, a posttest, and a delayed retention test. During the first session, students completed pretest measures that assessed individual differences in motivation, attitudes toward technology, prior self-explanation ability, and prior reading comprehension ability.

During the following 8 sessions, students completed the initial strategy training (~2 hours) and then spent the remainder of their time interacting with the extended practice module in either iSTART-Regular or iSTART-ME. In contrast to previous work [5], [16], all students were exposed to similar types of feedback as they progressed through the systems, with iSTART-ME providing a small amount of additional modeling and implicit feedback through examples and rewards. Session 10 included a posttest that incorporated measures similar to the pretest. The eleventh session occurred 1 week after the posttest. In this session, students completed a retention test that contained measures similar to the pretest and posttest (i.e., self-explanation ability and attitudinal measures).

At pretest, students provided ratings on their expectations of and attitudes towards technology. To assess prior expectations of technology, each student indicated the relative importance of the following statement, "I expect computer systems to be helpful," for related work see [2]. This rating was on a scale from 1 (strongly disagree) to 6 (strongly agree), and is the only pretest measure of students' expectations of computer helpfulness. Students' reading comprehension ability was assessed using the Gates-MacGinitie Reading Test [17]. Self-explanations were scored using the automated iSTART assessment algorithm.

3 Results

This study investigates how students' prior expectations of technology relate to learning outcomes from two learning environments. We first examined how individual differences influenced performance within these two systems (game and non-game) by examining the relation between students' pretest rating of prior expectations and pretest, posttest, and retention measures of learning outcomes (self-explanation quality). Analyses indicated no relation between expectations and students' self-explanation quality at pretest or posttest (see Table 1). However, these correlations revealed that students' prior expectations of system helpfulness had a significant positive relation with their self-explanation quality on the retention test.

Table 1. Correlations between Prior Expectations and Learning Outcomes across Conditions

Dependent Measure	Prior Expectations of Helpfulness
Pretest Self-Explanation Scores	.181
Posttest Self-Explanation Scores	.078
Retention Self-Explanation Scores	.247*
*$p < .05$; ** $p < .01$	

The positive relation between prior expectations and retention self-explanation scores suggests that students' expectations may impact long-term learning outcomes. Additionally, we were interested in assessing how these long-term impacts may vary as a function of condition. A second set of correlations examined the relation of prior expectations and learning outcomes in the two conditions separately (see Table 2). These results indicated that students assigned to the non-game condition (iSTART-Regular) did not demonstrate a significant relation between prior expectations and learning outcomes. However, students in the game condition (iSTART-ME) showed a significant positive correlation between their prior expectations of helpfulness and their retention self-explanation scores. These findings suggest that the long-term effects may be due to the characteristics of a system (e.g. interface and game features), rather than the content and domain being covered (i.e., both systems covered the same content and used the same assessment algorithm).

Table 2. Correlations between Prior Expectations and Learning Outcomes

Non-Game (iSTART-Regular)	**Prior Expectations of Helpfulness**
Posttest Self-Explanation Scores	- .127
Retention Self-Explanation Scores	- .062
Game (iSTART-ME)	
Posttest Self-Explanation Scores	.274
Retention Self-Explanation Scores	.473 **
*$p < .05$; ** $p < .01$,	

Table 2 shows a significant positive relation between students' prior expectations and retention outcomes for students in the game condition. Further examining this relation, a hierarchical linear regression found that for students in the game condition, prior expectations was a significant predictor of retention outcomes, over and above pretest self-explanation scores, $F(1,38) = 10.67$, $p < .05$, $R^2=.37$. Specifically, after controlling for pretest self-explanation scores ($\beta = .381$, $p < .05$), students' prior expectations ($\beta=.394$, $p<.05$, $R^2=.15$) significantly predicted retention self-explanation outcomes.

To investigate the potential impact of individual differences on learning outcomes across systems, two separate 2 x 2 mixed-factor ANOVAs compared the self-explanation performance at posttest and retention for the two expectation groups (low vs. high, using a median split on prior expectations) as a function of condition (game vs. non-game). These statistical analyses revealed no significant interactions between expectation group and condition for posttest self-explanation scores, $F(3,79)=1.04$, $p=.376$, but a marginally significant interaction between expectation group and condition for retention self-explanation scores, $F(3,79)=2.632$, $p=.056$.

Follow-up analyses were conducted to examine the potential effects within each condition. A one-way ANOVA on the posttest outcomes within the game condition demonstrated that students with low expectations performed marginally worse on posttest self-explanation than students with high expectations, $F(1,38)=3.19$, $p=.08$ (see Figure 3). Additionally, on the retention outcomes, students with low expecta-tions generated significantly worse self-explanations than students with high expecta-tions, $F(1,38)= 6.579$, $p<.05$ (see Figure 4). A similar ANOVA on the non-game con-dition found that there were no significant differences between the low and high ex-pectations groups for posttest self-explanation scores, $F(1,38)=.040$, $p=.85$ (see Figure 3) or retention self-explanation scores, $F(1,41)=.003$, $p=.95$ (see Figure 4).

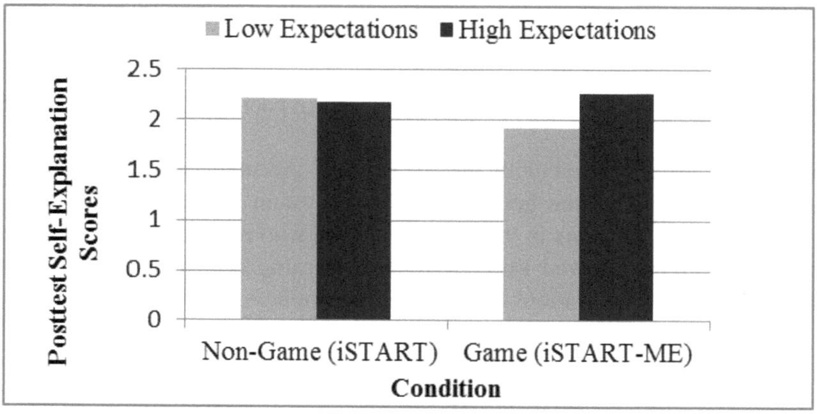

Fig. 3. Mean Posttest Self-Explanation Scores per Condition

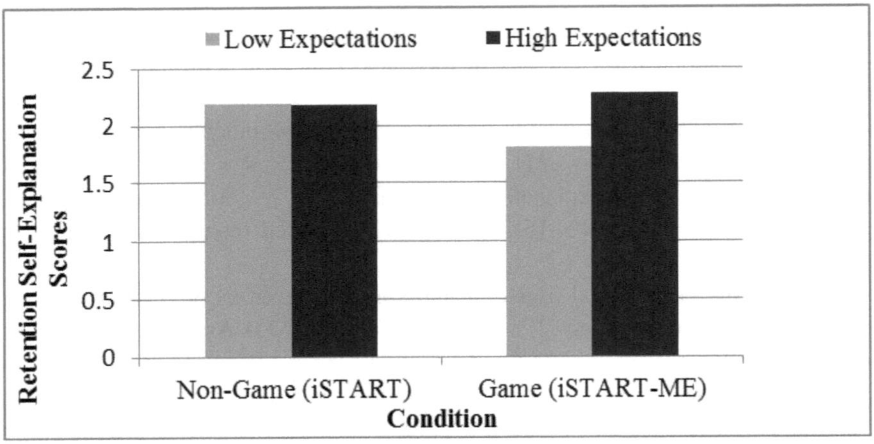

Fig. 4. Mean Retention Self-Explanation Scores per Condition

The null results for the non-game condition indicated that students' prior expectations did not impact overall learning outcomes. In contrast, results for the game condition indicated that students with low expectations of technology performed significantly worse at retention compared to students with high expectations of technology. These findings indicate that the influence of students' expectations on long-term learning outcomes may vary as a function of system characteristics

4 Conclusions and Implications

The current study investigated how system characteristics influence the impact of students' prior expectations on immediate and long-term learning outcomes. The results presented here indicate that overall skill retention is significantly affected by an interaction between students' prior expectations and characteristics of a system. These findings build upon two different bodies of work; the importance of students' perceptions and expectations [2], [3], [6] and the impact of game-based features in ITSs [7-8].

Our results are congruent with the Technology Acceptance Model; specifically, students' expectations of the helpfulness of the system impacted their interactions with the system [6]. Students in the game condition who reported low expectations of computer helpfulness showed lower long-term learning outcomes compared to students who had high expectations of computer helpfulness. However, this relation did not emerge within the non-game condition. Students with low expectations may have disliked the added level of complexity that accompanies the incorporation of game elements, while students with higher prior expectations may have viewed the added game-based features as helpful toward achieving the learning objectives.

In the current study, the primary difference between conditions was that one was a game-based ITS (iSTART-ME) and the other was a non-game-based ITS (iSTART-Regular). Although the non-game system does incorporate some game features (e.g., points and a qualitative feedback bar), these features are fixed and no other options are offered to the student. In contrast, the game-based system offers many features. iSTART-ME expands upon the features in iSTART-Regular by allowing users to choose to interact with multiple practice environments, mini-games, personalized characters, changeable pedagogical agents, and editable background themes.

It is important to note that iSTART-Regular does include some game-based fea-tures, which indicates that incorporating one or two game features is not sufficient to contribute to the overall effect on learning outcomes. Instead, the current study may suggest that the variety of game-based features within iSTART-ME required students to interact more within the system; therefore, their prior expectations may have played a bigger role in overall learning outcomes. However, future work is needed to investigate how specific features (e.g., variety, choice, and control) may be influencing the impact that students' prior expectations have on their learning outcomes. Additionally, studies are planned that will examine the efficacy of these systems within ecological settings.

The current findings demonstrate that students' prior expectations can impact learning and that these effects may be more likely when users are engaged in systems with game-based elements. These results are especially important for AIED developers who are implementing game-based features into systems. These elements are intended to engage students' interest in the learning environment. However, individual differences in prior expectations of technology may impact the effectiveness of the features.

Acknowledgments. This research was supported in part by the Institute for Educational Sciences (IES R305G020018-02; R305G040046, R305A080589) and National Science Foundation (NSF REC0241144; IIS-0735682). Any opinions, findings, and conclusions or recommendations expressed in this material are those of the authors and do not necessarily reflect the views of the IES or NSF.

References

1. Murray, T.: Authoring Intelligent Tutoring Systems: An Analysis of the State of the Art. International Journal of Artificial Intelligence in Education (IJAIED) 10, 98–129 (1999)
2. Jackson, G., Graesser, A., McNamara, D.: What Students Expect have More Impact than what They Know or Feel. In: Proceedings of the 14th Annual Meeting of Artificial Intelligence in Education, AIED, Brighton, UK, pp. 73–80 (May 2009)
3. Saadé, R., Bahli, B.: The Impact of Cognitive Absorption on Perceived Usefulness and Perceived Ease of Use in On-Line Learning: An Extension of the Technology Acceptance Model. Information and Management 42, 317–327 (2005)
4. Cordova, D., Lepper, M.: Intrinsic Motivation and the Process of Learning: Beneficial Effects of Contextualization, Personalization, and Choice. Journal of Educational Psychology 88, 715–730 (1996)
5. Corbett, A., Anderson, J.: Locus of Feedback Control in Computer-Based Tutoring: Impact on Learning Rate, Achievement and Attitudes. In: Proceedings of the Conference on Human Factors in Computing Systems, ACM CHI 2001, Seattle, WA, pp. 245–252 (2001)

6. Davis, D., Bagozzi, P., Warshaw, R.: User Acceptance of Computer Technology: A Comparison of Two Theoretical Models. Management Science 35, 982–1003 (1989)
7. Rai, D., Beck, J.: Math Learning Environment with Game-Like Elements: An Experimental Framework. International Journal of Game Based Learning 2, 90–110 (2012)
8. Rowe, J.P., Shores, L.R., Mott, B.W., Lester, J.C.: Integrating Learning and Engagement in Narrative-Centered Learning Environments. In: Aleven, V., Kay, J., Mostow, J. (eds.) ITS 2010, Part II. LNCS, vol. 6095, pp. 166–177. Springer, Heidelberg (2010)
9. McNamara, D., Levenstein, I., Boonthum, C.: iSTART: Interactive Strategy Trainer for Active Reading and Thinking. Behavioral Research Methods, Instruments, and Computers 36, 222–233 (2004)
10. Chi, M., Bassok, M., Lewis, M., Reimann, P., Glaser, R.: Self-explanations: How Students Study and Use Examples in Learning to Solve Problems. Cognitive Science 13, 145–182 (1989)
11. Landauer, T., McNamara, D., Dennis, S., Kintsch, W.: Handbook of Latent Semantic Analysis. Lawrence Erlbaum Associates Publishers (2007)
12. Jackson, G., Boonthum, C., McNamara, D.: iSTART-ME: Situating extended learning within a game-based environment. In: Proceedings of the Workshop on Intelligent Educational Games at the 14th Annual Conference on Artificial Intelligence in Education, AIED, Brighton, UK, pp. 59–68 (2009)
13. Bell, C., McNamara, D.: Integrating iSTART into a High School Curriculum. In: Proceedings of the 29th Annual Meeting of the Cognitive Science Society, pp. 809–814. Cognitive Science Society, Austin (2007)
14. McNamara, D., Jackson, G., Graesser, A.: Intelligent Tutoring and Games (iTaG). In: Proceedings of the Workshop on Intelligent Educational Games at the 14th Annual Conference on Artificial Intelligence in Education, AIED, Brighton, UK, pp. 1–10 (2009)
15. Jackson, G., McNamara, D.: Motivation and Performance in a Game-based Inteligent Tutoring System. Journal of Educational Psychology (in press)
16. Easterday, M.W., Aleven, V., Scheines, R., Carver, S.M.: Using Tutors to Improve Educational Games. In: Biswas, G., Bull, S., Kay, J., Mitrovic, A. (eds.) AIED 2011. LNCS, vol. 6738, pp. 63–71. Springer, Heidelberg (2011)
17. MacGinitie, W., MacGinitie, R.: Gates MacGinitie reading tests. Riverside, Chicago (1989)

Personalizing Embedded Assessment Sequences in Narrative-Centered Learning Environments: A Collaborative Filtering Approach

Wookhee Min, Jonathan P. Rowe, Bradford W. Mott, and James C. Lester

Department of Computer Science, North Carolina State University, Raleigh, NC 27695
{wmin,jprowe,bwmott,lester}@ncsu.edu

Abstract. A key challenge posed by narrative-centered learning environments is dynamically tailoring story events to individual students. This paper investigates techniques for sequencing story-centric embedded assessments—a particular type of story event that simultaneously evaluates a student's knowledge and advances an interactive narrative's plot—in narrative-centered learning environments. We present an approach for personalizing embedded assessment sequences that is based on collaborative filtering. We examine personalized event sequencing in an edition of the CRYSTAL ISLAND narrative-centered learning environment for literacy education. Using data from a multi-week classroom study with 850 students, we compare two model-based collaborative filtering methods, including probabilistic principal component analysis (PPCA) and non-negative matrix factorization (NMF), to a memory-based baseline model, *k*-nearest neighbor. Results suggest that PPCA provides the most accurate predictions on average, but NMF provides a better balance between accuracy and run-time efficiency for predicting student performance on story-centric embedded assessment sequences.

Keywords: Narrative-Centered Learning Environments, Embedded Assessment, Collaborative Filtering.

1 Introduction

Over the past several years there has been growing interest in narrative-centered learning environments, a class of game-based learning environments that contextualize learning and problem solving within interactive story scenarios. A key benefit of narrative-centered learning environments is their capacity to discreetly support students' learning processes by tightly integrating instructional and narrative elements. By leveraging the motivational characteristics of narrative and games, along with the adaptive pedagogy of intelligent tutoring systems, narrative-centered learning environments create educational experiences that are situated in meaningful contexts, found to be highly engaging, and dynamically personalized to individual students. Narrative-centered learning environments are under investigation in a range of domains, such as language learning [1], anti-bullying education [2], intercultural negotiation training [3], middle school science [4], and network security [5].

K. Yacef et al. (Eds.): AIED 2013, LNAI 7926, pp. 369–378, 2013.

A key challenge posed by narrative-centered learning environments is how to dynamically tailor story events to individual students [5–7]. Events in narrative-centered learning environments fulfill dual roles: they advance emerging plots in which students are active participants, and they serve pedagogical purposes such as providing feedback or assessments. In order to satisfy these dual roles, events take many forms. For example, a student found to have a misconception may be prompted to complete a quest that will help remediate his knowledge, or a student may find a virtual book accompanied by half-completed notes to be filled out, a form of embedded assessment. Because students often have considerable autonomy in narrative-centered learning environments, students may trigger events in many possible orders, including sequences that are sub-optimal for learning or engagement. In order to cope with this uncertainty, narrative-centered learning environments must be capable of dynamically personalizing event sequences to preserve the environment's ability to satisfy instructional and narrative objectives.

This paper investigates a method for personalizing event sequences in narrative-centered learning environments based on collaborative filtering. Frequently used in recommender systems, collaborative filtering techniques make predictions about individuals' actions based on the actions of others who behave similarly. We focus on personalizing a particular class of story events, story-centric embedded assessments, in the CRYSTAL ISLAND narrative-centered learning environment. CRYSTAL ISLAND features a mystery scenario about a spreading outbreak, and it has recently been extended to incorporate a curricular focus of middle-grade literacy education. Story-centric embedded assessments in CRYSTAL ISLAND evaluate students' reading comprehension skills, with a focus on complex informational texts and concept matrices, while simultaneously providing clues for solving the mystery. We examine several collaborative filtering algorithms for personalizing embedded assessment sequences. We compare two model-based collaborative filtering algorithms, probabilistic principal component analysis (PPCA) and non-negative matrix factorization (NMF), to a memory-based baseline model, *k*-nearest neighbor (kNN). Results suggest that PPCA provides the most accurate predictions on average, but NMF provides a better balance between accuracy and run-time efficiency.

2 Related Work

Narrative-centered learning environments couple salient features of stories (rich settings, believable characters, and compelling plots) and digital game environments (interactivity, rewards, and feedback) in order to increase student motivation, support meaning making, and guide complex problem solving. Interactions with narrative-centered learning environments can take several forms. Students may directly influence a narrative by completing actions in order to solve a problem [4, 5, 8], or they may indirectly influence events by providing guidance to autonomous virtual characters [2]. Multi-user virtual environments such as River City [4] use rich narrative settings to contextualize inquiry-based science learning scenarios with social and collaborative elements. Other work has utilized interactive narrative generation and agent behavior planning to create adaptive narrative experiences [1– 2].

Narrative-centered learning environments have begun to directly incorporate intelligent tutoring facilities, which provide support for coaching, feedback, and reflection that is tailored to individual students [1, 3, 5, 6, 7]. Many of these systems formalize models for personalizing story event sequences in terms of rule-based techniques, STRIPS-style planning algorithms, or probabilistic graphical models. In many cases, past approaches have involved hand-authoring problem domains [4–6], a process that can be labor-intensive, or supervised machine learning techniques that require training data collected in laboratory settings, such as Wizard of Oz experiments [7]. Our work is the first to use collaborative filtering for tailoring story-centric embedded assessments in narrative-centered learning environments, and the models are induced directly from student interaction data collected in classroom settings. Our approach is inspired by recent work on collaborative filtering-based drama management by Yu and Riedl [9].

Fig. 1. CRYSTAL ISLAND narrative-centered learning environment

3 CRYSTAL ISLAND

Over the past several years, our lab has been developing CRYSTAL ISLAND (Figure 1), a narrative-centered learning environment for middle school microbiology [8]. Designed as a supplement to classroom science instruction, CRYSTAL ISLAND's curricular focus has been expanded to include literacy education based on Common Core State Standards for reading informational texts. The narrative focuses on a mysterious illness afflicting a research team on a remote island. Students play the role of a visitor who is drawn into a mission to save the team from the outbreak. Students explore the research camp from a first-person viewpoint, gather information about patient symptoms and relevant diseases, form hypotheses about the infection and transmission source, use virtual lab equipment and a diagnosis worksheet to record their findings, and report their conclusions to the camp's nurse.

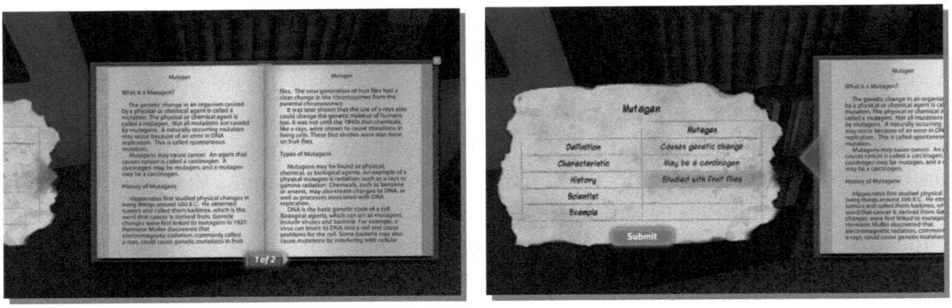

Fig. 2. (Left) An informational text stylistically formatted like a virtual book, and (Right) a concept matrix stylistically formatted as a scrap of note paper

As part of CRYSTAL ISLAND's curricular focus on literacy, students encounter books and articles throughout the camp that contain complex informational texts about microbiology concepts (Figure 2, left). Students read and analyze these texts, as well as complete associated concept matrices, to acquire knowledge necessary to diagnose the illness. Concept matrices (Figure 2, right) are framed within the narrative as partially completed notes written by one of the research team's scientists. Students learn that the scientist has fallen ill, and they must now "complete" the notes based on content in the informational texts. The concept matrices are story-centric embedded assessments that evaluate students' reading comprehension skills by requiring students to recognize and make connections among key ideas from the informational texts. Completing a concept matrix involves making several selections to populate blank cells based on the adjacent informational text.

Within the CRYSTAL ISLAND narrative environment, virtual books and articles have fixed physical positions. Because narrative-centered learning environments such as CRYSTAL ISLAND support many possible problem-solving paths, students encounter objects in many different orders. If the content of each book and article is static, students may encounter embedded assessments in orders that are sub-optimal for learning or solving the mystery. Instead, when a student opens a book or research article in the virtual environment, the informational text content should be dynamically selected and personalized to the student in terms of subject and difficulty level. In order to meet this objective, we have designed CRYSTAL ISLAND to draw on a pool of 27 informational texts and concept matrices that can be arbitrarily assigned as the contents of books and articles during run-time. The method that we use to personalize embedded assessment sequences is collaborative filtering.

4 Collaborative Filtering for Sequencing Embedded Assessments

Popularized by their use in recommender systems, collaborative filtering (CF) algorithms are used to predict user preferences about unseen items using ratings from similar users. The underlying assumption of CF is that if multiple users have similar past interests, they will also have similar preferences for items they have not yet encountered [10–11]. We investigate two model-based CF methods for personalizing story-centric embedded assessment sequences in the CRYSTAL ISLAND narrative-centered learning environment. The first is model-based techniques, which are particularly useful in domains with data sparsity, an inherent issue in sequencing story-centric embedded assessments. Similar to prefix-based collaborative filtering [9], our work focuses on recommending entire sequences of embedded assessments, rather than recommendations of individual assessments. Because the number of possible assessment sequences grows exponentially with sequence length, students will never experience the vast majority of assessment sequences, even in cases of large training data sets. In order to evaluate model-based CF techniques' ability to cope with the resulting data sparsity, we examine two dimension-reduction methods for personalizing story-centric embedded assessments: non-negative matrix factorization (NMF) and probabilistic principal component analysis (PPCA). In conjunction with each of NMF and PPCA, we employ expectation maximization (EM); through its iterative maximum likelihood estimation process, EM replaces missing values in the data set along with NMF and PPCA [12].

4.1 Non-negative Matrix Factorization

NMF is a decomposition technique for an observed matrix R populated by multivariate data. NMF involves finding two matrix factors, typically with reduced dimensionality relative to R, that approximate R by their multiplication [13].

$$R \approx W \times H . \quad (1)$$

The NMF algorithm is represented by Equation 1, where R is an $n \times m$ matrix denoting the observed input data, n is the number of different assessment sequences, and m is the number of observed users. The $n \times r$ matrix W is a basis model, which is calculated through the NMF algorithm, and the $r \times m$ matrix H is a coefficient matrix based on the basis model W.

NMF requires that two constraints be met by the input data matrix: (1) all values in R, W, and H are non-negative, and (2) r is smaller than either m or n. Because W is typically smaller in size than R due to the second constraint, a key aspect of the NMF algorithm lies in how W encodes the hidden structure in the matrix R. This is performed through an iterative process seeking the maximum likelihood estimate of the model's parameters [13–14].

4.2 Probabilistic Principal Component Analysis

The PPCA algorithm is a probabilistic extension of traditional principal component analysis, which finds the principal axes of a set of observed data vectors through iterative maximum likelihood estimation by the EM algorithm [15–16].

$$t = Wx + \mu + \varepsilon . \quad (2)$$

The PPCA technique is represented by Equation 2, where t denotes a d-dimensional observation vector; in our case, this is comprised of a single student's in-game assessment scores (Equation 3). The $d \times q$ matrix W contains principal components in its columns, x refers to a q-dimensional latent variable that is related to the observed data t by W, μ is a non-zero mean value, and ε is a Gaussian noise parameter. Because ε is normally distributed (i.e., it follows $N(0,\sigma^2 I)$), the distribution of the observation vector t given the latent variable x can be represented as $t|x \sim N(Wx + \mu, \sigma^2 I)$. Since the marginal distribution over the latent variable x follows a Gaussian distribution, the marginal distribution over t is also Gaussian [15].

$$Assessment\ Score = \frac{Number\ of\ assessments\ solved\ correctly\ so\ far}{Number\ of\ assessments\ attempted\ so\ far} * 100.0. \quad (3)$$

5 Empirical Evaluation

To evaluate the collaborative filtering approach for tailoring story-centric embedded assessment sequences, we analyzed student interaction data from a teacher-led deployment of CRYSTAL ISLAND in two rural school districts. Students used CRYSTAL ISLAND over several weeks in their Language Arts classrooms. CRYSTAL ISLAND was an instructional anchor in a curricular unit on reading comprehension, which included supplementary learning activities. Prior to beginning the unit, and immediately following the unit, students completed web-based pre- and post-study assessments to measure their reading comprehension skills. Each assessment was comprised of three distinct pairs of informational texts and concept matrices; they mirrored the embedded assessments in CRYSTAL ISLAND, but covered different microbiology topics and did not include the stylistic appearance of assessments in the narrative environment.

The data set for our analysis included interaction logs and pre/post measures for 850 students. There were 436 males and 414 females. On average, students played CRYSTAL ISLAND for approximately 92 minutes over several class periods, they attempted 9.9 embedded assessments, they correctly filled out 7.2 concept matrices, and they failed to complete 1.7 concept matrices (i.e., after three incorrect attempts, the student was given the correct answers and prompted to move on).

Prior to investigating collaborative filtering techniques for personalizing story-centric embedded assessment sequences, we investigated whether students achieved significant improvements in their reading comprehension skills as a result of the CRYSTAL ISLAND unit. Matched pairs t-tests comparing pre-study (M=0.60, SD=0.26) to post-study (M=0.74, SD=0.28) assessment scores indicated that students' learning gains were statistically significant, $t(863) = 16.21$, $p < .01$. Next, we investigated whether students' use of CRYSTAL ISLAND impacted their gains in reading comprehension skills. Table 1 presents findings from a multiple regression analysis, which treated pre-study assessment score and average in-game assessment score as predictor variables, and post-study assessment score as a dependent variable. The regression model explained a significant proportion of the variance in post-study assessment scores, *Adj.* $R^2 = .332$. Results indicate that students' in-game assessment performances predict their improvements across pre- and post-study assessments.

These findings provide the foundation for investigating personalized sequencing of embedded assessments in CRYSTAL ISLAND. Our examination of collaborative filtering consists of three stages. First, we transformed the interaction log data into a format suitable for collaborative filtering analysis. This involves extracting raw

Table 1. Multiple Regression Analysis Predicting Post-Study Assessment Scores

Dependent Variables	Independent Variables	*B*	*SE(B)*	*β*	*t*	*p*
Post-Study Assessment	Pre-Study Assessment	.511	.033	.476	15.620	< .001
	In-Game Assessment Score	.003	.000	.191	6.289	< .001

interaction logs from a MySQL database, filtering observations of students' in-game assessment performances, and constructing an assessment sequence matrix. The assessment sequence matrix, R, is comprised of n rows, one for each distinct sequence of embedded assessments, and m columns, one for each student. Each value in R is a student's in-game assessment score. Assessment scores range from 0 to 100. Any sequence not encountered by a student corresponds to a missing value in the matrix R.

Second, we reduced the sequencing task's dimensionality. The task's dimensionality grows exponentially with sequence length. Consequently, we reduced the number of considered sequences by focusing on a subset of the 27 informational texts in CRYSTAL ISLAND. We employed a Chi-square selection algorithm to choose five informational text/concept matrix pairs that were significantly correlated with solving the mystery. The five pairs consisted of the following topics: *Investigating an Illness*, *Salmonellosis*, *Microbes*, *Carcinogens*, and *Viruses*. Furthermore, while students could encounter story-centric embedded assessments in almost any order, the *Investigating the Illness* text was the first assessment for 735 of the students. In order to further reduce data sparsity, we considered only the 735 students who encountered the *Investigating an Illness* text as their first embedded assessment. This reduction produced an observation data matrix with 65 rows and 735 columns. Even with the steps taken to address data sparsity, 94.2% of the matrix values remained missing.

Third, we examined non-negative matrix factorization (NMF) and probabilistic principal component analysis (PPCA) across a range of reduced dimension values using 10-fold cross validation. Generating models for training involved the following: (1) replacing missing values for each student with the mean value of the student's non-missing assessment scores, (2) applying a collaborative filtering technique to the assessment sequence matrix, and (3) updating the missing values with new estimates if the distance between the original matrix and the new model-predicted matrix is decreased. Steps (2) and (3) are repeated until the distance is less than a threshold [14]. The validation step works similarly, except it uses a matrix inversion method instead of collaborative filtering, since it uses the previously trained model to predict scores for the validation set. Results from the evaluation are presented next.

6 Results

In order to evaluate the models' performance, we investigated their ability to minimize root mean square error (RMSE), which is defined in Equation 4.

$$RMSE = \sqrt{\frac{1}{|O|}\sum_{i,j\in O}(R_{i,j}^{v} - R_{i,j}^{v\prime})^2}\,. \tag{4}$$

In the above equation, O denotes all coordinates for observed values (i.e., non-missing values), $|O|$ is the number of observed coordinates, $R^{v}_{i,j}$ is the value at i^{th} row and j^{th} column in the validation set, and $R^{v\prime}_{i,j}$ is the estimated value at i^{th} row and j^{th} column according to the inference mechanism based on a generated model.

In addition to NMF and PPCA, we implemented a memory-based approach to collaborative filtering, *k*-nearest neighbor (kNN), as a non-trivial baseline. In implementing kNN, we utilized Euclidean distance as a distance metric, inferring users' ratings by averaging assessment performance scores among the k "nearest" users. Similar to the examinations of NMF and PPCA, we investigated the performance of kNN across a range of *k* values using 10-fold cross validation.

The RMSE results for each model are presented in Figure 3. RMSE values are displayed on the y-axis; lower RMSE values are better. The two model-based collaborative filtering approaches substantially outperformed kNN. PPCA yielded the lowest average *RMSE* (M = 0.42), followed by NMF (M = 0.89) and kNN (M = 14.93). NMF achieved its best performance with 50 dimensions, and PPCA achieved comparably good performance at 55 dimensions, with *RMSE* = 0.18.

Given the real-time performance requirements of narrative-centered learning environments, we also elected to investigate the running times of each algorithm across 10-fold cross validation. The results of this comparison are shown in Figure 4. Due to the wide range in run-times among the three algorithms, we charted run-time on a base-2 logarithmic scale along the y-axis. PPCA (M=1998179ms) proved to be considerably slower than NMF (M=1056ms), raising concerns about its utility for run-time settings. Possible methods for improving the run-time performance of PPCA include adjusting its termination threshold value, or restricting the maximum

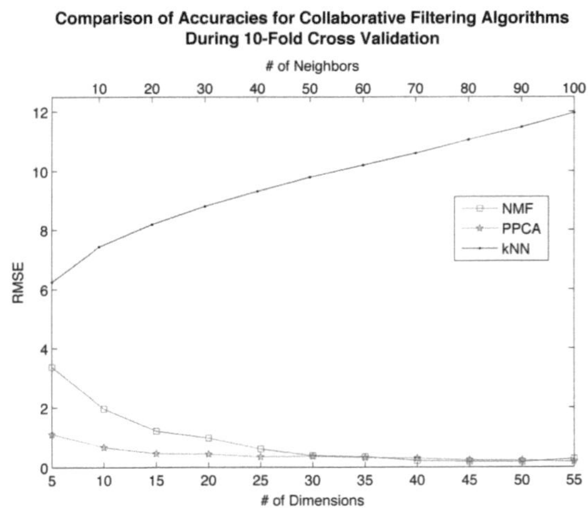

Fig. 3. RMSE values for the three CF algorithms plotted across parameter values. The bottom x-axis displays dimension values for NMF and PPCA. The upper x-axis displays k values for kNN.

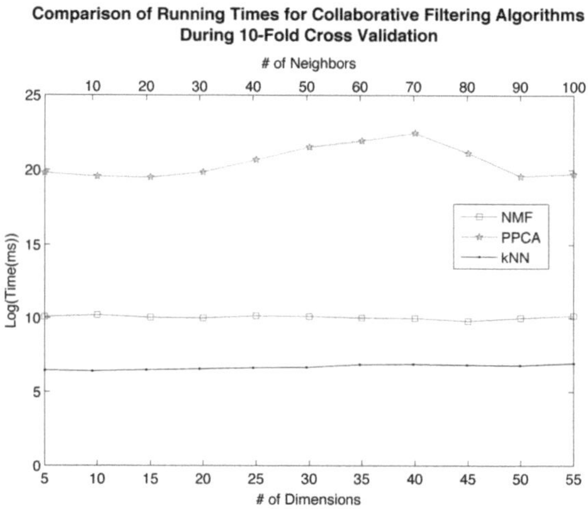

Fig. 4. Run-times (ms) for the three CF algorithms during cross validation. Run-times are plotted on a logarithmic scale along the y-axis. The test machine utilized an Intel i7-2600K processor and 16GB RAM.

number of iterations used during maximum likelihood estimation. In the current setting, the termination threshold value was set to 0.001 for both NMF and PPCA, and no limit was specified on the maximum number of iterations.

7 Conclusions and Future Work

Collaborative filtering algorithms show considerable promise for dynamically tailoring story events in narrative-centered learning environments. This paper introduces an effective approach to personalizing sequences of story-centric embedded assessments. Using data from classroom studies of a literacy-focused edition of the CRYSTAL ISLAND narrative-centered learning environment, an empirical evaluation demonstrated that model-based collaborative filtering techniques, such as non-negative matrix factorization and probabilistic principal component analysis, outperform baseline approaches for accurately predicting student performance on embedded assessments of reading comprehension skills. Further, results suggest that NMF techniques provide a superior balance between predictive accuracy and running time compared to PPCA. In the future, we intend to investigate alternate collaborative filtering techniques with improved scalability for larger data sets and longer assessment sequences. Additionally, we will incorporate collaborative filtering models into CRYSTAL ISLAND to evaluate the impacts of tailoring story-centric embedded assessment sequences in run-time narrative-centered learning environments.

Acknowledgments. The authors wish to thank colleagues from the IntelliMedia Group and East Carolina University for their assistance. This research was supported by the National Science Foundation under Grant DRL-0822200. Any opinions, findings, and conclusions or recommendations expressed in this material are those of the authors and do not necessarily reflect the views of the National Science Foundation. Additional support was provided by the Bill and Melinda Gates Foundation, the William and Flora Hewlett Foundation, and EDUCAUSE.

References

1. Johnson, W.L.: Serious use of a Serious Game for Language Learning. In: 13th International Conference on Artificial Intelligence in Education, pp. 67–74 (2007)
2. Aylett, R., Louchart, S.: If I were you: double appraisal in affective agents. In: 7th International Joint Conference on Autonomous Agents and Multiagent Systems, pp. 1233–1236 (2008)
3. Kim, Hill, Durlach, Lane, Forbell, Core, Marsella, Pynadath, Hart: BiLAT: A Game-Based Environment for Practicing Negotiation in a Cultural Context. International Journal of Artificial Intelligence in Education 19, 289–308 (2009)
4. Nelson, B.C., Ketelhut, D.J.: Exploring embedded guidance and self-efficacy in educational multi-user virtual environments. International Journal of Computer-Supported Collaborative Learning 3(4), 413–427 (2008)
5. Thomas, J.M., Young, R.M.: Annie: Automated Generation of Adaptive Learner Guidance for Fun Serious Games. IEEE Transactions on Learning Technologies 3(4), 329–343 (2010)
6. Mott, B.W., Lester, J.C.: Narrative-centered tutorial planning for inquiry-based learning environments. In: Ikeda, M., Ashley, K.D., Chan, T.-W. (eds.) ITS 2006. LNCS, vol. 4053, pp. 675–684. Springer, Heidelberg (2006)
7. Lee, S.Y., Mott, B.W., Lester, J.C.: Real-time narrative-centered tutorial planning for story-based learning. In: Cerri, S.A., Clancey, W.J., Papadourakis, G., Panourgia, K. (eds.) ITS 2012. LNCS, vol. 7315, pp. 476–481. Springer, Heidelberg (2012)
8. Rowe, J.P., Shores, L.R., Mott, B.W., Lester, J.C.: Integrating learning, problem solving, and engagement in narrative-centered learning environments. International Journal of Artificial Intelligence in Education 21(2), 115–133 (2011)
9. Yu, H., Riedl, M.O.: A sequential recommendation approach for interactive personalized story generation. In: 11th International Conference on Autonomous Agents and Multiagent Systems, pp. 71–78 (2012)
10. Resnick, P., Varian, H.R.: Recommender systems. Communications of the ACM 40(3), 56–58 (1997)
11. Goldberg, K., Roeder, T., Gupta, D., Perkins, C.: Eigentaste: A Constant Time Collaborative Filtering Algorithm. Information Retrieval 4(2), 133–151 (2001)
12. Rubin, D.B., Thayler, D.T.: EM algorithms for ML factor analysis. Psychometrika 47(1), 69–76 (1982)
13. Lee, D.D., Seung, H.S.: Algorithms for non-negative matrix factorization. In: Advances in Neural Information Processing, pp. 556–562 (2000)
14. Zhang, S., Wang, W., Ford, J., Makedon, F.: Learning from incomplete ratings using non-negative matrix factorization. In: 6th SIAM Conference on Data Mining, pp. 549–553 (2006)
15. Tipping, M.E., Bishop, C.M.: Probabilistic principal component analysis. Journal of the Royal Statistical Society, Series B 61, 611–622 (1999)
16. Roweis, S.: EM Algorithms for PCA and SPCA. In: Advances in Neural Information Processing Systems 10, pp. 626–632 (1998)

ReaderBench, an Environment for Analyzing Text Complexity and Reading Strategies

Mihai Dascalu[1,2], Philippe Dessus[2,3], Ştefan Trausan-Matu[1], Maryse Bianco[2], and Aurélie Nardy[2]

[1] Politehnica University of Bucharest, Computer Science Department, Romania
{mihai.dascalu,stefan.trausan}@cs.pub.ro
[2] LSE, Univ. Grenoble Alpes, France
[3] LIG-MeTAH, Univ. Grenoble Alpes, France
{philippe.dessus,maryse.bianco,aurelie.nardy}@upmf-grenoble.fr

Abstract. *ReaderBench* is a multi-purpose, multi-lingual and flexible environment that enables the assessment of a wide range of learners' productions and their manipulation by the teacher. *ReaderBench* allows the assessment of three main textual features: cohesion-based assessment, reading strategies identification and textual complexity evaluation, which have been subject to empirical validations. *ReaderBench* covers a complete cycle, from the initial complexity assessment of reading materials, the assignment of texts to learners, the capture of metacognitions reflected in one's textual verbalizations and comprehension evaluation, therefore fostering learner's self-regulation process.

Keywords: Text Cohesion, Reading Strategies, Textual Complexity, Latent Semantic Analysis, Latent Dirichlet Allocation, Support Vector Machines.

1 Introduction

In every instructional situation, reading textual materials and writing down thoughts are the core activities that represent both *causes* of learning (from learner's viewpoint) and *indicators* of learning (from teacher's viewpoint). Reading is a cognitive activity whose oral or written traces are usually analyzed by teachers in order to infer either learners' comprehension or reading strategies. Hence reading and writing are core activities that every teacher has to assess on a daily basis: reading materials have to be scaled or tailored to suit pupils' actual level, and reading strategies have to be analyzed for inferring learners' level of text processing and understanding.

Teacher's support of learners' reading and writing is difficult to be carried out on a larger scale, therefore he/she should take care of a small number of students. Moreover, assessing textual materials and verbalizations is a cognitively demanding and subjectivity-laden activity. We thus designed and implemented *ReaderBench*, a flexible computer-based environment that supports reading and writing activities of learners and of teachers in multiple educational scenarios.

The following section details some of the main predictors of reading comprehension, leading to the introduction of *ReaderBench*. The third section is centered on the

K. Yacef et al. (Eds.): AIED 2013, LNAI 7926, pp. 379–388, 2013.

analysis of textual cohesion, considered central within discourse analysis. Then we shift the point of interest towards reading strategies and assessing textual complexity. Each of the three latter sections is accompanied by a validation with *ReaderBench*.

2 Core Predictors of Reading Comprehension

Expert readers are strategic readers. They monitor their reading, being able to know at every moment their level of understanding. When faced with a difficulty, learners can call upon regulation procedures, also called *reading strategies* [1]. Reading strategies have been studied extensively with adolescent and adult readers using the think-aloud procedure that engages the reader to auto-explain at specific breakpoints while reading, therefore providing insight in terms of comprehension.

Four types of reading strategies are mainly used by expert readers [2]. *Paraphrasing* allows the reader to express what he/she understood from the explicit content of the text and can be considered the first and essential step in the process of coherence building. *Text-based inferences*, for example causal and bridging strategies, build explicit relationships between two or more pieces of information in texts. On the other hand, *knowledge-based inferences* build relationships between the information in text and the reader's own knowledge and are essential to the situation model building process. *Control strategies* refer to the actual monitoring process when the reader is explicitly expressing what he/she has or has not understood. The diversity and richness of the strategies a reader carries out depend on many factors, either personal (proficiency, level of knowledge, motivation), or external (textual complexity).

In addition, teachers need valid and reliable *measures of textual complexity* for selecting texts for the day-to-day instruction. Two approaches compete for the automated assessment of text complexity: 1/ using simple statistical measures that mostly rely on word difficulty (from already-made scales) and sentence length; 2/ using a combination of multiple factors ranging from lexical indicators as word frequency, to syntactic and semantic levels (e.g., textual cohesion) [3].

As an in-depth perspective, text cohesion, seen as the relatedness between different parts of texts, is a major determinant of text coherence and has been shown to be an important predictor of reading comprehension [4]. Cohesiveness understanding (e.g., referential, causal or temporal) is central to the process of building the coherence of a text at the local level, which, in turn, allows the textual content to be reorganized into its macrostructure and situation model at a more global level. High cohesion texts are more beneficial to low-knowledge readers than to high-knowledge readers [5]. Hence, textual cohesion is a feature of textual complexity (through some semantic characteristics of the read text) that might interfere with reading strategies (through the inferences made by a reader).

McNamara and colleagues devised two systems: while *CohMetrix* [5] addresses facets of textual complexity, *iStart* [6] is focused on reading strategies. *CohMetrix* provides a wide range of measures on textual features at five main levels: word (e.g., part-of-speech and frequency), syntax (e.g., percentage of nouns), text-base (e.g., co-reference and lexical diversity), situation model (e.g., cohesion and temporal indices), and genre and rhetorical structure (e.g., text genre).

iStart is the first implemented system that teaches and assesses self-explanations in accordance to the reading material, with various modules that train learners using the *Self-Explanation Reading Training* method [2]. One module shows how to use those techniques using a virtual student, while another module asks students to read texts and provide verbalizations, evaluates them and gives an appropriate feedback.

ReaderBench encompasses the functionalities of both *CohMetrix* and *iStart*, as it provides teachers and learners information on their reading/writing activities: initial textual complexity assessment, assignment of texts to learners, capture of meta-cognitions reflected in one's textual verbalizations, and reading strategies assessment. The main differentiators between *ReaderBench* and previous systems consist of the following: 1/ a generalized cohesion-based model of discourse that can be easily extended, in addition to plain essay- or story-like texts, to the analysis of chats and forums, with emphasis on collaboration assessment [7], 2/ different factors, measurements and the use of SVMs for increasing the validity of textual complexity assessment [8], 3/ multi-lingual support and the integration of specific Natural Language Processing (NLP) tools for both French and English, and 4/ a different educational purpose, as *ReaderBench* validation was performed on pupils (3rd to 5th grade), whereas *iStart* mainly targets high school and university students.

Moreover, the design of *ReaderBench* considers two dimensions. On one hand, the *flexibility* of the environment is highlighted through the following features: comparison of complexity levels of several texts, one to another, and the ease of editing reading materials from within *ReaderBench*, with the possibility to also add dynamic breakpoints for learners' verbalizations or summaries. Teachers can thus *manipulate* textual materials in order to reach desired features. Also learners can very quickly have an idea of the way they regulate their reading (strategies assessment). On the other hand, *extensibility* is reflected in the ease of training and of using additional LSA semantic vector spaces or LDA topic models or in the possibility to augment the features used for assessing textual complexity.

3 Cohesion-Based Discourse Analysis

Text cohesion, viewed as lexical, grammatical and semantic overt relationships, is defined within our implemented model in terms of: 1/ the *inverse distance* between textual elements; 2/ *lexical proximity* that is easily identifiable through words' identical lemmas and semantic distances [9, 10] within ontologies; 3/ semantic similarity measured through *Latent Semantic Analysis* (LSA) [11] and *Latent Dirichlet Allocation* (LDA) [12]. Additionally, specific NLP techniques are applied to reduce noise and improve the system's accuracy: tokenizing, splitting, part of speech tagging, parsing, stop words elimination, dictionary-only words selection, stemming, lemmatizing, named entity recognition and co-reference resolution [13].

In order to provide a multi-lingual analysis platform with support for both English and French, *ReaderBench* integrates both *WordNet* [14] and a transposed and serialized version of *WOLF* (*Wordnet Libre du Français*, `http://alpage.inria.fr/~sagot/wolf.html`). Due to the intrinsic limitations of *WOLF*, in which concepts are translated from English while their corresponding glosses are only partially translated, making a mixture of French and English definitions, only three frequently used semantic distances were applicable to both ontologies: path length, Wu–Palmer [9] and Leacock–Chodorow's normalized path length [10].

Afterwards, semantic models were trained using three specific corpora: "*TextEnfants*" [15] (approx. 4.2M words), "*Le Monde*" (French newspaper, approx. 24M words) for French, and Touchstone Applied Science Associates (TASA) corpus (approx. 13M words) for English. Moreover, improvements have been enforced on the initial models: the reduction of inflected forms to their lemmas, the annotation of each word with its corresponding part of speech through a NLP processing pipe, the normalization of occurrences through the use of term frequency–inverse document frequency [13] and distributed computing for increasing speedup [16].

LSA and LDA models extract semantic relations from underlying word co-occurrences and are based on the bag-of-words hypothesis [13]. Our experiments have proven that LSA and LDA models can be used to complement one other, in the sense that underlying semantic relationships are more likely to be identified, if both approaches are combined after normalization. Therefore, LSA vector spaces are generated after projecting the arrays obtained from the reduced-rank Singular Value Decomposition of the initial term-doc array and can be used to determine the proximity of words through cosine similarity [11]. From a different viewpoint, LDA topic models provide an inference mechanism of underlying topic structures through a generative probabilistic process [12]. In this context, similarity between concepts can be seen as the opposite of the Jensen-Shannon dissimilarity [13] between their corresponding posterior topic distributions.

Overall, in order to better grasp cohesion between textual fragments, we have combined information retrieval specific techniques, mostly reflected in word repetitions and normalized number of occurrences, with semantic distances extracted from ontologies or from LSA- or LDA-based semantic models.

In order to have a better representation of discourse in terms of underlying cohesive links, we introduced a *cohesion graph* that can be seen as a generalization of the previously proposed utterance graph [17]. We are building a multi-layered mixed graph consisting of three types of nodes: a central node, the *document* that can represent the entire reading material, nodes for *blocks* (paragraphs from the initial text) and for *sentences*, the main units of analysis. As edges, *hierarchical links* are enforced through inclusion functions (sentences within a block, blocks within the document) and *two types* of *links* are introduced between analysis elements of the same level. *Mandatory links* are established between adjacent paragraphs or sentences and are used for best modeling the information flow throughout the discourse, therefore making possible the identification of cohesion gaps. Additional *relevant links* are added to the cohesion graph for highlighting fine-grained and subtle relations between distant analysis elements. In our experiments, the use as threshold of the sum of mean and standard deviation of all cohesion values from within a higher-level analysis element provided significant additional links into the proposed discourse structure.

In contrast, as cohesion can be regarded as the sum of links that hold a text together and give it meaning, the mere use of semantically related words in a text does not directly correlate with its complexity. In other words, whereas cohesion in itself is not enough to distinguish texts in terms of complexity, the lack of cohesion may increase textual complexity, as a text's proper understanding and representation become more difficult to achieve. In order to better highlight this perspective, two measures for textual complexity were defined, later to be assessed: *inner-block cohesion* as the mean value of all the links from within a block (adjacent and relevant links between sentences) and *inter-block cohesion* that highlights semantic relationships at global document level.

As a *validation*, we have used 10 stories in French for which sophomore students in educational sciences (French native speakers) were asked to evaluate the semantic relatedness between adjacent paragraphs on a Likert scale of [1..5]; each pair of paragraphs was assessed by more than 10 human evaluators for limiting inter-rater disagreement. Due to the subjectivity of the task and the different personal scales of perceived cohesion, the average values of intra-class correlations per story were *ICC-average measures* = .493 and *ICC-single measures* = .167. In the end, 540 individual cohesion scores were aggregated and then used to determine the correlation between different semantic measures and the gold standard. On the two training corpora used (*Le Monde* and *TextEnfants*), the correlations were: Combined–*Le Monde* (r = .54), LDA–*Le Monde* (r = .42), LSA–*Le Monde* (r = .28), LSA–*TextEnfants* (r = .19), Combined–*TextEnfants* (r = .06), Wu–Palmer (r = -.06), Path Similarity (r = -.13), LDA–*TextEnfants* (r = -.13) and Leacock–Chodorow (r = -.40).

The previous results show that the proposed combined method of integrating multiple semantic similarity measures outperforms all individual metrics, that a larger corpus leads to better results and that Wu–Palmer, besides its corresponding scaling to the [0..1] interval (relevant when integrating measurements with LSA and LDA), behaves best in contrast to the other ontology based semantic distances. Moreover, the significant increase in correlation between the aggregated measure of LSA, LDA and Wu–Palmer, in comparison to the individual scores, proves the benefits of combining multiple complementary approaches in terms of the reduction of errors that can be induced by using a single method.

4 Reading Strategies

Starting from the four types of reading strategies introduced in section 2, our aim was to integrate automatic extraction methods designed to support tutors at identifying various strategies and to best fit with the categories aligned with [2]. We have tested various methods of identifying reading strategies (causality, control, paraphrasing, bridging, and knowledge inference) and we will focus solely on presenting here the alternatives that provided the best overall human–machine correlations.

In ascending order of complexity, the simplest strategies to identify are *causality* (e.g., "*parce que*", "*pour*") and *control* (e.g., "*je me souviens*", "*je crois*") for which cue phrases have been used. Additionally, as causality assumes text-based inferences, all occurrences of keywords at the beginning of a verbalization have been discarded, as such a word occurrence can be considered a speech initiating event (e.g., "*Donc*"), rather than creating an inferential link. Afterwards, *paraphrases*, that were considered repetitions of the same semantic propositions by raters, were automatically identified based on word lemmas and synonymy relationships from the lexicalized ontologies.

The strategies most difficult to identify are *knowledge inference* and *bridging*, for which semantic similarities have to be computed. An *inferred concept* is a non-paraphrased word for which the following three semantic distances were computed:

the distance from word w_1 from the verbalization to the closest word w_2 from the initial text (expressed in terms of semantic distances in ontologies, LSA and LDA) and the distances from both w_1 and w_2 to the textual fragments in-between consecutive self-explanations. The latter distances had to be taken into consideration for better weighting the importance of each concept, with respect to the whole text.

As *bridging* consists of creating connections between different textual segments from the initial text, cohesion was measured between the verbalization and each sentence from the reference reading material. If more than 2 similarity measures were above the mean value of all previous semantic similarities and exceeded a minimum threshold, bridging was estimated as the number of previous cohesive links between contiguous zones of cohesive sentences. This was an adaptation with regards to the manual annotation that considered two or more adjacent sentences, each cohesive with the verbalization, members of a single bridged entity.

Figure 1 depicts the cohesion measures with previous paragraphs from the story in the last column and the identified reading strategies for each verbalization marked in the grey areas, coded as follows: control, causality, paraphrasing [index referred word from the initial text], inferred concept [*] and bridging over the inter-linked cohesive sentences from the reading material.

We ran an experiment with pupils aged from 9 to 11 who had to read aloud a 450 word-long story and to stop in-between at six predefined markers and explain what they understood up to that moment. Their explanations were first recorded and transcribed, then annotated by two human experts (PhD in linguistics and in psychology), and categorized according to McNamara [2]'s scoring scheme. Disagreements were solved by discussion after evaluating each self-explanation individually. In addition, automatic cleaning had to be performed in order to process the phonetic-like transcribed verbalizations. Verbalizations from 12 pupils were transcribed and manually assessed as a preliminary validation. The results for the 72 verbalization extracts in terms of precision, recall and F1-score are as follows: *causality* ($P = .57$, $R = .98$, $F = .72$), *control* ($P = 1$, $R = .71$, $F = .83$), *paraphrase* ($P = .79$, $R = .92$, $F = .85$), *inferred knowledge* ($P = .34$, $R = .43$, $F = .38$) and *bridging* ($P = .45$, $R = .58$, $F = .5$). As expected, paraphrases, control and causality occurrences were much easier to identify than information coming from pupils' experience [18].

Moreover we have identified multiple particular cases in which both approaches (human and automatic) covered a partial truth that in the end is subjective to the evaluator. For instance, many causal structures close to each other, but not adjacent, were manually coded as one, whereas the system considers each of them separately. Moreover, "*fille*" ("daughter") does not appear in the text and is directly linked to the main character, therefore marked as an inferred concept by *ReaderBench*, while the evaluator considered it as a synonym. Additionally, when solely looking at manual assessments, high discrepancies between evaluators were identified due to different understandings and perceptions of pupil's intentions expressed within their metacognitions. Nevertheless, our aim was to support tutors and the results are encouraging (correlated also with the previous precision measurements and with the fact that a lot of noise existed in the transcriptions), emphasizing the benefits of a regularized and deterministic process of identification.

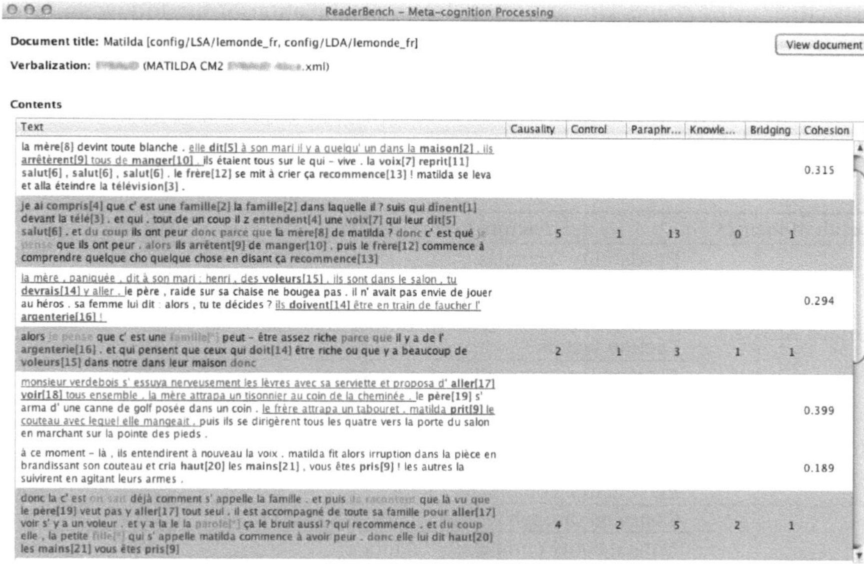

Fig. 1. Reading strategies analysis applied on verbalizations (grey) in *ReaderBench*

5 Textual Complexity

Assessing textual complexity can be considered a difficult task due to different reader perceptions primarily caused by prior knowledge and experience, cognitive capability, motivation, interests or language familiarity (for non-native speakers). Nevertheless, from the tutor perspective, the task of identifying accessible materials plays a crucial role in the learning process since inappropriate texts, either too simple or too difficult, can cause learners to quickly lose interest. We propose a multi-dimensional analysis of textual complexity, covering a multitude of factors depicted in Table 1 (extensive description in [8]) aggregated through the use of Support Vector Machines, which has proven to be the most efficient [19], as variables are not linearly separable.

Hence, besides shallow factors presented in [8], of particular interest is how morphological and semantic factors correlate to classic readability measures. Therefore, starting from the textual complexity model that already integrated these measures, surface metrics derived from automatic essay grading techniques, morphology and syntax factors [8], we have introduced new dimensions focused on semantics. Firstly, *cohesion* reflected in the strength of inner-block and inter-block links influences readability, as semantic similarities govern the understanding of a text. Secondly, a variety of metrics based on the span and the coverage of *lexical chains* [20] provide insight in terms of lexicon variety and of cohesion. Thirdly, *entity-density features* proved to influence readability as the number of entities introduced within a text is correlated to the working memory of the text's targeted readers. Finally, another dimension focuses on the ability to resolve referential relations correctly [21] as *co-reference inference features* also impact comprehension difficulty (e.g., the overall number of chains, the inference distance or the span between concepts in a single text). From a different perspective, *word complexity* was treated as a combination of the following factors: syllable count, distance between the inflected form, lemma and stem, whereas specificity is reflected in inverse document frequency from the training corpora, the distance in hypernym tree and the word polysemy count from the ontology.

Table 1. Textual complexity dimensions

Depth of metrics	Factors for evaluation	Avg. *EA*	Avg. *AA*
Surface Analysis	Readability formulas	.717	.995
	Fluency factors	.314	.579
	Structure complexity factors	.728	.993
	Diction factors	.550	.901
	Entropy factors (words vs. characters)	.313	.573
	Word complexity factors	.556	.918
Morphology & Syntax	Balanced CAF (Complexity, Accuracy, Fluency)	.755	.996
	Specific POS complexity factors	.570	.929
	Parsing tree complexity factors	.424	.806
Semantics	Cohesion through lexical chains, LSA and LDA	.544	.894
	Named entity complexity factors	.590	.929
	Co-reference complexity factors	.384	.730
	Lexical chains	.367	.704

As no corpus was available for French in order to train our complexity model, we have opted to automatically extract texts from TASA, using its Degree of Reading Power (DRP) score into six classes of complexity [22] of equal frequency, necessary for binary classification. This validation scenario consisting of approximately 1,000 documents was twofold: we wanted, on one hand, to prove that the *complete model* is *adequate* and *reliable* and, on the other, to demonstrate that *high level features* at semantic level *provide relevant insight* that can be used for automatic classification. As particular implementation aspects for increasing the effectiveness of SVMs, all factors were linearly scaled and a Grid Search optimization method of C and γ for the Gaussian kernel was enforced. In the end, k-fold cross validation [23] was applied for extracting the following performance features (see Table 1): *precision* or *exact agreement* (EA) and *adjacent agreement* (AA) [19], as the percent to which the SVM was close to predicting the correct classification.

Moreover, two additional measurements were performed. Firstly, an integration of all metrics from all complexity classes proved that the SVMs results are compatible with the DRP scores ($EA = .763$ and $AA = .997$), and that they provide significant improvements as they outperform any individual class precisions. The second measurement ($EA = .597$ and $AA = .943$) uses solely morphology and semantics measures in order to avoid a circular comparison between factors of similar complexity, as the DRP score is based on shallow factors. This result shows a link between low-level factors (also used in the DRP score) and in-depth analysis factors, which can also be used to accurately predict the complexity of a reading material.

6 Conclusion and Future Research Directions

ReaderBench is an environment integrating new ways to assess a wide range of cognitive processes involved in reading through the use of advanced NLP techniques. It provides a semantic insight and discourse structure through the combination of multiple semantic distances. Its flexibility (multilingual support) and extensibility (complexity factors easily incorporable) make its integration appropriate in various educational settings (e.g., understanding reading materials, lecture notes analysis). Further improvements, including chat/forum collaboration assessment, a human-rated corpus for textual complexity SVM training, *ReaderBench* will effectively support students in their learning activities. Moreover, speech-to-text functionality would enable its use with younger pupils and make the software more practicable. In addition, we envision controlled experiments performed with tutors and learners in classroom environments.

Acknowledgements. This research was supported by an *Agence Nationale de la Recherche* (DEVCOMP) grant, by the 264207 ERRIC–Empowering Romanian Research on Intelligent Information Technologies/FP7-REGPOT-2010-1 and the POSDRU/107/1.5/S/76909 Harnessing human capital in research through doctoral scholarships (ValueDoc) projects.

References

1. McNamara, D.S., Magliano, J.P.: Self-explanation and metacognition. In: Hacher, J.D., Dunlosky, J., Graesser, A.C. (eds.) Handbook of Metacognition in Education, pp. 60–81. Erlbaum, Mahwah (2009)
2. McNamara, D.S.: SERT: Self-Explanation Reading Training. Discourse Processes 38, 1–30 (2004)
3. Nelson, J., Perfetti, C., Liben, D., Liben, M.: Measures of text difficulty. Technical Report to the Gates Foundation (2011)
4. Tapiero, I.: Situation models and levels of coherence. Erlbaum, Mahwah (2007)
5. McNamara, D.S., Louwerse, M.M., McCarthy, P.M., Graesser, A.C.: Coh-Metrix: Capturing linguistic features of cohesion. Discourse Proc. 47(4), 292–330 (2010)
6. McNamara, D., Boonthum, C., Levinstein, I.: Evaluating self-explanations in iSTART: Comparing word-based and LSA algorithms. In: Landauer, T.K., McNamara, D., Dennis, S., Kintsch, W. (eds.) Handbook of Latent Semantic Analysis, pp. 227–241. Erlbaum, Mahwah (2007)
7. Trausan-Matu, S., Dascalu, M., Rebedea, T.: A system for automatic analysis of Computer-Supported Collaborative Learning chats. In: 12th Conf. ICALT, pp. 95–99. IEEE (2012)
8. Dascalu, M., Trausan-Matu, S., Dessus, P.: Towards an integrated approach for evaluating textual complexity for learning purposes. In: Popescu, E., Li, Q., Klamma, R., Leung, H., Specht, M. (eds.) ICWL 2012. LNCS, vol. 7558, pp. 268–278. Springer, Heidelberg (2012)
9. Wu, Z., Palmer, M.: Verb semantics and lexical selection. In: 32nd Annual Meeting of the Association for Computational Linguistics, pp. 133–138. ACL, Las Cruces (1994)

10. Leacock, C., Chodorow, M.: Combining local context and WordNet similarity for word-sense identification. In: Fellbaum, C. (ed.) WordNet: An Electronic Lexical Database, pp. 265–283. MIT Press, Cambridge (1998)
11. Landauer, T.K., Dumais, S.T.: A solution to Plato's problem: the Latent Semantic Analysis theory of acquisition, induction and representation of knowledge. Psychol. Rev. 104(2), 211–240 (1997)
12. Blei, D., Ng, A., Jordan, M.: Latent Dirichlet Allocation. Journal of Machine Learning Research 3(4-5), 993–1022 (2003)
13. Manning, C., Schütze, H.: Foundations of statistical Natural Language Processing. MIT Press, Cambridge (1999)
14. Miller, G.A.: WordNet. A Lexical Database for English. Comm. ACM 38(11), 39–41 (1995)
15. Denhière, G., Lemaire, B., Bellissens, C., Jhean-Larose, S.: A semantic space for modeling children's semantic memory. In: Landauer, T.K., McNamara, D.S., Dennis, S., Kintsch, W. (eds.) Handbook of Latent Semantic Analysis, pp. 143–165. Erlbaum, Mahwah (2007)
16. McCallum, A.K.: MALLET: A Machine Learning for Language Toolkit (2002), `http://mallet.cs.umass.edu`
17. Trausan-Matu, S., Dascalu, M., Dessus, P.: Considering textual complexity and comprehension in Computer-Supported Collaborative Learning. In: Cerri, S.A., Clancey, W.J., Papadourakis, G., Panourgia, K. (eds.) ITS 2012. LNCS, vol. 7315, pp. 352–357. Springer, Heidelberg (2012)
18. Graesser, A.C., Singer, M., Trabasso, T.: Constructing inferences during narrative text comprehension. Psychol. Rev. 101(3), 371–395 (1994)
19. François, T., Miltsakaki, E.: Do NLP and machine learning improve traditional readability formulas? In: Proc. First Workshop on Predicting and Improving Text Readability for Target Reader Populations (PITR 2012), pp. 49–57. ACL, Montréal (2012)
20. Galley, M., McKeown, K.: Improving word sense disambiguation in lexical chaining. In: 18th International Joint Conference on Artificial Intelligence (IJCAI 2003), Acapulco (2003)
21. Lee, H., Peirsman, Y., Chang, A., Chambers, N., Surdeanu, M., Jurafsky, D.: Stanford's multi-pass sieve coreference resolution system at the CoNLL-2011 shared task. In: 15th Conference on Computational Natural Language Learning, pp. 28–34 (2011)
22. McNamara, D.S., Graesser, A.C., Louwerse, M.M.: Sources of text difficulty: Across the ages and genres. In: Sabatini, J.P., Albro, E. (eds.) Assessing Reading in the 21st Century. R&L Education, Lanham (in press)
23. Geisser, S.: Predictive Inference. Chapman and Hall, New York (1993)

Cluster-Based Prediction of Mathematical Learning Patterns

Tanja Käser[1], Alberto Giovanni Busetto[1,2], Barbara Solenthaler[1], Juliane Kohn[4], Michael von Aster[3,4,5], and Markus Gross[1]

[1] Department of Computer Science, ETH Zurich, Zurich, Switzerland
[2] Competence Center for Systems Physiology and Metabolic Diseases, Zurich, Switzerland
[3] Center for MR-Research, University Children's Hospital, Zurich, Switzerland
[4] Department of Psychology, University of Potsdam, Potsdam, Germany
[5] Department of Child and Adolescent Psychiatry, German Red Cross Hospitals Westend, Berlin, Germany

Abstract. This paper introduces a method to predict and analyse students' mathematical performance by detecting distinguishable subgroups of children who share similar learning patterns. We employ pairwise clustering to analyse a comprehensive dataset of user interactions obtained from a computer-based training system. The available data consist of multiple learning trajectories measured from children with developmental dyscalculia, as well as from control children. Our online classification algorithm allows accurate assignment of children to clusters early in the training, enabling prediction of learning characteristics. The included results demonstrate the high predictive power of assignments of children to subgroups, and the significant improvement in prediction accuracy for short- and long-term performance, knowledge gaps, overall training achievements, and scores of further external assessments.

Keywords: feature processing, pairwise clustering, prediction, learning, dyscalculia.

1 Introduction

Recently, computer-assisted learning has entered different fields of education. Computer-based therapy systems for learning disabilities have gained particular attention. Such systems present inexpensive extensions to conventional one-to-one therapy by providing an adaptive and fear-free learning environment. The effectiveness of computer-based therapy programs has been proven by several user studies targeting children with dyslexia [3,6,13] and developmental dyscalculia (DD) [11,12,15]. To improve diagnostics and intervention outcomes, knowledge of performance profile, knowledge gaps and learning behaviours of the student as well as an accurate performance prediction are essential. This is particularly important for students suffering from learning disabilities as the heterogeneity of these children requires a high grade of individualization. Current tutoring

K. Yacef et al. (Eds.): AIED 2013, LNAI 7926, pp. 389–399, 2013.

systems use approaches such as Bayesian networks [16], knowledge tracing [4], and performance factors analysis [19] to assess the knowledge of the student.

Given the high diversity of students using a tutoring system, training individualization proves highly beneficial and has been the focus of recent improvements. Clustering is a family of approaches which are useful to detect small and homogeneous groups of learners. In fact, clustering [22] and co-clustering [23] approaches successfully improved post-test score predictions. The precision of a knowledge tracing model can be increased using clustering [18] and multiple classification models can also improve performance prediction within a system [5]. Furthermore, ensemble methods offer a way to increase prediction accuracy by training different types of student models [2,17]. Clustering can also be used to gain insight on learning characteristics of the students. Bootstrap aggregated clustering [14] identified different subtypes of children with dyslexia. Other authors used offline clustering followed by online classification to analyse and predict the students' input behaviours [1,10].

The present study aims at predicting and analysing children's mathematical performance on the basis of distinguishable learning patterns extracted from similar subgroups of students. Our approach is articulated in two steps: In a first step, we cluster children according to individual learning trajectories. Compared to previous approaches, we use the subgroup information not only to improve prediction accuracy, but also to provide a valuable tool for experts to analyse individual learning patterns. The second step consists of a supervised online classification during training, enabling prediction of future performance. Whereas existing contributions address the task of predicting short-term performance and external assessment results, we introduce a method which also predicts learning characteristics such as knowledge gaps and overall training achievement. The reported results demonstrate that the prediction accuracy of several learning characteristics can be significantly improved by taking subgroup information into account. They allow for a further training individualization and thus contribute to a better support for children with learning difficulties.

2 Method

Our model uses online and offline cluster information. Firstly, we cluster children after the complete training to identify subgroups with similar mathematical learning patterns. Secondly, we classify children to a particular subgroup after each training session to predict future performance. In the following, we first describe the experimental setup and specify the extracted features as well as the feature processing pipeline used for clustering and classification. We then explain clustering, classification and performance prediction in detail.

Experimental Setup. The training environment consists of Calcularis [11,12], a tutoring system for children with DD or difficulties in learning mathematics. The program transforms current neuro-cognitive findings into the design of different instructional games, which are classified into two parts. Part A focuses on the training of different number representations, while part B trains addition and

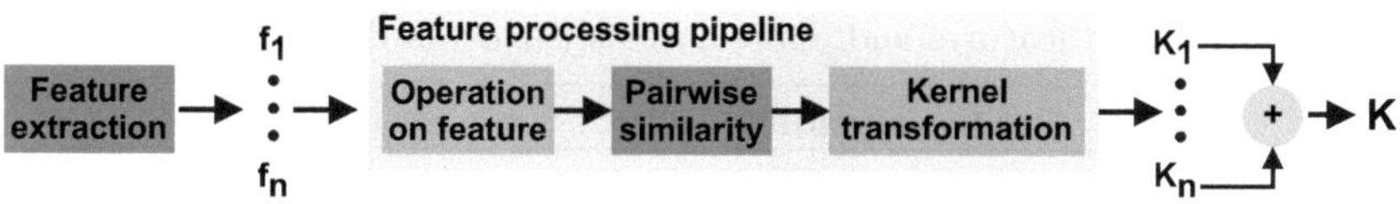

Operation		*Similarity measures*		*Kernel transformations*	
Inv:	$1/\mathbf{f}$	**JC:**	$(\mathbf{F_i} \cap \mathbf{F_j})/(\mathbf{F_i} \cup \mathbf{F_j})$	**JK:**	$2^S - 1$
LogInv:	$1/log(\mathbf{f})$	**L1:**	$\|\|\mathbf{f_i} - \mathbf{f_j}\|\|_1$	**GK:**	$exp(-S^2/(2 \cdot \sigma^2))$
Beta:	$betacdf(\mathbf{f}, .5, .5)^a$	**SD:**	$min(\mathbf{f_i} - \mathbf{f_j})^b$	**RK:**	$exp(-S/\sigma)$

[a] Cumulative distribution function of Beta distribution with $\alpha, \beta = 0.5$.
[b] Shortest path between skills on the skill net .

Fig. 1. Feature processing pipeline (top) and processing modules employed on feature **f** (**F** in case of a set feature) (bottom). The modules can be combined arbitrarily.

subtraction at different difficulty levels. All games in A and B are played in the number ranges 0-10, 0-100 and 0-1000 (A_{10}, A_{100}, A_{1000}, B_{10}, B_{100}, B_{1000}). The employed student model is a dynamic Bayesian network, consisting of a directed acyclic graph representing different mathematical skills s and their dependencies. The controller acting on the skill net is rule-based and allows forward and backward movements (increase and decrease of difficulty levels).

The data used in the presented analysis was collected by an on-going user study with 88 participants (68% females). 50 participants (72% females) were diagnosed with DD, and 38 participants (63% females) were control children (CC). All participants were German-speaking and visited the 2nd-5th grade of elementary school (mean age: 8.71 (SD 0.91), mean age CC: 8.06 (SD 0.48), mean age DD: 9.21 (SD 0.85)). The children trained with the program for 6 weeks with a frequency of 5 times per week, during sessions of 20 minutes. The collected log files contain 27 complete training sessions per child. On average, each child solved 1430 (SD 212) tasks during the 6 weeks.

Feature Extraction and Processing. We identified a set of recorded features, which describe local and global properties of the user's training performance. The set contains cumulative as well as per skill measures, and covers performance, error behaviour and timing. Table 1 lists the features, which are evaluated after each training session. Having continuous and discrete feature types as well as different scales, we process the features to make them comparable (Fig. 1, top). Depending on their nature, features are processed before calculating pairwise similarities s_{ij} (between all samples). The resulting similarity matrices $\mathbf{S_i}$ are transformed into a Kernel and summed up to obtain the similarity matrix $\mathbf{K}$. Finally, $\mathbf{K}$ is transformed to a distance matrix $\mathbf{D}$ using a constant shift ($\mathbf{D}$ = #features - $\mathbf{K}$). The employed processing modules are listed in Fig. 1 (bottom).

Clustering. An inherent property of the controller design of Calcularis is its adaptability. Rather than following a specified sequence of skills to the goal, learning paths are individually adapted for each child. Form and maxima of the network paths vary depending on the learning characteristics of a student

Table 1. Extracted features and abbreviations (bold) used in the following

Feature	Description
Highest **S**kills	Indices of highest skills per part (A and B).
Number of **P**assed **S**kills	Total number of skills passed.
Played **S**kills	Indices of played skills per part (A and B). Set feature.
Pass **T**imes	Accumulated time (from start of training) in seconds until passing a skill. Not passed skills are set to ∞.
Samples per **S**kill	Number of samples needed to pass a skill. Not passed skills are set to ∞.
Key **S**kills*	Indices of problem skills. Set feature.
Answer **T**imes	Mean answer time per skill. Not played skills set to ∞.
Performance **P**er **S**kill	Mean performance (correct trials/all trials) per skill. Not played skills are set to 0.

* Key skill s: If a user went back to a precursor skill at least once before passing s.

(see Fig. 4). These variations suggest that clustering the children on the basis of their trajectories identifies subgroups of children with similar mathematical learning profiles. Furthermore, the use of the trajectory features allows for modelling the development of mathematical learning over time.

Children are clustered after 27 training sessions using trajectory features. These features take into consideration how far the children came during the training (and how fast they arrived there) as well as how they reached this point. The selected features are **PT** evaluated per part and number range (6 dimensions: A_{10}, B_{10}, A_{100}, B_{100}, A_{1000}, B_{1000}) and **PS** (set features for part A and B). **PT** is processed using **LogInv** $\rightarrow$ **L1** $\rightarrow$ **GK** which yields the similarity matrix $\mathbf{K}_1$, while the pipeline **JC** $\rightarrow$ **JK** used for **PS** results in $\mathbf{K}_2$ and $\mathbf{K}_3$. The combined similarity matrix $\mathbf{K}$ ($\mathbf{K} = \mathbf{K}_1 + \mathbf{K}_2 + \mathbf{K}_3$) is finally transformed to the distance matrix $\mathbf{D}$ ($\mathbf{D}$ = 3 - $\mathbf{K}$) used for clustering.

As the measurements are characterized by relations, we performed pairwise-clustering (PC) [9] on $\mathbf{D}$. Through a kernel transformation, dissimilarity values can be interpreted as distances between points in a (usually higher-dimensional) Euclidean space. As shown by the Constant Shift Embedding transformation, PC exhibits a cost which is equivalent to that of K-means in the Euclidean embedding of the similarity data [21]. The optimal number of clusters is determined by the Bayesian Information Criterion (BIC) [20], calculating the effective number of parameters as the normalized trace of the kernel transformation matrix [8].

Classification. We classify students after each training session and use the according cluster information for perfomance prediction. The features used for clustering represent global measures and are thus not optimized for early classification. As all children start the training at the lowest skill level (A_{10}), their trajectories tend to be similar during early training and do not provide information about future performance. Therefore, we use additional features taking into account local differences. While **HS**, **NPS**, **PS** and **KS** are cumulative features, **PT**, **SS**, **AT** and **PPS** are evaluated per skill. All features and their processing pipelines are displayed in Fig. 2. The obtained similarity matrices $\mathbf{K}_i$ are

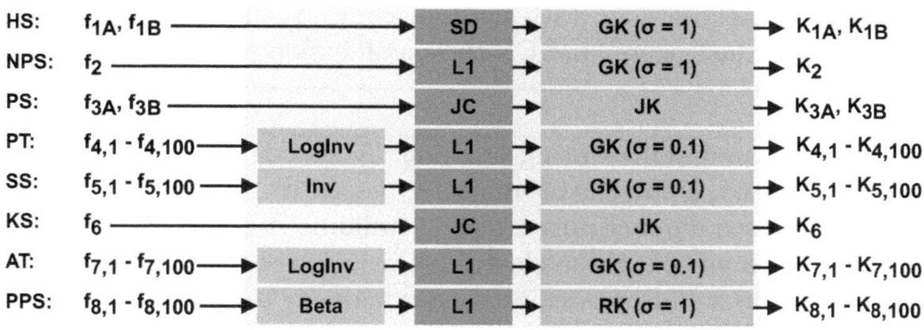

Fig. 2. Extracted features and according processing pipelines

transformed to distance matrices $\mathbf{D_i}$ through a constant shift ($\mathbf{D}_i = 1 - \mathbf{K}_i$). Feature processing yields a set of more than 400 distance matrices. Feature selection is performed by ranking the features according to their degree of correlation to the correct labels (of the clustering). An optimal matrix $\mathbf{T}$ is computed, which is a square-matrix containing the pairwise hamming distances between the labels of the samples: $\mathbf{T}(i,j) = 0$, if the samples i and j belong to the same cluster, and $\mathbf{T}(i,j) = 1$ otherwise. For each matrix $\mathbf{D_i}$, we compute the distance dt to the optimal matrix with the Frobenius norm: $dt = ||(\mathbf{T} - \mathbf{D_i})||_F$. The features are then sorted in ascending order by their distance dt. For classification, the best combination b of the 10 features with minimal distance to the optimal matrix $\mathbf{T}$ (2^{10} possibilities) is used. The distance matrix $\mathbf{D}$ is obtained by adding up the distance matrices $\mathbf{D_i}$ of the features $\mathbf{f_i}$ contained in b. Classification is performed by using a k-nearest neighbours scheme on $\mathbf{D}$. The best combination b and the optimal k are found using a 9-fold cross validation. The classification accuracy is computed on the same folds (not nested).

Performance Prediction. The cluster information can be used to predict the student's performance. We identified a set of interesting features (see Tab. 2) that we like to predict. These features can be attributed to four different areas:

1. *Long-term training performance* (**PAS**, **NR**, **HS**): End level reached within the tutoring system.
2. *Short-term training performance* (**NSS**, **NSR**): Prediction of student responses.
3. *Individual knowledge gaps* (**KS**, **KNR**): Identification of particular deficient areas of knowledge.
4. *External test results* (**EPT**): Prediction of external post-test scores. In the **HRT** [7], children are provided with a list of 40 addition (subtraction) tasks ordered by difficulty. The goal is to solve as many tasks as possible within 2 minutes. The mean scores were 21.4 (53% correct) for addition and 19.6 (49% correct) for subtraction. In the **AT** [15], children are presented serially 20 addition (subtraction) tasks and there is no time limit. The mean scores were 16.6 (83% correct) for addition and 14.5 (72% correct) for subtraction.

Prediction of features is performed using cluster information (as described in Tab. 2). The prediction of long-term training performance is interesting for

Table 2. Predicted features along with error measures. $\mathbf{f_p}$ denotes the predicted value, $\mathbf{f_t}$ the actual value of the feature, and CE the classification error: $\#(\mathbf{f_p} \neq \mathbf{f_t})/\#played$.

	Description	Error measures
PAS	Indices of passed skills during training. A skill is predicted as passed, if the cluster majority passed it.	**JC**
NR	Indices of passed number ranges during training. A range is predicted as passed, if the cluster majority passed it.	**JC**
HS	Indices of highest skills passed by cluster majority during training (separately for part A and B).	**SD**
NSS	# samples needed to pass a skill (cluster mean). Predicted only for skills passed by cluster majority.	median($\mathbf{L1}/\|\mathbf{f_t}\|$)
NSR	# samples needed to pass a number range (cluster mean). Predicted only for ranges passed by cluster majority.	median($\mathbf{L1}/\|\mathbf{f_t}\|$)
EPT	Absolute and relative (#correct tasks/#tasks) post test score (cluster mean): **HRT+**, **HRT-**, **AT+**, **AT-**.	**L1**
KS	Indices of key skills. A skill is classified as key skill, if the cluster majority has problems.	CE, Recall, Precision
KNR	Indices of key number ranges. A range is classified as key number range, if it contains at least one key skill.	CE, Recall, Precision

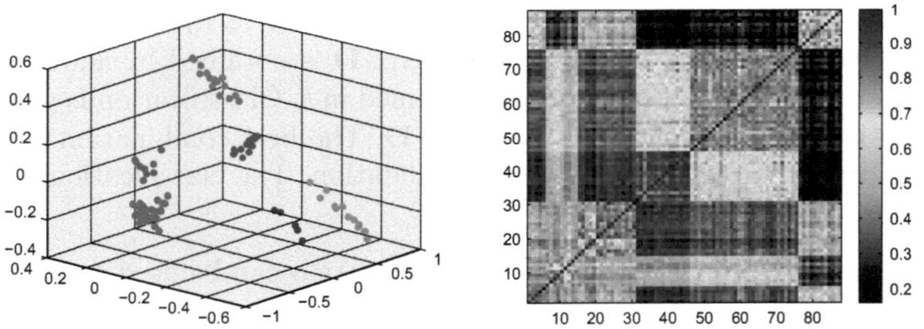

Fig. 3. Resulting clusters in 3 dimensions (left) and according similarity matrix (right). High similarities are displayed in red.

analysis as the predicted features are correlated to the learning trajectories. The identification of knowledge gaps helps to find subtypes of mathematical learning patterns and can be used to increase the degree of individualization (e.g., putting more emphasis on the training of key number ranges). Prediction of external test results is especially important for model validation. The prediction of short-term performance can be used to improve adaptation (e.g., minimizing frustration).

3 Results and Discussion

Clustering. The best BIC score was reached for k = 6 clusters. This result is supported by the clear separability of the transformed data in three dimensions (Fig. 3, left) and the clearly visible clusters on the diagonal of the similarity matrix (Fig. 3, right). Furthermore, the six clusters (C1-C6) can be interpreted

Table 3. Data per cluster (**C1 - C6**): Number of children **NC** (%), mean age **AG** (SD), number of passed skills **NPS**, probability of having problems **PP** in different number ranges of the training. + denotes the number ranges passed during training.

		C1	C2	C3	C4	C5	C6
NC	all	13 (14.77)	5 (5.68)	16 (18.18)	9 (10.23)	30 (34.09)	15 (17.05)
	CC	0 (0.00)	2 (40.00)	5 (31.25)	4 (44.40)	16 (53.30)	11 (73.30)
	DD	13 (100.0)	3 (60.00)	11 (68.75)	5 (55.60)	14 (46.70)	4 (26.70)
AG	all	9.26 (0.87)	8.18 (0.42)	8.60 (0.67)	8.52 (1.29)	8.78 (0.93)	8.53 (0.87)
	CC	-	8.06 (0.03)	8.10 (0.49)	7.52 (0.27)	8.16 (0.53)	8.11 (0.44)
	DD	9.26 (0.87)	8.26 (0.58)	8.82 (0.64)	9.32 (1.21)	9.49 (0.78)	9.67 (0.71)
NPS	A, B	12, 9	12, 14	15, 12	19, 22	22, 25	22, 30
PP	A_{10}	0.80^+	0.95^+	0.79^+	0.31^+	0.39^+	0.19^+
	B_{10}	0.68^+	0.20^+	0.57^+	0.11^+	0.14^+	0.14^+
	A_{100}	1.00	1.00	0.94^+	0.91^+	0.89^+	0.49^+
	B_{100}	0.99	0.98^+	0.99	0.96^+	0.87^+	0.30^+
	A_{1000}	x	x	x	0.98	0.72^+	0.56^+
	B_{1000}	x	x	x	0.98	0.99	1.00^+

regarding the characteristics and distinct learning patterns of the samples (Tab. 3), which are reflected in the training trajectories (Fig. 4). The children assigned to C1 have only passed the number range from 0-10. The difficulties with number representation (part A) as well as procedural knowledge (part B) imply an early disorder of numerical functions. All children of this group were diagnosed with DD. Children in C2 have passed the number range 0-100 for part B, but exhibit difficulties in part A. This learning pattern suggests problems with domain-specific functions such as quantity comparison and symbolic representation. In contrast to C2, children in C3 passed the number range 0-100 for part A, but not for B. This observation indicates intact number processing, but difficulties in understanding and executing procedures. The clusters C4 and C5 have passed the number range 0-100 for both parts and the number range 0-1000 for part A, respectively. C6 is the best performing cluster, with children having passed all number ranges and thus finished the training. The performance differences between clusters C4-C6 are probably due to differences in capacity and availability of domain-general functions (attention, working memory, processing speed). Notably, C4-C6 contain DD children (26.7% in C6). This fact can be attributed to age differences: DD children in C6 attend the 4th or 5th grade of elementary school. The interpretation of learning patterns confirms the usefulness of trajectory information for clustering.

Classification. During training, we classify the children to a particular subgroup depending on their current training status. As expected, classification accuracy increases with the number of training sessions (Fig. 5, left). Five sessions are already sufficient for the introduced method (blue) to cluster 50% of the

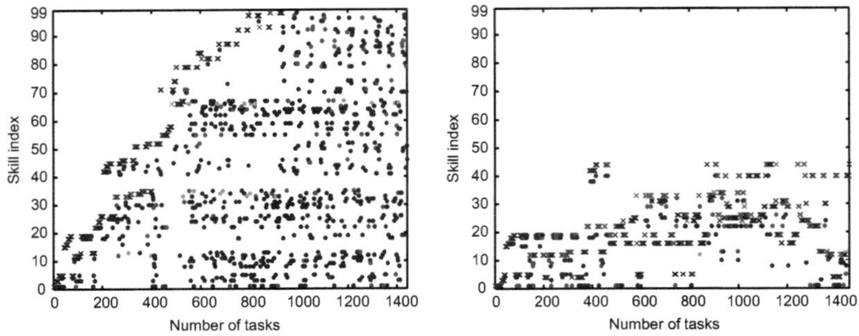

Fig. 4. Example trajectories of two children from clusters C6 (left) and C1 (right). A cross denotes a task played at the actual difficulty level while a dot denotes a random repetition. Red stands for a wrong answer, blue for correct, green for neutral.

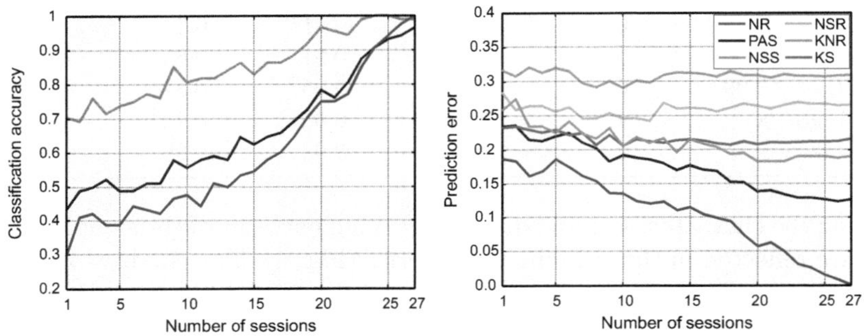

Fig. 5. Classification accuracy (left) and performance prediction for selected features (right) over time. Accuracy using offline features (red), the introduced method (blue) and portion of children classified correctly or to a direct neighbour cluster (light blue).

children correctly (chance: $16.\bar{6}\%$). Considering that some neighbouring clusters are close to each other (for instance, C1 and C2 are statistically distinguishable but similar), the assignment of a child to a direct neighbour of the correct cluster will not significantly deteriorate prediction quality. The estimation of the percentage of children assigned to the correct cluster or its direct neighbour (light blue) yields a success rate higher than 70% already after five sessions. The classification with the global features used for clustering (red) performs worse for small numbers of sessions, and equally well after 20 sessions. This behaviour highlights the importance of using local features for classification at an early stage in the training.

Performance Prediction. Student's performance in the four selected areas was predicted as described in Tab. 2. Figure 6 (left) shows the prediction errors after 27 sessions (offline prediction) on one to ten clusters. Most errors were significantly reduced (indicated by a two-sided t-test corrected for multiple comparisons with Bonferroni-Holm) by using the cluster information (Fig. 6, right). **NSS** and **NSR** do not show a high cluster dependency. However, as

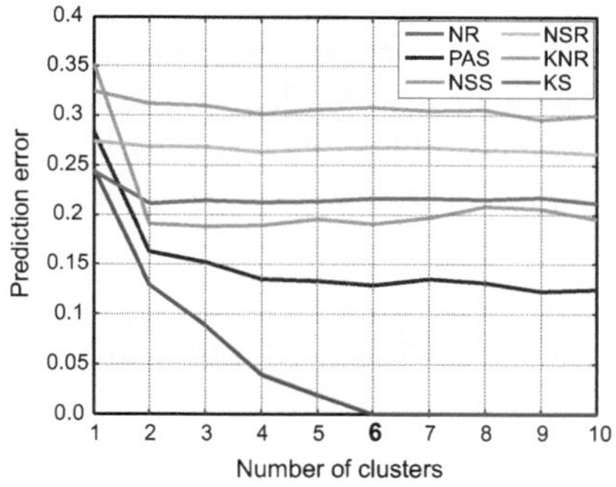

Feat.	Error_1	Error_6
PAS	0.28	0.13*
NR	0.25	0.00*
HS	2.69, 5.72	0.34*, 1.34*
NSS	0.32	0.31
NSR	0.27	0.26
HRT+	4.70 (0.12)	3.69* (0.09*)
HRT-	5.67 (0.14)	4.50* (0.11*)
AT+	3.26 (0.16)	2.61* (0.13*)
AT-	2.98 (0.15)	2.33* (0.12*)
KS	0.24, 0.10, 0.95	0.22*, 0.33*, 0.73*
KNR	0.35, 0.90, 0.55	0.19*, 0.82*, 0.74*

* $p - value < 0.01$

Fig. 6. Offline prediction errors (error measures from Tab. 2) plotted by the number of clusters (left) and listed for one and six clusters (right). For **EPT** features, absolute and relative errors (in brackets) are given and the numbers for **KS** and **KNR** denote classification error, recall and precision. The **HS** error is given for part A and B.

these features are predicted for skills (number ranges) passed by the cluster majority, the number of skills (number ranges) for which we can predict **NSS** (**NSR**) depends on **PAS** (**NR**). The high prediction accuracy of the long-term training performance (**PAS**, **NR**, **HS**) shows that clustering the children based on trajectory features is indeed meaningful. Furthermore, the accurate prediction of post-test results **EPT** demonstrates the correlation between achievement in external assessments and in-tutor performance and thus proves the validity of the student model. The promising results in the identification of knowledge gaps (**KS, KNR**) provide a valuable tool in the analysis of learning patterns and allow experts to elaborate individualized learning strategies. The accurate predictions of knowledge gaps together with the good prediction of short-term training performance (**NSS, NSR**) enable a tutoring system to better adapt the training to individual children. This, however, requires online performance prediction. Online prediction errors for the relevant features were computed after each session. As expected, the prediction errors depend on the classification accuracy (Fig. 5, right), i.e. prediction accuracy increases over the course of the training (due to their cluster independency, this does not hold for **NSS** and **NSR**). A good prediction accuracy is reached already after few trainings and allows to draw conclusions about short-term performance and knowledge gaps.

Conclusion. In this work, clustering was applied to learning trajectories of students to determine subgroups in a data set obtained from 88 children (50 children with DD and 38 controls). The computed BIC score suggested that six clusters are optimal. Moreover, the different clusters could be interpreted according to theory about mathematical development and DD. The online classification of the children to a particular subgroup has shown to be an inherent problem in the beginning of the training, but by using local features the classification accuracy was notably improved, enabling accurate prediction of student's future performance. Student's performance was predicted in four important areas. The results have demonstrated that the prediction accuracy can be significantly increased by taking subgroup information into account. The usefulness of clustering for the analysis of learning pattern and further training individualization contribute to a better support for children with learning difficulties.

Acknowledgments. The work was funded by the CTI-grant 11006.1 and the BMBF-grant 01GJ1011.

References

1. Amershi, S., Conati, C.: Combining Unsupervised and Supervised Classification to Build User Models for Exploratory Learning Environments. Journal of Educational Data Mining, 18–71 (2009)
2. Baker, R.S.J.d., Pardos, Z.A., Gowda, S.M., Nooraei, B.B., Heffernan, N.T.: Ensembling predictions of student knowledge within intelligent tutoring systems. In: Konstan, J.A., Conejo, R., Marzo, J.L., Oliver, N. (eds.) UMAP 2011. LNCS, vol. 6787, pp. 13–24. Springer, Heidelberg (2011)
3. Baschera, G.M., Gross, M.: Poisson-Based Inference for Perturbation Models in Adaptive Spelling Training. International Journal of AIED 20(4), 333–360 (2010)
4. Corbett, A.T., Anderson, J.R.: Knowledge tracing: Modeling the acquisition of procedural knowledge. UMUAI 4, 253–278 (1994)
5. Gong, Y., Beck, J.E., Ruiz, C.: Modeling multiple distributions of student performances to improve predictive accuracy. In: Masthoff, J., Mobasher, B., Desmarais, M.C., Nkambou, R. (eds.) UMAP 2012. LNCS, vol. 7379, pp. 102–113. Springer, Heidelberg (2012)
6. Gross, M., Vögeli, C.: A Multimedia Framework for Effective Language Training. Computer & Graphics 31, 761–777 (2007)
7. Haffner, J., Baro, K., Parzer, P., Resch, F.: Heidelberger Rechentest (HRT): Erfassung mathematischer Basiskomptenzen im Grundschulalter (2005)
8. Haghir Chehreghani, M., Busetto, A.G., Buhmann, J.M.: Information theoretic model validation for spectral clustering. In: Proc. AISTATS, pp. 495–503 (2012)
9. Hofmann, T., Buhmann, J.M.: Pairwise data clustering by deterministic annealing. IEEE Trans. Pattern Anal. Mach. Intell. 19(1), 1–14 (1997)
10. Kardan, S., Conati, C.: A framework for capturing distinguishing user interaction behaviours in novel interfaces. In: Proc. EDM, pp. 159–168 (2011)
11. Käser, T., Kucian, K., Ringwald, M., Baschera, G.M., von Aster, M., Gross, M.: Therapy software for enhancing numerical cognition. In: Interdisciplinary Perspectives on Cognition, Education and the Brain, vol. 7, pp. 219–228 (2011)
12. Käser, T., Busetto, A.G., Baschera, G.-M., Kohn, J., Kucian, K., von Aster, M., Gross, M.: Modelling and optimizing the process of learning mathematics. In: Cerri, S.A., Clancey, W.J., Papadourakis, G., Panourgia, K. (eds.) ITS 2012. LNCS, vol. 7315, pp. 389–398. Springer, Heidelberg (2012)
13. Kast, M., Meyer, M., Vögeli, C., Gross, M., Jäncke, L.: Computer-based Multisensory Learning in Children with Developmental Dyslexia. Restorative Neurology and Neuroscience 25(3-4), 355–369 (2007)

14. King, W., Giess, S., Lombardino, L.: Subtyping of children with developmental dyslexia via bootstrap aggregated clustering and the gap statistic: comparison with the double-deficit hypothesis. Int. J. Lang. Comm. Dis. 42(1), 77–95 (2007)
15. Kucian, K., Grond, U., Rotzer, S., Henzi, B., Schönmann, C., Plangger, F., Gälli, M., Martin, E., von Aster, M.: Mental Number Line Training in Children with Developmental Dyscalculia. NeuroImage 57(3), 782–795 (2011)
16. Mislevy, R.J., Almond, R.G., Yan, D., Steinberg, L.S.: Bayes nets in educational assessment: Where the numbers come from. In: Proc. UAI, p. 518 (1999)
17. Pardos, Z.A., Gowda, S.M., Baker, R.S., Heffernan, N.T.: The sum is greater than the parts: ensembling models of student knowledge in educational software. SIGKDD Explor. Newsl. 13(2), 37–44 (2012)
18. Pardos, Z.A., Trivedi, S., Heffernan, N.T., Sárközy, G.N.: Clustered knowledge tracing. In: Cerri, S.A., Clancey, W.J., Papadourakis, G., Panourgia, K. (eds.) ITS 2012. LNCS, vol. 7315, pp. 405–410. Springer, Heidelberg (2012)
19. Pavlik, P.I., Cen, H., Koedinger, K.R.: Performance factors analysis - a new alternative to knowledge tracing. In: Proc. AIED, pp. 531–538 (2009)
20. Pelleg, D., Moore, A.: X-means: Extending k-means with efficient estimation of the number of clusters. In: Proc. ICML, pp. 727–734 (2000)
21. Roth, V., Laub, J., Kawanabe, M., Buhmann, J.M.: Optimal cluster preserving embedding of non-metric proximity data. IEEE Trans. Pattern Anal. Mach. Intell. 25(12), 1540–1551 (2003)
22. Trivedi, S., Pardos, Z.A., Heffernan, N.T.: Clustering students to generate an ensemble to improve standard test score predictions. In: Biswas, G., Bull, S., Kay, J., Mitrovic, A. (eds.) AIED 2011. LNCS, vol. 6738, pp. 377–384. Springer, Heidelberg (2011)
23. Trivedi, S., Pardos, Z.A., Sárközy, G.N., Heffernan, N.T.: Co-clustering by bipartite spectral graph partitioning for out-of-tutor prediction. In: Proc. EDM, pp. 33–40 (2012)

Integrating Perceptual Learning with External World Knowledge in a Simulated Student

Nan Li, Yuandong Tian, William W. Cohen, and Kenneth R. Koedinger

School of Computer Science
Carnegie Mellon University
5000 Forbes Ave., Pittsburgh PA 15213 USA
{nli1,yuandong,wcohen,koedinger}@cs.cmu.edu

Abstract. Systems for smart authoring of automated tutors, like SimStudent, have been mostly applied in well-defined problem-solving domains where little real-world background knowledge is needed, like math. Here we explore the generality of these methods by considering a very different task, article selection in English, where little problem-solving is done, but where complex prior perceptual skills and large amounts of background knowledge are needed. This background knowledge includes the ability to parse text and the extensive understanding of semantics of English words and phrases. We show that good performance can be obtained by coupling SimStudent with appropriate broad-coverage linguistic tools. Performance can be improved further on this task by extending one of the learning mechanisms used by SimStudent so that it will accept less-accurate production rule conditions, and prioritize learned production rules by accuracy. Experimental results show that the extended SimStudent successfully learns the tutored article selection grammar rules, and can be used to discover a student model that predicts human student behavior as well as the human-generated model.

Keywords: simulated student, English article system, learner modeling.

1 Introduction

General theories and functioning simulations of how students learn have multiple uses. They can help educators to improve the understanding within domains, as well as to aid the authoring and evaluation of alternative instructional designs. To get a better understanding on how human students acquire knowledge, a lot of efforts (e.g., [2,17,21]) have been made to build intelligent agents that model the process of human learning in math and science.

SimStudent [17] is one such learning agent. It has been demonstrated in multiple domains such as fraction addition, equation solving, and stoichiometry [13]. Additionally, it has been shown that by integrating perceptual learning into skill learning, SimStudent can be used to find better student models than human-generated models [14]. However, most of these domains are well-defined problem-solving domains, where little real-world background knowledge is needed.

K. Yacef et al. (Eds.): AIED 2013, LNAI 7926, pp. 400–410, 2013.

In this paper, we explore the generality of the proposed approach in a linguistic domain, article selection in English, where no complex problem solving is needed, but where complex perceptual knowledge and large amounts of background knowledge are needed. Perceptual learning in this world-knowledge rich domain requires an extensive understanding of semantics of English words and phrases and in particular, sentence parsing. There has been a long-standing interest in the natural language processing community to learn how to parse sentences correctly. Therefore, we apply one of the extensively-used linguistic tools, the Stanford parser [8], to the sentences in the problems, and integrate the perceptual representations (parse trees) of the sentences into SimStudent.

In addition, although linguistic theory has long assumed that knowledge of language is characterized by a categorical system of grammar, many previous studies have shown that language users reliably and systematically make probabilistic syntactic choices [7]. To incorporate this probabilistic aspect, we further extend SimStudent to accept less-accurate production rule conditions, and learn to prioritize learned rules by accuracy.

Experimental results show that the extended SimStudent can successfully learn how to select the correct article given a reasonable number (i.e., 60) of problems. Moreover, we use the extended SimStudent to discover human student models. The model generated by the extended SimStudent is as good as the human-generated model in predicting human student behavior.

2 English Article System

Before describing our simulated student, let us first take a look at the domain. The learning task is to acquire the English article system. There are more than 40 grammar rules to decide which article to choose.

In the current study, we took the problems from a previous study on human students [22]. There are six most-frequently used grammar rules taught in the study, as shown in Table 1. Each problem consists of one or two sentences and an empty space to be filled with an article that best completes the sentence (e.g., *Clocks measure ___ time.*). There are three choices available, *a/an*, *the* and *no article*. In the clock example, since time is uncountable, *no article* should be selected based on the rule "generic-noncount".

Priorities exist among these six grammar rules. For example, in the problem *He drives ___ same car as he did last year*, both the condition of the rule

Table 1. Grammar rules in selecting appropriate articles

Rule Name	Content	Article
generic-singular	Use "a/an" when a singular count noun is indefinite.	a/an
generic-noncount	Use "no article" with a noncount noun that is indefinite.	no article
generic-plural	Use "no article with a plural noun that is indefinite.	no article
number-letter	Use "a/an" for single letters and numbers.	a/an
already-mentioned	Use "the" when the noun has already been mentioned.	the
same	Use "the" with the word "same".	the

- Skill generic-noncount (e.g., Clocks measure ___ time.)
- Perceptual information:
  - Noun the article is pointing at (time)
- Precondition:
  - Is uncountable (time)
- Operator sequence:
  - Select "no article"

- Skill same (e.g., He drives ___ same car as he did last year.)
- Perceptual information:
  - The word after the article (same)
- Precondition:
  - Is same (same)
- Operator sequence:
  - Select "the"

Fig. 1. The production rules "generic-noncount" and "same" in a readable format. The rule "same" has a higher priority than the skill "generic-noncount" and "generic-singular". If the word after the article is same, "the" will be selected no matter whether the noun the article is pointing at is countable or not.

"generic-singular" and the condition of the rule "same" are satisfied, but since the rule "same" has a higher priority, the article *the* should be selected.

3 A Brief Review of SimStudent

SimStudent is an intelligent agent that inductively learns skills to solve problems from demonstrated solutions and from problem solving experience. It is a realization of programming by demonstration [12] and employs inductive logic programming [19] as one of its learning mechanisms. For more details, please refer to [17]. Recently, in order to build a more human-like intelligent agent, we have developed a model of representation learning, and integrated it into SimStudent's skill acquisition mechanism [13].

In terms of tutoring strategy, SimStudent learns by interacting with a tutor, which can be either a human tutor or an automated tutor. Given a problem, if SimStudent does not know how to solve it, it will ask the tutor to demonstrate the next step. If SimStudent knows how to proceed, it will propose the next step, and ask for feedback from the tutor.

SimStudent learns skills as production rules. Figure 1 shows example production rules for skill "generic-noncount" and "same" in a readable format. A production rule shows "where" (i.e., perceptual information) to look for useful information, "when" (i.e., precondition) to apply the skill, and "how" (i.e., operator sequence) to proceed. For example, the rule shown in the left side of Figure 1 means given the noun that the article is pointing at (i.e., *time*), if the noun is uncountable, then select *no article.*

SimStudent has three learning components, where each of them acquires one part in the production rules. The first component is a perceptual information (i.e., "where") learner that acquires the path to identify the useful information from its environment given a perceptual hierarchy. In our case, the environment is a graphical user interface. Each sentence is filled in a row of cells, leaving an empty cell to be filled in by SimStudent or the tutor. In the example skill

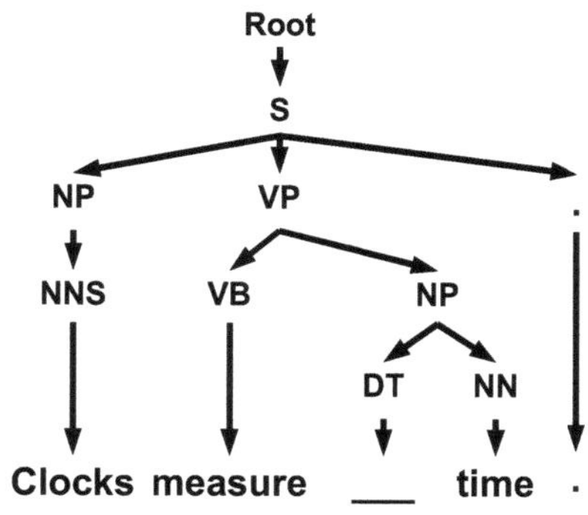

Fig. 2. The parse tree of "*Clocks measure* ___ *time.*" generated by the Stanford parser.

"generic-noncount", if no linguistic tool is used, the perceptual hierarchy provided to SimStudent becomes a flat list, and SimStudent may fail to learn how to identify the noun that the article is pointing at. As we will see later, with the parse trees generated by the parser, SimStudent can learn the path to identify the noun. The second part of the learning mechanism is a precondition (i.e., "when") learner, which acquires the description of desired situations in applying the skill given a set of feature predicates. The quality of the preconditions acquired largely depends on the set of feature predicates given to the precondition learner. As we will show later, SimStudent can automatically generate feature predicates based on the parse trees of the sentences. The last component is the operator sequence (i.e., "how") learner. Given all of the demonstrated steps, the learning mechanism searches for the shortest operator sequence that could explain all of the records, using iterative-deepening depth-first search.

As we can see, the prior knowledge given to SimStudent (e.g., the perceptual hierarchy, the feature predicates, operator function) affects the learning effectiveness of SimStudent. Moreover, we want this prior knowledge to be acquired rather than programmed, since the more knowledge engineering needed, the less human-like SimStudent is. Previous studies [5] have shown that one of the key differences between experts and novices is their different representations of the world. Therefore, we have extended SimStudent to support representation learning, and integrated it into skill learning [13]. By integrating representation learning and skill learning, we can learn a tree-structured representation of the problem, automatically generate feature predicates based on the representation [15], and reduce the need of domain-specific operator functions. The representation learning mechanism used is an extended version of a probabilistic context-free grammar (pCFG) learner. For more details, please refer to [13].

4 Perceptual Learning with External World Knowledge

In spite of the promising results we have shown, the domains we have tested so far are all well-defined domains (e.g., fraction addition, equation solving, stoichiometry), where the perceptual representation captured by a pCFG can be learned without large amounts of external world background knowledge. On the other hand, article selection in English is quite different, as complex prior perceptual knowledge as well as large amounts of world knowledge is needed.

Therefore, we use an existing linguistic tool, the Stanford parser, to automatically generate the parse structure of the input sentence for SimStudent. The parse tree for the clock example is shown in Figure 2. We give these parse trees to SimStudent as the perceptual hierarchies. Based on these hierarchies, SimStudent learned that the noun that the article is pointing to is the last sibling of the article in the subtree. In the example, the non-terminal node *NP* has two children, hence, the word *time* is the noun that the article is pointing at.

Moreover, SimStudent automatically generated a set of feature predicates based on the parse tree. For example, in the parse tree shown in Figure 2, each non-terminal symbol (e.g., *NN*) is associated with a feature predicate (e.g., *(is-NN ?val0 ?val1)*). Given the parse tree, *(is-NN time Clocks-measure-time)* returns true. Topological based feature predicates such as (e.g., *(is-child-of ?val0 ?val1 ?val2)*) can also be generated, but were not used in article selection.

Lastly, we use Wiktionary[1], which is a collaborative project for creating a free lexical database in every language, complete with meanings, etymologies, and pronunciations, to generate two feature predicates (i.e., *(is-countable ?val)*, *(is-uncountable ?val)*) that evaluate whether a noun is countable or not. Note that since one word may have multiple senses, it can be both countable and uncountable at the same time.

5 SimStudent with Probabilistic Conflict Resolution

As mentioned above, although grammar rules are often modeled as a categorical system, previous studies have shown that people systematically make probabilistic choices [7]. To incorporate this feature, we developed two conflict resolution strategies that prioritize rules based on accuracy. SimStudent associates each production rule with a utility. When multiple production rules are applicable, the production rule with the highest utility is applied first.

To implement the conflict resolution strategy, we lowered the accuracy requirement of the preconditions learned by FOIL, so that preconditions that are less accurate are also included in the production rule. This modification allows SimStudent to learn more general production rules. Therefore, there are more situations where more than one production rules are applicable. However, some of them may be incorrect.

Next, SimStudent computes the utility associated with each production rule based on the correctness of the rule's application history. We designed two ways of computing the utility. The first approach is developed based on ACT-R's conflict resolution strategy [3], where the utility associated with production rule i, U_i, is calculated based on the following equation.

[1] `http://www.wiktionary.org/`

$$U_i = P_i G - C_i,$$

where, P_i is the probability of success of the production rule i, C_i is the average cost of the production rule, and G is a goal value. Please refer to [3] for details.

In the above approach, P_i considers all successful applications are equally important. One interesting question to ask is whether the importance of the rule application result decays as time passes. Hence, in the second approach, instead of directly computing the probability of success, SimStudent weighs recent successes more than the past ones. Each time a rule is applied correctly, it is given a constant reward, R, and the utilities of all other rules decay by another constant, d. In case of an incorrect application, the same constant value, R, is removed from the utility function. Therefore, the utility of production rule i at time t, $U_{i,t}$, is calculated by

$$U_{i,t} = D_{i,t}G - C_i,$$
$$D_{i,0} = 0,$$
$$D_{i,t+1} = (-1)^{failure}R + dD_{i,t},$$

where $D_{i,t}$ is the decayed success rate at time t, $failure$ is an integer that equals to 1 if the rule application is incorrect, and 0 if correct, R is the reward/punishment given to the production rule, and d is the rate of decaying.

6 Experimental Results

To evaluate the effectiveness of the proposed approach, we carried out two experiments to test, 1) whether the extended SimStudent can learn the six grammar rules; and 2) whether the extended SimStudent can predict human student behavior just as well as human-generated models.

6.1 Experimental Design

We used data collected from Wylie et. al's [22] recent study on second language learning. The study was conducted at the University of Pittsburgh's English Language Institute. Students *(N=99)* were adult English language learners *(mean age = 27.9, SD=6.6)* and participated as part of their regular grammar class. Data collection was completed within one 50-minute class period. Pre- and post-test items were identical in the form of the practice problems that students had seen during tutoring without feedback and hints. All of the student behaviors were recorded during the process, and encoded with rules applied to the problems and whether students answers are correct.

SimStudent was taught by an automated tutor that simulates the tutor used by human students, and was trained on the same 60 problems that were provided to human students. The production rules acquired were evaluated on 12 problems given to human students as test problems.

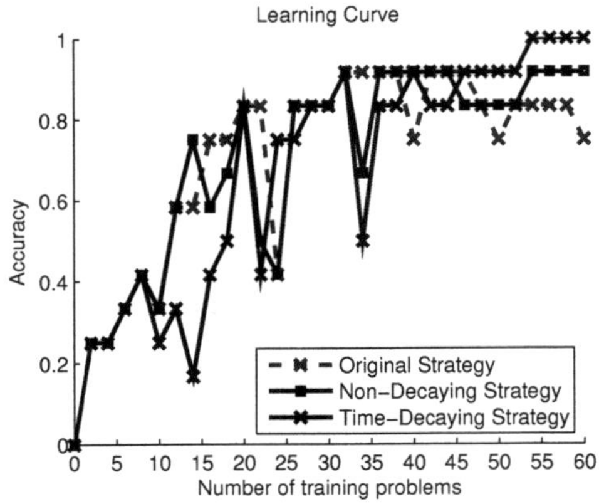

Fig. 3. Learning curves of SimStudents in article selection

6.2 Speed of Learning

We evaluated four versions of SimStudent, 1) the original SimStudent without external world knowledge and the new conflict resolution strategy[2], 2) the extended SimStudent with external world knowledge using the original conflict resolution strategy, 3) the extended SimStudent with external world knowledge using the non-decaying conflict resolution strategy, 4) the extended SimStudent with external world knowledge using the time-decaying conflict resolution strategy. In order to rule out the effect of other parameters, we set G and C_i to be the same across all production rules, so that the production rule priorities are decided by P_i and $D_{i,t}$. We report the average accuracy of SimStudent's first attempts at each step over 12 test problems.

Since the original SimStudent without external world knowledge considered that all words in the sentence form a flat hierarchy, it failed to learn how to identify the noun that the article is pointing at. In fact, it learned overly-general production rules, and could not finish training in a reasonable amount of time. Therefore, the learning curve of the original SimStudent is not reported here, and should be much flatter than the extended one.

As we can see in Figure 3, all three SimStudents learn reasonably well, reaching accuracies of more than 0.75 given 60 problems. This result indicates that by integrating perceptual learning with external world knowledge, the extended SimStudent is able to successfully learn the six grammar rules. Among the three SimStudents, the extended SimStudents using the proposed conflict resolution strategies are better than the SimStudent using the original strategy. A careful inspection of the data showed that although all SimStudents learned the rule "generic-plural" and the rule "already-mentioned", the SimStudent with the original conflict resolution strategy failed to learn that the rule "already-mentioned" is preferred over the rule "generic-plural". For example, when given

[2] The conflict resolution strategy of the original SimStudent is to fire the most recently activated non-buggy production rule.

the problem, *Some planes appeared, and then ___ planes landed in a field*, the SimStudent with the original conflict resolution strategy decided to apply the "generic-plural" rule, and selected *no article*. This suggests better conflict resolution strategies can further improve SimStudent's learning effectiveness.

The extended SimStudent using the time-decaying conflict resolution strategy learns the fastest. It reaches an accuracy of 1.00 given 60 training problems. The extended SimStudent using the non-decaying conflict resolution strategy is slightly worse than the one using the time-decaying strategy.

6.3 Fit to Human Student Data

The second experiment is to test whether the extended SimStudent can be used to discover models of human students. A student model is a set of *knowledge components (KC)* encoded in intelligent tutors to model how students solve problems. Applying the approach described in [14], we use SimStudent to automatically generate a student model. Each production rule or each disjunction in a rule corresponds to one KC. We compare the SimStudent-generated model with the best human-generated model constructed by domain experts. To evaluate how well the student model fits with human data, we used the Additive Factor Model (AFM) [4] to validate the coded steps. AFM is an instance of logistic regression that predicts the probability of a student making an error on the next step given each student, each KC, and the KC by opportunity interaction as independent variables. We use Akaike information criterion (AIC) and a 10-fold cross validation (CV) to test how well the generated model predicts the correctness of human student behavior without overfitting.

SimStudent successfully recovers the KCs associated with the six grammar rules. Moreover, it splits the rule "number-letter" into two KCs, one for "number" and one for "letter". The SimStudent-generated model is as good as the human-generated model both in terms of AIC (6221.39 vs. 6221.49) and the root mean-squared error in cross validation (0.3769 vs. 0.3777). This suggests that SimStudent finds as good a student model as the human-generated one. Moreover, we have carried out an in-depth study using Focused Benefits Investigation (FBI) [9] to better understand the difference between the two models. Results show that among the 19 KCs in the human-generated model, 15 of them are improved, in terms of RMSE, in the SimStudent-generated model.

7 Related Work

In this paper, we extend perceptual learning with external world knowledge in a simulated student. Previous work on article selection (e.g., [22]) has shown that learning in this domain contains challenges that cause some effective instructional strategies (e.g., self-explanation) in math and science to become less effective. Recent efforts such as the Fawlty tutor [10] have attempted to teach correct article usage by building an intelligent tutoring system. To better understand the cause of this phenomenon and to better teach students, we constructed a learning agent that models knowledge acquisition for article selection. This required extending our model of perceptual learning with external world knowledge, and integrating it into a simulated student. Other research on ill-defined domains [16] is also related to our work, but focuses on other learning tasks.

There have been recent efforts (e.g., [2,17,21]) in developing intelligent agents that model student learning, but most of the existing works have been done in well-defined domains, where little real-world knowledge is needed. There has also been considerable research on learning within agent architectures [11,1,20], and other efforts to incorporate machine learning to aid intelligent tutoring system authoring [18]. Unlike those theories, SimStudent puts more emphasis on knowledge-level learning (cf., [6]) than speedup learning. Moreover, to the best of our knowledge, none of them have focused on integrating representation learning with skill learning as we have done with SimStudent.

8 Conclusion

In future work, in addition to predicting the probability of success of human students, we would also like to see what causes human students to make certain types of errors by manipulating SimStudent's prior representation knowledge. Furthermore, in this study, we explored the six most frequently used grammar rules in article selection. There are many other cases that are not covered by these six rules. Future studies should explore other less frequently used grammar rules in this domain. Finally, we would like to carry out controlled simulation studies in article selection to get a better understanding of why self-explanation is no more effective than simple practice in this domain.

Constructing an intelligent agent that simulates human-level learning is an essential task in education. Previous effort has shown that by integrating a representation learning algorithm into an intelligent agent, SimStudent, as an extension of the perception module, the extended SimStudent is able to achieve comparable performance without requiring any domain-specific operator function as input in well-defined domains. In this paper, we further evaluated the generality of the approach in a world-knowledge rich domain, we extended representation learning with external world knowledge, and integrated it into SimStudent. Results show that given a reasonable number (e.g., 60) of training examples, the extended SimStudent successfully learns six frequently-used article selection rules, and can be used to find student models that predict human student behavior as well as a human-generated model.

Acknowledgements. We thank Ruth Wylie for helpful discussion, and the National Science Foundation (#SBE-0354420) for funding of the Pittsburgh Science of Learning Center.

References

1. Anderson, J.R.: Rules of the Mind. Lawrence Erlbaum Associates, Hillsdale (1993)
2. Anzai, Y., Simon, H.A.: The theory of learning by doing. Psychological Review 86(2), 124–140 (1979)
3. Belavkin, R.V., Ritter, F.E.: OPTIMIST: A New Conflict Resoution Algorithm for ACTR. In: Proceedings of the 6th International Conference on Cognitive Modeling, Pittsburgh, PA, pp. 40–45 (2004)
4. Cen, H., Koedinger, K., Junker, B.: Learning factors analysis – A general method for cognitive model evaluation and improvement. In: Ikeda, M., Ashley, K.D., Chan, T.-W. (eds.) ITS 2006. LNCS, vol. 4053, pp. 164–175. Springer, Heidelberg (2006)
5. Chase, W.G., Simon, H.A.: Perception in chess. Cognitive Psychology 4(1), 55–81 (1973)
6. Dietterich, T.G.: Learning at the knowledge level. Machine Learning 1(3), 287–315 (1986)
7. Hay, J., Bresnan, J.: Spoken syntax: The phonetics of giving a hand in new zealand english. In: The Linguistic Review: Special Issue on Exemplar-Based Models in Linguistics, pp. 321–349 (2006)
8. Klein, D., Manning, C.D.: Accurate unlexicalized parsing. In: Proceedings of the 41st Annual Meeting on Association for Computational Linguistics, Stroudsburg, PA, USA, pp. 423–430 (2003)
9. Koedinger, K.R., McLaughlin, E.A., Stamper, J.C.: Automated student model improvement. In: Proceedings of the 5th International Conference on Educational Data Mining, Chania, Greece, pp. 17–24 (2012)
10. Kurup, M., Greer, J.E., McCalla, G.I.: The fawlty article tutor. In: Frasson, C., McCalla, G.I., Gauthier, G. (eds.) ITS 1992. LNCS, vol. 608, pp. 84–91. Springer, Heidelberg (1992)
11. Laird, J.E., Rosenbloom, P.S., Newell, A.: Chunking in soar: The anatomy of a general learning mechanism. Machine Learning 1, 11–46 (1986)
12. Lau, T., Weld, D.S.: Programming by demonstration: An inductive learning formulation. In: Proceedings of the 4th International Conference on Intelligence User Interfaces, pp. 145–152 (1999)
13. Li, N., Cohen, W.W., Koedinger, K.R.: Efficient cross-domain learning of complex skills. In: Cerri, S.A., Clancey, W.J., Papadourakis, G., Panourgia, K. (eds.) ITS 2012. LNCS, vol. 7315, pp. 493–498. Springer, Heidelberg (2012)
14. Li, N., Cohen, W.W., Koedinger, K.R., Matsuda, N.: A machine learning approach for automatic student model discovery. In: EDM, pp. 31–40 (2011)
15. Li, N., Schreiber, A., Cohen, W.W., Koedinger, K.R.: Creating features from a learned grammar in a simulated student. In: Proceedings of the 20th European Conference on Artificial Intelligence (2012)
16. Lynch, C., Ashley, K.D., Pinkwart, N., Aleven, V.: Concepts, structures, and goals: Redefining ill-definedness. International Journal Artificial Intelligence in Education 19(3), 253–266 (2009)
17. Matsuda, N., Lee, A., Cohen, W.W., Koedinger, K.R.: A computational model of how learner errors arise from weak prior knowledge. In: Proceedings of Conference of the Cognitive Science Society (2009)
18. Mitrovic, A., Martin, B., Suraweera, P., Zakharov, K., Milik, N., Holland, J., Mcguigan, N.: Aspire: An authoring system and deployment environment for constraint-based tutors. International Journal of Artificial Intelligence in Education 19(2), 155–188 (2009)

19. Muggleton, S., de Raedt, L.: Inductive logic programming: Theory and methods. Journal of Logic Programming 19, 629–679 (1994)
20. Taatgen, N.A., Lee, F.J.: Production compilation: A simple mechanism to model complex skill acquisition. Human Factors 45(1), 61–75 (2003)
21. Vanlehn, K., Ohlsson, S., Nason, R.: Applications of simulated students: an exploration. Journal of Artificial Intelligence in Education 5, 135–175 (1994)
22. Wylie, R., Koedinger, K., Mitamura, T.: Analogies, explanations, and practice: Examining how task types affect second language grammar learning. In: Aleven, V., Kay, J., Mostow, J. (eds.) ITS 2010, Part I. LNCS, vol. 6094, pp. 214–223. Springer, Heidelberg (2010)

Using the Ecological Approach to Create Simulations of Learning Environments

Graham Erickson[1], Stephanie Frost[2], Scott Bateman[3], and Gord McCalla[2]

[1] Dept. of Computing Science, U. of Alberta, Edmonton, Canada
gkericks@ualberta.ca
[2] ARIES Lab., Dept. of Computer Science, U. of Saskatchewan, Saskatoon, Canada
stephanie.frost@usask.ca, mccalla@cs.usask.ca
[3] Dept. of Computer Science, U. of Prince Edward Island, Charlottetown, Canada
sbateman@upei.ca

Abstract. Simulated pedagogical agents have a long history in AIED research. We are interested in simulation from another, less well explored perspective: simulating the entire learning environment (including learners) to inform the system design process. An AIED system designer can carry out experiments in the simulation environment that would otherwise be too costly (or time consuming) with real learners using a real system. We suggest that an architecture called the "ecological approach (EA)"[1] can form the basis for creating such simulations. To demonstrate, we describe how to develop a proof-of-concept simulated ITS prototype, modelled in the EA architecture. We also show how to factor in data from two human subject studies (done for other purposes) to gain a degree of cognitive fidelity. An experiment is carried out with the prototype. The approach is general and can apply to learning systems with a wide variety of "pedagogical styles" (not just ITSs) at various stages of their life cycle. We conclude that simulation is a critically needed methodology in AIED.

Keywords: simulated learning environments, simulated learners, design of elearning systems, ecological approach.

1 Introduction

This paper is about the simulation of learning environments. The designer of a learning environment can use simulation to observe the impact of various design decisions under many combinations of circumstances: novice vs advanced learners, a few students vs many students, system vs learner control, etc. Simulations can allow learning system designers to easily experiment with many aspects of their systems without the need for expensive human subject studies, a similar role to mathematical models and physical models (like wind tunnels) for engineers when building physical artifacts. Simulations can be done at the outset of system design, or interleaved with human subject studies as a learning system iteratively evolves, or even during actual deployment in order to explore particular issues or to discover possible causes of various observed phenomena.

K. Yacef et al. (Eds.): AIED 2013, LNAI 7926, pp. 411–420, 2013.

In order to gain useful insights from a simulation, however, it must be possible to capture the key aspects of the learning system to be simulated. For a learning system this means, particularly, capturing the system's "pedagogical style" and capturing key aspects of the learners who will use the system. The simulated system can then interact with the simulated learners and the resulting performance can be measured in various ways to make predictions about how a real world version of the system might behave.

In this paper, we show how the ecological approach (EA) architecture [1] can serve as the framework for building learning systems of many different pedagogical styles. We discuss how a system designer can map a proposed learning system into the EA architecture. We then describe a prototype simulation that serves as a "proof of concept" of the feasibility of the approach. In particular we show how a specific pedagogical style (an ITS) can be implemented, and how the behaviour of the simulated learners can be informed by performance characteristics captured by human subject studies done for other purposes, providing a degree of cognitive fidelity with actual learners. We then discuss the result of an experiment run using the proof of concept prototype, that allows the extraction of a prediction about how the proposed learning system might function if actually built and used by real learners. We conclude the paper with a discussion of the role of simulation in the design of AIED systems, and why we feel that simulation must be in the arsenal of design methodologies available to AIED system designers, especially if we are to reduce the long development times normally associated with building "intelligent" learning systems (which can stretch to years or even decades).

2 The Ecological Approach

The *ecological approach* (EA) is an architecture for the design of learning environments that allows the capture of learner actions appropriately scoped to the content with which the learners are interacting. The architecture assumes that the learning content is packaged into *learning objects* (LOs) and that the learners are each represented by a *learner model* that contains both static attributes (the *characteristics* part of the model) and clickstream data gathered as they interact with the LOs (the *episodic* part). After each interaction by a learner with a LO, an *instance* of the learner model is attached to the LO as "metadata". Over time, many instances build up around each LO and can be the basis of reasoning for many purposes, such as recommending LOs that have been successful for learners who are similar to a given learner, finding out which LOs are useful or not, and so on. The approach is called ecological because as the metadata builds up naturally over time, the system can carry out its purposes with increasing precision, essentially "evolving" its capabilities in response to what has actually happened in the environment and what it is trying to do.

The ecological architecture also has the ability to represent many different styles of learning system. The concept of learning object is very general, and can include text, graphics, simulations, interactive pages, forums, etc. The learning objects and the learner models can contain many different attributes. Learners can interact in many different ways with LOs or with each other. No specific pedagogy is assumed: LOs can be presented in sequence, as in a traditional ITS; LOs can be recommended according to various recommender algorithms, collaborative or feature-based or hybrid; learners can help each other select content or to overcome impasses; and so on. The designer of a learning system can thus build a system using the EA architecture that matches his or her desired pedagogical style. This can be a system to be used with real learners, but more importantly for the purposes of this paper it can also be a simulation. We provide a "proof of concept" for this in the next section.

3 Building a Proof of Concept Prototype

In this section we show the development of a "proof of concept" prototype simulation created for a particular educational scenario. We demonstrate how the designer of a learning system can model his or her proposed system in the EA architecture (section 3.1) and then run experiments to answer questions about the proposed system (section 3.2). The goal is to provide a case study of our approach to simulation and its potential role in helping the process of learning system design.

3.1 Mapping to the Ecological Approach Architecture

For the proof-of-concept prototype, we developed the scenario of a designer building an intelligent tutoring system (ITS) for the introductory programming domain (a common one for an ITS). The stage of design is preliminary. The designer's purpose in building the simulation is to explore issues about the ordering of concepts and their effects on learning. In what follows, we talk about "the designer" and show the steps the designer takes as the simulation is being developed in order to illustrate the process in some detail. The simulation described below was actually designed and implemented by the authors, not some hypothetical designer, and the experiments using the simulation were actually carried out by the authors too.

In a traditional ITS, the content is typically packaged into modules that are related to one another by pre-requisite relations. The system typically also keeps learner models for each learner with both profile information and information gleaned during a learner's interactions with the ITS. As a learner interacts with a module, they are observed and evaluated as to how well they understand the content, and this information is incorporated into the learner model. Based on the learner model and the pre-requisite information, the ITS then recommends another module appropriate to the learner, and so on until some termination conditions are satisfied, ideally that the learner (as evidenced in their model) has mastered the important content.

An ITS can be easily mapped into the EA architecture. Each content module can be represented as a learning object. Prerequisites are kept as part of the information in each learning object. The learner profile for each learner is represented in the learner characteristics part of the learner model. Traces of learner interaction with learning objects are gathered in the episodic part. Algorithms are created to support the learner's interaction with a learning object, to evaluate the learner's performance, and to help in the selection of the next learning object. These all have to be emulated in a simulation of an ITS.

For the ITS simulation in this scenario, the designer can model the learning objects on the actual concepts in a typical introductory programming course, available readily from a course outline of an existing course. In the simulation, the designer also decides that (for his or her purpose) each learning object (LO) need only contain three elements: its level in the Bloom taxonomy [2], a set of parent LOs (that are prerequisites to this LO), and a set of child LOs (for which this LO is a prerequisite). Since this is a simulation, the learning objects need no other content. A similar process could be used to model almost any domain.

Having mapped the domain into learning objects, consistent with the EA architecture the designer also needs to model important attributes of each learner (the *characteristics*), to represent how each learner interacts with a learning object (the *behaviour function*), and to determine how successful (or not) a learner's interaction with a learning object is in pedagogical terms (the *evaluation function*). In this proof-of-concept prototype, the designer decides that he/she doesn't need to capture specific characteristics of the learners. Such characteristics (e.g. learning styles, gender) need only be added if certain attributes are deemed to generate important differences in learners' interactions relative to the designer's purpose.

To provide some realism to the behaviour function, the designer re-uses data collected in a study carried out by Bateman [3] exploring the workplace web browsing behaviour of 25 graduate and undergraduate research students. In the Bateman study a web browser plug-in called SaskWatch [3] logged each user's fine-grained actions for an entire year. By counting the number of times a user has performed a particular action divided by the number of minutes of system use, various rates for that user can be computed: *copyRate*, *cutRate*, *keypressRate*, *mouseClickRate*, *scrollRate*, *searchRate*, *changeLearningObjectRate*, *browseRate*. (Note: we only used a subset of the very large SaskWatch dataset.) For example, if a user had 3 mouse-clicks and used the system for 4 minutes, then their *mouseClickRate* is 0.75. Rates above 1 represent a user performing the action more than once per minute. Since the SaskWatch data set is so large, only a representative sample of each user's data is used. This collection of rates can then fuel a model of actual human browsing behaviour.

After obtaining each SaskWatch user's rates for each action, the designer creates a histogram for each rate across the population of users. This provides a distribution of the values for each rate. For example, the *browseRate* histogram showed that most users had a fairly short time between viewing pages, but indeed there were a few users with longer browse rates. Next, the designer fits a curve to each histogram so that the distribution of rate values can be represented by a function of the form $f(x) = a/(b*x) + c$, where a, b, c are constants and x is the rate value (for example, 0.75 *mouseClickRate*). Then $f(x)$ is the portion of the population who should have that rate. Next, each function is normalized to a probability density function so that the x-axis becomes the density (and not the actual rate value). To do this, $f(x)$ is integrated across its domain. The domain of $f(x)$ is the range of rate values given in the histogram. Using the probability density function, the cumulative distribution function, $F(x)$, is obtained. This gives the proportion of the population with a rate less than or equal to x. If $F(x)$ is inverted to obtain $F^{-1}(x)$, this will give rates that mimic the density described by the original $f(x)$. Learner interaction attributes can then be assigned using an initialization process structured like this:

for each rate, R: (ex: browseRate, mouseClickRate, *etc.)*
for each learner agent, L:
draw a uniform random number x
set $L.R = F^{-1}(x)$

Using this approach while there may be no real learner whose collection of web browsing attributes exactly matches a given simulated learner, the *population* of simulated learners will browse the learning objects in way that is statistically similar to the actual human web browsing activity logged by SaskWatch. At the design phase for which the proof-of-concept simulation is aimed, this allows the simulated learners to behave with some cognitive fidelity in the absence of other data about real learners. Of course, this approach ignores possible dependencies among the various rates. An alternative if there were more than 25 users in the study, would be to capture in a user model each user's behaviour over all the rates, and then design the artificial population to match the distribution of the user models rather than the specific rates. Later in the system life cycle, it might be possible to capture finer grained differences in how different users interact differently with specific learning objects, which would bring even more cognitive fidelity.

The designer also needs to capture how well a given simulated learner has understood a given learning object: that is, the evaluation function needs to be designed. For this, the designer decides to draw on another experiment carried out by Peckham and McCalla [4], who found patterns correlating learners' browsing behaviour with their success at answering questions at various levels of Bloom's taxonomy as they interacted with written material on-line. Since the simulated learning objects have Bloom levels, and since the simulated learners have been equipped with browsing behaviours (based on the SaskWatch data), this behaviour need simply be mapped onto Peckham's patterns, which then can predict the level of success in understanding the learning object.

Here are some details. Participant data were clustered into 4 groups of reading/scanning/scrolling behaviour: Light Reading, Light Medium Reading, Heavy Medium Reading or Heavy Reading. The Light Reading students spent the smallest proportion of time reading and the highest proportion of time scanning/scrolling. This proportion gradually changes all the way up to Heavy Reading, with the highest proportion of time spent reading and very little scanning/scrolling.

Peckham's study uncovered significant correlations between this behaviour and the score on comprehension questions, depending on the Bloom level of the LO. This correlation can be re-used in the simulation model to determine a score (degree of mastery of the concept). For example, consider a particular LO with a low Bloom level. Peckham's study shows that students with Light Reading behaviour achieved full marks or close to full marks on lower level Bloom questions, while students with Heavy Reading actually scored poorly: most scored 0 marks, with none achieving more than half marks (Peckham speculated heavy readers were confused by the material, and wasted too much time). Thus, in the simulation model, if a simulated learner exhibiting Light Reading behaviour interacts with a LO with a low Bloom level, the simulation model can assume that the learner will score high marks. Similarly, whenever a simulated learner exhibiting Heavy Reading behaviour comes across the same LO, the simulation model can assume that the interaction will end up with a poor score for the learner. A stochastic element is added to this score calculation, to account for the many other unknown factors that could impact a learner's score.

Thus, the proof-of-concept simulation has been equipped with simulated learning objects and simulated learners who interact with these learning objects. The modelling is based on real world data, but is still limited. The system designer could easily add in additional sophistication. For example, he or she might say that learners will achieve a higher score if they have already consumed prerequisite LOs. Or, higher scores might result when the learner's preferred learning style matches the style of the LO (which would require adding learning style attributes to both learners and learning objects). Even without data from human subject studies to inform the behaviour function, commonsense assumptions could be used. This is the approach taken by Champaign [5] to make a number of interesting predictions about learning systems. We emphasize that it is not necessary to deeply model the whole learner or the whole learning environment, only the parts relevant to the questions being asked by the designer. The stage of design will also be a big factor. In early stages of designing a learning system there will not be any data gleaned from an actual system deployed with real learners to inform the simulation, so re-purposing data gathered in other studies, as we have done here, is a plausible alternative. Later in the system life cycle, after various versions of the actual learning system have been built and tested with human subjects, real data would be available to any simulation modelling the designer wants to undertake.

Having created the simulation model in terms of the ecological architecture, the designer can then run experiments using the proof-of-concept prototype to show what happens when the model is used under various assumptions about how the next learning object is to be selected. This is discussed in the next section.

3.2 Running Experiments Using the Simulation

In the proof-of-concept scenario, the designer wishes to run the simulation to determine the impact on learning of various approaches to selecting the next learning object. To this end, an experiment is created where the simulation is run under three different conditions: *unstructured*, *semi-structured*, and *structured*.

The unstructured condition is a baseline, where learners select the next LO at random. In the semi-structured and structured conditions learners are not allowed to choose a LO unless they have "mastered" the pre-requisite LOs (i.e. the score is computed to be high after an interaction). Once an LO has been selected, in the structured condition learners must keep attempting to complete the LO until it has been mastered. In the semi-structured condition, learners can choose to abandon an LO in favour of another LO (whose pre-requisites they have mastered). In all conditions learners are not allowed to choose LOs that they have already mastered.

The experimental data includes a record of all learner-LO interactions and the resulting scores under the three conditions. From this data, the designer can choose among a wide variety of measurements of success: the average score for all LOs, the score for only leaf LOs (where 'leaf' means the LOs at the end of the course), the score for only mastered LOs (as opposed to the LOs not attempted or attempted and failed). These measurements can be compared across the three conditions. Note that the fine-grained data about learner-LO interaction collected in the EA would also allow other unanticipated patterns to be "mined" from this same data, should the designer wish to explore other issues.

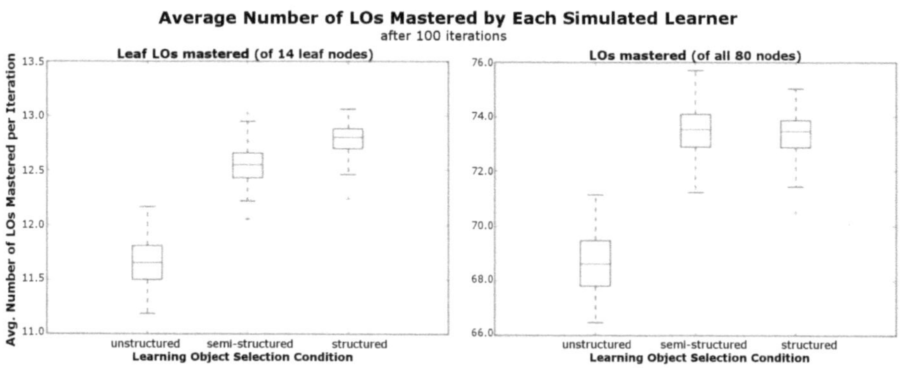

Fig. 1. Results of the Simulation (Box plot)

To illustrate, Figure 1 summarizes experimental results of the scenario. The experiment consisted of 100 runs (or iterations) of a simulated course with 400 learners. Out of the 80 LOs in the course, 14 were leaf objects. The red line shows the mean number of mastered leaf LOs (left) or the mean number of LOs mastered among all LOs (right), for each learner. The extent of the boxes represents the upper and lower quartile. The extent of the capped lines represent the max. and min. value still within 1.5 interquartile range. Outliers are marked by blue crosses.

The results show (unsurprisingly) that the unstructured condition is undesirable: structuring clearly is useful. Moreover, it is interesting that the semi-structured environment is marginally better than the structured environment for mastered LOs, but that this is substantially reversed for mastered leaf LOs. One hypothesis is that the structured environment reaches more leaf nodes because by not providing as much choice learners end up traversing the prerequisite tree more deeply (right down to the leaf LOs) in the same number of iterations.

These results can inform the system designer who presumably would decide to incorporate some version of structuring into the actual ITS to be used by real learners. Of course, the designer may decide to run any number of other simulations. It doesn't cost much once the simulation environment has been set up. For example, the designer could change the Bloom levels or pre-requisite requirements of a few key LOs and run the simulation again to get an idea of the impact. Another possible experiment would be to create other structuring conditions; e.g. instead of following the prerequisite structure so closely, the Bloom level could be more of a factor, perhaps favouring lower Bloom level LOs over higher ones when there is a choice. All of these could be done very easily, without changing any of the basic abstractions informing the simulation. But, it also is not too hard to start making the simulated learners more sophisticated (adding new characteristics), or to change the behaviour or evaluation functions, or to give additional attributes to the learning objects. With more effort, even the traditional ITS architecture could be changed. Thus, the designer could incorporate a LO recommendation engine, perhaps using the behaviour of the learner to help personalize the recommendation. Or the designer could create a collaborative environment, with protocols for the simulated learners to interact with one another (as Champaign [5] has done in one of his experiments). The ecological approach can support the modelling of virtually any kind of learning environment.

4 Research Context and Discussion

Over 15 years ago VanLehn et al. [6] outlined three main uses for simulation in the design of learning systems: (i) to provide a practice environment for human teachers; (ii) to provide simulated students who act as peers for human students; or (iii) to provide an environment for pilot testing instructional design issues. The second of these uses has had by far the most follow-up research in the intervening years. In fact, there have been many systems where simulated humans can take an explicit role in the learning environment, for example as learning companions [7], or as animated pedagogical agents [8], or as "teachable agents" in a reciprocal learning context [9], or even as tutors [10].

Our work is strongly aimed at the third use - to enable deep exploration of design choices when building a learning system. There has been some research in this context over the years. One branch is about cognitive modelling, e.g. Ohlsson et al.'s [11] simulations to provide insight into how students learn subtraction, and Matsuda et al.'s [12] increasingly sophisticated versions of SimStudent to capture fine-grained models of human skill acquisition. Another branch, recently championed by Champaign [5], does take a system level view to building simulated learning environments to answer specific pedagogical questions (based on commonsense assumptions about learners). Nobody to our knowledge has tried to provide a general framework for doing such simulations that could apply to the design of any system to support learning. This is the main contribution of our research.

We have argued that the ecological approach architecture allows systems of many pedagogical styles to be represented through mapping into learning objects, learner models, and appropriate interaction strategies. In a case study we shed light on how to actually build a "proof-of-concept" simulation of a learning system (an ITS in this case). An especially original aspect is the re-use of human subject data from other studies to inform the learner modelling and interaction behaviour. This may be the best that is possible early in the life cycle of a learning system. But after gaining insight from the simulation(s), the designer will eventually build a real system for human learners, so simulations developed later in the life cycle could use data gathered from actual learners.

Of course, our work provides only a proof-of-concept. Much more work has to be done to be completely convincing about the abstraction into the ecological architecture, its generality and power, and even the value of simulation itself. However, we strongly feel that the designers of learning systems need to add simulation to the arsenal of available tools. Simulation allows total designer control over any experiment. Measurements inaccessible in human subject studies can be made. Simulated learners are plentiful and cheap and are not required to give informed consent! Simulation allows a space involving a vast number of parameters to be explored with relative ease. Many questions (such as issues around load limits or appropriate response times) can be answered without needing cognitive fidelity in the learner models. Even if cognitive fidelity is desirable, there are so many sources of fine-grained user data being generated these days (e.g. from the PSLC data shop, https://pslcdatashop.web.cmu.edu/) that appropriate data could be found to inform the models (data re-purposing), as we have demonstrated here. Further, it is not necessary to model every detail of the learning process; valuable information can be gained simply by modelling characteristics most relevant to the questions being asked by the designer. This is a key point. We feel that simulation modelling may be most valuable for rejecting certain designs early in the design process, but if it is fairly easy to create a simulation then it can be used throughout the system life cycle, to test specific hypotheses (as Ohlsson et al. [11] did) or to gather data that can be mined for informative patterns. This is easier to do if both the simulation and the actual learning system share the same architecture (e.g. the EA architecture).

Perhaps the most convincing argument for simulation, however, is the nature of our field. The development time for a fully deployed learning system is often measured in decades, in no small part because of the huge cost in time and money of running human subject studies at each design cycle. Simulation can change that. As we begin to roll out learning environments meant for hundreds of thousands of learners (e.g. MOOCs, cognitive tutors, etc.), it will be important to test them first in simulation where we do not risk huge numbers of "drop outs" and to be able to continue to explore through simulation various hypotheses as these environments evolve over time. As AIED goes even further and begins to study lifelong learning, we will need some way to test lifelong learning techniques in less than a lifetime: simulation is a clear and promising possibility.

Acknowledgements. We would like to thank the Natural Sciences and Engineering Research Council of Canada for funding this research through a Discovery Grant to the last author.

References

[1] McCalla, G.: The Ecological Approach to the Design of e-Learning Environments: Purpose-based Capture and Use of Information about Learners. Journal of Interactive Media in Education (2004), `http://jime.open.ac.uk/jime/article/view/2004-7-mccalla`
[2] Bloom, B.: Taxonomy of Educational Objectives, Cognitive and Affective Domains. Longman Group, United Kingdom (1969)
[3] Bateman, S.: Using Group Interaction History in the Wild. In: The Doctoral Colloquium of the 2010 ACM Conf. Conference on Computer Supported Cooperative Work, Savannah, GA, pp. 523–524 (2010)
[4] Peckham, T., McCalla, G.: Mining Student Behavior Patterns in Reading Comprehension Tasks. In: Yacef, K., Zaïane, O., Hershkovitz, H., Yudelson, M., Stamper, J. (eds.) 5th Int. Conf. on Educational Data Mining, Greece, pp. 87–94 (2012)
[5] Champaign, J.: Peer-Based Intelligent Tutoring Systems: A Corpus-Oriented Approach. Ph.D. Thesis, University of Waterloo, Waterloo, Canada (2012)
[6] VanLehn, K., Ohlsson, S., Nason, R.: Applications of Simulated Students: An Exploration. Int. J. Artificial Intelligence in Education 5, 135–175 (1996)
[7] Chan, T.W.: Learning Companion Systems. In: Frasson, C., Gauthier, G. (eds.) Intelligent Tutoring Systems: At the Crossroads of Artificial Intelligence and Education, pp. 6–33. Ablex (1990)
[8] Johnson, L., Rickel, J., Lester, J.: Animated Pedagogical Agents: Face-to-Face Interaction in Interactive Learning Environments. Int. J. of Artificial Intelligence in Education 11, 47–78 (2000)
[9] Leelawong, K., Biswas, G.: Designing Learning by Teaching Agents: The Betty's Brain System. Int. J. Artificial Intelligence in Education 18(3), 181–208 (2008)
[10] Graesser, A., Chipman, P., Haynes, B., Olney, A.M.: AutoTutor: An Intelligent Tutoring System with Mixed-Initiative Dialogue. IEEE Transactions on Education 48, 612–618 (2005)
[11] Ohlsson, S., Ernst, A.M., Rees, E.: The Cognitive Complexity of Doing and Learning Arithmetic. Research in Mathematics Education 23, 441–467 (1992)
[12] Matsuda, N., Cohen, W.W., Sewall, J., Lacerda, G., Koedinger, K.R.: Predicting Students Performance with SimStudent that Learns Cognitive Skills from Observation. In: Luckin, R., Koedinger, K.R., Greer, J. (eds.) Proc. 12th Int. Conf. on AIED, pp. 467–476 (2007)

Using Data-Driven Discovery of Better Student Models to Improve Student Learning

Kenneth R. Koedinger[1], John C. Stamper[1], Elizabeth A. McLaughlin[1], and Tristan Nixon[2]

[1] Human-Computer Interaction Institute, Carnegie Mellon University
[2] Carnegie Learning, Inc.

Abstract. Deep analysis of domain content yields novel insights and can be used to produce better courses. Aspects of such analysis can be performed by applying AI and statistical algorithms to student data collected from educational technology and better cognitive models can be discovered and empirically validated in terms of more accurate predictions of student learning. However, can such improved models yield improved student learning? This paper reports positively on progress in closing this loop. We demonstrate that a tutor unit, redesigned based on data-driven cognitive model improvements, helped students reach mastery more efficiently. In particular, it produced better learning on the problem-decomposition planning skills that were the focus of the cognitive model improvements.

Keywords: data mining, machine learning, cognitive modeling.

1 Introduction

Much instruction is designed by intuition, drawing on the experiences and self-reflections of instructional designers or subject-matter experts. However, conscious access to our own knowledge is quite limited – estimated to be only about 30% of what we know [3]. The techniques of Cognitive Task Analysis (CTA), such as structured interviews of experts, can reveal such hidden knowledge. Furthermore, course redesign based on such analysis has been shown to improve student learning beyond that achieved by the original courses [3]. We have seen that greater levels of automation in CTA can be achieved by "mining" the log data from users of educational technology. By employing AI and statistical methods, better cognitive models have been discovered across multiple domains, and with student data from multiple technologies (intelligent tutors, online courses, games) [8]. This work is part of a related set of efforts to use data to discovery models of student knowledge and skill [1, 2]. One benefit of this data-driven approach to CTA is that it supplements human qualitative judgment with automated quantitative metrics that rigorously test purported cognitive model improvements. A critical next step is to the "close the loop" by using the improved cognitive models to redesign instruction and then to compare, in a controlled experimental study, whether the redesign produces better student learning than the original.

K. Yacef et al. (Eds.): AIED 2013, LNAI 7926, pp. 421–430, 2013.

Past experiments testing the benefits for student learning of CTA-based course redesigns have had impressive results, but have typically taken a broad strokes approach to redesign [10; 3]. The redesigned "treatment" course usually differs from the original "control" course in many ways not all of which are clearly attributable to cognitive model improvements or to the insights obtained from CTA. One exception is a tightly controlled experiment within an algebra story problem symbolization tutor where the treatment differed from the control only in the replacement of one problem type (simpler story problems) with another (symbolic substitution problems) [6]. Prior CTA, employing the Difficulty Factors Assessment technique, had discovered the cognitive skills of composing symbolic expressions (e.g., if w=40x and y=800-w, then y=800-40x) as a particularly difficult component in learning to model story problems in algebraic symbols. The treatment was designed to isolate practice on these skills and led to improved learning over the control, including transfer from symbolic substitution to story problems [6].

The Difficulty Factors Assessment is a paper-based predecessor of our current educational technology data mining techniques for CTA; and while the symbolization study is a nice example of closing the loop, it does not provide direct evidence that data mining can be leveraged to produce better student learning. That is the goal of the current paper. Before presenting the experiment, we first review the CTA that led to the recommended improvements.

2 Using Educational Technology Data for Cognitive Task Analysis

In [11], we presented a data-driven method for researchers to use data from educational technologies to identify and validate improvements in a cognitive model. For statistical modeling purposes, we used a simplification of a cognitive model made up of hypothesized components of knowledge or skills that students must acquire to be successful on target assessment tasks or activities. These knowledge components (KCs) identify latent variables in a logistic regression model called the Additive Factors Model (AFM) [11], which is a generalization of item-response theory [12]. The method involves a wash-rinse-repeat iteration: 1) inspect learning curve visualizations and best-fitting parameters of AFM for a given set of knowledge components (a KC model), 2) hypothesize changes to the KC model based on identified problematic KCs, and 3) refit AFM with the new KC model and return to step 1.

This method was applied to a publicly available data set from DataShop [5] called "Geometry Area (1996-97)." This data was generated by students using a Cognitive Tutor for learning geometry. A screen shot from a newer version of the tutor can be seen in Fig.1. The data included 5,104 student steps completed by 59 students. Using the visualizations available in DataShop, we identified potential improvements to the best existing KC model at the time we started, called Textbook-New, had 10 KCs. Three of the learning curves for these KCs are shown in Fig. 2. The lines represent the error rate (y-axis) averaged over all students for the first 20 practice opportunities for each KC. Most of the KCs in this model have reasonably smooth learning curves, like circle-area (some roughness in the learning curve can result from noise rather than a bad KC and particularly so when there are fewer observations being averaged, which

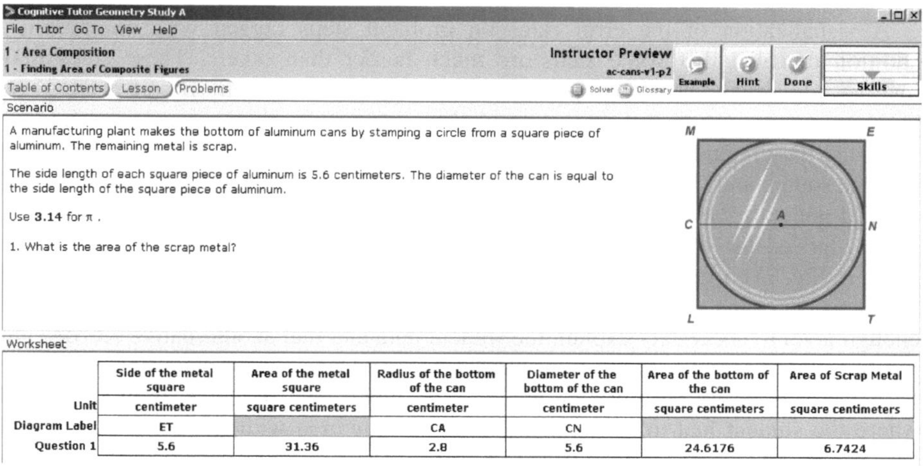

Fig. 1. A scaffolded "composite area" problem from the original Geometry Cognitive Tutor. In the lower table, the student fills in all cell values except the row and column labels. The columns for the areas of the metal square and the bottom of the can are given to scaffold student reasoning toward finding the composite area of scrap metal. These square and circle columns (2 and 5) are absent in an unscaffolded composite area problem.

is common at higher opportunity numbers.) The compose-by-addition curve is particularly jagged with upward blips at opportunities 12 and 15-18 where the curve jumps from about 25% to about 50%. Assuming there are particular problem steps that are more likely to occur at these opportunities (which is the case in this data set), those steps appear to have some knowledge demand that the other steps do not. The compose-by-addition KC involves "composite area problems", that is, problems where the area of a composite shape must be found by combining (adding or subtracting) the areas of two constituent regular shapes (e.g., what's left when a circle is cut from a square). In addition to the bumpy curve, the AFM parameter estimates indicate that compose-by-addition has no apparent learning (the slope parameter estimate is 0), yet it is associated with difficult tasks (the intercept parameter is 1.04 in log-odds, corresponding to a 26% error rate). The rough curve, flat slope, and non-trivial error rate are indications of a poorly defined KC.

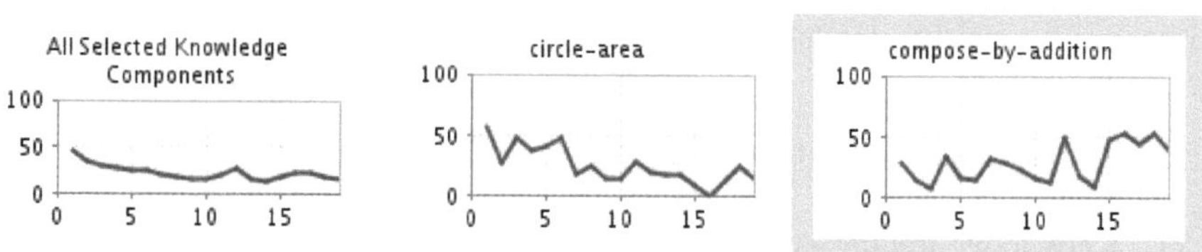

Fig. 2. Example learning curves where Y-axis is the error rate averaged across students (and KCs) and the X-axis is learning opportunities. Most curves, like the one for circle-area KC, are reasonably smooth and decreasing as indicated in the overall curve on the left. The curve for "compose-by-addition" is not smooth, with large jumps in the error rate particularly at opportunities 12 and 15.

A visualization of the error rates on problem steps tagged with compose-by-addition revealed that some steps are much harder than others. These steps may involve additional knowledge-demands that make them harder. By inspecting the problem content, we found that some of the composite problems were "scaffolded" such that they included columns that cued students to find the component areas first (see the square and circle columns in Fig. 1) [4]. Other problems were "unscaffolded" and did not start with such columns, thus students had to pose these sub-goals themselves. Indeed the blips in error rate for compose-by-addition (seen in the learning curve in Fig. 2) correspond with a high frequency of these more difficult unscaffolded problems. This analysis suggested that the compose-by-addition KC was not at a fine enough level to accurately explain the student data and that an alternative KC decomposition is needed. To improve the model, we split compose-by-addition into three KCs, one representing "*compose-by-addition*" with scaffolding present, a second where the student had to "*decompose*" a composite area without scaffolding, and a third where the student needs simply to "*subtract*" in order to execute a decomposition plan (formulated in a prior question within the same problem). In the new "DecomposeArith" KC model, the 20 steps that were previously labeled with the compose-by-addition KC are relabeled -- six with the new decompose KC, eight with the new subtract KC, and six keep the compose-by-addition KC label. The DecomposeArith model results in smoother, declining learning curves and, when fit with AFM, yields a significantly better prediction of student performance than the original.

To further validate the hypothesized model improvements, we performed a parallel analysis on a second Geometry Area data set also available in DataShop called "Geometry Area Hampton 2005-2006 Unit 34." The original Textbook student model associated with this data set had 13 KCs and when the steps for compose-by-addition were split into the three KCs as suggested above, a new DecomposeArith model was created with 15 KCs. Using AFM, we confirmed that this new model better predicts student data, reducing BIC (15,375 to 15,176) and root mean square error (RMSE) on test set fit in cross validation (.408 to .404) and thus supporting the existence of the new KCs.

The next step was to use the discovered model to improve the instruction in the cognitive tutor unit.

3 Redesigning the Geometry Cognitive Tutor

An improved cognitive model can be used in multiple possible ways to redesign a tutor:

1) Resequencing – position problems requiring fewer KCs before ones needing more
2) Knowledge tracing – add/delete skill bars for better cognitive mastery
3) Creating new tasks – add problems to focus practice on new KCs
4) Changing instructional messages, feedback or hint messages

We applied the improved model to the Geometry area unit of a high school geometry course. The improved model's new KCs are related to the planning of problem decomposition. We added three new skills to the tutor that differentiate unscaffolded decomposition, scaffolded, and simple addition/subtraction. These new skills resulted in changes to knowledge tracing and led to the creation of new tasks. In particular, students in the new version are not given credit for the difficult decomposition planning step via success on simpler scaffolded or subtraction steps, but only through success on unscaffolded composition steps.

We also added new problems to better target these newly identified skills. In our first attempt at redesign (briefly described in [11]), we identified four types of problems: unscaffolded, table scaffolded, area scaffolded, and problem statement scaffolded. Table scaffolded problems reflect the current setup in the tutor and include columns for intermediate areas (as in Fig. 1). Unscaffolded problems remove the columns for intermediate areas. Area scaffolded problems give the areas of the component shapes. Problem statement scaffolded problems have the same table as the unscaffolded problems but provide an explicit hint in the problem statement directing the student to first find the component areas. During the implementation of this first redesign attempt [11], we experienced some issues with the parameter settings and knowledge tracing algorithm which resulted in students never mastering all skills. We also found that the problem statement scaffolded problems did not seem to help the students learn the KCs, so we removed this type of problem in the next design iteration.

More importantly, inspired by related work [6], we realized there was an opportunity to better support students' learning of the hardest skill, the decomposition planning skill that recognizes a composite area is being sought and sets sub-goals to find it by first finding the component areas. We called this the "know to pose" skill and it always appeared with other skills on problem steps in the first redesign. The design challenge was to create a problem (or step) that makes visible and isolates just this "know to pose" skill. Our solution, shown in Fig. 3, was to ask students to come up with a plan to solve an unscaffolded composite area problem and recognize a correct description of such a plan.

In general, changes in skills can lead to changes in the feedback and hint messages the tutor provides. Thus, the new problems also come with new, more focused, context-sensitive instruction that follows directly from the cognitive model improvements.

To implement the new tutor, we needed to set the Bayesian Knowledge Tracing parameters for the new KCs. We set them by hand based on the available data, while recognizing the possibility of introducing differences between the experimental conditions. Given the introduction of more KCs, we wanted to avoid students in the treatment spending more time than the control, so we tried to err in the direction of more lenient settings (i.e., a higher initial probability of knowing a new KC). As it turned out, these settings were not too low as treatment students better learned decomposition skills than control students.

We also implemented a "minimizing" problem-selection algorithm which would help focus student practice by selecting problems with the fewest unmastered skills. This new algorithm is in contrast with the standard algorithm which selects problems that maximize a student's opportunity to practice unmastered skills.

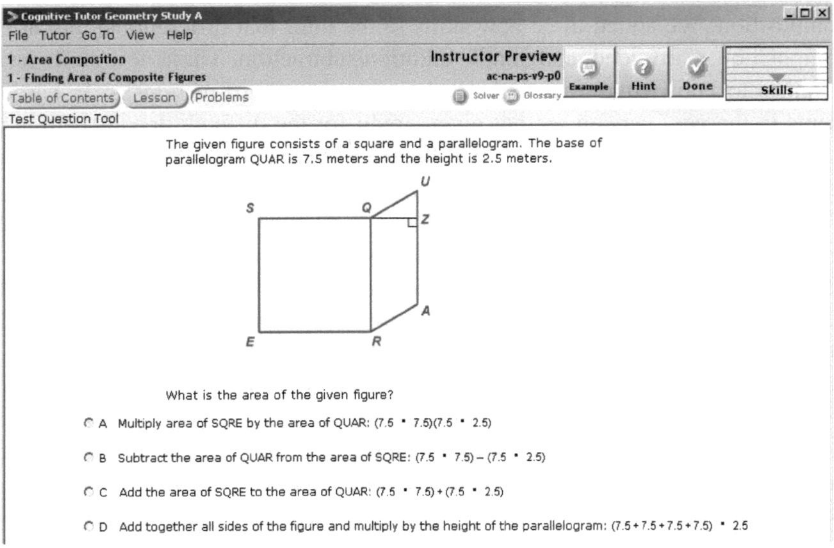

Fig. 3. Example of new problem type to isolate the know-to-pose KC. Students need to perceive the desired irregular area as being composed of areas of regular shapes and then devise a decomposition plan for solving for the irregular area. They do not need to execute the plan, but rather recognize a description of it.

4 Experiment

We performed an *in vivo* experiment comparing the redesigned tutor ("treatment") with the existing tutor ("control"). The study was run with 103 students (52 control, 51 treatment) as part of regular geometry classes in a local suburban high school in the Fall of 2011. Due to absenteeism, seven students did not complete the posttest and were excluded from our analyses leaving 96 students (48 control, 48 treatment).

Pre- and post-test measures were paper and pencil and included two versions (A and B) and two orders (four forms) with 12 problems each (5 area, 6 composition, and 1 compare - a qualitative judgment of the relative area of two related figures). The forms (A1, A2, B1, and B2) were randomly assigned for both pre and posttest. For each version, the cover stories, constants and sequence of problems varied but the shapes remained the same.

The treatment had one problem type, unscaffolded problems, that are harder than the table scaffolded problems used in the control and are more genuinely representative of the desired problem solving. The treatment also had two other problem types, area scaffolded and decomposition planning (as in Fig. 3), that are less complex, involving fewer steps but better isolating the critical decomposition skills. The intention was that these problems would more efficiently focus student learning on these skills, minimize distraction from and time spent on other skills, and better prepare students for unscaffolded problem solving practice. Thus, we hypothesized students would learn decomposition skills more effectively and more efficiently, that is, at a faster rate.

As shown in Fig. 4a, indeed, the treatment students mastered the required skills in much less time on average (20.9 minutes) than the control (28.4 minutes; see Fig. 1a). An ANCOVA with pre-test as a covariate found this difference to be statistically reliable ($F(1, 93) = 4.6$, $p = .03$) and an effect size (Cohen's *d)* of .6 indicates that it is substantial. Interestingly, despite taking 26% less time, the treatment students solved more problems (14.0 per student) than control students (10.4). We discuss later the reasons behind the treatment's faster completion of problems. We confirmed that all students mastered all knowledge components (8 in the treatment and 6 in the control) according to the Cognitive Tutor's Bayesian Knowledge Tracer ($p_{known} > .95$).

We must be cautious in using the tutor data alone to conclude that treatment students learned at a faster rate. The mastery criteria employed by the two tutors was different, based on different cognitive models. The post-tests, however, were the same and provide a more clearly comparable assessment of student achievement and its transfer from the computer environment to paper. We find, indeed, that the treatment did just as well on the posttest (M = 86.6% correct) as the control (M = 85.5%). An ANCOVA with pre-test as a covariate finds no reliable post-test difference by condition ($F(1, 93) = 1.03$, $p=.31$). The cognitive model differences in the two tutors suggest we should see a different pattern of performance on the post-test, with better performance of the treatment on composition problems. As Fig. 4b shows we find just such a pattern. We performed a MANOVA with condition as a factor and two separate post-test sub-scores, one for the decomposition problems and one for the pure area problems, as the dependent variables. Indeed the condition by problem-type interaction apparent in Fig. 4 is significant ($F(1, 94) = 4.05$, $p = .047$).

In fact, treatment students better performance on the composition items on the post-test may be underestimated in that many of the items were easier scaffolded composition problems. One of the problems in particular (the PIZZA problem) was an unscaffolded composition problem (it seeks the area after removing a circle inscribed in a square). We expected it to be the hardest problem on the test and indeed it was (pretest = 59%, average all pretest = 80%). The pre to post results are striking: the control shows little difference, a 5% gain (.50 to .55), whereas the treatment has an 18% gain (.67 to .85). This difference is consistent with the hypothesis that the redesigned tutor enables better learning of the challenging problem decomposition skills.

Toward better explaining the faster learning rate in the treatment, we also disaggregated the instructional time into time spent on composition steps versus other steps (e.g., finding area, entering givens, doing algebra). On average, treatment students spent less time on other steps (10.2 minutes) than control students (24.0 minutes). However, treatment students actually spent more time on composition steps (10.7 minutes) than the control students (4.5 minutes). A MANCOVA with pretest as a covariate and instructional time on decompose steps and other steps as the dependent measures confirmed the condition by step-type interaction to be significant, $F(1, 93) = 140$, $p < .0001$. These time differences are largely a consequence of different numbers of assigned steps. In particular, treatment students did fewer other steps on average than the control (173 vs. 224) and more composition steps (40.8 vs. 29.1). These differences reflect the cognitive model differences in the two tutors and, in particular, the model-based design of problems in the treatment to efficiently isolate decomposition skills and to minimize time spent on other skills.

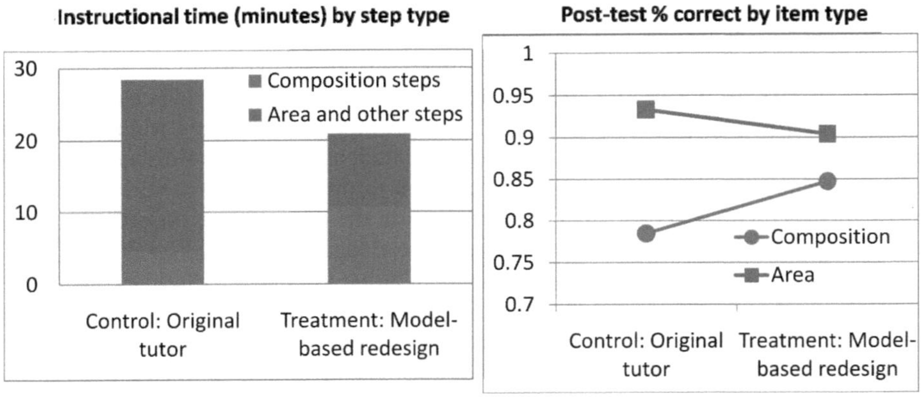

(a) (b)

Fig. 4. Students using the redesigned tutor reached mastery a) in significantly less time (21 vs. 28 minutes) while actually spending more time on the critical decomposition skills and b) better learned these decomposition skills as demonstrated by better post-test performance on composition problems

5 Discussion and Conclusion

Following our past demonstrations that better cognitive models of students can be discovered from data [8; 11], we have tested the hypothesis that using an improved model to redesign an adaptive tutor yields better student learning. The evidence supports the hypothesis. In particular, we found students using the redesigned tutor reached mastery (as demonstrated within the tutor and on a post-test) in significantly less time than students using the original tutor. Despite needing less overall time, the redesigned tutor had treatment students spending more time than control students on the difficult problem decomposition planning skills that were identified by way of a semi-automated Cognitive Task Analysis process. These students performed better on the targeted composition problems on the post-test.

It appears from the post-test results, that the treatment may not have gotten optimal practice on some area skills. For example, the treatment did not do as well on trapezoid area problems on the post-test. Unlike immediately prior units that differentiate individual area skills (e.g., rectangle vs. circle vs. trapezoid), this composite area unit had a single "individual area" KC for all regular shapes. We know from prior model search that this merged KC is too coarse and would benefit from being split into more specific KCs. Doing so, we suspect, would yield further improvements in student learning from this composition unit. Students using such a further redesigned unit should still do many fewer area steps overall than in the current control, but would get more as-needed practice on harder area skills, like trapezoid area, than the current treatment.

A related limitation of the current "close-the-loop" demonstration is that the redesigns follow from a KC model that, while validated statistically, was proposed from human inspection of learning curve data [13]. It would further strengthen the argument for this approach to have other demonstrations of close-the-loop success in other domains where LFA has achieved KC model discoveries through more automatic methods [8].

It may be tempting to conclude that "students learn what they spend time on", but this simple statement is dangerously misleading. It depends critically on how we categorize student activities. *All* of the problems that both groups solved in this study were composition problems, and the control group spent more time on these problems overall. Thus, by the simple statement, they should have learned the decomposition skills better. They did not. A finer grained cognitive analysis of student activity tells a different story -- one that matches the data! We need to categorize problem-solving steps, not problems, and we need to do so with respect to their cognitive demands, recognizing that different contexts for the same action require students to acquire different knowledge [13]. Our prior model discovery revealed a different skill is needed for unscaffolded composition steps than for scaffolded ones.

The phrase "how we categorize student activities" is another way of saying "cognitive model". Students learn the elements (the knowledge components) of the cognitive model they spend time practicing. However, the structure of that model is not obvious. Knowledge components are not directly observable and most are not open to conscious reflection, despite our strong feelings of self-awareness of our own cognition [3]. They can, however, be inferred and discovered from student performance data across multiple tasks [cf., 7] via a statistical comparison of alternative categorizations, that is, of alternative cognitive models.

Thus, it is a great opportunity for AI and Education not only in mining educational technology data to discover better cognitive models, but in closing the loop by redesigning systems based on the resulting insights and testing them toward achieving better student learning.

Acknowledgement. This work was supported by LearnLab, the Pittsburgh Science of Learning Center (NSF award 0836012). We thank Gail Kusbit, Steve Ritter, and the rest of LearnLab for their help on this project.

References

1. Barnes, T.: The Q-matrix Method: Mining Student Response Data for Knowledge. In: Beck, J. (ed.) Proceedings of AAAI 2005: Educational Data Mining Workshop (2005)
2. Beheshti, B., Desmarais, M., Naceur, R.: Methods to find the number of latent skills. In: Yacef, K., Zaïane, O., Hershkovitz, H., Yudelson, M., Stamper, J. (eds.) Proceedings of the 5th International Conference on Educational Data Mining, Chania, Greece, pp. 81–86 (2012)
3. Clark, R.E., Feldon, D., van Merriënboer, J., Yates, K., Early, S.: Cognitive task analysis. In: Spector, J., Merrill, M., van Merriënboer, J., Driscoll, M. (eds.) Handbook of Research on Educational Communications and Technology, Mahwah, NJ, pp. 577–593 (2007)
4. Corbett, A.T., Anderson, J.R.: Knowledge tracing: Modeling the acquisition of procedural knowledge. User Modeling and User-Adapted Interaction, 253–278 (1995)
5. Koedinger, K.R., Baker, R.S.J.d., Cunningham, K., Skogsholm, A., Leber, B., Stamper, J.: A Data Repository for the EDM commuity: The PSLC DataShop. In: Romero, Ventura, Pechenizkiy, Baker (eds.) Handbook of Educational Data Mining. CRC Press (2010), `http://learnlab.org/datashop`

6. Koedinger, K.R., McLaughlin, E.A.: Seeing language learning inside the math: Cognitive analysis yields transfer. In: Ohlsson, S., Catrambone, R. (eds.) Proceedings of the 32nd Annual Conference of the Cognitive Science Society, pp. 471–476. Cognitive Science Society, Austin (2010)
7. Koedinger, K.R., Corbett, A.C., Perfetti, C.: The Knowledge-Learning-Instruction (KLI) framework: Bridging the science-practice chasm to enhance robust student learning. Cognitive Science 36(5), 757–798 (2012)
8. Koedinger, K.R., McLaughlin, E.A., Stamper, J.C.: Automated Student Model Improvement. In: Yacef, K., Zaïane, O., Hershkovitz, H., Yudelson, M., Stamper, J. (eds.) Proceedings of the 5th International Conference on Educational Data Mining, Chania, Greece, pp. 17–24 (2012)
9. Lee, R.L.: Cognitive task analysis: A meta-analysis of comparative studies. Unpublished doctoral dissertation, University of Southern California, Los Angeles (2003)
10. Lovett, M., Meyer, O., Thille, C.: The Open Learning Initiative: Measuring the effectiveness of the OLI statistics course in accelerating student learning. Journal of Interactive Media in Education (2008), http://jime.open.ac.uk/2008/14
11. Stamper, J.C., Koedinger, K.R.: Human-machine student model discovery and improvement using DataShop. In: Biswas, G., Bull, S., Kay, J., Mitrovic, A. (eds.) AIED 2011. LNCS, vol. 6738, pp. 353–360. Springer, Heidelberg (2011)
12. Wilson, M., de Boeck, P.: Descriptive and explanatory item response models. In: de Boeck, P., Wilson, M. (eds.) Explanatory Item Response Models, pp. 43–74. Springer (2004)
13. Zhu, X., Simon, H.A.: Learning mathematics from examples and by doing. Cognition and Instruction 4(3), 137–166 (1987)

Wheel-Spinning: Students Who Fail to Master a Skill

Joseph E. Beck and Yue Gong

Worcester Polytechnic Institute
{josephbeck,ygong}@wpi.edu

Abstract. The concept of mastery learning is powerful: rather than a fixed number of practices, students continue to practice a skill until they have mastered it. However, an implicit assumption in this formulation is that students are capable of mastering the skill. Such an assumption is crucial in computer tutors, as their repertoire of teaching actions may not be as effective as commonly believed. What if a student lacks sufficient knowledge to solve problems involving the skill, and the computer tutor is not capable of providing sufficient instruction? This paper introduces the concept of "wheel-spinning;" that is, students who do not succeed in mastering a skill in a timely manner. We show that if a student does not master a skill in ASSISTments or the Cognitive Tutor quickly, the student is likely to struggle and will probably never master the skill. We discuss connections between such lack of learning and negative student behaviors such as gaming and disengagement, and discuss alterations to ITS design to overcome this issue.

Keywords: mastery learning, student modeling, wheel-spinning.

1 Introduction

Intelligent Tutoring Systems (ITS) are generally effective learning environments for computer-assisted problem solving. ITS are capable of providing assistance to students who are stuck with problem solving, and have been found to be better than traditional paper and pencil homework for helping students learn. Compared to more traditional methods of instruction, ITS typically perform much better on experimenter-defined measures [e.g., 1], and somewhat better on standardized instruments. Although it is tempting to assume all students benefit from using an ITS, this assumption does not necessarily hold as an ITS is not a strong choice for all learners.

In the mastery learning [2] framework, as implemented in many ITS, the student does not see a fixed number of problems, but continues to solve problems until he achieves mastery of the associated skills. In other words, once the student finishes solving a problem, possibly with the assistance of the computer, if he has not yet mastered the related skill, the computer presents another problem. There has been a long history of work in on mastery learning with computer-based education [3], and this model makes intuitive sense and certainly realizes the maxim of "practice makes perfect," particularly as most tutors provide assistance to the student in the form of hints or breaking the problem into steps. However, a bit of thought reveals some hidden weaknesses in the model. If a student requires assistance to solve the first two

K. Yacef et al. (Eds.): AIED 2013, LNAI 7926, pp. 431–440, 2013.

problems, presenting a third with the hope the student will learn the skill could very well be a sensible strategy. If the student has been unable to solve twenty problems, and required considerable help on all of them, it is probably rather optimistic to believe that the twenty-first problem will enable the student to suddenly acquire the skill (in the data set we analyze, there is only a 1.4% chance such a student will ever master the skill, at least within the data collected for this study).

The assumption that students will eventually acquire skills with enough practice is not just part of tutorial decision making, as knowledge tracing [4] assumes a constant probability of learning the skill on every problem-solving attempt. However, not all students are able to acquire skills within an ITS, and some spend a considerable amount of time stuck in the mastery learning loop without any learning occurring. Aside from simply wasting the learner's time, such an experience is presumably frustrating as learners are repeatedly presented with problems they are clearly unable to solve. We refer to this phenomenon as "wheel-spinning," referring to a car stuck in mud or snow; its wheels are spinning rapidly, but it is not going anywhere. Similarly, students are being presented with many problems, but are not making progress towards mastery. Later, we will discuss possible connections with other negative behaviors such as gaming.

2 Describing Wheel-Spinning

We define wheel-spinning as a student who spends too much time struggling to learn a topic without achieving mastery. Some students will begin working with an ITS already understanding the material. Other students will master the skill relatively quickly, perhaps with the assistance of the ITS's coaching. Neither group is problematic. We are concerned with students who spend too much time without mastering the skill. This definition has two concepts that must be operationalized:

1. What does it mean to *master* a topic?
2. How much time is *too much*?

The answer to both of these questions will vary somewhat by system, as the idea of mastery is a vague concept and can be instantiated in a variety of ways. One approach, proposed by Corbett and Anderson (1995), was to estimate the student's knowledge, and when the probability a student knew a skill exceeds 0.95, then the student is considered to have mastered the skill. An approach used in the ASSISTments system is to consider a student to have mastered the skill upon getting three questions in a row correct. With respect to time, an ideal amount will also vary by system. An ITS whose problems require 10 minutes to solve should probably require fewer problems for mastery than one that requires 20 seconds per problem.

For our mastery criterion, we decided to use the simpler approach of three correct responses in a row. The knowledge tracing model-fitting process is rather slow on large data sets, and there is concern about its ability to disambiguate student knowledge due to issues of identifiability [5]. Also, if others wish to replicate our work on other data sets, a mastery criterion that does not require subscribing to a particular student modeling framework will be easier to work with. We also assume that once students master a skill, they are unable to unmaster it. To be clear, we believe that forgetting does exist, and a real-world adaptive system needs to account for it. However, our goal here is to understand how learners perform during initial mastery, and whether they are able to achieve such in a reasonable amount of time. Forgetting what was learned, while an important topic, is not central to this research question.

For how much time is a reasonable amount to master, we selected 10 practice opportunities. Although this cutpoint is somewhat arbitrary, we will see (see Fig. 1) that the results are not that sensitive to the exact threshold selected. Furthermore, one of the systems we are analyzing, ASSISTments, has a feature which "locks out" learners after they have made 10 attempts at a skill in a single day, and requires them to try again on a later day. We are not sure what impact this feature could have on the data, or what students might be doing after being locked out (e.g., asking someone for help). Therefore, we used 10 practice opportunities as a threshold for mastering in a reasonable time frame. See Fig. 1 for a visual representation of wheel-spinning behavior in the Cognitive Algebra Tutor (CAT) and in ASSISTments.

In Fig. 1, the x-axis represents how many practice opportunities a student has had on a particular skill, and the y-axis represents the cumulative probability a student has mastered, i.e. gotten three problems in a row correct, the skill. By definition, no student has mastered a skill on the first two practice attempts. On the third practice attempt, approximately 35% of students in both the CAT and ASSISTments have mastered the skill. To achieve mastery this quickly, these students made no mistakes on their first three problems; therefore, these students did not benefit from any of coaching available on this skill. In other words, these students answered the questions without requiring assistance, and were essentially using the tutor as fancy paper and pencil homework; therefore, the ITS should not receive credit for having helped these students.

After three practice opportunities, both CAT and ASSISTments show a gradual rise in the percentage of students having mastered the skill. After 6 practice opportunities, 59% of students in the cognitive tutor and 55% of students in ASSISTments have mastered a skill. Finally, after 10 practice opportunities 69% of students in CAT and 62% of students in ASSISTments have mastered the skill. Although we selected 10 practice opportunities somewhat arbitrarily, and based on a possible artifact in the ASSISTments data set, this threshold is past the "elbow" of the mastery curves for both systems, and inspecting Fig. 1demonstrates that the proportion of students having mastered the skill would not change noticeably if the threshold were increased beyond 10. Therefore, we are satisfied with our threshold for wheel-spinning, at least for a first analysis of this problem.

It is interesting to compare the curves for the CAT and ASSISTments. Although, initially, both tutors had approximately equal numbers of students who already knew the skill, one possible implication is that the CAT is doing a better job of helping students achieve mastery than ASSISTments. Such comparisons should be made with caution, as there are a variety of factors that could influence differences in the curves between systems. First, problems could vary in difficulty. A system with relatively easier problems would show more students achieving mastery than one with harder questions. Making problems easier is probably not a good way of reducing wheel-spinning. However, since both systems have approximately 34% of students immediately mastering the skill, easier problems is an unlikely explanation. Second, patterns of usage can differ. For example, if students solve problems in a particular skill in large batches in ASSISTments, but only a few per day in CAT, students will have more opportunities for learning outside of the tutor. Thus, we cannot conclude that CAT is better than ASSISTments at providing assistance that prevents wheel-spinning, but can conclude that some combination of CAT and how it is deployed appears to work better than ASSISTments. One stark conclusion from the graph, however, is that a substantial number of students have problems with wheel-spinning, and this issue is not particular to one ITS, as it occurs in two widely-used computer tutors with differing pedagogical approaches.

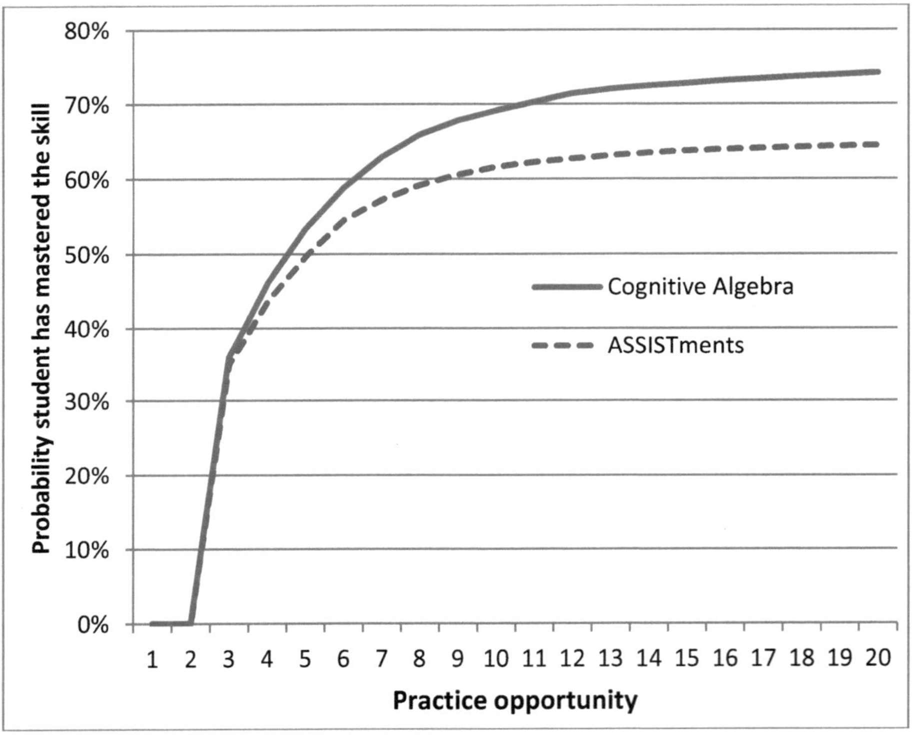

Fig. 1. Graph of wheel-spinning in ASSISTments and Cognitive Algebra Tutor

3 Modeling Wheel-Spinning

Given that wheel-spinning is at best non-productive and possibly irritating for the student, we would like to detect this behavior as rapidly as possible. If we can predict that a student is likely to spin his wheels, we can perform some other tutorial action that is more instructional in nature.

Our approach is to consider each student-skill pair, and look at cases where the student either masters the skill, or after seeing 10 problems has failed to master it (wheel-spinning). Data after the tenth encounter or after the student has mastered the skill are ignored. This definition has an asymmetry, as a student who only sees 7 problems but fails to master the skill, is of indeterminate wheel-spinning, and is not included in this analysis; whereas a student who did master it in 7 attempts is included. Thus, this approach undercounts wheel-spinning, and estimates it occurs in 9.8% of the data. We construct a logistic regression model to predict which category the student will master the skill or wheel-spin. In order to determine how quickly we can categorize students, we build a separate model for each number of practice opportunities the student has had on the current skill. In other words, we construct a model for when the student begins practicing the skill (has seen 0 problems), when he has seen 1 problem, 2 problems, etc. We take this approach for two reasons. First, we want to see how accuracy changes as we accumulate more data about the student. Second, what is important could change over time. Requesting a bottom-out hint (the answer to the problem) on the first item might not be problematic, but requesting such assistance on the fourth problem could be a strong negative indicator. We had 258,990 problems solved by 5997 students. After removing indeterminate data, our data set consists of 131,909 problems solved by 5026 students. This analysis used data collected between September 2010 and July 2011, with students primarily from the northeast United States. We only have student self-reported ages, and 75% of the students asserted they were 12 to 15 years of age on January 1, 2011.

The dependent variable is whether or not a student will wheel-spin on this skill. The first three independent variables track student performance on the skill in question, and the next three look at his performance across all skills:

- Prior number of correct responses by the student on this skill
- Response times on this skill. We first transform response times for each item into a Z score for that item (to account for some problems taking longer than others). We then took the geometric mean, γ * prior_average + (1- γ) * new_observation, with $\gamma = 0.7$. The geometric mean is a method of summarizing sequential data, but provides lesser weight to older observations, as prior observations are decayed by γ at each time step.
- How many times the student reached a bottom out hint on this skill.
- How often the student was rapidly guessing, computed across all skills, defined as submitting responses less than 2 seconds apart on successive items. We took the geometric mean in the same manner as for response time.
- How often the student gave a rapid response, computed across all skills, defined as responding in a time frame that suggests a reading rate of over 400 words per minute. We took the geometric mean of this feature.
- How often the student reached a bottom out hint on 3 consecutive problems, computed across all skills; a 1 indicates the student requested the answer on 3 consecutive problems. We took the geometric mean of this feature.
- The name of the current skill.

We fit this model using logistic regression in SPSS. The first six terms were covariates, and final term was entered as a fixed effect (i.e., one parameter per skill). Note that we were unable to have user identity as a factor in this model, as that exceeded SPSS's capabilities; therefore statistical reliability would be somewhat overstated due to non-independence of student trials [6], and we therefore do not report statistical reliability. Table 1 summarizes the model's accuracy. Each row denotes how well the model is doing after seeing the student solve a given number of problems on the skill. The second column indicates the percentage of the student-skill pairs that resulted in wheel spinning. When students first began a skill, 9.8% of the data included wheel spinning. For students who had not mastered a problem by the fifth attempt, 38.5% of the data indicated wheel spinning. The third column is R^2, a metric of model fit, which ranges from 0 (unable to predict the data) to 1 (perfect accuracy). Note that even before the student begins solving a problem on the skill, the model is able to account for 13% of the variation in wheel-spinning. The model is able to make use of the last four features listed above, the student's gaming behavior on other problems, and the identity of the current skill, since those do not depend on the student's performance on the current skill.

Table 1. Model performance for predicting wheel-spinning

# problems on this skill	Wheel-spinning %	Nagelkerke R^2	False positive%	False negative%
0	9.8%	0.13	0.3%	98.2%
1	9.8%	0.28	1.0%	88.6%
2	9.8%	0.39	1.6%	73.9%
3	20.5%	0.37	4.7%	60.5%
4	28.5%	0.41	9.2%	47.3%
5	38.5%	0.45	15.3%	33.7%
6	53.2%	0.44	27.0%	21.2%
7	67.5%	0.65	28.2%	10.2%
8	83.5%	0.85	3.9%	4.6%

The fourth column denotes false positives, that is, cases where the model predicts the student will wheel-spin, but in fact the student masters the skill within the first 10 practice opportunities. The model has a fairly low false percentage rate, mostly due to the imbalanced classes as, initially, wheel-spinning is a small minority of the data. The false positive rate continues to rise as wheel-spinning students constitute a larger and larger percentage of the dataset. However, in general, if the model asserts a student will wheel-spin, it is usually correct.

The fifth column denotes false negatives, the case where the model predicts the student will master the skill, but instead he wheel-spins. Initially, this rate is extremely high, mostly due to the model being unwilling to predict wheel-spinning, the minority class, on the basis of little data about the student's knowledge of this skill. The model does not do a good job at catching most of the cases when the student will wheel-spin, and is a bit conservative in its predictions. Thus, as an early warning system for preventing students from having frustrating problem-solving sequences without mastery, the detector still needs additional work. However, after students have solved 2 problems on a skill, it does a relatively good job at detecting wheel-spinning, and is potentially able to save students some frustration.

One question is what is model's source of power? Plotting the β values estimated by the logistic regression, the impact of the features is relatively stable across the models. The importance of the number of consecutive correct responses increases as the number of problems seen increases. This result makes intuitive sense; for example, a student with 0 correct in a row on the second problem is not in as much difficulty as a student with 0 correct in a row on the sixth problem, as the latter student has few remaining opportunities to get 3 right in a row. The student's normalized response time becomes relatively less important the more problems that are seen. Initially students who take relatively more time than average to complete a problem have a lower chance of wheel-spinning. This relationship is a bit surprising, but could perhaps be due to fast responses being ambiguous and indicating either the student is very skillful (and is likely to master the skill), or the student is just entering a random response (and is likely to wheel-spin). In general, the features related to performance on other skills become markedly less important the more problems the student solved on this skill. Again, this result makes intuitive sense as the fewer data available about this skill, the more useful data about the student's performance on other skills will be.

Beyond predicting wheel-spinning, we also explored its relationship with the negative behavior of gaming. We found that the 2491 students who never exhibited wheel-spinning had a mean gaming score of 0.013; the 366 students who always exhibited wheel-spinning had a mean gaming score of 0.163. Thus, students who wheel-spin are also likely to game. But does this relationship hold within a particular student; that is, when a student wheel-spins is he more likely to game than when he masters a skill? For the 1207 students who sometimes exhibited wheel-spinning, their mean gaming score was 0.104 when wheel spinning vs. only 0.017 when they mastered skills in a timely manner. These numbers are similar to the corresponding gaming values for students who always wheel-spun or always mastered quickly. This result strongly suggests that gaming and wheel-spinning are related. However, it leaves unresolved the direction of causality.

4 Contributions

The primary contribution of this paper is to identify a new problem in student modeling that is actionable by the tutorial decision-making module of an ITS. Most efforts in student modeling (e.g. [5, 7, 8]) and the 2010 KDD Cup on Educational Data Mining, focus on predicting student behavior at the level of individual responses. Although this approach clearly validates the student model, a reasonable question is why this problem is an interesting one in the first place, particularly from the standpoint of building an effective, adaptive ITS. Imagine our models had half of the error rate of the current state of the art, would that appreciably improve the performance of computer tutors? It is unclear what tutorial decisions would be affected by such better models, beyond slight refinements in the mastery learning model for when to consider the student done with a skill. In contrast, a strong model of wheel-spinning has clear implications for how to adapt instruction to the student. Consider Fig. 2 as one possible model for an ITS to incorporate a wheel-spinning detector, by modifying the typical ITS mastery learning cycle to not always present another problem in the event of a student mistake. If the student is likely to wheel-spin, there is little point in providing another problem to the student as he is unlikely to master the skill. As problem solving is, statistically, a futile exercise for this learner at this time, doing something other than problem solving seems warranted. There are a variety of possible methods of instruction, including intervention by the teacher, peer tutoring, or incorporating stronger instruction into the ITS itself (e.g. [9]). We do not have sufficient data to prescribe a particular solution to wheel-spinning, but are willing to conclude that more problem solving is not a viable approach. In addition, wheel-spinning can be computed from log files and does not require human coders to train a model, and it also accounts for a moderate percentage (10% to 35%) of behavior.

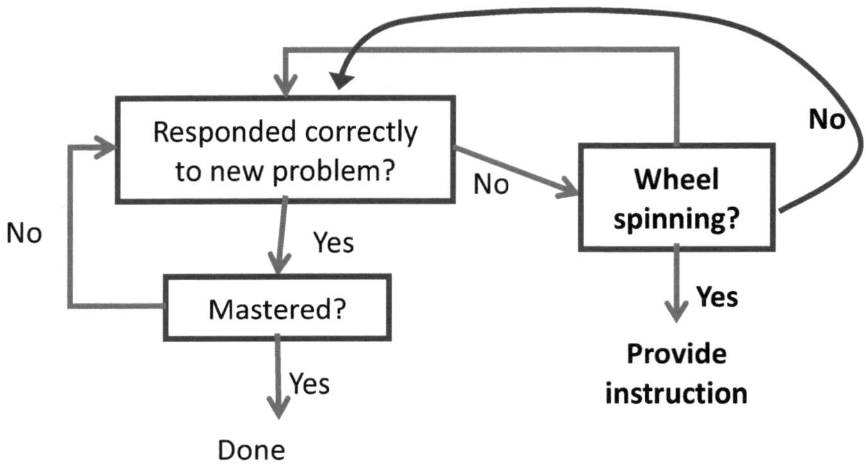

Fig. 2. Possible process model for incorporating wheel-spinning into an ITS

Finally, this paper provides a new approach for evaluating the impact of an intelligent tutoring system using Fig. 1 as a visualization. We can separate students into three categories. First, there are the 35% of the students in both CAT and ASSISTments who mastered the material with no mistakes; as they knew the skill before starting they did not directly benefit from the tutoring components. Second, there are the 9.8% (lower bound) to 35% (upper bound) of students who wheel-spun, they did not benefit from the tutor. The third group of students are those who *potentially* benefitted from the tutor, a group comprising 30% to 55% of the student population. We cannot determine whether these actually students benefitted or not, as perhaps they would have mastered the skill with simple pencil and paper practice. However, the upper bound on the percentage of students who could have been helped by the existing tutor is surprisingly low.

5 Conclusions and Future Work

This work is an initial attempt to model and understand wheel-spinning, and there are several unanswered questions. First, what does wheel-spinning look like in other systems? We have examined two mathematics tutors and found broadly similar patterns of behavior. Does this problem exist in other tutorial domains? A second question is what is the proper unit of measure for the x-axis? This work used the number of problems, but perhaps total time spent would be a better indicator?

The second dimension of future work involves understanding the nature of wheel-spinning, and how generalizable the detector is. We constructed a set of predictive features based upon our beliefs as to what would be predictive, but there are hopefully additional predictors that can be brought to bear on this problem. A related issue is whether the predictors are consistent across tutoring systems; how well would a detector for ASSISTments work on CAT, and vice versa? Would such a detector generalize to a non-mathematics domain? One likely important step in this process is the proper normalization of the data, similar to what was done for response time.

The third area of work involves exploring the relationship between wheel-spinning and negative behaviors such as gaming [10] and off task behavior [11]. We found that gaming and wheel-spinning were correlated behaviors, but it is a question as to the direction of causality, as there are three plausible models:

- Gaming causes wheel-spinning. Students are not taking problems seriously and requesting hints they perhaps do not need. As a result of help requests being scored as incorrect responses, students wheel-spin and do not achieve mastery.
- Wheel-spinning causes gaming. Students who do not understand the material are unable to solve the problems and become frustrated. Such students have no way to proceed other than requesting many hints, since many ITS do not have strong instructional components.
- Gaming and wheel-spinning are symptoms that are affected by a common cause.

These models have very different implications, as the first model suggests trying to affect the student's mood directly is a viable approach. The second model suggests that instruction is more likely to be beneficial. In reality, there is probably a mixture of both behaviors going on. It is interesting to note that the first work on remediating gaming had a positive effect [10], but included components that both attempted to discourage gaming, but also added instructional support beyond what was previously available in the tutor. Controlled studies that provide instruction to students who are likely to wheel-spin would be useful for disambiguating which of the two candidate hypotheses is closer to reality.

We see two clear consequences of this work. First, it is perhaps not wise to use all data for model-fitting purposes when training a student model. Since most student models assume a fixed probability of learning a skill, long sequences of problems by wheel-spinning students are likely to underestimate the learning rate for the average student. The distribution of learning rates can be thought of as bimodal with a group of wheel-spinning student-skill pairs clustered near 0. Thus, work on detecting contextual factors that affect learning [e.g., 12] is a welcome development.

The second consequence is that ITS designers should develop some fallback for failures of mastery learning. The simplified mastery learning cycle of "present problems until mastery" does not work for many learners, even with the assistance available in two popular tutors. Some modification or automated intervention is warranted if we wish to avoid frustrating learners.

Acknowledgements. This work was supported by the National Science Foundation (grant DRL-1109483) to Worcester Polytechnic Institute. The opinions expressed are those of the authors and do not necessarily represent the views of the Foundation.

References

1. Koedinger, K.R., et al.: Intelligent Tutoring Goes To School in the Big City. International Journal of Artificial Intelligence in Education 8, 30–43 (1997)
2. Bloom, B.S.: Human characteristics and school learning. McGraw-Hill (1976)
3. Frick, T.W.: A comparison of three decision models for adapting the length of computer-based mastery tests. Journal of Educational Computing Research 6(4), 479–513 (1990)
4. Corbett, A., Anderson, J.R.: Knowledge tracing: Modeling the acquisition of procedural knowledge. User Modeling and User-Adapted Interaction 4, 253–278 (1995)
5. Beck, J.E., Chang, K.-M.: Identifiability: A Fundamental Problem of Student Modeling. In: International Conference on User Modeling, Corfu, Greece (2007)
6. Menard, S.: Applied Logistic Regression Analysis. Quantitative Applications in the Social Sciences. Sage Publications (2001)
7. Pardos, Z., et al.: Analyzing fine-grained skill models using bayesian and mixed effect methods. In: Thirteenth Conference on Artificial Intelligence in Education. IOS Press (2007)
8. Chi, M., et al.: Instructional Factors Analysis: A Cognitive Model For Multiple Instructional Interventions. In: Proceedings of Educational Data Mining (2011)
9. de Koning, K., et al.: Model-based reasoning about learner behaviour. Artificial Intelligence 117, 173–229 (2000)
10. Baker, R.S.J.d., et al.: Adapting to When Students Game an Intelligent Tutoring System. In: Ikeda, M., Ashley, K.D., Chan, T.-W. (eds.) ITS 2006. LNCS, vol. 4053, pp. 392–401. Springer, Heidelberg (2006)
11. Baker, R.S.J.d.: Modeling and Understanding Students' Off-Task Behavior in Intelligent Tutoring Systems. In: Proceedings of ACM CHI 2007: Computer-Human Interaction (2007)
12. Baker, R.S.J.d., Goldstein, A.B., Heffernan, N.T.: Detecting the Moment of Learning. In: Aleven, V., Kay, J., Mostow, J. (eds.) ITS 2010, Part I. LNCS, vol. 6094, pp. 25–34. Springer, Heidelberg (2010)

A Matrix Factorization Method for Mapping Items to Skills and for Enhancing Expert-Based Q-Matrices

Michel C. Desmarais and Rhouma Naceur

École Polytechnique de Montréal,
C.P. 6079, succ. Centre-ville
Montréal (Québec) H3C 3A7, Canada
{michel.desmarais,rhouma.naceur}@polymtl.ca

Abstract. Uncovering the right skills behind question items is a difficult task. It requires a thorough understanding of the subject matter and of the cognitive factors that determine student performance. The skills definition, and the mapping of item to skills, require the involvement of experts. We investigate means to assist experts for this task by using a data driven, matrix factorization approach. The two mappings of items to skills, the expert on one side and the matrix factorization on the other, are compared in terms of discrepancies, and in terms of their performance when used in a linear model of skills assessment and item outcome prediction. Visual analysis shows a relatively similar pattern between the expert and the factorized mappings, although differences arise. The prediction comparison shows the factorization approach performs slightly better than the original expert Q-matrix, giving supporting evidence to the belief that the factorization mapping is valid. Implications for the use of the factorization to design better item to skills mapping are discussed.

Keywords: student models, skills assessment, alternating least squares matrix factorization, latent skills, cognitive modeling.

1 Introduction

Mapping items to latent skills is a notoriously difficult task and intelligent help to alleviate this difficulty would obviously be desirable. Although the complete automation of uncovering the skills behind question items for cognitive engineering purpose is beyond reach in the current state of research, means to help determine the number of skills and the common skills between items is a reasonable endeavour in the mid-term, and significant advances have been made recently. We review the state of the art towards this goal in recent years, and demonstrate how a matrix factorization technique can yield promising results to this end.

K. Yacef et al. (Eds.): AIED 2013, LNAI 7926, pp. 441–450, 2013.

2 Skills Modeling, Q-Matrices, and Matrix Factorization

Because of its importance, the problem of mapping items to underlying skills has been widely studied, and is still an ongoing topic of investigation in psychometrics and in educational data mining (see, for eg., [8,11,10,6,4,3,1] for recent contributions).

In the past ten years, a few groups of researchers have looked at *linear models* of item to skills mapping and of skills assessment, with promising results. We build upon this work which is briefly reviewed below.

2.1 Linear Models

Linear models of skills are familiar to most teachers. An exam's weighted sums of individual score items, broken down by topic (skill), implicitly constitute a linear model model. Also highly familiar in the psychometric field is the Q-matrix formalism, investigated by Tatsuoka and her colleagues in the early 1980's, which maps skills to items [14,15]. This formalism can also be considered a close parent of linear models.

Linear models were put to the task of assessing student skills mastery [2,19,18,17]. In the 2010 KDD Cup, a tensor model was developed to model student skills and the mapping of items to skills. Thai-Nghe et al. used a multi-relational matrix and tensor-based factorization to model skills and learning curves to predict student success [18,17]. A comparison with the widely recognized Bayesian Knowledge Tracing approach showed that it compares favorably [18].

The success of linear models and factorization methods raises the question of whether these methods could also be successful in deriving Q-matrices that maps items to skills. A few studies have shown that a mapping can, indeed, be derived from data [20,5]. Winters et al. showed that item topic extraction can be obtained from different data mining techniques, one of which is matrix factorization [20]. However, only very distinct topics like French and mathematics can yield adequate mapping. This study was later corroborated by Desmarais [5] who also used simulated data to show that the low discrimination power of some topics might be explained by their lower weight in terms of skill factors, when compared to other factors such as item difficulty and student ability. Recent work by Lan et al. [9] combine a factor analysis framework, named SPARFA, with Bayesian techniques to uncover skills behind task and to label these skills from tags and from the question item texts.

The factorization methods in the studies mentioned above rely on the standard matrix operators ("dot product"), and therefore can be considered as *compensatory models* of skills: each skill required adds to the chances of success of an item. Barnes, Stampers, and other colleagues [1,13] introduced a different algorithm to implement *conjunctive models* of skills, where any required skill missing will induce a failure to the item. We will borrow from this work and from [7] to implement both conjunctive and compensatory models in the current study. The foundations of these models is explained next.

2.2 Results Matrix, Q-Matrix, and Skills Matrix

Student test data can be represented in the form of a results matrix, **R**, with m row items by n column students. We use the term *item* to represent exercises, questions, or any task where the student has to apply a skilled performance to accomplish it correctly. If a student successfully answers an item, the corresponding value in the results matrix is 1, otherwise it is 0. Intermediate values could also be used to indicate partial success.

A results matrix **R** can be decomposed into two smaller matrices:

$$\mathbf{R} \approx \mathbf{Q}\,\mathbf{S} \tag{1}$$

The process of matrix factorization is to determine the matrices **Q** and **S** from **R**. The **Q** matrix is equivalent in form to the Q-matrix developed in the cognitive modeling field [15,14], although various semantics apply to each formalism, such as the *conjunctive* or *compensatory* versions explained below. This matrix is an m items by k skills matrix that defines which skills are necessary to correctly answer an item. It allows a "compressed" representation of the data that assumes the item outcome results are determined by the skills involved in each item and the skills mastered by each student. The k skills by n student matrix **S** represents the student skills mastery profiles. The product of **Q** and **S** yields an estimated results matrix $\hat{\mathbf{R}}$. The goal of factorization algorithms is to minimize $||\hat{\mathbf{R}} - \mathbf{R}||$.

As mentioned above, the Q-matrix (**Q**) can take different interpretations. A *conjunctive* Q-matrix assumes *all* skills in an item row are necessary for success, whereas a *disjunctive* Q-matrix assumes *any* skill is sufficient, and finally a *compensatory* Q-matrix assumes each skill *adds* to item success, which can be interpreted as increasing the chances of success if each item is either succeeded or failed. Equation (1) corresponds to the *compensatory* version of the Q-matrix, but it can be transformed into a *conjunctive* version through negation of the **R** and **S** matrices [7].

3 Comparing a Q-Matrix Induced from Data with an Expert Defined Matrix

Given the factorization obtained from equation (1), the question we address here is how to compare the matrix **Q** obtained from item outcome data, with an expert defined Q-matrix, in the hope that this comparison can help validate and improve the expert matrix.

3.1 Comparison Issues and Principle of the Proposed Method

One issue with the factorization of equation (1) is the interpretation of the **Q** matrix obtained. Although factorization techniques allow, or require, the specification of the number of skills, k, the skills appear in matrix **Q** in some unpredictable order. Moreover, the matrix can contain numerical values of various signs and amplitude that may not lend themselves to a sharp interpretation.

Another issue has to do with the factorization technique used. Some techniques, such as non-negative matrix factorization (NMF), lead to non unique and to local minima solutions. Experience shows that these solutions can be widely different, worsening the problem of interpretation and comparison with the expert Q-matrix.

To alleviate these issues, we rely on the principle of starting the factorization process with an initial matrix $\mathbf{Q}$ set to the expert Q-matrix. Many factorization algorithms could be used, as long as this condition can be met. The initial condition ensures that the matrix $\mathbf{Q}$ obtained after minimizing $||\hat{\mathbf{R}} - \mathbf{R}||$ will minimally diverge from the initial one, thereby rendering the comparison with, and enhancement of the expert's Q-matrix more feasible.

3.2 Alternate Least-Square Factorization (ALS)

The factorization method we use is the Alternate Least-square (ALS). Starting with the results matrix $\mathbf{R}$ and an initial Q-matrix, $\mathbf{Q}_0$, a least-squares estimate of the skills matrix $\hat{\mathbf{S}}_0$ can be obtained by:

$$\hat{\mathbf{S}}_0 = (\mathbf{Q}_0^{\mathrm{T}}\,\mathbf{Q}_0)^{-1}\,\mathbf{Q}_0^{\mathrm{T}}\,\mathbf{R} \tag{2}$$

The initial matrix $\mathbf{Q}_0$ will be the expert defined Q-matrix. Then, a new estimate of the Q-matrix, $\hat{\mathbf{Q}}_1$, is again obtained by the least-squares estimate:

$$\hat{\mathbf{Q}}_1 = \mathbf{R}\,\hat{\mathbf{S}}_0^{\mathrm{T}}\,(\hat{\mathbf{S}}_0\,\hat{\mathbf{S}}_0^{\mathrm{T}})^{-1} \tag{3}$$

And so on for estimating $\hat{\mathbf{S}}_1$, $\hat{\mathbf{Q}}_2$, etc. Alternating between equations (2) and (3) yields progressive refinements of the matrices $\hat{\mathbf{Q}}_i$ and $\hat{\mathbf{S}}_i$ that more closely approximate $\mathbf{R}$ in equation (1). In our experiments, the convergence at a delta of 0.001 occurs after 7–8 iterations and in a fraction of a second for factorizing a matrix of dimension 20×536. This performance makes the technique many times more efficient than factorizations that rely on gradient descent, for example.

It is worth mentioning that, by starting with non negative matrices $\mathbf{Q}_0$ and $\mathbf{R}$, the convergence process will generally end with positive values for both matrices $\mathbf{Q}_i$ and $\mathbf{S}_i$. The vast majority of values obtained are between -0.5 and 1.5 if both the results matrix and the initial Q-matrix have {0,1} values. No regularization terms are used in the current implementation of the algorithm to force non-negative or integer values.

4 Experiments and Data

We use the ALS method described above to compare an expert defined Q-matrix and a factor Q-matrix. Unless otherwise mentioned, factorization is based on the conjunctive model of skills (see [7]), which essentially consists in using the negation of the $\mathbf{R}$ matrix instead of the raw values.

The data comes from Tatsuoka's fraction algebra problems [16] which is available through the R package CDM [12]. It is composed of 20 question items and 536 respondents (see table 1 in [4] for a description of the problems and of the skills).

When cross-validation experiments are performed, they consists in breaking down the data into 8 sets of 67 students each. Training is done on 7 of the 8 sets and testing on the remaining set.

4.1 Visual Comparison of Q-Matrices

Figure 1 shows three versions of the Q-matrices. The left matrix is the one defined by the expert, as provided in [12]. Dark cells represent the required skills. The middle matrix is derived from the full data set. The gradients of colors represent the values that range between -0.5 and 1.5, where the darker color indicate higher values. The right matrix is the rounded version of the middle matrix: Real values of the middle matrix are rounded to 0 or 1.

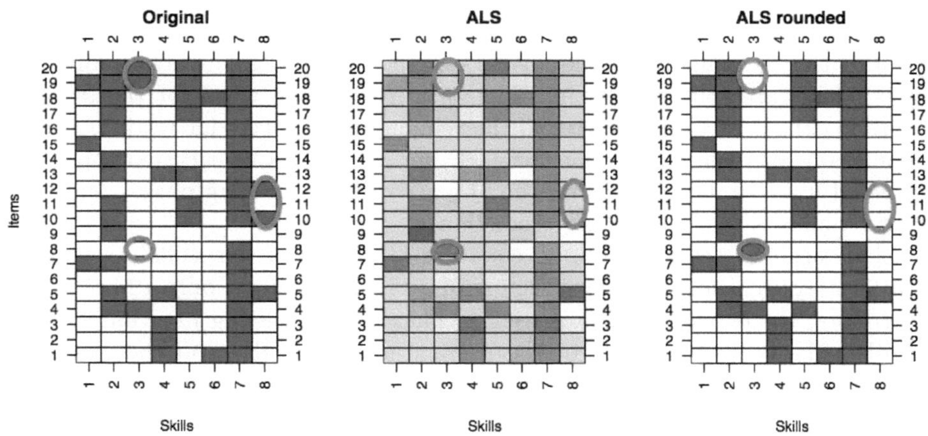

Fig. 1. Three Q-matrices of Tatsuoka's fraction algebra items

Five cells differ between the expert (left) and the ALS factorization (right) matrices. They are highlited by three ellipses. Except for cell (8,3), all of the differences are cells missing on the ALS matrix. We could bring back the missing values by tweaking the threshold to the 0/1 function, but that would come at the cost of creating false positives. Their absence in the ALS factorized matrix suggests that the corresponding skills may not contribute to the response outcome as much as the other skills. Equally interesting are the different color brightnesses in the true positive, suggesting that some skills may be more important than others. Finally, we note that the differences all come from only 2 skills (see [4] for a description of all skills):

(3): simplify before subtracting (eg. $3\frac{1}{2} - 2\frac{3}{2}$, $4 - 1\frac{4}{3}$, $4\frac{1}{3} - 1\frac{5}{3}$),
(8): reduce answers to simplest form (eg. $4\frac{3}{5} - 3\frac{4}{10}$, $4\frac{1}{2} - 2\frac{7}{12}$, $1\frac{1}{8} - \frac{1}{8}$).

The high level of discrepancies between the matrices for these two skills may hint at some issues with these particular skills. This observation is congruent with different analyis by DeCarlo of Tatsuoka's Q-matrix and based on the DINA latent factor model which identifies Skill 3 as a source of error: "Together, these results suggest that the Q-matrix might be misspecified, in that Skill 3 should not be included" (in [4], p. 20).

4.2 Validity of the ALS Q-Matrix

The ALS method clearly meets the criteria of interpretation and ease of comparison with an expert defined Q-matrix. However, does the ALS Q-matrix represent a "better" mapping of skills to items than the expert's, or even a "good" mapping at all?

Let us define the goodness of a Q-matrix by its ability to make accurate predictions. Accordingly, we compare the expert Q-matrix and the ALS Q-matrix over their performance for predicting response outcomes.

A cross-validation simulation is conducted and consists in predicting, in turn, each of the 20 items given the answers of the other 19 items. The individual respondents are split into 8 bins. The data from 7 bins serve for the training (deriving the ALS Q-matrices) and the remaining bin serves for testing. 8-folds simulations are conducted, one for each bin. The skills of each examinee are assessed from 19 items based on the Q-matrix of the training phase. The item that remains is used for testing prediction.

Skills are assessed according to equation (2). However, for skills assessment, the Q-matrix requires response vectors of 20 items, whereas only 19 are given. Therefore, the expected value is used in place of the missing item outcome to predict: the geometric mean of the average item difficulty and the examinee ability over the 19 given items is used (the value is not rounded to 0/1). Then, the predicted item outcome is computed according to equation (1).

To assess the performance of the original, expert Q-matrix, the same process as described above is used, except that there is no training phase. The expert Q-matrix is used in place of the ALS Q-matrix derived from training.

The results of the simulation are reported in figure 2. Results from both conjunctive and compensatory models are reported. The predictions based on expected values are also reported. Expected values are computed according to the method described above when assigning the value of the item to predict for the ALS Q-matrix predictions. Note that the average success rate is 53%, and therefore a *0-rule* type of prediction (predicting all 1s) would yield 47% MAE.

The lower MAEs of the ALS Q-matrix, compared to the Original expert Q-matrix in both the conjunctive and compensatory models, provide support for the validity of the ALS Q-matrix. Not surprisingly, the expert Q-matrix performs better under the conjunctive model than the compensatory. This is expected to the extent that it was designed by experts as a conjunctive rather than a compensatory model. However, the ALS Q-matrix predictions have practically the same accuracy for both models.

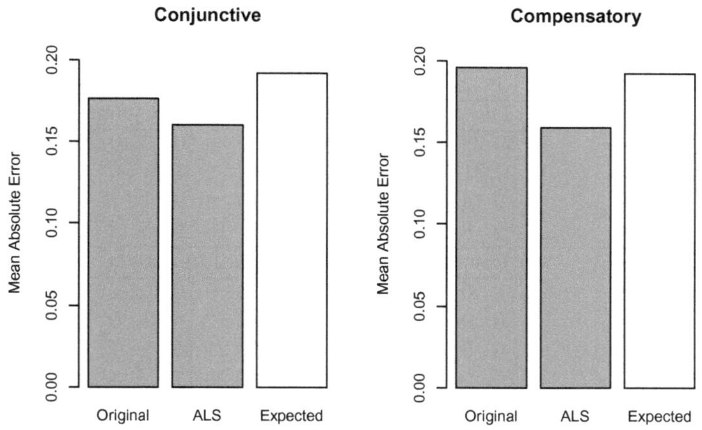

Fig. 2. Mean Absolute Error (MAE) predictive accuracy of Q-matrices with conjunctive and compensatory models. Predictions based on expected values is also provided for comparison. Standard deviation for ALS is 0.012 for the 8-folds simulation and 0.013 for the Original. A paired t-test of the conjunctive model shows the difference is statistically significant ($p = 0.001$, pairing is per fold).

Turning to the question of whether the expert and ALS Q-matrices are "good" at all, we compare the predictive performance of ALS Q-matrices derived from the expert Q-matrix with ALS Q-matrices derived from random starting points.

We computed the MAE of ALS Q-matrices for randomly generated initial Q-matrices. The MAE for this experiment based on 10-folds is 0.159 (sd. 0.001), which is practically the same as the ALS Q-matrices obtained when the starting Q-matrix is the expert one. However, convergence is slower, requiring between 8 and 14 iterations.

The fact that the MAE is relatively similar regardless of the initial Q-matrix further supports the belief that the ALS Q-matrix obtained from starting with the expert one is valid and could be regarded as a legitimate improvement.

4.3 Convergence/Divergence from Original Matrices

It is comforting to believe that there is one "true" Q-matrix for a given set of items and skills, and that, given a close approximation of this matrix, there exists a means to converge towards this true matrix and avoid divergence away from it. If the ALS factorization method allowed such outcome, it would truly offer useful guidance for the design of Q-matrices by reliably indicating the "faulty" cells regardless of which they are in the matrix.

To explore this conjecture, we design an experiment where perturbations are introduced in the Original expert Q-matrix, and perform ALS factorization on this corrupted matrix. If we had started with a perfect Q-matrix, we would like the method to detect the perturbations and return the original Q-matrix. If we

Table 1. Discrepancies as a function of the number of perturbations

Number of perturbations	Number of discrepancies																
	0	1	2	3	4	5	6	7	8	9	10	11	12	13	14	15	16
	(1) Discrepancies with original ALS Q-matrix																
1	42	50	28	16	9	10	2	2	1	0	0	0	0	0	0	0	0
2	11	27	31	30	26	10	8	6	4	3	2	1	1	0	0	0	0
3	3	9	14	25	24	20	20	11	12	10	6	2	1	1	1	1	0
4	1	2	8	15	12	19	25	20	19	11	10	9	5	3	0	0	1
	(2) Discrepancies with Original Q-matrix																
1	0	0	0	0	0	47	55	33	17	8	0	0	0	0	0	0	0
2	0	0	0	0	0	18	20	36	45	22	12	5	1	0	1	0	0
3	0	0	0	0	0	5	21	29	35	27	21	15	5	1	1	0	0
4	0	0	0	0	1	3	7	15	34	27	28	17	18	4	4	1	1

had started with a close approximation, we would expect the ALS Q-matrix derived from the corrupted matrix to still converge towards the same, hopefully "best" Q-matrix as the one obtained without perturbations.

Table 1 reports the results of this experiment. From 1 to 4 random perturbations are introduced in the Original expert matrix, $\mathbf{Q}_0$. With 1 perturbation, all 160 values of the 20 items $\times$ 8 skills Q-matrix are changed. With 2 and more perturbations, 160 random samples of combinations of values in the Q-matrix are changed. The table reports the number of discrepancies of the derived ALS Q-matrix between (1) the original ALS Q-matrix and (2) between the Original Q-matrix. Each row contains 160 values and the frequency of discrepancies from 0 to the observed maximum of 16 are reported. A line is drawn at the value of 5 discrepancies as a reminder of the original number of discrepancies.

We observe that with 1 perturbation, 42 of the 160 ALS Q-matrix derived are identical to the one derived with the unperturbed expert Q-matrix, and 50 show 1 discrepancy. This leaves 68 ALS Q-matrices that have 2 or more discrepancies, i.e. more discrepancies than perturbations introduced.

This trend increases with the number of perturbations: with 4 perturbations induced, only 28 ALS Q-matrices show 4 or less discrepancies, which leaves 132 with more discrepancies than the number of perturbations introduced.

Comparing the ALS Q-matrices with the Original expert Q-matrix, we see that for 1 perturbation, 47 of the 160 ALS Q-matrices derived correspond to the Original Q-matrix. For these matrices, the perturbation was removed. For the remaining 113, they show 6 to 9 discrepancies. However, given that for 1 perturbation, only 5 ALS Q-matrices diverge from the original ALS Q-matrix, this means that the overwhelming bulk of the discrepancies introduced are in fact changes towards the original ALS Q-matrix. The same argument can be made for 2 and for 3 perturbations, albeit to a lesser extent. Therefore, small perturbations still result in inducing ALS Q-matrices that converge towards the original ALS Q-matrix induced with the expert Q-matrix as a starting point.

However, starting at 4 perturbations, we see more divergences that are not aligned with the original ALS Q-matrix. Nevertheless, even at this number of perturbations, the large majority of the 160 cells remain intact, and so does the majority of the 56 cells which have a value of 1.

5 Discussion

The ALS factorization method offers a promising means of deriving Q-matrices from data given an expert defined Q-matrix to start with. One important advantage of this method is that it lends itself to an unambiguous comparison with the initial expert Q-matrix, and consequently to a clear interpretation.

The fact that the ALS Q-matrix derived generates slightly better predictive item outcome performance supports the hypothesis that the discrepancies between the this matrix and expert matrix are potentially valuable hints towards improving the expert Q-matrix.

The exploration of the space of Q-matrices through the experiment with perturbations showed that, up to 2 or 3 changes in an initial Q-matrix of the ALS factorization, the changes induced converge towards the original ALS factorization. This result suggests that a small number of errors will not affect the method's capacity to derive "better" Q-matrices (as defined by their predictive power) and make useful hints for enhancements.

In spite of these encouraging results, this study is limited to a single expert Q-matrix. Generalization to different dimensions of Q-matrices and different domains remain unknown and further studies are called for. Furthermore, a more in-depth, qualitative, and domain expert analysis of the discrepancies would be highly useful to better understand the results and assess the value of the method.

References

1. Barnes, T.: Novel derivation and application of skill matrices: The Q-matrix method. Handbook on Educational Data Mining (2010)
2. Cetintas, S., Si, L., Xin, Y.P., Hord, C.: Predicting correctness of problem solving in ITS with a temporal collaborative filtering approach. In: Aleven, V., Kay, J., Mostow, J. (eds.) ITS 2010, Part I. LNCS, vol. 6094, pp. 15–24. Springer, Heidelberg (2010)
3. De La Torre, J.: An empirically based method of q-matrix validation for the dina model: Development and applications. Journal of Educational Measurement 45(4), 343–362 (2008)
4. DeCarlo, L.T.: On the Analysis of Fraction Subtraction Data: The DINA Model, Classification, Latent Class Sizes, and the Q-Matrix. Applied Psychological Measurement 35, 8–26 (2011)
5. Desmarais, M.C.: Conditions for effectively deriving a q-matrix from data with non-negative matrix factorization. In: Conati, C., Ventura, S., Calders, T., Pechenizkiy, M. (eds.) 4th International Conference on Educational Data Mining, EDM 2011, Eindhoven, Netherlands, June 6-8, pp. 41–50 (2011)
6. Desmarais, M.C.: Mapping question items to skills with non-negative matrix factorization. ACM KDD-Explorations 13(2), 30–36 (2011)

7. Desmarais, M.C., Beheshti, B., Naceur, R.: Item to skills mapping: Deriving a conjunctive Q-matrix from data. In: Cerri, S.A., Clancey, W.J., Papadourakis, G., Panourgia, K. (eds.) ITS 2012. LNCS, vol. 7315, pp. 454–463. Springer, Heidelberg (2012)
8. Koedinger, K.R., McLaughlin, E.A., Stamper, J.C.: Automated student model improvement. In: Proceedings of the 5th International Conference on Educational Data Mining, pp. 17–24 (2012)
9. Lan, A.S., Waters, A.E., Studer, C., Baraniuk, R.G.: Sparse factor analysis for learning and content analytics. arXiv preprint arXiv:1303.5685 (2013)
10. Li, N., Cohen, W.W., Matsuda, N., Koedinger, K.R.: A machine learning approach for automatic student model discovery. In: Proceedings of the 4th International Conference on Educational Data Mining, pp. 31–40 (2011)
11. Liu, J., Xu, G., Ying, Z.: Data-driven learning of q-matrix. Applied Psychological Measurement 36(7), 548–564 (2012), http://apm.sagepub.com/content/36/7/548.abstract
12. Robitzsch, A., Kiefer, T., George, A., Uenlue, A., Robitzsch, M.: Package CDM (2012), http://cran.r-project.org/web/packages/CDM/index.html
13. Stamper, J.C., Barnes, T., Croy, M.J.: Extracting student models for intelligent tutoring systems. In: AAAI 2007, pp. 1900–1901. AAAI Press (2007)
14. Tatsuoka, K.K.: Rule space: An approach for dealing with misconceptions based on item response theory. Journal of Educational Measurement 20, 345–354 (1983)
15. Tatsuoka, K.: Cognitive Assessment: An Introduction to the Rule Space Method. Routledge Academic (2009)
16. Tatsuoka, K.: Analysis of errors in fraction addition and subtraction problems. Computer-based Education Research Laboratory, University of Illinois (1984)
17. Thai-Nghe, N., Drumond, L., Horváth, T., Nanopoulos, A., Schmidt-Thieme, L.: Matrix and tensor factorization for predicting student performance. In: Verbraeck, A., Helfert, M., Cordeiro, J., Shishkov, B. (eds.) CSEDU 2011 - Proceedings of the 3rd International Conference on Computer Supported Education, Noordwijkerhout, Netherlands, May 6-8, vol. 1, pp. 69–78. SciTePress (2011)
18. Thai-Nghe, N., Horváth, T., Schmidt-Thieme, L.: Factorization models for forecasting student performance. In: Conati, C., Ventura, S., Pechenizkiy, M., Calders, T. (eds.) Proceedings of EDM 2011, The 4th International Conference on Educational Data Mining, Eindhoven, Netherlands, July 6-8, pp. 11–20 (2011), http://www.educationaldatamining.org
19. Toscher, A., Jahrer, M.: Collaborative filtering applied to educational data mining. Tech. rep., KDD Cup 2010: Improving Cognitive Models with Educational Data Mining (2010)
20. Winters, T.: Educational Data Mining: Collection and Analysis of Score Matrices for Outcomes-Based Assessment. Ph.D. thesis, University of California Riverside (2006)

Maximum Clique Algorithm for Uniform Test Forms Assembly

Takatoshi Ishii[1], Pokpong Songmuang[2], and Maomi Ueno[1]

[1] University of Electro-Communications, Tokyo, Japan
{ishii,ueno}@ai.is.uec.ac.jp
[2] Thammasat University, Pratumthani, Thailand

Abstract. Educational assessments occasionally require "uniform test forms" for which each test form consists of a different set of items, but the forms meet equivalent test specifications (i.e., qualities indicated by test information functions based on item response theory). We propose two maximum clique algorithms (MCA) for uniform test forms assembly. The proposed methods can assemble uniform test forms with allowance of overlapping items among uniform test forms. First, we propose an exact method that maximizes the number of uniform test forms from an item pool. However, the exact method presents computational cost problems. To relax those problems, we propose an approximate method that maximizes the number of uniform test forms asymptotically. Accordingly, the proposed methods can use the item pool more efficiently than traditional methods can. We demonstrate the efficiency of the proposed methods using simulated and actual data.

Keywords: test assembly, uniform test forms, maximum clique problem, item response theory.

1 Introduction

Educational assessments occasionally require "uniform test forms" for which each form consists of a different set of items but which still must have equivalent specifications (e.g., equivalent amounts of test information based on item response theory, equivalent average test score, equivalent time limits). For example, uniform test forms are necessary when a testing organization administers a test in different time slots. To achieve this, uniform test forms are assembled in which all forms have equivalent qualities so that examinees who have taken different test forms can be evaluated objectively using the same scale.

Recently, automatic assembly for test forms has become popular. Automatic assembly assembles test forms to satisfy given test constraints (e.g., number of test items, amount of test information, average test score) to provide equivalent qualities [16,22,9,3,1,2,14,4,24,7,23,8,21,20,6].

In these studies, a test assembly is formalized as a combinational optimization problem. For example, van der Linden [23] proposed the big-shadow-test method using linear programming (LP). This method sequentially assembles uniform

K. Yacef et al. (Eds.): AIED 2013, LNAI 7926, pp. 451–462, 2013.

test forms by minimizing qualitative differences between a current assembled test form and the remaining set of items in an item pool. Although this method assembles uniform test forms in a practically acceptable time, it presents two problems. First, qualitative differences increase with the assembled order of test forms. Secondly, this method does not maximize the number of uniform test forms from the item pool.

To alleviate or ameliorate the first problem, Sun et al. [21] proposed a Genetic Algorithm (GA) for uniform tests assembly that simultaneously assembles uniform test forms as minimizing the differences among the qualities of assembled test forms and user-determined values. Furthermore, Songmuang and Ueno [20] applied the Bees Algorithm to uniform test forms assembly and to improve the performance of the method proposed by Sun et al. [21]. Although these methods [23,21,20] showed effective performance for minimizing the qualitative differences among assembled test forms, no method maximizes the number of uniform test forms from the item pool. These methods do not allow the item pool to be used efficiently to the greatest degree possible.

To maximize the number of test forms, Belov and Armstrong [8] proposed a uniform tests assembly method based on Maximum Set-Packing Problems. Moreover, Belov proposed a random test assembly method [6] to improve the tractability of maximizing the number of uniform test forms. However, these methods [8,6] cannot assemble uniform test forms with overlapping items (i.e., two test forms are allowed to have a common item called an overlapping item). In the non-overlapping conditions, each item is used only at once on assembled test forms. Therefore, the non-overlapping condition strongly restricts the number of assembled test forms. Consequently, the non-overlapping condition interrupts the efficient uses of the item pool.

The goal of this paper is to propose a uniform test forms assembly method that maximizes the number of assembled test forms with overlapping conditions. To achieve this goal, we apply the Maximum Clique Algorithm (MCA). MCA is an algorithm that solves the Maximum Clique Problem. We propose an exact method based on Maximum Clique Problem (ExMCP) for the maximum number of uniform test forms from the item pool.

The unique feature of ExMCP is to generalize Belov and Armstrong's method [8] to maximize the number of uniform test forms with an overlapping condition. Therefore, theoretically, ExMCP can assemble a greater number of test forms than when using traditional methods (e.g., [23,21,8,20]). In fact, ExMCP is expected to use the item pool more efficiently than traditional methods do.

However, the computational time and space costs of ExMCP increase exponentially with the number of "feasible test forms" (i.e., a set of those test forms which satisfy all test constraints except for the overlapping constraint from a given item pool). Therefore, it is difficult to use ExMCP for a large item pool.

To relax this problem, we propose RndMCP by approximating ExMCP using a random search approach (e.g., [19]). RndMCP maximizes the number of uniform test forms asymptotically from the item pool with overlapping conditions, and assembles a greater number of test forms than those of traditional methods (e.g., [23,8]). In addition, RndMCP searches the maximum number of uniform test forms more efficiently than traditional random search methods do [21,20] because the search space of RndMCP is more restrictive than those of the traditional methods.

Moreover, some experiments were conducted to evaluate the proposed methods. The results demonstrate that the proposed methods assemble a greater number of uniform test forms than the traditional methods do.

2 Maximum Clique Algorithm for Uniform Test Forms Assembly

In this section, we propose new methods to maximize the number of assembled uniform test forms with overlapping conditions.

2.1 Maximum Clique Problem

We apply the Maximum Clique Algorithm (MCA) to assemble the maximum number of uniform test forms. The MCA is an algorithm to solve the Maximum Clique Problem (MCP), which is a well-known combinational optimization problem in graph theory [15,11].

As described in this paper, a graph is represented as a pair $G = \{V, E\}$, where V denotes a set of vertices, and E denotes a set of edges.

Maximum Clique Problem searches a special structure called "Maximum Clique" from a given graph. "Clique" is a set of vertices in which each pair of vertices is connected. The "Maximum Clique" is the clique which has the maximum number of vertices in the given graph.

2.2 Maximum Clique Algorithm for Uniform Test Forms Assembly

In our study, the maximum number of uniform test forms is assembled to solve the maximum clique problem.

We assemble the following "Uniform test forms":

1. Any test form satisfies all test constraints.
2. Any two test forms satisfy the overlapping constraint. (i.e., any two test forms have fewer overlapping items than the allowed number in the overlapping constraint).

Accordingly, the maximum number of uniform test forms assembly can be described as the maximum clique extraction from a graph:

$$V = \left\{ \begin{array}{l} s : s \in S, \text{“Feasible test form”}, s \\ \quad \text{satisfies all test constraints} \\ \quad \text{excepting the overlapping constraint} \\ \quad \text{from a given item pool} \end{array} \right\}$$

$$E = \left\{ \begin{array}{c} \{s', s''\} : \text{The pair of } s' \text{ and } s'' \text{ satisfies} \\ \text{the overlapping constraint} \end{array} \right\}.$$

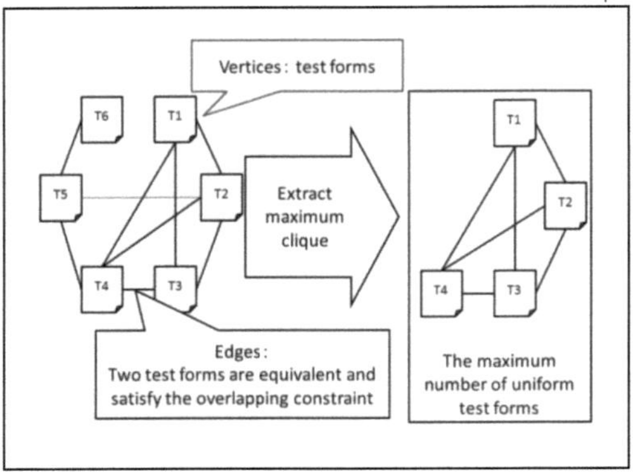

Fig. 1. MCA for Uniform Tests Assembly

This maximum clique problem searches the maximum set of feasible test forms in which any two test forms satisfy the overlapping constraint (i.e., this set is the maximum uniform test forms). Therefore, this optimization problem theoretically maximizes the number of uniform test forms. Figure 1 presents an example of uniform test forms assembly using the maximum clique problem. The graph G has six feasible test forms T1–T6 with nine satisfactions of overlapping constraint and the maximum number of uniform test forms $C_{max} = \{\text{T1}, \text{T2}, \text{T3}, \text{T4}\}$.

Belov and Armstrong's method [8] is a special case of this maximum clique problem when $E = \{ \{ \text{v,w} \}$: v and w have no overlap items ($v \cap w = \emptyset$) $\}$. Therefore, our method generalizes Belov and Armstrong's method by relaxing the overlapping constraint.

2.3 Exact Solution: ExMCP

We propose a uniform tests assembly algorithm, "ExMCP", which exactly solves the maximum clique problem described in *Maximum Clique Algorithm for Uniform Test Forms Assembly*. Therefore, ExMCP theoretically maximizes the number of uniform test forms.

ExMCP consists of the following three steps:

Step 1: (assembling feasible test forms)
Step 1 assembles all feasible test forms. We use branch and bound technique (e.g., [3]) to assemble the feasible test forms using test constraints except for the overlapping constraint. Finally, Step 1 stores the feasible test forms into a system memory.

Step 2: (generating a graph that corresponds to a set of feasible test forms with overlapping items)
Step 2 generates the corresponding graph by counting overlapping items among each pair of feasible test forms. The feasible test forms are represented as vertices and satisfactions of the overlapping constraint are represented as edges. Thereby, only if a pair of test forms has fewer common items than

the overlapping constraint do two vertices representing the pair of test forms have an edge.

Step 3: (extracting the maximum clique from the graph)
Step 3 extracts the maximum clique from the graph generated in Step 2. The extracted maximum clique represents the maximum number of uniform test forms that satisfy all test constraints including the overlapping constraint. To obtain the maximum clique, we use Nakanishi and Tomita's algorithm [17], which is the fastest exact algorithm in MCA.

ExMCP guarantees to extract the maximum number of uniform test forms with overlapping conditions from all combinations of feasible test forms from an item pool. However, the computational time and space costs are $O(2^F)$ and $O(F^2)$, where F is the number of feasible test forms from an item pool. Consequently, ExMCP is not available for large item pools.

2.4 Approximate Solution: RndMCP

To relax the computational costs problem, we approximate ExMCP using a random search approach. This method is designated as "RndMCP", which maximizes the number of uniform test forms asymptotically.

Although RndMCP consists of three steps similar to those of ExMCP, RndMCP repeats the three steps using a random search approach until it satisfies the three following constraints for computational costs:

$\mathbf{C_1}$ is the number of feasible test forms assembled in Step 1,
$\mathbf{C_2}$ is the time limit of Step 3,
$\mathbf{C_3}$ is the total time limit of the test assembly.

Details of the steps are the following.

Step 1: (assembling feasible test forms randomly)
Step 1 randomly assembles feasible test forms. Step 1 continues this step until the number of feasible test forms reaches $\mathbf{C_1}$. Finally, Step 1 stores the feasible test forms into the system memory.

Step 2: (generating a graph that corresponds to a set of feasible test forms with overlapping items)
Step 2 generates the corresponding graph by counting the overlapping items among feasible test forms similarly to ExMCP.

Step 3: (extracting the maximum clique)
Although Step 3 extracts the maximum clique from the graph similarly to ExMCP, the computation time of this step is limited by $\mathbf{C_2}$.

Step 4: (controlling the computation time)
Step 4 compares the current largest clique and the result of Step 3. Step 4 stores the larger clique as the largest clique. If the computation time is less than $\mathbf{C_3}$, then jump to Step 1.

The computational time cost of RndMCP is $\mathbf{C_3}$, and the space cost of RndMCP is $O({\mathbf{C_1}}^2)$. By controlling the computational time and space costs, RndMCP relaxes the computational costs problem in ExMCP.

RndMCP repeatedly extracts the maximum number of uniform test forms from subsets that are sampled randomly from all of feasible test forms. Therefore, it asymptotically assembles the maximum number of uniform test forms.

Moreover, this method searches the maximum number of uniform test forms more efficiently than the traditional random search methods [21,20] do because the search space of RndMCP is more restrictive than that of the traditional methods. The traditional methods have $O(2^F)$ search space size, but RndMCP (and ExMCP) has $O(2^{0.19171F})$ search space because this depends on Nakanishi and Tomita's MCA [17]. (This size is an upper bound of the search space size of maximum clique algorithm and might be more restricted when MCA research progresses)

3 Experiments and Results

We demonstrate the respective performances of the proposed methods using two experiments.

We used item response theory (IRT) to measure the quality of test forms similarly to most previous studies of test form assembly (e.g., [25,10,5,4,23,20]). We use simulated item pools in the first experiment and actual item pools in the second experiment.

The items in the simulated and actual item pools have discrimination parameter a and the difficulty parameter b in item response theory. In the simulated item pool, the discrimination parameter a is distributed as $a \sim U(0,1)$, and the difficulty parameter b is distributed as $b \sim N(0,1^2)$. The actual item pools use the Synthetic Personality Inventory (SPI) examination [18], which is a popular aptitude test in Japan. Table 2 presents details of the actual item pools.

We compared the performances of ExMCP and RndMCP with those of the traditional methods [23,21,20]. For that comparison, we used CPLEX [12] for the liner programming method in Linden's method. Table 1 shows details of computational environment for all experiments.

3.1 Results for the Simulated Item Pool

In the previous section, we described that ExMCP theoretically maximizes the number of uniform test forms. In this experiment, we present the performances of proposed methods experimentally using the simulated item pools.

We compare the number of assembled test forms with ExMCP, RndMCP, and the traditional methods [23,21,20].

We use six simulated item pools and three constraints. The item pools have the total quantities of items $I = 70, 80, 90, 100, 110$, and 120. The three constraints have common test constraints as follows:

1. The test length was four.
2. The allowed quantities of overlapping items were $0, 1$and 2.

Table 1. Computation Environment

CPU	Intel(R) Xeon(R) E5640 2.67 GHz
System Memory	12.0 GB
OS	Windows 7 SP1 64bit

Table 2. Details of the Actual Item Pool

Item Pool	Parameter a			Parameter b		
Size	Range	Mean	SD	Range	Mean	SD
87	0.15∼0.67	0.35	0.134	-2.09∼4.55	0.73	1.625
93	0.19∼0.69	0.43	0.122	-3.92∼3.61	-0.79	1.196
104	0.13∼1.10	0.59	0.213	-0.18∼4.55	1.50	1.188
141	0.24∼1.09	0.64	0.155	-1.41∼3.91	0.60	0.855
158	0.15∼3.08	0.44	0.255	-4.00∼4.00	-1.12	1.434
175	0.12∼0.93	0.39	0.139	-2.93∼3.12	-0.25	1.113
220	0.16∼0.92	0.46	0.155	-4.00∼2.82	-1.28	1.098

Table 3. Constraints of the Information Function

Constraint	Information Function (Lower /Upper Bound)				
ID	$\theta = -2.0$	$\theta = -1.0$	$\theta = 0$	$\theta = 1.0$	$\theta = 2.0$
1	0.1/0.2	0.2/0.3	0.4/0.5	0.2/0.3	0.1/0.2
2	0.0/0.2	0.1/0.3	0.3/0.5	0.1/0.3	0.0/0.2
3	0.0/0.4	0.1/0.5	0.3/0.7	0.1/0.5	0.0/0.4

In addition, the three constraints have different information constraints among the constraints. The information constraint is described by the lower and upper bounds of the test information function $I(\theta_k)$. Those information constraints are listed in Table 3. These restrict the number of feasible test forms (and assembled test forms) to ID: 1 < ID: 2 < ID: 3.

For the traditional methods [23,21,20], we determined the target values of information function $T(\theta_k)$ as

$$T(\theta_k) = \frac{(Lowerboundsofinformationfunction) + (Upperboundsofinformationfunction)}{2}.$$

The time limitation of test assembly is 6 hr for all methods except for RndMCP.

For RndMCP, we determined the respective computational cost constraints $\mathbf{C_1}$ as 100000, $\mathbf{C_2}$ as 60 s, and $\mathbf{C_3}$ as 1400 s.

Table 4 presents the quantities of test forms assembled by the proposed methods and the traditional methods for the item pool sizes, the overlapping constraint (maximum number of overlap items) and information constraints. In the table, "BST" denotes Linden's method [23],"GA" denotes Sun's method[21], "BA" denotes Songmuang's method[20], "EM" denotes the proposed ExMCP, and "RM" denotes the proposed RndMCP.

In many cases, ExMCP failed the test assembly because it did not complete the calculations in 6 hr (†). Moreover, it was unable to assemble uniform test

Table 4. Results for the Simulated Item Pool

Item Pool Size	Overlap Constraint	Constraint ID: 1					Constraint ID: 2					Constraint ID: 3				
		BST	GA	BA	EM	RM	BST	GA	BA	EM	RM	BST	GA	BA	EM	RM
70	0	1	0	1	1	1	6	6	7	8†	7	7	7	7	8†	8
	1	2	0	1	2	2	17	26	48	66†	67	17	58	59	0‡	99
	2	3	0	2	3	3	17	66	214	736†	735	17	274	278	0‡	1767
80	0	2	1	2	2	2	7	8	8	9†	9	7	8	8	0‡	9
	1	11	2	11	12†	11	20	40	64	100†	100	20	74	78	0‡	131
	2	20	4	69	88†	88	20	82	242	1462†	1404	20	347	301	0‡	2825
90	0	2	1	2	2	2	8	7	8	10†	10	8	8	9	0‡	10
	1	13	3	11	13†	12	22	40	71	122†	119	22	83	86	0‡	156
	2	22	3	78	107†	107	22	81	251	1949†	1846	22	321	336	0‡	3634
100	0	2	1	2	2	2	8	7	8	10†	10	9	9	9	0‡	11
	1	13	3	11	12†	13	25	36	76	131†	130	25	88	87	0‡	173
	2	25	3	87	118†	118	25	80	292	2325†	2170	25	312	346	0‡	4288
110	0	2	1	2	2	2	8	8	9	10†	10	10	9	10	0‡	11
	1	13	3	11	13†	13	27	34	79	138†	137	27	86	92	0‡	195
	2	27	2	91	123†	123	27	70	308	2632†	2413	27	271	356	0‡	4938
120	0	2	2	2	2	2	9	6	9	11†	11	10	10	11	0‡	13
	1	13	2	10	13†	13	30	29	82	152†	150	30	92	102	0‡	229
	2	30	4	95	129†	127	30	68	336	2913†	2617	30	269	407	0‡	6006

†: The maximum number of uniform test forms detected in 6 hr.
‡: A memory insufficiency problem interrupted the test construction.

forms because the computational environment had insufficient system memory (‡). In † cases, ExMCP detected a greater number of uniform test forms than any other method in the given time limitation. In all cases, RndMCP assembled higher quantities of uniform test forms than the traditional methods did [23,21,20]. In addition, the computational time of RndMCP is less than the other random search methods (e.g., [21,20]). The computational time of RndMCP is $\mathbf{C_3} = 1400$ s, and the time limitations of the other random search methods are 6 hr. Results show that RndMCP provides more accurate results than the other random search methods do. Moreover, the difference of quantities of assembled test forms between the proposed method and the traditional methods increase with the number of assembled test forms (or the scale of assembly).

The results can be summarized as shown below.

1. ExMCP assembles the maximum number of uniform test forms, but it entails a computational cost problem.
2. Even when ExMCP fails a uniform test forms assembly by computational cost problem, RndMCP assembles a greater number of uniform test forms than the traditional methods do. Actually, RndMCP relaxes ExMCPś computational costs problem.
3. RndMCP assembled more quantities of uniform test forms in a shorter time than the other random search methods (e.g., [21,20]) did. Results show that RndMCP provides more accurate results than the other random search methods do.
4. The differences of the number of assembled test forms between the proposed methods and traditional methods increase with the number of feasible test forms (or the scale of test assembly). For large scale assembly, the proposed methods are more efficient than the traditional methods are.

3.2 Results for Actual Item Pool

We assemble uniform test forms using actual item pools to demonstrate the effectiveness of RndMCP in actual situations. ExMCP cannot assemble the test forms in an actual situation because the computational environment has insufficient resources.

We use six actual item pools that have total numbers of items I = 87, 93, 104, 141, 158, 175, and 220. The distributions of item parameters a and b in the item pool are given in Table 2.

We use the same test constraints as in *Results for the Simulated Item pool.* For RndMCP, we determine the computational costs constraint $\mathbf{C_1} = 100000$, $\mathbf{C_2} = 30$ s, and $\mathbf{C_3} = 6$ hr. All other assembly methods are also given 6 hr for calculation times.

Table 5. Results for the Actual Item Pool

Item Pool Size	Overlap Constraint	Constraint ID: 1				Constraint ID: 2				Constraint ID: 3			
		BST	GA	BA	RM	BST	GA	BA	RM	BST	GA	BA	RM
87	0	0	0	0	0	3	3	4	4	3	3	4	4
	1	0	0	0	0	16	10	19	29	14	11	20	27
	2	0	0	0	0	21	36	139	307	21	39	140	309
93	0	0	0	0	0	4	5	5	6	5	5	5	6
	1	0	0	0	0	23	16	33	51	23	16	33	51
	2	0	0	0	0	23	43	211	658	23	54	208	721
104	0	2	2	2	2	6	5	8	10	12	15	15	18
	1	6	5	9	10	26	26	71	131	26	171	140	369
	2	26	14	83	121	26	59	275	2088	26	590	394	8442
141	0	10	3	9	10	18	19	21	27	26	31	27	35
	1	35	5	70	150	6	122	188	589	35	506	239	1014
	2	35	20	268	2307	10	185	393	11426	35	1511	386	19095
158	0	0	0	0	0	6	1	5	6	6	4	7	8
	1	0	0	0	0	22	12	24	40	39	42	75	131
	2	0	0	0	0	39	50	137	316	39	94	279	4877
175	0	2	0	2	2	6	6	7	9	6	6	8	10
	1	12	1	13	15	43	53	96	186	43	65	100	193
	2	43	2	128	234	43	102	303	7030	43	103	283	7413
220	0	2	0	2	2	7	5	8	10	9	8	10	13
	1	8	2	7	17	54	20	87	177	54	57	124	282
	2	54	8	75	136	54	44	309	5889	54	114	334	9938

Table 5 presents the quantities of test forms assembled using the proposed method and the traditional methods for the item pool size, the overlapping constraint and information constraints.

Similar to simulated experiments, in all cases, RndMCP assembled greater quantities of uniform test forms than the traditional methods did [23,21,20]. Moreover, the difference quantities of assembled test forms between the proposed method and the traditional methods increase continuously with the number of assembled test forms.

The results can be summarized as follows:

1. RndMCP assembles a greater number of uniform test forms than the traditional methods do.
2. RndMCP assembled greater quantities of uniform test forms than the other random search methods (e.g., [21,20]) did during an equal time period. Results show that RndMCP provides more accurate results than the other random search methods do.
3. The differences of the number of assembled test forms between the proposed methods and traditional methods increase along with the number of feasible test forms (or the scale of test assembly).

The results show that RndMCP uses an item pool more efficiently than the traditional methods do.

4 Conclusion

We proposed two uniform test forms assembly methods, ExMCP and RndMCP, based on the Maximum Clique Algorithm. The proposed methods exactly or asymptotically maximize the quantities of uniform test forms with an overlapping condition.

ExMCP generalizes Belov's method [8] for overlapping conditions. Furthermore, it maximizes the number of uniform test forms with overlapping conditions. However, ExMCP presents computational costs problems. RndMCP approximates ExMCP using a random search approach to relax this computational costs problem. RndMCP assembles a greater number of uniform test forms than the traditional methods (e.g., [23,21,20]) do. Moreover, RndMCP provides more accurate results than other random search methods (e.g., [21,20]) do.

To demonstrate these features, we conducted two experiments using simulated and actual data. Both experiments show that proposed methods assemble a greater number of uniform test forms than the traditional methods do. Moreover, the differences of the number of assembled test forms between proposed methods and the traditional methods increases with the number of feasible test forms (or the scale of test assembly). This result shows that the proposed methods can assemble a greater number of uniform test forms than the traditional methods can.

In simulated experiments, more cases exist in which ExMCP cannot assemble uniform test forms because of computational cost problems. However in those cases, RndMCP assembles a greater number of uniform test forms than the traditional methods do. This result shows that RndMCP relaxes the computational cost problems of ExMCP.

In simulated experiments, the computational time of RndMCP is less than that of the other random search methods. In actual experiments, RndMCP assembles a greater number of test forms than the traditional methods do, given equal time limitations. Therefore, RndMCP provides more accurate results than other random search methods (e.g., [21,20]) do.

Results show the salient benefits of using the proposed methods.

References

1. Ackerman, T.A.: An alternative methodology for creating parallel test forms using the irt information function. Paper presented at the Annual Meeting of the National Council on Measurement in Education, San Francisco, CA, March 30 (1989)
2. Adema, J.J.: Methods and models for the construction of weakly parallel tests. Applied Psychological Measurement 16(1), 53–63 (1992)
3. Ameda, J.J.: Implementations of the branch-and-bound method for test construction problems. Project Psychometric Aspects of Item Banking, Department of Education, University of Twente, Research Report 89-6 (1989)
4. Armstrong, R.D., Jones, D.H., Kunce, C.S.: Irt test assembly using network-flow programming. Applied Psychological Measurement 22(3), 237–247 (1998)
5. Armstrong, R.D., Jones, D.H., Wang, Z.: Automated parallel test construction using classical test theory. Journal of Educational Statistics 19(1), 73–90 (1994)
6. Belov, D.I.: Uniform test assembly. Psychometrika 73(1), 21–38 (2008)
7. Belov, D.I., Armstrong, R.D.: Monte carlo test assembly for item pool analysis and extension. Applied Psychological Measurement 29, 239–261 (2005)
8. Belov, D.I., Armstrong, R.D.: A constraint programming approach to extract the maximum number of non-overlapping test forms. Computational Optimization and Applications 33, 319–332 (2006)
9. Boekkooi-Timminga, E.: Simultaneous test construction by zero-one programming. Methodika 1, 101–112 (1987)
10. Boekkooi-Timminga, E.: The construction of parallel tests from irt-based item banks. J. Educat. Statist. 15, 129–145 (1990), reports
11. Garey, M.R., Johnson, D.S.: Computers and Intractability; A Guide to the Theory of NP-Completeness. W. H. Freeman & Co., New York (1990)
12. ILOG: ILOG CPLEX User's Manual 11.0
13. Ishii, T., Songmuang, P., Ueno, M.: A method to extract the maximum number of test forms using maxclique. In: The 23rd Annual Conference of the Japanese Society for Artificial Intelligence (2009)
14. Jeng, H., Shih, S.: A comparison of pair-wise and group selections of items using simulated annealing in automated construction of parallel tests. Psychological Testing 44(2), 195–210 (1997)
15. Karp, R.M.: Reducibility among combinatorial problems. Complexity of Computer Computations 40(4), 85–103 (1972)
16. Lord, F.M.: Applications of Item Response Theory to Practical Testing Problems, 1st edn. Routledge (July 1980)
17. Nakanishi, H., Tomita, E.: An $o(2^{0.19171n})$-time and polynomial-space algorithm for finding a maximum clique. Information Processing Society of Japan SIG Technical Report 2008(6), 15–22 (2008)
18. Recruit: Synthetic Personality Inventory (SPI), `http://www.spi.recruit.co.jp/`
19. Solis, F.J., Wets, R.J.B.: Minimization by random search techniques. Mathematics of Operations Research 6(1), 19–30 (1981)
20. Songmuang, P., Ueno, M.: Bees algorithm for construction of multiple test forms in e-testing. IEEE Transactions on Learning Technologies 4, 209–221 (2011)
21. Sun, K.T., Chen, Y.J., Tsai, S.Y., Cheng, C.F.: Creating irt-based parallel test forms using the genetic algorithm method. Applied Measurement in Education 21(2), 141–161 (2008)
22. Theunissen, T.J.J.M.: Binary programming and test design. Psychometrika 50(4), 411–420 (1985)

23. van der Linden, W.J.: Liner Models for Optimal Test Design. Springer (2005)
24. van der Linden, W.J., Adema, J.J.: Simultaneous assembly of multiple test forms. Journal of Educational Measurement 35(3), 185–198 (1998)
25. van der Linden, W.J., Boekkooi-Timminga, E.: A maximin model for irt-based test design with practical constraints. Psychometrika 54(2), 237–247 (1989)

The Effect of Interaction Granularity on Learning with a Data Normalization Tutor

Amali Weerasinghe, Antonija Mitrovic, Amir Shareghi Najar, and Jay Holland

Intelligent Computer Tutoring Group
University of Canterbury, Christchurch, New Zealand
{amali.weerasinghe,amir.shareghinajar}@pg.canterbury.ac.nz,
{tanja.mitrovic,jay.holland}@canterbury.ac.nz

Abstract. Intelligent Tutoring Systems (ITSs) have proven their effectiveness in many instructional domains, ranging in the complexity of domain theories and tasks students are to perform. The typical effect sizes achieved by ITSs are around 1SD, which are still low in comparison to the effectiveness of expert human tutors. Recently there have been several analyses done in order to identify the factors that contribute to success of human tutors, and to replicate it in ITSs. VanLehn [6] proposes that the crucial factor is the *granularity of interaction*: the lower the level of discussions between the (human or artificial) tutor and the student, the higher the effectiveness. We investigated the effect of interaction granularity in the context of NORMIT, a constraint-based tutor that teaches data normalization. Our study compared the standard version of NORMIT, which provided hints in response to errors, to a version which used adaptive tutorial dialogues instead. The results show that the interaction granularity hypothesis holds in our experimental situation, and that the effect size achieved is consistent with other reported studies of a similar nature.

Keywords: effectiveness of ITSs, interaction granularity hypothesis, empirical study, tutorial dialogues, NORMIT.

1 Introduction

One-to-one human tutoring is widely considered to be the most effective form of tutoring. Students' learning gains increase by two standard deviations when tutored by expert human tutors compared to traditional classroom instruction [1]. Researchers have been trying to identify the factors that contribute to the success of human tutors, and replicate it in ITSs. One of the frequently discussed factors is interactivity, since human tutoring is highly interactive. ITSs are also interactive: typically students are engaged in problem solving, and receive guidance in the form of feedback, adaptive problem selection and other interventions.

Many questions related to interactivity have been posed in the ITS literature. Koedinger and Aleven [2] investigate the assistance dilemma, which refers to the problem of balancing assistance giving and withholding in order to optimise student learning. Information might be provided to the student; for example, the student might be given advice how to solve a particular problem step. On the other hand, information might

K. Yacef et al. (Eds.): AIED 2013, LNAI 7926, pp. 463–472, 2013.

be elicited: the student might be asked a series of questions leading to the correct action. Similarly, worked-out examples might be given to the student, but if the student is prompted to self-explain the examples to him/herself, learning is greatly enhanced [3-5]. Cognitive tutors, for example, provide immediate positive and negative feedback on each step, instructions on how to complete the step on demand, adaptive problem selection and other forms of interactive guidance.

In a recent paper, VanLehn [6] examines several hypotheses that aim to explain the effectiveness of human tutoring and concludes that only two provide viable explanations. Human tutors provide frequent feedback which allows students to repair their knowledge. They also provide adaptive scaffolding in terms of tutorial dialogues. VanLehn proposes that the crucial factor for the effectiveness of instruction is the *interaction granularity*. Human tutoring has no limitation on interaction granularity as human tutors intervene very frequently and also at various levels. On the other extreme, if there is *no tutoring* provided whatsoever, the student is solving problems with no feedback and needs to do a lot of reasoning which often is unproductive because of lack of knowledge. In between those two extremes, VanLehn discussed three types of computer-based tutoring. In *answer-based tutoring* (such as in Computer-Aided Instruction), the student only submits the final answer for the problem without intermediate steps and therefore only limited feedback can be given. ITSs typically provide *step-based tutoring*, as they react (or may react) on each step of the solution, which represents a finer grain size. Dialogue-based ITSs represent *sub-step tutoring*, and are characterised with an even finer level of interaction granularity compared to step-based ITSs. Tutorial dialogues allow the ITS to obtain more information about the student's reasoning in comparison to step-based tutoring.

The interaction granularity hypothesis predicts that the effectiveness of tutoring increases as the granularity of interaction decreases (i.e. the grain size becomes smaller). VanLehn conducted a large meta-review of reported studies, each of which compared two instructional conditions that differ in the interaction granularity level keeping other factors the same. The meta-review confirmed the hypothesis, with the limitation that in some types of comparisons the number of studies was small.

Using the interaction granularity criterion, the studies we have performed can be classified into several groups. Some studies compared step-based to answer-based tutoring (e.g. [7]) or no tutoring [8]. We also performed studies comparing various forms of step-based tutoring to one another [9], or various forms of sub-step tutoring [10]. In this paper we report on a study that compares step-based to sub-step tutoring. Section 2 presents the step-based constraint-based tutor for data normalization, while Section 3 discusses the substep-based version of the same ITS. We then present the design of our study in Section 4, followed by the results in Section 5 and conclusions.

2 NORMIT

NORMIT [5, 11] is a constraint-based tutor that teaches data normalization, a technique which consists of refining an existing relational database schema in order to ensure that all relations are of high quality [12]. Normalization is a hard topic for students [5, 13], as it requires theoretical knowledge of the relational data model, functional dependencies (FDs), normal forms and the related algorithms.

Data normalization is a procedural technique, consisting of a sequence of tasks to analyze the quality of a database. Each problem consists of a relation schema and a set of given FDs. For example, problem 13 is defined on relation R(A, B, C, D, E) (typically the semantics of the attributes is not given) and the set of FDs: {A → BC, CD → E, AC → E, B → D, E → AB} (see Figure 1).

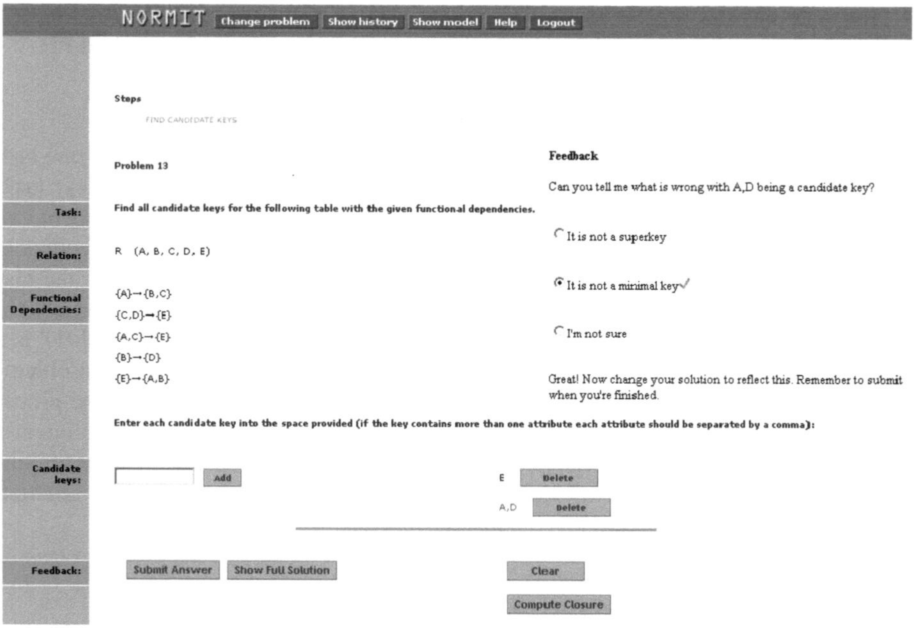

Fig. 1. A screenshot of NORMIT

The normalization procedure as implemented in NORMIT consists of eleven tasks described below. Please note that we refer to elements of the procedure as *tasks* rather than *steps*, as each of them contains a number of actions the student has to perform, including in some cases relatively complex algorithms. The first eight tasks are necessary to determine the highest normal form the relation is in. If the relation is not in Boyce-Codd Normal Form (BCNF), the student needs to apply the relational synthesis algorithm to derive an improved database schema via tasks 9-11.

1. Identify the candidate keys for the given table. There may be one or more keys in a table; e.g. in problem 13 there are four candidate keys: A, E, BC and CD.
2. Find the closure of a given set of attributes. For example, to make sure that E is a candidate key, the student can check that closure contains all attributes of R.
3. Identify prime attributes. Prime attributes are those attributes that belong to any candidate key. In problem 13, all attributes are prime.
4. Simplify FDs by applying the decomposition rule, if necessary. For example, A → BC is replaced with two FDs: A → B and A → C.
5. Determine the normal forms for the given relation.

6. If the student specified that the relation is not in 2NF, he/she needs to identify FDs that violate that form (i.e. partial FDs).
7. If the student specified that the relation is not in 3NF, he/she needs to identify FDs that violate that form (i.e. transitive FDs).
8. If the student specified that the relation is not in BCNF, he/she will be asked to identify FDs that violate that form.
9. For relations that are not in BCNF, reduce LHS of FDs. This task checks whether some of the attributes on the LHS can be dropped while still having a valid FD.
10. Find minimal cover (i.e. the minimal set of FDs).
11. Decompose the table by using the minimal cover.

NORMIT teaches data normalization in a task-by-task manner, showing only one task at a time which the student needs to complete before moving on to the next task. Figure 1, for example, shows the candidate keys task of problem 13. The student can submit a solution at any time, which the system then analyses and presents feedback. At any point during the session, the student may change the problem, review the history of the session, examine the student model or ask for the full solution. The system currently contains 50 problems and new problems can be added easily. NORMIT is a constraint-based tutor, and its knowledge base is represented as a set of 82 (problem-independent) constraints. Each constraint is relevant for a particular task of the procedure. Some constraints are purely syntactic, while others compare the student's solution to the ideal solution (generated by the problem solver). The short-term student model consists of a list of violated/satisfied constraints for the current attempt, while the long term model records the history of usage for each constraint.

3 The Model for Adaptive Tutorial Dialogues

In previous work [14] we developed a general model of adaptive tutorial dialogues, which we used to provide tutorial dialogues in NORMIT. This model consists of three parts: an error hierarchy, a set of tutorial dialogues and rules for adapting them. The error hierarchy categorises all error types in a particular domain. Each leaf in the hierarchy is associated with one or more violated constraints, which are covered by a single tutorial dialogue. The error types are grouped into higher-level categories, with the top three levels of the error hierarchy being domain-independent. At the top level of the hierarchy, errors are classified into syntax or semantic ones. Semantic errors are further classified into several groups, such as missing components or extra components in the solution.

The student model is extended with the information about the errors the student made during interaction. This new component of the student model stores the frequency of the student making a mistake corresponding to each node of the error hierarchy. When a student submits a solution to the current problem, a set of violated constrains (if any) is determined. The information about violated constraints is then used to update the violation frequencies for the relevant nodes in the hierarchy. If the student's solution contains several errors, the most suitable error for discussion is selected from the error hierarchy. The model identifies the error that was most frequent and the corresponding dialogue is then used for discussion with the student.

Tutorial dialogues (the second component of our model of tutorial dialogues), are hand-crafted for each error type. For syntax errors, dialogues are very simple, and consist of a single feedback message (the same message used as the hint[1] in the original version of NORMIT). For semantic errors, tutorial dialogues consist of four levels of prompts. Each prompt contains a question and a set of three options for the student to respond. For example, the tutorial dialogue in Figure 2 is used when the solution contains an incorrect candidate key, such as AD for problem 13. The first-level prompt (*NORMIT1*) presents a conceptual question. If the student fails to answer correctly, the model poses another question at the same level ("*What do we mean by a candidate key being a minimal set of attributes?*"). The tutor reveals the correct answer if the student cannot identify it.

The second level presents a *reflective prompt*, asking why the solution is incorrect (*NORMIT2*, shown in Figure 1). If the student fails to answer correctly, the tutor makes the reasoning process more explicit. In this scenario, the tutor says "*Let's see ... Check carefully whether all the attributes of AD are needed to determine all the other attributes*". The student needs to press the Continue button to proceed, after which the next prompt is revealed: "*Do we need all the attributes of AD to determine all the other attributes?*"

The third level provides a *corrective action prompt* which helps the student to correct the error (*NORMIT3*). Finally, the *conceptual reinforcement prompt* provides another opportunity to learn the corresponding domain concept (*NORMIT4*). This level uses different types of questions such as simple questions, fill-in-the-blank (*NORMIT4*) or true-false questions, to keep the student engaged. The first and last levels focus on problem-independent details and support the acquisition of conceptual knowledge. On the other hand, the second and third levels discuss problem-specific details.

NORMIT1: You seem to be having some difficulty with candidate keys. Let's look at candidate keys in detail. What is a candidate key?

Student1: *A candidate key is a minimal set of attributes that determines all the attributes*

NORMIT2: Great, can you tell me what's wrong with AD being a candidate key?

Student 2: *It is not a minimal key*

NORMIT3: Good job! Now tell me the extra attributes for AD?

Student3: *D*

NORMIT4: Well done! Now try to answer this question so that you'll remember what you learnt.
A .... is a ....key with extra ....

Student4: *superkey, candidate key, attributes*

NORMIT5: Great job! Please make the changes and submit the solution when you're done.

Fig. 2. An example tutorial dialogue

The last component of the model of tutorial dialogues is adaptation rules, which enable individualization of the selected dialogue. The rules use the student model and the session history to decide on the timing, selection and the dialogue content. The

[1] NORMIT offers six levels of feedback [5].

number of prompts a student receives depends on the accuracy of his/her answer and the number of times an error is made. If an error is made for the first time, a student receives a reflective prompt. If answered correctly (as in the situation illustrated in Figure 1), the student is allowed to resume problem solving. If the same error is made two times, the student receives two prompts: reflective and corrective action prompt. If the same error is repeated three times or more, the student must go through the entire dialogue starting from the conceptual prompt. At any level, an incorrect answer will trigger another prompt to be presented as there is no evidence the student has the relevant knowledge. Adaptation rules also deal with situations when students abandon problems, or are inactive for a period of time. In such cases, the current state of the student's solution is evaluated and a dialogue is initiated.

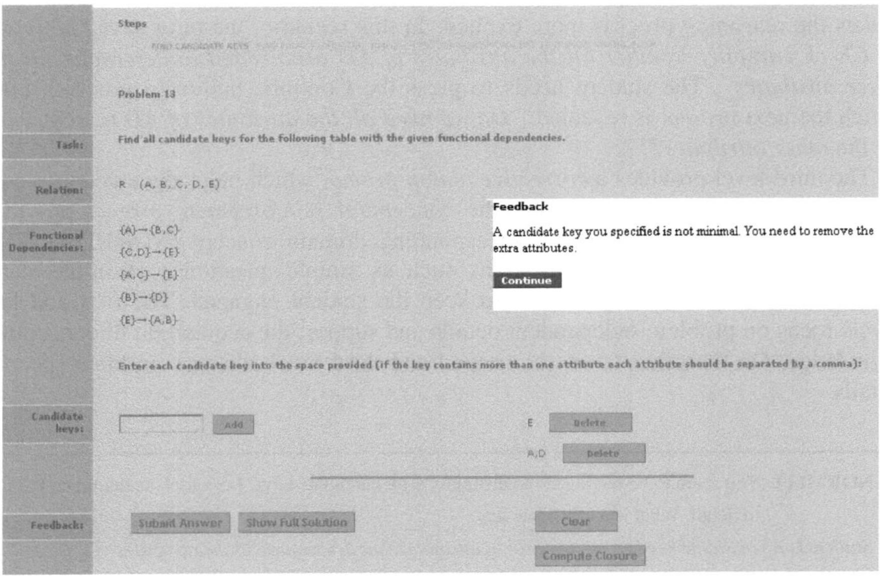

Fig. 3. A screenshot of problem 13 for a participant in the Hint group[2]

4 Study

Our goal was to investigate the effect of interaction granularity on learning data normalization. We conducted a study in October 2012 at the University of Canterbury, involving volunteers from an introductory database course. The study was conducted during a regular lab session (100 minutes long) in the eleventh week of the course, by which time the students had already learnt about data normalization in lectures. Participants were randomly assigned to two groups. Error selection was done in the same way in both groups, as described in Section 3. The Dialogue group received adaptive tutorial dialogues in response to errors, while the Hint group received non-interactive

[2] The problem-solving area (left pane) was disabled when feedback/dialogues were presented.

hint messages (Figure 3). In addition to hints/dialogues, both conditions received error-flag feedback: the incorrect part of the solution corresponding to the selected error was highlighted in red (AD in Figures 1 and 3). Both groups could also request the solution for the current task.

The Hint group received non-interactive hint messages. A hint message is attached to a constraint, and is provided as feedback when the constraint is violated. The theory of learning from performance errors [15] specifies that effective feedback should tell the user where the error is, what constitutes the error (perform blame allocation), and refer to the underlying domain concept. NORMIT highlights the incorrect part of the student's solution, while the feedback message specifies what is wrong. In Figure 3, the hint informs the student that the highlighted candidate key is not minimal.

The study consisted of three phases: pre-test, interaction and post-test. The tests were of similar complexities and consisted of four questions each. The first two questions focused on procedural knowledge whereas the remaining two were for conceptual knowledge.

5 Results

37 students participated in the study. Data about one participant was excluded, as the student spent only 5 minutes working with NORMIT, resulting in 18 students in each group. Some students have not completed the post-test. Table 1 reports the statistics for students who submitted both tests. The groups had similar performances on the pre- and post-test. Both groups improved significantly between the pre- and post-test. In the pre-test, we also asked the students about how interested they were in learning data normalisation, on the Likert scale from 1 (not interested at all) to 5 (very interested). The Mann-Whitney U-test revealed no significant differences between the two groups on this question.

Table 1. Performance of the students who submitted both tests

	Hint (17)	**Dialogue (15)**	**p**
Pre-test (%)	66.91 (25.36)	63.33 (22.89)	.34
Post-test (%)	82.35 (18.78)	89.17 (16.95)	.14
Improvement pre-to-post	t=-2.18, p=.022	t=-5.57, p<.01	
Gain	15.44 (29.16)	25.83 (17.97)	.11
Interest	3.35 (0.49)	3.13 (0.92)	.48

Table 2 provides additional statistics about the study. There was no difference in learning time, the number of attempted and solved problems, the total number of attempts (i.e. submissions) and learnt constraints. Learnt constraints are those that the student did not know at the beginning of the session, but learnt during the session. There was also no significant difference in the number of interventions (in the form of hints or adaptive dialogues) the two conditions received. The effect size (Cohen's *d*) based on the learning gain 0.42, which is a medium size effect.

Table 2. Basic statistics for all participants

	Hint (18)	Dialogue (18)	p
Time (min)	70.22 (21.06)	73.89 (13.72)	.27
Attempted problems	10.28 (5.21)	9.50 (4.62)	.32
Solved problems	9.33(4.97)	8.28 (4.11)	.25
Total attempts	109.22 (62.10)	99.44 (44.73)	.29
Learnt constraints	3.28 (3.00)	4.05 (2.99)	.22
No. of hints/dialogues	35.67 (22.57)	33.89 (18.15)	.39

Table 3 presents some details about the dialogues. Approximately one third of the dialogues were single-level ones; in those situations the Dialogue group participants received the same feedback (i.e. hints) as their peers. The remaining dialogues were multi-level dialogues. In such cases, the students saw on average 7.11 dialogues with only one prompt (because they successfully answered the prompt, as explained in Section 3) and 14.84 multi-prompt dialogues. The average number of prompts in the muti-prompt dialogues was 2.74. The average success rate in answering prmopts was 71%. The students received more problem-specific prompts (28.78) than problem-independent prompts (18.33), which was to be expected as that is the result of adaptation rules.The success rate on two types of prompts is comparable.

Table 3. Dialogue analyses

Single-level dialogues seen	11.89 (7.79)
Multi-level dialogues seen	22 (12.77)
Single-prompt dialogues	7.11 (4.01)
Multi-prompt dialogues	14.84 (9.57)
No of prompts in a multi-prompt dialogues	2.74 (0.30)
Total number of questions answered	47.11 (28.78)
% of prompts answered correctly	64.9 (17.61)
% of prompts answered incorrectly	19.9 (9.03)
% of prompts answered with a More Help request	15.2 (19.20)
Total number of problem-independent prompts	18.33 (13.69)
% of problem-independent prompts answered correctly	67.616 (17.68)
Total number of problem-specific prompts	28.78 (15.63)
% of problem-specific prompts answered correctly	64.29 (23.84)

We performed a finer analysis of the learning gains, looking at two types of questions (conceptual/procedural) in the tests (Table 4). There was no difference between the pre-test performances on both types of questions. The performance of the Dialogue group on the procedural questions is marginally significantly higher than that of the Hint group, but there is no significant difference on the gains. The Dialogue group improved significantly between pre and post-test on both types of questions, while the Hint group only improved significantly on conceptual questions. The effect size on procedural questions is 0.35, while the effect size for conceptual questions is 0.21. Therefore, tutorial dialogues enabled the students to significantly improve both conceptual and procedural knoweldge, while the hints resulted in a significant improvement of conceptual knowledge only.

Table 4. Comparison of the two groups on two types of questions

Procedural questions	**Hint (17)**	**Dialogue (15)**	**p**
Pre-test (%)	64.71 (23.48)	63.33 (35.19)	p= .44
Post-test (%)	70.59 (30.92)	83.3 (24.40)	t = -1.30, p = .10
Improvement pre-to-post	p = .29	t = -2.102, p = .03	
Gain	5.88 (42.87)	20 (36.84)	p = .16
Conceptual questions	**Hint (17)**	**Dialogue (15)**	**p**
Pre-test (%)	69.12 (34.83)	63.33 (35.19)	p = .3
Post-test (%)	94.12 (14.06)	95 (14.02)	p = .43
Improvement pre-to-post	t = -3.36, p < .01	t = -3.67, p < .01	
Gain	25 (30.62)	31.67(33.36)	p = .28

6 Conclusions

The interaction granularity hypothesis states that the effectiveness of tutoring increases as the granularity of interaction decreases. We conducted a study comparing two versions of the data normalization tutor, a step-based and a substep-based version. The Hint group (providing step-based tutoring) received non-interactive messages on their errors, while their peers in the Dialogue group received adaptive, interactive dialogues that discuss their errors (substep-based tutoring). The same mechanism was used in both conditions to select an error for presenting feedback or an adaptive dialogue in the case of multiple errors in the student's submission. In other words, if two students with identical interaction histories submit identical solutions, the error selected for discussion will be the same although the two students are from two different conditions. The main difference between the two groups lies in the instructional intervention in response to the selected error. While the Hint group participant received a single feedback message for the error, the participant from the Dialogue group was engaged in an interactive, adaptive dialogue for the same error. Additionally, in both conditions the selected error was flagged, and both groups had access to the solution for the current task of the procedure. As the performances of both groups improved significantly from pre- to post-test, both interventions (hints and dialogues) assisted the students to acquire knowledge about data normalization.

Further analysis of the effect of interactions with NORMIT on acquiring conceptual and procedural knowledge revealed interesting results: (i) the Dialogue group improved significantly both on conceptual knowledge and procedural knowledge; (ii) the Hint group significantly improved only on conceptual knowledge. The effect size on the procedural knowledge gain is 0.35, while for conceptual knowledge it is 0.21. The differences in gains between the Dialogue and Hint groups are not statistically significant, due to the small size of the study, but the trends are consistent with the interaction granularity hypothesis. The Hint group was presented with a non-interactive feedback message about the selected error; the hints were pre-specified messages of conceptual nature. Hints discuss the underlying domain concepts that are relevant for the incorrect part of the student's solution (identified via error flagging). The students from the Hint condition, however, need to reason about feedback. They were not told explicitly how to correct the error, unless they accessed the solution for the current task.

On the other hand, the Dialogue group participants were engaged in a discussion about both relevant domain concepts and the problem-solving procedure. This condition received more scaffolding via adaptive dialogues. The dialogues approach the error from multiple aspects, such as why the student's solution is incorrect, how to correct it and corresponding domain knowledge. The student involved in a tutorial dialogue is more engaged than a student who receives a hint message. As dialogues were adaptive, the number of prompts depended on the history of the individual tutoring session. Therefore, the granularity of the interaction was significantly lower for the Dialogue group than the Hint group. The effect size of our study (0.42) is of the same magnitude as the effect sizes reported for studies of similar nature in [6], thus providing another supporting evidence for the interactivity granularity hypothesis.

References

1. Bloom, B.S.: The 2-sigma problem: the search for methods of group instruction as effective as one-to-one tutoring. Educational Researcher 13, 4–16 (1984)
2. Koedinger, K., Aleven, V.: Exploring the assistance dilemma in experiments with cognitive tutors. Educational Psychology Review 19, 239–264 (2007)
3. Chi, M.T.H., De Leeuw, N., Chiu, M.H., LaVancher, C.: Eliciting self-explanations improves understanding. Cognitive Science 18, 439–477 (1994)
4. Aleven, V., Koedinger, K.R.: An effective metacognitive strategy: Learning by doing and explaining with a computer-based Cognitive Tutor. Cognitive Science 26, 147–179 (2002)
5. Mitrovic, A.: The effect of explaining on learning: a case study with a data normalization tutor. In: Looi, C.-K., McCalla, G., Bredeweg, B., Breuker, J. (eds.) Proc. Artificial Intelligence in Education, pp. 499–506. IOS Press (2005)
6. VanLehn, K.: The relative effectiveness of human tutoring, intelligent tutoring systems and other tutoring systems. Educational Psychologist 46(4), 197–221 (2011)
7. Suraweera, P., Mitrovic, A.: An Intelligent Tutoring System for Entity Relationship Modelling. Artificial Intelligence in Education 14(3-4), 375–417 (2004)
8. Amalathas, S., Mitrovic, A., Ravan, S.: Decision-making tutor: providing on-the-job training for oil palm plantation managers. Research and Practice in Technology Enhanced Learning 7(3), 131–152 (2012)
9. Mitrovic, A.: Fifteen years of Constraint-Based Tutors: What we have achieved and where we are going. User Modeling and User-Adapted Interaction 22(1-2), 39–72 (2012)
10. Weerasinghe, A., Mitrovic, A., Thomson, D., Mogin, P., Martin, B.: Evaluating a General Model of Adaptive Tutorial Dialogues. In: Biswas, G., Bull, S., Kay, J., Mitrovic, A. (eds.) AIED 2011. LNCS, vol. 6738, pp. 394–402. Springer, Heidelberg (2011)
11. Mitrovic, A., Mathews, M., Holland, J.: Exploring two strategies for teaching procedures. In: Cerri, S.A., Clancey, W.J., Papadourakis, G., Panourgia, K. (eds.) ITS 2012. LNCS, vol. 7315, pp. 499–504. Springer, Heidelberg (2012)
12. Elmasri, R., Navathe, S.B.: Fundamentals of database systems. Addison-Wesley (2010)
13. Phillip, G.C.: Teaching database modeling and design: areas of confusion and helpful hints. Journal of Information Technology Education 6, 481–497 (2007)
14. Weerasinghe, A., Mitrovic, A., Martin, B.: Towards individualized dialogue support for ill-defined domains. Artificial Intelligence in Education 19(4), 357–379 (2009)
15. Ohlsson, S.: Learning from Performance Errors. Psychological Review 103(2), 241–262 (1996)

Revealing the Learning in Learning Curves

R. Charles Murray, Steven Ritter, Tristan Nixon, Ryan Schwiebert,
Robert G.M. Hausmann, Brendon Towle, Stephen E. Fancsali, and Annalies Vuong

Carnegie Learning, Inc.
Frick Building, Suite 918
437 Grant Street, Pittsburgh, PA 15219
{cmurray,sritter,tnixon,rschwiebert,bhausmann,btowle,
sfancsali,avuong}@carnegielearning.com

Abstract. Most work on learning curves for ITSs has focused on the knowledge components (or *skills*) included in the curves, aggregated across students. But an aggregate learning curve need not have the same form as subsets of its underlying data, so learning curves for subpopulations of students may take different forms. We show that disaggregating a skill's aggregate learning curve into separate learning curves for different student subpopulations can reveal learning: 70% of the skills that did not show learning and were identified as candidates for improvement did show learning when disaggregated. This phenomenon appears to be in part a characteristic of mastery learning. Disaggregated learning curves can reconcile an apparent mismatch between the tutor's *runtime* assessment of student knowledge and the *post hoc* assessment provided by the aggregate learning curve. More precise learning curves can be used to refine Bayesian knowledge tracing parameters and to improve skill model assessment metrics.

Keywords: Knowledge tracing, learning curves, Bayesian networks, student modeling.

1 Introduction

The fundamental assumption behind Cognitive Tutors is that knowledge can be decomposed into discrete knowledge components – i.e., *skills* – and that learning is best modeled through these skills [1]. These skills act as parameters in our cognitive models. If we correctly identify the skills that students are actually learning, we should see improvement (reduced errors and latency) as students gain more experience with those skills. To the extent that the skills we are modeling are not aligned with what students are learning, we will not see learning on those skills [2].

These skill-based cognitive models are used in two ways. First, within a tutor at runtime, we use the cognitive model as the basis for Bayesian Knowledge Tracing (BKT) [3] to assess whether individual students have mastered the material. Second, we use learning curves, aggregated across students, to test whether the skills we are modeling correspond to the skills that students are learning.

K. Yacef et al. (Eds.): AIED 2013, LNAI 7926, pp. 473–482, 2013.

Figure 1 shows a learning curve for the skill "Write absolute value equation" in the Cognitive Tutor's 2010-2011 Algebra I curriculum. This skill corresponds to the knowledge required to answer a prompt like "Enter an absolute value equation to represent all points that are 5 units from zero on the number line" with the answer "$|x|=5$." The X-axis represents *opportunities*, or encounters with the skill. The left-hand Y-axis shows the percentage of students who were correct at each opportunity, and the right-hand Y-axis shows the number of students contributing to the data. The figure shows that students averaged 27% correct on their first encounter with this skill, and that performance rapidly increased to approximately 90% correct by the third encounter. The number of students drops off as BKT determines that students have mastered the skill. Thus, the right-hand side of the aggregate learning curve is dominated by students who require a relatively large number of opportunities to master the skill.

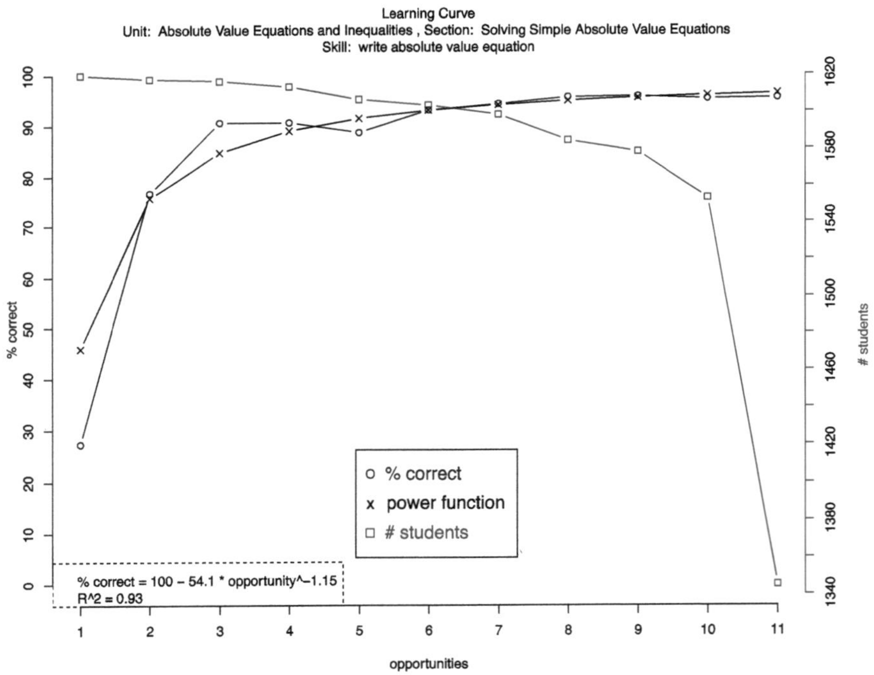

Fig. 1. An aggregate learning curve, aligned by opportunity number, that approximates a power function

Learning curves necessarily use data averaged over many students. Otherwise, a curve for a single student's performance would oscillate between 100% and 0% for correct and incorrect attempts, and the curve would be unduly influenced by factors in the student's environment other than knowledge of the skill itself. Ideally, by averaging across a large enough population of students, we minimize the effect of irrelevant factors and highlight the underlying trajectory of learning as a function of practice.

A ubiquitous finding for a wide variety a wide variety of cognitive tasks, as well as perceptual motor tasks and other phenomena, is that performance appears to follow the power law of practice [4]: performance improves rapidly at first and continues to improve but at a diminishing rate in a power function, where performance is a function of some power of the amount of practice (e.g., the number of opportunities): $E=E_0*n^{-\alpha}$, where E=error rate, E_0 (the intercept) is initial error rate, n is the opportunity number, and the exponent α controls the rate of change, equivalent to the linear slope when the data is plotted on log-log axes. For our learning curves, we transform the error rate into percentage correct as $C=100\text{-}E = 100 - E_0*n^{-\alpha}$. The fitted power function for the skill in Figure 1 is $C=100\text{-}54.1*n^{-1.15}$ with fit $R^2=0.93$. The α (exponent) value of *-1.15* indicates good learning, with percentage correct improving rapidly at first and then approaching an asymptote of 100%.

Given these considerations, it might seem reasonable that a learning curve that more closely approximates a power function would be more likely to accurately represent student learning [e.g., 2, 4]. Similarly, a learning curve that does not fit a power function well, or that fits with very small α (indicating little improvement over time) would indicate that students are not improving on actions labeled with that skill.

However, as we show in this paper, aggregate learning curves are not always a reliable guide to whether skills accurately model student learning. When averaging over different students who begin with different levels of knowledge and/or learn at different rates, we may see aggregate learning curves that appear to show little student learning even though BKT identifies the students as mastering the skills at runtime. In this paper, we: (1) illustrate this phenomenon; (2) demonstrate that it is frequent enough in our data to be a concern and (3) present disaggregated and mastery-aligned learning curves which more accurately reflect patterns of student performance.

2 Background

Cognitive Tutors use Corbett and Anderson's [3] Bayesian Knowledge Tracing (BKT) algorithm at runtime to estimate the probability that each skill is known, or *p_known*. The BKT algorithm uses four parameters to estimate *p_known* for each skill: *p_initial*, the probability that a student knows the skill prior to using it in the tutor; *p_learn*, the probability that the skill will transition from *unknown* to *known* following usage in the tutor; *p_guess*, the probability of correct performance when the skill is *unknown*; and *p_slip*, the probability of incorrect performance when the skill is *known*. Mastery learning is implemented by requiring students to solve problems until *p_known* for each skill in the section has reached 0.95.

Skills vary in difficulty (*p_initial* and *p_learn*), and also in how likely student problem-solving performance will accurately reflect skill knowledge (*p_guess* and *p_slip*), so the four BKT parameters may be calibrated differently for each skill. Modeling student learning involves making two types of decisions. First, we must identify the skills that best explain student learning [6]. Second, we assign BKT parameters to each skill [7]. For both of these processes, our initial decisions can be refined by testing these decisions against data collected from students using the tutor. For each skill, we generate a learning curve of the average percentage correct across all students for each opportunity to use a skill.

Although it has long been known that aggregate learning curves do not necessarily have the same form as the subsets of the underlying data [4, 8, 9], the existence of a learning curve approximating a power law is often taken as an indication that the skill model is an accurate representation of student learning. For example, Anderson et al. [2] take the power function relationship found when partitioning data by production rule rather than exercise as an indication that the production rule is the fundamental element of learning. Corbett and Anderson [3] partitioned data for a general rule (i.e., skill) into two more specific rules, providing a better model of student learning.

3 Related Work

Some modeling work has focused on how individual differences can be incorporated into aggregate models. Baker et al. [10] increased accuracy using machine learning trained on 23 features of the tutorial state to customize parameters for *p_guess* and *p_slip* to student subpopulations based upon their feature profiles. Pardos and Heffernan (2010) increased accuracy by learning values for *p_initial* customized per individual student across all skills. In plans for future work, Pardos and Heffernan [11] anticipate aspects of this investigation by considering whether clusters of student parameters can be found, and speculating that a model customized to both skill and student attributes would likely be better still. Martin et al. [5] suggest applying learning curves to subsets of a model, and generate separate learning curves for students with differing initial ability.

The approach discussed here partitions performance data both by skill and by student subpopulation. We show that partitioning data for particular skills by student subpopulation – i.e., disaggregating it – can reveal student learning that is hidden in aggregate learning curves. For this paper, we partition students based upon the number of opportunities it takes for them to reach "mastery" as assessed by the tutor at runtime, but other metrics for partitioning students (e.g., [5, 10, 11]) are likely to work as well. Disaggregated learning curves may lead to more accurate student modeling at runtime by providing data for refining BKT parameters such as *p_initial* and *p_learn*. By aligning disaggregated learning curves at the point of mastery in *mastery-aligned learning curves*, we reveal patterns of student performance as they reach runtime mastery.

4 Disaggregating Learning Curves by Student Subpopulations

Figure 2 shows a standard aggregate learning curve for a skill that shows little student learning. This skill is from the Cognitive Tutor 2010-2011 Algebra II curriculum and corresponds to the knowledge required to write a composed linear function such as "*1.6(19g)*" to represent the number of kilometers a driver can go on *g* gallons of gas

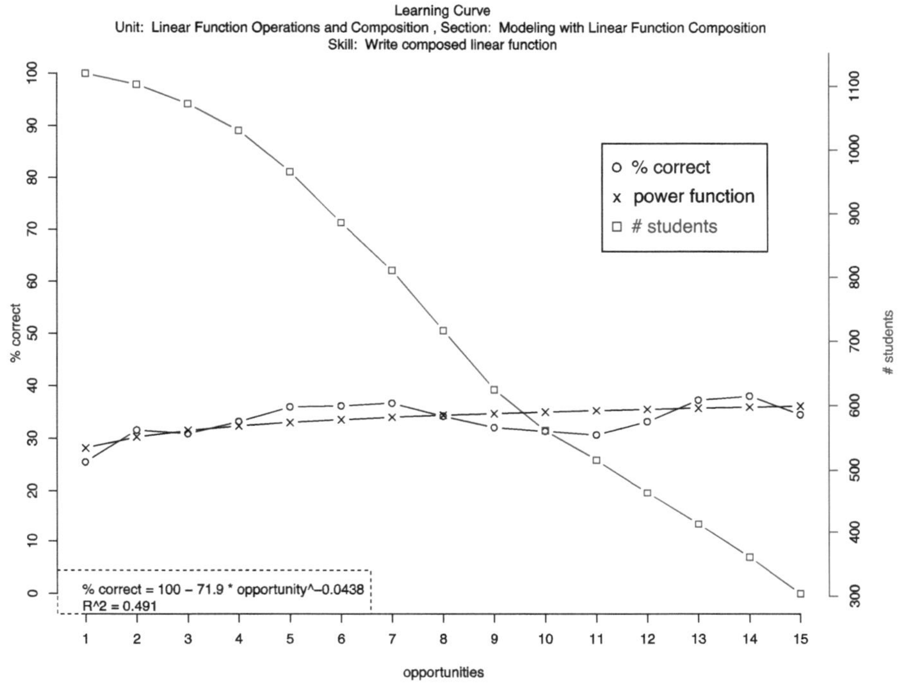

Fig. 2. An aggregate learning curve that shows little student learning

in a car that gets 19 miles/gallon, using a conversion factor of 1.6 kilometers/mile. For this skill, students initially average about 26% correct and, after 15 opportunities, they still average just a little over 30% correct. The fitted power function's α value *-0.0438* makes a relatively flat learning curve, which seems to indicate poor learning. However, the fact that the number of students drops off fairly quickly (from 1100 students at opportunity 1, to 300 students at opportunity 15) indicates that, at runtime, the tutor (using BKT) considered most students to have mastered this skill.

4.1 Disaggregating a Learning Curve That Does Not Show Learning

Figure 3, using the same performance data as Figure 2, shows that the apparent lack of learning in Figure 2 is due to averaging the learning curves of students who have different initial knowledge or learn at different rates. Each learning curve in Figure 3 represents a subpopulation of students who were judged by the tutor at runtime to have mastered the skill in the same number of opportunities, except for the bottom right curve, which represents students who took 15 or more opportunities to reach mastery. We limit the number of opportunities shown for each curve to those required to reach mastery because learning curves degrade as the number of students decreases [5]. These curves are somewhat noisier than the single aggregate curve due to the lower N in each curve.

Each of the disaggregated learning curves does appear to show learning except for the curve for students who needed 15 or more opportunities (some of whom may never reach mastery), which is cut off. The curve at the upper left shows that the only way to reach mastery in 3 opportunities is by perfect performance.

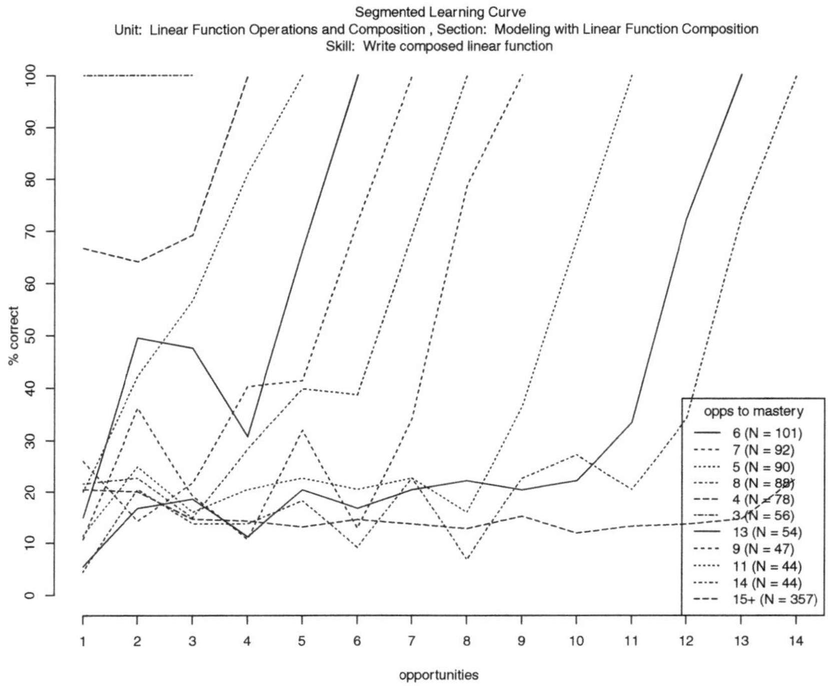

Fig. 3. Learning curves disaggregated by the number of opportunities that it takes each subpopulation to reach mastery (*p_known* = 0.95), aligned by opportunity number

4.2 Mastery-Aligned Disaggregated Learning Curves

Aggregate learning curves like those shown in Figures 1 and 2 align students at first opportunity. An alternative, which we call *mastery-aligned learning curves*, aligns students at the point of mastery. Figure 4 shows mastery-aligned disaggregated learning curves for the same skill illustrated in Figures 2 and 3. Each disaggregated curve still represents a set of students who have mastered the skill in a particular number of opportunities, as in Figure 3. However, in mastery-aligned learning curves, they are aligned at the point of first mastery. In the figure, *m* is the opportunity at which mastery was achieved, *m-1* is the preceding opportunity, etc. The curve that is cut off for students who took 15 or more opportunities to reach mastery (some of whom may not reach mastery) simply shows their first 14 opportunities.

Curves aligned by mastery make it easier to visualize whether different student subpopulations follow a similar path as they approach mastery, as would be the case if the students have similar rates of learning (corresponding to BKT parameter *p_learn*) but different initial knowledge (corresponding to *p_initial*). In these curves, student subpopulations' performance profiles look mostly similar as they approach mastery.

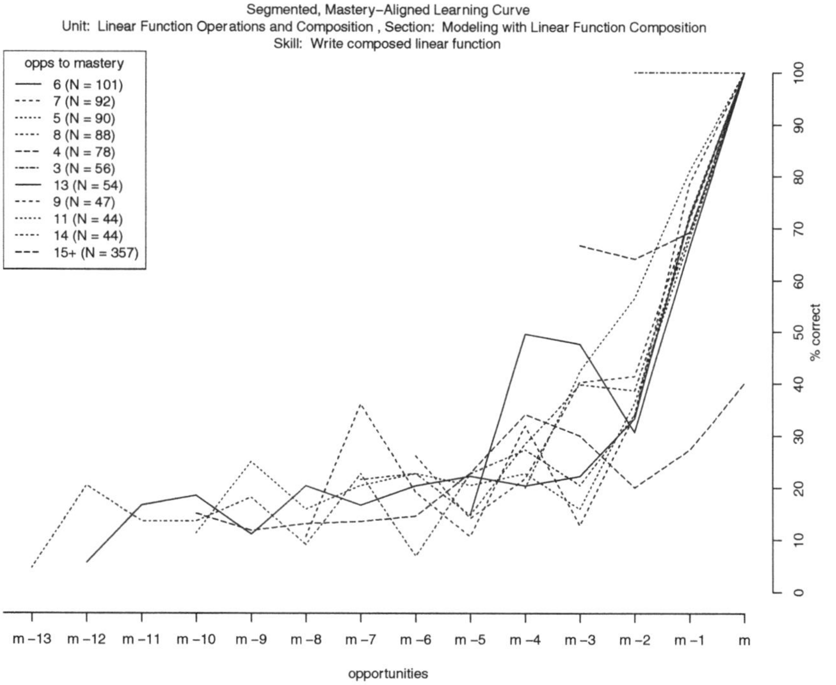

Fig. 4. Mastery-aligned disaggregated learning curves, aligned by the opportunity (*m*) at which each subpopulation first achieves mastery

5 Results

To investigate the frequency with which aggregate learning curves fail to show learning even when students appear to be learning at runtime, we studied the impact on the Cognitive Tutor 2010-2011 Algebra I curriculum, for which we had performance data for 15,414 unique students on 881 skills.

Skills that are most likely to be better modeled by disaggregated learning curves are those that the tutor (at runtime) thinks most students are learning, but that don't show learning in their aggregate learning curves. We set criteria that a learning curve does not show learning if the fitted power function's exponent α is greater than -0.1 – i.e., if the fitted power function is relatively flat or even decreasing in terms of percentage correct – and conversely, a learning curve does show learning for $\alpha \leq -0.1$.

Table 1. Skills in Algebra 1

All skills	881
Skills that are not premastered	720
Non-premastered skills with aggregate learning curves that don't show learning	375
Candidate skills for disaggregation: Tutor thinks students are learning, not premastered, don't show learning on aggregate curve, don't have multiple maxima, at least 250 students	166
Candidate skills that show learning when disaggregated	117

One reason that a skill may not show learning is that students already know it (performance on the learning curve starts out at or above 95%), so there is not much learning left to do – we call these *premastered*. Another reason may be that knowledge that is modeled as a single skill may actually consist of more than one skill [3], or the skill may be poorly modeled in some other way. Learning curves for composite and poorly modeled skills often show fluctuating performance – i.e., multiple local maxima – as students alternate between practicing two or more distinct skills with different learning trajectories.

Therefore, we selected for disaggregation skills that (1) the tutor thinks students are learning, operationalized as at least 75% of students achieve mastery within 12 opportunities; (2) do not show learning in the aggregate curve, as indicated by a fitted power function exponent of $\alpha > -0.1$; (3) are not premastered; and (4) do not have multiple local maxima. In addition, (5) we limited our selection to skills with at least 250 students, both for stable statistical properties and to have enough data points to smooth out random fluctuations in the curves. As shown in Table 1, this process identified 166 skills (approximately 23% of skills that are not premastered) that were potentially misidentified by their aggregate learning curves as not showing learning.

For each of these 166 skills, we created disaggregated learning curves by grouping students into subpopulations according to the number of opportunities it took them to reach mastery, as assessed by the runtime BKT parameters. We then computed the power function fit for each of these curves. We classified a skill as showing learning if at least 75% of its students were represented by a disaggregated learning curve that showed learning. This had the effect of weighting the disaggregated curves so that, for instance, a learning curve representing 20 students would not count as much as a learning curve representing 200 students. Using these criteria, 117 of the 166 skills, or 70%, showed learning when their skills were disaggregated. Overall, at least 117 skills (those for which we had enough data) of 720 skills that students didn't already know, or approximately 16%, had been misidentified as showing no learning.

6 Discussion

Aggregation of learning curve data is particularly problematic when different student subpopulations show different learning patterns. Learning for subpopulations can be affected by such factors as initial knowledge (modeled at runtime by *p_initial*), as others have found [e.g., 5, 11], and different probabilities of learning (*p_learn*). Both of these factors appear to influence our learning curves.

In addition, and importantly, one fundamental effect on the aggregate learning curve appears to be a *characteristic of mastery learning* itself: Mastery learning depresses performance increases in learning curves aggregated across student subpopulations. The reason is that the best performing students are removed from the aggregate population as they start performing well (when they graduate), at least for skills that are critical for graduating from the section, leaving only students who are performing less well. We discuss this phenomenon in detail in another paper [12].

7 Conclusions and Future Work

We have shown that aggregate learning curves do not always accurately represent student learning. We present disaggregated learning curves and mastery-aligned learning curves as alternative representations. Disaggregated learning curves can reconcile an apparent mismatch between the tutor's *runtime* assessment of student knowledge and the *post hoc* assessment provided by the aggregate learning curve. These representations have the potential to provide information to improve runtime student modeling and to improve our ability to detect flaws in cognitive models.

Although the disaggregated learning curves described here are calculated post hoc, they represent different underlying patterns of student learning. If the runtime system could identify a particular student's membership in one of the underlying subpopulations, we could better model the path of that student's learning (or, perhaps, identify that the student is unlikely to master the skill in a reasonable amount of time). Similarly to Pardos and Heffernan [11], we could imagine the runtime system making a quick estimate of the student's likely path and then adapting accordingly.

A second application of this work would be to better automate the process of identifying places where the instructional system itself could be improved. We have developed a series of "attention metrics," which are heuristics for automatically examining data to identify elements of the Cognitive Tutors that deserve attention by our developers. One of the attention metrics assesses whether whether students are learning the skills that we expect them to be learning. If aggregate learning curves are used to detect skills that students are not learning, we generate a significant number of false positives. Using disaggregated and mastery-aligned learning curves should provide more accurate metrics for whether students are learning particular skills.

References

1. Anderson, J.R.: Spanning seven orders of magnitude: a challenge for cognitive modeling. Cognitive Science 26, 85–112 (2002)
2. Anderson, J.R., Conrad, F.G., Corbett, A.T.: Skill acquisition and the LISP tutor. Cognitive Science 14, 467–505 (1989)
3. Corbett, A.T., Anderson, J.R.: Knowledge tracing: Modeling the acquisition of procedural knowledge. User-Modeling and User-Adapted Interaction 4, 253–278 (1995)
4. Newell, A., Rosenbloom, P.S.: Mechanisms of skill acquisition and the law of practice. In: Anderson, J.R. (ed.) Cognitive Skills and Their Acquisition, pp. 1–55. Lawrence Erlbaum Associates, Hillsdale (1981)
5. Martin, B., Mitrovic, A., Koedinger, K.R., Mathan, S.: Evaluating and improving adaptive educational systems with learning curves. User Modeling and User-Adapted Interaction 21, 249–283 (2011)
6. Koedinger, K., McLaughlin, E., Stamper, J.: Automated student model improvement. In: Proceedings of the 5th International Conference on Educational Data Mining (EDM 2012), pp. 17–24 (2012)
7. Ritter, S., Harris, T.K., Nixon, T., Dickison, D., Murray, R.C., Towle, B.: Reducing the knowledge tracing space. In: Proceedings of the 2nd International Conference on Educational Data Mining, pp. 151–160 (2009)
8. Heathcote, A., Brown, S.: The power law repealed: The case for an exponential law of practice. Psychonomic Bulletin & Review 7, 185–207 (2000)
9. Anderson, R.B.: The power law as an emergent property. Memory & Cognition 29, 1061–1068 (2001)
10. Baker, R., Corbett, A.T., Aleven, V.: More Accurate Student Modeling through Contextual Estimation of Slip and Guess Probabilities in Bayesian Knowledge Tracing. In: Woolf, B.P., Aïmeur, E., Nkambou, R., Lajoie, S. (eds.) ITS 2008. LNCS, vol. 5091, pp. 406–415. Springer, Heidelberg (2008)
11. Pardos, Z.A., Heffernan, N.T.: Modeling individualization in a Bayesian networks implementation of knowledge tracing. In: De Bra, P., Kobsa, A., Chin, D. (eds.) UMAP 2010. LNCS, vol. 6075, pp. 255–266. Springer, Heidelberg (2010)
12. Nixon, T., Fancsali, S.E., Ritter, S.: The complex dynamics of aggregate learning curves. In: Proceedings of the 6th International Conference on Educational Data Mining (EDM 2013) (2013)

Deliberate System-Side Errors as a Potential Pedagogic Strategy for Exploratory Virtual Learning Environments

Alyssa M. Alcorn[1], Judith Good[2], and Helen Pain[1]

[1] University of Edinburgh, School of Informatics, UK
{a.alcorn,helen.pain}@ed.ac.uk
[2] University of Sussex, School of Informatics, UK
j.good@sussex.ac.uk

Abstract. This paper describes an exploratory study of system-side errors (i.e. expectation- or rule-violations) in a *virtual environment* (VE), and the subsequent reactions of young children with *autism spectrum conditions* (ASC). Analysis of existing video from 8 participants interacting with the ECHOES VE showed that they frequently detected and reacted to system-side errors, engaging in social and communicative behaviours targeted by ECHOES. Detecting errors requires children to compare the VE's state to their "mental model" of its behaviour, determining where the two are discrepant. This is equivalent to learners identifying mistakes in their *own* knowledge and then re-aligning with the system-as-expert. This paper explores the implications of these results, proposing a taxonomy of discrepant event types, and discussing their location with respect to the learner and/or system. In addition to considering these results' significance for this user group and context, it relates the research to existing work that uses erroneous examples.

Keywords: Virtual environments, discrepancy, system error, learner error, learning, model, Autism, children, social communication, initiation, evaluation, HCI, design.

1 Introduction

Virtual learning environments and other adaptive systems have tended to focus their efforts on identifying and correcting errors in the learner's understanding or procedural knowledge. The knowledge shared by learner and system increases, with false or incomplete ("buggy") learner knowledge decreasing as a proportion of the total. Depending on the domain and the system, this may take the form of explicitly correcting steps in a learner's work or more subtly promoting relevant information and strategies (see [1] for a range of examples).

While the system's[1] domain knowledge must exceed the learner's in order to scaffold his/her progress, there is an important difference between an infallible system and one

[1] *System* is used in this paper as a generic term that encompasses adaptive learning environments, VEs, intelligent tutoring systems, serious games, and related projects that utilize technology for some teaching or practice function.

K. Yacef et al. (Eds.): AIED 2013, LNAI 7926, pp. 483–492, 2013.

that *overall* knows more, but makes occasional errors (as would a human teacher). If there are mistakes[2], they are generally presented as a deliberate teaching device, such as inviting learners to identify incorrect steps in worked mathematics examples [2, 3]. Occasional *system-side errors* that are *not* explicitly announced as problem-solving tasks may provide an opportunity for the learner to engage in metacognition, articulating his or her knowledge in order to address them. When errors constitute a relatively small proportion of the system-learner interactions, learners can take advantage of these metacognitive opportunities, and continue to benefit from the system's overall expertise.

This paper describes a study of system-side errors[3] in existing video data from the ECHOES virtual environment (VE). ECHOES was designed to help support young children with *autism-spectrum conditions* (ASC) to practice foundational social communication skills through exploratory play (see Section 2, and [4, 5])[4]. Its content, and thus the errors, are highly visual and focus on cause-and-effect relationships and patterns rather than factual knowledge. This cause-and-effect knowledge is never explicitly taught, but acquired over the course of the child's exploration. The system-side errors were a completely unintentional byproduct of the AI planner, rather than a deliberate design choice. Indeed, the characteristics of autism mean that expectation-violating aspects would generally be considered a poor, potentially upsetting choice for this user group (see Section 2). Nevertheless, the errors were highly effective in motivating children to engage the positive social communication behaviours that ECHOES tried to promote. In particular, children initiated to the human researcher and the ECHOES virtual character (VC) about the content of the system errors, sometimes explicitly indicating what *should* have happened instead (i.e. they were able to correct the system's error).

This error-detection process is inherently metacognitive [6], in that children had to compare their knowledge, expectations of, or predictions about the VE's contents and "rules" (i.e. their *mental model* of the system) to its actual behaviour, identifying mismatched aspects. This process of comparing models to identify *discrepancies* is arguably equivalent to learners identifying and correcting "bugs" in their own knowledge[5] by comparing themselves to an expert.

The ECHOES video analysis reported in this paper forms the basis for a more general discussion of discrepancy detection, including a taxonomy of discrepancy types and their possible sources in either a learner's mental model, or in a system. This paper explores the implications of these results for this particular user group and context, but also their relationship to existing work that uses erroneous examples.

2 The ECHOES Technology-Enhanced Learning Project

The ECHOES project developed a technology-enhanced learning environment targeted primarily at young children with ASC (aged 5-7 years), but with the potential to

[2] The terms 'error' and 'mistake' are used interchangeably in this paper.

[3] *Errors* do not mean error messages, or system freezes/crashes. They are errors in that the system violated its patterns of object or VC behaviour, or acted counter to activity goals.

[4] See `www.echoes2.org`

[5] More accurately, the learner corrects the mental model "for next time", as in most cases the process or interaction cannot actually be altered to reflect the correct action or information.

also be used by typically developing (TD) children [4, 5]. ECHOES includes a programme of game-like activities set in a "Magic Garden" VE, and was designed to support exploration and scaffolding of foundational social and communicative skills, such as turn-taking, and gaze- and point-following.

The ASC comprise a set of lifelong neuro-developmental conditions, characterised by notable and pervasive difficulties in communication and social interaction, plus the presence of repetitive behaviours and/or interests, sometimes manifested as a strong desire for routine and sameness [7]. Multiple VEs have already been developed to support children with ASC in learning specific skills (e.g. as discussed in [8]). The predictability, repeatability, and relative simplicity of VEs (compared to human-human interaction) are given as reasons why they are particularly suited to, and motivating for, this population, and may also be a useful research tool.

A young child using the ECHOES VE stands or sits in front of a 42" multi-touch screen, immersed in the visuals and sounds of the Magic Garden and physically involved in the interactions. ECHOES learning activities were developed with input from stakeholders, and draw strongly on educational and psychological theory. Activities encourage experimentation and play by deliberately introducing novel elements and behavioral fantasy, such as "pulling" on flower heads to transform them into bubbles or bouncy balls. The child has an autonomous, childlike VC (Andy) as a guide and playmate, demonstrating actions and offering encouragement. The underlying AI plans Andy's behaviour both deliberatively and in reaction to child actions (see [9]). Sound output is present, but dialogue is pre-recorded with no text-to-speech capability. There is also no capacity for speech recognition or sound input.

The system was designed such that children use it alongside an adult (researcher or teacher) who manages inter-activity transitions and gives limited system commands (such as for Andy to repeat an instruction) through a smaller, secondary screen (see Figure 1, Left). The adult does not direct the child's use of ECHOES. Instead, he/she plays an essential role in providing additional support for the child's complex communicative and emotional regulation needs (e.g. reformulating the VC's directions to include key instructional phrases or sign language familiar to that child). These cannot yet be met by an adaptive system in a rapid, robust, and appropriate fashion. Furthermore, an early ECHOES study [5] discovered that children frequently extended their interaction with the system to include the nearby adult, sharing their discoveries or seeking additional information.

28 children with ASC from four UK school sites participated in the summative evaluation of ECHOES (results in preparation). The goal was to assess a range of social and communication skills before, during, and after six to eight weeks of using the ECHOES environment. Children completed several 10-20 minute sessions with ECHOES per week, gradually encountering more complex material. Video data was the primary record of the child's communication and social behaviour. Each session was recorded by digital camcorder, positioned to capture the study environment

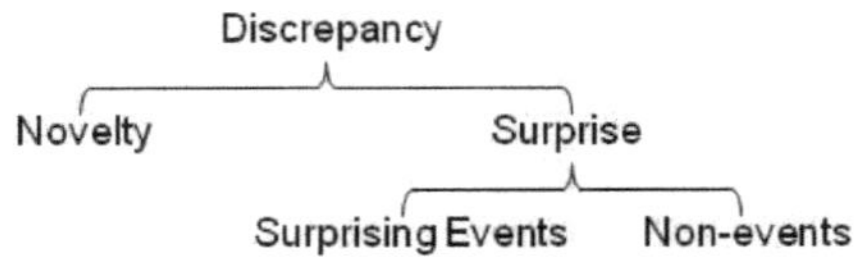

Fig. 1. *(Left)* ECHOES evaluation set-up. The researcher sits near the child, at the control monitor (not visible). *(Right)* Taxonomy of discrepancy types and their relationships, based on [10].

(see Figure 1, Left). This paper re-analyses a subset of the evaluation video data in order to explore the type and quantity of discrepancies and child reactions that were present (see [10]).

3 Types of Discrepancy

The ECHOES system included a range of errors in which the VE or VC appeared to make mistakes, compared to the pattern established by previous interactions. Participating children perceived many of these occurrences as *discrepant* from their expectations. In the current analysis, *discrepancy* has a child-centred definition. It is not an inherent property of mental models or environments, but exists via the process of the child making a comparison and detecting a mismatch between the mental model of the environment and some current aspect; if the child makes no comparison or fails to detect a difference, *then no discrepancy is present,* because the child's mental model agrees with the environment's current behaviour.

Many mistakes are examples of *surprise*— where something is known about the current aspect (it is part of the mental model), but it does not behave as expected. *Surprising events* include aspects that are present, but whose appearance or behavior is not as expected or predicted (i.e. in accordance with the mental model). In a *non-event,* some aspect of the environment violates expectations by unexpectedly or unpredictably being absent, being inactive or unresponsive, or failing to occur. A final type of discrepancy may occur when the current aspect is *novel*: one which is unknown (i.e. not yet part of the model). In other words, it does not fit the child's model because it extends the model. A taxonomy of discrepancy is mapped in Figure 1, Right. Subsequent discussion of discrepancy in this paper excludes novelty because it does not involve any element of error by either learner or system.

Several examples of surprises and child reactions are described below, all of which are drawn from the data set and results described in Section 4.

- *Surprising event 1:* The child and Andy are completing a turn-taking activity. Unexpectedly, Andy walks off-screen and does not return. Andy is always programmed to stay onscreen during activities. After watching the side of the screen for a few seconds, the child makes a social reference to the researcher (i.e. gazing to seek information), and then looks back to the screen.

- *Surprising event 2:* Andy demonstrates a ball-sorting activity for the first time, putting multiple balls into the boxes of the same colour. After the child takes several turns, Andy tries to put a yellow ball in the red box (see Figure 2). It rolls off the top instead of dropping in. The child explicitly corrects Andy, pointing to the yellow box and excitedly shouting "Right here!"
- *Non-event 1:* In a flower-picking activity, Andy asks for the child's help and then indicates one of the three available flowers with a combination of gaze and pointing. The child tries touching all three flowers in turn: the flower indicated by Andy should fly into the basket when touched, but does not (i.e. apparently no available choice is correct). The child reacts by ceasing to touch the screen and leaning in to look very closely at Andy's face (i.e. social referencing; seeking information).
- *Non-event 2:* The Magic Garden fades in to start a new activity. There is an unusually long pause without Andy entering (i.e. long compared to previous activities), but background sound effects continue (i.e. the system is not frozen). The child reacts by asking the researcher "Where's Andy?"

Fig. 2. Andy incorrectly sorts a ball (as described in Event example 2)

These qualitative examples illustrate the range of discrepancy-reaction pairs which were present in the current ECHOES dataset. The quantitative analysis described in Section 4 aimed to investigate their frequency and extent across the current participants, and whether the pattern varied across discrepancy types.

4 An Analysis of System-Side Errors in ECHOES

4.1 Method

Participants. The subset of ECHOES participants included in the discrepancy video analysis (n=8, 1 female, 7 male) were from two sites of the ECHOES summative evaluation study (in preparation). Each child had a previous diagnosis of an ASC by a paediatrician, child psychiatrist, or other professional. Their data was selected for additional analysis due to the children demonstrating at least phrase-language use and having sufficiently complete video samples (at least 30 minutes worth)[6]. All but one of the children in this group appear to have some degree of intellectual disability in addition to their ASC diagnosis, as evidenced by the discrepancy between their calendar ages (range= 5-8 yrs, mean= 6 yrs, 5 mo.) and verbal-mental ages[7] (VMA; range =2-5 yrs, 10mo., mean=3 yrs. 9 mo.).

Video Annotation. Each child's video samples were annotated for discrepancy-reaction pairs by the first author using ELAN [12], and in accordance with the categories described in Section 3 (see [10] for further details of the taxonomy and the annotation process). As noted in Section 3, discrepancy has a child-centred definition. As the child's understanding of the environment is generally private, with explicit statements of expectation or prediction relatively rare, observable child reactions are the only evidence for discrepancy detection. Thus, the unit of analysis is the *discrepancy-reaction pair*, not discrepancy alone.

The main source of information when inferring the presence of discrepancy-reaction pairs is knowledge of what the child has been exposed to in the environment (and how often). The annotator must consider the evidence a child might have about what is in the environment and how it "should" work. Surprises that could objectively be considered violations of the system's usual patterns (e.g. the VC making mistakes, or failing to appear) often signalled video sections that included discrepancy-reaction pairs, as did the introduction of a new activities or objects. Finding additional discrepancies involved observing the child's interaction with the environment, looking for cause-effect relationships between the system content and the child's behaviour.

Annotations noted whether child reactions were *initiations* (i.e. purposeful and spontaneous behaviours directed to a social partner), or *non-social reactions* (i.e. self-directed or undirected). The annotation recorded the target of the initiation (researcher or Andy) and also whether it was *primary* (the first reaction to that instance of discrepancy) or *secondary* (a subsequent initiation to the same instance of discrepancy). These categories aid in identifying reciprocal interactions about discrepancy.

Annotation data was exported from ELAN as tab-delimited text and further analysed in a standard spreadsheet program. Analysis focused on counting the instances in various categories, rather than seeking comparisons between participating children or between reactions to discrepancy as compared to other environmental events.

4.2 Results and Analysis

The spreadsheet analysis yielded 50 surprising event-reaction pairs and 71 non-event-reaction pairs from 347 minutes of video data. These totals include both primary

[6] The video data captured a variety of learning activities, as new material was introduced throughout. It consisted of three 15 minute samples from early, middle, and late sessions with the VE (45 minutes total per child). One participant had only 33 minutes of data due to missed sessions. Samples excluded non-analysable video (e.g. system crashes, child rest breaks) and learning activities in which the VC was not present.

[7] As calculated from their scores on the British Picture Vocabulary Scale (BPVS; [11]), a standardized measure of receptive language ability.

social reactions (initiations) and non-social reactions. Each child had between 9 and 22 pairs (mean=15.12, SD=4.12); it is encouraging that all children in the group both noticed and reacted to discrepancies, rather than reactions being concentrated in a few children only. Considering again the often severe social and communicative challenges that people with ASC may face (Section 2), perhaps the most notable result is that 54% of child reactions to surprising events and 69% of reactions to non-events were directed to the researcher or the VC (i.e. were initiations; mean= 61.05% of reactions). Furthermore, 33 out of these 121 discrepancy-reaction pairs (27.27%) formed the first in a *sequence* of child initiations about that same instance. Some of these sequences developed into reciprocal interactions, often verbal dialogues with the researcher.

Existing literature about the behavioural rigidity and insistence on sameness that frequently characterise ASC (see Section 2) suggests that participants might become severely emotionally dysregulated when they detect a discrepancy. However, there were few instances of obvious frustration and zero instances of the child "melting down" because the environment was breaking its own rules. The affect of the initiations was overwhelmingly positive or neutral with frequent smiles and laughter, as children appeared to find many of the system errors to be humorous.

5 Discussion

The results from the ECHOES video analysis are encouraging in and of themselves with respect to the specific user group, all of whom spontaneously engaged in social behaviours that are considered difficult for people with ASC [7], but are developmentally crucial. The current system, user group, and cause-and-effect type content are all undeniably specialised and may not be directly comparable to other teaching contexts, however, the underlying metacognitive process of discrepancy detection remains the same across contexts. It requires the learner to consider the current information or procedure in light of what he already knows (i.e. in comparison to his mental model), and to conclude that something "does not fit". Thus, the following sections use the current dataset as a starting point from which to theorise about discrepancy detection, system-side errors, and their potential as a pedagogic strategy.

5.1 Locating the Source of Errors

The discrepancy categories described and taxonomised in Section 3 (see also [10]) identify the *type* of mismatch between a mental model and the actual system/environment, but these categories are independent of the mismatch's *location*. In other words, they say nothing about whose error or misconception led to the mismatch. For example, several children using ECHOES requested help with unresponsive or "broken" digital objects that were in fact functional, but unable to detect their inappropriate touch screen actions (e.g. scratching or hitting). This was not a problem with the system, but with the child's mental model of the object (or rather, the actions by which it could be affected). From the child's view, there was a discrepancy between the action's expected result and the object's failure to respond (an example of a non-event).

For any given piece of system content for which the learner has a mental model, there are four possible combinations of errors and correct knowledge, only some of which afford discrepancy-detection. Table 1 explains these combinations. The location of an error matters when determining a pedagogic strategy. The end goal is usually to reach state A, alignment of learner and system knowledge. Most pedagogic strategies work towards state A from state C, learner-side errors, with the expert applying correct knowledge in order to support the learner in correcting the item. However, as the current video data illustrates, system-side errors (state B) can also galvanise learners to metacognitively reflect on their models, locate errors, and even offer correction (i.e. move toward state A). Correcting errors in teachable agent system (e.g. [13]) appears to have elements of both B and C, because the learner corrects "the agent's" mistakes, which are apparently external to the user (i.e. a system-side or at least system-*like* error, as in B), but she is actually reflecting on and amending her *own* externalized domain knowledge (a learner-side error, as in C). *Compound Errors* (state D) will not necessarily lead to this constructive metacognition and resolution, as the learner and the system may not be in a position to correct one another. Table 1 supports the taxonomy of discrepancy types briefly outlined in Section 3 and further expanded in [10] as, taken together, they provide a high-level description of a discrepancy's type and location. Deliberate system-side errors or erroneous examples appear to still be an "emerging" area for educational technologies, and while unlikely to be applicable to all domains, may prove to be a useful lens through which to describe and compare work in this area.

Table 1. Possible locations of discrepancy between learners' mental models of some kind *X* and a specific instance *x* in the system

	System behaves **correctly or consistently**[8] on *x*.	System behaves **incorrectly or inconsistently** on *x*.
Learner's mental model **correct** regarding *X*.	**A.** Learner-domain alignment (no error; no discrepancy to detect)	**B.** System-side error (Learner may detect error as a source of discrepancy)
Learner's mental model **incorrect** regarding *X*.	**C.** Learner-side error (Learner may detect error via metacognition or may require system's direction)	**D.** Compound error (2 sources of discrepancy, 4 possible outcomes with respect to detection/ non-detection)[9]

8 Behaviour is in accord with domain "facts" or "rules", (however represented), or behaviour consistent with the system's own procedures (outside of the targeted teaching material).

9 One discrepancy may result from the learner's error and another from the system's. The outcomes depend on whether or not the learner detects either of those errors.

5.2 Extending System-Side Errors: Domains, Users, Unanswered Questions

As other authors have already acknowledged [2, 3], a long list of foundational questions remain to be resolved before any system could be designed that employs deliberate errors and/or facilitates discrepancy detection in a truly adaptive way. Although the current research provides a framework in which to better understand the nature of such errors, further research is needed to address general questions regarding when and how often to deliberately introduce system-side errors, and whether or not they are equally appropriate for all types of learners or all levels of domain proficiency. Instead of providing answers, the current work is an example of how the general strategy of system-side errors motivating metacognition could be successful in a very different type of situation than has previously been investigated, or to which adaptive systems are most often applied. The main areas of difference are as follows:

- Learners' young age and significant additional support needs
- Exploratory system, not focused on explicit problem-solving or content-rehearsal
- Errors are "unannounced" rather than presented as a specific exercise, example, or teaching opportunity. This is of course due to the fact that the system-side errors in ECHOES were not a deliberate design decision; see Section 1.
- Domain content is non-propositional (social communication skills).
- Errors are also non-propositional, and constitute disrupted cause-and-effect relationships, or alterations of sensory or temporal aspects of the environment

The ECHOES video analysis illustrates a very different case of system-side errors than those in existing mathematics-focused work (e.g. [2, 3]), but arguably draws on the same underlying metacognitive processes of model-comparison and discrepancy detection. Presenting learners with deliberate errors may be a more widely applicable strategy than it initially appears.

6 Conclusion

In summary, the ECHOES dataset illustrates that occasional system-side errors can motivate children to spontaneously reflect on their mental model of an environment, and to spontaneously articulate information to social partners about discrepancies between their models and the system, and how these might be remedied. This appears to be an equivalent metacognitive process to learners correcting their own errors. In the context of ECHOES, these system-side errors brought clear benefits for learners, suggesting that use of errors to promote metacognition and content practice can be usefully extended to very different content and user groups than have previously been investigated. The taxonomy of discrepancy types and table of error locations presented in this paper attempt to abstract away from the ECHOES context, and suggest a means of describing discrepancies that may be useful in comparing and synthesizing work in this emerging area of educational technologies and pedagogic strategy.

Acknowledgements. This research was undertaken as part of a PhD thesis by the first author, funded by the University of Edinburgh and the Scottish Informatics and Computer Science Alliance. It includes materials from the ECHOES project (funded by ESRC/EPSRC TEL; RES-139-25-0395). The ECHOES environment was designed and developed by the ECHOES team, including the authors (see www.echoes2.org), with contributions from various stakeholders. Special thanks to the participating schools, staff, and children. Their time and enthusiasm made this work possible.

References

1. Du Boulay, B., Luckin, R.: Modelling human teaching tactics and strategies for tutoring systems. Int. J. of Artificial Intelligence in Education 12(3), 235–256 (2001)
2. Tsovaltzi, D., McLaren, B.M., Melis, E., Meyer, A.K.: Erroneous examples: effects on learning fractions in a web-based setting. Int. J. Technology Enhanced Learning 4(3/4), 191–230 (2012)
3. McLaren, B.M., et al.: To Err Is Human, to Explain and Correct Is Divine: A Study of Interactive Erroneous Examples with Middle School Math Students. In: Ravenscroft, A., Lindstaedt, S., Kloos, C.D., Hernández-Leo, D. (eds.) EC-TEL 2012. LNCS, vol. 7563, pp. 222–235. Springer, Heidelberg (2012)
4. Porayska-Pomsta, K., Frauenberger, C., Pain, H., Rajendran, G., Smith, T., Menzies, R., Foster, M.E., Alcorn, A., Wass, S., Bernadini, S., Avramides, K., Keay-Bright, W., Chen, J., Waller, A., Guldberg, K., Good, J., Lemon, O.: Developing technology for autism: an interdisciplinary approach. Personal and Ubiquitous Computing 16(2), 117–127 (2011)
5. Alcorn, A., et al.: Social communication between virtual characters and children with autism. In: Biswas, G., Bull, S., Kay, J., Mitrovic, A. (eds.) AIED 2011. LNCS, vol. 6738, pp. 7–14. Springer, Heidelberg (2011)
6. Flavell, J.H.: Metacognition and cognitive monitoring: A new area of cognitive–developmental inquiry. American Psychologist 34(10), 906–911 (1979)
7. DSM-IV: Diagnostic and statistical manual of mental disorders. American Psychiatric Association Washington, DC (1994)
8. Rajendran, G.: Virtual environments and autism: a developmental psychopathological approach. J. of Computer Assisted Learning (2013), doi:10.1111/jcal.12006
9. Foster, M., Avramides, K., Bernardini, S., Chen, J., Frauenberger, C., Lemon, O., Porayska-Pomsta, K.: Supporting Children's Social Communication Skills through Interactive Narratives with Virtual Characters. In: Proceedings of the International Conference on Multimedia, pp. 1111–1114 (2010)
10. Alcorn, A.M., Pain, H., Good, J.: Discrepancies in a Virtual Learning Environment: Something "Worth Communicating About" for Young Children with ASC? In: International Conference on Interaction Design and Children (IDC 2013), New York (in Press, 2013)
11. Dunn, L.M., Dunn, D.M., Whetton, C.W., Burley, J.: The British Picture Vocabulary Scale, 2nd edn. NFER Nelson, Windsor (1997)
12. Max Planck Institute for Psycholinguistics. ELAN Linguistics Annotator, version 4.4.0. Max Planck Institute for Psycholinguistics, The Language Archive, Nijmegen, The Netherlands (2012), `http://tla.mpi.nl/tools/tla-tools/elan/`
13. Biswas, G., Leelawong, K., Schwartz, D., Vye, N.: Learning by teaching: A new agent paradigm for educational software. Applied Artificial Intelligence: An International Journal 19, 363–392 (2005)

The Effects of Culturally Congruent Educational Technologies on Student Achievement

Samantha Finkelstein[1], Evelyn Yarzebinski[1], Callie Vaughn[2], Amy Ogan[1], and Justine Cassell[1]

[1] Human-Computer Interaction Institute
[2] Language Technologies Institute Carnegie Mellon University
5000 Forbes Avenue, Pittsburgh PA, 15289
{slfink,eey2,cllvaughn,aeo,justine}@cs.cmu.edu

Abstract. Dialectal differences are one explanation for the systematically reduced test scores of children of color compared to their Euro-American peers. In this work, we explore the relationship between academic performance and dialect differences exhibited in a learning environment by assessing 3rd grade students' science performance after interacting with a "distant peer" technology that employed one of three dialect use patterns. We found that our participants, all native speakers of African American Vernacular English (AAVE), demonstrated the strongest science performance when the technology used AAVE features consistently throughout the interaction. These results call for a re-examination of the cultural assumptions underlying the design of educational technologies, with a specific emphasis on the way in which we present information to culturally-underrepresented groups.

Keywords: culture, dialect, peer models.

1 Introduction

Despite the typically standardized nature of mainstream school experiences, children begin their educational journey with unique cultural backgrounds that impact how they speak, collaborate with their peers, interact with authority figures, and talk about school-relevant topics such as science [1; 2]. Indeed, students may encounter cultural and language mismatches with their teachers as early as pre-school [3], with teachers mistaking cultural difference as deficits, unwittingly perpetuating an academic achievement gap [4].

Increasingly, the persistently lower test scores of students of color as compared to their Euro-American peers have been attributed in part to dialectal differences between students [4; 5; 6]. For example, some (but not all) African American students may come to school speaking a stigmatized, non-standard dialect of English referred to as African American Vernacular English (AAVE) [7], which has a unique phonology, morphology, and syntax that is regularized across users [8; 9]. Though the exact mechanisms behind the phenomenon are unclear, students who come to school speaking this dialect consistently score lower on indices of emergent literacy skills

K. Yacef et al. (Eds.): AIED 2013, LNAI 7926, pp. 493–502, 2013.

than their predominantly Mainstream American English (MAE)-speaking peers [10; 11; 12]. Researchers and teachers alike are unsure of how to address these sensitive issues in a classroom, and whether to insist students transition to a mainstream dialect, teach in the students' native dialect, or provide instruction in code-switching (switching between dialects in different contexts) [13]. Unfortunately, insufficient evidence currently exists to fully understand how these different language ideologies might affect the learning and well-being of students who speak with non-standard dialects – a necessary step in supporting them academically, while not denying them access to key parts of their identity [14; 15].

We believe that educational technologies that employ culturally-congruent designs [16] can not only provide insight about culture's role in learning, but also significantly reduce the achievement gap. Previous research documents the importance of language similarities in learning, with students learning best from teachers who have similar accents to their own [17] or when allowed to work on material with a partner in their native language [18]. The majority of previous culturally-sensitive educational technologies, however, have exclusively focused on modeling surface level traits such as skin color, ignoring deeper cultural phenomena associated with communication [19]. There is therefore a need for experimental manipulations of language practices within educational technologies to examine the effect of dialect congruence between the student and technology. As such, in this work, we address this substantial lacuna with what we belief to be the first comparison of student learning in the context of technology that speaks one of the three dialectal patterns discussed above: exclusively Mainstream American English (MAE), exclusively AAVE, or code-switching.

2 Related Work

A limited number of educational technologies have addressed the discontinuity between students' home culture and their school environment by integrating commonly perceived aspects of minority culture, such as rap songs or cornrow hairstyles, into educational software [20;21;22]. For example, Culturally Situated Design Tools teaches transformation geometry with plaited symbols that can be rotated to re-create examples of African American cornrow hairstyles [20]. Gilbert et al. [21] similarly developed AADMLSS, in which students watch an embodied virtual agent solve a series of math problems grounded in neighborhood tasks, with mathematical explanations provided through rap songs. These ideas are also employed in Lyric Reader [22] which uses child-appropriate rap to promote literacy. Despite the positive qualitative results of these technologies, most have been compared against a "worksheet" control, rather than a similar technology that exclusively manipulates the presence of the intended cultural stimuli, such as corn rows or rap lyrics.

Also noteworthy is research on cultural sensitivity with virtual agents, such as Hayes-Roth's description of how agents from different cultural backgrounds could use language to embody deep-seated cultural differences [23]. There have been some studies which have included dialect as one index of culture, although it was not manipulated as distinct from skin color, and no information about the frequency or features of the non-standard dialects were discussed [24]. More commonly, studies investigating the impact of cultural differences in agents neglect to manipulate dialect at all, such as Baylor et al. [25], who found that varying agent age, gender, and ethnicity (including African American) affected both student perceptions of the agent's intelligence, and their learning. However, the authors did not manipulate dialect, nor did they report whether AAVE was used for the voice of the African American agents.

In our previous work, we addressed some of these issues by examining performance in a collaborative bridge-building task where students were either partnered with a human classmate, or a virtual peer who code-switched between speaking AAVE during science collaboration and MAE during a presentation to the teacher task [26]. While most students reduced their use of AAVE during the presentation task, those who were partnered with a code-switching agent demonstrated a significantly greater reduction of AAVE during formal presentation. However, this earlier work only examined one particular dialect switching pattern (AAVE for collaboration, MAE for presentation), motivating our current work to experimentally compare the effects of three dialect switching patterns in an agent, patterns whose benefits are currently being debated [27].

3 Methodology

We worked with 29 3rd grade students at a low SES (99% free or reduced lunch) 100% African American urban charter school to address whether students who speak with a non-standard dialect would demonstrate greater science proficiency after interacting with an educational technology that used the same dialect features in its own speech. We eliminated six students from the analysis due to data loss. Classroom observations determined that all students spoke AAVE to varying degrees, and dialect use was sometimes openly called out and stigmatized by the teacher.

We designed what we call a Distant Peer paradigm, in which children were partnered with an agent throughout the study to make audio recordings of a social task (an introduction about the student's interests) and a science task (providing scientific hypotheses about a pair of fictional creatures). Children believed their agent partner attended "a local school just like [theirs]," had completed the task a few days earlier, and would be later receiving the recordings the children created (like a pen pal). The agent partner was represented by a gender-ambiguous African American character ("Jamie") shown on individual laptops (see Figure 1). Jamie's voice was pre-recorded by a confederate who was bidialectal in AAVE and MAE, with recordings pitch-shifted to sound like a child. Children were randomly assigned to condition: (1) MAE, with an agent partner who spoke in MAE during both the social and science tasks; (2) AAVE, a partner who used AAVE in both tasks; and (3) code-switching, a partner who code-switched from AAVE in the social task to MAE in the science task. We emphasize that the only difference between the AAVE and code-switching agents is the dialect in which children heard the agent's initial four minute social introduction, allowing us to examine if science performance would be affected by the agent's dialect even in previous social dialogue unrelated to the task.

Fig. 1. Procedure: (1) listen to agent's social recording; (2) produce a social recording; (3) produce a first science recording; (4) listen to agent's science recording; (5) produce a second science recording. Order of creature sets A and B were counter-balanced.

In the science task, students were given pictures of fictional species in identical eco-systems. They were asked to "record [their] best hypotheses" about how the creatures might behave and interact within their environment for four minutes, both before and after hearing the peer science model, as shown in Figure 1. The open-ended nature of this task allowed students to monologue freely, allowing us to observe the students' use of dialect features and assess their science talk.

Jamie's social and science monologues were identical in both content and prosody across all condition [see previous work, 28], and differed only in presence of AAVE dialectal features (e.g. MAE: "the creatures don't have any claws" vs. AAVE: "the creatures don't have no claws.") For ease of exposition, specifics of Jamie's AAVE and science talk are described further in section 4.

4 Data Annotation

We focus our analysis on students' science talk and dialect use during the two four-minute science recordings students created (before and after hearing the agent model). The data was annotated by coders who were blind to condition. They achieved Cohen's Kappa agreement ratings of over .7 for each feature described below.

Our science annotation scheme was based on Linn et al.'s categorization of contribution, support, and complexity in science reasoning [29], as well as McNeill's description of claims and appropriate reasoning in science explanations [30]. Our science coding manual was reviewed and iterated upon with our science teacher advisor to obtain construct validity.

We first segmented students' monologues into units, defined as individual contributions that captured cohesive components of students' scientific ideas, as described in [31]. Each contribution was then coded for the presence of the following non-mutually-exclusive features: (1) claims, (2) reasoning, and (3) scientific integration (defined as integration of scientific ideas based in prior knowledge, analogies within ecology, or inferences about functionality.) Contributions that included at least one of each of these features (e.g. "the first creature is probably a carnivore because it looks fast and has sharp teeth and can use them to attack other animals for food") we called

"Strong Scientifically-Reasoned Arguments" (SSRAs) based on prior literature about elementary school level science arguments [29; 30]. Coders' inter-rater reliability for SSRAs was ($\kappa = .92$).

AAVE features were coded using the scheme proposed and validated by Renn [32], with slight modifications. We coded for morphosyntactic features, including multiple negation, copula deletion, and zero plural (see [37] for full list), as well as one phonetic feature, nasal fronting, identified as particularly relevant in children's code-switching [38]. While Renn additionally proposed two other phonetic features characteristic of AAVE, we primarily focus our analyses on morphosyntax because this has been shown to be more under children's control than their phonology, and therefore more likely able to be dampened when children code-switch [38]. We operationalize amount of dialect use with the Density Dialect Measure (DDM), calculated by dividing the total number of coded AAVE features used over the total number of words and multiplying by 100 as in [7].

Jamie's monologues in the AAVE condition included a subset of the 27 morphosyntactic features present in [32], because it would not have been realistic to fit examples of each feature into such small speech samples. The speech samples did contain a number of phonetic AAVE features because they were recorded by a natural bidialectal speaker, but we did not code for all of these features in our participants because of the difficulty of successfully annotating difficult phonetic features such as vowel quality. Jamie's monologues in the AAVE condition averaged a DDM of 13.3 and was designed to be substantially higher than our participants' ($M = 1.5$), such that there would be a clear distinction between MAE and AAVE conditions.

Jamie's science monologue included six examples of SSRAs, alongside other scientifically-relevant content, such as observations ("it looks like the creature has gills"), comparisons ("one creature looks like it can stand up on both legs, but the other one looks like it can only swim"), and questions "I wonder which one is more dangerous…").

5 Results

We operationalize students' science talk strength as the number of Strong Scientifically Reasoned Arguments (SSRAs) students provided in each four minute science recording. Jamie provided six examples of SSRAs (as well as other kinds of age-appropriate talk such as observations and comparisons of creatures) in the agent's 4 minute-long monologue. We first performed paired-samples t-tests to determine whether listening to Jamie's science talk recordings increased students' likelihood of producing on-task science contributions, SSRAs, reasoning, and scientific integration (ecological analogies, functionality, and prior knowledge) between their first and second science recordings, regardless of condition. As shown in Table 1, across all students the number of on-task science contributions, the number of SSRAs, and the amount of reasoning significantly increased from the first to second science recording. The incorporation of scientific integration did not change.

Table 1. Comparison of Students' Science Talk in First and Second Monologue

	Science 1 *M (SD)*	Science 2 *M (SD)*	*t*	*df*
# Contributions	15.35 (5.80)	18.65 (7.46)	-2.67*	22
# SSRAs	0.30 (.77)	1.83 (1.52)	-4.22***	22
# Reasoning	1.43 (2.62)	4.09 (3.07)	-4.46***	22
# Scientific Integration	2.91 (2.41)	3.96 (3.28)	-1.52	22

In order to test the hypothesis that students' ability to produce SSRAs would improve differentially based on condition, we ran a Repeated Measures ANOVA comparing the count of SSRAs in the first and second recording, with a between-subjects factor of condition. Results showed a significant main effect of science recording, $F(1, 20) = 26.06$, $p < .001$, showing that, as above, students increased their production of SSRAs after hearing a model. In addition, a significant interaction between condition and recording ($F(2, 20) = 6.887$, $p < .01$), revealed with Bonferroni post-hoc analyses that students in the AAVE condition showed a significantly higher increase than the MAE condition in production SSRAs from time one to time two ($p < .05$). The code-switching condition was not significantly different from either the AAVE or MAE condition at $\alpha = .05$, with gains between the other two conditions.

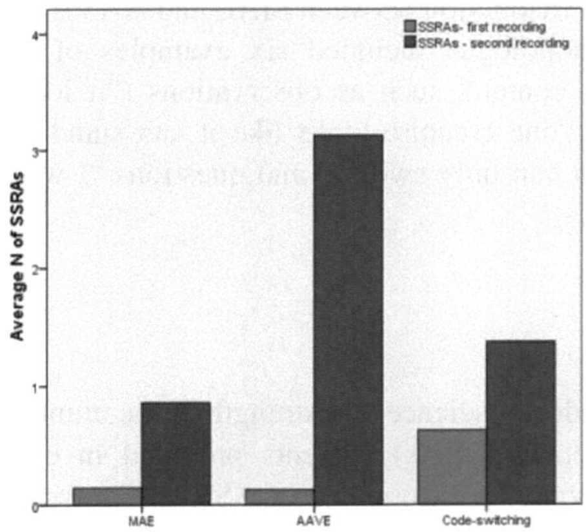

Fig. 2. Left: Relationship between students' initial DDM during the first science task and their subsequent performance on the second science task. **Right**: SSRAs produced by condition before and after interacting with Jamie.

A Repeated Measures ANOVA compared students' DDMs in the first (m – 1.5, range = 0 to 3.11) and second (m = 1.3, range = 0 – 4.5) science recording, with a between-subjects factor of condition. We clarify that demonstrating a DDM of 0 in these particular tasks does not mean that these students are not speakers of AAVE, as students may use the dialect in different contexts. There was no significant DDM difference between students' first or second recording, with no effect of condition. While not significant, students in the MAE condition trended to reduce their AAVE (M_Δ = -.0039), students in the code-switching condition trended to increase their AAVE (M_Δ = .0024), and students in the AAVE condition trended to stay the same (M_Δ = .0002). We reiterate that Jamie's DDM at 13.3 was substantially higher than our participants'.

6 Discussion

Though the vast majority of technologies are designed to communicate information to students using a mainstream dialect, the results of this work demonstrate that the strongest improvements in science talk were seen among students who heard the technology speak in AAVE – the children's native dialect. We additionally found that students' own dialect patterns did not change from their first science recording to their second. This has important implications, as teachers worry that allowing the vernacular dialect into their classroom will perpetuate the consistent use of the vernacular among students, and make them even less likely to use the standard [27]. However, our study did involve children only hearing very limited samples of the agent's speech in monologue, and we may see stronger effects on students' dialect use over greater periods of time spent interacting with the system, or during continuous dialogues with the system. Furthermore, we note that code-switching is a very complex linguistic process, and that the dialectal model we provided was a simplified instantiation of this process. Future analyses will continue to iterate our language model to better represent the intricacies of fluid switching behaviors seen among actual bidialectal students.

Because of the complex relationship between dialect and education, we propose three potential explanations for our result that AAVE-speaking students demonstrate increased success with AAVE speaking technology. The first is that there is a reduction of cognitive load when working with systems that communicate in students' native dialect, as supported by previous research that demonstrates students learn best from teachers who share their accent [17]. Students fluent in the mainstream dialect may be able to expend less effort during a learning task translating the provided information into a format they can better understand. It may also be that students are better able to demonstrate learning if they feel comfortable producing it in their native dialect, as they may be after hearing an example of the information provided in such dialect. The second explanation could be that students felt an increased rapport, or sameness, with the agent in our system who spoke in their own dialect, as students typically learn from those who are more similar to themselves [33]. Our previous work examined the acoustic features of students' recordings by condition, and found that those with an AAVE-speaking agent spoke more loudly, more quickly, and with more pitch fluctuation during the social introduction task compared to their peers who had an MAE-speaking agent. This leads us to believe that students felt more comfortable with an AAVE-speaking partner, which may have facilitated learning. The final explanation is that students may have been attending more closely to a technology who spoke in AAVE due to a novelty effect, as they have likely never experienced a system to communicate in this dialect before. Future studies which analyze the use of this technology over time will provide more insight about how these potential explanations affect students' overall learning, and clarify the role that each plays in the students' educational process.

7 Conclusion and Future Work

In this work, we provide, to our knowledge, the first example of an educational technology that experimentally manipulates different dialectal patterns and investigates subsequent academic performance. We exposed AAVE-speaking 3rd graders to an educational technology that used one of three dialect switching patterns, and conclude with two primary results: (1) students demonstrate improvement in science talk after listening to a science model from a peer educational technology, and (2) improvement is greatest among AAVE-speaking children with a peer that speaks in AAVE.

Our future work will incorporate our results into our virtual peer technology [26], and investigate more complex models of dialect switching, as this is a complicated and socially-driven phenomenon. Within these evaluations we will additionally examine transfer, retention, and longitudinal effects of learning with culturally sensitive technologies, as well as the long-term social benefits of culturally similar peer technologies, such as improved self-efficacy.

We believe the results of this work provide two primary lessons. The first is that we can design technologies to provide insight into complex and sensitive phenomena which are not yet fully understood. The second is that we make culturally-charged decisions in the design of every aspect of our technologies, and these may have significant impacts on users from underrepresented populations. As it is unreasonable to expect young children to be able to accurately articulate how sensitive topics such as race, identity, and cultural affiliation in educational environments may affect their learning, developers can work towards culturally sensitive technologies by experimentally manipulating aspects of our work, and monitoring the effects on children. This process not only provides insight about how to best design technologies for our target audiences to promote educational and socio-emotional success, it also acts to serve as the ground on which we begin to identify what (and how) cultural factors play into students' experiences. This study demonstrates the critical effects of small decisions within a system, and calls for developers to question the assumptions they put forth in the development of their own systems.

Acknowledgements. This work was supported in part by The Heinz Foundation (# C2902 and # E0510), the Graduate Training Grant awarded to Carnegie Mellon University by the Department of Education (# R305B090023), and the National Science Foundation (# 0946825). Many additional thanks to the RAs of the ArticuLab who've helped with this project!

References

1. Gutiérrez, K.D., Rogoff, B.: Cultural ways of learning: Individual traits or repertoires of practice. Educational Researcher 32(5), 19–25 (2003)
2. Lee, C.D.: Bridging home and school literacies: Models for culturally responsive teaching, a case for African American English. In: Handbook of Research on Teaching Literacy Through the Communicative and Visual Arts, pp. 334–345 (1997)
3. Michaels, S.A.: Sharing time: children's narrative styles and differential access to literacy. Doctoral dissertation, University of California, Berkeley (1991)
4. Atkinson, J.L.: Are We Creating the Achievement Gap? Examining How Deficit Mentalities Influence Indigenous Science Curriculum Choices. In: Cultural Studies and Environmentalism, pp. 439–446 (2010)
5. Morrison, F.J., Bachman, H.J., Connor, C.M.: Improving literacy in America: Guidelines from research. Yale University Press (2005)
6. Gann, R.R.: Connecting early language and literacy to later reading (dis)abilities: Evidence, theory, and practice. In: Handbook of Erly Literacy Research, pp. 97–110 (2001)
7. Craig, H.K., Thompson, C.A., Washington, J.A., Potter, S.L.: Phonological Features of Child African American English. Journal of Speech, Language and Hearing Research 55, 623–635 (2003)
8. Green, L.J.: African American English: a linguistic introduction. Cambridge University Press (2002)
9. Rickford, J.R., Labov, W.: African American vernacular English: Features, evolution, educational implications, p. 157. Blackwell, Oxford (1999)
10. Connor, C., Craig, H.: African American preschoolers' language, emergent literacy skills, and use of African American English: A complex relation. Journal of Speech, Language, and Hearing Research 49, 771–792 (2006)
11. Charity, A.H., Scarborough, H.S., Griffin, D.M.: Familiarity with school English in African American children and its relation to early reading achievement. Child Development 75(5), 1340–1356 (2004)
12. Scarborough, H.S.: Connecting early language and literacy to later reading (dis)abilities: Evidence, theory, and practice. In: Neuman, S.B., Dickinson, D.K. (eds.) Handbook of Early Literacy Research, pp. 97–110. Guilford, New York (2001)
13. Ball, A.F., Farr, M.: Language varieties, culture, and teaching the English. In: Handbook of Research on Teaching the English Language Arts, pp. 435–445. Lawrence Erlbaum, Mahwah (2003)
14. Terry, N.P., Connor, C.M., Thomas-Tate, S., Love, M.: Examining relationships among dialect variation, literacy skills, and school context in first grade. Journal of Speech, Language and Hearing Research 53(1), 126 (2010)
15. Connor, C.M.: Language and literacy connections for children who are African American. Perspectives on Communication Disorders and Sciences in Culturally and Linguistically Diverse Populations 15, 43–53 (2008)
16. Mohatt, G., Erickson, F.: Cultural differences in teaching styles in an Odawa school: A sociolinguistic approach. Culture and the Bilingual Classroom: Studies in Classroom Ethnography 105 (1981)
17. Gill, M.M.: Accent and stereotypes: Their effect on perceptions of teachers and lecture comprehension (1994)
18. Webb, L., Webb, P.: Introducing discussion into multilingual mathematics classrooms: An issue of code switching? Pythagoras (67), 26–32 (2011)

19. Cassell, J.: Social practice: Becoming enculturated in human-computer interaction. In: Stephanidis, C. (ed.) UAHCI 2009, Part III. LNCS, vol. 5616, pp. 303–313. Springer, Heidelberg (2009)
20. Eglash, R., Bennett, A., O'Donnell, C., Jennings, S., Cintorino, M.: Culturally situated design tools: Ethnocomputing from field site to classroom. American Anthropologist 108(2), 347–362 (2006)
21. Gilbert, J.E., Arbuthnot, K., Hood, S., Grant, M.M., West, M.L., McMillian, Y., Eugene, W.: Teaching algebra using culturally relevant virtual instructors. The International Journal of Virtual Reality 7(1), 21–30 (2008)
22. Pinkard, N.: Rappin'Reader and Say Say Oh Playmate: Using children's childhood songs as literacy scaffolds in computer-based learning environments. Journal of Educational Computing Research 25(1), 17–34 (2001)
23. Hayes-Roth, B., Maldonado, H., Moraes, M.: Designing for diversity: Multi-cultural characters for a multi-cultural world. In: Proceedings of IMAGINA, pp. 207–225 (2002)
24. Moreno, K.N., Person, N.K., Adcock, A.B., Eck, R.N.V., Jackson, G.T., Marineau, J.C.: Etiquette and efficacy in animated pedagogical agents: The role of stereotypes. In: AAAI Symposium on Personalized Agents, Cape Cod, MA (2002)
25. Baylor, A.L., Kim, Y.: Simulating instructional roles through pedagogical agents. International Journal of Artificial Intelligence in Education 15(1), 95–115 (2005)
26. Cassell, J., Geraghty, K., Gonzalez, B., Borland, J.: Modeling culturally authentic style shifting with virtual peers. In: Proceedings of the 2009 International Conference on Multimodal Interfaces, pp. 135–142. ACM (2009)
27. Ogan, A., Finkelstein, S., Cassell, J.: Starting where the teachers are: Culturally-Sensitive Educational Technology Through a Teacher's Lens (in preparation)
28. Finkelstein, S., Scherer, S., Ogan, A., Morency, L.P., Cassell, J.: Investigating the influence of virtual peers as dialect models on students' prosodic inventory. In: Workshop on Child, Computer and Interaction (WOCCI 2012). ISCA, Oregon (2012)
29. Linn, M.C.: The knowledge integration perspective on learning and instruction. In: The Cambridge Handbook of the Learning Sciences, pp. 243–264 (2006)
30. McNeill, K.L., Krajcik, J.S.: Supporting Grade 5-8 Students in Constructing Explanations in Science: The Claim, Evidence, and Reasoning Framework for Talk and Writing. Pearson, Upper Saddle River (2011)
31. Chi, M.T.: Quantifying qualitative analyses of verbal data: A practical guide. The Journal of the Learning Sciences 6(3), 271–315 (1997)
32. Renn, J.: Acquiring stylel The development of dialect shifting among African American children. Doctoral dissertation, The University of North Carolina at Chapel Hill (2010)
33. Schunk, D.H.: Peer models and children's behavioral change. Review of Educational Research 57(2), 149–174 (1987)

ITS and the Digital Divide: Trends, Challenges, and Opportunities

Benjamin D. Nye

Institute for Intelligent Systems, University of Memphis
Memphis, TN 38152
benjamin.nye@gmail.com

Abstract. This paper analyzes the state of current intelligent tutoring systems (ITS) research for applications in the developing world. Recent data shows a rapidly narrowing digital divide, with internet and computing device access rising sharply in less developed countries. Tutoring systems could be a transformative technology in these areas, where shortages of teachers and materials are persistent problems. However, the unique challenges and opportunities for ITS in this context are not well-explored. This paper identifies barriers to adoption distinct to the developing world, then presents the results of a systematic mapping study of recent ITS literature (2009-2012) that looks at the level of focus given to each barrier. This study finds that only a small percentage of peer-reviewed publications and architectures address even one of the barriers preventing adoption in these contexts. Implications and strategies being used to target these barriers are discussed.

Keywords: Intelligent Tutoring Systems, Digital Divide, Systematic Mapping Study, Mobile Learning, Barriers to Adoption.

1 Introduction

Recent studies show that the digital divide is narrowing rapidly, driven by the expansion of broadband access in developing countries. Between 2005 to 2011, the percentage of households with internet access in developing countries doubled from less than 10% to over 20% and are projected to reach 50% or more by 2015 (International Telecommunication Union, 2012, p. 10). This level of growth would add nearly 1.75 billion internet users, 500 million more than the combined population of all developed countries (Population Reference Bureau, 2012). Because these areas struggle with shortages of qualified teachers and traditional educational resources such as textbooks, intelligent tutoring systems (ITS) have the opportunity to play a pivotal role supporting and supplementing their educational needs.

The ability of existing ITS architectures to address these challenges is unclear. Potential barriers for successful adoption of ITS in developing countries must be better understood, such as constraints due to data costs, mobiles as a primary internet and communication technology (ICT), language support, and cultural

K. Yacef et al. (Eds.): AIED 2013, LNAI 7926, pp. 503–511, 2013.

values. To examine these issues, this research considers the current state of ITS research regarding its applications in the developing world. This study consists of three parts:

1. Identify barriers for ITS adoption in the developing world
2. Systematically review the level of ITS research focus on each barrier
3. Summarize current ITS research targeting each barrier

Below, Section 2 examines trends in technology access in developing countries and identifies barriers that significantly impact ITS suitability in these areas. Section 3 presents a systematic mapping study of the ITS literature examining the prevalence of recent research (2009-2012) that addresses barriers to ITS adoption. Only recent research was considered, to limit the review to potentially active projects. Section 4 examines possible opportunities for ITS based on these findings.

2 Barriers to ITS in the Developing World

To identify barriers that primarily impact the developing world, barriers noted in developing countries were contrasted against barriers encountered in most developed countries. Barriers for most developed countries were drawn from Balanskat et al. (2006), Bingimlas (2009), Goktas et al. (2009), Lowther et al. (2008), and Riasati et al. (2012). These reviews focus primarily on formal settings in the US and Europe. Research in these contexts emphasized teacher and school factors, such as time constraints, in-service training, administrative support, match to teachers' pedagogical views, and teacher beliefs on ICT. Developing countries share these barriers, but have additional challenges as well.

Barriers in developing world contexts were drawn from Gulati (2008), who reviewed barriers specific to developing nations at that time, and Cassim and Eyono Obono (2011), who presented barriers relevant to the KwaZulu Natal province of South Africa. Evaluations of ITS interventions in developing countries were also considered, including a multiple-user math tutoring in India (Brunskill et al., 2010), literacy tutors in Ghana (Mills-Tettey et al., 2009), math tutoring in India (Banerjee et al., 2007), and Cognitive Tutor field studies in Latin America (Ogan et al., 2012).

Based on this review, six barriers to adoption were distinct to the developing world: 1. Students' basic ICT skills, 2. ICT hardware availability, 3. Data costs, 4. Internet reliability, 5. Language, and 6. Lack of culturally appropriate content. Of these, lack of ICT hardware remains the primary barrier in the developing world. As mobile phones are the primary computing platform in these areas, lack of software targeting these devices is a related problem. Regional infrastructure, such as unreliable access to electricity and internet, poses a barrier, though appropriate hardware (e.g., laptops and mobile devices) should mitigate power disruptions with no added cost over desktops. Language barriers and culturally appropriate content were also considered significant issues. Data costs and basic ICT skills by learners were not a major factor in classroom settings but posed major hurdles for individual ICT use.

3 Systematic Mapping Study: Recent ITS Literature Addressing Barriers

A systematic study of recent ITS publications was conducted to identify the prevalence of literature that notes problems or solutions related to each barrier. Systematic mapping studies are similar to systematic reviews, except that they seek to classify research topics rather than outcomes. This study covers papers published no earlier than January 1, 2009 that were indexed on or before January 1, 2013. This time frame was chosen to limit the review to potentially active projects, since projects with no publications in the last 4 years are likely inactive. This review followed guidelines for systematic mapping studies contained in Petersen et al. (2008).

This analysis is one aspect of a larger mapping study that considers recent developments in ITS, with a special focus on barriers to adoption. Developing world barriers and most developed country barriers are presented in separate papers because the developing world barriers presented here are seldom relevant for traditional ITS settings. Moreover, a large scale review of ITS work related to the developing world has never been conducted so these topics require extra background to explain their significance and potential solutions.

3.1 Mapping Study Methodology

The primary aim of this study was to examine how much of the recent ITS literature addresses each barrier in the developing world. Citations were aggregated from Thomson-Reuters Web of Science, ACM Digital Library, IEEE Xplore, and ERIC. Searches for publications were based on the search term: "intelligent tutoring system" OR "intelligent tutoring systems." This generated a citation set of 2647 journal and conference papers to review. Short papers and demonstrations were included in this review, as these papers occasionally address aspects of an ITS that are otherwise unpublished.

Inclusion criteria were based on the following question: "Does the paper describe original research on ITS design, enhancements to an existing ITS design, studies using an existing ITS, or analysis of data collected in a study using an ITS?" For this study, an ITS was defined as a system with an inner loop that provides feedback intelligently as defined in VanLehn (2006). Each paper meeting inclusion criteria was evaluated based on seven boolean classification criteria based on each barrier:

1. Student Basic ICT Skills: Does the ITS research address usability by learners without basic computer experience or skills?
2. Hardware (Sharing): Does the ITS research address lack of hardware or multiple users sharing a single computing device?
3. Hardware (Mobile): Does the ITS address mobile devices, such as a mobile application or mobile version of a website?
4. Data Costs: Does the ITS research address reduced or optimized data transmission over a telecommunications carrier?

5. Internet: Does the ITS research address unreliable internet connectivity?
6. Language: Does the ITS design address multiple language support or describe features to facilitate language localization?
7. Culture: Does the ITS design include cultural features, cultural content, or features to facilitate cultural localization?

As these are not focal topics of the ITS community, criteria were applied broadly. Papers that addressed these topics in any fashion were included, even if they briefly noted the barrier as an obstacle (e.g. "due to insufficient computers, students had to share"). This determination was based upon the full text of the paper. However, raw publication counts are biased toward groups who publish more extensively. For an alternative perspective, papers were grouped into families of architectures as a secondary analysis. If any paper based on an architecture met the criteria, architecture was classified as meeting that criteria (i.e. a Boolean union).

3.2 Mapping Study Results

Based on the study criteria, 815 papers on ITS were identified. Table 1 shows the results of the mapping study on developing world barriers. The first row shows the raw results, which are the percentage of ITS publications that address each barrier. The second row displays the results for unique ITS architecture families (e.g., Cognitive Tutor, AutoTutor, etc.). The final row displays the results for "Major" ITS architectures, those with more than 10 papers published during the study period. These architectures are highly influential and account for 290 of 815 papers on tutoring systems. This analysis, despite covering a greater breadth than Blanchard (2012), also shows a strong WEIRD (Western, Educated, Industrialized, Rich, Democratic) bias. Approximately 75% of papers had a first author in such a country and, if data was used, it was collected from that population.

Table 1. Percentages of ITS Addressing Developing World Barriers

	N	Student ICT	Hardware Sharing	Mobile	Data Costs	Internet Reliability	Culture	Multiple Languages
All ITS Papers	815	2.21%	0.98%	5.77%	0.49%	0.73%	4.90%	3.93%
ITS Families	374	4.01%	1.34%	8.55%	1.07%	1.34%	5.88%	5.35%
Major ITS	12	16.7%	8.33%	33.3%	8.33%	25%	41.7%	16.7%

Overall, a very small number of recent ITS papers approached any of these topics (<10% for most categories and samples, excepting papers from major ITS families discussing mobile access, internet reliability, culture, and language). Even fewer papers addressed these topics in any depth. In comparison, over 45% of papers in the sample addressed student motivation (e.g., affect, games, etc.), and over 14% considered student affect alone. Based on these results, ITS research appears to have given these barriers little attention and would probably struggle in the developing world as a result. The following subsections briefly summarize the current literature on how ITS and other educational technologies are approaching these barriers.

Student Basic ICT Skills. Research on basic computing skills for students indicates significant differences between individual use and classroom use. Pilots of Cognitive Tutor and LISTEN Reading Tutor in the developing world found that students were able to navigate the software fairly quickly (Casas et al., 2011; Mills-Tettey et al., 2009). However, a study on mobile access in South Africa showed a much higher barrier to basic web use (Gitau et al., 2010). In many ways, this is a support issue: users can learn how to use ITS, but setting up a device is difficult. One solution is to simplify the system: Savvopoulos and Virvou (2010) approached elderly populations with low ICT skills by providing tutoring over interactive TV. However, mobile devices are the prevalent independent platform. On mobile platforms, community support such as libraries and schools may be pivotal to help install and setup ITS for home use.

Hardware Sharing. Sharing devices is a key technique for reducing barriers due to lack of hardware. From an ITS perspective, sharing a computer is a disruptive paradigm: most tutoring systems assume a 1:1 mapping of users to computers. Recent findings from the Cognitive Tutor project show that computer sharing accounts for over 60% of use in some areas, with students leaving their machines and sharing a single machine (Ogan et al., 2012). LISTEN and other groups have had similar experiences: computer sharing, even when enough hardware is available, is characteristic of developing world ICT usage (Mills-Tettey et al., 2009; Banerjee et al., 2007). This has serious implications for the user model, which assumes that each machine was measuring the work of one person. Ogan et al. (2012) suggests modeling the classroom as a network of connected user models rather than individual models. Unfortunately, software techniques for disentangling multiple users sharing an input are not mature. Moreover, a software solution would reduce the power of knowledge assessments by adding uncertainty about user identity. User models that account for collaboration are worth exploring, but they may only offer a partial solution.

Existing ITS that share hardware have focused on using multiple inputs instead. MultiLearn+ split a laptop display into quadrants, each with their own keypad (Brunskill et al., 2010). Single Display Groupware went further, with a whole class sharing a single projection and one mouse per student (Alcoholado et al., 2012). The latter paradigm was problematic due to the complexity of managing dozens of mouse cords, but might be effective using wireless mice, clickers, or other input devices. Notably, neither of these field studies indicated that students exchanged or shared input devices extensively under these conditions. Using a single machine also facilitates modeling collaboration, since the data for multiple users is already in a single system. As such, embracing computer sharing might also mitigate some of the user modeling issues.

Mobile ITS. Despite the expansion of mobile technology in the developing world, mobile ITS research was most prevalent in Western Europe (Virvou et al., 2012) and East Asia (Chu et al., 2010). In the US, the Tactical Language and Culture Training System (TLCTS) for language learning supports limited mobile access, but it is unclear how much of the original immersive ITS environment is retained (Johnson, 2010). Most of this research was designed for PDA's and higher-end smartphones, making it unlikely to transfer easily. Voice input is a common feature for mobile ITS focusing on language learning. Kumar et al. (2012) demonstrated that a speech-driven ITS was effective in India, but handling accents required a corpus of local speech. In the same paper, they proposed an ambitious plan to use speech recognition for mobile sharing that could have significant implications. A second variant of mobile ITS are ubiquitous e-learning systems for universities, such as EDUCA in Mexico (Cabada et al., 2011). These systems provide strong outer loops using adaptive curricula and inner-loop functionality for subsets of the system. These mobile web gateways are a strong cross-platform delivery method, but they rely on data significantly. Finally, a few mobile learning environments incorporate local data transmission using Bluetooth protocols. While no systems with full ITS capabilities used this approach, it has been incorporated into adaptive learning systems (Puntambekar et al., 2009; Munoz-Organero et al., 2012).

Data Costs. Data costs primarily impact mobile learning. Literature shows three main solutions: don't rely on data, use data in batches, and use data locally. Cognitive Tutor, EDUCA, and Learning Pills embody these concepts, respectively (Ogan et al., 2012; Cabada et al., 2011; Munoz-Organero et al., 2012). Cognitive Tutor avoided these barriers because it can be installed and run as a standalone application on a PC. EDUCA allows users to download ITS units as modules, enabling users to download them using cheap or free WiFi access rather than communicating wirelessly at runtime. Finally, Learning Pills relies on Bluetooth OBEX protocols to allow an instructor's machine to directly transmit data to students' phones in the classroom. The latter two approaches are more feasible for mobile devices than a large installer and can be combined, as they have complementary scope.

Internet Reliability. Internet reliability matters most in a classroom setting, since a short disruption would be a minor hiccup for independent work. However, losing internet in a class setting will wreck any lesson plan that relies on it. The systematic study provided few solutions for internet unreliability. Nedungadi and Raman (2012) employed asynchronous communication for robustness against internet problems in a mobile context, but this is only useful for web homework or independent study. As a result, web-reliant ITS are probably a bad fit for most developing world classrooms. However, web-based ITS could still be effective outside of a school setting if their data usage is handled appropriately.

Cultural and Language Localization. Culture and language are combined because the literature seldom addresses culture without addressing language. Localization expands beyond language to icons, graphics, and mother media. Localization and supporting users with different native languages have been addressed by a few medium to large ITS architectures. All of these ITS were localized manually. Cognitive Tutor was localized into Spanish and Portugese by working with local teachers to revise each problem (Ogan et al., 2012). REAP (REAder-specific Practice) was extended to Portugese by researchers who created an equivalent vocabulary list and extended the ITS (Silva et al., 2011). TLCTS (Tactical Language and Culture Training System) worked on the opposite issue: localizing training scenarios to support US soldiers' learning of different cultures (Johnson, 2010). These accounts all involve skilled local or expert involvement in the project. It is unclear if more efficient alternative practices are possible. Design patterns that separate graphics and text as replaceable assets can ease this process, but local knowledge is the primary barrier. Crowd-sourcing services have been used to tag other ITS content, but these techniques have not been explored for ITS localization (Parent and Eskenazi, 2010).

4 Conclusions: Opportunities for ITS

Intelligent tutoring systems have new opportunities to expand into the developing world, due to changes in ICT availability as well recent research seeking solutions to developing world barriers. While only a small portion of recent ITS research has addressed these barriers, these papers have outlined possible solutions to many of these issues. The present paper summarized these barriers and existing solutions to allow later projects to leverage these solutions. While these barriers were examined from the standpoint of ITS, they are also relevant to other educational technologies. This means that some of the solutions presented may also be valuable in other contexts.

A key finding was that barriers to classroom use are quite different from home use, which calls for different models of ITS for these settings. For classroom use, shared laptops running installed ITS software show promise. For independent use, mobile ITS applications downloaded at community centers or peer-to-peer over Bluetooth might be more accessible. In either context, language and cultural localization are important to ITS adoption. Future research may address such questions as: How do multiple-input devices impact user models? How might existing ITS be adapted for the mobile interfaces and hardware capabilities? Can parts of localization be automated? Because developing nations have pressing educational needs and studies on ITS provide a culturally biased sample due to under-representation of these areas (Blanchard, 2012), increased focus on tutoring systems for the developing world seems warranted.

References

Alcoholado, C., Nussbaum, M., Tagle, A., Gomez, F., Denardin, F., Susaeta, H., Villalta, M., Toyama, K.: One mouse per child: Interpersonal computer for individual arithmetic practice. Journal of Computer Assisted Learning 28(4), 295–309 (2012)

Balanskat, A., Blamire, R., Kefala, S.: The ICT Impact Report: A Review of Studies of ICT Impact on Schools in Europe. European Schoolnet (2006)

Banerjee, A., Cole, S., Duflo, E., Linden, L.: Remedying education: Evidence from two randomized experiments in India. The Quarterly Journal of Economics 122(3), 1235–1264 (2007)

Bingimlas, K.: Barriers to the successful integration of ICT in teaching and learning environments: A review of the literature. Eurasia Journal of Mathematics. Science and Technology Education 5(3), 235–245 (2009)

Blanchard, E.G.: On the WEIRD nature of ITS/AIED conferences: A 10 year longitudinal study analyzing potential cultural biases. In: Cerri, S.A., Clancey, W.J., Papadourakis, G., Panourgia, K. (eds.) ITS 2012. LNCS, vol. 7315, pp. 280–285. Springer, Heidelberg (2012)

Brunskill, E., Garg, S., Tseng, C., Findlater, L.: Evaluating an adaptive multi-user educational tool for low-resource environments. In: ICTD 2010, London, UK (2010)

Cabada, R.Z., Estrada, M.L.B., Parra, L.E., Garcia, C.A.R.: Interpreter for the deployment of intelligent tutoring systems in mobile devices. In: ICALT 2011, pp. 339–340. IEEE Press, Washington, DC (2011)

Casas, I., Goodman, P.S., Pelaez, E.: On the design and use of a cognitive tutoring system in the math classroom. In: Technology for Education (T4E) 2011, pp. 9–17. IEEE Press, Piscataway (2011)

Cassim, K.M., Eyono Obono, S.D.: On the factors affecting the adoption of ICT for the teaching of word problems. In: Ao, S.I., Douglas, C., Grundfest, W.S., Burgstone, J. (eds.) World Congress on Engineering and Computer Science 2011, vol. 1, pp. 269–276. Newswood Limited, San Francisco (2011)

Chu, H.C., Hwang, G.J., Tsai, C.C., Tseng, J.C.R.: A two-tier test approach to developing location-aware mobile learning systems for natural science courses. Computers and Education 55(4), 1618–1627 (2010)

Gitau, S., Marsden, G., Donner, J.: After access: Challenges facing mobile-only internet users in the developing world. In: SIGCHI 2010, pp. 2603–2606. ACM Press, New York (2010)

Goktas, Y., Yildirim, S., Yildirim, Z.: Main barriers and possible enablers of ICTs integration into pre-service teacher education programs. Educational Technology and Society Society 12(1), 193–204 (2009)

Gulati, S.: Technology-enhanced learning in developing nations: A review. International Review of Research in Open and Distance Learning 9(1), 1–16 (2008)

International Telecommunication Union: Measuring the Information Society, Geneva, Switzerland (2012)

Johnson, W.L.: Serious use of a serious game for language learning. International Journal of Artificial Intelligence in Education 20(2), 175–195 (2010)
Kumar, A., Reddy, P., Tewari, A., Agrawal, R., Kam, M.: Improving literacy in developing countries using speech recognition-supported games on mobile devices. In: SIGCHI 2012, pp. 1149–1158. ACM Press (2012)
Lowther, D.L., Inan, F.A., Strahl, J.D., Ross, S.M.: Does technology integration "work" when key barriers are removed? Educational Media International 45(3), 195–213 (2008)
Mills-Tettey, G.A., Mostow, J., Dias, M.B., Sweet, T.M., Belousov, S.M., Dias, M.F., Gong, H.: Improving child literacy in africa: Experiments with an automated reading tutor. In: ICTD 2009, pp. 129–138. IEEE Press, Piscataway (2009)
Munoz-Organero, M., Munoz-Merino, P.J., Kloos, C.D.: Sending learning pills to mobile devices in class to enhance student performance and motivation in network services configuration courses. IEEE Transactions on Education 55(1), 83–87 (2012)
Nedungadi, P., Raman, R.: A new approach to personalization: Integrating e-learning and m-learning. Educational Technology Research and Development 60(4), 659–678 (2012)
Ogan, A., Walker, E., Baker, R.S., Rebolledo Mendez, G., Jimenez Castro, M., Laurentino, T., de Carvalho, A.: Collaboration in cognitive tutor use in latin america: field study and design recommendations. In: SIGCHI 2012, pp. 1381–1390. ACM Press, New York (2012)
Parent, G., Eskenazi, M.: Clustering dictionary definitions using amazon mechanical turk. In: 2010 NAACL HLT Workshop on Creating Speech and Language Data with Amazon's Mechanical Turk, pp. 21–29. Association for Computational Linguistics, Stroudsburg (2010)
Petersen, K., Feldt, R., Mujtaba, S., Mattsson, M.: Systematic mapping studies in software engineering. In: EASE, pp. 1–8. IET Publications (2008)
Population Reference Bureau: 2012 World Population Data Sheet, Washington, DC (2012)
Puntambekar, D.M., Gondal, S., Agrawal, M.: Province of multiuser m-learning environment using artificial intelligence: bluetooth techniques. In: AH-ICI 2009, pp. 1–5 (2009)
Riasati, M.J., Allahyar, N., Tan, K.E.: Technology in language education: Benefits and barriers. Journal of Education and Practice 3(5), 25–30 (2012)
Savvopoulos, A., Virvou, M.: Tutoring the elderly on the use of recommending systems. Campus-Wide Information Systems 27(3), 162–172 (2010)
Silva, A., Mamede, N., Ferreira, A., Baptista, J., Fernandes, J.: Towards a serious game for portuguese learning. In: Ma, M., Fradinho Oliveira, M., Madeiras Pereira, J. (eds.) SGDA 2011. LNCS, vol. 6944, pp. 83–94. Springer, Heidelberg (2011)
VanLehn, K.: The behavior of tutoring systems. International Journal of Artificial Intelligence in Education 16(3), 227–265 (2006)
Virvou, M., Alepis, E., Troussas, C.: A mobile expert system for tutoring multiple languages using machine learning. In: ICEEE 2012, pp. 128–133. IPM, India (2012)

A Hypergraph Based Framework for Intelligent Tutoring of Algebraic Reasoning

Miguel Arevalillo-Herráez[1] and David Arnau[2]

[1] Department of Computer Science, University of Valencia, Spain
[2] Department of Didactics of Mathematics, University of Valencia, Spain
{miguel.arevalillo,david.arnau}@uv.es

Abstract. The translation of word problems into equations is one of the major difficulties for students regarding problem solving. This paper describes both a domain-specific knowledge representation and an inference engine based on hypergraphs that permits intelligent student supervision of this stage of the solving process. The framework presented makes it possible to simultaneously: a) represent all potential algebraic solutions to a given word problem; b) keep track of the student's actions; c) provide automatic remediation; and d) determine the current state of the resolution process univocally. Starting from these ideas, we have designed an intelligent tutoring system (ITS). An experimental evaluation supports the use of this ITS in practice.

Keywords: intelligent tutoring systems, problem solving, algebra, knowledge representation, hypergraph.

1 Introduction

The stage of translating a word problem into equations is particularly difficult when students are introduced in the algebraic way of solving word problems [1-2]. Many interactive learning environments have been developed to support the resolution of word problems. However, none of these systems has been able to analyse the student's interaction and use the results of the analysis to simultaneously: supervise the complete resolution of an algebra-based word problem, provide meaningful feedback and make tutoring decisions. For example, *MathCAL* [3] is only able to handle typical arithmetical problems. *Ms Lindquist* [4] is capable of supervising the construction of algebraic expressions, but it is not able to guide the algebraic resolution of a problem. *PAT* [5] allows the algebraic resolution of a problem, but imposes restrictions on the equations format.

In this paper, we present an Intelligent Tutoring System (ITS) that uses a domain-specific knowledge representation mechanism which makes it possible to represent all potential solutions of a word problem, without making any assumption on the resolution path that a student may follow in the resolution process. This knowledge representation mechanism uses a description language based on trinomial graphs, as described by Fridman [6]. Trinomial graphs were initially used as an abstract notation

K. Yacef et al. (Eds.): AIED 2013, LNAI 7926, pp. 512–521, 2013.

to describe relations between quantities in word problems. However, we have implemented a reasoning engine that is able to work on this representation. This has made it possible to build an ITS that is able to track the student's action and provides automatic feedback according to the current state of the resolution process.

The major contribution presented in this paper is the use of a domain specific approach for word problem knowledge representation. The use of domain specific approaches has also been applied to other ITS in different application fields e.g. [7]. Most existing methods are based on general architectures to represent domain knowledge. These are the constraint based approach [8] and the model tracing method, which is based on ACT-R cognitive architectures [9]. In the former, knowledge is represented as a set of constraints that the problem solution must satisfy. The latter represents domain knowledge as a set of production rules that are used by a model tracer module to determine whether a sequence of rule executions matching the student's input exists.

The description language presented in this paper constitutes a powerful and more flexible mechanism than other more general alternative knowledge representation approaches to: a) represent the expert's knowledge on the solution for a word problem; b) track the student's actions and represent the current state of the student's solution; and c) provide automatic feedback to a student input. This allows a straight forward construction of an ITS with an inner loop [10]. The key issue is the minimization of the declarative knowledge linked to a problem that the specific representation permits.

The remainder of the paper is organized as follows. Section 2 outlines the aims and philosophy of the application. The description language used for knowledge representation is described in Section 3. Next, section 4 explains how student inputs are processed by the ITS; section 5 presents an automatic problem solver module; and section 6 describes the Graphical User Interface (GUI). Then, section 7 describes an empirical study that confirms its educational potential. Finally, in Section 8 some conclusions are drawn and further work is briefly explained.

2 Aims and Philosophy

The ITS presented in this paper focuses on the translation stage of the problem solving process. The usual steps involved are part of the Cartesian method generally used in algebraic word problem solving [1]. Briefly, this consists of: (a) identifying the appropriate unknown quantities and the existing relations between them and other known quantities or previously determined ones and (b) expressing a set of n equations with n unknowns. Less attention is paid to the algebraic manipulation of the symbolic expressions, which are automatically done by the ITS without requiring the student's intervention.

3 Expert Knowledge Representation

While common graphs are limited to modeling binary relations or other relations that can ultimately be reduced to binary form, hypergraphs are able to represent n-ary relations, by having edges ("hyperedges", but we will use the more usual word "edge" instead) that may connect any number of vertices. When all edges have n vertices the hypergraph is called an n-uniform hypergraph.

Algebraic knowledge on a word problem can easily be represented as a function of known quantities, unknown quantities and relations between them. In fact, Fridman [6] showed that the structure of the solution of a given word problem can be expressed as a set of interconnected ternary relations by trinomial graphs. A trinomial graph extends the concept of a 3-uniform hypergraph, allowing for the distinction between known and unknown elements by using a different representation for each. In particular, known quantities are represented by dark circles, unknowns by clear ones, and ternary relations are represented by arcs that pass by the three vertices involved. Moreover, in a trinomial graph there is at least one unknown element in each edge and relations are linked between them by at least one unknown quantity. This is the basis for the knowledge representation mechanism showed in this paper to represent the structure of the solution.

To be able to represent n-ary relations among quantities univocally and explicitly, we have extended Fridman's notation based on trinomial graphs. For example, edges with just two vertices to account for the binary relation of equality, or edges with n vertices linked to represent the additive conceptual scheme that describes the relation whole/parts. As an example, the structure of the solution for the word problem "Louis, John and Robert earned 960 € for painting a house. As they did not work the same time, Louis received 24 € less than John and the tenth part of what Robert earned. How much did each one earn?" could be represented by the hypergraph in Fig. 1. The nodes with the labels *Ml*, *Mj* and *Mr* represent the money earned by Louis, John and Robert, respectively. The straight horizontal edge represents the existing relation between these quantities and the total of money ($960 = Ml + Mj + Mr$). The lower edge represents the relation between the money earned by Louis and John ($Ml = Mj - 24$). The upper edge represents the relation between the money earned by Louis and Robert ($Ml = Mr/10$). To identify the quantity at the left side of the relation, directed edges are used. To indicate the operator that relates the variables, a label is added at the side of the arrow used to indicate the direction of the edge. This extended notation of Fridman's trinomial graph allows the construction of a reasoning engine that is able to track the student actions and produce automatic remediation, as described in section 4.

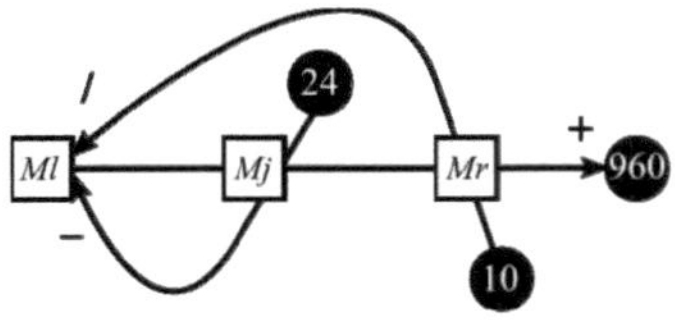

Fig. 1. Problem structure using hypergraphs

4 Tracking of Student Actions

During the tutoring process, the student's inputs need to be checked for correctness. This analysis requires the collaboration between two major components. On the one hand, the knowledge base stores the current state of the resolution process for the word problem at hand. In addition, this module records all previous mistakes made by the student. On the other hand, a reasoning engine updates the knowledge base and provides automatic feedback, according to the student's inputs received from the GUI.

When a problem is loaded into the user interface, the hypergraph is imported from the problems database into the knowledge base. In addition, a value field is created for each node and only nodes with a value are considered defined quantities. Initially, this field is only filled up for numeric (known) values, with the same value as its corresponding label. All other nodes are not assigned a value. However, this value may be defined as specified in section 6, by using the GUI component to either assign it a symbol or an algebraic expression. The hypergraph then evolves according to the actions taken by the student to allow for an adequate supervision of the problem resolution. To this end, every action is processed by an inference engine, which updates the hypergraph so that it always represents the current stage of the resolution process. This is done according to the following rules:

1) The definition of a quantity by using a symbol is always accepted as valid, and the corresponding node is immediately marked as defined. In addition, the value of the node is filled with the symbol.
2) If a quantity is defined by using an expression, the validity of the expression needs to be tested. To this end, all different edges in the hypergraph with exactly one undefined quantity are visited. For each such edge, the reasoning engine determines whether the known quantities are the same as those in the expression. If this is the case, the correctness of the operator and the order of the operands are validated against the information contained in the edge. If they are correct, the undefined node in the edge becomes defined by taking the user's expression as its value. In addition, the current state of the resolution process is updated by removing the edge from the graph. Otherwise, automatic feedback can easily be provided. If all edges are visited and no such edge is found, the quantities in the expression introduced by the student are not related. This algorithm is illustrated in the form of a flowchart in Fig. 2.
3) Another way to remove an edge from a hypergraph is by defining an equation. The construction of an equation implies using a non-visited relation in which all vertices have already been defined. In this case, the student's expression is checked against the remaining edges that do not have any light vertex, accepting it and removing the edge from the hypergraph only if it matches one. Again, if the quantities are related, but either the operator used or the position of the operands were incorrect, automatic, feedback can easily be generated. The resolution process is only considered ended when all edges have been treated and hence removed from the hypergraph.

This type of processing allows the student to take any valid path that yields a correct solution, without imposing any restrictions on neither the number of symbols/equations used nor the order of the actions taken to translate the problem into equations. No system intervention occurs unless an incorrect input is processed by the engine. When this happens, the student's incorrect input is stored for final reporting purposes. In addition, the system supports multiple hypergraphs for the same problem, by maintaining multiple concurrent instances of the knowledge base.

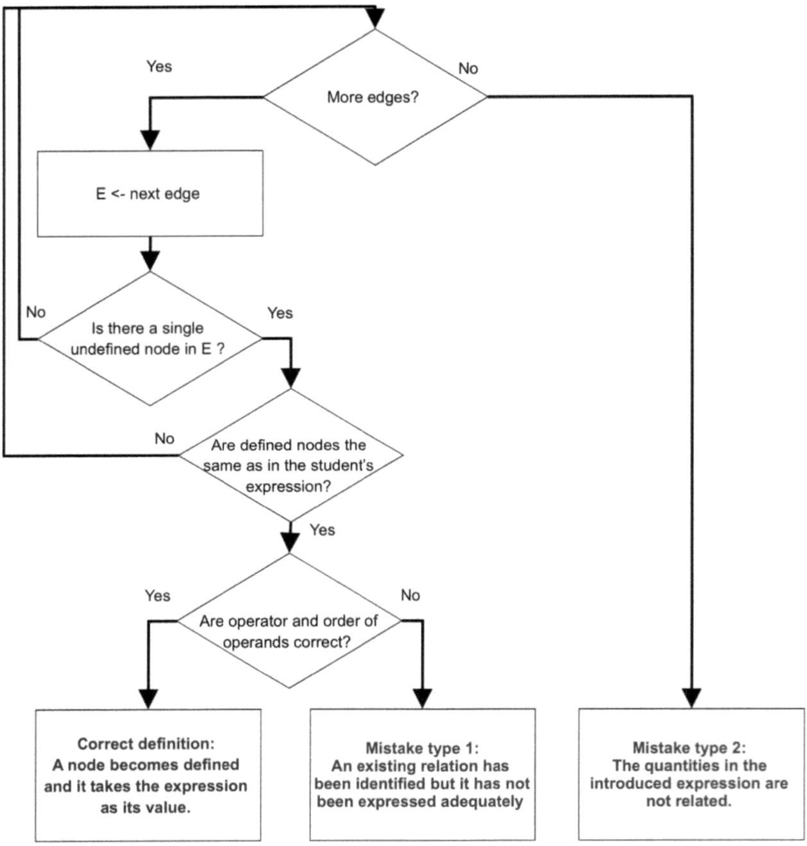

Fig. 2. Flowchart of the algorithm that processes the expressions introduced by a student

5 Problem Solver

The same principles have been applied to construct a problem solver module that is able to automatically work out a solution from the corresponding hypergraph stored in the problem database. In this case, the problem solver is responsible for defining the quantities according to a deterministic and systematic approach that permits to express the word problem as a set of n equations with n unknowns.

The edges with exactly one undefined node can directly be solved, by defining the remaining node. The value that results from introducing the value fields of the already defined nodes in the relation represented in the edge is assigned to the undefined node. Then, the edge is removed from the hypergraph. The algorithm works by iteratively exploring the hypergraph for this type of edges. If no such edges exist and undefined nodes are still present in the graph, the edge with the highest number of defined nodes is selected. A random choice is taken if there is a draw between several edges. Then, a symbol is assigned to the value field of one undefined node that belongs to the edge, and the iterative process continues. Once all nodes have been defined, the remaining edges (if any) give raise to the final system of equations. Each edge defines an equation that is set up by assigning two value fields to any of its nodes: a value defined previously and a value obtained by applying the relation in the concerned remaining edge.

****** STEP 1 ****** **Defining letter x to Money earned by Louis (*Ml*)**	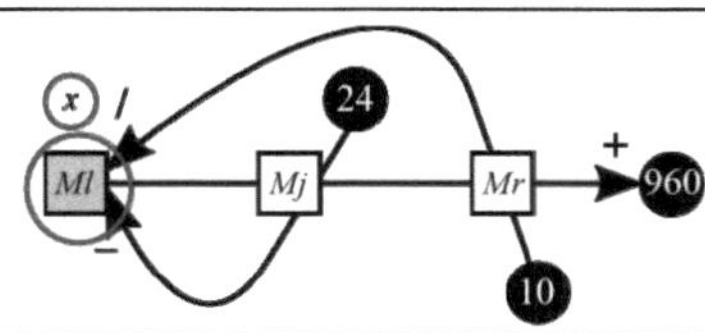
****** STEP 2 ****** **Using expression *Ml* = *Mj*-24 with 1 unknowns** **Known values after using expression:** **x-> Money earned by Louis (*Ml*)** **x+24-> Money earned by John (*Mj*)**	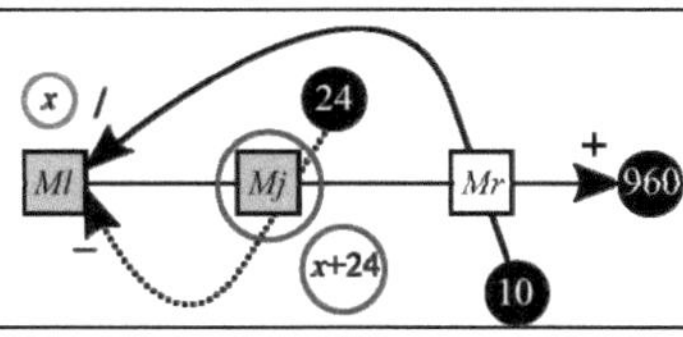
****** STEP 3 ****** **Using expression *Ml* = *Mr*/10 with 1 unknowns** **Known values after using expression:** **x-> Money earned by Louis (*Ml*)** **x+24-> Money earned by John (*Mj*)** **x*10-> Money earned by Robert (*Mr*)**	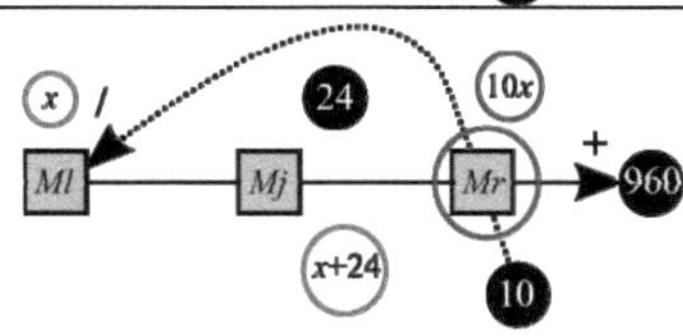
-- **---- FINAL PROBLEM RESULT ----** **--** **x-> Money earned by Louis (*Ml*)** **x+24-> Money earned by John (*Mj*)** **x*10-> Money earned by Robert (*Mr*)** **Finding problem solution requires solving** **960=x+x+24+x*10**	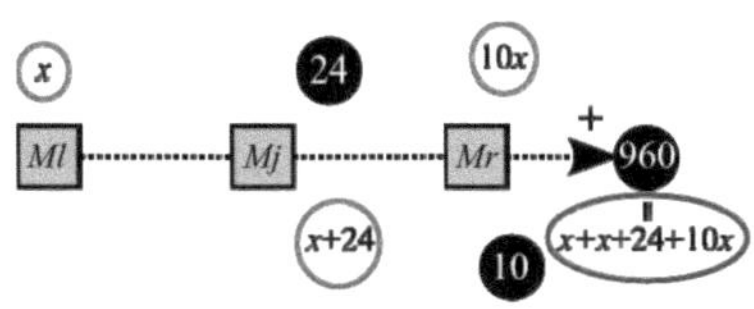

Fig. 3. Step by a step resolution by the problem solver

Fig. 3 shows a tracing of how the problem solver algorithm would work given the example represented by the hypergraph shown in Fig. 1. The program output is shown on the left. On the right, the knowledge base just before taking each action is displayed. At step 1, the automatic solver does not find any edge with just one undefined node and thus defines one by using a symbol. Any of the three undefined nodes would have been a valid alternative. Then, the solver selects one of the two edges with two defined nodes, and uses it to give value to the undefined node in that edge. This same process is repeated with the other edge, until all nodes become defined. Finally, the remaining edge gives rise to the final equation that defines the problem solution.

Note that this implementation can easily be adapted to generate all multiple paths that a user could adopt to solve the word problem, by replacing the choice of the next node to be defined by a backtracking approach to explore the entire solution space.

6 The Graphical User Interface

The graphical user interface has been carefully designed to facilitate the learning of the algebraic approach to problem solving, focusing on the translation of the problem statement into equations (a more detailed description can be found in [11-12]). With the aim of forcing a structured resolution, quantities need first be defined before they are used as part of a relation. To implement this restriction, the student is not allowed to type the expressions directly. Instead, these are built by using a calculator-like graphical component that contains a button for each arithmetic operator and one more for each quantity that has already been defined.

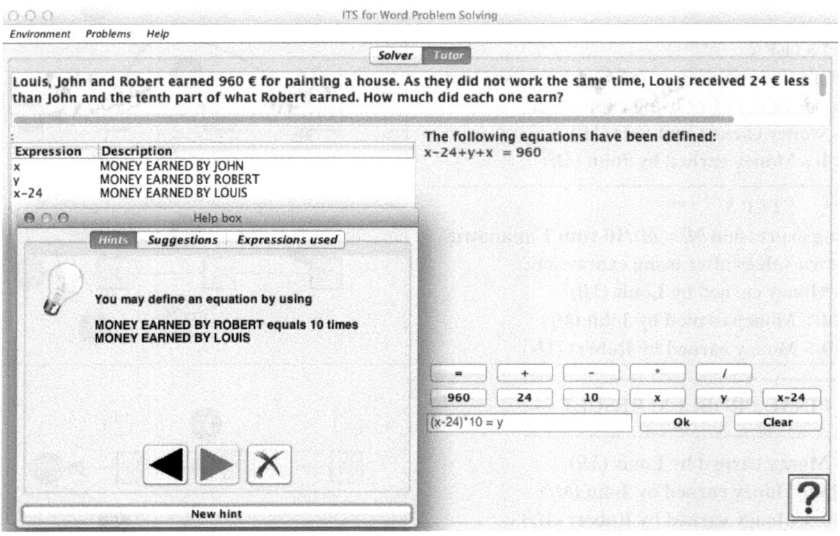

Fig. 4. A screenshot of the GUI

Fig. 4 shows a screenshot of the GUI. At the top of the screen, the statement for the word problem is displayed. The bottom part appears divided into two sections. The left side is used to define new quantities, either by using a letter (symbol) or as a function of other quantities that have been previously defined. To visually help identifying previously defined quantities, these are displayed on a table that includes both their values and the descriptions assigned by the student. Each time that a new quantity is defined, a new entry is added to the table and a new button is created so that the new quantity may be used to define another one or to build an equation as part of the problem solution. Equations are built by using the calculator on the right side panel that contains the equal symbol and the same buttons as the component used to define new quantities in terms of previously defined quantities.

The user may request hints by pressing on the question mark button placed at the bottom right hand side corner of the GUI. In this case, the system uses the problem solver module and offers the next action as a suggestion. Help is offered in a progressive way. On a first request, the system makes an attempt to get the user focused on the particular stage of the resolution process. In the situation depicted in Fig. 4, this first message would suggest the user sets an equation. If further help was requested, a second message with specific instructions to perform the task would be generated. By using the problem solver engine, both the problem's constraints and the state of the resolution are taken into account. Fig. 4 shows a floating window with an example message that includes specific instructions for a potential next action.

7 Evaluation

To judge on the success of the tutoring system as a tool to learn the process of solving word problems an experimental study has been devised. A group of 36 students of a Bachelor Education degree at a public university in Spain was randomly divided into a control and an experimental group. They belonged to two natural groups of a subject that has the aim to deliver a sufficient level in mathematics to allow them to teach in primary education. The aim was to determine whether the use of the ITS helped in gaining competence on algebraic problem solving.

The experiment was run over five lecture sessions. In the first session (100 minutes), the students in both groups had to solve on paper a collection of 10 word problems that were characterized by being usually solved in the algebraic way (pre-test). At the beginning of the second session, two different problems from the ones that had been used so far were solved in order to instruct the students in the use of the ITS. This demonstration, which lasted 30 minutes, was carried out for both the experimental and control group in order to avoid any possible bias. For the rest of the session and the two following ones (sessions second, third and fourth), which lasted 60 minutes each, the students were given five problems per session. The students in the control group were asked to solve the problems on paper, without any external help. The students in the experimental group were asked to solve them using the ITS. During the fifth and last session (100 minutes), students were handed a second test (post-test) consisting of 10 problems with mathematical structures that were isomorph to the ones in the pre-test. Each participant was assigned a score in the pre-test and the post-test, according to the number of problems that had been set out correctly at each stage.

Table 1. Differences between groups and testing times in the scores obtained by the students. CG = Control group; EG = Experimental group. Data are expressed as mean (SD).

	Pre-test results	**Post-test results**
CG (n=18)	4.33 (2.03)	4.78 (2.18)
EG (n=18)	4.00 (2.74)	6.06 (2.51)

For evaluation purposes, all variables were checked for normality (K-S normality test) and homoscedasticity (Levene's test). Standard statistical methods were used to obtain the mean as a measurement of the central trend and the standard deviation (SD) as a measurement of dispersion (see Table 1). A mixed model [group (2; control and experimental) x type of test (2; pre and post-test)] ANOVA was performed to determine the effect of the new software in the scores obtained by the students (dependent variable). Post-hoc analyses with Bonferroni correction were applied in the case of significant main or interaction effects. The ANOVA showed a main effect of the testing time (pre-test and post-test) in the scores ($F(1,34) = 30.17$, $p<.001$), as well as an interaction effect of the testing time and group on the tests scores ($F(1,34)=12.53$, $p=.001$). In the control group, significant differences between the pre and post tests were not found ($F(1,34)=1.91$, $p=.176$). However, the experimental group significantly improved its score in the post-test ($F(1,34)=40.79$, $p<.001$), which would imply that the practice would have meant a significant effect only in the group which had used the ITS.

8 Conclusions and Future Work

In this paper, a novel knowledge representation approach to support ITSs for the learning of algebra has been presented. This knowledge representation has been used to build an ITS to train students on the translation of word problems into algebraic language. Most existing applications with a similar purpose use general approaches. The use of more specific representations that exploit specific domain particularities may result in additional benefits. In this particular case, the use of a description language based on hypergraphs permits to separate the declarative knowledge from the procedural one necessary to solve a problem. The procedural knowledge needed to solve a problem algebraically as well as the tutoring actions are embedded in the program. The independence between procedural and declarative knowledge permits the ITS to admit the incorporation of new problems without the need of being reprogrammed. Moreover, it provides a) greater simplicity to model all different algebraic solutions to a given word problem; and b) higher flexibility to provide automatic feedback based on a simple analysis of the student's input. In addition, the existence of a problem solver based on the same description language facilitates solution modeling by the expert.

Results from the empirical study highlight that when recreating a solo work situation without human tutoring, the use of the ITS produces a significant increase in the number of correct resolutions when, after the practice, word problems are solved in the algebraic way.

Currently, the student selects the word problem from a drop down menu in the GUI, according to the teacher's instructions. As a next step, we are working on a problem selection module to allow the system to make this selection automatically, according to the student progress and the type of mistakes previously made. We are also working on the implementation of a knowledge base acquisition tool to facilitate the introduction of knowledge by the expert. This is a common component in most expert systems and in this case would consist of an intuitive graphical tool to guide the construction of the trinomial graphs required by the reasoning engine.

Acknowledgements. This work has been partly supported by the Spanish Ministry of Economy and Competitiveness through projects EDU2012-35638 and TIN2011-29221-C03-02; by the Vicerrectorado de Convergencia Europea y Calidad of the University of Valencia, through projects DocenTIC UV-SFPIE_DOCE12-81047 and Finestra Oberta UV-SFPIE FO12-80215; and by the Vicerrectorado de Investigación of the University of Valencia through project UV-INV-PRECOMP12-80109.

References

1. Filloy, E., Rojano, T., Puig, L.: Educational Algebra. A Theoretical and Empirical Approach. Springer, New York (2008)
2. Croteau, E.A., Heffernan, N.T., Koedinger, K.R.: Why are Algebra Word Problems Difficult? Using Tutorial Log Files and the Power Law of Learning to Select the Best Fitting Cognitive Model. In: Lester, J.C., Vicari, R.M., Paraguaçu, F. (eds.) ITS 2004. LNCS, vol. 3220, pp. 240–250. Springer, Heidelberg (2004)
3. Chang, K.E., Sung, Y.T., Lin, S.F.: Computer-assisted learning for mathematical problem solving. Computers & Education 46(2), 140–151 (2006)
4. Heffernan, N.T., Koedinger, K.R.: Intelligent Tutoring Systems are Missing the Tutor: Building a More Strategic Dialog-Based Tutor. In: Rose, C.P., Freedman, R. (eds.) Building Dialogue Systems for Tutorial Applications, Papers of the 2000 AAAI Fall Symposium, pp. 14–19. AAAI Press, Menlo Park (2000)
5. Koedinger, K.R., Anderson, J.R.: Illustrating Principled Design: The Early Evolution of a Cognitive Tutor for Algebra Symbolization. Interactive Learning Environments 5(1), 161–179 (1998)
6. Fridman, L.M.: Los grafos trinomiales como metalenguaje de los problemas. Matemáticas. Revista del Departamento de Matemáticas de la Universidad de Sonora 17-18, 51–59 (1990)
7. Do, N., Pham, T.-L.: Knowledge representation and algorithms for automatic solving integral problems. In: Proc. 6th Int. Computer Science & Education (ICCSE), pp. 730–735 (2011)
8. Mitrovic, A., Martin, B., Suraweera, P.: Intelligent tutors for all: the constraint based approach. IEEE Intelligent Systems 22(4), 38–45 (2007)
9. Anderson, J.R., Bothell, D., Byrne, M.D., Douglass, S., Lebiere, C., Qin, Y.: An integrated theory of the mind. Psychological Review 111(4), 1036–1060 (2004)
10. VanLehn, K.: The behavior of tutoring systems. International Journal of Artificial Intelligence in Education 16(3), 227–265 (2006)
11. Arevalillo-Herráez, M., Arnau, D., González-Calero, J.A., Ayesh, A.: Domain specific knowledge Representation for an Intelligent Tutoring System to Teach Algebraic Reasoning. In: Cerri, S.A., Clancey, W.J., Papadourakis, G., Panourgia, K. (eds.) ITS 2012. LNCS, vol. 7315, pp. 630–631. Springer, Heidelberg (2012)
12. Arnau, D., Arevalillo-Herráez, M., Puig, L., González-Calero, J.A.: Fundamentals of the design and the operation of an intelligent tutoring system for the learning of the arithmetical and algebraic way of solving word problems. Computers & Education 63, 119–130 (2013)

Learner Differences and Hint Content

Ilya M. Goldin[1] and Ryan Carlson[2]

[1] Human-Computer Interaction Institute, Carnegie Mellon University, Pittsburgh, USA
goldin@cmu.edu
[2] Language Technologies Institute, Carnegie Mellon University, Pittsburgh, USA
ryancarlson@cmu.edu

Abstract. Because feedback affects learning, it is central to many educational technologies. We analyze properties of hint feedback in an intelligent tutoring system for high school geometry. First, we examine whether feedback content or feedback sequence is a better predictor of student performance after feedback. Second, we investigate whether linguistic features of hints affect performance. We find that students respond to different hint types differently even after accounting for student proficiency, skill difficulty, and prior practice. We also find that hint content, but not linguistic features affects performance. The findings suggest that tutoring system developers should focus on individual learner differences and feedback content.

1 Introduction

Feedback plays a key role in learning. Formative feedback helps students understand their present level of performance, the level of performance they should target, and how they can rise to the target level [1, 2]. As a consequence, feedback is implemented in many kinds of educational technologies, including directive intelligent tutoring systems (ITS), exploratory environments such as simulations, and educational games.

As system designers, we hope to develop feedback techniques that are effective for all learners. Otherwise, we would either need to accept that our systems are effective for some students only, or we would have to develop technologies that adapt to learner differences. Indeed, some feedback techniques can be implemented broadly, such as goal-setting feedback (which reminds students of the problem objective) and condition-violation feedback (which points out when a student applies a rule inappropriately) [3]. Hints in an ITS are a kind of feedback; because learners may differ in what they know, contingent tutoring varies hint specificity according to estimated student mastery of the target skill [4]. Nonetheless, after taking into account student mastery (as well as skill difficulty and history of successful and unsuccessful prior practice), students may still differ in how likely they are to respond correctly after different types of hints [5]. Students also differ metacognitively, such as in tendency to seek hints rather than respond incorrectly [4, 6], and their errors in hint-seeking [7, 8].

Our broad aim is to understand why hints may be less effective for some students than others, and if adaptation to student differences is necessary. Student mastery, skill difficulty and history of prior practice may affect success after hints, and effectiveness of

K. Yacef et al. (Eds.): AIED 2013, LNAI 7926, pp. 522–531, 2013.

hints in different positions in a hint sequence may differ across students [5]. We examine whether hint content bears on hint effectiveness more so than position in a sequence. Because hints are often expressed as texts, we also examine whether linguistic properties influence hint effectiveness. Our method is to mine log data of an ITS for geometry. We build models that predict performance after feedback to ask whether including features of hint content and linguistic properties improves predictive accuracy. (Learning after hints is arguably more important than performance [9], but learning is unlikely if a hint is not helpful.) Thus, we build successively more comprehensive models so that we do not falsely claim that students differ, and that we do not propose building adaptive technologies that are not truly needed.

Our first contribution is to build more comprehensive models, i.e., models that improve on prior work in being conservative about a claim of individual differences among learners. We also discuss a lesson learned from this experience in log data analysis, which is a prominent methodology in this age of "big data". Specifically, prior work [5] categorized hints based on the position of each hint in an ordered hint sequence. Hint position is an automatically generated indicator that only correlates in part with feedback content. Instead, we manually categorize the hint messages before fitting statistical models. To be conservative about the claim of individual differences, we posit three hypotheses that could plausibly explain away prior findings:

1. Recategorizing hints based on content rather than categorizing based on the position of a hint in a hint sequence will improve models' predictive power.
2. Recategorizing will account for the prior finding of differential effectiveness of various types of hints, which was due to the position-based indicator. Allowing for individual differences will not improve prediction of student performance.
3. Barring (2), the prior finding was due not to differences among learners but to variability in the hint wording across a variety of problems. Allowing for more distinct hint types will predict performance just as well as allowing for learner differences.

Second, we compare the effect of feedback on performance with a baseline of unaided performance. In our dataset, hints are delivered on a student's request. Rather than requesting a hint after an error, a student may try to solve the problem again. Such unaided (no-hint) attempts may lead to good performance on their own, e.g., if students accidentally make mistakes and know how to correct a "slip," or if they take the opportunity to reflect. Relatively long attempts, potentially signifying reflection, have been positively associated with learning outcomes [10]. However, reflection is possible in the presence of feedback, not just in its absence. We hypothesize:

4. The information contained in hints will help a student make progress on a problem more effectively than attempting the problem without a hint.

Third, because students can only use hints that they can comprehend, we identify features of hint texts that may affect learner performance: hint readability [11, 12] and idea density [13]. This investigation can improve our understanding of (4) and can suggest what to modify to improve tutoring systems. We hypothesize:

5. Incorporating linguistic features of hints will improve models' predictive power beyond the above features and interactions.

Below, we address data and models, followed by results, discussion, and future work.

2 Methods

We fit models of hint effectiveness to a dataset of 51 9th grade students using the Geometry Cognitive Tutor ITS as part of regular instruction (about twice a week for five weeks) [14]. The students worked through 170 geometry problems, consisting of 1666 problem steps. Each student only saw a subset of the 170 problems.

In this ITS a student may make multiple attempts to complete a problem step. Completing a step requires a correct response; giving a correct response on the first attempt means that this student will never see a hint. On each attempt, a student may supply a correct answer, an incorrect answer, or may ask for a hint.

2.1 Hint Types

Most problem steps are supported by sequences of three levels of hints. Hint sequences are meant to guide the student to the answer and to provide multiple opportunities to retrieve appropriate principles. In this tutoring system, hints were designed such that first-level hints generally point to relevant features of the problem and define key terms, e.g., "In this problem, you have triangle ABC. You know the measure of two of the angles in this triangle, namely, angles DAB and BCD." Second-level hints state geometry principles using terminology consistent with the first hint and often tie them back into the problem, e.g., "The sum of the measures of the interior angles of a triangle is 180 degrees." Third-level hints are "bottom-out" hints that provide the answer so that even a student who cannot solve the problem can progress through the tutoring process, e.g., "m∠ABC = 180 - m∠DAB - m∠BCD."

For each hint that GCT displays, it logs the hint's position in the hint sequence, e.g., "2 of 3" for the second of three hints. In general, hint position constitutes an automatic indicator of hint content because hint sequences are similar by design, but some hint sequences violate the "features, principle, bottom-out" design pattern. For example, there are sequences of just one hint, e.g., "Some useful information is highlighted in the problem statement", with associated on-screen highlighting. Being the only hint in a sequence, this hint would have hint position of 1, but since it points to known quantities, it is more appropriately thought of as a "bottom-out" level-3 hint. We also identified four-hint sequences in which two hints pointed out problem features. We manually recoded hints according to their content (features, principle, or bottom-out) rather than their position in the sequence.

To facilitate hint-type recoding, we created hint templates that removed problem-specific references in the hint text, eliminating spurious distinctions between different hints. For example, we converted hint "m∠ABC=90–m∠DEF" to template "#Angle1=#Num–#Angle2". This particular template summarized over 70 distinct texts, which were shown to learners over 400 times. Thus, generalizing across hint texts, such as by substituting placeholders for angle names and measures and collapsing semantically equivalent phrases, allowed us to recode hint types and extract new features (sec 2.2) efficiently. In effect, each template served as a conjecture that all matching hint texts were equally effective. In all, over 6000 distinct hint texts were collapsed to 117 hint templates. Both authors coded all templates, and came to agreement on all cases. About one third of the hint texts were recategorized. (Nonetheless, we did not manipulate order of hints in an experiment, so our analysis of hint-type differences is correlational, not causal.)

2.2 Linguistic Features of Hints

Linguistic aspects of hint texts may influence how students comprehend all types of hints, potentially affecting performance. For instance, textbook authors often target specific reading levels and consider readability metrics to help calibrate their texts. We consider three linguistic measures to investigate Hypothesis (5), described above: propositional idea density, Flesch Reading Ease, and Coh-Metrix L2 Reading Index.

Propositional idea density, computed using CPIDR [15], uses part of speech tagging to count the verbs, adjectives, adverbs, prepositions, and conjunctions in a text. The algorithm then computes the fraction of these words out of the total number of words. This provides a rough tally of ideas in a text. We expect hints with high idea density to be more difficult to understand [13], which should hurt performance.

Flesch Reading Ease is based on the number of sentences (S), words (W), and syllables (Y) in a text [11]. Higher values indicate easier-to-read texts.

$$\mathbf{FleschReadingEase} = 206.835 - \left(1.015 \times \frac{W}{S}\right) - \left(84.6 \times \frac{Y}{W}\right)$$

Coh-Metrix L2 Reading Index [12] aims to improve on Flesch Reading Ease by using psycholinguistic and cognitive models of reading to ground readability in theory. The Index combines three measures. First, word frequency (F) from the CELEX database is used with the intuition that the most common words are likely easier to understand. Second, a syntax similarity index (T) measures parallel constructions at the phrase and part-of-speech level. Hints containing similar syntactic structures may lower cognitive load on the user, potentially freeing her to think about the content of the hint. Third, content word overlap (C) tracks non-stopwords across sentence boundaries. In hints with two sentences, for example, the second often introduces few new concepts, instead referring back to concepts from the first, which may make that second sentence easier to read. Higher values indicate easier-to-read texts.

$$\mathbf{CohMetrixReadingIndex} = -45.032 + (22.2 \times F) + (61.3 \times T) + (52.2 \times C)$$

2.3 Models

To gauge hint effectiveness, our models predict whether a student will answer a problem correctly with and without feedback. To this end, the models include the unique ID of each student, the relevant knowledge components (KCs) for the problem step, linguistic features about the feedback text (Sec. 2.2), the quantity of prior successes and failures, and the attempt type. The attempt type indicates whether the student's attempt on a step follows directly after a particular kind of hint, after a first incorrect attempt, or after a second incorrect attempt. Given this, the model-fitting procedure estimates parameter values that represent the significance of each of these pieces of information. Formally, the models are multilevel mixed effects logistic regressions.[1]

$$logit(\Pr(Y=1)) = \alpha + \theta_p + \lambda_h + \sum_{j \in KC} (\beta_j + \gamma_j s_{pj} + \rho_j f_{pj})$$

Equation 1: ProfHelp (Proficiency with Help) model

$$logit(\Pr(Y=1)) = \alpha + \theta_p + \lambda_{ph} + \sum_{j \in KC} (\beta_j + \gamma_j s_{pj} + \rho_j f_{pj})$$

Equation 2: ProfHelp-ID (Individual Differences) model

$$logit(\Pr(Y=1)) = \alpha + \theta_p + \lambda_h + \omega_h + \sum_{j \in KC} (\beta_j + \gamma_j s_{pj} + \rho_j f_{pj})$$

Equation 3: ProfHelp-LF (Linguistic Features) model

The ProfHelp model implements the hypothesis that feedback is equally effective for all students; the ProfHelp-ID model implements the hypothesis of individual differences in hint effectiveness across students; the ProfHelp-LF model implements the hypothesis that linguistic features explain hint effectiveness. The ProfHelp-LF-ID model (not shown; includes $\lambda_{ph} + \omega_h$) posits that both individual differences and linguistic features explain hint effectiveness. In the models, $Y = 1$ indicates a correct response by a student on a problem step, and $Y = 0$ indicates an incorrect response or hint request. The probability that a student responds correctly, $\Pr(Y = 1)$, is determined by adding parameters. Parameter α is a global intercept, indicating the average probability of a correct response in these data. The properties of the problem-step to which the student is responding (i.e., the "item" in Item Response Theory) are expressed via intercept β_j, denoting the easiness of the jth knowledge component (KC_j), and via slopes γ_j and ρ_j, the weights on the observed frequency of successful (s_{pj}) and unsuccessful (f_{pj}) prior practice by the same learner p on the same KC_j. The properties of the student are summarized by θ_p, the baseline proficiency for each student p, which is the incremental change in probability of solving each problem-step correctly on a first attempt. Unlike parameters above, θ_p is a partially pooled parameter: to compensate for unbalanced and sparse data per student, each individual student's proficiency is shifted ("shrunk") towards the average of all students.

Relative to these parameters, λ_h in ProfHelp denotes the incremental change in probability of solving a problem-step on an attempt after the first. For example, λ_2 represents the change to probability of success on an attempt directly following a principle-stating hint, and λ_4 on an attempt following one previous incorrect attempt. An analogous

[1] Models were fit using Markov Chain Monte Carlo simulation, as in [5].

interpretation is that λ_h represents average proficiency with level-h hints. ProfHelp-ID extends λ_h into λ_{ph} to generate an individual proficiency estimate for each pupil p and attempt type h. Put another way, ProfHelp-ID fits a main effect of performance after different actions h, such as different kinds of hints or unaided performance, as well as an interaction between pupil p and performance after action h. Similar to θ_p, the λ_{ph} estimates are pooled within the corresponding λ_h. Lacking additional data about learners, we cannot explain their individual differences. Still, if incorporating λ_{ph} should improve model fit, then we can argue that differences exist.

The ProfHelp-LF model aims to *explain* [16] hint effects, rather than only *describe* them via the intercepts λ_h and $\lambda_{p,h}$. This model adds parameter $\boldsymbol{\omega}_h$, a vector of slopes (weights) on the hint properties described under Hint Features above. For ease of interpretation and model stability, all covariates were centered, and the Flesch and Coh-Metrix scores were additionally standardized. This meant that other parameters could be interpreted with reference to a hint text of "average readability", "average idea density" and so forth. Instances not following hints (i.e., first attempts and attempts following incorrects) were coded as having a zero for each hint-property covariate so that $\boldsymbol{\omega}_h$ did not affect those instances.

2.4 Dataset

To fit the models, we created a dataset from the log data. The dataset included an instance for each attempt by a student to solve a problem step if it (1) was the first attempt on a problem step, or (2) directly followed the first time the student saw a hint text on a problem step, or (3) directly followed a first or a second attempt on a problem set that had an incorrect outcome. We omitted 20 instances that used hints that were not meaningful for this study (e.g., "You have completed this problem. Please select Done from the Tutor menu to move to the next problem"). Each instance had features corresponding to student ID, KC ID, prior practice counts, and attempt type.

After recoding and templatizing, the attempt-type feature could take on one of three sets of values: attempts following a hint position, as in the original dataset; attempts following a hint recategorized as feature-pointing, principle-stating, or bottom-out, following the hint design pattern; or attempts following a hint identified by template ID, 1 through 117. Each of these three definitions of attempt-type had two additional levels indicating attempts that followed a first incorrect attempt or a second incorrect attempt. We omitted attempts following further incorrect attempts.

The manual recoding meant that a student's attempts on a problem step sometimes included multiple hint texts that were all assigned the same hint type. Unless a step was terminated early (e.g., due to a software crash), exactly one attempt on a problem step has the outcome of correct. This means that on the recoded dataset, the models were sometimes fit with both positive and negative examples for the same feature vector (i.e., student identifier p, attempt type h, KC identifier j, etc.), implying that they were guaranteed to make incorrect predictions on some instances.

3 Results and Discussion

We tested our hypotheses by fitting multilevel Bayesian models to the data and comparing fits in terms of Deviance Information Criterion (DIC). Similar to Akaike Information Criterion (AIC), DIC estimates what the prediction error would be on held-out data, rewarding models for low deviance (estimated error) but penalizing those with more parameters. This helps us find the most parsimonious model that summarizes the data with the fewest explanatory factors to guard against overfitting. DIC takes into account that in Bayesian models with pooling, the effective number of parameters is itself estimated. (Our informal rule of thumb is that DIC differences of 10 imply a significant model improvement. Because of the scale of the deviance term, it is inappropriate to compare proportion of change from model to model.)

Table 1. Model fit. $DIC = deviance + number\ of\ parameters\ in\ model$ (lower is better)[2].

Model	Hint-Type Indicator	Deviance	Effective Parameters	DIC
ProfHelp	Position	23876	166	24042
ProfHelp	Recategorized	23221	159	23380
ProfHelp	Template	22416	Inf.	Inf.
ProfHelp-ID	**Recategorized**	**22988**	**274**	**23262**
ProfHelp-LF	Recategorized	23320	151	23471
ProfHelp-LF-ID	Recategorized	23092	268	23360

Hypothesis (1) stated that recategorizing hint texts will improve the model's predictive ability over using the position-based indicator. Hypothesis (1) is confirmed. DIC for ProfHelp with the position-based indicator is higher than with the recoded indicator due to a reduction in both deviance (error in predicting student performance) and in the effective number of parameters.

Hypothesis (2) stated that allowing for individual differences in addition to recategorizing will not improve predictive accuracy. Hypothesis (2) is disconfirmed. DIC for ProfHelp-ID with the recoded indicator is lower than for ProfHelp with the recoded indicator due to a reduction in deviance. The increase in effective parameters with ProfHelp-ID is as expected due to the interaction λ_{ph}, which may add about 250 parameters: 51 students × 5 attempt types (attempts after each of 3 hint types, after a first incorrect attempt, and after a second incorrect attempt).

Hypothesis (3) stated that variability in hint effectiveness found in [5] was due not to individual differences but to variability in the hint texts themselves, and that accounting for distinct hint texts will have similar predictive accuracy to allowing for individual differences. Hypothesis (3) is disconfirmed. Because fitting a parameter for each hint text would likely lead to overfitting, the one-per-template hint-type indicator reduced dimensionality by allocating one parameter for each hint template. In fact,

[2] By including attempts after incorrects, DIC values are not comparable to results in [5].

there are only 119 possible parameters λ_h in ProfHelp with the one-per-template indicator (117 templates plus attempts after a first and a second incorrect) compared to over 250 possible levels for λ_{ph} in ProfHelp-ID with recoding. Although the former model has lower deviance than any other, the Bayesian estimate of the effective number of parameters (pD) is infinite in 51 of 200 MCMC samples, implying that the one-per-template indicator overfits the data. Even if hint templates may explain individual differences, ProfHelp-ID describes student performance more parsimoniously.

Hypothesis (4) stated that information contained in hints will help students more effectively than attempting problems without hints. Hypothesis (4) is disconfirmed, but with a caveat. Under ProfHelp-ID, mean posterior λ_h estimates are -2.04, -2.15, and 1.06 logits for attempts after feature-pointing, principle-stating and bottom-out hints, respectively, and -1.02 and -1.38 logits for attempts after one and two incorrect attempts, respectively. Bottom-out hints, which almost always state the answer, unsurprisingly correlate more positively with performance than hints that only lead a student towards an answer. Further, students are more likely, on average, to answer correctly if they try again than if they ask for a hint. The caveat is that these are only correlational, not causal relationships: it is unlikely that hints cause students to answer incorrectly, and more likely that students request hints when they feel they require assistance. Thus, proficiency after incorrects likely represents proficiency on attempts where students reasonably expect that they will succeed.

Hypothesis (5) stated that linguistic features of hints will further improve predictions. Hypothesis (5) is rejected: ProfHelp-LF and ProfHelp-LF-ID perform worse than ProfHelp-ID in terms of both deviance and DIC. Nonetheless, ProfHelp-LF and ProfHelp-LF-ID do arrive at fairly consistent estimates of ω_h. Under ProfHelp-LF-ID, which has lower DIC of these two models, the effect of propositional idea density (-0.72) and the effect of Flesch Reading Ease (0.07) both include 0 in the 95% posterior credible interval, implying that these are not reliable predictors of student performance after a hint. The effect of a one-unit change in the Coh-Metrix Reading Index is -0.20, with 0 outside the 95% CI, implying that hint texts that are more difficult to read have a positive effect on student performance. Average effectiveness of different attempt types λ_h is similar under ProfHelp-LF-ID and ProfHelp-LF-ID.

This analysis has limitations. First, in this dataset, hint sequences always have the same order, so the differential effects of hint types cannot be teased apart. Second, because hints are presented only on request, we cannot measure the effect of help for those students who avoid seeking help when they should [7]. Third, we cannot know if students actually read the hints. Fourth, with no data about students other than anonymous identifiers, we cannot explain their behaviors. While these are limitations of the dataset, not the ProfHelp models, it remains for future work to answer definitively whether a first display of a type of hint is differently effective across students.

4 Conclusion

The chief finding is that we cannot rule out a claim of individual differences in proficiency with hints, despite our conservative approach to allowing the claim. This result depends on a manual coding of hint type because the position-based indicator added noise into our model. Our experience suggests that researchers should use log data cautiously. Further, bottom-out hints correlate more positively with performance than other hints, and feature-pointing and principle-stating hints correlate more negatively than one or even two attempts without hints, but these are likely correlations due to students only asking for hints when really struggling, and not as often as they should.

The findings also suggest that student performance is fairly robust to the complexity and readability of the hint texts. Only one of our three metrics significantly impacted performance: more difficult-to-read hints were more effective. Another interpretation may be that the CohMetrix Reading Index is related to text coherence [12], and learners with high prior knowledge benefit more from low-coherence texts [17], which would imply that the ProfHelp models do not adequately capture prior knowledge. If in fact they do not, that would also explain the finding that viewing hints is less effective than additional attempts without hints because learners with high prior knowledge would outperform the model's prediction on attempts following incorrects. This suggests a path to future investigations and model refinements.

While these findings leave unanswered research questions, they also have implications for the design of educational systems. Even if the effectiveness of feature-pointing and principle-stating hints is underestimated by the ProfHelp models due to the correlations with when and how often students request hints, they may still be not as effective as desired, which suggests a need to redesign these formats. Even though the causes of individual differences with hints require investigation, it is clear that educational technologies need to measure and monitor individual proficiency with different types of feedback, even if only to ensure equitable instruction for all learners. If future research identifies the need for an adaptive, personalized approach to feedback, the ProfHelp-ID model can serve as a component.

Some issues for future work are (1) to replicate the individual differences analysis on other datasets, e.g., from other ITSs and educational technologies; (2) to address the confounds of fixed-order hint presentation and differences in hint-seeking behavior (e.g., by shuffling hints within problem steps and sometimes offering hints proactively); (3) to investigate the relationship between feedback effectiveness and metacognitive and motivational constructs such as help-seeking tendency [6]; and (4) to measure effect of feedback on learning in addition to performance [9].

References

1. Cizek, G.J.: An Introduction to Formative Assessment. In: Andrade, H., Cizek, G.J. (eds.) Handbook of Formative Assessment, pp. 3–17. Routledge, New York (2010)
2. Hattie, J., Timperley, H.: The Power of Feedback. Review of Educational Research 77, 81–112 (2007)
3. McKendree, J.: Effective feedback content for tutoring complex skills. Human-Computer Interaction 5, 381–413 (1990)
4. Wood, H., Wood, D.: Help seeking, learning and contingent tutoring. Computers and Education 33, 153–170 (1999)

5. Goldin, I.M., Koedinger, K.R., Aleven, V.A.W.M.M.: Learner Differences in Hint Processing. In: Yacef, K., Zaïane, O., Hershkovitz, A., Yudelson, M., Stamper, J. (eds.) Proceedings of 5th International Conference on Educational Data Mining, Chania, Greece, pp. 73–80 (2012)
6. Goldin, I.M., Koedinger, K.R., Aleven, V.A.W.M.M.: Hints: You Can't Have Just One. In: Proceedings of 6th International Conference on Educational Data Mining (under review)
7. Aleven, V., Mclaren, B., Roll, I., Koedinger, K.: Toward meta-cognitive tutoring: A model of help seeking with a Cognitive Tutor. International Journal of Artificial Intelligence in Education 16, 101–128 (2006)
8. Roll, I., Aleven, V., McLaren, B.M., Koedinger, K.R.: Improving students' help-seeking skills using metacognitive feedback in an intelligent tutoring system. Learning and Instruction 21, 267–280 (2011)
9. Beck, J.E., Chang, K.-M., Mostow, J., Corbett, A.T.: Does Help Help? Introducing the Bayesian Evaluation and Assessment Methodology. In: Woolf, B.P., Aïmeur, E., Nkambou, R., Lajoie, S. (eds.) ITS 2008. LNCS, vol. 5091, pp. 383–394. Springer, Heidelberg (2008)
10. Shih, B., Koedinger, K., Scheines, R.: Unsupervised discovery of student learning tactics. In: Proceedings of 3rd International Conference on Educational Data Mining (2010)
11. Flesch, R.: A new readability yardstick. Journal of Applied Psychology 32, 221 (1948)
12. Crossley, S., Allen, D.B., Mc-Namara, D.S.: Text readability and intuitive simplification: A comparison of readability formulas. Reading in a Foreign Language 23, 84–101 (2011)
13. Kintsch, W., Keenan, J.: Reading rate and retention as a function of the number of propositions in the base structure of sentences. Cognitive Psychology 5, 257–274 (1973)
14. Salden, R.J.C.M., Aleven, V.A.W.M.M., Renkl, A., Schwonke, R.: Worked Examples and Tutored Problem Solving: Redundant or Synergistic Forms of Support? In: Love, B.C., McRae, K., Sloutsky, V.M. (eds.) Proceedings of the 30th Annual Conference of the Cognitive Science Society. Cognitive Science Society, Austin (2008)
15. Brown, C., Snodgrass, T., Kemper, S.J., Herman, R., Covington, M.A.: Automatic measurement of propositional idea density from part-of-speech tagging. Behavior Research Methods 40, 540–545 (2008)
16. Wilson, M., de Boeck, P.: Descriptive and explanatory item response models. In: de Boeck, P., Wilson, M. (eds.) Explanatory Item Response Models: A Generalized Linear and Nonlinear Approach, pp. 43–74. Springer, New York
17. McNamara, D.S., Kintsch, E., Songer, N.B., Kintsch, W.: Are good texts always better? Interactions of text coherence, background knowledge, and levels of understanding in learning from text. Cognition and Instruction 14, 1–43 (1996)

Guided Skill Practice as an Adaptive Scaffolding Strategy in Open-Ended Learning Environments

James R. Segedy, Gautam Biswas, Emily Feitl Blackstock, and Akailah Jenkins

Institute of Software Integrated Systems, Department of Electrical Engineering and Computer Science, Vanderbilt University, 1025 16th Avenue South, Nashville, TN, 37212, U.S.A.
{james.segedy,gautam.biswas,emily.a.feitl,
akailah.t.jenkins}@vanderbilt.edu

Abstract. While open-ended learning environments (OELEs) offer powerful learning opportunities, many students struggle to learn in them. Without proper support, these learners use system tools incorrectly and adopt suboptimal learning strategies. Typically, OELEs support students by providing hints: suggestions for how to proceed combined with information relevant to the learner's situation. However, students often ignore or fail to understand such hints. To address this problem, we present an alternative approach to supporting students in OELEs that combines suggestions and assertions with guided skill practice. We demonstrate the feasibility of our approach through an experimental study that compares students who receive suggestions, assertions, and guided skill practice to students who receive no such support. Findings indicate that learners who received the scaffolds approached their tasks more systematically.

Keywords: Open-ended learning environment, scaffolds, guided practice.

1 Introduction

Advances in technology have provided learning technology researchers the affordances for designing computer-based learning environments that provide students with opportunities to take part in authentic, complex problem solving tasks. These environments, generally called open-ended learning environments (OELEs) [1-2], are learner-centered; they provide students with a learning context and a set of tools for exploring, hypothesizing, and building solutions to problems. Examples include hypermedia environments and environments for modeling and simulation [3-4].

OELEs place high cognitive demands on learners [2]. To be successful, learners must understand how to execute: (1) cognitive processes for accessing and interpreting information, constructing problem solutions, and assessing constructed solutions; and (2) metacognitive processes for coordinating the use of cognitive processes and reflecting on the outcome of solution assessments. This presents significant challenges to novice learners; they may have neither the proficiency for using the system's tools nor the experience and understanding necessary for explicitly regulating their learning behaviors. Not surprisingly, research has shown that novices often struggle to succeed in OELEs (*e.g.*, [2], [5]). Without adaptive scaffolds, these

K. Yacef et al. (Eds.): AIED 2013, LNAI 7926, pp. 532–541, 2013.

learners tend to use tools incorrectly and adopt suboptimal learning strategies [6-7]. For the purposes of this article, adaptive scaffolds in OELEs refer to actions taken by the learning environment, based on the learner's interactions, intended to support the learner in successfully completing their task [8].

While several OELEs have been developed and used with learners, relatively few provide adaptive scaffolds. Instead, these systems include non-adaptive scaffolded tools (*e.g.*, lists of guiding questions) designed to provide support for learners who choose to use them. Systems that do provide adaptive scaffolds usually do so in the form of hints: suggestions for how to proceed combined with information relevant to the learner's situation. However, researchers have found that learners, perhaps due to misunderstandings or incomplete knowledge, often ignore such hints [1], [9-10], instead continuing to employ sub-optimal learning behaviors. In this paper, we present an alternative approach to adaptive scaffolds in OELEs that combines suggestions and assertions with guided skill practice. We demonstrate the feasibility of our approach through an experimental study that compares students who receive suggestions, assertions, and guided skill practice to students who receive no such support.

2 Background

The importance of adaptive scaffolding in intelligent computer-based learning environments is well-recognized, and several computer-based learning environments incorporate adaptive scaffolds by providing suggestions and making assertions). VanLehn [11], for example, discusses a *Point, Teach, and Bottom-out strategy* for scaffolding in intelligent tutoring systems (ITSs). Pointing hints direct attention to specific problem features, *suggesting* that students consider those features; teaching hints *assert* knowledge components and how to apply them; and bottom-out hints *assert* how to solve the current problem step.

Several OELEs also utilize suggestions and assertions in order to scaffold students. Ecolab [12], for example, is an OELE in which students learn about ecology by building and executing simulations of food chains and food webs. The learning task is broken down into activities of different difficulty levels, and learners are allowed to choose from among these activities. When learners select an activity that the system feels is too easy or too difficult for them, the system suggests a more appropriate activity. It also asserts information in order to help students who incorrectly construct food chains and food webs (*e.g.*, "Caterpillars do not eat thistles"). TheoryBuilder [4], an OELE for learning through model-building, helps learners plan their learning activities by providing a set of guiding questions. The system recognizes specific suboptimal behaviors, such as choosing not to create a plan for how to construct a model, and responds by suggesting alternative approaches (*e.g.*, creating a plan before embarking on the task).

Suggestions and assertions provide learners with information that may allow them to overcome the challenges associated with learning in OELEs. However, research with OELEs has found that students often ignore suggestions and assertions provided by the learning environment. For example, Segedy, Kinnebrew, & Biswas [10] analyzed video data from students using Betty's Brain, finding that 77% of the suggestions and assertions delivered by the system were ignored by students. Similarly, work by Clarebout & Elen [1] found that students working in an OELE followed the system's suggestions only 20% of the time. Finally, work with PrimeClimb [9] used eye tracking to measure how long students spent reading system-delivered suggestions and assertions. Results showed that students fixated on the content for far less than the expected reading time calculated for those hints.

One challenge in relying solely on suggestions and assertions for scaffolding is that it pre-supposes students' ability to understand and take advantage of the information provided in the scaffolds. This is particularly problematic when a scaffold encourages the use of a cognitive skill that the learner is unfamiliar with or unable to perform correctly. For example, an OELE for modeling and simulation may encourage students to compare their simulation of a science process to a written description of that process. This suggestion constitutes a problem for low-ability readers, and their difficulty in reading may lead to frustration.

Such a problem can be dealt with in multiple ways depending on the learning goals for which the system is designed. For example, the goal of most ITSs is to help students develop declarative and procedural understanding of how to solve specific classes of problems. Thus, when students reach an impasse, ITSs use bottom-out hints (as previously described) in order to "essentially [convert] a too-challenging problem step into an annotated example" [13]. This strategy is effective; it provides students with opportunities to study the example and infer procedural information required for solving future problems.

OELEs, on the other hand, expect students to learn by exploring, testing, and developing abilities for explicitly setting goals, establishing plans for achieving goals, monitoring progress toward achieving goals, and using the evaluation of progress in achieving goals to regulate and improve their approach to completing tasks. Additionally, activities within an OELE often focus on learning a particular process or topic (*e.g.*, climate change), and students are expected to learn about that process in addition to learning how to solve complex problems. This last aspect of OELEs makes the bottom-out hint strategy difficult to implement, as it could compromise the system's learning goals by giving away aspects of the domain content.

A more effective scaffolding strategy for OELEs may involve *dynamically modifying* the learning task when learners demonstrate that they are unable to succeed. These modification scaffolds, unlike suggestions and assertions, do not operate by communicating information to the learner; rather, they alter aspects of the learning task itself. In doing so, they seek to maintain the learner's engagement by adapting the task to their needs and abilities. A good example of a computer-based learning environment that employs modification scaffolds is AutoTutor [14], which teaches science topics by posing questions and then holding natural language dialogues with learners as they attempt to answer those questions. When students are unable to answer one of AutoTutor's questions, the system *modifies* the learning task: it breaks down the larger question into a series of smaller questions. To illustrate this process, consider the example AutoTutor-Learner dialogue from [14]; it shows AutoTutor asking a learner the following question: *The sun exerts a gravitational force on the earth as the earth moves in its orbit around the sun. Does the earth pull equally on the sun? Explain why.*

In the example, the learner indicates that she doesn't know the answer, and this prompts AutoTutor to alter the learning task by asking the learner a simpler question: *How does Newton's third law of motion apply to this situation?* Again, the learner cannot answer the question, prompting AutoTutor to ask an even simpler question: *Newton's third law refers to the forces exerted by one body on another _____?* When the learner successfully responds with *body*, AutoTutor continues by posing another question, and this dialogue continues until the learner and AutoTutor co-construct an answer to the original question, with AutoTutor continuing to adjust the learning task based on the needs of the learner.

Few (if any) OELEs employ modifications to scaffold students, and to the best of our knowledge, no empirical studies have examined the effect of modification scaffolds on students' learning activities in OELEs. In this paper, we investigate a specific type of modification scaffold, *guided practice*. Our approach recognizes when students repeatedly fail to take advantage of system hints, and then temporarily modifies the learning task by requiring students to practice the skills targeted by those hints. This paper presents an experiment designed to test the effectiveness of guided practice scaffolds using Betty's Brain [15], an OELE for science learning.

3 Overview of Betty's Brain

The Betty's Brain learning environment [15] presents students with the task of teaching a virtual agent, Betty, about science topics by constructing a causal map that represents relevant science phenomena as a set of entities connected by directed links, which represent causal relations. Once taught, Betty can use the map to answer causal questions and explain those answers. The goal for students using Betty's Brain is to teach Betty a causal map that matches a hidden, expert model of the domain.

The students' learning and teaching tasks are organized around three activities: (1) reading hypertext resources, (2) building the map, and (3) assessing the correctness of the map. The hypertext resources describe the science topic under study (*e.g.*, climate change) by breaking it down into a set of sub-topics. Each sub-topic describes a system or a process (*e.g.*, the greenhouse effect) in terms of entities (*e.g.*, absorbed heat energy) and causal relations among those entities (absorbed heat energy *increases* the average global temperature). As students read, they need to identify causal relations and then explicitly teach those relations to Betty by constructing a causal map.

Learners can assess the quality of their constructed map in two ways. First, they can ask Betty to answer a question. After Betty answers the question, learners can ask Mr. Davis, another pedagogical agent that serves as a mentor, to evaluate her answer. If the portion of the map that Betty uses to answer the question matches the expert model, then Betty's answer is correct. Learners can also have Betty take a quiz on one or all of the sub-topics in the resources. Quiz questions are selected dynamically by comparing Betty's current causal map to the expert map. Since the quiz is designed to reflect the current state of the student's map, a set of questions is chosen (in proportion to the completeness of the map) for which Betty will generate *correct* answers. The rest of the quiz questions produce either *incorrect* or *incomplete* answers.

These answers can be used to infer which causal links are correct and which causal links may need to be revised or removed from the map.

Should learners be unsure of how to proceed in their learning task, they can ask Mr. Davis for help. Mr. Davis responds by asking the learner about what they are trying to do, and he provides information and examples based on learners' responses.

4 Method

The present experimental study tested the effectiveness of incorporating a guided practice scaffold into Betty's Brain. The guided practice scaffold was used in conjunction with suggestions and assertions in a *knowledge construction* (KC) support module, which scaffolded students' understanding of how to construct causal maps by identifying causal relations in the resources. Participants were divided into two treatment groups. The experimental group used a version of Betty's Brain that included the KC support module and a *causal link discovery tutorial* (Figure 1) that they could access at any time. The tutorial allowed students to practice identifying causal relations in text passages and provided correctness feedback after each solution attempt. The control group used a version of Betty's Brain that included neither the support module nor the tutorial. Our hypothesis was that students who worked with the KC support module would gain a better understanding of the skills related to knowledge construction. Thus, we predicted that they would: (1) be more accurate in editing their causal maps, and (2) more often edit their maps based on recent reading activities.

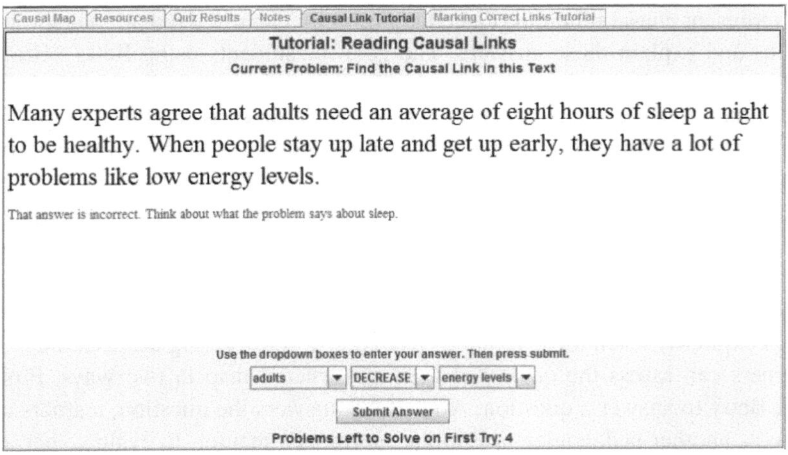

Fig. 1. Causal Link Discovery Tutorial

For students in the experimental group, the KC module activated when three out of a student's last five map edits were incorrect, at which point Mr. Davis informed students that they seemed to be having trouble and offered some suggestions for improving. In addition, Mr. Davis monitored students' activities, offering suggestions and assertions to students when they performed uninformed or shortcut edits. *Uninformed edits* describe causal map edits that are not connected to recent reading activities, and *shortcut edits* refer to adding a link between two concepts that, in the expert map, are connected by a chain of links.

Should students continue to make several incorrect map edits despite the suggestions and assertions from Mr. Davis, the KC module activated a second tier of support: guided practice. During guided practice, students were moved to the causal link tutorial and were not permitted to access any other portion of the program. Students completed the tutorial session once they solved five problems correctly on the first try. At this point, Mr. Davis brought them to the resources activity, highlighted a paragraph, and asked them to identify a causal link from that paragraph. This last step attempted to illustrate the connection between the skill practice and the overall task of teaching Betty. Once they successfully identified a link, the KC support module was deactivated and students were once again allowed to navigate the program freely.

4.1 Participants

Forty-one seventh grade students from four middle Tennessee science classrooms, taught by the same teacher, participated in the study. Because use of Betty's Brain relies on students' ability to independently read and understand the resources, the system is not suited to students with limited English proficiency or cognitive-behavioral problems. Therefore, while all students were encouraged to participate, data from ESL and special education students were not analyzed. We also excluded data from students who missed more than two class periods. The final sample included 20 students in the experimental group and 15 students in the control group.

4.2 Topic Unit and Text Resources

Students used Betty's Brain to learn about climate change. The expert map (Figure 2) contained 22 concepts and 25 links representing the greenhouse effect, human activities affecting the global climate, and impacts on climate. The resources were organized into one introductory page, three pages covering the greenhouse effect, four pages covering human activities, and two pages covering impacts on climate. Additionally, a dictionary section defined key terms contained in the resources. The text was 4,188 words with a Flesch-Kincaid reading grade level of 8.4.

4.3 Learning and Performance Assessments

Learning was assessed using a pre-post test design. Each test consisted of five questions that asked students to consider a given scenario and explain its causal impact on climate change (*e.g.*, explain how an increase in carpooling would affect the amount of carbon dioxide in the air). Scoring was based on the causal relations students used to explain their answers. These relations were compared to the causal relations that would be used to derive the answer from the expert map. For each expert causal link, learners either received 0 points (if they did not use the link), 1 point (if they did use the link, or half of a point (if they used a link that was related to the expert link;

e.g., fossil fuel use increases pollution instead of carbon dioxide). The maximum combined score for the five questions was 16. Two coders independently scored a subset of the written tests with at least 85% agreement, at which point they split and individually scored the remainder of the tests.

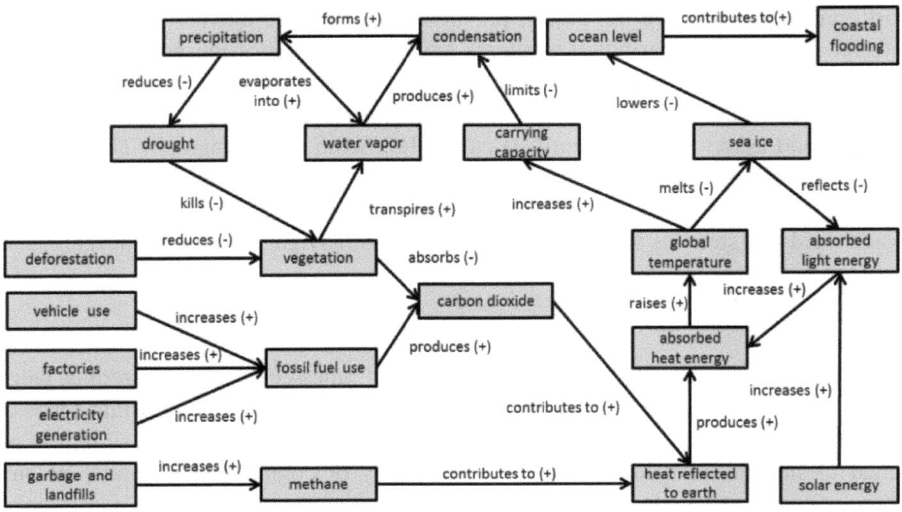

Fig. 2. Climate Change Expert Map

Performance was assessed by analyzing the knowledge construction activities students employed while using Betty's Brain. For each student, we calculated a measure of *map edit effectiveness* and four measures of *map edit support*. Map edit effectiveness was calculated as the percentage of causal link additions, removals, and modifications that improved the quality of Betty's causal map, where causal map quality is defined as the number of correct links minus the number of incorrect links in the map. Map edit support was defined as the percentage of causal map edits that were *supported* by previous resource accesses. An edit was "supported" if students had previously accessed pages in the resources that discuss the concepts connected by the manipulated link. A further constraint was added: an action could only support another action if both actions occurred within the same time window, and we calculated support in relation to four time windows: 10, 5, 3, and 2 minutes.

4.4 Procedure

Study duration was 9 school days. During the first 60-minute class period, students completed the pre-test. During the second and third class periods, researchers introduced students to causal modeling, reasoning with causal models, and identifying causal relations in text passages. During the fourth class period, students were introduced to the system. Students in each treatment group then spent four class periods using their respective versions of Betty's Brain with minimal intervention by the teachers and the researchers. On the ninth day, students completed the post-test.

5 Results

Results of the pre-post tests are displayed in Table 1. A repeated measures ANOVA performed on the data revealed a significant effect of time ($F = 9.541$, $p < 0.01$). However, the analysis failed to reveal a significant interaction between time and treatment, indicating that while all students learned as a result of using the system, the experimental manipulation was not associated with differences in pre-post gains. This may be partially attributed to the small sample size and large variations in performance within groups. However, one positive aspect of this finding is that while students in the experimental group spent 17% of their time in guided practice, they seemed to learn just as much as control group students.

Table 1. Means (and standard deviations) of pre-post test scores

	Pre-test Score	Post-test Score	Gain Score
Control Group	5.07 (2.03)	6.10 (2.64)	1.03 (1.99)
Exp Group	3.85 (2.54)	5.13 (3.37)	1.28 (2.33)

Results of the effectiveness and support calculations for both experimental groups are shown in Figure 3. Students in the experimental group exhibited higher map edit effectiveness (51.9% vs. 45.7% for the control group students). However, an ANOVA performed on the data revealed only a slight trend for an effect of condition on map edit effectiveness ($F = 3.074$, $p = .089$).

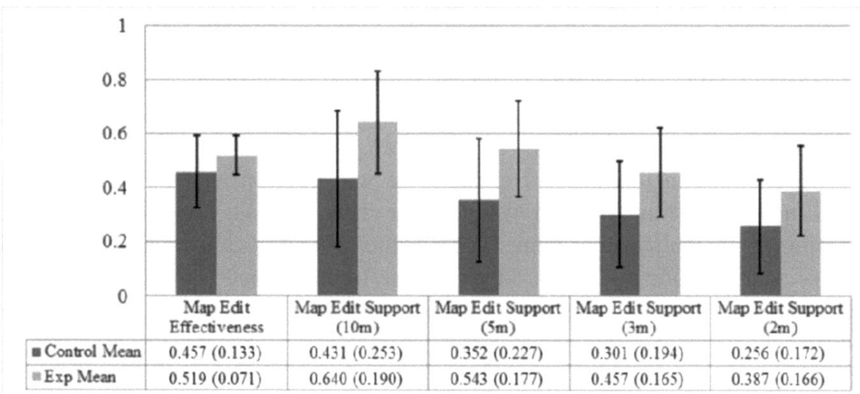

Fig. 3. Means (and standard deviations) of effectiveness and support measures

Students in the experimental group also performed a higher proportion of map edits that were supported by recent reading activities. In all four time windows used to calculate support, the experimental group students achieved a higher level of average support. ANOVAs performed on the data revealed significant effects of condition on map edit support with a window of ten minutes ($F = 7.787$, $p = .009$), five minutes ($F = 7.824$, $p = .009$), three minutes ($F = 6.639$, $p = .015$), and two minutes ($F = 5.140$, $p = .030$).

6 Discussion and Conclusions

Open-ended learning environments provide opportunities for learners to take part in authentic, complex problem solving tasks. However, the complexity of such tasks places high cognitive demands on learners, and the success of such environments may rely on the adaptive scaffolds that the system provides to learners. In this paper, we have presented preliminary data in support of the potential for including *guided practice modification scaffolds* as part of effective scaffolding strategies in OELEs. Our approach recognizes when students repeatedly fail to take advantage of hints and then intervenes with a *guided practice tutorial*. While in the tutorial, students must practice skills related to identifying causal relations from reading materials.

The results of our experimental study showed that students who received scaffolding that consisted of both hints and guided practice were more effective in constructing their causal maps; their causal map edits were both more likely to be correct and more likely to be related to recently accessed resource pages. The results suggest that students in the experimental condition may have gained a better understanding of how to find causal links in the resources. Moreover, these students may have learned the importance of connecting their information seeking activities (*i.e.*, reading) to the construction of their causal maps.

However, the results presented in this paper are not conclusive. Students in the experimental group did not show larger learning gains when compared to the control group. Additionally, while students in the experimental group were more accurate in their map edits, this difference did not reach statistical significance. Moreover, the experiment tested the effectiveness of the entire scaffolding module, including both hints and guided practice. Future studies will need to separately test the effects of these scaffolds in OELEs. Finally, the data analysis was performed at a relatively course-grained level; the metrics used to compare experimental groups evaluated students' overall use of the system. Future analyses will need to analyze the immediate effect of scaffolds in OELEs.

As we continue in this line of research, we will develop and improve upon skill tutorials in Betty's Brain. We will also combine these tutorials with techniques we are developing for the online measurement of students' use of cognitive and metacognitive processes as they work in OELEs. Ideally, these measurements will allow us to better detect when students need support and in relation to which cognitive or metacognitive process.

Acknowledgements. This work has been supported by Institute of Educational Sciences CASL Grant #R305A120186 and the National Science Foundation's IIS Award #0904387.

References

1. Clarebout, G., Elen, J.: Advice on tool use in open learning environments. Journal of Educational Multimedia and Hypermedia 17, 81–97 (2008)

2. Land, S.M.: Cognitive requirements for learning with open-ended learning environments. Educational Technology Research and Development 48, 61–78 (2000)
3. Azevedo, R., et al.: The effectiveness of pedagogical agents' prompting and feedback in facilitating co-adapted learning with metatutor. In: Cerri, S.A., Clancey, W.J., Papadourakis, G., Panourgia, K. (eds.) ITS 2012. LNCS, vol. 7315, pp. 212–221. Springer, Heidelberg (2012)
4. Jackson, S.L., Krajcik, J., Soloway, E.: The design of guided learner-adaptable scaffolding in interactive learning environments. In: Karat, C., Lund, A., Coutaz, J., Karat, J. (eds.) Proceedings of the SIGCHI Conference on Human Factors in Computing Systems (CHI 1998), pp. 187–194. ACM Press, New York (1998)
5. Mayer, R.E.: Should there be a three-strikes rule against pure discovery learning? American Psychologist 59, 14–19 (2004)
6. Azevedo, R., Hadwin, A.: Scaffolding self-regulated learning and metacognition – Implications for the design of computer-based scaffolds. Instructional Science 33, 367–379 (2005)
7. Kinnebrew, J.S., Biswas, G.: Identifying learning behaviors by contextualizing differential sequence mining with action features and performance evolution. In: Proceedings of the 5th International Conference on Educational Data Mining (2012)
8. Puntambekar, S., Hübscher, R.: Tools for scaffolding students in a complex learning environment: What have we gained and what have we missed? Educational Psychologist 40, 1–12 (2005)
9. Muir, M., Conati, C.: An analysis of attention to student – adaptive hints in an educational game. In: Cerri, S.A., Clancey, W.J., Papadourakis, G., Panourgia, K. (eds.) ITS 2012. LNCS, vol. 7315, pp. 112–122. Springer, Heidelberg (2012)
10. Segedy, J.R., Kinnebrew, J.S., Biswas, G.: Supporting student learning using conversational agents in a teachable agent environment. In: van Aalst, J., Thompson, K., Jacobson, M.J., Reimann, P. (eds.) The Future of Learning: Proceedings of the 10th International Conference of the Learning Sciences (ICLS 2012): Short Papers, Symposia, and Abstracts, vol. 2, pp. 251–255. ISLS (2012)
11. VanLehn, K.: The behavior of tutoring systems. International Journal of Artificial Intelligence in Education 16, 227–265 (2006)
12. Luckin, R., Hammerton, L.: Getting to know me: Helping learners understand their own learning needs through metacognitive scaffolding. In: Cerri, S.A., Gouardéres, G., Paraguaçu, F. (eds.) ITS 2002. LNCS, vol. 2363, pp. 759–771. Springer, Heidelberg (2002)
13. Roll, I., Aleven, V., McLaren, B.M., Koedinger, K.R.: Improving students' help-seeking skills using metacognitive feedback in an intelligent tutoring system. Learning and Instruction 21, 267–280 (2011)
14. Graesser, A.C., McNamara, D.: Self-regulated learning in learning environments with pedagogical agents that interact in natural language. Educational Psychologist 45, 234–244 (2010)
15. Leelawong, K., Biswas, G.: Designing learning by teaching agents: The Betty's Brain system. International Journal of Artificial Intelligence in Education 18, 181–208 (2008)

Intelligent Augmented Reality Training for Assembly Tasks

Giles Westerfield[1], Antonija Mitrovic[2], and Mark Billinghurst[1]

[1] Human Interface Technology Laboratory NZ
[2] Intelligent Computer Tutoring Group
University of Canterbury, Christchurch, New Zealand
giles.westerfield@gmail.com,
tanja.mitrovic@canterbury.ac.nz,
mark.billinghurst@hitlabnz.org

Abstract. We investigate the combination of Augmented Reality (AR) with Intelligent Tutoring Systems (ITS) to assist with training for manual assembly tasks. Our approach combines AR graphics with adaptive guidance from the ITS to provide a more effective learning experience. We have developed a modular software framework for intelligent AR training systems, and a prototype based on this framework that teaches novice users how to assemble a computer motherboard. An evaluation found that our intelligent AR system improved test scores by 25% and that task performance was 30% faster compared to the same AR training system without intelligent support. We conclude that using intelligent AR tutor can significantly improve learning compared to traditional AR training.

Keywords: augmented reality, intelligent tutoring, assembly skills.

1 Introduction

Augmented Reality (AR) allows the user's view of reality to be combined with virtual content that appears to be spatially registered in the real world [1]. One area of particular interest is the use of AR to assist with training for manual assembly and maintenance tasks. Whether a person is putting together furniture or repairing a car engine, these types of tasks are inherently spatial in nature, and can be difficult to teach without supervision. Many systems include instruction manuals containing diagrams that detail the necessary steps to be performed, but these can be difficult to interpret. Video tutorials can be more effective, but the user must repeatedly switch between the video and the real-world environment.

AR has the capacity to deliver hands-on training where users receive visual instructions in the context of the real world objects. Instead of reading a paper manual, a person could look at a car engine while the AR display shows the parts that need to be adjusted and the sequence of steps required. Earlier research in this area has largely involved procedural tasks where the user follows visual cues to perform a series of steps, with the focus on maximizing the user's efficiency while using the AR system.

K. Yacef et al. (Eds.): AIED 2013, LNAI 7926, pp. 542–551, 2013.

Boeing developed one of the first industrial AR applications [2], which assisted with assembling aircraft wire bundles, with the goal of improving worker efficiency and lowering costs. Henderson and Feiner [3] developed an AR application to support military mechanics conducting routine maintenance tasks inside an armored vehicle turret. They found that the use of AR allowed the subjects to locate components 56% faster than when using traditional untracked head-up displays (HUDs) and 47% faster than using standard computer monitors.

Baird and Barfield [4] studied the assembly of components on a computer motherboard. Participants were asked to perform the task using printed materials, slides presented on a computer monitor, or screen-fixed textual instructions on opaque and see-through HMDs. The test subjects completed the assembly task significantly faster and with fewer errors when using the HMD displays. However, they did not employ spatially-registered AR and users had to follow a rigid series of assembly steps.

While there has been much research into the use of AR to assist with assembly and maintenance, existing systems generally focus on improving user performance while using the AR interface as opposed to teaching the user how to perform the task without assistance. Most systems guide the user through a fixed series of steps and provide minimal feedback when the user makes a mistake, which is not conducive to learning. The learning experience is the same for every user, and there is little regard for whether learning is actually taking place.

In contrast, Intelligent Tutoring Systems (ITSs) provide customized instruction to each student [5]. ITSs have been applied successfully to a variety of topics, such as physics, algebra and database design [6-8]. However, until now, there has been little research investigating how ITSs can be combined with AR technology for training. ITSs have been created for a wide variety of domains, but the interfaces employed are normally text-based or 2D graphical applets, which limit their ability to convey spatial or physical concepts. There have been a few studies investigating the combination of ITSs with Virtual Reality such as [9-11], but very few examining the combination of ITSs with AR. The integration of AR interfaces with ITSs creates new possibilities for both fields and could improve the way we acquire practical skills.

A few projects claim to have created intelligent AR applications, but in practice these systems are minimally intelligent and do not employ domain, student and pedagogical models to provide adaptive tutoring. For example, Qiao et al. [12] developed an AR system that teaches users about the instruments in a cockpit. Their system detects which cockpit component the user is looking at and then displays relevant information describing the component's function. This context-based interface is very different from the kind of intelligence that is employed in the ITSs.

Feiner et al. [13] developed a prototype that employed knowledge-based AR. Their system used an intelligent Intent-Based Illustration System to dynamically generate graphics based on the communicative intent of the AR system at any particular moment. While this system is intelligent in how it generates the graphics for the user, it is neither intelligent from a training or tutoring standpoint nor adaptive.

The primary focus of our research is to explore the combination of AR with ITSs for an assembly task. We present the architecture of our intelligent AR system and its components in the next Section. Our research question is whether intelligent AR-based training enables users to learn and retain assembly skills more effectively than traditional AR training approaches. To address this question, we performed an evaluation study described in Section 3. The results strongly support our conclusion that using an intelligent AR tutor can significantly improve the learning outcome over traditional AR training.

2 The Architecture and Development of MAT

We developed the Motherboard Assembly Tutor (MAT), an intelligent AR system for training users how to assemble components on a computer motherboard, including identifying individual components, installing memory, processors, and heat sinks. Figure 1 shows the system's architecture, which is designed to be as modular as possible so that it can be easily adapted for new assembly and maintenance tasks. The display elements and the domain model must be customized for each type of task, but the underlying software architecture, scaffolding algorithms and other back-end processing remains the same.

The communication module relays information between the AR interface and the ITS. The ITS controls what the user sees via the interface, and the AR interface tells the ITS what the user is doing. The AR interface encapsulates the video capture, tracking system, display and keyboard input. It uses 3D graphics, animations, audio and text, which are blended with the student's view of reality via a head-mounted display. The interface uses a camera to observe the student's behaviour, and the communication module sends the necessary data to the ITS via XML remote procedure calls over a TCP/IP network connection. The ITS analyzes the data, provides feedback about student performance and decides what material to present next. We describe the ITS first, followed by the description of the AR interface.

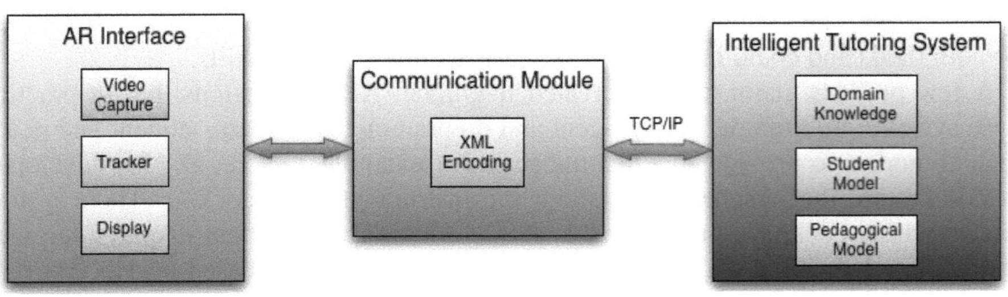

Fig. 1. The architecture of MAT

2.1 Developing the Intelligent Support

The intelligent tutoring support was developed in ASPIRE, an authoring system and deployment environment for constraint-based tutors [14]. The first stage of the authoring process involved describing characteristics of the task and composing an ontology of the relevant domain concepts. In the case of the motherboard assembly tutor, the assembly task is procedural in nature consisting of 18 steps to be completed, such as opening the processor enclosure and inserting the processor in the correct orientation. Each concept in the domain ontology has a number of properties and relationships to other domain concepts. For example, in the case of a memory slot, an important property is an indicator of whether the slot is open or not, since the slot must be opened before the memory can be installed. This property is represented as a Boolean value. There are 14 domain concepts in the ontology.

Next, we specified the solution structure by indicating which ontology concepts are involved with each problem-solving step. For example, installing computer memory involves four steps: (1) Identifying and picking up the memory component, (2) opening the locking levers at the ends of the memory slot, (3) aligning the memory with the slot in the correct orientation, and (4) pushing the memory down into the slot until it locks. Each of these steps has at least one concept associated with it, and each concept has properties that are used to determine whether the student's solution is correct. In the case of the *open locking levers* step, the ITS uses the Boolean *isOpen* property of the *MemorySlot* concept to determine whether the slot has been successfully opened or not. The value of the Boolean property is set via the AR interface, which is described in the next section.

The following step was to create the interface that the students would use. ASPIRE supports text-based and graphical interfaces, and also communicates over a network via a remote procedure call (RPC) protocol, which allows it to communicate with an external AR interface. In the case of the motherboard assembly tutor, the AR front-end communicates with ASPIRE directly over a network.

We then specified a set of problems with their solutions. The problem structure describes steps that apply to all motherboards, while a particular problem and associated solutions apply to a specific brand and model of motherboard. ASPIRE allows multiple solutions to be specified for each problem. In the case of motherboard assembly, there is often only one way to correctly install each component, but this is not always the case. For example, a memory module can be inserted into one of several slots, and a heat sink can sometimes be installed in more than one orientation. Accepting these different configurations as correct solutions gives the student more flexibility when solving the problem and enhances learning.

Using the information provided in the domain ontology, problem/solution structures and the set of problems with solutions, ASPIRE generated the domain model consisting of 275 constraints. We tailored the constraints by changing the feedback messages that ASPIRE generates automatically, so that the feedback is more useful for the students.

2.2 AR Interface Design

The AR interface presents problems and other information from the ITS to the student. The tracking module calculates the pose of the computer motherboard and its components relative to the camera affixed to the head-mounted display. This serves two fundamental purposes: (1) It allows the display module to render 3D graphics in an AR view of the real world, and (2) the tracker sends information about the relative positions of the motherboard components to the ITS, which allows it to analyze the user's behavior, provide feedback and make changes to the teaching approach as necessary. The bulk of the work performed in the tracking module is handled by the underlying osgART software library [15], which uses the used the ARToolkit marker tracking approach [16].

All of the graphics are generated by the OpenSceneGraph[1] computer graphics library (OSG), which has been integrated into the osgART software package. OSG is based on the standard OpenGL[2] API, and provides a robust scene graph structure. In addition to built-in support for materials, textures, lighting and shaders, OSG has a set of plug-ins that allow it to handle a wide variety of file formats for image s, 3D models and sound. We created accurate 3D models of the components to be installed on the computer motherboard, including memory, processor, graphics card, TV tuner card and heatsink. Models were also produced for relevant parts of the motherboard itself, such as the processor enclosure and memory securing mechanisms. Other 3D models, such as arrows, were created to guide the user through the tutoring process.

Figure 2.a shows a first-person view of the display for the TV tuner installation task. The insertion animation is not visible in the picture. The models were then animated to illustrate the proper installation procedures. For example, the graphics card is visibly pushed downward into the PCI express slot, and the processor enclosure is opened before the processor is inserted. The animations were embedded into the exported 3D model files, which can be loaded directly into the display module by the appropriate plug-in in the OpenSceneGraph software library.

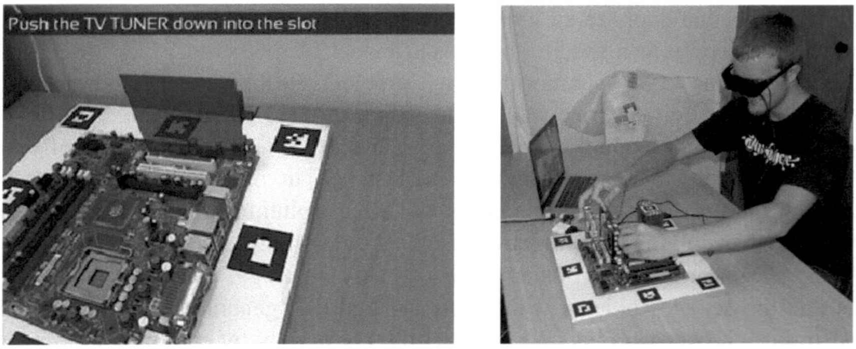

Fig. 2. a)First-person view of the AR display for part of the TV tuner installation task. The red-colored 3D model indicates where the component should go. b) A participant using the tutor.

In addition to the spatially-registered 3D models that are anchored to a position within the scene, we developed a screen-aligned head-up display (HUD) for displaying text messages from the ITS. As the user looks around, the HUD components always stay in the same place on the screen. The ITS messages consist of instructions and positive/negative feedback. The text is displayed across the top of the screen and is highlighted with a semi-transparent background that changes color based on the

[1] www.openscenegraph.org

[2] www.opengl.org

message type. Instructions are blue (such as in Fig. 2a), positive feedback is green and negative feedback is red. The HUD also utilizes text-to-speech technology to read the messages to the user, via the Microsoft Speech API.

The hardware setup for the AR interface consists of a head-mounted display, a camera, a MS Windows computer and the ARToolkit fiducial markers used for tracking (Fig. 2b). An Intel motherboard was selected for use with the computer assembly, as well as five generic hardware components to be installed: memory, processor, graphics card, TV tuner card and heatsink. At least one unique marker was attached to each component to enable the system to identify and track its position. The motherboard itself was mounted on a sturdy wooden surface and surrounded with a configuration of eight separate markers. This group of markers works together with the tracking system to limit the effects of marker occlusion as users look around and move their arms during the installation procedures. As long as the camera can see at least one of the eight markers, the tracking system is able to determine the relative position and orientation of the motherboard.

The HMD and camera combination chosen for the project is the Wrap 920AR model produced by Vuzix[3], which has a resolution of 1024x768 pixels with a 31-degree horizontal field of view. It supports stereoscopic viewing, and the front of the display is outfitted with two cameras for stereo video capture at 640x480 at 30 frames per second. The device connects to a computer via the standard VGA interface and also delivers audio via earbud headphones.

3 Study

We conducted a study in which we compared the intelligent AR system with a traditional AR tutor. The goal of the study was to determine the difference in knowledge retention between the two approaches. The evaluation was split into two phases: a training phase and a testing phase (without the tutor) that measured the extent to which the participants retained the knowledge they acquired.

The traditional AR training proceeds linearly through the assembly steps like slides in a slideshow. It does not customize the experience to each individual student: it simply shows the student what needs to be done for each step. In contrast, the intelligent AR system controls the ordering of the assembly steps and can make decisions about what material to present next based on the student's performance. Both tutors have the same interface and provide the same visual and oral instructions for each step, so the only differences lie in the features directly related to the ITS. Whether using the intelligent or traditional tutor, the student indicates that he/she is finished with the current step by pressing a button. If the solution is incorrect, the intelligent tutor prevents the student from proceeding to the next step and provides a specific feedback message, while the traditional tutor always proceeds regardless.

There were 16 participants who were randomly allocated to one of the conditions. The experimental group used the intelligent AR tutor, while the control group used the traditional AR tutor. Great care was taken to select participants with minimal

[3] http://www.vuzix.com/consumer/produces\wrap920ar.html

experience with computer hardware assembly. To measure this, all participants were given a written pre-test asking them to identify the five hardware components and their position on the motherboard. The participants also rated their prior hardware experience on a scale from one (not experienced) to seven (very experienced). All of the participants were university students aged 18-45 (11 males and 5 females).

Following the pre-test, the participants were given an orientation to the AR tutor (intelligent or traditional) and its operation procedures. After they put on the head-mounted display, the tutor guided them through the process of identifying and installing five motherboard components: memory, processor, graphics card, TV tuner card and heatsink. After all of the components were assembled, the tutoring phase was complete and the participants were given a written post-test that was similar to the pre-test to measure how well they learned from the tutor. The two written tests covered the same material, but were not identical.

Immediately after the written post-test, the participants were asked to perform a physical post-test in which they attempted to assemble the motherboard components once more, this time without the help of the tutor. The aim of the physical post-test was to measure how well the participants retained the physical assembly knowledge gained from the tutoring process. Given only the name of each component, the participants had to correctly identify and install them one by one. In addition to qualitative observations, a number of quantitative measures were taken during this process, including task completion time and error counts.

Finally, the participants completed a questionnaire, which prompted them to provide detailed feedback regarding their experience with the tutor. In addition to asking about prior hardware experience, the questionnaire contained a variety of questions with Likert-scale ratings. These asked the participants to indicate whether they thought the tutor was effective, whether they were satisfied with the 3D AR content, whether they thought the AR training system was more effective than other types of media such as videos or paper manuals, and whether they felt physically or mentally stressed during the tutoring process. Participants also had the opportunity to provide additional written feedback.

4 Results

Table 1 summarizes the written pre-test and post-test scores for the two groups. The maximum score on each tests was 10 marks. There was no significant difference between the two groups on the pre-test performance. There was also no significant difference in the times both groups spent on working with the tutoring systems. The performance of both groups increased significantly between the pre- and the post-test, yielding $t(7) = 7.165$, $p < .0002$ for the experimental group, and $t(7) = 5.291$, $p < .002$ for the control group. Both of these values are significantly less than the Bonferroni-corrected α value of .0083 (.05/6), which makes a very strong case for the effectiveness of both AR tutors.

The post-test performance of the experimental group is significantly higher than that of the control group ($t(14) = 3.374$, $p < .005$). This is less than the Bonferroni-corrected value of .0083 (.05/6), so the intelligent AR tutor produced a significantly better learning outcome than the non-intelligent AR tutor. There is also a significant difference between the normalized learning gains of the two groups ($t(14) = 2.198$, $p < .05$). The effect size (Cohen's d) is 0.981, which is a significant improvement.

Table 1 also reports the number of errors made and the total completion time to install all five motherboard components during the physical post-test. The errors generally fit into two categories: failing to match a name with the correct component, or incorrectly performing an installation procedure. There was no significant difference on the number of errors made, but the experimental group participants completed the task significantly faster than their peers ($t(14) = 2.9$, $p < .02$).

Table 1. Mean and standard deviations for two groups

Group	Pre-test	Post-test	Normalized Gain	Time (s)	Errors
Exper.	2.50 (2.27)	9.13 (1.13)	0.66(0.26)	56.56 (11.31)	0.50 (0.93)
Control	2.63 (1.92)	6.63 (1.77)	0.40 (0.21)	81.13 (21.11)	1.00 (0.93)

The questionnaire feedback was positive for both tutors. Most participants felt that the visual step-by-step instructions were very helpful, allowing them to proceed at their own pace. The immersive first-person experience provided by the head-mounted display was engaging, and the system as a whole was interesting and fun to use. Some of these responses can be attributed to the novelty factor associated with AR, but the fact remains that the participants generally found the tutors to be both effective and entertaining. Many of the experimental group participants found the ITS feedback very helpful. One criticism stemmed from the fact that the textual instructions were screen-aligned in typical HUD fashion. Reading the text required the participants to shift their focus from looking into the scene to looking at the text displayed on the surface of the screen. It may have been more natural to use spatially-registered text that appeared within the scene to keep the students immersed in the AR environment. Other criticisms addressed the tracking performance. The virtual content would sometimes jiggle or disappear entirely when the tracking system was unable to obtain enough information about the markers. These issues could be addressed with a more robust tracking approach, perhaps one that utilizes multiple cameras and tracks the natural features of the motherboard components without markers.

While the participants found determining the correct position of the components to be relatively easy, determining the proper orientation was more difficult. This was partially due to a lack of orientation cues in some of the virtual content shown. The memory and processor are essentially symmetrical in shape, and it can be difficult to determine which direction the virtual rendering is facing when there are no distinguishing features. In these cases, it would be helpful to have some additional AR cues to help the student infer the correct orientation. One idea would be to attach virtual arrows to the motherboard slot as well as the actual component to be inserted, prompting the student to line up the arrows with each other. When this type of orientation mistake occurred, the intelligent AR tutor was able to detect the error and inform the student that the orientation was incorrect. The participant was required to correct the mistake before being allowed to proceed. The traditional tutor was unable to observe or correct errors, and they often went unnoticed by the student. In these cases, the student typically made similar mistakes during the post-test. This supports the claim that the ITS feedback improved the learning outcome over the traditional AR training approach, particularly where it was easy to make a mistake.

The results of the study confirm the overarching hypothesis that the use of ITSs with AR training for assembly tasks significantly improves the learning outcome over traditional AR approaches.

5 Conclusions

Augmented Reality has been repeatedly shown to improve education and training through visualization and interactivity, but most AR training systems are not intelligent. In this paper we have shown how to combine an AR interface with an Intelligent Tutoring System to provide a robust and customized learning experience for each user. To demonstrate this we created a prototype application that teaches users how to assemble hardware components on a computer motherboard. An evaluation found that our intelligent AR system improved test scores by 25% and that task performance was 30% faster compared to the same AR training system without intelligent support. From these results, we conclude that using the ITS approach can significantly improve the learning outcome over traditional AR training.

There are many future research directions that could be explored. For example, the intelligent AR tutor could be extended by integrating a virtual character into the tutoring environment. Research has shown that virtual characters can be beneficial in tutoring situations as they increase student motivation [17-19]. A 3D virtual character would allow the ITS to inhabit the world with the user, where it could give verbal instructions, make gestures and demonstrate installation procedures.

Tracking is another area in which the intelligent AR tutor can be improved. The current solution uses a fiducial marker-based approach, which has limited accuracy, poor resistance to occlusion and obtrusive markers. There are a number of better tracking approaches such as natural feature tracking or using multiple cameras to reduce the effect of occlusion. Stereoscopic cameras and depth mapping could be used to determine the three-dimensional shapes of objects. This would allow the system to generate a model of the environment on the fly, and adapt to new scenarios such as different brands of computer motherboards and components. It could also enable more complex training tasks that require more robust tracking.

Finally, more user studies need to be conducted in a wider range of training domains. Our results have shown the value of using an intelligent AR tutor in training for motherboard assembly, but it would be good to examine the educational benefits in other assembly or maintenance tasks.

References

1. Azuma, R.T.: A survey of augmented reality. Presence: Teleoperators and Virtual Environments, 355–385 (1997)
2. Caudell, T., Mizell, D.: Augmented reality: an application of heads-up display technology to manual manufacturing processes. In: Proc. 25th Hawaii Int. Conf. System Sciences, vol. 2, pp. 659–669 (1992)

3. Henderson, S.J., Feiner, S.: Evaluating the benefits of augmented reality for task localization in maintenance of an armored personnel carrier turret. In: Proc. 8th Int. Symp. Mixed and Augmented Reality, pp. 135–144. IEEE (2009)
4. Baird, K.M., Barfield, W.: Evaluating the effectiveness of augmented reality displays for a manual assembly task. Virtual Reality 4(4), 250–259 (1999)
5. Psotka, J., Mutter, S.A.: Intelligent Tutoring Systems: Lessons Learned. Lawrence Erlbaum Associates (1988)
6. VanLehn, K., Lynch, C., Schulze, K., Shapiro, J.A., Shelby, R., Taylor, L., Treacy, D., Weinstein, A., Wintersgill, M.: The Andes Physics Tutoring System: Lessons Learned'. Artificial Intelligence in Education 15, 147–204 (2005)
7. Koedinger, K.R., Anderson, J.R., Hadley, W.H., Mark, M.A.: Intelligent tutoring goes to the big city. Artificial Intelligence in Education 8, 30–43 (1997)
8. Mitrovic, A.: Fifteen years of Constraint-Based Tutors: What we have achieved and where we are going. User Modeling and User-Adapted Interaction 22(1-2), 39–72 (2012)
9. Mendez, G., Herrero, P., de Antonio, A.: Intelligent virtual environments for training in nuclear power plants. In: Proc. 6th Int. Conf. Enterprise Information Systems (2004)
10. Evers, M., Nijholt, A.: Jacob - An animated instruction agent in virtual reality. In: Tan, T., Shi, Y., Gao, W. (eds.) ICMI 2000. LNCS, vol. 1948, pp. 526–533. Springer, Heidelberg (2000)
11. Fournier-Viger, P., Nkambou, R., Nguifo, E.: Exploiting partial problem spaces learned from users' interactions to provide key tutoring services in procedural and ill-defined domains. In: Dimitrova, V., Mizoguchi, R., du Boulay, B., Graesser, A. (eds.) Proc. 14th Int. Conf. Artificial Intelligence in Education, pp. 383–390 (2009)
12. Qiao, Y., Xie, X., Sun, T.: Design for the cockpit intelligent tutoring system based on augmented reality. In: Proc. Int. Symp. Computational Intelligence and Design, vol. 2, pp. 224–227 (2008)
13. Feiner, S., Macintyre, B., Seligmann, D.: Knowledge-based augmented reality. Communications of ACM 36, 53–62 (1993)
14. Mitrovic, A., Martin, B., Suraweera, P., Zakharov, K., Milik, N., Holland, J., McGuigan, N.: ASPIRE: an authoring system and deployment environment for constraint-based tutors. Artificial Intelligence in Education 19(2), 155–188 (2009)
15. Looser, J., Grasset, R., Seichter, H., Billinghurst, M.: OSGART-A pragmatic approach to MR. In: 5th IEEE and ACM Int. Symp. on Mixed and Augmented Reality, pp. 22–25 (2006)
16. Kato, H., Billinghurst, M.: Marker tracking and HMD calibration for a video-based augmented reality conferencing system. In: Proc. 2nd IEEE and ACM Int. Workshop on Augmented Reality, pp. 85–94 (1999)
17. Johnson, W.L., Rickel, J.W., Lester, J.C.: Animated pedagogical agents: Face-to-face interaction in interactive learning environments. Artificial Intelligence in Education 11(1), 47–78 (2000)
18. Liu, Z., Pan, Z.: An emotion model of 3d virtual characters in intelligent virtual environment. In: Tao, J., Tan, T., Picard, R.W. (eds.) ACII 2005. LNCS, vol. 3784, pp. 629–636. Springer, Heidelberg (2005)
19. Gulz, A., Haake, M.: Design of animated pedagogical agents—A look at their look. Human-Computer Studies 64(4), 322–339 (2006)

Users at the Center of Designing Informal Learning Experiences

Maria Roussou

Makebelieve Design & Consulting and University of Athens, Greece
maria@makebelieve.gr

Abstract. Designing interactive learning experiences for informal educational settings, such as museums, presents challenges due to the particularities of context. In this presentation, the implications of applying user modeling and human computer interaction methods in the design of informal digital learning experiences will be highlighted. The discussion will be based on the example of the CHESS project and its formative and summative evaluation effort in two museums.

1 Overview

The design of learning experiences is a challenging undertaking. Designing interactive learning experiences for informal educational settings, such as museums, presents even greater challenges due to the particularities of context. The informal learning context differs from that of formal education in key areas, which can largely influence and complicate the design of an interactive system. To name just a few: the target audience is heterogeneous with diverse goals, expectations, and abilities; interaction with the learning content unavoidably takes the form of brief encounters rather than longitudinal exposure to it; the connection of the virtual to physical objects and space is crucial and must be seamless; visitor mobility in the physical space may entail navigation, orientation and location-based subsystems, all of which can further complicate and disrupt the visitor's immersive experience; personalization of learning is inevitably in conflict with the inherently social activity of visiting a museum, thus placing additional tension on how to support individualized learning while also facilitating social interaction.

A possible way to overcome these challenges is through a general shift in practice to designing personalized interactive experiences *with* rather than *for* users of digital systems. The successful application of digital technology for learning must be guided by an understanding of how people use technology and how this technology is able to fit to their personal interests and aspirations, learning styles, existing knowledge and mental models, as well as their current (at the time of use) mood and preferences. This presentation will draw from the experience of designing, developing, and evaluating a prototype personalized mobile storytelling system (the CHESS system) for two very different museums, the world renowned Acropolis Museum, displaying the remains of the archaeological site of the Acropolis of Athens, Greece, and the Cité de l'espace in Toulouse, France, an edutainment center focused on space and its conquest.

K. Yacef et al. (Eds.): AIED 2013, LNAI 7926, pp. 552–553, 2013.

The CHESS system employs mixed reality and pervasive games techniques, ranging from interactive stories to augmented reality, on mobile devices (Pujol et al., 2012).

The on-going evaluation of the CHESS prototype at the two museums has highlighted many issues and challenges, including:

- The issues in applying human computer interaction methods, such as participatory design, to the design of informal digital experiences
- The problems of using personas to model visitors and to initialize personalization (Roussou et al., 2013)
- The tension between achieving an immersive story while providing interactivity and adaptivity (Vayanou et al., 2012; Roussos et al., 1996)
- The challenges in evaluating learning in such interactive user experiences (Roussou et al., 2008; Roussou, 2009).

Acknowledgments. CHESS (Cultural Heritage Experiences through Socio-personal interactions and Storytelling) is an on-going project co-funded by the European Commission within the 7th Framework Programme (FP7/2007-2013) under grant agreement n° 270198. For more information see www.chessexperience.eu.

References

1. Pujol, L., Roussou, M., Poulou, S., Balet, O., Vayanou, M., Ioannidis, Y.: Personalizing interactive digital storytelling in archaeological museums: the CHESS project. In: 40th Annual Conference of Computer Applications and Quantitative Methods in Archaeology (CAA). Amsterdam University Press, Southampton (2012) (to appear)
2. Roussou, M., Katifori, A., Pujol, L., Vayanou, M., Rennick-Egglestone, S.: A Life of Their Own: Museum Visitor Personas Penetrating the Design Lifecycle of a Mobile Experience. In: CHI 2013 Extended Abstracts on Human Factors in Computing Systems Proceedings, pp. 547–552. ACM, New York (2013), doi:10.1145/2468356.2468453
3. Roussou, M., Oliver, M., Slater, M.: Exploring Activity Theory as a Tool for Evaluating Interactivity and Learning in Virtual Environments for Children. Cognition, Technology & Work 10(2), 141–153 (2008), doi:1007/s10055-006-0035-5
4. Roussou, M.: A VR Playground for Learning Abstract Mathematics Concepts. IEEE Computer Graphics and Applications 29(1), 82–85 (2009), doi:http://doi.ieeecomputersociety.org/10.1109/MCG.2009.1
5. Roussos, M., Johnson, A.E., Leigh, J., Vasilakis, C.A., Moher, T.G.: Constructing Collaborative Stories within Virtual Learning Landscapes. In: Paiva, A., Brna, P. (eds.) European Conference of AI in Education, Lisbon, Portugal, pp. 129–135 (1996)
6. Vayanou, M., Karvounis, M., Kyriakidi, M., Katifori, A., Manola, N., Roussou, M., Ioannidis, Y.: Towards Personalized Storytelling for Museum Visits. In: 6th International Workshop on Personalized Access, Profile Management, and Context Awareness in Databases (PersDB 2012), Istanbul, Turkey (2012), http://persdb2012.cs.umn.edu (retrieved)

Games, Motivation, and Integrating Intuitive and Formal Understanding

Douglas B. Clark

Vanderbilt University, Department of Teaching and Learning, Nashville, TN, 37203
doug.clark@vanderbilt.edu

Abstract. A central goal of education involves helping students develop deep understandings of complex models at the heart of core learning goals. Interestingly, an analogous goal of commercial recreational digital games involves helping players develop deep understandings of the models at the heart of those games. Given that games can motivate players to engage voluntarily over extended periods of time in developing understandings of complex game models, one may ask whether and how one might foster similar engagement with educational concepts and models. Much fanfare has accompanied claims about games' potential for engagement and motivation, but many of those claims have focused on a shallow idea of "fun". This talk takes a deeper view of motivation and learning by considering motivation and games through the lens of research on motivation to learn in classrooms. The talk then considers how research from the learning sciences, psychology, and science education can expand this motivation framework to scaffold the integration of intuitive and formal understanding through games for learning. Discussion of these ideas is framed in terms of examples from commercial game design and from our ongoing research and development of games to support physics learning. This talk builds on a submitted paper [3].

1 Overview

Digital games provide a promising medium for education [7, 10]. Much fanfare has accompanied claims about games' potential for engagement and motivation, but many of those claims have focused on a shallow idea of "fun". This talk goes beyond that shallow idea of "fun" to analyze the affordances of commercial game design conventions in terms of Paul Pintrich's [11] synthesis of research on motivation to learn. Researchers have outlined important arguments and frameworks for conceptualizing the design of games for learning [c.f., 1, 6, 13]. The current talk builds on these arguments and frameworks by proposing that Pintrich's framework provides a productive lens for examining how popular game design conventions currently scaffold motivation to learn as well as how game design conventions might be augmented to more effectively scaffold motivation to learn in the future.

Pintrich's work on motivation and learning is widely acknowledged as foundational in the fields of psychology, motivation, and conceptual change. Pintrich's synthesis of the literature makes clear that motivating students to learn does not focus on a

K. Yacef et al. (Eds.): AIED 2013, LNAI 7926, pp. 554–556, 2013.

shallow sense of "fun." Pintrich highlights the importance of numerous principles for supporting motivation to learn including building adaptive self-efficacy and competence beliefs, fostering adaptive attributions and control beliefs, and maintaining high levels of perceived value. Pintrich clarifies the importance of scaffolding students' perceptions of their potential to succeed, their perceptions of control over their environment, and their actual progressive success and mastery. This talk explores the affordances of game design conventions through Pintrich's synthesized framework and design principles, thus positioning Pintrich's framework as a powerful and generative tool for thinking about motivation to learn, game design, and game design conventions.

The talk begins with a brief overview of research supporting the general proposition that digital games as a medium provide affordances for learning. We then outline Pintrich's framework and design principles. Building on this outline, we analyze how game design conventions currently scaffold motivation to learn and how these conventions might more effectively scaffold motivation to learn. The talk concludes with a discussion of implications in terms of teachers, design, future research, and expanded learning goals. This talk builds on a submitted paper on this topic [3] as well as other papers more generally focusing on games and science learning [2, 3, 4, 5, 8]. Clark will gladly send these articles if emailed.

References

1. Annetta, L.A.: The I's have it: A framework for serious educational game design. Review of General Psychology 14(2), 105–112 (2010)
2. Clark, D.B., Martinez-Garza, M.: Prediction and explanation as design mechanics in conceptually-integrated digital games to help players articulate the tacit understandings they build through gameplay. In: Steinkuhler, C., Squire, K., Barab, S. (eds.) Games, Learning, and Society: Learning and Meaning in the Digital Age, pp. 279–305. Cambridge University Press, Cambridge (2012)
3. Clark, D.B., Martinez-Garza, M., Killingsworth, S.: Beyond Fun: Pintrich, Motivation to Learn, and Games for Learning (submitted)
4. Clark, D.B., Martinez-Garza, M., Biswas, G., Luecht, R.M., Sengupta, P.: Driving Assessment of Students' Explanations in Game Dialog Using Computer-Adaptive Testing and Hidden Markov Modeling. In: Ifenthaler, D., Eseryel, D., Xun, G. (eds.) Game-based Learning: Foundations, Innovations, and Perspectives, pp. 173–199. Springer, New York (2012)
5. Clark, D.B., Nelson, B., Chang, H., D'Angelo, C.M., Slack, K., Martinez-Garza, M.: Exploring Newtonian mechanics in a conceptually-integrated digital game: Comparison of learning and affective outcomes for students in Taiwan and the United States. Computers and Education 57(3), 2178–2195 (2011)
6. Gee, J.P.: What video games have to teach us about learning and literacy. Palgrave Macmillan, New York (2003/2007)
7. Honey, M.A., Hilton, M. (eds.): Learning Science Through Computer Games and Simulations, National Research Council. National Academy Press, Washington, DC (2010)
8. Kinnebrew, J., Killingsworth, S., Clark, D.B., Biswas, G., Martinez-Garza, M., Krinks, K., Sengupta, P.: Data Mining and Modeling in Digital Games for Science Learning. IEEE Transactions on Learning Technologies (accepted with revisions)

9. Martinez-Garza, M., Clark, D.B.: Teachers and Teaching in Game-Based Learning Theory and Practice. In: Khine, M., Saleh, I. (eds.) Approaches and Strategies in Next Generation Science Learning, pp. 147–163. IGI Global, Hershey (2013), doi:10.4018/978-1-4666-2809-0.ch008
10. National Research Council: National Research Council Workshop on Games and Simulations, Washington, D.C., October 6-7 (2009)
11. Pintrich, P.R.: A motivational science perspective on the role of student motivation in learning and teaching contexts. Journal of Educational Psychology 95(4), 667 (2003)
12. Sengupta, P., Kinnebrew, J., Basu, S., Biswas, G., Clark, D.: Integrating Computational Thinking with K12 Science Education Using Agent-Based Computation: A Theoretical Framework. Education & Information Technologies (accepted with revisions)
13. Squire, K.: Video games and learning: teaching and participatory culture in the digital age. Teachers College Press, New York (2011)

Lessons from Project LISTEN: What Have We Learned from a Reading Tutor That Listens?

Jack Mostow

Carnegie Mellon University, School of Computer Science, Pittsburgh, PA 15213-3890
mostow@cs.cmu.edu

Abstract. For 20+ years, Project LISTEN (www.cs.cmu.edu/~listen) has made computers listen to children read aloud, and help them learn to read. Along the way we have learned lessons about children, reading, speech technology, intelligent tutors, educational data mining, and doing AIED research in schools.

1 Some of the Research Questions Project LISTEN Has Studied

Nobel laureate Herbert Simon's annual talk on how to do research advised incoming PhD students to pick research questions (not merely topics) both significant (i.e., that people care about) and right-sized (not too hard). Questions we have studied include[1]:

What ought a Reading Tutor do?	AAAI94*, *CALICO* 99, ICMI02, **STLL 08**
Do children like a feature?	AIED05, SLaTE11
Which system features matter?	SIGDial11
What should the Reading Tutor listen for, why, and how?	Eurospeech93&03, ESCA99, HMC00, AAAI94*, ICSLP98&02&06, AIED01&05&07, ICAAI03, EDM08, Interspeech09&11, SLaTE09&11, ITS10, *TSLP 11*, FLAIRS12, Chen 12, ISADEPT12, *IJAIED 13*
How much is it used, and why?	Kant 04, **IERI 07**
Do Reading Tutor gains beat…	
classroom instruction?	*ETS 02,* **STLL 08**
human tutors?	*JECR 03*
independent reading?	*JECR 07*
ELL instruction in ...	Canada? IDEC07&09; Ghana? *ITID 10;* India? Dev10
How to model word meaning?	SSSR09, EACL12
How to generate… questions?	Aist 01*, AIED03, QG09&11, BEA12
examples?	BEA11, *JNLE 12*
instruction?	AAAI99, *IJAIED 01,* ITS04&06, AIED09
How to model students?	ITS02&04&06&08*, UM03&07, *TICL 04,* AIED05&07, *IJAIED 06,* EDM07&08&10&11&12*, ICWS09, LSA10, *TSLP 11*
What practice helps most?	**FF 01**, **FLET 08,** ITS08*, SSSR12
Could EEG help?	AIED11*, Tan 12, NAACL12
How to mine student data?	*JNLE 06,* ITS06, **HEDM 10**, EDM10&11, FLAIRS12*

[1] www.cs.cmu.edu/~listen lists *articles*, **chapters**, conferences, theses, and awards*.

K. Yacef et al. (Eds.): AIED 2013, LNAI 7926, pp. 557–558, 2013.

2 Some of the Secret Weapons Project LISTEN Has Used

Dr. Simon advised students to find "secret weapons" to attack problems in novel ways. Project LISTEN has used speech recognition to attack illiteracy, as well as:

- **Reframing:** replay of a tutoring session as browsing it [**HEDM 10**]; tracking a reader's position as guiding it [SLaTE11, FLAIRS12]; understanding children's questions as training them to ask predictable ones [SLaTE09]; joint cognitive and student modeling as topic modeling [EDM12]
- **Humans:** Wizard of Oz tests to evaluate and extend a tutor [AAAI94*, ICMI02]
- **Devices:** EEG to detect students' mental states [AIED11, *IJAIED 13*]
- **Randomness:** randomize tutor decisions to test effects [AIED03&13, ITS04&06]
- **Corpora:** adult narrations to score children's reading prosody [*TSLP 11*]; Google N-grams to build example contexts [BEA11, *JNLE* 12]; children's oral reading to mine [Chen 12, ISADEPT12, FLAIRS12*]
- **Databases:** WordNet to generate vocabulary factoids and questions [Aist 01*, *IJAIED 01*]; dictionary to generate vocabulary questions [QG11]
- **Features:** hasty responses to model disengagement [ITS04]
- **Representations:** DBNs to model scaffolding [EDM06]; SCONE mental states to generate questions [AIED09]; maps from prosody to graphics [SLaTE11]; search space of parameterizations [EDM11]
- **Analysis Methods:** learning decomposition [ITS06&08, AIED07, EDM07]; Bayesian knowledge tracing [ITS08*]; regularization [*TSLP 11*]; incorporating logistic regression into DBN to trace multi-skill steps [EDM11&12*]

Acknowledgments. The research reported here was supported most recently by the Institute of Education Sciences, U.S. Department of Education, through Grants R305B070458, R305A080157, and R305A080628, and by the National Science Foundation under Grants 1121873 and 1124240. Any opinions, findings, and conclusions or recommendations expressed in this publication are those of the author and do not necessarily reflect the views or official policies, either expressed or implied of the Institute, the U.S. Department of Education, the National Science Foundation, or the United States Government. I thank the educators and students who helped generate our data, the many LISTENers over the years who contributed to the work cited here, and Chad Lane for suggesting a table format to improve readability.

The AIED Industry and Innovation Track

W. Lewis Johnson[1] and Ari Bader-Natal[2]

[1] Alelo Inc.
12910 Culver Bl., Suite J, Los Angeles, CA 90066 USA
[2] The Minerva Project
1145 Market St., San Francisco, CA 94103 USA

Abstract. The new Industry and Innovation Track of the AIED 2013 conference includes submissions from commercial and entrepreneurial organizations that are putting AIED technologies into practice. As digital tutors enter the main stream, and demand increases for advanced capabilities such as automated assessment and personalized learning, there is increasing interest in learning products that incorporate artificial intelligence technologies. The Industry and Innovation Track is intended to attract innovators, practitioners, and technology adopters to the AIED conference to share lessons learned and best practices, and draw on emerging technologies and methods. It includes regular papers and posters, as well as late-breaking reports from fast-moving efforts.

Keywords: Innovation, technology transition, adoption-based research.

1 Introduction

Education is in the midst of a period of rapid technological change. New types of online learning resources such as Khan Academy videos (Khan Academy, 2013) and massive open online courses (MOOCs) offer the potential for "flipping" conventional classroom instruction, enabling new paradigms of blended learning, or eliminating brick-and-mortar instruction altogether. As more learning moves on line there is a growing need for tools to track learner progress, personalize curricula, and provide feedback. These are all topics that the AIED community has researched over a number of years, often in research laboratory environments. There is now an unprecedented opportunity to put AIED-based methods into practice on a large scale. This can lead to improved learning solutions. It can also inform AIED research through access to real data and experience with real learning problems.

The Industry and Innovation Track of AIED aims to bring together researchers, practitioners, and innovators in the education space to share experiences related to putting AIED technologies into practice. We recruited a program committee of industry leaders and individuals experienced with applying learning technologies, who could bring an industry perspective to the evaluation process. Because commercial efforts tend to move rapidly and aim for quick results, we included a late-breaking reports category with a reduced time between submission and publication.

Like many learning innovations, the AIED Innovation and Industry Track is an iterative work in progress. The number of contributions this year is relatively small,

K. Yacef et al. (Eds.): AIED 2013, LNAI 7926, pp. 559–560, 2013.

but includes several interesting contributions from a cross-section of industrial research laboratories, government agencies and commercial enterprises engaged in educational innovations. We will draw lessons from this pilot effort and use them to grow the industry-and-innovation component of the AIED conference in future years.

2 Contributions

Two contributions to the Industry and Innovation Track are included in this proceedings volume. Melinda Gervasio and Karen Myers of SRI International report on an automated capability for assessing procedural skills, developed to support training for a software system in widespread use across the US Army. Jeremiah Folsom-Kovarik and Robert Wray report on their work on adaptive assessment algorithms, which will enable adaptive assessment in real-world training settings where calibration data is sparse. A third paper by Brian Vogt of the US Army was also accepted, on the topic of a methodology for assessing scenarios in the UrbanSim strategy game. Unfortunately Mr. Vogt is unable to attend AIED and present the paper.

There are also three late-breaking reports, which will be published in a separate volume at the conference. Brian Duffy and team at Team Carney report on a case study of gamification of traditional courseware. Lewis Johnson gives an interim report on Alelo's Tactical Interaction Simulator, and current efforts to integrate it into instruction at the Defence Forces Language School in Australia. Finally Jennifer Sabourin and team at the SAS Institute report on their SAS® Read Aloud app for early reading, and discuss opportunities for incorporating intelligent technologies to further improve and understand early literacy reading.

Reference

1. Khan Academy, A free world-class education for anyone anywhere (2013), `http://www.khanacademy.org/about` (retrieved)

Drill Evaluation for Training Procedural Skills

Karen Myers, Melinda Gervasio, Christian Jones, Kyle McIntyre, and Kellie Keifer

SRI International, Menlo Park, CA
firstname.lastname@sri.com

Abstract. The acquisition of procedural skills requires *learning by doing*. Ideally, a student would receive real-time assessment and feedback as he attempts practice problems designed to exercise the targeted skills. This paper describes an automated assessment and feedback capability that has been applied to training for a complex software system in widespread use throughout the U.S. Army. The automated assessment capability uses soft graph matching to align a trace of student actions to a predefined gold standard of allowed solutions, providing a flexible basis to evaluate student performance, identify problems, give hints, and suggest pointers to relevant tutorial documentation. Collectively, these capabilities facilitate self-directed learning of the training curriculum.

Keywords: procedural skills, automated assessment, relaxed graph matching.

1 Introduction

Today's workers require a broad and growing set of *procedural skills,* which involve learning multistep procedures to accomplish a task. Procedural skills apply to both physical environments (e.g., how to repair a device, how to build a shed) and online environments (e.g., how to create a pivot table in Excel).

This paper reports on a system called Drill Evaluation for Training (DEFT) that was developed to facilitate the learning of procedural skills related to the use of a complex piece of software. More specifically, DEFT provides an automated assessment capability to evaluate students' performance as they learn how to use the Command Post of the Future (CPOF)—a collaborative geospatial visualization environment system used extensively by the U.S. Army to develop situational awareness and to plan military operations. Although a powerful tool, CPOF can be difficult to learn; furthermore, CPOF skills decay rapidly when not in regular use. Because soldiers have limited availability for formal training sessions, achieving and maintaining necessary skills presents a significant challenge.

DEFT addresses the training problem for CPOF through automated support for assessing learned skills and providing targeted feedback designed to further student understanding. An automated capability of this type would reduce the burden on instructors in classroom settings, thus enabling them to provide more personalized attention to individual students. It would also enable students to pursue independent supplemental training beyond a formal classroom setting.

We begin the paper with background on CPOF and its training curriculum, followed by a technical overview of DEFT. We then present results of a user study that

K. Yacef et al. (Eds.): AIED 2013, LNAI 7926, pp. 561–570, 2013.

assessed the usability and utility of DEFT for CPOF training. We close with a discussion of related work, a summary of contributions, and directions for future work.

2 Command Post of the Future (CPOF)

CPOF is a state-of-the-art command and control (C2) visualization and collaboration system. The CPOF software is part of the U.S. Army's Battle Command System, and as such is standard equipment for virtually every Army unit. Since its inception in 2004, thousands of CPOF systems have been deployed. Its usage spans organizational echelons from Corps to Battalion in functional areas that include intelligence, operations planning, civil affairs, and engineering. CPOF is used extensively to support C2 operations for tasks covering information collection and vetting, situation understanding, daily briefings, mission planning, and retrospective analysis [4].

CPOF uses geospatial, temporal, tabular, and quantitative visualizations specifically tailored to information in the C2 domain. Users can collaborate synchronously in CPOF by interacting with shared products. The ability to dynamically incorporate new information is critical to the success of any C2 operation; CPOF's "live" visualizations continually update in response to changes sourced from user interactions or underlying data feeds, thus ensuring that data updates flow rapidly to users.

The U.S. Army offers the Battle Staff Operations Course (BSOC) to provide instruction to students on basic CPOF interaction skills. Much of what is taught in the BSOC is procedural, i.e., determining what steps to perform and in what order to achieve a particular result. The following provides a portion of an exercise from the BSOC course materials: *Create a 2D map. Create a notional unit; name it A10 #X 1v2. Edit the size, type, and affiliation. Place the unit on the 2D map.*

An analysis of an examination used to test student mastery of BSOC material showed that 69% of the questions required demonstration of procedural skills; another 6% involved true/false or multiple-choice questions; the remaining 25% required short-answer responses. Similar exercises are used within the course itself to enable students to apply the classroom knowledge in a hands-on fashion. This predominance of procedural skills within the BSOC curriculum motivated the development of DEFT, as having an ability to automatically assess student performance could dramatically alter the manner in which CPOF training is conducted.

3 DEFT Technical Components

DEFT performs real-time monitoring of students as they attempt to complete exercises (see Fig. 1). While a student works on an exercise, DEFT logs a trace of the student's actions. That trace is compared to a representation of allowed solutions to the exercise (the *gold standard*) to create assessment information that identifies conceptual errors or mistakes, provides guidance in the form of hints to help the student complete a task, and suggests links to contextually relevant training materials.

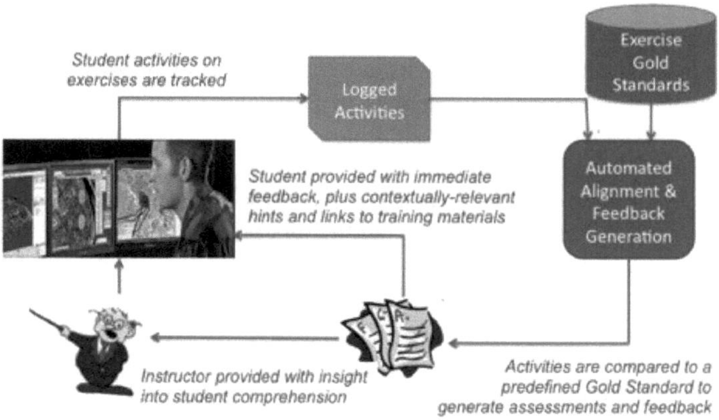

Fig. 1. Automated assessment in DEFT

3.1 Gold Standard Representation

The *gold standard* defines the space of acceptable solutions to an exercise. For BSOC exercises, there can be numerous solutions that involve different actions and orderings between them, along with significant variability in the specific objects that are created or manipulated. This richness precludes an explicit enumeration of gold standard solutions as a collection of totally ordered actions.

Instead, we represent the gold standard as one or more traces obtained through demonstrations of correct solutions to an exercise, augmented with *annotations* that define allowable variations from the trace. A gold standard defines a partial ordering on the steps of a trace, where a step can be a (parameterized) CPOF action, a class of actions, or set of options, each of which is itself a partially ordered set of steps. The annotations take the form of constraints over steps or parameters. Currently, DEFT supports action ordering constraints, parameter equality constraints, parameter value constraints (between parameters and constant values), and a limited set of query constraints. Query constraints capture requirements on the application state or on object properties that cannot be determined from the arguments of the actions themselves. The abstractions provided by this scheme can yield compact representations of large solution spaces.

We anticipate that instructors will play a critical role in gold standard development by providing solution traces and annotating them. However, we can also leverage automated reasoning and machine learning techniques to facilitate the process. For example, we can apply heuristics to determine default annotations and generalize over parameters and actions from multiple examples.

3.2 Alignment

The automated assessment capability in DEFT centers on determining a mapping from the student's submitted response for an exercise to the predefined gold standard for that exercise. We have framed this alignment problem as a form of *inexact semantic graph matching* in which a similarity metric based on graph edit distance is used to rate the quality of the mappings. Graph edit distance measures the number—more generally, the cumulative cost—of graph editing operations needed to transform the student response into an instance consistent with the gold standard. Intuitively, finding the lowest-cost alignment corresponds to DEFT finding the specific solution the student is most likely to have been attempting.

To use this graph matching approach in DEFT, we represent the gold standard as one or more *solution graphs*, with each graph representing a family of possible solutions to the exercise. Actions and their parameters are nodes; parameter roles within actions are links; and required conditions within the solution (e.g., action orderings, values of textual or numerical parameters) are constraints. The student response is represented similarly as a *response graph*.

Alignment involves finding the mapping between the response and a solution graph with the lowest edit distance cost. We associate costs that impose a penalty in the score for missing the respective action, parameter, constraint, and so on. Alignment to the closest solution allows DEFT to generate an assessment that identifies differences between the response and the gold standard, which translate both to specific errors the student has made (e.g., out-of-order actions, incorrect action parameter values, missing or extra actions) and to the corrections needed.

The alignment capability in DEFT builds on a pattern-matching algorithm that was developed originally for link analysis applications [10]. While this algorithm provided a reasonably good fit for solving the alignment problem, we developed a set of performance optimizations linked to the structure of our specific matching problem that significantly prune the overall search space.

3.3 Student Interface

DEFT's student interface serves two functions. First, it provides a framework for exercise administration: presenting exercises for selection, supporting navigation through the exercises, and making available contextually relevant hints and documentation links. Second, it presents students with visual feedback on their solutions that shows problems detected by the automated assessment capability.

A user who selects an exercise is presented with background information from the BSOC training materials, including a statement of the learning objectives and links to relevant study materials. The user begins the exercise by clicking on a *Start* button on the bottom of the screen. The exercise is presented to the student incrementally as a sequence of numbered tasks. For example, Fig. 2 shows the three tasks that compose an exercise related to Spot Reports. The user interacts with CPOF to complete each task in turn, with instrumentation logging his actions. Upon completing a task, the user clicks on a *Next* button to proceed to the next task.

Users are presented with context-sensitive hints (accessed via the light bulb icon) and documentation links (accessed via the question mark icon) to facilitate their completion of tasks. DEFT uses hint sequences, with initial hints providing high-level guidance and subsequent hints progressively disclosing more complete directions for the task. Clicking on a documentation link displays the relevant section of the online CPOF documentation in a Web browser. After completing all tasks, the user can click on the *'How did I do?'* button to view the DEFT assessment of his performance.

DEFT provides real-time feedback but at the level of exercises rather than individual steps. For the BSOC exercises, it is impossible to know whether a particular step is correct in isolation, as there can be multiple ways to complete subtasks within an exercise. In particular, it is important to interpret actions *in context*.

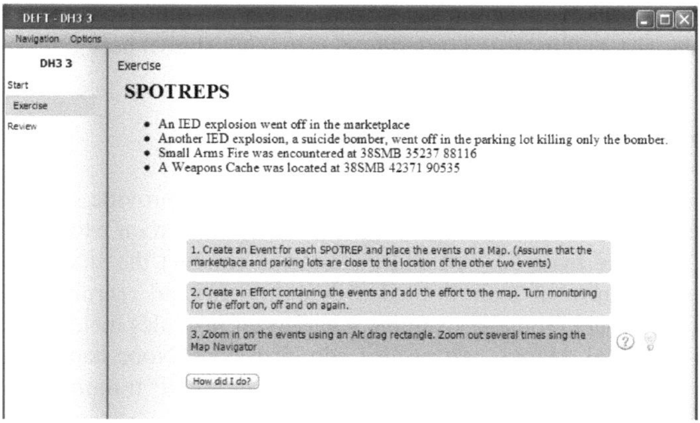

Fig. 2. Student interface: task structure for an exercise

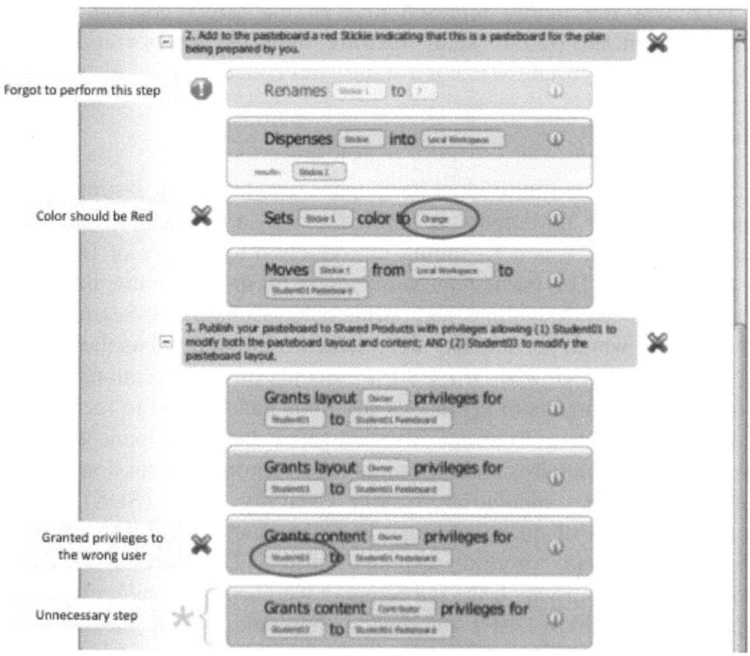

Fig. 3. Sample feedback from a fragment of a BSOC exercise

Fig. 3 shows sample feedback generated by DEFT. An icon to the right of each subtask indicates whether the subtask was completed successfully (green checkmark), contained mistakes (red x), or triggered warnings (yellow checkmark). An icon to the left of a step denotes a specific type of problem with that step. Hovering on the icon presents a textual description of the problem (the yellow boxes in the figure). Possible problem types include incorrect step values (red X and red circle on incorrect value), a missing step (red exclamation mark beside a grayed-out step), an unnecessary step (yellow asterisk), and incorrect ordering of steps (not shown here).

4 User Study

We conducted a user study to evaluate DEFT's ability to provide students with correct and comprehensible feedback regarding their performance on exercises derived from the BSOC training material. We had intended to conduct the study with active duty soldiers but, because of their limited availability, instead recruited ten participants without military backgrounds, spanning a variety of job roles including administrative assistants, technical editors, and project administrators. None had previous exposure to CPOF so they were given a two-hour hands-on CPOF training session the week before the study.

Typical BSOC students would have had minimal CPOF exposure; their facility with computers would vary, with most being comfortable using computers and a few having more advanced skills. Thus, other than their lack of military backgrounds, our subject pool was reasonably representative of the target population. Because BSOC training concentrates on the use of software rather than on operational content, the lack of a military background was not a significant concern.

4.1 Methodology

The user study comprised ten individual participant sessions, each lasting two hours. Each session involved the participant, a facilitator, and a note-taker; and was conducted in three parts. First was a 15-minute introduction to the use of DEFT to perform exercises in CPOF. The participant was guided by the facilitator in performing an exercise and introduced to the hints and online help mechanisms. Second was a 75-minute session during which participants were asked to think aloud as they performed exercises on their own and viewed DEFT's assessments of their solutions. They were also presented with assessments of erroneous solutions handcrafted to include various types of errors. Finally was a 30-minute debrief where the participant was asked to complete two brief questionnaires and then engaged in an open discussion. First was a standard questionnaire for calculating System Usability Scale (SUS) scores [3]; second was a compilation of questions regarding computer usage. The open discussion was structured around "product response cards" [2], a set of 55 adjectives (positive and negative) from which the participants were asked to select five that best described what they thought of DEFT and then to elaborate on their selections.

4.2 Results

Demographics. All ten participants self-reported being "comfortable" or "very comfortable" with the use of computers. On the questions regarding computer and software use, on a scale of 0 to 4 (0 = never, 4 = very often), they averaged 3.22 on online activities, 2.73 on office applications (e.g., word processing, spreadsheets), 1.67 on games, and 0.56 on advanced computer use (e.g., programming, sound/video editing). Six reported having taken a programming class at some point, but none were active programmers. All reported having taken a computer-based training or online course.

Automated Assessment. Each participant completed two to three exercises and viewed two to three additional assessments within the time allotted. Performance on the exercises varied greatly, with some completing exercises with few errors or none at all, while others struggled on all exercises. The instructions in the exercises were intentionally designed to elicit some errors and all the participants committed at least a few errors. DEFT's automated assessment module correctly identified all the errors during the study except in two situations where the system crashed due to CPOF instrumentation issues in the prototype system. All the participants were able to correctly interpret the error feedback on their solutions and, in the cases where they were asked to repeat an exercise, to correct their mistakes. Everyone was also able to interpret assessments of the handcrafted erroneous solutions but required more effort to do so because of the additional need to interpret someone else's solution.

However, based on the results of the think-aloud sessions and the discussions afterwards, it was apparent that most participants found the assessment visualizations too busy or too long. Several stated that they would prefer a simple textual rendering, with a few suggesting just a summary of the results. One participant found DEFT's focus on error feedback (i.e., only errors were pointed out) to be particularly harsh and suggested providing positive feedback as well. Many also wanted not just to be told what they had done wrong but also to be directed on how to fix it.

The perceived deficiencies of the assessment visualization were surprising, given that we had designed them in close collaboration with CPOF instructors. However, we realized that instructors and students have distinct needs. For an instructor, who needs to see the performance of an entire classroom, seeing individual user responses and high-level assessments in the form of markups (checkmarks, Xs, and circled elements) is especially valuable. In contrast, students already know what they did and are more interested in the assessment along with guidance on how to fix identified errors.

Exercise Administration. The study provided the opportunity to evaluate DEFT's exercise administration functionality. Participants found the DEFT workflow of loading an exercise, performing a sequence of tasks, and getting an assessment to be straightforward. However, a few expressed a desire for more immediate feedback to guide them through an exercise. In a number of situations, a participant started floundering and was then unable to make progress without intervention from the facilitator.

DEFT's task-specific hints and links to online help were perceived by all participants to be valuable and everyone relied on them at some point. Although a few tasks involved CPOF concepts that the participants had not been or were only briefly exposed to during their CPOF training, most were able to use the hints and help to accomplish the tasks anyway. Most participants preferred the brevity and directness of hints, often finding the online CPOF documentation to be overwhelming.

Usability and Usefulness. The SUS scores ranged from 35 to 90, with a mean of 61.25 and a median of 62.5 (scores that can be interpreted to mean roughly "average"). There are too few participants to draw statistically significant conclusions. However, together with our observations during the think-aloud sessions and the open discussions with the participants, these results indicate that although the participants found DEFT easy to use, gaps remain in its exercise administration and automated assessment capabilities.

In the product response cards exercise, participants were asked to choose the five words best describing what they thought of DEFT. The results (Fig. 4) reveal that participants had a predominantly positive response to DEFT, with several describing it as "useful", "straightforward", "relevant", and "valuable". A few participants found DEFT "frustrating"; further probing revealed that their reaction was at least partly due to their lack of familiarity with CPOF and with military terminology in the exercises.

Across the board participants expressed their belief that DEFT was a valuable training tool. They appreciated its tight integration with the training application (CPOF, in this case). All the participants readily suggested examples where they thought a tool like DEFT could be useful for training. These included various procedures they had encountered in their work, such as accounting processes, website navigation, webpage creation, and timecard management; as well as more unusual suggestions such as learning a new language or how to play an instrument.

Fig. 4. Tag cloud depicting subjective participant response to DEFT, with word size reflecting the number of times it appeared in participants' Top 5 lists

4.3 Discussion

The user study provided valuable feedback and encouraging results regarding DEFT as a training tool for procedural tasks. It is notable that although the participants in the study were complete novices in both the application (CPOF) and the domain (military operations), they were able to use DEFT to complete real training exercises in CPOF. And in spite of the difficulty in performing a task (encountered by most of the participants at some point during the study), the participant response to DEFT was predominantly positive. However, as a prototype system whose primary focus has been on automated assessment, DEFT has room for improvement. In particular, to be an effective tool for self-directed learning, it needs to provide more student-focused interactions, including a tighter integration between performance, assessment, and correction, as well as more comprehensive and focused explanatory feedback.

5 Related Work

Example-tracing tutors [1] assess procedural skills by comparing student actions against a *behavior graph* that represents all acceptable ways of achieving a task, much like DEFT compares student solutions against a *gold standard*. Both behavior graphs and our gold standards capture a range of solutions by allowing alternative actions, ranges of values used in actions, and alternative action orderings. However, because an example-tracing tutor's primary task is to *teach* a procedural skill, its assessment is focused on recognizing what the student is trying to do and ensuring that the student remains on track to successfully accomplishing a task. In contrast, DEFT is designed primarily to *assess* how well a student has performed a skill and is thus focused on identifying key mistakes in the student solution.

This distinction also applies when comparing DEFT to model-tracing [6,9] and constraint-based tutors [7]. In addition, model-tracing tutors are designed for domains such as math and physics where automated problem-solvers can be developed; they are less applicable to open-ended domains like CPOF. Meanwhile, constraint-based tutors are designed for tasks where the challenge is not in the selection of actions and parameter values but in the selection of values that satisfy potentially complex constraints. Although CPOF requires capturing such constraints as well, the variety of actions available to accomplish a task requires evaluating the procedures themselves.

In *programming*, assessment can be performed entirely on the end product (the program): whether it produces the correct results, meets complexity and style criteria, is efficient, and so on [5] To some extent, such assessment can be performed on the final information products in CPOF but the real-world need for efficient operation and adherence to best practices further demands assessment of how products are created.

6 Conclusion and Future Work

Several CPOF instructors enthusiastically endorsed our automated assessment and feedback capability, noting benefits of the technology on several levels. In a classroom setting, it would enable high achievers to progress more rapidly, potentially exploring challenge concepts beyond the baseline skills required for the entire cohort; for weaker students, the technology would provide real-time, personalized feedback. The instructors were also excited by the prospect of being able to track individual and aggregate student performance to help them identify concepts that are problematic for students and to adjust their instruction accordingly. Finally, the technology opens the door to supporting student-directed acquisition of skills outside of the classroom.

DEFT is currently a research prototype. Given the encouraging results from the user study and the strong desires expressed by CPOF trainers for a capability of this type, we believe that it would be valuable to continue this line of work with the objective of generating a fully operational assessment and feedback capability that could be deployed to facilitate self-directed CPOF training.

To date, gold standards for the BSOC exercises have been hand-coded by members of our research team. Ideally, curriculum developers would be able to construct gold standards on their own. For this, we envision a tool that would enable an instructor to demonstrate the procedural structure of an exercise solution, augmented with an annotation mechanism for specifying the companion constraints that define allowed variations from the demonstration. We believe that it would be feasible to develop such an authoring tool, leveraging learning by demonstration technology we have deployed previously within CPOF to enable automation of routine tasks [8].

Although our focus was on CPOF skills, the assessment capabilities in DEFT are not CPOF-specific and could be readily applied to other procedural training tasks.

Acknowledgments. This material is based upon work supported by the United States Air Force and DARPA under Contract No. FA8750-09-D-0183. Any opinions, findings and conclusions or recommendations expressed in this material are those of the authors and do not necessarily reflect the views of the United States Air Force and DARPA. The authors thank Chris Bonheim and the training staff from the U.S. Army Tactical Mission Command, who provided valuable input into the design of DEFT. Approved for Public Release, Distribution Unlimited.

References

1. Aleven, V., McLaren, B., Sewall, J., Koedinger, K.: A New Paradigm for Intelligent Tutoring Systems: Example-tracing Tutors. Intl. J. of AI in Education 19(2), 105–154 (2009)
2. Benedek, J., Miner, T.: Measuring Desirability: New Methods for Evaluating Desirability in a Usability Lab Setting. In: 2nd Conf. of the Usability Professionals Assoc. (2002)
3. Brooke, J.: SUS—a quick and dirty usability scale. In: Jordan, P.W., Thomas, B., Weerdmeester, B.A., McClelland, A.L. (eds.) Usability Evaluation in Industry, pp. 188–194. Taylor & Francis, London (1996)
4. Croser, C.: Commanding the Future: Command and Control in a Networked Environment. Defense & Security Analysis 22(2), 197–202 (2006)
5. Douce, C., Livingstone, D., Orwell, J.: Automatic Test-based Assessment of Programming: A Review. ACM Journal of Educational Resources in Computing 5(3) (2005)
6. Koedinger, K.R., Anderson, J.R., Hadley, W.H., Mark, M.A.: Intelligent Tutoring Goes to School in the Big City. Intl. J. of AI in Education 8, 30–43 (1997)
7. Mitrovic, A.: NORMIT: A Web-enabled Tutor for Database Normalization. In: Intl. Conf. on Computers in Education, pp. 1276–1280 (2002)
8. Myers, K., Kolojejchick, J., Angiolillo, C., Cummings, T., Garvey, T., Gaston, M., Gervasio, M., Haines, W., Jones, C., Keifer, K., Knittel, J., Morley, D., Ommert, W., Potter, S.: Learning by Demonstration for Collaborative Planning. AI Magazine 33(2), 15–27 (2012)
9. VanLehn, K., Lynch, C., Schulze, K., Shapiro, J.A., Shelby, R., Taylor, L., Treay, D., Weinstein, A., Wintersgill, M.: The Andes Physics Tutoring System: Lessons Learned. Intl. J. of AI in Education 15(3), 678–685 (2005)
10. Wolverton, M., Berry, P., Harrison, I., Lowrance, J., Morley, D., Rodriguez, A., Ruspini, E., Thomere, J.: LAW: A Workbench for Approximate Pattern Matching in Relational Data. In: 15th Conf. on Innovative Applications of AI, pp. 143–150 (2003)

Adaptive Assessment in an Instructor-Mediated System

Jeremiah T. Folsom-Kovarik, Robert E. Wray, and Laura Hamel

Soar Technology, Inc.
{jeremiah,wray,lhamel}@soartech.com

Abstract. *Instructor-mediated* training systems give end users direct control over content, increasing acceptance but introducing new technical challenges. Decreased opportunity for parameter estimation limits the utility of item-response or Bayesian approaches to adaptive assessment. We present four adaptive assessment algorithms that require little data about test item characteristics. Two algorithms present about half as many items as random selection before producing accurate skill estimates. These algorithms enable adaptive assessment in training settings where calibration data is sparse.

Keywords: assessment, adaptive training, instructor-mediated design.

1 Introduction

Instructor-mediated design is a pattern the authors use to help ensure training systems fit practitioner needs. The goal is to reduce technical barriers to instructors' control over the content and operation of a training system. Giving instructors direct control over systems can improve acceptance and effectiveness. It can reduce costs, turnaround time for changes, and errors introduced during communication between end users and developers. However, when adaptive elements are complex, instructor-mediated design can place technical burdens on instructors or, more likely, result in incompleteness and incorrectness. To enable instructor-mediated design for adaptive training, adaptation should be simple and transparent.

Well-studied Bayesian and item response theory approaches to adaptive assessment [1, 2] have drawbacks for some use cases. They require specification of multiple important values that are nuisance parameters from an instructor point of view, such as prior beliefs about learner ability and item discrimination or difficulty. Principled machine learning of such parameters necessitates large amounts of empirical data, on the order of 1800 people or more answering each test item [3]; there is a possibility of incorrect outcomes before the model saturates; and the learned parameters are sensitive to small changes in item content or context [4]. Approximate methods can reduce but not eliminate these requirements. Whether they are learned from data or set by developers, the number and precision of model parameters in these approaches are barriers to transparency, instructor acceptance, and quick changes to content.

To combine adaptive assessment with instructor-mediated design, we investigated transparent selection algorithms that could adapt to individual students without requiring large amounts of calibration data. We developed simulated students to empirically

K. Yacef et al. (Eds.): AIED 2013, LNAI 7926, pp. 571–574, 2013.

evaluate the algorithms and found a simple algorithm can choose effectively between skills to test, an important task for real-world adaptive training and assessment.

2 Adaptive Readiness Assessment

We are exploring the challenge of readiness assessment in the context of a US Navy course that trains mid-career officers. Officers at mid-career may have very different prior experience, so it is important to identify specific knowledge and skill gaps quickly. Other requirements make a traditional test design less effective:

1. Test items are authored by instructors with only face validation prior to use. Therefore, there is no opportunity to characterize individual items before presenting them. Further, the test item pool is small.
2. Instructors define relationships between tested skills. We seek to help expert instructors express their understanding rather than fit their experience into a skill taxonomy we define. Therefore, it is not practical to rely on precise weights in a skill network or apply inference methods to interpret test items.
3. Because materials quickly become outdated in a changing tactical environment, we estimate that each item might be presented to between 50 and 500 students before being retired. Approaches that calibrate test items online over time will not have enough learners to estimate item characteristics.

In order to address these needs, we studied four adaptive assessment algorithms. Candidate algorithms were chosen for their minimal instructor input requirements, potential to work with small amounts of data, and their transparency to instructors.

Least Confidence: This algorithm asks more questions about skills for which the system has least certainty (whether because of mixed student performance or possible problems with test items). Sample variance of ability estimates is an easily calculated proxy for estimate certainty, and its meaning is accessible to instructors. For each student, sample variance was calculated for each skill ability estimate and the skill with the highest sample variance was selected for testing.

Neighbor Divergence: This algorithm uses the skill tree topology to compare ability estimates of each skill with those of related skills. Local outliers in ability estimates may indicate errors introduced by, for example, a lucky guess. Each skill is compared with its parents, children, and siblings in order to find the average absolute difference between abilities at the node and its neighbors. The node with the greatest difference from its neighbors is selected.

Overall Divergence: This algorithm, a variation on Neighbor Divergence, also concentrates on outliers in ability estimate means, but compares node estimates to the overall (domain) ability estimate for each learner. The skill with the ability estimate most different from the overall estimate is selected for further testing.

Population Divergence: This algorithm finds the mean ability estimate for each skill across all students and chooses test items to test the skill whose ability estimate differs most from the population. Ability often (not universally) clusters around a unimodal distribution, meaning that exceptional estimates are more likely to represent sampling error than estimates that are closer to the center of the distribution.

Baselines: We compared the adaptive algorithms to two baselines that bracket the results. *Random* ordering bounds the low end of performance. Because item selection is not systematic currently, it may be an apt estimate of today's efficiency. To find the upper bound on performance, *perfect knowledge* selection uses true underlying ability (which is known for simulated students) to choose the most apt question at all times.

3 Method

One hundred simulated students were used for each experimental run. A run consisted of a cycle of selecting a test item for a student, evaluating the student's response, and updating ability estimates until all test items were presented. To reflect a basic level of practice, items were dichotomous and tests estimated ability by percentage correct.

The fundamental evaluation metric was the number of items needed to reduce mean absolute error (MAE) of all ability estimates as compared to the true underlying values. In order to summarize change over time into an accuracy threshold that identifies fast improvement and is comparable across different test conditions, we present a normalized metric: the percentage of the entire item pool an algorithm needs to remove half of the error that is possible to remove. For example, in a simulation with MAE of 0.5 before asking any questions and 0.1 after asking all questions in the pool, we would count the questions each algorithm presents before error drops below 0.3.

Each test targeted multiple skills, arranged into hierarchies with topology varying by experiment. Each item tested only one skill. Because we do not expect to have enough data to characterize individual items (as above), item difficulty depended only on skill. Item selection represented a decision of which skill to test.

We assigned each simulated student a single, hidden ability in each skill. Student abilities affected the probability of answering an item according to a logistic curve, so that even proficient students had a chance of slipping. Additional sources of variance included chance of guessing correctly, skill difficulty, and accuracy of prior ability estimates. Prior ability scores were generated with a wide variance for each skill to emulate information from other sources such as collateral tests or instructor inputs.

4 Results and Discussion

We focused on algorithm performance for a skill hierarchy with skills arranged at varying depths from the root of a tree. This topology is common and reflects observed usage in the current assessment system. Two candidate algorithms significantly outperformed the rest (two-tailed Welch's t-tests, $p < 0.01$ each): neighbor divergence and overall divergence. Comparing mean differences pairwise against the perfect-knowledge baseline showed that neighbor divergence eliminated 53% of wasted item presentations, while overall divergence eliminated 49%.

We next examined these two algorithms in tests of sensitivity to different skill relationships. In a highly interconnected graph, with multiple parents for each skill node and therefore larger neighborhoods and smaller distinctions between student abilities, the two algorithms' performance did not degrade. In a flat topology with all skills direct children of a root node, the two algorithms also performed equally. We detected one difference in experiments using multiple unrelated skill trees. This topology challenged the overall divergence algorithm. Its single-value model was not sufficient when a student could be good at skills in one tree and simultaneously poor in another. However, in this case the neighbor divergence approach still worked well. It was able to differentiate between a student who scored poorly on a skill cluster and one who scored poorly on a single skill and might deserve a second chance there.

The results are stable over a range of simulation parameters and conditions. With additional experiment runs, we found that adding the ability to assess multiple skills in a single test item presentation benefitted all algorithms proportionally. On the other hand, removing noise in prior estimates slowed the random baseline but improved the adaptive algorithms. When prior estimates were reasonably accurate, random selection could not find the few inaccurate estimates but the adaptive algorithms could.

In conclusion, the results of our experiments suggest that two adaptive algorithms, neighbor divergence and overall divergence, can control adaptive assessment in training settings that do not offer large amounts of empirical data, calibration time, or formal expertise to fully characterize skill relationships and individual test items. At the same time, the algorithms are simple to explain and are likely to garner acceptance and adoption from practitioners in need of quick and efficient assessment.

We will implement the best-performing neighbor divergence algorithm in our readiness assessment system. In that setting, it will be possible to evaluate with real instructors and students how efficiently and accurately it identifies skill gaps.

Acknowledgement. This work is supported in part by the Office of Naval Research via contracts N00014-10-C-0526 and N00014-11-M-0504. The views and conclusions contained in this document are those of the authors and should not be interpreted as representing the official policies, either expressed or implied, of the Department of Defense or Office of Naval Research. The U.S. Government is authorized to reproduce and distribute reprints for Government purposes notwithstanding any copyright notation hereon.

References

1. van der Linden, W.J., Pashley, P.J.: Item Selection and Ability Estimation in Adaptive Testing. In: van der Linden, W.J., Glas, C.A.W. (eds.) Elements of Adaptive Testing, pp. 3–30. Springer, New York (2010)
2. Pardos, Z.A., Heffernan, N.T., Anderson, B., Heffernan, C.L.: Using Fine-grained Skill Models to Fit Student Performance with Bayesian Networks. In: Christobal, R., et al. (eds.) Handbook of Educational Data Mining, pp. 417–426. CRC Press, Boca Raton (2010)
3. Cook, L.L., Eignor, D.R.: IRT Equating Methods. Educational Measurement: Issues and Practice 10(3), 37–45 (2005)
4. Davey, T., Lee, Y.H.: Potential Impact of Context Effects on the Scoring and Equating of the Multistage GRE Revised General Test. Technical report GREB-08-01, ETS GRE Board, Princeton, NJ (2011)

Development of an Affect-Sensitive Agent for Aplusix

Thor Collin S. Andallaza and Ma. Mercedes T. Rodrigo

Ateneo Laboratory for the Learning Sciences,
Department of Information Systems and Computer Science,
Ateneo de Manila University, Loyola Heights, Quezon City, Philippines
{tandallaza,mrodrigo}@ateneo.edu

Abstract. We compared two versions of an affect-sensitive embodied conversational agent for Aplusix, an intelligent tutoring system for algebra. The initial agent, Grimace v.1, was able to detect and respond to user affect, but it responded too quickly and too frequently. The second version of the agent, Grimace v.2 was less sensitive compared to the first version, in that it provided fewer interventions to engaged students, more evaluations of engagement, fewer evaluations of boredom. In a field test of the agent, students generally preferred version 2 over version 1.

Keywords: affect, Aplusix, embodied conversational agent, intelligent tutoring systems, learning, motivation.

1 Introduction

Embodied conversational agents (ECAs) are computer programs that are capable of autonomous action within their environment [9] and are able to interact with users or other agents in a manner similar to human face-to-face conversation [3].

In recent years, the intelligent tutoring systems (ITSs) community has been adopting ECAs to address the non-cognitive aspects of learning (e.g. [5], [8]). Our study's objective was to create an emotionally intelligent ECA for Aplusix, an ITS for algebra [4]. A full description of Aplusix and the data it logs is available in [1] and [7]. In our study, we attempted to answer the following questions:

1. What is the appropriate timing of the agent's interventions given an observed affective state?
2. How do we determine the effectiveness of the agent in improving student learning and the learning experience?

2 Methods

We aimed to create detectors for engaged concentration, boredom, and confusion based on the human observations and the Aplusix log dataset described in Lagud and Rodrigo [6]. We divided the log data into terciles, according to number of steps taken per problem. Per student, we computed average number of steps per problem

K. Yacef et al. (Eds.): AIED 2013, LNAI 7926, pp. 575–578, 2013.

per level of difficulty. We then redivided the log data into terciles, this time based on duration or length of time it took to solve each problem. Per student, we computed average duration per level of difficulty. The two sets of terciles described three distinct groups of student described in [6]. Students who took the least number of steps and least amount of time to solve a problem were more engaged, while those who took the most number of steps or the most time were bored or confused.

For the model to inform an ECA's interventions, it has to provide the ECA with criteria by which to evaluate whether a phenomenon of interest has taken place. In practical terms, the criteria takes the form of threshold values. Once the count of a user action exceeds (or goes below) a defined threshold, the ECA should intervene. We created two models—two sets of threshold values—for confusion, boredom, and engaged concentration with varying levels of sensitivity. The first model, Grimace v.1, used as basis data at the per problem type level. On the other hand, the second model, Grimace v.2, the unit of analysis was the student. Unfortunately, the details of how each model was computed are outside the scope of this paper. Note, though, that v.1 is more sensitive than v.2 in that it detected changes in affect more quickly and consequently responded more frequently.

2.1 Field Testing of the Models

The agents were tested with first year high school students from a public school in Metro Manila. The population consisted of 39 males and 51 females with ages ranging from 12 to 14, an average age of 12.53, and a modal age of 12. The students were taking up introductory algebra at the time of the experiment, but none were familiar nor have used Aplusix in the past. These students were randomly assigned into one of three groups – a control group, which used Aplusix without the agent, an experimental group which used Aplusix along with Grimace v.1, and an experimental group which used Aplusix with Grimace v.2.

The experiment began with a pre-test consisting of 10 factoring problems, which were sample problems of level B1 (factorization with integer coefficients) difficulty from Aplusix. After the pre-test, the students were each given a handout on how to use Aplusix and were allowed to ask questions regarding the software. The students were then asked to interact with Aplusix (and with the agent for experimental groups) for 45 minutes, answering problems of level B1. During this time, the agent generated interaction logs of the session. Following the interaction was a post-test containing a different set of 10 factoring problems, which again were sample problems taken from Aplusix. Finally, for the experimental groups, an Agent Perception Survey based on a study by Baker [2] was given to evaluate the agent. The survey contained a set of eight statements which described the agent, and the students were asked to rate from 1-6 how much they disagreed or agreed with each statement.

3 Results

Throughout the experiment, we were able to collect a total of 45,402 transactions between the students and the two agents, with 22,121 transactions between the stu-dents and Grimace v.1 and 23,281 between the students and Grimace v.2.

3.1 Appropriate Timing of Responses

We analyzed two properties for each affective state: the incidence or percentage of time that the agent detected of a state and the frequency with which the agent intervened. The incidence of each affective state, was computed by taking the number of times the agent reported that state and dividing it by the number of affective states reported by the agent in total. The frequency of interventions for an affective state was computed by getting the number of times the agent intervened given a detected affective state and dividing it by the total number of times the agent reported that affective state in total.

Results revealed that for both Grimace v.1 and v.2, boredom was the most frequently detected affective state. However, Grimace v.2 evaluated students as bored significantly fewer times than Grimace v.1 ($t(58) = 2.45$, two-tailed $p = 0.02$). Moreover, Grimace v.2 evaluated students as engaged significantly more frequently than the Grimace v.1 ($t(58) = -3.12$, two-tailed $p = 0.003$).

The analysis of the frequency of interventions showed that Grimace v.1 intervened the most when students were engaged ($M = 0.82$, $SD = 0.012$), while Grimace v.2 intervened the most when students were bored ($M = 0.56$, $SD = 0.21$). An independent samples two-tailed t-test revealedthat the difference between the frequency values of the two agents was only significantly different for engaged concentration ($t(58) = 19.29$, $p < 0.01$).

3.2 Impact on Learning

The pre-test mean scores of all three groups fell under the same range, i.e. the intervals of all groups overlap ($M = 2.3$, 95% CI [1.22, 3.48] for the control group; $M = 1.77$, 95% CI [0.72, 2.82] for the Grimace v.1 group; $M = 1.77$, 95% CI [0.89, 2.65] for the Grimace v.2 group). This meant that there is no significant difference in their prior knowledge. The post-test mean scores were higher across all groups however they still overlapped ($M = 6.7$, 95% CI [5.62, 7.78] for the control group; $M = 6.77$, 95% CI [5.63, 7.77] for the Grimace v.1 group; $M = 6$, 95% CI [4.84, 7.16] for the Grimace v.2 group). In addition, a One-Way Analysis of Variance (ANOVA) of the learning gains (computed as post-test score – pre-test score) of each group ($M = 0.55$, $SD = 0.35$ for the control group, $M = 0.58$, $SD = 0.32$ for the old agent group, and $M = 0.52$, $SD = 0.33$ for the new agent group) indicated no significant difference learning gains among the groups ($F(2,87) = 0.25$, $p = 0.78$).

3.3 Impact on Learning Experience

There was a difference in the learning experiences among the groups. A t-test of scores of self-reported responses to the Agent Perception Survey did not show significant differences per individual criterion. However, we noted that the overall trend per criterion was in favor of Grimace v.2. A paired t-test showed a significant difference ($t(7) = -4.50$, $p = 0.002$) in the mean scores for each statement, showing an overall preference for the new agent.

Acknowledgements. We thank the Ateneo Laboratory for the Learning Sciences for its unique contributions to our research, in particular Marc Armenta and Paul Contillo for their assistance during our field testing. We thank Dr. Joseph Beck of Worcester Polytechnic Institute in Worcester, MA and Dr. Ryan Baker of Columbia University in New York, NY for their valuable insights and support. We thank Department of Science and Technology Philippine Council for Industry, Energy, and Emerging Technology Research and Development (PCIEERD) for making this research a reality through the grant entitled, "Development of Affect-Sensitive Interfaces".

References

1. Andallaza, T.C.S., Jimenez, R.J.M.: Design of an Affective Agent for Aplusix. Undergraduate thesis, Ateneo de Manila University, Quezon City (2012)
2. Baker, R.S.J.d.: Designing Intelligent Tutors That Adapt to When Students Game the System. Doctoral Dissertation, Carnegie Mellon University, Pittsburgh (2005)
3. Cassell, J., Bickmore, T., Campbell, L., Vilhjálmsson, H., Yan, H.: Human conversation as a systems framework: Designing embodied conversational agents. In: Embodied Conversational Agents, pp. 29–63. The MIT Press, USA (2000)
4. Chaachoua, H., Nicaud, J., Bronner, A., Bouhineau, D.: APLUSIX, a Learning Environment for Algebra, Actual Use and Benefits. In: 10th International Congress on Mathematics Education (2004)
5. Graesser, A., D'Mello, S., Strain, A.: Computer Agents that Help Students Learn with Intelligent Strategies and Emotional Sensitivity. Philippine Computing Journal Dedicated Issue on Affect and Empathic Computing 6(2), 1–8 (2011)
6. Lagud, M.C.V., Rodrigo, M.M.T.: The affective and learning profiles of students using an intelligent tutoring system for algebra. In: Aleven, V., Kay, J., Mostow, J. (eds.) ITS 2010, Part I. LNCS, vol. 6094, pp. 255–263. Springer, Heidelberg (2010)
7. Nicaud, J.F., Bouhineau, D., Chaachoua, H.: Mixing microworld and CAS features in building computer systems that help students learn algebra. Intl. Journal of Computers for Mathematical Learning 9(2), 169–211 (2004)
8. Rebolledo-Mendez, G., du Boulay, B., Luckin, R.: Motivating the learner: An empirical evaluation. In: Ikeda, M., Ashley, K.D., Chan, T.-W. (eds.) ITS 2006. LNCS, vol. 4053, pp. 545–554. Springer, Heidelberg (2006)
9. Wooldridge, M., Jennings, N.: Intelligent agents: Theory and practice. The Knowledge Engineering Review 10(2), 115–152 (1995)

Assessment and Learning of Qualitative Physics in Newton's Playground

Matthew Ventura, Valerie Shute, and Yoon Jeon Kim

Florida State University, Tallahassee FL
{mventura,vshute,yk06c}@fsu.edu

Abstract. This study investigated the learning and assessment efficacy of a physics video game we developed called Newton's Playground. 165 8th and 9th graders played Newton's Playground for roughly five hours. Findings include significant pre-post physics gains and notable correlations between performance in Newton's Playground and physics pretest knowledge. Suggestions are given on how to develop assessments in video games to enhance learning.

Keywords: stealth assessment, qualitative physics, learning in games.

There is growing evidence of video games supporting learning (e.g., Tobias & Fletcher, 2011; Wilson et al., 2009). However, learning in games has historically been assessed indirectly and/or in a post hoc manner. We need to understand more precisely how and what kinds of knowledge and skills are being acquired in games. This paper introduces a way to assess learning in video games called "stealth assessment" (Shute & Ventura, in press). Similar to other performance-based assessment in games (e.g., DiCerbo & Behrens, 2012), stealth assessment refers to evidence-based assessments that are woven directly and invisibly into the fabric of the gaming environment. During game play, students naturally produce rich sequences of actions while performing complex tasks. Evidence needed to assess the skills is thus provided by the players' interactions with the game itself. In this paper we describe our stealth assessment of qualitative physics in a game we created called Newton's Playground.

1 Newton's Playground

Research into what's called "folk" physics demonstrates that many people hold erroneous views about basic physical principles that govern the motions of objects in the world, a world in which people act and behave quite successfully (Reiner, Proffit, & Salthouse, 2005). Recognition of the problem has led to interest in the mechanisms by which physics students make the transition from folk physics to more formal physics understanding (diSessa, 1982) and to the possibility of using video games to assist in the learning process (Masson, Bub, & Lalonde, 2011).

We developed a game called Newton's Playground (NP) to help middle school students understand qualitative physics (Ploetzner, & VanLehn, 1997). We define qualitative physics as a nonverbal understanding of Newton's three laws, balance,

K. Yacef et al. (Eds.): AIED 2013, LNAI 7926, pp. 579–582, 2013.

mass, conservation of momentum, kinetic energy, and gravity. NP is a 2D game that requires the player to guide a green ball to a red balloon. The player can nudge the ball to the left and right (if the surface is flat) but the primary way to move the ball is by drawing/creating simple machines on the screen that "come to life" once the object is drawn. Everything obeys the basic rules of physics relating to gravity and Newton's three laws of motion. The 74 problems (split into 7 playgrounds) in NP require the player to draw/create four simple machines: inclined plane/ramps, pendulums, levers, and springboards.

For example, in the "golf problem" (see Figure 1), the player must draw a pendulum on a pin (i.e., little circle on the cloud) to make it swing down to hit the ball. In the depicted solution, the player also drew a ramp to prevent the ball from falling down a pit. The speed of (and importantly, the impulse delivered by) the swinging pendulum is dependent on the size/mass distribution of the club and the angle from which it was dropped to swing.

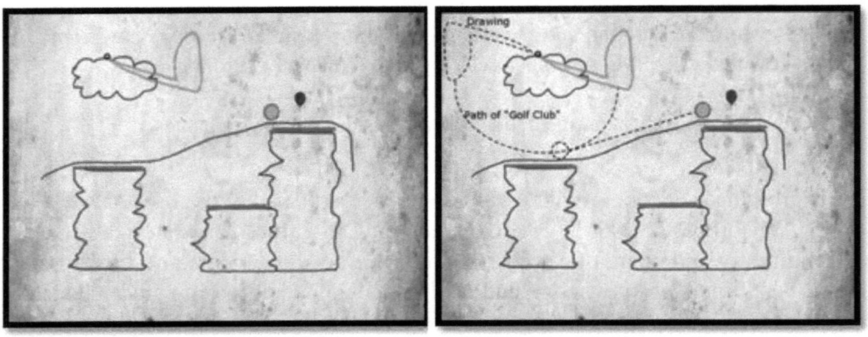

Fig. 1. Golf problem in NP (left is solution; right is path of motion)

NP displays silver and gold trophies in the top right hand part of the screen which represent progress in the game. A silver trophy is obtained for any solution to a problem. Players can also receive a gold trophy if a solution is under a certain number of objects (the threshold varies by problem, but is typically < 3). A player can receive one silver and one gold trophy per problem.

2 The Present Study

This study aims to show how playing NP can improve understanding of qualitative physics (i.e., simple machines). Additionally, we examine how performance in NP relates to existing understanding of qualitative physics. Establishing the validity of the stealth assessment in NP lays the foundation for developing diagnostic support mechanisms in NP (e.g., feedback). We have two hypotheses in this study. First, players will learn qualitative physics as a function of playing NP. Second, performance in NP will relate to existing qualitative physics knowledge. There are two main indicators from log files that we predict will be related to qualitative physics knowledge: (1) number of gold trophies per agent, (2) number of silver trophies per agent.

3 Method

3.1 Sample

165 8th and 9th grade students (76 male, 91 female) enrolled at the Florida State University School participated in the study. Each student was paid $25 for participation.

3.2 Procedure

Students played NP for around 4 hours (split into five 45-minute sessions over the course of 2 weeks). We tested around 20 students at a time in a large computer lab. Students were not allowed to talk or look at other student's gameplay. We administered our qualitative physics pretest at the beginning and a posttest at the end of the study (both online). After completing the pretest, the students were told about NP and that the person with the most gold trophies at the end of the study would receive a special prize (an extra $25). Proctors were instructed to tell players to watch the agent tutorial videos if they were stumped on a problem.

3.3 Measures

Working with a physics professor, we developed a qualitative physics test consisting of 24 pictorial multiple choice items. Its purpose is to assess implicit knowledge of Newton's three laws, balance, mass, conservation of momentum, kinetic energy, and gravity (see Masson, Bub, & Lalonde, 2011; Reiner, Proffit, & Salthouse, 2005). We split the qualitative physics test into two forms that were counterbalanced between pretest and posttest (Form A = 12 items; Form B = 12 items).

4 Results

Reliability for the qualitative physics test was acceptable (Form A: $\alpha = .72$; Form B: $\alpha = .73$). Regarding overall learning as a function of NP gameplay, we found a significant difference between the pretest and posttest (t (154) = 2.12, $p < .01$). Table 1 displays the correlations among the indicators and pretest knowledge. The gold trophies per agent relate significantly to the pretest. Silver springboard use relates to pretest.

Table 1. Correlations between pretest scores and NP trophies

	Posttest	PSg	SBg	LEg	RAg	PSs	SBs	RAs	LEs
Pretest	.60**	.34**	.41**	.23**	.24**	-.02	.15	.09	-.04

* = p < .05; ** = p < .01 (PS = pendulum strike; SB = springboard; LE = lever; RA = ramp; g = gold; s = silver)

5 Discussion

This study is the first of its kind to show that specific behavior in a video game can be used for assessment purposes. We found that performance related to creating and using various agents in NP correlated to qualitative physics knowledge. Additionally, we found preliminary evidence that playing NP can lead to improved understanding of qualitative physics knowledge without any explicit instruction.

Regarding future research, the stealth assessment in NP has the potential to be useful for diagnostic and support purposes. For example, if a student has trouble using a particular agent, certain gameplay features could inform the most likely reasons why that's the case. For instance, a player's lever solution may have failed because: (a) the wrong mass of an object was used on one side of the lever, (b) the fulcrum was positioned inaccurately, and/or (c) the size/length of the lever was too short or too long. Based on this information, NP can give feedback as to how to correctly draw agents of force and motion.

Acknowledgements. We would like to thank the Bill and Melinda Gates Foundation for their funding of this project. We would also like to thank Matthew Small, Lubin Wang, and Don Franceschetti for their work on this project.

References

DiCerbo, K.E., Behrens, J.T.: Implications of the digital ocean on current and future assessment. In: Lissitz, R., Jiao, H. (eds.) Computers and their Impact on State Assessment: Recent History and Predictions for the Future, pp. 273–306. Information Age Publishing, Charlotte (2012)

diSessa, A.A.: Unlearning Aristotelian physics: A study of knowledge-based learning. Cognitive Science 6, 37–75 (1982)

Masson, M.E.J., Bub, D.N., Lalonde, C.E.: Video-game training and naive reasoning about object motion. Applied Cognitive Psychology 25, 166–173 (2011)

Ploetzner, R., VanLehn, K.: The acquisition of qualitative physics knowledge during textbook-based physics training. Cognition and Instruction 15, 169–205 (1997)

Reiner, C., Proffit, D.R., Salthouse, T.: A psychometric approach to intuitive physics. Psychonomic Bulletin and Review 12, 740–745 (2005)

Shute, V.J., Ventura, M.: Measuring and supporting learning in games: Stealth assessment. White paper for MIT series. Published by the MacArthur Foundation (in press)

Tobias, S., Fletcher, J.D. (eds.): Computer games and instruction. Information Age Publishers, Charlotte (2011)

Wilson, K.A., Bedwell, W., Lazzara, E.H., Salas, E., Burke, C.S., Estock, J., ... Conkey, C.: Relationships between game attributes and learning outcomes: Review and research proposals. Simulation & Gaming 40(2), 217–266 (2009)

The PHP Intelligent Tutoring System

Dinesha Weragama and Jim Reye

School of Electrical Engineering & Computer Science
Queensland University of Technology, Brisbane, Australia
{d.weragama,j.reye}@qut.edu.au

Abstract. Teaching introductory programming has challenged educators through the years. Although Intelligent Tutoring Systems that teach programming have been developed to try to reduce the problem, none have been developed to teach web programming. This paper describes the design and evaluation of the PHP Intelligent Tutoring System (PHP ITS) which addresses this problem. The evaluation process showed that students who used the PHP ITS showed a significant improvement in test scores.

Keywords: Intelligent Tutoring Systems, PHP, program analysis.

1 Introduction

Although programming is a fundamental component of any Computer Science course, many beginning students find it a very difficult subject. Intelligent Tutoring Systems (ITSs) are a possible means of reducing this problem. Researchers have developed many ITSs that teach programming (Corbett, 2000; Holland, Mitrovic, & Martin, 2009; Johnson, 1990; Sykes & Franek, 2004; Weber & Brusilovsky, 2001). However, none of them address teaching web development in any form. Developing web pages requires the use of certain skills which are not required for stand-alone programming. This research concentrates on building such an ITS to teach the PHP scripting language for developing web pages.

Since programming is a practical subject, an ITS to teach programming must include programming exercises. The tutor should be capable of analyzing solutions to such exercises and providing appropriate feedback. A major challenge faced at this time is that a programming exercise rarely has a unique solution. This is demonstrated in Table 1 which shows two possible solutions to a programming exercise that requires the student to write a program segment to display consecutive numbers from 1 to 10 using a looping construct.

This paper discusses the PHP Intelligent Tutoring System, which is an ITS designed to solve the problem described above. Section 2 looks at how the knowledge base is designed to analyze computer programs written by students. Section 3 discusses the evaluation process used and the results of the evaluation. Finally, section 4 concludes the paper and discusses future improvements.

K. Yacef et al. (Eds.): AIED 2013, LNAI 7926, pp. 583–586, 2013.

Table 1. Two solutions to displaying consecutive numbers from 1 to 10 using a looping construct

Program a	Program b

`for($i=1;$i<=10;$i++)`
`{`
`   echo($i);`
`}`
	`$i=1;`
	`while($i<=10)`
	`{`
	`   echo($i);`
	`   $i++;`
	`}`

2 Program Analysis

As discussed earlier, a programming exercise rarely has a unique solution. Any ITS that teaches programming needs to be able to identify semantically equivalent solutions to such exercise. This problem is handled in the PHP ITS using concepts of first order predicate logic to model states and changes of state. The knowledge base used here consists of a set of predicates and associated rules and actions (Weragama & Reye, 2012a).

When a student submits a solution to an exercise, it is first converted to an Abstract Syntax Tree (AST). The AST is then walked through, node by node, creating facts or activating actions that correspond to the functionality of each node. The knowledge base also contains a set of rules which are activated based on facts that are created in the system using the process above. The set of facts that exist after all the nodes of the AST have been processed is known as the final state.

This final state is compared against the overall goal for that particular exercise. This overall goal consists of a set of predicates that should exist once the student's solution has been analyzed (Weragama & Reye, 2012b). The overall goal for the exercise described above is given in Fig. 1. Any arguments of predicates written using uppercase prefixes signify variables in predicate logic that are existentially quantified.

Goal: ∀ j [(1≤j≤10)→ OnPage(j,j)]
Constraints: LoopBodyOK(FORID1)
Conditions of Subplan(LoopBodyOK(ForId1)),
PRECOND: HasForVariable(FORID1,VARID_i)
∧ HasValue(VARID_i,VALUE_i)
POSTCOND: OnPage(VALUE_i,VALUE_i)

Fig. 1. Overall goal for example exercise

The overall goal is divided into three components: the goal, constraints and conditions of subplan. The *goal* is the required final outcome of execution of the program. In this case, the predicates corresponding to the goal specify that the outcome should happen for all values of j between 1 and 10. An *OnPage* fact is created each time anything is displayed on the web page, so the goal here specifies that the value of j is displayed for all the above values. The *constraints* are used to specify structural requirements of the program. In this case, the presence of the *LoopBodyOK* predicate indicates that a loop has been used to achieve the execution goal. The *conditions of subplan* are only used when the exercise requires the use of PHP functions or loops. When a loop is encountered, any conditions of subplan are checked to see if the pre-conditions are satisfied. If so, all the statements within the loop are processed to create the relevant facts. When this is completed, the conditions of the sub-plan are checked to see whether the post-conditions are satisfied. If the post-conditions are satisfied, the loop is taken to be correct and the *LoopBodyOK* fact is created to indicate this. If either the pre-conditions or the post-conditions are not satisfied, an error in the loop is identified.

Once the final state of the program is obtained, this state is checked to see whether all the predicates in the overall goal are present in the final state. If they are, the program is identified as correct. If they are not, an error is identified and feedback is provided based on which sub-goal was not satisfied.

The handling of alternative solutions to exercises is inherent within the analysis process described above. Rules are sometimes used to convert between equivalent expressions. Another method used for this purpose is to include several alternative conditions of subplan.

The current knowledge base of the PHP ITS has functionality to handle assignment statements, selection structures, arrays, PHP functions, PHP form processing and certain types of loops.

3 Evaluation

The PHP ITS was developed using the knowledge base described above and was evaluated with postgraduate students enrolled in a unit to study PHP at the Queensland University of Technology in 2012. Thirty four students in total took part in the evaluation. No control group was used since the evaluation was conducted on university courses which counted towards credit, and so it was deemed unethical to allow one group of students access to the system while depriving the other.

The students were required to first complete a pre-test. They then used the PHP ITS to solve exercises during their own time. The students were not given any lectures or tutorials. At the end, the students completed a post-test and a questionnaire regarding the system. Fig. 2 shows the average student score for the pre-and post-tests. It can be seen that there was a visible increase in test scores after using the system.

A one-tailed paired t-test with a 95% confidence interval was carried out between the pre- and post-test marks in order to check whether the increase was significant. A p-value of less than 0.001 was obtained indicating that the post-test results were significantly higher than the pre-test results. These results indicate that the PHP ITS could be a useful resource in teaching web development to beginning students.

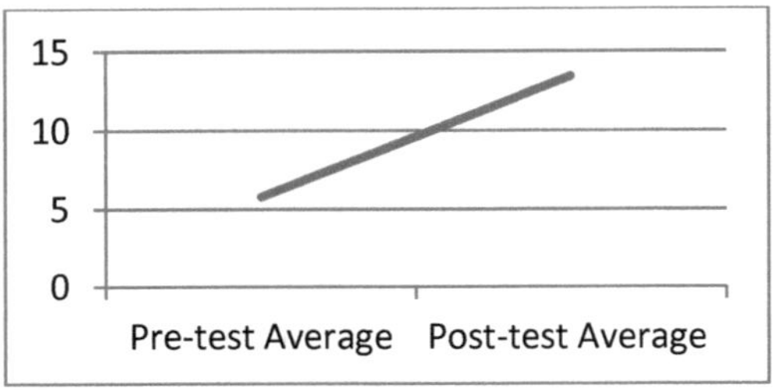

Fig. 2. Average student score for pre-and post- test

4 Conclusion

The students' feedback during the evaluation showed that it was necessary to incorporate more PHP constructs into the program analysis process. Although this would make the PHP ITS stronger, it can still be used in its present form to teach introductory web development to beginners as indicated by the above results. This fact is strengthened further by the feedback comment given by one student "I enjoy (sic) the ITS, with a few improvements it will just keep getting stronger".

References

1. Corbett, A.T.: Cognitive Mastery Learning in the ACT Programming Tutor. AAAI Technical Report SS-00-01. Cognitive Mastery Learning in the ACT Programming Tutor (2000)
2. Holland, J., Mitrovic, A., Martin, B.: J-LATTE: a Constraint-based Tutor for Java. Paper Presented at the 17th International Conference on Computers in Education, Hong Kong (2009)
3. Johnson, W.L.: Understanding and debugging novice programs. Artificial Intelligence 42(1), 51–97 (1990), doi:10.1016/0004-3702(90)90094-G
4. Sykes, E., Franek, F.: Presenting JECA: A java error correcting algorithm for the java intelligent tutoring system. Paper Presented at the IASTED International Conference on Advances in Computer Science and Technology, St. Thomas, Virgin Islands, USA (2004), `http://citeseerx.ist.psu.edu/viewdoc/download?doi=10.1.1.137.303&rep=rep1&type=pdf`
5. Weber, G., Brusilovsky, P.: ELM-ART: An adaptive versatile system for web-based instruction. International Journal of Artificial Intelligence in Education 12(4), 351–384 (2001), `http://www.ijaied.org/pub/965/file/965_paper.pdf`
6. Weragama, D., Reye, J.: Design of a knowledge base to teach programming. In: Cerri, S.A., Clancey, W.J., Papadourakis, G., Panourgia, K. (eds.) ITS 2012. LNCS, vol. 7315, pp. 600–602. Springer, Heidelberg (2012), `http://dx.doi.org/10.1007/978-3-642-30950-2_83`
7. Weragama, D., Reye, J.: Designing the Knowledge Base for a PHP Tutor. In: Cerri, S.A., Clancey, W.J., Papadourakis, G., Panourgia, K. (eds.) ITS 2012. LNCS, vol. 7315, pp. 628–629. Springer, Heidelberg (2012), `http://dx.doi.org/10.1007/978-3-642-30950-2_94`

The Interplay between Affect and Engagement in Classrooms Using AIED Software

Arnon Hershkovitz[1], Ryan S.J.d. Baker[1], Gregory R. Moore[2], Lisa M. Rossi[2], and Martin van Velsen[3]

[1] Teachers College, Columbia University, New York, NY
ah3096@columbia.edu, baker2@exchange.tc.columbia.edu
[2] Worcester Polytechnic Institute, Worcester MA
{gregmoore,lrossi}@wpi.edu
[3] Carnegie Mellon University, Pittsburgh, PA
martinv@andrew.cmu.edu

Abstract. Affect has been hypothesized to play a significant role in triggering engagement/disengagement during learning. In this paper, we study the inter-relationships between students' affect (boredom, confusion, frustration, engaged concentration) and their engaged and disengaged behaviors (off-task, on-task solitary, on-task conversation, gaming the system). We study these relationships in the context of four different software programs, involving students of different ages, in order to increase confidence in the generalizability of the findings. Understanding these relationships might assist in maintaining students' engagement over time.

Keywords: Affect, disengagement, quantitative field observations.

1 Introduction

Disengaged behaviors have been shown to lead to poorer learning outcomes in both computer-based learning and traditional curricula. Recent research has suggested that affect - emotion experienced in context – can contribute to student disengagement [1-2]. In this paper, we study these relationships in the context of four different learning systems, used by four different populations; the systems are all being used as part of routine instruction. By studying this relationship across multiple data sets, a more nuanced understanding of affect-engagement patterns during routine learning may be achieved, potentially contributing to the improvement of both theoretical knowledge and practical applications.

2 Measuring Disengagement and Affect during Learning

Engagement and disengagement are challenging to measure. We followed the paradigm of studying specific behaviors which are indicative of engagement or disengagement, and which are associated with differences in students‘ learning outcomes: a) **Off-task**

K. Yacef et al. (Eds.): AIED 2013, LNAI 7926, pp. 587–590, 2013.

behavior, where a student disengages from the learning task; b) **On-task solitary work** within the learning system; c) **On-task conversation**, where the student talks to an instructor or peer about the educational software or its domain, rather than interacting solely with the educational software; and d) **Gaming the system**, where students engage in behaviors such as systematic guessing or help requests in order to obtain answers without thinking through the learning material.

The four affective states studied in this paper are known to be common during learning, and have been demonstrated or hypothesized to have strong links to learning: a) **Boredom**, b) **Confusion**, c) **Frustration**, and d) **Engaged concentration**, the affective state associated with Csikszentmihalyi's construct of flow [3].

We study the fine-grained temporal relationships between affect and disengagement using quantitative field observations (QFO) of student affect and disengaged behaviors conducted by trained field coders who observe students' interaction with the educational software [cf. 1]. The same protocol as in [1] was used; the observers based their judgment on the student's work context, actions, utterances, facial expressions, body language, and interactions with teachers or fellow students.

3 Data Sets, Likelihood of Transitions, Co-occurrences

To increase the generalizability of our results, we studied these issues within four learning enviroments (*The Chemistry Virtual Laboratory*, *Cognitive Tutor Algebra*, *Cognitive Tutor Geometry*, and *ASSISTments*) that differ by populaion (middle school to undergraduates), region (rural and urban Pennsylvania, urban Massachusetts), learning topic (Chemistry, Mathematics), and learning software design (simulation-based virtual laboratory, intelligent tutoring systems). Students were observed during natural use of these systems, in the schools' computer labs, classes lasted 45-60 minutes. Overall, 518 students were observed in 58 class sessions.

D'Mello's Likelihood (L) [1] was used to determine how likely a transition (or a co-occurrence) is to occur, from one base state to another. D'Mello's L can be a value between $-\infty$ and 1. We calculate L values at the student-level for each transition/co-occurrence and each learning environment. We can determine if a given transition is significantly more/less likely than chance (i.e., above/below 0), using the two-tailed t-test for one sample. Significance for a given transition/co-occurrence can be calculated across learning environments using Stouffer's Z. As a substantial number of statistical analyses are made, we adjust for potential Type I errors using a False Discovery Rate (FDR) post-hoc correction, using the QVALUE software package within R. This procedure gives a q-value, which can be interpreted the same way as a p-value. All Z values reported below as significant had $q<0.05$; all values reported as marginal had $q<0.1$.

4 Results

Co-occurences of Behavior and Affect. Off-task was more likely than chance to co-occur with Boredom, across environments ($Z = 8.31$) and in all but one system, Cognitive

Tutor Geometry, a finding that replicated previous findings that used self-reported questionnaires [4]. Off-task was less likely than chance to co-occur with Engaged Concentration (Z = -11.01) and with Confusion (Z = -7.79) across environments, a finding that was true in each environment. Off-task was less likely than chance to co-occur with Frustration across environments (Z = -4.32) and in two systems (Cognitive Tutor Algebra, ASSISTments).

On-task was more likely than chance to co-occur with Engaged Concentration, across environments (Z = 18.15) and in each system separately, in line with flow theory [3] Across systems, On-task was more likely than chance to co-occur with Confusion (Z = 2.73) and Frustration (Z = 3.18). Taken separately, these relationships were found only in ASSISTments. On-task was less likely than chance to co-occur with Boredom, across environments (Z = -5.16) and in two systems (Cognitive Tutor Algebra, ASSISTments).

On-task Conversation was more likely than chance to co-occur with Confusion, across environments (Z = 4.63) and in two systems (Chemistry Virtual Lab and ASSISTments). It is possible that students seek on-task conversation to relieve their confusion, or alternatively, perhaps students become confused during on-task conversation, due to the cognitive disequilibrium arising from confronting different ideas. On-task Conversation was less likely than chance to co-occur with Boredom, across environments (Z = -4.04) and in two systems (Chemistry Virtual Lab, Cognitive Tutor Algebra).

Behavior to Affect Transition. Across environments, only two transitions were significantly different from chance: On-task behavior was somewhat surprisingly more likely than chance to be followed by Boredom (Z = 2.77) (taken separately, this finding was seen only in Cognitive Tutor Algebra), and less likely than chance to be followed by Engaged Concentration (Z = -3.30) (which holds also for two systems, Cognitive Tutor Geometry and ASSISTments). These findings might imply that it can be difficult to keep students attentive over significant periods of time, even when using advanced AIED systems. Two relationships were marginally significant across environments. The transition from Off-task to Bored was marginally less likely than chance (Z = -2.18), and the transition from On-task Conversation to Frustrated was marginally less likely than chance (Z = -2.07), which highlights the importance of on-topic social interactions with teacher/peers.

Affect to Behavior Transition. Only one transition was significant different from chance across environments (but not in any system separately): the transition from Frustration to On-task Conversation, which was less likely than chance to occur (Z = -2.28). Note that the converse relationship was also marginally significant, suggesting that frustration neither follows nor precedes on-task conversation.

5 Conclusions

Several interesting patterns emerge from this study. Across environments, off-task behavior was found to more likely than chance to co-occur with Boredom, and less likely than chance to co-occur with the other affective states. This may suggest that off-task behavior plays some positive role in regulating negative affect during learning, disrupting "vicious cycles" where a student who becomes bored is highly likely to remain bored.

On-task solitary behavior was associated with a greater degree of future boredom and less engaged concentration. This might be explained by confusion and frustration co-occurring more than chance with on-task solitary behavior. By contrast, frustration neither preceded nor followed on-task conversation. On-task conversation was also found more likely to co-occur with confusion and less likely to co-occur with boredom. These relationships confirm reports that episodes of on-task conversation are a normal and beneficial part of "individual" use of educational software.

Acknowledgements. This research was supported by grant "Toward a Decade of PSLC Research: Investigating Instructional, Social, and Learner Factors in Robust Learning through Data-Driven Analysis and Modeling," National Science Foundation award #SBE-0836012.

References

1. Baker, R.S.J.d., D'Mello, S.K., Rodrigo, M.M.T., Graesser, A.C.: Better to be frustrated than bored: The incidence, persistence, and impact of learners' cognitive-affective states during interactions with three different computer-based learning environments. International Journal of Human-Computer Studies 68(4), 223–241 (2010)
2. Sabourin, J., Rowe, J.P., Mott, B.W., Lester, J.C.: When off-task is on-task: The affective role of off-task behavior in narrative-centered learning environments. In: Biswas, G., Bull, S., Kay, J., Mitrovic, A. (eds.) AIED 2011. LNCS, vol. 6738, pp. 534–536. Springer, Heidelberg (2011)
3. Csikszentmihalyi, M.: Flow: The Psychology of Optimal Experience. Harper & Row, New York (1990)
4. Pekrun, R., Goetz, T., Titz, W., Perry, R.P.: Academic emotions in students' self-regulated learning and achievement: A program of qualitative and quantitative research. Educational Psychologist 37(2), 91–105 (2002)

Towards Automated Analysis of Student Arguments

Nancy L. Green

University of North Carolina Greensboro
Greensboro, NC 27402 USA
nlgreen@uncg.edu

Abstract. This paper presents the approach to automated analysis of student argument diagrams to be used in the Genetics Argumentation Inquiry Learning (GAIL) system. Student arguments are compared to expert arguments automatically generated using an existing argument generator developed previously for the GenIE Assistant project. A prototype argument analyzer was implemented for GAIL. Weaknesses in student arguments are identified using non-domain-specific, non-content-specific rules that recognize common error types.

Keywords: Educational Argumentation Systems, Genetics Education.

1 Introduction

We are developing the Genetics Argumentation Inquiry Learning (GAIL) system for improving undergraduate biology students' argumentation skills in the domain of genetics. As in many educational argumentation systems, GAIL will provide the learner with tools for representing arguments in diagrams due to the cognitive benefit of diagrams (Kirschner et al. 2003; Scheuer et al. 2010; Pinkwart and McLaren 2012). In addition, educational systems can exploit the learner's argument diagram as a source of information for providing educational feedback. The top left-hand side of GAIL's graphical user interface (GUI) presents a problem, e.g., to make an argument for the claim that J.B., an imaginary patient, has the genetic condition called cystic fibrosis. Below that are possible hypotheses, data about the patient and his biological family members, and biomedical principles that may be relevant to the current problem. The learner can drag these elements into the argument diagramming workspace in the center of the screen to construct an argument in a Toulmin-influenced (1998) box-and-arrow notation; a vertical arrow from the *data* points upward to the *claim/conclusion* and the *warrant* is attached at a right-angle to the arrow. With this approach, GAIL circumvents the challenge of understanding unrestricted text input.

This paper describes our planned approach to automatic analysis of argument diagrams constructed by learners in GAIL. Expert models for argument analysis will be automatically constructed by GAIL using an argument generator module similar to the argument generator developed for the GenIE Assistant (Green et al. 2011). The expert model will contain all acceptable arguments that can be automatically generated for a given claim from an underlying knowledge base (KB) representing the problem domain. The generated argument structures contain KB elements. Text elements

K. Yacef et al. (Eds.): AIED 2013, LNAI 7926, pp. 591–594, 2013.

provided to the learner through GAIL's GUI are linked internally to KB elements. The inputs to GAIL's argument analyzer will be the learner's argument and the expert model. The analyzer will compare the user's argument to the generated expert arguments to identify acceptable learner arguments and weaknesses in the learner's argument. Weaknesses in student arguments are identified using non-domain-specific, non-content-specific rules that recognize common error types. The error types are based on those observed in a pilot study.

In some previous educational argumentation systems, the student's diagram is compared to a manually-constructed expert model to provide problem-specific support. However, expert models are expensive to construct and may not cover all possible solutions or errors (Scheuer et al. 2012). In GAIL's approach the expert model is constructed automatically. Other systems use simulation of reasoning to evaluate formal correctness but do not provide problem-specific support (Scheuer et al. 2012). GAIL's approach is similar in that it reasons like an expert to generate an argument. Unlike those systems, however, GAIL's approach will provide both problem-specific support on weaknesses in the student's argument and evaluation of argument quality.

2 Generation of Expert Arguments

Generation of expert arguments in GAIL will be done following the approach to argument generation used in the GenIE Assistant, a proof-of-concept system for generating genetic counseling patient letters (Green et al. 2011). GenIE's internal components include (1) *domain models*, causal models of genetic conditions (Green 2005), (2) an *argumentation engine* that uses computational definitions of *argumentation schemes* (Walton et al. 2008) to guide search in the domain model for data and warrant needed to support a particular claim, and (3) a *letter drafter* that organizes and expresses the arguments as English text using natural language generation techniques. GAIL's expert arguments will be produced using a similar approach to the GenIE Assistant's domain models and argumentation engine. However, the natural language generation module, the letter drafter, will not be needed to generate expert arguments.

Computational definitions of argumentation schemes are used by the GenIE Assistant's argumentation engine to construct a genetic counselor's arguments for the diagnosis and genotypes of family members. The argumentation schemes are formalized in a structure including *claim*, *data*, and *warrant*. Since the argumentation engine and schemes do not encode domain-specific or patient case-specific content, they can be used to generate arguments in any domain whose domain knowledge can be represented in terms of causal variables. An argument for a given claim is automatically constructed by searching the domain model and data about the patient's case for information fitting GenIE's argumentation schemes instantiated with the claim. The schemes support abductive reasoning, reasoning from cause to effect, reasoning from negative evidence, and reasoning by elimination of alternatives. The GenIE Assistant's argumentation engine can construct complex arguments involving multiple pieces of evidence and chains of arguments. The same approach will be used in GAIL to generate expert arguments for a given claim.

3 Pilot Study

A formative evaluation of GAIL's prototype user interface was done in fall 2011 through spring 2012 with a total of 10 paid undergraduate volunteers, the first seven of which were biology students and the last three computer science students. Each participant was given several problems to construct arguments for or against claims about a hypothetical patient with cystic fibrosis. However, none of the first seven students created acceptable arguments. At that point in the study, it was decided to modify the materials and procedure. First, the problems were reduced in number (eliminating an argument involving conjunction). Second, when the participant submitted a response the research assistant reviewed it using a checklist of error types created by the author after reviewing the arguments created by the first group of participants. If the participant's response contained any of those types of errors then the research assistant gave feedback and asked the student to revise his or her argument. After three tries, the student was told to proceed to the next problem in the set.

The distribution of error types is shown in Table 1. A Type 1 error was an argument whose claim did not match the claim for which the student was asked to give an argument. Type 2 was an argument where the data was not evidence for the claim. Type 3 was an argument where the warrant did not relate the data to the claim. Type 4 was an argument where the opposite type of link was required. Type 5 was a chained argument in which a subargument was missing or incorrect. Type 6 errors involved incorrect use of conjunctions. Type 7 was omission of the warrant. In Table 1, Group 1 comprises the first seven students, who were given no feedback. Group 2 comprises the last three students, who were given feedback and three tries on each problem. The number of errors on each try for each student in Group 2 was totaled and the average was computed by dividing by nine (i.e., three students with three tries each). From the first group, it can be seen that the most frequent errors (in descending frequency) were incorrect data, incorrect warrant, and incorrect claim. Although the quantity of errors in the first and second groups cannot be compared, it should be noted that the top three error types in Group 1 remained the top three in Group 2.

Table 1. Average number of errors per error type per person in each group

Error Type	Group 1	Group 2
1:Incorrect claim	1.9	0.8
2:Incorrect data	2.6	0.3
3:Incorrect warrant	2	1
4:Incorrect pro/con	0.9	0.3
5:Incorrect/missing chained claim	1.4	0
6: Incorrect/missing conjunction	0.9	NA
7: Missing warrant	0.1	0.4

4 Argument Analyzer

Implemented in Prolog, the prototype argument analyzer determines if a student's argument diagram represents an acceptable argument and if not, identifies its weaknesses. The analyzer presupposes that the argument generator has generated all acceptable arguments for the given claim from the KB elements corresponding to the elements in GAIL's GUI that the user could have used in his diagram. (In addition, the GUI prevents certain types of syntactic errors from occurring.) The algorithm to determine acceptability merely checks whether the user's argument matches one of the acceptable arguments. If the user's argument does not match an acceptable argument, its weaknesses are identified using pattern-matching rules motivated mainly by the types of errors seen in the study described in the previous section. The rules are non-domain-specific and non-problem-specific. For example, if the user's data and claim match the expert's, but the warrant does not, the analyzer identifies the problem as an unacceptable warrant (Type 3). The prototype argument analyzer implementation outputs an error message for each error detected. However, in the future implementation of GAIL, the argument analyzer output would be used by the as yet unimplemented Pedagogical Feedback Generator, responsible for selecting which error(s) to highlight and providing appropriate feedback. We are currently running a think-aloud user study to understand why students make errors in argumentation. Future work remains to finish the implementation of GAIL and to evaluate its effectiveness.

Acknowledgments. Graduate students B. Wyatt and C. Martensen implemented the prototype of GAIL's user interface described here; Martensen ran the user study in fall 2011-spring 2012; both received support from a UNCG Faculty Research Grant.

References

Green, N.: A Bayesian network coding scheme for annotating biomedical information presented to genetic counseling clients. Journal of Biomedical Informatics 38, 130–144 (2005)

Green, N., Dwight, R., Navoraphan, K., Stadler, B.: Natural language generation of transparent arguments for lay audiences. Argument and Computation 2(1), 23–50 (2011)

Kirschner, P.A., Buckingham Shum, S.J., Carr, C.S. (eds.): Visualizing Argumentation. Springer, London (2003)

Pinkwart, N., McLaren, B.M. (eds.): Educational Technologies for Teaching Argumentation Skills. Bentham Science Publishers, Sharjah (2012)

Scheuer, O., Loll, F., Pinkwart, N., McLaren, B.M.: Computer-Supported Argumentation: A Review of the State of the Art. Computer-Supported Collaborative Learning 5(1), 43–102 (2010)

Scheuer, O., McLaren, B.M., Loll, F., Pinkwart, N.: Automated Analysis and Feedback Techniques to Support and Teach Argumentation: A Survey. In: Pinkwart, McLaren (eds.) Educational Technologies for Teaching Argumentation Skills (2012)

Toulmin, S.E.: The uses of argument. Cambridge University Press, Cambridge (1998)

Walton, D., Reed, C., Macagno, F.: Argumentation Schemes. Cambridge University Press, Cambridge (2008)

Automatic Detection of Concepts from Problem Solving Times

Petr Boroš, Juraj Nižnan, Radek Pelánek, and Jiří Řihák

Faculty of Informatics, Masaryk University Brno
{boros,niznan,xpelanek,thran}@mail.muni.cz

Abstract. Intelligent tutoring systems need to know a mapping between particular problems and general domain concepts. Such mapping can be constructed manually by an expert, but that is time consuming and error prone. Our aim is to detect concepts automatically from problem solving times. We propose and evaluate two approaches: a model of problem solving times with multidimensional skill and an application of spectral clustering. The results show that it is feasible to construct a problem-concept mapping from solely the problem solving times and that the results of the analysis can bring an interesting insight.

1 Introduction

One of the functions of intelligent tutoring systems is to provide students feedback on their skills and to adaptively select suitable problems. To this end, the system needs to understand its target domain, e.g., to have a mapping between particular problems and general domain concepts (e.g., fractions, linear functions, trigonometry). Such mapping can be constructed manually by an expert, but that is time consuming and error prone. Thus it is desirable to construct and validate such mappings automatically.

In this work we study techniques to automatically determine concepts from problem solving times. To this end, we propose and evaluate two approaches. The first approach is a multidimensional extension of the model of problem solving times, which we introduced in previous work [3]. This model is analogous to the Q-matrix approach [1], the main difference is that a standard Q-matrix is used with discrete values (0/1), whereas in our setting we use continuous values. The second approach is to determine the concepts by a clustering technique, particularly by the spectral clustering method [4]. For evaluation we use data from the Problem Solving Tutor [3].

The results show that it is feasible to automatically detect concepts (i.e., similarity between problems) from problem solving times. We present a specific example which shows an interesting and useful output of the automatic detection of concepts. The two studied methods, although using completely different approaches, give similar overall results. The approach based on multidimensional model is less stable than spectral clustering, but can be naturally used for validation and improvement of a Q-matrix provided by an expert.

K. Yacef et al. (Eds.): AIED 2013, LNAI 7926, pp. 595–598, 2013.

2 Techniques for Detection of Concepts

In the following we assume that we have a set of students, a set of problems, and data about problem solving times: t_{sp} is a logarithm of time it took a student s to solve a problem p. The first approach is based on a previously described model of problem solving times [3]. The basic structure of the model is simple – it assumes a linear relationship between the logarithm of a time and a skill: $t_{sp} = b_p + q_p\theta_s + \epsilon$, where t_{sp} is the logarithm of a problem solving time for a student s and a problem p, b_p is the basic difficulty of a problem p, q_p is a discrimination factor of a problem p, θ_s is a skill of a student s, and ϵ is Gaussian noise. A more detailed discussion of the model is given in [3].

Here we consider an extension of this model with k dimensional skills: $t_{sp} = b_p + \boldsymbol{q_p}^T\boldsymbol{\theta_s} + \epsilon$, where $\boldsymbol{q_p}$ is a k dimensional discrimination vector and $\boldsymbol{\theta_s}$ is a k dimensional skill vector. The model is analogical to widely used Q-matrix models [1]. The main difference is that standard Q-matrices are typically used in the setting of test questions with binary response (0 – incorrect, 1 – correct), with the Q-matrix entries and student skills being also binary (the model specifies probability of a correct answer using noisy and/or function).

In our setting it is natural to allow both Q-matrix values (discrimination factors) and skills to be continuous. The estimation of the parameters can be done by stochastic gradient descent, analogically to the model with one dimensional skill [3]. The main complication with respect to the one dimensional case is a suitable initialization of the gradient descent.

The second approach is spectral clustering, which is a popular clustering technique based on linear algebra [4]. The main principle of the algorithm is the following. At first, a similarity graph for the data is created; construction of this graph is specific to a domain of application. At second, a Laplacian matrix of the similarity graph is constructed and its first n eigenvectors are computed. At third, the eigenvectors are used to transform original data into points in R^n; these points are clustered using the standard k-means algorithm (an illustration is provided in Fig. 1.).

Note that only the first step is problem specific, the other two steps are generic. In our case for each pair of problems we define their similarity as a Spearman's correlation coefficient of times of shared students (those who solved both problems). Based on the computed similarity matrix, we construct k-nearest-neighbours graph (connecting each node with k most similar nodes); where k is one half of the number of problems. For our data the spectral clustering method is quite stable and not susceptible to details (e.g., a choice of k or an exact version of the algorithm).

3 Evaluation

We evaluated the described techniques over data from the Problem Solving Tutor (`tutor.fi.muni.cz`) [3]. To evaluate the identification of concepts we performed the following experiment. We mix data from the Problem Solving Tutor for two different types of problems and remove information about the type of the problem from the data. Then we let an algorithm analyze the data and cluster problems into two groups. The performance is measured by the number of correctly clustered problems (reported below as percentage of all problems). For the experiment we used 8 most solved problem types from the Problem Solving Tutor. The experiment was performed on all pairs of these problem types. For each pair we consider only data about students who solved at least 10 problems from both problem types. On average the data for each problem pair contain 150 problem instances and 150 students.

The overall mean performance of spectral clustering is 86.5%, the model with two skills achieves very similar overall results (85.9%). We also evaluated clustering using only the standard k-means algorithm (each problem is represented as a vector of correlation coefficients with other problems), the performance in this case was slightly worse (83.5%). All of these techniques are partially stochastic, so we measured the performance over multiple runs. Spectral clustering yields very consistent results, whereas the model based classification (which uses stochastic gradient descent with randomized initialization) has in few cases large variance.

The performance differs for individual problems. Results are very good (over 90%, up to 99%) for problems which strongly depend on logical reasoning skills and thus the noise in the data is low. On the other hand, results are poor for a geometric puzzle, where the noise in data is quite high since the puzzle is based more on insight and luck than on skill.

We analyzed one of the problems in more detail – a Binary crossword problem. The goal is to fill a grid with zeros and ones in such a way that all specified conditions are met (see Fig. 1.). This setting can be used for easy problems for practicing basics of binary numbers (a) and logic operations (b), but also for more challenging problems where the specified conditions are given in self-referential crossword manner, which leads to quite entertaining practice of binary numbers and logic operations (c, d).

There are 55 instances of Binary crosswords and they can be naturally divided to three main groups: examples based on knowledge of binary notation, examples which use logical operations, and the self-referential crossword examples which usually combine different types of conditions and require deeper thinking. The Problem Solving Tutor contains manually created classification of examples into these three types (binary numbers, logic operations, and crosswords). We used the spectral clustering method to compute 3 clusters and compared the results with the manual labeling of examples – the agreement of the classifications was about 80%. Most differences can be intuitively explained, and in fact in most cases the misclassification brings an useful insight, often showing inappropriateness of the manual labeling.

One of the advantages of spectral clustering is the possibility to use the computed eigenvectors to plot data in a low dimensional space. In Fig. 1. we can see that instances a, b, c, which are typical examples of their groups, are placed in the middle of their clusters. Instance d has a form of a self-referential crossword but strongly uses the concept of logic operations and the location of this

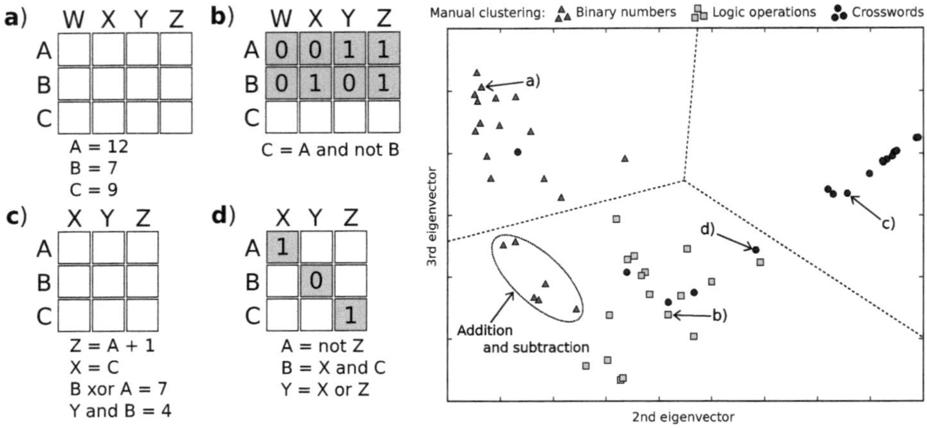

Fig. 1. Examples of Binary crossword problems and projection of all problems onto a plane by spectral clustering (with algorithmically determined clusters)

example corresponds to this observation. Another similar example is a circle in Binary number cluster which also has a form of crosswords, but solving requires only ability to write binary numbers. Interesting results were obtained for examples based on addition and subtraction of binary numbers. These examples were manually labelled as "binary numbers", but Fig. 1. suggests that these examples are slightly different then other binary numbers examples and are closer to the "logic operations" cluster.

This kind of analysis can be done also using the model with multiple skills. In this case it is natural to initialize the model according to the provided labeling, fit the model to data, and then check which problems deviate most from the initialization (thus performing a Q-matrix validation [2]). We have performed this analysis for the Binary crossword problem, the results are similar to the above presented results obtained through spectral clustering.

References

1. Barnes, T.: The q-matrix method: Mining student response data for knowledge. In: American Association for Artificial Intelligence 2005 Educational Data Mining Workshop (2005)
2. De La Torre, J.: An empirically based method of q-matrix validation for the dina model: Development and applications. Journal of Educational Measurement 45(4), 343–362 (2008)
3. Jarušek, P., Pelánek, R.: Analysis of a simple model of problem solving times. In: Cerri, S.A., Clancey, W.J., Papadourakis, G., Panourgia, K. (eds.) ITS 2012. LNCS, vol. 7315, pp. 379–388. Springer, Heidelberg (2012)
4. Ng, A.Y., Jordan, M.I., Weiss, Y., et al.: On spectral clustering: Analysis and an algorithm. In: Advances in Neural Information Processing Systems, vol. 2, pp. 849–856 (2002)

Educational Potentials in Visually Androgynous Pedagogical Agents

Annika Silvervarg[1], Magnus Haake[2], and Agneta Gulz[1]

[1] Department of Computer Science, Linköping University, Sweden
{annika.silvervarg,agneta.gulz}@liu.se
[2] Department of Cognitive Science, Lund University, Sweden
magnus.haake@lucs.lu.se

Abstract. We report a study on student's attitudes to a visually androgynous in comparison to a male and a female Teachable Agent (TA). Results were that overall the androgynous agent was preferred over the female and male agents. A visually androgynous agent does not embody categorical gender attributes. At the same time it does not have to be *genderless* but instead represent *both* maleness and femaleness so that students can chose for themselves. Androgyny, in this sense, is potentially a way to have femaleness and maleness represented, with corresponding educational benefits such as role modelling and identification, without risking negative reinforcement of gender stereotypes.

Keywords: pedagogical agent, teachable agent, androgyny, visual appearance.

1 Introduction

The impact of role models and identification in educational contexts is well established. Bandura [1] highlights the significance of similarities between a role model and a learner and points out gender as a crucial dimension. A number of studies have explored the impact of visual gender in terms of male versus female pedagogical agents. For instance, the use of virtual coaches portrayed as young females increased the willingness of female students to choose technically oriented courses and helped increase their self-efficacy [2]. But there were drawbacks. The female student's positive attitudes seemed to stem from a conception of a female engineer being less competent than a "real, typical male engineer". They reasoned along the line "If she is able to do it, I can do it!" [2]. Thus the short-term pedagogical benefits of recruitment and boosted self-efficacy in female students were accompanied by a long-term pedagogical drawback in reproducing and reinforcing – not changing – gender stereotypes and prejudices. In the study presented in this paper a humanlike visually androgynous agent was compared with a female and a male agent in terms of students' attitudes toward the agents. The rationale for the study was the following question: Is it possible to retain the benefits of gender in pedagogical agents, in terms of identification and role models, but avoid or diminish the drawbacks in terms of reinforcement of gender stereotypes including a high amount of abuse towards female agents [4].

K. Yacef et al. (Eds.): AIED 2013, LNAI 7926, pp. 599–602, 2013.

2 Study

The pedagogical agent is a Teachable Agent (TA), i.e. a digital tutee, situated in an educational math game that trains basic arithmetic skills with a focus on grounding base-ten concepts in spatial representations [3]. The TA engages in on-task activities with the student – board games and multiple choice conversations regarding math as trained in the game – as well as in free off-task conversation in natural language in a social chat.

The study explored the following questions: How would a visually androgynous vs. a visually gender stereotypical TA affect students' attitudes towards the TA (i) as their tutee?" and (ii) as their social chat partner?

The three agent representations used in the study are shown in Fig. 1. All three representations were pre-validated in terms of gender perception by 38 students from the target group. Agent interests, conversational style, etc., were identical and designed to be gender neutral. Also all agent names were gender neutral. Importantly the agents are humanlike. We were not interested in androgynous agents in the form of artifacts, animals or robots (which can all be designed to be genderless or as avoiding gender).

Fig. 1. The agents' visual representation: female, androgynous, and male

2.1 Method

44 female and 64 male students of age 12-14 participated. Since all were not present at both lessons, the analysis included 37 females and 46 males. The students played the math game and interacted with two different TAs during two separate 45 minute lessons spaced a week apart from each other. In the first lesson all students played with the visually androgynous agent, in the second they were randomly assigned the female or the male agent. A combination of data from questionnaires and computer-generated logs were used. The questionnaire focused on the experience of chatting with the agent and the perception of the agent. It also contained a question about the agent's visual appearance: "[Agent name] looked like" with the scale: Definitely like a girl, A little like a girl, Neither girl nor boy, A little like a boy, Definitely like a boy. For the second session the questionnaire was extended with free format questions. At the top of the page the name and picture of the two agents the student had encountered were placed and below this the following questions: "Who did you prefer to have as your tutee? WHY?" and "Who did you prefer to chat with? WHY?"

2.2 Results

Perception of Visual Androgyny. Most students perceived the visually androgynous agent as not clearly a boy nor clearly a girl, but as "neither girl nor boy", "a little like a girl" or "a little like a boy". There was no significant difference in the scores for boys (M = 2,62, SD = 1,33) compared to girls (M = 3,05, SD = 1,36); t(84) = 1,50, p = 0,14.

In the chat conversation with their digital tutees, students could potentially ask their tutee about its gender. (Androgynous agents were assigned the same gender as the agent in the second session.) However, the visually androgynous agent was asked about its gender by only 15% of the students. Simultaneously it was obvious from classroom observations and from the free format questionnaire answers, that the students generally themselves assigned a gender to it. In other words, even though a majority of students did not perceive a clear gender – boy or girl – in their androgynous tutee agent, they did not ask her/him about her/his gender – but assigned one, by their own decision.

These results are important. They indicate that perceiving an agent as visually androgynous is compatible with assigning a gender (male or female) to it, but with this assignment being personal rather than imposed by external information.

Preference of Agent as Tutee. The analysis of which agent students preferred as their tutee was undertaken for the two conditions androgynous agent vs. female agent, and androgynous agent vs. male agent, and with regard to student gender. The data was coded as follows: 1 stands for a preference for the androgynous agent 0 stands for a preference for the female or male agent, and 0,5 stands for "it does not matter" (or the like). Means were then calculated for the different groups, see Fig. 2.

All groups show a significant preference for the androgynous agent (M = 0.64, SD = 0.46) over the gendered (female and male) agents; t(76) = 2.74, p = 0.007). Girls significantly preferred the androgynous agent (M = 0.78, SD = 0.43) over the female agent; t(17) = 2.75, p = 0.014. For boys, this preference was marginally significant (M = 0.68, SD = 0.41; t(19) = 1.93, p = 0.069). Girls significantly preferred the androgynous agent before the male agent (M = 0.74, SD = 0.44); t(16) = 2.22, p = 0.041, whereas for boys (M = 0.43, SD = 0.50) there was no significant result; t(21) = -0.65, p = 0.53.

Preference of Agent as Chat Partner. Preference for chat partner was coded the same way as that regarding preference of tutee, and the results are shown to the right in Fig. 2. The androgynous agent was preferred (M=0.67, SD=0.43) over the female and male agents for the group as a whole; t(67)=2.00, p=0.002. Boys preferred the androgynous over the female agent (M=0.81, SD=0.30); t(17)=2,1, p=0.0005, while girls showed no such significant preference t(16)=2.12, p=0.23. Girls preferred the androgynous (M=0,82, SD=0,37) before the male agent, t=2.16, p=0.007, while boys showed no such significant preference, t(18)=2.10, p=0.63.

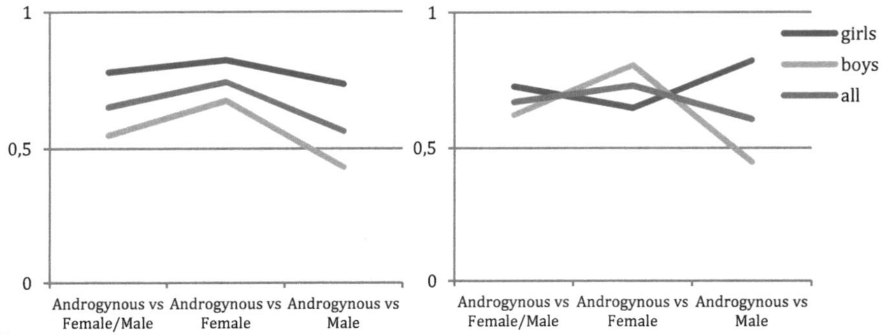

Fig. 2. Left: Means for student preference for tutee. Right: Means for student preference of chat partner. 1=androgynous agent, 0=gendered agent (female or male).

3 Conclusions

At the outset of the paper we discussed educational benefits as well as drawbacks with clearly gendered pedagogical agents and asked: Can we retain the benefits and avoid or diminish the drawbacks? Can we have the cake and eat it too? On these questions we want to give cautious affirmative answers. Visually androgynous characters can, as indicated in our study, be well received (a primary condition that has to be fulfilled). A main result was that girls consistently preferred the visually androgynous character both before the female character and the male character. Boys preferred an androgynous agent before a female, but preferred an androgynous and male agent equally.

Importantly, visually androgynous agents, as constructed in the present study, combine possibilities for identification on the basis of gender – known to be pedagogically valuable due to role modeling effects – with increased freedom for the students themselves to construct and ascribe gender. Simultaneously one can avoid or diminish the drawback of reproduction of gender stereotypes, since a visually androgynous character does not embody categorical gender.

References

1. Bandura, A.: Self-efficacy: the exercise of control. Freeman, New York (1997)
2. Baylor, A., Rosenberg-Kima, R., Plant, E.: Interface agents as social models: The impact of appearance on females' attitude toward engineering. In: Proc. of CHI 2006, Montreal, Canada (2006)
3. Pareto, L., Haake, M., Lindström, P., Sjödén, B., Gulz, A.: A Teachable Agent Based Game Affording Collaboration and Competition: evaluating math comprehension and motivation. Educational Technology Research and Development (2012)
4. Silvervarg, A., Raukola, K., Haake, M., Gulz, A.: The Effect of Visual Gender on Abuse in Conversation with ECAs. In: Nakano, Y., Neff, M., Paiva, A., Walker, M. (eds.) IVA 2012. LNCS, vol. 7502, pp. 153–160. Springer, Heidelberg (2012)

Plan Recognition for ELEs Using Interleaved Temporal Search

Oriel Uzan, Reuth Dekel, and Ya'akov (Kobi) Gal

Dept. of Information Systems Engineering,
Ben-Gurion University,
Beer-Sheva, Israel
{uzanu,dekelr,kobig}@bgu.ac.il

Abstract. Exploratory Learning Environments (ELE) provide a rich educational environment for students, but challenge teachers to keep track of students' progress and to assess their performance. This paper proposes an algorithm that decomposes students complete interaction histories to create hierarchies of interdependent tasks that describe their activities in ELEs. It matches students' actions to a predefined grammar in a way that reflects students' typical use of ELEs, namely that students solve problems in a modular fashion but may still interleave between their activities. The algorithm was empirically evaluated on peoples interaction with two separate ELEs for simulating a chemistry laboratory and for statistics education. It was separately compared to the state-of-the-art recognition algorithm for each of the ELEs. The results show that the algorithm was able to correctly infer students' activities significantly more often than the state-of-the-art, and was able to generalize to both of the ELEs with no intervention. These results demonstrate the benefit of using AI techniques towards augmenting existing ELEs with tools for analyzing and assessing students' performance.

1 Introduction

Exploratory Learning Environments (ELE) are open-ended software in which students build scientific models and examine properties of the models by running them and analyzing the results[1]. ELEs are generally used in classes too large for teachers to monitor all students and provide assistance when needed, and are becoming increasingly prevalent in developing countries where access to teachers and other educational resources is limited [4]. Thus, there is a need to develop tools of support for teachers' understanding of students' activities. Such tools can provide support for teachers and education researchers in analyzing and assessing students' use of ELEs. However, there are several aspects to students' interactions with ELEs that make it challenging to recognize their activities. Students can engage in exploratory activities involving trial-and-error, they can repeat activities indefinitely, and they can interleave between activities. For example, an ELE for teaching chemistry, called VirtualLabs, allows students to design and carry out their own experiments for investigating chemical processes [6] by simulating the conditions and effects that characterize scientific

K. Yacef et al. (Eds.): AIED 2013, LNAI 7926, pp. 603–606, 2013.

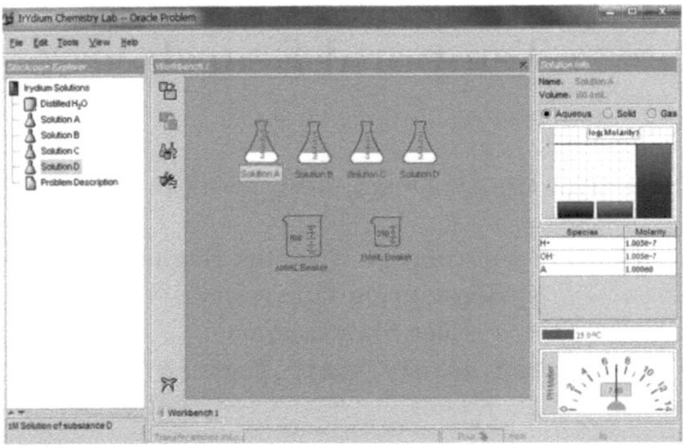

Fig. 1. Snapshot of VirtualLabs

inquiry in the physical laboratory. A snapshot of a student's interaction with VirtualLabs when solving the Oracle problem is shown in Figure 1.

This paper presents a plan recognition algorithm that meets these challenges. It works offline, and decomposes students' complete interaction history with the software into hierarchies of interdependent tasks that best describe their work with the software. It matches students' actions to a grammar in a way that reflects the aspects of students' work in ELEs described above. The algorithm was evaluated in an extensive empirical study that involved seven different types of problems and 68 instances of students' interactions in two different ELEs. It was compared to two state-of-the-art algorithms for recognizing students' plans in the ELEs. It was able to correctly recognize significantly more plans than did both of the state-of-the-art algorithms [2,5].

2 Methodology and Results

Our algorithm, called Plan Recognition via Interleaved Sequential Matching (PRISM), provides a tradeoff between the following two complementary aspects of students' interactions with ELEs. First, students generally solve problems in a sequential fashion, by which we mean that actions that are (temporally) closer to each other are more likely to relate to the same sub-goal. Second, students may interleave between activities relating to different sub-goals. The complexity of the algorithm is, in practice, polynomial in the size of the log and the recipe database.

We evaluated the algorithm on real data consisting of students' interactions. To demonstrate the scalability of the PRISM algorithm we evaluated it on two different ELEs: the VirtualLabs system as well as an ELE for teaching statistics and probability called TinkerPlots [3] used worldwide in elementary school and colleges. In TinkerPlots, students build models of stochastic events, run the models to generate data, and analyze the results. It is an extremely flexible application, allowing for data to be modeled, generated, and analyzed in many ways using an open-ended interface.

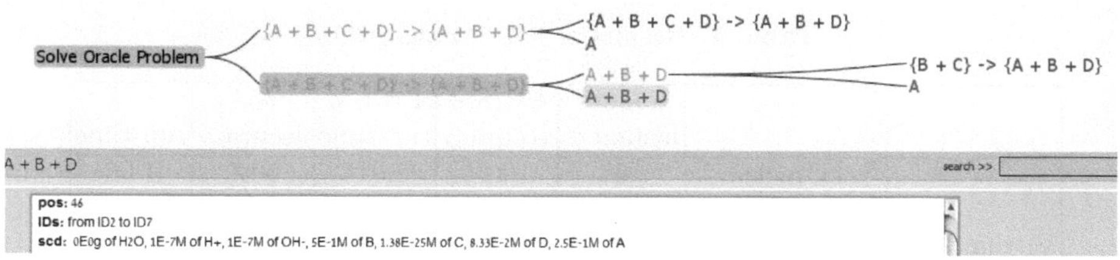

Fig. 2. Visualization of Oracle Plan

For VirtualLabs, we used four problems intended to teach different types of experimental and analytical techniques in chemistry, taken from the curriculum of introductory chemistry courses using VirtualLabs in the U.S. One of these was the oracle problem in which students had to guess the nature of interaction between different chemical processes. Another, called "Coffee", required students to add the right amount of milk to cool a cup of coffee down to a desired temperature. The third problem, called "Unknown Acid" required students to determine the concentration level and Ka level of an unknown solution. The fourth problem, called "Dilution", required students to create a solution of a base compound with a specific desired volume and concentration. For TinkerPlots, we used two problems for teaching probability to students in grades 8 through 12. The first problem, called "ROSA", required students to build a model that samples the letters A, O, R, and S and to compute the probability of generating the name ROSA using the model. The second problem, called "RAIN", required students to build a model for the weather on a given day, and compute the probability that it will rain on each of the next four consecutive days.

We compared PRISM to the best algorithms from the literature for each ELE: the algorithm of Gal et al. [5] for TinkerPlots, and the algorithm of Gal and Amir [2] for VirtualLabs. For each problem instance, a domain expert was given the plans outputted by PRISM and the other algorithm, as well as the student's log. We consider the inferred plan to be "correct" if the domain expert agrees with the complex and basic actions at each level of the plan hierarchy that is outputted by the algorithm. The outputted plan represents the student's solution process using the software.

Figure 2 shows the visualization of one of the plans that were presented to domain experts. The visualization is meant to facilitate the analysis of the expert by including additional information from the log. It does not perform any inference over the output of PRISM. The visualization groups all trees in the student's plans as children to a single root node "Solve Oracle problem". Complex nodes are labeled with information about the chemical reactions that occurred during the activities described by the nodes. The coloring of the labels indicate the type of chemical reaction that has occurred.

Table 1 summarizes the performance of the PRISM algorithm according to accuracy and run time of the algorithm (in seconds on a commodity core i-7 computer). The column "SoA" (State-of-the-art) refers to the appropriate algorithm from the literature for each problem. All of the reported results were

Table 1. Results of PRISM algorithm

		num of instances	PRISM accuracy	PRISM run-time	SoA accuracy	SoA run-time
Virtual Labs	Oracle	6	100%	8.015	50%	1.06
	Unknown Acid	7	100%	31.589	57%	0.8
	Camping	2	100%	0.929	100%	0.4
	Coffee	9	100%	17.567	67%	0.4
	Dilution	4	100%	1.529	75%	0.54
TinkerPlots	Rosa	23	87%	55.22	78%	3.34
	Rain	17	82%	3.049	71%	0.54
Average			91%	25.841	71%	1.537

averaged over the different instances in each problem. As shown in the table, the PRISM algorithm was able to recognize significantly more plans than did the state-of-the-art ($p < 0.001$ using a proportion based Z test). The instances that the algorithms failed to recognize are false negatives that represent bad matches in the plan recognition process. We note that PRISM was significantly slower than the state-of-the-art approaches. This is not surprising given its worst case complexity. Although PRISM is, in practice, polynomial in the size of the log and recipes, the algorithm by Gal and Amir is only polynomial in the size of recipes (which is significantly smaller than the log size). However, PRISM is designed to run off-line after the completion of the student's interaction. Therefore an average run time of 25 seconds is a "low price to pay" given the significant increase in performance and its ability to generalize across different ELEs.

References

1. Amershi, S., Conati, C.: Automatic recognition of learner groups in exploratory learning environments. In: Ikeda, M., Ashley, K.D., Chan, T.-W. (eds.) ITS 2006. LNCS, vol. 4053, pp. 463–472. Springer, Heidelberg (2006)
2. Amir, O., Gal, Y.: Plan recognition in virtual laboratories. In: Proceedings of the 22nd International Joint Conference on Artificial Intelligence, IJCAI (2011)
3. Konold, C., Miller, C.: TinkerPlots Dynamic Data Exploration 1.0. Key Curriculum Press (2004)
4. Pawar, U.S., Pal, J., Toyama, K.: Multiple Mice for Computers in Education in Developing Countries. In: Conference on Information and Communication Technologies and Development, pp. 64–71 (2007)
5. Reddy, S., Gal, Y., Shieber, S.M.: Recognition of users' activities using constraint satisfaction. In: Houben, G.-J., McCalla, G., Pianesi, F., Zancanaro, M. (eds.) UMAP 2009. LNCS, vol. 5535, pp. 415–421. Springer, Heidelberg (2009)
6. Yaron, D., Karabinos, M., Lange, D., Greeno, J.G., Leinhardt, G.: The ChemCollective–Virtual Labs for Introductory Chemistry Courses. Science 328(5978), 584 (2010)

ExploreIT! An Adaptive Tutor in an Informal Learning Environment

Stephen B. Blessing, Jeffrey S. Skowronek, and Ana-Alycia Quintana

University of Tampa, 401 W. Kennedy Blvd., Tampa, FL 33606
{sblessing,jskowronek}@ut.edu,
anaalycia.quintana@spartans.ut.edu

Abstract. We created an application for the Apple iPad that families at a children's museum used as they toured the museum. The application provided activities and explanation at various exhibit areas along with adaptive quizzes. We investigated their retention of the museum content and their attitudes toward the intervention. We found that content that provides an over-arching narrative to the museum experience along with the adaptive quizzes resulted in families enjoying the activities more, staying longer at the museum, and the children learning more information.

Keywords: informal learning, adaptive tutor, iPad.

1 Introduction

Adaptive and intelligent tutors have met with success in classroom settings [1-2]. Children spend much of their time outside of classroom settings, however. While some researchers have started to bring such technologies into these settings [3], there is still much work to be done in exploring this area. In an informal setting such as a museum, the museum goer may only interact with the tutor for a couple of hours. The techniques employed in a classroom-based tutor over the course of a semester can still be employed in the informal setting. The tutor can adapt and personalize the content, as well as motivate the student. We designed an iPad-based adaptive tutor, ExploreIT, for the Glazer Children's Museum, located in Tampa, Florida. We believe such tutors will provide a more engaging museum visit for the family, resulting in a richer and more powerful learning experience for the child.

Research in informal settings has centered on examining discourse styles between parent and child [4-6]. Two distinct styles emerge, high and low elaborative. High elaborative parents ask many questions, providing opportunities for their children to embellish on descriptions of the past. High elaborative parents view recall as an instrument for storytelling Conversely, low elaborative parents view memory as an instrument used to retrieve information. Low elaborate parents ask yes or no type questions and will often repeat the same question until the child provides an exact, specific answer [7].

K. Yacef et al. (Eds.): AIED 2013, LNAI 7926, pp. 607–610, 2013.

We wanted to increase the interaction between parent and child, enabling elaborative storytelling. The iPad suggests activities, providing prompts for the caregiver. We manipulated how strong of a narrative existed within these prompts, akin to recent ITS work with narrative tutors [8]. We are interested to see if providing such narrative in an informal setting would raise the elaboration across families and if that would increase learning.

2 Pilot Project

Eleven families from the Tampa Bay area participated. A family consisted of at least one parent and one child aged 4-6. A research assistant gave each family an iPad. The application contained 4 activity suggestions for each of 4 exhibit areas. The content of the activities could be presented matter-of-factly, without a narrative (the Semantic condition) or it could be presented wrapped in a story about Peter the Parrot needing to prepare for a trip (the Episodic condition). Figure 1 shows a screenshot. The left-hand side contained buttons to select the activities. The top section contained blue text listing the main activity. The parent read this blue text to the child. The middle section contained suggestions to the parent for ways to change the activity or additional activities that could be done. The bottom section contained background information for the parent concerning the educational and psychological objectives of the activity.

The assistant randomly determined in which condition to put the family, either the Episodic (6 families) or the Semantic (5 families). The family toured the museum exhibits on their own. We required families to do all 16 activities. Within an exhibit

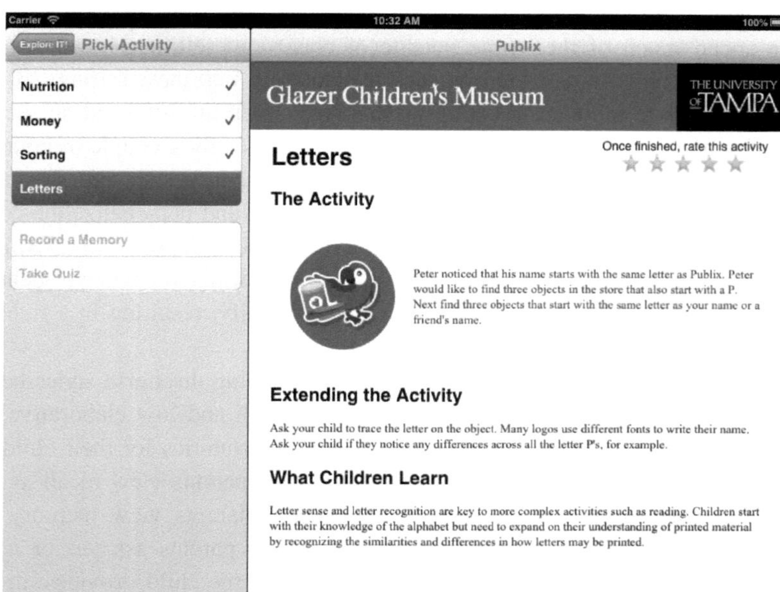

Fig. 1. Screenshot of the ExploreIT iPad application

area, all 4 activities had to be done to take a quiz. The quiz had to be completed in order to earn a virtual badge for that area. The quizzes contained 4 items, one for each activity. The quiz adapted itself to the child, providing harder questions when the child did well, and easier questions if the child did poorly. The assistant gave the family a 10-question attitudinal survey upon completion of their tour, and the child received a squishy brain ball at that time.

3 Results

The families in the Episodic condition spent more time on average (M = 94.18 min, SD = 19.79) in the museum those in the Semantic condition (M = 67.84 min, SD = 23.30). While not a significant difference ($t(9)$=2.03, p =.073, d = 1.23), it is firmly in the predicted direction and Cohen's d indicates a large effect size. The families in the Episodic condition rated the tasks as more enjoyable (M = 3.67, SD = 0.55) than those in the Semantic condition (M = 3.05, SD = 0.38). While not a significant difference ($t(9)$=2.11, p =.064, d = 1.30) it is a large effect size.

Each student received 4 questions within each of the 4 exhibits. Questions had 3 difficulty levels. If the student got two questions right in a row, they went up in difficulty level. If they got two wrong in a row, they went down a level. Children in the Episodic condition received higher difficulty questions (M = 2.43 min, SD = 0.13) on average than those in the Semantic condition (M = 2.18 min, SD = 0.47). This is not statistically significant ($t(9)$ = 1.28, p = .232, d =0.89), but still a relatively large effect. However, the difference in percent correct across the 16 questions between the Episodic condition (M = .75, SD = .08) and the Semantic condition (M = .65, SD = .03) is statistically significant, $t(9)$ = 2.71, p = .024, d = 1.82.

Families answered 7 Likert-scale items on the questionnaire. Families in the Episodic condition (M = 5.81, SD = 1.04) were more favorable than those in the Semantic condition (M = 5.29, SD = 0.54), though not significantly so ($t(9)$ = 0.92, p = .387, d = 0.62). Both groups had the same high level of enthusiasm on the last question, which asked how much they would like to see ExploreIt expanded to all the exhibit areas (6.67 v. 6.50 for the Episodic and Semantic conditions, respectively).

4 Discussion

These results address the question we had at the outset, does providing a narrative increase retention of museum concepts? As assessed by the adaptive quizzes, children in the Episodic condition retained more information. The families in the Episodic condition stayed longer, liked their visit more, and most importantly, the children learned more while answering more challenging questions. These findings support that the novel episode provided a form of elaborative conversation that enhanced learning, perhaps independent of parent conversational style.

Based on this initial study, we have three further issues we would like to investigate. First, we would like to personalize the narrative more to each child. More personalization should result in more learning. Second, we want to know to what extent the narrative was used by the families as they did the activities. We intend to more fully examine protocols from the visits in the future. Lastly, we are interested in how special populations might use this iPad app and how they would react to the activities. Past research has suggested that children with ADHD benefit from having a story woven around to-be-remembered information [9].

Acknowledgements. We received The University of Tampa Dana Foundation Grant and The University of Tampa David Delo Research Professor Grant to assist in this research. We thank the staff at the Glazer Children's Museum for their assistance.

References

1. Mitrović, A., Mayo, M., Suraweera, P., Martin, B.: Constraint-based Tutors: A Success Story. In: Monostori, L., Váncza, J., Ali, M. (eds.) IEA/AIE 2001. LNCS (LNAI), vol. 2070, pp. 931–940. Springer, Heidelberg (2001)
2. Ritter, S., Anderson, J.R., Koedinger, K.R., Corbett, A.: Cognitive Tutor: Applied Research in Mathematics Education. Psychonomic Bulletin and Review 14, 249–255 (2007)
3. Lane, H.C., Noren, D., Auerbach, D., Birch, M., Swartout, W.: Intelligent Tutoring Goes to the Museum in the Big City: A Pedagogical Agent for Informal Science Education. In: Biswas, G., Bull, S., Kay, J., Mitrovic, A. (eds.) AIED 2011. LNCS, vol. 6738, pp. 155–162. Springer, Heidelberg (2011)
4. Leichtman, M.D., Pillemer, D.B., Wang, Q., Koreishi, A., Han, J.J.: When Baby Maisy Came to School: Mothers' Interview Styles and Preschoolers' Event Memories. Cognitive Development 15, 99–114 (2000)
5. Reese, E., Newcombe, R.: Training Mothers in Elaborative Reminiscing Enhances Children's Autobiographical Memory and Narrative. Child Development 78, 1153–1170 (2007)
6. Tessler, M., Nelson, K.: Making Memories: The Influence of Joint Encoding on Later Recall by Young Children. Consciousness and Cognition: An International Journal (1994)
7. Reese, E., Haden, C.A., Fivush, R.: Mother–child Conversational Interaction about the Past: Relationships of Style and Memory Over Time. Cognitive Development 8, 403–430 (1993)
8. Rowe, J.P., Shores, L.R., Mott, B.W., Lester, J.C.: Integrating Learning and Engagement in Narrative-Centered Learning Environments. In: Aleven, V., Kay, J., Mostow, J. (eds.) ITS 2010, Part II. LNCS, vol. 6095, pp. 166–177. Springer, Heidelberg (2010)
9. Skowronek, J.S., Leichtman, M.D., Pillemer, D.B.: Long-term Episodic Memory in Children with Attention-Deficit/Hyperactivity Disorder. Learning Disabilities Research & Practice 23, 25–35 (2008)

Diagnosing Errors from Off-Path Steps in Model-Tracing Tutors

Luc Paquette, Jean-François Lebeau, and André Mayers

Université de Sherbrooke, Québec, Canada
{Luc.Paquette,Andre.Mayers}@USherbrooke.ca

Abstract. Model-tracing tutors were shown to be effective for the tutoring of problem solving tasks, but they usually lack the capability to provide feedback on learners' off-path steps. In this paper, we define a method, inspired by Sierra, to diagnose many of the learners' errors from their off-path steps. This method is implemented in Astus, a model-tracing tutor authoring framework. We show how Astus diagnose errors from off-path steps and use the resulting diagnostic to generate negative feedback.

Keywords: Model-tracing, off-path steps, error diagnosis, negative feedback.

1 Introduction

Model-tracing tutors (MTTs) [1] were shown to be effective for the tutoring of problem-solving tasks [2, 3]. They provide pedagogical feedback to the learners by flagging their steps as correct or incorrect and by offering next-step hints. However, MTTs lack the capability to provide pedagogical feedback for steps that are not predicted by the model (off-path steps) and simply consider them as erroneous.

To increase the amount of steps for which a tutor can provide relevant feedback, we designed a method to automatically diagnose many of the learners' procedural errors by analyzing their off-path steps. This method is inspired by Sierra [4], a theory explaining the origin of the learners' procedural errors, and is implemented with Astus [5], a MTT authoring framework whose knowledge representation system was designed to facilitate the generation of pedagogical interventions.

2 Error Diagnostics

We took inspiration from Sierra [4] and designed a method allowing Astus to diagnose many of the learners' errors during problem solving. We have shown in a previous paper [6] that Astus's knowledge representation system is compatible with the assumptions formulated in Sierra and that it can automatically disrupt procedural knowledge components to model erroneous behaviors analogous to those resulting from Sierra's impasse and repair process. In this paper, we briefly show how our Sierra inspired method is used to diagnose many of the learners' errors.

K. Yacef et al. (Eds.): AIED 2013, LNAI 7926, pp. 611–614, 2013.

Astus's procedural knowledge is modeled using goals and procedures that together form a procedural graph. Goals are achieved by the execution of procedures (primitive or complex). Primitive procedures reify steps in the learning environment and complex ones are scripts (sequence, selection, iteration) producing a set of sub goals.

During the tutor's execution, goals and procedures are instantiated in order to produce an episodic tree containing all the completed (C) or currently executing (E) goals (rectangles) and procedures (ovals) as well as goals waiting (W) to be expended. The episodic tree is used to match the learner's steps and indicate whether they are correct or not. When a learner commits a step, the tutor searches the episodic tree in order to find a match. If no match is found, the step is considered off-path.

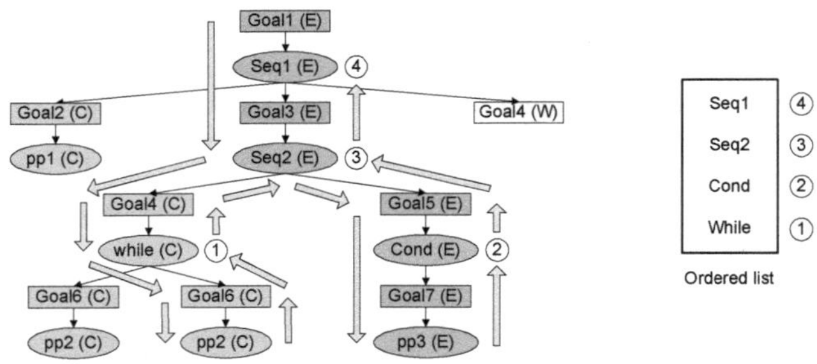

Fig. 1. Construction of a list of all the procedures that might have been incorrectly executed

When an off-path step is committed, Astus attempts to diagnose the learner's error by manipulating the content of the episodic tree. The tutor searches the tree to identify all the complex procedures that might have been incorrectly executed. This is achieved with the help of a depth-first search on the currently executing procedures and the procedures completed by the learner's last step. The result is an ordered list of procedures with the first ones being closest to the correct steps (Figure 1).

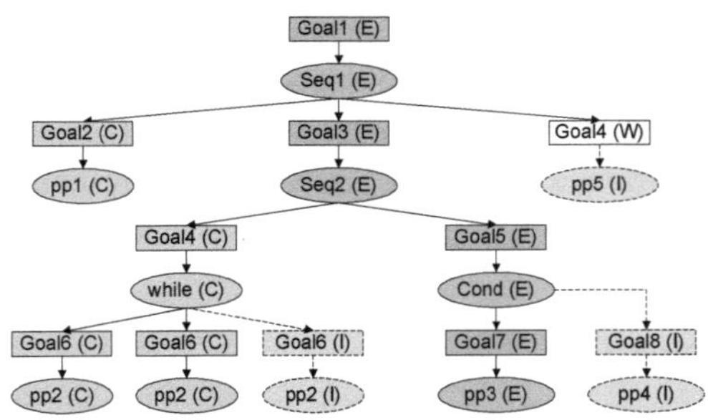

Fig. 2. Result of the interpolation. The interpolated goals and procedure are marked with an (I).

Once all the relevant procedures have been identified, the steps resulting from their incorrect executions are interpolated. For example (figure 2), the learner might repeat the sub goal (Goal6) of a completed *While* procedure, achieve the wrong sub goal (Goal8) for a *Conditional* procedure or try to achieve a sub goal (Goal4) that is still waiting for the completion of a previous one.

Once Astus has finished its interpolation, it tries to find a match for the learner's off-path step. If such a match is found, the branch of the episodic tree containing the interpolated step is used as a diagnostic of the learner's error. The tutor can use this diagnostic to react to the learners step by, for example, providing negative feedback.

3 Feedback Generation

When Astus recognizes an off-path step, it provides negative feedback as an automatically generated text message. To achieve this behavior, we use Astus's capability to generate messages by examining the content of the task's model, a process we used to generate next-step hints [5]. We illustrate the process of generating negative feedback using an example from a tutor for the insertion of elements in an AVL tree.

When trying to insert the value 18 into an existing AVL tree, a learner might encounter a node containing the value 15. He/she than has to decide on which side of this node to continue the insertion process. Figure 3 shows part of the episodic tree that might be instantiated for such a task. The procedure *PCCheckInsertSide* is a complex procedure of type *conditional* determining if the value should be inserted to the left or to the right of the current node. As the value 18 is greater than 15, the goal *GInsertRight* is instantiated by *PCCheckInsertSide* and the learner has to insert to the right of the current node.

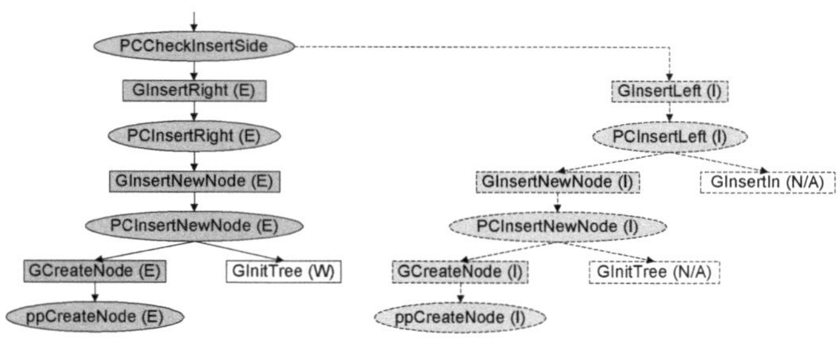

Fig. 3. Part of the episodic tree for inserting the value 18 and the interpolated branch

According to the episodic tree, the next step for the learner is to create a new node (*ppCreateNode*) to the right of the current one. If he/she instead create a new node to the left, Astus will search the episodic tree to diagnose this off-path step. Starting from the procedure *PCCheckInsertSide* (figure 3), Astus instantiates the goal *GInsertLeft* to interpolate the effect of incorrectly executing *PCCheckInsertSide*. This interpolation will be used as a diagnosis for the learner's error as it leads to an instance of the primitive procedure *ppCreateNode* that corresponds to the learner's step.

To produce feedback on errors, Astus associates a message template to every type of error that it can diagnose. In the above example, the source of the error is the conditional procedure *PCCheckInsertSide*. As the learner did not fully understand when to insert to the left or to the right, he/she incorrectly chose to insert 18 to the left of the current node (*GInsertLeft*). Using this diagnostic, Astus can provide feedback to the learner by instantiating the corresponding template:

```
You should [correct sub goal name] instead of [used sub
goal name] since [condition for the correct goal].
```

Using the content of the procedure that was incorrectly executed:

```
Conditional PCCheckInsertSide achieves GCheckInsertSide {
    if 'insertValue' lesserThan 'node->content'
        goal 'GInsertLeft' with 'node', 'insertValue'
    if 'insertValue' greaterThan 'node->content'
        goal 'GInsertRight' with 'node', 'insertValue'
}
```

Thus resulting in the instantiation of the following text message:

```
You should insert to the right instead of insert to the
left since the value to insert is greater than the
content for the node.
```

Although the messages generated by Astus explain the learners' errors using relevant information, their readability is currently limited by the use of templates. Using natural language processing techniques would greatly improve their quality.

4 Conclusion

In this paper, we showed how Astus can diagnose many errors from the learners' off-path steps. This is achieved by interpolating the erroneous execution of the model's procedural knowledge in order to match the learner's off-path steps. Once a diagnosis has been made, Astus is able to provide negative feedback to help the learner by automatically generating text messages relevant to the error. Our future work will include validating the accuracy of our diagnoses, the coverage of our diagnostic method and the effectiveness of our negative feedback.

References

1. Anderson, J.R., Boyle, C.F., Corbett, A., Lewis, M.W.: Cognitive Modeling and Intelligent tutoring. Artificial Intelligence 42, 7–49 (1990)
2. Koedinger, K.R., Anderson, J.R., Hadley, W.H., Mark, M.A.: Intelligent Tutoring Goes to School in the Big City. International Journal of Artificial Intelligence in Education 8, 30–43 (1997)
3. VanLehn, K., et al.: The Andes Physics Tutoring System: Lessons Learned. International Journal of Artificial Intelligence in Education 15(3), 1–47 (2005)
4. VanLehn, K.: Mind Bugs: The Origin of Procedural Misconceptions. MIT Press (1990)
5. Paquette, L., Lebeau, J.-F., Beaulieu, G., Mayers, A.: Automating Next-Step Hints Generation Using ASTUS. In: Cerri, S.A., Clancey, W.J., Papadourakis, G., Panourgia, K. (eds.) ITS 2012. LNCS, vol. 7315, pp. 201–211. Springer, Heidelberg (2012)
6. Paquette, L., Lebeau, J.-F., Mayers, A.: Automating the Modeling of Learners' Erroneous Behaviors in Model-Tracing Tutors. In: Masthoff, J., Mobasher, B., Desmarais, M.C., Nkambou, R. (eds.) UMAP 2012. LNCS, vol. 7379, pp. 316–321. Springer, Heidelberg (2012)

Understanding the Difficulty Factors for Learning Materials: A Qualitative Study

Keejun Han, Mun Y. Yi, Gahgene Gweon, and Jae-Gil Lee

Knowledge Service Engineering Department,
Korea Advanced Institute of Science and Technology (KAIST), Daejeon, South Korea
{keejun.han,munyi,ggweon,jaegil}@kaist.ac.kr

Abstract. Difficult materials overwhelm learners whereas easy materials deter advanced knowledge acquisition. Toward the goal of automatic assessment of learning materials, we conducted a laboratory experiment involving 50 college students recruited from two universities in Korea using 115 PowerPoint files. On the basis of the qualitative analysis results, we propose a model of learning difficulty, distinguishing measurable factors from non-measurable factors. The most influential factors for the easiest and the hardest learning materials are also identified and compared. The study findings have implications for educational service providers who need to automatically classify learning materials based on their innate difficulties.

Keywords: Learning material difficulty, Recommender system, PowerPoint slides, Difficulty factors, Coding analysis.

1 Introduction

Toward the goal of automatic assessment of learning materials, this paper reports the findings of a laboratory experiment conducted to identify the factors that underlie the difficulty of PowerPoint slides from college students because of its commonality and popularity as educational source. In short, the objective of the study reported in this paper was to discover the factors that determine the difficulty of learning materials in general, and PowerPoint slides in specific, on the basis of user comments. The findings have significant implications for the development of an autonomous difficulty classifier, which can be easily incorporated into search engines and online learning service platforms.

The oldest method for measuring the difficulty of a document was to set up mathematical formulas that utilize lexical features of the document [1, 2]. There are also alternative approaches of applying machine learning techniques to estimate the difficulty of a document [3,4,5]. However, those approaches have limited value in assessing the difficulty of learning materials, particularly of PowerPoint slides, because they only focus on the textual sources of documents. Thus, the difficulty dimensions we propose in this paper can be considered more complete as they are applicable to the learning materials that consist of both textual and graphical sources.

K. Yacef et al. (Eds.): AIED 2013, LNAI 7926, pp. 615–618, 2013.

2 Method

We conducted a laboratory experiment involving 50 college students recruited from two universities in Korea. Each participant examined five PowerPoint files while thinking aloud about the difficulty aspects of each slide. In the end of each session, they were asked to choose the easiest and hardest learning materials out of five. All participants' utterances were recorded and transcribed.

The average age of the participants was 21.3. The youngest participant was 18 years old, and the oldest was 32. Participants have been using PowerPoint slides for 4.74 years on average. The shortest period of using PowerPoint slides was 1 year, and the longest was 12 years.

Thirty transcripts were analyzed by two coders; their inter-coder reliability was 0.87. Overall, the iterative coding process identified a total number of 41 difficulty factors out of 3150 initial units of utterances obtained from the 50 transcripts.

We further conducted a card-sorting study to empirically examine the mapping between the 41 difficulty factors, which were derived from the coding analysis, and the 7 principal categories (groups of similar factors), which were mainly theorized by the authors until that time with the help from prior research on difficulty. Two types of measurements, agreement and correlation proposed in [6], were calculated in order to evaluate the results of the card sorting study. The agreement scores for each category ranged from 0.5 to 0.84, with the average score of 0.64, showing that those categories were reasonably well understood across the participants. A correlational analysis conducted between the 41 difficulty factors and their corresponding category identified by the participants showed that 32 factors (78%) had a correlation value greater than 0.75, which is considered high [6]. The remaining 9 factors had a correlation value between 0.6 and 0.7. In addition, 39 out of 41 factors were placed in only one or two categories, implying that each category is highly distinct.

3 Results

After card-sorting, we further distinguished the 41 factors into those that are automatically measurable by computer versus not. This distinction was made so that researchers who are building automatic classifier for learning material difficulty could consider using these measurable factors. The distribution of the automatically measurable factors and non-measurable factors over the 7 principal categories are presented as follows:

- Detailedness: Factors that represent how comprehensible and concrete the slides are.
  - Measurable: Highlighting important terms, Presence of examples, Presence of formula, Presence of tables, Presence of visual materials, Presence of external links, Brief summary for visual materials
  - Non-measurable: Detailedness of visual materials, Detailedness of text, Presence of animation effects

- Structural Completeness: Factors that represent how comprehensible & concrete the slides are.
    - Measurable: Presence of a summary, Presence of sub-titles, Presence of bullets, Presence of numbering, Presence of grocery terms, Presence of a table of contents, Presence of Q&A
- Relevancy: Factors that capture how appropriate the slide components are.
    - Measurable: Title relevancy, Visual material relevancy, Similarity between slides and its origin
    - Non-measurable: Animation effect relevancy
- Flow: Factors that represent how logically coherent the slides are.
    - Measurable: Similarity between adjacent slides
    - Non-measurable: A logical order of contents
- Readability: Factors that indicate how well the text is comprehensible.
    - Measurable: Term difficulty, Topic difficulty in a domain
- Length: Factors that capture the size of the presentation.
    - Measurable: The length of slides, The number of words in a page, The number of tables, The number of formula, The number of examples, The number of external links, Topic coverage, The number of visual materials
    - Non-measurable: The number of animation effects
- Formatting Style: Factors that capture the appearance of slides.
    - Measurable: Font size, Language used
    - Non-measurable: The number of colors used, Background color, Text color, Visual attractiveness of visual components (figures, graphs, animations), Visual attractiveness of non-visual components

We further examined the factors that were most frequently mentioned regarding whether a given PowerPoint slide material was easy or difficult. Table 1 shows the top factors that contributed in determining each difficulty level, as well as the frequency of each factor. Recall that we had fifty participants. Therefore, a frequency of 15 for a given factor means that 30% of the participants listed that factor as a determinant.

Certain factors are listed as being influential for both easy and difficult levels of learning materials. Such factors differed in terms of its value. For example, the top factor for both levels of difficulty is "topic difficulty in a domain." For the "easy" list, this means that the topic itself was not difficult, whereas for the "difficult" list, the topic itself was difficult. Another example is "presence of visual materials." In the "easy" list, this factor tells us that if there are visual elements in a learning material, it tends to be easy. However, in the "difficult" list, this factor means that absence of visual elements makes a learning material difficult. Half of the factors that made the top lists are unique to each difficulty level. Therefore, different factors should be accounted for depending on the difficulty level.

Table 1. Top N Influential Difficulty Factors for the Easiest and Hardest Learning Materials

Difficulty factor for **easiest** learning material	Freq	Difficulty factor for **most difficult** learning material	Freq
Topic difficulty in a domain	15	Topic difficulty in a domain	14
Presence of visual materials	14	Number of words in a page	14
Summary for visual materials	13	Presence of visual materials	10
Presence of examples	13	Highlighting important terms	8
Highlighting important terms	8	Number of visual materials	7
Presence of Q&A	8	Term difficulty	7
The number of example	7	Summary for visual materials	6

4 Conclusion

In this research, we conducted a qualitative study to identify the factors that affect the difficulty of learning materials, in particular PowerPoint slides. Going through the coding and card-sorting processes, we developed a model of difficulty factors over the seven principal categories of learning difficulty. Further, through the difficulty factor comparison analysis, we identified top influential factors for determining whether a given learning material is relatively easy or difficult. Our proposed model of difficulty factors can benefit online educational service providers who want to automatically sort their learning materials in terms of the material's innate difficulty.

Acknowledgement. This work was supported by the National Research Foundation of Korea (NRF) grant funded by the Korea government (MEST) (No. 2011-0029185).

References

1. Flesch, R.: A new readability yardstick. Journal of Applied Psychology 32, 221–233 (1948)
2. Dale, E., Chall, J.S.: A formula for predicting readability. Educational Research Bulletin 27, 1–20 (1948)
3. Peterson, S.E., Ostendorf, M.: A machine learning approach to reading level assessment. Computer Speech and Language 23, 89–106 (2008)
4. Chen, W., Persen, R.: A Recommender System for Collaborative Knowledge. In: Artificial Intelligence in Education (2009)
5. White, S.: Mining the Text: 34 Text Features That Can Ease or Obstruct, Text Comprehension and Use. Literacy Research and Instruction 51(2), 143–164 (2012)
6. Spencer, D.: Card sorting: Designing usable categories. Rosenfield Media (2009)

Mobile Testing for Authentic Assessment in the Field

Yoshimitsu Miyasawa and Maomi Ueno

University of Electro-Communications, Tokyo, Japan
{miyasawa,ueno} @ai.is.uec.ac.jp

Abstract. We have developed a mobile testing system using computerized adaptive testing for assessing learning at museums, parks, and other sites in the field. Computerized adaptive testing is a form of computer-based testing that progressively estimates an examinee's ability from his/her answer history and uses that ability to present test items making ability estimation even more accurate. Field-testing, however, requires activities such as observing and searching at specific positions within a site, which requires the learner to move about to get to those positions. Moreover, the time that can be spent taking such an on-site test is usually limited, which means that the test may end before a sufficient number of test items can be answered thereby decreasing the accuracy of ability estimation. In response to these issues, we formalize for field-testing purposes an optimization problem called the traveling purchaser problem (TPP) that incorporates graph theory and propose an computerized adaptive testing system using TPP.

Keywords: mobile device, computerized adaptive testing, item response theory.

1 Introduction

Knowledge does not exist on its own; rather, it is embedded in situations [6]. It is known, moreover, that knowledge is acquired in conjunction with past experiences [10]. These observations suggest that testing should be embedded in situations to authentically assess learning. Recent advances in mobile technologies are making it possible to estimate ability in a manner not possible by paper-based testing. Specifically, they are making it possible to perform assessments that require actions like observing and searching in the field such as at museums as opposed to tests that simply assess knowledge related to facts and procedures [8]. Taking, for example, e-learning and learning using mobile devices, systems have been developed to support these forms of learning in the field in terms of formative evaluation and self/peer assessment [1]. A testing system using the Global Positioning System (GPS) has also been developed for administering tests that require actions like observing and searching in the field[8]. This system takes into account the fact that test items require certain actions at a specific position and therefore identify the examinee's present position to present test items corresponding to that position. However, the test items presented by this system are fixed, that is, the same test items are presented to all examinees.

K. Yacef et al. (Eds.): AIED 2013, LNAI 7926, pp. 619–623, 2013.

A more effective presentation format has recently been achieved through Computerized Adaptive Testing (CAT). CAT progressively estimates the examinee's ability from his/her answer history and uses an item bank to present test items that maximize the amount of information with regard to that ability[4]. Furthermore, by selecting test items most applicable to ability under a time-limit constraint, the accuracy of estimating ability can be improved for tests having a time limit [5,3]. Improvement in the accuracy of estimating the examinee's ability is one advantage that can be expected from CAT, and incorporating CAT in mobile testing systems should be able to improve the accuracy of ability estimation in anywhere/anytime testing [9,2].

Testing in the field, however, requires actions like observing and searching at specific positions within a certain site, which means that the examinee must move about to get to those positions. In other words, positions at which the examinee must respond to test items are scattered throughout a site, which means that wasted time from unnecessary back-and-forth movements can be incurred. Moreover, as the time that can be spent for taking a test is generally limited, there is always the possibility that the test will end before a sufficient number of test items have been answered thereby decreasing the accuracy of ability estimation.

The purpose of this study is to make tests in the field more efficient and improve the accuracy of estimating an examinee's ability. Specifically, we propose a CAT system using the traveling purchaser problem (TPP), which is an optimization problem combined with graph theory.

The TPP is defined as follows[7]. Let nodes and edges within a graph denote stores and distance traveled, respectively. Each store sells products that need to be purchased but the number of products and their prices differ from store to store. The task here is to find a route that returns to the purchaser's point of departure minimizing the total cost of products and distance travelled. For the purposes of our study, we change products and shops defined in TPP to test items and the positions where those test items are presented, respectively, with the aim of finding the optimal route in a mobile test. In TPP, however, the number of products is given as a constraint, but since it is our desire to give time as a constraint in our study, we cannot use TPP in its existing form.

We therefore propose TPP having a time-limit constraint and propose an CAT system using this modified form of TPP as an optimization problem. The advantage of this approach is that we can raise the efficiency of testing that considers movement in the field and therefore improve the accuracy of estimating the examinee's ability. In this paper, we also report on experiments that show the proposed system to be more accurate in measuring performance compared to previous systems.

2 CAT Incorporating TPP with a Time-limit Constraint

With the aim of using TPP with time as a constraint for testing conducted in the field, we formalize this type of TPP as an optimization problem in the following way. Let the set of positions that present test items be denoted as $S := \{v_1, \ldots, v_n\}$ and the set of all items as $K := \{p_1, \ldots, p_m\}$. Let the set of all positions be denoted as $S_0 := \{S \cup o\}$, where o is the point of departure. Graph $G = (V, E)$ is an undirected graph, where $V := S_0$ represents the set of nodes and $E := \{[v_i, v_j] : v_i, v_j \in S, i < j\}$ the set of edges. Let the item information of test item p_k be denoted as b_k, the time required to answer test item p_k (required response time) as t_k, and the travel time between positions v_i, v_j as d_{ij}. T is the test time limit. The order of presenting items is called a route. For a certain route, if item p_k of position v_i is included in the route, $z_{ik} = 1$, and if not, $z_{ik} = 0$. Furthermore, if the route between positions v_i and v_j is included, $x_{ij} = 1$, and if not, $x_{ij} = 0$. D is the constant 0.00001. The optimal route can now be found from the following optimization problem:

$$\text{Maximize } w = \sum_{v_i \in S} \sum_{p_k \in K} b_k z_{ik} - D \sum_{(i,j) \in L} d_{ij} x_{ij} \tag{1}$$

subject to

$$\sum_{v_i \in S} \sum_{p_k \in K} t_k z_{ik} + \sum_{(i,j) \in L} d_{ij} x_{ij} < T \tag{2}$$

Solving this optimization problem determines which test items to present to the examinee.

3 Mobile Testing System

We here describe the mobile testing system that we developed as part of this study. This system consists of a navigation function and an item view function. The navigation function displays on a map the examinee's present location and the positions presenting test items as shown in 1. The item view function displays test items to the examinee as shown in Fig. 2.

4 Evaluation of the System

In this section, we describe a experiment that we conducted at a temple site within the Tokyo to evaluate the validity of the proposed system. In this experiment, we conducted a test using the proposed method and a test using time-constrained CAT ([5,3]). Different two groups of five students in the same university examined each test. The number of test items was 80. The questionnaire given to subjects after each test consisted of the two following questions. Subjects were asked to reply to these questions on a six-level basis. Question 1: travel time was not overly long but appropriate compared to test item response timeD Question 2: the order of moving from one position to another was the optimalD In addition, the system estimated travel time and the number of moves.

Fig. 1. Screen shot of navigation function

Fig. 2. Screen shot of computerized adaptive testing

Results of the experiment are listed in Table 1. The values shown for item information in the table indicates the average value and the variance (in parentheses) of item information over all subjects. The symbols ** and * in the table signify a significant difference in t-test results at a significance level of 1% and 5%, respectively. The results of this experiment show that the average item information of the proposed method was significantly higher than that of time-constrained CAT, Namely, the accuracy of estimating ability was significantly higher by the proposed method than by time-constrained CAT. The above experimental results demonstrate the effectiveness of the proposed method.

Table 1. The result of the Experiment

	Proposed Method	Time-constrained CAT
Item information**	4.24(0.236)	2.03(0.253)
Travel time*	110(787)	238(8833)
Number of moves*	4.0(0.5)	5.8(1.7)
Number of test items**	18.2(13.7)	9.0(4)
Question 1**	4.8(0.2)	3.4(0.3)
Question 2*	4.6(0.3)	3.2(0.7)

References

1. Hsiu Chen, C.: The implementation and evaluation of a mobile self- and peer-assessment system. Computers & Education 55(1), 229–236 (2010)
2. Huang, Y.M., Lin, Y.T., Cheng, S.C.: An adaptive testing system for supporting versatile educational assessment. Computers & Education 52(1), 53–67 (2009)
3. van der Linden, W.J.: Linear Models for Optimal Test Design (Statistics for Social and Behavioral Sciences). Springer (2005) [Hardcover]
4. van der Linden, W.J., Glas, C.A.: Computerized adaptive testing: Theory and practice (July 2000)

5. van der Linden, W.J., Scrams, D.J., Schnipke, D.L.: Using response-time constraints to control for differential speededness in computerized adaptive testing. Applied Psychological Measurement 23(3), 195–210 (1999)
6. Quine, W.V.O.: Word and Object (Studies in Communication), 1st edn. The MIT Press (March 1964)
7. Ramesh, T.: Travelling purchaser problem. Opsearch 18, 78–91 (1981)
8. Santos, P.R., Pérez-Sanagustín, M., Hernández-Leo, D., Blat, J.: Questinsitu: From tests to routes for assessment in situ activities. Computers & Education 57(4), 2517–2534 (2011)
9. Triantafillou, E., Georgiadou, E., Economides, A.A.: The design and evaluation of a computerized adaptive test on mobile devices. Computers & Education 50(4), 1319–1330 (2008)
10. Wittgenstein, L.: Philosophical Investigations. Wiley-Blackwell (2009) (an imprint of, 4th revised edition)

Field Observations of Engagement in Reasoning Mind

Jaclyn Ocumpaugh[1], Ryan S.J.d. Baker[2], Steven Gaudino[3], Matthew J. Labrum[3], and Travis Dezendorf[3]

[1] Worcester Polytechnic Institute, Worcester, MA
[2] Teachers College, Columbia University, New York, NY
[3] Reasoning Mind, Houston, TX
jocumpaugh@wpi.edu, baker2@exchange.tc.columbia.edu,
{sjg,Matthew.Labrum,Travis.Dezendorf}@reasoningmind.org

Abstract. This study presents Quantitative Field Observations (QFOs) of educationally relevant affect and behavior among students at three schools using Reasoning Mind, a game-based software system designed to teach elementary-level mathematics. High levels of engagement are observed. Possible causes for these high levels of engagement are considered, including the interactive pedagogical agent and other design elements.

Keywords: Affect Modeling, Intelligent Tutoring System, Boredom, Frustration, Engaged Concentration.

1 Introduction

Reasoning Mind (RM) is a hybrid mathematics program that combines extensive teacher training with a game-based AIED system. It is used by around 100,000 students a year in the Southern United States. Developed for elementary and middle school students, the RM system graphically represents student learning activity modules in a virtual "RM City," where activities take place in different virtual buildings. An interactive pedagogical agent named "Genie" guides students through both the city and the activities. On successful completion of the activities, students are rewarded with points that they may use to furnish their own space within the environment. Student and teacher reports indicate that students find both the pedagogical and artistic designs of this system highly engaging, but to date, no quantitative study of student engagement has been conducted. In this paper, we use Quantitative Field Observations (QFOs) to evaluate student engagement with the RM software. We demonstrate that key measures of behavior and affect reflect anecdotal reports from students and teachers who have used the system—that students engage in a high degree of on-task behavior and engaged concentration, as intended by the software designers.

2 Methods and Results

Quantitative Field Observations (QFOs) were collected using the BROMP method [1]. In this method, which has previously been used in multiple studies of student engagement [cf. 2-5] trained coders record synchronized observations of educationally relevant

K. Yacef et al. (Eds.): AIED 2013, LNAI 7926, pp. 624–627, 2013.

behavior (on task, on task conversation, off task, gaming the system, and other) and affect (boredom, confusion, delight, engaged concentration/flow, frustration, and other) using an Android application designed for these purposes.

BROMP coders follow a strict protocol. In order to avoid bias towards dramatic events in the classroom, QFOs occur in a pre-determined order. Each student is observed individually, and observers avoid looking directly at that student in order to disguise who is being currently observed. Because behavior and affect are considered orthogonal in this coding scheme, they are coded separately. The observer has up to 20 seconds to complete an observation. If a student presents more than one behavior or affect during that window, only the first is recorded. In ambiguous cases, or when a student leaves the room, "other" is selected. During the QFOs for this study, BROMP training was conducted, and an acceptable inter-rater reliability was obtained (Kappa=.58-.72 for affect, Kappa=.63-.79 for behavior). As the secondary coders were being trained during data collection, only data from the trainer is included in our results.

Students from three different schools in the Texas Gulf Coast region were observed. Two schools were in urban areas with large class sizes (around 25 students each). Both served predominantly ethnic minority populations: one with a large Hispanic population and another with a large African-American population. Both served communities with a median income below the state average, reflected by substantial populations (57% and 96%) of economically disadvantaged students, defined as those who received free or reduced price lunch. A third, suburban charter school had smaller class sizes (approximately 15 students each), a majority White population, a median income slightly above the state average, and fewer economically disadvantaged students (16%). For each of the three schools, two classes were observed.

Table 1. Summary of Classroom Observation Data

BROMP Category		**N**	**%**
behavior	on task	243	82%
	on task conversation	20	7%
	off task	31	10%
	gaming	2	1%
affect	boredom	27	10%
	confusion	24	9%
	delight	9	3%
	engaged concentration	194	71%
	frustration	19	7%

Results are given in Table 1. The overall incidence of behavior and affect indicates high engagement. Students were on-task 82% of the time, in on-task conversation 7% of the time, off-task 10% of the time, and gaming the system 1% of the time. The total of 89% on-task (in either fashion) is higher than values observed in Cognitive Tutor classrooms in US suburban middle schools [cf. 4] and in traditional US classrooms [cf. 6-7]. Affect patterns also indicate high engagement. There was a high proportion of engaged concentration (71% of the time), while boredom was fairly uncommon, occurring in only 10% of observations.

3 Discussion and Conclusion

Within this paper, we use quantitative field observations to examine the frequency of engaged and disengaged student behaviors and affective states in students using Reasoning Mind, a popular AIED system. These numbers reflect patterns that suggest high student engagement with this learning system, despite the largely economically disadvantaged urban populations investigated, findings that should be explored further in future research.

It is worth asking which design factors have influenced these outcomes. Some potential hypotheses include the scaffolding curricular techniques in RM, the use of Genie (the embodied pedagogical learning agent who guides students through RM City), and RM's game-like features. The designers of RM have spent considerable effort to replicate curricular techniques used by Russian teachers, both in the software design and in the extensive teacher training they require. Thus, students alternate between units of theory and units of practice. It is possible that this activity switching may reduce disengagement.

Anecdotal evidence suggests that students are quite attached to Genie, who regularly receives (and answers) email on topics beyond the scope of the learning software, including jokes, requests for friendship, and confessions about students' home life. On the basis of these reports, it seems that the effect of Genie deserves more careful consideration, as the success of this agent's design may contribute significantly to the high levels of engagement observed.

Finally, we should consider the many game-like elements in its design, including a point system that rewards students for speed drills and puzzles. Once sufficient points have been accumulated, students may furnish their own virtual space within RM City or buy virtual books. Particularly at a young age, this kind of autonomy is likely very appealing.

Acknowledgements. This research was supported by grant #OPP1048577 from the Bill & Melinda Gates Foundation. We also thank George Khatcharyan and Caitlin Watts for their support in data collection.

References

1. Ocumpaugh, J., Baker, R.S.J.d., Rodrigo, M.M.T.: Baker-Rodrigo Observation Method Protocol (BROMP) 1.0. Training Manual version 1.0. Technical Report. EdLab, New York, Ateneo Laboratory for the Learning Sciences, Manila (2012)
2. Rodrigo, M.M.T., Baker, R.S.J.d., Lagud, M.C.V., Lim, S.A.L., et al.: Affect and Usage Choices in Simulation Problem Solving Environments. In: Proceedings of Artificial Intelligence in Education 2007, pp. 145–152 (2007)

3. Rodrigo, M.M.T., Baker, R.S.J.d.: Comparing Learners' Affect While Using an Intelligent Tutor and an Educational Game. Research and Practice in Technology Enhanced Learning 6(1), 43–66 (2011)
4. Baker, R.S.J.d., Corbett, A.T., Koedinger, K.R., Wagner, A.Z.: Off-Task Behavior in the Cognitive Tutor Classroom: When Students "Game The System". In: Proceedings of ACM CHI 2004: Computer-Human Interaction, pp. 383–390 (2004)
5. Baker, R.S.J.d., Gowda, S.M., Wixon, M., Kalka, J., Wagner, A.Z., et al.: Sensor-free automated detection of affect in a Cognitive Tutor for Algebra. In: Proc. of the 5th International Conference on Educational Data Mining, pp. 126–133 (2012)
6. Lloyd, J.W., Loper, A.B.: Measurement and Evaluation of Task-Related Learning Behavior: Attention to Task and Metacognition. School Psychology Review 15(3), 336–345 (1986)
7. Lee, S.W., Kelly, K., Nyre, J.E.: Preliminary report on the relation of students' off-task behavior with completion of school work. Psychological Reports 84, 267–272 (1999)

Analyzer of Sentence Card Set for Learning by Problem-Posing

Tsukasa Hirashima and Megumi Kurayama

Graduate School of Engineering, Hiroshima University, Japan
tsukasa@lel.hiroshima-u.ac.jp

Abstract. MONSAKUN is software for learning by problem-posing in arithmetical word problems where a learner poses a problem by selecting and combining sentence cards from a given set of sentence cards. It is not easy task to prepare the sets of the sentence cards manually because it is necessary to evaluate all combinations. This paper describes an analyzer of a set of sentence cards. Experimental evaluation of the analyzer is also reported.

Keywords: Learning by Problem-Posing, Arithmetical Word Problem, Sentence Integration, Dummy Sentence Card.

1 Introduction

We have already developed several environments for learning by problem-posing that realize automatic assessment of posed problems by learners [1, 2]. We call this automatic assessment facility "agent-assessment" in comparison with "teacher-assessment", "self-assessment" and "peer-assessment" [3]. MONSAKUN [4] is a support system for learning by problem-posing where a learner poses a problem by selecting and combining sentence cards from a given set of sentence cards. A set of sentence cards includes necessary sentence cards and unnecessary sentence cards. We call the unnecessary sentence cards as "dummy cards". Because learner's behavior of problem-posing depends on the combination of necessary and unnecessary ones, to prepare an adequate set of sentence cards to each problem-posing task is an indispensable task to realize learning by problem-posing. In this paper, we introduce a method to analyze a set of the sentence cards. We evaluated the analyzer implemented by the method by using 48 sets of sentence cards that were practically used in problem-posing exercise in an elementary school, and found several defects that we should improve the card sets.

2 MONSAKUN

2.1 Task Model of Problem-Posing

Targeting arithmetical word problems that can be solved by one addition or subtraction, we have already proposed a task model of problem posing composed of following four

K. Yacef et al. (Eds.): AIED 2013, LNAI 7926, pp. 628–631, 2013.

tasks, (1) deciding calculation operation structure, (2) deciding story operation structure, (3) deciding story structure, and (4) deciding problem sentences [4]. It is necessary for learners to complete these tasks to pose a correct problem though the execution order of the tasks is not decided in the model. Problem-posing tasks in MONSAKUN are designed based on this model.

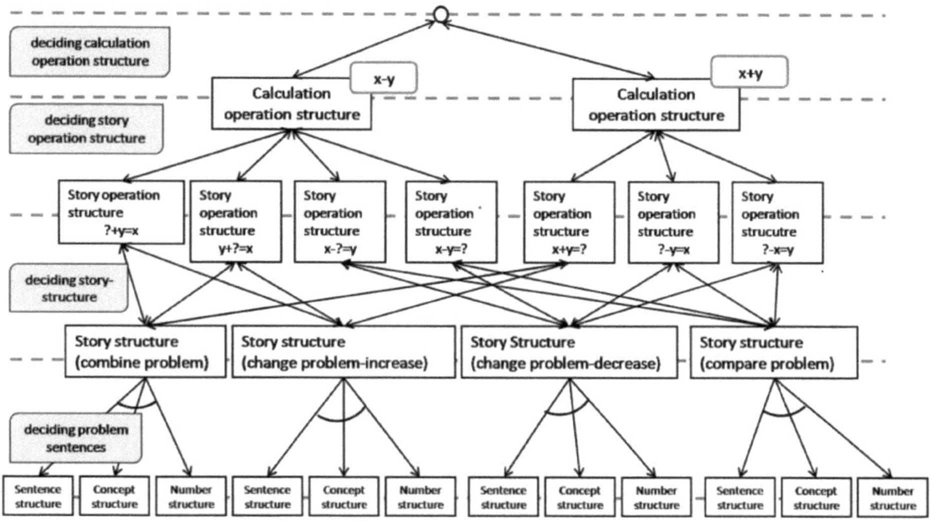

Fig. 1. Task Model of Problem-Posing

2.2 Overview of MONSAKUN

The problem-posing interface MONSAKUN is shown in Figure 2. In MONSAKUN, several sentence cards are provided to a learner. The learner poses a problem by selecting and ordering some of them. Then, MONSAKUN assigned a story operation structure or calculation operation structure is provided to the learner. This assignment is the condition that the posed problem should satisfy.

A sentence card is put into a blank in the problem-combination area. There are three blanks in Figure 2, a learner should select three cards from the card set at right side and arrange them in a proper order. A learner can move a card by drag & drop method in the interface. When a learner pushes "Check the Problem" under the problem-composition area, the system diagnoses the combination of sentences. The results of the diagnosis and message to help the learner's problem-posing is presented by another window.

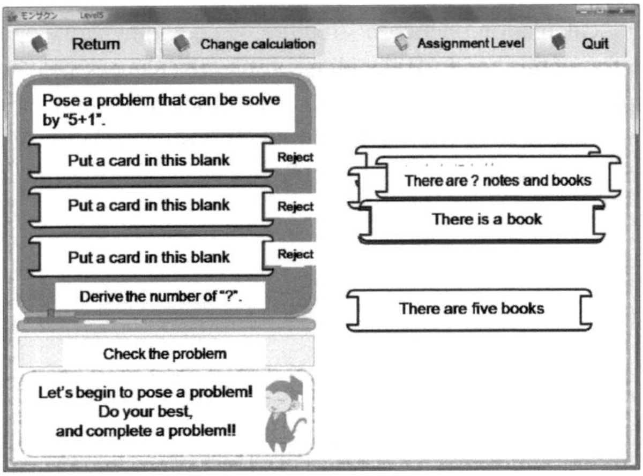

Fig. 2. MONSAKUN interface

3 Analyzer of Sentence Card Set

3.1 Card Set Analysis

Figure 1 shows tasks that learners must perform for problem-posing by the MONSAKUN. The specific purpose of the problem-posing activity is to enable learners to make proper decisions through these tasks. Decisions learners need to make depend heavily on the characters of card sets given. For example, setting the same concept for all the card sets available will make unnecessary a decision by learners on unifying the concept in the deciding problem sentences. Thus, it is of crucial importance for a card set developer to understand what kind of problem-posing activities the learners will engage in by using a card set made available. However, as the number of possible problems to be posed (including wrong problems) is determined by the permutation of the sentence cards, the number increases in series as the number of cards in a card set increases. Therefore, a tremendous amount of work will be required for a card set developer to manually check all the possible problems to be posed.

3.2 Analysis Flow

A card set developer enters a story structure, a story operation structure and a card set in the system. The developer selects from among 4 story-structures (multiple choices allowed) and selects addition or deduction and enters any value between 1 and 9 for the story operation structure. For the card set, the developer selects pre-arranged sentence card forms, which followed by the concepts and numerical values used for the cards, and adds them to the card set. A card set developer can enter card sets by repeating such steps.

The system creates all the possible combinations based on the card set entered, by considering each combination as a problem posed by learners, and performs check similar to that actually performed by the MONSAKUN and classifies the combinations based on the check results. The results are displayed on windows which can be switched per classification

3.3 Experimental Evaluation of Analyzer

By using the analyzer, we have examined 48 sets of sentence cards that were practically used in problem-posing exercise in an elementary school. Only one story that specified in problem-posing task can be correctly generated from 42 out of 48 card sets. Then, from 6 card sets, it is possible to make a solvable problem covered by other story specified in problem-posing task. The developer of the card sets had not noticed the 6 cards sets. The analyzer also detected that in several card sets learner could not make several types of mistakes because of enough kinds of dummy card were prepared. We confirmed that these information was useful to prepare and sophisticate the sets of sentence cards.

4 Conclusion

In this study, we have developed a system to analyze possible problems to be posed from sentence card set based on the task model of problem-posing. Our major future issues include the development of a system to automatically generate effective card sets.

References

[1] Nakano, A., Hirashima, T., Takeuchi, A.: Problem-Making Practice to Master Solution-Methods in Intelligent Learning Environment. In: Proc. of ICCE 1999, pp. 891–898 (1999)
[2] Hirashima, T., Yokoyama, T., Okamoto, M., Takeuchi, A.: Learning by Problem-Posing as Sentence-Integration and Experimental Use. In: Proc. of AIED 2007, pp. 252–261 (2007)
[3] Yamamoto, S., Waki, H., Hirashima, T.: An Interactive Environment for Learning by Problem-Changing. In: Proc. of ICCE 2010, pp. 1–8 (2010)
[4] Hirashima, T., Kurayama, M.: Learning by Problem-Posing for Reverse-Thinking Problems. In: Biswas, G., Bull, S., Kay, J., Mitrovic, A. (eds.) AIED 2011. LNCS, vol. 6738, pp. 123–130. Springer, Heidelberg (2011)

Modelling Domain-Specific Self-regulatory Activities in Clinical Reasoning

Susanne P. Lajoie[1], Eric Poitras[1], Laura Naismith[1], Geneviève Gauthier[2], Christina Summerside[1], Maedeh Kazemitabar[1], Tara Tressel[1], Lila Lee[1], and Jeffrey Wiseman[1]

[1] ATLAS Laboratory, Department of Educational and Counselling Psychology, McGill University, 3700 McTavish St, Montreal, QC H3A 1Y2, CA
[2] Department of Educational Psychology, University of Alberta, 5-154 Education North, Edmonton, AB T6g 2R1, CA
susanne.lajoie@mcgill.ca

Abstract. BioWorld is a computer-based learning environment that supports medical students in their clinical reasoning about virtual cases. We model the regulatory processes sudents use in the context of BioWorld in an effort to see when they ask for tutorial guidance and how guidance can be improved. BioWorld provides assistance using an artificial physician to deliver hints when students request a consult. We analyzed the concurrent think aloud protocols and log-file trace data collected from 30 students who solved 3 cases with BioWorld. Our findings highlight the antecedents and functions of regulatory activities involved in help-seeking. We discuss the implications for tailoring the content of the hints provided by the consult tool to the specific needs of different students.

Keywords: Models of Learners, Metacognition, Tasks and Problem-Solving Processes, Domain-Specific Learning Applications.

1 Introduction

An important challenge in developing professional expertise in medical problem solving is the acquisition of skills that mediate proficiency. BioWorld is a computer-based learning environment designed to develop professional competence in clinical reasoning using cognitive apprenticeship as an instructional framework [1]. Students practice clinical reasoning and receive feedback on their problem-solving in the context of working with virtual patient cases. In this paper, we model how novices regulate clinical reasoning when asking for a consult in BioWorld.

The current study explicitly looks at self-regulation with respect to students' help-seeking behavior where students ask for help from an artificial physician that provides hints. We synthesized models of self-regulation and problem-solving in order to provide a domain-specific account of how novices use skills to regulate problem-solving [2-4]. In the initial stages of problem-solving, the *forethought* phase involves novices' attempts to orient and plan the steps involved in diagnosing the disease by formulating an action plan to test a hypothesis. The *performance* phase refers to the steps

K. Yacef et al. (Eds.): AIED 2013, LNAI 7926, pp. 632–635, 2013.

involved in executing the action plan, such as ordering a lab test, searching through the library, identifying a relevant symptom, and requesting a consult. In the *reflection* phase, novices evaluate and elaborate on the outcomes of the clinical process, in doing so, checking the available evidence as well as justifying the hypothesis. In the following section, we provide an overview of the methodological and analytical techniques that were used to study how novices engaged in these regulatory activities.

2 Modelling Skills in Regulating Problem-Solving

A sample of 30 second-year medical students solved three cases (Pheochromocytoma, Diabetes Mellitus Type 1, and Grave's disease) using BioWorld. Twenty-nine consult requests were sampled for the purposes of this analysis. A consult request was defined as clicking on the consult tool button with the aim of receiving a hint from the artificial physician in BioWorld. For the purpose of this analysis no hints were available when students asked for help. The actual feedback was disabled in an effort to study the regulatory activities that occurred both before and after students needed help, allowing us to gain a better understanding of why students requested consults. The log-files were examined for the behaviors that occurred before and after requesting help; these behaviors served as the boundaries of our unit of analysis when coding the concurrent think-aloud protocols.

2.1 Characteristics of Help-Seeking Behaviors

We examined the time taken prior to asking for a consult relative to the total amount of time taken to solve the case (i.e., consult request time / case solution duration). The resulting percentage indicates that students requested help during the later stages of problem solving. On average 83% of the time taken to solve the case had elapsed ($SD = 18.0\%$) prior to asking for help. We compared the case solution duration to the length of time between the activities that occurred prior to and following each consult request (i.e., time duration between activity following and prior to consult request / total amount of time taken to solve the case). The resulting value suggests that students spent 10% of their overall problem solving behavior requesting a consult ($SD = 7.1\%$).

Help-seeking varied across cases. In particular, 52% of consults were requested while diagnosing a rare disease (i.e., Pheochromocytoma) with lower frequency of help-seeking when solving more common diseases, such as Diabetes mellitus Type 1 and Grave's disease (i.e., 28% and 21%, respectively). It is noteworthy that 72% of consult requests were preceded by ordering a lab test. The students' consult requests were most commonly followed by either: (a) submitting the final diagnosis (28%), (b) changing their conviction in regards to their hypotheses (21%), or (c) reading a topic in the library (14%). These patterns suggest that students requested consults while reasoning about the implications of a lab test towards their own hypotheses as well as gathering additional information regarding either the tests or a particular disease.

2.2 Antecedent and Consequent Activities during Help-Seeking

The results show significant differences across the frequencies of regulatory activities that occurred before and after asking help in BioWorld. Students engaged in orientation activities 3.2 times more often before, as opposed to after, asking for help (f_{before} = 19 vs. f_{after} = 6; $\chi^2(1) = 6.67$, $p < .05$). The most frequent skills that students demonstrated during the orienting phase were identifying important information, such as the vital signs and symptoms and formulating their differential diagnoses (a.k.a. hypotheses) (f_{before} = 10 and 9 vs. f_{after} = 4 and 1, respectively).

Students were 1.9 times more likely to engage in planning activities before requesting a consult (f_{before} = 43 vs. f_{after} = 23; $\chi^2(1) = 6.06$, $p < .05$). The descriptive statistics suggest that students preferred initially to formulate an action plan (f_{before} = 22 vs. f_{after} = 8) and organize thoughts by self-questioning (f_{before} = 16 vs. f_{after} = 6).

Students were 2.1 times more likely to engage in the monitoring phase while regulating their clinical activities before they requested a consult (f_{before} = 33 vs. f_{after} = 16; $\chi^2(1) = 5.90$, $p < .05$). Before students requested a consult, the descriptive statistics suggest that students were more likely to notice instances of confusion pertaining to their hypotheses (f_{before} = 11 vs. f_{after} = 8). Students were also more likely to obtain a non-pertinent lab test as opposed to a pertinent one before they asked for help (f_{before} = 15 and 5 vs. f_{after} = 3 and 0).

After requesting a consult, students were in the evaluation phase 2 times more often than before they had asked for help (f_{before} = 12 vs. f_{after} = 24; $\chi^2(1) = 4.00$, $p < .05$). In evaluating the outcomes of the clinical process, the descriptive statistics suggest that students were more likely to either: (a) justify the correct diagnosis as more probable or the incorrect diagnosis as less probable (f_{before} = 1 vs. f_{after} = 6) as well as the incorrect diagnosis as more probable or the correct diagnosis as less probable (f_{before} = 0 vs. f_{after} = 2); and (b) give up or quit solving the case (f_{before} = 0 vs. f_{after} = 5).

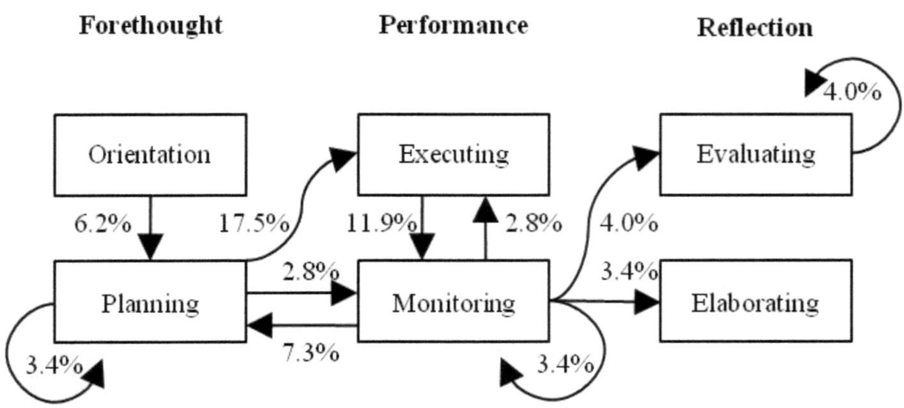

Fig. 1. State Transitions across Phases of Self-Regulation while Seeking Help

The use of monitoring activities served as a hub for the regulation of clinical reasoning while seeking help with BioWorld. Figure 2 shows the ten most frequent transitions that occurred between the different regulatory activities. The results show that 20.9% of these transitions had monitoring activities as their starting point, while 18.1% resulted in monitoring activities. These transitions clustered together in that students first engaged in orientation (6.2% of all transitions), and then moved to formulate a plan (17.5% of all transitions), execute the plan (11.9% of all transitions), and make adjustments while monitoring progress (7.3% of all transitions). Based on the outcomes of the monitoring activities, students shifted from the performance by engaging in the reflection phase or re-orienting their efforts to solve the problem.

3 Discussion

This aim of this study was to model regulatory activities in problem-solving during help-seeking in the context of BioWorld. Help-seeking accounted for a tenth of the time taken to solve the problem. The findings show that students most often requested help while solving the most complex case, Pheochromocytoma. Help-seeking activities occurred most often after ordering a lab test. A non-pertinent lab test was an indication to students that their diagnosis was incorrect and that they needed to evaluate and regulate their clinical reasoning processes. Students interpreted the outcomes of the lab test correctly, but needed assistance to reorient themselves when facing an impasse. Students often engaged in planning the clinical process by self-questioning and formulating an action plan and as such future hints will support these activities. Furthermore, students often gave up after requesting help and thus our hints will be designed to encourage reflection and motivational support to students who are experiencing frustration while solving the problem. These findings are indicative of the need to assess the reasons why students request help in order to ensure that the artificial physician tailors each hint to the specific needs of different students.

References

1. Lajoie, S.P.: Developing professional expertise with a cognitive apprenticeship model: Examples from avionics and medicine. In: Ericsson, K.A. (ed.) Development of Professional Expertise: Toward Measurement of Expert Performance and Design of Optimal Learning Environments, pp. 61–84. Cambridge University Press, New York (2009)
2. Lajoie, S.P., Lu, J.: Supporting collaboration with technology: Does shared cognition lead to co-regulation in medicine. Metacognition and Learning 7, 45–62 (2012)
3. Zimmerman, B.: Investigating self-regulation and motivation: Historical background, methodological developments, and future prospects. American Educational Research Jounal 45(1), 166–183 (2008)
4. Meijer, J., Veenman, M., van Hout-Wolters, B.: Metacognitive activities in text-studying and problem-solving: Development of a taxonomy. Educational Research and Evaluation 12(3), 209–237 (2006)

Pilot Test of a Natural-Language Tutoring System for Physics That Simulates the Highly Interactive Nature of Human Tutoring

Sandra Katz[1], Patricia Albacete[1], Michael J. Ford[2], Pamela Jordan[1], Michael Lipschultz[3], Diane Litman[1,3], Scott Silliman[1], and Christine Wilson[1]

[1] Learning Research and Development Center, University of Pittsburgh, Pittsburgh PA, USA
{katz,palbacet,pjordan,scotts,clwilson}@pitt.edu
[2] School of Education, University of Pittsburgh, Pittsburgh PA, USA
mjford@pitt.edu
[3] Dept. of Computer Science, University of Pittsburgh, Pittsburgh PA, USA
{dlitman,lipschultz}@cs.pitt.edu

Abstract. This poster describes Rimac, a natural-language tutoring system that engages students in dialogues that address physics concepts and principles, after students have solved quantitative physics problems. We summarize our approach to deriving decision rules that simulate the highly interactive nature of human tutoring, and describe a pilot test that compares two versions of Rimac: an experimental version that deliberately executes these decision rules within a Knowledge Construction Dialogue (KCD) framework, and a control KCD system that does not intentionally execute these rules.

Keywords: Natural-language dialogue, human tutoring, interaction hypothesis.

1 Introduction

Much research has been devoted to identifying features of tutorial dialogue that can explain its effectiveness [1], so that these features can be simulated in natural-language tutoring systems. One hypothesis is that the highly interactive nature of tutoring itself promotes learning—that is, the "Interaction Hypothesis" [2]. Although this hypothesis is supported by some research, several studies indicate that it is underspecified. That is, it is not how much interaction takes place during tutoring that is important, nor the granularity of interaction—for example, whether the student and tutor discuss a step towards solving a problem, or the sub-steps that lead to that step. Instead, what matters most is how *well* the interaction is carried out (e.g., [3]).

This refinement of the Interaction Hypothesis raises the question, *which linguistic mechanisms support learning from human tutoring?* We address this question by identifying co-constructed discourse relations in tutorial dialogues whose frequency predicts learning; specifying the context in which these relations occur; using this knowledge to formulate decision rules to guide automated tutorial dialogues; implementing these rules in a natural-language tutoring system; and testing the effectiveness of this decision rule-based system, relative to a system that does not intentionally execute these rules [4].

K. Yacef et al. (Eds.): AIED 2013, LNAI 7926, pp. 636–639, 2013.

Table 1. Examples of co-constructed discourse relations during physics tutoring

Bi-directional relations and definitions (S=Speaker)	Examples (T=tutor; S=student)
Whole:Part (Part:Whole) S2 names a part of an object that S1refers to; or S1 names a part of an object named in S2.	**S:** acceleration would be plus **T:** right, the x-component of the acceleration would be plus
Process:Step (Step:Process) S2 presents a step that follows from the process or line of reasoning described by S1; or S2 describes the line of reasoning that leads to the step described by S1.	**S:** the acceleration is zero **T:** so then m*a=0=Fnet=T-W and hence T=W.
Condition:Situation (Situation:Condition) S1 presents a condition or set of circumstances, and S2 states the situation that stems from those conditions; or, S1 presents a situation and S2 states the conditions or circumstances that explain it.	**T:** when do kinematics equations apply? **S:** when the acceleration is constant

We used Rhetorical Structure Theory [5] to identify and tag co-constructed discourse relations in a large corpus of instructional dialogues between human physics tutors and students, via typed interaction ([6], study 2). A sample of these relations are defined and illustrated in Table 1. Any relation can be delivered didactically, by the student or tutor, instead of interactively. For example, the co-constructed Condition:Situation (conditional) relation shown in Table 1 could have been stated didactically by the tutor as, "Kinematics equations apply when the acceleration is constant." We focused on the potential relationship between *co-constructed* discourse relations and learning because these relations operationalize vague notions such as "interactivity" and "cooperative execution" during tutoring (e.g., [2], p.199).

We found that the frequency of several types of co-constructed relations in the tagged corpus predicted learning gains from pretest to posttest. Moreover, the types of co-constructed discourse relations that predict learning vary based on students' ability level. These correlational analyses of co-constructed discourse relations and learning, and the decision rules that stem from them, are described in detail in [4]. In this poster, we: (1) illustrate these decision rules, which are implemented in Rimac, a natural-language tutoring system that guides reflective dialogues about the concepts associated with quantitative physics problems, and (2) describe the design of a pilot evaluation of Rimac that we are currently conducting, and planned analyses.

2 Methods

2.1 Deriving Decision Rules to Guide "Highly Interactive" Dialogues

We conducted correlational analyses between the frequency of discourse relation types (Table 1) and three measures of student learning: overall gain score from pretest to posttest, gain score on qualitative test items, and gain score on quantitative items.

We divided students into ability groups to investigate whether better-prepared students (high pretesters) might benefit from co-constructing different types of discourse relations with their tutor than less well-prepared students (low pretesters). These analyses, coupled with an analysis of the discourse context in which potentially effective relations occur, enabled us to formulate nine decision rules to drive "highly interactive" tutorial dialogues [4]. Two examples of these decision rules are:

Rule 1: **When the student provides a step in a line of reasoning, the tutor may provide the missing steps, rather than ask about each step individually.** This decision rule stems from several correlations involving the Step:Process relation. For example, for the set of students taken as a whole, the frequency of tutor extensions of the student's line of reasoning predicted overall gain [$r(14)=.65$, $p<.01$]. Tutors typically did this when the student answered a question correctly but not completely, or had difficulty figuring out the next step in a solution or discussed line of reasoning.

Rule 2: **If the student answers a question incorrectly, if possible show why it is incorrect by stating the conditions under which it *would* be correct.** This rule is mainly motivated by a correlation between the frequency of co-constructed conditional relations and qualitative gains among low pretest students [$r(7)=.68$, $p< .05$].

2.2 Pilot Evaluation of Rimac

We implemented the nine derived decision rules in the experimental version of Rimac, using a Knowledge Construction Dialogue (KCD) framework (e.g., [7]), but not in a control version whose dialogues are otherwise the same in content and structure. For example, in the following dialogue excerpt, the computer tutor (T) applies Rule 2 (boldfaced segment) in the experimental (decision-rule) driven version:

> **T:** When an object is slowing down, how does the final velocity (vf) compare to the initial velocity (vi) for any interval of time? (smaller, larger, etc.)?
> **S:** Larger
> **T: If the object is speeding up then its final velocity is larger than its initial velocity.** But when an object is slowing down its velocity is getting smaller all the time. So for any interval of time the final velocity is smaller than the initial velocity.

The standard KCD dialogue excerpt is the same, except for the omission of the boldfaced segment and the connector "but;" that is, it simply corrects the student. The research platform is illustrated further at https://sites.google.com/site/rimacdemo [8].

Data collection for this pilot study is in progress, in physics classes at six high schools in the mid-western USA. Approximately 250 students are participating in the field trials, which take place during two physics lab periods, each lasting approximately 1.5 hrs. in conjunction with the course units on kinematics and dynamics.

3 Plans for Data Analysis

We will verify that the two conditions did differ significantly, in terms of frequency of rule firings and other linguistic indicators of a high level of "interactivity." We will then determine if there is a significant difference in the amount of learning gains (from pretest to posttest) between conditions, and investigate whether there is an interaction between student ability and dialogue condition: for example, is the highly interactive version more helpful for low ability students (as measured by pretest and SAT scores), whereas the standard version better supports high ability students?

Acknowledgements. This research is supported by the Institute of Education Sciences, U.S. Department of Education, through Grant R305A10063 to the University of Pittsburgh. The opinions expressed are those of the authors and do not necessarily represent the views of the Institute or the U.S. Department of Education. We thank Stefani Allegretti, Kevin Krost, and Tyler McConnell for their contributions.

References

1. Bloom, B.S.: The 2 Sigma Problem: The Search for Methods of Group Instruction as Effective as One-to-One Tutoring. Educational Researcher 13, 4–16 (1984)
2. Van Lehn, K.: The Relative Effectiveness of Human Tutoring, Intelligent Tutoring Systems, and Other Tutoring Systems. Educational Psychologist 46(4), 197–221 (2011)
3. Chi, M., VanLehn, K., Litman, D., Jordan, P.: An Evaluation of Pedagogical Tutorial Tactics for a Natural Language Tutoring System: A Reinforcement Learning Approach. International Journal of Artificial Intelligence in Education 21, 83–113 (2011)
4. Katz, S., Albacete, P.: A Tutoring System that Simulates the Highly Interactive Nature of Human Tutoring. Educational Psychology (Special Issue on Advanced Learning Technologies) (in press)
5. Mann, W.C., Thompson, S.: Rhetorical Structure Theory: Toward a Functional Theory of Text Organization. Text 8(3), 243–281 (1988)
6. Katz, S., Allbritton, D., Connelly, J.: Going Beyond the Problem Given: How Human Tutors Use Post-Solution Discussions to Support Transfer. International Journal of Artificial Intelligence and Education 13(1), 79–116 (2003)
7. Rosé, C., Jordan, P., Ringenberg, M., Siler, S., VanLehn, K., Weinstein, A.: Interactive Conceptual Tutoring in Atlas-Andes. In: Moore, J.D., Redfield, C.L., Johnson, W.L. (eds.) Artificial Intelligence in Education, pp. 256–266. IOS Press, Amsterdam (2001)
8. Jordan, P., Albacete, P., Ford, M.J., Katz, S., Lipschultz, M., Litman, D., Silliman, S., Wilson, C.: The Rimac Tutor - A Simulation of the Highly Interactive Nature of Human Tutorial Dialogue. In: Lane, C., Yacef, K., Mostow, J., Pavlik, P. (eds.) AIED 2013. LNCS (LNAI), vol. 7926, pp. 928–929. Springer, Heidelberg (2013)

Authoring Expert Knowledge Bases for Intelligent Tutors through Crowdsourcing

Mark Floryan and Beverly Park Woolf

Department of Computer Science, University of Massachusetts, Amherst,
140 Governors Dr. Amherst, MA USA
{mfloryan,bev}@cs.umass.edu

Abstract. We have developed a methodology for constructing domain-level expert knowledge bases automatically through crowdsourcing. This approach involves collecting and analyzing the work of numerous students within an intelligent tutor and using an intelligent algorithm to coalesce data to construct the domain model. This evolving expert knowledge base (EEKB) is then utilized to provide expert coaching and tutoring with future students. We can compare the knowledge created in human crafted expert knowledge bases (HEKB) with knowledge resulting from our knowledge acquisition algorithm to judge quality. We find that our EEKB models have qualities that rival that of the human crafted knowledge bases and can be generated in significantly less time. We have built four unique knowledge bases using this methodology. This paper provides a pithy high-level overview of our approach along with some findings.

Keywords: Expert knowledge bases, crowd-sourcing authoring tools, ill-defined domains, collaboration.

1 Introduction

This research investigates whether the process of authoring domain models for intelligent tutoring systems (ITS) can be simplified and automated. Specifically, this project tests whether authoring tools based on crowdsourcing can support development of large-scale, real-world tutors.

Our tutor Rashi provides support in ill-defined domains by leveraging an expert knowledge base (EKB). One clear expense in building intelligent tutors like Rashi is the development of these domain models. For example, extensive interviews or "think aloud" protocols with subject matter experts (SMEs) are required to develop domain models [1]. Thus, the primary goal of our research is to provide techniques for improving the development time of these domain models. This paper presents an approach to domain knowledge base construction that leverages the large corpus of data available when students work within tutors. We present the concept of an evolving expert knowledge base (EEKB), which is structurally equivalent to an expert knowledge base (EKB), but is generated by crowdsourcing [4][5] the actions of students using Rashi.

K. Yacef et al. (Eds.): AIED 2013, LNAI 7926, pp. 640–643, 2013.

2 Knowledge Acquisition Algorithm

Rashi is an existing well-vetted inquiry learning system that has been used by several thousand students. The system provides case descriptions for students to investigate problems, along with information about how to approach problems [2]. Rashi is domain independent and applications in several domains have been created and tested (e.g., biology, forestry and art history). This research focuses primarily on the Human Biology domain. The system contains a *content knowledge base* (i.e., an expert system) with knowledge of individual cases and human biology in general. In the Human Biology Tutor, students evaluate virtual patients and generate hypotheses about their medical condition. Students create hypotheses and establish relations between observable data and hypotheses in their notebook.

In addition, Rashi contains an algorithm for generating an Evolving Expert Knowledge Base (EEKB). This algorithm works by accepting input from multiple students that represent actions within the tutor. The algorithm contains two handler methods, one that deals with analyzing evidence of existing nodes (concept, hypothesis, data, etc.) and another that does the same for edges (relationships, etc.). The algorithm searches for matches to incoming pieces of evidence and adds or updates the probabilistic confidence of EEKB entries appropriately. Entries representing the same topics are automatically combined to produce a unified graph representing student knowledge as a whole.

3 Methodology

We tested our approach by utilizing five years worth of Rashi data, garnered from four unique classroom settings. These settings provide a strong randomization of student age (middle school through college), student background (private and public school students, etc.), and level of pedagogical intervention.

Four of our medical cases provided sufficient data to analyze our approach. We ran the data for each case through our knowledge acquisition algorithm. To judge the quality of an evolving expert knowledge base (EEKB), we compare it directly to a human created expert knowledge base (HEKB). We utilize two distinct but related metrics: precision and recall. Precision is the information in the EEKB that is 'true' according to an HEKB built in the same domain, while recall is the breadth of knowledge created:

$$Precision\,(EEKB, HEKB) = |\,EEKB \cap HEKB\,| \;/\; |\,EEKB\,|$$

Where EEKB is the automatically generated graph and HEKB is the human generated graph

$$Recall\,(EEKB, HEKB) = |\,EEKB \cap HEKB\,| \;/\; |\,HEKB\,|$$

Where EEKB is the automatically generated graph and HEKB is the human generated graph

We observe how the generated model changes over time. We took snapshots of the state of the EEKB every 100 inputs and measured both precision and recall.

4 Results

We see that precision consistently hovers around 90 percent (figure 1). As the knowledge base begins to reach a saturation point, we see that precision begins to decline.

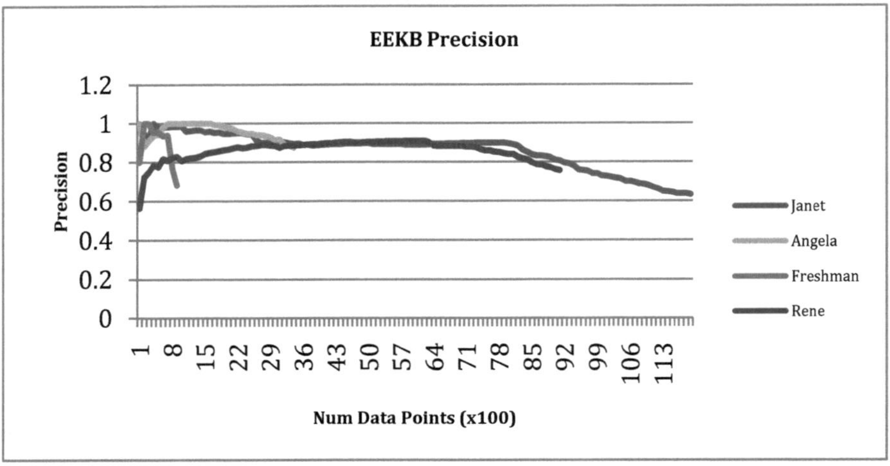

Fig. 1. Precision over time for all four EEKB models generated

EEKB recall over time is slightly different in that the raw numbers seem quite low (figure 2). The generated EEKB models reached a maximum of 23 percent recall; however, past research suggests that students only explore 15-25% of our HEKB [3].

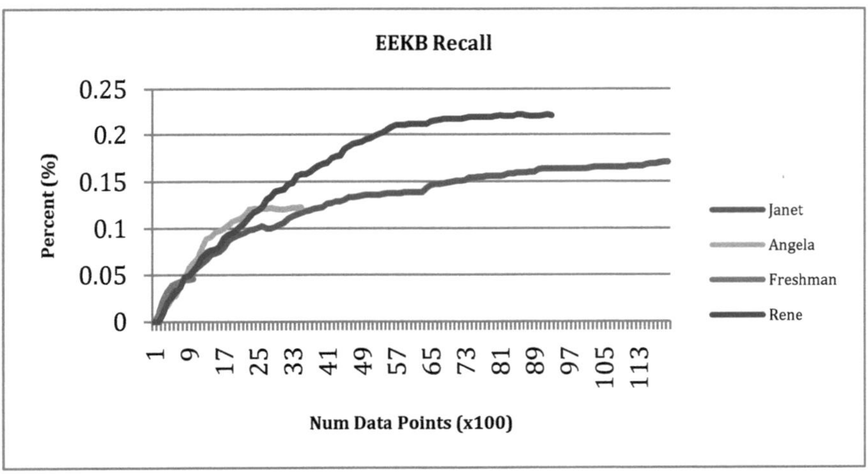

Fig. 2. Recall over time for all four EEKB models generated

Lastly, we find that these models can be generated in significantly less time. Particularly, our algorithm requires roughly 300 hours of parallel student work, as opposed to an equivalent 400 hours of estimated expert work.

5 Conclusions

In conclusion, we present a novel approach for efficiently creating domain models within intelligent tutors without requiring extensive programming or tedious human interviews. Students, especially when sampled in mass quantities, are capable of creating precise knowledge. In addition, because the student to teacher ratio is high, students have more capability for parallelization without being asked to perform additional work (i.e., the students were going to use Rashi as a learning activity anyway). Although our results show low recall, we have data suggesting that students generally don't explore most of the knowledge base [3] and that our particular model represents a set of potential topics largely outside the scope of the given case. Thus, this leads us to believe that 1) it is difficult to create a domain model that encompass an accurate scope of practical student interest and 2) constructing models of this form from student data may be the best approach to converging quickly on a domain model most relevant to the students in question.

Future work will involve testing this method to introduce more medical cases and then designing tools to evaluate how well our method transfers to cases in other domains.

Acknowledgements. This research was funded by an award from the National Science Foundation, NSF 0632769, IIS CSE, Effective Collaborative Role-playing Environments, (PI) Beverly Woolf, with Merle Bruno and Daniel Suthers. Any opinions, findings, conclusions or recommendations expressed in this material are those of the authors and do not necessarily reflect the views of the funding agencies.

References

1. Aleven, V., McLaren, B., Sewall, J., Koedinger, K.: A New Paradigm for Intelligent Tutoring Systems: Example-Tracing Tutors. International Journal of Artificial Intelligence in Education 19(2), 105–154 (2009)
2. Dragon, T., Floryan, M., Woolf, B., Murray, T.: Recognizing Dialogue Content in Student Collaborative Conversation. In: Aleven, V., Kay, J., Mostow, J. (eds.) ITS 2010, Part II. LNCS, vol. 6095, pp. 113–122. Springer, Heidelberg (2010)
3. Floryan, M., Dragon, T., Woolf, B.P.: When Less is More: Focused Pruning of Knowledge Bases to Improve Recognition of Student Conversation. In: Cerri, S.A., Clancey, W.J., Papadourakis, G., Panourgia, K. (eds.) ITS 2012. LNCS, vol. 7315, pp. 340–345. Springer, Heidelberg (2012)
4. Siorpaes, K., Hepp, M.: Games with a purpose for the semantic web. IEEE Intelligent Systems 23(3), 50–60 (2008)
5. Kittur, A., Chi, E.H., Suh, B.: Crowdsourcing User Studies With Mechanical Turk. In: Proceedings of the ACM CHI Conference, Florence, Italy (2008)

Towards Providing Feedback to Students in Absence of Formalized Domain Models

Sebastian Gross[1], Bassam Mokbel[2], Barbara Hammer[2], and Niels Pinkwart[1]

[1] Clausthal University of Technology, Department of Informatics, Julius-Albert-Str. 4, 38678 Clausthal-Zellerfeld, Germany
{sebastian.gross,niels.pinkwart}@tu-clausthal.de
[2] Bielefeld University, CITEC Center of Excellence, Universitaetsstr. 21-23, 33615 Bielefeld, Germany
{bmokbel,bhammer}@techfak.uni-bielefeld.de

Abstract. In this paper, we propose the provision of feedback in Intelligent Tutoring Systems in absence of a formalized domain model. In a Wizard of Oz experiment, a human tutor gave feedback to students based on sample solutions applying two strategies which aimed to encourage learners' self-reflection. We discuss possibilities to automate the methods of feedback provision using domain-independent proximity measures.

Keywords: intelligent tutoring systems, feedback provision, machine learning.

1 Introduction

Various studies demonstrated that feedback plays a significant role in instruction and that feedback has to be well designed to have a positive impact on learning to guide learners and support the learning process [7]. ITS research on feedback provision included aspects such as how feedback should be phrased (e.g., response accuracy, correct answer, hints, examples), when feedback should be provided (e.g., immediately, or after some time has elapsed), or which pedagogical theory of learning it should be based on. For instance, Zakharov et al. [9] implemented pedagogical strategies based on the theory of learning from performance errors in EER-Tutor, a Constraint-Based Tutor for database design.

Most ITS approaches rely on formalized domain knowledge or models in order to provide feedback. In ill-defined domains where no such formalized knowledge exists, student solutions cannot be analyzed by comparing them to a domain model. The ITS literature knows several approaches that aim to compensate for that fact. For instance, Nkambou and colleagues [6] proposed a hybrid approach for supporting tutoring services in astronaut training by combining an expert-system and data mining approaches. Example based learning has shown to be effective in supporting learning also in ill-defined domains. In the NavEx tutor, annotated program code examples were provided to students in order to give explanations to learners instead of providing bare solutions [1]. In summary, most

K. Yacef et al. (Eds.): AIED 2013, LNAI 7926, pp. 644–648, 2013.

approaches either use formalized knowledge modelled in rules or constraints, or require an effort-intensive preparation of appropriate examples.

In this paper, we propose two feedback provision strategies that rely on supporting learner's self-reflection using example-based instructions. The proposed strategies are based on (dis-)similarities among student solutions and can thus potentially be applied independently of the domain being taught and without manually prepared example solutions by identifying appropriate examples in sets of student solutions using machine learning techniques.

2 Feedback Provision in Absence of Domain Models

Assume that for a given problem, formalized domain models are not available, but a set of student solutions and a means to identify similarities among these solutions are. A newly submitted solution of a student can then be analyzed and compared to the existing set of solutions using the proximity measure, and a highly similar solution from the existing set (which we call *counterpart*) can automatically be determined. It is assumed that the student solution differs partially from its counterpart, but implements the same problem solving strategy. Then, a fine-grained comparison between the two can be used to provide feedback. Here, we distinguish two feedback strategies:

F1 *Highlighting* of parts in the student solution which differ from its counterpart, without showing the counterpart to the learner.
F2 *Contrasting* parts in the student solution, revealing parts of its counterpart.

Feedback strategy **F1** is designed to guide learners towards reflecting on their solution and explaining it. Without showing the counterpart, the learner is required to reason the highlighted aspects of her solution, thus identifying potential mistakes. Feedback strategy **F2** requires a learner to understand the contrasted part, to identify the corresponding part in her own solution, and to compare both parts in order to find a possible mistake. Combining strategies **F1+F2** simultaneously supports a learner in identifying similarities by highlighting and contrasting dissimilar parts of her solution and its counterpart, and may thus help the learner to focus on specific differences.

Implementing the same strategy but differing in parts could be an indication of a mistake or a misconception. In a set of student solutions, however, we usually can not guarantee that the counterpart solution is correct (unless, of course, using a domain model). At first sight, this vagueness of correctness seems to be a crucial drawback of the approach. Yet, with suitable feedback messages accompanying the highlighting or contrasting, this issue can be addressed. Feedback messages can be formulated as self reflection prompts which have shown to be an effective form of intervention [2]. For example, students can be asked not only to reflect their own solution but also on the contrasted solution which could (also) be erroneous to identify misconceptions. Modelled in a procedure of peer interactions students can then help each other to improve their solutions [8].

3 Evaluation of Feedback Provision Strategies

We conducted a field study in an introductory university programming course over a period of 23 days in order to evaluate the proposed feedback strategies. To make students believe that feedback was generated by an ITS, the study was conducted as a Wizard of Oz experiment where a human tutor provided feedback (as described in Sec. 2) to students. Applying strategy **F2** means that a student has to match a contrasted part to an appropriate part in her solution, which might have been difficult in our setting (1st semester non-computer science students being introduced to Java programming). We therefore decided to apply strategy **F2** simultaneously with strategy **F1**. Thus, we tested both strategy **F1** and the combination **F1+F2** in the experiments.

We used an online submission and assessment system which enabled students to submit solutions to a task of a specific lecture in the curriculum. Students were able to request feedback and access the provided feedback via this system. Overall, during the 23 days, students were able to request feedback 4 times. The task students had to solve (and could get feedback on) was part of the regular set of class exercises. A set of sample solutions implementing typically used problem solving strategies for the given task was prepared in advance. Based on these sample solutions, the tutor generated and provided feedback to students' requests in Wizard of Oz manner, and recorded the process of feedback generation and provision regarding effort and potential helpfulness. He applied the strategies **F1** and **F1+F2** choosing freely between the two strategies. To simulate a deterministic system behavior, we defined standards of how feedback should be generated. The human tutor was instructed to strictly adhere to the rules that (**i**) feedback had to be consistent over time and between different students, specifically, it was not allowed to consider former feedback that had been given to a particular learner, and (**ii**) feedback had to consist of parts of sample solutions and highlights in the student solutions only. The human tutor violated rule (**i**) only once where a student obviously did not understand the given feedback. This student just copied and pasted code of the contrasted sample solution without transforming names of variables. Furthermore, the student wrote comments in the program code asking what the sample code meant. Rule (**ii**) was not violated by the tutor, although one of the student solutions did not fit any of the sample solutions. In this case, the tutor generated feedback using smaller parts of several sample solutions.

Feedback was requested 30 times from 22 different students. Upon generating feedback, the human tutor rated on a 5 point scale whether he thought that based on his tutoring expertise the provided feedback was appropriate or not (1 = not appropriate, 5 = very appropriate). On average, the expert rated the feedback with 4.33 (sd = 0.802) points. Overall, the human tutor needed about 10 hours for generating and providing feedback for 30 requests. This means that, on average, 20 minutes were required for each feedback provision.

4 Automation of Feedback Provision

The evaluation illustrated that feedback generation by a human tutor means a huge amount of work. In a realistic scenario, students will want to request feedback on demand and usually expect immediate replies. Therefore, our long-term goal is to define a proximity measure to compute the (dis)similarity of two solutions in such a way, that the outcome reflects the specific syntactical and semantical relationships we are interested in. Then, the best matching sample solution for a given student solution would be the one with the highest similarity. Based on the identified sample, appropriate feedback can be generated as described in Sec. 2. Hence, defining a meaningful measure is essential to enable automatic feedback. First steps to evaluate possible choices for proximity measures have been presented in [4, 3]. Domain-independent measures in the literature can be categorized according to the form of representation in which the subjects (i.e. solutions) are considered, distinguishing three degrees of structural complexity: (**A**) a finite-dimensional *vector* consisting of numerical features and statistics of the solution, where typical proximity measures would be distances in the underlying vector space; (**B**) a symbolic *sequence*, where the (dis-)similarity can be calculated, e.g., by the normalized compression distance (NCD) or alignment measures, common in bioinformatics or text processing [4]; (**C**) an annotated tree or *graph*, where proximities can be structure kernels [5].

We are currently developing an approach to incorporate more structural and morphological aspects into a proximity measure which is based on classical string similarity. According to relationships and dependencies in the syntax (e.g. dependencies between Java expressions), we decompose each solution into meaningful units, before calculating an average (dis-)similarity between the units via established proximity measures. This is subject of ongoing work.

Acknowledgement. This work was supported by the German Research Foundation (DFG) under the grant "FIT - Learning Feedback in Intelligent Tutoring Systems." (PI 767/6 and HA 2719/6).

References

[1] Brusilovsky, P., Yudelson, M.: From webex to navex: Interactive access to annotated program examples. Proc. of the IEEE 96(6), 990–999 (2008)

[2] Chi, M.T.H., Bassok, M., Lewis, M.W., Reimann, P., Glaser, R.: Self-explanations: How students study and use examples in learning to solve problems. Cognitive Sci. 13(2), 145–182 (1989)

[3] Gross, S., Mokbel, B., Hammer, B., Pinkwart, N.: Feedback provision strategies in intelligent tutoring systems based on clustered solution spaces. In: DeLFI 2012: Die 10. e-Learning Fachtagung Informatik, pp. 27–38. Köllen (2012)

[4] Mokbel, B., Gross, S., Lux, M., Pinkwart, N., Hammer, B.: How to quantitatively compare data dissimilarities for unsupervised machine learning? In: Mana, N., Schwenker, F., Trentin, E. (eds.) ANNPR 2012. LNCS, vol. 7477, pp. 1–13. Springer, Heidelberg (2012)

[5] Neuhaus, M., Bunke, H.: Edit distance-based kernel functions for structural pattern classification. Pattern Recognition 39(10), 1852–1863 (2006)
[6] Nkambou, R., Fournier-Viger, P., Nguifo, E.M.: Learning task models in ill-defined domain using an hybrid knowledge discovery framework. Know.-Based Syst. 24(1), 176–185 (2011)
[7] Shute, V.J.: Focus on formative feedback. Review of Educational Research 78(1), 153–189 (2008)
[8] Topping, K.: Peer assessment between students in colleges and universities. Rev. of Educational Research 68(3), 249–276 (1998)
[9] Zakharov, K., Mitrovic, A., Ohlsson, S.: Feedback micro-engineering in eer-tutor. In: Proc. AIED 2005, pp. 718–725. Press (2005)

Enhancing In-Museum Informal Learning by Augmenting Artworks with Gesture Interactions and AIED Paradigms

Emmanuel G. Blanchard, Alin Nicolae Zanciu, Haydar Mahmoud, and James S. Molloy

Department of Architecture, Design and Media Technology,
Aalborg University at Copenhagen, Denmark
{emmanuel.g.blanchard,alin.zanciu,deeninteractive,
jamesstuartmolloy}@gmail.com

Abstract. This paper presents a computer-supported approach for providing 'enhanced' discovery learning in informal settings like museums. It is grounded on a combination of gesture-based interactions and artwork-embedded AIED paradigms, and is implemented through a distributed architecture.

Keywords: Museum exhibition, informal learning, enhanced discovery learning, augmented artwork, gesture-based interaction, distributed system.

1 Introduction

There is a growing interest of museum curators for technologies that would make their institutions more interactive. Rather than totally reshaping museum experiences, curators expect smooth transitions towards more interactivity while preserving the informal learning nature of museum experiences, characterized as opportunities for visitors to freely decide "*where to go, what to do, and how long to do it*"[7]. Several initiatives already investigate in-museum educational support through technology [5] but very few of them integrate personalization or adaptation mechanisms (see [7, 9] for counter examples). In order to embed additional features and information in artworks, visually-Augmented Reality (AR) is probably the most commonly explored practice nowadays (e.g. [8]). However the use of additional devices such as smartphones to convey AR is stated to disrupt museum experiences [6] and using the body as a control method to trigger visitor-artwork interactions is a proposed alternative to overcome this focus shift [6]. We thus believe that gesture-based interaction is an interesting-yet-unexplored approach for more inclusive in-museum adaptive educational experiences through "*enhanced discovery learning*" [1]. Consequently, in this paper, we discuss a gesture-based Intelligent Tutoring System (ITS) where artworks are augmented to allow personalized and adaptive learning experiences

2 Overall Description

In an enhanced museum exhibition, several artworks are augmented with an installation that we refer to a 'station'. The goal of a station is to provide artwork-embedded

K. Yacef et al. (Eds.): AIED 2013, LNAI 7926, pp. 649–652, 2013.

gesture-based adaptive learning opportunities for visitors. It also transmits recordings of visitor activities to a central server through wifi for future adaptations. Our system aims at keeping visitor navigation unconstrained and consequently preserving the informal learning nature of museum experiences, which is why we adopted this distributed architecture approach as did previous works with similar objectives (e.g. [2]).Technically speaking, a station consists of a computer controlling both a *Microsoft Kinect 3D camera* for monitoring gestures (i.e. pointing at specific areas) and a projector for displaying visual cues of these gestures and additional visual information (e.g. informative texts, guidance, visual hints).

In a typical interaction scenario, a visitor first registers to the system and is provided with a color sequence that he later has to enter to be recognized by stations. He can then physically navigate through the museum exhibition the way (s)he wants. When he chooses to interact with a station, informative text is displayed along with a related enigma. By moving his/her right hand, the user is controlling a projected visual cue and can select an area of the artwork that, (s)he thinks, is the answer to the enigma. If (s)he identifies the correct area, new text is provided to introduce the next enigma until no more enigma is available for the painting or the user quits the station. In the current implementation of the system, the painting is displayed by the projector, but an alternative version is possible where visual cues are directly projected on artworks (or copies of it in case artifacts are light-sensitive). Fig. 1 presents the system architecture along with details of a station installation (left) and the graphical user interface including informative text and an enigma (right).

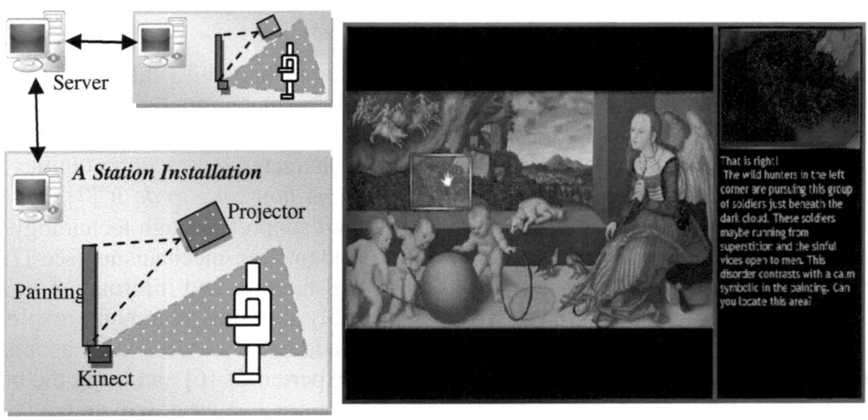

Fig. 1. Distributed architecture of the ITS (left), and interface of a station (right). The displayed artwork, « *Melancholia* » is visible at the *National Gallery of Denmark* - http://www.smk.dk-.

Using concept maps, we have designed a two 2-level process to elicit expert knowledge. The first level consists in eliciting general information about the main theme of an exhibition, and is aimed at providing a framework to ensure that experts use consistent grounding in their various artwork descriptions. The second level focuses on the elicitation of knowledge specific to a particular artwork and consequently describes interactive opportunities for each station. This elicitation process results in one XML file per painting that structures all the knowledge presentation variants and allows a decision module to choose the most adequate one according to users' personal characteristics and past experiences.

The whole system is organized as an "*enhanced discovery learning*" activity [1], which is achieved by implementing several paradigms and mechanisms:

Cycle of Expertise. Enigmas and knowledge are organized around a '*cycle of expertise*' [4], a scaffolding technique that consists of providing knowledge and skills to raise the level of expertise of an individual, having him/her using these acquired knowledge and skills to achieve more and more challenging activities that lead him/her to discover and learn more advanced knowledge and skills, and so on.

Provision of Visual Hints. Failing to solve an enigma does not result in a dead end since frames and other visual cues can be generated after a certain time as visual hints for visitors to continue their discovery of the painting.

Personalization and Adaptation. The personalization mechanism currently considers the following user characteristic categories: language (*English versus Danish*) and age group (*children versus adults*). Presented information and enigmas are also adapted to previous station experiences i.e. when a visitor interacts with a station, keywords describing the experienced content are registered in the visitor's profile that is used to select the most appropriate text variant in future station-user interaction.

3 Evaluation and Conclusion

A proof-of-concept evaluation was performed in a laboratory environment. The sample consisted of 30 people in the test group (interaction with the system) and 29 in the control one (interaction with a real scale copy of a painting along with explanatory text aside of it). Both conditions provided similar informative content with the system making it more interactive and progressive in the test condition. Both test and control groups essentially consisted of Danish undergraduate students.

Analyses of a post test questionnaire revealed that test subjects (18/30) more frequently provided a deep analysis of the painting than control subjects (10/20) ($\chi2(1)=4.9$ $p<.05$). One potential explanation is that test subjects spent significantly more time interacting with the painting ($M=291.1$ $SD=122.2$) than did control ones ($M=67.6$ $SD=66.1$), $t(57)=8.7$ $p<.0005$ even though they were free to leave the experiment at any time. Using 5-point Likert scales, test participants reported the system to be easy and intuitive to use (6 found it very intuitive, 16 intuitive, 7 neutral, and 1 not very intuitive), and very fun and interesting (17 found it very interesting, 10 interesting, and 3 neutral). 19 out of 30 participants thought the system improved their connectedness/attachment to artworks and among those 19 persons, only 5 thought that a similar effect could have been achieved by means other than the in-museum gesture based approach we used (e.g. online/mobile app.). Indeed, 28 out of 30 described this way of interacting with artworks as innovative. Eventually, 29 out of 30 people would like to see the system in museums, and 22 out of 30 (others having no opinion) think this would have a positive impact on their will to visit an exhibition.

We also asked participants to provide their overall opinion about the project as free comments, and 26 of them were clearly positive. Participants described our system as "*a good way to learn about the painting. It is not always that someone reads the little plaques next to the painting*", and implicitly acknowledged its constructivist nature since they saw it as "*a good way for, step-by-step, acquiring information about paintings.*" The gesture-based interaction paradigm made it "*a lot more fun to interact with a painting than just looking at it [and made it] easier to remember details*". Participants also found it "*nice to be more active in a museum visit*", which helped them "*to remember far more details about the work than [they] otherwise would*" and "*made [them] think about the work in more depth*". Few people also rightfully pointed out dangers of abusing such interactive installations, and suggested to limit this "*great experience for some paintings that are 'important' or 'hard to understand*'.

Conveying AIED support through gesture-based interactions that trigger artwork-embedded information is a winning combination to support in-museum informal and unconstrained learning. The critical reception of our prototype demonstrated a strong interest for this innovative approach that has the potential of attracting a new generation of museum visitors, while renewing the interest of a more traditional audience. This is a very encouraging start when considering that the system can be improved in many ways such as including the visitors' cultural origin in the adaptation process [3].

References

1. Alfieri, L., Brooks, P.J., Aldrich, N.J., Tenenbaum, H.R.: Does discovery-based instruction enhance learning? J. Educational Psychology 103(1), 1–18 (2011)
2. Blanchard, E., Frasson, C.: An autonomy-oriented system design for enhancement of learner's motivation in E-learning. In: Lester, J.C., Vicari, R.M., Paraguaçu, F. (eds.) ITS 2004. LNCS, vol. 3220, pp. 34–44. Springer, Heidelberg (2004)
3. Blanchard, E.G., Ogan, A.: Infusing cultural awareness into intelligent tutoring systems for a globalized world. In: Nkambou, R., Bourdeau, J., Mizoguchi, R. (eds.) Advances in Intelligent Tutoring Systems. SCI, vol. 308, pp. 485–505. Springer, Heidelberg (2010)
4. Gee, J.P.: Good videogames + good learning: Collected essays on video games, learning, and literacy. Peter Lang Publishing, New York (2007)
5. Hatala, M., Tanenbaum, K., Wakkary, R., Muise, K., Mohabbati, B., Corness, G., Budd, J., Loughin, T.: Experience structuring factors affecting learning in family visits to museums. In: Cress, U., Dimitrova, V., Specht, M. (eds.) EC-TEL 2009. LNCS, vol. 5794, pp. 37–51. Springer, Heidelberg (2009)
6. Kortbek, K.J., Grønbæk, K.: Communicating art through interactive technology: New approaches for interaction Design in art museums. In: NordCHI 2008, pp. 229–238. ACM Press (2008)
7. Lane, H.C., Noren, D., Auerbach, D., Birch, M., Swartout, W.: Intelligent tutoring goes to the museum in the big city: A pedagogical agent for informal science education. In: Biswas, G., Bull, S., Kay, J., Mitrovic, A. (eds.) AIED 2011. LNCS, vol. 6738, pp. 155–162. Springer, Heidelberg (2011)
8. Mannion, S.: Augmented reality for culture. Presentation recorded during the 2011 InsideAR: Augmented Reality Conference, Munich, Germany, `http://www.youtube.com/watch?feature=player_embedded&v=jijJbIrKJY0#!` (last accessed January 28)
9. Wang, Y., Aroyo, L., Stash, N., Sambeek, R., Schuurmans, Y., Schreiber, G., Gorgels, P.: Cultivating personalized museum tours online and on-site. J. Interdisciplinary Science Reviews 34(2), 141–156 (2009)

Measuring Procedural Knowledge in Problem Solving Environments with Item Response Theory

Manuel Hernando, Eduardo Guzmán, and Ricardo Conejo

E.T.S. Informática, Universidad de Málaga,
Bulevar Louis Pasteur, 25. Campus de Teatinos,
29071, Málaga, Spain
{mhernando,guzman,conejo}@lcc.uma.es

Abstract. In this paper, a new data-driven model to measure procedural knowledge is described. The model is based on Item Response Theory. The main idea behind this new model is to establish an analogy between the testing and the problem solving environment. For this purpose, we model each problem (or exercise) solution path as a directed graph where nodes are states of the problem and edges, transitions between states (i.e. the actions accomplished by the student). We can match this model with testing by seeing each node as a question and each edge as choices within the questions.

Keywords: Problem Solving Environments, Student Modeling, Procedural Knowledge Estimate, Item Response Theory.

1 Introduction

The way learners acquire knowledge has changed in the last few years with the arrival of new technologies and computer-aided systems. Individualized learning, which is more effective than traditional methods [1], can be achieved through a combination of traditional methods and computer-aided ones. In order to offer students the best strategy to acquire some concepts or skills, we need to maintain a student model that represents his/her knowledge. Using that information an Intelligent Tutor System could guide students to reach a certain goal. Updating and maintaining this model is a difficult issue in the field. Students' models have to be updated as students interact with the system, so it is necessary to infer the student's model through his/her actions.

There are different strategies for representing student models in the AIED literature; most of them assume procedural-declarative distinction. Declarative knowledge refers to the knowledge of relevant principles and concepts of a certain subject that can be applied in new tasks [2]. Procedural knowledge is the acquisition of skills related to step-by-step actions in solving problem context [3]. Declarative knowledge is usually assessed with testing systems, while procedural knowledge is mainly assessed through problem solving environments.

In testing systems, the Item Response Theory (IRT) [4] constitutes probably the most successful and well founded of all the strategies. Otherwise, most of procedural

K. Yacef et al. (Eds.): AIED 2013, LNAI 7926, pp. 653–656, 2013.

assessment strategies are based on Bayesian networks. These networks can be, in the worst case scenario, NP-hard which is certainly not desirable. In this paper we present a new technique that uses IRT to estimate procedural knowledge in a problem-solving environment. To this end, problem solution path is ideally modeled as a directed graph in which nodes are states of the problem and edges are transitions between states.

2 Procedural Assessment through Item Response Theory

IRT [4] is one of the best-known strategies for declarative knowledge assessment. According to how the models update the inferred student knowledge in terms of their response IRT-based models could be [5]: dichotomous and polytomous models. Dichotomous models consider only two possible scores, i.e. either correct or incorrect. A characteristic curve, called *Item Characteristic Curve* (ICC), models each item. This curve expresses the probability that student with a certain knowledge level will answer the item correctly; polytomous models have a characteristic curve per choice in an item called *Operating Characteristic Curve* (OCC) [6],which expresses the probability that a student with a certain knowledge level will select this answer [7].

In our approach, each problem is internally modeled as a directed graph the nodes of which are states of the exercises and arcs are the transitions between states. Figure 1 shows an example of a possible graph that represents the addition of $\frac{9}{14}$ and $\frac{3}{10}$. In this figure, we can see that there is more than one path to reach the correct solution$\frac{33}{35}$.

To apply the IRT to estimate the student's knowledge when applying procedural skills, we have made an analogy between problem solving and testing. To do this matching we understand each state of problem solving as an item in testing, and each possible next step from a state to another, as choices of the item. Accordingly, the process of solving a problem by a student could be considered as a branched test where he/she is answering items about the procedures applied to solve this problem. Let us consider the node at the top of the graph presented in Figure 1. This node could be understood as an item such as *How can we go on one step?*, and choices of this item could each be arcs for other nodes of the graph. While solving a problem, there are states where a student could make more than one decision, and therefore, we cannot consider the correctness of a step in isolation. There is usually more than just one way to reach a solution and, generally, they are not all equally good (e.g. adding fractions by multiplying denominators is not as correct as using the least common denominator but it is not incorrect), and even other steps could lead to incorrect solutions. We have chosen an IRT-based polytomous model to assess procedural knowledge since each step could provide relevant information for the assessment. Therefore, each step in problem solving will have its own characteristic curve, like options in polytomous traditional models. The student model is updated during problem solving by the product of the characteristic curves corresponding to the steps he/she is following. In our model, each characteristic curve is called a *Step Characteristic Curve* (SCC). That means that each edge of the problem graph has a characteristic curve associated with it and while a student is "navigating" through the graph, his/her knowledge estimates are updated by means of IRT using the SCC associated to each arc he/she is navigating through.

In this work, for modeling the SCCs we have used the proposal by Thissen and Steinberg for multiple-choice items [8]. The formula of each observable category is shown below, where X_i represents the item and h the response selected in this item:

$$P(X_i = h|\theta) = \frac{e^{a_h\theta+c_h}}{\sum_{k=0}^{m_i} e^{a_k\theta+c_k}} + d_h\frac{e^{a_0\theta+c_0}}{\sum_{k=0}^{m_i} e^{a_k\theta+c_k}} \quad (1)$$

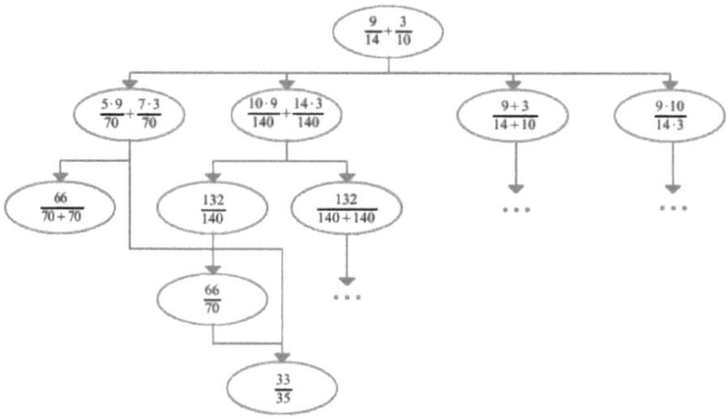

Fig. 1. Example of an exercise graph

3 Experimentation

We have conducted an experiment in order to determine whether or not our approach could be useful for procedural knowledge assessment. The experiment was carried out in January 2013 with a sample of 23 undergraduate students from a course of Project Management taught in the ninth semester of the M.Sc. in Computer Science at the University of Málaga (Spain). These students were previously instructed in project investment with a two-hour lecture and a two-hour training problem solving session. Our hypothesis is that the results of measuring the performance of students while solving a problem with our proposal should be similar to those results obtained through a test with items asking about procedural principles.

The experiment was conducted in a two-hour laboratory session and comprised two different phases. Firstly, the students had to solve two project investment problems. Secondly, a test was posed, the goal of which was to assess the same procedural skills evaluated through the test. The two problems posed to students required calculus of some financial indexes in the project investment domain. The test had 15 multiple choice items related to the calculation of these indexes focusing on procedural steps needed to reach the correct result.

We calculated the student's procedural knowledge from the evidence obtained in the two different ways, i.e. in the test and in the problems applying our proposal. Both calibration and assessment were made using the model explained in Section 2 for both the test and our model. Once the calibration and the assessment of test and problem solving were complete, we compared the results of both techniques. We have accomplished correlation tests in order to verify if both estimations were similar. Results show that the correlation between test results and our approach results were different to 0 with 90% confidence obtaining a correlation coefficient of 0.3435.

4 Conclusions and Future Work

In this paper, we have presented a new approach for assessing procedural knowledge. This proposal applies the IRT (commonly used to assess declarative knowledge) to assess procedural knowledge in problem solving environments. The main idea behind this proposal is to map a problem with a test. As a result, the process of solving a problem can be seen as a graph the node of which are states and its arc the result of applying procedural knowledge which also leads to new states. In our model each state can be modeled with an item, the choices of which are the set of possible transitions from the source state to another new state, obtaining as a result, what in the testing literature is known as a branched test. We have conducted an experiment in order to explore the performance of our model. To this end, we have constructed a test in which items were focused on procedural skills and we have compared its results with those obtained using our model. The evidence suggests that our model can be used for assessment purposes in a problem solving environment and, consequently, as a tool for updating the student model.

Acknowledgements. This work is part of DEDALO project which is financed by the Andalusian Regional Ministry of Science, Innovation and Enterprise (P09-TIC-5105).

References

1. Bloom, B.S.: The search for methods of group instruction as effective as one-to-one tutoring. Educational Leadership 1, 4–17 (1984)
2. Rittle-Johnson, B., Koedinger, K.R.: Designing Knowledge Scaffolds to Support Mathematical Problem Solving. Cognition and Instruction 23(3), 313–349 (2005)
3. Bisanz, J., LeFevre, J.: Strategic and nonstrategic processing in the development of mathematical cognition. In: Bjorklund, D. (ed.) Children's Strategies: Contemporary Views of Cognitive Development, pp. 213–244. Lawrence Erlbaum Associates, Inc., Hillsdale (1990)
4. Embretson, S.E., Reise, S.P.: Item response theory for psychologists. Lawrence Erlbaum, Mahwah (2000)
5. Guzmán, E., Conejo, R., de-la Cruz, J.L.P.: Adaptive testing for hierarchical student models. User Model. User-Adapt. Interact. 17, 119–157 (2007)
6. Dodd, B.G., De Ayala, R.J., Koch, W.R.: Computerized adaptive testing with polytomous items. Applied Psychological Measurement 19, 5–22 (1995)
7. Guzmán, E., Conejo, R.: A model for student knowledge diagnosis through adaptive testing. In: Lester, J.C., Vicari, R.M., Paraguaçu, F. (eds.) ITS 2004. LNCS, vol. 3220, pp. 12–21. Springer, Heidelberg (2004)
8. Thissen, D., Steinberg, L.: A response model for multiple choice items. Psychometrika 49, 501–519 (1984)

Analysis of Emotion and Engagement in a STEM Alternate Reality Game

Yu-Han Chang, Rajiv Maheswaran, Jihie Kim, and Linwei Zhu

University of Southern California,
Information Sciences Institute,
Marina del Rey, CA 90292
{ychang,maheswar,jihie}@isi.edu, vic90228@gmail.com

Abstract. Alternate reality games (ARGs) are a promising new approach for increasing student engagement; however, automated methods for analyzing and optimizing game play are non-existent. We captured the player communication generated by a recent STEM-focused ARG that we piloted in a Los Angeles charter high school. We used shallow sentiment analysis to gauge the levels of various emotions experienced by the players during the course of the game. Pre/post-game surveys gauged whether the game narratives had any effect on student engagement and interest in STEM topics.

1 Introduction

Alternate Reality Games (ARGs) are a relatively new genre that has shown promise for engaging students in STEM learning activities. These transmedia experiences typically draw participants into fictional narratives, where players interact via various forms of social and traditional media, and frequently become part of the storyline themselves. They differ from traditional virtual reality computer games, where the entire story takes place in a fictional online world. In ARGs, the game world overlaps with the real world. Players visit real places, research the real world wide web, communicate with other players and fictional characters using real social media, phone, text messaging, and occasionally live encounters in the real world. For education, this novel game format has the potential to literally bring science activities and learning into the normal lives of students, emphasizing STEM relevance to the students context, surroundings, and community. The ARG brings the game space into the physical daily reality of students [1,3].

In this paper, we describe a pilot ARG we designed and implemented at USC Hybrid High in Fall 2012. We describe the ways in which we were able to capture player data, both by observing the players in game, and by validating these observations through pre and post game tests. In order for ARGs to truly support educational objectives, we need to be able to unobtrusively measure and understand the performance of players within the game, using only their in-game, visible interactions, such as website visitation and forum postings. Individual player assessment enables puppetmasters to tweak the game play to maximize

K. Yacef et al. (Eds.): AIED 2013, LNAI 7926, pp. 657–660, 2013.

Fig. 1. (Top Left) The main characters in the game: William, Isa, and Rudy, (T. Right) The final story element in the game, where Fortinbras' CEO is arrested. (Bottom Left) Special trip to Space X facilities, (B. Center) Mysterious poster at USC Hybrid High, (B. Right) Device used to thwart Fortinbras.

engagement and educational outcome for each learner. Clearly AI and other computational techniques are needed to reach this goal, and this short paper only presents a summary of a small step in this direction.

USC Hybrid High ARG Pilot: Operation Daylight. In Fall 2012, we fielded a pilot alternate reality game, "Operation Daylight," at USC Hybrid High, a new charter high school with approximately 100 ninth graders in its inaugural class. The population is almost entirely minority and receive free/reduced lunches. The game focuses on π, an organization set up centuries ago to defend science. Its most recent incarnation, i4, needs students from USC Hybrid High to be their next generation, and the game begins with i4 recruiting and training students from the school. In the process, the students complete STEM-related activities to advance up the i4 recruitment ladder.

Gradually, the students uncover an evil plot by Fortinbras Industries that threatens their protagonist recruitment agents, the fictional characters Rudy Vanzant and Isa Figueroa, played by local actors in a variety of video sequences. This requires the students to put their newly learned skills to real use in order to save their friends Rudy and Isa. Figure 1 shows some of the elements used in the game. The game ran for approximately five weeks at USC Hybrid High, from 10/18/12 to 11/21/12. It was a completely optional activity that students could engage in if they chose to, with both online, at-school, and out-of-school elements. Students drove over 27,670 page views to the i4 website and posted 1394 messages to the i4 forum.

2 Methodology and Results

We used well-established scales for measuring student interest in STEM topics developed by OECD's Programme for International Student Assessment (PISA) [2]. Pre and post game surveys were developed using these scales, and administered to students at USC Hybrid High one week before the game commenced and one week after the game concluded. The surveys included approximately thirty questions where students would respond "Strongly Agree", "Agree", "Disagree", or "Strongly Disagree." The survey also included questions that established basic demographic information, as well as self-reported aspects of game play. In addition to the survey data, we also collected in-game data such as forum visits, messages posted, videos and pictures posted. We also used the Linguistic Inquiry and Word Count (LIWC) text analysis tool to process the messages [4] and detect whether they expressed a positive or negative sentiment, or whether the message contained anxiety, fear, or happiness.

Fifty-nine out of the 94 survey respondents indicated that they had heard of i4 and the Operation Daylight game. Twenty-three of the 29 students who signed up on the Operation Daylight website filled out surveys. Among students who played the game, they overwhelmingly thought the game increased their interest in science (48%) or did not change their already positive interest in science (47%). No one ended up having less interest in science.

These responses are corroborated with the students' answers to the OECD science interest questions. Figure 2 shows how the students' science interest levels changed from the beginning of the game to the end of the game, conditioned how often they visited the i4 forum, and on the average length of their posts on the forum. In these graphs, 0 corresponds to "Strongly disagree" (dislike science), and 3 corresponds to "Strongly agree" (like science). We see that there is a correlation between more visits and higher science interest level, as well as between longer posts and higher interest levels. There also appears to be a correlation between longer posts and a larger amount of increase in science interest.

Figure 3 shows that there is a correlation between forum activity and the major game events, such as the main characters being abducted. This suggests

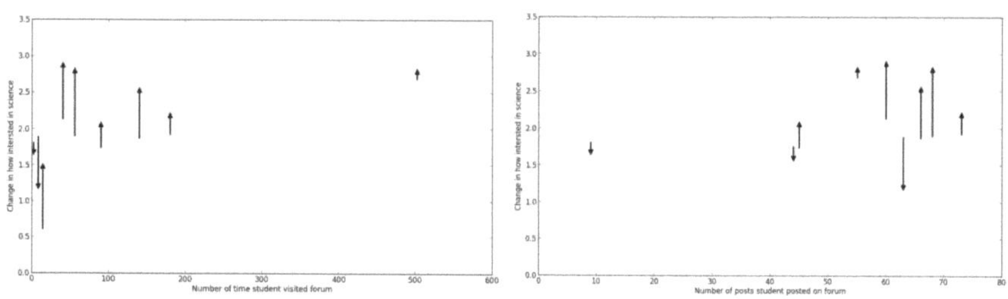

Fig. 2. (Left) Number of visits vs. change in science interest levels, (Right) Average length of forum postings vs. change in science interest levels.

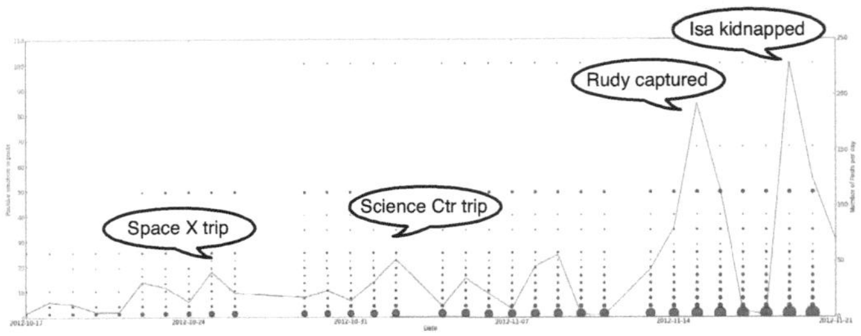

Fig. 3. Time showing the level of forum activity over the course of the game. The thin blue line denotes the number of posts in the forum on each day, the red circles denote how many of those messages contained a particular fraction of positive words.

that these ARG story elements might promote the higher science interest levels described above. We also analyze the number of messages that contained certain percentages of message words that indicate positive or negative attitude, anxiety, fear, or sadness. It turned out that there is no clear pattern between the story elements and the production of particular categories of words, contrary to our expectation. For example, the abduction of the main character did not obviously produce more messages of fear or negativity. Generally the proportional levels of positive words stays constant during the game, and the levels of negative words stays quite low. The proportions of messages with varying levels positive words are also shown in Figure 3. Due to lack of space here, a longer version of this paper will be posted at our website, http://cb.isi.edu.

Acknowledgements. This work was supported by NSF Award #:1224088.

References

1. Klopfer, E.: Augmented learning: Research and design of mobile educational games. MIT Press (2008)
2. Marsh, H.W., Hau, K.-T., Cordula, A., Jurgen, B., Peschar, J.L.: Oecd's brief self-report measure of educational psychology's most useful affective constructs: Cross-cultural psychometric comparisons across 25 countries. International Journal of Testing 6(4), 311–360 (2006)
3. Moseley, A., Whitton, N., Culver, J., Piatt, K.: Motivation in alternate reality gaming environments and implications for learning. In: 3rd European Conference on Games Based Learning. Academic Conferences Limited (2009)
4. Pennebaker, J.W.: Putting stress into words: Health, linguistic, and therapeutic implications. Behaviour Research and Therapy 31(6), 539–548 (1993)

Higher Automated Learning through Principal Component Analysis and Markov Models

Alan Carlin, Danielle Dumond, Jared Freeman, and Courtney Dean*

{acarlin,ddumond,jfreeman,cdean}@aptima.com

Abstract. This paper reports a hybrid method for data-driven instructional design, a method that combines Principle Components Analysis (PCA), Hidden Markov Models (HMM), and Item Response Theory (IRT). PCA is used to identify instructional objectives as well as potential student states, HMMs are used to identify dynamics between states, and IRT is used to construct measurements of state. We report on the architecture of the system along with preliminary results.

Keywords: HMM, IRT, learning path, PCA, learner knowledge assessment.

1 Introduction

Instructional design is entering a period of transformation, one in which this intellect-driven process becomes increasingly data-driven. Traditionally, the design of curricula, courses, and assessments has been driven by a human designer alone, drawing on expert knowledge of the domain and instructional methods to define topics of instruction, measures of student achievement, and an instructional sequence. This instructional design strategy has several shortcomings.

- It assumes that the expert will partition the domain into topics appropriate for the learner, though there is ample evidence that expert knowledge is structured differently from that of novices [3], and that experts disagree significantly about the structure of some domains [5].
- It assumes that the expert will define appropriate measures of student knowledge and skill, though this is logically contingent on partitioning the domain well.
- It assumes that a fixed sequence of instructional topics is sufficient for all learners, though prior knowledge strongly determines learning [4].
- It requires a great deal of time from the expert, though that time is often scarce.

Data-driven aids for instructional design would help to overcome these challenges. Research concerning such aids is growing (c.f., the International Educational Data Mining Society) as data sources arise from intelligent tutoring systems (c.f., the PSLC

* This work was funded by the Office of Naval Research. The opinions expressed here are the authors' and do not necessarily reflect the policy of ONR.

K. Yacef et al. (Eds.): AIED 2013, LNAI 7926, pp. 661–665, 2013.

DataShop), serious games and simulations, and internet courses. Specifically, data-driven instructional design aids might mine these data to recommend to the designer:

- The instructional topics that are most distinct to students, and thus may be the most accessible partitioning of the domain;
- The minimal set of measures required to assess student knowledge and skill on the instructional topics; and
- The sequences of instruction that most efficiently support learning by students.

This paper reports a hybrid method for data-driven instructional design (see Figure 1). Raw input consists of test items and their features. Principle Components Analysis (PCA) casts the data into fundamental components of the domain. The set of student states consists of elements identifying a level of expertise for each component. Item Response Theory (IRT; [2]) is used to define the individual measurements of the state. Hidden Markov Models (HMM; [1]) represent the student's measured progress through the state space. A proof of concept study, reported here, indicates the promise of this hybrid method. We call this method HAL, for Higher Automated Learning.

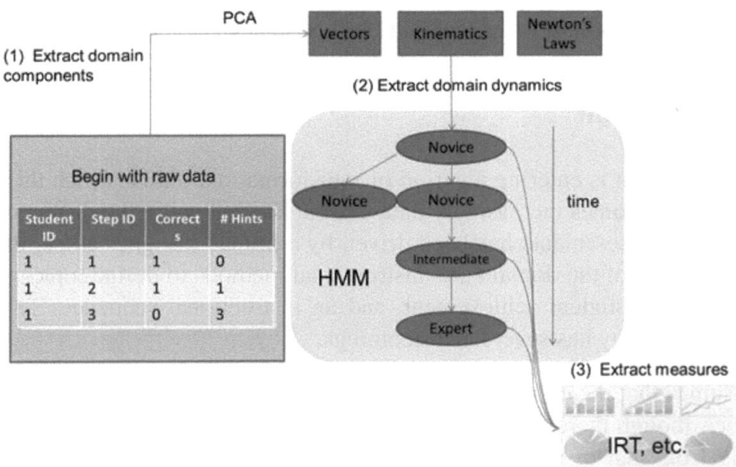

Fig. 1. The methodology for Higher Automated Learning (HAL)

2 Principal Component Analysis

PCA was used to identify the components of learning, where components here are the similarity or natural grouping of problems based on student performance. PCA uses eigenvectors to transform a set of observations of possibly correlated variables into linearly uncorrelated variables called principal components. In HAL, PCA was applied to the Andes data set [6], specifically to data about problems and performance by 77 students.

We calculated a measure of student performance (p) as:

$$p = \frac{correct\ steps - incorrect\ steps - hints}{total\ problem\ steps}$$

The resulting matrix was then transformed into principal components via Singular Value Decomposition. Homework problems were re-plotted as points on the two primary components that accounted for 54% of the variance in the data. In Figure 2 we compare expert-labeled classes of problems (vector vs. wave items) to the components discovered by PCA. To reduce noise, we would, in future applications, analyze problems of similar difficulty to each other (as assessed using IRT). PCA approximately re-created the expert classes from scratch without using the provided labels.

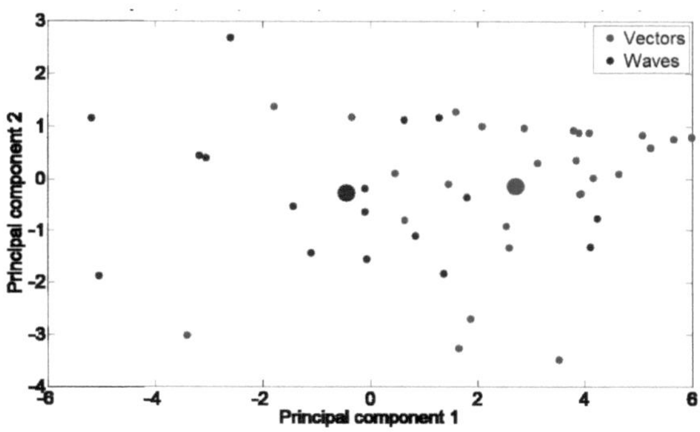

Fig. 2. First principle component roughly separates vector (red) from wave problems (blue)

3 Markov Models

Given the PCA partitioning of the problem space, we can now examine how students transition through that space. Based on this analysis, we will both understand student behaviors and be positioned to optimize student learning paths. A Markov Model is a good tool for modeling student *transitions*, and the HMM framework is a standard method to develop the transition model parameters. In the model, student state is partially observable, so we propose Item Response Theory (IRT) as a framework to understand the *measures* (observations) of student state.

To demonstrate that transition models and observation models are complementary, we constructed a Markov chain consisting of three states per principal component, representing the student progressing on a curriculum. The transition model was learned from student performance results on Vectors problems. The observation model was parameterized based on IRT, the IRT model was assigned parameters θ and β such that a student at a high level of proficiency has an 80% chance of getting an item correct, and a student at a low level has a 20% chance.

An instructional policy was automatically generated. This policy chooses a remediation for the student on the current topic in Andes based on its assessment of student progress. Three remediations are available, one for students who are currently at a high proficiency, one for medium, and one for low. However, the true state of the student is hidden, so the instructor must infer the best possible remediation based on observations of the student. Our experimental hypothesis was that transition and observation models in combination outperform each model in isolation.

To test this hypothesis, we conducted a simulation of instruction in which different instructional strategies leveraged none, one, or both of the transition model (TM) and observation model (OM). We tried four instructional strategies, **Myopic** (neither model; intervention is based on the success or failure of the last item), **Measurement** (OM only; intervention is based on the history of measurements, but does not take into account the transition model), **Learning Path** (TM only**;** intervention is based on the transition model in the Markov chains, but does not account for measurements produced by IRT), and **HAL Combined** (both TM and OM; intervention is based on combining information produced by Markov chains and IRT).

The model was run on 10,000 simulated students performing the Vectors portion of the Andes curriculum. Students were modeled as being in a high, medium, or low state of comprehension, and intervention options (items) could be selected to target each state. An intervention was deemed incorrect if it was targeted at a student in a high state of comprehension when the student was actually in a low state, and vice versa. If the intervention was intermediate and the student was in a low or high state, the intervention was scored as 30% correct. Results show that the combined approach works best, Learning Path nearly as well (middle column). To show that Measurement could outperform Learning Path in different domains with different amounts of noise in the model parameters, we simulated artificial Markov parameters that introduced more noise in the transition model and subtracted noise from the IRT model (3rd column). The combined approach works best in this case as well.

Strategy	**% correct (Vectors)**	**% correct (Artificial)**
Myopic	48.1%	62.1%
Measurement Only	62.5%	68.6%
Learning Path	74.3%	32.2%
Combined HAL	76.5%	69.8%

4 Conclusion

The preparation of effective instruction is a manual, intellectually intense process that produces sound courses only at great expense, and courses that are optimal for individual students only rarely. HAL can partially automate instructional design to improve and individualize instruction. It does so by applying PCA, IRT, and HMMs to empirically define student states, measures of them, and models of their dynamics. The pilot study described here shows the promise of this hybrid technique.

References

1. Baum, L.E., Eagon, J.A.: An inequality with applications to statistical estimation for probabilistic functions of Markov processes and to a model for ecology. Bulletin of the American Mathematical Society 73, 360 (1967)

2. Birnbaum, A.: Some latent trait models and their use in inferring an examinee's ability. In: Lord, F.M., Novick, M.R. (eds.) Statistical Theories of Mental Test Scores. Addison–Wesley, Reading (1968)
3. Cooke, N.M., Schvaneveldt, R.W.: Effects of computer programming experience on network representations of abstract programming concepts. International Journal of Man-Machine Studies 29, 407–427 (1988)
4. Ohlsson, S.: Deep learning: How the mind overrides experience. Cambridge University Press, Cambridge (2011)
5. Shanteau, J.: Competence in experts: The role of task characteristics. Organizational Behavior and Human Decision Processes 53, 252–266 (1992)
6. VanLehn, K., Lynch, C., Schulze, K., Shapiro, J.A., Shelby, R., Taylor, L., Treacy, D., Weinstein, A., Wintersgill, M.: The Andes Physics Tutoring System: Lessons Learned. International Journal of Artificial Intelligence and Education 15, 147–204 (2005)

Evaluation of a Meta-tutor for Constructing Models of Dynamic Systems

Lishan Zhang, Winslow Burleson, Maria Elena Chavez-Echeagaray, Sylvie Girard, Javier Gonzalez-Sanchez, Yoalli Hidalgo-Pontet, and Kurt VanLehn

Arizona State University, Computing, Informatics, and Decision Systems Engineering, Tempe, AZ, 85281, U.S.A.
{lishan.zhang,winslow.burleson,mchaveze,sylvie.girard, javiergs,yhidalgo,kurt.vanlehn}@asu.edu

Abstract. While modeling dynamic systems in an efficient manner is an important skill to acquire for a scientist, it is a difficult skill to acquire. A simple step-based tutoring system, called AMT, was designed to help students learn how to construct models of dynamic systems using deep modeling practices. In order to increase the frequency of deep modeling and reduce the amount of guessing/gaming, a meta-tutor coaching students to follow a deep modeling strategy was added to the original modeling tool. This paper presents the results of two experiments investigating the effectiveness of the meta-tutor when compared to the original software. The results indicate that students who studied with the meta-tutor did indeed engage more in deep modeling practices.

Keywords: meta-tutor, intelligent tutoring systems, empirical evaluation.

1 Introduction

Modeling is both an important cognitive skill [1] and a potentially powerful means of learning many topics [5]. The Affective Meta-Tutoring (AMT) system teaches students how to construct system dynamics models. Such models are widely used in professions, often taught in universities and sometimes taught in high schools.

1.1 The Modeling Language

In our modeling language, a model is a directed graph with one type of link. Each node represents both a variable and the computation that determines the variable's value. There are three types of nodes.

- A *fixed value* node represents a constant value that is directly specified in the problem. A fixed value node has a diamond shape and never contains incoming links.
- An *accumulator* node accumulates the values of its inputs. That is, its current value is the sum of its previous value plus or minus its inputs. An accumulator node has a rectangular shape and always has at least one incoming link.

K. Yacef et al. (Eds.): AIED 2013, LNAI 7926, pp. 666–669, 2013.

- A *function* node's value is an algebraic function of its inputs. A function node has a circular shape and at least one incoming link.

The students' task is to draw a model that represents a situation that is described in the form of a relatively short text. During construction, students can use the *Check* button to evaluate the correctness of the current tab or the *Give up* button to ask the system to fill out the tab automatically.

1.2 The Target Node Strategy

The meta-tutor teaches students a goal reduction procedure for constructing models. It is called the Target Node Strategy. The basic idea is to focus on one node at a time (the target node) and completely define it before working on any other node. This process decomposes the whole problem of modeling a system into a series of atomic modeling problems, one per node. Like Pyrenees [2], it teaches students that if they just master this one difficult but small skill, then the rest of the problem solving is straight forward. In addition, the meta-tutor complains if students appear to be guessing too much or giving up too early, just as the Help Tutor did [3].

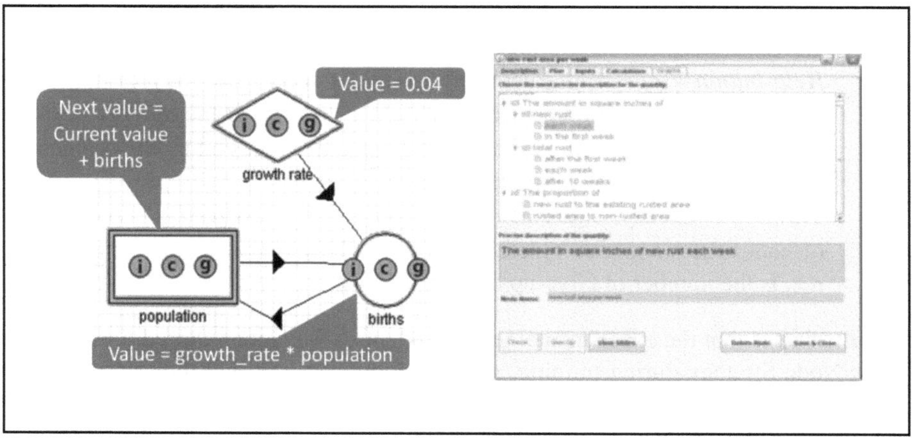

Fig. 1. The left image is the example of model, with gray callouts added to explain the contents of nodes. The right image is the example of a node editor.

2 Evaluation

2.1 Experiment Design

The experiment was designed as a between-subject single treatment experiment with a control condition, where the meta-tutor was off, and an experiment condition, where the meta-tutor was on. The difference between the conditions occurred only during a training phase where students learned how to solve model construction problems. In order to assess how much students learned, a transfer phase followed the training phase. During the transfer phase, all students solved model construction problems with almost no help: the meta-tutor, the Check button and the Give-up button were all turned off, except in the Description tab where the Check button remained enabled to facilitate grounding. Because system dynamics is rarely taught in high school, no pre-test was included in the procedure. We conducted two experiments with 44 students participating in the first experiment and 34 students in the second experiment.

2.2 Hypotheses and Measures

Hypothesis 1 is that the meta-tutored students will use deep modeling more frequently than the control students during the *transfer* phase. We used the three measures below to assess it.

- The *number of the Run Model button presses* per problem.
- The *number of extra nodes* created, where extra nodes are defined as the nodes that can be legally created for the problem but are not required for solving the problem.
- The *number of problems completed* during the 30 minute transfer period.

Hypothesis 2 is that meta-tutored students will use deep modeling more frequently than the control group students during the *training* phase. The three dependent measures used to evaluate this hypothesis are described below:

- *Help button usage:* was calculated as $(n_{wc} + 3n_{gu})/n_{rn}$, where n_{wc} is the number of Check button presses that yielded red, n_{gu} is the number of Give-up button presses, and n_{rn} is the number of nodes required by the problem.
- *The percentage of times the first Check was correct.*
- *Training efficiency:* was calculated as $3n_{cn} - n_{gu}$ where n_{cn} is the number of nodes the student completed correctly ($3n_{cn}$ is the number of tabs), and n_{gu} is the number of Give-up buttons presses.

Hypothesis 3 is that the experimental group students, who were required to follow the Target Node Strategy during training, would seldom use it during the transfer phase. To evaluate this hypothesis, we calculated the proportion of student steps consistent with the target node strategy.

2.3 Results

Table 1 summarizes the results of experiment 1 and experiment 2.

3 Conclusion and Future Work

Although we achieved some success in encouraging students to engage in deep modeling, there is much room for improvement. If the meta-tutor had been a complete success at teaching deep modeling, we would expect to see students supported by the meta-tutor working faster than the control students. The stage is now set for the last phase of our project, where we add an affective agent to the system [4], in order to encourage engagement and deep modeling.

Table 1. Results of Experiment 1 and 2: E stands for the meta-tutor group, and C stands for the control group. Reliable results are bold.

Measure (predicted dir.)	*Experiment 1 (N=44)*	*Experiment 2 (N=33)*
Transfer phase (Hypothesis 1)		
Run model button usage (E<C)	E<C (p=0.31, d=0.32)	E≈C (p=0.98, d=-0.0093)
Extra nodes (E<C)	**E<C (p=0.02, d=0.80)**	E<C (p=0.47, d=0.26)
Probs completed (E>C)	E≈C (p=0.65, d=0.04)	E<C (p=0.09, d=−0.57)
Training phase (Hypothesis 2)		
Help button usage (E<C)	**E<C (p=0.04, d=0.68)**	**E<C (p=0.02, d=0.89)**
Correct on 1st Check (E>C)	Missing data	**E>C (p=0.015, d=0.98)**
Efficiency (E>C)	E<C (p=0.05, d=−0.70)	E>C (p=0.59, d=0.19)
Transfer phase use of Target Node Strategy (Hypothesis 3)		
Usage (E=C)	Missing data	E≈C (p=0.59, d=−0.19).

Acknowledgements. This material is based upon work supported by the National Science Foundation under Grant No. 0910221.

References:

1. CCSSO: The Common Core State Standards for Mathematics, Downloaded from `http://www.corestandards.org` (October 31, 2011)
2. Chi, M., Van Lehn, K.: Meta-cognitive strategy instruction in intelligent tutoring systems: How, when and why. Journal of Educational Technology and Society 13(1), 25–39 (2010)
3. Roll, I., Aleven, V., McLaren, B.M., Ryu, E., Baker, R.S.J.d., Koedinger, K.R.: The Help Tutor: Does Metacognitive Feedback Improve Students' Help-Seeking Actions, Skills and Learning? In: Ikeda, M., Ashley, K., Chan, T.-W. (eds.) ITS 2006. LNCS, vol. 4053, pp. 360–369. Springer, Heidelberg (2006)
4. Girard, S., Chavez-Echeagaray, M.E., Gonzalez-Sanchez, J., Hidalgo-Pontet, Y., Zhang, L., Burleson, W., VanLehn, K.: Defining the behavior of an affective learning companion in the Affective Meta-Tutor project. In: Chad Lane, H., Yacef, K., Mostow, J., Pavlik, P. (eds.) AIED 2013. LNCS (LNAI), vol. 7926, pp. 21–30. Springer, Heidelberg (2013)
5. Treagust, D.F., Chittleborough, G., Mamiala, T.: Students' understanding of the role of scientific models in learning science. International Journal of Science Education 24(4), 357–368 (2002)

Identification of Effective Learning Behaviors

Paul Salvador Inventado[1,2], Roberto Legaspi[1], Rafael Cabredo[1,2],
Koichi Moriyama[1], Ken-ichi Fukui[1], Satoshi Kurihara[1], and Masayuki Numao[1]

[1] The Institute of Scientific and Industrial Research, Osaka University,
8-1 Mihogaoka, Ibaraki, Osaka, 567-0047, Japan
[2] Center for Empathic Human-Computer Interface, College of Computer Studies,
De La Salle University, 2401 Taft Avenue, Manila, Philippines

Abstract. Self-regulated learners have been shown to learn more effectively. However, it is not easy to become self-regulated because learners have to be capable of observing and evaluating their thoughts, actions and behaviors while learning. In this work, we used Q-learning to reveal the effectiveness or ineffectiveness of a learning behavior that carries over learning episodes. We also showed different types of effective learning behavior discovered and how they were differentiated. Providing learners with knowledge about learning behavior effectiveness can help them observe how strategy selection affects their performance and will help them select more appropriate strategies in succeeding learning episodes for better future performance.

1 Introduction

Self-regulated learning is a self-initiated process wherein learners manage their thoughts, feelings and actions to achieve their goal [1]. Research shows that it is not only important for students to know different learning strategies but also how to evaluate them [2]. This enables students to select and adapt their learning strategies effectively. However, this is not easy due to the cognitive load required for learning, monitoring and adapting strategies simultaneously.

In our previous work [3], we developed a software called Sidekick Retrospect which took desktop screenshots and webcam video stills while students learned so they can later review and annotate what transpired. However, post-experiment interviews revealed that students' observations and reflections usually focused on one aspect of their learning and did not consolidate realizations from other learning episodes. Knowledge of other effective learning behaviors during the session would expand the students' knowledge for selecting strategies and possibly improve future performance. In this paper, we present a data driven approach for uncovering the students' effective learning behaviors in a session that may carry over learning episodes which they can then use to better adapt their strategies.

2 Data and Pre-processing

Annotated learning behavior data from our previous work [3] was taken from two students who wrote conference papers and two students who made power

K. Yacef et al. (Eds.): AIED 2013, LNAI 7926, pp. 670–673, 2013.

point presentations about their research. They all processed and performed experiments on collected data, searched for related literature and created a report or document. Although their topics were different, they performed similar types of activities. Two hours of annotated learning behavior data in five separate learning episodes were collected from each student consisting of 7,160 instances with four features– time stamp, activity (e.g., using a browser, reading a paper), intention (goal or non-goal related) and affective state (see [3] for more details).

Manually observing students' intentions and activities from the data revealed six common strategies– information search using a search engine (IS), viewing information sources (e.g., books, websites) (IV), changing information sources (CS), seeking help from peers (HS), knowledge application (i.e., paper writing, presentation creation, data processing) (KA) and off-task activities (OT).

Using the intention, activity and affect features of the data set, adjacent instances were merged when they referred to the same strategy and affective state. Time stamp features were then replaced with the new instance's duration. The merged data had an average of 54.35 (N=20; σ=27.71) instances per session.

3 Discovering Effective Learning Behaviors

We defined learning behaviors as learning strategies performed in a particular context wherein context was described by seven features– current strategy, current affect, strategy in previous instance, affect in previous instance, dominant learning strategy, dominant affective state and duration. A strategy or affect was dominant when students did or experienced it the most within the past five minutes, which was the average maximum duration of instances. These features were chosen because activities, affect and time have effects on learning [3,4].

Effective learning behavior involves using the best learning strategy in a particular context. The best learning strategy is one in which students engage in goal related activities that bring them closer to their goals. Thus, all strategies except OT are potentially effective. Delight and engaged were good indicators of students moving towards their goal while confusion indicated cognitive disequilibrium wherein the student needed to exert more cognitive effort to understand a concept and remove misconceptions [4]. Although confusion is essential, too much could cause students to become frustrated, or worse, disengaged (i.e., boredom or shifting to OT). We can express the utility of each strategy by assigning them with reward values. Non-OT strategies resulting in delight or an engaged state: 3, confusion: 2, frustration: 1, boredom: -1 and neutral: 0. OT strategies regardless of the resulting affect are assigned -2. These reward values can then be multiplied to the affect's duration to account for its temporal effects.

The reward value reflected the strategy's immediate effects, but the effectiveness of a learning behavior needs to account for the strategy's rewards and those that follow it (i.e., return). We estimated the return of a strategy in a given context by incrementally applying Q-learning's action-value function [5]

$$Q(s_t, a_t) \leftarrow Q(s_t, a_t) + \alpha[r_{t+1} + \gamma \max_a Q(s_{t+1}, a) - Q(s_t, a_t)]. \quad (1)$$

The expected return of performing action a_t (i.e., learning strategy) in state s_t (i.e., context) was updated using its old expected return value, r_{t+1} (i.e., reward value of a strategy resulting to the next instance's affective state) and $maxQ(s_{t+1}, a)$ (i.e., the return value of the best action to take in the next instance's context). γ was set to 0.9 to give importance to future rewards while α was set to 0.5 so it can learn from new data but partially account for noise.

Q-learning was applied on each students' sessions separately resulting in four learning policies. A policy consisted of context-strategy pairs wherein different strategies could be associated with the same context. Strategies with higher returns can be considered effective learning behavior because they worked better than others (see Table 1). We can also assume that these behaviors may carry over learning sessions because they were observed from different sessions.

Four types of effective learning behaviors were observed– feeling engaged and using the same strategy (Prolonged strategy behavior - PSB), changing strategies while feeling engaged (Flow behavior - FB), confusion leading to change in strategies (Cognitive disequilibrium handling behavior - CDHB) and feeling bored or performing OT then shifting to a learning related strategy (Resume learning behavior - RLB) (see Table 2 for examples). Effective PSB and CDHB were logical and explainable as they described when to continue performing a strategy or change it and mostly discouraged shifts to OT. FB and RLB always led to goal related strategies however these were situation dependent. It was difficult to identify if these were effective or just usual behavior.

In each student's policy, there was an average of 166.75 (N=4; σ=72.78) learning behaviors, but effective learning behaviors could only be identified in 30.42% (N=4; σ=7.43%) of the data. The remaining 69.58% had only one strategy associated to each context so an effective strategy could not be identified. It is likely that there are other strategies that will be more effective and that learning behavior effectiveness will change as more data is observed or if a student's behavior changes. The advantage of the Q-learning algorithm is that it can incrementally update its estimates with more data thus having an up-to-date learning behavior effectiveness measure. Despite its incremental nature however, it is still limited by a student's actions. It will be beneficial to help the student find other strategies that can be used and in turn will facilitate the search for more effective learning strategies. Possible strategies can be taken from other students' policies or from an expert's background knowledge.

Table 1. Learning Behavior Returns

Context	Next Strategy	Normalized Return [0,100]
CO KA < 5min, NE OT, CO KA	IV	26.8
CO KA < 5min, NE OT, CO KA	OT	13.1
CO IV <5min, CO IV, CO IV	OT	28.2
CO IV <5min, CO IV, CO IV	CS	16.5

*Legend: **DE**lighted, **EN**gaged, **NE**utral, **CO**nfused

Table 2. Examples of Effective Learning Behaviors

Type	Context	Next Strategy	Normalized Return
PSB	EN KA < 5min, CO KA, CO KA	KA	75.6
FB	EN IS < 5min, EN KA, EN KA	KA	68.7
CDHB	CO KA < 5min, NE OT, CO KA	IV	26.8
RLB	DE OT < 5min, EN KA, EN KA	KA	46.0

4 Conclusion and Future Work

Our work describes an approach that automatically identifies effective learning behaviors. The results show that it is capable of discovering such behaviors and can be used to help students identify which learning behaviors should be retained or adapted. The Q-learning algorithm used in our work makes the approach capable of improving with more data and handle changes in a student's behavior.

However, effective behavior discovered by the system are based on the student's actions. Students have to explore other strategies so that both they and the system can benefit from observing its effects. There is also a need to evaluate how information regarding effective learning behavior can impact learning.

Ideally, learning systems will be able to use this approach for helping students distinguish effective learning behavior which is essential for self-regulation. It can also be used to identify when certain strategies would be more appropriate and support the self-monitoring and self-control processes of self-regulation.

Acknowledgements. This work was supported in part by the Management Expenses Grants for National Universities Corporations from the Ministry of Education, Culture, Sports, Science and Technology of Japan (MEXT) and JSPS KAKENHI Grant Number 23300059. We would also like to thank all the students who participated in our data collection.

References

1. Zimmerman, B.J.: Becoming a Self-Regulated learner: An overview. Theory into Practice 41(2), 64–70 (2002)
2. Zimmerman, B.J.: Self-regulated learning and academic achievement: An overview. Educational Psychologist 25(1), 3–17 (1990)
3. Inventado, P.S., Legaspi, R., Numao, M.: Student learning behavior in an unsupervised learning environment. In: Proceedings of the 20th International Conference on Computers in Education, pp. 730–737 (2012)
4. D'Mello, S., Graesser, A.: Dynamics of affective states during complex learning. Learning and Instruction 22(2), 145–157 (2012)
5. Sutton, R.S., Barto, A.G.: Reinforcement Learning: An Introduction (1998)

Modeling the Process of Online Q&A Discussions Using a Dialogue State Model

Shitian Shen and Jihie Kim

University of Southern California Information Sciences Institute
4676 Admiralty Way, Marina del Rey, CA, U.S.A.
shtians@usc.edu, jihie@isi.edu

Abstract. Online discussion board has become increasingly popular in higher education. As a step towards analyzing the role that students and instructors play during the discussion process and assessing students' learning from discussions, we model different types of contributions made by instructors and students with a dialogue-state model. By analyzing frequent Q&A discussion patterns, we have developed a graphic model of dialogue states that captures the information role that each message plays, and used the model in analyzing student discussions, presenting several viable ap-proaches including CRF, SVM, and decision tree for the state classification. Such analyses can give us a new insight on how students interact in online discussions and kind of assistance needed by the students.

Keywords: online discussions, dialogue transition, speech act, CRF.

1 Introduction

Online discussion boards, an application of social network on education, provides a platform for students and instructors to share their ideas or to discuss their question not only in traditional courses but also in web-based courses. Such tools can help students solve their problems opportunely, as well as improving instructors' work efficiency. As the discussion board usage increases, we want to understand how students interact with instructors and peers, and how they learn through such interaction.

There has been prior work on discussion analysis including use of speech act framework in modeling online discussions [2]. Some people focus on the roles that students play such as asking problems or answering other's questions [6,7]. There has also been work on machine classification of student online discussions [5,7] and results have been used to find meaningful dialogue patterns including features for critical thinking. Hidden Markov Model provides the framework for modeling the dialogue structure with hidden states [1,8]. They are closely related to our work, and we extend the existing framework by mapping interactions in discussions into a Q&A dialogue state model where state for each message illustrates the status and function of the given message in the Q&A process (discussion thread) [3,9]. Particularly, we identified six distinctive and frequent states in the discussion process and applied machine classifiers for state classification.

K. Yacef et al. (Eds.): AIED 2013, LNAI 7926, pp. 674–678, 2013.

2 State Transition Model of Q&A Discussions

We use discussion corpus from undergraduate operating systems courses. The courses contain programming projects, and students use discussions to share problems and get help from the instructor and other students. Figure 1 shows an example discussion thread with a sequence of message. User A, B and C represents the participants. User A initiates the thread by describing the problem and asks for help. User B asks for more details related to the problem and User A provides some information. User B then gives a possible solution and User A complains that it doesn't solve the problem. User C offers another answer, and User A asks a related question. User C provides an additional suggestion. Finally, User A acknowledges the help with thanking.

Table 1. A Q&A State Model: Definitions and Examples

State	Definition	Example	Count	Kappa
Problem (P)	Original problem is proposed by information seeker	I stuck in a weird problem…..	251	0.98
Problem Understandin g (PU)	1.Providers ask related questions for understanding original question; 2.Seekers answer the related questions and supply more details related to original issues.	1.What kind of exception do you have? 2. It's seg fault afterwarods	49	0.96
Solving (S)	Information providers supply answer or suggestions for solving original question	You can try to reduce the memory	447	0.99
Solution Appreciation (SA)	Seekers solve problem and acknowledge the help from providers	It works, Thanks.	25	0.92
Solution Objection (SO)	Seekers find the answer doesn't work and may ask for more help.	It doesn't work, any ideas?	18	0.88
Solution Understandi ng (SU)	Seekers may be confused about answer and ask questions for understanding.	What's the race condition, can you explain it?	108	0.97

Through analyses of the discussion corpus, we identified six distinctive and frequent states: *Problem presenting, Problem understanding, Solving, Solution understanding, Solution objecting,* and *Solution appreciation*, the definition of which can be refer to table 1 and generate a graphic model as described in figure 2. User roles are relevant to characterizing the states: information *seeker* and information *provider*, and often the role of a user stays the same within a short discussion thread [10]. Comparing with the work in [8], an apparent difference and the unique contribution in our work is that we explore the discussion model, showed in figure 2, by adding four different states with the purpose of demonstrating the processing of discussion more clearly.

Table 1 presents a description of each state and examples. The state information is annotated manually and the last column shows the Kappa values for agreement between two annotators. The table also shows the distribution of the states. We can find that almost 50 percent of states belong to *S*. There is a small number of *SO*s.

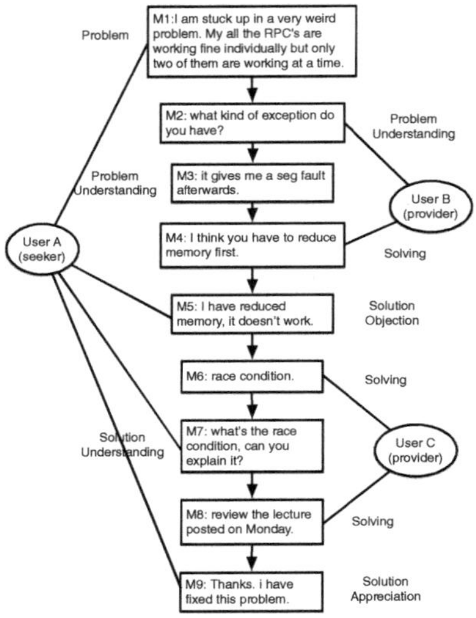

Fig. 1. An example of discussion thread

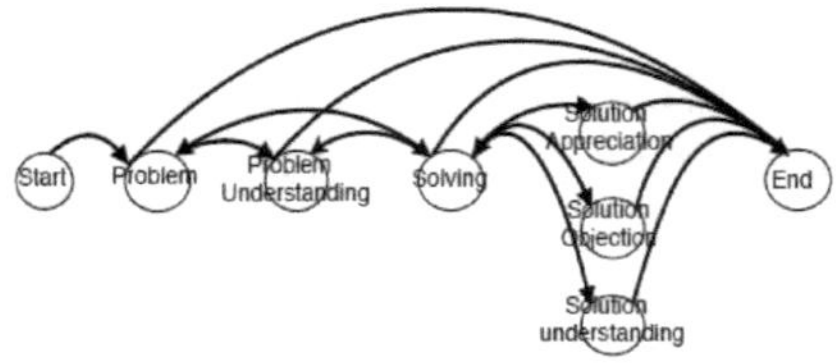

Fig. 2. State transition model for Q&A discussions

Table 2. State transition matrix frequencies

	P	PU	S	SA	SO	SU
P	-	14	220	-	-	-
PU	-	20	19	-	-	-
S	9	16	101	22	17	92
SA	-	-	4	4	-	3
SO	-	-	13	-	-	-
SU	-	-	90	-	-	10

Table 2 shows the frequency of state transitions. We can find that *S* is a bridge between the first two states and the last three states. The first two states (*P* and *PU*) discusses about the problem to be solved, while the last three are the feedback to the solution, and *S* connect the two parts. *S* dominates in the corpus. A S often directly follows a *P*, but there are cases where the Q&A process goes through a *PU*.

3 Automatic Discussion State Classification

236 threads and 899 posts are used for constructing the state transition model.

Data preprocessing, normalization, and feature generation

Student discussion data is highly noisy due to variances and informal nature of student written messages. The data pre-processing steps convert some of the informal expressions. The features for state classification are generated from (a) the message content, (b) neighboring messages, and (c) the message/author locational information:

-F1: n grams features within current message
-F2: position of the current message, such as the first message, the last message
-F3: position of participants, like the first author, the last author
-F4: n grams features within the previous message
-F5: position of the previous message
-F6: position of previous author

Classification results

Table 3. Classification Results

	Precision/Recall/F-measure (%)					
Model	P	PU	S	SA	SO	SU
CRF	98.1/95.3/**96.7**	32.0/20.6/**25.0**	86.4/90.6/88.5	43.1/38.8/40.8	23.3/12.4/16.2	62.2/74.0/**67.5**
SVM	100/93.8/**96.7**	15.8/36.7/22.1	88.7/91.1/**90.0**	42.1/63.0/**53.6**	24.1/56.7/**31.2**	53.8/90.6/**67.5**
J48	99.6/94.1/**96.7**	10.1/28.7/15.8	83.0/89.0/85.2	22.5/48.8/29.1	10.8/23.3/14.3	47.6/80.1/59.5
LR	87.2/87.5/87.3	12.1/22.7/15.8	85.8/87.9/85.2	41.0/56.3/29.1	22.8/15.0/14.3	41.8/59.6/59.5

We use Mallet [4] to create a CRF model. Other machine learning methods such as SVM, decision tree, are also used in our practice by employing Weka [9]. Table 3 shows precision, recall and F-measure scores for different classifiers. Linear CRF, SVM perform better than logistic regression and decision tree. It seems that the relation between states and features are not fully captured through a non-linear function directly. Although SVM and decision tree regard messages individually, both methods make use of dependencies among neighboring messages as some of the features capture previous message content and location information. Because of the small size for state *PU*, *SA* and *SO*, the precision and recall for these three states is low, especially for decision tree, which is sensitive for the features and instances. The precision and recall for state *SA* is relatively high. A possible reason is that its features include useful cue words including "thanks", "it works" that appear regularly. On the other hand, although we have 108 instances for state *SU*, the precision and recall for it is not so high. We may need further examples due to its variances. Another reason is that *SU* often contains a question for the solution, which may use similar key words as in *P*, thus it's challenging to completely distinguish *SU* from *P*.

4 Conclusion

We have presented a graph model for analyzing the discussion process and developed approaches for message state classification and thread characterization. The state information is used in analyzing frequent patterns and time intervals, and identifying different roles that instructors and students play in the Q&A process. Thread classification for resolved vs. unresolved problem is supported by the state information. As a next step, we plan to collect more data in order to obtain the more reliable classifica-tion result and explore additional improvement, including topic-based analysis of student problems. We plan to evaluate usefulness of the information with instructors.

Acknowledgement. This work is supported by the National Science Foundation, REESE Program (award #1008747).

References

[1] Boyer, K.E., Ha, E.Y., Wallis, M.D., Phillips, R., Vouk, M.A., Lester, J.C.: Discovering tutorial dialogue strategies with hidden Markov models. In: Proc. AIED (2009)

[2] Fossati, D., Di Eugenio, B., Ohlsson, S., Brown, C., Chen, L.: Generating proactive feedback to help students stay on track. In: Aleven, V., Kay, J., Mostow, J. (eds.) ITS 2010, Part II. LNCS, vol. 6095, pp. 315–317. Springer, Heidelberg (2010)

[3] Kim, J., et al.: Mining and assessing discussions on the web through speech act analysis. In: Workshop on Web Content Mining with Human Language Technologies at ISWC (2006)

[4] McCallum, A.: MALLET: a machine learning for language toolkit (2002), http://mallet.cs.umass.edu

[5] McLaren, B., et al.: Using Machine Learning Techniques to Analyze and Support Mediation of Student E-Discussions. In: Proceedings of AIED (2007)

[6] Mu, J., Stegmann, K., Mayfield, E., Rose, C., Fischer, F.: The ACODEA framework: Developing Segmentation and Classification Schemes for Fully Automatic Analysis of Online Discussions. In: Proc. CSCL (2012)

[7] Ravi, S., Kim, J.: Profiling Student Interactions in Threaded Discussions with Speech Act Classifiers. In: Proceeding of AIED (2007)

[8] Seo, S.W., Kang, J.-H., Drummond, J., Kim, J.: Using Graphical Models to Classify Dialogue Transition in Online Q&A Discussions. In: Biswas, G., Bull, S., Kay, J., Mitrovic, A. (eds.) AIED 2011. LNCS (LNAI), vol. 6738, pp. 550–553. Springer, Heidelberg (2011)

[9] Witten, I.H., Frank, E.: Data Mining: Practical machine learning tools and techniques, 2nd edn. (2005)

[10] Yoo, J., Kim, J.: Predicting Learner's Project Performance with Dialogue Features in Online Q&A Discussions. In: Cerri, S.A., Clancey, W.J., Papadourakis, G., Panourgia, K. (eds.) ITS 2012. LNCS, vol. 7315, pp. 570–575. Springer, Heidelberg (2012)

An Authoring Tool for Semi-automatic Generation of Self-assessment Exercises

Baptiste Cablé, Nathalie Guin, and Marie Lefevre

Université de Lyon, CNRS
Université Lyon 1, LIRIS, UMR5205, F-69622, France
{baptiste.cable,nathalie.guin,marie.lefevre}@liris.cnrs.fr

Abstract. In this article we propose a semi-automatic generator of self-assessment exercises. This work is part of the CLAIRE project the aim of which is to design a collaborative authoring platform for pedagogic content. The proposed generator of exercises allows the author (usually a teacher) to create a model of exercise according to his/her pedagogic objectives. This model is automatically instantiated to produce several different exercises that evaluate the same skills. The learner's answer is automatically and instantly evaluated by the system. He/she thus receives immediate feedback on his/her skills. The distinctive feature of this generator is that the proposed types of exercise are independent of the domain, which allows them to be used for many different subjects and levels. In addition, domain knowledge is used to facilitate the author's task when the model of exercises and the diagnostic are designed.

Keywords: semi-automatic generation of exercises , authoring tool, self-assessment, automatic diagnostic.

1 Introduction

The CLAIRE project [1] (Community Learning through Adaptive and Interactive multichannel Resources for Education) aims at creating an open-source platform for collaborative authoring in the field of higher education. It contains a generator of self-assessment exercises that allows execution of the exercises and automatic diagnostic of the learner's answers. In order to allow the learner to autonomously check his/her level of proficiency in what has been learned on the course, every exercise should have a different version at every new attempt of the learner. However, it is difficult to ask the author to write many versions of each exercise. Thus, we propose using a generator of exercises.

Several generators of exercises exist but none of them match all the features we require: the exercise is different every time; the author has total control of the exercise content and is ensured that the exercise matches his/her pedagogic goals; the generator of exercises can be used in different subjects and levels; the answer diagnostic is automatic and immediate; designing an exercise is not excessively time-consuming for the author; designing an exercise requires no technical skill. This article describes the solution that we propose in the context of CLAIRE.

K. Yacef et al. (Eds.): AIED 2013, LNAI 7926, pp. 679–682, 2013.

The article is structured as follows: section 2 is a succinct state of the art of the generators of exercises. Our proposition is explained in section 3. Lastly, section 4 concludes the article and describes the further directions of our research.

2 Generators of Exercises: State of the Art

We can classify the generators of exercises in three types. The first one contains the **automatic generators** like in the microworld APLUSIX [2]. With this kind of generators, many exercises are created automatically but the author has no real flexibility.

The second class of generators of exercises contains the **manual generators**. They allow the author to define precisely the content of the exercise and all his/her preferences. Such a generator can be found with the authoring tool GenEval [3]. Unfortunately, we cannot use a manual generator of exercises in order to meet our need for a large number of different interactive self-assessment exercises.

Semi-automatic generators of exercises combine the advantages of the two previous classes of generator. The most relevant work regarding our needs is the GEPPETOp (GEneric models and Processes to Personalize learners' PEdagogical activities according to Teaching Objectives - Paper) approach [4] that makes it possible to define and generate exercises in a semi-automatic way and which can be used in many fields. GEPPETOp is designed to produce paper exercises and requires some improvements to feet our context: we want to generate interactive exercises with automatic diagnostic.

3 The Generator of Exercises of CLAIRE

3.1 Architecture

The architecture of our proposition is presented in figure 1. The upper block is composed of the levels of representation of the exercises. The mechanisms that manipulate these exercise representations are in the central block. The lower block contains the resources and the knowledge used in the exercise creation process.

The resources are the "raw material" needed to build the exercises. They can be, for example, texts, pictures or multiple choice questions. Each resource is characterized and enriched by metadata such as a caption or annotations on different zones of a picture. The domain knowledge (see 3.2) is knowledge concerning a subject and is independent of the type of exercise.

The author creates the model of exercises[1] using a dedicated tool based on the knowledge of types of exercise[2]. This exercises model creation tool helps

[1] A model of exercises contains constraints and preferences of the author about the content of the generated exercise. For example: "I want a cloze test with one of these texts, removing the following words: if, then, else, switch.".

[2] What is called "type of exercise" is the form of the question. For example, the following types of exercise can be found: "right or wrong", "cloze test" or "translation".

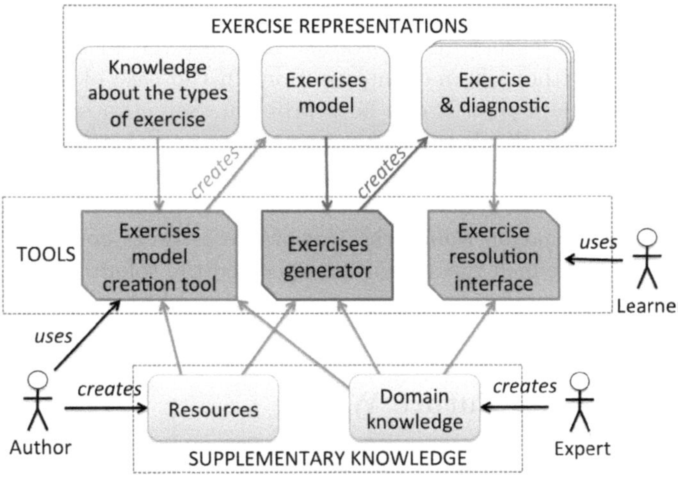

Fig. 1. The architecture of our approach

create the model, especially using the domain knowledge. It also generates some exercise examples to check that the exercises are created as expected. Finally, this tool facilitates access and choice of the resources and allows the author to create new ones.

The generator receives as input a model of exercises that it instantiates to generate output exercises (and their diagnostic) without human intervention. The exercises follow the model and thus the author's preferences. The exercises are given to the user through the resolution interface. This tool formats and displays the exercise, collects the learner's answer and gives him feedback on it.

3.2 Domain Knowledge

The domain knowledge is specific to a subject, a context or a field but it is independent of the type of exercise in which it may be used. For example, it can consist of the list of the key words of the C programming language, a way of detecting the gender of a noun (in foreign language), the value of a constant, etc. Depending on the type of knowledge, the form can vary: constant value, computation formula, rule, enumeration, etc.

Such knowledge is used at two different levels. Firstly, it facilitates the exercises model creation because this knowledge can be used instead of defining it again and again for each model of exercises of the domain. Moreover, it reduces the risk of author errors. Secondly, the domain knowledge can be used for the diagnostic of the learner's answer (cf. 3.3).

The creation of domain knowledge is independent of the creation of the models of exercises and not every author will wish to spend time on it. This task is performed by an expert in the domain who has the technical skills to create domain knowledge.

3.3 Diagnostic

In our approach, the learner answers online and receives an instant diagnostic of his/her answer without human intervention. In the case of an exercise with many possible right answers, it can be a problem. Sometimes, it is difficult to ask the author to provide all the right answers because they can be too many. To solve this issue, rather than generating a solution to the exercise (when the exercise is generated), we generate a model of solution that covers all the right solutions. This information about the acceptable answers comes (1) from the model of exercises in which the author has specified the tolerance and variations of the answer or (2) from the resource that is used which encloses a model of the acceptable solutions.

4 Conclusion and Future Work

In this article we present the self-assessment exercises generator of the CLAIRE platform. This generator is semi-automatic and it creates interactive exercises with automatic diagnostic. This generator allows an author to create a model of exercises which is instantiated by a generator to create many exercises that evaluate the same learner skills. The learner answers the exercise through a computer interface and obtains an immediate diagnostic of his/her answer. This solution is an interesting compromise between the authoring tools to create an exercise in total accordance with the author's choices and the automatic generators able to create many exercises of the same type on a given theme.

The first experiments we carried out in the laboratory allowed us to validate the architecture of the generator. It will soon be tested when CLAIRE is fully operational. This will allow a larger scale validation in real conditions.

The generator of exercises being independent of the domain, domain knowledge does not exist at the beginning. Its acquisition is thus a very important issue. At present, only manual creation is supported and carried out by an expert. We would like the author, especially if he/she is not a computer scientist, to be assisted in the definition of domain knowledge as he/she builds activities.

References

1. CLAIRE: Web Site, `http://www.projet-claire.fr/` (online; accessed April 2013)
2. Bouhineau, D., Chaachoua, H., Nicaud, J.F.: Helping teachers generate exercises with random coefficients. International Journal of Continuing Engineering Education and Life-Long Learning 18(5-6), 520–533 (2008)
3. David, J.P., Cogne, A., Dutel, A.: Hypermedia exercises prototyping and modelising. In: Diaz de Ilarraza Sanchez, A., Fernandez de Castro, I. (eds.) CALISCE 1996. LNCS, vol. 1108, pp. 252–260. Springer, Heidelberg (1996)
4. Lefevre, M., Jean-Daubias, S., Guin, N.: Generation of pencil and paper exercises to personalize learners work sequences: typology of exercises and meta-architecture for generators. In: Proceedings of World Conference on E-Learning in Corporate, Government, Healthcare, and Higher Education 2009, Vancouver, Canada, pp. 2843–2848. AACE (October 2009)

Open Learner Models to Support Reflection on Brainstorming at Interactive Tabletops

Andrew Clayphan, Roberto Martinez-Maldonado, and Judy Kay

School of Information Technologies, The University of Sydney, NSW, 2006, Australia
{andrew.clayphan,judy.kay}@sydney.edu.au,
roberto@it.usyd.edu.au

Abstract. Brainstorming is a widely-used group technique to enhance creativity. Interactive tabletops have the potential to support brainstorming and, by exploiting learners' trace data, they can provide Open Learner Models (OLMs) to support reflection on a brainstorming session. We describe our design of such OLMs to enable an individual to answer core questions: C1) how much did I contribute? C2) at what times was the group or an individual stuck? and C3) where did group members seem to 'spark' off each other? We conducted 24 brainstorming sessions and analysed them to create brainstorming models underlying the OLMs. Results indicate the OLM's were effective. Our contributions are: i) the first OLMs supporting reflection on brainstorming; ii) models of brainstorming that underlie the OLMs; and iii) a user study demonstrating that learners can use the OLMs to answer core reflection questions.

Keywords: Open Learner Models, Brainstorming, Reflection.

1 Introduction and Related Work

Brainstorming is a technique to help produce creative solutions to a problem [5]. It starts with an idea generation phase, *storming*, followed by assessing and grouping the ideas. To be effective, core rules should be followed to reduce members social inhibitions and stimulate idea generation: the focus should be on the *quantity* of ideas; everyone should contribute; there should be *no early evaluation*; particularly *no criticism*; and *un-usual or divergent ideas are welcomed.* All should contribute fully and equally, with discussion limited to cases where people are *stuck* and cannot create ideas.

Multi-touch interactive tabletops can support free flow of ideas by providing a shared group interface so that people can generate many ideas in parallel [4]. A less explored potential of interactive tabletops is to show key information about group and individual performance as Open Learner Models (OLMs) [2]. OLMs can serve several roles, including support for reflection [3], formative assessment, and to facilitate collaborative interaction. It has been shown that there is value in providing multiple OLM representations to support higher levels of reflection, because different learners prefer different forms of OLMs, particularly to meet differing concerns [6]. Research has explored OLM visualisations at interactive tabletops in research settings and in classrooms for teacher use [1,7].

K. Yacef et al. (Eds.): AIED 2013, LNAI 7926, pp. 683–686, 2013.

2 Open Learner Model Design

To enable learners to answer our core questions, we designed the OLMs in Figure 1. *Item 1*: number of ideas each person created (C1). *Item 2*: each idea is a dot, its colour indicating authorship, vertical axis shows its final category, coloured rectangles show when the group was stuck (2a) and coloured bars for individuals (2b), yellow bars show where one person's idea followed closely after another's and both went into the same category (2c) (C2,3). *Item 3*: ideas created by each learner, every 30 seconds (C1,2). *Item 4*: cumulative count of ideas generated (C2). *Item 5*: indicators of group members talking. We expect discussion when a group is stuck (C2,3). *Item 6*: all ideas in their final categories, author, and creation time.

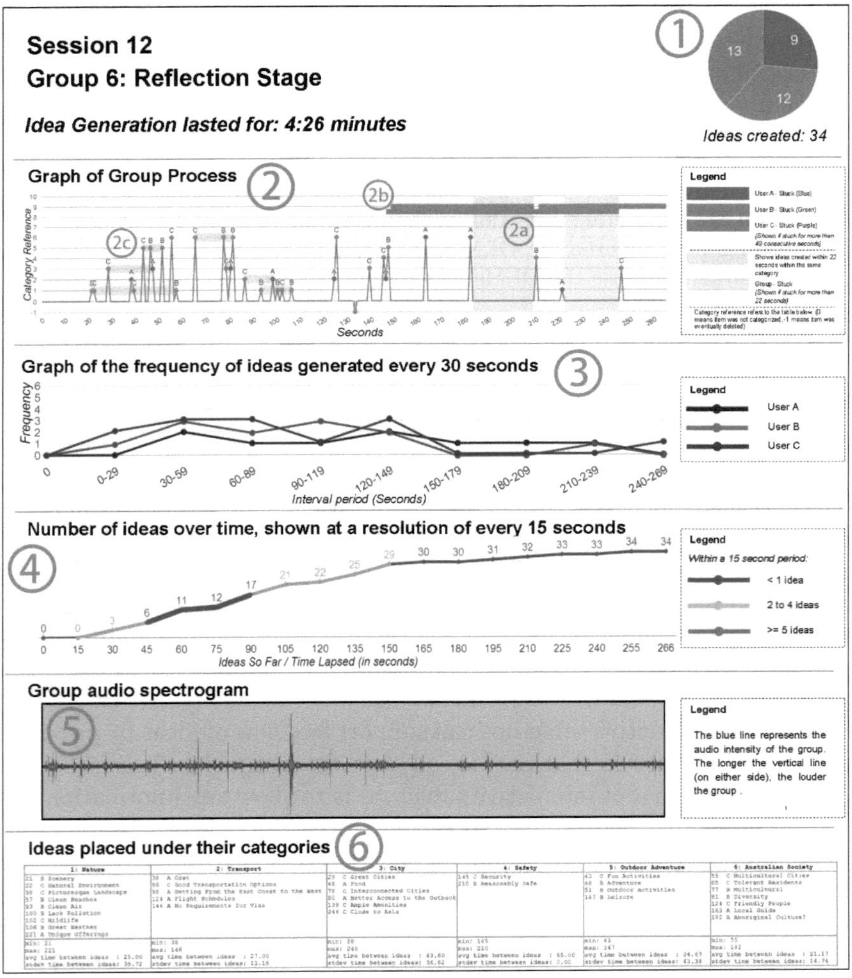

Fig. 1. OLM visualisations

3 Evaluation and Results

An interview/think-aloud study was conducted with 15 participants. OLMs were presented on large laminated sheets. Participants answered a series of questions on a 6-point Likert scale (6 for strongly agree). Q1: I could work out how much was my contribution; Q2: I could figure out when we made the most ideas in the session; Q3: I could see who created each idea; Q4: I could see when the group was talking; Q5: I could figure out when the group got stuck; Q6: I could figure out when I got stuck in the session; Q7: I could figure out the times when the group created a burst of ideas that ended out in the same category; Q8: I could figure out periods when the group was on a roll; Q9: I could see how the ideas were categorised; Q10: I thought the group did a good job in the brainstorm; and Q11: I thought I did a good job in the brainstorm.

Participants answered these questions by studying OLMs from 3 anonymised brainstorming sessions, as follows: 1) Pretend to be the learner who produced 13 ideas in a group that made 34; 2) Study the OLM from a high performing group (created 80 ideas), reviewing earlier answers; 3) Pretend to be a learner with 52 ideas in a group with 98; and 4) Open-ended questions about including the OLM for reflection.

Learners strongly agreed that the OLM visualisations provided key information about the group brainstorm ($\geq$4.20 across the Likert scores). As participants worked, over half commented on good understandability, especially by the third group OLMs.

Table 1. Summary of responses. Item number is as in Figure 1. Item rows shows most commonly used items for each question. Bold shows statistically significant change from Step 1 to 2 (Q10,11), and from Step 1 to 3 (Q1-9).

		Contributions				Stuck		Sparking			Others impact	
Questions		Q1	Q2	Q3	Q4	Q5	Q6	Q7	Q8	Q9	Q10	Q11
Step 1 34 idea group	Likert	5.07	5.53	4.87	5.40	5.67	5.87	4.20	5.00	5.20	4.40	4.73
	Item	1,3	4,3	2,6	5,2	2,4	2,3	2,6	4,2	6,2	1,2	3, 2
Step 2	Likert										**3.40**	**4.40**
Step 3 98 idea group	Likert	5.53	4.93	5.33	5.20	5.27	5.40	**5.20**	5.20	5.27	5.20	5.60
	Item	1,6	4,2	6,2	5	2,4	2,3	2,6	4,3	6,2	1,4	1, 3

4 Discussion and Conclusions

C1: who contributed?: Participants initially judged equality by referring to Items 1 and 3. After seeing additional OLMs, participants switched focus to numbers of ideas produced. For Q1, participants use Items 1, 3 & 6. for Q2, 12 people used Item 4 – number of ideas over time, checking the colour scheme. A small number used Item 3, identifying when most ideas were generated was high by all members. For Q3, Items 2 and 6 were used.

C2: when was the group or individuals stuck?: For Q5 and Q6 participants used Items 2, 3 & 4, with Item 2's timeline, shaded regions and horizontal bars proving the most useful to identify stuck periods. These indicators (the shading, bars and coloured segments) can be the basis for group discussion and reflection about what caused the group to be unproductive.

C3: where group members 'sparked' off of each other?: For Q7, Item 2 was used, but with a mixed response. 8 participants said the yellow highlight in Item 2 was obvious, but 4 other participants found it unclear or did not notice it, instead scanning across the grey line of each row. 3 participants mentioned Item 6. To determine when a large number of ideas were created, regardless of category, most participants shifted to Item 4. Overall, Item 2 was the most used.

Impact of OLMs from different groups: On seeing the high performing group, participants altered their assessment of how well they and the their group had performed. For Q10, 8 participants downgraded their responses leading to a statistically significant difference, and for Q11, 5 participants downgraded their responses.

In summary, we designed a set of OLM visualisations to help individuals reflect on group and individual performance and processes for group brainstorming. Our study indicates learners found the OLMs generally easy to understand and could answer our questions. The study enabled us to learn how people use the visualisations to answer each of our questions. This is a foundation for creating an enhanced form of tabletop brainstorming system, which can help people reflect on a session using our OLMs to answer the series of questions that will enable each group member to assess the level of their own contribution, the times the group was stuck and whether they sparked off each other.

References

1. Al-Qaraghuli, A., Zaman, H.B., Olivier, P., Kharrufa, A., Ahmad, A.: Analysing tabletop based computer supported collaborative learning data through visualization. In: Badioze Zaman, H., Robinson, P., Petrou, M., Olivier, P., Shih, T.K., Velastin, S., Nyström, I. (eds.) IVIC 2011, Part I. LNCS, vol. 7066, pp. 329–340. Springer, Heidelberg (2011)
2. Bull, S., Kay, J.: Student Models that Invite the Learner In: The {SMILI} Open Learner Modelling Framework. IJAIED, International Journal of Artificial Intelligence 17(2), 89–120 (2007)
3. Bull, S., Kay, J.: Metacognition and Open Learner Models. In: The 3rd Workshop on Meta-Cognition and Self-Regulated Learning in Educational Technologies, at ITS 2008 (2008)
4. Clayphan, A., Kay, J., Weinberger, A.: Enhancing brainstorming through scripting at a tabletop. In: Educational Interfaces, Software, and Technology 2012: 3rd Workshop on UI Technologies and Educational Pedagogy (2012)
5. Isaksen, S.: A review of brainstorming research: Six critical issues for inquiry. Creative Research Unit, Creative Problem Solving Group-Buffalo (1998)
6. Mabbott, A., Bull, S.: Alternative views on knowledge: Presentation of open learner models. In: Lester, J.C., Vicari, R.M., Paraguaçu, F. (eds.) ITS 2004. LNCS, vol. 3220, pp. 689–698. Springer, Heidelberg (2004)
7. Martinez Maldonado, R., Kay, J., Yacef, K., Schwendimann, B.: An Interactive Teacher's Dashboard for Monitoring Groups in a Multi-tabletop Learning Environment. In: Cerri, S.A., Clancey, W.J., Papadourakis, G., Panourgia, K. (eds.) ITS 2012. LNCS, vol. 7315, pp. 482–492. Springer, Heidelberg (2012)

Predicting Low vs. High Disparity between Peer and Expert Ratings in Peer Reviews of Physics Lab Reports

Huy V. Nguyen and Diane J. Litman

University of Pittsburgh, Pittsburgh, PA, 15260
{huynv,litman}@cs.pitt.edu

Abstract. Our interest in this work is to automatically predict whether peer ratings have high or low agreement in terms of disparity with instructor ratings, using solely features extracted from quantitative peer ratings and text-based peer comments. Experimental results suggest that our model can indeed outperform a majority baseline in predicting low versus high rating disparity. Furthermore, the reliability of both peer ratings and comments (in terms of peer disagreement) shows little correlation to disparity.

Keywords: peer review, rating disparity, peer reliability, topic models.

1 Introduction

To address instructor workload and provide students with more opportunities to develop their writing and evaluation skills, instructors are increasingly using other students in the class to review and rate student papers. Given instructor concerns about the possible low validity of peer-generated grades, research has been conducted to understand when peer grading is likely to be both reliable and valid (see [3] for a short survey). Nevertheless, from the perspective of individual students some disparity between instructor and peer grades is unavoidable. Even when there is a large positive correlation between instructors and peers (across student papers), there may still be outlier peers. Our research goal is to automatically classify peers into groups of low and high rating agreement with instructors, using only information from quantitative and qualitative peer feedback. Such a classifier could be used to better understand the validity of peer assessment, and to enhance current peer-review technology systems by flagging peer outliers whose work should be reviewed by instructors.

2 Peer Review Data

The data used in this study are peer and expert reviews of the same formal report assignment collected in Physics Lab classes at the University of Pittsburgh during 2010–2011. In each class, students were asked to describe experiments they conducted and the obtained results. For this writing task, students were required to organize their reports into sections including abstract, introduction and theory (introduction), experimental setup (experiment), data analysis and questions (analysis),

K. Yacef et al. (Eds.): AIED 2013, LNAI 7926, pp. 687–691, 2013.

Table 1. Size of datasets

Report Section	Abstract	Introduction	Experiment	Analysis	Conclusion
# Instances	362	361	362	280	362

Table 2. Means of rating disparity in the low and high groups

Mean disparity	Abstract	Introduction	Experiment	Analysis	Conclusion
Low group	0.37	0.30	0.38	0.40	0.30
High group	1.51	1.39	1.53	1.65	1.61

Left to right: reviewer, rating, comment. Nimning is an expert.

AM795712 7 *Experiment 2's part is a little lengthy [...] but everything is explained clearly. Experiment 3 and 4 were perfect.*

ATgirl 7 *Really nice job! [...] I understood everything you were saying.*

dude12 7 *A lot of equations you could probably get rid of some of the basic ones, other than that it was very good.*

sureshot58 1 *This section was basically all equations. There was little to no theory in this section. [...] Try to explain more of the symbols in each equation as many of them are unclear.*

Nimning 6 *You provide most of the critical equations which are used in this experiment. [...] You are also good at balancing the equation and the description of the theory.*

Fig. 1. An example instance (for the Introduction of a student report)

and conclusion. Student reports were submitted to SWoRD [2] to be assigned randomly to peers in the class for reviewing. Student reviewers were asked to evaluate each section of the reports from their peers by providing written comments and ratings using a 7-point scale (in which 7 means excellent). The number of peers per student report varied from 1 to 7, with a mean of 2.7 [1]. In addition to peer reviewers, all classes had one or two experts review and rate each student paper; most experts were the class TAs while the others were hired graduate students. This setting makes the data ideal for our study as we can use the expert ratings as a gold standard to assess the validity of the peer ratings (in terms of agreement to expert ratings). Fig. 1 is an example of a set of ratings and comments given by 4 peers and an expert to a student report section; we use the term instance for the set of reviews for a single student report section. Because different grading rubrics were given for different report sections, we study the rating disparity between peer reviewers and experts using the 5 datasets shown in Table 1 [2], each corresponding to a report section.

3 Predicting Low vs. High Rating Disparity

Binary Classification Task. For each instance, we first compute the absolute difference between the means of the peer and expert ratings. Within each dataset, these absolute differences (**Rating Disparity**) are then used to label each instance as either **Low** (for values below the median) or **High** (for values above the median). Values equal to the

[1] Some students did not do their reviewing, while others were assigned bonus reviews.

[2] Two classes did not require an analysis section in the report, and there were some data missing, so the number of instances is not the same among sections.

median are given the label of the smaller group to make the two classes as balanced as possible. For classification, we aim to predict whether the rating disparity of an instance is Low or High. As shown in Table 2, the means of rating disparity of the high groups is higher than those of the low groups (significant in all section with $p < 0.01$). Using rating agreement between peers and experts as a proxy for peer rating validity, our model predicts low versus high validity to an extent. We however leave the measurement in [3] of validity as the target variable of prediction for future work.

Features. To develop a model for predicting binary rating disparity, we represent each instance in terms of a set of automatically computable features. First, we extract the number of peer reviewers (**#Peers**) per instance, motivated by previous findings that assigning more reviewers yields greater validity. Second, we calculate the mean (**Mn**) and standard deviation (**Std**) of the peer ratings. The mean reflects our intuition that extreme ratings are more likely to result in higher deviation from expert ratings, while the standard deviation tests whether there is a relationship between rating reliability (low standard deviation) and rating validity (low disparity). Third, as an alternative method of quantifying peer reliability, we compute topic diversity in peer comments based on topic modeling. In probabilistic topic models, documents are random mixtures over latent topics, which are represented as a probability vector whose elements are the probabilities that the document belongs to the corresponding topics. Topic diversity among documents can be measured as the distance between topic distributions using Euclidean distance (**Euc**) and Kullback–Leibler divergence[3] (**KL**). For each dataset, a standard implementation[4] of LDA [1] runs over all peer comments. Each report section forms a set of peer comments whose inter-comment topic diversity is quantified by the average distance of all comment pairs in the set.

4 Results and Discussion

Table 3 shows prediction accuracies and kappa using Weka[5] J48 decision tree algorithm to learn three models from different feature sets. Compared to the majority class baseline results, the first feature set yields significantly higher accuracies for all report sections, demonstrating that low versus high rating disparity between peers and experts is predictable using the number of peer reviews in conjunction with the rating features. Examination of the learned trees shows that the mean peer rating is the most predictive feature. The Pearson's product-moment correlation coefficients in Table 4 further show that peers and experts agree more when peers give high grades. Turning to the next feature set, the results in Table 3 show that features derived from peer comments (rather than peer ratings) also significantly outperform the majority baseline, but only for three of the five sections. However, the final columns indicate that topic features do not further improve the use of rating features alone.

---

[3] A non-symmetric measure of the difference between 2 probability distributions - Wikipedia

[4] GibbsLDA++: `http://gibbslda.sourceforge.net`. Number of topics is set to 50.

[5] `cs.waikato.ac.nz/ml/weka`. Experiments with logistic and SVM obtained no better results.

Table 3. Prediction performance using 10-fold cross validation

Section	Majority	#Peers + Mn + Std		#Peers + Euc + KL		All Features	
	Acc.(%)	Acc.	*K*	Acc.	*K*	Acc.	*K*
Abstract	54.98	61.66 *	0.22	56.27	0.13	61.06 *	0.21
Introduction	50.69	60.40 *	0.21	61.62 *	0.23	59.91 *	0.20
Experiment	51.10	63.15 *	0.26	58.16 *	0.15	62.82 *	0.26
Analysis	51.07	62.43 *	0.24	51.07	0.0	62.07 *	0.23
Conclusion	54.42	67.02 *	0.32	59.17 *	0.16	66.86 *	0.32

* denotes significantly better than majority baseline ($p < 0.05$). The majority baseline's kappa is 0.

Table 4. Correlation coefficients between Mn and Rating Disparity ($p < 0.01$)

Section	Abstract	Introduction	Experiment	Analysis	Conclusion
Mn	-0.21	-0.37	-0.38	-0.4	-0.35

Table 5. Correlation coefficients between topic diversity values and Std ($p < 0.01$)

Section	Abstract	Introduction	Experiment	Analysis	Conclusion
Euc	0.38	0.38	0.45	0.39	0.45
KL	0.34	0.28	0.31	0.29	0.36

Finally, to explore the relation between the reliability of peer ratings and of peer comments, the results in Table 5 show that the two topic diversity metrics both positively correlate to the standard deviation of peer ratings. However, there is no correlation between any of these features (Euc, KL, or Std) and Rating Disparity. Fig. 1 illustrates such a case: although the peer ratings have a high standard deviation of 3, the mean of 5.5 is close to the expert rating and is of low disparity.

5 Conclusion

We present preliminary results in predicting binary rating disparity between peers and experts, using only features computed from information typically available during peer review (namely, peer ratings and comments). The mean of peer ratings appears as the most predictive feature in our learned models, although topic features are also predictive in some datasets. Experimental results suggest that peer rating is likely more valid when it is high. Further, neither rating disagreement nor topic diversity (reliability) directly relates to rating disparity (validity) in our data. In the future, we hope to further improve predictive accuracy by adding features extracted from student papers themselves, and will study different rating validity measurements including the measurement used in [3], and the raw difference between peer and expert rating.

Acknowledgements. This work is supported by LRDC Internal Grants Program, University of Pittsburgh. We thank C. Schunn for providing us with the data and feedback regarding this paper. We thank the reviewers for their many helpful comments.

References

1. Blei, D.M., Ng, A.Y., Jordan, M.I.: Latent Dirichlet allocation. The Journal of Machine Learning Research 3, 993–1022 (2003)
2. Cho, K., Schunn, C.D.: Scaffolded writing and rewriting in the discipline: A web-based reciprocal peer review system. Computers and Education 48(3), 409–426 (2007)
3. Cho, K., Schunn, C.D., Wilson, R.W.: Validity and reliability of scaffolded peer assessment of writing from instructor and student perspectives. Journal of Educational Psychology 98(4), 891–901 (2006)

Linguistic Content Analysis as a Tool for Improving Adaptive Instruction

Laura K. Varner , G. Tanner Jackson, Erica L. Snow, and Danielle S. McNamara

Department of Psychology, Learning Sciences Institute, Arizona State University, Tempe, AZ, 85287

{Laura.Varner,TannerJackson,Erica.L.Snow,Dsmcnama}@asu.edu

Abstract. This study investigates methods to automatically assess the features of content texts within an intelligent tutoring system (ITS). Coh-Metrix was used to calculate linguistic indices for texts (n = 66) within the reading strategy ITS, iSTART. Coh-Metrix indices for the system texts were compared to students' (n = 126) self-explanation scores to examine the degree to which linguistic indices predicted students' self-explanation quality. Initial analyses indicated no relation between self-explanation scores on a given text and its linguistic properties. However, subsequent analyses indicated the presence of robust text effects when analyses were separated for high and low reading ability students.

Keywords: Natural Language Processing, Readability, Tutoring, ITS, Text Characteristics, System Adaptability.

1 Introduction

Coh-Metrix [1] is a computational text analysis tool that was developed, in part, to provide stronger measures of text difficulty [2]. To account for multiple text dimensions, Graesser and colleagues (2011) developed the *Coh-Metrix Easability Components* [3]. These components offer a detailed glance at the primary levels of text difficulty and are aligned with an existing multilevel framework [4]. Additionally, Coh-Metrix offers general readability formulas (e.g., *Flesch-Kincaid Grade Level, FKGL)* as well as fine-grained linguistic indices that relate to lower and higher-level aspects of texts, from basic text properties to lexical, syntactic, and cohesive measures.

1.1 iSTART

iSTART trains adolescent students to use self-explanation (SE) and reading comprehension strategies [5]. Training in iSTART is divided into three modules: introduction, demonstration, and practice. In the modules, students receive instruction, watch demonstrations of SEs, and practice applying strategies to texts. iSTART scores students' SEs (from 0 to 3) using a natural language assessment algorithm [6] that utilizes a combination of word-based measures and latent semantic analysis. In iSTART, students have the opportunity to read and self-explain complex texts

K. Yacef et al. (Eds.): AIED 2013, LNAI 7926, pp. 692–695, 2013.

assigned by the teacher, experimenter, or system curriculum. One research goal has been to identify student characteristics and text features associated with performance [2], [7]. By doing so, our objective is to develop algorithms that intelligently guide text assignment and feedback during training.

2 Current Study and Results

We build upon previous work investigating reader characteristics, text difficulty, and students' performance. Our goal is to use readability and linguistic measures to identify interactions between student and text characteristics on SE performance.

Participants in the current study were 126 high-school students randomly assigned to one of two versions of iSTART. Half ($n = 65$) of the students interacted with the original iSTART system and the other half ($n = 61$) interacted with a game-based version called iSTART-ME (motivationally enhanced) [8]. In both conditions, students completed the same SE tasks and were assessed with the same algorithm; therefore, the two conditions were collapsed for the current analyses.

2.1 Global Analyses

The SE scores for each text were combined to produce a mean *text SE score*. Thus, each text had an overall mean SE score, which reflected the average score that all students received on that text. Further, Coh-Metrix was used to calculate text difficulty and linguistic measures for each content text.

Correlations between text SE scores and text difficulty measures indicated that text difficulty was not related to students' overall SE quality. Follow-up analyses were conducted for low and high reading ability students to examine the influence of text characteristics on SE quality. A median split on the pretest comprehension scores (Gates-MacGinitie) was used to categorize students as either low or high reading ability. Mean text SE scores were compiled separately to produce a mean score for low ability students and a mean score for high ability students.

2.2 Low Reading Ability Students

A stepwise regression analysis using the readability measures as predictors of SE scores yielded a significant model, $F(1, 58) = 6.01$, $p < .05$; $R^2 = .10$, retaining only one predictor: FKGL [$\beta = -.31$, $t(1, 58)= -2.45$, $p < .05$].

In addition to the standard readability measures, analyses examined which fine-grained linguistic properties interacted with reading ability to influence SE quality. A stepwise regression analysis was conducted on low ability students' SE scores from the battery of linguistic indices provided by Coh-Metrix; this yielded a significant model with four predictors, $F(4, 58) = 4.96$, $p < .01$; $R^2 = .27$ (see Table 1).

Table 1. Linguistic measures predicting self-explanation scores

Variable	β	SE β	B	ΔR^2
Final Model For Low Ability				**.27****
Logical Connectives	.44	.00	.01**	.07*
Average Syllables per Word	-.24	.29	-.57	.08*
MED (all words)	-.31	1.19	-2.90*	.06*
Agentless Passives	-.25	.01	-.02*	.06*
Final Model For High Ability				**.34****
Lexical Diversity	.28	.00	.00*	.17**
Modifiers per Noun Phrase	-.34	.20	-.62**	.10**
Logical Connectives	.29	.00	.01*	.08*

** $p < .01$; * $p < .05$

2.3 High Reading Ability Students

A stepwise regression analysis examining the six readability measures as predictors of SE scores yielded a significant model, $F(2, 57) = 6.23$, $p < .01$; $R2 = .19$, with two predictors: Deep Cohesion [$\beta = .39$, $t(1, 57) = 3.06$, $p < .01$, R^2 change = .08] and Narrativity [$\beta = .34$, $t(2, 57) = 2.65$, $p < .05$, R^2 change = .10].

A stepwise regression using the Coh-Metrix linguistic measures was significant and included three predictors, $F(3, 57) = 9.29$, $p < .001$; $R2 = .34$ (see Table 1). Thus, high reading ability students produce higher SE scores for texts with varied word choices, logically connected ideas, and simple syntax constructions.

3 Conclusions

The current study investigated a method for assessing text difficulty measures that showed significant relations to students' SE performance. Additionally, we examined whether these text effects differed for students with low and high reading skills. The results of our initial analyses suggested that characteristics of training texts had no effect on students' SE scores. However, when reading skill was considered, significant text effects were identified for low and high ability students. Low reading ability students benefited from lower grade level texts with simple words and explicit cohesive devices. Conversely, high ability students generated better SEs for texts that had explicit and deep cohesion, varied word choice, and simple syntax. Overall, these results suggest that automated indices of text difficulty can provide valid representations of system content, particularly using specific linguistic indices.

These results have implications for the development of adaptive content in computerized systems. This study indicated that text difficulty accounted for less variance in low ability students' SE scores than those of high ability students. Thus, low reading ability students may be affected by a number of non-linguistic factors not addressed in this study, such as text genre. Future studies should investigate methods for representing these features. Further, the results suggest that the analysis of text difficulty at multiple levels produced different results among the low and high ability students. Thus, developers of computerized learning environments may want to consider how to assess content at the appropriate level for individual students. Overall, these results, along with previous research, support the need for computerized systems to match characteristics of their users with characteristics of reading material. The current work provides a foundation on which to develop new methods that can intelligently adapt text types based on the needs of the readers.

Acknowledgments. This research was supported in part by the Institute for Educational Sciences (IES R305G020018-02; R305G040046, R305A080589) and National Science Foundation (NSF REC0241144; IIS-0735682). Any opinions, findings, and conclusions or recommendations expressed in this material are those of the authors and do not necessarily reflect the views of the IES or NSF.

References

1. McNamara, D., Graesser, A.: Coh-Metrix: An Automated Tool for Theoretical and Applied Natural Language Processing. In: McCarthy, P., Boonthum-Denecke, C. (eds.) Applied Natural Language Processing and Content Analysis: Identification, Investigation, and Resolution, pp. 188–205. IGI Global, Hershey (2012)
2. Duran, N., Bellissens, C., Taylor, R., McNamara, D.: Quantifying Text Difficulty with Automated Indices of Cohesion and Semantics. In: McNamara, D.S., Trafton, G. (eds.) Proceedings of the 29th Annual Meeting of the Cognitive Science Society, pp. 233–238. Cognitive Science Society, Austin (2007)
3. Graesser, A., McNamara, D., Kulikowich, J.: Coh-Metrix: Providing Multilevel Analyses of Text Characteristics. Educational Researcher 40, 223–234 (2011)
4. Graesser, A., McNamara, D.: Computational Analyses of Multilevel Discourse Comprehension. Topics in Cognitive Science 2, 371–398 (2011)
5. McNamara, D., Levinstein, I., Boonthum, C.: iSTART: Interactive Strategy Trainer for Active Reading and Thinking. Behavioral Research Methods 36, 222–233 (2004)
6. McNamara, D., Boonthum, C., Levinstein, I., Millis, K.: Evaluating Self-explanations in iSTART: Comparing Word-based and LSA Algorithms. In: Landauer, T., McNamara, D., Dennis, S., Kintsch, W. (eds.) Handbook of Latent Semantic Analysis, pp. 227–241. Erlbaum, Mahwah (2007)
7. Bellissens, C., Jeuniaux, P., Duran, N., McNamara, D.: Towards a Textual Cohesion Model that Predicts Self-Explanations Inference Generation as a Function of Text Structure and Readers' Knowledge Levels. In: Proceedings of the 29th Annual Meeting of the Cognitive Science Society, pp. 233–238. Cognitive Science Society, Austin (2007)
8. Jackson, G., Dempsey, K., McNamara, D.: The Evolution of an Automated Reading Strategy Tutor: From Classroom to a Game-enhanced Automated System. In: Khine, M., Saleh, I. (eds.) New Science of Learning: Cognition, Computers and Collaboration in Education, pp. 283–306. Springer, New York (2010)

Situational Interest and Informational Text Comprehension: A Game-Based Learning Perspective

Lucy R. Shores and John L. Nietfeld

Department of Curriculum & Instruction, North Carolina State University, Raleigh, NC 27695
{lrshores,jlnietfe}@ncsu.edu

Abstract. Motivated by disturbing national educational statistics, the newly adopted Common Core State Standards [1] prioritize reading instruction across the content areas. This will significantly increase students' exposure to informational texts that are notorious for low comprehension rates and less than engaging content. Given the substantial literature supporting the positive relationship between situational interest and reading comprehension [2,3], this study will address whether game-based learning environments generate situational interest and, more importantly, whether the produced situational interest increases students' reading comprehension for informational texts. Using an explanatory sequential mixed methods design, eighth-grade students' situational interest and comprehension of texts embedded within a science game-based learning environment will be measured. Implications for this research include the design of intelligent game-based learning environments, the extent to which game elements generate situational interest, and techniques for capitalizing on this situational interest by intelligently and automatically integrating texts to challenge each reader.

Keywords: Game-Based Learning, Situational Interest, Reading Comprehension.

1 Introduction

The Common Core State Standards, now widely adopted across the nation, identify both a set of English Language Arts and Mathematics skills necessary for postsecondary and occupational success [1]. Within the English Language Arts framework, reading across the subject areas is emphasized, and higher-order skills associated with comprehending informational texts are prioritized [1].

While these standards are new to the field, reading comprehension research has been meticulously studied and provides a myriad of evidenced-based best practices. One well-researched area is how comprehension and learning from text is affected by student motivation, and more specifically, student interest [2-4]. Generally, when students are interested in the text, they experience heightened levels of cognitive and affective processing, which yields deeper understanding and greater levels of comprehension [2,3,5]. However, we cannot expect all students to be *personally* interested in all aspects of all subjects. Instead, *situational interest* encompasses

K. Yacef et al. (Eds.): AIED 2013, LNAI 7926, pp. 696–699, 2013.

temporary interest elicited primarily through contextual attributes [2,5]. In other words, the actualization, intensity, and duration of situational interest are dependent upon the presence of aspects in the environment that, when interpreted by an individual, inherently produce a cognitive and affective response [2,3]; therefore, situational interest is "under the direct control of educators" and potentially instrumental for addressing the divergence between ideal and observed states of student motivation [2,5]. While the majority of situational interest and comprehension research has focused on text- and classroom-based manipulations, instructional technologies focused on deeper learning and engagement provide opportunities to investigate how these contexts affect comprehension.

Specifically, work focused on the development of digital, intelligent game-based learning environments, an instructional technique juxtaposing elements of games and educational content, is rapidly populating research agendas and classrooms. Rationale for this movement is provided through theoretical discussions and empirical findings supporting intelligent game-based learning as an effective method for encouraging sustained engagement and producing significant learning gains through adaptive, inquiry experiences [6,7]. Despite some apprehension for the current state of games for learning [8], the 2012 Horizon Report expects game-based learning to experience widespread adoption in the next two to three years [9].

Nonetheless, research investigating the effect of environmental contexts (e.g., hands-on activities, games) known to promote situational interest on reading comprehension is limited [10]. Furthermore, best-practices for designing such learning contexts should be better understood [8], as hastily integrating identified sources of situational interest can undermine the benefits of this state and even lead to a negative effect on learning. The proposed study has five main thrusts: 1) determine the efficacy of utilizing a game-based learning environment as a vehicle for evoking situational interest for informational texts, 2) investigate the influence situational interest has on reading comprehension within a game-based learning environment, 3) identify a set of generalizable game features and design principles that contribute to heightened states of situational interest, and 4) propose methods to optimize situational interest by intelligently integrating texts that challenge each reader.

2 Crystal Island: Lost Investigation

CRYSTAL ISLAND: LOST INVESTIGATION (Figure 1), a game-based learning environment for eighth-grade science and literacy, is derived from North Carolina's standard course of study for microbiology and revolves around a central problem solving narrative. Prior to playing CRYSTAL ISLAND: LOST INVESTIGATION students view a two-minute introductory video setting the stage for the underlying narrative where the student is cast as an investigator sent to Crystal Island to diagnose a mysterious illness plaguing researchers that have been stationed there to study the indigenous flora and fauna. Once game interaction begins, the student must interview sick team members, read relevant documents, test potentially contaminated objects, synthesize information, and accurately diagnosis the illness before it spreads. Several complex informational texts are embedded within the narrative and the generation of inferences and application of the texts' main ideas is imperative for game success.

Fig. 1. Crystal ISLAND game world (left) and informational text (right)

3 Current Investigation

Eighth-grade students ($N \approx 325$) from a large, socioeconomically diverse middle school will be invited to participate in the study. Students will be randomly assigned to one of three conditions: game-based learning, classroom-based learning, reading only. Students in the game-based condition will interact with CRYSTAL ISLAND: LOST INVESTIGATION. Students in the classroom-based learning condition will complete a series of activities similar to those presented in the gaming environment separated by reading sessions. The purpose of this condition is to understand how the gaming environment affects situational interest and comprehension beyond more traditional classroom-based conditions. Finally, students in the reading only condition will simply read the passages provided in the other conditions without context. A select group of students will be asked to participate in follow-up, semi-structured interviews to expand upon and triangulate the quantitative data.

Specifically, this study will employ both quantitative and qualitative methods to answer the following research questions: 1) Do game-based learning environments trigger and sustain greater levels of situational interest than classroom-based conditions?, 2) Does situational interest generated through game-based learning affect and predict reading comprehension for texts embedded within the environment? 3) What components of game-based learning environments lead to greater levels of situational interest?

Reading comprehension will be assessed through multiple-choice questions written to measure both fact- and application-level understanding of the text. *Reading ability* will be measured using the Woodcock-Johnson and will be controlled for during analysis. *Situational interest* will be measured following each reading passage using methods similar to those used by [10]. *Reading motivation*, as measured by the Motivation for Reading Questionnaire [11], and *science interest*, as measured by the Science Interest Survey [12], will be used to control for prior and personal interests. *Prior knowledge* will be assessed through a researcher-constructed 20-item, multiple-choice test. The Perceived Interest Questionnaire [13] will be used to measure overall situational interest. ANCOVA and multiple regression procedures will be conducted to determine differences in comprehension and situational interest between conditions and reveal the predictive power of situational interest for comprehension. Moreover, multilevel modeling techniques will be used to understand how situational interest behaves during the interaction. Follow-up interviews will provide a qualitative perspective to expand upon and triangulate the quantitative data as suggested by [3].

With respect to the artificial intelligence and educational community, findings from this investigation could provide a foundation for intelligently adapting to students' individual differences in order to optimize situational interest. Furthermore, when interested, readers tend to demonstrate deeper comprehension [2,5]; therefore, informed by learner models, intelligent learning environments, such as game-based learning, could leverage situational interest and make intelligent, real-time decisions regarding the presentation texts appropriately challenging for each student.

Acknowledgments. The authors wish to thank members of the IntelliMedia Group for their assistance. This research was supported by the Next Generation Learning Challenges with funding from the Bill & Melinda Gates and William and Flora Hewlett foundations. Any opinions, findings, and conclusions expressed in this material do not necessarily reflect the views of the funding sources.

References

1. National Governors Association Center for Best Practices, Council of Chief State School Officers: Common Core State Standards for English Language Arts. NGACBP, CCSSO, Washington D.C. (2010)
2. Schraw, G., Lehman, S.: Situational Interest: A Review of the Literature and Directions for Future Research. Edu. Psych. Review 13, 23–51 (2001)
3. Renninger, K.A., Hidi, S.: Revisiting the Conceptualization, Measurement, and Generation of Interest. Edu. Psychologist 46, 168–184 (2011)
4. Kintsch, W.: Learning From Text. Cog. and Instruction 3, 87–108 (1986)
5. Hidi, S.: Interest, Reading, and Learning: Theoretical and Practical Considerations. Edu. Psych. Review 13, 191–209 (2001)
6. Rowe, J., Shores, L., Mott, B., Lester, J.: Integrating Learning, Problem Solving, and Engagement in Narrative-Centered Learning Environments. Intl. J. of Artificial Intelligence in Edu. 21, 115–133 (2011)
7. Barab, S., Thomas, M., Dodge, T., Carteaux, R., Tuzun, H.: Making learning fun: Quest Atlantis, a game without guns. Edu. Tech. Research and Development 53, 86–107 (2005)
8. Mayer, R., Johnson, C.: Adding Instructional Features that Promote Learning in a Game-Like Environment. J. Edu. Comp. Res. 42, 241–265 (2010)
9. Johnson, L., Smith, R., Willis, H., Levine, A., Haywood, K.: The 2012 Horizon Report. The New Media Consortium, Austin, Texas (2012)
10. Rotgans, J.I., Schmidt, H.G.: Situational interest and academic achievement in the active-learning classroom. Learning and Instruction 21, 58–67 (2011)
11. Wigfield, A., Guthrie, J.: Relations of children's motivation for reading to the amount and breadth or their reading. J. Edu. Psych. 89, 420–432 (1997)
12. Lamb, R.L., Annetta, L., Meldrum, J., Vallett, D.: Measuring Science Interest: RASCH Validation of the Science Interest Survey. International Journal of Science and Mathematics Education 10, 643–668 (2012)
13. Schraw, G.: Situational interest in literary text. Contemp. Edu. Psych. 22, 436–456 (1997)

Learner-Created Scenario for Investigative Learning with Web Resources

Akihiro Kashihara and Naoto Akiyama

Graduate School of Informatics, The University of Electro-Communications, Japan
akihiro.kashihara@inf.uec.ac.jp

Abstract. Web brings about a lot of opportunities for learners to investigate a topic with Web resources to learn. Such investigative learning process involves creating a scenario that explains what to and how to investigate with Web resources. However, it is quite difficult for the learners to create their own learning scenario concurrent with knowledge construction from the contents of the resources. The main issue addressed in this paper is how to scaffold learning scenario creation. This paper presents a model of investigative learning, which induces learners to create the learning scenario by decomposing the topic into sub-topics to be learned while searching and learning the Web resources. This paper also demonstrates an interactive learning scenario builder, which provides a scaffold for the learners to build their own scenario in learning with Web resources.

Keywords: Learning scenario, investigative learning, scaffolding, Web.

1 Introduction

Web recently brings about a lot of opportunities for learners to investigate any topics to learn, which allows them to construct a wider, deeper, and timely knowledge from a great variety of Web resources [3, 4]. Since Web includes not only reliable/structured resources but also unreliable/unstructured ones, the learners need to sort out the resources suitable for learning, and to reconstruct the contents learned by themselves [1].

In undertaking the task of investigating a topic with Web resources, the learners would integrate and construct knowledge learned at each resource, and find out related topics to be further investigated which can be viewed as the sub-topics. In this way, the investigation task involves decomposing the topic into sub-topics. Wider and deeper decomposition of the topic would make investigative learning process more structured and fruitful.

In learning with a textbook, on the other hand, learners are usually provided with the learning scenario indicating the topics and their sequence to be learned. The learners are allowed to follow the scenario to learn the topics. In investigative learning with Web resources, however, it is necessary for learners to create their own scenario while investigating and learning [2, 3]. Such learner-created scenario would be also useful to reflect on their constructed knowledge after investigative learning process.

K. Yacef et al. (Eds.): AIED 2013, LNAI 7926, pp. 700–703, 2013.

But, it is quite difficult for the learners to create their own scenario concurrent with knowledge construction from the contents of the resources. Since they tend to pay more attention to navigation and knowledge construction for learning the topic [2], they often miss finding out related topics to be further investigated, which results in an insufficient investigation [3].

The main issue addressed in this paper is how to promote decomposing the topic to be investigated while searching and learning Web resources to scaffold learning scenario creation. Our approach to this issue is to model the investigative learning process and to induce learners to decompose the topic into sub-topics as modeled and to define the investigation task. In this model, the learning scenario is represented as a tree of topics investigated (called topic tree), which is composed of parent-children relations between topic and the sub-topics.

This paper also demonstrates an interactive learning scenario builder (iLSB for short), which allows the learners to build their own scenario during investigative learning process and to reflect on their knowledge constructed with the scenario after investigative learning process.

2 Model of Investigative Learning with Web Resources

In order to scaffold learning scenario creation, this paper proposes a model of investigative learning with Web resources. This model includes three phases, which are (i) search for Web resources, (ii) navigational learning, and (iii) learning scenario creation.

In the phase (i), learners who undertake a task of investigating a topic could use a search engine such as Google with a keyword (called topic keyword) representing the topic to gather Web resources suitable for learning the topic, and navigate across these resources. In the phase (ii), they could then navigate the Web pages included in these resources to learn the contents and construct knowledge about the topic. Such knowledge construction with navigation is called navigational learning. In navigational learning process, they could find out related topics to be further investigated, which can be viewed as the sub-topics. In the phase (iii), the learners are expected to build a topic tree by decomposing the topic into the sub-topics, each of which could be investigated and learned in the next phases (i) and (ii). These three phases are repeated until the topic decomposition does not occur anymore.

In this model, the topic decomposition results in the topic tree including parent-children relations between topic and the sub-topics, which corresponds to the learning scenario. The root of the tree represents the initial topic in investigative learning process. Creating the scenario corresponds to defining how to investigate the initial topic.

The created scenario allows the learners to keep track of the topics to be investigated during searching and learning with Web resources, which could prevent them from getting lost in hyperspace provided with the resources [2, 3]. After investigative learning process, it also allows the learners to reproduce their knowledge construction process and to reflect on their knowledge constructed. Without the created scenario, it would be quite difficult to understand how their knowledge has been constructed.

3 iLSB: Interactive Learning Scenario Builder

In order to scaffold the investigative learning process as modeled, we have developed iLSB, which is implemented as an add-on for Firefox. iLSB provides learners with the three scaffolds, which are search engine (such as Google) on Firefox, keyword repository for storing keywords representing the contents learned about topics, and topic tree representing parent-children relations between topic keywords.

Figure 1 shows the user interface of iLSB. The search engine (page browser) and the topic tree are displayed as tabbed pages on Firefox. The keyword repository is also displayed in the left-side bar.

iLSB first requires the learners to input an initial topic as topic keyword, which is then located in the root of the topic tree. iLSB next allows the learners to use the search engine with the topic keyword to find out and navigate across Web resources fruitful for learning the topic. In navigational learning with these resources, they are allowed to browse the Web pages with the page browser to extract keywords from the browsed pages, which represent the contents learned about the topic. The keyword repository allows them to put the extracted keywords and to make inclusive relations among them to classify, which represent knowledge constructed. Although the constructed knowledge would intrinsically include a greater variety of relations, iLSB currently deals with only inclusive relations. In the keyword repository, the learners could become aware of sub-topics insufficiently learned or crucial for investigating the topic, which should be further investigated. They are then allowed to mouse-drag

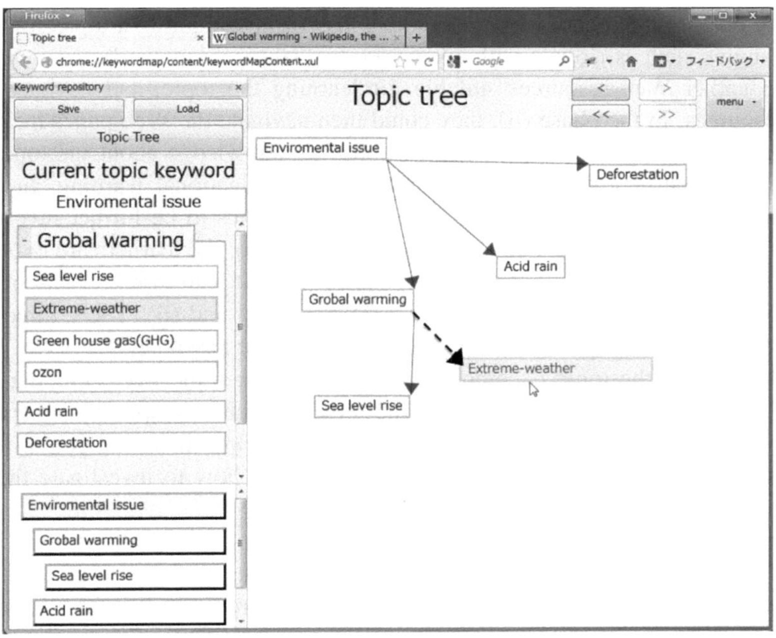

Fig. 1. User Interface of iLSB

the keywords representing the sub-topics to drop them on the topic tree and to make the parent-children relations from the root. The next task for the learners is to investigate these children topics by means of the three scaffolds.

Mouse-clicking a topic keyword in the topic tree, it is set up as the current topic investigated. The keyword repository also changes the current topic keyword synchronously, which displays the keywords extracted in learning the current topic. In other words, each topic keyword has its own sub-repository for storing the keywords extracted.

These functions of iLSB allow learners to build their own topic tree to make learning scenario creation process explicit. iLSB would accordingly make investigative learning process more structured.

4 Conclusion

This paper has proposed a model of investigative learning with Web resources, and demonstrated iLSB that provides learners with a scaffold for creating the learning scenario as modeled. The learning scenario creation is defined as decomposing topic to be investigated into the sub-topics to build a tree of topics investigated.

We have conducted a case study with iLSB. The results indicate the possibilities that iLSB makes investigative learning process more structured, and that it allows learners to promote reflection on knowledge constructed.

In future, we will conduct more detailed evaluation with iLSB to refine the model and functionality of iLSB. We will also address an issue of how to scaffold learning scenario building with adaptive aids.

Acknowledgments. This work is supported in part by Grant-in-Aid for Scientific Research (B) (No.23300297 and No.22300284) from the Ministry of Education, Science, and Culture of Japan.

References

1. Henze, N., Nejdl, W.: Adaptation in open corpus hypermedia. International Journal of Artificial Intelligence in Education 12(4), 325–350 (2001)
2. Hill, J.R., Hannafin, M.J.: Cognitive Strategies and Learning from the World Wide Web. Educational Technology Research and Development 45(4), 37–64 (1997)
3. Jonassen, D.H.: Computers as Mindtools for Schools: Engaging Critical Thinking, 2nd edn. Prentice-Hall (2000)
4. Kashihara, A., Ito, M.: Fadable Scaffolding with Cognitive Tool. In: Cerri, S.A., Clancey, W.J., Papadourakis, G., Panourgia, K. (eds.) ITS 2012. LNCS, vol. 7315, pp. 662–663. Springer, Heidelberg (2012)

Towards Identifying Students' Causal Reasoning Using Machine Learning

Jody Clarke-Midura[1] and Michael V. Yudelson[2]

[1] Graduate School of Education, Harvard University
50 Church Street, Suite 422, Cambridge, MA 02138 USA
jody@post.harvard.edu
[2] Human-Computer Interaction Institute, Carnegie Mellon University
5000 Forbes Ave., Pittsburgh, PA 15213 USA
yudelson@cmu.edu

Abstract. Causal reasoning is difficult for middle school students to grasp. In this research, we wanted to test the possibility of using machine learning for modeling students' causal reasoning in a virtual environment designed to assess this skill. Our findings suggest it is possible to use machine learning to emulate student pathways that are able to predict their causal understanding.

Keywords: Virtual learning environment, performance assessment, causal reasoning, machine learning.

1 Introduction

Building on years of research that has documented the ways in which causal understanding is challenging for students [7-9], we designed a virtual performance assessment that relies on students' ability to distinguish non-causal from causal data in a scientific investigation. We developed a rubric to quantify the extent interaction with evidence in the scenario provides students with the causal evidence to solve the problem. The purpose of this research is exploratory. We want to test the ability to examine students' pathways and determine whether or not they should have drawn certain conclusions based on the type of evidence they encountered. In this paper, we discuss the methodological approach for developing and testing our causal reasoning rubric.

2 Related Work

Digital media, such as virtual environments, games, and simulations, allow for the capturing the student learning data impossible to record in traditional classrooms. As students interact with the digital environment, their actions can be captured unobtrusively as log data. Numerous researchers have been exploring various ways to use log data to model and understand students' inquiry learning in relatively structured

K. Yacef et al. (Eds.): AIED 2013, LNAI 7926, pp. 704–707, 2013.

simulations [2,4,5], intelligent tutoring systems [1], and more open environments such as virtual environments and games [3,4,6,10].

3 The Environment

The virtual performance assessment (VPA) is a 3-D immersive virtual environment that has the look and feel of a videogame. Each participant takes on the identity of an avatar, a virtual persona that can move around the 3-D context (Fig. 1). Students investigate what caused a frog to grow two extra limbs. There are 5 competing hypotheses for how this may have happened. Students walk around and gather data, run lab tests, talk to non-player characters, and conduct scientific research. Each action results in access to information that supports, rejects, or is neutral to each of the 5 competing hypotheses. There are 92 unique actions that are possible in the environment.

Fig. 1. Screen shots of the Virtual Performance Assessments (VPA)

4 Methods

We developed a rubric that indicated the level to which an action supported, rejected, or was neutral to each of the 5 causal factors. We then wanted to create a composite score that should indicate based on the actions they carried out whether or not they were exposed to evidence that should have led them to the right causal factor. This would indicate their ability to tease out the causal from non-causal information. We used two approaches to devise rubric scores: expert-set rubrics and machine learned rubrics (seeded with expert rubrics). The quality of the rubrics was verified by regressing the final student in-game score to the two summative metrics: sum of all accept rubric scores and sum of all reject rubric scores.

5 Data

Our sample contains logs of 1,986 middle school students in grades 7-8,, spread across 40 teachers and 138 classrooms. Actions within the software were logged as individual events including the type of action, location, and time stamp.

6 Results

Machine learning procedure fitting 92 distinct action rubric scores was able to move away from the initial expert-seeded point. As a result the amount of variance on the dependent variable explained is improved from 47% in the expert rubric model to 66% in the learned rubric model. Table 1 is a summary of regressions that were based on expert rubrics as well as the learned rubric scores. We can see that in both cases the sums of accept and reject scores remain robust positive predictors and students consistently benefit more from positive evidence supporting the right claim than from evidence against it. The fact that coming across evidence against the correct final claim has a significant positive effect is reassuring. That could be thought of an indicator that students, in fact, are capable of thinking critically overall.

Table 1. Regression model parameters for expert and learned rubric scores

Parameter	Estimate (p-value)	
	Expert rubrics	Learned 92 rubrics
Intercept	6.15 (0.00)***	0.70 (0.58)
Sum of accept scores	0.99 (0.00)***	0.88 (0.00)***
Sum of reject scores	0.56 (0.00)***	0.49 (0.00)***
Prediction of pesticides	-0.65 (0.70)	1.19 (0.38)
Prediction of aliens	-4.60 (0.01)*	-2.63 (0.08).
Prediction of pollution	-3.02 (0.07).	0.40 (0.77)
Prediction of parasites (correct)	0.14 (0.94)	2.09 (0.14)
Prediction of genetic mutation	-2.32 (0.13)	0.64 (0.60)
Prediction of "I don't know"	-0.29 (0.85)	1.83 (0.13)
DV variance explained (%)	46.77	65.56

Influence of initial claims students make before entering the exploration game seem to change a lot between the models. However, only *aliens* claim has a significant negative effect in the model with expert rubric scores and remains negative but marginally significant in the learned rubric scores model. There was no supporting evidence in the VPA for aliens and 31 out of 92 actions are against it. Students with lower abilities to engage in causal reasoning may have developed their own tacit theories that diverge from scientific views [7]; or have difficulty giving up their theories even when they discover counter evidence [8,9]. Students who entered with a prediction of aliens were able to determine causal from non-causal and build emerging models as they carried out their investigation.

7 Conclusions

The automated procedure we designed to learn rubrics for student actions, despite potentially complex solution space, has proven to be robust to subjective skews in prior assumptions. We tested the machine learning methodology on a new dataset with no expert solution. The percent of final student score explained we achieved in this case was comparable to the solution for the original discussed in this paper.

Acknowledgements. This work was supported by the Institute of Education Sciences (Grant# R305A080141) and The Bill & Melinda Gates Foundation.

References

1. Roll, I., Aleven, V., Koedinger, K.R.: The invention lab: Using a hybrid of model tracing and constraint-based modeling to offer intelligent support in inquiry environments. In: Aleven, V., Kay, J., Mostow, J. (eds.) ITS 2010, Part I. LNCS, vol. 6094, pp. 115–124. Springer, Heidelberg (2010)
2. Quellmalz, E.S., Timms, M.J., Silberglitt, M.D., Buckley, B.C.: Science Assessments for All: Integrating Science Simulations Into Balanced State Science Assessment Systems. Journal of Research in Science Teaching 49(3), 363–393 (2012)
3. Rowe, J., Lester, J.: Modeling User Knowledge with Dynamic Bayesian Networks in Interactive Narrative Environments. In: Proceedings of the Sixth Annual Artificial Intelligence and Interactive Digital Entertainment Conference (AIIDE 2010), Palo Alto, California, pp. 57–62 (2012)
4. Sao Pedro, M., Baker, R., Gobert, J., Montalvo, O., Nakama, A.: Leveraging Machine-Learned Detectors of Systematic Inquiry Behavior to Estimate and Predict Transfer of Inquiry Skill. User Modeling and User-Adapted Interaction: The Journal of Personalization Research 23(1), 1–39 (2013)
5. Sao Pedro, M.A., Baker, R.S.J.d., Montalvo, O., Nakama, A., Gobert, J.D.: Using Text Replay Tagging to Produce Detectors of Systematic Experimentation Behavior Patterns. In: Proceedings of the 3rd International Conference on Educational Data Mining, pp. 181–190 (2010)
6. Sil, A., Shelton, A., Ketelhut, D.J., Yates, A.: Automatic Grading of Scientific Inquiry. In: Proceedings of the NAACL-HLT 7th Workshop on Innovative Use of NLP for Building Educational Applications (BEA-7), Montreal, Quebec, Canada (2012)
7. Perkins, D.N., Grotzer, T.A.: Dimensions of causal understanding: The role of complex causal models in students understanding of science. Studies in Science Education 41, 117–166 (2005)
8. Kuhn, D.: The skills of argument. Cambridge University Press (1991)
9. Chinn, C.A., Brewer, W.F.: The role of anomalous data in knowledge acquisition: A theoretical framework and implications for science instruction. Review of Educational Research 63(1), 1–49 (1993)
10. Shute, V.J.: Stealth assessment in computer-based games to support learning. In: Tobias, S., Fletcher, J.D. (eds.) Computer Games and Instruction, pp. 503–524. Information Age Publishers, Charlotte (2011)

Social Personalized Adaptive E-Learning Environment: Topolor - Implementation and Evaluation

Lei Shi, George Gkotsis, Karen Stepanyan, Dana Al Qudah, and Alexandra I. Cristea

Department of Computer Science, University of Warwick, CV4 7AL Coventry, UK
{lei.shi,gkotsis,kstepanyan,d.al-qudah,
acristea}@dcs.warwick.ac.uk

Abstract. This paper presents a quantitative study on the use of Topolor - a prototype that introduces Web 2.0 tools and Facebook-like appearance into an adaptive educational hypermedia system. We present the system design and its evaluation using system usability scale questionnaire and learning behavior data analysis. The results indicate high level of student satisfaction with the learning experience and the diversity of learning activities.

Keywords: adaptive educational hypermedia, e-learning system, evaluation, learning behavior analysis, social learning.

1 Introduction

Adaptive Educational Hypermedia System (AEHS)[1] makes educational hypermedia adaptive and personalized. Web 2.0 tools enable learners to create, publish and share their study, and facilitate interaction and collaboration. The integration of Web 2.0 tools into AEHS may offer novel opportunities for learner engagement and user modeling. However, there has been a lack of empirical design and evaluation to elaborate methods for the integration. The goal of this research, therefore, is to investigate 1) the potential benefits to integrate Web 2.0 tools into AEHS, and 2) the balance between adaptation and social interaction in an AEHS. In this paper, we present the design and evaluation of an AEHS, Topolor, for web-based personalized learning environment that takes into account social interactions between learners.

2 The Topolor System

Topolor [2,3] is an adaptive personalized e-learning system developed at the University of Warwick. It is built on Yii Framework (http://yiiframework.com) and hosted on Github (https://github.com/aslanshek/topolor). The first version of Topolor (http://www.topolor.com) was launched in November 2012, and has been used as an online learning environment for MSc level students at the University of Warwick.

2.1 System Architecture

Topolor adopts a layered architecture (Fig. 1): the *storage layer* is a persistence infrastructure representing the physical storage of entities within the system; the *runtime layer* parses adaptation strategies for presenting adaptive user interface.

K. Yacef et al. (Eds.): AIED 2013, LNAI 7926, pp. 708–711, 2013.

Storage Layer. The main difference from other system architectures is the *Affiliate Model*, designed for social annotation and collaborative learning. a) *Concept Model* presents the smallest knowledge unit containing metadata and concrete learning content. b) *Course Model* presents a self-contained module containing organized *Concept Models*. c) *Affiliate Model* is affiliated to a *Course Model* or a *Concept Model*. It can be instantiated to tag, share, comment, question, note and to-do. This mechanism can help learners easily interact with each other. d) *User Model* stores learner's preference and knowledge space. It's built on a well-established concept of overlay model [4]. e) *Group Model* presents a relatively isolated set of learners having the same learning goals. f) *Adaptation Model* contains adaptation strategies that determine if and how to present entities such as courses, concepts, and learning peers.

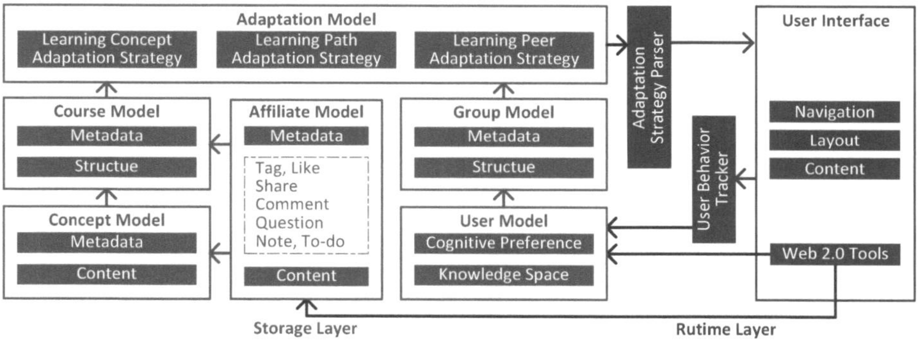

Fig. 1. The System Architecture of Topolor

Runtime Layer. a) *Adaptation Strategy Parser* analyzes adaptation strategies to determine if and how to present learning topics, learning paths and peers. b) *User Behavior Tracker* monitors user activities and updates user models. c) *User Interface* consists of the navigation menu, the layout and the content controller. The core components are the Web2.0 tools for social annotation, discussion and collaboration.

2.2 Implementation

Topolor is implemented using mainly PHP, HTML, CSS, SQL and JavaScript. Fig. 2 shows the screenshot of the 'Topolor Home' and 'Module Center' sub-systems in Topolor. The numbers in the screenshot highlight the features and functionalities.

1. Topolor – Home page (Facebook-like appearance)
   a. Left menu: to check messages, Q&A list, notes list and to-do list.
   b. Learning peer list: to send messages to recommended learning peers.
   c. Information flow wall: to share, comment on and favorite posts.
   d. Posting tool: to post learning status, messages, questions, notes and to-dos.
2. Topolor – Module page
   a. Learning topic adaptation. Topics are recommended according to the number of tags, which are the same as the topic that the learner is currently learning.
   b. Learning peer adaptation & Messaging tool. Peers are recommended according to the number of questions they asked or correctly answered. By clicking on the avatar, the message box will pop up for sending messages.

c. Web2.0 tools. Learners can a) comment on this topic, b) ask questions with tags, c) create/edit/tag/share notes, and d) create/edit/tag to-do.
d. By clicking the button 'previous' or 'next', a learner can review the prerequisite topic or go to the next topic according to the recommended learning path.
e. Quiz. When clicking the button 'Take a Quiz', s/he will be redirected to the quiz sub-system, where s/he can answer the quiz related to this topic.

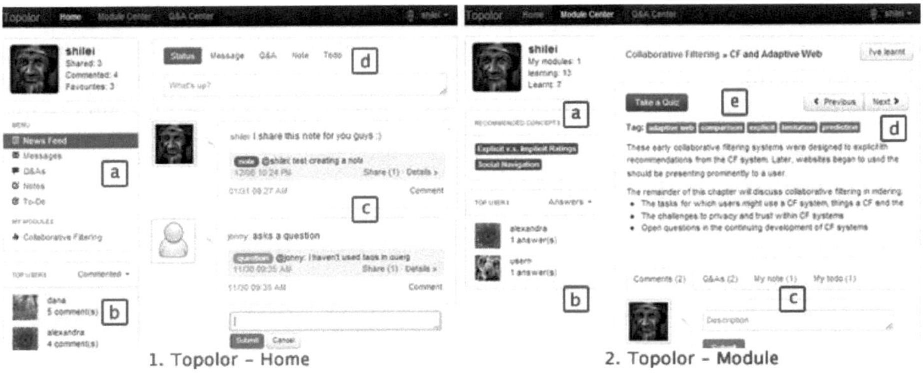

Fig. 2. The Screenshot of Topolor: 1. Home page; 2. Module page

3 Evaluation

21 postgraduate students studying computer science at the University of Warwick attended an intensive online course on "Collaborative Filtering". Before the online course, a 'functionality list' was handed out to each student, to inform them about the existing functionalities and to make sure that as many functions as possible are tested.

3.1 Usability of Topolor

The online course lasted for two hours, after which the students were asked to fill in an optional SUS [5] questionnaire for the system usability evaluation. We received 10 (out of 21) students' responses. The SUS score for the Topolor system was 75.75 out of 100 (σ=12.36, median=76.25). The results' *Cronbach's alpha* value was 0.85 (>0.8), meaning the questionnaire results were reliable. Therefore, we claim that the usability of Topolor meets our initial expectations. We received some qualitative feedbacks from the students as well. Consistently, their responses were positive and supported the SUS result. The qualitative feedback included a description of the system as "similar to known Social Network Sites; fast and responsive". A student claimed s/he liked the process of asking and answering questions. Another student appraised the system for "providing updates about who else is learning the topic".

3.2 Learning Behavior Analysis

During the 2-hour session, a logging mechanism kept track of distinct user actions. Out of the 21 students, 4 students had performed less than 10 actions, and 1 student had performed only the social interaction actions. After the exclusion of these 5 students, 16 students ended up with a total sum of 2,175 actions (with an average of 136 actions and a standard deviation of 71 actions per student). In total, 41 different types of raw actions were identified from the log data. These actions were annotated following a higher-level categorization that divided the actions into a) assessment, b) auxiliary, c) social interaction, d) navigation, and e) reading, shown in Fig. 3.

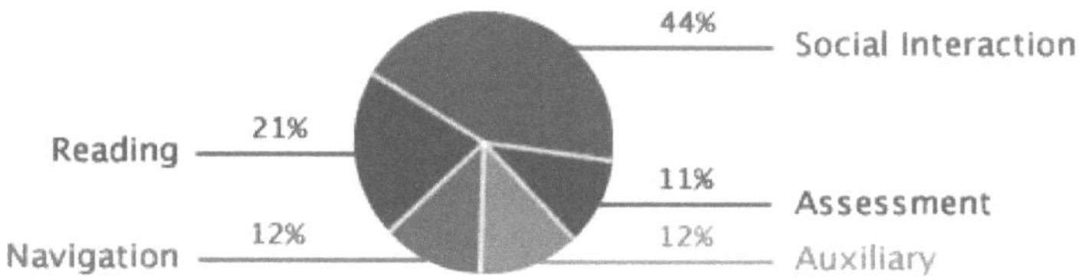

Fig. 3. The proportions and categorizations of learner actions

4 Conclusion

In this paper, we have presented the design and evaluation of the Topolor system; reported a quantitative case study on its usability using SUS questionnaire and learning behavior data analysis. The significant discrepancies between Topolor and other e-learning systems are 1) Topolor provides the *Affiliate Model* for more convenient social interaction; and 2) Topolor emphasizes that learner familiarity of Web2.0 tools promotes engagement, participation and collaboration. The results from both the system usability evaluation and the learning behavior analysis are positive, which encourages us to continue working in this direction. We believe that the fact that a lot of provided features had a look and feel familiar to the popular Facebook environment, promoted the student engagement, participation and collaboration. It is important to take into consideration the familiarity in designing such systems.

Acknowledgements. This research is partially supported by the Blogforever Project, funded by the European Commission FP7 (Contract No. 269963).

References

1. Brusilovsky, P.: Adaptive Educational Hypermedia: From generation to generation (Invited talk). In: Proc. of Hellenic Conference on Information and Communication Technologies in Education, Athens, Greece, pp. 19–33 (2004)
2. Shi, L., Al Qudah, D., Qaffas, A., Cristea, A.I.: Topolor: A Social Personalized Adaptive E-Learning System. In: Weibelzahl, S., Carberry, S., Micarelli, A., Semeraro, G. (eds.) UMAP 2013. LNCS, vol. 7899, pp. 338–340. Springer, Heidelberg (2013)
3. Shi, L., Stepanyan, K., Al Qudah, D., Cristea, A.I.: Evaluation of Social Interaction Features in Topolor - A Social Personalized Adaptive E-Learning System. In: 13th IEEE International Conference on Advanced Learning Technologies (accepted, 2013)
4. Brusilovsky, P., Millán, E.: User models for adaptive hypermedia and adaptive educational systems. In: Brusilovsky, P., Kobsa, A., Nejdl, W. (eds.) Adaptive Web 2007. LNCS, vol. 4321, pp. 3–53. Springer, Heidelberg (2007)
5. Brooke, J.: SUS-A quick and dirty usability scale. In: Usability Evaluation in Industry, pp. 189–194 (1996)

Adaptive Testing Based on Bayesian Decision Theory

Maomi Ueno

University of Electro-Communications, Tokyo, Japan
ueno@ai.uec.ac.jp

Abstract. To propose a new CAT(Computerized Adaptive Testing) algorithm, we regard selecting an item from an item bank as a decision making in Bayesian theory and propose a new item selection criterion we call "expected value of test information" (EVTI). The unique features of EVTI are that it 1) maximizes the prediction utility of an examinee's ability estimation and 2) generates a decision tree with an item selection order based on the examinee's responses. The CAT references the tree and then instantaneously selects and presents the optimal item from an item bank. Simulation results showed that the proposed method performed better than conventional methods.

Keywords: Educational assessment, e-testing, e-assessment, test theory, EVSI, Bayesian statistics, decision theory, adaptive testing, item response theory.

1 Introduction

Since the early days of CAT(Computerized Adaptive Testing), the maximum information method [1] based on item response theory (IRT) has been commonly used. This method selects the optimal item that maximizes the test information (Fisher information measure) at the current estimated ability based on IRT derived from an item bank. However, item selection based on Fisher information has its own share of problems. One is that it tends to select only items with high values of item discrimination parameters. Consequently, it selects mostly similar items from an item bank, which results in item selection bias. Another problem is serious estimation errors at the beginning of the test [2]. Because errors in the initial ability estimates are typically quite significant, item selection criteria that ignore them tend to favor items with optimal measurement properties at an incorrectly estimated ability value. In response to this second problem, Chang and Ying (1996) [2] proposed using Kullback-Leibler information as test information. In a similar vein, Veerkamp and Berger (1997) [3] proposed using a likelihood-weighted Fisher information measure. Van der Linden (1998) proposed a posterior-weighted information criterion using posterior distribution instead of the likelihood function in a likelihood-weighted Fisher information measure [4]. Although these new item selection algorithms are effective in that they solve the problems and improve the accuracy of examinee ability estimation, unfortunately they all result in extremely high computational costs because they need a numerical integration over an ability parameter. Therefore, none of these algorithms have been put to actual practical use. In this paper, we propose a new, less expensive CAT algorithm based on Bayesian decision theory. The proposed framework assumes

K. Yacef et al. (Eds.): AIED 2013, LNAI 7926, pp. 712–716, 2013.

adaptive item selection as a decision process using expected value of sample information (EVSI)[5], which is the expected utility of a selected item. In Bayesian decision theory, EVSI is the expected increase in utility that the user can obtain from gaining access to a sample of additional observations before making a decision. In this study, we propose a new item selection criterion, expected value of test information (EVTI), to maximize prediction utility. We expect EVTI to increase the item selection accuracy in CAT because, unlike previously proposed criteria, it maximizes the prediction of estimators. Furthermore, the proposed algorithm generates a decision tree, which has an item selection order based on examinee's responses, to maximize the EVSI. The CAT instantaneously selects the next item according to the decision tree. There are three key advantages to our proposals:1.The method has less item selection bias than Fisher information-based methods., 2.The method has no estimation errors at the beginning of the test. 3. Item selection according to a decision tree reduces computational costs compared to conventional methods. We performed simulation experiments to compare the performances of the proposed method and conventional item selection methods.

2 CAT Based on Bayesian Decision Theory

2.1 Decision Theory and EVSI

In decision theory, the expected value of sample information (EVSI) [8] is often used to evaluate the value of observation. EVSI is the expected increase in utility that a user can obtain from gaining access to a sample of additional observations before making a decision. Let $d \in D$ be the decision being made, chosen from decision space *D*, and let $Ut(d, x)$ be the utility of selecting decision *d* from *x*. We write $x \in X$ as an uncertain state with true value in space *X* and write $z \in Z$ as an observed sample.

EVSI is formally defined as

$$EVSI = \int_Z \max_{d \in D} \int_X Ut(d, x) p(z|x) p(x) dx dz - \max_{d \in D} \int_X Ut(d, x) p(x) dx \quad (1).$$

2.2 Item Selection Criterion EVTI

We use the EVSI framework to propose a new item selection criterion in CAT. Namely, we regard item selection as a decision making and $d \in D$ in (1) can be interpreted as an item being selected, $j \in R_k$. The purpose of CAT is to increase the prediction accuracy of the examinee ability estimate. Therefore, we set x and $Ut(d, x)$ as θ and the log-predictive score $\ln p(\theta|U_{i1}, \cdots, U_{ik}, U_j)$. As a result, the expected value of test information (EVTI) is defined as

$$\begin{aligned} EVTI = \\ \max_{j \in R_k} \Big[\int_\theta & [\ln p(\theta|U_{i1}, \cdots, U_{ik}, U_j = 0)]\, p(U_j = 0|\theta) p(\theta|U_{i1}, \cdots, U_{ik}, U_j = 0) + \\ & [\ln p(\theta|U_{i1}, \cdots, U_{ik}, U_j = 1)]\, p(U_j = 1|\theta) p(\theta|U_{i1}, \cdots, U_{ik}, U_j = 1)\, d\theta - \\ \int_\theta & [\ln p(\theta|U_{i1}, \cdots, U_{ik})] p(\theta|U_{i1}, \cdots, U_{ik})\, d\theta \Big] \end{aligned} \quad (2).$$

EVTI is defined as the expected increase of the log-predictive score for θ when we select item *j*. However, the computational cost of EVTI is still heavy for direct calculation. Therefore, we propose an off-line algorithm that constructs a decision tree with an item selection order based on examinee responses. The decision tree generation algorithm is as follows.

1. k = 1. Randomly select an item as the initial item, i_1, from the item bank and determine i_1 as the root.
2. The *k*-th nodes expand into children nodes having items to maximize EVTI for cases $U_{ik} = 0$ and $U_{ik} = 0$.
3. If a stopping criterion is met, the nodes expand into a child node that has the estimate $\hat{\theta}|U_{i1}, \cdots, U_{ik}$.
4. k + 1. Go to line 2 until there are no nodes that satisfy a stopping criterion.

In this algorithm, the first item is randomly selected to construct as many different trees as possible. This is an off-line algorithm, so although it takes a lot of time to construct a tree, the CAT can instantaneously select the optimal item to the examinee according to his/her responses.

3 Numerical Experiments

In this section, we compare the proposed item selection method with four conventional methods based on IRT (2-parameter logistic model).

- Maximum information (MI) method [1]
- Maximum global information (MGI) method [2]
- Maximum likelihood-weighted information (MLWI) method [3]
- Maximum expected posterior weighted-information (MEPWI) method [4]

We used Bayesian parameter estimation as the item parameter estimation in this experiment. The ability estimation method was EAP estimation. The prediction accuracies were compared using mean squared errors (MSEs) between the predicted ability parameters and true values.

We used 27 different item banks prepared with the following details:

– I = 100, 500, and 1000.
– The values of *a* are generated randomly from three conditions: *a* ∈[0, 0.3], [0.3, 0.6], and [0.6, 1]. We call these sets "low *a*", "medium *a*", and "high *a*", respectively.
– The values of *b* are generated randomly from three conditions: *b*∈ [–3, –1], [–1, 1], and [1, 3]. We call these sets "low *b*", "medium *b*", and "high *b*", respectively.

The simulation data of 5000 examinee responses (1-0) were randomly generated using the 2-parameter logistic model. We compared the prediction accuracy MSEs of the proposed method with the conventional methods listed above. The CAT provided items until the stopping criterion $|\hat{\theta}_k - \hat{\theta}_{k+1}| < 0.001$. The results are shown in Table 1. The proposed method and the maximum expected posterior weighted-information (MEPWI) method had the best performances. The performance of the proposed method was slightly better than that of MEPWI, but there were no significant statistical differences because both predict the examinee's next response using Bayesian estimation. The key difference is that the proposed method uses a log-predictive score for θ while MEPWI uses Fisher information. The column "Number of items" shows the number of items that were presented until the CAT satisfied the stopping criterion. The proposed method presented fewer items than the others, indicating that it improves the CAT efficiency.

The column "High *a* (SD)" indicates the average number of item selections that are included in the 20 percent high *a* parameter items in the item bank. The results also show that the proposed method provides the least bias in terms of item selection, thereby easing the item selection bias problem.

The column "Time" means the computation time for one item selection. EVTI had a computation time of much less than 1.0 (represented by <<1.0). These results demonstrate that the proposed method dynamically improves upon the computation time of the conventional methods. It provides the best estimation accuracy and the most efficient item selection, thus making it suitable for putting the CAT algorithm into actual practice.

Table 1. Comparison of item selection methods

Method	MSE (SD)	Number of items (SD)	Time (SD)/sec	High *a* (SD)
Item Bank I = 100				
MI	1.54 (.82)	43.06 (24.82)	5.99 (19.47)	241.09 (64.66)
MGI	1.55 (.82)	43.26 (23.84)	5.65 (12.89)	242.07 (69.36)
MLWI	1.56 (.82)	45.76 (25.05)	4.87 (15.21)	259.06 (67.41)
MEPWI	1.42 (.79)	29.21 (19.63)	7.13 (10.98)	157.88 (95.19)
EVTI	1.37 (.36)	28.74 (21.71)	<<1.0	146.88 (127.90)
Item Bank I = 500				
MI	1.74 (.93)	191.50 (124.91)	6.29 (22.84)	240.40 (35.27)
MGI	1.75 (.95)	194.78 (127.91)	19.12 (19.53)	223.96 (28.97)
MLWI	1.88 (.91)	203.65 (122.02)	8.36 (5.22)	252.94 (16.64)
MEPWI	1.60 (.87)	72.50 (63.56)	46.38 (79.16)	80.79 (61.12)
EVTI	0.78 (.32)	68.42 (59.04)	<<1.0	78.90 (65.75)
Item Bank I = 1000				
MI	2.12 (.93)	484.85 (286.68)	11.20 (44.35)	312.10 (45.57)
MGI	2.06 (.97)	467.15 (302.96)	22.20 (78.16)	308.71 (45.78)
MLWI	2.09 (.94)	488.00 (289.19)	9.81 (26.31)	320.61 (43.53)
MEPWI	1.80 (.87)	95.08 (164.10)	83.88 (120.52)	103.58 (113.63)
EVTI	1.74 (.84)	92.37 (158.48)	<<1.0	98.76 (70.84)

References

1. Birnbaum, A.: Some Latent Trait Models and Their Use in Inferring an Examinee's Ability. In: Lord, F.M., Novick, M.R. (eds.) Statistical Theories of Mental Test Scores, pp. 395–479. Addison-Wesley (1968)

2. Chang, H.-H., Ying, Z.: A global information approach to computerized adaptive testing. Applied Psychological Measurement 20(3), 213–229 (1966)
3. Veerkamp, W.J.J., Berger, M.P.F.: Some New Item Selection Criteria for Adaptive Testing. Journal of Educational and Behavioral Statistics 2(2), 203–226 (1997)
4. van der Linden, W.J.: Bayesian item selection criteria for adaptive testing. Psychometrika 63(2), 201–216 (1998)
5. Raiffa, H., Schlaifer, R.: Applied Statistical Decision Theory. Harvard Business School Publications (1961)

Trust-Based Recommendations for Scientific Papers Based on the Researcher's Current Interest

Shaikhah Alotaibi and Julita Vassileva

Department of Computer Science, University of Saskatchewan, 176 Thorvaldson Bldg., 110 Science Place, Saskatoon, SK, Canada
Shaikhah.otaibi@usask.ca, jiv@cs.usask.ca

Abstract. Social reference management systems, such as Mendeley, Zotero or CiteUlike offer many services to their users: finding and managing references, finding other users, grouping users with similar research interests. Harnessing these systems to build personalized recommendations could be useful both for novice researchers (graduate students) and for experienced researchers to keep them updated in their areas. We propose a trust-based hybrid recommender system that infers the user's ratings of papers and builds a social trust network for an area of recent research interest. We will evaluate the accuracy of predicting the most relevant papers for the current interest and experience level of the researcher and the user satisfaction of the system.

Keywords: recommender system, personalization, trust and reputation, user modeling, hybrid approach, digital library, information retrieval, social network.

1 Introduction

With the increasing number of digital libraries with vast amount of published papers, researchers face a challenge of finding papers that fulfill their needs and finding other researchers who share the same research interest. Now, most researchers use social reference management systems such as Mendeley, CiteUlike or Zotero, which help them to find, bookmark or save locally, annotate and manage the papers that they need for research. These systems also allow researchers communicate and share their collections with other researchers. To alleviate the effect of data overload, many recommender systems have been built. In this paper, we propose a personalized recommender system that suggests the most related papers to read based on users' shared data in a social reference management system. Our objective is to both improve the quality of the paper recommendations and to increase user satisfaction with the recommendations. The evaluation of the proposed algorithm will use standard metrics of precision and recall, as well as a comparison to the existing methods that use either citation analysis or usage analysis of the papers. A user study will follow to evaluate the user satisfaction with the implemented algorithm using Mendeley.

K. Yacef et al. (Eds.): AIED 2013, LNAI 7926, pp. 717–720, 2013.

2 Overview of the Proposed Approach

Our algorithm work at two layers: the papers' layer connects papers through citation and the researchers' layer connects researchers through their social relationships. Each researcher in the second layer is connected to his/her papers in the first layer through his/her papers in the library (published and bookmarked papers). In order to collect the candidate papers (CP), we start from the papers in the active researcher's library and the libraries of other researchers with whom the active researcher is connected to. Then the algorithm cascades to include papers that have citation connections in the papers' layer (papers that reference or cite papers in the library).

In the second layer, a social model of each user is built that represents the mutual relationships of trust between the researchers in the online social network and the overall reputation of researchers. We use three types of trust evidence as follows: the active researcher A trusts another researcher B if the two researchers have significant overlap in their libraries, thus representing the trust of A trust in B's interests and trust his criteria for bookmarking papers. Second, the trust value of B can also be increased if B is the author of some papers in A's library (authority trust). The third evidence of trust is when A's trust in B' knowledge in specific topic. This trust is computed when B has more papers about the same topic in his library than A. These three different values of trust are combined to produce one value that is used in the recommendation. In addition, we consider the reputation of the author of the paper (represented by a measure such as the h-index). That is necessary to avoid a bias in the recommendation against new papers, because recently published papers usually do not have enough citations. We also include the researchers' ratings of the papers which could be explicit or implicit. Explicit ratings are those assigned directly by the researchers to the papers. Implicit ratings are inferred by our algorithm. We use three kinds of implicit ratings. First, if the researcher adds a paper to his/her library, we interpret this as an implicit positive rating. We use binary ratings (1 for papers in the researcher's library, and 0 otherwise). Second, similar to [1] we generate implicit ratings based on the citations of the paper. If paper cites other papers, this means it rates them positively. Last, if the candidate paper is in the library of other researcher who is trusted by the active researcher, as explained in the next paragraph, we consider this also as an implicit positive rating of the paper.

We need first to construct the researcher's profile to reflect his/her interests. It is important also to model the expertise of the user, since the reading goals of junior researchers and senior researchers are different. Senior researchers are distinguished from junior by the number of publications authored by them and by their goals. Senior researchers have already a publication record that reflects their interests and it can be used to bootstrap their profiles. Their goal is to keep up to date with new interesting research in the area. In contrast, junior researchers have no publication record of their own (in this our approach differs from [2] which requires at least one publication for junior researchers). Their interests can be inferred from the list of their bookmarked (saved in their libraries) papers. Their goal is to learn about the area, and they need to be guided through review papers and important "milestone" papers in the field. We use the researcher's papers (published or bookmarked) in the researcher's library to construct the researcher's profile feature vector using lexical analysis of the texts of papers (title, abstract and keywords) and the TF/IDF metric. In order to keep the profile in line with the most recent research interests of the researcher, we attach a time-stamp with each added term to the feature vector. Then, the timestamp is updated each time a new paper containing this term is added to the library. By using that, we can keep track of recent research by monitoring which terms have recent timestamps. To the best of our knowledge, this idea of updating researcher's interest has not been proposed before. After the researcher profile is constructed, the papers that could be recommended (CPs) are collected. Then the filtering begins on the citation layer: the content similarity between the CP and the researcher's profile is computed to select the most related papers to the researcher's current interest. Then, a score for each CP is computed by checking if the researchers trusted by the user have the paper in their libraries evaluating the CP quality based on the implicit and explicit ratings they have given to the CP, the citation count of the CP and in general how many other researchers have this paper in their library (readership measure), reputation of the author of the CP (using the h-index). Each of these criteria is assigned a weight; for example, the citation count is given higher weight for older papers whereas the readership is given a higher weight for recent papers. After the weights are assigned, the ranking of the CP is computed. Fig. 1 shows the steps of obtaining the list of recommended papers. Researchers will be shown their libraries with the papers ranked using our algorithm in addition to a ranked list of new papers.

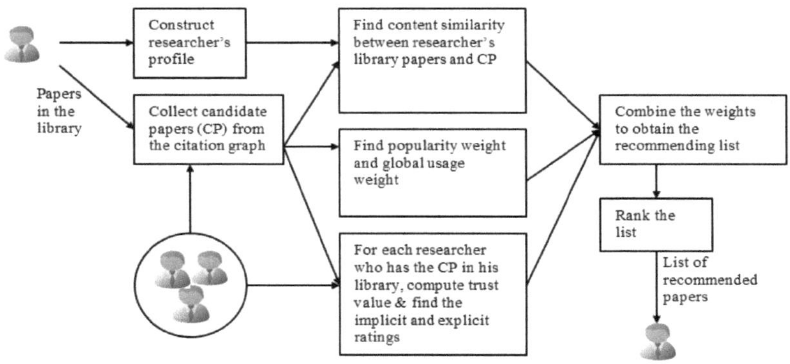

Fig. 1. The steps of obtaining the recommended list of papers

3 Related Work

Torres et al. [1] has introduced the notion of implicit rating by considering all of the papers appearing in a paper's reference list as a positive rating of these papers. They developed TechLens and its extension TechLens+ that use the implicit ratings. Other methods of inferring implicit ratings of a paper is through the usage data (i.e. the clickstream and number of downloads) [3]. Some hybrid recommender systems, such as Papyres [4], use explicit ratings for ten different qualities of a paper which are orthogonal to the semantic content of the paper (i.e. originality, readability). This approach helps in finding papers with certain qualities, i.e. the most readable papers or more well-organized papers. ScienStein [5] is also a hybrid recommender system that is similar to our approach. It uses two ways of implicit rating: by using the citations and by monitoring users' actions (i.e. annotation, highlighting text, downloading or printing the paper, sending it to a friend) to infer the user preferences that are then used to provide the recommendations. The system also allows users to rate the papers explicitly, but unlike to our approach, the trust and reputation relationships have not been used.

Our approach extends the ideas proposed in the previous work by including trust between the active researcher and the researchers who are connected with him/her. There exists other previous work that uses models of trust. PubRec [6] computes trust in researchers with respect to different topic categories depending on how many papers they have in a topic category. A two-layers approach similar to our approach is proposed in [7], where the paper recommendation is based on reviews of people who are trusted by the active user. However, only one trust dimension is used, considering as trusted - those users that rate similarly the same papers. Instead, we use three evidence types of trust: interest and authority, knowledge and rating similarity.

4 Summary and Future Work

The main contribution of our approach is that it combines content-based and collaborative filtering, citation-based and usage-based methods, implicit and explicit ratings, and a three-level trust model to generate recommendations suited for both junior and senior researchers. We are currently implementing the algorithm. It will be first evaluated for accuracy using a dataset and after that in an empirical study to evaluate the system and the user satisfaction in Mendeley.

References

1. Torres, R., McNee, S.M., Abel, M., Konstan, J.A., Riedl, J.: Enhancing digital libraries with TechLens+. In: Proc. ACM/IEEE-CS, pp. 228–236. ACM, New York (2004)
2. Sugiyama, K., Kan, M.-Y.: Scholarly paper recommendation via user's recent research interests. In: Proc. AGC/DL, pp. 29–38. ACM, New York (2010)
3. Pohl, S., Radlinski, F., Joachims, T.: Recommending related papers based on digital library access records. In: Proc. of ACM/IEEE-CS, pp. 417–418. ACM, New York (2007)
4. Naak, A., Hage, H., Aimeur, E.: Papyres: A Research Paper Management System. In: IEEE Conference on E-Commerce Technology and the Fifth IEEE Conference on Enterprise Computing, E-Commerce and E-Services, pp. 201–208 (2008)
5. Beel, J., Hentschel, C.: Scienstein – A Research Paper Recommender System. In: Proc. ICETiC, Virudhunagar (India), pp. 309–315 (2009)
6. Pera, M., Ng, Y.-K.: A personalized recommendation system on scholarly publications. In: Proc. ACM-CIKM, pp. 2133–2136. ACM, New York (2011)
7. Hess, C., Stein, K., Schlieder, C.: Trust-enhanced visibility for personalized document recommendations. In: SAC 2006, pp. 1865–1869. ACM, New York (2006)

Modelling Students' Knowledge of Ethics

Mayya Sharipova and Gordon McCalla

ARIES Lab, Dept. of Computer Science, University of Saskatchewan
{m.sharipova,gordon.mccalla}@usask.ca

Abstract. To accurately model and represent student knowledge is a challenging task, and it is especially difficult for ill-defined domains, characterized by uncertainty and ambiguity. We propose a way to represent students' positions as they analyze case studies in the Professional Ethics domain. We designed our representation with the goal not only to model students' knowledge, but also to encourage positive behaviour in students, and increase the quality of their case analyses. As our experiment demonstrates our representation was successful in stimulating certain desired actions in students, but didn't seem to significantly affect the quality of students' case analyses.

Keywords: ethics education, ill-defined domain, student model, LSA.

1 Introduction

Adequate assessment of students' knowledge in an ethics class has always been challenging. How can we tell that a student has "learned" ethics, and what distinguishes a student who did well in ethics from a student who did poorly?

Goldin, Ashley and Pinkus [1] developed an instrument for assessing students' case analyses in bioengineering ethics. The assessment of the student's performance is based on how well the student has grasped higher-level moral reasoning skills. The core of these skills is the student's ability to label, define, and apply general and professional ethics concepts to the case study.

Lynch et al. [2] adopted a more quantifiable perspective on the assessment of argumentation skills of students. Their assessment is based on the structure of the argument diagrams that students make in the LARGO system. They found out that different characteristics of students' argument diagrams are predictive of students' aptitude and expertise. Although their study was designed for the legal argumentation, the similar ill-defined nature of the legal domain makes the discussion of Lynch et al.'s paper applicable to the ethics domain as well.

Goldin et al.'s approach is largely based on human evaluation, and Lynch et al.'s method is more of an assessment of the structure of students' arguments rather than their content. This paper proposes a new way to organize computer modelling of learners' knowledge of ethics based on the content of their arguments. Students are assessed by a computer system called Umka as they analyze an ethical case study. The assessment is then fed back to the students in a visualization that helps the students to judge the worth of their arguments. This visualization is the core contribution of this paper.

K. Yacef et al. (Eds.): AIED 2013, LNAI 7926, pp. 721–724, 2013.

2 The Visualization

We have developed a system called Umka where learners analyze a given case study (Figure 1). They do an individual analysis in which they propose actions to resolve dilemma(s) in a case study and provide arguments why a particular action is good or bad. In a follow-up collaborative stage, students can access the analyses of other students, read and comment on each other's arguments, and incorporate each other's arguments into individual analyses if necessary.

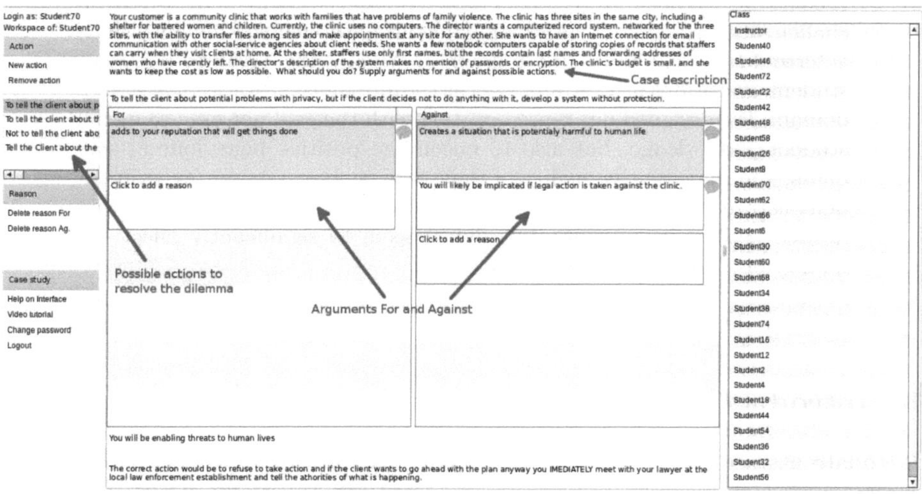

Fig. 1. A screenshot of the Umka system

As learners analyze the case study, we wanted to show them how they are doing. We have come up with a visualization that represents a student's position as a circle (Figure 2). Three things are reflected in this visualization:

1. The size of the circle reflects the breadth of the student's position, which is determined by the number of different arguments the student has for and against a particular action in a case study.
2. The darkness of the circle reflects the well-formedness of the student's position. The more the arguments and comments of the student are accepted by others, the more well-formed is his position, and the darker is his circle.
3. The distance between circles of different students reflects the distance or contrast in their positions. The more distant are two circles, the more different are the positions of the two respective students.

Students should aim to achieve a big and dark circle for each position they take, indicating that they have reached a broad and well-formed position about a given ethical dilemma through interaction with other students. To calculate the number of diverse arguments in a student's position, and the semantic distance between positions of students, we used latent semantic analysis (LSA) [3].

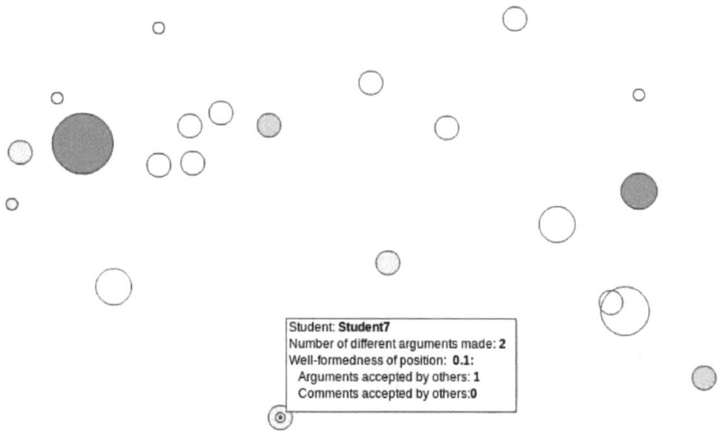

Fig. 2. The visualization. A student sees his/her position as a red circle, and positions of other students - as blue circles.

3 Experiments and Results

3.1 Hypotheses and Experiment

We expected that the proposed visualization in the Umka system would stimulate personal reflection, and collaboration between students. Our expectations can be distilled into the two following hypotheses:

Hypothesis 1: The visualization positively affects students' behaviour. Students will interact more with each other, introduce more arguments, and look for positions of other students that are broad (big), well-formed (dark) or very different from their own (distant).

Hypothesis 2: The visualization positively affects the quality of students' ethical analysis. Students will make more arguments and more contrasting arguments, and better arguments overall.

To validate our hypotheses we conducted an experiment with 44 students taking a "Computer Systems Ethics" seminar at a local public institution. We randomly divided students into two groups: 1) treatment group - those who used the Umka system with the visualization 2) control group - those who used Umka without the visualization.

3.2 Results

Our experiments confirmed our first hypothesis. Students tend to view positions of other students that are broad, well-formed or contrasting, presumably looking for more ideas, confirmed ideas or diverse opinions. We also observed two other positive effects of the visualization: 1) statistically significant increase in students' interaction with each other - the number of comments per student was significantly higher; and 2) increase in students' revisions of their arguments - students added and revised their arguments more often than in the system without the visualization, but this could not be confirmed statistically.

For the second hypothesis, we noticed that students who used Umka with the visualization had more arguments, and more diverse arguments per student than students who used Umka without the visualization, but these differences were not statistically significant. Talking about the difference in the quality of arguments between the control and treatment groups, we noticed that students in the treatment group had more issues raised in their analyses than the control group. Since this evaluation was essentially qualitative, it was not useful to calculate the statistical significance of it. Thus, although the data is trending in the right direction, our second hypothesis could not be statistically verified by our experiments.

We have also calculated the accuracy of LSA for comparing students' arguments with each other. The accuracy ranged from 0.4 to 0.7, which was comparable to the performance of other tutoring systems that used LSA.

4 Conclusion

In this paper we have proposed a novel way to model students' knowledge of ethics through visualization. We have demonstrated that such an open model stimulates more students' interaction and arguments, and there is some evidence (although not statistically significant evidence) that these arguments are better. We believe the approach described in this paper is an initial demonstration that the computer modelling of learners' knowledge and skills in the ill-defined domain of ethics is not only possible, but also can be organized in a way to further develop these knowledge and skills in learners. The approach may also generalize to other ill-defined domains involving argumentation.

Acknowledgements. The authors wish to thank the Natural Sciences and Engineering Research Council of Canada for their funding of this research project.

References

1. Goldin, I., Ashley, K., Pinkus, R.: Assessing case analyses in bioengineering ethics education: Reliability and training. In: Proceedings of International Conference on Engineering Education, San Juan, Puerto Rico (2006)
2. Lynch, C., Pinkwart, N., Ashley, K., Aleven, V.: What do argument diagrams tell us about students aptitude or experience? A statistical analysis in an ill-defined domain. In: Intelligent Tutoring Systems for Ill-Defined Domains: Assessment and Feedback in Ill-Defined Domains, p. 56 (2008)
3. Landauer, T., McNamara, D., Dennis, S., Kintsch, W.: Handbook of Latent Semantic Analysis. Lawrence Erlbaum Associates Publishers (2007)

System Comparisons: Is There Life after Null?

Natalie B. Steinhauser[1], Gwendolyn E. Campbell[1], Sarah Dehne[2]
Myroslava O. Dzikovska[3], and Johanna D. Moore[3]

[1] Naval Air Warfare Center TSD, Code 4651
12350 Research Parkway, Orlando, FL 32826-3275
{Natalie.Steinhauser,Gwendolyn.Campbell}@navy.mil
[2] Kaegan Corporation, Orlando, FL
Sarah.Dehne.ctr@navy.mil
[3] Human Communication Research Center, University of Edinburgh
{M.Dzikovska,J.Moore}@ed.ac.uk

Abstract. It is common practice to compare gain scores in order to determine the effectiveness of adding features to a training system. Here we argue that relying on one measure of overall system effectiveness may result in overlooking valuable lessons available from a comparison of different versions of a system. To illustrate our point, we present the results of comparing a Natural Language Processing (NLP) based adaptive feedback system to a system that does not utilize NLP capabilities. We show that, while there were no learning gain differences between the two systems, the correlates to gain were different. In the non-NLP system, only student performance during the training was correlated to learning gain. In the adaptive system, more variables correlated with learning, including measures of system capability and student satisfaction. This level of analysis suggests that the two systems are not equivalent and points us towards modifications that may improve effectiveness.

Keywords: Intelligent Tutoring Systems, Adaptive feedback, Natural Language Processing, Effectiveness evaluation.

1 Introduction

When new training systems are created or additional features are added, it is common practice for researchers to compare the systems on learning gain or effect sizes [1]. Comparing systems in this way allows the researcher to determine if there is value added in implementing their system or the new feature. However, is it fair to the system to rely so heavily on one measure of its relative effectiveness? It is not clear how to interpret a null result in this case. Here, we describe a study in which a Natural Language Processing (NLP)-enabled adaptive tutoring system was compared to a system which does not utilize NLP capabilities. The goal of the study was to investigate the value added of incorporating NLP capability into a computer tutoring system.

2 Method

2.1 Data Collection

A four hour lesson, based on overcoming misconceptions and conceptual change, was implemented into the Basic Electronics and Electricity Tutorial Learning Environment II

K. Yacef et al. (Eds.): AIED 2013, LNAI 7926, pp. 725–728, 2013.

(BEETLE II) intelligent tutoring system (ITS) for data collection in this study [2]. The BEETLE II incorporates (1) pre-authored lesson material in the form of a self-paced page-turning slides, (2) A circuit simulator for building and manipulating circuits, and (3) a text-based dialogue box where the tutor and student communicate.

Two versions of BEETLE II were built and compared: an adaptive NLP-enabled version and a non-NLP version. The learning environment, lesson materials, activities and questions were exactly the same in the two versions. The only thing that differed was the type of feedback the students received after answering each question.

The NLP-enabled version of BEETLE II uses a deep wide-coverage parser and a domain-specific interpreter in order to build semantic representations of student input. When a student makes a mistake, the system provides context-specific remediations, gradually increasing the specificity of the remediation, and finally giving the answer away if the student could not improve it after 3 attempts ("bottom-out")[2]. In the non-NLP version of BEETLE II, the system did not attempt to provide any feedback on the accuracy of student answers and simply gave a neutral acknowledgement, followed by a bottom-out after each student answer.

After reviewing the informed consent paperwork, all participants filled out a demographic questionnaire and took a pre-test consisting of 22 multiple choice questions. The participants ran through two lessons in BEETLE II. During the lessons, the computer tutor instructed the student to read slides, build circuits, and asked the student open-ended questions about the material. After every student answer, BEETLE II would provide feedback to the student based on the condition they were assigned to. After the students completed the lessons, they took a post-test which included 21 multiple choice questions and completed the Report on the Enjoyment, Value, and Usability of an Intelligent Tutoring System (REVU-IT) questionnaire [3].

Participants were randomly assigned to either the NLP adaptive or non-NLP condition. There were 35 participants in the adaptive feedback condition whose ages ranged from 18 to 37 years (M = 21). The non-NLP feedback condition consisted of 38 participants aging from 18 to 42 years (M= 21.5).

2.2 Coding Student Utterances

All of the transcripts were coded on several dimensions so that student verbal behavior with the computer tutor could be studied. Two independent raters were able to reliability code accuracy (kappa= 0.69). Each statement was coded as either (a) (fully) correct, (b) (fully) incorrect, (c) incomplete but without any errors (partially correct some missing), (d) Complete but with some errors (partially correct some errors), (e) Incomplete and containing both some correct pieces and some errors (partially correct), or (f) Irrelevant.

Next, we looked for instances where students displayed evidence of using repetitive words and syntactic structures when interacting with the computer tutor. We labeled this behavior “mimicking” [5]. Each time a student re-used a particular statement, we further classified it according to the original source (either one of the student’s own earlier statements or a statement made earlier by the tutor) and the outcome of the student’s re-use (successful or unsuccessful in producing an acceptable answer.) Two independent raters reliably coded the transcripts (kappa = 0.62).

Further, we computed an automated measure of interpretation quality by extracting from the logs the number of student utterances that the system was unable to interpret (which we will call "uninterpretables".) We also calculated the % student or the proportion of the entire tutorial dialogue that was contributed by the student.

3 Results

3.1 Learning Gain

Pre- and post-test scores were calculated in terms of percentage correct. A learning gain score was then calculated for each participant using the formula: (post-test score – pre-test score)/ (1- pre-test score). The adaptive NLP group had a mean learning gain of 0.61 (SD = 0.15). The non-NLP group had a mean learning gain of 0.65 (SD = 0.21). Unfortunately, there was not a significant difference in learning gain between the two groups ($t = 0.88$, $p = 0.38$).

3.2 Correlates to Learning Gain by Condition

A lack of a significant difference in learning gains between the two conditions means that we were not able to provide evidence supporting our hypothesis that adding NLP capability to a tutoring system should improve the effectiveness of that system. However, this is not the same thing as providing evidence that the two systems are equivalent. One way to look more deeply into the comparability (or lack thereof) between the two systems is to see if the same variables moderate the effectiveness of each system by calculating correlations between those variables and learning gain scores within each condition. Hence, we ran correlations with system performance variables and variables from other categories of measures that are likely, based on past research, to predict learning gain.

In the Adaptive NLP-enabled version of BEETLE II, % accurate classification (r= .39, p=.022), % student dialogue (r=.37, p=.031), % correct (r=.42, p=.011), % self mimicking (r=.45, p=.007), % self successful mimicking (r=.40, p=.018), lesson material satisfaction (r=.36, p=.035), simulator satisfaction (r=.55, p=.001), tutor satisfaction (r=.43, p=.010), and overall satisfaction (r=.39, p=.023) were positively correlated with learning gain. Negative correlates included % uninterpretable (r= -.38, p=.026), % incorrect (r= -.47, p=.005), % partially correct (r= -.54, p=.001), and % tutor unsuccessful mimicking (r= -.56, p=.001). Non-significant correlations included % partially correct some missing, % partially correct some error, % self unsuccessful mimicking, and % tutor successful mimicking. In the Non-NLP condition, the only significant correlates to learning gain were % correct (r=.35, p=.03), % incorrect (r= -.41, p<.05), and % partially correct (r=-.34, p=03).

4 Discussion

In our study, a statistical comparison of the average learning gains of our NLP and non-NLP enabled tutoring systems did not support our hypothesis. However, we were able to show distinct differences between the two systems by calculating correlations between potential moderator variables and student learning gains within conditions. Only answer accuracy was correlated to learning gain in the non-NLP enabled system. On the other hand, it appears as if many other factors are correlated with learning gain in the NLP-based adaptive feedback system and thus these correlations do suggest candidate manipulations that may increase the effectiveness of the more advanced system. For example, the significant negative correlation between % uninterpretables and learning gain and the positive correlation between % accurate classification and gain are consistent with the hypothesis that improving the natural language interpretation capability may result in an overall improvement in learning gains.

Other student language-based correlations describe the students with the highest learning gains as the ones who are doing a larger percentage of the talking during the lessons, answering more questions correctly, and generating and reusing effective syntactic and lexical structures when communicating with the computer tutor. It is possible that modifications designed to increase the likelihood of students exhibiting these behaviors may positively impact the effectiveness of the system as well.

In summary, while null results are always discouraging, they should not be interpreted as indicating that two systems are equivalent and that there is nothing more to learn from a data collection effort. Other analyses may help support an argument that the two systems are not equivalent and may even suggest ways in which a system's effectiveness could potentially be improved.

References

1. Van Lehn, K.: The relative effectiveness of human tutoring, intelligent tutoring systems, and other tutoring systems. Educational Psychologist 46(4), 197–221 (2011)
2. Dzikovska, M.O., Bental, D., Moore, J.D., Steinhauser, N.B., Campbell, G.E., Farrow, E., Callaway, C.B.: Intelligent tutoring with natural language support in the BEETLE II system. In: Wolpers, M., Kirschner, P.A., Scheffel, M., Lindstaedt, S., Dimitrova, V. (eds.) EC-TEL 2010. LNCS, vol. 6383, pp. 620–625. Springer, Heidelberg (2010)
3. Dzikovska, M.O., Moore, J.D., Steinhauser, N., Campbell, G.: Exploring User Satisfaction in a Tutorial Dialogue System. In: Proceedings of SIGdial 2011 (2011)
4. Campbell, G.E., Steinhauser, N.B., Dzikovska, M., Moore, J.D., Callaway, C.B., Farrow, E.: The "DeMAND" coding scheme: A "common language" for representing and analyzing student discourse. In: Dimitrova, V., Mizoguchi, R., du Boulay, B., Graesser, A. (eds.) Artificial Intelligence in Education, pp. 665–667. IOS Press, Amsterdam (2009)
5. Steinhauser, N.B., Campbell, G.E., Taylor, L.S., Caine, S., Scott, C., Dzikovska, M.O., Moore, J.D.: Talk like an Electrician: Student dialogue mimicking behavior in an Intelligent Tutoring System. In: Biswas, G., Bull, S., Kay, J., Mitrovic, A. (eds.) AIED 2011. LNCS, vol. 6738, pp. 361–368. Springer, Heidelberg (2011)

Question Generation and Adaptation Using a Bayesian Network of the Learner's Achievements

Michael Wißner[1], Floris Linnebank[2], Jochem Liem[2], Bert Bredeweg[2], and Elisabeth André[1]

[1] Human Centered Multimedia, Augsburg University, Germany
{wissner,andre}@informatik.uni-augsburg.de
[2] Informatics Institute, University of Amsterdam, The Netherlands
{f.e.linnebank,j.liem,b.bredeweg}@uva.nl

Abstract. This paper presents a domain independent question generation and interaction procedure that automatically generates multiple-choice questions for conceptual models created with Qualitative Reasoning vocabulary. A Bayesian Network is deployed that captures the learning progress based on the answers provided by the learner. The likelihood of concepts being known or unknown on behalf of the learner determines the focus, and the question generator adjusts the contents of its questions accordingly. As a use case, the Quiz mode is introduced.

Keywords: Question Generation, Learner Models, Bayesian Networks, Conceptual Knowledge.

1 Introduction

The DynaLearn project (http://www.DynaLearn.eu) has developed an Interactive Learning Environment (ILE) that supports learners in manipulating conceptual knowledge using Qualitative Reasoning technology [1]. Learners learn by creating conceptual models using the software (an example is shown in Figure 1). However, the ILE can also be used to have learners learn from interacting with an existing model (e.g. made by a teacher, domain expert or maybe a peer). One of the instruments developed for this is the *Quiz*-mode, essentially a question/answering interaction that engages a learner to discover the knowledge captured in an already existing model.

In DynaLearn, specific constraints apply: The question generation has to proceed automatically, be domain independent and adapt to the ongoing learning on behalf of the learner. To illustrate the components and ideas presented, consider the architecture and interaction flow for the Quiz-mode as shown in Figure 2. Everything starts with the learners working on a model, which they *Build* and *Simulate*. Then the Quiz option can be activated and the *Bayesian Network* (BN) for knowledge tracing is built from the *QR model & simulation* (dashed line) (Section 2.1). Next, the *Generate questions* component constructs a *Question list* (Section 2.2). The *Question request* influences this process and as it

K. Yacef et al. (Eds.): AIED 2013, LNAI 7926, pp. 729–732, 2013.

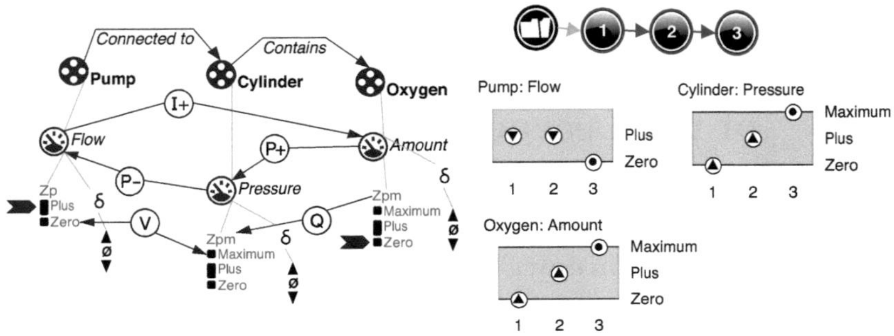

Fig. 1. An example model describing oxygen flow (LHS) along with its simulation results: State-graph and value histories (RHS)

contains those concepts that are least understood by the learner. The *Select question* takes a specific *Question* from the list based on its type (preferring the least asked question types for variety) and difficulty (trying to present a gentle learning curve to the learner). The *Dialogue history* keeps record of all asked questions and can thus support the selection task and prevent obvious repetition. The selected question is then presented to the learner in the form of a multiple-choice question (*Express question*). *Check answer* assesses the answer given by the learner. An answer is either correct or incorrect, and with that information the *Bayesian Network* is updated as well as the *Dialogue history.* The new state of the BN is analyzed by *Determine focus* to establish the next Question request, again based on the now least known concept. The latter feeds into *Generate questions* to steer the next round of the Quiz mode. Each Quiz lasts for a number of interaction rounds until either the system determines that the learner's knowledge of the current model is sufficient, or there are no more questions to ask.

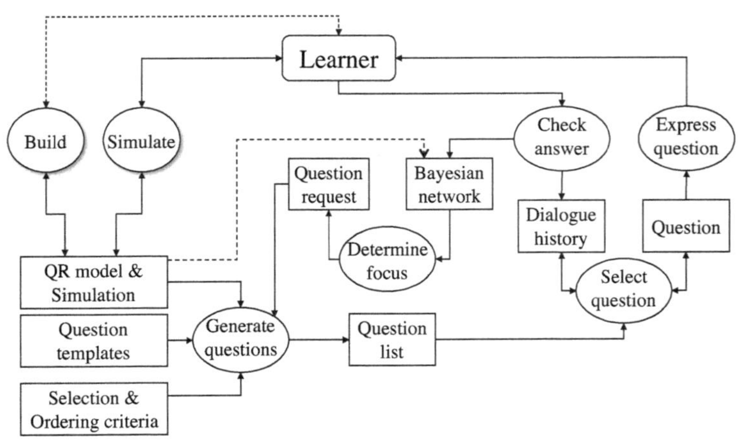

Fig. 2. System Architecture and Data Flow

2 Implementation

2.1 Question Generation

The question generator is based on QUAGS [2]. It is implemented addressing two requirements. First, the component is domain independent. It uses generic ingredient types as the basis to generate questions. These generic types are instantiated with domain specific concepts and therefore the questions are in fact about the domain itself. Second, the number of questions that can be generated for a specific conceptual model and its simulation is enormous. For instance, the Cerrado succession model [3] easily allows for over 72000 questions to be generated. Many of these questions are rather simple and do not necessarily address the key concepts in the model (for instance, asking for the value of each quantity in each state). The generator has two features to ensure that relevant questions are generated and that the total number of questions stays small. One concerns the notion of a focus (Question Request in Figure 2). The generator accepts a focus and adjusts the generation of questions accordingly. In addition, the generator has intrinsic mechanisms that limit the number of questions it will generate (N<16), and that ensures that those generated questions address the most relevant domain facts in the simulation. So, even in the absence of a focus, a limited set of relevant questions will be generated. Finally, QUAGS is augmented to generate multiple choice questions.

2.2 Knowledge Tracing with the BN

From the conceptual model a BN is created to track the learner's performance. Following Millán et al. [4], entities can be regarded as the subject nodes, quantities as the topic nodes and every ingredient associated with a quantity can be regarded as a concept node. That is, for learners to understand an entity, they must know all of its quantities, and to know a quantity, they must understand all the concepts *directly related to it.*

To represent the learner's knowledge of these different concepts, each concept node in our BN can be either *known* or *unknown.* Thus our approach follows ideas as presented by Corbett and Anderson [5]. While their model does not implement *forgetting*, it does take the possibility of *guesses* (a learner does not know the answer but answers correctly) and *slips* (a learner answering wrong despite knowing the answer) into consideration. To represent this in our model, each concept node is given a child node representing one question, and the possibility of guesses and slips is modeled in this question node. Finally, all entity nodes are connected to the node *Model*, which represents the learner's knowledge about the model as a whole and is used to determine whether a model is sufficiently understood by the learner.

However, there is one problem: Imagine an extension of the model shown in Figure 1, but with two containers (a cylinder and a scuba tank), connected by a hose, and the cylinder being filled with oxygen from a pump. This brings up the issue of *recurring concepts*: If a student learns something about one container, they will have learned something about the other as well. Therefore, the idea of *answer collectors* is introduced, which adds an additional layer to the network (between the concept nodes and their question nodes). In case of a concept with multiple instances, each of them will have an answer collector which propagates the evidence from the question node to all the instances. This way, if learners answer a question about one of the instances, their knowledge of all the instances will increase, although the answer collectors will have more impact on "their" instances than on the others.

3 Conclusion

Being able to ask relevant questions is an important requirement for an ILE. We have presented a set of components for creating this functionality within the DynaLearn ILE. The question generation functionality is domain independent. It has a mechanism to ensure that questions are meaningful, and that the total number of questions stays within limits. A BN is used to track the learner's performance and steer the question generator.

Further improvements could address alternative methods for updating the learner's knowledge: Multiple question nodes could be connected to a concept and their exact number would be dependent from the type of concept (more questions for more important concepts). Also each concept currently makes an equal contribution to its quantity's understanding. The approach could be extended to allow for adding weights to concept nodes in the BN, e.g. making magnitudes more important than derivatives. Future research could also address the re-usage of the BN across multiple models of the same domain, since a single QR model can be a part of a bigger domain a learner is supposed to cover. Our BN setup has the basics to incorporate these extensions.

Acknowledgments. This research is co-funded by EC FP7, Project no. 231526, http://www.DynaLearn.eu. Our implementation uses SMILE and GEeNIe from the Decision Systems Laboratory, Univ. of Pittsburgh, http://genie.sis.pitt.edu/.

References

1. Bredeweg, B., Linnebank, F., Bouwer, A., Liem, J.: Garp3 – workbench for qualitative modelling and simulation. Ecological Informatics 4, 263–281 (2009); Special Issue: Qualitative models of ecological systems
2. Goddijn, F., Bouwer, A., Bredeweg, B.: Automatically generating tutoring questions for qualitative simulations. In: Proc. of the 17th Int. Workshop on Qualitative Reasoning, pp. 87–94 (2003)
3. Salles, P., Bredeweg, B.: Modelling population and community dynamics with qualitative reasoning. Ecological Modelling 195, 114–128 (2006)
4. Millán, E., Pérez-de-la-Cruz, J.L., Suarez, E.: Adaptive bayesian networks for multilevel student modelling. In: Gauthier, G., VanLehn, K., Frasson, C. (eds.) ITS 2000. LNCS, vol. 1839, pp. 534–543. Springer, Heidelberg (2000)
5. Corbett, A.T., Anderson, J.R.: Knowledge tracing: Modeling the acquisition of procedural knowledge. UMUAI 4, 253–278 (1995)

Towards Empathic Virtual and Robotic Tutors

Ginevra Castellano[1], Ana Paiva[2], Arvid Kappas[3], Ruth Aylett[4], Helen Hastie[4], Wolmet Barendregt[5], Fernando Nabais[6], and Susan Bull[1]

[1] University of Birmingham, UK
[2] Inst de Engenharia de Sistemas e Computadores Investigação e Desenvolvimento, Portugal
[3] Jacobs University Bremen GmbH, Germany
[4] Heriot-Watt University, UK
[5] Goeteborgs Universitet, Sweden
[6] YDreams-Informatica S.A., Portugal
g.castellano@bham.ac.uk

Abstract. Building on existing work on artificial tutors with human-like capabilities, we describe the EMOTE project approach to harnessing benefits of an artificial embodied tutor in a shared physical space. Embodied in robotic platforms or through virtual agents, EMOTE aims to capture some of the empathic and human elements characterising a traditional teacher. As such, empathy and engagement, abilities key to influencing student learning, are at the core of the EMOTE approach. We present non-verbal and adaptive dialogue challenges for such embodied tutors as a foundation for researchers investigating the potential for empathic tutors that will be accepted by students and teachers.

Keywords: Virtual and robotic tutor, affect recognition, adaptive behaviour.

1 Introduction

Artificial tutors are being developed with the ability to perceive emotions experienced by learners, and to incorporate these into pedagogical strategies [1]. For example, determining the appropriateness of affective interventions by means of empathic strategies as a response to a learner's emotional state [2]; and strategies for keeping students in an affective state that promotes learning [3]. The presence of a tutor, embodied as a 2D or 3D character, has shown some positive learning effects, in particular in student engagement [4]. Recent research on artificial companions has demonstrated the key role that embodiment plays in user perception of an artificial entity: experiments comparing robots with their virtual representations demonstrated that the robotic embodiment was preferred by users in terms of social presence [5], enjoyment [6] and performance [7]. Possible reasons were identified with reference to size, realism, shared physical space, physical presence and perceived social presence [8], which may facilitate the establishment of a social bonding with the artificial entity.

Robot features affecting children's learning and behaviour have also been explored [9]; effects of supportive behaviour of a robotic tutor on children's learning performance and motivation have been considered [10]; and home robots have been found

K. Yacef et al. (Eds.): AIED 2013, LNAI 7926, pp. 733–736, 2013.

more effective for children's learning concentration, learning interest and academic achievement than other types of instructional media [11]. Studies on robotic companions in real world classroom environments [12] indicate that robotic platforms are promising tools for experimental learning.

Automatic recognition of a user's affective state is of primary importance for a virtual agent or robot to establish an affective loop with the user, through generation of an appropriate response [13]. Non-verbal behaviours play a key role in Human-Agent and Human-Robot Interaction, helping the user maintain a social relationship with the robot or agent [14]. Despite advances in expressive behaviour of virtual agents [15], expressive mechanisms for social robots are still, in general, quite limited.

The above opens up opportunities for novel contributions in artificial tutors. This paper introduces some of the central issues to be considered in the design of embodied virtual and robotic agents that take an empathic approach. We present the EMOTE project's approach to addressing the unique challenges, setting out areas underpinning future directions for research into empathic adaptive virtual and robotic tutors.

2 Embodied Empathic Virtual and Robotic Tutors with EMOTE

"Two students are learning about ecology models. They aim to create a model of how acid rain impacts the level of fish in a local stream both in winter, when it contains a lot of cold water, and in summer, when its water level is low and much warmer. They find grasping how the processes affect each other quite difficult and, when completing structured learning activities at their own computers, they get tired and frustrated.

Another option is to work on the activity together at the multi-touch table with the robot tutor Emys. Emys calls up a graphical representation of the processes on the table and asks the children to link them together to create their model. During this activity, Emys tracks their choices and asks questions that set them on the right track while physically pointing at items on the table that scaffold their learning. The students ask Emys questions using buttons on the table and related gestures. Emys encourages the children when they seem uncertain and praises when they succeed. Through their non-verbal responses and progress in the task, Emys confirms that they now understand how to construct this model much more clearly, and suggests a follow-up activity that involves collecting field data to input into the model and offers to come with them on a visit to the stream. They agree and Emys migrates to their phones for the trip."

Following from the vision above, the EMOTE project's aim is to (1) facilitate the building of tutors that enrich learning experiences by:

(a) monitoring the learner's abilities and difficulties throughout learning;
(b) modelling affect-related states experienced by the learner during the learning task and the interaction with the tutor;
(c) providing appropriate feedback to the learner by means of contextualised empathic reactions, adaptive dialogue and personalised learning strategies

and (2) demonstrate the practical (technical and learning) possibilities of achieving this, realised across virtual and robotic embodiments. Figure 1 gives examples of tabletop learning situations with students interacting with the Emys robotic tutor; and gesture/pointing interaction by the Nao robot. Future researchers will then be able to build on the findings as applicable to their own contexts.

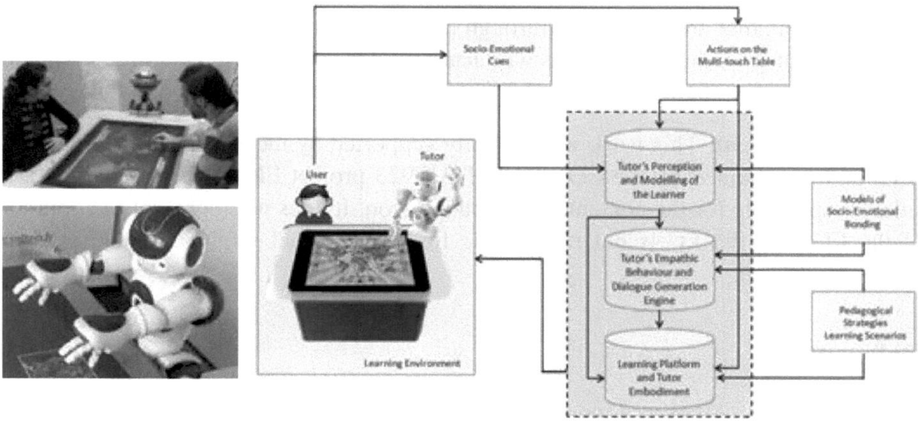

Fig. 1. Tabletop interaction examples and core tutor components

We recommend the following as crucial to the success of embodied empathic virtual and robotic tutors, that may not necessarily apply in other tutor contexts:

- an empathy model allowing tutor understanding of learners' affective states in interaction with both a virtual and robotic embodied tutor.
- Robotic tutors that have perceptive capabilities to engage in empathic interactions with learners in a shared physical space.
- Modelling learner affective states that may emerge during the learning process and related to the interaction with a robotic tutor.
- Development of a set of cues that should create social bonding despite the fact that not all features will be anthropomorphic (for example: emblematic highly synthetic sounds as used in toys and sci-fi movies ("R2-D2").
- Establishing a new paradigm for optimisation of dyadic bonding (by systematically evaluating the role of features such as shared gaze, synchronisation of gestures and sensitivity to certain movements on the side of the human).

Figure 1 also shows the tutor's core components for addressing the unique challenges of an empathic virtual and robotic tutor: the learning interaction (shown here with user, robotic tutor and tabletop), providing information through actions on the multi-touch table, and socio-emotional cues. Along with models of socio-emotional bonding, these contribute to the tutor's perception of learners and learner modelling, allowing, in turn, empathic tutor behaviour based on a dialogue generation engine, also informed by pedagogical strategies. Actions of the embodied tutor will feed back to the learning environment and further influence the tutor's guidance.

3 Summary

The challenges for building successful empathic virtual and robotic tutors are substantial. The EMOTE project's aims include defining and creating a new generation of artificial tutors that are embodied (through a robotic platform and a virtual character) and engage in empathic interactions with learners. This paper presented initial steps in identifying unique challenges for embodied empathic virtual and robotic tutors.

Acknowledgement. This work was partially supported by the European Commission (EC) and was funded by the EU FP7 ICT-317923 project EMOTE. The authors are solely responsible for the content of this publication. It does not represent the opinion of the EC, and the EC is not responsible for any use that might be made of data appearing therein.

References

1. Burleson, W.: Affective Learning Companions: Strategies for Empathetic Agents with Real-Time Multimodal Affective Sensing to Foster Meta-Cognitive and Meta-Affective Approaches to Learning, Motivation, and Perseverance, PhD Thesis, MIT (2006)
2. Robison, J., McQuiggan, S.W., Lester, J.: Evaluating the Consequences of Affective Feedback in Intelligent Tutoring Systems. In: Proceedings of ACII, Amsterdam, pp. 37–42 (2009)
3. Robison, J., McQuiggan, S.W., Lester, J.: Modeling Task-Based vs. Affect-Based Feedback Behavior in Pedagogical Agents: An Inductive Approach. In: AIED 2009, pp. 25–32. IOS Press (2009)
4. McQuiggan, S.W., Lester, J.C.: Modeling and Evaluating Empathy in Embodied Companion Agents. International Journal of Human-Computer Studies 65, 348–360 (2007)
5. Kidd, C.: Sociable Robots: The Role of Presence and Task in Human-Robot Interaction (2003)
6. Pereira, A., Martinho, C., Leite, I., Paiva, A.: iCat the Chess Player: the influence of embodiment in the enjoyment of a game. In: Proceedings of 7th International Joint Conference on AAMAS, Estoril, Portugal, pp. 1253–1256 (2008)
7. Bartneck, C.: eMuu-An Embodied Emotional Character for the Ambient Intelligent Home (2002)
8. Hoffmann, L., Krämer, N.C.: How Should an Artificial Entity be Embodied? Comparing the Effects of a Physically Present Robot and its Virtual Representation. In: Proceedings of Workshop on Social Robotic Telepresence, HRI (2011)
9. Okita, S.Y., Ng-Thow-Hing, V., Sarvadevabhatla, R.K.: Learning Together: ASIMO developing an interactive learning partnership with children. In: Proceedings IEEE Int. Symposium on Robot and Human Interactive Communication, pp. 1125–1130 (2009)
10. Saerbeck, M., Schut, T., Bartneck, C., Janse, M.D.: Expressive Robots in Education: varying the degree of social supportive behavior of a robotic tutor. In: Proceedings of the International Conference on Human Factors in Computing Systems, pp. 1613–1622 (2010)
11. Han, J., Jo, M., Jones, V., Jo, J.H.: Comparative Study on the Educational Use of Home Robots for Children. Journal of Information Processing Systems 4(4) (2008)
12. Leite, L., Castellano, G., Martinho, A., Pereira, C., Paiva, A.: Modelling Empathic Behaviour in a Robotic Game Companion for Children: an Ethnographic Study in Real-World Settings. In: Proc. ACM/IEEE Int. Conference on Human-Robot Interaction (2012)
13. Castellano, G., et al.: Affect Recognition for Interactive Companions: Challenges and design in real-world scenarios. Journal on Multimodal User Interfaces 3(1-2), 89–98 (2010)
14. Breazeal, C.: Emotion and Sociable Humanoid Robots. International Journal of Human-Computer Studies 59, 119–155 (2003)
15. Pelachaud, C.: Multimodal Expressive Embodied Conversational Agents. In: Proceedings of ACM International Conference on Multimedia, pp. 683–689 (1995)

Can Online Peer-Review Systems Support Group Mentorship?

Oluwabunmi Adewoyin and Julita Vassileva

Department of Computer Science
University of Saskatchewan, Canada
Oluwabunmi.adewoyin@usask.ca,
jiv@cs.usask.ca

Abstract. As we are entering the age of open social e-learning environments, group (peer) mentorship becomes an increasingly important mode of learning. The academic peer review system can be viewed as a group mentorship system. Peer reviews have been used for over a century by the research community to provide not only quality control for publishing new research contributions, but also as a way to provide constructive feedback to the authors and help them to improve their work. There are two critical questions that need to be addressed in both peer-review and group peer mentorship: 1) how to motivate reviewers (mentors) to give serious, detailed and constructive feedback, 2) how to find good reviewers (mentors) for a particular author (mentee). This research addresses the above questions in the context of a group online peer-mentorship system aimed at improving the writing skills of university students using a conference peer review model.

Keywords: Group Mentorship, Peer Review, Online Mentorship.

1 Introduction

Since its inception in the 18th century, peer review has become a veritable means of judging the quality of a product or an entity by a community of peers. In the research community, it is a process whereby an author's scholarly work is subjected to scrutiny by peers, who ideally are equally or more knowledgeable in the field. Researchers believed that the peer review system gives a sense of control to their community, and provides feedback that helps improve the quality of published papers. In addition, peer review helps in mentoring researchers, as authors, to further develop their work and knowledge by providing competent peer-criticism. It also helps them develop their ability, as reviewers, to provide fair and constructive criticism of peer's work by seeing the other reviews of the same paper that they have reviewed. Researchers have recently benefitted from the use of web-based conference management systems like EasyChair, Precision Conference and OpenConf, in the peer review of their academic papers.

Mentorship is the relationship between mentor and mentee for the purpose of career or psychosocial benefits. It cuts across different endeavors of life. For example, relationship between graduate students and their academic supervisors and also

K. Yacef et al. (Eds.): AIED 2013, LNAI 7926, pp. 737–741, 2013.

relationship between students and their more knowledgeable peers can be considered mentoring relationships e.g. peer-help systems [4]. One-to-one mentoring matches one mentor to a mentee and it encourages the development of individual relationship between the mentor and the mentee, if the mentoring goes on smoothly. However, it is relatively costly and not time effective. Also, there is possibility of the population of mentees scaling above the available mentors.

Research has shown that group mentoring offers great motivation for positive interaction among the participants [2]. Also, it saves cost and time by engaging more mentees at a time than in one-to-one mentoring. In addition, group mentoring helps to bridge the communication gap that might occur between shy mentees and their mentors as they leverage on their other group members to initiate discussion with their mentors. In situations where mentors are reluctant to check on their mentees out of fear of being intrusive, group mentoring offers mentors a safe ground on which they can check on the group performances and provide collective feedbacks to them. Currently, there are many online mentorship systems that basically do manual pairing of mentors with mentees in one-to-one mentorship (e.g. MentorNet, CyberMentor and myWISEmentor). Therefore, the area of group online mentorship is still relatively new and not well-researched [1].

Peer review system can be viewed as a group peer mentorship system. Besides its usefulness in the research community, peer review is also useful among employees and students, particularly for group peer mentoring (see Table 1).

Table 1. Learning Domains in Peer Review System

Goal	Mentors	Submissions	Reviews	Learning Domain
Improving research and criticism skills	Peers, senior researchers (Program committee members)	Research papers	Peer-reviews of research papers	Academic research
Improving argumentation and writing skills	Peer students	Essays on given topics	Peer-reviews of essays	University / High school learning in Literature, Social Sciences, Philosophy, Ethics
Improving reading summarization skills	Peer students	Summaries / presentations presenting compilation of materials on different topics	Peer-reviews of the summaries or presentations	Graduate level university classes
Improving programming skills	Peer students, open source developers	Documented source code solutions to a programming assignment	Peer-reviews of submitted program source code	Programming, Software Engineering
Seeking career advice	Mentors, peers	Questions or requests for advice, with situation descriptions	Advice from mentors and/ or peers	Professional development, human resources

In a typical peer review system, users can take role as authors, reviewers or both. Authors are allowed to submit their papers and these papers are assigned to reviewers. Reviewers are able to see the other reviews of their assigned papers, modify their reviews and discuss each paper with other reviewers assigned to the paper. Authors are provided with the reviews of their papers and with the decision of either acceptance or rejection. Finally, authors of accepted papers can re-submit the revised papers, taking into account any suggestions given by the reviewers. The question is if these features are sufficient to support online group mentorship. We believe that the features of a typical peer review systems are necessary, but not sufficient to support online group mentorship. Users in a group mentorship system are mentors and mentees. Information about the skills and competence of the mentors, as well as information about the problems and goals of the mentees are used to match mentors to mentees, which is different from the topic-based or bidding-based matching of papers with reviewers in online peer-review systems. The following are the additional questions we want to explore in order for the peer review system to support group online mentorship. **Q 1**: How is the group composed? **Q 2**: How large should the group be? **Q 3**: Should the group members be anonymous or not? **Q 4**: What are the incentives for group members to give high quality feedback to their colleagues? **Q 5**: How do we measure the success of the session?

2 Proposed Solutions to the Questions

To support the group online mentorship system, we propose the following solutions, which we will evaluate in our future research. **Q1:** Peers would be grouped based on their competence. An initial calibration test would be given to all the peers to judge their competence. The test results, in addition to their profile information, will constitute their user model. Also in each group, diversity would be embraced. For example, we do not want peers with low competence to review one another. So, peers with high competence would be grouped with peers that are weaker. We believe that more competent peers would serve as mentors to their less experienced peers in the same group. Also, each group would comprise a senior peer, who provides authoritative feedback on the group performance. **Q2:** Each group would not be too small, in order to save cost and time and not too large because research in optimal group formation has revealed that large group size may negatively affect group cohesion [3]. Therefore, we propose a maximum of 10 members in each group. **Q3:** Peers will remain anonymous in each group, but they will have pseudonyms so they can build continuous identities over multiple sessions and reputation. Also, the senior peer will not be anonymous in order to reinforce their feedback on peer reviews, in case of conflict, and the overall group performance. **Q4:** We propose intrinsic and extrinsic motivations, to encourage peers to give high quality feedback.

(a) *Intrinsic*: We propose that peers in the role of reviewers should get feedback from the authors on the reviews they gave them and also see the reviews given by other reviewers on the same paper. This, we believe, will allow peers to learn from others and will also motivate them to improve on the quality of review they give. We propose also that peers as reviewers should provide feedback on the quality and usefulness of the other reviews on the same paper, given by other peers in their group.

(b) *Extrinsic:* All feedbacks listed in (a) will contain a numeric component. The results for each peer, in their roles as reviewer will be tallied and presented in a public display, thus serving as a public reputation or a leader-board.

Q5: In order to judge the overall success of the review session, we propose that peers provide the evaluation of learning from other reviews and peers as authors also evaluate the learning from all received reviews.

To implement these solutions, we have proposed the mechanism shown in Fig.1and are currently applying it in a fourth year undergraduate class on Ethics and IT at the University of Saskatchewan, where students need to learn argumentation and good writing skills (the application listed in row 2,Table 1). Future work will include developing a peer-mentoring system in 'a particular domain, e.g. graduate students and faculty as their committee members, for young faculty or girls interested in science, technology, engineering and mathematics (STEM) fields.

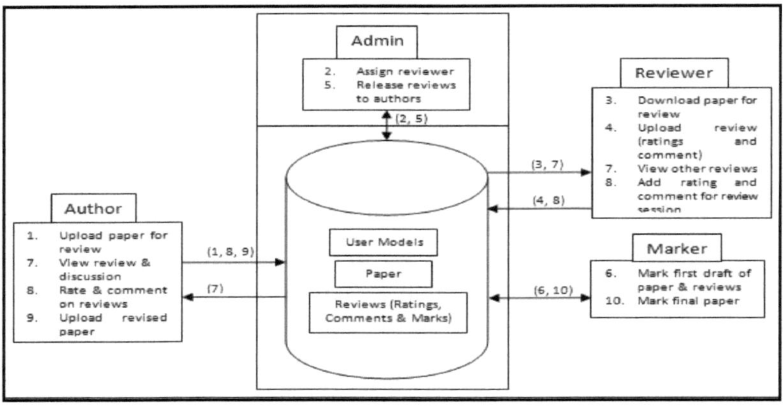

Fig. 1. Workflow of the Group Mentorship System

3 Conclusion

We see untapped potential in using the mechanism of peer-review, with some modifications, to support online group mentorship. These systems are gaining importance with the increase of open social learning environments, where learners can access high-quality learning materials in a wide variety of domains and topics, but currently lack guidance, support, and mentorship that can help them set learning goals, and plan their learning process. Through peer feedback and the feedback from more experienced mentors, they can get direction.

References

1. Adewoyin, O., Vassileva, J.: Recommendation, Trust and Reputation Management in a Group Online Mentorship System. In: Kravcik, M., Santos, O.C., Boticario, J.G., Perez-Marin, D. (eds.) UMAP 2012. CEUR Workshop Proceedings, pp. 53–58 (2012) ISSN 1613-0073
2. Lawrence, E.C., Levy, M., Martin, N., Strother-Taylor, J.: Case Studies in Youth Mentoring, One-on-One and Group Mentoring: An Integrated Approach. U.S. Department of Education, Office of Safe and Drug-Free Schools, Mentoring Resource Center (2008), http://educationnorthwest.org/webfm_send/216 (accessed: March 25, 2012)

3. McKisack, C., Waller, G.: Factors Influencing the Outcome of Group Psychotherapy for Bulimia Nervosa. International Journal of Eating Disorder 22(1), 1–13 (1997)
4. Vassileva, J., Greer, J., McCalla, G., Deters, R., Zapata, D., Mudgal, C., Grant, S.: A Multi-Agent Approach to the Design of Peer-Help Environments. In: Lajoie, S., Vivet, M. (eds.) Artificial Intelligence and Education, pp. 38–45. IOS Press, Amsterdam (1999)

Emotions Detection from Math Exercises by Combining Several Data Sources

Olga C. Santos, Sergio Salmeron-Majadas, and Jesus G. Boticario

aDeNu Research Group, Artificial Intelligence Dept. Computer Science School, UNED
C/Juan del Rosal, 16, Madrid 28040, Spain
{ocsantos,jgb}@dia.uned.es, ssalmeron@bec.uned.es

Abstract. Emotions detection and their management are key issues to provide personalize support in educational scenarios. Literature suggests that combining several input sources can improve the performance of affect recognition. To gain a better understanding of this issue, we carried out a large scale experiment in our laboratory where about 100 participants performed several mathematical exercises while emotional information was gathered from different input sources, including a written emotional report. As a first step, we have explored emotions detection from traditional methods by combining analysis of user behavior when typing this report with sentiment analysis on the text. Moreover, an expert labeled these reports. All these data were used to feed several machine learning algorithms to infer user's emotions. Preliminary results are not conclusive, but lead some light on how to proceed with the analysis.

Keywords: Emotions, Sentiment analysis, Machine learning, Mathematics.

1 Introduction

Affective support can improve the learning performance in educational scenarios, especially when dealing with activities on math as math may awaken different emotions in the learner [1]. For this support, the first step is to properly gather changes in the affective states of the learners while carrying out the educational tasks [2]. Literature shows different input sources from where to obtain affective information of users, such as questionnaires, physiological measures, keyboard and mouse inputs, interactions, facial expressions, posture analysis, pressure on the mouse, etc. Moreover, think aloud methods (which ask participants to make explicit what is implicitly present in the tasks being performed) can be used to give meaning to learners' actions while solving math problems [3]. However, despite the potential benefits of combining different kinds of input sources to improve the performance of affect recognition [4], we have not found in the literature approaches that are based on collecting a wide range of emotional data sources to obtain an extended affect analysis based on the combination of all of them.

In our current research (framed in the MAMIPEC project) we explore the application of affective computing to develop accessible and personalized learning systems that consider a user context where appliances and devices are included in a jointly

K. Yacef et al. (Eds.): AIED 2013, LNAI 7926, pp. 742–745, 2013.

manner to conform a richer and more sensitive user interaction led by affective educational oriented recommendations [5]. In particular, we are considering the following input sources: 1) personality questionnaires, such as the Five Factor Model [6], 2) the Self-Assessment Manikin (SAM) scale [7] to measure valence (pleasantness of the emotion) and arousal (strength of the emotion) dimensions, 3) facial action units computed with Kinect device, 4) webcam video, 5) heart and breath parameters from physiological sensors, 6) mouse movements and keystrokes, and 7) eye tracking.

So far, we have carried out several experiments in our laboratory with nearly 100 participants. In this paper we report on the individual mathematical activities organized by our research group in the Madrid Week of Science (November 2012), which involved 71 participants. All the aforementioned input sources, except the eye tracker, were used to gather data. In order to analyse these data we have used machine learning techniques following an incremental approach. Thus, we have started the analysis of emotions detection from the emotional reports that participants were asked to type throughout the experience. To this we have combined traditional emotions gathering methods: the analysis of keystrokes interactions [8] and sentiment analysis techniques [9] with subjective methods for expressing affective states such as the SAM, as pointed out in other works [10]. This paper focuses on reporting the analysis carried out so far, which includes some preliminary results. To conclude, a discussion of the results and the outline of on-going work are provided.

2 Preliminary Analysis and Results

For the experiment reported in this paper, 71 participants came to our lab and were asked to perform 3 different mathematical tasks: i) average level problems, ii) time-limited problems with insufficient time, and iii) easy and entertaining exercises. Each task consisted of a 6 problem set. For each problem, 4 possible answers were presented, but only one was correct. After each problem, participants were asked to use the SAM scale of 9 points (i.e. from 1 to 9) to provide the valence and arousal perceived by them after answering each problem. Moreover, after each set of problems (i.e. task) was finished they were asked to put in writing what emotions they felt while they were carrying out the task. The idea was to get similar information as the one that can be obtained with the think aloud method, provided that users do not talk as they were solving problems because this would have introduced noise in the physiological measures. Besides, by having the participants typing their emotions about the task, we were able to perform interaction analysis on their keystrokes.

In addition, emotional reports were labelled by an expert to identify participants' valences from the written text (i.e. intrinsic attractiveness -positive valence-, aversiveness -negative valence-, no valence –neutral-, or ambivalence –both positive and negative valence-). Furthermore, the average SAM scores (valence and arousal) given by each participant for the mathematical problems of each task were computed. All these labels, namely SAM averages and the expert emotional validation of the reports per each task were use to feed the machine learning algorithms. Data mining was applied on the data collected from the emotional report. We used MPQA Opinion

Corpus affective database[1] to carry out a sentiment analysis on the text and counted the terms with positive valence and negative valence, producing a similar categorization as the expert (positive, negative, neutral and ambivalence). Since the database is in English and our texts were in Spanish, we used Google translator, which in our view was a reasonable approach as the translation per word is supposed to be sufficient accurate. In turn, we analysed the keystrokes interaction that took place while typing the emotional report. Typical indicators such as typing speed, average time among key pressed or pressing specific keys such as "del" were computed from the key interactions logged using the keyboard hook provided by kSquared.de[2].

Our first target using different machine learning algorithms and various mining options was to look for correlations among the indicators involved, namely text mining scores, keyboard interactions, SAM values and experts labelling. Weak correlations (around 0.3) appeared between text mining scores and the expert's evaluation and SAM valence average values (slightly better if automated binning was used).

Being able to compute user's emotional valence without requesting users to neither fill in the SAM scale nor get the expert evaluation is our ultimate goal. We have studied several alternatives to this end covering supervised and unsupervised machine learning approaches. We started using clustering techniques such as k-means to see if there were hidden associations in the collected data but no correlations were found. Other alternatives were also investigated, such as using prediction trees and naïve bayes algorithms on the input data in order to find out if there was a match with the expert's labelling or the tags generated from the SAM valences given by participants. Applying these techniques to the keystroke analysis reported around 60% success rate, and that rate was slightly improved when the text mining data was attached. However, the best success rates (roughly 70%) were achieved by filtering out the text mining records with less than a difference of 3 in the frequency of affective words (i.e. positive words minus negative words counted from the MPQA database). This result suggests that there is an open issue in coping with neutral and ambivalence texts. As another alternative, we computed the overall emotion experienced by each participant during the activity by grouping all the records by user id, calculating the mean of their values. This last approach gave us prediction rates up to 63%.

3 Discussion and On-Going Work

There are some issues that may have affected this experience and its results. In particular, note that we have used SAM scores and the expert's valence as labels for setting up the machine learning data sets. The expert commented that she was having some doubts while assigning the valence to texts, which might be one reason for the weak correlation that was found with SAM values. To clarify this issue and obtaining a more exact expert labeling we are currently involving three more experts in the evaluation of texts. Hopefully with the revised labeling from this new analysis, we will be able to check if there are correlations among experts' values, SAM values and

[1] `http://mpqa.cs.pitt.edu/`

[2] `http://ksquared.de/blog/2011/07/java-global-system-hook/`

sentiment analysis. Another conclusion from the analysis done is that adding the keyboard interaction information did not help much to improve the performance of data mining algorithms. As an alternative approach, we are investigating ways to transform the keystrokes indicators computed into emotional information. Moreover, results gathered suggested that neutral and ambivalence expressions are harder to identify as algorithms performance improved when they were removed, thus additional effort should be put into better characterizing these cases. We also expect that by adding to these data information the rest of the input sources that were gathered in the experiment (e.g. facial expressions, physiological sensors, personality questionnaires…) the mining analysis will be able to find useful correlations among some of them.

Acknowledgments. Authors would like to thank experiments' participants, MAMIPEC project (TIN2011-29221-C03-01) colleagues and the Spanish Government for its funding.

References

1. Goetz, B.T., Frenzel, A.C., Hall, N.C., Pekrun, R.: Antecedents of academic emotions: Testing the internal/external frame of reference model for academic enjoyment. Contemporary Educational Psychology 33(1), 9–33 (2008)
2. Shen, L., Wang, M., Shen, R.: Affective e-Learning: Using "Emotional" Data to Improve Learning in Pervasive Learning Environment. Educational Technology & Society (ETS) 12(2), 176–189 (2009)
3. Tai, M., Woolf, B.P., Arroyo, I.: Using the Think Aloud Method to Observe Students' Help-seeking Behavior in Math Tutoring Software. In: Proceedings of the 2011 IEEE 11th International Conference on Advanced Learning Technologies (2011)
4. Zeng, Z., Pantic, M., Roisman, G.I., Huang, T.S.: A survey of affect recognition methods: audio, visual and spontaneous expressions. IEEE Trans. Pattern Anal. Mach. Intell. 31(1), 39–58 (2009)
5. Santos, O.C., Boticario, J.G., Arevalillo-Herráez, M., Saneiro, M., Cabestrero, R., del Campo, E., Manjarrés-Riesco, A., Moreno-Clari, P., Quirós, P., Salmeron-Majadas, S.: MAMIPEC - Affective Modeling in Inclusive Personalized Educational Scenarios. Bulletin of the Technical Committee on Learning Technology 14(4), 35–38 (2012)
6. Goldberg, L.R.: The structure of phenotypic personality traits. American Psychologist 48(1), 26–34 (1993)
7. Bradley, M.M., Lang, P.J.: Measuring Emotion: The Self-Assessment Manikin and the Semantic Differential. J. of Behavior Therapy and Experimental Psychiatry 25(I), 49–59 (1994)
8. Zimmermann, P., Guttormsen, S., Danuser, B., Gomez, P.: Affective computing–a rationale for measuring mood with mouse and keyboard. International Journal of Occupational Safety and Ergonomics 9(4), 539–551 (2003)
9. Pang, B., Lee, L.: Opinion Mining and Sentiment Analysis. Now Publishers Inc. (2008)
10. Epp, C., Lippold, M., Mandryk, R.L.: Identifying emotional states using keystroke dynamics. In: Annual Conference on Human Factors in Computing Systems, pp. 715–724 (2011)

Illustrations or Graphs: Some Students Benefit from One over the Other

Michael Lipschultz and Diane Litman

Computer Science Department, University of Pittsburgh
{lipschultz,litman}@cs.pitt.edu

Abstract. We examine whether there are differences between students regarding the utility of learning from visual representations (illustrations or graphs) within the context of a typed natural language-based conceptual physics tutoring system. Showing half of the students only illustrations and the other half only graphs, we found that novices benefited from illustrations, whereas non-novices showed no difference.

Keywords: ITS, graphics, dialogue, conceptual physics, student modeling.

1 Introduction

1-on-1 human tutoring is a very effective method of instruction [8]. Intelligent tutoring systems (ITSs) have been developed to provide similar, but computer-based, tutoring; they too are effective at improving student knowledge [11]. ITSs use various representations to convey information, such as through natural language (NL) or through visuals. Our ITS presents visuals within the context of a NL-based tutoring system. Other systems using both tend to present them together. The NL representation may be expository with the visuals showing the concepts being explained [1] or may be more interactive in the form of a dialogue accompanied by a static image [5] or an interactive simulation [4]. These systems present only one kind of visual, which may not be best for students [7,9].

Research suggests novices will benefit from concrete illustrations because they are relatable for those students [7]. Non-novices will benefit more from abstract representations, such as graphs, because the concepts are presented without problem-specific context and so are easier to learn in a context-free way [7]. Therefore, we believe that adapting visual representations to students will improve learning. Some ITSs make use of multiple visual representations, but do not adapt representation selection to learners [10].

We present here the first step towards adapting visuals to learners, by showing either illustrations or graphs during the course of typed dialogue conceptual physics tutoring. We hypothesize novices will learn more when seeing illustrations over graphs during tutoring (hypothesis H1) and that skilled students will learn more when seeing graphs during tutoring over illustrations (hypothesis H2). We find evidence supporting H1, but not for H2.

K. Yacef et al. (Eds.): AIED 2013, LNAI 7926, pp. 746–749, 2013.

Problem Statement: A kangaroo can jump about 1.50 m straight up. What is the magnitude of the take-off velocity?

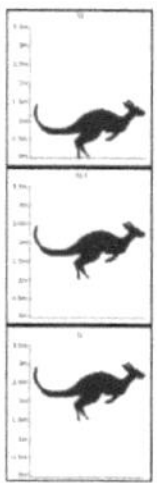

(a) Illustration

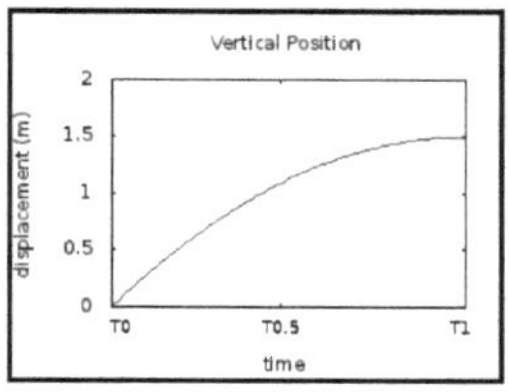

(b) Graph

Tutor$_1$: The figure shown represents the kangaroo's position in the vertical direction. The x-axis is time and the y-axis is vertical position. At what time was the kangaroo's velocity greatest?
Student$_1$: at T1 (top of jump)
Tutor$_2$: I don't think that's right. The kangaroo is moving fastest when it first takes off (at T0). We can see this in the figure. Velocity is the change in position over the change in time. So let's take a look at the change in position at three instances during the jump: beginning, middle, and end.

(c) Start of 1st reflection dialogue

Fig. 1. The first tutoring problem. The problem statement is at the top. Subfigures 1a and 1b show the basic visuals for each condition. Subfigure 1c shows the beginning of the first reflection dialogue.

2 Methods

The experiment compared two conditions: one where students saw only illustrations during tutoring and the other where students saw only graphs. Tutoring consisted of 2 problems and 3 reflection questions per problem, within the Rimac tutoring system [6], which consists of a problem-solving component (Andes [11]) and a post-problem discussion component.

29 college students without college physics were recruited and randomly assigned to one of the conditions. Students in both conditions filled out a background survey, completed the Paper Folding Test (PFT, a standard spatial reasoning test [3]), and read a short text on kinematic physics (the domain tutored).

Students took a pretest (one of two counterbalanced isomorphic tests), consisting of 31 multiple choice questions, to measure their incoming physics knowledge. 5 questions were **problem-solving** or numeric and 26 were **conceptual** questions. Of the conceptual questions, 8 did not include visuals, 9 involved **illustrations**, and 9 involved **graphs** (graph and illustration questions were isomorphic). From these, we have five measures of learning: overall, problem-solving, conceptual, score-illustration, and score-graph.

We trained students to use Rimac, then began tutoring. With the help of a walkthrough dialogue, students first solved a physics problem in Andes [11]. Figure 1 shows the first problem statement. After solving the problem, they began the reflection dialogue, where they reflected on concepts involved in the problem. During this dialogue, up to 7 visuals relevant to each student's condition are shown to help explain concepts (modified versions of Figures 1a, 1b). Figure 1c shows the start of a reflection dialogue. After completing the last reflection dialogue, they repeat for another problem and three reflection dialogues. Both problems and all six reflection questions were approved by physics teachers. At the end, students took a post-test.

3 Results

T-tests confirmed conditions were balanced on pretest score (p=0.943) and PFT (p=0.524). Based on [7], we believed PFT should correlate with score-graph on the pretest but not score-illustration on the pretest. Both correlate (p-values 0.033 and 0.023), suggesting PFT may not measure the spatial reasoning used.

Of the 29 students who participated in the study, 7 did not show learning gains, 5 in the illustration condition and 2 in the graphs. In the following analysis, we consider only the 22 students who had learning gains (including all 29 gave similar, but not significant or trend patterns).

We ran 5 ANCOVAs (1 for each measure of learning) to identify main and interaction effects. For each, the dependent variable was the post-test score, the covariate was the pre-test score, and the independent variables were condition (illustration or graph) and overall pretest score (median split: high or low). Although no main effects, there was a condition-pretest interaction effect for all ANCOVAs, except problem-solving, see Table 1.

H1 is confirmed. For each of the four significant interactions, low pretesters who saw illustrations scored higher than low pretesters seeing graphs.

H2 is not supported. For overall, conceptual, and score-graph, those who saw illustrations scored higher than those who saw graphs. For score-illustration, those who saw graphs scored higher than those who saw illustrations. Comparing this to score-graph, we see that during tutoring better performance on score-graph came from those who saw illustrations and better performance on score-illustration came from those who saw graphs.

Table 1. Pretest score and condition interactions. Cells contain the adjusted post-test scores (percentages out of the total number of questions for that subset of the test, e.g. out of nine for graphs) from the ANCOVAs, with 95% confidence intervals beneath.

Test	Pretest=High		Pretest=Low		Signif. Interaction?
	Illus.	Graph	Illus.	Graph	
N	2	4	7	9	
Overall	0.876 (0.647, 1.106)	0.865 (0.662, 1.069)	0.784 (0.632, 0.935)	0.655 (0.555, 0.755)	Y
P Solving	0.815 (0.476, 1.166)	0.550 (0.474, 1.108)	0.525 (0.376, 0.910)	0.544 (0.307, 0.619)	N
Conceptual	0.876 (0.674, 1.078)	0.870 (0.695, 1.045)	0.817 (0.691, 0.943)	0.694 (0.604, 0.784)	Y
Graphs	0.828 (0.656, 1.001)	0.785 (0.614, 0.957)	0.801 (0.690, 0.911)	0.634 (0.550, 0.718)	Y
Illustrations	0.878 (0.630, 1.127)	0.916 (0.709, 1.124)	0.798 (0.650, 0.946)	0.702 (0.582, 0.821)	Y

4 Conclusions and Future Work

Half of the students saw only illustrations and the other half only graphs within a NL-based conceptual physics ITS. We found that novices benefit from illustrations, but no difference existed for non-novices. Therefore, non-novices might benefit from seeing both representations, alternated according to a schedule, which others have found helps learning [10].

We are now developing a student model for predicting which visual is more beneficial using features found useful in similar tasks [9,2,7] that were collected in this pilot study. With a student model, we plan on evaluating whether an adaptive tutoring system shows greater learning gains than a non-adaptive one in another study.

Acknowledgments. We thank Wenting Xiong, Huy Viet Nguyen, the rest of the Itspoke team, the Rimac team, Jingtao Wang, and Vincent Aleven for their contributions. This research was supported by IES Grant R305A10063 to the University of Pittsburgh. The opinions expressed are those of the authors and do not represent the views of IES or the U.S. DoE.

References

1. Albacete, P.L., VanLehn, K.: Evaluation the effectiveness of a cognitive tutor for fundamental physics concepts. In: Proc. Cog. Sci. Society (2000)
2. Chi, M., VanLehn, K., Litman, D.: Do micro-level tutorial decisions matter: applying reinforcement learning to induce pedagogical tutorial tactics. In: Aleven, V., Kay, J., Mostow, J. (eds.) ITS 2010, Part I. LNCS, vol. 6094, pp. 224–234. Springer, Heidelberg (2010)
3. Ekstrom, R., French, J., Harman, H.: Manual for kit of factor referenced cognitive tests. Educational Testing Service, Princeton (1976)
4. Graesser, A.C., Chipman, P., Haynes, B.C., Olney, A.: AutoTutor: an intelligent tutoring system with mixed-initiative dialogue. IEEE Trans. Educ., 612–618 (2005)
5. Graesser, A.C., Lu, S., Jackson, G.T., Mitchell, H.H., Ventura, M., Olney, A., Louwerse, M.M.: AutoTutor: A tutor with dialogue in natural language. Behavior Research Methods 36(2), 180–192 (2004)
6. Katz, S., Jordan, P., Litman, D., The Rimac Project Team: Rimac: A natural-language dialogue system that engages students in deep reasoning. SREE (2011)
7. Kozhevnikov, M., Motes, M.A., Hegarty, M.: Spatial visualization in physics problem solving. Cognitive Science 31(4), 549–579 (2007)
8. Kulik, C.L.C., Kulik, J.A., Bangert-Drowns, R.L.: Effectiveness of mastery learning programs: A meta-analysis. Review of Educational Research 60(2), 265–299 (1990)
9. Meltzer, D.E.: Relation between students problem-solving performance and representational format. Am. J. Phys. 73, 463 (2005)
10. Rau, M., Rummel, N., Aleven, V., Pacilio, L., Tunc-Pekkan, Z.: How to schedule multiple graphical representations? A classroom experiment with an intelligent tutoring system for fractions. In: ICLS, pp. 64–71 (2012)
11. VanLehn, K., Lynch, C., Schulze, K., Shapiro, J., Shelby, R., Taylor, L., Treacy, D., Weinstein, A., Wintersgill, M.: The Andes physics tutoring system: Lessons learned. IJAIED, 147–204 (2005)

Prosodic Entrainment and Tutoring Dialogue Success

Jesse Thomason, Huy V. Nguyen, and Diane Litman

University of Pittsburgh, Pittsburgh PA 15213

Abstract. This study investigates the relationships between student entrainment to a tutoring dialogue system and learning. By finding the features of prosodic entrainment which correlate with learning, we hope to inform educational dialogue systems aiming to leverage entrainment. We propose a novel method to measure prosodic entrainment and find specific features which correlate with user learning. We also find differences in user entrainment with respect to tutor voice and user gender.

1 Introduction

Spoken dialogue systems offer students one-on-one instruction from a computer tutor. Entrainment occurs when speakers unconsciously mimic one another's voices, diction, and other behaviors [2]. In tutoring dialogues, [7] found entrainment from students with high pre-test scores correlated with learning gain, and [4] found such correlations to learning and negative emotional states. If a system encouraged entrainment from users, as the system in [6] did to improve speech recognition, it might reduce negative states and encourage learning.

Knowing which entrainment features are correlated with learning gain would inform this strategy. We searched an existing intelligent tutoring dialogue system corpus to find such correlations with speech features. There is no standard for measuring prosodic entrainment, though several methods exist. We calculated entrainment with both a recent metric [3] and a new metric we propose.

2 Data and Post-hoc Experiment

Our data comes from an experiment using the ITSPOKE tutoring dialogue system [1]. Each student interacted with either a pre-recorded or synthesized tutor voice. They verbally responded to tutor questions for 5 problem dialogues over one or more sessions. Pre- and post- test scores were recorded. We considered only students who experienced no technical problems, and completed all problem dialogues and a post-experiment survey, which gave us 29 total students. We hypothesized we would find that entrainment:

1 - *positively correlated with learning gain.* Past literature suggests correlations with both learning [4,7] and task success [3].

2 - *was higher for students interacting with the pre-recorded tutor voice.* If true, this would inform a system that elicits entrainment or accommodates.

K. Yacef et al. (Eds.): AIED 2013, LNAI 7926, pp. 750–753, 2013.

3 - *was higher for males.* Psychological research suggests that males entrain more than females when they are in a subservient role of conversation [5]. A system utilizing entrainment may need to consider student gender.

2.1 Entrainment Features

We used openSMILE[1] to extract prosodic features. Specifically, we considered the mean, min, max, and standard deviation of the speech signal amplitude (RMS) and pitch (F0) of every utterance. We captured entrainment on each feature f in two ways. In each, we consider the pre-recorded and synthesized tutor voices as their own speakers.

In the first method, we speaker-normalized each feature value via z-scores and used the metric proposed by [3]. In our domain, it defines entrainment between the student s and tutor t on feature f as $ent(s,t) = -|s_f - t_f|$ where speaker$_f$ is the speaker's mean for f over the dialogue. We denote this entrainment calculation metric **Avg**.

Additionally, we proposed a metric to capture changes in exchange-level similarity throughout a dialogue. For each student s, we divided the dialogue into N consecutive exchanges. Each exchange was a pair of student/tutor utterances where the student s was directly responding to the tutor t. These formed a sequence of exchanges $(n_1, \ldots, n_N)$ where each $n_i = (f_{ti}, f_{si})$, the tutor and student raw feature values on the turns of exchange i. We denote the sequence of the tutor's feature values from the i to jth exchange as $T_i^j = (f_{ti}, f_{ti+1}, \ldots, f_{tj})$ and the student's as $S_i^j = (f_{si}, f_{si+1}, \ldots, f_{sj})$. We give a similarity score which considers preceding exchanges[2] when scoring the current exchange. Specifically, we define $\text{sim}(j) = \text{linreg}_{r^2}(T_3^k, S_3^k), 3 \leq k \leq j$, where linreg_{r^2} is the fit coefficient r^2 of a linear regression between the two sequences. We calculate the entrainment on f for this student/tutor pair as $ent(s,t) = \text{linreg}_r(j, \text{sim}(j)), 3 \leq j \leq N$, where linreg_r is the fit coefficient r of the linear regression between the similarity scores and the number of consecutive exchanges that yielded them. Figure 1 outlines this calculation. We expect $ent(s,t)$ to be more positive on feature f when the student is converging to the tutor's feature f values over the course of the dialogue. We denote this entrainment calculation metric **Reg**.

2.2 Experimental Methods and Results

We judged student learning using normalized learning gain, $NLG = \frac{post-pre}{1-pre}$, then found all significant correlations between our calculated entrainment scores and learning. As in [7], we performed correlation tests for students in high- and low-pretest groups as well. We divided these groups by the median pre-test score (students with median score were not considered). Table 1 summarizes the correlations found between entrainment[3] and learning in these groups.

---

[1] `http://opensmile.sourceforge.net/`

[2] We start with 3 exchanges because a regression is trivial on 2 and undefined on 1.

[3] We denote entrainment scores for a feature by that feature's abbreviated name. Thus, *RMS Max* denotes the entrainment values for the loudness maximum feature.

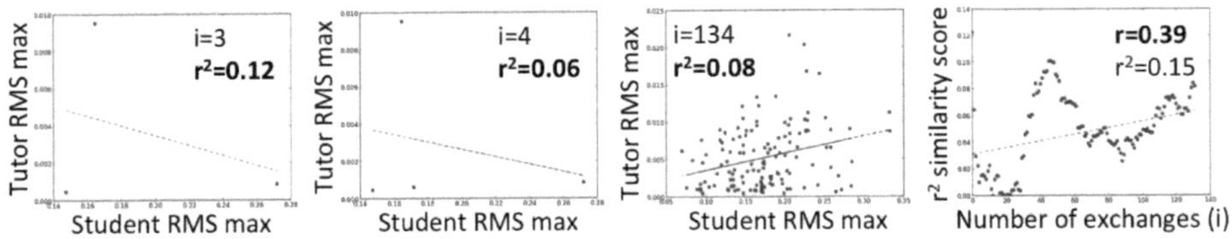

Fig. 1. Each tutor-student exchange was plotted as a point. The similarity r^2 of the linear regression between tutor and student was calculated for the 3rd through Nth exchange. The entrainment score was calculated as the correlation coefficient r of the regression between these similarity scores and the number of exchanges that took place to form them.

Table 1. Correlations of student learning (NLG) with entrainment scores for all students and for low- and high-pretest groups. * denotes significance ($p < 0.05$), while $^+$ denotes a trend ($p < 0.1$).

Group	Metric	Direction	Entrainment
all	Avg	↗	F0 Min$^+$, F0 Max$^+$, F0 Stddev$^+$
low	Reg	↗	RMS Min*
high	Avg	↗	F0 Mean*, F0 Stddev*
high	Reg	↗	F0 Max*

We used Welch's two-tailed t-tests to determine if there were significant differences between users' mean entrainment in the pre-recorded (15 students) and synthesized (14 students) voice conditions or between male (12 students) and female (17 students) mean entrainment. Table 2 summarizes differences found between mean entrainments in those pairs.

Table 2. Differences in entrainment means between students in the pre-recorded versus synthesized condition and between male and female students. * denotes significance ($p < 0.05$), while $^+$ denotes a trend ($p < 0.1$).

Metric	Direction	Entrainment
Avg	pre>syn	F0 Stddev$^+$
Reg	pre>syn	F0 Mean$^+$, F0 Min$^+$
Avg	male>female	RMS Max*, RMS Min*

3 Discussion and Future Work

Returning to our hypotheses, our results suggest the following.

1 - *support.* Learning gain positively correlated with entrainment for several pitch features when considering all students, significantly so for high-pretesters alone, and for the loudness min feature significantly so for low-pretesters alone.

2 - *partial support.* The means of several pitch entrainments in the pre-recorded condition were found higher than those in the synthesized condition.

3 - *support.* Male mean entrainment was significantly higher than female mean entrainment on loudness min and max features.

We support existing claims that entrainment correlates with student performance in intelligent spoken tutor dialogue systems. Our results suggest student entrainment correlates with learning and that tutor voice and gender both affect entrainment. Our new metric for capturing prosodic entrainment in a turn-taking scenario does not require normalization and could be deployed in a live system, unlike that of a recent work [3]. We find that the entrainment correlations it detects complement those detected by the metric used in [3]. Thus the new metric, which captures changes in similarity over time, might be useful in tandem with metrics similar to that of [3], which measure average dialogue similarity.

In the future, we will further analyze differences between our new entrainment metric and those established. We will also explore lexical entrainment. Students may reset their entrained behaviors on new problems or new sessions with the tutor, so we will investigate finer-grained entrainment calculations.

Acknowledgments. We thank the ITSPOKE group for their helpful feedback and the reviewers for their suggestions.

References

1. Forbes-Riley, K., Litman, D., Silliman, S., Tetreault, J.: Comparing Synthesized versus Pre-Recorded Tutor Speech in an Intelligent Tutoring Spoken Dialogue System. In: Proc. 19th International Florida Artificial Intelligence Research Society, Melbourne Beach, FL, pp. 509–514 (2006)
2. Lakin, J.L., Jefferies, V.E., Cheng, C.M., Chartrand, T.L.: The chameleon effect as social glue: Evidence for the evolutionary significance of nonconscious mimicry. Springer Journal of Nonverbal Behavior 27(3), 145–162 (2003)
3. Levitan, R., Gravano, A., Willson, L., Benus, S., Hirschberg, J., Nenkova, A.: Acoustic-Prosodic Entrainment and Social Behavior. In: Proc. Conference of the North American Chapter of the Association for Computational Linguistics: Human Language Technologies (NAACL HLT), pp. 11–19. ACM, Montreal (2012)
4. Mitchell, C.M., Boyer, K.E., Lester, J.C.: From Strangers to Partners: Examining Convergence within a Longitudinal Study of Task-Oriented Dialogue. In: Proc. 13th Annual Meeting of the Special Interest Group on Discourse and Dialogue, pp. 94–98. ACM, Seoul (2012)
5. Pardo, J.S.: On phonetic convergence during conversational interaction. Journal of the Acoustical Society of America 119(4), 2382–2393 (2006)
6. Raux, A., Eskenazi, M.: Non-Native Users in the Let's Go!! Spoken Dialogue System: Dealing with Linguistic Mismatch. In: Proc. NAACL HLT, pp. 217–224 (2004)
7. Ward, A., Litman, D.: Dialog convergence and learning. In: Proc. 13th International Conference on Artificial Intelligence Education, Los Angeles, CA (2007)

Assistance in Building Student Models Using Knowledge Representation and Machine Learning

Sébastien Lallé[1,2], Vanda Luengo[1], and Nathalie Guin[2]

[1] LIG METAH, Joseph Fourier University, Grenoble, France
[2] Université de Lyon, CNRS Université Lyon 1,
LIRIS, UMR5205, F-69622, France
{sebastien.lalle,vanda.luengo}@imag.fr,
Nathalie.Guin@liris.univ-lyon1.fr

Abstract. We propose a method and a first authoring tool to assist the design and implementation of diagnostic techniques. This method is independent from the domain and allows building more than one technique at once. The method is based on knowledge representation and a semi-automatic machine learning algorithm. We tested the method in two domains, surgery and reading English. Techniques built with our method beat the majority class in terms of accuracy.

Keywords: Knowledge diagnostic, authoring tool, machine learning.

1 Introduction

In Technology Enhanced Learning (TEL) systems, knowledge diagnostic is the process of inferring a student model using traces collected from a TEL system during the interactions with the learner. Traces are the record of all actions or interactions of the student with the TEL system. Knowledge diagnostic can be used to adapt the behavior of a TEL system to the learner, like providing feedback or choosing the next exercise to practice. A diagnostic technique is a way to do knowledge diagnostic (i.e. infer a student model), like knowledge tracing [4] or constraint-based [12].

A complex and expensive task is the design and the implementation of diagnostic techniques. Actual methods usually require manual work and strongly depend on a particular diagnostic technique. The problem we address is to propose a more generic method to build and evaluate more than just one diagnostic technique.

The content of this paper is organized as follows: previous work and motivations, presentation of our methodology of assistance, experimental results and conclusion.

2 Related Work and Motivations

There are two main approaches for building diagnostic techniques: manually through authoring tools, and automatically though machine learning. Firstly, authoring tools are environments allowing building a TEL system without programming everything. Some include the design of a diagnostic technique: rules in Eon [11], Model Tracing

K. Yacef et al. (Eds.): AIED 2013, LNAI 7926, pp. 754–757, 2013.

in CTAT [1], and Constraint-based in ASPIRE [9]. These systems often require to design several components of the TEL system (like the interface), and using existing components like complex interfaces is limited. They support only one diagnostic technique. Secondly the goal of machine learning is to instantiate a generic diagnostic technique to a given domain using students' traces. The result is an instantiated or learned diagnostic technique. Some authors discussed this approach for bug libraries [13], Item-to-Item Theory [5], cognitive modeling [7][2]. The main issues of the results of unsupervised algorithms are their interpretability for humans, their plausibility, and thus their utility. These algorithms can learn only one diagnostic technique.

None of these approaches allow building different kinds of diagnostic. This paper addresses this issue. Our proposition is based both on authoring tools and machine learning, aiming to reduce implementation cost but also to keep the interpretability and the utility of the instantiated diagnostic techniques. Motivations include easing the implementation of diagnostic techniques, the comparison of techniques over several datasets, and the choice of one technique for an existing or a new TEL system.

3 Semi-automatic Machine Learning Method

We present in this section our methodology, which we implemented in a first platform. The problem is to assist a designer to instantiate a set of diagnostic techniques for his/her domain, as defined in introduction, thanks to traces. The set of techniques is generic (independent to the learning domains). Instantiate them means to find in traces the different variables required to infer a student model. For instance, what are the skills of the domain, the steps involving each skill?

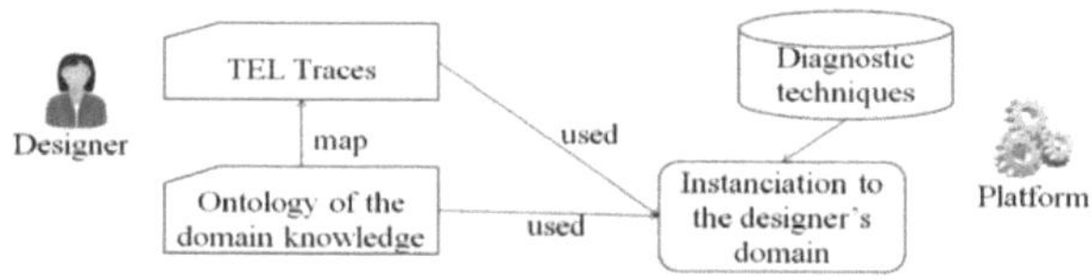

Fig. 1. Schema of the interaction between the user and the platform

We addressed two problems. First, the format of traces is unknown and traces may be incomplete. We propose to add semantic to the traces with an ontology of the domain knowledge. Then, design each diagnostic technique independently may be too fastidious for a designer. We propose a machine learning algorithm to instantiate a set of generic techniques using traces. The set of techniques is stored into the platform using a common representation. Currently the techniques are: Knowledge Tracing [4], Additive Factor Model [3], Constraint-based [12], and Control-based [8].

First we propose to the designers to define an ontology of the domain knowledge, and the ontology is mapped to the traces. The ontology does not depend on a diagnostic technique, and does not have to be complete. The goal is to describe variables in the traces and complete the traces. We impose two main classes in the ontology: observable elements and knowledge elements. All new classes inherit of one of these two. The second step is to map the ontology to the traces. Classes or individuals in the ontology are associated by the designer to variables or elements in the traces. Several variables in the traces can be associated to one class in the ontology.

The machine learning algorithm works in three steps. First it associates the variables in the traces to the variables required by each diagnostic technique, using the ontology and the mapping from the ontology to the traces. Thus, each variable of each technique is mapped to the corresponding elements in the traces. Then it extracts all possible values of the variables in the traces. Finally it learns the required parameters such as the probabilities of the Hidden Markov Model used by Knowledge Tracing. The results depend on the ontology. Our assistance is iterative: user shall start with a basic ontology and complete it until results (the learned techniques) are satisfying. We show below how the platform directly helps to evaluate the learned techniques.

4 Experiments and Results

We applied our approach in two domains, using students' traces. The first set of traces was collected with TELEOS [8] in orthopedic surgery. We got 2695 correct or incorrect interactions (actions) with the tutor. The second set of traces were collected with the Reading Tutor [10]. We got 240,204 words read fluently or not by a student.

We computed and compared in cross validation how well the instantiated technique fit the traces, by measuring their predictive accuracy, i.e. the percent of good predictions at time *t* of the student's answer at time *t+1* (like correct or not). Almost all accuracies beat the majority class (correct actions for TELEOS, words read fluently for Reading Tutor), meaning that the learned diagnostic techniques are more accurate than always predicting the majority class (Table 1).

Table 1. Results for TELEOS and Reading Tutor. 95% confidence intervals in parentheses.

Diagnostic techniques	Knowledge Tracing	Additive Factor Model	Constraint-based	Control-based	Majority class
TELEOS	71% (±2,7%)	70% (±2,8%)	73% (±3,6%)	75% (±3,3%)	54%
Reading Tutor	78% (±3,2%)	78% (±3,9%)	72% (±4,1%)	74% (±3,5%)	74%

5 Conclusion

We proposed a methodology and a first platform for assisting the design and development of different knowledge diagnostic techniques. Our work is independent both from the domain and the diagnostic techniques, allowing building and comparing more than one diagnostic technique. This is new as far as we know. Our method is based on a semi-automatic machine-learning algorithm, driven by an ontology. Results showed accuracies over the majority class in two domains, surgery and reading.

Unlike existing tools, our method is independent from each diagnostic technique, and aims to increase interpretability and utility of learned techniques thanks to the semi-automatic approach. The tradeoff is that a manual work for building the ontology is still required. Choosing a diagnostic technique depends on the goal of the designer, in term of pedagogical strategies implemented in the TEL system, and it is not clear when and why a technique is better than another, as shown in [6]. Our assistance platform can make easier to try, test and compare different techniques.

Future work includes evaluating our platform on more domains, improving the interface of our platform to test its usability, and assisting the design of the ontology.

This work was supported by a PhD scholarship from the Rhone-Alpes Region in France. We thank project LISTEN and TELEOS for the data used in our study.

References

1. Aleven, V., McLaren, B.M., Sewall, J., Koedinger, K.R.: The cognitive tutor authoring tools (CTAT): Preliminary evaluation of efficiency gains. In: Ikeda, M., Ashley, K.D., Chan, T.-W. (eds.) ITS 2006. LNCS, vol. 4053, pp. 61–70. Springer, Heidelberg (2006)
2. Beck, J.E., Woolf, J.E., Beal, C.R.: ADVISOR: a machine-learning architecture for intelligent tutor construction. In: 17th AAAI Conference on Artificial Intelligence, pp. 552–557 (2000)
3. Cen, H., Koedinger, K., Junker, B.: Comparing two IRT models for conjunctive skills. In: Woolf, B.P., Aïmeur, E., Nkambou, R., Lajoie, S. (eds.) ITS 2008. LNCS, vol. 5091, pp. 796–798. Springer, Heidelberg (2008)
4. Corbett, A.T., Anderson, J.R.: Knowledge tracing: Modeling the acquisition of procedural knowledge. User Modelling and User-Adapted Interaction 4, 253–278 (1995)
5. Desmarais, M.C., Meshkinfam, P., Gagnon, M.: Learned student models with item to item knowledge structures. User Modeling and User-Adapted Interaction 16(5), 403–434 (2006)
6. Gong, Y., Beck, J.E., Heffernan, N.T.: How to Construct More Accurate Student Models: Comparing and Optimizing Knowledge Tracing and Performance Factor Analysis. International Journal of Artificial Intelligence in Education 21(1), 27–46 (2011)
7. Gonzales-Brenes, J., Mostow, J.: Dynamic Cognitive Tracing: Towards Unified Discovery of Student and Cognitive Models. In: 5th International Conference on Educational Data Mining, pp. 49–56 (2012)
8. Minh Chieu, V., Luengo, V., Vadcard, L., Tonetti, J.: Student modeling in complex domains: Exploiting symbiosis between temporal Bayesian networks and fine-grained didactical analysis. International Journal of Artificial Intelligence in Education 20(3), 269–301 (2010)
9. Mitrovic, A., Suraweera, P., Martin, B., Zakharov, K., Milik, N., Holland, J.: Authoring constraint-based tutors in ASPIRE. In: Ikeda, M., Ashley, K.D., Chan, T.-W. (eds.) ITS 2006. LNCS, vol. 4053, pp. 41–50. Springer, Heidelberg (2006)
10. Mostow, J., Aist, G.: Evaluating tutors that listen: An overview of Project LISTEN. In: Smart Machines in Education, pp. 169–234. MIT/AAAI Press (2001)
11. Murray, T.: Eon: Authoring tools for content, instructional strategy, student model, and interface design. In: Authoring Tools for Advanced Technology Learning Environments, pp. 309–340 (2003)
12. Ohlsson, S.: Constraint-based student modeling. NATO ASI Series F Computer and Systems Sciences 125, 167–189 (1994)
13. Sison, R., Shimura, M.: Student modeling and machine learning. International Journal of Artificial Intelligence in Education 9(1-2), 128–158 (1998)

Tracking and Dynamic Scenario Adaptation System in Virtual Environment

Kahina Amokrane-Ferka[1], Domitile Lourdeaux[1], and Georges Michel[2]

[1] UTC, HEUDIASYC UMR CNRS 7253
Compiegne, France
[2] AFPA, France
{kahina.amokrane,domitile.lourdeaux}@hds.utc.fr,
Georges.Michel@afpa.fr

Abstract. Technological maturity allows, nowadays, to plan increasingly complex applications. However, on the one hand, such complexity increases the difficulty to propose simultaneous, pedagogical and narrative control as well as some freedom of actions. On the other hand, that complexity makes difficult the tracking of a learner's path. To overcome this limitation, we propose in this paper **1**) a tracking system of learners' actions along with analysis and automatic diagnosis tools of learners' performances and **2**) a scripting model for training in virtual environments combining both a pedagogical control and the emergence of pertinent learning situations.

Keywords: Virtual reality, Serious games, Adaptive scripting, Knowledge Representation.

1 Introduction

Our goal is to propose models to control the dynamic adaptation of a training system, whose objective is twofold. On the one hand, it allows players to freely explore the Virtual Environment (VE) and learn from their errors without constraints or activity guidance. On the other hand, it allows the system to dynamically *control* the learning situations and the total coherence of the scenario.

To adapt the scenario to the learner's behaviors, it is necessary to be able to finely understand what they are doing. Therefore, we propose a learner tracking system based on plan recognition techniques. It is based on the finalized activity that contains mainly the observed procedure in situ, the compromises made by the operators and frequent errors. Our system allows to determine the task performed by the player and committed errors, from observable actions and the effects left in the VE, based on a reference model. In return, our system scripts the VE basing on pedagogical and contextual rules and on two calculated parameters: complexity and severity. These two parameters allow us to select virtual characters behaviors. Note that the application consists of training of babysitters.

K. Yacef et al. (Eds.): AIED 2013, LNAI 7926, pp. 758–761, 2013.

2 Our Proposal

2.1 Task Recognition and Reference Model

Our approach consists in proposing an emergence of relevant learning situations and allows to put the learner in front of varied and controlled situations. We prefer to guide the player through a non-intrusive scripting, to favor an exploratory approach and learning by trial and error. Therefore, the reference model must contain the finalized activity (not only the prescribed procedure but also real, degraded, stressful and complex situations).

To recognize the task performed by the player and the committed errors, we based on formal plan recognition techniques[2]. An approach based on heuristics, proposed in [4] and we adapt it to our needs. This recognition system takes as an input the actions or observable effects in the VE, the reference model; and produces on outputs the tasks performed and errors made by the player. In our system, we distinguished between errors and violations. The errors concern those of CREAM model [3]. The violations concern safety related errors, action errors, target object errors and view point errors[1].

To describe finalized activity, that contains principally the observed procedure in situ, the compromises made by the operators and frequent errors, we proposed, with ergonomists, HAWAI-DL [1]. HAWAI-DL allows ergonomists to do activity analysis and our modules to interpret them. Even if the activity is described previously, but thanks to the hierarchical representation of the activity and the concept of hyperonymous tasks, the player has the freedom to choose his path to reach his goal, crossing from one branch of this tree to another or from one hyperonymous task to another.

2.2 Scripting Using Pedagogical, Contextual and Motivation Concepts

Our system allows a progressive and adaptive learning. To this end, it is based on difficulty levels dynamically adapted during the session. Furthermore, we adapted the learning situations and their difficulties in real time during the session. However, even if giving the learner a total freedom in his choices makes the serious game more attractive, it does not ensure learning. To have the two sides, we added a set of pedagogical and contextual rules, that are based on learning situations defined by the AFPA, according to professional didactics. But these situations are very limited and constrained, do not allow to create unexpected, surprising and unusual situations. To overcome such a limitation, we took into account the main learning situations. Then, we identified several **complexity levels** of situations and events. This complexity level depends on learners actions, nominal task and principal pedagogical situations. To create unique and unexpected game situations, we identified several **severity levels** of actions and events consequences. This severity levels depend on the historical of learner's actions and errors. These complexity and severity levels are recalculated dynamically during the session according to player's activity and learning situations. These two elements allow to play on learner s intrinsic motivation and allow to increase his commitment in history. Complexity and severity also allow to control the generation of virtual characters behaviors (i.e., children). Among a set of possible situations, our system eliminates situations that are not valid, those that have already occurred, and determined those that are more appropriate.

2.3 Trace and Its Replay

As we are in the case of very complex activities, and which require to react quickly, we have not the time to analyze and understand in real time. Naturally, our system provides a trace which allows the trainer and the learner to go back on what have been done, to analyze it and understand all the cause and effect relationships. This trace does not only contain the activity performed by the player, but also all the committed errors, feedbacks and all Performance Criteria (PC) and their values. For each session, a trace is saved in xml format. At the trace replay time, the player can revise everything he did during a session [1].

3 Results

The evaluation of our approach is performed by AFPA learners for real training sessions. The tests were performed in two sessions, with 14 learners for each and during one week. The methodology used is the one which compares two groups: one used our system to learn (experimental group), another learn without our system (Control group). The evaluation considers principally the usability of the feedbacks that we proposed and the PC. At the end of the experiments, a satisfaction questionnaire is filled out by each learner of the group.

The Figure 1 and 2 summarize some comparison results between the two groups regarding the evolution of PC before and after using our system by experimental group and the results of control group, respectively. The results of this experiment show positive effects after the use of our system for learning skills related to child safety. If we consider the differences between the pre-test and post-test results, which means the learning gain at the end of the training

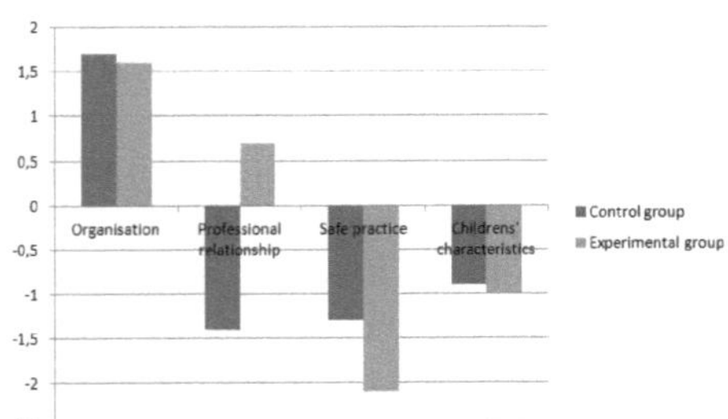

Fig. 1. PC evolution (pres test)

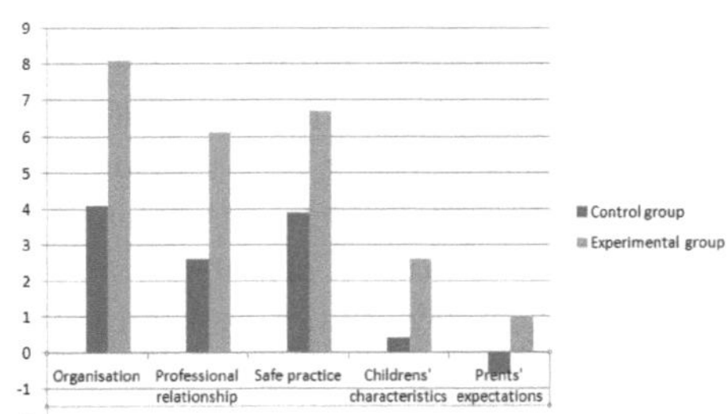

Fig. 2. PC evolution (post test)

week, positive tendency appears in the experimental group. The experimental group gets a larger learning gain for all the criteria and a significant difference occurs on the "Safe Practice" criterion which is fundamental to the child Safety. The questionnaire shows that learners are very satisfied by using our system to learn.

4 Conclusion

In our work, we proposed a serious game equiped with a learner tracking and dynamic scenario adaptation system, which allows to: 1) infer the task performed by the player, 2) determine committed errors and necessary feedbacks (consequences and scenario adaptation), 3) calculate the Performance Criteria, and 4) produce the trace.

Our reference model is tree-based one, which gives the player the freedom to choose paths to achieve his objectives. Furthermore, we added a set of pedagogical and contextual rules based on the professional didactic, which represent key points of our system. To maintain the motivation of the player, we added two concepts: complexity and severity. Dynamic adaptation of the complexity allows to learn concepts in a progressive manner. Thus, the dynamic adaptation of the severity level allows to prevent consequences and to punish the player if he committed this error previously.

For the generation of children's behaviors, our system relies on the world state, the complexity and severity. To allow the player and the trainer to go back on what have been done, a replay of the trace of each session is possible. During this replay, feedbacks and Performance Criteria are displayed.

Acknowledgments. We should like to thank DGCIS which funded this project. We also wish to thank D. Dufour, J. THIERY from UTC, M. ANDRIBET and trainer of AFPA and C. LE MAITRE, K. GUENNOUN from Virtuofacto. Our thought is especially dedicated to Regis Courtalon, the Virtuofacto CEO, who unfortunately left us.

References

1. Amokrane, K., Lourdeaux, D., Burkhardt, J.M.: HERA: Learner Tracking in a Virtual Environment. International Journal of Virtual Reality 7(3), 23–30 (2008)
2. Cohen, P.R., Perrault, C.R., Allen, J.F.: Beyond questionanswering. DTIC Research Report ADA100432 (1981)
3. Hollnagel, E.: The phenotype of erroneous actions. International Journal of Man-Machine Studies 39, 1–32 (1993)
4. El-Kechaï, N., Després, C.: A plan recognition process, based on a task model, for detecting learner's erroneous actions. In: Ikeda, M., Ashley, K.D., Chan, T.-W. (eds.) ITS 2006. LNCS, vol. 4053, pp. 329–338. Springer, Heidelberg (2006)

How to Use Multiple Graphical Representations to Support Conceptual Learning? Research-Based Principles in the Fractions Tutor

Martina A. Rau[1], Vincent Aleven[1], and Nikol Rummel[2]

[1] Human-Computer Interaction Institute, Carnegie Mellon University, Pittsburgh, USA
[2] Universität Bochum, Institute of Education, Germany
{marau,aleven}@cs.cmu.edu, nikol.rummel@rub.de

Abstract. Multiple graphical representations are ubiquitous in educational materials because they serve complementary roles in emphasizing conceptual aspects of the domain. Yet, to benefit robust learning, students have to understand each representation and make connections between them. We describe research-based principles for the use of multiple graphical representations within intelligent tutoring systems (ITSs). These principles are the outcome of a series of iterative classroom experiments with the Fractions Tutor with over 3,000 students. The implementation of these principles into the Fractions Tutor results in robust conceptual learning. To our knowledge, the Fractions Tutor is the first ITS to use multiple graphical representations by implementing research-based principles to support conceptual learning. The instructional design principles we established apply to ITSs across domains.

Keywords: Multiple graphical representations, ITSs, classroom evaluation.

1 Introduction

Multiple graphical representations are used in all science and math domains [1] because they serve complementary roles to illustrate conceptual aspects of the domain content. Yet, multiple representations do not automatically enhance learning [2]). To benefit from them, students need to understand each individual representation, become fluent in using them, and make connections between them.

ITSs provide novel opportunities for supporting students' learning with multiple graphical representations because they can provide individualized support for students' interactions with the representations. However, these opportunities are under-researched, leaving developers of ITSs without guidance on how best to implement instructional support for learning with multiple graphical representations.

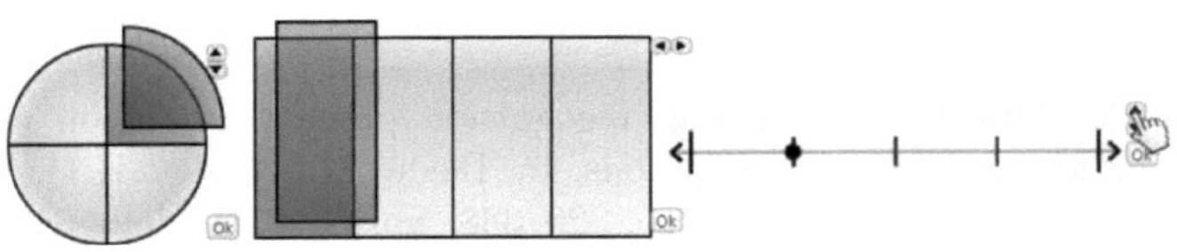

Fig. 1. Interactive representations used in Fractions Tutor: circle, rectangle, number line

K. Yacef et al. (Eds.): AIED 2013, LNAI 7926, pp. 762–765, 2013.

2 Principles for the Use of Multiple Graphical Representations

In this paper, we present a set of instructional design principles for the effective use of multiple graphical representations within ITSs. These principles are the outcome of a sequence of classroom experiments with over 3,000 students in grades 4-6. As part of these experiments, we iteratively improved an ITS for fractions that focuses on conceptual learning [3]. The Fractions Tutor uses multiple interactive, abstract graphical representations (see Fig. 1), provided in addition to text and symbols.

2.1 Use Multiple Graphical Representations to Support Conceptual Learning

A vast literature documents the advantages of dual representations on students' learning [2]: text paired with one graphical representation leads to better learning than text alone. However, it remains an open question whether this advantage extends to *multiple graphical* representations compared to a *single graphical* representation, each provided in addition to text and symbols.

In several experiments, we found that multiple graphical representations lead to better learning of robust conceptual knowledge [3-5], compared to a single graphical representation. Yet, we also found that the advantage of multiple graphical representations on students' conceptual learning depends on what types of instructional support they receive to understand the individual graphical representations, and to make connections between the graphical representations.

2.2 Use Prompts to Support *Understanding* of Graphical Representations

To benefit from multiple graphical representations, students need to conceptually understand how each graphical representation depicts information. We investigated the use of menu-based reflection prompts to support students in making sense of how each graphical representation depicts the concepts of numerator and denominator. In a classroom experiment with 132 students [6], we compared versions of the Fractions Tutor with or without such prompts. Results show that students only benefited from multiple graphical representations when reflection prompts were provided.

2.3 Interleave Topics to Support *Understanding* of Graphical Representations

A vast literature documents the advantages of interleaving learning tasks [e.g., 7]: students learn better when frequently alternating between topics (e.g., when topics a and b are interleaved, a-b-a-b, rather than blocked, a-a-b-b). However, in multi-representational ITSs, problems can vary on two dimensions: topics and graphical representations. Should we interleave topics while blocking representations (e.g., a1-b1-a2-b2, where a and b are topics, and 1 and 2 are representations)? Or should we interleave representations while blocking topics (e.g., a1-a2-b1-b2)?

We investigated this question in a classroom experiment with 158 students [14]. Results show a significant advantage of interleaving topics while blocking graphical representations on students' understanding of graphical representations. This finding demonstrates that interleaving topics while blocking graphical representations is a further means to support students' understanding of graphical representations.

2.4 Interleave Representations to Support *Fluency* with Graphical Representations

Building on the previous experiment, we investigated whether combining interleaved practice with topics *and* interleaved practice with graphical representations supports students in developing fluency with individual graphical representations. Interleaving graphical representations requires students to repeatedly load their knowledge about each graphical representation from long-term memory into working memory. This should strengthen their knowledge about each graphical representation, help them recall this knowledge later on, and thereby promote fluency-building processes.

We investigated this hypothesis in a classroom experiment with 587 students [5]. All students worked on the same tutor problems which were provided in different sequences: graphical representations were either blocked or interleaved. Results show that students learn better when graphical representations are interleaved (in addition to topics being interleaved).

2.5 Support *Connection-Making* between Multiple Graphical Representations

Successful learning of conceptual knowledge of the domain depends on students' ability to make connections between multiple graphical representations. In a classroom experiment with 599 students, we investigated the complementary effects of two types of support for connection making on students' conceptual learning [3]. Sense-making support aims at helping students understand the correspondences between pairs of graphical representations (e.g., circle and number line) based on their structural components [8]. We implemented two types of sense-making support: worked examples [9] which required students to make connections between graphical representations themselves, and with auto-linked graphical representations, where the system automatically presented students with these correspondences [10]. Fluency-building support helps students gain experience in relating graphical representations based on their perceptual properties [11].

Our results demonstrate that only students who received both sense-making support and fluency-building support for connection-making benefited from multiple graphical representations. Furthermore, worked examples were the more effective type of support for sense-making of connections. Only the condition that received worked examples combined with fluency-building support significantly outperformed a single-representation control condition on conceptual knowledge of fractions.

3 Conclusions

We describe a set of instructional design principles for the effective use of multiple graphical representations within ITSs. These principles are the outcome of a series of controlled experiments conducted in real classrooms. The implementation of these principles in the Fractions Tutor results in robust learning of conceptual domain knowledge. Our research shows how the use of an ITS as a research platform can be instrumental to establishing instructional design principles.

Acknowledgements. We thank the NSF REESE-21851-1-1121307, and the IES R305A120734, Ken Koedinger, Richard Scheines, Brian Junker, Mitchell Nathan, Zelha Tunc-Pekkan, Jay Raspat, Mike Ringenberg, Datashop and CTAT.

References

1. NMAP: Foundations for Success: Report of the National Mathematics Advisory Board Panel. U.S. Government Printing Office (2008)
2. Ainsworth, S.: DeFT: A conceptual framework for considering learning with multiple representations. Learning and Instruction 16, 183–198 (2006)
3. Rau, M.A., Aleven, V., Rummel, N., Rohrbach, S.: Sense Making Alone Doesn't Do It: Fluency Matters Too! ITS Support for Robust Learning with Multiple Representations. In: Cerri, S.A., Clancey, W.J., Papadourakis, G., Panourgia, K. (eds.) ITS 2012. LNCS, vol. 7315, pp. 174–184. Springer, Heidelberg (2012)
4. Rau, M.A., Aleven, V., Rummel, N.: Intelligent tutoring systems with multiple representations and self-explanation prompts support learning of fractions. In: Dimitrova, V., et al. (eds.) Proceedings of the 2009 Conference on Artificial Intelligence in Education: Building Learning Systems that Care: From Knowledge Representation to Affective Modelling, pp. 441–448. IOS Press, Amsterdam (2009)
5. Rau, M.A., Rummel, N., Aleven, V., Pacilio, L., Tunc-Pekkan, Z.: How to schedule multiple graphical representations? A classroom experiment with an intelligent tutoring system for fractions. In: Van Aalst, J. (ed.) The Future of Learning: Proceedings of the 10th ICLS, pp. 64–71. ISLS, Sydney (2012)
6. Rau, M.A., Aleven, V., Rummel, N.: Interleaved practice in multi-dimensional learning tasks: which dimension should we interleave? Learning and Instruction 23, 98–114 (2013)
7. de Croock, M.B.M., Van Merrienboër, J.J.G., Paas, F.G.W.C.: High versus low contextual interference in simulation-based training of troubleshooting skills: Effects on transfer performance and invested mental effort. Computers in Human Behavior 14, 249–267 (1998)
8. Seufert, T.: Supporting Coherence Formation in Learning from Multiple Representations. Learning and Instruction 13, 227–237 (2003)
9. Renkl, A.: The worked-out example principle in multimedia learning. In: Mayer, R. (ed.) Cambridge Handbook of Multimedia Learning, pp. 229–246. Cambridge Univ. Press (2005)
10. van der Meij, J., de Jong, T.: Supporting Students' Learning with Multiple Representations in a Simulation-Based Learning Environment. Learning & Instruction 16, 199–212 (2006)
11. Kellman, P., Massey, C., Roth, Z., et al.: Perceptual learning and the technology of expertise: studies in fraction learning and algebra. Pragmatics & Cognition 16, 356–405 (2008)

Using HCI Task Modeling Techniques to Measure How Deeply Students Model

Sylvie Girard, Lishan Zhang, Yoalli Hidalgo-Pontet, Kurt VanLehn,
Winslow Burleson, Maria Elena Chavez-Echeagaray, and Javier Gonzalez-Sanchez

Arizona State University, Computing, Informatics, and Decision Systems Engineering,
Tempe, AZ, 85281, U.S.A.
{sylvie.girard,lzhang90,yhidalgo,kurt.vanlehn,
winslow.burleson,helenchavez,javiergs}@asu.edu

Abstract. User modeling in AIED has been extended in the past decades to include affective and motivational aspects of learner's interaction in intelligent tutoring systems. In order to study those factors, various detectors have been created that classify episodes in log data as gaming, high/low effort on task, robust learning, etc. In this article, we present our method for creating a detector of shallow modeling practices within a meta-tutor instructional system. The detector was defined using HCI (human-computer interaction) task modeling as well as a coding scheme defined by human coders from past users' screen recordings of software use. The detector produced classifications of student behavior that were highly similar to classifications produced by human coders with a kappa of .925.

Keywords: intelligent tutoring system, shallow learning, robust learning, human-computer interaction, task modeling.

1 Introduction

Advances in student modeling in the past two decades enabled the detection of various cognitive [1], meta-cognitive [2], and affective [4] processes during learning based on classification of episodes in log data. Steps have been taken toward detecting when learning occurs [1] and to predict how much of the acquired knowledge students can apply to other situations [2]. However, an obstacle in such research is the lack of generality of the detectors for tutoring systems involving problem solving tasks, especially when trying to gain an understanding of the user's cognitive or metacognitive processes while learning. While some of the indicators used in the literature are common to any intelligent tutoring system, others are closely linked to the activities and pedagogical goals of a specific application. The adaptation of such indicators from one application to another often necessitates a detailed analysis of the new domain and how the tutoring system guides learners to acquire its skills and knowledge. We view the specificity of detectors as unavoidable, so the best solution is to develop good methods for analyzing the new tutoring system and designing the detectors. This short article describes our method and its application to AMT.

K. Yacef et al. (Eds.): AIED 2013, LNAI 7926, pp. 766–769, 2013.

AMT teaches students how to create and test a model of a dynamic system. The instruction is divided into three phases: (1) an introduction phase where students learn basic concepts of dynamic system model construction and how to use the interface; (2) a training phase where students are guided by a tutor and a meta-tutor to create several models; and (3) a transfer phase where all scaffolding is removed from software and students are free to model as they wish. The tutor gives feedback and corrections on domain mistakes. The meta-tutor requires students to follow a goal-reduction problem solving strategy, the Target Node Strategy [6], which decomposes the overall modeling problem into a series of "atomic" modeling problems whose small scope encourages students to engage in deep modeling rather than shallow guess-based modeling strategies. To assess students, the project needed detectors that detect shallow and deep modeling practices both with and without the meta-tutor.

2 Task Modeling: Analysis of User's Actions on Software

A task model is a formal representation of the user's activity in an interactive system. It is represented by a hierarchical task tree to express all sub-activity that enables the user to perform the planned activity. The tasks need to be achieved in a specific order, defined in the task tree by the order operators. In AMT, every modeling activity follows the same procedure involving the same help features, task flow, and meta-tutor interventions. With a single task model of a prototypical modeling task, it is therefore possible to account for all of the user's activity in software. The task modeling language K-MAD and its task model creation and simulation environment, K-MADe [3] were chosen because they enable the creation and replay of scenarios of student's actions and they enable a formal verification of the model.

The task model developed with K-MADe was used to define the episode structure. This established the unit of coding to be used in the next phase. Screen videos representing the learners' use of the AMT software with and without the meta-tutor were recorded during an experimental study described in [6]. These videos were studied to determine how much shallow vs. deep modeling occurred and the contexts, which tended to produce each type. A coding system was then created for video recordings of the learners' behavior. Three iterations of design for this coding scheme were performed, ending with a coding scheme that reached a multi-rater pairwise kappa of .902. The final coding scheme mapped learners' behavior to six classifications, which were implemented as the following depth detectors:

- GOOD_METHOD: The students followed a deep method in their modeling. They used the help tools appropriately, including the one for planning each part of the model.
- VERIFY_INFO: Before checking their step for correctness, students looked back at the problem description, the information provided by the instruction slides, or the meta-tutor agent.
- SINGLE_ANSWER: The student's initial response for this step was correct, and the student did not change it.

- SEVERAL_ANSWERS: The student made more than one attempt at completing the step. This includes guessing and gaming the system:
  - o The user guessed the answer, either by clicking on the correct answer by mistake or luck, or by entering a loop of click and guessing to find the answer.
  - o The user "games the system" by using the immediate feedback given to guess the answer: series of checks on wrong answers that help deduce the right answer.
- UNDO_GOOD_WORK: This action suggests a modeling misconception on the students' part. One example is when students try to run the model when not all of the nodes are fully defined.
- GIVEUP: The student gave up on finding how to do a step and clicked on the "give up" button.

Another detector was defined as a linear function of the six episode detectors. It was intended to measure the overall depth of the students' modeling, therefore providing an outcome measure in the transfer phase in future experimental studies. It considered two measures (GOOD_ANSWER, VERIFY_INFO) to indicate deep modeling, one measure (SINGLE_ANSWER) to be neutral, and three measures (SEVERAL_ANSWERS, UNDO_GOOD_WORK, and GIVE_UP) to indicate shallow modeling.

Once the coding scheme reached a sufficient level of agreement between coders, the task model was used to adapt the coding to students' actions on the software. The episodes that were coded for depth by human analysts in the sample video were analyzed by creating scenarios from the task model within K-MADe. The validation of six detectors' implementation involved three human coders, who watched a sample of 50 episodes, paying attention to the depth of modeling exhibited by the student's actions, and chose the classification that best represented the depth of the learner modeling at the time of the detected value. A multi-rater and pairwise kappa was then performed, reaching a level of inter-reliance of .925.

3 Conclusion and Future Work

In this paper, a method to create a detector of deep modeling within a meta-tutor using HCI task modeling and video coding schemes was described. The main outcome of this process was the creation of detectors inferring the depth of students' modeling practices while they learn on a meta-tutoring system, reaching a multi-rater and pairwise kappa score of .925. One use of the detectors was to consider the proportion of shallow versus deep learning as an outcome measure in the transfer phase. This was used as a dependent measure of shallow learning in an experimental study investigating the effectiveness of the meta-tutor versus the original interface, described in [6]. The second use of the detectors was to help drive the behavior of an affective learning companion in the current phase of the AMT project [5]. A limitation of the method however is the applicability to different types of tutoring systems. In AMT, a single task model was able to represent the entirety of a users' learning activity. In tutoring systems that teach a set of skills through different pedagogical approaches for diverse types of learning tasks, the creation of such task models might prove more costly and may not be completely adapted to the creation of detectors that need to be adapted to each task specifically.

Acknowledgements. This material is based upon work supported by the National Science Foundation under Grant No. 0910221. We would like to thank Sybille Caffiau for consulting in the project and sharing her expertise in task modeling of interactive systems.

References

1. Baker, R.S.J.d., Goldstein, A.B., Heffernan, N.T.: Detecting the moment of learning. In: Aleven, V., Kay, J., Mostow, J. (eds.) ITS 2010, Part I. LNCS, vol. 6094, pp. 25–34. Springer, Heidelberg (2010)
2. Baker, R.S.J.d., Gowda, S.M., Corbett, A.T., Ocumpaugh, J.: Towards automatically detecting whether student learning Is shallow. In: Cerri, S.A., Clancey, W.J., Papadourakis, G., Panourgia, K. (eds.) ITS 2012. LNCS, vol. 7315, pp. 444–453. Springer, Heidelberg (2012)
3. Caffiau, S., Scapin, D., Girard, P., Baron, M., Jambon, F.: Increasing the expressive power of task analysis: Systematic comparison and empirical assessment of tool-supported task models. Interacting with Computers 22(6), 569–593 (2010)
4. D'Mello, S.K., Lehman, B., Person, N.: Monitoring affect states during effortful problem solving activities. International Journal of Artificial Intelligence in Education 20(4), 361–389 (2010)
5. Girard, S., Chavez-Echeagaray, M.E., Gonzalez-Sanchez, J., Hidalgo-Pontet, Y., Zhang, L., Burleson, W., VanLehn, K.: Defining the behavior of an affective learning companion in the affective meta-tutor project. In: Chad Lane, H., Yacef, K., Mostow, J., Pavlik, P. (eds.) AIED 2013. LNCS (LNAI), vol. 7926, pp. 21–30. Springer, Heidelberg (2013)
6. Zhang, L., Burleson, W., Chavez-Echeagaray, M.E., Girard, S., Gonzalez-Sanchez, J., Hidalgo-Pontet, Y., VanLehn, K.: Evaluation of a meta-tutor for constructing models of dynamic systems. In: Chad Lane, H., Yacef, K., Mostow, J., Pavlik, P. (eds.) AIED 2013. LNCS (LNAI), vol. 7926, pp. 666–669. Springer, Heidelberg (2013)

Auto-scoring Discovery and Confirmation Bias in Interpreting Data during Science Inquiry in a Microworld

Janice Gobert, Juelaila Raziuddin, and Kenneth R. Koedinger

Worcester Polytechnic Institute, Worcester, Massachusetts
{jgobert,juelaila}@wpi.edu
Carnegie Mellon University, Pittsburgh, Pennsylvania
koedinger@cmu.edu

Abstract. Many students have difficulty with inquiry and difficulty with interpreting data, in particular. Of interest here is confirmation bias, i.e., when students won't discard a hypothesis based on disconfirming results, which is in direct contrast to when students make a discovery, having originally made a scientifically inaccurate hypothesis. The goal of the present study is to better understand these two data interpretation patterns and autoscore them. 145 eighth grade students engaged in inquiry with a state change microworld. Production rules were written to produce model-tracing in order to identify when students either made a discovery or engaged in confirmation bias. Interesting to note was an emerging pattern wherein many of the same students made discoveries across the four inquiry tasks. These data are important for performance assessment of inquiry and suggest that students may need adaptive scaffolding support while engaging in data interpretation.

Keywords: Science inquiry, model tracing, production rules, discovery, confirmation bias.

1 Overview

Students have difficulty with inquiry learning in general (de Jong & van Joolingen, 1998). Regarding interpreting data, one critical inquiry skill, students have difficulty with confirmation bias, that is, they won't discard a hypothesis based on negative results (Klayman & Ha, 1987; Dunbar, 1993; Klahr & Dunbar, 1988; Dunbar, 1993). Additionally, they draw conclusions based on confounded data (Klahr & Dunbar, 1988; Kuhn, Schauble & Garcia-Mila, 1992; Schauble, Glaser, Duschl, Schulze & John, 1995), change ideas about causality many times (Kuhn, Schauble & Garcia-Mila, 1992), don't relate outcomes of experiments to theories being tested (Schunn & Anderson, 1999), and reject theories without disconfirming evidence (Klahr & Dunbar, 1988).

In prior work, it has been shown that a cognitive model can be constructed (Koedinger, Suthers, & Forbus, 1999; Schunn & Anderson, 1998, 1999) and used to perform automated performance assessment of some inquiry skills (Gobert & Koedinger, 2011). Here we extend the work of Gobert & Koedinger (2011), who

K. Yacef et al. (Eds.): AIED 2013, LNAI 7926, pp. 770–773, 2013.

wrote production rules (Koedinger, Forbus, & Suthers, 1998) to produce model-tracing (Koedinger & Corbett, 2006) to provide a proof of concept that production rules could be used to score students' inquiry processes. In the present study, we extend this earlier work by Gobert and Koedinger in order to better understand students' reasoning during the interpreting data phase of inquiry. Specifically, using the model tracer, we sought to identify both students who made scientific discoveries and those who demonstrated confirmation bias. Discovery refers to students who originally made a scientifically inaccurate hypothesis but then 'discovered' a scientific phenomenon as indicated by appropriate experimental trials and correct interpretation of these data. Confirmation bias students, on the other hand, were those who originally made a scientifically inaccurate hypothesis and held on to their false hypothesis, as represented in their data interpretation even though their trials generated scientifically accurate data. Identifying confirmation biases during inquiry is critical to scaffolding students' inquiry real time, the goal of the Science Inq-ITS project (www.inq-its.org; Sao Pedro et al, 2011; Gobert et al, 2012).

In this study 145 eighth grade students were given pre- and post-tests for inquiry skills and domain knowledge. Four Phase Change activities were used; students made hypotheses (using our hypothesis widget), collected data using our microworlds (generating log data), interpreted their data (using our data interpretation widget), and communicated their findings (using open response format). In the hypothesizing phase, students were asked to identify variables (independent (size of container, amount of substance, level of heat and status of the cover of the flask) and dependent variables (time, melting point, and boiling point)) and their relationships. Next, students conducted experiments for their hypothesis. Data were collected and displayed in a table. In the analyzing phase, students used our data interpretation widget to interpret their findings relative to their hypothesis, and were asked to warrant their claims with evidence from trials. Lastly, students communicated their findings by explaining their data and drawing conclusion supported by evidence from the collected data.

2 AI-Based Scoring and Summary of Results

Our model tracer, applied to students' log data, coded: whether students' initial hypotheses were scientifically accurate, whether their experimental trials were relevant to their hypotheses, whether their trials demonstrated controlled for variables strategy (Chen & Klahr, 1999), and whether their final interpretation in the widget was either supported or unsupported by their trials. Their open responses (4 tasks), reflecting communicating findings skills (NRC, 2011) were coded by hand to score the accuracy and level of details relevant to the task. These data were also used to examine students' reasoning and to check whether students returned to their original, in correct hypothesis (i.e., another demonstration of confirmation bias) or whether their discoveries were reflected in their explanations when they communicated their findings as a summative activity during inquiry.

Of the instances identified by our model tracer as reflecting scientific discoveries made by the students, 73% of the open responses also reflected this discovery. For example, students' explanations on the task in which they made discoveries were more detailed and thorough describing variables, observations, and effects of each level of independent variable on the dependent variable. Their scores for level of details and accuracy were high (max of 2) and consistently high thereafter, in subsequent tasks. An example of a scientific discovery open response was *"I found that as the amount of the substance decreases, so does the time it takes for the ice cube to melt and the water to boil. I noticed that though it took less time to melt and boil, the temperatures at which the ice melted and the water boiled remained the same"*. In the other 27% of instances, although the model tracer identified that the student had collected the appropriate data and had entered a "scientifically accurate" interpretation, their open response explanation did not reflect an accurate understanding of the data they had collected. For instance, the explanations reflected their observations during experimentation but did not explain the effects of the independent variable on the dependent variable. In general, explanations were shorter and incomplete and/or inaccurate. An example of such open response is *"it will change the conclusion depending on the grams of the substance"*. Of the instances that were identified by our model tracer as reflecting confirmation biases, 80% of these also reflected this confirmation bias in their explanation(s). These students scored lower on level of detail and understanding; for example, *"The level of heat changes the boiling point by more heat melts the ice faster and less ice takes more time to melt ice"*. The other 20% reflected a scientifically accurate explanation of the phenomena, suggesting that they may have learned about the phenomenon as a result of their inquiry, even though their interpretation, entered into our interpretation widget, was scientifically inaccurate; these instances also may reflect productive failure (Kapur, 2009). An example is *"in the experiment i found out that the size of the container does not affect the time it takes the ice to melt but the size of the ice does determine the time it takes to melt"*.

Taken together these data are important for understanding inquiry processes more deeply, specifically involving interpreting data; they are also important for performance assessment. Lastly, these data suggest that students who engage in confirmation bias are in need of adaptive scaffolding while engaging in interpreting since individualized adaptive scaffolding in real time is when tutoring is most effective (Koedinger & Corbett, 2006).

References

1. Chen, Z., Klahr, D.: All Other Things Being Equal: Acquisition and Transfer of the Control of Variables Strategy. Child Development 70(5), 1098–1120 (1999)
2. de Jong, T., van Joolingen, W.R.: Scientific discovery learning with computer simulations of conceptual domains. Review of Educational Research 68(2), 179–201 (1998)
3. Dunbar, K.: Concept discovery in a scientific domain. Cognitive Science: A Multidisciplinary Journal 17(3), 397–434 (1993)

4. Gobert, J., Koedinger, K.: Using model-tracing to conduct performance assessment of students' inquiry skills within a Microworld. Presented at the Society for Research on Educational Effectiveness as Part of a Symposium, Supporting Elementary and Middle-School Students' Development of Science Reasoning Skills, Washington, D.C., September 8-10, (2011)
5. Gobert, J., Sao Pedro, M., Baker, R.S., Toto, E., Montalvo, O.: Leveraging educational data mining for real time performance assessment of scientific inquiry skills within microworlds. Journal of Educational Data Mining (in press)
6. Kapur, M.: Moving beyond the pedagogy of mathematics: Foregrounding epistemological concerns. In: Kaur, B., Yeap, B.H., Kapur, M. (eds.) Mathematical Problem Solving. World Scientific, Singapore (2009) (in press)
7. Klahr, D., Dunbar, K.: Dual search space during scientific reasoning. Cognitive Science 12(1), 1–48 (1988)
8. Klayman, J., Ha, Y.-W.: Confirmation, disconfirmation, and information in hypothesis testing. Psychological Review 94(2), 211–228 (1987)
9. Koedinger, K., Corbett, A.: Cognitive Tutors: Technology Bringing Learning Sciences to the Classroom. In: Sawyer, R. (ed.) The Cambridge Handbook of the Learning Sciences, pp. 61–77. Cambridge University Press, New York (2006)
10. Koedinger, K., Suthers, D., Forbus, K.: Component-Based Construction of a Science Learning Space. International Journal of Artificial Intelligence in Education (IJAIED) 10, 292–313 (1998)
11. Kuhn, D., Schauble, L., Garcia-Mila, M.: Cross-domain development of scientific reasoning. Cognition and Instruction 9(4), 285–327 (1992)
12. National Research Council, A Framework for K-12 Science Education: Practices, Crosscutting Concepts, and Core Ideas. Committee on a Conceptual Framework for New K-12 Science Education Standards. Board on Science Education, Division of Behavioral and Social Sciences and Education. The National Academies Press, Washington, DC (2011)
13. Schauble, L., Glaser, R., Duschl, R., Schulze, S., John, J.: Students' understanding of the objectives and procedures of experimentation in the science classroom. Journal of the Learning Sciences 4(2), 131–166 (1995)
14. Schunn, C.D., Anderson, J.R.: Scientific Discovery. In: Anderson, J.R. (ed.) The Atomic Components of Thought, pp. 385–428. Lawrence Erlbaum Associates, Inc., Mahwah (1998)
15. Schunn, C.D., Anderson, J.R.: The generality/specificity of expertise in scientific reasoning. Cognitive Science 23(3), 337–370 (1999)
16. Sao Pedro, M., Baker, R., Gobert, J., Montalvo, O., Nakama, A.: Using Machine-Learned Detectors of Systematic Inquiry Behavior to Predict Gains in Inquiry Skills. User Modeling and User-Adapted Interaction (2011), doi:10.1007/s11257-011-9101-0

A Teaching-Style Based Social Network for Didactic Building and Sharing

Carla Limongelli, Matteo Lombardi, Alessandro Marani, and Filippo Sciarrone

"Roma Tre" University
Department of Computer Science and Automation
AI-Lab
Via della Vasca Navale, 79 - 00146 Rome, Italy
{limongel,sciarro}@dia.uniroma3.it,
{mat.lombardi,ale.marani}@stud.uniroma3.it

Abstract. Nowadays, teachers tend to build their own didactic local repository composed by learning objects retrieved from web repositories or, in most cases, by self-made didactic material. In this way they do not share their teaching experience, loosing a precious shortcut to a fast professional update and to an improvement of their teaching activity. In this paper we address the problem of helping teachers to retrieve didactic material from a repository through a didactic social network where teachers with similar Teaching Styles, can help each other in retrieving educational material. To this aim a teaching-styles based social network is built following the Grasha TS paradigm. We present a first evaluation of the network embedded in a web application.

1 Introduction

Today the Internet is full of Social Networks (SNs), i.e., communities of people where one can enter, chat, ask for a problem resolution or for everyday life, post new threads. This phenomenon is giving a strong impulse to researchers in this area ([1]). The main added value of a SN is the synergy caused by the peer to peer communication: a community of users grows faster than individuals. In the educational field, there is a lot of repositories where teachers can share their experience and retrieve didactic materials to reuse as well. Among all, worth mentioning are *Merlot* and *Desire2Learn*[1] that provide thousands of learning objects and where registered members can share their expertise and receive peer feedback. Unfortunately, none of these didactic repositories allows for an intelligent management of the teaching activity: there is not an intelligent profiling system that helps teachers to build their didactic strategy and share their expertise with peers. Here we propose a cluster-based didactic SN where teachers can share their experience and can be recommended to retrieve new didactic material. We group teachers on the basis of their Teaching Styles (TS), so that they can rely on the support of peers belonging to the same cluster each

[1] http://www.merlot.org, http://www.desire2learn.com

K. Yacef et al. (Eds.): AIED 2013, LNAI 7926, pp. 774–777, 2013.

of them representing their community of peers. To this aim, we use a revised version of the k-means clustering algorithm, taking into account the TS as proposed by Grasha [4]. Our research question is if such a cluster-based network can help teachers to retrieve more suitable didactic material (compliant with her own TS), than a *dummy* retrieval were such a help is not given. We built a pilot system in order to test this approach.

2 A Teaching-Style Based Social Network of Teachers

In the literature there is more research on student's modeling [7,2,6,8,10] than on teacher's modeling [4,3,5,9]. We believe that a teacher centered approach should be addressed as well, in order to give teachers a personalized support taking into account their own pedagogy, styles of teaching, and teaching experience. Our model takes into account all these components in a dynamic way and it is based on Grasha TS [4] which express teacher attitudes, rather than Felder and Silverman TS [3], that describe the style of teaching concerning a given didactic material. To represent a teacher it is necessary to know both her way of teaching and her teaching experience. Our Teacher Model has two components: an *educational* component given by (TS) and an *ontological* one, given by all her own courses during her teaching activity, i.e., the Teaching Experience (TE). In this work we address the TS component of a TM, building a TS-based SN of teachers with similar teaching attitudes. Here we consider the Grasha TS Model, that is composed by the following five TS [4]: Expert (E), Personal Model (PM), Formal Authority (FA), Delegator (D), Facilitator (F). Each style is in the range $[1.0, 7.0]$. In addition, Grasha identifies four groups of teachers, depending on their primary and secondary TS as illustrated in the left-hand side of Tab. 1. Each group represents a network of similar teachers. The idea behind this work

Table 1. On the left-hand table: Grasha TS partition into four cluster of teachers. For each cluster primary TS and secondary TS are defined. On the right-hand table: TS Classification Matrix.

TS	C_1	C_2	C_3	C_4
Primary	E, FA	PM, E, F	F, PM, E	D, F, E
Secondary	PM, F, D	F, D	FA, D	FA, PM

Cluster	E	PM	FA	D	F
C_1	1	0	1	0	0
C_2	1	1	1	0	0
C_3	1	1	0	0	1
C_4	1	0	0	1	1

is to build the four Grasha clusters $C_i, (i = 1, \cdots, 4)$ of teachers, depending on their TS, taking into account that Grasha does not quantify primary and secondary TS, but he rather provides generically *high values* for primary TS and *low values* for the secondary ones. The problem is then to quantify these *high* and *low* values. To this aim we first represent a teacher by means of an array of five components, and secondly we use an adapted version of k-means algorithm. Following the classification given in the right-hand side of Tab. 1, we can represent primary and secondary TS into a binary matrix with 4 rows (clusters) and 5 columns (TS), with 1 for primary TS and 0 for secondary ones. We call it *Classification Matrix*: this matrix is a constant for the new clustering algorithm. We compute centroids by attributing to primary TS the maximum value among the primary TS of all points in the cluster, including the centroid, dually attributing to secondary TS the minimum value among the secondary TS of all points in the cluster. Let TS_j a point representing a given teacher TS: $TS_j[h], h = 1, \cdots, 5$ represents the h-th value for a given TS. The adapted k-means algorithm is shown below:

for each C_i with $i = 1, \cdots, 4$
  if (ClassificationMatri$x[C_i, TS_j[h]] = 1$**)**
    then $c_i^{new}[h] \longleftarrow max(TS_j[h], c_i^{old}[h]), \forall j \in C_i$
    else $c_i^{new}[h] \longleftarrow min(TS_j[h], c_i^{old}[h]), \forall j \in C_i$

where functions max and min compute respectively the maximum and minimum value of TS in all points of the cluster including the centroid. In this way we obtain four significant centroids that, once they have reached the optimal value of the cluster for the set of the input data, they will no longer move. This means that an update will be done only in case is found a better value for a given TS, than the current centroid value. In this way the centroid itself will represent a *dummy* teacher with optimal values for primary and secondary TS in that cluster. The centroid will no longer change once it reaches its optimal value and the pedagogical difference among clusters will be clear, also in case of a single teacher per cluster.

3 Evaluation and Final Remarks

The evaluation involved a sample of 20 teachers, 10 from University and 10 from technical high school, randomly selected. They were asked to retrieve didactic material from the local repository. We evaluated two retrieval modalities:

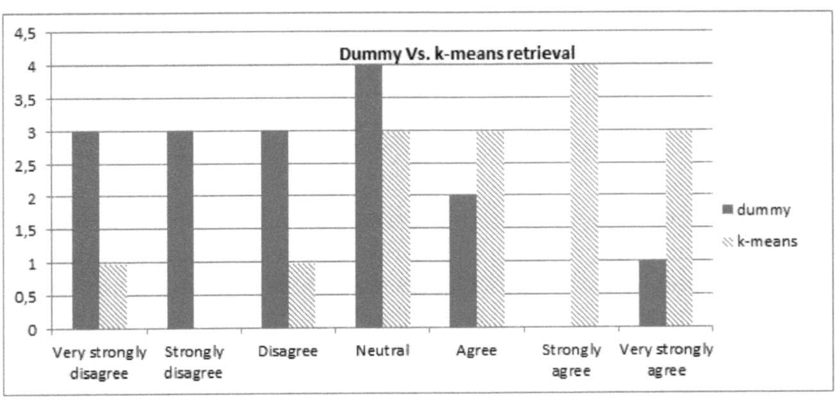

Fig. 1. Experimental results for the retrieval assessment

dummy retrieval Vs. *intelligent retrieval*. In the first case the learning material was retrieved and proposed without taking into account the clustering technique while in the second modality the learning materials were proposed to the teacher starting from the SNs ,i.e., from the four clusters built exploiting the revised k-means algorithm. Experimental results are shown in Fig. 1. The dummy retrieval modality, histograms with dashed color, has its distribution shifted towards low levels of the Likert scale with respect to the intelligent retrieval modality, represented by full-color histograms. Most users have appreciated the contribution of the social mechanism. We presented a SN of teachers built through a revised version of the k-means algorithm, taking into account teachers TS and measuring its added value in the retrieval of learning materials from web repositories. The first indication is promising and we plan to add web 2.0 instruments inside the network to strengthen the social aspects together with a more extensive evaluation.

References

1. Akcora, C.G., Carminati, B., Ferrari, E.: User similarities on social networks. J. Social Network Analysis and Mining, 1–21 (2013)
2. Limongelli, C., Sciarrone, F., Vaste, G.: LS-PLAN: An effective combination of dynamic courseware generation and learning styles in web-based education. In: Nejdl, W., Kay, J., Pu, P., Herder, E. (eds.) AH 2008. LNCS, vol. 5149, pp. 133–142. Springer, Heidelberg (2008)
3. Felder, R.M., Silverman, L.K.: Learning and teaching styles in engineering education. Engineering Education 78(7), 674 (1988)
4. Grasha, A.: Teaching with Style: A Practical Guide to Enhancing Learning by Understanding Teaching and Learning Styles. Alliance Publishers (1996)
5. Limongelli, C., Miola, A., Sciarrone, F., Temperini, M.: Supporting teachers to retrieve and select learning objects for personalized courses in the Moodle-LS environment. In: IEEE Computer Society (ed.) Proc. of the 12th IEEE Int. Conf. on Advanced Learning Technologies, pp. 518–520. IEEE Computer Society (2012)
6. Limongelli, C., Sciarrone, F., Starace, P., Temperini, M.: An ontology-driven olap system to help teachers in the analysis of web learning object repositories. Information Systems Management 27(3), 198–206 (2010)
7. Limongelli, C., Sciarrone, F., Temperini, M., Vaste, G.: Lecomps5: A web-based learning system for course personalization and adaptation. In: Nunes, M.B., McPherson, M. (eds.) Proc. of E-Learning 2008, Amsterdam, The Nederlands, vol. 1, pp. 325–332 (2008)
8. Limongelli, C., Sciarrone, F., Temperini, M., Vaste, G.: Adaptive learning with the ls-plan system: a field evaluation. IEEE Transactions on Learning Technologies 2(3), 203–215 (2009)
9. Limongelli, C., Sciarrone, F., Temperini, M., Vaste, G.: The Lecomps5 framework for personalized web-based learning: a teacher's satisfaction perspective. Computers in Human Behavior 27(4), 1310–1320 (2011)
10. Sterbini, A., Temperini, M.: Supporting assessment of open answers in a didactic setting. In: IEEE Computer Society (ed.) Proc. of the 12th IEEE Int. Conf. on Advanced Learning Technologies, pp. 678–679. IEEE Computer Society (2012)

Turn-Taking Behavior in a Human Tutoring Corpus

Zahra Rahimi and Homa B. Hashemi

Intelligent Systems Program
University of Pittsburgh
Pittsburgh, PA
{zar10,Hashemi}@pitt.edu

Abstract. Analysis of turn-taking in tutoring dialogues can be helpful to understand the procedure of tutoring and also the influence with regard to demographics between students and the tutor. In this research, we analyze turn-taking behavior between students in a human-human spoken tutoring system. Our approach is to learn turn-taking models using dialog activity state sequences and then we measure the association of these models with students' demographic features (gender and education). The experimental results show that female students speak simultaneously longer with the tutor than male students, female activities are less than male activities and also the tutor speaks longer with students who have lower pre-test score.

1 Introduction

The goal of this research is to analyze turn-taking behavior between students and tutor in human tutoring dialogues with regards to their demographic features (gender and education). Grothendieck et. al [3] showed that different traits are correlated with a speakers derived turn-taking style. This research and other studies on analyzing turn-taking models have been done on multi-party conversations [4,1], and also in telephone conversations [6]. However the analysis of turn-taking on human tutoring data has not previously been attempted. This analysis can be useful for predicting influence with regard to demographics between students and tutor and also for understanding tutoring procedure which can help to design tutoring systems in a way that lead to improvement in learning of students. Friedberg [2] has conducted a study on analyzing turn-taking of tutoring [5] before, but her main focus was on identifying prosodic cues that are useful in predicting student turn boundaries. This research is similar to the work done by Grothendieck et. al, [3] in which they analyze turn-taking behaviors of speakers with regard to demographic attributes on Switchboard-1 corpus. The main contribution of this paper is to analyze turn-taking behavior of students and tutor on ITSPOKE data [5] based on the proposed approach in [3]. In this report, we first describe the turn-taking models that we have used and then present experiments and statistical results over the human-human tutoring data of ITSPOKE.

2 Tutoring Turn-Taking Models

In this section, we describe the approach proposed in [3] to train state sequence models using extracted activity state sequences from dialogs.

K. Yacef et al. (Eds.): AIED 2013, LNAI 7926, pp. 778–782, 2013.

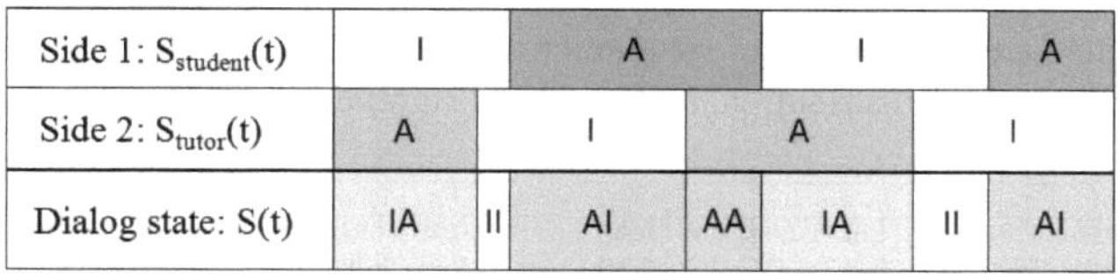

Fig. 1. Sample dialog activity state sequence [3]

Dialog States: Each conversation can be modeled with a sequence of speech and silence states over time. So, the observed activity of each speaker is denoted with two states of Active(A) when she is talking and Inactive(I) when she is silent.

As shown in figure 1, each speaker is modeled with a sequence of activity states (SAS). For instance, the first row of figure 1 ($S_{student}(t)$) shows the SAS of a student which is I A I A.

In a two-sided dialog, SAS of both participants combine and produce four new states which are AA, AI, IA and II (such as $S(t)$ as shown in the last row of figure 1). AA happens when both speakers talk together, AI is when the first participant is speaking and the other is silent, IA is when the other participant is active and the first is silent and II happens when both of the participants are inactive (silent). In our experiments, the first participant is always student and the second speaker is tutor.

Using this low-level notation, a two-sided dialog is modeled with a sequence of states which also contains turn-taking behavior of a conversation. For instance, the sequence of AI II IA shows that II is a switching pause. But in sequence AI II AI, after the pause the first speaker continue speaking, so II is an internal pause.

In order to extract state sequences from dialogs, first we separate two channels and then use Sphinx toolkit (released by Carnegie Mellon University) to segment audio files into activity states. We segmented the corpus by 200 ms as threshold [1].

State Sequence Models: We use a semi-Markov process to model each activity state sequence with history of length 2 [3]. Consider the state sequence of $S(t)$. As the first parameter of the model, we calculate state transition probabilities $P(X_i|X_{i-2}, X_{i-1})$ by counting their occurrences in the sequence.

As the second parameter, we calculate the probability of duration of the state conditioned on its preceding and succeeding states. Consider d_i as the duration of state X_i, then conditional state duration distribution is $f(d_i|X_{i-1}, X_i, X_{i+1})$ which is modeled via log-normal distribution. We call the combination of these two sets of trained parameters over $S(t)$ as $D(t)$.

3 Experiments

In our experiments we use the ITSPOKE tutoring corpus [5] which is an human-human tutoring audio corpus. This corpus consists of dialogues of 18 university students working with a tutor on physics problems.

Unigram Turn-Taking Model. In our experiment, for each student i, we extract her activity state sequence for each physics problem j which denoted as $S_{ij}(t)$. Then we aggregate all of her conversations to construct $S_i(t)$.

[1] We also tried 2 sec. like [3] but the conclusions were the same.

Table 1. Parameters are: probability of state, relative time in state, mean and standard deviation of durations via log-normal distribution, and statistical significant of differences between means

State	P_F	$T_F\%$	μ_F	σ_F	P_M	$T_M\%$	μ_M	σ_M	Sig.
AA	0.10	2.31	-0.96	1.10	0.09	1.63	-1.04	1.11	**0.007**
AI	0.16	7.64	-0.04	0.94	0.20	9.24	0.02	0.85	**0.001**
IA	0.34	33.18	0.71	0.95	0.31	30.95	0.73	0.94	0.148
II	0.39	56.86	-0.12	1.43	0.41	58.17	-0.02	1.40	$\approx \mathbf{0}$

(a) Unigram model parameters on gender

State	P_H	$T_H\%$	μ_H	σ_H	P_L	$T_L\%$	μ_L	σ_L	Sig.
AA	0.08	1.97	-1.07	1.13	0.11	2.11	-0.99	1.09	**0.032**
AI	0.19	9.49	0.02	0.85	0.19	8.99	-0.01	0.9	0.138
IA	0.31	30.17	0.66	0.93	0.31	32.37	0.72	0.95	$\approx \mathbf{0}$
II	0.42	58.38	-0.04	1.35	0.39	56.53	-0.1	1.43	**0.005**

(b) Unigram model parameters on education

As the first experimental results, we aggregated all the state sequences of students to build $S(t)$ and then trained the state sequence model ($D(t)$). We show probability of the state with P_{state}, the relative time spent on the state with $T_{state}\%$. The results show that $T_{II} = 57\%$ which means that 57% of the time tutor and student are silent. Looking closer to the corpus reveals that during the conversation students are mostly thinking or typing the answers of questions. Also, $T_{AI} = 8\%$ and $T_{IA} = 32\%$ which means that tutor talks around four times more than students. Moreover, the state of AA happens very rarely ($T_{AA} = 2\%$ and $P_{AA} = 9.5\%$). This may be because of the tutoring domain in which participants might not begin speaking while the other is active.

Turn-Taking Model Conditioned on Gender. In this set of experiments, we manually divided students based on gender and analyzed the turn-taking style of each group. Here there are 8 female students and 10 male students. The parameters of unigram models for both female and male students are shown in table 1a. The comparison of parameter values of these two groups shows that female students have more and longer AA states than male students. Also comparing the AI states show that female students speak less than male students.

In the next set of experiments, we train trigram models $D_F(t)$ and $D_M(t)$ for all the dialogs of female and male students. The parameters of these models for the state sequences that we can infer information from are shown in table 2a. For instance, the second row in this table shows that probability $P(IA|AI, AA) = 0.88$ for male students and log-normal mean state duration of state AA conditioned on AI and IA for male students is -1.44. It is noteworthy to mention that these results are also compatible with unigram based results. As the table shows, we can conclude that mean duration of AA state based on its previous and following states are higher in female students than men. Also, female students are less active than male students.

Turn-Taking Model Conditioned on Education. In the next set of experiments, we manually divided students based on their score on pre-test problems. The pre-test data in ITSPOKE corpus is available for 14 students. We divided students into two groups of *High* (students with pre-test score greater than 0.4) and *Low* (students with pre-test score less than or equal to 0.4). 0.4 is the mean of pre-test scores. Here there are 6 students with high score and 8 students with low score.

The parameters of unigram model for students in high and low groups are shown in table 1b. The comparison of parameter values of these two groups shows that the tutor speaks longer with students with lower pre-test score. Also, these students have more and longer AA states and less and shorter II states than students with higher pre-test scores.

Table 2. Parameters are: State transitions, probability of state P, log-duration means μ, and statistical significance of differences between means

State	P_F	P_M	μ_F	μ_M	Sig.
AI **AA** AI	0.134	0.117	-0.082	-0.160	0.298
AI **AA** IA	0.863	0.880	-1.278	-1.440	**0.001**
IA **AA** AI	0.546	0.575	-1.422	-1.358	0.203
IA **AA** IA	0.450	0.423	-0.191	-0.216	0.438
AA **AI** AA	0.363	0.346	-0.294	-0.229	0.312
AA **AI** II	0.615	0.643	-0.444	-0.376	0.237
II **AI** AA	0.234	0.153	-0.380	-0.481	0.084
II **AI** II	0.747	0.827	0.215	0.205	0.625
AI **II** AI	0.442	0.562	0.642	0.725	**0.038**
AI **II** IA	0.555	0.437	-0.228	-0.245	0.699
IA **II** AI	0.257	0.280	-0.207	-0.114	**0.025**

(a) Gender

State	P_H	P_L	μ_H	μ_L	Sig.
AI **AA** AI	0.118	0.128	-0.164	-0.119	0.626
AI **AA** IA	0.878	0.869	-1.441	-1.358	0.148
IA **AA** AI	0.551	0.579	-1.488	-1.336	**0.010**
IA **AA** IA	0.446	0.418	-0.251	-0.172	**0.032**
AA **IA** AA	0.243	0.263	0.544	0.423	0.137
AA **IA** II	0.745	0.733	0.431	0.636	$\approx$ **0**
II **IA** AA	0.137	0.173	0.208	0.344	**0.016**
II **IA** II	0.857	0.821	0.782	0.852	$\approx$ **0**
AI **II** AI	0.585	0.497	0.608	0.769	$\approx$ **0**
AI **II** IA	0.414	0.500	-0.235	-0.326	0.054
IA **II** AI	0.254	0.296	-0.088	-0.213	**0.009**

(b) Education

Then, we train model $D_H(t)$ and $D_L(t)$ for all the dialogs of students with high and low pre-test scores, respectively. The parameters of these models are shown in table 2b. These results also show that the tutor speaks longer with students with lower pre-test score than students with higher pre-test score. Furthermore, when the tutor is talking, students with lower pre-test scores have significantly longer regions of double activity (middle AA state) than students with higher pre-test score. The analysis of II states shows that the switching pauses for students with lower pre-test score is shorter but their internal pauses is longer than students with higher pre-test score.

4 Conclusion and Future Work

This study presented some analysis over turn-taking behavior in spoken human-human tutoring dialogues. Some interesting points emerge from our learned turn-taking parameters over state sequences: female students speak simultaneously longer with the tutor than male students, female activities are less than the male activities, the tutor speaks longer with students with lower pre-test score and these students have longer double activity states (AA) and shorter double pause (II) states. There are different interesting directions for future work such as predicting students' social correlates from their turn-taking behavior, studying influence over tutoring conversations based on turn-taking behaviors, and analyzing turn-taking behaviors in multi-party study groups.

Acknowledgments. Special thanks to Dr. Diane Litman for her guidance and help and significant comments on this research.

References

1. Cristani, M., Pesarin, A., Drioli, C., Tavano, A., Perina, A., Murino, V.: Generative modeling and classification of dialogs by a low-level turn-taking feature. Pattern Recognition 44, 1785–1800 (2011)
2. Friedberg, H.: Turn-taking cues in a human tutoring corpus. In: ACL HLT 2011, p. 94 (2011)
3. Grothendieck, J., Gorin, A., Borges, N.: Social correlates of turn-taking style. Computer Speech & Language 25(4), 789–801 (2011)

4. Laskowski, K.: Modeling norms of turn-taking in multi-party conversation. In: ACL, pp. 999–1008 (2010)
5. Litman, D., Rosé, C., Forbes-Riley, K., VanLehn, K., Bhembe, D., Silliman, S.: Spoken versus typed human and computer dialogue tutoring. International Journal of Artificial Intelligence in Education 16(2), 145–170 (2006)
6. Raux, A., Eskenazi, M.: Optimizing the turn-taking behavior of task-oriented spoken dialog systems. ACM Trans. Speech Lang. Process. 9(1), 1–23 (2012)

An Automatic Marking System for Interactive Exercises on Blind Search Algorithms

Foteini Grivokostopoulou and Ioannis Hatzilygeroudis

University of Patras, School of Engineering Department of Computer Engineering & Informatics, 26500 Patras, Hellas, Greece
{grivokwst,ihatz}@ceid.upatras.gr

Abstract. In this paper, we present a web-based automatic marking system that aims to assist the tutor in assessing the performance of students in interactive exercises related to breadth-first search (BFS) and depth-first search (DFS) algorithms. The system has been tested on a number exercises for BFS and DFS search algorithms and its performance has been compared against that of an expert tutor. The experimental results are quite promising.

Keywords: Web-based e-learning system, automated marking, e-assessment, blind search algorithms.

1 Introduction

Student assessment via tests is an important and complex part of learning process. Automatic assessment can assist the tutor in evaluating student's work and also enable more regular and prompt feedback [3][5][9]. In an artificial intelligence (AI) course, a fundamental topic is "search algorithms". It is considered necessary for students to get a strong understanding of the way search algorithms work and also of their implementation for solving various problems. Usually in an AI course, for teaching a search algorithm and evaluating the students' comprehension, the tutor creates and gives a set of assignments asking the students to provide their hand-made solutions. Afterwards, the tutor has to mark all students' answers, present the correct ones and discuss the common errors. This process is time demanding for the tutor. So, an automatic marking system, which helps the tutor reduce the time spent in marking and use this time efficiently for more creative work, is desirable. Moreover, the automatically marking system allows every student to have his/her test immediately evaluated. In this paper, we present a system that has been developed to support automatic marking of student answers to interactive exercises concerning blind search (i.e. BFS and DFS) algorithms.

2 Related Work

There are a number of automatic assessment systems recently developed to aid in assessing student answers to exercises in various courses. The most common field, where automatic assessment is widely used, is assessing programming exercises [2].

K. Yacef et al. (Eds.): AIED 2013, LNAI 7926, pp. 783–786, 2013.

For example, BOSS system [7] is a web based tool facilitating the online submission and processing of programming assignments. QuizPACK [4] is a good example of a system that assesses program evaluation skills. Other applications include exercises on algorithms. TRAKLA2 [8] is a system for automatically assessing visual algorithm simulation exercises and provides automatic feedback and grading. In [1], a work that deals with teaching AI searching algorithms is presented. It is a visualization tool for helping students to learn artificial intelligence searching algorithms. However, this system does not support automatic marking of student answers or error feedback.

Furthermore, in our previous works, systems that automatically mark exercises about logic have been developed. AutoMark-NLtoFOL [10] is a web-based system that automatically marks student answers in exercises related to converting Natural Language (NL) into First Order Logic (FOL). Also, in [6] a system for automatic marking FOL to CF (clause form) conversion exercises is presented. In addition, the systems provide feedback on errors made by students through interactions with them.

3 Automatic Marking

An automatic marking mechanism has been developed that marks a student's answers to an interactive test. Each test consists of a number of BFS and DFS interactive exercises. The student's answer to an interactive exercise is stored as the sequence of the selected nodes (states). For example, the following node sequence: N1-N2-N3-N4-N5-N6 corresponds to the following state transitions: (S1-S2) (S2-S3) (S3-S4) (S4-S5) (S5-S6), where Si is the state corresponding to node Ni.

A student's answer is characterized in terms of *completeness* and *accuracy* as follows: *Complete-Accurate* (C-A), *Complete–Inaccurate* (C-I), *Incomplete–Accurate* (I-A), *Incomplete–Inaccurate* (I-I) and *Superfluous* (S-F). An answer is *complete* if all nodes and transitions of the correct answer appear in the student's answer; otherwise, it is *incomplete*. An answer is *correct* when all nodes and transitions of the student's answer are correct; otherwise it is *inaccurate*. Case S-F tries to capture superfluous answers; represents cases where nodes and corresponding transitions in the answer are more than the required. We also consider that existence of only one error in an answer may be due to inattention. We distinguish the following types of *single-error answers*: SE1 (a node is missing compared to the correct sequence), SE2 (there is an extra node-state compared to the correct sequence), SE3 (two consecutive nodes-states have been switched between each other compared to the correct sequence).

Marking is based on the similarity between the student's answer and the correct answer on a 1-100 scale. We consider that a student's answer NS_i includes s_i states (nodes) and n_i transitions (actually $s_i = n_i+1$), whereas the correct answer NS_{ic} includes s_{ic} states (nodes) and n_{ic} transitions (actually $s_{ic} = n_{ic}+1$). Both NS_i and NS_{ic} are sequences of nodes (states). We use a simple similarity formula to calculate similarity sim_i of NS_i to NS_{ic}:

$$sim_i = \sum_{j=1}^{n_{ic}} m_j \quad (1) \qquad \text{where} \quad m_j = \begin{cases} 1, if\ NS_{ic}(j) = NS_i(j) \\ 0, \qquad\qquad otherwise \end{cases} \qquad (2)$$

Then, mark M_i for answer NS_i is $M_i = \frac{sim_i * 100}{n_{ic}}$ (3)

If NS_i and NS_{ic} have not the same length, then we start tracing both sequences from both start and end node of each of them and each time we meet identical nodes at the same position in the two sequences we put $m_j = 1$, otherwise $m_j = 0$. For any missing or extra nodes in NS_i, we put $m_j = 0$. Finally, given a test including a number of q interactive exercises, the test score is calculated as the average mark of answers:

$$Test\_Score = \frac{\sum_{i=1}^{q} M_i}{q}$$

Test_Score is a real number between 0 and 100 and gives the score that a student has achieved in a test for blind search algorithms. The above is the basic mechanism, followed to all answers with less than seven transitions.

The algorithm for marking an answer NS_i, based on the above ideas, is as follows:

1. If $n_{ic} \leq 6$, M_i is calculated via formulas (1)-(3)
2. If $n_{ic} > 6$
   - 2.1 If NS_i is of type I-A, $M_i = (n_i/n_{ic})*100$
   - 2.2 If NS_i is of type C-I
     - 2.2.1 If NS_i is of type SE3, $M_i = ((n_{ic}-3)*100+3*40)/n_{ic}$
     - 2.2.2 M_i is calculated via formulas (1)-(3)
   - 2.3 If NS_i is of type I-I
     - 2.3.1 If NS_i is of type SE1, $M_i = ((n_{ic}-2)*100+2*40)/n_{ic}$
     - 2.3.2 M_i is calculated via formulas (1)-(3)
   - 2.4 If NS_i is of type S-F
     - 2.4.1 If NS_i is of type SE2, $M_i = 100*0.8$
     - 2.4.2 M_i is calculated via formulas (1)-(3)
   - 2.5 (Type C-A) $M_i = 100$.

For example, consider that the correct answer is: A-C-B-D-E-G-L-K-N (where A, B, C etc represent nodes-states) and the answer of a student is: A-C-B-D-E-G-L-N. The mechanism detects the student's answer as I-I and also as a SE1. According to the marking algorithm, $M_1 = ((8-2)*100+2*40)/8 = 85$.

4 Evaluation

We conducted an evaluation study for the automatic marking during the Artificial Intelligence course in our department. The participants were 10 undergraduate students enrolled in the course. An assignment on DFS and BFS algorithms was given to them. More specifically, the students were asked to take a number of tests on the BFS and DFS algorithms and then submit their answers. All students' answers were sent to the automatic marking tool for marking. After that, they were also marked by the tutor. The tests marked by the tutor and the tool were 10, each one containing five exercises, thus giving a total number of 50 marked answers. The results indicate a good agreement between expert and system marking. Also, at the end of the test, students were asked to complete an online questionnaire about the system.

The results show that most of the students gave positive responses. The students in general found their marks to be fair and the feedback provided by the system helpful in understanding their errors. Moreover, 70% of the students agreed that the system assisted them in learning BFS and DFS algorithms.

5 Conclusions and Future Work

In this paper, we present a new mechanism for automatic assessment of students' tests on BFS and DFS exercises in a consistent manner. The automatic marking mechanism is used to mark the student's answers based on the similarity between student's answer and the correct answer. Evaluation results show good agreement with the expert-tutor. However there are some points that the system could be improved. First, the system does not take into account in calculating the test score the difficulty levels of the exercises. Also, a more sophisticated similarity measure could be used.

Acknowledgements. This work was supported by the Research Committee of the University of Patras, Greece, Program "KARATHEODORIS", project No C901.

References

1. Naser, A.: Developing Visualization tool for teaching AI searching algorithms. ITJ 7(2), 350–355 (2008)
2. Ala-Mutka, K.: A Survey of Automated Assessment Approaches for Programming Assignments. Computer Science Education 15, 83–102 (2005)
3. Barker-Plummer, D., Dale, R., Cox, R., Etchemendy, J.: Automated Assessment in the Internet Classroom. In: Proc. AAAI Fall Symp. Education Informatics, Arlington, VA (2008)
4. Brusilovsky, P., Sosnovsky, S.: Individualized exercises for self-assessment of programming knowledge: An evaluation of QuizPACK. ACM J. Education Resources Computing 5(3), 6 (2005)
5. Charman, D., Elmes, A.: Computer Based Assessment: A guide to good practice, vol. 1. University of Plymouth (1998)
6. Grivokostopoulou, F., Perikos. I., Hatzilygeroudis, I.: An Automatic Marking System for FOL to CF Conversions. In: Proc. of IEEE International Conference on Teaching, Assessment and Learning for Engineering (TALE), Hong Kong, pp. H1A-7–H1A-12 (2012)
7. Joy, M., Griffith, N., Boyatt, R.: The Boss Online Submission and Assessment System. ACM Journal on Educational Resources in Computing 5(3), 2 (2005)
8. Malmi, L., Karavirta, V., Korhonen, A., Nikander, J., Seppala, O., Silvasti, P.: Visual algorithm simulation exercise system with automatic assessment: TRAKLA2. Informatics in Education 3(2), 267–288 (2004)
9. Mehta, S.I., Schlecht, N.W.: Computerized assessment technique for large classes. Journal of Engineering Education 87, 167–172 (1998)
10. Perikos, I., Grivokostopoulou, F., Hatzilygeroudis, I.: Automatic Marking of NL to FOL Conversions. In: Proc. of 15th IASTED International Conference on Computers and Advanced Technology in Education (CATE), Napoli, Italy, pp. 227–233 (2012)

Game Penalties Decrease Learning and Interest

Matthew W. Easterday and Yelee Jo

School of Education and Social Policy, Northwestern University

Abstract. Penalties are frequently used in games and rarely in tutors, creating a dilemma for designers seeking to combine games and tutors to maximize fun and learning. On the one hand, penalties can be frustrating and waste instructional time, on the other, they may increase excitement and prevent gaming. This study tested the effects of penalties on learning and interest. In a randomized, controlled experiment with a two-group, between subjects design, 100 University students played two versions of a game with an embedded tutor, with and without penalties that forced students to replay parts of the game. Results showed that penalties decreased learning and interest. These findings suggest a minimize penalties principle for designing cognitive games.

Keywords: intelligent tutoring, educational games, serious games, penalties.

1 Introduction

Can *cognitive games*—educational games with embedded intelligent tutors, promote learning as effectively as tutors [1] and be as fun to play as games? Unfortunately, tutors and games take conflicting approaches to assistance. Tutors provide more assistance than games, providing scaffolding and feedback on each *step*, providing hints and minimizing penalties. If an entertainment game like *Halo* adopted such tutoring strategies, it would look quite odd: not only would it tell you whether you've hit or been hit by an enemy, it would tell you what kind of weapon to choose, which enemy to target, how to point the weapon, when to shoot, the enemy's weakness, etc.; being hit wouldn't reduce your health; and after missing an enemy, the enemy would patiently wait for you try again. These conflicting approaches make it unclear whether cognitive games can simply combine tutors with games to maximize learning and fun—adding tutors may increase learning at the expense of fun.

To explore the cognitive game design space at the intersection of tutors and games, Easterday et. al. [2] compared two cognitive games: a high-assistance, low penalty *tutored game* and a low-assistance, high-penalties *hardcore game* (Figure 1). Intuitively, we might predict a tradeoff with the tutored cognitive game better for learning, and the hardcore-game generating greater interest. In fact, the tutored-game led to greater learning and competence, which in turn increased interest. So if hardcore game conventions are not effective (feedback is good for learning after all), how might a high penalties/high feedback *walkthrough* game fare? In this study, we examine the role of minimal and harsh penalties in cognitive games.

K. Yacef et al. (Eds.): AIED 2013, LNAI 7926, pp. 787–790, 2013.

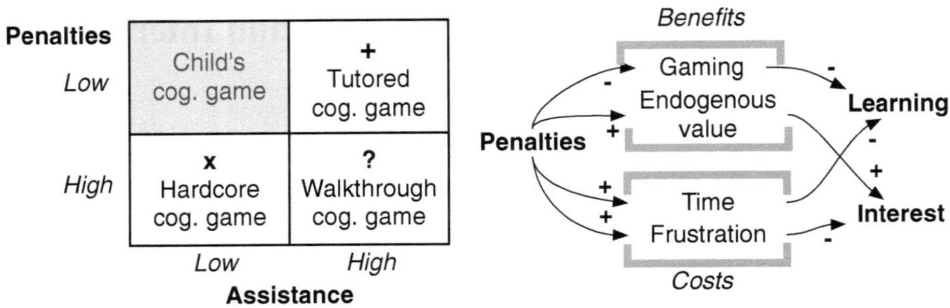

Fig. 1. Cognitive game design space (left) and possible causal effects penalties (right)

Hypotheses. In this study, we compared how two cognitive games with either *harsh* or *minimal penalties* affected learning and interest. The *harsh penalty* version required students to replay parts of the game after an error, while the *minimal penalty* version allowed immediate error correction. The outcome measures were *learning*, which measured the policy analysis skills taught by the game, and *interest*, as measured by the Intrinsic Motivation Inventory [3]. Assuming that penalties make games more challenging, there are several plausible hypotheses:

1. *Null*: Penalties have a minor, floor, or ceiling effect on learning and interest.
2. *Reduced gaming*: Penalties increase learning by reducing gaming (caused by low levels of interest), but have little effect on low levels of interest.
3. *Tutored game*: Penalties decrease learning and interest because they waste instructional time and are unnecessary for generating interest.
4. *Walkthrough game*: Penalties increase interest by making the game more challenging and do not harm learning because they do not affect the assistance provided.
5. *Hardcore game*: Penalties decrease interest by making the game too challenging.

We predicted support for either the *null* or *hardcore cognitive game hypothesis* based on the motivational importance game designers place on penalties and our previous finding that a *minimal penalties* version of the cognitive game increased learning and aspects of interest more than "game-like" version with minimal feedback and penalties [2]–possibly suggesting that lack of feedback in the game-like version decreased learning and masked the motivational effects of penalties.

2 Method

Design. Learners played the anime-adventure game *Policy World* that taught them 4 policy analysis skills: *comprehending* causal claims in text, *evaluating* evidence for claims, *diagramming* claims, and *synthesizing* evidence across claims. The study used a two-group, between subjects, randomized, controlled, experimental design that compared a *harsh penalties* version with a *minimal penalties* version of the game. During training, the harsh penalties version of Policy World erased learners' progress upon making a mistake. When the learners made errors on an analysis step for a particular causal claim, they were sent back to the first analysis step. When learners received 5 debate strikes, they had to replay the level. The minimal penalties version allowed learners to correct errors with no loss of progress.

Participants. 100 university students were recruited through campus flyers and email. Students were compensated $16 for completing the study and an additional $4 for beating posttest 1 and an additional $4 for beating posttest 2.

Procedure. Students first took a pretest on either the drinking age (5 causal claims) or obesity (7 causal claims). During the pretest, students were allowed to search and analyze as many or as few reports as they liked before continuing to the debate. Students were then randomly assigned to the *harsh* or *minimal penalties* training. Each group completed 3 training problems on video game violence (4 causal claims), organic foods (5 causal claims), and vaccines (4 causal claims). During training, harsh penalties students received penalties for errors while minimal penalties students did not. Since it was possible that harsh penalties students might take much longer on training, they were allowed to advance to the test levels after 1 hour on the training levels. After training, students completed the intrinsic motivation inventory survey [3] with sub-scales measuring perceived competence, effort, pressure, choice, value and interest. Finally, students played two test levels without penalties or tutoring. The debate test (on cap-and-trade, with 8 causal claims) was a debate-only level that provided a completed diagram (to test hypotheses about debate skills outside the scope of this paper). Students then took a posttest identical to, and counterbalanced with, the pretest.

3 Results

Table 1. Both groups learned analysis but the minimal penalties group learned more

		Pretest		Posttest	
Analysis skill	**Penalties**	**M**	**SD**	**M**	**SD**
Comprehend	*Harsh*	2.68	1.92	3.50	1.79
	Minimal	2.24	1.82	4.26	1.64
Evaluate	*Harsh*	1.72	1.58	2.38	1.59
	Minimal	1.68	1.63	3.10	1.72
Diagram	*Harsh*	2.26	1.77	3.36	1.79
	Minimal	1.94	1.68	4.08	1.68
Synthesize	*Harsh*	2.76	2.19	4.00	2.06
	Minimal	2.66	2.50	4.60	2.34

Table 2. The ANOVA showed a significant increase on all analysis skills for both groups and a greater increase on 3 out of 4 skills for the minimal penalties group

	Test (pre/post)				Penalty				Test-penalty interaction			
	df	**F**	**p**	**GES**	**df**	**F**	**p**	**GES**	**df**	**F**	**p**	**GES**
Comprehend	1 98	53.4	7.5E-11 *	0.138	1 98	0.28	0.60	0.002	1 98	9.53	2.6E-03 *	0.028
Evaluation	1 98	36.4	2.9E-08 *	0.094	1 98	1.51	0.22	0.011	1 98	4.86	3.0E-02 *	0.014
Diagram	1 98	70.9	3.2E-13 *	0.183	1 98	0.48	0.49	0.003	1 98	7.31	8.1E-03 *	0.022
Synthesize	1 98	39.2	9.8E-09 *	0.110								

Analysis 1: Do penalties affect learning? To examine how penalties affect learning we examined students' pre/post test differences in analysis skills across the minimal/harsh penalties groups using a two-way, repeated measures (mixed) ANOVA. Both groups improved on all skills. The minimal penalty group showed significantly greater improvement than the harsh penalty group on comprehension, evaluation and diagramming and a (not significantly) greater improvement on synthesis, (Table 1-2).

Analysis 2: Do penalties affect intrinsic motivation? To examine how penalties affect interest we asked students to complete a well-validated interest questionnaire, the intrinsic motivation inventory [3], immediately after the three training levels and analyzed the results with pair-wise t tests. Table 3 shows that the minimal penalties group felt significantly more competent, found the game more interesting and more valuable for learning about policy.

Table 3. Penalties decreased perceived interest, competence and value

	Harsh		Minimal						
	M	SD	M	SD	t	df	p	ll	ul
Interest	3.44	1.32	3.93	1.24	1.89	97.62	0.061 .	-0.02	0.99
Effort	4.83	1.06	4.83	1.09	-0.02	97.88	0.985	-0.43	0.42
Choice	3.41	0.82	3.50	0.87	0.57	97.59	0.567	-0.24	0.43
Competence	3.45	1.43	4.17	1.20	2.71	94.91	0.008 **	0.19	1.24
Pressure	3.74	1.64	3.74	1.06	0.01	84.13	0.988	-0.54	0.55
Value	3.88	1.56	4.41	1.34	1.80	95.91	0.075 .	-0.05	1.10

4 Discussion

The results show that penalties decrease learning and interest in cognitive games. While these results contradict possible intuitions about the motivational effects of penalties, they are consistent with the effects on learning of previous work on combining tutors and games, which found that greater assistance also increased learning and motivation through similar mechanisms[2]. Thus, as the main contribution of this work, we propose a *minimize penalties principle*—that cognitive games should reduce penalties to increase learning and interest. This means that we can embed tutors in games to increases learning and interest with *no tradeoff*.

References

1. VanLehn, K.: The relative effectiveness of human tutoring, intelligent tutoring systems, and other tutoring systems. Educational Psychologist 46(4), 197–221 (2011)
2. Easterday, M.W., Aleven, V., Scheines, R., Carver, S.M.: Using Tutors to Improve Educational Games. In: Biswas, G., Bull, S., Kay, J., Mitrovic, A. (eds.) AIED 2011. LNCS (LNAI), vol. 6738, pp. 63–71. Springer, Heidelberg (2011)
3. University of Rochester: Intrinsic Motivation Inventory (IMI) (Web page) (1994), http://www.psych.rochester.edu/SDT/measures/IMI_description.php (retrieved)

An Evaluation of the Effectiveness of Just-In-Time Hints

Robert G.M. Hausmann, Annalies Vuong, Brendon Towle, Scott H. Fraundorf, R. Charles Murray, and John Connelly

Carnegie Learning, Inc.
Frick Building, Suite 918
437 Grant Street, Pittsburgh, PA, 15219
{bhausmann,avuong,btowle,sfraundorf,cmurray,jconnelly}@carnegielearning.com

Abstract. The present study evaluates the effectiveness of *Just-In-Time Hints* (*JITs*) by testing two competing hypotheses about learning from errors. The *tutor-remediation hypothesis* predicts that students learn best when a tutoring system immediately explains why an entry is incorrect. The *self-remediation hypothesis* predicts that learning is maximized when learners attempt to correct their own errors. The *Cognitive Tutor* was used to test these hypotheses because it offers both JITs, which map onto the tutor-remediation hypothesis, and flag feedback, which maps onto the self-remediation hypothesis. To evaluate the effectiveness of JITs, we conducted a naturalistic experiment where learning from older versions of the software, which did not include specific JITs, was contrasted with a later version that included the JITs. The results suggest JITs reduced the frequency of errors; however, this observation was qualified by an aptitude-treatment interaction whereby high- and low-prior knowledge students differentially benefited from JIT availability.

Keywords: Just-in-time help, feedback, naturalistic experimentation, aptitude-treatment interaction.

1 Introduction

One core belief of the intelligent tutoring system (ITS) community is that intelligent tutoring systems are effective because they provide contextually relevant assistance on individual steps, typically in the form of a hint [1]. Either the student can request a hint, or the system can provide assistance based on the student's recent performance. In the case where the system knows about a common student misconception and automatically delivers a hint based on the current (wrong) entry, we refer to that as a *just-in-time* hint, or a *JIT* for short.

A review of the learning literature suggests two hypotheses about maximizing the probability a student will learn from an error. The first, which we call the *tutor-remediation hypothesis,* posits that learning occurs during the explicit remediation of an error. For example, Anderson *et al.* found that students who received explanatory feedback made fewer errors than students who received only error-flagging feedback.

K. Yacef et al. (Eds.): AIED 2013, LNAI 7926, pp. 791–794, 2013.

Students who received explanatory feedback also took less time to complete the task, although the differences did not persist on a long-term assessment [2].

The second hypothesis, which we call the *self-remediation hypothesis*, places more emphasis on students generating their own explanations for mistakes. In general, learning is more effective when students are required to generate or process the to-be-learned material on their own, rather than having it done for them [3].

2 Method

Both the tutor-remediation and self-remediation hypotheses inform the design of intelligent tutoring systems. The *Cognitive Tutor* employs "just-in-time hints," which map onto the tutor-remediation hypothesis. It also offers immediate "flag feedback," which maps onto the self-remediation hypothesis. Although the *Cognitive Tutor* incorporates both features into its design, the relative strength of including a JIT on a specific problem-solving step is an open question. How much learning improvement might we expect from providing a JIT over and above the mere flagging of an incorrect entry? Moreover, does the effectiveness of a JIT depend on student factors, such as the strength of the student's current understanding? The purpose of our study is to contrast the above hypotheses while looking for an aptitude-treatment interaction [4].

To test the learning improvements provided by a JIT, we needed to compare one group of students presented with a JIT in response to a particular set of inputs, to another group of students not presented with a JIT in response to the same inputs. We elected to do this via a natural experiment; in the course of ongoing *Cognitive Tutor* development, we typically add JITs for inputs that are believed to require them. The result is that students using the tutor in year N+1 will see JITs for inputs that did not provide JITs for students in year N. Thus, our method was to identify JITs that:

1. were contained in sections of the tutor that did not change appreciably at the same time the JIT was added; and,
2. had sufficiently detailed student information logged in our database in the year the JIT was added, as well as in the following year.

These conditions led us to study JITs added in 2008 or 2009. From a random sample of one-third of all schools that used *Cognitive Tutor*, we included all 320 students who produced input that did or could have triggered one of the target JITs. We can thus compare students from the year before the JIT was added to students from the following year, with a high degree of confidence that any changes in student performance were due to the addition of the JIT and not to any confounding factors.

3 Results

To better understand the effectiveness of JITs, we analyzed the percentage of errors (i.e., the number of errors / total number of transactions) between the point at which students did or would have triggered a JIT and the point at which they mastered the skill. Students who did not receive a JIT (M = 26%, SD = 16%) made proportionally more errors on subsequent transactions than students who received a JIT (M = 20%; SD = 14%), $t(434) = 3.32$, $p < .01$, d =.40). This result suggests that JITs were helpful in reducing errors, and it also supports the tutor-remediation hypothesis.

To further clarify this result, we conducted an analysis to determine whether high- versus low-knowledge students differentially benefit from the availability of JITs. We explored this using the estimated probability that the student knows a skill, or *p_known*, given past performance. At the moment she received (or would have received) a JIT, the tutor's runtime engine computes this probability, which is represented as the current value of *p_known* in the Bayesian Knowledge Tracing (BKT) algorithm. A student whose probability of mastery was above the median value was considered *High Prior Knowledge* (High PK), whereas a student who was below the median was labeled *Low Prior Knowledge* (Low PK).

We conducted a 2x2 ANOVA to examine an aptitude (High PK vs. Low PK) by JIT availability (No JIT vs. JIT) interaction. There was a significant main effect for prior knowledge, confirming that our two groups were indeed different, $F(1, 432) = 84.18$, $p < .01$. There was no main effect for the version of the system, $F < 1$. More importantly, the main effects were qualified by a marginally significant interaction and a large effect size, $F(1, 432) = 2.90$, $p < .10$, $\eta_p^2 = .17$.[1] High prior knowledge students took slightly longer to master their skills when they did not see a JIT, whereas the reverse was true for the low prior knowledge students (see Figure 1). The low prior knowledge students who saw a JIT required slightly more interactions with the tutor to master their skills than did students who did not see the JIT. This evidence suggests that JITs' effectiveness may depend on students' having sufficient knowledge to comprehend the JIT's intended message.

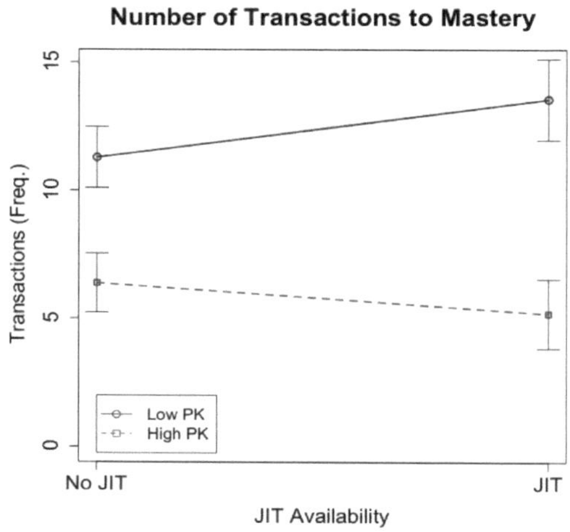

Fig. 1. The interaction between prior knowledge and the exposure to a JIT on the average number of transactions needed to master a skill. Error bars indicate standard error of the mean.

[1] The effect size indicator, partial eta squared (η_p^2), can be interpreted as small when $\eta_p^2 < .06$, medium when $.06 < \eta_p^2 < .14$, and large when $\eta_p^2 > .14$.

4 Discussion

This paper makes two contributions to the ITS literature. First, it demonstrates that the benefits of including a JIT in a sequence of problem-solving steps are contingent on the student's current level of understanding. If students have a sufficiently high understanding of the step, then it is likely that a JIT will help them master the skill more quickly. However, if understanding has not yet reached a certain level, then the JIT is not as effective. The second contribution is methodological. The present analyses represent a "natural experiment" because we were able to manipulate the presence or absence of a JIT depending on the year the software was used. This is analogous to a between-groups experimental design; however, various features of the tutor change between versions because of on-going attempts to improve the software.

To more broadly generalize about the effectiveness of JITs on learning, we would like to extend our sample to include various types of JITs. For example, it would be interesting to extend these analyses by categorizing the types of JITs themselves, such as those that provide simplistic (e.g., "You entered the coordinates with x and y reversed.") versus conceptually rich (e.g., "Remember that you need to count the area of the base twice, once for the top of the cylinder and once for the bottom.") feedback messages. Different types of JITs may be differentially effective, and certain types may depend more heavily on the strength of the student's current understanding.

In conclusion, we found more evidence in favor of the tutor-remediation hypothesis. Students who were exposed to JITs were more effective in remediating their local errors; however, the long-term impact on learning may be contingent upon the student's current understanding of the skill. Additional work in this area will help build systems that better understand how to use ongoing skill estimates and how to provide students with they help they need.

Acknowledgements. The authors would like to thank the schools that allowed us to collect log files from their students. More importantly, we wish to thank all of the anonymous students who used our software. Special thanks go to Leslie Hausmann for her valuable comments on an earlier draft of this paper.

References

[1] Wood, H., Wood, D.: Help seeking, learning and contingent tutoring. Computers & Education 33, 153–169 (1999)

[2] Anderson, J.R., Corbett, A.T., Koedinger, K.R., Pelletier, R.: Cognitive tutors: Lessons learned. The Journal of the Learning Sciences 4, 167–207 (1995)

[3] Schmidt, R., Bjork, R.: New Conceptualization of Practice: Common Principles in Three Paradigms Suggest New Concepts for Training. Psychological Science 3, 207–217 (1992)

[4] McNamara, D.S., Kintsch, E., Songer, N., Kintsch, W.: Are good texts always better? Interactions of text coherence, background knowledge, and levels of understanding in learning from text. Cognition and Instruction 14, 1–43 (1996)

Repairing Deactivating Negative Emotions with Student Progress Pages

Dovan Rai[1], Ivon Arroyo[2], Lynn Stephens[2], Cecil Lozano[3], Winslow Burleson[3], Beverly Park Woolf[2], and Joseph E. Beck[1]

[1] Department of Computer Science, Worcester Polytechnic Institute
{dovan,josephbecj}@wpi.edu
[2] Department of Computer Science, University of Massachusetts, Amherst
{Ivon,Lynn,Bev}@cs.umass.edu
[3] School of Computing and Informatics, Arizona State University
{ceci.lozano,winslow.burleson}@asu.edu

Abstract. We report on two studies that suggest that showing reports of student progress at key moments of deactivating negative emotions (boredom or lack of excitement) can help improve students' affective state and learning behavior while using an adaptive math tutoring system. The studies involved 160 middle-school students in public schools in Arizona and California who reported higher levels of interest and excitement and also demonstrated more positive engagement behavior when using the intervention progress pages.

Keywords: affect, engagement behavior, metacognition, open learner modeling.

1 Motivation

One major factor that biases students' academic success is their emotions and their general affective experience while learning. Research has shown that students' affect (e.g., confidence, boredom, and confusion) is a strong predictor of achievement [6]. Given the pivotal role that affect plays in education, both in short term performance outcomes and in long term life-long career choices, researchers have developed affect-aware technologies that can automatically detect and respond to student affect [1, 3, 5]. While modeling affect, a critical first step in providing adaptive support tailored to students' affective needs, very little work exists on systematically exploring the impact of affective pedagogical interventions on students' performance, learning, affect and attitudes, i.e., how to respond to students' emotions, such as frustration, anxiety, boredom and hopelessness, as they arise. The research described here starts to fill this gap by analyzing the value of tailoring different types of interventions for negative affective states, such as deactivating emotions, and responding to these specific states.

2 Metacognitive Support and the Student Progress Page

This research was conducted within a well-tested intelligent mathematics tutor for grades 5-12 developed at UMass-Amherst and named Wayang Outpost.[1] Prior research

[1] Wayang Outpost is described in detail at http://wayangoutpost.com/

K. Yacef et al. (Eds.): AIED 2013, LNAI 7926, pp. 795–798, 2013.

showed positive evidence for the impact of basic progress charts on post-tutor affective and performance outcomes, which showed individual student progress on the last 5 problems [2]. One possibility is that such meta-cognitive support would help to address students' deactivating negative emotions (e.g., boredom and lack of engagement).

We extended this metacognitive support by creating a Student Progress Page (SPP) that supports students to observe their performance and the tutor's assessment and feedback (Figure 1). The page lists mathematics topics (rows) and provides sophisticated meta-cognitive scaffolding to support students to reflect on the tutor's inferences about their effort (column 2) and knowledge (column 3). One hypothesis of this research is that providing meta-cognitive support through the Student Progress Page will generate cascading effects: it should enhance students' affective state (interest and excitement), which should increase student engagement and productive behaviors such as spending time on help, which should lead to higher learning.

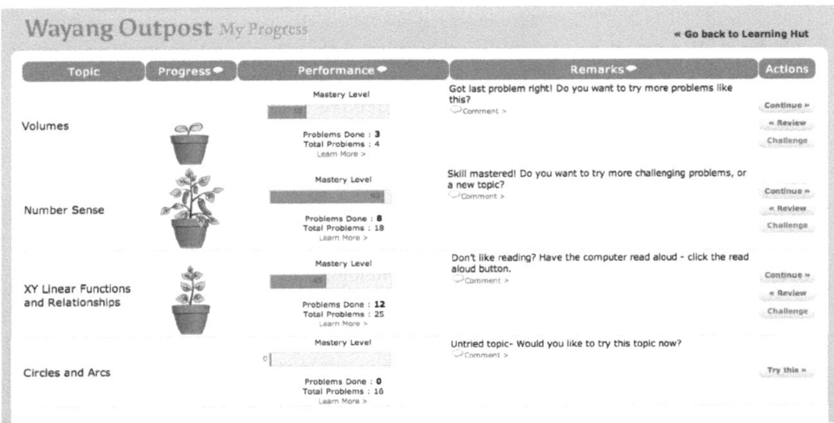

Fig. 1. The Student Progress Page (SPP) encourages students to reflect about their progress on each topic (column 1) and to make informed decision about future choices. The plant (column 2) demonstrates an assessment of student effort and the mastery bar (column 3) records students' presumed knowledge. The tutor comments about student behavior (column 4) and offers students the choice to continue, review or challenge themselves (column 5).

Verpoortan (2011) makes argument that this crisscrossing between content-related and self-related dimensions may cultivate awareness and coordination of the various personal and contextual dimensions of learning. We propose that the SPP provides many of the benefits predicted for open student models [4]: promote meta-cognitive activities; support learners to take greater control and responsibility over their learning; encourage learner independence; and increase learner trust in an adaptive educational environment.

3 Experiments and Results

We conducted two studies (a pilot study in May 2012 and a main study in January 2013) with middle school students from public schools in Arizona and California. All students had the progress page available via the "my progress" button. In addition, all students were asked "How interested are you right now? Very Bored … Very Interested", or "How excited are you right now? Very excited … Not excited at all", every five minutes but only after a problem was completed. The main difference between conditions was that students in the experimental condition were invited to see the progress page immediately after they reported low levels of excitement or interest (boredom). Students could accept the offer, or reject it and continue. In both studies, students were randomly assigned to an experimental or a control condition and used Wayang Outpost over three class sessions within a week.

Affective Outcomes. We considered all student reports of excitement and interest, and because students were not "forced" to answer, we eliminated cases where students skipped the report. We calculated mean values for "interest" and "excitement" for each student across her self-reports. Then, we averaged those means across students in each experimental group (31 total students in the pilot study and 83 students in the main study). Significant differences were observed in the mean "excitement" reported between experimental and control groups in the pilot study and "interest" in the main study (see Table 1). The results from both studies study show that students' deactivating emotions improved in conditions where the software decided when to show students the progress reports, as compared to the control condition where this progress page was available but not offered at key moments.

Table 1. Students' mean deactivating emotions within the tutor (Pilot Study) using a scale from 1 (minimum) – 5 (maximum). Numbers in bold type indicate significant values.

	Emotion	Experimental	Control	p-value
		Mean (SD)	**Mean (SD)**	
Pilot Study	Interest	3.71 (0.57) N=15	3.69 (0.56) N=16	0.93
	Excitement	3.86 (0.64) N=15	3.12 (0.84) N=16	**0.01****
Main Study	Interest	3.85 (0.76) N=43	3.47 (0.87) N=40	**0.04***
	Excitement	3.73 (0.73) N=40	3.39(1) N=43	0.08

Engagement Behavior. We used log data from the main study to make inference about student engagement and labeled each series of student actions by an engagement state. Students in the experimental group showed a tendency towards more positive behavior, e.g., requesting more help to solve problems and demonstrating less negative behavior, e.g., quick-guessing and giving up. We calculated the mean number of problems that students solved on first attempt with no help (SOF), that students solved once incorrectly but corrected themselves with no need for help (ATT), solved with hints (SHINT), quick-guessed (GUESS), or abandoned without giving the correct answer (GIVEUP).

We generated an *EngagedBehavior* measure for each student, by adding the total number of problems where students reflected an engaged behavior (SOF, ATT and SHINT) and subtracted the ones that reflected a disengaged behavior (GUESS and GIVEUP).

$$EngagedBehavior = SOF + ATT + SHINT - GUESS - GIVEUP \quad (1)$$

EngagedBehavior was found to be significantly correlated with the mean level of "Interest" reported by each student (correlation = 0.37**). We also found that students in the experimental group demonstrated significantly higher instances of *EngagedBehavior* as shown in table 2.

Table 2. Engagement Behavior and Hints asked (Main Study). Numbers in bold type indicate significant values.

	Experimental (N = 44)	**Control (N = 44)**	**p-value**
	Mean (SD)	Mean (SD)	
Hints asked	24 (22)	16 (16)	**0.05***
EngagedBehavior	12 (14)	6 (15)	**0.05***

We observed that SPP, as metacognitive support, enhances both emotions and engagement behavior. We assume that better affective states and engagement behavior should lead to higher learning. However, we were not able to measure learning gain in our main study due to technical issues. We would like to test this hypothesis again in our next study. We also realize the need for richer interaction data (e.g. eye tracking data) and qualitative assessments to infer metacognitive gains along with affective gains that lead to effective learning outcomes.

References

1. Arroyo, I., Cooper, D.G., Burleson, W., Woolf, B.P., Muldner, K., Christopherson, R.: Emotion sensors go to school. In: Proceedings of the 14th International Conference on Artificial Intelligence in Education, pp. 17–24 (2009)
2. Arroyo, I., Ferguson, K., Johns, J., Dragon, T., Meheranian, H., Fisher, D., Barto, A., Mahadevan, S., Woolf, B.P.: Repairing disengagement with non-invasive intervention. In: Proceedings of the 13th International Conference on Artificial Intelligence in Education, pp. 195–202 (2009)
3. Baker, R., D'Mello, S., Rodrigo, M., Graesser, A.: Better to be frustrated than bored: The incidence, persistence, and impact of learners' cognitive-affective states during interactions with three different computer-based learning environments. International Journal of Human-Computer Studies 68(4), 223–241 (2010)
4. Bull, S.: Preferred features of open learner models for university students. In: Cerri, S.A., Clancey, W.J., Papadourakis, G., Panourgia, K. (eds.) ITS 2012. LNCS, vol. 7315, pp. 411–421. Springer, Heidelberg (2012)
5. D'Mello, S., Graesser, A.: Language and discourse are powerful signals of student emotions during tutoring. IEEE Transactions on Learning Technologies (2012)
6. Pekrun, R., Goetz, T., Daniels, L., Stupinsky, R., Perry, R.: Boredom in achievement settings: exploring control–value antecedents and performance outcomes of a neglected emotion. Journal of Educational Psychology 102(3), 531–549 (2010)
7. Verpoorten, D.: A first approach to Learning Dashboards in formal learning contexts (2011), http://dspace.learningnetworks.org

Searching for Predictors of Learning Outcomes in Non Abstract Eye Movement Logs

Janice D. Gobert, Ermal Toto, Michael Brigham, and Michael Sao Pedro

Learning Sciences and Technologies Program, Worcester Polytechnic Institute
{jgobert,toto,mbrigham1223,mikesp}@wpi.edu

Abstract. We present a study that addressed if providing students with scaffolding about how to "integrate" science text and animations impacts content learning. Scaffolding was delivered by a pedagogical agent and driven by student's eye gaze movements (compared to controls). We hypothesized that students in the pedagogical agent condition would engage in richer learning as evidence by a more "integrated" pattern from text to animation and back, etc. In addition to eye gazes we collected pre- and post test knowledge about the domain, and open responses to explanation-type questions. We are currently analyzing these data.

Keywords: Eye tracking, pedagogical agent, plate tectonics, science learning.

1 Introduction

Previous research has shown that pedagogical agents can be effective in directing students' to acquire knowledge from diagrams representing electrical circuits, as evidenced by higher post-test conceptual scores (Ozogul, et al., 2011). Although not used in the aforementioned study, eye-tracking data have been successfully used to understand and create accurate models of user actions (Conati et al., 2005). In the present study, we explore if a pedagogical agent (compared to a control group), driven by eye-tracking data, can be used to effectively promote students' acquisition and integration of information from animations and text, and whether better integration leads to better performance on open response questions and post-test gains (compared to pre-test). We are currently analyzing these data specifically to: 1) test whether the pedagogical agent directed students to "interweave" their knowledge acquisition from text and animations, 2) examine which propositions in the text and viewing areas in the animations were attended to in each condition, and, 3) and examine the post-test conceptual items and explanations in each condition. This is being done with the goal finding useful data that could be incorporated in an online scaffolding system driven by eye tracking traces.

2 Method

2.1 Participants

This study consisted of 30 volunteer middle school students from central Massachusetts who had no prior classroom exposure to plate tectonics. Students' names were entered in a drawing for a gift card as compensation for participation in the study.

K. Yacef et al. (Eds.): AIED 2013, LNAI 7926, pp. 799–802, 2013.

2.2 Materials

Plate Tectonics Activity. In this study, we used four animations and corresponding textual descriptions that were developed in earlier work (Gobert & Pallant, 2004) including: a cross section of the earth, continental-continental convergence, oceanic-continental convergence, and oceanic-oceanic convergence. An example is shown in Figure 1. Reading regions and viewing regions were defined a priori for each of the four screens, also shown in Figure 1.

Eye Tracking System. The computer set-up was augmented with a Mirametrix S1 eye-tracking system to record. We were specifically interested in the order in which students acquired information from sections of the text (defined in Figure 1 as reading regions RR1-6) and their corresponding viewing regions within each animation (VR1-VR6). Backend code was written in C to identify which paragraph or area of the animation the student was looking at and to determine if all the prerequisite regions had been examined. For example, if a student tried to read the second paragraph (RR2) without viewing region 1 (VR1), then, in the scaffolded condition, a message was displayed by Rex, our pedagogical agent. A patent application is in place for this process (Gobert & Toto, 2012).

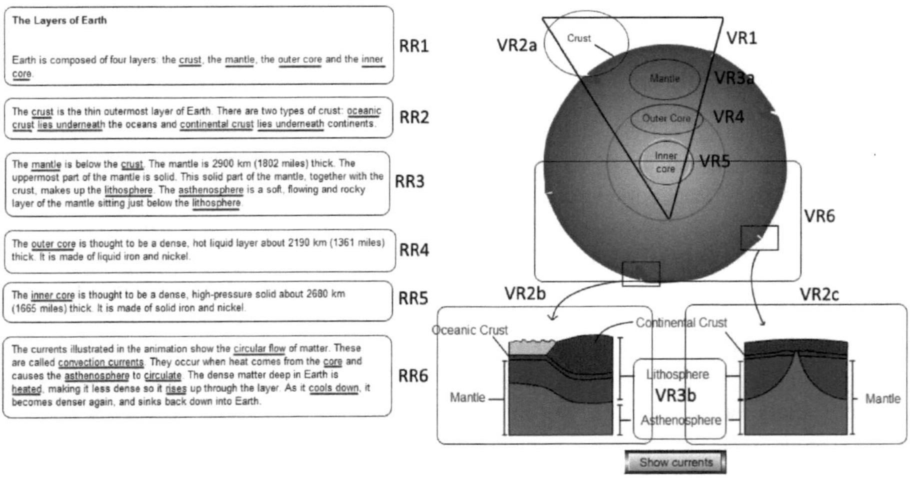

Fig. 1. Example of plate tectonics screen and the eye tracking regions

Pre- and Post-tests. To measure content gains, we constructed 10 multiple-choice and 4 open response questions used as both pre- and post- tests. The tests were composed of questions addressing both spatial/static and causal/dynamic concepts. Static questions tested the participants' understanding of the spatial/static layout of the earth, while dynamic questions tested causal and dynamic concepts about plate tectonics-related phenomena. The open response tasks (4) asked students to write detailed explanations about each screen; for example, the first was: "*Write a detailed explanation describing the different layers of the earth and the processes that happen inside the* *earth. Include all the information about these layers that you can so that a friend who did not do this activity could lean about it?"*

2.3 Procedure

Participants completed a pre-test used to assess each participant's prior knowledge of the domain; this was done in small groups in a computer lab. Using a random number generator, each participant was randomly assigned to either the Rex or control condition (no Rex) and escorted to the eye tracker workstation located in another lab. Once seated at the computer, the eye tracker was adjusted to account for the height and distance of the participant from the monitor. Participants were asked to limit the movement of their head as much as possible during the calibration and data collection session to improve accuracy of the eye tracker. The eye tracker was then calibrated to the individual participant using the software supplied by the manufacturer, Mirametrix. To verify calibration, each participant was then recorded for approximately 10 seconds reading the webpage www.thisafterthat.com, which was chosen for its large text and spacing. If the calibration was sufficiently inaccurate or the eye tracker was not following the participant's eyes, the calibration process was repeated up to 3 times. The final calibration numbers were recorded for each participant and a note was included if the participant wore glasses. Students then viewed and read each of the screens, namely, Layers of the Earth, Continental-Continental Convergence, Oceanic-Continental Convergence, Oceanic-Oceanic Convergence. For those in the control condition, Rex, who was on the lower right portion of the screen, did not generate text. For those in the scaffolded condition, if the prerequisite reading and viewing regions were not viewed/read, such as reading the second paragraph without reading the first, then a scaffolding message was displayed by Rex. After each student was finished with the eye-teaching portion of the task, they were moved to another work station in the same lab and asked to answer the post-test questions and answer the four open response questions.

3 Data Scoring and Analyses

3.1 Labeling of Eye-Tracking Data

As previously stated, the interface is split into regions (see Figure 1). Particular key words (high in semantic value) in the reading regions and parts of images (high in semantic value) were labeled. A human coder watched video playbacks of each student's eye gaze traces and labeled segments of those playbacks with screen regions. As such, the process of manually coding the videos of eye tracking traces generated an output file with three columns: 1) timestamp of the action, 2) interface region, 3) specific area within reading region/viewing region, and 4) current simulation/screen being coded. The timestamps are based on the coder's reaction to observing the students' actions rather than the actions themselves. When factoring the video playback speed, coders' reactions aligned with the actual student actions.

3.2 Scoring of Conceptual Data

Scoring of multiple choice pre- and post-test data was done automatically within the learning environment Science Assistments (Gobert et al., 2012), now referred to as Inq-ITS (www.inq-ITS). Scoring of open response data was done by hand; coders scored each open response tasks according to a two rubrics: one reflecting the inclusion of correct spatial/static information from the text, and one reflecting the inclusion of causal/dynamic information from the text (fuller description of a similar coding scheme can be seen in Gobert & Clement, 1999; Gobert, 2000).

3.3 Data Analysis

We are in the process of analyzing the effects of scaffolding by Rex on the various measures: eye tracking gazes, open responses, and pre-post test gains. Specifically we are: 1) testing whether the pedagogical agent directed students to "interweave" their knowledge acquisition from text and animations, 2) examining which propositions in the text and viewing areas in the animations were attended to in each condition, and, 3) and examining the post-test conceptual items and explanations in each condition. With these data, we will be able to evaluate the efficacy of Rex in guiding students' knowledge acquisition patterns as they read and viewed the animations, and whether such scaffolding lead to: more "interwoven" knowledge acquisition processes, higher post-test gains, and better explanations, as indicated by a larger amount of semantic information reflecting both spatial/static and causal/dynamic information.

References

1. Conati, C., Merten, C., Muldner, K., Ternes, D.: Exploring eye tracking to increase bandwidth in user modeling. In: Ardissono, L., Brna, P., Mitrović, A. (eds.) UM 2005. LNCS (LNAI), vol. 3538, pp. 357–366. Springer, Heidelberg (2005)
2. Gobert, J.D.: A typology of models for plate tectonics: Inferential power and barriers to understanding. International Journal of Science Education 22(9), 937–977 (2000)
3. Gobert, J.D., Clement, J.: Effects of student-generated diagrams versus student-generated summaries on conceptual understanding of causal and dynamic knowledge in plate tectonics. Journal of Research in Science Teaching 36(1), 39–53 (1999)
4. Gobert, J.D., Pallant, A.: Fostering students' epistemologies of models via authentic model-based tasks. Journal of Science Education and Technology 13(1), 7–22 (2004)
5. Gobert, J.D., Toto, E.: An Instruction System with Eyetracking-based Adaptive Scaffolding. US Patent application 13/774,981 (February 22, 2013)
6. Gobert, J.D., Sao Pedro, M., Baker, R., Toto, E., Montalvo, O.: Leveraging educational data mining for real time performance assessment of scientific inquiry skills within microworlds. Journal of Educational Data Mining 4(1), 111–143 (2012)
7. Ozogul, G., Reisslein, M., Johnson, A.M.: Effects of visual signaling on pre-college students' engineering learning performance and attitudes: Peer versus adult pedagogical agents versus arrow signaling. In: Proceedings of the 118th Annual Conference and Exposition of the American Society for Engineering Education (2011)
8. Brigham, M., Levine, E.: Eye Tracking and Prompts for Improved Learning. Interactive Qualifying Project Report, Worcester Polytechnic Institute (2012)

Erroneous Examples as Desirable Difficulty

Deanne M. Adams[1], Bruce M. McLaren[2], Richard E. Mayer[1], George Goguadze[3], and Seiji Isotani[4]

[1] University of California, Santa Barbara, U.S.A.
[2] Carnegie Mellon University, U.S.A.
[3] Leuphana University Lüneburg, Germany
[4] The University of São Paulo, Brazil
bmclaren@cs.cmu.edu

Abstract. Erroneous examples, an unusual and challenging form of learning material, are arguably a type of desirable difficulty for students that could lead to deeper learning. In a series of studies we have done over the past three years involving web-based math instruction, the learning benefits of erroneous examples we have observed occured on delayed tests, as occurs in the desirable difficulties literature. This short paper briefly reviews the literature, summarizes our results, and speculates on how an adaptive version of our materials could better leverage desirable difficulties theory and lead to deeper student learning.

Keywords: erroneous examples, interactive problem solving, adaptation of problems, self-explanation, decimals, mathematics education.

1 Introduction

Erroneous examples are step-by-step descriptions of how to solve a problem in which one or more of the steps are incorrect. In the studies we have done with erroneous examples over the past three years, focused on learning decimals using web-based, interactive materials, middle school students are prompted to find, explain, and fix error(s) in order to more deeply learn how to solve decimal problems.

Presenting students with challenge is central to the notion of learning with erroneous examples. Research on *desirable difficulties* has shown that it is possible to achieve long-term benefits if lessons are designed (or altered) to make them more challenging during learning [1, 2]. Examples of desirable difficulties include mixing the order of tasks for practice (rather than providing tasks in *blocked* fashion); varying the frequency and timing of feedback (rather than providing immediate feedback); and varying tasks with a focus on generalizability. These changes to standard instructional practice have been shown to slow the rate of improvement in students' understanding during the learning process but lead to long-term benefits [1, 2].

The erroneous examples we work with can be viewed as presenting desirable difficulties for students in two ways. First, they are an unusual and challenging form of problem, in which students must find, explain, and correct errors, as opposed to the more standard practice of simply solving problems. Although this characteristic is not

K. Yacef et al. (Eds.): AIED 2013, LNAI 7926, pp. 803–806, 2013.

cited in the original definition of desirable difficulties [1], this type of challenge, which we believe promotes deeper cognitive processing, is also arguably a form of desirable difficulty. Second, the erroneous examples intervention of the present study provides the third type of challenge from Schmidt and Bjork's original desirable difficulties – varying of tasks – by prompting students to grapple with both erroneous examples and problems to solve in the intervention.

The domain we have focused on is decimals. A variety of studies have shown that students often have difficulty mastering decimals and have common and persistent misconceptions [3, 4], as well as problems that extend even into adulthood [5]. For instance, students often treat decimals as if they are whole numbers (e.g. they think 0.15 is greater than 0.8, since 15 is greater than 8, i.e., longer decimals are larger) or they think that all decimals are less than zero.

2 Research on Erroneous Examples

Research on erroneous examples derives from work on *correct* worked examples, which has attracted much attention in the literature and in empirical studies, e.g., [6]. The idea behind worked examples is that they free working memory, which has a limited capacity, which can be used to support learning of new knowledge. Erroneous examples may tax working memory somewhat during learning, but they also may engage students in a different form of active learning, particularly when coupled with self-explanation [7]. Erroneous examples may help students become better at evaluating and justifying solution procedures, which may, in turn, help them learn material at a deeper level. Empirical research in erroneous examples is nascent, but with encouraging results. For instance, Siegler [8] found that self-explaining both correct and incorrect examples (of mathematical equality) is more beneficial than self-explaining correct examples only. Grosse and Renkl [9] studied whether explaining both correct and incorrect examples can help university students learn mathematical probabilities. Their studies also showed learning benefits of erroneous examples but the benefit was only for learners with higher prior knowledge and for far transfer learning only. When errors were highlighted, on the other hand, low prior knowledge individuals did significantly better, while high prior knowledge students did not benefit, presumably because they were already able to identify the error on their own.

3 Our Erroneous Examples Studies and Results

Providing students with interactive erroneous examples is the approach that we take in our research. By *interactive* we mean that students are prompted to actively engage with the examples. More specifically, our computer-based materials first prompt a student to review an error made by a fictitious peer, next request that the student explain the error (from a multiple-choice list), then correct the error and explain how to solve problems of this type (again from a multiple-choice list). At every step the student's action is evaluated for correctness.

We have conducted two previously published studies with interactive erroneous examples [10, 11]. In the first study [10] an interactive erroneous examples condition did not lead to learning benefits compared to a worked examples condition and problem solving condition. We attributed this result to two things: (1) A cognitively taxing self-explanation step, in which students were prompted to complete explanations of incorrect steps by filling in two phrases of a sentence, using pull-down menus. Students struggled with this task, possibly undercutting the intended benefit we intended. (2) We did not prompt students to correct the errors and produce the correct answers themselves, a step we now believe to be a critical component of interactive erroneous examples.

Our second study [11] was conducted after revising the interactive erroneous examples along these two dimensions (i.e., simplifying the self-explanation step by prompting for only a single sentence completion phrase and prompting students to correct errors). With 100+ students in each of two conditions – interactive erroneous examples and supported problem solving – an effect was found: students who worked with the interactive erroneous examples did significantly better than the problem solving students on a delayed posttest (but not on an immediate posttest).

Our third study, which will be published in a forthcoming journal article, employed the same materials as described in [11] but entailed a much larger population of students. More specifically, our latest results are a combination of the [11] results and the running of the study five more times at three additional schools over the course of a year. The total number of subjects per condition is more than three times that of [11] – over 300 students per condition. In addition, a third condition of 82 students, in which subjects were presented with erroneous examples in adaptive fashion, based on a Bayes Net assessment of their misconceptions on the pretest, was included in the final three versions of the study. These results indicate, once again, that students who worked with the interactive erroneous examples did significantly better than the problem solving students on a delayed posttest (but not on an immediate posttest). Surprisingly, the adaptive condition did not lead to significantly better learning results than the other two conditions on either the immediate or delayed posttest.

4 Discussion and Conclusion

Our results provide evidence that working with interactive erroneous examples can help students learn mathematics, delivering a learning experience similar to other types of desirable difficulties, one that facilitates deeper understanding over time instead of immediately.

However, the adaptive erroneous examples condition, which we hypothesized would be even better than the erroneous examples condition, did not result in higher learning gains. A blocked format of material presentation may have had a negative affect on the adaptive condition. In this condition many students displayed one (or two) prominent misconception(s) on the pretest and thus received a large number of problems of similar type(s), i.e., the blocking was very prominent in the adaptive condition. Thus, a modification to the adaptive algorithm to provide more problem variability (and thus more desirable difficulty) could make a big difference.

Acknowledgements. The U.S. Department of Education (IES), Award No: R305A090460, provided support for this research. We also thank the Pittsburgh Science of Learning Center, NSF Grant # 0354420, for technical support of our work.

References

1. Schmidt, R.A., Bjork, R.A.: New conceptualization of practice: Common principles in three paradigms suggest new concepts for training. Psych. Science 3(4), 207–217 (1992)
2. Bjork, E.L., Bjork, R.A.: Making things hard on yourself, but in a good way: Creating desirable difficulties to enhance learning. In: Gernsbacher, M.A., Pew, R.W., Hough, L.M., Pomerantz, J.R. (eds.) Psychology and the Real World: Essays Illustrating Fundamental Contributions to Society, pp. 56–64. Worth Publishers, New York (2011)
3. Irwin, K.C.: Using everyday knowledge of decimals to enhance understanding. Journal for Research in Mathematics Education 32(4), 399–420 (2001)
4. Sackur-Grisvard, C., Léonard, F.: Intermediate cognitive organizations in the process of learning a mathematical concept: The order of positive decimal numbers. Cognition and Instruction 2, 157–174 (1985)
5. Stacey, K., Helme, S., Steinle, V., Baturo, A., Irwin, K., Bana, J.: Preservice teachers' knowledge of difficulties in decimal numeration. Journal of Mathematics Teacher Education 4, 205–225 (2001)
6. Renkl, A., Atkinson, R.K.: Learning from worked-out examples and problem solving. In: Plass, J.L., Moreno, R., Brünken, R. (eds.) Cognitive Load Theory. Cambridge University Press, Cambridge (2010)
7. Fonseca, B., Chi, M.T.H.: The self-explanation effect: A constructive learning activity. In: Mayer, R., Alexander, P. (eds.) The Handbook of Research on Learning and Instruction, pp. 270–321. Routledge Press, New York (2001)
8. Siegler, R.S.: Microgenetic studies of self-explanation. In: Granott, N., Parziale, J. (eds.) Microdevelopment, Transition Processes in Development and Learning, pp. 31–58. Cambridge University Press (2002)
9. Grosse, C.S., Renkl, A.: Finding and fixing errors in worked examples: Can this foster learning outcomes? Learning and Instruction 17(6), 612–634 (2007)
10. Isotani, S., Adams, D., Mayer, R.E., Durkin, K., Rittle-Johnson, B., McLaren, B.M.: Can erroneous examples help middle-school students learn decimals? In: Kloos, C.D., Gillet, D., Crespo García, R.M., Wild, F., Wolpers, M. (eds.) EC-TEL 2011. LNCS, vol. 6964, pp. 181–195. Springer, Heidelberg (2011)
11. McLaren, B.M., Adams, D., Durkin, K., Goguadze, G., Mayer, R.E., Rittle-Johnson, B., Sosnovsky, S., Isotani, S., van Velsen, M.: To err is human, to explain and correct is divine: A study of interactive erroneous examples with middle school math students. In: Ravenscroft, A., Lindstaedt, S., Kloos, C.D., Hernández-Leo, D. (eds.) EC-TEL 2012. LNCS, vol. 7563, pp. 222–235. Springer, Heidelberg (2012)

Repairing Disengagement in Collaborative Dialogue for Game-Based Learning

Fernando J. Rodríguez, Natalie D. Kerby, and Kristy Elizabeth Boyer

Department of Computer Science, North Carolina State University, Raleigh, NC 27695
{fjrodri3,ndkerby,keboyer}@ncsu.edu

Abstract. Successfully promoting engagement within learning environments is a subject of increasing attention within the AI in Education community. Evidence is mounting that game-based learning environments hold great potential to engage students, but disengaged behavior is still observed. Devising adaptive strategies to re-engage students in the learning task is a key open research question. Toward that end, this paper examines the collaborative behavior of pairs of middle school students solving game-based computer science problems. We examine the dialogue moves that were used by a more engaged learner to repair a partner's disengagement and consider the implications that these strategies may have for designing collaborative game-based learning environments.

Keywords: Engagement, Collaboration, Dialogue, Game-Based Learning.

1 Introduction

A growing body of empirical findings has revealed the importance of supporting learner engagement. Disengagement has been associated with decreased learning, both overall and with respect to local learning outcomes [1, 2]. Targeted interventions can positively impact engagement, for example, by influencing students to spend more time on subsequent problems [3]. A promising approach to support engagement involves adding game elements to learning environments [4, 5] or creating game-based learning environments with engaging narratives [6]. However, even with these effective systems, some disengaged behaviors are negatively associated with learning, and the relationships between engagement and learning are not fully understood.

Collaboration also holds great promise for supporting engagement and can be combined with game-based learning environments [7]. Results have demonstrated the importance of well-timed help for collaborators [8] and the promise of pedagogical agents that support self-explanation [9]. In the problem-solving domain of computer science, a combination of hints and collaboration support may be particularly helpful [10]. However, many open questions remain. This paper examines the dialogue moves that were used by a more engaged learner to repair a partner's disengagement and considers the implications that these patterns may have for the design of collaborative game-based learning environments.

K. Yacef et al. (Eds.): AIED 2013, LNAI 7926, pp. 807–810, 2013.

2 Description of Study and Data

The corpus was collected within a computer science elective course for middle school students (ages 11 to 14). Participants included 18 males and 2 females, though the female pair was absent on the day the present corpus was collected. (This gender disparity is an intrinsic problem in many technology electives and is an important component of our related research.) Students worked in pairs to solve three game-based tasks using a drag-and-drop visual programming language (Fig. 1).

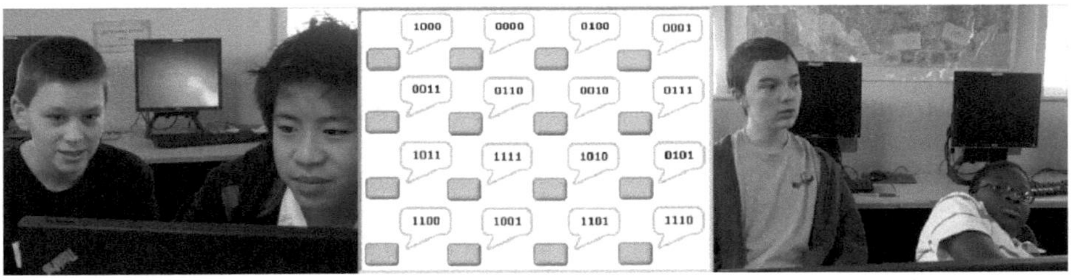

(a) Engaged pair (b) Software interface (c) Disengaged pair

Fig. 1. Collaborative setup and interface

Students took turns controlling the keyboard and mouse [7]. In computer science education, this is often referred to as *pair programming*: the *driver* actively creates the solution, while the *navigator* provides feedback [11]. Students were asked by a researcher to switch roles every 6 minutes. The maximum allowed time was 40 minutes, with two pairs finishing sooner. Video was recorded using a tripod-mounted camera recording at 640x480 resolution. The nine videos were divided into 5-minute segments to facilitate annotation. Of the total 65 segments, 25 were randomly selected for annotation and serve as the basis for the results presented here (a subset was necessary due to the time requirement of manual annotation, in this case approximately 8 minutes per minute of video). Each segment was annotated for student disengagement by observing for one of three signs of disengagement: posture, gaze, and dialogue. The judge paused the video, annotated the start time of the disengagement event, then continued and annotated the end time, rewinding as needed.

An inter-annotator reliability study was conducted for presence of disengagement, and who (self, partner, or instructor) appeared to facilitate re-engagement. Twelve of the 65 video segments were randomly selected and assigned to two judges, and the tagged segments were subsequently discretized into one-second intervals. The Kappa for disengagement was 0.59 (87.25% agreement). For the events on which both judges agreed that disengagement had occurred, the tag for who facilitated re-engagement resulted in a Kappa of 0.60 (78.57% agreement).

3 Results

Overall, drivers spent an average of 16.4% of their time disengaged (σ=16.6%), compared to 42.6% for navigators (σ=24.1%). Overall, 76.8% of re-engagements were self re-engagements. However, the collaborative role plays an important part: drivers had an 87.7% probability of self re-engaging, while navigators had a 68.7% probability of self re-engaging. These findings indicate that repairing one's own disengaged state is more challenging for the partner who is not actively at the controls. In order to examine strategies that are effective at repairing disengagement of one's partner, we consider all instances where the driver re-engaged a disengaged navigator through dialogue. There are 22 such instances. Four are questions addressed to the collaborative partner, such as, "OK, now where?" These questions re-engaged the navigator in part because attending to the speaker is a social dialogue norm. Two utterances served as exclamations, e.g., "What the heck?" In these cases, the driver was expressing surprise with an event in the learning environment, which drew the disengaged student's attention back to the task. The remaining utterances were fragments, such as, "Pick up current tile...," though one utterance explicitly reminded the disengaged student about short time remaining, "So we only have a couple of minutes."

To examine these re-engagement events in context, we consider two excerpts (Table 1). In Excerpt A, the navigator gets stuck and raises his hand for help, briefly becoming disengaged before his partner asks for feedback. In Excerpt B, the navigator engages in off-topic dialogue with another team. Meanwhile, the driver makes a plan and then calls for the navigator's attention. These excerpts suggest that within a collaborative game-based learning environment, providing both students with a sense of control is particularly important. To accomplish this goal with a single-computer game-based environment, each student could be provided with different responsibilities and complementary information, even if this additional information is external to the game environment. Additionally, intelligent learning environments may leverage strategic dialogue moves to re-engage disengaged students, a direction that holds particular promise given recent advances in automatic tracking technologies.

Table 1. Dialogue excerpts

Timestamp	Role	Dialogue Excerpt A
19:25	**Navigator:**	OK, if prime, number is prime. Dang!
		[*Navigator notices instructor nearby, raises hand*]
19:34	**Navigator:**	Uh...
Disengaged		[*Navigator looks away from screen, leans back on seat*]
19:38	**Driver:**	OK, now where?
Re-engaged		[*Navigator points at program block*]
19:40	**Navigator:**	Put it there.
		Dialogue Excerpt B
		[Note: students are discussing '@' symbols]
26:01	**Navigator:**	OK, @'s. Do you want more @'s... (inaudible)
26:08	**Driver:**	One two three four five
Disengaged		[*Navigator looks away to talk to another student*]
26:14	**Driver:**	I have an idea. You (taps navigator's shoulder)
Re-engaged		
26:16	**Navigator:**	Me?

4 Conclusion and Future Work

Supporting engagement within a collaborative game-based learning environment may be particularly important for the collaborator who is not at the controls. These learners may cycle rapidly in and out of attending to the learning environment. Because of strong social norms associated with human dialogue, strategic moves by a partner can serve to re-engage a student. Promising future work includes exploring the extent to which these strategic moves may be leveraged within an adaptive dialogue system. It is also important for future work to examine the duration of engagement and effectiveness of interventions. Additionally, it is important to integrate automated methods of measuring disengagement. Finally, addressing issues of diversity and groupwise differences is an essential direction in order to develop game-based learning environments that support engagement and learning for all students.

Acknowledgements. The authors wish to thank Joseph Grafsgaard and Alexandria Vail for their contributions. This work is supported in part by NSF through grants CNS-1138497 and CNS-1042468. Any opinions, findings, conclusions, or recommendations expressed in this report are those of the participants and do not necessarily represent the official views, opinions, or policy of the National Science Foundation.

References

1. Forbes-Riley, K., Litman, D.: When does disengagement correlate with learning in spoken dialog computer tutoring? In: Biswas, G., Bull, S., Kay, J., Mitrovic, A. (eds.) AIED 2011. LNCS, vol. 6738, pp. 81–89. Springer, Heidelberg (2011)
2. Cocea, M., Hershkovitz, A., Baker, R.: The impact of off-task and gaming behaviors on learning: immediate or aggregate? In: Proceedings of AIED, pp. 507–514 (2009)
3. Arroyo, I., Ferguson, K., Johns, J., Dragon, T., Meheranian, H., Fisher, D., Barto, A., Mahadevan, S., Woolf, B.P.: Repairing Disengagement With Non-Invasive Interventions. In: Proceedings of AIED, pp. 195–202 (2007)
4. Jackson, G.T., Dempsey, K.B., McNamara, D.S.: Short and Long Term Benefits of Enjoyment and Learning within a Serious Game. In: Biswas, G., Bull, S., Kay, J., Mitrovic, A. (eds.) AIED 2011. LNCS, vol. 6738, pp. 139–146. Springer, Heidelberg (2011)
5. Rai, D., Beck, J.E.: Math Learning Environment with Game-Like Elements: An Incremental Approach for Enhancing Student Engagement and Learning Effectiveness. In: Cerri, S.A., Clancey, W.J., Papadourakis, G., Panourgia, K. (eds.) ITS 2012. LNCS, vol. 7315, pp. 90–100. Springer, Heidelberg (2012)
6. Rowe, J., Shores, L., Mott, B., Lester, J.C.: Integrating Learning, Problem Solving, and Engagement in Narrative-Centered Learning Environments. IJAIED, 115–133 (2011)
7. Meluso, A., Zheng, M., Spires, H.A., Lester, J.: Enhancing 5th graders' science content knowledge and self-efficacy through game-based learning. Computers & Education Journal 59, 497–504 (2012)
8. Chaudhuri, S., Kumar, R., Howley, I., Rosé, C.P.: Engaging Collaborative Learners with Helping Agents. In: Proceedings of AIED, pp. 365–272 (2009)
9. Hayashi, Y.: On Pedagogical Effects of Learner-Support Agents in Collaborative Interaction. In: Cerri, S.A., Clancey, W.J., Papadourakis, G., Panourgia, K. (eds.) ITS 2012. LNCS, vol. 7315, pp. 22–32. Springer, Heidelberg (2012)
10. Holland, J., Baghaei, N., Mathews, M., Mitrovic, A.: The Effects of Domain and Collaboration Feedback on Learning in a Collaborative Intelligent Tutoring System. In: Biswas, G., Bull, S., Kay, J., Mitrovic, A. (eds.) AIED 2011. LNCS, vol. 6738, pp. 469–471. Springer, Heidelberg (2011)
11. Nagappan, N., Williams, L., Ferzli, M., Wiebe, E., Miller, C., Balik, S., Yang, K.: Improving the CS1 Experience with Pair Programming. In: Proceedings of the SIGCSE Conference, pp. 359–362 (2003)

An Exploration of Text Analysis Methods to Identify Social Deliberative Skill*

Tom Murray, Xiaoxi Xu, and Beverly Park Woolf

School of Computer Science, Commination Dept.
University of Massachusetts, Amherst, MA
tmurray@cs.umass.edu

Abstract. We report on text processing and machine learning methods with the goal of building classifiers for social deliberative skill, i.e. the capacity to deal productively with heterogeneous goals, values, or perspectives. Our corpus includes online deliberative dialogue from three diverse domain contexts. We use the LIWC and CohMetrix linquistic analysis tools to generate feature sets for machine learning. We report on our evaluation of various machine learning algorythms, feature selection methods, and cross-domain training methods.

1 Introduction

A key human capacity is the ability to negotiate situations involving differing opinions where a resolution of ideas is sought, e.g., in dispute resolution, collaborative problem solving, bargaining, and civic deliberation processes. The need for this deliberative capacity, which we call social deliberative skill (SD-skill), is seen in all realms of human activity from international politics, to collaborative work, to mundane familial squabbles. As communication, collaboration, and deliberation occur increasingly on the internet we believe that there is great potential to design software that supports skillful deliberation through gentle prompts and scaffolds, especially for groups of interlocutors who, acknowledging that deliberation in complex and stressful situations can be challenging, are interested in putting some attention and effort on the quality of their communication. Our overall research goals are to better *understand, assess, and support* SD-skills in online contexts. Our evaluation of software features designed to support SD-skills is reported elsewhere (Stephens, et al. 2103 in submission). Evaluation of SD-skills in that study used a hand-coding scheme. Here we focus on our attempts to use machine learning to assess or model SD-skills based on participant text. Automated assessment will not only facilitate *data analysis* by allowing us to assess more data faster, but, if done in real time, can be used in visualization tools for SD-skills and other important dialogue and deliberation metrics. We have prototyped a Facilitators Dashboard tool that gives facilitators, teachers, or participants a birds-eye view of conversation metrics, as described in (Murray et al., 2013, in submission).

* An extended version of this paper is available on the first author's web site.

K. Yacef et al. (Eds.): AIED 2013, LNAI 7926, pp. 811–814, 2013.

2 Background

Social Deliberative Skills. We frame SD-skills in terms of these capacities (see Murray et al., 2013 submitted): perspective taking (includes cognitive empathy, reciprocal role taking); perspective seeking (includes social inquiry, question asking skills); perspective monitoring (includes self-reflection, meta-dialogue); and perspective weighing (related to "reflective reasoning" and includes comparing and contrasting the available views, including those of participants and external sources and experts). SD-skills overlaps with but is distinct from other cognitive constructs that have been studied in depth, including collaboration skills, metacognition, reflective reasoning, social intelligence, argumentation skills, and critical thinking . We differentiate our research from others that focus on *argumentation*, which aims to help learners generate logical, well-formed, well-supported explanations and justifications (Andriessen et al., 2003), usually framed in objective rather than intersubjective terms. That is, they are about finding the right answer or the most efficient and effective solution to a technical or scientific question—but don't address, as we do, the *skills need in those moments during deliberation or collaboration containing opportunities for mutual understanding and mutual recognition.*

Text Classification. Text analysis has been used successfully for a wide variety of purposes, including to: grade essays (Shermis & Burstein 2003), analyze content for conceptual understanding (Lintean et al., 2011), score text sophistication, writing quality, and reading grade level (McNamara et al., 2010), and score deliberative, argumentative, and question-answering quality (Rose et al. 2008; Ravi & Kim 2007). Past research exploring linguistic and discourse features in dialogues has proven moderately successful in predicting complex phenomena such as personality type, status, deception behavior, metacognition, speech acts, intention, and affect states . Therefore, it is plausible to expect that a linguistic and discourse analysis of deliberation dialogues would provide valuable insights into predictors that are diagnostic of deliberation dynamics and skills. Our research question is whether such methods can be used to predict SD-skills.

Our primary goal is to build domain-independent classifier models that will predict what we call Total-SD-skill, and, later, individual SD-skill components (the total skill is a summation of individual skill occurrences). Perhaps the most prominent machine learning method used in natural language processing, information retrieval, and document/text classification is the 'bag of words" unigram method, in which the feature set for the learning algorithm consist of an unordered set of all the words in a document (preprocessed with stemming etc. as necessary). However, we have much more information available with which to build our predictive models, including deep and surface text classification metrics previously researched. In particular, CohMetrix (Graesser et al., 2011) and LIWC (Linguistic Inquiry Word Count; Pennebaker et al., 2007) are two highly cited and used text analysis in systems in domains related to dialogue and collaborative learning. We hypothesize that using LIWC and CohMetrix outputs as feature inputs to machine learning models would increase their accuracy and efficiency vs bag-of-words methods. Thus we can do a two-step analysis, in which we extract the CohMetrix and/or LIWC features, and then use these features as inputs to machine learning methods.

3 Method and Results

Coding: We have developed and refined a 30-category hierarchical coding scheme for human raters to code segments of the text according to speech act type (which, for our purposes, is sometimes equivalent to SD-skill indicators) showing inter-rater Cohen's Kappa statistics of 71% on average in these domains (Murray et al, 2012). For this paper we focus on a Total-SD-skill metric that is true if any of 17 codes associated with higher quality deliberation is true (including: perspective taking, asking clarifying questions, mediation actions, and meaning generation and repair actions, weighing alternatives, citing sources, changing ones mind, and apologizing). **Corpora**: Table 1 shows descriptive statistics for the three domains we have coded, civic deliberation postings from a neighborhood civic engagement online discussion forum; email exchanges from a faculty listserv where two research communities were engaged in a negotiation discussion; and postings from 7 online discussions on controversial issues from three college classrooms.

Table 1. Descriptive Statistics for Three Domains

Domain	Posts	Seg-ment	Partic-ipants	SD-Skill seg	% SD-Skills	Words/ Post	Posts / Partic	Seg. / post
Civic deliberation	51	396	31	225	57%	352	1.6	7.8
Faculty negotiation	72	438	16	231	53%	195	4.5	6.1
College discussions	768	1783	90	565	32%	88	8.5	2.3

Results. Results can only be sketched in this short paper. Early work looked at correlations between LIWC and CohMetrix measurements and the individual and Total-SD-Skill manual classifications. There were a number of small correlations, such as LIWC "Assent" 8.5% (R-squared) with AGREE speech acts; and CohMetrix SecondPersonPronoun 4.4% with INTERSUBJECTIVE speech acts. The top 20 correlations were in the 1% to 4% range. Though there was not obvious strong correlation between individual LIWC/CohMetrix measure and manual codes, there were a number of smaller correlations that indicated that a machine learning algorithm might combine these to predict the codes.

In our first attempts at building a model for Total-SD-skill we used standard SVM (support vector machine) methods and found that none of the models using LIWC and CohMetrix measurements did as well as the unigram bag-of-words features (we tried using the full set of LIWC and CohMetrix measures and a subset of measures highly correlated with Total-SD-skill). (Note that in this document we used 10-fold cross validation where applicable on all machine-learning methods, unless otherwise stated; SVM used unigram features TF-IDF settings). As expected, we found that trying to predict individual SD-skills was much more challenging than predicting Total-SD-skill, so we focused on Total-SD-skill. Next we compared several machine learning methods: SVM (Cortes & Vapnik, 1995), Naïve Bayes (Rish, 2001), and L1 Regularized Logistic Regression (Tibshirani, 1996) (trying various tuning parameters for each to arrive at a best-guess parameter set). The best performance was obtained using the LI RLR method using the LIWC and CohMetrix measures as features. L1 RLR is purported to have superior generalizability, interpretability, and scalability vs. other methods.

Next we turn to the question of whether some deliberative domains make better training sets for a domain-independent model (see Xu et al., 2013 submitted). We hypothesized that domains that have least skew (imbalanced frequency distributions) might serve as better training sets. Results include: (1) Overall using the **Civic domain** as the training set did much better than using the Faculty domain, the Classroom domain, or all of the data as the training set. This was true for all three learning algorithms and all four performance measures (accuracy, precision, recall, and F2). Our hypothesis that the domain with the least skew would serve as the best cross-domain training set was confirmed. (2) Overall the **L1 RLR algorithm** significantly outperformed Naïve Bayes and SVM (this was true when the Civic or Faculty domains were used to train). This confirms our expectation that L1 RLR has performance characteristics addressing for the modeling challenges we face. (3) From #1 and #2 above we see that the **best model for domain-independent** prediction, i.e. prediction that worked best averaged over all three domains, was L1 RLR using the Civic domain for training: accuracy 51%, precision 49%, recall 82%, and F2 71%. (4) ***Cross-training*** proved to have advantages. For precision, recall, and F2-measure (but not accuracy) using the Civic domain as a training set outperformed using the *same* domain to train as was tested on. I.E. for performance on the Faculty domain by itself, training with Civic was better than training with Faculty. Similarly with the Classroom domain. (5) These overall results for binary classification of Total-SD-skill, accuracy 51%, precision 49%, recall 82%, and **F2 71%**, are encouraging for our exploratory study, but not particularly impressive for a binary classifier.

References

1. Graesser, A.C., Dowell, N., Moldovan, C.: A computer's understanding of literature. Scientific Study of Literature 1(2) (2011)
2. Ravi, S., Kim, J.: Profiling student interactions in threaded discussions with speech act classifiers. IOS Press (2007)
3. Lin, X., Sullivan, F.: Computer contexts for supporting metacognitive learning. In: Voogt, J., Knezek, G. (eds.) International Handbook of Information Technology in Primary and Secondary Education, pp. 281–298. Springer Science+Business Media, LLC (2008)
4. McNamara, D.S., Crossley, S.A., McCarthy, P.M.: Linguistic features of writing quality. Written Communication 27(1), 57–86 (2010)
5. Murray, T., Wing, L., Woolf, B., Wise, A., Wu, S., Clark, L., Osterweil, L.: A Prototype Facilitators Dashboard: Assessing and visualizing dialogue quality in online deliberations for education and work. Submitted to Elearn 2013 (in submission, 2013)

Impact of Different Pedagogical Agents' Adaptive Self-regulated Prompting Strategies on Learning with MetaTutor

François Bouchet, Jason M. Harley, and Roger Azevedo

McGill University, SMART Laboratory, Montreal, Canada
francois.bouchet@mcgill.ca

Abstract. Extended interactions with a pedagogical agent (PA) assisting students to enact cognitive and metacognitive self-regulated processes requires the system to adapt the types and frequency of scaffolding. We compared learners' perception of PAs' prompts with MetaTutor, a hypermedia adaptive learning environment, with 40 undergraduates randomly assigned to one of three conditions: non-adaptive prompting (NP), frequency-based adaptive prompting (FP) and frequency and quality-based adaptive prompting (FQP). Results indicate learners are unable to reliably perceive differences in the number of prompts received, though these differences are reflected in positive outcomes in terms of SRL processes enacted and learning gains, and negative outcomes in terms of self-reported satisfaction. Preliminary results indicated that more frequent, but adaptive prompting is an efficient scaffolding strategy, despite negatively impacting learners' satisfaction.

Keywords: pedagogical agents, intelligent tutoring systems, adaptivity, user perception, self-regulated learning, metacognition.

1 Need for Adaptive Prompt Frequency

ITSs' core ability is to provide individualized instruction, feedback, and scaffolding based on a dynamic assessment of learners' emerging understanding of the content, use of learning strategies, and metacognitive judgments to help learners develop cognitive skills [1, 2]. This paper assessed the impact of different pedagogical agents' (PAs) adaptive prompting of self-regulated learning (SRL) processes during learning with MetaTutor [3], a multi-agent ITS designed to track, detect, model, and foster cognitive and metacognitive processes, in which 4 PAs help students learn about the circulatory system, using 38 pages with text and diagrams, accessible through a table of contents [3]. PAs scaffold by prompting students to engage into SRL processes, which they can also self-initiate through a palette of actions (in which case PAs simply accompany their deployment through a dialogical interaction). More specifically, we investigate: (1) how the frequency changes affect learners' use of SRL processes and (2) whether learners perceived changes in the frequency of prompts they received.

K. Yacef et al. (Eds.): AIED 2013, LNAI 7926, pp. 815–819, 2013.

2 Method

40 undergraduates (62.5% female) were randomly assigned to 3 experimental conditions: non-adaptive prompt (NP, from a larger sample of 58), frequency-based prompt (FP) and frequency and quality-based prompt (FQP, cf. Table 1). As learners in FP and FQP were similar, they were sometimes grouped to have two samples of an identical size. In the *NP condition*, learners received a moderate, but constant amount of prompts from the PAs (~ 1 every 10 min.) to engage in SRL processes. In the *FP and FQP conditions*, they received more prompts at first (~ 3.5 every 10 min.), but the probability of each prompt category (monitoring and strategy) being triggered decreased after each received prompt and after each self-initiated enactment of an SRL process. In the *FQP condition*, the probability of each prompt category to be triggered could also increase (1) if learners did not comply to a PA's non-mandatory prompt (e.g., a suggestion to open an image), or (2) if learners' metacognitive judgment was inaccurate (e.g., evaluating a page irrelevant to the active sub-goal as relevant).

Table 1. Pre-test and post-test means and standard deviations across conditions

	NP (n = 20)		**Original NP (n = 58)**		**FP (n = 8)**		**FQP (n = 12)**	
	M	*SD*	*M*	*SD*	*M*	*SD*	*M*	*SD*
Pre-test score (out of 1)	0.67	0.20	0.69	0.23	0.72	0.20	0.68	0.23
Post-test score (out of 1)	0.83	0.10	0.82	0.16	0.86	0.16	0.85	0.17

Table 2. Definition of variables used for the data analyses

Variable	**Definition**
Prop_Learn_Gain	(post-test score – pre-test score) / (1 – pre-test score), where scores are calculated only over questions relevant to the 2 initial sub-goals
Strategy_Processes	Ratio per period of 10 min. of SRL strategy processes (summary, coordination of information sources, re-reading, note-taking) deployed (agent and user-initiated), normalized over the session time
Monitoring_Processes	Same as above for monitoring processes (feeling of knowing [FOK], judgment of learning [JOL], content evaluation [CE], prior knowledge activation [PKA], monitoring progress to goals [MPTG])
User-init_SRL_first30 (*)	Ratio per period of 10 min of user-initiated SRL processes (monitoring and strategy) during the first 30 min. of the session
User-init_SRL_last30	Same as (*) during the last 30 min.
Agent-init_SRL_first30	Same as (*) for agent-initiated processes
Agent-init_SRL_last30	Same as (*) for agent-initiated processes during the last 30 min.

The experiment involved two sessions: the first one (40 min. long) was used to collect information about participants and for them to take a pre-test on the circulatory system. In the second session (90 min. long), participants activated prior knowledge, set up two sub-goals and then spent 60 min. browsing through the content. At the end, participants were given a post-test and asked to complete a questionnaire about the PAs. In addition to the variables described in Table 3, we used participants' replies to 2 sets of post-session questions on the quality PAs' feedback (from 1 [very dissatisfied] to 7 [very satisfied]), and the prompts frequency (more, less, or neither more nor less). In FP and FQP conditions, participants were asked if they noticed changes in the prompts frequency (and if yes, if it was an increase, a decrease or irregular variations). Only Mary (monitoring) and Sam (learning strategies) are considered here.

3 Results

Evolution of the Probability of Activation of Rules. The probability of activation of strategy and monitoring rules decreased throughout the session: more in FP than in FQP (as the probabilities could increase), and more for monitoring than for strategy processes. The proportion of user-initiated processes in the probability of activation of processes was lower at the end of the session for learners in FQP than in FP.

Table 3. Summary of Follow-Up ANOVA results and means and std. dev. of variables used

Variable					NP		FP&FQP	
	df	*F*	*p*	η_p^2	*M*	*SD*	*M*	*SD*
Prop_Learn_Gain	1, 38	2.44	0.127	0.06	40.51	34.53	58.24	37.22
Strategy_Processes	1, 38	18.71	0.00**	0.33	0.12	0.11	0.32	0.20
Monitoring_Processes	1, 38	60.60	0.00**	0.62	0.12	0.06	0.28	0.07

Comparison of SRL Processes Across Conditions. An omnibus MANOVA to compare two conditions (NP vs. FP&FQP) regarding three variables indicated a significant multivariate difference between them for strategy and monitoring processes, Wilk's Lambda = 0.31, $F(3, 36) = 26.78$, $p < .01$, $\eta_p^2 = .69$ (cf. Table 3).

Evolution of the Number of User and Agent-Initiated Prompts. A repeated measures ANOVA revealed a significant main effect of condition on user-initiated SRL behavior, $F(1,38) = 7.64$, $p < .01$, $n^2_p = 0.17$, but no main effect for time or interaction between condition and time. Another repeated measures ANOVA revealed a significant main effect of time, $F(1,38) = 32.79$, $p < .01$, $n^2_p = 0.46$, a main effect of condition $F(1,38) = 71.23$, $p < .01$, $n^2_p = 0.65$, and an interaction of condition and time $F(1,38) = 22.48$, $p < .01$, $n^2_p = 0.37$, on learners' agent-initiated SRL behavior. Moreover, Table 4 shows that in the FP&FQP conditions, although the number of agent-initiated SRL processes in the last 30 min. is inferior by 40% on average to the one in the first 30 min., the number of user-initiated ones increased (75% of the learners in FP&FQP conditions initiated more SRL processes in the last 30 min. than in the first 30). In the NP condition, learners initiated overall less processes.

Perception of the Agent-Initiated Prompts Frequency Evolution. Overall, participants in FP&FQP did not perceive the decrease in the number of prompts received from Mary and Sam (cf. upper Table 5). Although a majority perceived a frequency change, as many learners reported an increase as those correctly reporting a decrease (even in FP where, by design, the probability of activation could only decrease).

Satisfaction with PAs' Feedback Quality and Quantity. A one-way ANOVAs revealed a significant difference between conditions for Sam, $F(1,38) = 6.40$, $p < .05$, $n^2_p = .14$, where participants in the NP condition ($M = 4.65$, $SD = 1.63$) reported higher levels of satisfaction with Sam than those in the FP&FQP conditions ($M = 3.45$, $SD = 1.36$). No significant difference existed between the NP ($M = 4.60$, $SD = 1.57$) and FP & FQP ($M = 4.00$, $SD = 1.92$) for Mary $F(1,38) = 1.17$, $p > .05$, $n^2_p = 0.03$. The lower part of Table 5 shows a majority of participants in conditions FP&FQP would have liked less prompts from Sam, while a majority of participants in condition NP were fine with their frequency. Their opinion about Mary was mixed.

Table 4. Comparison across conditions of user and agent-initiated processes during the session

Variable	NP		FP & FQP	
	M	*SD*	*M*	*SD*
User-init_SRL_first30 / _last30	0.90 / 0.95	1.15 / 1.16	1.82 / 2.22	1.60 / 1.48
Agent-init_SRL_first30 / _last30	0.95 / 0.82	0.58 / 0.62	3.47 / 2.05	1.00 / 1.00

Table 5. Proportion of self-reported perception of prompts frequency and satisfaction about it

	Mary (monitoring)			Sam (strategy)		
Perceived frequency of prompts	**FP**	**FQP**	**FP&FQP**	**FP**	**FQP**	**FP&FQP**
Did not change	37.5	16.7	25	25	8.3	15
Decreased	25	33.3	30	37.5	33.3	35
Varied	25	16.7	20	0	33.3	20
Increased	12.5	33.3	25	37.5	25	30
Would have wanted prompts		**NP**	**FP&FQP**		**NP**	**FP&FQP**
Less frequently		5	40		20	70
More frequently		25	30		25	5
Neither more nor less frequently		70	30		55	25

4 Conclusion and Future Directions

In this paper, we tested the impact of varying the dynamic prompting delivered by MetaTutor's PAs on learners' performance with the system. Preliminary data shows that learners in the FP&FQP conditions enacted consistently more monitoring and strategy SRL processes and had (non sig.) higher proportional learning gains than in the control NP one. The decrease in agent-initiated processes was compensated by a (non sig.) increase in user-initiated ones. Overall, learners did not perceive the prompts variations, but it negatively affected their perception of the quality of the feedback provided by the PAs. Current work focuses on increasing sample size to analyze the impact of the feedback quality on SRL processes enactment.

References

1. Graesser, A.C., Conley, M.W., Olney, A.M.: Intelligent tutoring systems. In: Graham, S., Harris, K. (eds.) APA Educational Psychology Handbook: Applications to Learning and Teaching, Washington, DC, vol. 3, pp. 451–473 (2012)
2. Woolf, B.P.: Building intelligent interactive tutors: Student-centered strategies for revolutionizing e-learning. Morgan Kaufmann (2008)
3. Azevedo, R., Moos, D.C., Johnson, A.M., Chauncey, A.D.: Measuring cognitive and metacognitive regulatory processes during hypermedia learning: Issues and challenges. Educational Psychologist 45, 210–223 (2010)

Class Distinctions: Leveraging Class-Level Features to Predict Student Retention Performance

Xiaolu Xiong, Joseph E. Beck, and Shoujing Li

Department of Computer Science
Worcester Polytechnic Institute
100 Institute Road, Worcester, MA
{xxiong,josephbeck,sli}@wpi.edu

Abstract. This paper describes our experiments and analysis of utilizing class-level features to predict student performance for retention tests. There are two aspects that make this paper interesting. First, instead of focusing on short-team performance, we investigated student performance after a delay of at least 7 days. Second, we explored several class-level features that can be captured in intelligent tutoring systems (ITS), and we showed that some of them have encouraging predictive power. With the help of class-level features, the prediction result indicated an improvement from an R^2 of 0.183 with a normal feature set to an R^2 value of 0.224.

Keywords: Educational data mining, Feature selection, Knowledge retention, Intelligent tutoring system.

1 Introduction

Currently, most ITS present a sequence of problems and, if the student performs well, decide that the student has mastered the skill. Similarly, researchers of educational data mining have investigated the prediction of student behavior on the immediate next action, in other words, student short-term performance [3]. Although performing well on a group of problems is an indicator of mastery, it is by far not the only criteria.

Inspired by the notion of robust learning [1] and the design of the enhanced ITS mastery cycle proposed by Wang and Beck [4], we developed and deployed a system called the Automatic Reassessment and Relearning System (ARRS) to make decisions about when to review each skill the student mastered. ARRS is an extension of the ASSISTments system (www.assistments.org). The idea of ARRS is if a student masters a problem set with three correct responses in a row, such mastery is not necessarily an indication of long-term retention. Therefore, ARRS will present the student with a reassessment test on the same skill at expanding intervals: firstly 7 days after mastery, then 14 days, 28 days and 56 days after the very first test. If a student fails the reassessment test, ASSISTments will give him an opportunity to relearn the skill. Relearning means that the student must again demonstrate mastery by responding correctly to three items in a row. Once a student relearns a skill, he will receive another reassessment test at the same time delay at which he previously responded incorrectly.

K. Yacef et al. (Eds.): AIED 2013, LNAI 7926, pp. 820–823, 2013.

2 Intuition and Approach

In general, student modeling uses data about a student's performance in order to assess his degree of knowledge. However, consider a situation where all of a student's classmates respond incorrectly to a particular item. When this student encounters the item, we would not expect him to respond correctly based on his peers' performance. Strangely, most student modeling approaches would not take advantage of this information, even though it is presumably relevant to understanding this student's knowledge. We formed a hypothesis that the class performance and student individual performance are not independent and can be used to enhance our models. However, in the study of ARRS data, we initially noticed that the number of attempted problems before students achieve mastery has great influence on the one-week delayed performance [5].

2.1 Modeling Retention

At a minimum, students require 3 correct attempts to master a skill. If a student gets the first item wrong, he could master the skill in 4 attempts. We refer to the number of problems required as the *mastery speed* that represents a combination of how well the student knew this skill originally, and how quickly he can learn the skill. We observed that, in general, the slower the *mastery speed*, the lower the probability that the student can answer the problems in the retention test correctly. Students who mastered a skill in 3 or 4 problems had an 82% chance of responding correctly on the first retention test, while students who took over 8 attempts to master a skill only had a 59% chance of responding correctly on the first retention test. Finally, there is a group of students who tried but failed to master the skill, and who, predictably, did the worst.

2.2 Modeling Class-Level Effects

To test our hypothesis of class-level features, we selected the following three features to capture different class-level information: (1) *class_id*: classes were created by teachers who are using the ASSISTments, and represent each distinct class a teacher has. By modeling *class_id* as a factor, we are estimating an overall effect of the classroom. (2) *class_prior_performance*: measures the class' performance on prior reassessment tests on same skill. For each reassessment test, the performance is represented by using the percentage of correctness of tests that have been answered in the same class, on the same skill, and have been answered before the student attempts this retention item. (3) *class_other_skill_performance*: measures the class' performance on all reassessment tests on all other skills. This feature is permitted to use data from the future, and is thus not realistic in an actual system, but provides an upper bound for how well such information could work.

3 Model Results

To train our model, we used 42,332 instances of a student using the ARRS system and attempting the first retention test for each skill. We separated these pieces of data into

33,866 instances for the training set and 8,466 for the testing set. The testing set was selected by randomly choosing 20% of the dataset, so there is an issue of non-independence as the same student appears in both sets. We first employed the *mastery speed*, as well as three other basic features, to establish a baseline for our modeling work. These features forced on item and skill information, including: (1) *on_grade*, whether this skill is typically taught in the same grade-level of the student. (2) *grade_diff*, the binned value of grade difference and (3) *item_easiness*. We fitted this base model using multinomial logistic regression; we got an R^2 of 0.183.

To investigate how our class-level features could impact our predictions on student retention test performance, we started from our base model, described previously, and added to it a representation of the class' performance. We experimented with using the *class_id* as a factor, prior performance on this skill's retention test, and all performance on all retention tests that did not involve this skill. Table 1 provides the results for each of these models. We provide both the classic R^2 metric, as well as the Nagelkerke (pseudo) R^2 for comparison purposes as other logistic regression results reported have used Nagelkerke [2].

Table 1. Class-level model performance

Model	R^2 on training set	R^2 on testing set
Base model + *class_id*	0.158 (Nagelkerke: 0.215)	0.159
Base model + *class_prior_performance*	0.155 (Nagelkerke 0.204)	0.153
Base model + *class_other_skill_performance*	0.145 (Nagelkerke 0.185)	0.142
Base model	0.143 (Nagelkerke 0.183)	0.142

From the above results, we can see that new model with *class_id* and *class_prior_performance* performed slightly better than the base model. The importance of *class_id* in the prediction may suggest that there seems to be an overall class effect that differs from average performance on other skills, which is modeled by *class_other_skill_performance*. One question is whether combining the two features would be fruitful in improving accuracy? Somewhat surprisingly, a model using both *class_id* and *class_prior_performance* achieved an R^2 value of 0.165 (Nagelkerke 0.224). Thus, whatever *class_id* represents, it is relatively distinct from *class_prior_performance* as the R^2 increases noticeably when both are modeled.

4 Contributions, Future Work and Conclusions

This paper makes three contributions. Firstly, this paper identifies speed of mastery as a useful new feature relevant to robust learning. Secondly, this paper explored and identified class-level effects as being worth modeling. Our analysis adopted class-level features in order to account for influences that will affect all members of the class. The third contribution of this paper is by employing class id in our prediction; we adopted a generic approach for intuitively "clustering" students. Our approach of clustering requires little additional information, no complex processing, and it is easy to understand our clusters and the semantics behind them.

For examining class-level effects and predicting retention, we used a classifier with features that were known to be predictive, such as *mastery speed*. There are many follow-up problems that we are interested in: Are there better ways of using the class-level data? How well has this teacher's classes done in preceding years? Does this teacher's students systematically under- or over-perform on retention tests? Exploring these avenues to discover class-level impacts on performance is an interesting future direction.

This paper has presented a problem of predicting whether students will retain information after a delay of 7 days. We found that mastery alone is insufficient to predict retention, and the ease with which students achieve mastery is critical. However, the cognitive meaning of this statement is unclear. Do students who achieve mastery quickly already understand the skill, and have retained it from prior instruction, or are they simply learning quickly, and quick learners also retain better. Understanding what speed of mastery means is a difficult problem. One other clear conclusion is that class matters, and the performance of the students' peers is useful for predicting his performance.

References

1. Baker, R.S.J.D., Gowda, S.M., Corbett, A.T., Ocumpaugh, J.: Towards automatically detecting whether student learning is shallow. In: Cerri, S.A., Clancey, W.J., Papadourakis, G., Panourgia, K. (eds.) ITS 2012. LNCS, vol. 7315, pp. 444–453. Springer, Heidelberg (2012)
2. Gong, Y., Beck, J.E., Heffernan, N.T.: Comparing knowledge tracing and performance factor analysis by using multiple model fitting procedures. In: Aleven, V., Kay, J., Mostow, J. (eds.) ITS 2010, Part I. LNCS, vol. 6094, pp. 35–44. Springer, Heidelberg (2010)
3. Pardos, Z.A., Heffernan, N.T.: Using HMMs and bagged decision trees to leverage rich features of user and skill from an intelligent tutoring system dataset. Journal of Machine Learning Research W & CP (2010)
4. Wang, Y., Beck, J.E.: Using Student Modeling to Estimate Student Knowledge Retention. In: Proceedings of the 5th International Conference on Educational Data Mining, pp. 176–179 (2012)
5. Xiong, X., Li, S., Beck, J.: Will you get it right next week: Predict delayed performance in enhanced ITS mastery cycle. In: The 26th International FLAIRS Conference (accepted)

Estimating the Effect of Web-Based Homework

Kim Kelly[1], Neil Heffernan[1], Cristina Heffernan[1],
Susan Goldman[2], James Pellegrino[2], and Deena Soffer Goldstein[2]

[1] Worcester Polytechnic Institute
[2] University of Illinois –Chicago
{kkelly,nth}@wpi.edu

Abstract. Traditional studies of intelligent tutoring systems have focused on their use in the classroom. Few have explored the advantage of using ITS as a web-based homework (WBH) system, providing correctness-only feedback to students. A second underappreciated aspect of WBH is that teachers can use the data to more efficiently review homework. Universities across the world are employing these WBH systems but there are no known comparisons of this in K12. In this work we randomly assigned 63 thirteen and fourteen year olds to either a traditional homework condition (TH) involving practice without feedback or a WBH condition that added correctness feedback at the end of a problem and the ability to try again. All students used ASSISTments, an ITS, to do their homework but we ablated all of the intelligent tutoring aspects of hints, feedback messages and mastery learning as appropriate to the two practice conditions. We found that students learned reliably more in the web-based homework condition and with an effect size of 0.56. Additionally, teacher use of the homework data lead to a more robust and systematic review of the homework. Future work will further examine modifications to WBH to further improve learning from homework and the role of WBH in formative assessment.

Keywords: intelligent tutoring systems, immediate feedback, homework, effect size, formative assessment.

1 Introduction

Several studies have shown the effectiveness of intelligent tutoring systems when used in the classroom [7], [9], reporting effect sizes up to 0.78. The few studies that have explored the effectiveness of ITS when used as homework were very encouraging [9]. Yet, complex tutoring systems are not suited for nightly homework. Computer aided instruction (CAI), which gives all students the same questions with immediate end-of-question feedback is more applicable as teachers can easily create the content from textbooks or worksheets. Kulik and Kulik's [4] meta-analysis reviewed CAI and reported an effect size of 0.3 for simple computer based immediate feedback systems. However, these studies were not in the context of homework use and did not focus on how teachers use the data to respond to student performance.

Despite the relatively low effect sizes reported in Kulik and Kulik [4], web-based homework (WBH) holds promise for improving learning from homework by tailoring

K. Yacef et al. (Eds.): AIED 2013, LNAI 7926, pp. 824–827, 2013.

practice to individual performance. Doing so enables individuals to get corrective feedback so they can focus on areas where they are not successful. Shute [6] reviews the plethora of studies and theoretical frameworks developed around understanding the role of feedback for students as well as teachers. Black and William [1] have focused on formative assessments, with an eye on informing the teacher and giving feedback to students. The cognitive science literature suggests that letting students practice the wrong skill repeatedly on their homework is detrimental to learning. In this study we look to measure the effect on learning by comparing simple WBH to a traditional homework (TH) condition representing the type of practice that millions of students perform every night in America and probably around the world. Additionally, we explore how the teacher can use the data to modify and improve instruction.

2 Experimental Design

Participants were 63 seventh grade students, who completed the activities included in the study as part of their regular math class and homework. Students were assigned to conditions by blocking on prior knowledge. All students were given a pre-test and lesson on negative exponents. That night, students completed their homework using ASSISTments. The assignment was designed in triplets, with three morphologically similar questions in a row. Additional challenge questions were included to maintain ecological validity.

Students in the WBH condition were given correctness-only feedback at the end of the problem. If a student answered a question incorrectly, he/she was given unlimited opportunities to self-correct, or he/she could press the "show me the last hint" button to be given the answer. It is important to emphasize that this button did **not** provide a hint; instead it provided the correct response, which was required to proceed to the next question. Students in the TH condition used ASSISTments in "test mode" to simulate traditional homework practice without any feedback.

The following day all students took PostTest1 and then participated in the homework review process. Students in the WBH condition left the room and completed an unrelated assignment. Students in the TH condition reviewed their homework in a very prevalent and traditional fashion. They were given the answers to the homework, time to check their work, and the opportunity to ask questions. The groups of students switched and the teacher used the item report, generated by ASSISTments to review the homework with students in the WBH condition. Common wrong answers and obvious misconceptions guided the discussion. The next day, all students took PostTest2. All of the study materials, data and videos are available in Kelly [3].

3 Results

Several scores were derived from the data collected by the ASSISTments system. Student's HW Average was calculated based on the number of questions answered correctly on the first attempt divided by the total number of questions on the assignment (20). Partial Credit HW Score was calculated by dividing the number of questions answered without being given the answer by the number of total questions on the homework assignment (20). Time Spent was calculated using the problem log data generated in ASSISTments and is reported in minutes. Times per action are truncated at five minutes.

Learning Gains from Homework: An ANCOVA showed that students in the WBH condition reliably outperformed those in the TH condition on both PostTest1 (F(1,60)=4.14, p=0.046) and PostTest2 (F(1,60)=5.92, p=0.018) when controlling for pre-test score. See Table 1 for means and standard deviations. If the difference was reliable we computed a Hedge corrected effect size [2]. The effect sizes do not take into account pretest. The key result for posttest2 of 0.56 effect size had a confidence interval of between 0.07 and 1.08. Unexpectedly, correctness-only feedback was found to be time efficient. Students in both conditions spent the same amount of time to complete their homework (F(1,60)=0.002, p=0.96).

Table 1. Means, standard deviations (in parenthesis), and effect size for each measure by condition. *Notes a reliable difference.

	TH	WBH	*p*-value	Effect Size
Pre-Test	9% (17)	7% (14)	0.78	NA
PostTest1	58% (27)	69% (21)	0.046*	0.52
PostTest2	68% (26)	81% (22)	0.018*	0.56
HW Average	61% (20)	60% (15)	0.95	NA
Partial Credit HW Score	61% (20)	81% (18)	0.0001*	1.04
Time Spent (mins)	22.7 (9.6)	23.2(6.2)	0.96	NA

Learning Gains from Homework Review: To address the second research question of the effectiveness of using the data to support homework review, a paired t-test revealed that students in both conditions did reliably better on PostTest2 than on PostTest1 (t(62)=3.87, p<0.0001). However, an ANCOVA revealed that when accounting for PostTest1 scores, there is not a reliable difference by condition in the gains from PostTest1 to PostTest2 (F(1,60)=2.18, p=0.15). This suggests that both methods of reviewing the homework lead to substantially improved learning.

Observational Results: In addition to examining the effects of immediate feedback on learning, this study explored the qualitative changes to the homework review process the following day in class. An observational analysis of the video recordings of the teacher reviewing the homework revealed that while the time spent in the WBH condition was often longer than the TH, it was also far more focused than the TH. Specifically, when students were in the TH condition, on average two minutes passed before any meaningful discussion took place. Whereas, when students were in the WBH condition, homework review began immediately with the teacher reviewing what she perceived to be the most important learning opportunities. Additionally, students in the TH condition reviewed fewer questions than the WBH condition and they tended to ask the same types of questions or even the same exact question that was already reviewed. In the WBH condition, the teacher was able to ensure that a variety of question types and mistakes were addressed.

4 Contributions and Future Work

In this fast-paced educational world, it is important to ensure that time spent in class and on homework is as beneficial as possible. The randomized-controlled study presented here provides some strong evidence that web-based homework systems that provide correctness-only feedback and data to teachers are useful tools to improve learning on homework without additional time, suggesting a new use for ITS.

Acknowledgment. The authors would like to acknowledge support from the Bill and Melinda Foundation via EDUCAUSE as well as IES grants R305C100024 and R305A120125.

References

1. Black, P., Wiliam, D.: Inside the black box: Raising standards through classroom assessment. Granada Learning (2006)
2. CEM (2013), http://www.cemcentre.org/evidence-based-education/effect-size-calculator (accessed January 28, 2013)
3. Kelly, K.: (2012), http://www.webcitation.org/6E03PhjrP contains the materials Browse, http://web.cs.wpi.edu/~nth/PublicScienceArchive/Kelly.htm to view the materials
4. Kulik, C.C., Kulik, J.A.: Effectiveness of computer-based instruction: An updated analysis. Computers in Human Behavior 7, 75–94 (1991)
5. Rochelle: The IES Grant (2013), http://ies.ed.gov/funding/grantsearch/details.asp?ID=1273 (accessed January 28, 2013)
6. Shute, V.: Focus on Formative Feedback. Review of Educational Research 78(1), 153–189 (2008), http://www.ets.org/Media/Research/pdf/RR-07-11.pdf
7. Singh, R., Saleem, M., Pradhan, P., Heffernan, C., Heffernan, N.T., Razzaq, L., Dailey, M.D., O'Connor, C., Mulcahy, C.: Feedback during Web-Based Homework: The Role of Hints. In: Biswas, G., Bull, S., Kay, J., Mitrovic, A. (eds.) AIED 2011. LNCS, vol. 6738, pp. 328–336. Springer, Heidelberg (2011)
8. VanLehn, K.: The relative effectiveness of human tutoring, intelligent tutoring systems, and other tutoring systems. Educational Psychologist 46(4), 197–221 (2011)
9. VanLehn, K., Lynch, C., Schulze, K., Shapiro, J.A., Shelby, R., Taylor, L., Treacy, D., Weinstein, A., Wintersgill, M.: The Andes physics tutoring system: Lessons Learned. International Journal of Artificial Intelligence and Education 15(3), 1–47 (2005)

A Markov Decision Process Model of Tutorial Intervention in Task-Oriented Dialogue

Christopher M. Mitchell, Kristy Elizabeth Boyer, and James C. Lester

Department of Computer Science, North Carolina State University, Raleigh, North Carolina, USA
{cmmitch2,keboyer,lester}@ncsu.edu

Abstract. Designing dialogue systems that engage in rich tutorial dialogue has long been a goal of the intelligent tutoring systems community. A key challenge for these systems is determining when to intervene during student problem solving. Although intervention strategies have historically been hand-authored, utilizing machine learning to automatically acquire corpus-based intervention policies that maximize student learning holds great promise. To this end, this paper presents a Markov Decision Process (MDP) framework to learn an intervention policy capturing the most effective tutor turn-taking behaviors in a task-oriented learning environment with textual dialogue. The model and its learned policy highlight important design considerations, including maintaining tutor engagement during student problem solving and avoiding multiple consecutive interventions.

Keywords: Tutorial Dialogue, Markov Decision Processes, Reinforcement Learning.

1 Introduction

The effectiveness of tutorial dialogue has been widely established [1, 2]. In recent years, reinforcement learning (RL) has proven useful in the analysis and creation of tutorial dialogue system behaviors in structured interactions [3, 4]. Extending this prior work, this paper presents a novel application of RL to a corpus of textual tutorial dialogue. In particular, the focus here is automatically learning intervention strategies from a fixed corpus of human-human task-oriented tutorial dialogue with unrestricted turn-taking. The presented approach and policy results can inform the development of tutorial dialogue systems whose policies are acquired automatically based on fixed corpora.

The corpus analyzed in this paper consists of 66 text-based tutorial dialogues between first-year university students and experienced tutors as the students worked to solve introductory computer science problems. Each student-tutor pair collaborated using the JavaTutor remote interface [5], which supports textual communication between the tutor and student as well as giving the tutor a real-time synchronized view of the student's workspace. Over the course of a 40-minute session, each student endeavored to build a working program using the Java programming language.

K. Yacef et al. (Eds.): AIED 2013, LNAI 7926, pp. 828–831, 2013.

In order to measure the effectiveness of each session, students completed a pre-test and post-test. Students scored significantly higher on the post-test than the pre-test ($p < .001$). We computed normalized learning gain, which can range from -1 to 1. In the present study normalized learning gains ranged from -0.29 to 1 (mean = 0.42; median = 0.45; st. dev. = 0.32).

2 Building the Markov Decision Process and Policy Learning

From the tutors' perspective, the decision to intervene was made based on the state of the interaction as observed through the two information channels in the interface: the textual dialogue pane and the synchronized view of the student's workspace. In order to use a MDP framework to derive an effective intervention policy, we describe a representation of the interaction state as a collection of features from these information channels.

A Markov Decision Process is a model of a system in which a policy can be learned to maximize reward [6]. It consists of a set of states S, a set of actions A representing possible actions by an agent, a set of transition probabilities indicating how likely it is for the model to transition to each state $s' \in S$ from each state $s \in S$ when the agent performs each action $a \in A$ in state s, and a reward function R that maps real values onto transitions and/or states, thus signifying their utility.

The goal of this analysis is to model tutor interventions during the task-completion process, so the possible actions for a tutor were to intervene (by composing and sending a message) or not to intervene. Hence, the set of actions is defined as $A = \{TutorMove, NoMove\}$. We chose three features to represent the state of the dialogue, with each feature taking on one of three possible values. These features, described in Figure 1, combine as a triple to form the states of the MDP as (Current Student Action, Task Trajectory, Last Action). In addition, the model includes 3 more states: an *Initial* state, in which the model always begins, and two final states: one with reward +100 for students achieving higher-than-median normalized learning gain and one with reward -100 for the remaining students, following the conventions established in prior research into reinforcement learning for tutorial dialogue [3, 4].

Current Student Action	Task Trajectory	Last Action
Task: Working on the task	***Closer***: Moving closer to the final correct solution	***TutorDial***: Tutor message
StudentDial: Writing a message to the tutor	***Farther***: Moving away from correct solution	***StudentDial***: Student message
NoAction: No current student action	***NoChange***: Same distance from correct solution	***Task:*** Student worked on the task

Fig. 1. The features used to define the states of the Markov Decision Process

Using these formalizations, one state was assigned to each of the log entries collected during the sessions and transition probabilities were computed between them when a tutor made an intervention (*TutorMove*) and when a tutor did not make an intervention (*NoMove*). An excerpt from the corpus with these assigned states is shown in Figure 2.

Event	Tutor action and state transition
1. *Student is declaring a String variable named "aStringVariable".*	*NoMove* ↓ (Task, NoChange, Task)
2. *Tutor starts typing a message*	*TutorMove*
3. *1.5 seconds elapse, task action is complete.*	↓
4. **Tutor message:** That works, but let's give the variable a more descriptive name	(NoAction, Closer, TutorDial)
5. *Tutor starts typing a message*	*TutorMove*
6. *Student starts typing a message*	↓
7. **Student message:** ok	
8. **Tutor message:** Usually, the variable's name tells us what data it has stored	(NoAction, Closer, TutorDial)

Fig. 2. An excerpt from the corpus with state, action, and transition labels

In order to learn a tutorial intervention policy, we used a policy iteration algorithm [6] on the MDP. Some noteworthy patterns emerge in the intervention policy learned from the corpus. For example, in seven of the eight states where the student is actively engaged in task actions, i.e., matching the pattern (*Task*, *, *), the policy recommends that the tutor make a dialogue move. On its surface this policy may seem counterintuitive, since the student may be making task progress and there is a risk of interruption by the tutor. However, the policy suggests that sessions in which the tutor remained engaged in the problem-solving process by making dialogue moves as the student was working were more likely to produce high normalized learning gains.

Among the states in which no action is currently being taken by the student and the last action was a tutor message, i.e., matching the pattern (*NoAction*, *, *TutorDial*), we find that the policy recommends that a tutor not make another consecutive dialogue move, regardless of how well the student is progressing on the task. It is possible that consecutive tutor dialogue moves would present more information than a student could effectively process, thus leading to high cognitive load or disengagement for the student and, in turn, lower learning gains. While this could be interpreted as a recommendation for the tutor to be less talkative, the just-mentioned recommendation regarding continual tutor engagement during task completion would seem to contradict this interpretation. Instead, it is more likely that an effective tutor will compose messages such that they engage the student in dialogue or provide succinct guidance for the student to make progress on the task without additional intervention. Further investigation of the consequences of these recommendations will be addressed in future work.

3 Discussion and Conclusion

The model presented here demonstrates a novel approach to automatically determining an intervention policy for tutorial dialogue with unrestricted turn-taking from a fixed corpus using a reinforcement learning-based approach. The resulting policy provides insight into the effectiveness of tutor intervention decisions with respect to the success of a tutorial dialogue. We note the gap between the recommended action in the learned policy and the actual actions taken by tutors in the corpus: tutors follow the recommended *(Task, *, *)* policy only 11% of the time, while following the recommended (*NoAction*, *, *TutorDial*) policy slightly more than 43% of the time. Avoiding policies prevalent in sessions with lower learning gain is one of the key advantages of using reinforcement learning.

Further exploration of the state space via simulation and utilizing a more expressive representation of state are highly promising directions for future work. Other directions for future work include undertaking a more fine-grained analysis of the timing of interventions, which could inform the development of more natural interactions, as well as allowing for more nuanced intervention strategies. Additionally, these models should be enhanced with a more expressive representation of both dialogue and task. It is hoped that these lines of investigation will yield highly effective machine-learned policies for tutorial dialogue systems.

Acknowledgements. This work is supported in part by the National Science Foundation through Grants DRL-1007962 and CNS-1042468. Any opinions, findings, conclusions, or recommendations expressed in this report are those of the participants, and do not necessarily represent the official views, opinions, or policy of the National Science Foundation.

References

1. Bloom, B.: The 2 sigma problem: The search for methods of group instruction as effective as one-to-one tutoring. Educational Researcher 13, 4–16 (1984)
2. VanLehn, K., Graesser, A.C., Jackson, G.T., Jordan, P., Olney, A., Rosé, C.P.: When Are Tutorial Dialogues More Effective Than Reading? Cognitive Science 30, 3–62 (2007)
3. Chi, M., VanLehn, K., Litman, D.: Do Micro-Level Tutorial Decisions Matter: Applying Reinforcement Learning to Induce Pedagogical Tutorial Tactics. In: Aleven, V., Kay, J., Mostow, J. (eds.) ITS 2010, Part I. LNCS, vol. 6094, pp. 224–234. Springer, Heidelberg (2010)
4. Tetreault, J.R., Litman, D.J.: A Reinforcement Learning Approach to Evaluating State Representations in Spoken Dialogue Systems. Speech Communication 50(8), 683–696 (2008)
5. Grafsgaard, J.F., Fulton, R.M., Boyer, K.E., Weibe, E.N., Lester, J.L.: Multimodal Analysis of the Implicit Affective Channel in Computer-Mediated Textual Communication. In: Proceedings of the International Conference on Multimodal Interaction, pp. 145–152 (2012)
6. Sutton, R., Barto, A.: Reinforcement Learning. MIT Press, Cambridge (1998)

Didactic Galactic: Types of Knowledge Learned in a Serious Game

Carol Forsyth[1], Arthur Graesser[1], Breya Walker[1], Keith Millis[2], Philip I. Pavlik, Jr.[1], and Diane Halpern[3]

[1] The University of Memphis, Institute for Intelligent Systems, Memphis, TN
{cmfrsyth,graesser,bswlker2,ppavlik}@memphis.edu
[2] Northern Illinois University, Psychology Department, Dekalb, IL
kmillis@niu.edu
[3] Claremont McKenna College, Psychology Department, Claremont, CA
diane.halpern@claremontmckenna.edu

Abstract. Operation ARA is a serious game that teaches scientific inquiry using natural language conversations. Within the context of the game, students completed up to two distinct training modules that teach either didactic or applied conceptual information about research methodology (e.g., validity of dependent variables, need for control groups). An experiment using a 4-condition between-subjects pretest-interaction-posttest design was conducted in which 81 undergraduate college students interacted with varying modules of Operation ARA. The four conditions were designed to test the impact of the two distinct modules on different types of learning measured by multiple-choice, short answer, and case-based assessment questions. Results revealed significant differences on training condition and learning gains on two of the three types of questions.

Keywords: Intelligent Tutoring Systems, reasoning, serious games, learning.

1 Introduction

Cognitive scientists often make distinctions as to whether knowledge is acquired, stored and used. Different types of training and assessment may be required for one to completely understand a new topic, depending in part as to whether it is shallow versus deep. The current study examined the learning of didactic, factual information versus conceptually applied knowledge about research methodology by interacting with a serious game.

1.1 Types of Knowledge Acquisition and Test Questions

Previous research suggests that basic didactic information, including vocabulary, facts, and simple procedures, may be learned through iterative presentation and practice over an extended period of time rather than in a single session [1,2] . However, understanding didactic information in research methodology does not directly

K. Yacef et al. (Eds.): AIED 2013, LNAI 7926, pp. 832–835, 2013.

translate to the learner being able to apply the knowledge within a case-based reasoning framework [3,4]. To obtain this deeper-level understanding, students may need to complete tasks which require making fine-grained discriminations among alternatives [3-5] constructing explanations, or generating questions about difficult conceptualizations [6]. These two very separate types of knowledge acquisition (didactic factual recall versus conceptual applications) may be reflected in performance on different types of test questions. Specifically, a continuum from shallow to deep-level questions may start out with recognition-oriented questions exemplified in most multiple-choice questions, move on to recall-oriented questions that elicit words or sentences in an answer [6,7], and progress to a deep level captured by performance on case-based test questions where students apply their knowledge on concrete practical problems. The current study utilizes three different types of questions to capture knowledge on a continuum from a shallow to a deep level, in the context of a serious game called OperationARA.

1.2 Operation ARA: A Serious Game

Operation ARA is a serious game that teaches research methodology through a number of pedagogical components, including natural language conversation [8]. Operation ARA encompasses training of both didactic and applied knowledge of 21 core concepts of research methodology. The two types of instruction (i.e. didactic and applied) are given across three separate modules of the game (i.e. Cadet Training, Proving Ground, Active Duty), however the focus is on the first two modules only. In the Cadet Training module, students learn didactic knowledge by focusing primarily on the definition and importance of the concepts in research methodology. They read an E-Text, answer multiple-choice questions, and hold natural language tutorial conversations with pedagogical artificial agents. In the Proving Ground module, students apply their knowledge by analyzing summaries of research cases and identifying flaws that are aligned with core concepts of research methodology. This paper explores the relationship between (a) learning procedures that emphasize either didactic knowledge (Cadet Training) or application (Proving Ground) and (b) measures that either emphasize relatively low-level didactic information (multiple choice questions), intermediate (short answer) or higher-level conceptual knowledge (case study analysis).

2 Methods

The participants were 81 undergraduate students (N=81) enrolled in an Introduction to Psychology course who completed the study across the course of a semester. Participants were given course credit for their completion but not performance of the study. They participated in a 4 condition, between-subjects pretest-training -posttest study. The conditions included 1) interaction with Cadet Training only, 2) interaction with Proving Ground only, 3) interaction with both Cadet Training and Proving Ground, and 4) a control condition with no interaction.

Participants were randomly assigned to one of the four conditions. After completing a pretest, students in the experimental conditions interacted with ARA and subsequently completed the posttest. Participants in the control condition had no interaction with the game. Two versions of the test were created and counterbalanced over pretest and posttest. Each test had a total of 50 questions, including 21 multiple-choice questions, 21 short-answer questions, and 8 questions which required deep application. Learning gains were computed by subtracting the proportional pretest scores from the proportional posttest scores for the multiple-choice, short-answer, and case-based questions, respectively.

2.1 Planned Comparisons

The hypotheses were tested by planned comparisons. The first hypothesis was that the Cadet Training module learning gains would lead to greater learning gains on the MC questions than the other conditions. Using contrast coefficients, the Cadet Training Only module and Cadet Training with Proving Ground conditions were compared against the Proving Ground only and Control conditions. The mean MC learning gains for conditions with the Cadet Training module was .08 and -.01 for conditions without it. The contrast was statistically significant (t (77) = 2.64, p <.01) with a medium effect size of .60 (Cohen's d= .60).

Next, we tested the second hypothesis that predicted the Proving Ground module would lead to greater scores than the Cadet Training on the short answer questions. Using contrast coefficients, the Proving Ground module and the Cadet Training plus Proving Ground conditions were compared to the Cadet Training only and control conditions. For the short-answer questions, the mean learning gains for conditions with the Proving Ground module was .04 and .01 for conditions without it. The contrast comparisons revealed a non-significant difference, (t (77) =.88, p=.19).

Finally, we tested the third hypothesis that predicted the group who received both the Cadet Training and Proving Ground would perform better on the case-based questions than any other group. The mean learning gains were .14 for the condition including both the Cadet Training and Proving Ground modules, and .06 for the other groups. The contrast comparison between the condition with both modules and the three other groups (i.e. Cadet Training only, Proving Ground only, and Control) was significant, (t (77) = 1.66, p=.05) with a small effect (Cohen's d= .38).

3 Conclusions

Our analyses revealed effects of different types of training on learning. Specifically, the Cadet Training module which emphasized didactic learning significantly affected factual recall as assessed by multiple choice questions, compared to the other conditions. Though statistically non-significant, the Proving Ground module which emphasizes application showed a small impact on short answer questions. This module may have been more difficult as it requires a deeper-level understanding of the core concepts taught within Operation ARA. Participants who received both the Cadet

Training and Proving Ground module performed better on the case-based reasoning questions. These results suggest that students must first learn the didactic and then the conceptually applied information in order to achieve a deep-level understanding of the topics of research methodology taught in the game. Future studies hope to assess these findings with a more fine-grained assessment containing questions that reflect the intricate levels of shallow to deep questions made available by more current taxonomies[6].

Acknowledgements. This research was supported by the Institute for Education Sciences, U.S. Department of Education, through Grant R305B070349. The opinions expressed are those of the authors and do not represent views of the Institute or the U.S. Department of Education.

References

1. Pavlik, P.I., Anderson, J.R.: Forgetting Effects on Vocabulary Memory: An Activation-based Model of the Spacing Effect. Cog. Sci. 29, 559–586 (2006)
2. Cepeda, N.J., Pashler, H., Vul, E., Wixted, J.T., Rohrer, D.: Distributed Practice in Verbal Recall Tasks: a Review and Quantitative Synthesis. Psyc. Bull. 132, 354–380 (2006)
3. VanLehn, K., Graesser, A.C., Jackson, G.T., Jordan, P., Olney, A., Rose, C.P.: When are Tutorial Dialogues more Effective than Reading? Cog. Sci., 313–362 (2007)
4. Anderson, J.R., Corbett, A.T., Koedinger, K.R., Pelletier, R.: Cognitive Tutors: Lessons Learned. J. of Learn. Sci. 4, 167–207 (1995)
5. Graesser, A.C., Conley, M., Olney, A.: Intelligent Tutoring Systems: Applications to Learning and Teaching. In: Harris, K.R., Graham, S., Urdan, T. (eds.) APA Psyc. Handbook 2012, vol. 3, pp. 451–473. American Psychological Association, Washington, D.C (2012)
6. Graesser, A.C., Ozuru, Y., Sullins, J.: What is a Good Question? In: McKeown, M.G., Kucan, L. (eds.) Threads of Coherence in Research on the Development of Reading Ability, pp. 112–141. Guilford, New York (2009)
7. Bloom, B.S.: Taxonomy of Educational Objectives: The Classification of Educational Goals. In: Handbook I: Cog. Dom. McKay, New York (1956)
8. Millis, K., Forsyth, C., Butler, H., Wallace, P., Graesser, A., Halpern, D.: Operation ARIES!: A Serious Game for Teaching Scientific Inquiry. In: Oikonomou, A., Ma, M., Lakhmi, J. (eds.) Serious Games and Ed. Apps. Springer, London (2011)

A Comparison of Two Different Methods to Individualize Students and Skills

Yutao Wang and Neil Heffernan

Worcester Polytechnic Institute
{yutaowang,nth}@wpi.edu

Abstract. One of the most popular methods for modeling students' knowledge is Corbett and Anderson's [1] Bayesian Knowledge Tracing (KT) model. The original Knowledge Tracing model does not allow for individualization. In this work, we focus on comparing two different individualized models: the Student Skill model and the two-phase model, to find out which is the best for formulating the individualization problem within a Bayesian networks framework.

Keywords: Student Modeling, Knowledge Tracing, Student Skill Model, Individualization.

1 Introduction

One of the most popular methods for modeling students knowledge is Corbett and Anderson's[1] Bayesian Knowledge Tracing model. The original Knowledge Tracing model does not allow for individualization. Recently, Pardos and Heffernan [3] built a two phase individualization method where they trained four parameters per student at a pre-process, then took those values and put into a per skill model to learn how the user parameters interacted with the skill. This model is part of the final model that won the 2010 KDD Cup on educational data mining. The assumption this model made, which is we can learn student parameters first without any knowledge of skills seems unreasonable. Wang and Heffernan's [4] work further explored the individualization of student parameters to allow the Bayesian network to keep track of four student parameters and four skill parameters simultaneously in one step in a model called the Student Skill model (SS), which seems more appealing to our desire for elegance. The goal of this paper is to answer two questions that this new individualization model raised. First, is this approach better than the two phase model that won the KDD Cup? And second, under what circumstances is it better?

1.1 Two Individualization Models

Fig.1. shows Pardos and Heffernan's two phased model. To train this model, the first step was to learn student parameters by using the Prior Per Student [2] model by training on all skill data for an individual student one at a time. The second step was to include all of the student specific parameter information into a model, shown in Fig. 1 to learn skill related parameters.

K. Yacef et al. (Eds.): AIED 2013, LNAI 7926, pp. 836–839, 2013.

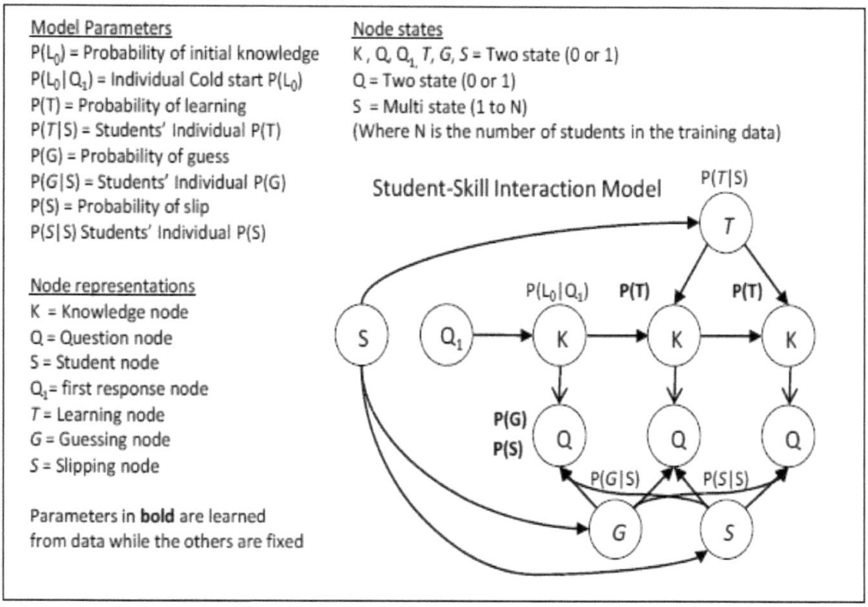

Fig. 1. The Two Phase Model. Pardos &Heffernan [3]

The second model that allows for individualization is called the Student Skill(SS) model[4]. It can learn four student parameters and four skill parameters simultaneously in a single phase process. The model is shown in Fig. 2.

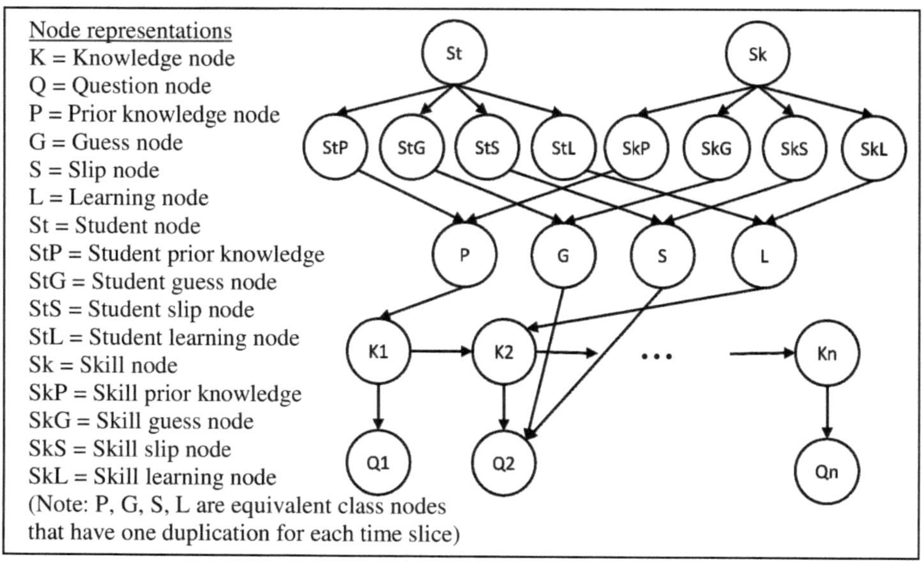

Fig. 2. The Student Skill model

2 Experiments

The two models were compared in both simulated and real data experiments. Given limited space, only the real data result is reported, simulation result is similar.

The data used in the analysis came from the ASSISTments platform, a freely available web-based tutoring system for 4th through 10th grade mathematics. We randomly pulled out data of one hundred 12-14 year old 8th grade students and fifty skills from the school year September 2010 to September 2011. There are in total 53,450 problem logs in the dataset. The dataset was randomly split into four bins in order to perform a four-fold cross-validation. For each student, we made a list of the skills the student had seen and split that list of skills randomly into four bins, placing all the data for that student for that skill into the respective bin. There were four rounds of training and testing where at each round a different bin served as the test set, and the data from the remaining three bins served as the training set. Both models were trained and tested on the same dataset.

The accuracy of the prediction was evaluated in terms of the Root Mean Squared Error (RMSE). Lower value means higher accuracy.

2.1 General Data Experiment

The purpose of the general data experiment was to determine which of the two individualization models works better in a real world Intelligent Tutoring System datasets. The cross-validation results are shown in Table 1.

Table 1. RMSE of SS vs 2-phase

	SS	2-phase
Fold 1	0.447	0.452
Fold 2	0.438	0.451
Fold 3	0.422	0.420
Fold 4	0.445	0.446

The average RMSE of the Student Skill model is 0.438, which is better than the Two Phase model 0.442. However, paired t-test result has $p > 0.05$, which indicates that the result is not statistically reliable.

2.2 Filtered Data Experiment

The assumption we tried to verify in this experiment is that, in the first phase of the two phase model, when the model tries to determine which are the student parameters without knowing the skill information, the students that have done only easy skills will be more likely to get "better" parameters (better here means indicating he/she is a good student) than the students who have done only hard skills, and this inaccuracy in estimating student parameters would affect the Two Phase model's results, and causes a difference in model performance compared to the Student Skill model.

We filtered our dataset according to our assumption through the following steps and then compared the two models again on this filtered dataset.

a) Group skills to hard/medium/easy using percent correctness, in order to ensure that skills are very different, we threw out the medium group and kept only the hard and easy group skills;
b) Find student group A that contains students who have done both hard and easy skills;
c) Find student group B who have done only hard skills;
d) Find student group C who have done only easy skills;
e) Randomly select equal numbers of students from all three groups and use the data logs that are from only the hard and easy skills to build the dataset.

The cross-validation results are shown in Table 3.

Table 2. RMSE result of SS vs 2-phase in Filtered Real Data Experiment

	SS	2-phase
Fold 1	0.423	0.428
Fold 2	0.425	0.423
Fold 3	0.419	0.427
Fold 4	0.423	0.423

The average RMSE of the Student Skill model is 0.423, which is better than the Two Phase model 0.426. The paired t-test on the prediction residual of all of the data points has $p < 0.05$, which indicates that the two models do perform differently in the situation we filtered the data to make.

3 Conclusion

In this paper, we were able to show that the two different individualized Knowledge Tracing models perform similarly in general, yet different under certain circumstances.

References

1. Corbett, A.T., Anderson, J.R.: Knowledge Tracing: Modeling the Acquisition of Procedural Knowledge. User Modeling and User-Adapted Interaction 4, 253–278 (1995)
2. Pardos, Z.A., Heffernan, N.T.: Modeling Individualization in a Bayesian Networks Implementation of Knowledge Tracing. In: Proceedings of the 18th International Conference on User Modeling, Adaptation and Personalization, pp. 225–266 (2010)
3. Pardos, Z.A., Heffernan, N.T.: Using HMMs and bagged decision trees to leverage rich features of user and skill from an intelligent tutoring system dataset. Journal of Machine Learning Research W & CP (in press)
4. Wang, Y., Heffernan, N.T.: The Student Skill Model. In: Cerri, S.A., Clancey, W.J., Papadourakis, G., Panourgia, K. (eds.) ITS 2012. LNCS, vol. 7315, pp. 399–404. Springer, Heidelberg (2012)

On the Benefits (or Not) of a Clustering Algorithm in Student Tracking

Reva Freedman and Nathalie Japkowicz

Northern Illinois University, Department of Computer Science
{rfreedman,njapkowicz}@niu.edu

Abstract. This study proposes a first step toward the automated realization of student tracking, i.e., dividing a class of students into several streams according to criteria such as overall strength, specific abilities, etc. Our study is based on a database of 214 students who took a 64-question multiple choice exam. We examine a family of tracking schemes based on the k-means algorithm but differing in feature selection and attribute weighting. We compare these schemes to a naïve scheme based solely on overall grades and a human-based scheme that applies k-means to content-based features assigned by experienced teachers.

Keywords: student tracking, unsupervised learning, clustering algorithms.

1 Introduction

This study proposes a first step toward the automated realization of student tracking (also known as streaming; we use both terms). Tracking consists of dividing a class of students into several streams according to a desired measure of ability.

The data was obtained from 64 multiple-choice items on a final exam administered to all 214 students in a beginning C++ class at Northern Illinois University in May 2009 [1]. For each algorithm we clustered students into three groups, representing a typical university situation where three classrooms are available for sections of a class. We compared three clustering schemes:

1. A naïve scheme, which consists of dividing students into three categories according to the overall grade they received on the exam.
2. A set of more sophisticated schemes based on the k-means algorithm but differing in feature selection and attribute weighting. We tried to stream together students who failed the same questions and were successful on the same questions while still considering their overall strength. Each of these schemes not only optimizes the students' overall strength but also ensures that the variance obtained on the answers to all the questions in each stream is minimized.
3. A human-based scheme that applies the k-means algorithm to a set of ten features assigned by human instructors based on the content of the exam questions.

K. Yacef et al. (Eds.): AIED 2013, LNAI 7926, pp. 840–843, 2013.

2 Methodology

The naïve approach was implemented manually from the data in Figure 1. The y-axis represent the grade and the x-axis represents the 214 students, ranked from lowest grade to highest. Since there is no natural break in this graph, we divided the students into three roughly equal categories, making sure to include all the students who received the same grade in the same category and locally maximizing the gaps from one group to the next. Group 1 contained 67 students (47-107 points out of 200), group 2 contained 74 students (109-142 points) and group 3 also contained 74 students (143-197 points).

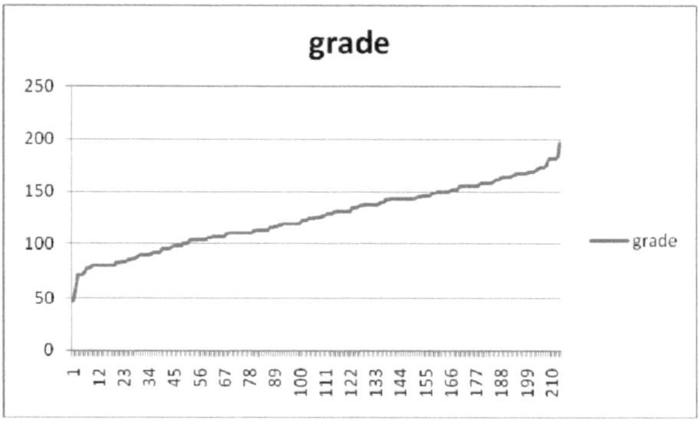

Fig. 1. Grade distribution in the database

In the sophisticated approach, we started by using one correct/incorrect feature for each question. We also tried including the overall grade at various weights. Finally we looked at using subsets of the questions, such as the half of the questions on which the students did best and the half on which they did worst.

The human-based approach depended on qualitative knowledge obtained from course instructors. Each question was labeled as to which category (or categories) of knowledge it required, including arrays, functions, I/O, math, objects, pointers, references, strings, "structs," and control structures. The categories were derived from a popular textbook [2]. We calculated a subscore showing the student's performance on each of the 10 types of questions. Since students need to learn each topic, we treated the 10 subscores equally in spite of the differing number of questions in each. We then used k-means to derive clusters from a vector consisting of the 10 subscores. Thus the human-based approach used intelligence, albeit indirectly, through the assignment of topics, while the others did not.

3 Results and Discussion

We used both internal and external measures to evaluate these three types of clustering. For internal measures, we used both entropy and purity [3]. Lower values are preferable for entropy, which measures the level of uncertainty in the clustering, while higher values are preferable for purity, which assesses the extent to which a cluster contains only one class of data.

In addition, we evaluated the naïve and sophisticated schemes under the assumption that the human-based scheme supplied the correct cluster for each student. This approach provided two statistics. The success rate is the percent of students that a given clustering scheme assigned to the same cluster as the human-based scheme, i.e., the percent that the test scenario got "right." Finally, the kappa statistic discounts the success rate by the number of matches expected to be correct by chance. For both of these metrics, higher values indicate a more accurate clustering scheme.

Table 1 shows a comparison of the naïve strategy and members of the sophisticated family against the human-based strategy, sorted by entropy. The first three columns indicate the number of instances in each cluster. (The human-based scheme had 78, 50 and 86, respectively.) Q&G stands for Questions and Grade. The number appearing after Grade is the coefficient used to increase the weight of the grade. Worst Q, Middle Q and Best Q correspond to the 32 questions on which the students performed worst (i.e., the most difficult questions), the central 32 questions, and the 32 questions on which the students performed best (i.e., the easiest questions).

Table 1. Performance of other tracking schemes vs. the human-based one

	C1	C2	C3	Entropy	Purity	Success	Kappa
Naïve	67	74	73	0.8197	0.7477	0.7477	0.6223
Q&G5	52	89	73	1.0488	0.6449	0.6355	0.4618
Q	65	78	71	1.0700	0.6636	0.6636	0.4984
Q&G	70	76	68	1.0768	0.6542	0.6542	0.4840
Worst Q	90	67	57	1.1201	0.6495	0.6495	0.4742
Middle Q	67	60	87	1.1777	0.6402	0.6402	0.4523
Best Q	44	47	123	1.3684	0.5841	0.5327	0.2730

The naïve strategy is closer to the human-based one than are any of the sophisticated approaches, as measured by both success and kappa. Furthermore, the difference between the naïve strategy and the others is well marked, suggesting that naïve is well ahead of the sophisticated strategies. Still, it is far from the human-based strategy, as shown by the success rate. The poor performance of Best Q is consistent with the intuition that questions on which everyone does well do not do a good job of differentiating students.

We also graphed each result to enable us to make a qualitative estimate of the spread between the clusters. Figures 2 and 3 show the results obtained for the naïve and human strategies, respectively. Each point represents a student. The x-axis indicates the grade the student obtained on the exam, sorted from worst to best, and the y-axis represents the cluster that student is in (1 = weakest, 2 = average, 3 = strongest). As expected, the naïve scheme does not allow for any overlap while the human scheme does. Qualitatively speaking, these schemes are therefore not closely related, whereas the sophisticated schemes (graphs not shown) also yield overlapping graphs and can therefore be thought of as qualitatively closer to the human-based one.

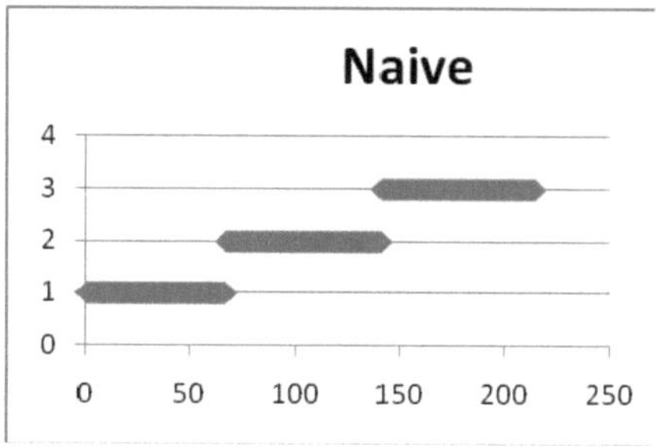

Fig. 2. Naïve clusters

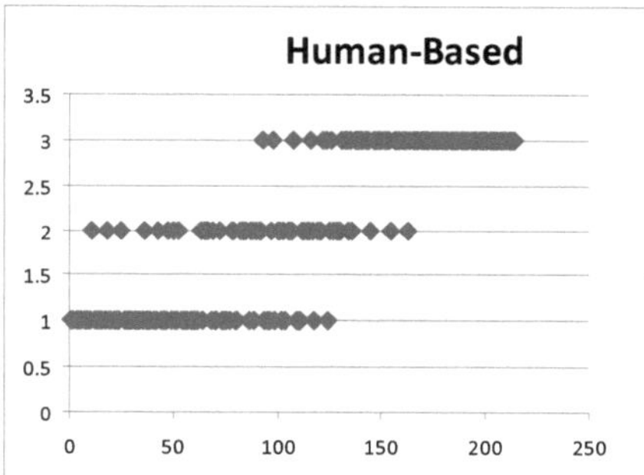

Fig. 3. Human-based clusters

4 Conclusions

This paper compared three schemes for student streaming based on final exam questions: a naïve scheme based solely on students' exam results, a set of more sophisticated schemes based on applying k-means to the correct/incorrect pattern of individual questions, and an approach applying k-means to factors labeled by humans. Although none of the sophisticated approaches did as well quantitatively as the naïve approach with respect to the human scheme, qualitatively speaking, the overlapping nature of their graphs suggests some closeness, which we plan to investigate further.

Acknowledgements. Georgia Brown, Amy Byrnes, Kurt McMahon and Margie Musich of NIU helped to elucidate the behavior of the human-based scheme.

References

1. Lulis, E., Freedman, R.: Validating an instructor rating scale for the difficulty of CS1 test items in C++. Journal of Computing Sciences in Colleges 21(2), 85–91 (2011)
2. Deitel, H., Deitel, P.: C++ How to Program. Prentice Hall, Upper Saddle River (2003)
3. Liu, B.: Web Data Mining: Exploring Hyperlinks, Contents, and Usage Data, 2/e. Springer, Heidelberg (2011)

Programming Pathways: A Technique for Analyzing Novice Programmers' Learning Trajectories

Marcelo Worsley and Paulo Blikstein

Stanford University, Graduate School of Education, Stanford, CA, USA
{mworsley,paulob}@stanford.edu

Abstract. Introductory computer science courses are a valuable resource to students of all disciplines. While we often look at students' end products to judge their proficiency, little analysis is done on the most integral aspect of learning to programming, the process. We also have a hard time quantifying how students' programming changes over the course of a semester. In order to address these we show how a process-oriented analysis can identify meaningful trends in how programmers develop proficiency across various assignments.

Keywords: Machine Learning, Computational Thinking, Programming.

1 Introduction

We are seeing a shift in who is using computers, and in who is doing computer programming. A variety of disciplines are realizing that the skills of computational thinking and debugging, for example, are applicable to nearly every domain. There is something about the process of learning computer programming that facilitates one's ability to think constructively about any number of tasks. Despite the importance of the process, most computer science curricula rely on a final code submission and course examinations in order to validate student learning. In order to get back to processes, this work closely analyzes student learning processes for a class of introductory programming students. Furthermore, the analysis demonstrates how we can use techniques from computer science to automatically identify important changes that take place in the process that students use to complete their assignments.

2 Previous Work

Traditional work in computer programming assessment has focused on learning outcomes (Cooper, Cassell, Cunningham, Moskal 2005; Olds, Moskal and Miller 2005), and designing the right environment for enabling students to achieve those learning outcomes (Moskal, Lurie, Cooper 2004; Goldman 2004). Ironically, initial work in computer science education was heavily centered on process based assessments. For example, from Soloway and Spohrer (1989) we observe that more expert programmers are "planners," who make large, low frequency code updates. The trend towards process recently re-emerged (Jadud 2005, Blikstein 2011 and Piech et al. 2012).

K. Yacef et al. (Eds.): AIED 2013, LNAI 7926, pp. 844–847, 2013.

These three studies utilized snapshots of student compilations as the basis of their analysis. This study borrows elements from Jadud, Blikstein and Piech et al., but differs in that we look at changes in students' programming process over a set of assignments, instead of just looking at one assignment, as

3 Methods

This work was intended to automatically detect the evolution of student programming strategies and knowledge throughout an introductory programming class. In order to do this, we focused on studying "tinkering," or bricoleur, and "planning" (Turkle and Papert, 1991). We operationalized "tinkerer" and "planner" to be related to the number of characters or lines that a student adds, removes or modifies between snapshots. We are not concerned with absolute labels of tinkering and planning, but are looking for relative changes for each student and to tinkering and planning episodes.

Data comes from four programming assignments that seventy-four students, from a research-1 university, completed during the course of several weeks of their class. These assignments do not represent the entirety of the assignments for this course. Two early assignments were omitted because the nature of the programming environments varied greatly from later assignments.

We first extract the number of lines added, lines removed, lines modified, characters added, characters removed and absolute value of characters modified between successive snapshots, a value that we collectively refer to as the "update characteristics." These values exclude comments and are based on computing the line-by-line difference between snapshots. "Modified" was used for lines that are at least 70% the same as the line in the previous snapshot.

The extracted values are z-transformed across all students for a given assignment. In order to compute the similarity between students' sets of snapshots, we used dynamic time warping, and then scaled all sequences to be of the same length before computing the Euclidean distance between a given pair of snapshots. We then observe whether each student's programming pattern for Assignment 3 was most similar to that of Assignment 1, Assignment 2. Similarly, we record if Assignment 4's updates are more similar to that of Assignment 1, Assignment 2 or Assignment 3. Each student is assigned to a group based on their completion of the last two assignments, with the options: Assignment 1 - Assignment 1, Assignment 1 - Assignment 2, Assignment 1- Assignment 3, Assignment 2 - Assignment 1, Assignment 2-Assignment 3, Assignment 2-Assignment 2. For ease of interpretation we'll give each group a name (Table 1).

Table 1. Proportion of Students in Each Cluster

Cluster	1- 1	1- 2	1-3	2-1	2-2	2- 3
Name	ALPHA	BETA	DELTA	GAMMA	ZETA	OMEGA
Proportion	0.35	0.15	0.22	0.12	0.08	0.08

4 Results and Discussion

Table 1 shows the relative sizes of each group. Comparing clusters across assignment scores, we do not see any significant differences. However, when we compare examination scores (Table 2) we see a clear hierarchy, with OMEGA at the top and ZETA at the bottom[1]. The first thing that we note is that the data is normally distributed with the two smallest groups, ZETA and OMEGA occupying the two extremities. We also present data about help seeking frequency, disaggregated by month, for each group. ZETA, the worst performing group, is the most frequent attender of help during the first two months (Help 1 and Help 2) of the course, but fall to the least frequent attenders during the last month (Help 3). OMEGA, the highest performing group quickly transitions into being frequent help seekers (Help2), and both GAMMA and ALPHA become more frequent help seeking attenders[2].

Table 2. Ranking of Groups Across Variables

Rank	Midterm	Final	Help 1	Help 2	Help 3	Update Vector[3]
1	OMEGA	OMEGA	ZETA	ZETA	BETA	ALPHA
2	GAMMA	GAMMA	GAMMA	OMEGA	OMEGA	ZETA
3	DELTA	ALPHA	BETA	BETA	GAMMA	OMEGA
4	ALPHA	DELTA	DELTA	GAMMA	ALPHA	DELTA
5	BETA	BETA	OMEGA	ALPHA	DELTA	BETA
6	ZETA	ZETA	ALPHA	DELTA	ZETA	GAMMA

In an effort to characterize each groups progress over the course of the class, we present their change in update characteristics between Assignment 1 and Assignment 4 in the "Update Vector" column. ALPHA, ZETA and OMEGA share similar update vectors and DELTA, BETA and GAMMA share similar update vectors. These similarities are startling, given that ALPHA, ZETA and OMEGA occupy different parts of the performance spectrum, and the help seeking spectrum.

Looking closer we saw that students with different levels of expertise get differential benefits from help and differential benefits from their overall update approach. Additionally, we see that students use their code updates differently. Some use their updates as a way for checking syntax. Other students use updates to make their code more efficient. The other important difference is that students change in different ways. Some groups change in terms of average update size, but not in the overall approach. This was largely the case of ALPHA and ZETA. Alternatively some groups: DELTA, GAMMA, BETA and OMEGA; changed in their *sequence* of small

[1] ZETA was outscored on the final exam by ALPHA, GAMMA and OMEGA ($t(30)$ - 2.6896 $p < 0.012$, $t(13)= 3.586$ $p < 0.003$, $t(10)=2.1778$ $p<0.04$) and on the midterm ($t(30)=2.5264$ $p<0.02$, $t(13)=2.254$ $p < 0.04$, $t(10) = 2.386$ $p< 0.04$), as well as by DELTA ($t(20) = 2.221$ $p< 0.04$).

[2] GAMMA attended fewer help sessions that ZETA in month 1 and month 2 ($t(20)=2.20$ $p< 0.0049$) and month 2 ($t(20)=2.786$ $p < 0.0114$).

[3] Similarity was computed using the f-statistics across all six items in the update vector.

and large changes, or tinkering and planning episodes, but maybe not in the average size of those updates.

Thus as we consider these types of analysis in future work, and study, in greater depth how different resources and actions impact traditional outcome based measures, we have to consider that students may change in different ways and look to better explain these different processes.

5 Conclusion

In this paper we presented an algorithm for studying changes in programming styles among novice programmers. We showed how using a process-oriented analysis was a meaningful approach. We also showed how looking at changes in students' programming update characteristics, relative to themselves, may provide the most useful lens for studying programming proficiency, as measured through assignment grades and test scores. In future research we will expand this work to a larger population of users and combine this analysis with additional qualitative data to more closely corroborate our interpretation of the data, especially as it relates to planning and tinkering.

References

1. Blikstein, P.: Using learning analytics to assess students' behavior in open-ended programming tasks. In: 2011 Learning Analytics Knowledge Conference (LAK 2011), pp. 110–116. ACM, New York (2011)
2. Cooper, S., Cassel, L., Moskal, B., Cunningham, S.: Outcomes-based computer science education. In: 36th SIGCSE Technical Symposium on Computer Science Education (SIGCSE 2005), pp. 260–261. ACM, New York (2005)
3. Goldman, K.: A concepts-first introduction to computer science. In: 35th SIGCSE Technical Symposium on Computer Science Education (SIGCSE 2004), pp. 432–436. ACM, New York (2004)
4. Jadud, M.: Methods and tools for exploring novice compilation behaviour. In: 2nd International Workshop on Computing Education Research (ICER 2006), pp. 73–84. ACM, New York (2006)
5. Moskal, B., Lurie, D., Cooper, S.: Evaluating the effectiveness of a new instructional approach. In: 35th SIGCSE Technical Symposium on Computer Science Education (SIGCSE 2004), pp. 75–79. ACM, New York (2004)
6. Soloway, E., Spohrer, J.: Studying the novice programmer. L. Erlbaum Assoc. Inc., Hillsdale (1988)
7. Turkle, S., Papert, S.: Epistemological Pluralism and Revaluation of the Concrete. In: Papert, I.H.A.S. (ed.) Constructionism, pp. 161–192. Ablex Publishing Co., Norwood (1991)
8. Piech, C., Sahami, M., Koller, D., Cooper, S., Blikstein, P.: Modeling how students learn to program. In: 43rd ACM Technical Symposium on Computer Science Education (SIGCSE 2012), pp. 153–160. ACM, New York (2012)

Knowledge Maximizer: Concept-Based Adaptive Problem Sequencing for Exam Preparation

Roya Hosseini[1], Peter Brusilovsky[1], and Julio Guerra[2]

[1] University of Pittsburgh, Pittsburgh, USA
{roh38,peterb}@pitt.edu
[2] Universidad Austral de Chile, Valdivia, Chile
jguerra@inf.uach.cl

Abstract. To support introductory Java programming students in preparing for their exams, we developed Knowledge Maximizer as a concept-based problem sequencing tool that considers a fine-grained concept-level model of student knowledge accumulated over the semester and attempts to bridge the possible knowledge gaps in the most efficient way. This paper presents the sequencing approach behind the Knowledge Maximizer and its classroom evaluation.

Keywords: problem sequencing, concept-based student model.

1 Introduction

Exam preparation is a challenging task for college students. For many courses, students need to review the content that was studied over the whole semester within a short time frame, identify possible knowledge gaps and misconceptions, and remediate these gaps. An adaptive problem-sequencing tool, based on a fine-grained concept-level student model, could be very helpful in this context. By reflecting students' progress over the whole semester, the student model can distinguish between: 1) concepts that were learned well and need not be practiced again; 2) concepts that were not mastered and need to be reviewed; 3) and concepts that were missed and may need a thorough review. Based on this model, an adaptive problem-sequencing tool can individually guide each student through the exam preparation process.

While concept-level adaptive sequencing is a relatively mature and well-known approach [1; 2], there are still no instances of its use in the context of exam preparation. This context, however, is different from the traditional sequencing that carries a student through the course. Exam-time sequencing implies that a student has a relatively complete knowledge of course materials and little time to improve it. Instead of gradual coverage of concepts, exam-time sequencing should focus on bridging knowledge gaps while trying to maximize the number of concepts that are assessed and mastered by completing each suggested problem. To explore sequencing in this interesting context, we developed Knowledge Maximizer, a concept-based problem sequencing tool for Java programming exam preparation. This paper presents the sequencing approach of Knowledge Maximizer and the results of its classroom study.

K. Yacef et al. (Eds.): AIED 2013, LNAI 7926, pp. 848–851, 2013.

2 The Knowledge Maximizer

The goal of the Knowledge Maximizer (KM) is to provide the learner with a sequence of questions to help address gaps in Java knowledge as quickly as possible. To this end, KM uses an overlay student model in conjunction with a concept-level model of Java knowledge represented in the form of Java ontology. The learning content in KM comprises 103 parameterized self-assessment questions (activity) indexed by ontology concepts. The indexing distinguishes *prerequisite* and *outcome* concepts for each activity. To select and rank the 10 most important activities, KM uses the following factors:

How prepared is the student to do the activity? The activities for which the student has less knowledge of prerequisite concepts are not appropriate suggestions. We calculate the learner knowledge for each of the prerequisite concepts in an activity to see how well the student is prepared to do it. Eq.1 shows the formula:

$$K = \frac{\sum_{i}^{M_r} k_i w_i'}{\sum_{i}^{M_r} w_i'} \qquad w_i' = \log(w_i) \qquad \text{Eq. (1)}$$

where K is the learner's knowledge level about the prerequisites of the activity; w_i' is the log-smoothed weight for the concept; k_i is the level of the learner's knowledge about the ith concept and M_r is the set of prerequisite concepts for the activity. More knowledge of prerequisite concepts for an activity (higher K) makes it a better candidate for selection by the optimizer. Due to the short duration of the course and the complexity of the Java concepts, we do not take knowledge decay into account in Eq.1.

What is the impact of the activity? The formula for this impact is shown as Eq.2 where M_o is the set of outcome concepts for the activity (i.e., concepts that are mastered by the student while working with the activity). Impact I of a certain activity measures how well it addresses the current lack of knowledge. An activity with a higher impact factor is a better candidate for selection by the optimizer.

Has the user already completed the activity? We define it as Eq.3 where $\overline{S}$ is the inverse success rate of the student in the activity; s is the number of the times the student has succeeded in the activity; and t is the total number of times the student has attempted to complete the activity.

$$I = \frac{\sum_{i}^{M_o} w_i'(1-k_i)}{\sum_{i}^{M_o} w_i'} \quad \text{Eq. (2)} \qquad \overline{S} = 1 - \frac{s}{t+1} \quad \text{Eq. (3)} \qquad R = K + I + \overline{S} \quad \text{Eq. (4)}$$

Having calculated these factors, we simply rank the activities using Eq. 4 where R is the rank of the activity which is obtained by summing over the values of K, I, and $\overline{S}$.

Fig. 1 shows the KM interface. The question with the highest rank is shown first. Users can navigate the ranked list of questions utilizing navigation buttons at the top. The right side of the panel shows the list of concepts covered by the question. The color next to each concept visualizes the student's current knowledge level (from red representing less knowledge to green representing more knowledge).

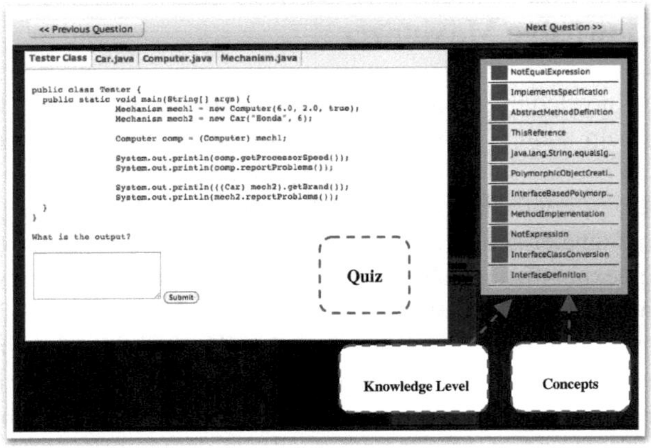

Fig. 1. The Knowledge Maximizer interface

3 The Evaluation

To assess the value of Knowledge Maximizer, we conducted a classroom study in the context of a Java-based undergraduate programming course at the School of Information Sciences, University of Pittsburgh. All students enrolled in this course were invited to use the KM during preparation for the final exam. The study began about a week prior to the final exam. Throughout the course, students used two other adaptive tools, QuizGuide, and Progressor+ to work with Java problems. Both tools reported student knowledge updates to the central student model server which was also used by KM. As a result, many students mastered a significant number of Java concepts by the time they started with KM and were ready to benefit from its "gap filling" nature.

In our analysis, we counted separately questions accessed from KM and questions accessed from QuizGuide or Progressor+. Attempts made from KM were made by 14 students while attempts made from QuizGuide/Progressor+ were made by 17 students. To assess whether KM was successful in "maximizing" students' progress towards the goal, we grouped questions into three different complexity levels based on the number of involved concepts: 1) Easy, 2) Moderate, and 3) Complex. Table 1 lists the number of attempts made to do easy, moderate, and complex questions from KM and from QuizGuide/Progressor+. The data reveals that the number of attempts to access complex questions was about 2.5 times greater in KM. Despite a remarkable increase in complex questions in KM, the success rates across all systems were comparable.

To compare the effect of KM and the other systems on the improvement of students' performance, we compared quiz grades obtained by the students in the second part of the course and their post-test results. Since in-class quizzes and post-tests have different numbers of questions, we used a percentage of the total as a relative score. We discovered that the average increase in performance percentage among the students who used QuizGuide/Progressor+ was 12% (0.68% to 0.8%) while KM users experienced an average increase of 19% (0.53% to 0.72%). Moreover, students who used KM "for real" (i.e., made at least 10 attempts using KM) achieved a 28% increase (0.48% to 0.76%). This provides some evidence (as much as could be collected in a non-controlled classroom situation where learning can happen outside of the systems) that KM acted as a strong exam preparation tool, surpassing the more traditional adaptive systems QuizGuide/Progressor+ not designed for exam preparation.

Table 1. Number of Attempts, success rates by System and complexity level

Complexity	KM (n=14)		QG,P+ (n=17)	
	Number of Attempts	Success rate	Number of Attempts	Success rate
Easy	27 (6.2%)	93%	1123 (34.6%)	73%
Moderate	189 (43.5%)	68%	1471 (45.3%)	61%
Complex	218 (50.2%)	46%	651(20.1%)	55%
Total	434	58%	3245	64%

4 Conclusion and Future Work

We have explored adaptive problem sequencing in KM to support exam preparation in a Java programming class. Results of our study revealed the ability of KM to generate challenging questions that shortened the path to students' learning goals. KM can be applied to any other domains with ontology and questions indexed by ontology concepts. Our future work will focus on improving KM by considering more parameters that affect the selections of questions, such as the timing factor.

Acknowledgement. This research was supported in part by the National Science Foundation under Grant No. 0447083. Julio Guerra is supported by a Chilean Scholarship (Becas Chile) from the National Commission for Science Research and Technology (CONICYT, Chile) and the Universidad Austral de Chile.

References

1. Brusilovsky, P.: A framework for intelligent knowledge sequencing and task sequencing. In: Frasson, C., McCalla, G., Gauthier, G. (eds.) ITS 1992. LNCS, vol. 608, pp. 499–506. Springer, Heidelberg (1992)
2. Kumar, A.N.: A Scalable Solution for Adaptive Problem Sequencing and its Evaluation. In: Wade, V., Ashman, H., Smyth, B. (eds.) AH 2006. LNCS, vol. 4018, pp. 161–171. Springer, Heidelberg (2006)

Worked Out Examples in Computer Science Tutoring

Barbara Di Eugenio[1], Lin Chen[1], Nick Green[1], Davide Fossati[2], and Omar AlZoubi[2]

[1] Computer Science, University of Illinois at Chicago
Chicago, IL, USA
{bdieugen,lchen43,ngreen21}@uic.edu
[2] Computer Science, Carnegie Mellon University in Qatar
Doha, Qatar
{dfossati,oalzoubi}@cmu.edu

Abstract. We annotated and analyzed Worked Out Examples (WOEs) in a corpus of tutoring dialogues on Computer Science data structures. We found that some dialogue moves that occur within WOEs, or sequences thereof, correlate with learning. Features of WOEs such as length also correlate with learning for some data structures. These results will be used to augment the tutorial tactics available to iList, an ITS that helps student learn linked lists.

Keywords: Tutoring dialogues, Tutoring strategies, Intelligent tutoring.

1 Introduction

Worked out examples (WOEs) demonstrate a step by step solution of a problem for the learner to study. Learning from WOEs has been studied in cognitive research [1,2], including in the context of Intelligent Tutoring Systems (ITSs) [3,4]. However, the conditions that trigger WOEs and how tutors structure WOEs have not been extensively investigated. Our domain of interest is introductory data structures in Computer Science (CS). Interestingly, one of the first papers on WOEs [7] also concerns learning in CS, specifically recursion in LISP programming. Within CS, [5,6] have employed WOEs for classroom instruction.

Our interest in exploring WOEs is two-fold. We believe that in order to deploy WOEs in an ITS, it is essential to uncover the conditions under which WOEs are effective. Additionally, in our previous work, we showed that certain Dialogue Moves (DMs) on the part of the tutor, or sequences thereof, correlate with learning gains [8]. Many of those findings have been implemented in the iList system, that helps students learn linked lists [9,10]. Still, the tutor interventions we deployed are not conditioned on the larger tutoring strategies the tutor uses. WOEs can provide one type of context to structure those tutor moves.

K. Yacef et al. (Eds.): AIED 2013, LNAI 7926, pp. 852–855, 2013.

2 WOEs, Their Features and Learning

Our corpus consists of 54 tutoring sessions with two human tutors on linked lists, stacks, and binary search trees. It had been previously annotated with Student Initiative (SI), and with 5 tutor moves: prompts (PT); positive and negative feedback (PF, NF); Direct Procedural Instruction (DPI) – the tutor provides insight into steps to solve the problem; Direct Declarative Instruction (DDI) – the tutor states facts about the problem [8]. The annotation of WOEs was superimposed on these preexisting annotations. Two coders marked beginning and end of WOEs.[1] We obtained excellent intercoder agreement ($\kappa = .82$) on 7 sessions that were double annotated. Each coder then annotated half of the remaining sessions. Fig. 1 shows a WOE excerpt from our corpus starting at TUT2 (it continues beyond TUT6, and it has been modified for space reasons). Fig. 1 also shows the moves each utterance is labelled with.

```
DDI              TUT1   Now a binary search tree must remain ordered.
DPI, WOE-START   TUT2   say we want to insert, um, six.
SI               ST     down there? [pointing to tree drawing]
PF               TUT4   right
SI               ST     five is smaller than six
DDI              TUT5   and the right child of five is null
DPI              TUT6   so we will insert six to its right
```

Fig. 1. A worked out example to insert a node into a binary search tree

Table 1 shows distributional statistics about WOEs, per topic: how many sessions (tutors were free to skip topics), and total number of WOEs; average number of WOEs, average lengths of WOEs in words and in utterances (standard deviations in parenthesis). Tutors use many more WOEs for lists and trees than for stacks; more frequent WOEs for trees are offset by longer WOEs for lists.

Table 1. Worked Out Examples Statistics

Topic	N	Total WOEs	Avg. WOEs	Avg. Words/WOE	Avg. Utts./WOE
Lists	52	180	3.5 (1.4)	498.3 (438)	48.3 (42.7)
Stacks	46	24	0.5 (0.5)	615.5 (115.6)	68.5 (17.1)
Trees	53	454	8.6 (2.7)	212.5 (223)	24.0 (24.5)

As in our previous work, we adopt a multiple regression approach, because it shows how much variation in learning gains is explained by the variation of features in the data. We previously included pre-test score, the length of the tutoring sessions, the DMs we annotated for, and DM *bigrams* and *trigrams*, i.e.

[1] Coders also marked nested WOEs, but since only 21 nested WOEs exist out of 658 total, we will not discuss them further.

DM sequences of length 2 or 3. In our best regression models (R^2=.415 for lists, R^2=.416 for stacks, and R^2=.732 for trees), significant features are pre-test score and trigrams of specific DMs (negative correlations between previous knowledge and learning gains are common: models that only include pre-test score result in R^2=.200 for lists, R^2=.296 for stacks, and an astounding R^2=.676 for trees).

We now add WOEs and their features to the regression. Simply adding the number of WOEs per session does not correlate with learning gains, other than for stacks; however, this correlation is negative. Next, we explore models where we differentiate between DMs within and outside of WOEs. We ran every regression model that results from the systematic combination of pre-score, length of dialogue, number of WOEs, length of WOEs in words and utterances, and then, for each DM, how many occur outside, and how many inside, a WOE. As a result, we obtain better regression models, but only for lists and stacks (see Table 2). Even if some correlations are only marginally significant, together they throw further light on WOEs. For trees, the best previous model includes pre-test and the DM trigram [PF,SI,DDI]. Using **only** the occurrences of this trigram of DMs within WOEs (as in Fig. 1), we obtain a slightly improved R^2 = .737.

Table 2. The most explanatory models include WOE features

Topic	Predictor	β	R^2	P
Lists	Pre-test	−0.442	.485	<.01
	WOE_Prompt	−.0006		= 0.073
	WOE_#Utterances	.002		= 0.092
	PF	.005		= 0.099
Stacks	Pre-test	−.37	.606	<.005
	WOE_PF	0.077		< .005
	WOE_Prompt	−.021		<.05
Trees	Pre-test	−.736	.737	<.0001
	WOE_[PF,SI,DDI]	.037		< .005

From the models shown in Table 2, we can confirm that WOEs can be a successful tutorial strategy, but we need to look "under the hood". First, effective features of WOEs depend on the specific topic; e.g., longer WOEs are effective only for lists. Positive feedback (PF) within and outside WOEs is important: PFs within WOEs marginally correlate with learning gains for stacks, and robustly correlate with learning as part of the sequence [PF,SI,DDI] for trees; PFs outside of WOEs correlate with learning gains for lists (this confirms our previous results on positive feedback). Surprisingly, for lists and stacks, prompts within WOEs are **negatively** correlated with learning gains. This seems to suggest that during WOEs, where the tutor is demonstrating a solution, students should not be invited to participate in problem solving, which is otherwise well known as conducive to learning. It turns out that, on average, more prompts occur in WOEs for stacks (11.1), than for lists (7.7), than for trees (3.3). This may in part be due to the respective difficulty of these data structures, with stacks being easiest, next lists, and then trees. This may also explain the negative correlation between number of WOEs and learning gains, for stacks.

3 Future Work

Our findings open various lines of inquiry for future work, such as, what the role of prompts within WOEs is. We also intend to analyze the internal structure of WOEs, and what may trigger a WOE. A preliminary analysis shows that DDIs are the most frequent DM that immediately precedes the start of a WOE (see TUT1 in Fig. 1) with 435 occurrences out of 658 (66%); in 113 cases (17%) the preceding DM is a DPI. This seems to suggest that most of the time the tutor sets the stage for a WOE with a DDI. We will integrate our findings within the probabilistic model that iList uses to generate its next move. This model is based on the "promise" of the current and previous student steps [10].

Acknowledgments. This work is supported by award NPRP 5-939-1-155 from the Qatar National Research Fund.

References

1. Sweller, J.: The worked example effect and human cognition. Learning and Instruction 16(2), 165–169 (2006)
2. Atkinson, R.K., Derry, S.J., Renkl, A., Wortham, D.: Learning from examples: Instructional principles from the worked examples research. Review of Educational Research 70(2), 181–214 (2000)
3. Renkl, A., Atkinson, R., Maier, U., Staley, R.: From example study to problem solving: Smooth transitions help learning. Journal of Experimental Education 70, 293–315 (2002)
4. Ringenberg, M., VanLehn, K.: Scaffolding problem solving with annotated, worked-out examples to promote deep learning. In: Ikeda, M., Ashley, K.D., Chan, T.-W. (eds.) ITS 2006. LNCS, vol. 4053, pp. 625–634. Springer, Heidelberg (2006)
5. Moura, I.C.: Worked-out examples in a computer science introductory module. In: Proceedings of the World Congress on Engineering, vol. II (2012)
6. Luukkainen, M., Vihavainen, A., Vikberg, T.: A software craftsman's approach to data structures. In: Proceedings of the 43rd ACM Technical Symposium on Computer Science Education, SIGCSE 2012, pp. 439–444 (2012)
7. Pirolli, P., Anderson, J.R.: The role of learning from examples in the acquisition of recursive programming skills. Canadian Journal of Psychology 39(2) (1985)
8. Chen, L., Di Eugenio, B., Fossati, D., Ohlsson, S., Cosejo, D.: Exploring Effective Dialogue Act Sequences in One-on-one Computer Science Tutoring Dialogues. In: BEA6, The 6th Workshop on Innovative Use of NLP for Building Educational Applications (2011)
9. Fossati, D., Di Eugenio, B., Brown, C., Ohlsson, S., Cosejo, D., Chen, L.: Supporting Computer Science curriculum: Exploring and learning linked lists with iList. IEEE Transactions on Learning Technologies 2(2), 107–120 (2009)
10. Fossati, D., Di Eugenio, B., Ohlsson, S., Brown, C., Chen, L.: Generating proactive feedback to help students stay on track. In: Aleven, V., Kay, J., Mostow, J. (eds.) ITS 2010, Part II. LNCS, vol. 6095, pp. 315–317. Springer, Heidelberg (2010)

Student Coding Styles as Predictors of Help-Seeking Behavior

Engin Bumbacher, Alfredo Sandes, Amit Deutsch, and Paulo Blikstein

Stanford University, Stanford, California
{buben,alfredos,adeut195,paulob}@stanford.edu

Abstract. Recent research in CS education has leveraged machine learning techniques to capture students' progressions through assignments in programming courses based on their code submissions [1, 2]. With this in mind, we present a methodology for creating a set of descriptors of the students' progression based on their coding styles as captured by different non-semantic and semantic features of their code submissions. Preliminary findings show that these descriptors extracted from a single assignment can be used to predict whether or not a student got help throughout the entire quarter. Based on these findings, we plan on developing a model of the impact of teacher intervention on a student's pathway through homework assignments.

Keywords: Computer Science Education, Machine Learning.

1 Introduction

Recent work in CS education has leveraged machine learning techniques to gain insight into the ways in which students approach a given programming assignment. Piech et al. [2] created a graphical model of how students in an introductory programming course progressed through a homework assignment. They were able to extract characteristic pathways, which can be used to predict their midterm grades.
Our own research examines the relationship between students' coding styles and their general help-seeking behaviors; we want to know when students learning to program get help, why they get help, and how the help impacts their progression. We hope that this work could be used to determine potential points on a student's learning path where help interventions would be most effective; this could transform into a technology feature for recommendation of "help" in tutor learning systems.

In this preliminary study, we used machine learning techniques to show that the evolution of a student's code in a single assignment could be predictive of whether or not that student sought help throughout the academic quarter. This suggests that student coding patterns might be indicative of relevant behavioral or cognitive processes of students learning to program that give rise to certain help-seeking behaviors.

2 Data Sources

We collected data from a Stanford introductory course on programming methodologies in Java. Every time a student tried to compile their program we collected text

K. Yacef et al. (Eds.): AIED 2013, LNAI 7926, pp. 856–859, 2013.

snapshots of their code, regardless of whether or not their code compiled. We had access to a subject pool of 370 students. The target assignment we analyzed contained 8,772 snapshots of code across all students. To measure help-seeking behavior, we collected tracking data from an on-campus homework help service, where teaching assistants (TAs) track student visits. Thus, help-seeking behavior here refers to whether or not a student got help. Over the span of the quarter, there were 1,148 visits in the help center from 172 distinct students. Of these students, 91 sought help 1 or 2 times, and 81 sought help three times or more.

For this study, we analyzed a single assignment in which students were tasked with writing a program that accepts an arbitrary list of numbers and outputs the maximum and minimum values.

3 Methods

Our basic methodology, from data preprocessing to classification, can be broken down into three stages: characterizing code snapshots, characterizing students based on the ensemble of their snapshots, and classification of TA help data.

3.1 Characterizing Code Snapshots

We created a set of both semantic and non-semantic features with which we tried to capture what we refer to as "coding styles". The non-semantic features are: number of lines of a code, number of comments, and number of comment blocks. The semantic features are: number of variable declarations, number of method declaration, and the number and nesting level of loops and conditional statements within the code. Through a preliminary examination of student code submissions, we found that these features best describe the constrained solution space of the target assignment.

As a metric for dissimilarity measures, we used a simple Euclidian distance. For the clustering step, the data was normalized by the mode of each feature.

3.2 Characterizing Students: Cluster-Based Student Feature Selection

We clustered a student's snapshots based on structure similarities representative of different possible program structures. This allowed us to characterize the progression of a student through the assignment as a progression through clusters. In the unsupervised learning step, these clusters were generated using kernelized k-means with Gaussian kernels [3]. The number of optimal clusters was determined by a combination of silhouette value maximization [4] and Davies-Bouldin index minimization [5]. Assigning each snapshot to the corresponding cluster, we defined the students with a new feature set consisting of: the number of different clusters visited, the total number of cluster changes, a measure of the variance of the number of successive snapshots within the same cluster, the time to solution, and the total count of clusters visited.

3.3 Classification of the TA Intervention Data

In order to classify the TA intervention data, we trained a nonlinear Support Vector Machine (SVM) with a Gaussian radial basis function kernel with the student feature data by means of 10-fold cross-validation. Given the highly non-linear feature space, kernelized SVM was best suited for the binary classification task [6]. We also ran a Naïve Bayes Classifier with less promising results (data available upon request).

4 Results

As shown in Table 1, the kernelized SVM trained on the student population features predicts whether a student got help or not performs with an accuracy of 66.5% with a precision of 63.6% and a recall of about 71%.

Table 1. Performance of Binary SVM Classifier

Accuracy	66.5%
Precision	63.6%
Recall	71.1%

Figure 1 shows the dissimilarity matrix after clustering the student snapshots into 16 clusters and arranging them according to the clusters. Each matrix entry m_{ij} represents the dissimilarity in terms of Euclidian distance between snapshot i and snapshot j, with black being a dissimilarity of zero. As can be seen, the snapshots are well separated into the clusters (which is further supported by the silhouette value of about 0.72 in Table 2). The selection model based on the Davies-Bouldin Index and the silhouette value suggests 16 clusters as a good representation (see Table 2).

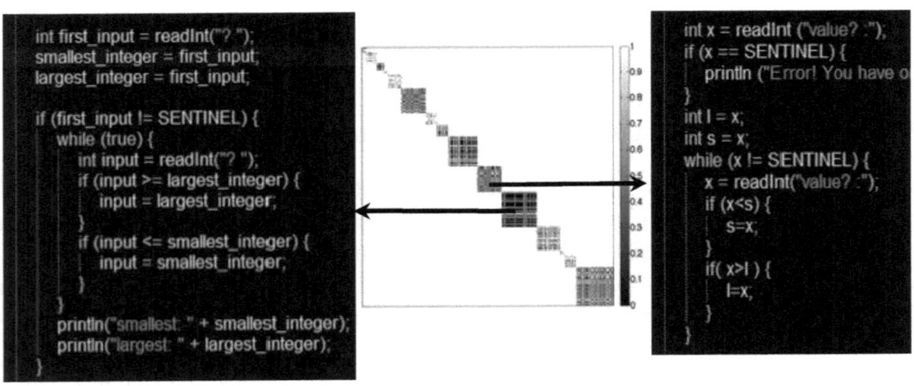

Fig. 1. Dissimilarity matrix of the k-means clusters, and 2 snapshots representative of their clusters

Table 2. Characteristics of the k-means clusters of code snapshots

Optimal choice of clusters:	16
Silhouette index:	0.72
DB-index:	0.43

To illustrate how codes within different clusters can differ from each other, we have added two code snapshots representative of their clusters in Figure 1. As can be seen, the code snapshot on the right of the dissimilarity matrix has two if statements nested within a loop; the code on the left has two if statements nested within a loop, which is in turn nested in another if statement.

5 Conclusions

Using a simple measure of a student's progress and representation of their code in a single assignment, we were able to predict with accuracy of about 66.5% the student's help-seeking behavior across the whole quarter. In light of the fact that the representation is very simplistic, and that we have excluded any complex measures entailing temporal dimensions, these results indicate that there is structure in the relationship between a student's progression through an assignment and their help-seeking behavior, and this relationship requires further exploration. Nonetheless, these results are especially interesting because they suggest that there are generalizable characteristics found in a small sample of code from one assignment early in the class that can be indicative for help seeking behavior across the entire quarter.

This project is the start of an extended investigation of student programming data. Based on the preliminary findings, we intend to integrate the TA help data and weekly survey data about motivation and perceived difficulty into a Markov model of assignment progress that can predict student grades and suggest critical points for intervention.

References

1. Blikstein, P.: Using Learning Analytics to Assess Students' Behavior in Open-Ended Programming Tasks. In: Proceedings of the Learning Analytics and Knowledge Conference (LAK 2011), Alberta, Canada (2011)
2. Piech, C., Sahami, M., Koller, D., Cooper, S., Blikstein, P.: Modeling how Students Learn to Program. In: Proceedings of the 43rd ACM Technical Symposium on Computer Science Education, Raleigh, NC, pp. 153–160 (2012)
3. Sewell, G., Rousseau, P.J.: Finding Groups in Data: An Introduction to Cluster Analysis. Wiley & Sons (2005)
4. Wang, K., Wang, B., Peng, L.: CVAP: Validation for Cluster Analyses. Data Science Journal 8, 88–93 (2009)
5. Petrovic, S.: A Comparison Between the Silhouette Index and the Davies-Bouldin Index in Labelling IDS clusters. In: Proceedings of the 11th Nordic Workshop of Secure IT Systems, Linkoping, Sweden, pp. 53–64 (2006)
6. Stanevski, N., Tsvetkov, D.: Using Support Vector Machine as Binary Classifier. In: Proceedings of the International Conference on Computer Systems and Technologies, Varna, Bulgaria (200)

Search-Based Estimation of Problem Difficulty for Humans

Matej Guid and Ivan Bratko

Faculty of Computer and Information Science, University of Ljubljana, Slovenia

Abstract. The research question addressed in this paper is: Given a problem, can we automatically predict how difficult the problem will be to solve by humans? We focus our investigation on problems in which the difficulty arises from the combinatorial complexity of problems. We propose a measure of difficulty that is based on modeling the problem solving effort as search among alternatives and the relations among alternative solutions. In experiments in the chess domain, using data obtained from very strong human players, this measure was shown at a high level of statistical significance to be adequate as a genuine measure of difficulty for humans.

Keywords: human problem solving, heuristic search, problem difficulty.

1 Introduction

In this paper, we address the research question: Given a problem, can we automatically predict how difficult the problem will be to solve by humans? This question is complex and concerns many aspects. It depends on the type of problem and on the human's knowledge about the problem domain. Our current investigation is focused on problems in which the difficulty arises from the combinatorial complexity of problems. We propose a measure of difficulty that is based on modeling the problem solving effort as search among alternatives and the relations among alternative solutions.

The basis for that is the AI formulation of problem solving as search: a given problem is reduced to finding a path in the state space. This typically leads to the problem of combinatorial complexity due to the rapidly growing number of alternatives. To overcome this problem, *heuristic search* is widely used. For the nodes in the state space heuristic estimates are determined, indicating how promising nodes are with respect to reaching a goal node, and this knowledge then guides the search.

Our experiments in this paper with the proposed measures of difficulty were carried out in a game playing domain (chess). Our method is based on heuristic search. In general, relatively little research has been devoted to the issue of problem difficulty. Some specific puzzles were investigated with this respect, including Tower of Hanoi [1], Chinese rings [2], 15-puzzle [3], Traveling Salesperson Problem [4], Sokoban puzzle [5], and Sudoku [6]. To the best of our knowledge, no related work deals with possibilities of using heuristic-search based methods for determining how difficult the problem is for a human.

K. Yacef et al. (Eds.): AIED 2013, LNAI 7926, pp. 860–863, 2013.

2 Method

Our basic idea is as follows: a given problem is difficult with respect to the task of accurate evaluation and finding the best solution, when different "solutions," which considerably alter the evaluation of the initial problem state, are discovered at different search depths. In such a situation a human has to analyze more continuations and search to a greater depth from the initial state to find actions that may greatly influence the assessment of the initial state, and then eventually choose the best continuation [7].

In the experiments, the chess program HOUDINI 1.5a (64-bit), one of the strongest chess engines, was used to analyze more than 40.000 positions from real games played in World Chess Championship matches, using the methodology presented in [8]. Each position was searched to a fixed depth ranging from 2 to 20 plies. The aim of the heuristic search performed by the engine was both (I) to obtain the data for experimental evaluation of our proposed difficulty measure called "difficulty score," and (II) to estimate players' errors in these positions. A large data set made it possible to obtain average players' deviations from best play across a wide range of positions with the same difficulty score.

2.1 Proposed Measure of Difficulty

In accordance with our hypothesis about what makes the problems difficult for a human, an algorithm for calculating the difficulty of a chess position had to satisfy the following properties:

1. A problem is difficult if several different sensible "solutions" appear with increasing depth of search. That is, different amounts of search produce different solutions of the problem.
2. The higher the magnitude of differences in the values of various "solutions" obtained at different search depths, the greater the difficulty of the problem.

A formal measure of difficulty that attempts to implement the principles above is given by the following formula.

$$\sum_{d=3}^{MAX} |E(best_d) - E(second\_best_d)| \times [best_d \neq best_{d-1}] \tag{1}$$

where $best_d$ is the move that the chess program suggests as best at d-ply search, $E(best_d)$ and $E(second\_best_d)$ are the evaluations of the best and the second best move (respectively) at depth d, and MAX is a user-defined parameters for the maximal search depth used by the program. The bracket value [] is 1 if the condition holds, otherwise it is 0. We call this measure the difficulty score. Figure 1 illustrates how the difficulty score is calculated.

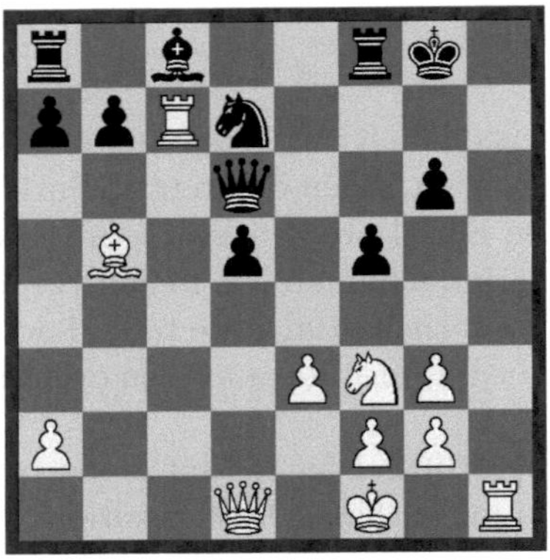

d	best	E1	second	E2	DS
2	Nf3-g5	123	Qd1-c2	80	–
3	Nf3-g5	107	Qd1-c2	103	0
4	Nf3-g5	117	Qd1-c2	103	0
5	Nf3-g5	117	Qd1-c2	103	0
6	Nf3-g5	117	Qd1-c2	103	0
7	Nf3-g5	117	Qd1-c2	103	0
8	Nf3-g5	98	Qd1-c2	98	0
9	**Qd1-c1**	**118**	**Nf3-g5**	**92**	**26**
10	Qd1-c1	163	Qd1-c2	128	26
11	Qd1-c1	178	Qd1-c2	166	26
12	**Qd1-d4**	**805**	**Qd1-c2**	**166**	**665**

Fig. 1. Euwe-Alekhine, 16th World Chess Championship, Game 14, position after Black's 19th move. The table on the right shows the values of $best_d$, $E(best_d)$, $second\_best_d$, $E(second\_best_d)$, and the difficulty score, respectively, for each search depth d in range from 2 to 12 plies. At $MAX = 12$, formula (1) thus assigns this position the difficulty score of 665. In the game Euwe, the contender for the title of World Champion, failed to find the strongest move 20.Qd1-d4, with a winning attack.

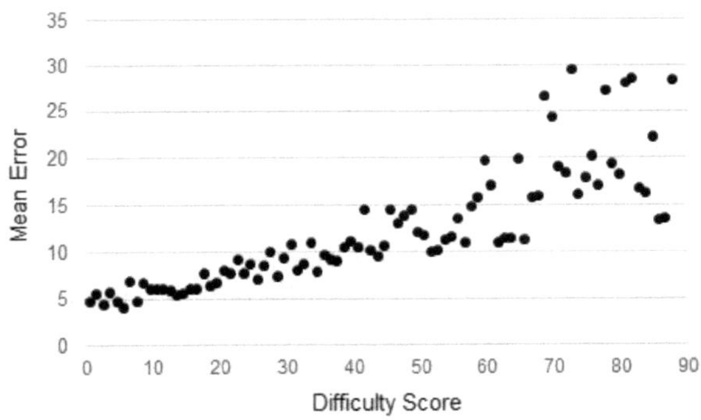

Fig. 2. The scatter plot above shows the relation between the predicted difficulty (obtained with formula (1), $MAX = 15$) and mean players' error in chess positions with corresponding difficulty scores. Each data point is represented by at least 30 examples.

3 Results

To evaluate the adequacy of our proposed measure of difficulty, we carried out the following experimental evaluation. If the difficulty score indeed measures the difficulty of a chess position for human chess players, then a high difficulty score of a given position should indicate a relatively high probability of a human player making a mistake in that position. Also, a higher difficulty score should indicate a more severe error. This was experimentally tested by observing the correlation between the difficulty scores of positions and the error scores of very strong chess players in these positions. As mistakes by very strong players are subject to chance it was appropriate to average the errors in *sets* of positions with similar difficulty scores.

Figure 2 shows the relation between the difficulty scores (that is the predicted difficulties of chess positions), and the players' mean errors in positions with (roughly) the same difficulty score. Ideally, the mean error should be a monotonically increasing function of difficulty score. Because of the randomness of human errors, this relation has to be tested statistically. A Spearman's correlation was run to determine the relationship between the difficulty scores and the mean errors. There was a very strong, positive monotonic correlation between Difficulty Score and Mean Error ($r = .93$, $n = 88$, $p < .001$).

4 Conclusions

Our approach to predicting the difficulty of problems for humans is based on modeling the problem solving as search. We proposed a concrete measure of difficulty, called difficulty score. It was experimentally shown to be statistically adequate as a genuine measure of difficulty for humans. The experiments were carried out in the domain of chess using the experimental data obtained from extremely strong human experts - world chess champions. It should be noted that despite high overall statistical significance of the proposed measure, the success of difficulty score as a reliable predictor of the difficulty of individual problems is open to further investigation. This will probably depend on the application. Also, the implementation by a concrete difficulty measure of the two basic assumptions about the measures' properties is open to refinements. For example, it might be better (I) to consider that decision changes become more and more important with increasing search depth, and (II) to take into account more than just two best solutions as it is done in formula (1).

References

1. Kotovsky, K., Hayes, J., Simon, H.: Why are some problems hard? Evidence from tower of Hanoi. Cognitive Psychology 17(2), 248–294 (1985)
2. Kenneth Kotovsky, H.A.S.: What makes some problems really hard: Explorations in the problem space of difficulty. Cognitive Psychology 22(2), 143–183 (1990)
3. Pizlo, Z., Li, Z.: Solving combinatorial problems: The 15-puzzle. Memory and Cognition 33(6), 1069–1084 (2005)
4. Dry, M., Lee, M., Vickers, D., Hughes, P.: Human performance on visually presented traveling salesperson problems with varying numbers of nodes. Journal of Problem Solving 1(1), 20–32 (2006)
5. Jarušek, P., Pelánek, R.: Difficulty rating of sokoban puzzle. In: Proc. of the Fifth Starting AI Researchers' Symposium (STAIRS 2010), pp. 140–150. IOS Press (2010)
6. Pelánek, R.: Difficulty rating of sudoku puzzles by a computational model. In: Proc. of Florida Artificial Intelligence Research Society Conference (FLAIRS 2011), pp. 434–439. AAAI Press (2011)
7. Guid, M., Bratko, I.: Computer analysis of world chess champions. ICGA Journal 29(2), 65–73 (2006)
8. Guid, M., Bratko, I.: Using heuristic-search based engines for estimating human skill at chess. ICGA Journal 34(2), 71–81 (2011)

Using Semantic Proximities to Control Contextualized Activities during Museum Visits

Pierre-Yves Gicquel, Dominique Lenne, and Claude Moulin

Heudiasyc CNRS
University of Technology of Compiegne
{pgicquel,dlenne,cmoulin}@utc.fr

Abstract. We present in this paper CALM (ContextuAlized Learning through Mobility), an ubiquitous learning environment for museum visits. This environment uses semantic proximities over a semantic model of the domain (cultural heritage) and context (e.g. position in the museum, activity) to offer contextualized activities. Our proposal aims to provide learners with situated interactions, while giving teachers the opportunity to integrate learning objectives that will influence the proposed interactions. To that end, we propose to use semantic rules that enables a loosely-based control of learning activities by the teacher.

1 Introduction

The development of mobile devices, such as smartphones and tablets, has led to the emergence of a new kind of learning environments: ubiquitous learning environments. However a conflict appears in the development of these environments. Indeed, one of the major interests of these environments is to preserve the authentic nature of the situations by granting the learner an important freedom during learning sessions. However, particularly for primary and secondary school learning, there is a need to provide the teacher with some degrees of guidance on learning situations. The problem is to determine how to offer this learning guidance while leaving some degree of freedom to the learners.

We present in this article elements of response to this question. Our application field is primary school visits to museums. Our proposal is CALM, an ubiquitous learning system based on a semantic model of the learning domain (Cultural Heritage) and a semantic model of the learning context (e.g. position in the museum, learners activity). We show how contextualized activities (games, suggestions of artworks) can be generated and controlled by using semantic proximities over the representation of artworks and context.

2 Semantic Proximities for Contextualized Activities

2.1 Semantic Model of Artworks

In order to represent the cultural aspects of artworks, we used three sources of knowledge: CIDOC-CRM[1], Getty-AAT[2] and ICONCLASS[3]. CIDOC-CRM is

[1] http://www.cidoc-crm.org/
[2] http://www.getty.edu/research/tools/vocabularies
[3] http://www.iconclass.nl

K. Yacef et al. (Eds.): AIED 2013, LNAI 7926, pp. 864–867, 2013.

the reference ontology for describing cultural heritage. Among others it defines the concepts of *work*, *person*, *historical event* and *place*.

However, CIDOC-CRM is a generic ontology. It does not include concepts for a fine description of artworks, such as the style or the theme. We then extended this model by including the ICONCLASS taxonomy, a classification of art themes and the Getty-AAT thesaurus (Art and Architecture Thesaurus) about art and architecture techniques and materials. An excerpt of the resulting semantic model of artworks is presented in figure 1.

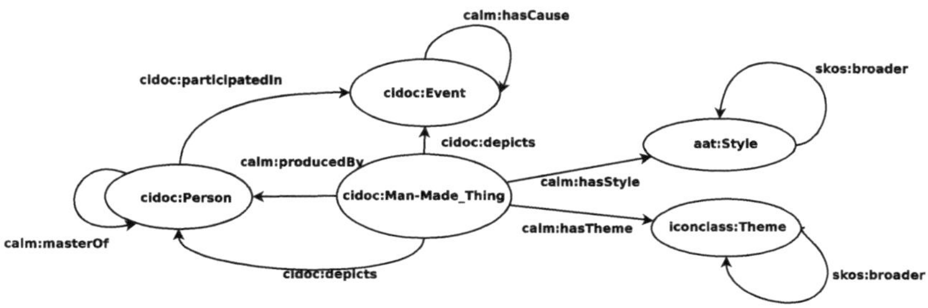

Fig. 1. Excerpt of the semantic model of artworks

2.2 Semantic Model of Context

We selected two categories of information for the representation of the visiting context: information on the location and information on the history of visit.

The location context is constituted of the set of instances representing artworks accessible to learners' perception. We built a semantic model of physical space in a museum, using the spatial ontology proposed by the DAIsy[1] laboratory. Our space model is a meshing of the different places in the museum. Each cell is associated to adjacent cells using the *daisy:adjacentTo* relation. The link between a cell and an artwork is provided by the *daisy:contains* relation, which combines one or more artworks to an instance of *daisy:Location*.

The historical context of the user aims at capturing the temporality of the visit. This context is modelled using the SEM (Simple Event Model) ontology [1]. An instance of *sem:Event* is added to the history context of the user during an interaction with an artwork *via* the mobile device (e.g. consultation of documents, games). This event describes the links between the learner and the instance that represents the element he is consulting (e.g artist, artwork, style).

2.3 Semantic Proximity between Instances

In order to offer relevant situated interactions to learners, we rely on a calculation of semantic proximities. The proximity between two objects (instances of

[1] `http://daisy.cti.gr/svn/ontologies/AtracoProject/AtracoSpatialOntology/Spatial.owl`

CIDOC-CRM) is based on the proximity between their features, that is to say the value of their properties. We described this proximity in [2].

For example, in order to compare two instances of *Person*, we compare the proximity of the properties of these instances, that is to say the proximity between their parents, teachers or students, their styles or the works they have created or owned. We construct a vector of proximities quantifying, for each property, the proximity of two instances. We note in the following $Prox_{Sem}(a, b)$ the proximity value between a and b.

2.4 Activities in Museum

The use of semantic proximity allows us to offer two types of activities: assisted browsing among museum documents and self-assessment with games.

When the learners are in a room, they choose a work, and can browse museum documents about the artwork, the artist, the style... In addition, for each category of elements (e.g. artist, work, style), the learners are provided with suggestions of elements of the same type, semantically close to the element they consider, and belonging to their location or history context. For instance, if the learner is considering "Mona Lisa", she may be suggested to consider "The Vitruvian Man". These suggestions are associated to justifications, generated automatically from the assertions of the knowledge base.

Fig. 2. Example of MCQ game

The second type of activities we propose are self-assessment games (figure 2). Three types of games are offered: MCQ, true-false questions and classification games (e.g. classification of works by date, style ....). These games are dynamically generated from the assertions of the knowledge base. For example, from the assertion: (*calm:Monalisa cidoc:createdBy calm:Davinci*) one question can be : Who is the author of Mona Lisa? Incorrect answers, also called distractors, are selected among the instances of the knowledge base which are semantically close to the correct answer (Da Vinci).

3 Pedagogical Control by the Teacher

The pedagogical control covers the entire visit and aims to ensure thematic consistency. It helps to attract learners' attention on relevant artworks or information according to the theme chosen by the teacher.

To this end, the teacher has to choose a number of resources in the museum knowledge base. For example, if the theme focuses on "The French First Empire", she will have to select the characters, places, events, styles and works related to this theme (e.g. Napoleon, Waterloo, Marie-Louise). This set of instances defines the theme of the visit and is noted T thereafter.

The calculation of contextualized suggestions is adjusted to fit the choice of T. The idea is to suggest elements semantically close to the set T, while remaining consistent with the item consulted by the learner. Taking into account the theme of the visit, the score of a suggestion s with respect to the entity e is:

$$Score(e,s) = \alpha * Prox_{Sem}(e,s) + \beta * Prox_{Sem}(s,T)$$

with $Prox_{Sem}(s,T)$ being the mean of proximities between s and every instance of T, and α and β such as $\alpha + \beta = 1$.

The mode of self-assessment games generation is also modified to take into account the theme of visit. Initially, questions and distractors are selected from the history and location context. Using pedagogical control, distractors are still chosen in the history and location context, but must be close to the set T to be selected.

4 Conclusion

We presented in this paper an ubiquitous learning system designed to assist a school group museum visit. Using a semantic representation of the context and cultural heritage we proposed various contextualized activities to help learners to navigate through the museum knowledge and to use the acquired knowledge through self-assessment activities and open questions. The originality of our proposal is based on the dual modelling, semantic and contextual, which allows us to provide the teacher with some control over the tour while allowing students a certain degree of freedom.

References

1. van Hage, W., Malais, V., Segers, R., Hollink, L., Schreiber, G.: Design and use of the simple event model (SEM). In: Web Semantics: Science, Services and Agents on the World Wide Web (2011)
2. Gicquel, P., Lenne, D.: Using semantic similarities to instrument informal learning activities in ubiquitous environments. In: 2012 IEEE 12th International Conference on Advanced Learning Technologies (ICALT), pp. 618–620 (2012)

Towards Evaluating and Modelling the Impacts of Mobile-Based Augmented Reality Applications on Learning and Engagement

Eric Poitras[1], Kevin Kee[2], Susanne P. Lajoie[1], and Dana Cataldo[1]

[1] ATLAS Laboratory, Department of Educational and Counselling Psychology
McGill University, 3700 McTavish St, Montreal, QC H3A 1Y2, CA
[2] Department of History, Ontario Augmented Reality Network
Brock University, St. Catharines, Ontario, L2S 3A1, CA
{eric.poitras,dana.cataldo}@mail.mcgill.ca, kevin.kee@brocku.ca,
susanne.lajoie@mcgill.ca

Abstract. Mobile augmented reality applications are increasingly utilized as a medium for enhancing learning and engagement in history education. Although these digital devices facilitate learning through immersive and appealing experiences, their design should be driven by theories of learning and instruction. We provide an overview of an evidence-based approach to optimize the development of mobile augmented reality applications that teaches students about history. Our research aims to evaluate and model the impacts of design parameters towards learning and engagement. The research program is interdisciplinary in that we apply techniques derived from design-based experiments and educational data mining. We outline the methodological and analytical techniques as well as discuss the implications of the anticipated findings.

Keywords: Affective Aspects of Learning, Data Mining and Machine Learning, Design and Formative Studies of AIED Systems, Ubiquitous Learning Environments.

1 Research Background

Digital technologies provide instructors with new and innovative media to represent historical information [1]. Augmented reality (AR) applications implemented on mobile platforms enable students to think and engage with history while studying real-life scenes augmented with virtual objects. iPhone applications such as the *Niagara 1812: Return of the Fenian Shadow* and *Queenston 1812: The Bomber's Plot* guide students in the context of walking tours with the aim of solving century-old mysteries pertaining to the War of 1812.

Researchers have made significant progress in fostering learning and engagement through mobile AR applications during the past decade [2-3]. However, the interactive properties of these applications are limited to adjusting the instructional content on the basis of the tracking data (i.e., the GPS coordinates and student keystrokes).

K. Yacef et al. (Eds.): AIED 2013, LNAI 7926, pp. 868–871, 2013.

This research program addresses this issue by evaluating and modelling the impacts of the mobile AR application design parameters towards learning and engagement. In doing so, the revised applications should be capable of individualizing instruction through the analysis of not only the tracking data, but also features extracted from the audio signal and discourse processes. In the following sections, we provide an overview of the theories and instructional approaches that guide our research, the paradigms that underlies the techniques used to collect and analyze data, and the anticipated contributions to research and practice.

2 Theoretical and Instructional Frameworks

Our conceptualization of learning and engagement is guided by the Benchmarks of Historical Thinking [4] and the Control-Value Theory of Emotions [5]. Peter Seixas identified several key historical thinking skills that are critical to gain deeper understanding of historical sources and events: namely, establishing historical significance, using primary source evidence, identifying continuity and change, analyzing cause and consequence, taking historical perspectives, and understanding the ethical dimension of historical interpretations [4]. Reinhard Pekrun outlined several emotional experiences that are of particular relevance to learning and instruction about history. These experiences may range from positive ones, such as enjoyment, hope, interest, relief, satisfaction, and pride, to more negative ones, including anger, anxiety, hopelessness, boredom, dissatisfaction, disappointment, shame, and guilt [5].

The mobile AR applications promote learning and engagement in accordance with instructional principles that ensure immersive, meaningful, and engaging experiences. Firstly, instruction is situated in the context of performing authentic and meaningful tasks [6]. The mobile AR applications guide learners through historic and heritage sites using GPS-based tracking. Secondly, instruction is provided as learners perform historical inquiries into several aspects of the historical event or issue under investigation [7]. The mobile AR applications enable learners to investigate the past by providing them with a series of problems to solve as well as feedback on their performance.

3 Methodological and Analytical Techniques

This research program collects and analyzes data for the purposes of evaluating and modelling learning and engagement. We focus on two research questions: (a) Does the use of mobile AR applications influence how learners think and feel about the past? and (b) How can we adjust the design parameters of the mobile AR applications in order to promote learning and engagement? On the basis of the Benchmarks of Historical Thinking and the Control-Value Theory of Emotions, we collect and analyze data in accordance with techniques derived from design-based experiments and educational data mining. In the following sub-sections, we outline the research paradigms that underlie these techniques and how they address the research objectives and questions.

3.1 Evaluating Learning and Engagement

Design experiments entail the study of how variations in design parameters impact educational outcomes [8]. We conduct design experiments in order to progressively refine the design parameters of the mobile AR applications and attain optimal outcomes with respect to learning and engagement. The experiments will also lead to improved instructional practices used in the context of the guided walking tours.

The experiments are conducted in the context of the guided walking tours, where learners use the mobile AR applications. The dependent variables under investigation are the components of learning and engagement as defined by the Benchmarks of Historical Thinking and the Control-Value Theory of Emotions. We also study how they are influenced by the instructional and contextual conditions that change throughout the study. Multiple data sources (i.e., self-report, tracking data, audio signal, and discourse processes) are analyzed according to both qualitative and quantitative perspectives to capture as accurately as possible how learners are thinking and feeling. The experiments are conducted in annual cycles in that the design parameters are continually revised on the basis of previous findings. The participants, experimenters, and stakeholders in the design experiments are involved in revising the design parameters with the aim of increasing the prevalence of desirable outcomes.

3.2 Modelling Learning and Engagement

Educational data mining is a field concerned with the study of analytical techniques and how they enable researchers to make inferences in relation to learner characteristics [9]. One of the most important applications of data mining is user modelling, where a representation of learner characteristics and states are implemented as part of an application for the purposes of personalizing instruction [10]. We aim to use these techniques to develop the user modelling capabilities of the applications.

These data mining techniques are used to classify states in relation to learning and engagement as defined by the Benchmarks of Historical Thinking and the Control-Value Theory of Emotions. In order to develop the prediction model, we analyze the discourse and audio features extracted from the data that was collected during the guided walking tours. We extract, select, and reduce the dimensionality of the speech characteristics (i.e., prosody and spectrum) and discourse features (i.e., terminology) at the utterance level. First, audio signal and text processing algorithms are applied to extract the audio features (i.e., pitch, energy, duration, and spectral) and discourse features (i.e., term tokens). Second, the dimensionality of the data is reduced through the comparison of a forward selection, backward elimination, and genetic algorithm for feature selection. Third, a series of classification experiments will be performed using the audio and discourse features as well as by fusion of the audio-discourse features both before and after the selection stage. These experiments will be performed using a Support Vector Machine classifier and by varying the type of kernel (i.e., dot, radial, polynomial, neural). The audio, discourse, and audio-discourse prediction models are evaluated using a 10-fold cross-validation procedure. The performance of these models is determined through classification accuracy, sensitivity, specificity, the positive and negative predictive value as well as the ROC curve.

4 Contributions to Research and Practice

This study aims to foster learning and engagement in users of mobile AR applications. In doing so, this research program stands to contribute to the learning sciences community in the areas of design-based research and educational data mining. Firstly, the use of educational methods, theories, and practices ensure that we design an optimal AR application in terms of teaching the subject matter in ways that actively engage students in learning. Secondly, the analytical techniques aim to develop a user model that once implemented, will provide instruction that is flexible and sensitive to individual differences. As such, the progressive refinement of the device stands to improve learning about the past through captivating and meaningful experiences.

Acknowledgements. We acknowledge the contributions of Dr. Peter Seixas and CEO of Furi Enterprises Thomas Madej to this work. Financial support from the Learning Environments Across Disciplines Research Partnership grant from the Social Sciences and Humanities Research Council of Canada is greatfully acknowledged.

References

1. Kee, K., Darbyson, N.: Creating and Using Virtual Environments to Promote Historical Thinking. In: Clark, P. (ed.) New Possibilities for the Past: Shaping History Education in Canada, pp. 264–281. UBC Press, Vancouver (2011)
2. Dede, C.: Immersive Interfaces for Engagement and Learning. Science 323(5910), 66–69 (2009)
3. Wu, H.-K., Lee, S.W.-Y., Chang, H.-Y., Liang, J.-C.: Current Status, Opportunities and Challenges of Augmented Reality in Education. Computers & Education 62, 41–49 (2013)
4. Seixas, P.: Assessment of Historical Thinking. In: Clark, P. (ed.) New Possibilities for the Past: Shaping History Education in Canada, pp. 139–153. UBC Press, Vancouver (2011)
5. Pekrun, R.: The Control-Value Theory of Achievement Emotions: Assumptions, Corollaries, and Implications for Educational Research and Practice. Educational Psychology Review 18, 315–341 (2006)
6. Sawyer, R.K., Greeno, J.: Situativity and Learning. In: Robbins, P., Aydede, M. (eds.) The Cambridge Handbook of Situated Cognition, pp. 347–367. Cambridge University Press, New York (2009)
7. Levstik, L.S.: Learning History. In: Mayer, R.E., Alexander, P.A. (eds.) Handbook of Research on Learning and Instruction, pp. 108–126. Routledge, New York (2011)
8. Collins, A., Joseph, D., Bielaczye, K.: Design Research : Theoretical and Methodological Issues. The Journal of the Learning Sciences 13(1), 15–42 (2004)
9. Baker, R.S.J.D., Yacef, K.: The State of Educational Data Mining in 2009: A Review and Future Visions. Journal of Educational Data Mining 1(1), 3–17 (2009)
10. Desmarais, M.C., Baker, R.S.J.D.: A Review of Recent Advances in Learner and Skill Modeling in Intelligent Learning Environments. User Modeling and User-Adapted Interaction 22, 9–38 (2012)

An Intelligent Tutoring System to Teach Debugging

Elizabeth Carter and Glenn D. Blank

Lehigh University, Computer Science and Engineering Department,
19 Memorial Drive West, Bethlehem PA 18015
eec209@lehigh.edu, glennblank@gmail.com

Abstract. Although several Intelligent Tutoring Systems (ITS) have been built to teach students how to write programs, few focus on teaching students the skills required to debug faulty code. Indeed, outside of general debugging advice, it is also a skill seldom outright taught in the classroom. This paper discusses a web-based ITS to teach introductory level Computer Science students debugging skills, using and teaching case-based reasoning.

1 Introduction

Debugging is an intrinsic and difficult part of Computer Science for the novice, for the expert, and for software designed to assist in the process. When an expert is debugging, they must apply their experiences with past defect encounters. When encountering a new difficulty the expert may fall back on general problem solving strategies or look for human, written and web resources in order to determine the cause for a given defect and how to resolve it; but a novice does not have these previous experiences to draw on. Computer systems for analyzing and correcting defective software perform static and/or dynamic analysis, use rules (ITS4) and/or patterns (FindBugs), but are limited by their static knowledge bases, not to mention the Halting problem. The novice's problem is evident—they lack the skills and information experts and software analysis systems have. If students had a resource that could assist them in acquiring the skills they required to debug their own programs more quickly, they would be more likely to succeed in their current and future course work. This paper discusses the motivation behind this work, an overview of the methodology adopted in this work, what this work contributes to the AIED community, and a research plan.

2 Motivation and Background

Debugging is a skill that is important to all programmers, especially novices, simply because novices are apt to make mistakes in their code with greater frequency than the expert. Rather than waste hours and much frustration following faulty hypotheses for their programming defects, it is crucial that novices pick up debugging skills early and continually in their coursework.

K. Yacef et al. (Eds.): AIED 2013, LNAI 7926, pp. 872–875, 2013.

The need for debugging instruction has received attention in both the Computer Science Education and the AIED communities [3-5]. Within Computer Science Education, some have designed courses around teaching debugging skills, either for the students' own benefit or with a view towards research in automating the debugging process [9]. Others have designed specific systems and tools to assist the novice with debugging their code; including novice centered IDEs such as BlueJ and DrJava.

Three tutoring systems have been proposed for teaching debugging and a paper exists describing experiments towards determining the correct design of a tutoring system for teaching debugging in object oriented environments. PROUST, designed in the early 1980s, sought to utilize intention-based analysis in order to understand the programmer's intentions within Pascal programs [2]. Intention-based analysis would be performed by matching the code to known coding plans through source code analysis and non-algorithmic descriptions of the program's intended outcome. However, it does not appear that this system was developed into a full-fledged ITS. Another system, DebugIT [4] produced an exercise based debugging practice system that guided students through debugging faulty code with limited hints and revealing answers. However, this system did not have all the components of an ITS, consisting of an exercise system and a limited pedagogical module. Additionally, a precursor to Amruth Kumar's Problets tutor [3] aimed to help students debug C++ pointer issues using model-based reasoning, with the models consisting of state diagrams.

3 Proposed Solutions and Methodology

We propose that the domain of debugging is inherently case-based. Case Based Reasoning (CBR) uses a cycle of actions: retrieve, reuse, revise, review, retain [1]. A case similar to the current situation is retrieved and selected for reuse, revised if necessary, reviewed after use to determine if it actually helped in the current situation, and then retained with revisions if appropriate. When debugging a program, the programmer experiences a similar cycle of actions—have I seen this error before? Will what I did before fix the error this time? What might I have to do differently this time to fix the error? How well did this solution work in this context? The similarities between the CBR cycle and the debugging reasoning cycle have inspired the use of CBR both as a way to represent and acquire debugging knowledge in our system and as a crucial aspect of the skill and knowledge that the system seeks to help novices learn in this domain.

In a system for teaching debugging, each defect pattern can be represented as a case with attributes for solution and symptoms. Similar cases can be selected according to the symptoms of the defect and the affected language construct. These patterns of debugging knowledge provide the starting point for the case-based knowledge acquired for an ITS for teaching debugging[1], developed as the first author's dissertation research. Development of the system has been broken into three phases.

---

[1] Please see `www.cse.lehigh.edu/~eec209/caseDef.html` for a more formal description of the cases utilized by this system.

Phase 1 of the system encompasses the core of the ITS. Each case in the system represents a programming defect, including symptom(s), solution, and other information required to identify case similarity. Each solution in the case base is an abstraction using a limited language consisting of actions and items. Actions included in this language are {add, remove, edit}; items consist of any valid Java construct (i.e. While loop, If block, Expression, ...). This abstraction is utilized throughout the system for feedback generation, exercise creation, and later for case acquisition. The pedagogical component provides two types of feedback for verbal and visual learning styles [5]. Phase 2 addresses the static case base and exercise system limitations of phase 1 by adding the ability to create exercises on demand (by using the case solutions) and acquiring cases from student solutions. Adding these cases will require greater granularity in case similarity computations—using the error message will no longer be sufficient to differentiate which suggested solution is correct. Phase 3 will take the system one step further. Where students really need debugging assistance is while they're working on their class assignments. Receiving assistance in situ may benefit students more than just studying debugging in an isolated manner.

The system is built as a Mono .Net web system with a MySQL backend. An analyzer module is responsible for preprocessing and output analysis. This part of the system gathers the abstract syntax tree data from the javac compiler and all other relevant data from javac, the Java runtime, and the FindBugs static analyzer. Any messages from these systems are transferred to the tutoring system and serve as a starting point for case based knowledge and similarity computations.

The tutoring system consists of four ITS modules: Domain, Pedagogical, Student, and Communication. The Domain module is realized as a CBR system with a hand coded set of cases representing syntax, runtime, and logic errors obtained from the specifications of these systems. The data from the analyzer module is parsed into symptoms and then used by the domain module to find similar cases in the case base. Students are modeled according to exercises attempted and cases encountered. The pedagogical module uses data from these two modules to determine the proper remediation for the student for a given error and number of attempts. Remediation is further differentiated according to details from the case and the student's preferred modality (verbal or visual).

4 Contributions to AIED Community

Although some work does exist in this community that touch on the debugging problem, only one full ITS has been built and evaluated [3], for a limited problem domain. This system seeks to tutor debugging more generally, and provide support for concepts throughout the CS1 course. Moreover, while there is existing work regarding dynamic exercise creation [8, 3], this system will dynamically break code to teach students debugging principles. Additionally, this system employs the use of multiple learning modalities. Although this too has been explored in other work it is not an approach that has been widely adopted and more stands to be learned about how learning styles affect the effectiveness of an ITS. Finally, this system employs CBR in its domain, student and pedagogical modules. Because of this, the knowledge that the system can model for the student will increase as the case base increases, as the system observes student work. Though there have been a few ITS utilizing CBR [6, 7], none have emphasized the parallels between cases and what students actually need to learn in the debugging domain, and none of the related systems encountered have used CBR to drive multiple modules of the ITS.

5 Future Work

This work is intended as both PhD research and as a springboard for continuing research. During the proposal process many interesting questions than can be pursued were identified, including: How could the system move beyond static analysis of code (already important for novices) to modeling dynamic aspects of debugging, perhaps by making use of Java Reflection libraries? Could peer assistance factor in to modeling the student and if so how? Could the system gather domain data automatically by crawling the Internet? Building on the framework of this system, the first author plans to continue studying these questions after her PhD is complete.

References[2]

1. Aamodt, A., Plaza, E.: Case-Based Reasoning: Foundational Issues, Methodological Variations, and System Approaches (1994), `http://www.iiia.csic.es/People/enric/AICom.html` (retrieved February 12, 2013)
2. Johnson, W.L., Soloway, E.: PROUST: Knowledge-Based Program Understanding. IEEE Transactions on Software Engineering SE-11(3), 267–275 (1985)
3. Kumar, A.N.: Model-Based Reasoning for Domain Modeling in a Web-Based Intelligent Tutoring System to Help Students Learn to Debug C++ Programs. In: Cerri, S.A., Gouardéres, G., Paraguaçu, F. (eds.) ITS 2002. LNCS, vol. 2363, pp. 792–801. Springer, Heidelberg (2002)
4. Lee, G.C., Wu, J.C.: Debug it: a debugging practicing system. Computers & Education 32(2), 165–179 (1999)
5. Moritz, S.H., Wei, F., Parvez, S.M., Blank, G.D.: From objects-first to design-first with multimedia and intelligent tutoring. SIGCSE Bull. 37(3), 99–103 (2005)
6. Soh, L.-K., Blank, T.: Integrating Case-Based Reasoning and Meta-Learning for a Self-Improving Intelligent Tutoring System. Int. J. Artif. Intell. Ed. 18(1), 27–58 (2008)
7. Weber, G., Mollenberg, A.: ELM-PE: A Knowledge-based Programming Environment for Learning LISP. In: Educational Multimedia and Hypermedia, Vancouver, British Columbia, Canada, June 25-30, pp. 557–562 (1994)
8. Williams-King, D., Aycock, J., Nunes de Castro, D.M.: Enbug: When Debuggers Go Bad. In: ITiCSE 2010, Bilkent, Ankara, Turkey, June 26-30 (2010)
9. Zeller, A.: Why Programs Fail. Elsevier, New York (2009)

[2] For more detailed references please see `www.cse.lehigh.edu/~eec209/dissRef.html`

Mobile Adaptive Communication Support for Vocabulary Acquisition

Carrie Demmans Epp

Dept. of Computer Science, University of Toronto
carrie@taglab.ca

Abstract. Language learners are often isolated because of their inability to communicate. Adaptive mobile communication support tools could be used to scaffold both their interaction with others and their vocabulary acquisition. I propose the exploration of a new tool that is designed to meet this need.

Keywords: Mobile Assisted Language Learning (MALL), Assistive and Augmentative Communication (AAC), Situated Learning.

1 Introduction

Current educational software fails to fully meet the needs of recent immigrants who do not speak the dominant language of their new homes. Many English language learners (ELL) struggle with obtaining oral fluency. This affects their ability to access employment and social support [1]. In many cases, ELL are isolated [2] and rely on mobile translators or family and friends to interact with their new environment.

An adaptive mobile assisted language learning (MALL) tool, called VocabNomad, will be studied since it could enable anytime-anywhere learning, increase the authenticity of learning activities, and reduce ELL isolation. To develop this tool, I explored ELL use of a communication support tool. I am improving upon this tool, using models of the learner and his/her context, to ensure that VocabNomad supports the user's emergent communication and vocabulary needs. I will then study VocabNomad use to determine its ability to a) effectively support ELL communication, by scaffolding their use of vocabulary and b) affect ELL vocabulary knowledge.

2 Related Work

The use of communication support technologies is common when people have limited communicative abilities. Using these support tools has allowed those with limited communicative abilities to cross the communication barrier that exists between them and those in their environment [3]. While these tools hold the potential to support language acquisition, they have not been exploited for this purpose. This may be due to their limited ability to support emergent user needs since they use pre-existing libraries of image-word pairs [4, 5] and, therefore, cannot support unexpected events.

K. Yacef et al. (Eds.): AIED 2013, LNAI 7926, pp. 876–879, 2013.

Asynchronous communication requires a different level of support for emergent user needs than synchronous communication since users have time to find additional support. Several MALL tools already support asynchronous communication; this includes ALEX [6], electronic translators, and dictionaries. However, few MALL tools support synchronous oral communication [7]. Call-in services [8] and translation tools can support oral communication. However, these are limited in their ability to support ELL. Call-in services can benefit travelers and help ELL but do not scaffold one's ability to communicate on one's own. While translation applications can support the comprehension and production of language, they typically only work well for specific domains and are limited in the scope of the support that they provide [9].

Existing adaptive MALL that support vocabulary acquisition use location [10, 11], algorithms that carefully time the repetition of studied words [12], and sometimes more advanced learner models [11] to adjust learning materials. However, none of these tools provide adequate support for emergent user needs. Dearman and Truong's Live Wallpaper [10] is the closest to providing support for emergent or unanticipated needs: it rapidly displays location-specific vocabulary to increase vocabulary exposure, but unlike dictionaries or phrasebooks, it does not allow ELL to use the vocabulary to scaffold their communication. None of the widely available communication support or MALL tools provide the context-sensitive scaffolding that is needed to allow ELL to communicate for themselves while supporting their vocabulary acquisition goals. VocabNomad can fill this gap.

3 VocabNomad: A MALL Tool that Supports Communication

VocabNomad is based on the educational theories of situated and incidental learning (i.e., fast mapping [13]). It is a dual-platform tool (i.e., mobile and web) that provides just-in-time (jit) support for the emergent vocabulary of ELL by applying information retrieval techniques to Internet-based corpora to generate collections of vocabulary that can support communication. Vocabulary entries (i.e., words or phrases) are paired with images that scaffold their meaning (Fig. 1). Both interfaces can be used to study and organize vocabulary. The mobile interface also allows users to support their communication by using vocabulary entries as prompts, by showing a message to someone, or by having the application speak on their behalf using text to speech.

VocabNomad tracks learner activities to create a model of his/her knowledge. It uses this learner model along with a context model that includes information about the user's location and time to adapt the provided vocabulary support. These two models refine the words that are displayed to ELL, ensuring that they are relevant to the user's current situation and that the user is exposed to new vocabulary items.

Fig. 1. Screen captures of the mobile (left) and web (right) clients

The algorithms used to drive adaptivity are being validated. Those used to provide jit vocabulary support were validated for their ability to support communication [14] and those that are being used to find visual representations of the meaning of vocabulary entries are being evaluated. Additional aspects of the system are also being evaluated. This includes the graphical user interface that will be used to communicate that two items are synonymous. Beyond this, the inclusion of features and their usefulness was verified through a formative evaluation that was performed with ELL who had recently immigrated to Canada [15]. Additional usability testing is ongoing.

4 VocabNomad's Effect on ELL

In order to explore the effectiveness of the approaches used by VocabNomad, two deployment studies will be performed. One will assess VocabNomad's effect on ELL communication and affective state. The other will assess its effect on vocabulary knowledge. To do this, they will both use a within subjects design with reversal, where the baseline measures will be taken when VocabNomad is not being used. Both studies will last a minimum of three weeks and have at least six participants.

To test VocabNomad's effect on the communicative success and affective state of ELL, the first study will collect self-report data using an experience sampling approach. Information about the success or failure of communication events will be collected and a short form of the Positive and Negative Affect Schedule that has been validated cross culturally, the I-PANAS-SF, and the Self-Assessment Manikin (SAM) will be used to collect measures of the user's affect. In addition to this, interviews will be used to explore the nature of participants' communication experiences in an English-language environment. This data, when combined, should reveal how well VocabNomad scaffolds ELL language production.

A second study that aims to determine VocabNomad's effect on vocabulary knowledge will also be performed. It will initially measure phonological knowledge, morphological knowledge, working memory, and recall. Standardized measures of vocabulary knowledge (i.e., PPVT-4), morphological knowledge, and phonological knowledge, will be performed in between phases and at the end of the study. Beyond this, an adaptive test of vocabulary knowledge will be developed so that it can be administered throughout the study. This test will aim to assess vocabulary knowledge based on the frequency of occurrence of words in spoken and written English and the frequency of exposure that the participant has had to words within VocabNomad. The test results will be used to test hypotheses related to the effectiveness of VocabNomad at promoting vocabulary acquisition by supporting situated learning and the fast-mapping process, which is a form of incidental learning.

The data from these studies should reveal the effectiveness of using an adaptive MALL tool to support vocabulary acquisition and communication within a second language environment. Understanding its effectiveness in this context can then help guide explorations into its use in foreign language or formal educational contexts.

References

1. Gordon, D.: "I'm Tired. You Clean and Cook." Shifting Gender Identities and Second Language Socialization. TESOL Quarterly 38, 437–457 (2004)
2. Siegel, P., Martin, E., Bruno, R.: Language Use and Linguistic Isolation: Historical Data and Methodological Issues. United States Census Bureau (2001)
3. McNaughton, D., Bryen, D.N.: AAC Technologies to Enhance Participation and Access to Meaningful Societal Roles for Adolescents and Adults with Develop-mental Disabilities Who Require AAC. Augmentative and Alternative Communication 23, 217–229 (2007)
4. Kim, G., Park, J., Han, M., Park, S., Ha, S.: Context-Aware Communication Support System with Pictographic Cards. In: MobileHCI, pp. 1–2. ACM, Bonn (2009)
5. Wisenburn, B., Higginbotham, D.J.: An AAC Application Using Speaking Partner Speech Recognition to Automatically Produce Contextually Relevant Utter-ances: Objective Results. Augmentative and Alternative Communication 24, 100–109 (2008)
6. Munteanu, C., Lumsden, J., Fournier, H., Leung, R., D'Amours, D., McDonald, D., Maitland, J.: ALEX: Mobile Language Assistant for Low-Literacy Adults. In: MobileHCI, pp. 427–430. ACM, Lisbon (2010)
7. Kukulska-Hulme, A., Shield, L.: An Overview of Mobile Assisted Language Learning: from Content Delivery to Supported Collaboration and Interaction. ReCALL 20, 271–289 (2008)
8. Shanghai: Immediate Translation Services - TripAdvisor, `http://www.tripadvisor.co.uk/Travel-g308272-c108779/Shanghai:China:Immediate.Translation.Services.html`
9. Star Trek-like "Phraselator" device helps police communicate, `http://www.networkworld.com/community/node/24034`
10. Dearman, D., Truong, K.N.: Evaluating the Implicit Acquisition of Second Lan-guage Vocabulary Using a Live Wallpaper. In: Conference on Human Factors in Computing Systems (CHI), pp. 1391–1400. ACM, Austin (2012)
11. Edge, D., Searle, E., Chiu, K., Zhao, J., Landay, J.A.: MicroMandarin: Mobile Language Learning in Context. In: Conference on Human Factors in Computing Systems (CHI), pp. 3169–3178. ACM, Vancouver (2011)
12. FullRecall - Software For Effective Memorization, `http://fullrecall.com/`
13. Carey, S.: Beyond Fast Mapping. Lang. Learn. Dev. 6, 184–205 (2010)
14. Demmans Epp, C., Djordjevic, J., Wu, S., Moffatt, K., Baecker, R.M.: Towards Providing Just-in-Time Vocabulary Support for Assistive and Augmentative Communication. In: International Conference on Intelligent User Interfaces (IUI), pp. 33–36. ACM, Lisbon (2012)
15. Demmans Epp, C., Baecker, R.M.: Employing Adaptive Mobile Phone Applica-tions for Scaffolding the Communication and Vocabulary Acquisition of Lan-guage Learners. In: LearnLab's Learning Science Workshop on the Use of Technology Toward Enhancing Achievement and Equity in the 21st Century, Pittsburgh, USA (2012)

Utilizing Concept Mapping in Intelligent Tutoring Systems

Jaclyn K. Maass and Philip I. Pavlik Jr.

Institute for Intelligent Systems and Department of Psychology, University of Memphis, Memphis, TN, USA
{jkmaass,ppavlik}@memphis.edu

Abstract. Concept mapping is a tool used in many classrooms and highly researched in the field of education. However, there are fewer concept mapping studies in the field of artificial intelligence in education, specifically within intelligent tutoring systems. Two studies highlight the important roles that concept maps and other non-linear organizers play in learning. Concept maps provide students with a macrostructure view of the information as well as allow students to easily see relationships between concepts. Students generating material for a concept map has shown high learning gains; however, students creating maps from scratch or students being provided a completed map has not seen such positive effects. The proposed study looks at the importance of the links, or relationships between concepts, within concept maps. We plan to provide students with partially filled in concept maps as note-taking devices to investigate how much and what kind of assistance or scaffolding is needed.

Keywords: concept map, intelligent tutoring system, scaffold, note-taking.

1 An Introduction to Concept Mapping

Concept mapping as a learning tool was first introduced by Novak and Gowin [1]. They showed that students could use concept maps to learn how to learn effectively. Since then, there have been many other studies showing the advantages of using concept mapping in the classroom, particularly within the science domain. The basic components of a concept map are nodes, which display the main ideas or concepts, and links which connect the nodes and depict the relationships between concepts. Each node-link-node connection is called a proposition [1].

There is a clear difference between concept maps, which are spatial in nature, and more traditional, linear outlines, which do not lend themselves toward comparison or explicit learning of relationships among concepts. Concept maps allow for faster and easier access to: the location of information within the larger arrangement [2], relationships between concepts [3], and the macrostructure of the information [4].

2 Combining Concept Mapping and Artificial Intelligence

Educational artificial intelligence materials have lacked an emphasis on the use of concept maps. There are two instances we will discuss here in terms of the different

K. Yacef et al. (Eds.): AIED 2013, LNAI 7926, pp. 880–883, 2013.

ways they utilized concept maps within intelligent tutoring system (ITS) structures. We will then suggest a different use for concept maps in ITS's to advance the field and aid in student learning.

An experiment by Chang, Sung & Chen [5] compared the effectiveness of two computerized concept mapping environments (and one pencil-and-paper based). The two computerized concept mapping conditions were "construct-on-scaffold" and "construct-by-self." For the construct-on-scaffold condition, an incomplete framework of a concept map was given in which some nodes and links were left as blanks for the students to fill in. This sort of framework was inspired by the notion of an "expert skeleton" map [6] in which the beginning of a concept map is set up by an expert and the rest of the map is to be completed by the learner. In the construct-by-self condition, students freely constructed maps with "no aid." However, in both conditions the program offered the aid of providing concept and relationship lists to add to the students' maps. Hint and evaluation tools were also available to students.

After controlling for the pre-test scores, differences in posttest scores were found to be significant between the three conditions. The construct-on-scaffold condition showed significantly more learning than the other two conditions, with no difference seen between the construct by self and the paper and pencil condition. This suggests that asking the students to create a concept map from a blank canvas was too much, even in a computerized environment with the additional help that the construct-by-self condition offered. We have seen across age groups, spanning to college aged students, similar evidence that without extensive training, novices struggle with creating concept maps without scaffolding [5, 7]. The task is seen as too time consuming and too cognitively demanding for students to accomplish; therefore, some form and amount of scaffolding appears to be necessary for effective concept mapping.

Another prominent study of an ITS implementing the use of concept maps is that of Betty's Brain [8-9]. The students' objective was to teach a novice computer agent, Betty, about river ecosystems. The students helped structure the domain knowledge they were trying to convey through the use of concept maps and other visual tools [8-9]. Another way in which concept maps were utilized within the system was through Betty's responses to student prompted questions; Betty explained her responses by highlighting her logical path through the student-created concept map. In a Betty's Brain study [9] three different versions of the system were used, two of which included concept mapping as a learning technique. All three groups showed learning gains, but the two in which students were learning by teaching (with concept maps and other tools) performed better than the third group.

Although these two studies highlight a few uses of concept maps in ITS's, there lacks more comprehensive studies of the different functions concept maps can play. For example, researchers have not yet studied the difference in generating links versus nodes, nor the different roles that each play within concept maps. In addition, although we know that scaffolding is necessary, we cannot be sure how much assistance to offer and when such scaffolding should be removed as the student progresses through a domain. The proposed study will look at some of these unexplored questions.

3 Our Proposal

The experiment we propose differs from previous work in how we treat the links within the concept maps. In the Chang, Sung, & Chen study [5], hints given were in the form of prompting students to complete the end node in a proposition by providing the linking words. This de-emphasized the importance of generating the links in a concept map. We propose an experiment to look deeper into the important role that links play within a concept map. Why might the links be worthy of such research? The simple answer is because of the relational properties that they contain. Relationships and structural information are important aspects in the transfer of knowledge [10], which is the end goal, and optimal outcome, of teaching students. Studies have repeatedly shown that novices do not do well at perceiving the relational or structural similarities between examples in different contexts [10-11]. Analogical reasoning, being able to apply relational properties between contexts, is an important aspect of learning, but students are not currently doing a very good job of this. It stands to reason, then, that students may benefit from having their attention directed more explicitly toward the relationships between concepts.

In order to explore this topic more deeply, we propose an experiment in which students are provided with one concept map for each domain that they are taught in an ITS. We would instruct them to use the concept map as a note-taking device throughout the learning session with the system. In order to not overwhelm the students by asking them to create a map from scratch, different levels of completed and partially completed maps would be provided to the student. The presence of provided nodes and the presence of provided links would vary between being fully filled in and being completely blank. In other words, the experiment would be a 2 (providing all of the links or none of the links) x 2 (providing all of the nodes or none of the nodes) design. In the blank links, blank nodes condition the students will still be given the layout of the concept map (i.e., they will not be creating a map from scratch). The two conditions of most interest are the full links, blank nodes condition and the blank links, full nodes condition. In both of these conditions we have a medium level of scaffolding, and if links serve the important purpose that we believe they do, forcing the students to generate them in the blank links, full nodes condition will encourage larger learning gains than in the full links, blank nodes condition. This hypothesis is supported by studies which have shown that providing students with completely pre-constructed, filled in concept maps does not show as much learning gains as when the students are given the opportunity to generate the material themselves [12].

The four conditions in this experiment would also provide a wide coverage of different amounts of scaffolding which would allow us to more fully look at the assistance dilemma. The assistance dilemma is the issue of how much assistance to provide to students; if you give too much assistance they are bored and not stimulated, but if you give too little assistance they are confused and overwhelmed [13].

These conditions could be set up as within-subjects if each student is provided with one of each type of concept map for each section of a domain that an ITS covers. Further experiments would look at the effect of using a concept map which grows progressively along with the lesson and which reduces the scaffolding as the student progresses. If our research reveals that explicit learning of relational features increases learning gains, this would be progress toward more transferable learning and may affect ITS's with and without concept maps.

References

1. Novak, J.D., Gowin, D.B.: Learning How to Learn. Cambridge University Press (1984)
2. Robinson, D.H., Skinner, C.H.: Why Graphic Organizers Facilitate Search Processes: Fewer Words or Computationally Efficient Indexing? Contemporary Educational Psychology 21, 166–180 (1996)
3. Winn, W.: Learning from Maps and Diagrams. Educational Psychology Review 3, 211–247 (1991)
4. O'Donnell, A.M., Dansereau, D.F., Hall, R.H.: Knowledge Maps as Scaffolds for Cognitive Processing. Educational Psychology Review 14 (2002)
5. Chang, K.E., Sung, Y.T., Chen, S.F.: Learning through Computer-Based Concept Mapping with Scaffolding Aid. Journal of Computer Assisted Learning 17, 21–33 (2001)
6. Novak, J.D., Cañas, A.J.: The Theory Underlying Concept Maps and How to Construct and Use Them, vol. 284. Florida Institute for Human and Machine Cognition, Pensacola (2008)
7. Reader, W., Hammond, N.: Computer-Based Tools to Support Learning from Hypertext: Concept Mapping Tools and Beyond. Computers & Education 22, 99–106 (1994)
8. Biswas, G., Leelawong, K., Schwartz, D.L., Vye, N., Vanderbilt, T.T.A.G.A.: Learning by Teaching: A New Agent Paradigm for Educational Software. Applied Artificial Intelligence 19, 363–392 (2005)
9. Leelawong, K., Biswas, G.: Designing Learning by Teaching Agents: The Betty's Brain System. International Journal of Artificial Intelligence in Education 18, 181–208 (2008)
10. Gentner, D.: Structure-Mapping: A Theoretical Framework for Analogy. Cognitive Science: A Multidisciplinary Journal 7, 155–170 (1983)
11. Gentner, D., Landers, R.: Analogical Reminding: A Good Match is Hard to Find. In: Proceedings of the International Conference on Systems, Man, and Cybernetics, Tucson, AZ (1985)
12. Cañas, A.J., Reiska, P., Novak, J.D.: Concept Mapping in e-Learning. STRIDE 122 (2010)
13. Koedinger, K.R., Pavlik Jr., P.I., McLaren, B.M., Aleven, V.: Is It Better to Give Than to Receive? The Assistance Dilemma as a Fundamental Unsolved Problem in the Cognitive Science of Learning and Instruction. In: Sloutsky, V., Love, B., McRae, K. (eds.) Proceedings of the 30th Conference of the Cognitive Science Society, Washington, D.C, pp. 2155–2160 (2008)

Discrepancy-Detection in Virtual Learning Environments for Young Children with ASC

Alyssa M. Alcorn

University of Edinburgh, School of Informatics, UK
a.alcorn@ed.ac.uk

Abstract. This PhD project lays the groundwork for a future VLE that adaptively introduces *discrepancies* (i.e. novel or rule-violating occurrences) in order to support young children with *autism spectrum conditions* (ASC) in practicing foundational social skills. This paper suggests a taxonomy of discrepancy types and briefly summarises a completed analysis of discrepancy-detection in existing video data from 8 children with ASC using the ECHOES VLE. It then describes planned future work, which will explore possible types of discrepancies for exploratory social content (as present in ECHOES) and address other key questions about how they might impact this group of learners, and be incorporated into the design of a future VLE. It also considers how the current work relates to existing literature on metacognition and use of erroneous worked examples in tutoring systems.

Keywords: Virtual environments, discrepancy, novelty, Autism, children, social communication, initiation, learning, evaluation, HCI, design.

1 Introduction and Background

The *autism spectrum conditions* (ASC) are a set of pervasive developmental conditions, characterized by notable difficulties in communication and social interaction, plus the presence of repetitive behaviours, which often manifest themselves as relatively narrow interests and a strong desire for sameness [1]. The predictability, relative simplicity of virtual environments (VEs) (compared to human-human interaction) are frequently given as reasons why they may be particularly suited to teaching specific skills to people with ASC and supporting daily-life tasks [2].

Recent observations from the ECHOES technology-enhanced learning project (see Section 2; [3]) suggest that VEs and virtual characters (VCs) may also support and motivate young children with ASC when their behaviour is *un*predictable. In an analysis of children with ASC working with ECHOES, it was noted that intermittent software errors[1] unpredictably altered the behaviour of both the VE and VC, violating child expectations about how the environment and its contents "should" behave. There were multiple examples of children clearly reacting to these errors by

[1] *Errors* do not mean error messages, or system freezes/crashes. They are errors in that the system violated its own patterns of object or VC behavior, or acted counter to activity goals.

K. Yacef et al. (Eds.): AIED 2013, LNAI 7926, pp. 884–887, 2013.

making spontaneous, social initiations, including shared positive affect, verbal comments, and social referencing. Such reactions are noteworthy: children with ASC[2] are particularly unlikely to share sharing objects and information for social purposes [1]. Supporting initiation is thus a prominent target of behavioural interventions. The current PhD project is empirically motivated by these initial observations of discrepancies in the ECHOES VE and the subsequent child reactions, a phenomenon unrecorded elsewhere in the ASC literature.

These errors or rule-violating occurrences are *discrepancies*. Discrepancies may result from a *novel* aspect: one which is as yet unknown (i.e. no expectations; not yet in the mental model). Alternatively, the aspect may be a *surprise*— one where something is known about it, but it does not behave as was expected (i.e. mismatch between mental model and environment). Surprise has two subcategories: *surprising events,* or discrepant aspects that are present but behave in unpredictable, expectation-violating ways, and *non-events,* in which aspects are discrepant by their unexpected absence, unresponsiveness, or failure to occur.[3]

Note that *discrepancy* is not an inherent property of the VE, but is defined in relation to individual children and their process of comparing the state of the environment to their mental model and detecting a "mismatch". Thus, the current unit of analysis is the *discrepancy-reaction pair,* not discrepancy alone. As the child's understanding of the environment is generally private, observable reactions are the main evidence for detection of a discrepancy.

2 The ECHOES Project

The first phase of the current project has been a re-analysis of existing video data from the ECHOES technology-enhanced learning project [3]. ECHOES uses exploratory, game-like learning activities to provide opportunities for young children with ASC (target chronological ages 5-7 years) to practice foundational social skills such as turn-taking and gaze- and point-following. The activities are set in a "Magic Garden", and accessed through a 42" touch-screen. Andy, an autonomous, childlike VC, functions as the child's guide and playmate in the VE. The AI plans Andy's behaviour both deliberatively and in reaction to the child's system actions (or non-actions). A researcher at a second monitor used a GUI for limited system control, mainly managing inter-activity transitions.

The broad goal of the ECHOES summative evaluation study (results in preparation) was to assess a variety of social and communication skills before, during, and after six to eight weeks of using the ECHOES environment. 28 children with ASC from four UK school sites each completed multiple 10-20 minute sessions of learning activities per week, gradually attempting more complex material over time. Video data was the primary record of the child's communicative and social behaviour, as

[2] By "children with ASC" we are not referring to those diagnosed with high-functioning autism or Asperger syndrome, as those children are likely to show a very different communication profile to the target group, and indeed may struggle to *limit* their initiations appropriately.

[3] A taxonomy of discrepancy, developed as part of this research programme, is proposed in [5].

automatic logging captured touch-screen actions only. Children frequently interacted with the researcher(s) as well as the system; thus video collection during the summative evaluation (results in preparation) captured as much as possible of the broader study environment (screen, child, and researcher).

3 Current Exploratory Work

The first phase of the PhD project has focussed on exploring whether the initially observed (unintentional) discrepancies are common across the current participant group and appear with relative frequency, as well as whether different discrepancy types lead to different quantities or types of reactions. These questions were addressed through re-analysing a subset of ECHOES videos from 8 children with ASC diagnoses (7 male, 1 female), all with phrase-language production or better. All but one child appears to have some intellectual disability in addition to ASC, as evidenced by the discrepancy between their calendar ages (range= 5-8 yrs, mean=6 yrs, 5 mo.) and verbal-mental ages[4] (range=2-5 yrs, 10mo., mean=3 yrs. 9 mo.).

A total 347 minutes of video was annotated by the author, using ELAN [8][5]. Annotations noted discrepancies, and whether child reactions were *initiations* (i.e. purposeful and spontaneous behaviours directed to a social partner), or were *non-social reactions*. Annotation yielded 239 discrepancies followed by observable child reactions (Novelty=118, Surprising events=50, Non-events=71), with a mean of 29.87 discrepancy-reaction pairs per child (SD=5.22). Across all categories and children, a mean 61.91% of reactions were social initiations to the human researcher or the VC (i.e. more than 3 out of 5), and included a range of verbal and non-verbal behaviours.

Children did not initiate equally across all discrepancy types: there was a strong inverse correlation between the percentage of a child's initiations that were about novel events versus about non-events (Spearman's Rho= -0.762, p= 0.037). Children's affect was positive or neutral overall, with them appearing to find many of the discrepancies humorous, rather than upsetting or disruptive.

4 Future Work

This PhD project will continue for two more years and will build on these initial results through a blend of theoretical and empirical work. One overarching goal is to better understand what discrepancy *means* to children with ASC in the context of a VE, and how this fits into their broader understanding of the world. Non-events will be a main focus, as these do not appear to have been explored in other literature.

While a small body of existing work on adaptive systems has begun to explore the use of erroneous worked examples to support metacognition and content learning

---

4 As calculated from the British Picture Vocabulary Scale [7], a measure of language ability.

5 45 minutes of video per child (three 15-minute samples from early, middle, and late sessions with the VE). Samples excluded any system crashes, child rest breaks and learning activities in which Andy was not present. One child had only 32:46 minutes of qualifying video.

[e.g. 4], this work has included older, typically developing (TD) children and explicit problem-solving. In those contexts and in the present one, many general questions remain unanswered regarding *when* and *how often* to introduce system-side errors (i.e. likely opportunities for discrepancy detection), and whether or not these are equally appropriate for all learners or all levels of domain proficiency. There is also, as yet, no common high-level vocabulary or framework for describing and comparing the type of errors being presented (and thus the type of discrepancies that are detectable). The following phases of this project will attempt to work both at this higher level (such as refining and extending the taxonomy of discrepancy types mentioned in section 1 and in [5]), and on lower-level questions that lay the foundations for building a future VE capable of adaptively introducing discrepancies in order to support young children in practicing social skills or other exploratory, non-propositional content.

The planned work will necessitate a mixture of methods, potentially including further ECHOES video analysis, examining other existent datasets, and designing small-scale virtual activities for explicit hypothesis testing about discrepancy-reaction pairs. Young children with ASC (developmentally 3-5 years, some verbal language) will continue to be the main participant group and target of the design recommendations. New empirical work will not compare TD children and those with ASC, nor examine collaborative learning. Nonetheless the current work on discrepancy-detection, especially as it relates to metacognition, may well be relevant for other groups of learners and other contexts beyond ASC, as discussed more fully in Alcorn et al. [8].

References

1. DSM-IV: Diagnostic and statistical manual of mental disorders. American Psychiatric Association Washington, DC (1994)
2. Rajendran, G.: Virtual environments and autism: a developmental psychopathological approach. J. of Computer Assisted Learning (2013), doi:10.1111/jcal.12006
3. Porayska-Pomsta, K., Frauenberger, C., Pain, H., Rajendran, G., Smith, T., Menzies, R., Foster, M.E., Alcorn, A., Wass, S., Bernadini, S., Avramides, K., Keay-Bright, W., Chen, J., Waller, A., Guldberg, K., Good, J., Lemon, O.: Developing technology for autism: an interdisciplinary approach. Personal and Ubiquitous Computing 16(2), 117–127.3 (2011)
4. Tsovaltzi, D., McLaren, B.M., Melis, E., Meyer, A.K.: Erroneous examples: effects on learning fractions in a web-based setting. Int. J. Technology Enhanced Learning 4(3/4), 191–230 (2012)
5. Alcorn, A.M., Pain, H., Good, J.: Discrepancies in a Virtual Learning Environment: Something "Worth Communicating About" for Young Children with ASC? In: International Conference on Interaction Design and Children IDC 2013, New York (in press, 2013)
6. Dunn, L.M., Dunn, D.M., Whetton, C.W., Burley, J.: The British Picture Vocabulary Scale, 2nd edn. NFER Nelson, Windsor (1997)
7. Max Planck Institute for Psycholinguistics. ELAN Linguistics Annotator, version 4.4.0. Max Planck Institute for Psycholinguistics, The Language Archive, Nijmegen, The Netherlands (2012), `http://tla.mpi.nl/tools/tla-tools/elan/`
8. Alcorn, A.M., Good, J., Pain, H.: Deliberate system-side errors as a potential pedagogic strategy for exploratory virtual learning environments. In: Chad Lane, H., Yacef, K., Mostow, J., Pavlik, P. (eds.) AIED 2013. LNCS (LNAI), vol. 7926, pp. 483–492. Springer, Heidelberg (2013)

Towards an Integrative Computational Foundation for Applied Behavior Analysis in Early Autism Interventions

Edmon Begoli[1], Cristi L. Ogle[2], David F. Cihak[1], and Bruce J. MacLennan[1]

[1] University of Tenneesee, Knoxville, TN 37996, USA
{ebegoli,dcihak,maclennan}@utk.edu
[2] Knox County Schools, Knoxville, TN 37902, USA
cristi.ogle@knoxschools.org

Abstract. Applied Behavior Analysis-based early interventions are evidence based, efficacious therapies for autism. They are, however, labor intensive and often inaccessible at the recommended levels. In this paper we present ongoing doctoral research aimed at development of the formal, computational representation for Applied Behavior Analysis (ABA) that could serve as a reasoning foundation for intelligent-agent mediated ABA therapies. Our approach is to formulate the representation of ABA dynamics and concepts as a process ontology expressed in a controlled natural language (CNL). As an ontology language, CNL is not only a machine interpretable, logically sound reasoning foundation, but also understandable and editable by human users.

Keywords: Applied behavior analysis, knowledge representation, autism, ontology, intelligent agents.

1 Introduction

Autism Spectrum Disorder (ASD) is a complex developmental disability characterized by impairments in social interaction and communication and by restricted, repetitive and stereotyped patterns of behavior [1]. It is a prevalent and challenging condition affecting 1 in 88 children [2].

While there is no known cure for ASD there are a number of interventions aimed at remediation of the symptoms of the disorder. Behavioral and developmental interventions, based on demonstrated efficacy [3, 4], have become the predominant treatments for improving social, adaptive and behavioral functions in children. This dissertation research focuses on a group of behavioral treatment interventions based on the principles of Applied Behavior Analysis (ABA) [5].

According to Foxx [3], Applied Behavior Analysis incorporates all of the factors identified by the US National Research Council as characteristic of effective interventions in educational and treatment programs for children who have autism (p. 821). With the prevalence rates of autim stated earlier and with high hourly demands for this therapy to be effective, ABA-based approaches are still largely inaccessible to most families in need [6].

K. Yacef et al. (Eds.): AIED 2013, LNAI 7926, pp. 888–891, 2013.

Within the field of computer science, socially assistive robotics [7], intelligent tutoring systems [8] and general use of intelligent agents have been investigated for autism therapies and early interventions. This is a nascent field and approaches are limited to research settings. Even within current inititiatives it is recognized that this interdisciplinary research area, which brings together psychologists, special education teachers, computer scientists and electrical engineers, needs an integrated approach that will be accessible to all participants in the process.

2 Hypothesis

The main hypothesis of this doctoral research is that the deterministic nature of behavioral interventions [9, p. 5] and the scripted structure of ABA-based therapies are well suited for computational formalization. As an outcome of the research, we intend to represent the structure and governing principles of ABA as a process ontology that could serve as a theoretical foundation for different modalities for implementation of intelligent-agent-mediated behavioral therapies. Furthermore, we intend to use controlled natural language as a human user friendly medium of formal knowledge representation and as an ontology language.

3 Approach

Our research approach to developing an ABA ontology is to follow the formal ontology engineering process specified by OnTO [10]. We have chosen the OnTO approach to ontology specification and validation for its comprehensive, formal and modular approach to domain analysis and ontology engineering. OnTO was also devised with customizability and collaborative development in mind, hence we selected its domain analysis and validation components as the most relevant to the research process while omitting aspects that are suitable primarily for industrial and engineering applications. In developing an integrative, multidisciplinary, usable ABA ontology, we recognize that we need to establish a theoretical formalism for ABA and to specify and describe the key elements of the process in a manner that is both machine and human readable.

3.1 β-Calculus — A Logic Formalism for ABA Dynamics

The β-calculus is a concept we are introducing. It is a formal way to express the dynamics and inference rules that govern ABA. In part the β-calculus will formalize the key concepts behind ABA: three-term contingency, prompting, fading, forward and backward chaining, and intra-trial intervals [9, p. 32-328]. Further, its inferential processes will support the dynamics of ABA: initiation of antecedants, consequences and evaluation of the progress of trials.

3.2 Controlled Natural Language as ABA Ontology Language

We use Attempto Controlled English (ACE) [11] to describe the ABA ontology. Attempto is a controlled natural language that supports writing of ontologies in a machine processable, logically sound but human understandable natural language. Writing well-formed Attempto expressions is supported by a set of tools developed for user friendly, collaborative and interactive authoring of ACE expressions by non-programming users. The advantage of ACE is not only its understandabilty but also its ability to process ACE expressions as logic statements and to translate them into other forms of knowledge or machine representation, such as RDF, OWL and OWL 2. Our choice of ACE as the ontology language is based on studies showing that controlled natural languages are effective, broadly understandable mediums for collaborative development and use of ontologies by a non-programming audience [12].

3.3 Validation

β-calculus is a logic formalism representing ABA dynamics, so the process of its derivation follows the validation rules and proof methods consistent with an axiomatic system. The ACE-encoded ABA ontology will be developed with the assistance of subject matter experts, and it will be validated against the ABA-related competency questions [13] that were developed by practicing behavioral therapists. Finally, to demonstrate translatability of the ACE-encoded ABA ontology, we intend to develop a small proof-of-concept translator from ACE expressions into executable Behavioral Markup Language (BML) scripts for intelligent agents.

4 Contribution and Expected Outcome

We expect this research to benefit Computer Science and other associated fields, including Psychology, Special Education and Artificial Intelligence. We specifically expect that:

1. The theoretical foundation and conceptual framework resulting from this research could serve as a foundation for development of interactive, flexible, intelligent-agent-mediated ABA-based therapies for children and adolescents with disabilities or special needs. We expect this framework to be applicable to the broad category of instructional applications ranging from traditional GUI-oriented to mixed reality and socially intelligent-agent-based therapies.
2. We will demonstrate how the cognitive gap between different, interrelated but mutually dependent fields can be effectively and formally bridged by the most universally undestood form of human expression: human language.

References

[1] American Psychiatric Association: Pervasive developmental disorders. In: Diagnostic and Statistical Manual of Mental Disorders (DSM-IV-TR), 4th edn., pp. 69–70. American Psychiatric Association, Washington, DC (2000)
[2] Baio, J.: Prevalence of autism spectrum disorders: Autism and developmental disabilities monitoring network, 14 sites, United States (2008); Morbidity and mortality weekly report. Surveillance Summaries 61(3). Centers for Disease Control and Prevention (2012)
[3] Foxx, R.: Applied behavior analysis treatment of autism: The state of the art. Child and adolescent psychiatric clinics of North America 17(4), 821–834 (2008)
[4] Voos, A.C., Pelphrey, K.A., Tirrell, J., Bolling, D.Z., Wyk, B.V., Kaiser, M.D., McPartland, J.C., Volkmar, F.R., Ventola, P.: Neural mechanisms of improvements in social motivation after pivotal response treatment: Two case studies. Journal of autism and developmental disorders, 1–10 (2012)
[5] National Research Council (US). Committee on Educational Interventions for Children with Autism: Educating children with autism. National Academies Press (2001)
[6] Wise, M., Little, A., Holliman, J., Wise, P., Wang, C.: Can state early intervention programs meet the increased demand of children suspected of having autism spectrum disorders? Journal of Developmental & Behavioral Pediatrics 31(6), 469–476 (2010)
[7] Feil-Seifer, D., Mataric, M.: Defining socially assistive robotics. In: IEEE 9th International Conference on Rehabilitation Robotics, ICORR 2005, pp. 465–468 (2005)
[8] Kay, J.: Ai and education: Grand challenges. IEEE Intelligent Systems 27(5), 66–69 (2012)
[9] Cooper, J., Heron, T., Heward, W.L.: Applied Behavior Analysis. Prentice Hall (2007)
[10] Suárez-Figueroa, M., Gómez-Pérez, A., Motta, E., Gangemi, A.: Introduction: Ontology engineering in a networked world. Ontology Engineering in a Networked World, 1–6 (2012)
[11] Kuhn, T.: Controlled English for Knowledge Representation. PhD thesis, Faculty of Economics, Business Administration and Information Technology of the University of Zurich (2010)
[12] Denaux, R., Dolbear, C., Hart, G., Dimitrova, V., Cohn, A.G.: Supporting domain experts to construct conceptual ontologies: A holistic approach. Web Semantics: Science, Services and Agents on the World Wide Web 9(2), 113–127 (2011)
[13] Gruninger, M., Fox, M.: The role of competency questions in enterprise engineering. In: Proceedings of the IFIP WG5, vol. 7, pp. 212–221 (1994)

Adaptive Scaffolds in Open-Ended Learning Environments

James R. Segedy

Institute of Software Integrated Systems, Department of Electrical Engineering and Computer Science, Vanderbilt University, 1025 16th Avenue South, Nashville, TN, 37212, U.S.A.
james.segedy@vanderbilt.edu

Abstract. Open-ended learning environments (OELEs) are learner-centered, and they offer students opportunities to take part in authentic and complex problem-solving tasks. However, learners typically struggle to learn with OELEs without proper adaptive scaffolds. This paper describes research and development related to designing real-time algorithms for diagnosing students' needs in OELEs and responding with appropriate adaptive scaffolds.

Keywords: Open-Ended Learning Environment, Adaptive Scaffolds, Problem Solving.

1 Introduction

Open-ended learning environments (OELEs) [1] are learner-centered, and they offer students opportunities to take part in authentic and complex problem-solving tasks by providing a learning context and a set of tools for exploring, hypothesizing, and building their own solutions to problems. Examples include hypermedia learning environments (e.g., [2]), modeling and simulation environments (e.g., [3-4]), and educational games featuring open worlds (e.g., [5]). While OELEs may vary in the particular sets of tools they provide, they often include tools for: (i) seeking and acquiring knowledge and information, (ii) applying that information to a problem-solving context, and (iii) assessing the quality of the constructed solution.

By the very nature of the choices they allow for learning and problem solving, OELEs provide opportunities for students to exercise higher-order reasoning skills that include: (i) *cognitive processes* for accessing and interpreting information, constructing problem solutions, and assessing constructed solutions; and (ii) *metacognitive processes* for coordinating the use of cognitive processes and reflecting on their understanding of the knowledge they are learning, their approach to generating solutions, and possible next steps for improving their problem-solving approach. This presents significant challenges to novice learners; they may have neither the proficiency for using system tools nor the understanding necessary for explicitly regulating their learning behaviors. Not surprisingly, research has shown that novices often struggle to succeed in OELEs [6-7]. Without *adaptive scaffolds*, these learners typically use tools incorrectly and adopt suboptimal learning strategies (e.g. [8]). Adaptive scaffolds in OELEs refer to actions taken

K. Yacef et al. (Eds.): AIED 2013, LNAI 7926, pp. 892–895, 2013.

by the learning environment, based on the learner's interactions, intended to support the learner in completing a task [9].

Developing adaptive scaffolds in OELEs is a difficult task for designers [10]; it requires systematic analysis techniques for diagnosing learners' needs and theoretically sound approaches for selecting adaptive scaffolds from a variety of potential scaffolding strategies. The open-ended nature of OELEs combined with the longer term nature of the problems presented in such environments further exacerbates the problem; since the environments are learner-centered, these systems typically do not restrict the approaches that learners take to solving their problems. Thus, interpreting and assessing students' learning behavior is inherently complex, and choosing an ideal scaffold for a particular learner in a particular situation is not a straightforward process.

While several OELEs have been developed and used with learners, relatively few of them provide adaptive scaffolds. Instead, these systems include non-adaptive scaffolded tools (*e.g.*, lists of guiding questions) designed to provide support for learners who choose to use them, and they expect learners to come to the learning environment with either: (i) sufficient cognitive and metacognitive skill proficiency, or (ii) the self-regulative capabilities necessary for independently seeking out missing knowledge and practicing underdeveloped skills. Such an approach alienates a large number of learners; while several students are able to productively learn in OELEs, many of their less capable counterparts instead experience significant confusion and frustration, greatly limiting the population of learners for which OELEs lead to meaningful learning [6], [11].

2 Approach and Contributions

Given the established need for developing and testing methods for selecting appropriate adaptive scaffolds based on real-time assessments of learner behaviors [10], the research that I have conducted and am continuing to conduct in this area represents a significant contribution to the AIED research community. My approach includes the following specific contributions:

1. The development of a theoretically grounded model of managing one's own learning processes in an OELE called *Betty's Brain* [12]. The model will draw upon research related to the structure of OELEs and their cognitive and metacognitive requirements [11], general models of self-regulated learning [13], and the interplay between cognition and metacognition [14].
2. The development of a novel technique for the online interpretation of students' behaviors in *Betty's Brain*. The technique will assess learners in terms of their proficiency in executing cognitive operations and their understanding of metacognitive strategies for managing their learning. To assess learners' cognitive operations, the module will analyze actions in terms of their effectiveness in moving the learner closer to completing their tasks. To measure learners' metacognitive strategy understanding, the module will assess sequences of learner actions in terms of how they could possibly cohere within a sensible learning strategy. The model developed in step 1 will drive the development of this new analysis technique.

3. The development and preliminary testing of a novel *adaptive scaffolding strategy* for *Betty's Brain*. The approach utilizes the analysis techniques developed in step 2 in order to identify and select a specific process or strategy to support, and it will include two tiers of support. The first tier will support students through suggestions and assertions in the form of *contextualized conversational feedback* [11] that explains the importance of the process, how to execute it, and how proper execution of the process will help in completing the learning task. These conversations will allow for a *mixed-initiative dialogue* between the learner and the OELE; together, they can discuss follow-up questions and jointly negotiate next steps for completing the learning task. Should students' performance not improve as a result of these conversations, a second tier of support, *guided practice* will require students to explicitly practice the use of the targeted process while receiving guidance and feedback. The scaffolding strategy should allow the OELE to adapt to the needs of students with both low and high prior knowledge and experience with the system by allowing students to practice under-developed skills necessary for achieving success within the environment. To the best of my knowledge, guided practice modification scaffolds have never been studied as part of a scaffolding strategy for OELEs; thus, this aspect of my research will provide novel data and analyses that will contribute to the field's understanding of the effect of guided practice scaffolds on student learning. This adaptive scaffolding strategy will be described in terms of a novel taxonomy for classifying and describing adaptive scaffolding approaches. The taxonomy, which will be developed as part of this research, describes adaptive scaffolds as consisting of one or more suggestions, assertions, and learning task modifications. *Suggestion scaffolds* provide information to learners for the purpose of prompting them to perform a specific behavior. *Assertion scaffolds* communicate information to learners as being true. Finally, *modification scaffolds* modify the requirements of the learning task (*e.g.*, adjusting task difficulty).

Moving forward with this research will require the development and testing of a preliminary version of the analysis techniques and scaffolding strategy outlined above. To accomplish this, I will employ video recorded one-on-one think-aloud protocol studies, which will be coded in order to assess: (i) the accuracy of the OELE's understanding of learners' cognitive and metacognitive skill proficiency and (ii) the effect of the adaptive scaffolds on students' understanding of and ability to make progress in completing their tasks. In addition, the scaffolding strategy will be validated experimentally by comparing students who use *Betty's Brain* with the scaffolds in place to students who use the system without the scaffolds. The experiments will attempt to address the following two research questions:

1. Is the incorporation of the adaptive scaffolding strategy associated with more effective problem-solving behaviors and increased learning of domain knowledge, cognitive skills, and metacognitive strategies?
2. Are students who receive the adaptive scaffolding more likely to employ effective cognitive skills and metacognitive strategies when the scaffolds are removed?

Acknowledgements. This work has been supported by Institute of Educational Sciences CASL Grant #R305A120186 and the National Science Foundation's IIS Award #0904387.

References

1. Jonassen, I., Land, S. (eds.): Theoretical Foundations of Learning Environments, 2nd edn. Routledge, New York (2012)
2. Azevedo, R., Landis, R.S., Feyzi-Behnagh, R., Duffy, M., Trevors, G., Harley, J.M., Bouchet, F., Burlison, J., Taub, M., Pacampara, N., Yeasin, M., Rahman, A.K.H.M., Tanveer, M.I., Hossain, G.: The effectiveness of pedagogical agents' prompting and feedback in facilitating co-adapted learning with metatutor. In: Cerri, S.A., Clancey, W.J., Papadourakis, G., Panourgia, K. (eds.) ITS 2012. LNCS, vol. 7315, pp. 212–221. Springer, Heidelberg (2012)
3. Leelawong, K., Biswas, G.: Designing learning by teaching agents: The Betty's Brain system. International Journal of Artificial Intelligence in Education 18, 181–208 (2008)
4. van Joolingen, W.R., de Jong, T., Lazonder, A.W., Savelsbergh, E.R., Manlove, S.: Co-Lab: Research and Development of an Online Learning Environment for Collaborative Scientific Discovery Learning. Computers in Human Behavior 21, 671–688 (2005)
5. McQuiggan, S.W., Rowe, J.P., Lee, S., Lester, J.C.: Story-Based Learning: The Impact of Narrative on Learning Experiences and Outcomes. In: Woolf, B.P., Aïmeur, E., Nkambou, R., Lajoie, S. (eds.) ITS 2008. LNCS, vol. 5091, pp. 530–539. Springer, Heidelberg (2008)
6. Mayer, R.E.: Should there be a three-strikes rule against pure discovery learning? American Psychologist 59, 14–19 (2004)
7. Shute, V.J., Glaser, R.: A Large-Scale Evaluation of an Intelligent Discovery World: Smithtown. Interactive Learning Environments 1, 51–77 (1990)
8. Segedy, J.R., Kinnebrew, J.S., Biswas, G.: Modeling learners' cognitive and metacognitive strategies in an open-ended learning environment. In: Advances in Cognitive Systems: Papers from the AAAI Fall Symposium, pp. 297–304. AAAI Press (2011)
9. Puntambekar, S., Hübscher, R.: Tools for scaffolding students in a complex learning environment: What have we gained and what have we missed? Educational Psychologist 40, 1–12 (2005)
10. Azevedo, R., Jacobson, M.J.: Advances in Scaffolding Learning with Hypertext and Hypermedia: A Summary and Critical Analysis. Educational Technology Research and Development 56, 93–100 (2008)
11. Land, S.M.: Cognitive requirements for learning with open-ended learning environments. Educational Technology Research and Development 48, 61–78 (2000)
12. Segedy, J.R., Kinnebrew, J.S., Biswas, G.: The Effect of Contextualized Conversational Feedback in a Complex Open-Ended Learning Environment. Educational Technology Research and Development 61, 71–89 (2013)
13. Winne, P.H.: Self-regulated learning viewed from models of information processing. In: Zimmerman, B.J., Schunk, D.H (eds), Self-Regulated Learning and Academic Achievement: Theoretical Perspectives, pp. 153–189. Erlbaum (2001)
14. Veenman, M.V.J.: Metacognition in science education: Definitions, constituents, and their intricate relation with cognition. In: Zohar, A., Dori, Y.J. (eds.) Metacognition in Science Education, pp. 21–36. Elsevier (2012)

Sorry, I Must Have Zoned Out: Tracking Mind Wandering Episodes in an Interactive Learning Environment

Caitlin Mills[1] and Sidney D'Mello[1, 2]

Departments of Psychology[1] and Computer Science[2], University of Notre Dame, Notre Dame, IN 46556, USA
{cmills4,sdmello}@nd.edu

Abstract. Mind wandering is the attentional shift from task-related thought to task-unrelated thoughts and can have disastrous effects on learning. Previous research has found that mind wandering is detrimental to comprehension during reading. However, to our knowledge, no research has investigated mind wandering during interactive educational learning environments. This paper discusses preliminary studies and a proposed line of research that aims to investigate models of mind wandering in the context of an interactive computerized learning environment. The proposed three-phase plan will develop a deep understanding of the factors that influence mind wandering with an eye towards developing intelligent learning environments that automatically detect and respond to minds when they begin to wander.

Keywords: mind wandering, learning, advanced learning technologies.

1 Introduction

Student engagement is an integral part of learning from an advanced learning technology (ALT). No matter how a student is receiving information (e.g., reading, listening, observing), some level of engagement must be devoted to the incoming information to achieve successful reception and integration with mental models. Otherwise, attentional lapses will occur, leaving the student's mind free to wander. This phenomenon of perceptual decoupling is known as mind wandering, zoning out, or day dreaming [1, 2]. Specifically, mind wandering occurs when there is an attentional shift away from the task-related information in the external environment towards task unrelated information in the internal environment [1].

Theory and evidence both suggest that mind wandering is ultimately detrimental during educational activities [3]. However, most studies on mind wandering have been largely limited to simple perceptual-motor tasks and sometimes during reading of non-academic narrative texts [4–6]. As such, there is little information about the incidence of mind wandering during interactions with ALTs. To alleviate this gap in the literature, the current research project aims to deeply understand the phenomenon of mind wandering during computer-based learning in order to eventually inform interventions that

K. Yacef et al. (Eds.): AIED 2013, LNAI 7926, pp. 896–899, 2013.

deter mind wandering. We propose a series of experiments that will explore mind wandering during learning at three levels. First, we will conduct a broad investigation to gain a basic understanding of mind wandering during an interactive learning session. Second, we will systematically hone in and manipulate factors that affect mind wandering based on the first study. Third, we will build models to predict mind wandering during learning. This will be completed using an interactive computer-based learning environment that teaches core concepts in scientific research methods.

2 Background and Previous Research

Relevant research endeavors on mind wandering during reading have provided valuable insight to inform the current research project. For example, we know that mind wandering occurs around 20 to 40 percent of the time during reading and negatively affects reading comprehension [5]. Some previous studies have focused on the effect of textual factors (e.g., difficulty) on mind wandering. For example, [4] found that mind wandering was reported more frequently and comprehension was negatively related to mind wandering when reading difficult texts compared to easy texts. Other research has focused on identifying behavioral patterns associated with mind wandering during reading. Previous research suggests that gaze durations and blinking patterns are different preceding instances of mind wandering compared to on-task reading [8, 9]. It is important to note, however, that the studies discussed so far were all conducted using non-academic texts, so there is still a question about how mind wandering is manifested in real-life educational tasks.

Our first steps along this research front were two studies that targeted reading academic texts about scientific reasoning concepts during a computerized reading task. The first study investigated how perceived choice and text difficulty affected mind wandering during reading academic texts [10]. Results indicated that participants mind wandered more when reading the difficult texts compared to the easy texts, but there was no effect of perceived choice on rates of mind wandering. The next study (in progress) examines how topic interest, text difficulty, as well as text presentation affect rates of mind wandering and learning. For example, does it matter if the text is presented one sentence at a time or in larger chunks of text?

However, one outstanding and unresolved issue is the severe paucity of evidence on the incidence of mind wandering beyond mere reading. We must go beyond reading to investigate mind wandering, because reading does not afford the same interactivity and multimodal information delivery as do current ALTs.

3 Future Research Plans

The next step for the proposed research endeavor is to extend the study of mind wandering to an interactive computer-based learning environment. The learning environment consists of the student engaging in a trialogue with two pedagogical agents in which they diagnose the flaws in research case studies through a series of conversational turns about research methods [11]. Two agents (tutor-agent and student-agent) and the human student will take turns stating their opinions about flaws in various research case studies. At the end of each study, flaws are diagnosed and explained by the pedagogical agents. This type of environment is ideal to investigate mind wandering because it affords opportunities for a variety of manipulations and events. For example, difficulty of the learning material, level of interactivity, and feedback can all be manipulated in this environment for experimental purposes.

3.1 Phase 1: Exploratory Pilot Study

The first step will be a pilot study in which students will interact with the learning environment. There will be no experimental manipulations during this pilot study. Students will first complete a pretest and then engage in a learning session that involves a series of trialogues with two pedagogical agents about four different research methods concepts. Finally, they will take a posttest to assess their learning. Pre- and posttests will consist of deep-reasoning questions previously tested for reliability. Mind wandering will be measured using auditory probes at specific points during learning. Probes will consist of beeps that students will respond 'yes' or 'no' to indicate if they are currently mind wandering (see [1]). Probes will occur during the agent interactions, as well before and after student responses. Data from this study will be analyzed to see what events are related to mind wandering, such as characteristics of the learning environment (e.g., topic, which agent recently spoke), learner characteristics (e.g., prior knowledge), and patterns of interaction during the learning session (e.g., response quality, verbosity). Galvanic skin response and gaze data will also be collected and analyzed for physiological and behavioral correlates of mind wandering.

3.2 Phase 2: Investigating Experimentally Manipulated Factors

Phase 2 will consist of two experiments that will systematically manipulate factors in the learning session. Ideally, these experimental manipulations will be influenced by the data from the exploratory study in Phase 1. One potential manipulation stems from previous research on the influence of text difficulty on mind wandering. For example, given the same content, will difficulty of the language used in the dialogue induce mind wandering? Another feasible manipulation might systematically manipulate the amount of interactivity or feedback that students receive. If the pedagogical agents give more informative feedback (e.g., manipulating specificity), is the student more likely to pay attention? These experimental manipulations will allow us to refine and develop a psychologically driven model for mind wandering, while also collecting valuable data from the behavioral and physiological measures.

3.3 Phase 3: Building and Testing Models of Mind Wandering

The final phase will attempt to build a model that predicts mind wandering using information from previous phases. Specifically, we will combine information from the different channels of data that will have been collected and analyzed. We will use machine learning to build a model that will link the environmental, behavioral, and physiological features within a learning session to signals of mind wandering.

4 Conclusion

It is the goal that future learning environments will have the tools necessary to detect and adaptively respond to mind wandering in order regain the student's attention to maximize engagement and learning. Following this research plan will allow us to take steps in the direction to accomplish this goal and take ALTs to the next level.

Acknowledgment. This research was supported by the National Science Foundation (NSF) (ITR 0325428, HCC 0834847, DRL 1235958). Any opinions, findings and conclusions, or recommendations expressed in this paper are those of the authors and do not necessarily reflect the views of NSF.

References

1. Smallwood, J., Schooler, J.: The restless mind. Psychological Bulletin 132, 946 (2006)
2. Schooler, J., Smallwood, J., Christoff, K., Handy, T., Reichle, E., Sayette, M.: Meta-awareness, perceptual decoupling and the wandering mind. Trends in Cognitive Sciences 15, 319–326 (2011)
3. Smallwood, J., Fishman, D., Schooler, J.: Counting the cost of an absent mind: Mind wandering as an underrecognized influence on educational performance. Psychonomic Bulletin & Review 14, 230–236 (2007)
4. Feng, S., D'Mello, S., Graesser, A.: Mind wandering while reading easy and difficult texts. Psychonomic Bulletin and Review (in press)
5. Schooler, J., Reichle, E., Halpern, D.: Zoning out while reading: Evidence for dissociations between experience and metaconsciousness. In: Thinking and Seeing: Visual Metacognition in Adults and Children, pp. 203–226. MIT Press, Cambridge (2004)
6. Smallwood, J., Davies, J., Heim, D., Finnigan, F., Sudberry, M., O'Connor, R., Obonsawin, M.: Subjective experience and the attentional lapse: Task engagement and disengagement during sustained attention. Consciousness and Cognition 13, 657–690 (2004)
7. Smallwood, J., Baracaia, S., Lowe, M., Obonsawin, M.: Task unrelated thought whilst encoding information. Consciousness and Cognition 12, 452–484 (2003)
8. Smilek, D., Carriere, J., Cheyne, J.: Out of Mind, Out of Sight Eye Blinking as Indicator and Embodiment of Mind Wandering. Psychological Science 21, 786–789 (2010)
9. Reichle, E., Reineberg, A., Schooler, J.: Eye Movements During Mindless Reading. Psychological Science 21, 1300–1310 (2010)
10. Mills, C., D'Mello, S., Lehman, B., Bosch, N., Strain, A., Graesser, A.: What Makes Learning Fun? Exploring the Influence of Choice and Difficulty on Mind Wandering and Engagement during Learning. In: Proceedings of 16th International Conference on Artificial Intelligence in Education (in press)
11. D'Mello, S., Lehman, B., Pekrun, R., Graesser, A.: Confusion can be beneficial for learning. Learning and Instruction (in press)

Intelligent Tutoring Systems for Collaborative Learning: Enhancements to Authoring Tools

Jennifer K. Olsen[1], Daniel M. Belenky[1], Vincent Aleven[1], and Nikol Rummel[1,2]

[1] Human Computer Interaction Institute, Carnegie Mellon University, Pittsburgh, PA, USA
{jkolsen,aleven}@cs.cmu.edu, dbelenky@andrew.cmu.edu
[2] Institute of Educational Research, Ruhr-Universität Bochum, Germany
nikol.rummel@rub.de

Abstract. Collaborative and individual instruction may support different types of knowledge. Optimal instruction for a subject domain may therefore need to combine these two modes of instruction. There has not been much research, however, on combining individual and collaborative learning with Intelligent Tutoring Systems (ITSs). A first step is to expand ITSs for collaborative learning. This paper investigates the expansion of the Cognitive Tutor Authoring Tools to include collaborative components for example-tracing tutors. The tools were enhanced to support flexible use of collaboration scripts so different learning goals can be supported. We introduce the collaboration features supported and describe an initial pilot study using the new features in a fractions ITS.

Keywords: Problem solving, collaborative learning, intelligent tutoring system.

1 Introduction

Intelligent Tutoring Systems (ITSs) have shown great success in increasing learning gains for individual learning [10], while collaborative learning has been shown to increase learning gains in some computer-supported settings [6]. Although there is evidence that a combination of individual and collaborative learning may be needed for optimal knowledge acquisition, there is not much research on how to combine the two modes [7]. To facilitate this kind of research, it would help to expand ITSs so they support both individual and collaborative learning. Specifically, it would help if ITSs could flexibly support *collaboration scripts,* which aim to support productive collaborative interactions within groups [3]. Prior research in computer-supported collaborative learning show that scripts can be effective means of structuring collaborations. Collaboration scripts can be defined by five components: learning goals, activity types, sequencing, role distribution, and representation types [3].

In our research, we investigate how an ITS authoring tool can flexibly incorporate these components to support collaborative learning for a wide range of learning goals. While there have been previous ITSs that include collaborative features [4-5], [9] and research has been done to standardize collaboration scripts across contexts [2], authoring tools for ITSs generally do not support a range of collaboration script features. In the current work, we extend a proven ITS authoring tool, Cognitive Tutor

K. Yacef et al. (Eds.): AIED 2013, LNAI 7926, pp. 900–903, 2013.

Authoring Tools (CTAT) [1], to support the authoring of collaboration scripts for example-tracing tutors. Example-tracing tutors are behaviorally similar to cognitive tutors, but instead of relying on a rule-based cognitive model, they use a generalized behavior graph to guide students during problem solving. We describe how we enhanced CTAT so example-tracing tutors support both individual and collaborative learning.

2 Collaborative CTAT Extension

We extended CTAT so an author can create tutors that allow students in two different locations to interact with the same problem synchronously. Our collaborative version of CTAT allows the five collaboration script components to be supported flexibly.

In the simplest form of collaboration supported by these tools, each student has identical views and allowed interactions. This set-up would support a low-scaffolded collaboration scenario. However, the tools also support more complex and varied forms of collaboration, in which the collaborating students have different views and interactions. As an example, consider a collaborative environment where unique information can be presented to each student. Such interaction can increase individual accountability and the effectiveness of the collaboration. The ability to divide the information supports scripts such as the "Jigsaw" script [4].

Another typical element of collaboration scripts that can be supported with our enhanced version of CTAT is the use of different interactions to create roles. Even though each student can view the entire problem, the interactions that the students can take can be specialized based on their role. In this case, a student would be able to view their partner's interactions but not be able to take over their partner's role. This integrated feature may help to support mutual discussions and improve learning. Peer tutoring roles could also be supported by only providing feedback on interactions to the student in the "tutor" role. Our enhanced version of CTAT also supports scripts where each student has a completely different view of the problem. This kind of script can encourage collaboration where students have varied perspectives of the problem, but the actions of one student can influence the other.

The challenge in enhancing the authoring tools to support these possibilities was to provide the flexibility needed to support a wide range of collaboration scripts. This goal was achieved by using multiple example-tracing tutor engines running in parallel, one for each student. The parallel tutor engines all receive all the input from each interface and send all output to all interfaces. This structure allows an author to develop tutors that support more complex collaboration scripts, as in the example below.

3 Collaborative Tutor Example

We created a collaborative tutor for fractions and pilot tested it with two fourth/fifth grade students for initial impressions. This work extends an existing ITS for learning fractions with graphical representations [8]. For our pilot, the students were asked to collaborate on four procedural and four conceptual problems while working in different rooms, communicating both through their interactions with the tutor and by talking to each other through an audio connection. The script elements used in these problems were unique information as seen in Figure 1 and roles as seen in Figure 2.

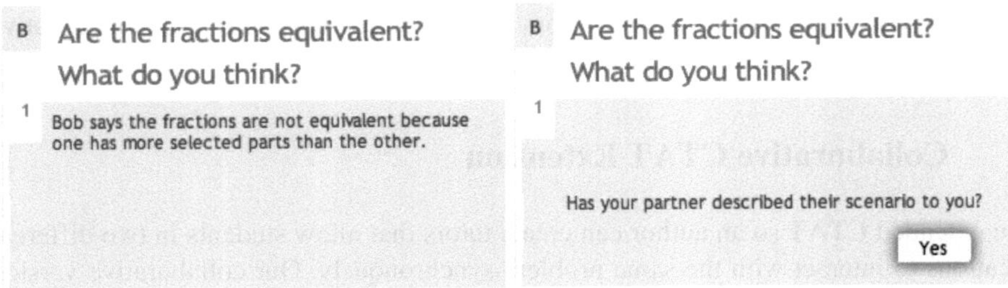

Fig. 1. Students are each provided with a unique story to share and are prompted to discuss

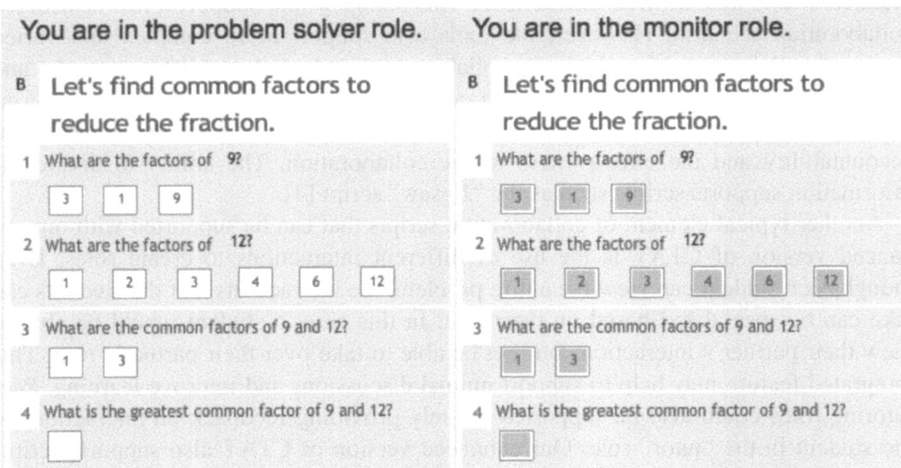

Fig. 2. Example of role assignment, where the gray indicates the component is inactive

First, each student was given unique information at the beginning of the problem and asked to share it to create individual accountability. Then they were assigned to either a monitor role, where they were accountable for asking their partner questions, or a problem solver role, where they were responsible for selecting or filling in the dyad's answers. The tutor also maintained key ITS features that have been shown to be critical to help learning, such as step-by-step guidance and hint levels [10].

4 Discussion, Conclusion and Future Work

The use of both individual and collaborative modes has been shown to be important in successful instruction [7], but how to combine the modes is not as well known. Currently, authoring tools do not flexibly support a range of collaboration script elements that would be needed to pursue this question. We extended CTAT to allow a range of collaborative scenarios to be supported. In an initial pilot, we demonstrated the feasibility of using features that support collaboration (e.g., providing unique information), helped spark a productive conversation between students, and found that the students enjoyed the collaboration. Future work will use these tools to develop a combined individual and collaborative tutor to test the basic hypothesis that optimal instruction often requires a combination of individual and collaborative learning.

Acknowledgments. We thank the Cognitive Tutor Authoring Tools team for their help. This work was supported by Graduate Training Grant # R305B090023 and by Award # R305A120734 both from the US Department of Education (IES).

References

1. Aleven, V., McLaren, B.M., Sewall, J., Koedinger, K.R.: A New Paradigm for Intelligent Tutoring Systems: Example-tracing Tutors. International Journal of Artificial Intelligence in Education 19, 105–154 (2009)
2. Kobbe, L., Weinberger, A., Dillenbourg, P., Harrer, A., Hämäläinen, R., Häkkinen, P., Fischer, F.: Specifying Ccomputer-Supported Collaboration Scripts. International Journal of Computer-Supported Collaborative Learning 2(2), 211–224 (2007)
3. Kollar, I., Fischer, F., Hesse, F.W.: Collaboration Scripts–A Conceptual Analysis. Educational Psychology Review 18(2), 159–185 (2006)
4. Kumar, R., Rosé, C.P., Wang, Y., Joshi, M., Robinson, A.: Tutorial Dialogue as Adaptive Collaborative Learning Support. Frontiers in Artificial Intelligence and Applications 158, 383 (2007)
5. Lesgold, A., Katz, S., Greenberg, L., Hughes, E., Eggan, G.: Extensions of Intelligent Tutoring Paradigms to Support Collaborative Learning. In: Dijkstra, S., Krammer, H.P.M., van Merrienboer, J.J.G. (eds.) Instructional Models in Computer-based Learning Environments, pp. 291–311. Springer, Heidelberg (1992)
6. Lou, Y., Abrami, P.C., d'Apollonia, S.: Small Group and Individual Learning with Technology: A Meta-Analysis. Review of Educational Research 71(3), 449–521 (2001)
7. Mullins, D., Rummel, N., Spada, H.: Are Two Heads Always Better Than One? Differential Effects of Collaboration on Students' Computer-Supported Learning in Mathematics. International Journal of Computer-Supported Collaborative Learning 6, 421–443 (2011)
8. Rau, M.A., Aleven, V., Rummel, N., Rohrbach, S.: Sense Making Alone Doesn't Do It: Fluency Matters Too! ITS Support for Robust Learning with Multiple Representations. In: Cerri, S.A., Clancey, W.J., Papadourakis, G., Panourgia, K. (eds.) ITS 2012. LNCS, vol. 7315, pp. 174–184. Springer, Heidelberg (2012)
9. Walker, E., Rummel, N., Koedinger, K.: CTRL: A Research Framework for Providing Adaptive Collaborative Learning Support. User Modeling and User-Adapted Interaction. The Journal of Personalization Research (UMUAI) 19(5), 387–431 (2009)
10. VanLehn, K.: The Relative Effectiveness of Human Tutoring, Intelligent Tutoring Systems, and Other Tutoring Systems. Educational Psychologist 46, 197–221 (2011)

Towards Automated Detection and Regulation of Affective States During Academic Writing

Robert Bixler[1] and Sidney D'Mello[1, 2]

Departments of Computer Science[1] and Psychology[2], University of Notre Dame, Notre Dame, IN 46556, USA
{rbixler,sdmello}@nd.edu

Abstract. This project focuses on developing methods to automatically detect and respond to emotions that students experience while developing writing proficiency with computerized environments. We describe progress that we have already made toward detecting affect during writing using keystroke analysis, stable traits, and task appraisals. We were able to distinguish boredom from engagement with an accuracy of 38% above random guessing. Our next goal is to improve the accuracy of our classifier. We plan to accomplish this through an exploration of higher level features such as sequences of character types. Ultimately we hope to develop a system capable of both detecting affect and influencing affect through interventions and experimentally testing this system.

Keywords: affect, keystroke, writing, boredom, engagement.

1 Introduction

Writing is a task that is performed in a variety of daily situations. Writing makes up a large portion of human communication and is increasingly being considered an important 21st century skill [1]. With this increased importance comes a need to not only understand the components of proficient writing, but also a desire to bolster the abilities of students whose writing proficiency may be lacking. This is especially pressing in light of the possibility that the average student possesses inadequate writing skills. A 2011 National Assessment of Educational Progress report declared that only 27% of 12th graders in the U.S. were considered to be "proficient" writers, which is a lower percentage of 12th graders than what was reported in 2007 [2].

In order to improve writing proficiency, it may be beneficial to delve deeper into the psychological processes involved in writing. Until now, most of the research on writing has focused on the cognitive aspects of writing, such as the classic cognitive process theory developed by Flower and Hayes or the more recent functional dynamic approach to the writing process developed by Rijlaarsdam and Bergh [3, 4]. Researchers have also proposed some automated systems to help students develop writing proficiency, such as Summary Street and Writing Pal [5, 6]. To date, however, the emphasis of research and technology is on the cognitive processes involved in writing. This might be insufficient because emerging evidence suggests that affective states continually arise and play an important role in the process of writing [7].

K. Yacef et al. (Eds.): AIED 2013, LNAI 7926, pp. 904–907, 2013.

For example, D'Mello and Mills tracked the emotions of writers in two studies and found that boredom, engagement/flow, anxiety, frustration, and happiness were the most frequent affective states experienced and some of these states were correlated with writing outcomes (quality of a written essay). Given this observation, we hypothesize that a system that can detect and respond to affect could have a significant impact on writing quality by helping writers upregulate positive affective states (e.g., engagement, curiosity) and downregulate negative states (e.g., boredom, anxiety). Developing and validating such an affect-sensitive system is the focus of the proposed project.

2 Previous Research (Affect Detection)

An affect-sensitive writing environment must first detect affect before it can respond to affect. Over the last decade, affect detection has progressed via a number of modalities including facial expression, speech, and physiology (see [8] for a review). Each modality has associated strengths and weaknesses, as well as certain situations in which they are more or less applicable. However, they all require physical sensors and this causes scalability issues. Taking a different approach, we focus on detecting a writer's affective states via keystroke analysis, a technique that is attractive for several reasons. First, collecting data is relatively unobtrusive. All that is needed is installed software to collect keystrokes and a keyboard. Second, keystroke analysis is scalable since every general purpose computer includes a keyboard. Third, the object of writing is to produce text, thereby making keystroke analysis ideal for affect detection in writing contexts. Finally, keystrokes are generated by a number of other tasks so any methods we develop could potentially be used in other domains as well.

Our first project involved detecting affect through keystroke analysis while participants completed an essay writing task. Forty-four participants typed three essays on a computer interface which logged each keystroke along with timing information. Immediately after the writing session, participants watched a video recording of their face and a screen capture video and provided self-judgments of their affective states at 15 second intervals [7].

We calculated 12 features (e.g. verbosity, smallest time difference between keystrokes) for each 15 second self-judgment interval from the keystroke logs and combined them with stable traits such as ACT scores and task appraisals such as subjects' interest in the writing task. We only used data from the boredom, engagement, or neutral, classes as these states comprised the majority of the affect labels (72.9%). We built a large number of models in which we varied classifiers, the affective states being discriminated, data manipulations such as downsampling and standardization, and chosen features. Our results indicated that the models built to distinguish engagement from boredom using task appraisals, stable traits, and both keystroke and timing features performed the best, with a kappa value of 0.374 and an accuracy of 87.0%. The models built to distinguish all three emotions from one another using task appraisals, stable traits, and both keystroke and timing features performed somewhat worse, with a kappa value of 0.171 and an accuracy of 56.3% [9].

3 Future Work

Our research is proceeding along two avenues: improving affect detection and designing affect-sensitive interventions. These are briefly discussed below.

3.1 Improving Affect Detection

Our immediate goal is to improve the classification rate of our automated affect detection models, with an overarching goal of establishing just how effective keystroke analysis can be for determining affect. We have been attempting to do this by analyzing sequences of keystroke events and using these as features. Our aim is to identify sequences of writing, editing, or varying lengths of pauses, and determine if we can use these higher level events as features. We are also working on improving affect detection by examining the broader context of essay composition. As of now, we only analyze each 15 second interval of data in isolation, but a further step that might prove beneficial is to implement features that depend on not only the current interval, but all the previous intervals as well. Another line of work involves exploring the generalizability of our affect detectors by performing cross-validation experiments across different essay topics and student characteristics. A limitation of our previous experiment was the narrow range of emotions that we focused on. During this stage we will expand the scope of our detection to include more affective states.

3.2 Designing Affect-Sensitive Interventions

The next step is to develop interventions to regulate affect. Appropriate interventions would transition a user into an affective state that is most conducive to their current writing task. Interventions will be selected from the literature along with new ones that we wish to try. Examples of interventions would be supplying writing advice or supportive statements when a participant is feeling confused or frustrated. We will then evaluate their ability to influence the affective state of the writer via formative testing. Each writer will perform one of the writing tasks used in the previous studies. Our system will attempt to detect certain affective states based on a running stream of the user's keystrokes, and once a target affective state is detected it will administer one of the interventions. If our system then detects a different affective state and overall writing outcomes improve, the intervention will be deemed successful.

3.3 Experimentally Testing Interventions

The third step is to compare a system that incorporates affect detection and intervention to a system that detects but does not respond to affect. Participants would be randomly assigned to one of two groups. Participants in the first group will complete two writing tasks without attempted intervention, while the second group will complete two writing tasks with a system that *does* attempt interventions. Each essay will be scored and compared to evaluate the effect of interventions on writing proficiency.

4 Conclusions

We have described a research project that aims at creating a scalable system that can detect and intervene to regulate a writer's affective state. We focus on affect detection during writing because it is a convenient domain to explore and because of the significant role that affect has been shown to have on writing. However, it is important to note that our methods may not be restricted to a writing context. Affect detection in other domains that involve tasks which generate keystrokes would conceivably also benefit from our research. It is our hope that our methods can be adopted for use in other domains as well. In addition to the important engineering goal of developing our proposed, another goal is that our research activities influence the cognitive process theory of writing to incorporate affect. If affect does play a part in the writing process, as some evidence shows, then hopefully the results of this research will help inform a new theory of writing, an affective-cognitive process theory of writing.

Acknowledgment. This research was supported by the National Science Foundation (NSF) (ITR 0325428, HCC 0834847, DRL 1235958). Any opinions, findings and conclusions, or recommendations expressed in this paper are those of the authors and do not necessarily reflect the views of the NSF.

References

1. Weigle, S.C.: Assessment of Writing. The Encyclopedia of Applied Linguistics (2012)
2. NAEP. The Nation's Report Card: Writing 2011 (2011)
3. Flower, L.A., Hayes, J.R.: A cognitive process theory of writing. College Composition and Communication 32, 365–387 (1981)
4. Rijlaarsdam, G., Bergh, H.: Writing Process Theory: A Functional Dynamic Approach. In: Macarthur, C.A., Graham, S., Fitzgerald, J. (eds.) Handbook of Writing Research, pp. 41–53. Guildford Press, New York (2006)
5. Wade-Stein, D., Kintsch, E.: Summary Street: Interactive computer support for writing. Cognition and Instruction 22(3), 333–362 (2004)
6. McNamara, D.S., Raine, R., Roscoe, R., Crossley, S., Jackson, G.T., Dai, J., Graesser, A.C.: The Writing-Pal: Natural language algorithms to support intelligent tutoring on writing strategies. In: Applied Natural Language Processing and Content Analysis: Identification, Investigation, and Resolution. IGI Global, Hershey (2012)
7. D'Mello, S., Mills, C.: Emotions during emotional and non-emotional writing (in review)
8. Calvo, R.A., D'Mello, S.K.: Affect detection: An interdisciplinary review of models, methods, and their applications. IEEE Transactions on Affective Computing 1(1), 18–37 (2010), doi:10.1109/T-AFFC.2010.1
9. Bixler, R., D'Mello, S.K.: Detecting Boredom and Engagement During Writing with Keystroke Analysis, Task Appraisals, and Stable Traits. In: Proceedings of the 2013 Annual Conference on Intelligent User Interfaces, IUI 2013 (in press, 2013)

Programming with Your Heart on Your Sleeve: Analyzing the Affective States of Computer Programming Students

Nigel Bosch[1] and Sidney D'Mello[1,2]

Departments of Computer Science[1] and Psychology[2],
University of Notre Dame, Notre Dame, IN 46556
{pbosch1,sdmello}@nd.edu

Abstract. Students learning computer programming must learn difficult concepts via complex problem-solving activities which elicit strong emotional responses. In this research we explore the affective states that occur while learning computer programming, the events that precede them, and the outcomes that are influenced by them. The data collected in current and future research will be used to create an affect-sensitive intelligent tutoring system which will be better able to maximize learning gains in novice computer programmers and improve their perception of computer science via intelligent handling of emotion.

Keywords: computer programming, affect, emotions, ITSs.

1 Introduction

Between the 2000-2001 and 2009-2010 school years, there was a net increase in the number of CS degrees granted, but the percentage of CS degrees compared to all degrees dropped from 9.4% to 7.8% [1]. This drop is surprising given the increasing demand for computer programmers and the growing influence of computer technology in everyday life. Efforts have been made to increase the retention rate of CS students, including tailoring coursework to the special interests of students, providing engaging assignments to improve learning gains, and giving extra opportunities for students to practice programming skills [2]. Researchers have also experimented with using statistical approaches, based on homework submission patterns and similar factors, to identify struggling students who may need special attention to succeed [3].

The low number of students graduating with CS degrees might partially be attributed to the fact that computer programming, which is an essential component of a CS degree, is a difficult skill to acquire because it requires advanced critical thinking, abstract reasoning, and analytical skills. Computer programming is challenging, and often disheartens students due to the impasses that arise. One of the often overlooked factors that contribute to the challenge of programming is the emotional toll that it can inflict on students [4]. Previous work has found that affective states are an important part of conceptual learning and complex problem solving [5] and that computer programming elicits affective states that can be important predictors of performance [6].

K. Yacef et al. (Eds.): AIED 2013, LNAI 7926, pp. 908–911, 2013.

Improved computer programming education that takes into account affective states and how they influence the learning experience for students could improve the enrollment, retention, and degree production of university computer science and engineering programs. Creating an affect-sensitive ITS to teach novices the basics of computer programming could potentially create a more positive and effective learning experience. This is the major goal of the proposed research project.

2 Previous Research

Over two decades ago, researchers were already exploring the factors that contribute to becoming a good computer programmer and good programming education [7]. Although a number of computerized learning environments to teach programming have emerged, they do not react intelligently in real-time to changes in student affect and do not adjust the material or instruction accordingly.

Recent research has indicated that frustration can be effectively predicted from the code compilation behavior of programming students [8], while a wide variety of sensors and techniques have been used to detect emotion in other contexts [9]. These affect detection techniques can be used to dynamically adjust feedback and instruction based on sensed affective states of computer programming students.

We have done some preliminary work to investigate affective states experienced by novice students while learning to program in the Python language [10]. A computerized learning environment delivered instructional material to 29 students with no prior programming exposure. The system provided them with a series of exercises designed to teach them the fundamentals of computer programming and to test what they had learned. We used a retrospective affect judgment protocol, in which students viewed videos of their face and on-screen interaction and provided affective judgments at approximately 100 points throughout a learning session. Flow/engagement, confusion/uncertainty, frustration, and boredom were the dominant affective states of students when they were not in the neutral state. These four states accounted for 71%, neutral 15%, while other affective states (curiosity, happiness, anxiety, surprise, anger, disgust, fear, and sadness) accounted for a mere 14% of the affect reports. We found that confusion/uncertainty and boredom had a negative impact on performance while flow/engagement had a positive effect. This suggests that confusion/uncertainty and boredom are negative states that an affect-sensitive ITS can focus on regulating.

We also explored some of the effects that instructional materials have on learning. Hints were available to students during problem-solving exercises, to help resolve mental impasses that they were likely to encounter. When using hints, participants did not experience significantly different levels of flow/engagement, but they did experience less boredom, frustration, and confusion/uncertainty.

3 Future Research Plans

To advance this research, we intend to design and implement an ITS that is capable of adapting intelligently to the affective state of novice students as they learn computer programming. This project will consist of three major parts: data collection and analysis, affect detection, and affect responding.

3.1 Data Collection and Analysis

The previous research we have conducted to monitor the affective states of novice programmers will be augmented with additional data collection with a larger sample of students to better explore the links between affective states and programmer actions. Additionally, we will look at how different types of system actions (e.g. feedback, hints, etc.) correlate with affect and performance. We will also explore the time spent on various components of the learning task (reading, typing, testing, off-task behavior, etc.) via refinements to our computerized learning environment to discern what relationships those components have on affective states and performance. The data collected will be analyzed similarly to our previous research and also with Hidden Markov Models (HMMs) to uncover latent (hidden) factors that give rise to time series consisting of student actions, system responses, and student affect.

3.2 Affect Detection

We will use machine learning techniques to build affect detectors that diagnose what affective states will arise based on contextual factors (e.g., problem difficulty), student actions (e.g., code executions, edits), and system responses (e.g., syntax errors, negative feedback). In addition, videos of the faces of students will be analyzed with facial feature detection computer vision algorithms. These facial features will be added as features to enhance the power of the affect detectors. Graphical models that explore the temporal dependencies among features and labels, such as conditional random fields, will also be investigated over more standard supervised learning techniques.

3.3 Affect Responding

We will create an ITS specifically tailored to the emotional needs of novice computer programming students by first integrating the aforementioned affect detectors in the computerized environment. The ITS will then be able to use this information to adjust the instructional material and feedback for students to maintain an emotional state better suited to learning, and to improve students' perceptions of the introductory programming experience. The affect-sensitive ITS will intervene to steer students back toward more productive affective states using interventions at crucial moments when a student is struggling with material but has not yet given up or disengaged. For example, after a student runs their code and encounters an error, it might be useful to provide some encouraging feedback and thus ameliorate affect. Finally, we will compare performance of students with and without affect-sensitive enhancements in the learning environment to determine the efficacy of affect sensitivity in this domain.

4 Conclusion

Computer science can be furthered in many ways through better education. ITS-based learning helps to alleviate problems of availability and cost, and continues to become more technologically advanced as the scientific method is applied to improving techniques. By developing an affect-sensitive computer programming ITS, we hope to improve the learning gains of novice computer programming students and better prepare them for programming education opportunities in the future while simultaneously deepening our understanding of the role of affect in learning.

Acknowledgment. This research was supported by the National Science Foundation (NSF) (ITR 0325428, HCC 0834847, DRL 1235958). Any opinions, findings and conclusions, or recommendations expressed in this paper are those of the authors and do not necessarily reflect the views of the NSF.

References

1. Snyder, T.D., Dillow, S.A.: Digest of Education Statistics 2011 (2012), http://nces.ed.gov/pubs2012/2012001_0.pdf
2. DeClue, T., Kimball, J., Lu, B., Cain, J.: Five focused strategies for increasing retention in Computer Science 1. Journal of Computing Sciences in Colleges 26, 252–258 (2011)
3. Tabanao, E.S., Rodrigo, M.M.T., Jadud, M.C.: Predicting at-risk novice Java programmers through the analysis of online protocols. In: Proceedings of the Seventh International Workshop on Computing Education Research, pp. 85–92. ACM, New York (2011)
4. Kinnunen, P., Simon, B.: Experiencing programming assignments in CS1: the emotional toll. In: Proceedings of the Sixth International Workshop on Computing Education Research, pp. 77–86. ACM, New York (2010)
5. Pekrun, R., Stephens, E.J.: Academic emotions. In: Harris, K.R., Graham, S., Urdan, T., Graham, S., Royer, J.M., Zeidner, M. (eds.) APA Educational Psychology Handbook. Individual differences and cultural and contextual factors, vol. 2, pp. 3–31. American Psychological Association, Washington, DC (2012)
6. Rodrigo, M.M.T., Baker, R.S., Jadud, M.C., Amarra, A.C.M., Dy, T., Espejo-Lahoz, M.B.V., Lim, S.A.L., Pascua, S.A.M.S., Sugay, J.O., Tabanao, E.S.: Affective and behavioral predictors of novice programmer achievement. SIGCSE Bull. 41, 156–160 (2009)
7. Shute, V.J., Kyllonen, P.C.: Modeling Individual Differences in Programming Skill Acquisition (1990)
8. Rodrigo, M.M.T., Baker, R.S.J.D.: Coarse-grained detection of student frustration in an introductory programming course. In: Proceedings of the Fifth International Workshop on Computing Education Research, pp. 75–80. ACM, New York (2009)
9. Calvo, R.A., D'Mello, S.: Affect Detection: An Interdisciplinary Review of Models, Methods, and Their Applications. IEEE Transactions on Affective Computing 1, 18–37 (2010)
10. Bosch, N., D'Mello, S., Mills, C.: What Emotions Do Novices Experience During their First Computer Programming Learning Session? (in review)

Supporting Lifelong Learning: Recommending Personalized Sources of Assistance to Graduate Students

David Edgar K. Lelei

ARIES Laboratory, Department of Computer Science, University of Saskatchewan
davidedgar.lelei@usask.ca

Abstract. Access to and effective use of relevant information and continuously learning is an integral part of graduate students' daily lives. However, when searching for learning materials, students face challenges selecting relevant information because of the tremendous increase of learning resources over the last few years. This research proposes a novel methodology that aids graduate students to find appropriate sources of information in their lifelong learning endeavors by using people-to-people recommender system (RS) techniques. The people-to-people RS aims to help graduate students by suggesting persons (peers/experts) to contact about the problems they are facing when the problems are not easily identifiable from static fact sheets (a.k.a, question and answer or frequently asked questions).

Keywords: Lifelong learning, Recommender systems, Graduate students.

1 Introduction

Lifelong Learning (LLL) refers to systematic and purposeful learning throughout a person's life involving formal (schools) and informal (work, recreation, leisure, social relations, family life) domains [1]. Though, the idea of LLL is not new, it is among the new themes of AIED research [2]. LLL as a concept has gone through a lot of changes over the years, including continuing education, adult learning, and higher education at both the undergraduate and graduate levels [3].

Graduate students generally experience challenges that go beyond their course work [4]. To address such challenges, students often seek information by asking people around them or searching online [5]. Even though advances in technology, especially the Web, enable universal and parallel accessibility to information, there are several challenges including information overload [6]. In addition, there are challenges whose solutions cannot be found online and would be better served by peers or expert help [7], such as answering situational questions or personal questions.

In an attempt to solve some of these learning challenges, researchers have developed and deployed various technological approaches. ITSs that support learning by providing environments for students to find help from others in the same university course [8], are used. Similarly, e-portfolios are employed to support and organize learning in schools and specifically LLL in a university context [9]. Furthermore, recommender systems have also been proposed in education [10].

K. Yacef et al. (Eds.): AIED 2013, LNAI 7926, pp. 912–915, 2013.

Recommender systems enable students to make informed decisions on what courses to take [11], help learners organize and structure their curriculum [12], recommend domain-based learning objects [13] and provide research papers to graduate students [6]. People-to-people RSs are a class of recommender technology whose focus is on recommending people to each other. Their application domains include areas where social networks and social matching are important, such as in education (e.g., I-Help, [7]), online dating, and online job seeking. When a person is expected to provide help as well as receive help, such RSs are called reciprocal RSs [14].

While there is much research that deploys recommender systems approaches to help students with their challenges such as [6, 11–15], most of this research focuses on supporting courses or learning objects recommendation. None considers recommendation in a dynamic context, such as dealing with lifelong learners' daily challenges. To address this gap, this research seeks to explore how people-to-people RS techniques can assist in finding and suggesting an expert or peer as a source of help to a lifelong learner facing challenges, in particular to a graduate student over the course of his or her graduate program. Like Bull et al. [15] the focus is on identifying factors that increase the efficacy of good recommendations. This project extends their research from a course context to a dynamic domain that extends to the entire life of graduate students.

2 Description of Our Approach

The RS will seek to predict and recommend the best person (helper) based on the characteristics of both the helper and the student. To meet this goal, the project can be broken into the four stages depicted by Figure 1 and described below:

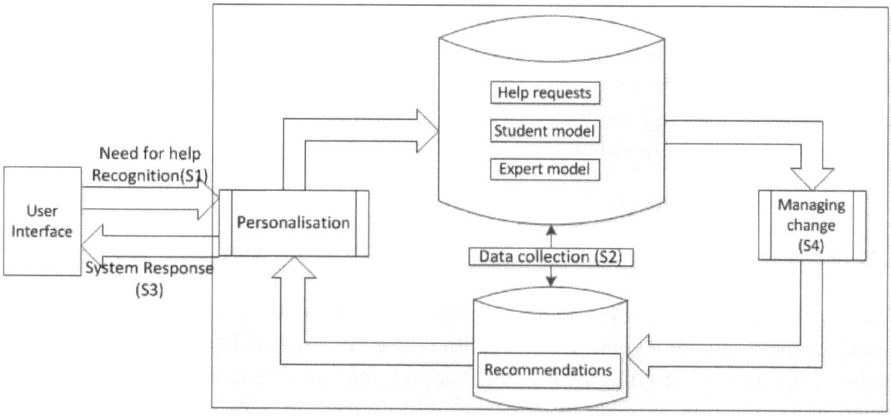

Fig. 1. Recommendation stages

S1: Recognizing the need for help. How can the system diagnose and recognise a student's need for help?

In the first stage, the system will diagnose a student's need for help by considering student information provided in explicit and implicit ways. Explicitly, a student can notify the system that he/she is in need of help by pressing a '*helpme*' button. The system then provides the student with a predefined list of challenges from which he/she can choose one. Implicitly, students' challenges can be inferred by monitoring their activities on the system and/or tracking their stated plans. An initial student model will be created based on the explicit or implicit request for help.

S2: Data Collection. What student, expert, and situational characteristics need to be collected, in order to, contextualize the need for help? How can such data be collected in the graduate studies context?

The second stage is about placing the request for help perceived from S1 into a proper context. This can be achieved by finding ways to improve the student model and problem context. Possible information sources include requesting the student to enter explicit initial information. Furthermore, information can be collected by considering the student's browsing behaviour, the time the student is seeking help, and referring to previous help requests/needs made by the same student and/or others in similar circumstances.

S3: System Response. What techniques can be used to find and suggest an appropriate expert or peer to deal with the student's issues? What factors need to be given higher consideration?

The third stage involves determining how the RS will respond to a request for help in accordance with the challenge facing the student. Two possibilities are considered: first, recommend a person straight away, or second, delay the recommendation and let the student wait. In order to build a model for finding a good helper, many factors will be considered. Such factors include availability, willingness, knowledge, social skill, compatibility, time constraints on getting an answer, knowing who seems to have helped resolve similar issues earlier, and considering later availability of a really good helper. Not every challenge is expected to need real time response, but if the help is needed in real time, and the "best" person is not currently available, then the system would have to find the next best person.

S4: Managing Change. How can the collected data in S2 be managed so that the system can update its knowledge? How can the profiles of the people in the system be maintained to keep up with the dynamic nature of lifelong learning challenges?

The fourth stage will involve managing the resulting models and data. A prominent aspect of the graduate student LLL domain is that of change. The models will have to evolve: first year grad students become second year grad students; people who have gotten help may now be able to dispense help on the same topic; courses and milestones have been achieved; and so on. It will be necessary track everybody who helped, what the help need was, and how the help was received by the person needing help (by asking for feedback from each participant after a help session). Over time, a knowledge base of helpers who would be useful for particular help needs is build.

3 Current Work and Future Research Plans

This research plan is a preliminary outline of the requirements for people-to-people RS focused on supporting graduate students. Current research work is focused on identifying the people-to-people RS system requirements. Next, a set of educational discussion forum datasets will be examined to find out if there are any relationships between older challenges and newer challenges. Furthermore, the dataset will be examined to determine the relationship between availability, time taken to respond, and individual characteristics of the helper and the person seeking help. The result of this analysis is expected to address the concerns at all stages of the RS, but especially to determine if a student's need for help can be implicitly identified.

References

1. Cropley, A.J.: Some Guidelines for the Reform of School Curricula in the Perspective of Lifelong Education. IROE 24, 21–33 (1978)
2. Underwood, J., Luckin, R.: Themes and Trends in AIED Research, 2000 to 2010. A report for the UK's TLRP Technology Enhanced Learning – AIED Theme (2011)
3. Jarvis, P.: Global Trends in Lifelong Learning and the Response of the Universities. Comparative Education 35, 249–257 (2010)
4. Darisi, T., Davidson, V.J., Korabik, K., Desmarais, S.: Commitment to Graduate Studies and Careers in Science and Engineering: Examining Women's and Men's Experiences. IJGST 2, 48–64 (2010)
5. George, C., Bright, A., Hurlbert, T.: Scholarly Use of Information: Graduate Students' Information Seeking Behaviour. Information Research 11, 1–19 (2006)
6. Tang, T.Y., McCalla, G.: A Multidimensional Paper Recommender: Experiments and Evaluations. IEEE Internet Computing 13, 34–41 (2009)
7. Greer, J.E., McCalla, G.I., Cooke, J., Collins, J., Kumar, V., Bishop, A., Vassileva, J.: The Intelligent Helpdesk: Supporting Peer-Help in a University Course. In: Goettl, B.P., Halff, H.M., Redfield, C.L., Shute, V.J. (eds.) ITS 1998. LNCS, vol. 1452, pp. 494–503. Springer, Heidelberg (1998)
8. Bull, S., Greer, J., McCalla, G., Kettel, L.: Help-Seeking in an Asynchronous Help Forum. In: AIED (2001)
9. Bozhko, Y., Heinrich, E.: Enhancing Eportfolio Systems to Better Support Lifelong Learning in Universities: Students' Perspective. In: EDMEDIA, pp. 1912–1917 (2011)
10. Manouselis, N., Drachsler, H., Vuorikari, R., Hummel, H.: Recommender Systems in Technology Enhanced Learning. In: RS Handbook, pp. 387–415 (2011)
11. Kolowich, S.: Recommended for You (2012), `http://www.insidehighered.com/News/2012/03/16/University-Builds-Course-Recommendation-Engine-Steer-Students-Toward-Completion`
12. Drachsler, H., Hummel, H.G.K., Koper, R.: Recommendations for Learners are Different: Applying Memory-Based Recommender System Techniques to Lifelong Learning. In: SIRTEL, pp. 18–26 (2007)
13. Santos, O.C., Boticario, J.G.: TORMES Methodology to Elicit Educational Oriented Recommendations. In: Biswas, G., Bull, S., Kay, J., Mitrovic, A. (eds.) AIED 2011. LNCS, vol. 6738, pp. 541–543. Springer, Heidelberg (2011)
14. Pizzato, L., Rej, T., Akehurst, J., Koprinska, I., Yacef, K., Kay, J.: Recommending People to People: The Nature of Reciprocal Recommenders with a Case Study in Online Dating. In: User Modeling And User-Adapted Interaction, pp. 1–42 (2012)
15. Bull, S., Greer, J., McCalla, G.: The Caring Personal Agent. IJAIED 13, 21–34 (2003)

Conceptual Scaffolding to Check One's Procedures

Eliane Stampfer and Kenneth R. Koedinger

Human Computer Interaction Institute, 5000 Forbes Ave
Pittsburgh, PA, 15213 USA
{stampfer,krk}@cs.cmu.edu

Abstract. Our tutoring system for fraction addition uses dynamic pictorial representations that reflect student-inputted quantities. However, students had difficulty interpreting the pictorial feedback. Surprisingly, we found that including symbolic numbers with the pictures decreased performance. We hypothesize that students' difficulty may stem from insufficient domain knowledge, or insufficient metacognitive skills to use conceptual knowledge to check their work.

Keywords: graphical representation; fraction addition; symbolic fractions.

One goal of education is to foster learning with deep understanding, and one demonstration of this understanding is to check the outcome of a procedure against conceptual knowledge. For example, while tempting to say 3/4 + 1/7 = 4/11, conceptual reasoning reveals the fallacy: 3/4 is greater than half while 4/11 is smaller. Pictorial representations of each fraction may speed these comparisons. Prior work found benefits for conceptually-based pictorial feedback above right/wrong immediate feedback for college students learning algebra [1]. However, [3] found that while 6th grader's math performance improved with pictorial scaffolds, 4th grader's performance decreased, likely because the younger students were confused by the representations. It appears that conceptual scaffolds have great potential but are not uniformly useful.

Our tutor uses *grounded feedback*: student inputs are in the to-be-learned representation, while a linked representation reflects students' inputs in a more concrete form. In our tutor, students input numeric symbols and the tutor displays corresponding fraction bars (see fig. 1). Grounded feedback allows students to see the consequences of their errors and thus may promote students' evaluation of their own work (e.g., a student may guess that 3/6 + 2/6 = 5/12, but the fraction bars show 5/12 is too small). The link direction ensures that students engage with the more difficult to-be-learned representation instead of directly manipulating the already-understood feedback representation.

Our prior work found learning gains for the grounded feedback tutor, but results also indicate that students found the feedback unclear. Participants in a think-aloud study used the fraction bar feedback to fix their own mistakes [5]. Further, a classroom study found learning gains [6]. However, the 90 5th grade students using the tutor in that study did not seem to use the fraction bars to check their work - they often clicked the "done" button when the fraction bars did not line up [6]. The next

K. Yacef et al. (Eds.): AIED 2013, LNAI 7926, pp. 916–919, 2013.

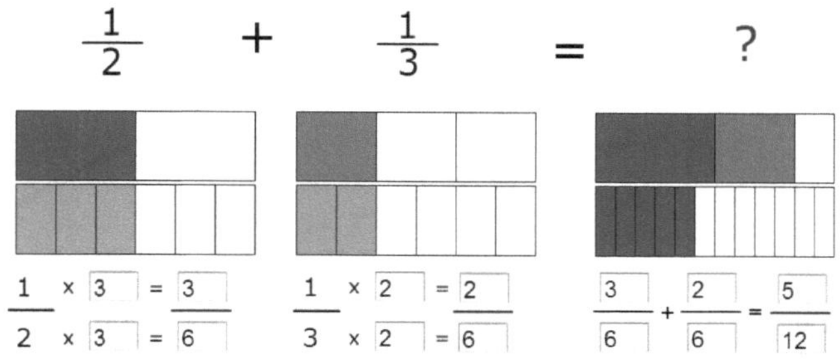

Fig. 1. Fraction Tutor. Top row of fractions and red and green fraction bars are given, second row of bars dynamically shows students' inputs as they are typed in boxes at the bottom.

year, a paper test with 5th graders assessed the difficulty of fraction addition and fraction equivalence questions in four formats: three included fraction bars, and one was a numbers-only control (equivalence items asked if one fraction was greater than, equivalent to, or smaller than another; addition examples in fig. 2) [7]. For both question types, students performed better with the bars than with numbers alone. However, while all three fraction-bar formats were equally helpful for fraction equivalence, they were significantly different from each other for fraction addition. As the salience of the numbers increased, scores decreased (fig. 3). Students' success with the fraction equivalence items and with the pictures-only addition items indicates proficiency at using the fraction bars to determine if two quantities are equal. Why didn't students use that skill for the other addition items? The incorrect addition items all used the common mistake of adding both numerators and both denominators. Perhaps the tempting misconception overrode the fraction bars' conceptual hint. Or, maybe students misunderstood the meaning of the equals sign and then considered the conceptual hint to be irrelevant. [2] found that 6th-8th grade students looking at a problem such as 3 + 4 = 7 were more likely to interpret the equals sign to mean 'write answer here' than 'both sides are equivalent.' Perhaps on the addition questions with numbers students interpreted the equals sign to mean 'put the answer here' instead of 'the two sides are equal'. In that case the fraction bars showing a sum that was not equal to the two addends would not alert the student that the answer was wrong.

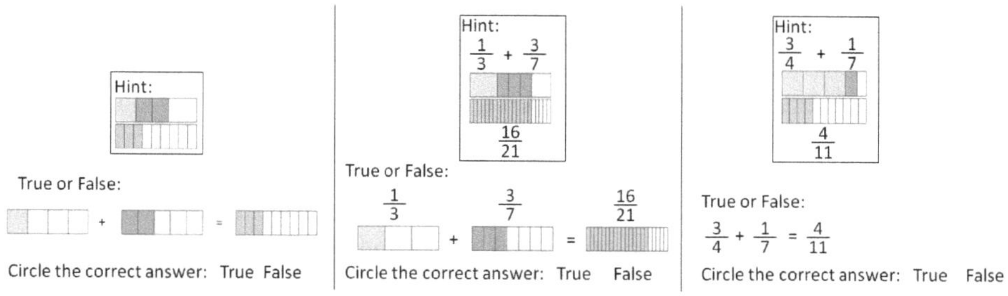

Fig. 2. Addition (from left): Pictures Only, Pictures & Numbers, Half Pictures & Numbers

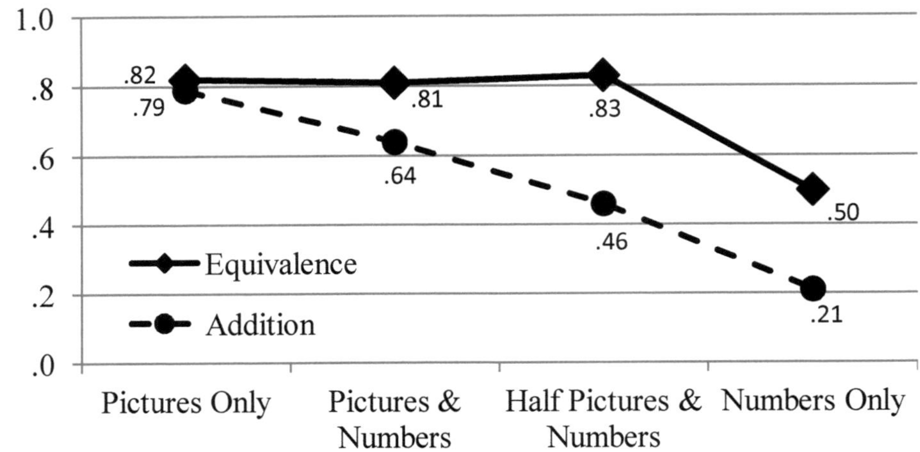

Fig. 3. Mean Scores (max. 1) on Fraction Equivalence and Addition Items by Scaffold Type

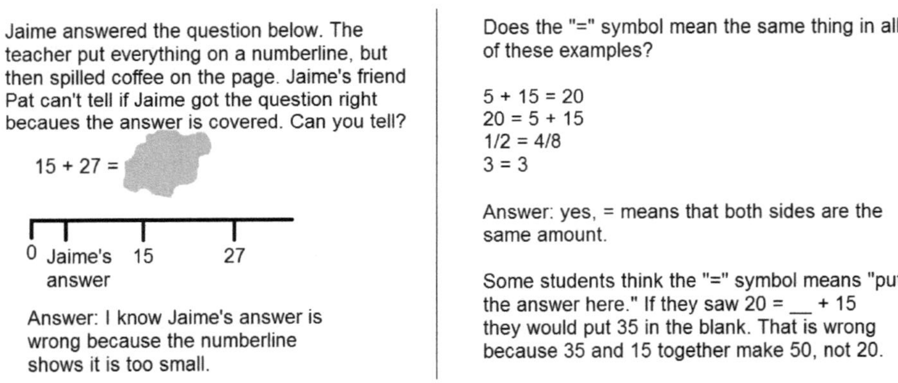

Fig. 4. Proposed Metacognitive Instruction (left) and Domain-specific Instruction (right)

This work leads to questions about the role of procedural and conceptual knowledge in problem solving. The premise of grounded feedback is that students can use their conceptual knowledge to identify errors that result from faulty procedures. However, doing that requires domain-specific skill to interpret the conceptual hint, and metacognitive skill to check one's work and fix errors before moving on. Our next study will attempt to find out if tutoring on those skills improves performance and learning with the grounded feedback tutor.

We propose a 2x2 study on grounded feedback with 1) metacognitive instruction (checking one's work with conceptual aids) and 2) domain-specific instruction (meaning of the equals sign). Figure 4 shows possible examples. The metacognitive instruction demonstrates using a conceptual aid, but does not explain why a number smaller than 15 cannot be the sum of 15+27. The domain-specific instruction explains the meaning of the equals sign, but does not demonstrate conceptual ways to check for inequalities. This experiment will determine if students need more domain-specific knowledge or more metacognitive knowledge (or both) to benefit more from the grounded feedback.

References

1. Nathan, M.J.: Knowledge and Situational Feedback in a Learning Environment for Algebra Story Problem Solving. Interactive Learning Environments 5, 135–159 (1998)
2. McNeil, N.M., Grandau, L., Knuth, E.J., Alibali, M.W., Stephens, A.C., Hattikudur, S., Krill, D.E.: Middle-School Students' Understanding of the Equal Sign: The Books They Read Can't Help. Cognition and Instruction 24(3), 367–385 (2006)
3. Rittle-Johnson, B., Koedinger, K.: Using cognitive models to guide instructional design: The case of fraction division. In: Moore, J., Stenning, K. (eds.) Proceedings of the 23rd Annual Conference of the Cognitive Science Society, pp. 857–862. Erlbaum, Mahwah (2001)
4. Stampfer, E., Long, Y., Aleven, V., Koedinger, K.R.: Eliciting Intelligent Novice Behaviors with Grounded Feedback in a Fraction Addition Tutor. In: Biswas, G., Bull, S., Kay, J., Mitrovic, A. (eds.) Proceedings of the 15th International Conference of Artificial Intelligence in Education, pp. 560–562. International AIED Society, Auckland (2011)
5. Stampfer, E., Koedinger, K.R.: Tradeoffs between Immediate and Future Learning. Presented at the European Association for Research on Learning and Instruction Special Interest Groups 6&7 Conference, Bari, Italy (2012)
6. Stampfer, E., Koedinger, K.R.: When seeing isn't believing: Influences of prior conceptions and misconceptions. Accepted to the 35th Meeting of the Cognitive Science Society (2013)

A Computational Thinking Approach to Learning Middle School Science

Satabdi Basu and Gautam Biswas

Institute of Software Integrated Systems, Vanderbilt University, Nashville, TN, U.S.A.
{satabdi.basu,gautam.biswas}@vanderbilt.edu

Abstract. Computational Thinking (CT) defines a domain-general, analytic approach to problem solving, combining computer science concepts with practices central to modeling and reasoning in STEM (Science, Technology, Engineering and Mathematics) domains. In our research, we exploit this synergy to develop CTSiM (Computational Thinking in Simulation and Modeling) - a cross-domain, visual programming and agent based, scaffolded environment for learning CT and science concepts simultaneously. CTSiM allows students to conceptualize and build computational models of scientific phenomena, execute the models as simulations, conduct experiments to verify the simulation behaviors against 'expert behavior', and use the models to solve real world problems.

Keywords: Computational Thinking, Science education, Visual Programming, Agent-based modeling and simulation, Learning by design, Scaffolding.

1 Introduction

Computational Thinking (CT) provides a domain-general approach to modeling phenomena, solving problems, and designing systems by drawing on core computer science concepts [9]. It supports practices like abstraction, decomposition, recursion, simulation, and verification, several of which are also central to the development of STEM expertise [5]. For example, formally representing scientific laws and phenomena resembles the object-oriented programming concepts of encapsulation, abstraction, and generalization. Conversely, the biological concepts of taxonomy and inheritance inspire the class inheritance concepts in CT. Research has also shown that novice misconceptions have similar patterns in science, math, and programming domains: they have both domain-specific and domain general roots (e.g., challenging concepts, and difficulties pertaining to conducting inquiry and problem solving) [6].

Exploiting the assumption that CT concepts are learnt best when anchored in real world problem contexts and that CT concepts parallel important aspects of science learning, several researchers have focused on leveraging the synergies between CT and scientific expertise [2,3,6]. Though research suggests that programming and computational modeling can serve as effective vehicles for learning challenging STEM concepts [2,3], we still know of no CT-based environments for science education that have been integrated into classrooms in any significant way.

K. Yacef et al. (Eds.): AIED 2013, LNAI 7926, pp. 920–923, 2013.

This motivates our research, which aims to develop a computer-based learning environment for synergistic teaching of CT and science concepts in middle school classrooms supported by an adaptive scaffolding framework. Developing such an environment involves several challenges including (1) selecting a pedagogical approach supporting science learning as well as CT practices, (2) designing an activity sequence progressing from conceptualization of a phenomena to problem-solving using the acquired knowledge, (3) designing an interface where the functionality of the environment is decomposed into manageable modules, (4) choosing a programming paradigm that makes the CT principles explicit without the challenges of learning a programming language syntax, (5) making explicit the computational commonalities across different science domains, and (6) diagnosing problems faced by students at varying levels of understanding and developing supporting tools and scaffolds to help them learn CT and science concepts simultaneously. The following sections describe our approach to addressing these challenges by developing the CTSiM (Computational Thinking in Simulation and Modeling) environment.

2 Research Methodology

In keeping with the core epistemic and representational scientific practice of 'modeling' [4], and a core CT practice of developing models and simulations of problems [9], our research adopts a *learning-by-design* pedagogy, as described below.

CTSiM is decomposed into multiple worlds [1,8] to make the learning process more manageable. In the *Conceptual Modeling (CM) World*, students develop initial abstractions of the phenomena being studied by identifying the types of agents involved, their properties and behaviors, and specifying how the properties and behaviors are related. We choose an agent-based paradigm since it is believed to leverage students' pre-instructional intuitions, and help learn emergent phenomena in science domains. In the *Construction (C) World*, students build executable computational models using a visual programming language, thus reducing students' challenges in learning programming language syntax. Some visual primitives are domain-specific, while others related to CT principles (conditionals, loops, operators) can be reused across domains. Each visual primitive is defined in terms of one or more domain-independent computational primitives, which is translated to NetLogo code to produce multi-agent simulations, which students visualize in the *Enactment (E) world*. Then, students design experiments in the *Envisionment (V) World* to compare their model behaviors with that of an 'expert' model, and demonstrate their understanding in the *Problem-solving (PS) World* by using their models to predict, explain and solve real-world problems.

For supporting students' tasks in CTSiM, various tools have been and will continue to be developed. These include (a) *a set of searchable hypermedia resources* with text, diagrams, videos, and simulations acting as a domain knowledge source for the phenomena being studied, (b) *a model-tracing tool* in the E-World that enables tracing the code command-by-command with the simulation to help students correlate their models with the resultant simulations, (c) *a code commenting-out tool* that enables students to test their code in parts, and (d) *a guided dynamic workflow* in the

V-World to help students design structured experiments, explicitly specify their goals, and use the comparison results effectively to verify and refine their models. The Resources and the Workflow can be used with any modeling task, while the other tools are specific to the agent-based computational modeling paradigm we employ.

In addition to providing these tools, open-ended systems like CTSiM need to provide scaffolding to help learners who may not be proficient in using the systems' tools or regulating their own learning. *Adaptive scaffolding* refers to actions taken by the learning environment, based on its interactions with the learner, with the intention to support the learner in completing a task [7]. However, providing adaptive scaffolds is challenging. It requires systematically diagnosing learners' needs by interpreting how learners at varying levels of understanding approach their tasks, and adapting dynamically to the learners' states. While several modeling, simulation, and problem-solving environments have been developed for science domains, few provide adaptive scaffolding derived from systematic interpretations of the learners' approach to the learning task. In CTSiM, we systematically analyzed the challenges faced by different students and categorized them broadly into modeling, programming, domain knowledge and agent-based thinking challenges [1]. Accordingly, adaptive scaffolding in CTSiM will focus on online detection of these challenges along with providing supporting strategies for the broad categories of challenges identified.

3 Expected Contributions of this Research

Given the dearth of learning environments that exploit the synergy between CT and science education, our research will significantly contribute to the AIED community. In particular, its contributions will include: (1) the development of a learning environment that fosters the development of model building and scientific reasoning on the one hand, and algorithm design and verification on the other; (2) the development of a multi-level Conceptual Modeling interface that makes explicit students' conceptions about the model structure; (3) the seamless integration of a visual programming and animation tool into a multi-agent modeling and simulation environment that improves the understanding of science topics in middle school classrooms; (4) the development of a limited set of domain-independent computational primitives such that all visual primitives can be defined in terms of one or more of them; (5) the development and testing of a guided dynamic workflow to help students experiment systematically, set goals for themselves, record observations, draw conclusions based on the observations, and monitor their own progress; (6) a systematic analysis and categorization of challenges students face while working with a CT based learning environment for science; and (7) the development and testing of an adaptive scaffolding framework based on detecting and overcoming the identified challenges.

4 Next Steps and Expected Results

In our first iteration of designing and implementing CTSiM, only the C, E, and V worlds were developed along with two curricular units for kinematics and ecology (these units can be tried out at http://www.teachableagents.org/downloadctsim.php). A preliminary research study conducted in 6th grade classrooms showed significant pre-post test learning gains in science, while demonstrating the need for scaffolds and supporting tools [1,8]. The study also showed that the verbal scaffolds provided were useful and helped reduce the average number of challenges over time and increase the learning gains. The next steps of our research will include: (1) incorporating more support through the CM and PS worlds, the 4 tools described in Section 2, and an adaptive scaffolding framework using a mixed-initiative dialogue between the students and a pedagogical agent; (2) developing more curricular units and making the computational commonalities across domains more explicit; (3) conducting experiments with and without the different tools and scaffolds to demonstrate their individual effects; and (4) conducting experiments to show learning gains for both science and CT concepts, transfer of CT skills across domains, and increased abilities to solve real world problems, construct their abstractions and model them algorithmically.

Acknowledgements. This work was supported by the NSF (NSF Cyber-learning grant #1237350).

References

1. Basu, S., Dickes, A., Kinnebrew, J.S., Sengupta, P., Biswas, G.: CTSiM: A Computational Thinking Environment for Learning Science through Simulation and Modeling. In: Proceedings of the 5th International Conference on Computer Supported Education, Aachen, Germany, pp. 369–378 (2013)
2. Guzdial, M.: Software-realized scaffolding to facilitate programming for science learning. Interactive Learning Environments 4(1), 1–44 (1995)
3. Hambrusch, S., Hoffmann, C., Korb, J.T., Haugan, M., Hosking, A.L.: A multidisciplinary approach towards computational thinking for science majors. In: Proceedings of the 40th ACM Technical Symposium on Computer Science Education (SIGCSE 2009), pp. 183–187. ACM, New York (2009)
4. Lehrer, R., Schauble, L.: Cultivating model-based reasoning in science education. In: Sawyer, R.K. (ed.) The Cambridge Handbook of the Learning Sciences, pp. 371–388. Cambridge University Press, New York (2006)
5. National Research Council, A framework for K-12 Science Education: Practices, Crosscutting Concepts, and Core Ideas. The National Academies Press, Washington, DC (2011)
6. Perkins, D.N., Simmons, R.: Patterns of misunderstanding: An integrative model for science, math, and programming. Review of Educational Research 58(3), 303–326 (1988)
7. Puntambekar, S., Hübscher, R.: Tools for scaffolding students in a complex learning environment: What have we gained and what have we missed? Educational Psychologist 40, 1–12 (2005)
8. Sengupta, P., Kinnebrew, J.S., Basu, S., Biswas, G., Clark, D.: Integrating Computational Thinking with K-12 Science Education Using Agent-based Computation: A Theoretical Framework. Education and Information Technologies 18(2), 351–380 (2013)
9. Wing, J.M.: Computational Thinking: What and Why? Link Magazine (2010)

Modes and Mechanisms of Game-Like Interventions in Computer Tutors

Dovan Rai

Department of Computer Science, Worcester Polytechnic Institute
dovan@wpi.edu

Abstract. Educational games intend to make learning more enjoyable, but potentially compromise learning by consuming both instructional time and student cognitive resources. Therefore, instead of creating an educational game, we are exploring different ways of integrating game-like elements in a computer tutor. We are experimenting with cognitive, metacognitive and affective modes of such game-like interventions. We are also exploring causal mechanisms of how different interventions lead to the desired learning outcomes.

1 Motivation

Games can not only enhance the affective aspects of learning, but also hold the potential to improve cognitive outcomes of learning. But despite this intuitive appeal of educational games, there is insufficient empirical evidence on the effectiveness of educational games [2]. Direct comparisons between computer tutors and educational games have found the tutors to be more effective [3,4]. However, computer tutors have had difficulties in maintaining students' interest for long periods of time, which limits their ability to generate learning in the long-term. Given the complementary benefits of games and tutors, there has been considerable effort to combine these two fields. However, fulfilling this vision is a challenge as it is difficult to effectively integrate educational content with game attributes, and to align sometimes conflicting cognitive and affective outcomes. For example, extraneous details in games can distract and overwhelm students by overloading their working memory [5]. Due to these limitations, there is a search for more efficient and effective alternatives to educational games. Researchers in computer tutors are trying to make tutors more fun by integrating game elements in tutors [3,4] and there have been efforts to study individual game attributes [6].

2 Research Questions

RQ1: What is the range of activities for game-like interventions? Game-like interventions (GLIs) can be used to teach content, act as affective hooks to engage students, or to represent student performance in a fun way. We have analyzed the

K. Yacef et al. (Eds.): AIED 2013, LNAI 7926, pp. 924–927, 2013.

different ways in which we can use GLIs and we have come up with three broad categories: cognitive, metacognitive and affective.

Cognitive Mode of Game-Like Intervention: Though the primary connotation of games is "fun," games also have cognitive affordances, which can make them effective teaching tools. We will work to identify game elements that carry these affordances, but avoid adding cognitive overload. For example, in *Monkey's Revenge* [7], a game-like math tutor, we use immediate visual feedback, collecting and building. Our approach is using game-like elements in a very cautious and minimalist way. For example: we want to exploit learning benefit of narrative by creating situated learning context but would not like the narrative to be too elaborate as that would distract learners.

Meta-Cognitive Mode of Game-Like Intervention: Unlike using GLIs to teach learning content, we are using this mode to communicate metacognitive information with learners. We created 'Student Progress Page' for students of *Wayang Outpost*, an intelligent math tutor. This page is a summary of student performance, effort and progress in different math skills along with strategic suggestions for learning. We are using game elements such as progress bars to demonstrate skill mastery. Similarly, students are given a plant for each math skill, as a representation for their math knowledge, which grows, give flowers and fruits and withers depending upon student's effort in the skill. We are not claiming to teach metacognitive skill, but we are trying to present metacognitive content in more intuitive way that triggers student to take more productive actions.

Affective Mode of Game-Like Intervention: In this mode, we are trying to use games solely to enhance affect while leaving the computer tutor as responsible for teaching. Our hypothesis is that enhanced student affect will result in more usage of tutor and, consequently, more learning. We make use of two strategies: affective repair and affective hook. With affective repair, when students show negative affective behavior such as boredom and frustration in computer tutor, they are given game-like learning activities. We expect the students to have more positive affective state when they go back to the tutor. To investigate the benefits of an affective hook, we are creating a game, *Mosaic*, where player solves math problems to generate geometrical shapes in a mosaic. In case the player makes certain number of mistakes, she is required to master the skill in the tutor to be able to continue the game. In this way, we use game as an affective hook, while the tutor is teaching the skill. Unlike cognitive mode of intervention, games here are just a platform to use math skills, not necessarily actively teach the content.

We will analyze pros and cons of these different modes, by examining outcome data such as learning gains, time on task and engagement. We assume that cognitive mode can generate higher learning gain as it directly involves teaching instead of supporting it via metacognitive and affective path. But this mode is also more susceptible to cognitive overload and demands more creative and careful implementation. Metacognitive and affective modes, even if they appear more superficial, are reusable across learning content and may produce learning benefits, particularly over the long-term.

RQ2: What are the causal mechanisms of learning outcomes in game-like interventions? It is one thing to find that GLIs result in increasing learning; we would also like to understand why and how? Why do certain students, but not others benefit from our interventions? If games generate learning gain, it is because they are better cognitive tools or are they effective because students are spending more time on task due to increased engagement?

We are using a causal modeling framework to integrate and analyze student data collected from surveys, logs and tests to understand the interrelationships between different student and tutor variables. We have found causal modeling superior approach to common statistical techniques such as correlation and multiple regression for generating a plausible set of hypotheses when using observational educational data sets [8]. We can use it not only to confirm our prior hypothesis such as whether the game-like intervention has generated the outcomes expected but also to explore different causal mechanisms of such outcomes. For example: game-like intervention can lead to higher learning outcome only for the students who had higher time on task, or it could be effective irrespective of time on task which suggests that games can enhance learning beyond improving learner engagement. On the other hand, games may enhance engagement but also add cognitive overload. There might not be significantly visible overall learning outcome. But if we are able to measure these mediating variables, we will be able to understand the actual causal mechanisms and effects.

3 Methodologies

We are taking an empirical, incremental and iterative approach. For each intervention, we are creating different versions of tutor with different degree of game-likeness and running randomized controlled studies so that we can identify effect and impact of each individual element. We would like to select the game-like elements that can enhance learning or at least do not distract or overload learners. We would repeat the experiments with different elements and details in an iterative manner till we find the optimal point of engagement and learning.

We have developed four different versions of 'Monkey's Revenge', which are pedagogically equivalent but have different degree of game-likeness. Based on a randomized controlled study with 252 students, we found that students reported more liking and satisfaction with a more 'game-like' tutor. 'Narrative' was found to be more effective than 'immediate visual feedback' as game-like element. Students also took an 11-item pretest and posttest and the students with the most game- like tutor were the only group to have significant learning gain and there was no reliable difference between the different versions of the tutor. We are working on running more controlled studies with newer versions of the tutor.

Based on a study with 160 middle school students, we found that the students who were offered 'Student Progress Page' at key moments of deactivating negative emotions (boredom and lack of excitement), reported significantly higher positive affect (more interest and more excitement) and demonstrated better engagement behavior (asking for tutor help to solve problems rather than making guesses and giving up) than the control group.

After we finish developing the game 'Mosaic', we would like to observe whether students are going to spend more time on tutor mastering the math skills required to solve problems in the game.

4 Conclusions and Future Work

Our goal is to create an alternative research approach to educational games: computer tutors with game-like interventions. We have created two systems, one in which we are using game-like elements in a math tutor and another where we use those elements not to teach but rather to represent student performance and progress. These two cognitive and metacognitive modes of game-like interventions have led to higher student liking and satisfaction and better affect and engagement behavior respectively. We have yet to empirically conclude whether such enhancements in affective states and engagement behavior lead to higher learning. Besides measuring learning outcomes of these various modes of game-like interventions, we would like to use rich educational data to explore causal mechanisms of how these interventions actually lead to different learning outcomes for different students.

References

1. Gee, J.P.: Good video games and good learning: Collected essays on video games, learning and literacy. Peter Lang., New York (2007)
2. O'Neil, H., Wainess, R., Baker, E.: Classification of learning outcomes: Evidence from the computer games literature. The Curriculum Journal 16(4), 455–474 (2005)
3. Easterday, M.W., Aleven, V., Scheines, R., Carver, S.M.: Using tutors to improve educational games. In: Biswas, G., Bull, S., Kay, J., Mitrovic, A. (eds.) AIED 2011. LNCS (LNAI), vol. 6738, pp. 63–71. Springer, Heidelberg (2011)
4. Jackson, G.T., McNamara, D.S.: Motivational impacts of a game-based intelligent tutoring system. In: Proceedings of the 24th International Florida Artificial Intelligence Research Society (FLAIRS) Conference, pp. 519–524 (2011)
5. Clark, R.E.: Games for Instruction? Presentation at the American Educational Research Association, New Orleans, LA (2011)
6. Wilson, K.A., Bedwell, W.L., Lazzara, E.H., Salas, E., Burke, S.C., Jamie, L., Estock, O.K.L., Conkey, C.: Relationships between game attributes and learning outcomes: Review and research proposals. Simulation & Gaming 40(2), 217–266 (2008)
7. Rai, D., Beck, J.E.: Math Learning Environment with Game-Like Elements: An Incremental Approach for Enhancing Student Engagement and Learning Effectiveness. In: Cerri, S.A., Clancey, W.J., Papadourakis, G., Panourgia, K. (eds.) ITS 2012. LNCS, vol. 7315, pp. 90–100. Springer, Heidelberg (2012)
8. Rai, D., Beck, J.E.: Exploring user data from a game-like math tutor: a case study in causal modeling. In: Proceesings of 4th International Conference on Educational Data Mining, pp. 307–311 (2011)

Interactive Event: The Rimac Tutor - A Simulation of the Highly Interactive Nature of Human Tutorial Dialogue

Pamela Jordan[1], Patricia Albacete[1], Michael J. Ford[2], Sandra Katz[1], Michael Lipschultz[3], Diane Litman[3], Scott Silliman[1], and Christine Wilson[1]

[1] Learning Research and Development Center
[2] School of Education
[3] Department of Computer Science
University of Pittsburgh, Pittsburgh PA, USA, 15260
pjordan@pitt.edu

Rimac is a natural-language intelligent tutoring system that engages students in dialogues that address physics concepts and principles, after they have solved quantitative physics problems. Much research has been devoted to identifying features of tutorial dialogue that can explain its effectiveness (e.g., [1]), so that these features can be simulated in natural-language tutoring systems. One hypothesis is that the highly interactive nature of tutoring itself promotes learning. Several studies indicate that our understanding of interactivty needs refinement because it cannot be defined simply by the amount of interaction nor the granularity of the interaction but must also take into consideration how well the interaction is carried out (e.g., [2]).

This need for refinement suggests that we should more closely examine the linguistic mechanisms evident in tutorial dialogue. Towards this end, we first identified which of a subset of co-constructed discourse relations correlate with learning and operationalized our findings with a set of nine decision rules which we implemented in Rimac [3]. To test for causality, we are conducting pilot tests that compare learning outcomes for two versions of Rimac: an experimental version that deliberately executes the nine decision rules within a Knowledge Construction Dialogue (KCD) framework, and a control KCD system that does not intentionally execute these rules.

In this interactive demo, participants will experience the two versions of the system that students have been using in high school classrooms during pilot testing. Students first take a pre-test, and then complete a homework assignment in which they solve four quantitative physics problems. In a subsequent class, they then use the Rimac system and finally during the next class meeting take a post-test. When working with the Rimac system, students are asked to first view a brief video that describes how to solve a homework problem and then are engaged in a reflective dialogue about that problem. See [4] for a more detailed description of the pilot study and planned analyses.

Demo participants will have the opportunity to experience exactly what the students experience when working with Rimac. They will see the video and engage in a reflective dialogue about that problem with the highly interactive

K. Yacef et al. (Eds.): AIED 2013, LNAI 7926, pp. 928–929, 2013.

version of the system. But in addition, as they progress through the interactive dialogue, the control dialogue will play along beside the interactive one in order to highlight the differences and illustrate when one of the nine rules that comprise the interactive version of the system has been applied.

Rimac was built using the TuTalk tutorial dialogue toolkit [5] but has been enhanced with additional dialogue features such as reformulation of student input (e.g., [6]). The dialogues are tutor-initiative only and are primarily short answer questions in order to keep the accuracy of automatic recognition high. The system does request student explanations at a few key points in the dialogues but does not attempt automatic recognition of student responses to these particular questions. Instead it always follows-up with multiple choice answers for the explanation question and a request that the student select the best match for the explanation he/she just provided. Demo participants will also see Rimac's method for handling explanation questions.

A web-viewable Interactive Event Presentation is available at https://sites.google.com/site/rimacdemo. Please note that it is best viewed using non-mobile devices. If you choose to use a mobile device, you will be instructed to download the Educreations app to view the worked example video.

Acknowledgements. This research is supported by the Institute of Education Sciences, U.S. Department of Education, through Grant R305A10063 to the University of Pittsburgh. The opinions expressed are those of the authors and do not necessarily represent the views of the Institute or the U.S. Department of Education.

References

1. Bloom, B.: The 2 sigma problem: The search for methods of group instruction as effective as one-to-one tutoring. Educational Researcher 13, 4–16 (1984)
2. Chi, M., VanLehn, K., Litman, D., Jordan, P.: An evaluation of pedagogical tutorial tactics for a natural language tutoring system: A reinforcement learning approach. International Journal of Artificial Intelligence in Education 21, 83–113 (2011)
3. Katz, S., Albacete, P.: A tutoring system that simulates the highly interactive nature of human tutoring. Educational Psychology (Special Issue on Advanced Learning Technologies) (in press)
4. Katz, S., Albacete, P., Ford, M.J., Jordan, P., Lipschultz, M., Litman, D., Silliman, S., Wilson, C.: Pilot test of a natural-language tutoring system for physics that simulates the highly interactive nature of human tutoring. In: Chad Lane, H., Yacef, K., Mostow, J., Pavlik, P. (eds.) AIED 2013. LNCS (LNAI), vol. 7926, pp. 636–639. Springer, Heidelberg (2013)
5. Jordan, P., Hall, B., Ringenberg, M., Cui, Y., Rosé, C.: Tools for authoring a dialogue agent that participates in learning studies. In: Proceeding of Artificial Intelligence in Education Conference, pp. 43–50 (2007)
6. Jordan, P., Katz, S., Albacete, P., Ford, M., Wilson, C.: Reformulating student contributions in tutorial dialogue. In: Proceedings of 7th International Natural Language Generation Conference, pp. 95–99 (2012)

AutoTutor 2013: Conversation-Based Online Intelligent Tutoring System with Rich Media (Interactive Event)

Qinyu Cheng, Keli Cheng, Haiying Li, Zhiqiang Cai, Xiangen Hu, and Art Graesser

University of Memphis
{qcheng,kcheng,hli5,zcai,xhu,graesser}@memphis.edu

Abstract. AutoTuto 2013 is an advanced version of the intelligent tutoring system, proven to be effective in empirical tests. AutoTutor 2013 is an agent-based online system with rich media among multiple agents and learners. AutoTutor delivers knowledge by means of multi-turns of conversions with the assist of the comprehensive media technology, including images, diagrams, audios, videos and other interactive presentations developed by Media Semantics Character Builder program.

Keywords: AutoTutor, trialog, conversation, intelligent tutoring system.

AutoTutor is an intelligent tutoring system integrated with conversations, animated agents and tutoring technologies. In this system, the conversation involves one human learner in the form of dialogs (human with one agent), trialogs (human with two agents), or conversation with even more agents. AutoTutor constructs a system consisting of questions by agents, possible diverse responses from learners, followed by corresponding feedback, hints, prompts or pumps by agents. Specifically, when it starts with an opening conversation followed by the main question, the system waits for the learner's response. If the learner provides an expected correct answer, system gives a positive closing remark and the conversation ends. If the response is not an expected answer or an expected misconception, the system delivers the corresponding hint in terms of the given answer. If the learner answers correctly, the conversation ends positively. Otherwise, the system prompts the learner. Agents assist learns several times in a loop like this, but eventually a smart agent will give up and assert the expected answer.

Varied media elements are seamlessly integrated in the system. The learner's response may trigger diverse media, such as images, diagrams, audios, videos and other interactive presentations developed by Media Semantics Character Builder program. The progress of the media element may also trigger conversation. For example, based on leaner's responses, a specific video may be triggered. While showing the video, the system may pause at the specific frame to interact with the learner by conversation.

We provide the full demo version to AIED Interactive Event. People will be able to go through all topics, take tests and interact with the agents through natural language conversation. An online demo is available at

http://x-in-y.com/dropbox/Fakewww/Qinyu/autoTutor2013/autoTutor2013.html

K. Yacef et al. (Eds.): AIED 2013, LNAI 7926, pp. 930–931, 2013.

Acknowledgments. This work was supported by Institute of Education Sciences (R305c120001) for the project of Center for the Study of Adult Literacy (CSAL): Developing Instructional Approaches Suited to the Cognitive and Motivational Needs for Struggling Adults. Any opinions, findings, and conclusions or recommendations expressed in this material are those of the authors and do not necessarily reflect the views of these funding agencies, cooperating institutions, or other individuals.

Interactive Event: Enabling Vocabulary Acquisition while Providing Mobile Communication Support

Carrie Demmans Epp, Stephen Tsourounis, Justin Djordjevic, and Ronald M. Baecker

Technologies for Aging Gracefully Laboratory (TAGlab),
Department of Computer Science, University of Toronto
{carrie,steve,justin,ron}@taglab.ca

We have developed an adaptive communication support tool that also supports vocabulary acquisition. This tool is called VocabNomad; it is one of the few mobile assisted language learning tools that aims to support the call for activities that are fundamentally different than those provided by paper and pencil or computer assisted language learning [1]. VocabNomad meets this call by trying to support the communication of immigrants who are isolated from their surrounding environment because of their limited English language proficiency. In the US, these English language learners (ELL) make up more than 20 percent of the population [2, 3].

VocabNomad is a dual-platform tool (i.e., Android and .NET web application) [4] that provides adaptive vocabulary support by exploiting contextual information (e.g., location) and information from a model of the learner's knowledge, background, and previous activities (i.e., a learner model) [5]. Relying on a mobile application that employs learner modeling provides VocabNomad with the potential to transform events that happen during everyday activities into learning opportunities. Thus, enabling anytime-anywhere learning [6, 7]. The scaffolding that VocabNomad provides for communication may also support the inclusion of ELL within society.

The main questions that we are trying to answer through studying the use of VocabNomad are whether a tool that employs just-in-time vocabulary support based on the user's context can improve the language-learning processes and outcomes of ELL. We are also hoping to determine if this type of support tool can improve their communicative success when speaking with others in English.

This interactive event will highlight VocabNomad's ability to use overlapping contextual information to refine the vocabulary support that is provided to users. We will also show the system's on-demand vocabulary support. This builds on the work of Dearman et al. [8] and uses Internet-based corpora and information retrieval techniques to meet emergent user needs [9].

Attendees will be able to experience the application from the perspective of two different users. The first will be that of a newly created user. The second will demonstrate how VocabNomad would behave for an ELL who has been using VocabNomad for some time.

Conference attendees will be able to search through the vocabulary that is provided, edit vocabulary entries through the device or web-based interfaces, and see the vocabulary that are recommended to users. Attendees will be shown the just-in-time incorporation of learning materials (e.g., visual representations of a word's meaning

K. Yacef et al. (Eds.): AIED 2013, LNAI 7926, pp. 932–933, 2013.

or simplified definitions) that can be used to scaffold the meaning of the provided vocabulary. They will also have the opportunity to see the recommendation of synonyms that are intended to expand the user's vocabulary knowledge. Beyond this, attendees will be able to hear the pronunciation models that are generated using speech synthesis, which learners can use to rehearse their own speech or to scaffold their communication with others.

An outline of the various operations that participants will be able to perform can be seen at http://sites.google.com/site/carriedemmansepp/publications/aied2013_ie.

Acknowledgements. This work was funded by the National Science and Engineering Research Council of Canada and GRAND.

References

1. Ballance, O.J.: MALL—Somewhere between the Tower, the Field, the Classroom, and the Market: A Reply to Professor Stockwell's Response. Language Learning & Technology (LLT) 17, 37–46 (2013)
2. Shin, H.B., Kominski, R.A.: Language Use in the United States: 2007. United States Census Bureau (2010)
3. Siegel, P., Martin, E., Bruno, R.: Language Use and Linguistic Isolation: Historical Data and Methodological Issues. United States Census Bureau (2001)
4. Demmans Epp, C., Baecker, R.M.: Employing Adaptive Mobile Phone Applica-tions for Scaffolding the Communication and Vocabulary Acquisition of Language Learners. In: LearnLab's Learning Science Workshop on the Use of Technology Toward Enhancing Achievement and Equity in the 21st Century, Pittsburgh, PA (2012)
5. Demmans Epp, C., Baecker, R.M.: VocabNomad: a Context-Sensitive Application for Mobile Assisted Language Learning. Young Researcher's Track Poster Session at Artificial Intelligence in Education (AIED). Auckland, New Zealand (2011)
6. De Jong, T., Specht, M., Koper, R.: A Reference Model for Mobile Social Software for Learning. International Journal of Continuing Engineering Education and Life-Long Learning 18, 118–138 (2008)
7. Liu, T.-Y.: A Context-Aware Ubiquitous Learning Environment for Language Listening and Speaking. JCAL 25, 515–527 (2009)
8. Dearman, D., Truong, K.N.: Evaluating the Implicit Acquisition of Second Language Vocabulary Using a Live Wallpaper. In: Conference on Human Factors in Computing Systems (CHI), pp. 1391–1400. ACM, Austin (2012)
9. Demmans Epp, C., Djordjevic, J., Wu, S., Moffatt, K., Baecker, R.M.: Towards Providing Just-in-Time Vocabulary Support for Assistive and Augmentative Communication. In: ACM International Conference on Intelligent User Interfaces (IUI), pp. 33–36. ACM, Lisbon (2012)

Authoring Problem-Solving ITS with ASTUS: An Interactive Event

Luc Paquette, Jean-François Lebeau, and André Mayers

Université de Sherbrooke, Québec, Canada
{luc.paquette,andre.mayers}@USherbrooke.ca
http://astus.usherbrooke.ca/aied2013_ie.pdf

1 ASTUS

Problem-solving or step-based ITS have been proven successful for well-defined domains, particularly in well-defined tasks, but their success is mitigated by their cost. Typically, the main factor behind the cost is the efforts needed to model the task domain. Different approaches have been investigated to reduce these efforts: Model-Tracing Tutors (e.g. Cognitive Tutors [1], Andes [2]), Constraint-Based Tutors (e.g. SQL-Tutor [3], ASPIRE [4]) and Example-Tracing Tutors (e.g. CTAT [5], ASSISTment [6]).

With ASTUS [7], we aim to offer to the ITS community a support for the development of tutors for well-defined tasks in a wide range of task domains. In such context, building a framework based on a generative model of the task domain was deemed the most interesting approach, as it appeared as the one leading to a comprehensive and flexible solution. A solution which includes, for instance, not only the capacity to show next-step hints, but to generate them by instantiating domain-independent templates using data extracted from knowledge components [8].

ASTUS's knowledge representation approach encodes tutored skills with glass-box components and the underlying ones (mental inferences and atomic actions in the learning environment) with black-box components. Thus, a model consists of formatted definitions and executable code. Using an authoring language (prototyped with a Groovy-based DSL), the model can be completely encoded in a single, coherent, easy-to-navigate file, much like a typical source file should be. Programming is needed to produce the learning environment's UI, and tools for debugging and visualization are available at runtime.

2 Interactive Event

In this interactive event, we present a brief overview of the ASTUS framework. Examples from tutors for the insertion of elements in an AVL tree and for the training of nurses will be shown. They will be used to explain ASTUS's knowledge representation system and to demonstrate the authoring process, the debugging tools available in ASTUS and the pedagogical feedback generated by the resulting tutors.

K. Yacef et al. (Eds.): AIED 2013, LNAI 7926, pp. 934–935, 2013.

ASTUS's knowledge representation system allows it to automatically generate pedagogical feedback using processes that are independent from the tutored task. The formalism used to model procedural and declarative knowledge allows the tutor to generate next-step hints by interpreting the model of the task [8] and to provide negative feedback on errors diagnosed from off-path steps. In addition, the reification of objects contained in the knowledge base as components of the learning environment allows ASTUS more flexibility when providing visual feedback such as flag feedback and interface highlight.

We will also present a brief overview of the tools included in ASTUS to facilitate the authoring process. Those tools include a graphical representation of procedural knowledge, an episodic tree to examine the tracing of the learners' steps and a browser for the content of the knowledge base.

3 Conclusion

As the ITSs move from the labs to the classrooms, the next logical step may be to largely move the authoring efforts from highly specialized graduate students to domain experts (including teachers), but we are interested in investigating an intermediate step that consists in a comprehensive, flexible and usable framework for programmers and people skilled in knowledge-based systems. We are aware that our solution, based on generative models, may be justified only in well-defined domains and that some ill-defined tasks, such as design-based ones, may be challenging at best. However, there is no such tool available for the ITS community that is explicitly designed to facilitate the experimentation of different pedagogical approaches.

References

1. Anderson, R.R., Corbett, A.T., Koedinger, K.R., Pelletier, R.: Cognitive Tutors: Lessons Learned. The Journal of the Learning Sciences 4(2), 167–207 (1995)
2. VanLehn, K., et al.: The Andes Physics Tutoring System: Lessons Learned. International Journal of Artificial Intelligence in Education 15(3), 1–47 (2005)
3. Mitrovic, A.: A Knowledge-Based Teaching System for SQL. In: Proceedings of ED-MEDIA 1998, pp. 1027–1032 (1998)
4. Mitrovic, A., et al.: ASPIRE: An Authoring System and Deployment Environment for Constraint-Based Tutors. International Journal of Artificial Intelligence in Education 19, 155–188 (2009)
5. Aleven, V., McLaren, B.M., Sewall, J., Koedinger, K.R.: Example-Tracing Tutors: A New Paradigm for Intelligent Tutoring Systems. International Journal of Artificial Intelligence in Education, Special Issue on "Authoring Systems for Intelligent Tutoring Systems", 105–154 (2009)
6. Razzaq, L., Heffernan, N.T.: Open Content Authoring Tools. In: Nkambou, R., Bourdeau, J., Mizoguchi, R. (eds.) Advances in Intelligent Tutoring Systems. Studies in Computational Intelligence, vol. 308, pp. 407–420. Springer, Heidelberg (2010)
7. Paquette, L., Lebeau, J.-F., Mayers, A.: Authoring Problem-Solving Tutors: A Comparison between ASTUS and CTAT. In: Nkambou, R., Bourdeau, J., Mizoguchi, R. (eds.) Advances in Intelligent Tutoring Systems. SCI, vol. 308, pp. 377–405. Springer, Heidelberg (2010)
8. Paquette, L., Lebeau, J.-F., Beaulieu, G., Mayers, A.: Automating Next-Step Hints Generation Using ASTUS. In: Cerri, S.A., Clancey, W.J., Papadourakis, G., Panourgia, K. (eds.) ITS 2012. LNCS, vol. 7315, pp. 201–211. Springer, Heidelberg (2012)

Interactive Event: From a Virtual Village to an Open Learner Model with Next-TELL

Susan Bull[1], Michael Kickmeier-Rust[2], Gerhilde Meissl-Egghart[3], Matthew D. Johnson[1], Barbara Wasson[4], Mohammad Alotaibi[1], and Cecilie Hansen[5]

[1] Electronic, Electrical and Computer Engineering, University of Birmingham, UK
[2] Knowledge Management Institute, Technical University of Graz, Austria
[3] Talkademy, Vienna, Austria
[4] Department of Information Science and Media Studies, University of Bergen, Norway
[5] Uni Health, Uni Research AS, Norway
s.bull@bham.ac.uk

1 Introduction

With the range of educational tools available it is now realistic for learner models to take account of broader information, and there are strong arguments for placing open learner models in the centre of environments with diverse sources of data [1],[2],[3]. This Interactive Event will demonstrate the Next-TELL approach to facilitating teachers' use of data from a variety of sources, and will allow participants to interact at all stages of this process. The Interactive Event will comprise three parts:

- Going to the Chatterdale village: an OpenSim mystery for language learners;
- Interaction with ProNIFA (probabilistic non-invasive formative assessment) to help teachers transform Chatterdale log data for an open learner model;
- Interaction with the Next-TELL Open Learner Model to explore learner model visualisations from automated and manual sources.

2 Chatterdale

Most of the inhabitants of Chatterdale have disappeared. Why has this happened? Where have they gone? This is the challenge faced by Austrian and Norwegian students entering the virtual village. Can they work together to solve this mystery?

The Interactive Event will introduce participants to Chatterdale. Members of the Next-TELL project will be in the village to greet and show participants around. Participants will leave log traces as they communicate and as their avatars move.

3 Learning Analytics with ProNIFA

ProNIFA uses smart data analysis to identify the probabilities that a range of language competencies are held. It offers statistics on usage (e.g. words, comments, time of engagement, hints used), while still allowing teachers to fine-tune the data.

K. Yacef et al. (Eds.): AIED 2013, LNAI 7926, pp. 936–937, 2013.

Participants will be able to automatically transform their Chatterdale log data using ProNIFA. How well did they communicate their goals in Chatterdale? Did they understand the main points, make inferences and understand details? How well did they use the clues? And do they know where everybody went? ProNIFA sends the competencies identified to the Next-TELL open learner model.

4 The Next-TELL Open Learner Model

The open learner model visualises competencies to students and teachers in various ways (e.g. skill meters, tables, word cloud, treemap), with reference to the Common European Framework of Reference for Languages [4]. Students and teachers can explore the learner models to better recognise their own, or their students' competencies; and they can compare the data from Chatterdale to that entering the learner model from other applications or manual input (e.g. self or peer assessments).

Will the Interactive Event participants be surprised at the language competencies identified for them? Does their open learner model encourage them to seek additional practice? Will they return to Chatterdale for more immersive experiences? Will they log in again after the Interactive Event, and use the open learner model discussion facility to communicate with others about their competencies?

With this example, the Next-TELL Interactive Event will illustrate methods of combining multiple data sources in an open learner model, to meet the challenges posed by the current wealth and speed of information available about learners.

Acknowledgement. This project is supported by the European Commission (EC) under the Information Society Technology priority of the 7th Framework Programme for Research and Development under contract no 258114 NEXT-TELL. This document does not represent the opinion of the EC and the EC is not responsible for any use that might be made of its content.

References

1. Morales, R., Van Labeke, N., Brna, P., Chan, M.E.: Open Learner Modelling as the Keystone of the Next Generation of Adaptive Learning Environments. In: Mourlas, C., Germanakos, P. (eds.) Intelligent User Interfaces, Information Science Reference, pp. 288–312. ICI Global, London (2009)
2. Mazzola, L., Mazza, R.: GVIS: A Facility for Adaptively Mashing Up and Representing Open Learner Models. In: Wolpers, M., Kirschner, P.A., Scheffel, M., Lindstaedt, S., Dimitrova, V. (eds.) EC-TEL 2010. LNCS, vol. 6383, pp. 554–559. Springer, Heidelberg (2010)
3. Bull, S., Wasson, B., Kickmeier-Rust, M., Johnson, M.D., Moe, E., Hansen, C., Meissl-Egghart, G., Hammermuller, K.: Assessing English as a Second Language: From Classroom Data to a Competence-Based Open Learner Model. In: ICCE (2012)
4. Council of Europe (nd). The Common European Framework of Reference for Languages, `http://www.coe.int/t/dg4/linguistic/Source/Framework_EN.pdf` (accessed June 1, 2012)

Interactive Event Visualization of Students' Activities Using ELEs

Ya'akov (Kobi) Gal

Dept. of Information Systems Engineering,
Ben-Gurion University
https://sites.google.com/site/aied13gal/

Exploratory Learning Environments (ELEs) are open-ended software in which students build scientific models and examine properties of the models [1,4]. Such software are generally used in classes too large for teachers to monitor all students and provide assistance when needed, and are becoming increasingly prevalent in developing countries where access to teachers and other educational resources is limited [6]. Thus, there is a need to develop tools of support for teachers' understanding of students' activities. Such tools can provide support for teachers and education researchers in analyzing and assessing students' use of ELEs.

We propose an interactive event demonstration of two visualization methods to present students' activities with ELEs to teachers and researchers. One of the methods visualized the plans that were inferred by plan recognition algorithms [3,7]. The second method visualized students actions over a time-line.

Both of these visualization methods have been shown to improve teachers' understandings of students' activities in a way that was not possible beforehand [2]. We will demonstrate that our visualization tools generalize across several ELEs (for both chemistry [8] and statistics [5]), inferring aspects of students' interactions that are important to teachers and researchers, such as interleaving of activities, exogenous actions and trial-and-error. These are the first tools developed to visualize students' activities in ELEs.

To demonstrate our approach we will use the following problems posed to students that use one of the ELEs in our interactive event for an introductory chemistry course. The software, called VirtualLabs [8] simulates a real chemistry lab and used in the instruction of college and high school chemistry courses worldwide. It allows students to design and carry out experiments which connect theoretical chemistry concepts to real world applications.

> Given four substances A, B, C, and D that react in a way that is unknown, design and perform virtual lab experiments to determine the correct reaction between these substances.

The flexibility of VirtualLabs affords two classes of solution strategies to this problem (and many variations within each). The first strategy mixes all four solutions together, and infer the reactants by inspecting the resulting solution. The second strategy mixes pairs of solutions until a reaction is obtained.

The *plan visualization* method presents students' interactions as a hierarchy of inferred activities called "plans". Students' plans are presented using an interactive interface that enables to explore the plan tree. The plan is presented as

K. Yacef et al. (Eds.): AIED 2013, LNAI 7926, pp. 938–939, 2013.

a tree. Each of the nodes in the tree represents a student's activity. The leaves of the plan represent the basic actions of the student that constitute students' interactions with VirtualLabs. The other nodes represent higher level activities that were inferred by the algorithm.

The *Temporal visualization* methods presents students' interactions using a timeline. The vertical axis displays the objects used by the student, while the horizontal axis displays students' actions in the order in which they were created. This student's interaction consisted of mixing solutions in flasks, and each arrow in the figure represents one of these mixing actions. The base of the arrow represents the source flask, while the head of the arrow indicates the recipient flask. Thicker arrows correspond to larger volumes of solution being mixed.

Our interactive event will demonstrate the efficacy of combining computational methods for recognizing users interactions with intelligent interfaces that visualize how they use flexible, open-ended software. It is a first step in creating systems that provide the right machine-generated support for their users. For teachers, this support consists of presenting students performance both after and during class. For students, this support will guide their problem-solving in a way that maximizes their learning experience while minimizing interruption.

The url for submission is `https://sites.google.com/site/aied13gal/`

References

1. Amershi, S., Conati, C.: Automatic recognition of learner groups in exploratory learning environments. In: Ikeda, M., Ashley, K.D., Chan, T.-W. (eds.) ITS 2006. LNCS, vol. 4053, pp. 463–472. Springer, Heidelberg (2006)
2. Amir, O., Gal, Y.: Plan recognition and visualization in exploratory learning environments
3. Amir, O., Gal, Y.: Plan recognition in virtual laboratories. In: Proceedings of the 22nd International Joint Conference on Artificial Intelligence, IJCAI (2011)
4. Cocea, M., Gutierrez-Santos, S., Magoulas, G.D.: S.: The challenge of intelligent support in exploratory learning environments: A study of the scenarios. In: Proceedings of the 1st International Workshop in Intelligent Support for Exploratory Environments on European Conference on Technology Enhanced Learning (2008)
5. Konold, C., Miller, C.: TinkerPlots Dynamic Data Exploration 1.0. Key Curriculum Press (2004)
6. Pawar, U.S., Pal, J., Toyama, K.: Multiple Mice for Computers in Education in Developing Countries. In: Conference on Information and Communication Technologies and Development, pp. 64–71 (2007)
7. Reddy, S., Gal, Y., Shieber, S.M.: Recognition of users' activities using constraint satisfaction. In: Proceedings of the First and Seventeenth International Conference on User Modeling, Adaptation and Personalization (2009)
8. Yaron, D., Karabinos, M., Lange, D., Greeno, J.G., Leinhardt, G.: The ChemCollective–Virtual Labs for Introductory Chemistry Courses. Science 328(5978), 584 (2010)

AutoMentor: Artificial Intelligent Mentor in Educational Game

Jin Wang[1], Haiying Li[1], Zhiqiang Cai[1], Fazel Keshtkar[1], Art Graesser[1], and David Williamson Shaffer[2]

[1] University of Memphis
{wjin,hli5,zcai,fkeshtkar,graesser}@memphis.edu
[2] University of Wisconsin-Madison
david.williamson.shaffer@gmail.com

Abstract. AutoMentor is an artificial intelligent mentor who guides groups of players to accomplish tasks through online interaction including chats and E-mails in a serious game called "Land Science". The architecture of AutoMentor consists of such analysis modules as speech act classifier, newness, relevance, epistemic network analysis and state transition network. The analyses of these modules make human mentor to be replaced by automated mentor agent. The forms of conversation among mentor agent and groups of students involve multi-logues and mutli-turns.

Keywords: AutoMentor, educational game.

AutoMentor is an artificial intelligent mentor who guides groups of players to accomplish tasks through online interaction including online chats and E-mails in a serious game "Land Science". Land Science game is a specific STEM computer game in which players play the role as members of a fictitious urban and regional planning firm solving land use issues. A key part of the game is that players interact with a professional human mentor who helps players take actions and guide them to finish all tasks. The AutoMentor is designed eventually to simulate human mentor who handles the entire conversation with groups of players. AutoSuggester is transitional product from human mentor to AutoMentor. AutoSuggester automatically generate suggestions for human mentors with respect to players' chatting message, activities and game states. The core of the AutoMentor is production rules. A production rule consists of two parts: a sensory precondition and an action. If a rule's precondition matches the current state of the game, then the corresponding rule will be triggered and fired. The architecture of AutoMentor consists of such analysis modules as speech act classifier, newness, relevance, epistemic network analysis and state transition network. The analyses of these modules make automated mentor possible and eventually replaces human mentor. The speech act classifier is used to classify players' input to category (e.g., metacognition, question, request, command, positive/negative feedback, etc.). The newness and relevance module is used to identify whether either an off-topic or a new topic occurs. The epistemic network analysis is

K. Yacef et al. (Eds.): AIED 2013, LNAI 7926, pp. 940–941, 2013.

used to identify whether or what skill, knowledge, identity, value and epistemic knowledge occur. With these comprehensive considerations, the forms of conversation among mentor agent and groups of students involve multi-logs such as dialog, trilog or even more, and mutli-turns between the mentor agent and multiple players.

We provide a demo version of AutoMentor to AIED Interactive Event. People will be able to go through all rooms, finish different tasks, and interact with the AutoMentor via natural language conversation. An online demo of AutoMentor is available at http://141.225.41.83/memphis/.

Acknowledgments. This work was supported by the National Science Foundation (0918409) for the project of AutoMentor: Virtual mentoring and assessment in computer games for STEM learning. Any opinions, findings, and conclusions or recommendations expressed in this material are those of the authors and do not necessarily reflect the views of these funding agencies, cooperating institutions, or other individuals.

Practical Ultra-Portable Intelligent Tutoring Systems(PUPITS): An Interactive Event

Cecily Heiner

Southern Utah University, Cedar City, Utah
cecilyheiner@suu.edu

Abstract. Intelligent tutoring systems have shown promise as personalized learning assistants that can increase learning by as much as a standard deviation over classroom teaching. However, typically, they are expensive to build, requiring extensive technical and educational expertise. They are often difficult to develop and deploy with simple modifications often requiring weeks of time to develop and favorable deployments requiring months of negotiations. This interactive event presents an alternative to such traditional large systems that we call Practical Ultra-Portable Intelligent Tutoring Systems(PUPITS).

Keywords: Practical Ultra Portable Tutoring Systems(PUPITS), educational data mining, embedded experiments, mammography, tutorial dialog.

1 Introduction

One of Benjamin Bloom's most cited papers describes a challenge known as "The 2 Sigma Problem"(Bloom 1984). The most commonly referenced portion of this challenge describes research showing that with expert human tutoring, a student can perform at two standard deviations above typical classroom performance. As a research community, we have made substantial progress on that challenge with many systems reporting a learning gain of at least one standard deviation. (Graesser 2001) A less commonly referenced challenge also contained in the Bloom paper is "*practical methods*" defined as "methods that the average teacher or school faculty can learn in a brief period of time and use with little more cost or time than conventional instruction". With respect to this challenge, the research community has made some efforts, but with less zeal and success. This interactive event aims to demonstrate an approach to building intelligent tutoring systems that can maintain the same degree of scientific integrity as existing intelligent tutoring systems by including features such as embedded experiments and fine grained data collection with a different kind of system architecture. Our architecture is more flexible and suitable for different kinds of learning scenarios and demonstrates more "practical methods" than existing systems.

In this interactive event, we will demonstrate two mini-intelligent tutoring systems with a common system architecture. Our essential software includes XAMPP lite and the client and server tutoring software developed with the typical web stack of HTML, CSS, JavaScript, MySQL, and PHP. Our essential hardware consists of a

K. Yacef et al. (Eds.): AIED 2013, LNAI 7926, pp. 942–943, 2013.

portable hard drive or thumb drive that contains the essential software as well as a laptop or desktop to act as the server machine host, as well as client machines that can be desktops, laptops, cell phones, or other computing devices with a browser. NFC tags or QR codes for faster browsing are optional, but recommended.

We aim to create systems that can run on a cell phone or tablet, so any text input is limited to less than 200 characters. This approach is a good alternative for educational settings where people are interacting with the system for approximately two minutes, for settings where reliable internet is not available, and for rapid prototyping.

2 Case Study 1: A Practical Ultra-Portable Tutoring System to Improve Mammography Rates in Utah

Breast cancer is the leading cancer killer of Utah women. One factor in the mortality rate is that Utah has an exceptionally low mammogram rate, one of the lowest in the nation. We are building a tutoring system to determine why women do not obtain mammograms and try to motivate them to change their behavior. It is important for the system to run in rural locations where they might (or might not) have reliable internet connectivity as well as at events and venues where there may be internet dead spots. We need to be able to collect data on multiple user-owned devices at once.

3 Case Study 2: A Practical Ultra-Portable Tutoring System to Classify Student Responses During Lectures

In educational environments, campus networks can be either flaky and/or overly locked down, preventing access to a desirable web site and lecture halls can be isolated in buildings or basements where there is not reliable wireless access. Nevertheless, many students have access to at least one portable computing device- a cell phone, notebook, or other alternative with wi-fi capability. The goal of this project is to provide quick interchange and classification of student responses, so that instructors can adjust the difficulty of a class up or down as they teach and provide additional examples as needed, without having lecture pace dictated by one or two obnoxiously vocal students and without jeopardizing the self-esteem of shy students who may not know the correct answer.

References

(see more-http://www.cecilyheiner.com/research/projects/)

1. Bloom, B.S.: The 2 Sigma Problem: The Search for Methods of Group Instruction as Effective as One-to-One Tutoring. Educational Researcher 13(6), 4–16
2. Graesser, A.C., VanLehn, K., Rosé, C.P., Jordan, P.W., Harter, D.: Intelligent Tutoring Systems with Conversational Dialogue AI Magazine, 39–50 (2001)

2nd Workshop on Intelligent Support for Learning in Groups

Jihie Kim[1] and Rohit Kumar[2]

[1] University of Southern California, Los Angeles, CA 90292
[2] Raytheon BBN Technologies, Cambridge, MA 02138
https://sites.google.com/site/islg2013/

Workshop Goals and Themes

Technological advances in the use of Artificial Intelligence for Educational (AIEd) applications over the past two decades have enabled the development of highly effective, deployable learning technologies that support learners across a wide-range of domains and age-groups. Alongside, mass access and adoption of revolutionary communication technologies have made it possible to bridge learners and educators across spatiotemporal divides.

On the other hand, research in collaborative learning has informed instructional principles that leverage the pedagogical benefits of learning in groups. Educational service providers including mainstream universities are deploying their courses to online learning platforms that allow students to share their learning experience with their peers. Large volumes of educational content including videos, presentations, books and games are accessible on mobile/tablet devices which enrich learning interactions by bringing students together.

Over the past few years, the AIEd research community has started investigating extension of the fundamental techniques (student modeling, model-based tutors, integrated assessment, tutorial dialog, automated scaffolding, data mining, pedagogical agents, and so on) to support learning in groups. The goal of this series of workshops is to provide a focused forum for bring this sub-community of AIEd researchers together to share recent advances in the field.

Building on its first instantiation last year [1], this workshop will comprise of papers describing advances in the state of the art AIEd techniques to improve the effectiveness of learning in groups. This year, the proposed workshop on Intelligent Support for Learning in Groups (ISLG) will be organized around the theme of "Quantifying Real-World Impact". Full (10 pages), Short (4 pages) and Position papers relevant to this theme and other topics of interest are will be presented at this workshop.

Reference

1. 1st Workshop on Intelligent Support for Learning in Groups (2012), https://sites.google.com/site/islg2012/

K. Yacef et al. (Eds.): AIED 2013, LNAI 7926, p. 944, 2013.

Towards the Development of a Generalized Intelligent Framework for Tutoring (GIFT)

Robert A. Sottilare and Heather K. Holden

U.S. Army Research Laboratory, Human Research and Engineering Directorate
{robert.sottilare,heather.k.holden}@us.army.mil

This workshop provides the AIED community with an in-depth exploration of the Army Research Laboratory's effort to develop tools, methods and standards for Intelligent Tutoring Systems (ITS) as part of their Generalized Intelligent Framework for Tutoring (GIFT) research project. GIFT is a modular, service-oriented architecture developed to address authoring, instructional strategies, and analysis constraints currently limiting the use and reuse of ITS today. Such constraints include high development costs; lack of standards; and inadequate adaptability to support tailored needs of the learner. GIFT's three primary objectives are to provide: (1) authoring tools for developing new ITS, ITS components (e.g., learner models, pedagogical models, user interfaces, sensor interfaces), tools, and methods based on authoring standards that support reuse and leverage external training environments; (2) an instructional manager that encompasses best tutoring principles, strategies, and tactics for use in ITS; and (3) an experimental testbed for analyzing the effect of ITS components, tools, and methods. GIFT is based on a learner-centric approach with the goal of improving linkages in the adaptive tutoring learning effect chain in Figure 1.

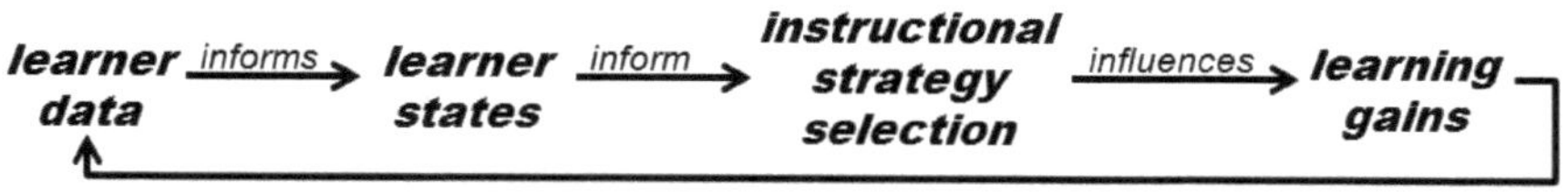

Fig. 1. Adaptive Tutoring Learning Effect Chain

The goal of GIFT is to make ITS affordable, effective, usable by the masses, and provide equivalent (or better) instruction than expert human tutors in one-to-one and one-to-many educational and training domains. GIFT's modular design and standard messaging provides a largely domain-independent approach to tutoring where domain-dependent information is concentrated in the one module making most of its components, tools and methods reusable across training domains. More information about GIFT can be found at **www.GIFTtutoring.org**.

The workshop is divided into five themes: **(1)** *Fundamentals of GIFT* (includes a tutorial on GIFT and a detailed demonstration of the latest release); **(2)** *Authoring ITS using the GIFT Authoring Construct*; **(3)** *Adapting Instructional Strategies and Tactics using GIFT*; **(4)** *Analyzing Effect using GIFT*; and **(5)** *Learner Modeling*. Themes include presentations from GIFT users regarding their experiences within the respective areas and their recommendations of design enhancements for future GIFT releases. Theme 5 is dedicated to discussing the outcomes of the learner modeling advisory board meeting conducted at the University of Memphis Meeting in September 2012.

K. Yacef et al. (Eds.): AIED 2013, LNAI 7926, p. 945, 2013.

Formative Feedback in Interactive Learning Environments

Ilya M. Goldin[1], Taylor Martin[2], Ryan Baker[3], Vincent Aleven[4], and Tiffany Barnes[5]

[1] Human-Computer Interaction Institute Carnegie Mellon University,
Pittsburgh, PA, USA
[2] Department of Instructional Technology & Learning Sciences,
Utah State University,
Logan, UT, USA
[3] Department of Human Development Teachers College Columbia University,
New York City, NY, USA
[4] Human-Computer Interaction Institute Carnegie Mellon University,
Pittsburgh, PA, USA
[5] Department of Computer Science North Carolina State University,
Raleigh, NC, USA

Educators and researchers have long recognized the importance of formative feedback for learning. Formative feedback helps learners understand where they are in a learning process, what the goal is, and how to reach that goal. While experimental and observational research has illuminated many aspects of feedback, modern interactive learning environments provide new tools to understand feedback and its relation to various learning outcomes.

Specifically, as learners use tutoring systems, educational games, simulations, and other interactive learning environments, these systems store extensive data that record the learner's usage traces. The data can be modeled, mined and analyzed to address questions including when is feedback effective, what kinds of feedback are effective, and whether there are individual differences in seeking and using feedback. Such an empirical approach can be valuable on its own, and it may be especially powerful when combined with theory, experimentation or design-based research. The findings create an opportunity to improve feedback in educational technologies and to advance the learning sciences.

At Formative Feedback in Interactive Learning Environments, we will explore these and other issues, including feedback content, timing, initiative, sequencing, modes of presentation, generation and sources of feedback, outcomes, research methods, computational models, help-seeking behaviors, interaction with learner and domain characteristics, differences of learning environments, personalization and adaptation, and systems implementation.

Program Committee: William Cope, Albert Corbett, Davide Fossati, Neil Heffernan, Pamela Jordan, Sandra Katz, Michael D. Kickmeier-Rust, Young-Jin Lee, Chas Murray, Susanne Narciss, Niels Pinkwart, Steve Ritter, Valerie Shute, John Stamper, Denise Whitelock, Caroline Wylie.

K. Yacef et al. (Eds.): AIED 2013, LNAI 7926, p. 946, 2013.

The First Workshop on AI-supported Education for Computer Science (AIEDCS)

Nguyen-Thinh Le[1], Kristy Elizabeth Boyer[2], Beenish Chaudry[3], Barbara Di Eugenio[4], Sharon I-Han Hsiao[5], and Leigh Ann Sudol-DeLyser[6]

[1] Clausthal University of Technology, Germany
[2] North Carolina State University, USA
[3] Indiana University, USA
[4] University of Illinois at Chicago, USA
[5] Columbia University, USA
[6] New York University, USA

Summary: The global economy increasingly depends upon Computer Science and Information Technology professionals to maintain and expand the infrastructure on which business, education, governments, and social networks rely. Demand is growing for a global workforce that is well versed and can easily adapt ever-increasing technology. For these reasons, there is increased recognition that computer science and informatics are becoming, and should become, part of a well-rounded education for every student. However, along with an increased number and diversity of students studying computing comes the need for more supported instruction and an expansion in pedagogical tools to be used with novices. The study of computer science often requires a large element of practice, often self-guided as homework or lab work. Practice as a significant component of the learning process calls for AI-supported tools to become an integral part of current course practices.

Designing and deploying AI techniques within computer science learning environments presents numerous challenges. First, computer science focuses largely on problem solving skills in a domain with an infinitely large problem space. Modeling possible problem solving strategies of experts and novices requires techniques that address many types of unique but correct solutions to problems. In addition, there is growing need to support affective and motivational aspects of computer science learning, to address widespread attrition of students from the discipline. AIED researchers are poised to make great strides in building intelligent, highly effective AI-supported learning environments and educational tools for computer science and information technology. Spurred by the growing need for intelligent learning environments that support computer science and information technology, this workshop will provide a timely opportunity to present emerging research results along these lines.

Program Committee: T. Barnes (NC State Univ., USA), P. Brusilovsky (Univ. of Pittsburgh, USA), D. Fossati (Carnegie Mellon Univ., Qatar), T. Hirashima (Hiroshima Univ., Japan), W. Jin (Univ. of West Georgia, USA), T. Kojiri (Kansai Univ., Japan), S. Kumar (Univ. of Tennessee, USA), C. Lane (Univ. of Southern California, USA), J. Lester (NC State Univ., USA), B. McLaren (Carnegie Mellon Univ., USA),

K. Yacef et al. (Eds.): AIED 2013, LNAI 7926, pp. 947–948, 2013.

P. Munoz Merino (Universidad Carlos III de Madrid, Spain), N. Pinkwart (Clausthal Univ. of Technology, Germany), K. Seta (Osaka Prefecture Univ., Japan), S. Sosnovsky (CeLTech, DFKI, Germany), J. Stamper (Carnegie Mellon Univ., USA), F. Yu (National Cheng Kung Univ., Taiwan), M. Yudelson (Carnegie Learning, USA).

The Fourth International Workshop on Culturally-Aware Tutoring Systems

Emmanuel G. Blanchard[1] and Isabela Gasparini[2]

[1] Department of Architecture, Design and Media Technology,
Aalborg University at Copenhagen, Denmark
Emmanuel.g.blanchard@gmail.com
[2] Department of Computer Science,
University of Santa Catarina State, Brazil
isabela.gasparini@udesc.br

1 Outline

The 4th international workshop on Culturally Aware Tutoring Systems (CATS2013) is a follow-up to the three previously successful CATS workshop editions, organized in conjunction with ITS2008, AIED2009, and ITS2010. It discusses the place of culture in AIED research. Considering culture in this field is important because it is known to have a strong impact on many cognitive and affective processes including those related to learning. Furthermore, people with different cultural backgrounds develop alternative interpretations and strategies and do not similarly appraise their environment, which naturally reflects in their interactions with AIED systems.

All previous CATS workshops have generated great discussions among the AIED community and were also occasions for people from related research fields (e.g., HCI, Autonomous Agent) to share their culture-related work with the AIED community. During CATS2013, particular emphasis is put on addressing the following topics:

- designing AIED systems to teach cultural knowledge and intercultural skills,
- enculturating AIED systems (i.e., developing AIED mechanisms that incorporate cultural features),
- considering cultural biases/imbalances in the AIED research production, and ways to deal with them.

The scientific quality of CATS2013 is ensured by a program committee of 21 members representing 11 different countries and 4 continents.

Acknowledgements. The organizers are particularly thankful to the members of the program committee: Ryan S.J.D. Baker, Benedict du Boulay, Jacqueline Bourdeau, Stefano A. Cerri, Vania Dimitrova, Birgit Endrass, Geneviève Gauthier, Monique Grandbastien, Seiji Isotani, Stan Karanasios, Paul Libbrecht, Samuel Mascarenhas, Riichiro Mizoguchi, Amy Ogan, Elaine Raybourn, Matthias Rehm, Katharina Reinecke, Ma Mercedes T. Rodrigo, Silvia Schiaffino, and Dhavalkumar Thakker.

K. Yacef et al. (Eds.): AIED 2013, LNAI 7926, p. 949, 2013.

First Annual Workshop on Massive Open Online Courses

moocshop

Zachary A. Pardos[1] and Emily Schneider[2]

[1] Massachusetts Institute of Technology, Cambridge, MA
[2] Stanford University, Stanford, CA
zp@csail.mit.edu, elfs@cs.stanford.edu
http://www.moocshop.org

The moocshop will survey the rapidly expanding ecosystem of Massive Open Online Courses (MOOCs). We will foster a cross-institutional and cross-platform dialogue in order to articulate and synthesize the plurality of challenges that arise when evaluating and designing MOOCs. While the forms and functions of MOOCs are currently evolving, we aim to develop a shared foundation for an interdisciplinary field of inquiry moving forward. Researchers, technologists, and course designers from universities and multiple platforms will share their approaches and perspectives on key topics, including analytics and data mining, assessment, pedagogy, platform design, data standards, and privacy for open datasets.

Other goals of the workshop include raising awareness of the similarities and differences between the various platforms to create opportunities for future standardization and collaboration and drawing on perspectives from research in other virtual learning environments such as intelligent tutoring systems. We will lay the foundation for a community of interest that will continue this dialogue after the workshop, feeding into subsequent offerings of the workshop and an online community for sharing up-to-date MOOC research findings.

Guest speaker: George Siemens, Athabasca University

Topics areas

- analytics and data mining
- pedagogy
- platform design
  - course features
  - instructor-facing features
    - authoring tools
    - dashboards
- privacy
- evaluation of efficacy
- accreditation, credentialing, certification
- modalities of use (present / future)
- assessment
- personalization
- student models
- data standards

K. Yacef et al. (Eds.): AIED 2013, LNAI 7926, p. 950, 2013.

Cross-Cultural Differences and Learning Technologies for the Developing World

Ivon Arroyo[1], Imran Zualkernan[2], and Beverly Park Woolf[3]

[1] Social Sciences and Policy Studies, Worcester Polytechnic Institute
[2] University of Sharjah, United Arab Emirates
[3] School of Computer Science, University of Massachusetts Amherst
iarroyo@wpi.edu, izualkernan@aus.edu, bev@cs.umass.edu

The LT4D workshop aims to provide a forum for a discussion of cross-cultural differences regarding the immersion of AIED systems and the rational introduction of learning technologies in the developing world. Focus of the workshop is to explicitly explore the economic, social, political and cultural constraints that shape affordances for learning technologies in the developing world.

Besides differences in socialization and cultural differences, well-intentioned introduction of learning technologies in developing countries can fail for mundane reasons such as teachers not willing to use the technology because of lack of comfort with technology, or simply lack of computers in sharp contrast to abundance of mobile devices. Such constraints cannot be ignored. Rather than blindly implanting technologies, based on a rationalized discussion of such issue and constraints, and possibilities for the immersion of learning technologies, the workshop then aims to provide future visions and roadmaps of such technologies for the developing world and subsequent practical implementation for technology enhanced learning.

Questions that will be addressed are: 1) Cross-cultural differences in educational outcomes of AIED systems or non-adaptive learning technologies across countries, developing vs. developed, or across developing countries; 2) issues of economic cost of adapting interactive learning environments (ILEs) to developing countries ; 3) examples of localization and cultural translation of systems and interfaces ; 4) issues of Social Inclusion: how to encourage and support both individuals and communities that are marginalized --economically, socially, or culturally; 5) sustainable projects and sustainability of learning technologies for the developing world; 6) how education and technology is used in the developing world; how is or should it be used?; 7) supporting Teacher Training via e-Learning in developing countries ; 8) how can Educational Data Mining help to support education and reveal information that would help developing countries ; 9) Differences in realities across the developing world? Is there a common ground, or are countries too different from each other? ; 10) issues of timing: are there key areas where learning technologies can have an immediate impact?; 11) models of adoption of learning technologies in the developing world ; 12) an analysis of great successes or drastic failures in applying ILEs to the developing world ; 13) opportunities for leap frogging and avoiding mistakes in the developed world.

K. Yacef et al. (Eds.): AIED 2013, LNAI 7926, p. 951, 2013.

Workshop on Scaffolding in Open-Ended Learning Environments (OELEs)

Gautam Biswas[1], Roger Azevedo[2], Valerie Shute[3], and Susan Bull[4]

[1] Vanderbilt University, USA
gautam.biswas@vanderbilt.edu
[2] McGill University, Canada
roger.azevedo@mcgill.ca
[3] Florida State University, USA
vshute@fsu.edu
[4] University of Birmingham, UK
s.bull@bham.ac.uk

1 Summary

Open-ended learning environments offer students opportunities to take part in authentic and complex problem-solving and inquiry tasks by providing a learning context and a set of tools for exploring, hypothesizing, and building their own solutions to problems. Also referred to as exploratory environments, examples include hypermedia learning environments, modelling and simulation environments, microworlds, scientific inquiry environments, and educational games featuring open worlds. By the very nature of the choices they provide for learning, exploration and problem solving, OELEs offer opportunities for students to exercise higher-order skills that include: (i) *cognitive processes* for accessing and interpreting information, constructing problem solutions, and assessing constructed solutions; (ii) *metacognitive and self-regulation processes* for coordinating the use of cognitive processes and reflecting on the outcome of solution assessments; and (iii) *emotional and motivational regulatory processes*, such as curiosity and persistence. This presents significant challenges to novice learners; they may have neither the proficiency for using the system's tools nor the experience and understanding necessary for explicitly monitoring and regulating their learning behaviours. Not surprisingly, research has shown that novices often struggle to succeed in OELEs. Without adaptive scaffolds, these learners typically use tools incorrectly, adopt sub-optimal learning strategies, and fail to regulate key cognitive, motivational, and emotional processes. Adaptive scaffolds in OELEs refer to actions taken by the learning environment, based on the learner's interactions, intended to support the learner in completing a task and understanding the topic.

Given the developing interest in this area, the workshop will include papers on: (1) Theoretical frameworks for Designing Scaffolding; (2) Implementing Adaptive Scaffolding; (3) Cognitive, Metacognitive and Self-Regulation models for Designing Scaffolds; and (4) Formative Assessments that support Students' Learning, Performance, and Learning-related Behaviours.

K. Yacef et al. (Eds.): AIED 2013, LNAI 7926, pp. 952–953, 2013.

Programme Committee: Vincent Aleven (Carnegie Mellon University), Bert Bredeweg (University of Amsterdam), Cristina Conati (University of British Columbia), Sergio Gutiérrez-Santos (London Knowledge Labs), Judy Kay (University of Sydney), Susanne Lajoie (McGill University), James Lester (North Carolina State University), Rose Luckin (London Knowledge Labs), Manolis Mavrikis (London Knowledge Labs), Bruce McLaren (Carnegie Mellon University), Ido Roll (University of British Columbia), James Segedy (Vanderbilt University), Phil Winne (Simon Fraser University).

AIED 2013 Simulated Learners Workshop

Gord McCalla[1] and John Champaign[2]

[1] Department of Computer Science, University of Saskatchewan
[2] Cheriton School of Computer Science, University of Waterloo

In their landmark paper VanLehn, Ohlsson and Nason [1] delineate three roles for simulated learners in learning systems: (i) to provide an environment in which human teachers can practise; (ii) to embed simulated learners as part of the learning environment; (iii) to provide an environment for exploring and testing learning system design issues. The second of these roles has been much explored in AIED, with the development of pedagogical agents [2] that can serve, for example, as learning companions [3] or disturbing agents, or even as tutors. In contrast, there is a paucity of research into either the first or third role for simulated learners. The main research touching on the first role is the development of teachable agents in a reciprocal learning context [4], but this is more of a pedagogical strategy for learners than it is a practice environment for teachers. As to the third role, even though VanLehn et al strongly argued that simulated learners could be used to provide both quick and deep insights about learners and pedagogy at the formative evaluation stage of the design of a learning system, there has not been much subsequent research into this role for simulated learners. There has been recent interest in opening up this third line of research again.

This workshop aims to be broadly integrative across all possible roles for simulated learners. Can research into one role inform issues affecting the other roles? In particular, can the lessons learned in building pedagogical agents, the main strand of simulated learner research, provide useful insight into other strands, and vice versa? Among the many questions and issues that could be discussed, here are a few important ones:

- how can simulated learners be deployed to support better learning environments?
- how much cognitive fidelity with real learners do simulated learners need to have? when is cognitive fidelity needed and when is it not?
- what advantages do simulated learners provide in comparison to real learners? what disadvantages?
- what is the role for entire simulated learning environments, including simulated learners?

References

1. VanLehn, K., Ohlsson, S., Nason, R.: Applications of Simulated Students: An Exploration. Int. J. Artificial Intelligence in Education 5, 135–175 (1996)

K. Yacef et al. (Eds.): AIED 2013, LNAI 7926, pp. 954–955, 2013.

2. Johnson, L., Rickel, J., Lester, J.: Animated Pedagogical Agents: Face-to-Face Interaction in Interactive Learning Environments. Int. Journal of Artificial Intelligence in Education 11, 47–78 (2000)
3. Chan, T.W.: Learning Companion Systems. In: Frasson, C., Gauthier, G. (eds.) Intelligent Tutoring Systems: At the Crossroads of Artificial Intelligence and Education, pp. 6–33. Ablex (1990)
4. Leelawong, K., Biswas, G.: Designing Learning by Teaching Agents: The Betty's Brain System. Int. J. Artificial Intelligence in Education 18(3), 181–208 (2008)

Workshop on Self-Regulated Learning in Educational Technologies (SRL@ET): Supporting, Modeling, Evaluating, and Fostering Metacognition with Computer-Based Learning Environments

Amali Weerasinghe[1], Benedict du Boulay[2], and Gautam Biswas[3]

[1] University of Canterbury, NZ
[2] University of Sussex, UK
[3] Vanderbilt University, USA

Learners need to acquire insight into their own learning as well as developing the skill to manage and regulate it. A key question for this workshop is whether instructional technology can be as effective in fostering such metacognitive skills as it is in teaching domain-specific skills and knowledge. This workshop will focus on modeling metacognitive and SRL skills, evaluating metacognitive and SRL behaviours, fostering metacognitive and SRL skills as well as exploring the relationships between metacognition and domain level learning and between metacognition, motivation and affect.

Programme Committee

- Roger Azevedo, McGill University, Canada
- Ryan Baker, Worcester Polytechnic Institute, USA
- Paul Brna, University of Leeds, UK
- Janice D. Gobert, Worcester Polytechnic Institute, USA
- Neil Heffernan, Worcester Polytechnic Institute, USA
- Michael J. Jacobson, University of Sydney, Australia
- Judy Kay, University of Sydney, Australia
- Susanne Lajoie, McGill University Canada
- James Lester, North Carolina State University, USA
- Gordon McCalla, University of Saskatchewan, Canada
- Amir Shareghi Najar, University of Canterbury, NZ
- Christina Steiner, University of Graz, Austria
- Philip Winne, Simon Fraser University, Canada
- Beverly Woolf, University of Massachusetts, USA

K. Yacef et al. (Eds.): AIED 2013, LNAI 7926, p. 956, 2013.

Author Index

MIX
Papier aus verantwortungsvollen Quellen
Paper from responsible sources
FSC® C105338

If you have any concerns about our products,
you can contact us on
ProductSafety@springernature.com

In case Publisher is established outside the EU,
the EU authorized representative is:
Springer Nature Customer Service Center GmbH
Europaplatz 3, 69115 Heidelberg, Germany

Printed by Libri Plureos GmbH
in Hamburg, Germany